Foreign Relations
of the
United States
1949

Volume VIII

The Far East:
China

United States
Government Printing Office
Washington : 1978

DEPARTMENT OF STATE PUBLICATION 8886

OFFICE OF THE HISTORIAN
BUREAU OF PUBLIC AFFAIRS

———

For sale by the
U.S. Government Book Store
Department of State
Washington, D.C. 20520 - (Buckram)
Stock Number 044–000–01689–3

PREFACE

This volume was prepared under the general supervision of E. Ralph Perkins and, at a later stage, of the late S. Everett Gleason, his successor as editor of *Foreign Relations*.

Francis C. Prescott, Ralph R. Goodwin, Herbert A. Fine, and Velma Hastings Cassidy compiled the documentation. Mr. Perkins, the late John G. Reid, and Mr. Prescott were responsible for preliminary planning and review. Work on the volume was then suspended for some years. Rogers P. Churchill, Mr. Reid, Fredrick Aandahl, and John P. Glennon were responsible for final editing and declassification.

Historians of the Department of Defense, including those of the Joint Chiefs of Staff, gave useful assistance which the editors acknowledge with appreciation. They also wish to recognize the cooperation of the Department of Defense and the Central Intelligence Agency, which facilitated declassification of papers for release in this publication. Thanks are also due to those foreign governments that kindly granted permission for publication of certain of their documents.

The Publishing and Reproduction Services Division (Paul M. Washington, Chief) was responsible for the technical editing of this volume.

The index was prepared by Mr. Prescott.

DAVID F. TRASK
The Historian, Office of the Historian
Bureau of Public Affairs

PRINCIPLES FOR THE COMPILATION AND EDITING OF
"FOREIGN RELATIONS"

The principles which guide the compilation and editing of *Foreign Relations* are stated in Department of State Regulation 2 FAM 1350 of June 15, 1961, a revision of the order approved on March 26, 1925, by Mr. Frank B. Kellogg, then Secretary of State. The text of the regulation, as further amended, is printed below:

1350 DOCUMENTARY RECORD OF AMERICAN DIPLOMACY

1351 *Scope of Documentation*

The publication *Foreign Relations of the United States* constitutes the official record of the foreign policy of the United States. These volumes include, subject to necessary security considerations, all documents needed to give a comprehensive record of the major foreign policy decisions within the range of the Department of State's responsibilities, together with appropriate materials concerning the facts which contributed to the formulation of policies. When further material is needed to supplement the documentation in the Department's files for a proper understanding of the relevant policies of the United States, such papers should be obtained from other Government agencies.

1352 *Editorial Preparation*

The basic documentary diplomatic record to be printed in *Foreign Relations of the United States* is edited by the Historical Office, Bureau of Public Affairs of the Department of State. The editing of the record is guided by the principles of historical objectivity. There may be no alteration of the text, no deletions without indicating where in the text the deletion is made, and no omission of facts which were of major importance in reaching a decision. Nothing may be omitted for the purpose of concealing or glossing over what might be regarded by some as a defect of policy. However, certain omissions of documents are permissible for the following reasons:

a. To avoid publication of matters which would tend to impede current diplomatic negotiations or other business.
b. To condense the record and avoid repetition of needless details.
c. To preserve the confidence reposed in the Department by individuals and by foreign governments.
d. To avoid giving needless offense to other nationalities or individuals.
e. To eliminate personal opinions presented in despatches and not acted upon by the Department. To this consideration there is one qualification—in connection with major decisions it is desirable, where possible, to show the alternative presented to the Department before the decision was made.

1353 *Clearance*

To obtain appropriate clearances of material to be published in *Foreign Relations of the United States*, the Historical Office:

a. Refers to the appropriate policy offices of the Department and of other agencies of the Government such papers as appear to require policy clearance.
b. Refers to the appropriate foreign governments requests for permission to print as part of the diplomatic correspondence of the United States those previously unpublished documents which were originated by the foreign governments.

CONTENTS

CONTENTS

POLITICAL AND MILITARY SITUATION IN CHINA [1]

I. NATIONALIST AND COMMUNIST MANEUVERS REGARDING CONDITIONS FOR PEACE; CHINESE GOVERNMENT APPEAL FOR FOUR-POWER MEDIATION AND UNITED STATES REFUSAL; COMMUNIST CAPTURE OF TIENTSIN AND PEIPING; RETIREMENT OF PRESIDENT CHIANG KAI-SHEK (JANUARY 1–23)

893.00/1–349 : Telegram

The Ambassador in China (Stuart) to the Secretary of State

NANKING, January 3, 1949—3 p. m.
[Received 11 :39 p. m.]

5. Although press is playing up Generalissimo's [2] New Year's statement [3] as indication his willingness step aside to permit peace, Lu Han, Governor Yunnan, who attended military discussions informs us intention Generalissimo's statement is "if Communists want peace they can have peace; if they want war they can have war".

STUART

___

893.00/1–349 : Telegram

The Ambassador in China (Stuart) to the Secretary of State

NANKING, January 3, 1949—3 p. m.
[Received January 4—10 :16 p. m.]

7. May I give my following reflections on Generalissimo['s] New Year message: My first reaction was favorable. It was dignified and conciliatory. There was less abuse of Communists than usual. In assuming blame for national distress Generalissimo was in best tradition and in indicating his readiness either to continue or retire he was in accord with new democratic concepts.

But on further thought the fatal flaws reveal themselves. It was too much a literary composition in grand manner. It had the gracious tone of a powerful ruler dealing with troublesome rebels. In this it ignored unpleasant realities: The virtual collapse of military capacity, the failure of latest monetary measures, the almost universal desire for peace and impossibility of it as long as he stays in office.

___

[1] Continued from *Foreign Relations*, 1948, vol. VII, pp. 1 ff.
[2] Chiang Kai-shek, President of the Republic of China.
[3] Department of State, *United States Relations With China* (Washington, Government Printing Office, 1949), p. 920.

The other flaw was more serious. In a sense he has made concessions but in doing so has not gone far enough. His stubborn pride, his anger over Communist war criminal list which he heads, influence of T. V. Soong [4] and other irreconcilables led him to retract his forthright decision made earlier in week to resign and leave Vice President [5] free to adopt any policy that might seem to him to be for national welfare. Yet the pressure was too strong and his original intention too definite for him to avoid any reference to his own willingness to retire. This will destroy whatever is left of will to fight among his troops. There was at once division of opinion among military officers. Position taken seems to be result of compromise among various groups in Kmt.[6] Each of Generalissimo's five conditions may be taken to represent emphasis of one of these factions. In attempting to reconcile them all he may further intensify internal disagreements. Communist reaction can be easily surmised. Their attitude will doubtless be uncompromising. Flushed with success and with victory in sight they want to complete task of eradicating once for all the evil influence of Kmt, precisely as Chen Li-fu [7] and his supporters have consistently argued regarding Communists. Whether by this Communists mean only present leadership and structural organization of Kmt or everything that stands in way their absolute control can only be learned from their future behavior. But it will seem that Kmt at any rate must succumb to dynamic purpose of Communists and because of its own shortcomings. Once Communists have eliminated this source of opposition they may propose some inclusive form of coalition and attempt political settlement with political resistance groups in outlying provinces.

In any event a movement was started on New Year's Day which would seem to be beginning of end of military conflict on national scale. Present indications are that Generalissimo looks forward to withdrawing when necessary to Taiwan and making that his base for continuing resistance.

STUART

---

[4] Governor of Kwangtung and former President of the Chinese Executive Yuan and Minister of Finance; brother-in-law of Generalissimo Chiang Kai-shek.
[5] Marshal Li Tsung-jen.
[6] Kuomintang (Nationalist Party).
[7] Chinese Minister without Portfolio and coleader of the so-called C–C clique in the Kuomintang.

893.00/1–349 : Airgram

The Consul General at Shanghai (Cabot) to the Secretary of State

SHANGHAI, January 3, 1949.
[Received January 14—1:50 p. m.]

A–1. Following is the substance of the more interesting statements made, in the course of a recent general conversation with an officer of this Consulate General, by Yeh Tu-yi, close Democratic League[8] associate of Lo Lung-chi:[9]

1. The Chinese Communists are firmly against any compromise involving the retention of Li Tsung-jen in a coalition government and the same applies to virtually all the top-ranking Nanking officials with the exception of Chang Chih-chung[10] and Shao Li-tze.[11] The Communists would probably not ever accept Madame Sun Yat-sen[12] in the government, owing to her membership in the Soong family, though they would treat her with deference. (According to another local source, fairly close to Madame Sun, she herself wishes to avoid any political role and to devote herself to expanding her humanitarian world; and she has turned down several requests for her future patronage and assistance in connection with programs being planned for activation under a Communist dominated regime.)

2. The retirement or ousting of the Generalissimo, the complete breakup of his regime, and the establishment of a Communist and liberal coalition government are necessary and inevitable; and the United States would do well to make the best of it.

3. The Chinese Communists are pleased over America's apparent rebuff of Madame Chiang Kai-shek.[13] Any steps by the United States toward repudiating Chiang's regime and hastening the advent of a coalition government would help strengthen the influence of the Democratic League and other anti-Nanking minor parties in the new setup and would better their prospects for winning over the Communists to a more friendly attitude toward the United States.

4. Ma Yin-ch'u, the noted liberal economist, is a likely candidate for Minister of Finance in the new government.

5. While the Democratic League leaders still at Shanghai (Lo Lung-chi, Chang Lan, Kuang Yen-pei, Yeh and one or two others) are closely watched, the reason that none of them has left for Manchuria or elsewhere is more concerned with the difficulty of travel than with their surveillance. In the case of Lo Lung-chi, also is the factor of Lo's still unrecovered health, as well as the fact that he is in love with the female liberal leader, Pu Hsi-lu, who is under arrest at Nanking and whom Lo wishes to stay near. (Lo himself recently

---

[8] Organized in 1940 as a federation of Chinese "liberal parties" to serve as a "third force" between the Nationalists and Communists.
[9] Leader of the Democratic League.
[10] Military and Political Affairs Director for Northwest China and Government representative during the 1946 negotiations with the Chinese Communist Party.
[11] Kuomintang member and Chinese Ambassador in the Soviet Union, 1939–42.
[12] Widow of the founder of the Kuomintang and the Chinese Republic; sister of Madame H. H. Kung and Madame Chiang Kai-shek and of T. V. Soong.
[13] For documentation regarding Madame Chiang Kai-shek's visit to the United States late in 1948, see Foreign Relations, 1948, vol. VIII, pp. 296 ff.

indicated with believed sincerity to another of this office's staff that he fears a trip to Manchuria would nullify the partial recovery he has made.)

6. The Shanghai Democratic Leaguers have, however, appointed as their unofficial delegate to the pre-PCC [14] meetings, Wu Nan, the well-known professor of Tsinghua University, Peiping (who, as reported in the Consulate General's A–69, October 20,[15] has already been serving as a liaison agent in transmitting Lo Lung-chi's proposals to the Democratic League representatives sent from Hong Kong to the meetings.)

7. Lung Yun, the former governor of Yunnan who recently escaped to Hong Kong in the disguise of an old woman, is definitely working with the Communists. He told Yeh over six months ago that he had instructed his troops leaving for Manchuria under Nanking's orders that they should go over to the Communist side at the first opportunity.

8. Shanghai Communists have been ordered not to see foreigners at present, especially Americans.

9. The Chinese Communists are all strongly behind Mao Tse-tung.[16] They are different from other Communists, they do not owe their position to Moscow; they are Chinese first and Communists second. There is a real chance of Mao becoming another Tito.[17]

10. Yeh has just received a report that Chou En-lai [18] recently left for Washington. (This rumor, which has also reached us from another source, is only reported to bring out the fact that, in imparting the story, Yeh displayed a patently eager interest revealing how much it would please him if the report were true.)

Yeh is believed to be a man of frank character and pro-American leanings, who has few illusions as to what his party would be up against as a minor group in a Communist dominated regime. However, his assertions should of course be taken with the thought in mind that, as a member of a party which seems to have committed its fortunes for better or worse to cooperation with the Communists in a coalition wherein the party would hope to maintain some influence as a moderating element potentially useful to the Communists in winning American economic assistance, he is presumably most anxious to see the complete collapse of the Generalissimo's regime and the failure of any movement to replace it with a new anti-Communist front of Nanking progressive elements and other groups not yet committed to cooperation with the Communists. Agreement by the Communists to accept Li Tsung-jen and other Nanking leaders in the coalition would probably be regarded somewhat differently and with

---

[14] Political Consultative Conference.
[15] Not found in Department of State files.
[16] Chairman of the Central Committee of the Chinese Communist Party.
[17] Marshal Josip Broz Tito, head of the Yugoslav Communist Party and State, who defected from Moscow leadership in June 1948.
[18] Member of the Central Committee and Politburo of the Chinese Communist Party and chief Communist representative during the 1946 negotiations.

mixed feelings by Yeh and his party—their relief at having a stronger opposition to the Communist domination of the coalition being likely to be offset by fear that the Nanking elements would eclipse their own party in prestige and in usefulness for winning favors from the Western democracies.

CABOT

800.76 Monitoring/1–449 : Telegram

The Ambassador in China (Stuart) to the Secretary of State

NANKING, January 4, 1949.
[Received January 4—6 :35 p. m.]

14. Embassy has thus far been able to monitor only garbled and incomplete version of CCP [19] New Year's editorial broadcast by North Shensi station December 3 [*31?*] and January 1 and 3, entitled "Carry Revolution to Very End!" This news editorial does not reply to Generalissimo's New Year's message of December 31. However, fact that North Shensi station twice rebroadcast its editorial seems to indicate that CCP may consider it as sufficient reply to Generalissimo's last statement. Following are more important sections which Embassy monitored.

"Chinese people will win final victory in liberation war. Not even our enemy doubts this." During 1946 "People's Liberation Army (PLA) adopted correct strategy of placing main emphasis on destroying enemy's certified [*fortified?*] cities". "Main Kmt forces annihilated north of Yangtze River. As result future PLA operation of crossing Yangtze and advancing southward to liberate all China has been greatly expedited. Chinese people also won great victories on political and economic front. Because of this there is absolutely no dispute about victory of Chinese PLA throughout entire country even among world opinion including all imperialist powers."

"Enemy will not expire of its own accord. Neither Chinese people nor forces of American imperialist aggression in China will voluntarily retire from scene. Precisely because they see that nationwide victory of PLA cannot be blocked by means of military struggle, they are daily attaching more and more emphasis to political struggle."

"Policy of American Government has turned from mere support of Kmt counter revolutionary war to struggle in two different forms. First is to organize remnants of Kmt military strength and so-called provincial forces to continued resistance to PLA south of Yangtze and in distant border provinces. Second is to organize opposition within revolutionary camp and exert all efforts to put halt to revolution or for revolution to take on moderated coloring so as not to encroach too much on the interests of imperialism and its stooges. British and French imperialists support this policy of American imperialism." If Chinese people are going to thwart American im-

---

[19] Chinese Communist Party.

perialist plans, "this means overthrowing the reactionary rule of Kmt and establishing democratic dictatorship dominated by alliance between workers and peasants so that China can be changed from semi-[colony?] into really individual state, so that Chinese people can be liberated from shackles of feudalism and bureaucratic capitalism, so that the country can be democratized and restored to peace, so that prerequisite conditions into industrialization can be created and so that society of exploitation of man by man can be developed into society of socialism. There are two roads ahead of us. Which one shall we choose."

Broadcast next listed names of eminent Chinese leaders recently named as war criminals and pointed out that record of each is connected with US imperialism and anti-Chinese activities. Broadcast then characterized as dangerous snakes Americans, some Kmt [liberals?] and [non-]Kmt liberals, and Sun Fo [20] who recently sought "honorable peace". "Since enemy is trying to use peace and infiltration into our revolutionary rank as means to preserve themselves and to strengthen their ground, and since the people's fundamental interests demand thorough eradication of all reactionary influences and expulsion of American imperialism, then all those who want us to take pity on enemy and to permit continued existence of reactionary forces are not people's friends but friends of enemy."

"Fury of Chinese revolution is forcing every social class to determine stand it will take. Changes are taking place in relative strength of China's social classes. The nearer people's war of liberation approaches victory, more closely revolutionary people and their friends stand together and under leadership of CCP determinedly expand revolutionary forces. Although Chinese reactionaries and their friends cannot stand together to form united front and quarrel with and desert one another, they do cooperate in one point which is to use all open and secret, direct and indirect methods to destroy revolutionary influence and preserve reactionary influence. But Chinese people and CCP will smash people's political schemings just like they have smashed enemy's military advances and carry great war of the PLA to very end in 1949. PLA will cross Yangtze and advance southward and score greater victories than in 1948."

STUART

893.001 Chiang Kai-shek/1-449 : Telegram

The Ambassador in China (Stuart) to the Secretary of State

NANKING, January 4, 1949.
[Received January 4—2:55 p. m.]

17. President Chiang Kai-shek's New Year's Day address was prominently reported by all Nanking vernacular papers. Immediately following Generalissimo's speech, talk of peace tendencies began to predominate in press. Following is summary of news and editorial comment appearing in Nanking papers up to and including January 3.

---

[20] President of the Chinese Executive Yuan; son of the late Sun Yat-sen.

Local tabloid reported that Chang Chih-chung had approached US and USSR Embassies to negotiate with Communists while official Kmt and pro-Government press firmly denied that either Embassy had been approached in an official capacity. Several tabloids also feature return to Nanking of Shao Li-tze, former Ambassador to USSR, and current advocator of peace at request of Sun Fo, predicting that he will confer with Chang Chih-chung on reopening peace negotiations. Official Kmt organ, however, prominently asserted Communists do not want peace as evidenced by their New Year's Day declaration but local tabloids argue Communist statement prepared before Generalissimo's speech delivered and eagerly await Communist reaction.

Official Kmt organ editorially warned against misinterpreting Generalissimo's speech as peace offer, recalling that "at start of Communist rebellion Chiang Kai-shek repeatedly invited Mao Tze-tung to Chungking to help work out a peace settlement". Paper added, "but Communists, directed by foreign masters and bent on ruining China, closed door to peace talks". People were urged to make up their minds to fight to finish and strengthen military power in order [to] force Communists to sincerely agree to political settlement. Pointing out that desire for peace cannot be one-sided, paper stressed danger of over-optimism and firmly asserted "willingness to resume peace talks with Communists does not mean Government is unable to continue fight nor that it is prepared to give up duty of saving nation".

Army organ lauded President's courage and unselfish attitude in offering resume peace talks "in order alleviate suffering of people". Paper expressed identical views of official party organ regarding government's ability to carry on war and appealed to people for added cooperation. C–C organ praised President's unconcern for his own future status, adding, "great statesmen are not concerned with their own positions but only with future of nation and welfare of people". Arguing that war is only a means to attain peace, paper felt there should be no reason for refusing peace negotiations "if Communists are sincerely desirous of peace". However, this organ insisted on preservation national independence, sovereignty and democratic form of government as only conditions for peace, stating "unconditional peace with Communists would mean surrender and loss of national independence". Other comment followed same line, placing full responsibility for peace or war on Communists and evincing some concern that Communists would not take Government's offer of peace negotiations seriously.

Sent Department 17, repeated Shanghai 9.

STUART

893.00/1–449 : Telegram

The Ambassador in China (Stuart) to the Secretary of State

NANKING, January 4, 1949—8 p. m.
[Received January 5—4 :28 a. m.]

25. On afternoon of January 3 Kan Chieh-hou [21] called on me on behalf of Vice President and made following report. I am convinced its factual authenticity in spite of his request that it be treated as absolutely confidential.

On New Year's Day, Generalissimo told Li Tsung-jen that he really intended to retire and would announce this very soon. He would expect Li to act for him while he was in prolonged retirement. He would stay first in Fenghua [22] and if military situation made it necessary he would withdraw to Taiwan. He would locate Navy and Air Force there and remove Government's movable assets there. If CP proves intractable he would return and carry on struggle. Generalissimo called on Li yesterday and repeated this. He also asked Li to persuade Pai Chung-hsi [23] to be more patient in regard to his own resignation since Li would soon be in control. Generalissimo thus showed his fear of Kwangsi clique.

Meanwhile, Pai sent his emissary to urge Li to join him in Hankow and from there to disavow Government policy and inaugurate move for peace. It should be noted that Pai did not know of Soviet issues described below.

In considering his course in advocating peace Li felt it necessary to know more of Soviet and CCP attitudes and mutual relations. Therefore he delegated Kan to learn what he could. Lin Chung-yung, Chairman Sino-Soviet Cultural Society, gave New Year's lunch which was attended by Miss Chiang, Secretary of Society, Chu Wu, Moscow-educated former Mayor to [of] Tihwa, son-in-law of Yu Yu-jen, [24] Wang Kun-lun, member Legislative Yuan and former Chairman of Society, and Kan, who had been trying to ingratiate himself with this group. Kan has also called on Roschin. [25] Incidents recorded below are composite of information obtained from Roschin and Chu.

Roschin told Kan that in January 1945, Generalissimo sent special representatives to Moscow to see Stalin [26] who told him "lots of things" but that after the man's return to China nothing had been heard from Generalissimo. Chu went into further detail. Delegate was

[21] Personal adviser to Vice President Li Tsung-jen.
[22] His native place in Chekiang.
[23] Military and Political Affairs Director for Central China.
[24] President of the Chinese Control Yuan.
[25] Maj. Gen. N. V. Roschin, Soviet Ambassador in China.
[26] Marshal Josif Vissarionovich Stalin, then Chairman of the Council of Commissars of the Soviet Union.

Chiang Ching-kuo,[27] to whom Stalin stated China's foreign policy would be independent and not under dictation of US, also Russia did not desire China to be on her side in next war but merely be neutral; USSR would approve of coalition including all "democratic" elements. Stalin is further alleged to have said that if above China policy could be assured he would tell CCP to come to an understanding with Generalissimo and would support Kmt Government. Such coalition government would safeguard Russian interest with respect to Chinese foreign policy. Chiang Ching-kuo thought he could get his father's approval for all this but there was no reply.

Roschin added that in May 1946 Generalissimo sent a man to call on him [28] proposing that he, Generalissimo, make trip to Moscow, to which Roschin agreed and an airplane was accordingly put at his disposal. But again nothing happened. Roschin said that after these experiences Russia was unwilling to take any further part in Chinese affairs. Chu version is that in December 1945, Chiang Ching-kuo called on Roschin and said that his father was now ready to consider the points made to Stalin and would be willing visit Moscow if it were not too late. Roschin promised to wire for instructions and hoped he would get reply in 4 days. When reply came in 3 days, Generalissimo's son said when notified of its favorable contents that situation had changed and Generalissimo would not make trip. Stalin then gave orders to USSR Embassy and Consulates not to meddle again in affairs of Chiang Government which he would like to see overthrown. Russia was afraid of China being an ally of US in next war and has hoped to exact promise of China's neutrality from Generalissimo, but having failed desired no further dealings with him.

At present—according to Chu—two schools of thought are held in Soviet Union and in CCP.

(1) If the progressive elements in Kmt are sincerely ready to cooperate with CCP and Soviet Union, they should be negotiating with them for peace, while testing Kmt by (a) evidence that they are not merely tools of US, (b) their willingness to come not as a devisive unit but into fusion of whole. This would give protection against US domination over Kmt without irritating US. (2) Neither USSR nor CCP, according to Chu, feel Kmt peace movement is sincere but has been instigated by US which, realizing that military situation is hopeless, is playing for time. CCP must, therefore, eradicate all such opposition by force, as only after this has been achieved can real coalition be effected. Even though US is offended, CCP must work for this objective by force before US has time to train and arm new Kmt troops. CCP must fight on until it can have sufficient guarantee. According to Chu, the second school of thought, namely that Kmt peace movement is insincere and instigated by US, is thought to be stronger in both Russia and among CCP.

---

[27] Son of Generalissimo Chiang Kai-shek.
[28] General Roschin then was Soviet Military Attaché in China.

Li feels himself to be in quandary. If in next few days General-issimo leaves Nanking and Li takes over, should he remain here as Acting President with prestige this gives him but with no final authority? Or should he act on Pai's advice and remove to Hankow where he will have no official position but can act independently? If he stays in Nanking and CCP armies come to Yangtze, ignoring his peace proposal, what should he then do? He would greatly appreciate American advice on his dilemma. I asked Kan to assure Li of my deep personal sympathy in these perplexities, but to express my fear that it would be difficult to obtain any explicit advice from Washington.

Chu stressed concern of Soviets that China be neutral in event of third World War. He intends to sound out Roschin as to validity of documents signed by Li, pledging China's neutrality, and thus strengthening guarantee already implicit in formation of coalition.

STUART

893.001 Chiang Kai-shek/1–549 : Telegram

The Ambassador in China (*Stuart*) *to the Secretary of State*

NANKING, January 5, 1949.
[Received January 4—11:29 p. m.]

26. North Shensi radio Chinese voicecast last night featured very strongly worded New China News Agency editorial which rejected New Year's Day "peace plot" by "China's No. 1 war criminal Chiang Kai-shek", on grounds that the Kmt reactionaries and "American imperialists" are only maneuvering to obtain respite for purpose of reconstructing their armed forces for further "imperialist aggression" against CCP. This news has not yet been broadcast.

Sent Department 26, repeated Shanghai 16.

STUART

893.001 Chiang Kai-shek/1–549 : Telegram

The Consul General at Shanghai (*Cabot*) *to the Secretary of State*

SHANGHAI, January 5, 1949.
[Received January 5—1:25 a. m.]

22. Although at previous meetings of Eighth Plenary Session Shanghai City Council keynote had been Shanghai self-defense, Council members eagerly seized upon Generalissimo's New Year message "advocating peace" as incentive for sending telegrams to President, to important leaders CCP and to various provincial and municipal authorities appealing for termination hostilities.

Telegram to President expresses gratification at his message, states that although peace desired by all "it must not impair the integrity of national sovereignty and must not be detrimental to the people's freedom of life" and hopes that "the gentlemen of the Chinese Communist Party" will out of love for country and respect for compatriots entertain same sincerity as President so peace talks can be opened.

Telegram to CCP leaders addresses them in courteous terms; referring to horrible plight of country with much suffering by all, telegram states that new hope has arisen because of President's New Year message advocating peace and saying that he is not concerned with own status but will follow consensus of people. Telegram continues, "to bring peace or war to the country and to bring disaster or blessing to the people now rest entirely with you. If you actually aspire to liberate the people, you should first alleviate their sufferings."

Council appeals on behalf of 6 million Shanghailanders to CCP to terminate hostilities and open sincere peace talks. Divergent views of both sides should be left to judgment of people which will bring fair solution. Telegram continues, "if you turn down the peace offer . . ."[29] this country will be thrown into a quagmire of complete hopelessness. Since the people have not done you any wrong, we do not know how you can face them. The people are tired of the civil war and are anxious to enjoy a breathing spell. We hereby advance our humble views and eagerly wait for your reply.["]

Telegram to provincial and municipal leaders requests them unanimously respond to appeal for cessation hostilities.

Sent Department, repeated to Nanking 18.

CABOT

893.00/1–549 : Telegram

The Consul General at Shanghai (Cabot) to the Secretary of State

SHANGHAI, January 5, 1949—3 p. m.
[Received January 5—12 :07 p. m.]

27. Local press reports Shanghai Self-Help and National Salvation Association sent identical telegrams January 4 to Central Govt and CCP headquarters Yenan, appealing for termination hostilities and calling on both sides to send delegates to Shanghai to "begin sincere consultations under the unbiased observation of the Chinese people and of representatives of friendly nations, so that all outstanding issues may be settled by political means". General purport this same as that of telegrams sent by Shanghai City Council preceding day (remytel to Dept 22, 5th, repeated to Nanking 18). Telegrams appear to be part of general peace offensive on part of C–C clique controlled

---

[29] Omission indicated in the source text.

552–963—78——2

forces Shanghai for purpose throwing onus on Communists if latter refuse comply with what is meant to appear to be overwhelming popular demand for peace based on terms in Gimo's [30] New Year declaration.[31]

Sent Dept 27, pouched Nanking.

CABOT

893.00/1–549 : Telegram

The Ambassador in China (Stuart) to the Secretary of State

NANKING, January 5, 1949—4 p. m.
[Received January 6—1 :37 a. m.]

37. According to report from Hong Kong, [Lung] Yun [32] is acting chairman KmtRC [33] while Marshal Li [34] in North China. C. Y. Li states Chang Lan [35] has arrived North China and says the Marshal also accompanied by Li Tse-lin, Mei Kung-ping, Chu Yun-shan, Mao Tun and Mason Wu. Li Tse-lin is KmtRC member and old associate Marshal Li recently living Macao; Mei Kung-ping is prominent KmtRC member; Chu Yun-shan is member Standing Committee Democratic League; Mao Tun is Leftist writer; Mason Wu (Wu Mao-sun) is Marshal Li's protégé.

STUART

893.00/1–549 : Telegram

The Ambassador in China (Stuart) to the Secretary of State

NANKING, January 5, 1949.
[Received January 6—2 :04 a. m.]

42. ReEmbtel 26 to Department, January 5, repeated Shanghai 16. Following broadcast from Communist-occupied territory heard Nanking night January 4:

"*North Shensi News*, January 4: A New China Agency reporter, commenting on New Year's message of China's No. 1 war criminal, i.e. one Chiang, head of a faction of the Kuomintang, states in brief as follows: With a view to preserving power of Chinese reactionaries

---

[30] Generalissimo Chiang Kai-shek, President of the Republic of China.
[31] In telegram No. 34, January 6, 8 a. m., the Consul General at Shanghai reported similar telegrams sent by business, labor, and educational organizations (893.00/1–649).
[32] Governor of Yunnan, 1927–45.
[33] Kuomintang Revolutionary Committee, with headquarters at Hong Hong.
[34] Marshal Li Chi-shen, Chairman of the KmtRC, had left Hong Kong on or about December 27, 1948, under auspices of the Chinese Communist Party and probably aboard the Soviet ship *Aldan*, according to despatch No. 1, January 4, from the Consul General at Hong Kong (893.00B/1–449).
[35] Titular leader of the Democratic League.

and aggressive influence of US in China, Chiang issued a peace-seeking message New Year's Day. From this message, treacherous plot of both Kuomintang and American imperialism is revealed to Chinese people. This plot was that so-called peace talks should by no means impair interests of four big families and of compradore and landowner classes and should preserve American special privileges in China. This is an attempt to take advantage of opportunity to rest and after recuperating to stage come-back and destroy the revolution. With regard to decisive battle to be fought in Nanking and Shanghai as mentioned in this message, Chiang stated that both militarily and economically Kuomintang's force exceeds that of Communist Party by several times to several tens of times.

"Reporter states that dealing with military phase alone and disregarding political and economic phases, People's Liberation Army has 3,000,000 men. Double this would be 6,000,000 and 20 times would be 60,000,000 men. Chiang accused his subordinates of being shaken in their faith because they merely saw the strength of the Liberation Army without seeing their own strength, which exceeds it several tens of times. Kuomintang members have all seen the more than 3,000,000 men in the People's Liberation Army, but none has seen Chiang's force which is several tens of times stronger than that of the Liberation Army. This is really extraordinary news. Question of whether the news has any sale in the market is answered by a United Press telegram from Shanghai which states that the reaction was cold. Chiang has lost his soul. He is merely a vampire. No one believes him any more."

Pouched Shanghai.

STUART

893.00/1–649 : Telegram

The Consul General at Peiping (Clubb) to the Secretary of State

[Extract]

PEIPING, January 6, 1949.
[Received January 7—1:19 a. m.]

11.

.   .   .   .

Communist North Shensi Chinese language broadcast January 5 contained following message addressed generals and officers Kuomintang forces defending North China by commanding officer of Northeastern field army of People's Liberation Army Lin Piao and Political Commissioner Lo Jung-huan.

"With Peiping, Tientsin and Tangku encircled, retreat your route overland has been cut. Although a few of you succeed in escaping by air or sea, absolute majority of you will be unable to escape fate of destruction. Chiang Kai-shek is too much occupied with saving himself while USA is also unable help you. Are you expecting receive further assistance? Well, there is no more such assistance to be expected. Do you wish break encirclement? There are lessons Kalgan and Hsuchow still fresh before you. At present there is only one way leading to life remaining you, that is to follow example General Cheng Tung-kuo, Changchun, and immediately order complete surrender your forces. So long as you will guarantee not kill war captives and common people and transfer intact all arms assets and warehouses and industrial and communication facilities where you are stationed to Liberation Army, we will accord you all lenient treatment similar to that given General Cheng Tung-kuo and protect lives and properties all your officers and men and their dependents.

"As far [for] Fu Tso-yi [36] himself, although he has been listed as major war criminal, this army will still provide opportunity for him to atone for past crimes through striving to perform meritorious services and will protect his life and property provided he surrenders with whole of his forces. If you should agree to this proposal, we hope you would immediately send your representatives to headquarters this army to make arrangements accordingly. Representatives of your generals and officers of any rank will be equally welcome. As this army is about to start general offensive against you, it is earnestly hoped that you will make decision immediately. Do not say you have not been forewarned. Lin Piao, commanding officer of Northeastern field army of Chinese People's Liberation Army, and Lo Jung-huan, political commissioner."

Sent Department, Nanking 10, Shanghai 13, Tientsin 6, January 6.

CLUBB

893.00/1–749

Memorandum by the Director of the Office of Far Eastern Affairs (Butterworth) to the Acting Secretary of State

[WASHINGTON,] January 7, 1949.

MILITARY SITUATION IN CHINA

The deterioration of the Chinese Nationalist military forces which began with the first phases of the Communist autumn offensive in Shantung and Manchuria has continued unabated with the shift in Communist military effort to north and central China.

Since the beginning of the battle for north and central China in November, the National Government has lost approximately 86,000 troops in north China, 230,000 in central China, and has an additional 100,000 besieged and written off southwest of Hsuchow.

Generally speaking, Nationalist units are surrounded, isolated, or so badly weakened that they can do little more than temporarily delay

---

[36] Commander in Chief of Rebellion Suppression Forces in North China.

the winning of any Communist military objective. The Communists enjoy a marked numerical superiority in both north and central China.

A tabulation of the manpower losses sustained by Nationalist forces and their present strength and disposition is attached.

[Annex]

STATUS OF REGULAR CHINESE NATIONALIST FORCES AS OF DECEMBER 31, 1948

A. Estimate of losses since the beginning of the battle for Hsuchow on November 9, 1948:

Central China—the most capable of the regular units in the area.	230, 000
North China—units of General Fu Tso-yi's command.	86, 000
Total losses	316, 000

B. Estimate of strength remaining:

Central China—

1. Nanking–Shanghai Defense Area, including 5 inferior armies north of the Yangtze and 9 armies deployed along the Yangtze.	150, 000
2. General Tu Yu-ming's army groups isolated and written off southwest of Hsuchow.	100, 000
3. General Pai Chung-hsi's troops in Hupeh.	50, 000
Total in Central China	300, 000

North China—

1. General Fu Tso-yi's command isolated in a number of cities along the Tientsin–Peiping–Suiyuan railroad.	286, 000
2. General Yen Hsi-shan's troops encircled at Taiyuan with sufficient equipment but with food shortages.	120, 800
3. Tsingtao forces isolated and incapable of effective offensive action.	51, 900
4. Sian Area—inferior troops incapable of affecting the course of operations in north or central China.	176, 000
Total in North China	634, 700

B[C]. Estimated total strength remaining in all the war areas of China: 934, 700

893.00B/1-748[9]

Memorandum by the Chief of the Division of Commercial Policy (Willoughby) to Mr. Paul H. Nitze, Deputy to the Assistant Secretary of State for Economic Affairs (Thorp)

[WASHINGTON,] January 7, 1948 [*1949*].

Subject: New China News Agency (Communist) Editorial of December 31, 1948 [37]

This editorial, translated in full in the FBIS [38] of January 5, 1949, deserves careful study and analysis for possible clues to developing trends of Chinese Communist policy.

The distinguishing characteristic of this editorial, as compared with other North Shensi broadcast material I have seen, is its polemic style. Never before, in anything I have seen, has there been any indication of the slightest doubt as to what Communist policy is or should be; but clearly in this editorial there is developed strong argumentation directed not against the Kmt, not against foreigners, but against what appear to be views believed to be held by elements in the Chinese Communist Party itself or in groups allied to it. Ostensibly it is put in the form of a warning not to be taken in by pleas of Kmt "liberals" and non-Kmt "liberals" for conciliatory policies of accommodation leading to peace; but obviously there is a fear that these pleas will strike a responsive chord among large sectors of Communist supporters—hence the warning: "We reiterate, the Chinese people's revolutionary Front *must be consolidated by unity.* Bad elements must not be allowed to break into our front." This is almost a confession of divided counsels.

Some points advanced deserve particular notice. It is admitted (1) that "the revolutionary front of China must be expanded", and (2) that "it must accommodate all those who are willing to participate in the present revolutionary mission". These two points are obviously presented as basic assumptions on which Party members are agreed. The disagreement thus must relate to the extent to which the Party must "accommodate" other elements in order to consolidate its control over China.

Now the line the editorial takes is that the "fundamental interests" of the people (in Communist eyes) require "the thorough destruction of all reactionary forces" (see earlier passages listing "war criminals"), and the "driving out of American aggressive influence". Note that the reference to "reactionary forces" is suitably vague, and that the reference to American influence is qualified by the word "aggressive". In general however the tone of the editorial is uncom-

[37] Not printed; for general summary, see telegram No. 14, January 4, from the Ambassador in China, p. 5.
[38] Foreign Broadcast Intelligence Service.

promising and much more violent than that of Mao's [39] December 1947 allocution; [40] and the impression given is that of an attack on Mao's more tolerant policy enunciated therein.

Note also the curious statement that "The revolutionary mission of the Chinese people requires a major military force and *an allied military force. Without the help of an allied military force, the enemy cannot be beaten*". This statement appears in juxtaposition with the immediately preceding admission of the need for broadening the support of the party among the Chinese people, and with the immediately following insistence that the Chinese people "at the height of the revolution" must "recognize and remember their friends."

This propounds a puzzle that has interesting implications. The reference to an "allied military force" may mean merely the local militia that is organized for service by the Communists wherever they move in; but it may also be intended to argue for a military alliance with the Soviet Union leading to Soviet intervention in the Chinese civil war. If taken in connection with the preceding reference to the need for broadening the base of Communist support, it has the first implication, if taken in connection with the following statement regarding the importance of "remembering friends" it appears to have the second implication.

But in view of the general impression given, of an attack on Mao's conciliatory policy of toleration, it seems to me that the second inference is more probable.

If this is correct, however, it has far-reaching consequences. If Mao's views are being seriously attacked, Mao's leadership would appear to have been challenged by persons or groups who hold the view that (1) an uncompromising Communist revolution must be enforced in China, with no concessions being made to non-Communist groups, and (2) that a close military alliance must be made with Russia, and the Russians invited in to help finish off the civil war. The alternative conclusion would be that Mao himself is reconsidering his policy and has permitted open discussion of alternatives. But since Mao's consistent policy over a long period of years has been one of denying the possibility of an immediate, thorough-going Communist revolution in China, and of adapting his tactics to what is practicable in the Chinese situation, it is difficult to believe that he is now reversing himself; and the fact that his policy of moderation has paid off in significant gains in the past year makes it even more unlikely. I therefore find it difficult to believe that this editorial is not an open attack on Mao by Russian-indoctrinated and Russian-controlled

---

[39] Mao Tse-tung, Chairman of the Central Executive Committee of the Chinese Communist Party.

[40] For summary, see memorandum of January 12, 1948, by the Chief of the Division of Chinese Affairs (Ringwalt), *Foreign Relations*, 1948, vol. VII, p. 29.

Chinese Communists, in an effort to bring Communist China under strict Russian control. If this is so, it is 1926–27 all over again, and the issues between Mao and Moscow are precisely those raised at that time.

The bearing of all this on policy matters under discussion is obvious. If the conclusion above is true it indicates that Moscow's effort to move in and take over Chinese Communist policy is beginning earlier than expected; that it has advanced sufficiently to force an open discussion of the questions involved; that apparently infiltration has already had considerable success among the propaganda services of the Chinese Communists; and that Mao probably will soon be faced with the alternatives of yielding control of policy to these elements or of fighting back.

If Mao fights back, he will undoubtedly have to seek strength wherever he can find it. Unless he is knocked out promptly by a Russian takeover, there should therefore be an excellent chance of success for the policy toward China recommended by CP [41] for the United States.

893.00/1–749 : Telegram

The Consul General at Shanghai (Cabot) to the Secretary of State

SHANGHAI, January 7, 1949.
[Received January 7—3 :58 p. m.]

63. Most Shanghai papers January 7 give prominent coverage Carsun Chang's [42] statement yesterday on peace possibilities. Chang states key to door of peace lies in reviving freedom of discussion political problems. Government ban on past peace discussions made it impossible for anyone to work for nonmilitary settlement. Chang urges that non-Kmt political leaders who in past have had close connections with CCP be invited join peace negotiations to utilize their knowledge Communist policies. Declares that some Communists including Chou En-lai and Tung Pi-wu [43] not unmindful of China's welfare and inclined towards negotiated peace. Believes official Communist silence on Government peace overtures may reflect contention in Communist leadership views. Communists well aware their own military and political capacities and realize they can't swallow whole country one gulp. Therefore still hope for peace parleys. Chang discounts possibilities of foreign mediation.

Sent Nanking 50, repeated Department 63.

CABOT

---

[41] Division of Commercial Policy.
[42] Leader of the Chinese Democratic Socialist Party, with headquarters at Shanghai.
[43] Chinese Communist member of the Chinese delegation to the San Francisco Conference to organize the United Nations in 1945.

893.00/1–749 : Telegram

The Consul General at Tientsin (Smyth) to the Secretary of State

TIENTSIN, January 7, 1949—3 p. m.
[Received 4 :47 p. m.]

20. In conversation with Mayor Tu last night he said situation very bad, saw no prospect holding out against Communists. He said Communists stepping up attacks and believed only thing now preventing entry into city was land mines laid just outside defense moat around city.

Mayor said worst situation was inside city. With factories, shops, etc., closing, more than 200,000 out of work with more thousands unemployed added daily. Also 100,000 refugees and 40,000 defeated troops from Manchuria. He said Government military had food for 3 months but food for civilians would not last many weeks.

Mayor said actions of Government military in city were disgraceful and getting worse. Most of his difficulties were with Government military who have no regard for civilians.

Mayor remarked universal desire all civilians for peace. He knew nothing about peace for all China but indicated peace for North China might be possible. He personally felt peace should be made as soon as possible to end people's sufferings.

Tempo action around Tientsin much increased last 2 nights, continuing today. Quite heavy mortar artillery, some small arms fire. Some wounded also in evidence from fighting at Huitui taken by Communists yesterday and from western outskirts.

Sent Department 20, repeated Nanking 21, Peiping 15, Shanghai 18.

SMYTH

893.00/1–749 : Telegram

The Consul General at Shanghai (Cabot) to the Secretary of State

SHANGHAI, January 7, 1949.
[Received January 7—1 :47 p. m.]

62. Peace offensive continues as Chinese National Federation of Chambers of Commerce issues appeal January 6 signed by chairman Wang Hsiao-lai calling on Government and Communist leaders for immediate cease-fire and peace negotiations. Also asks national civic, business, industrial and agricultural associations to send representatives to Shanghai to form national peace consultation body which will cooperate with minor political parties in nominating emissaries for purpose conveying public hope for peace to major party leaders. Appeal states, "his (Gimo's) personal future—his retirement or remaining in office—is immaterial. He will follow the will of the people".

China Press reports over 2,000 delegates attending peace rally held January 6 hear Shanghai City Council chairman Pan Kung-chan and others urge local populace to promote peace and defend city. "Peace is our sole aim and in case the Communists ignore the appeal of the people and continue their destruction work to the negligence of the people's lives and property, then the 6,000,000 people in Shanghai will have to concentrate their manpower and wealth and endeavor to protect their lives and properties with the spirit of a blessed martyr. If they (the Communists) want peace and to alleviate the sufferings of the people, they should lay down their arms in North China first and send delegates to Shanghai to talk peace." Pan concludes by asking local populace to contribute manpower and wealth toward concentrated effort protect Shanghai and to donate articles for comforting soldiers fighting at front.

Several vernacular papers report that over 100 local college professors will soon hold meeting to arrange peace telegram to Government and CCP and to prepare proposals for reforms conducive to the restoration of peace. Vernacular press also reports spokesman of Democratic Socialist Party as advocating impartial personages of various quarters to build "bridge of peace" between Kmt and CCP.

Sent Nanking as 48; repeated Department 62.

CABOT

893.00/1–849 : Telegram

The Consul General at Shanghai (Cabot) to the Secretary of State

SHANGHAI, January 8, 1949.
[Received January 8—1:34 p. m.]

66. *China Daily Tribune* January 8 reports Shanghai Bankers Associations address messages Generalissimo and Mao Tse-tung urging peace. Yesterday motor car floats accompanied by music parade through Shanghai streets distributing handbills, leaflets with motif of peace.

Sent Nanking 52, repeated Department 66.

CABOT

893.00/1–849 : Telegram

The Ambassador in China (Stuart) to the Secretary of State

NANKING, January 8, 1949—9 a. m.
[Received 7:52 p. m.]

58. Flushed with victory Communists are casting defiance at those who seek peace and giving every indication they will cease hostilities only on terms dictated by them. Meanwhile, Generalissimo's New

Year's statement has started growing and irresistible demand for peace and Kmt leaders, except Generalissimo, are in quandary how to move. Communists' publications of war criminal list, their vituperative New Year's Day broadcast (see Embtel 14, January 4), their first violent reaction to Generalissimo's New Year message (see Embtel 42, January 5) and their latest broadcast calling for repudiation by Nationalist Government of all treaties with US, add up to attitude of intransigence which offers little encouragement to Kmt peace seekers. Its effect on Generalissimo has, of course, been to confirm his opinion of incorrigibility of Communists and to sharpen his decision continue resistance. It is reported he massing what troops available for all out resistance in Nanking–Shanghai area. Meanwhile, Generalissimo moving large quantities gold, silver, other mobile assets to Taiwan and is apparently planning to make it an island fortress from which to continue fight against Communism. Appointment of Chen Cheng[44] and Chiang Ching-kuo[45] as Governor and Kmt Chief respectively of Taiwan, together with transfer air force headquarters, navy and industry to island, all confirm this intent. The effect of Generalissimo's New Year's Day speech, however, can not be undone. Regardless of cautious tone and even ambiguity of that statement, interpretation given it by press and public generally has snowballed into universal and powerful peace move throughout Nationalist territory. It is reported that at first rumors of peace, his hold over Kmt began to disintegrate and effect upon Nationalist troops along north Yangtze front can only be demoralizing to whatever fighting spirit may be left. It is difficult to see how even Generalissimo can combat or reverse this force now given public expression or regroup any semblance of Nationalist resistance to Communists once public disillusionment over chance of peace sets in. However, in his present plans, he will always have Taiwan to fall upon as outpost of continuing resistance.

This change of mind on Generalissimo's part (if indeed it represents a change at all) [will] leave Vice President and his peace-seeking Ministers in an intolerable position. Their earlier feverish political activity is now paralyzed by Generalissimo's growing conviction that negotiation with Communists is impossible and that continued resistance all the way to Taiwan is only course. The recent behavior of Pai Chung-hsi (see Embtel 2678, December 31[46]) has aroused Generalissimo's suspicions and it is reported that even Li Tsung-jen is under surveillance. All this would seem to increase dilemma of "peace group" in Cabinet and may lead to open break between Generalissimo

---

[44] Former Chinese Minister of War, Chief of the General Staff, and Director of Generalissimo Chiang Kai-shek's Northeast (Manchurian) Headquarters.

[45] Son of Generalissimo Chiang Kai-shek.

[46] *Foreign Relations*, 1948, vol. VII, p. 722.

and "peace Ministers" led by Li and Pai. Accordingly most likely immediate developments would appear to be resumption military pressure by Communists, further deterioration Nationalists' will to resist and condemned authority of Generalissimo as head of Government with resultant paralyzing effect on Li Tsung-jen and rest of peace party.

STUART

893.00/1–849 : Telegram

The Ambassador in China (Stuart) to the Secretary of State

NANKING, January 8, 1949—7 p. m.
[Received January 9—1 :06 p. m.]

61. I was called to Foreign Ministry this afternoon and handed an *aide-mémoire* by Wu Te-chen [47] suggesting that US Government along with British, French and Soviet Governments, act as intermediary for initiation of negotiations with Chinese Communist Party with view to attaining restoration of peace in China. Text of *aide-mémoire* follows:

"The Chinese people, true to their peaceful traditions, have always devoted themselves to the pursuit of international as well as domestic peace. In their long history, it was only when they were in the face of the danger of aggression that they took up arms in self-defense. For this reason, the people rose to resist the Japanese invaders, and later, through their close cooperation with their allies, World War II was carried to a successful conclusion. On the eve of victory, China took an active part in organizing and founding the United Nations in the hope that a foundation for world peace might thus be laid and international disputes settled by pacific means. For, it has long been the conviction of the Chinese people that it is only through the maintenance of peace that the continuity and development of human civilization can be ensured.

Following the surrender of Japan, the National Government immediately took steps to initiate and carry on peace negotiations with the Chinese Communist Party. Through the good offices personally offered by General Marshall [48] the Political Consulative Council was set up and a number of meetings took place. Unfortunately, the failure to reach a mutually satisfactory settlement led to a renewal of hostilities. Although these efforts proved abortive at the time, the Government and the people have never since abandoned the hope that hostilities may still be brought to an end.

---

[47] Vice President of the Chinese Executive Yuan and concurrently Minister for Foreign Affairs.
[48] General of the Army George C. Marshall was President Truman's special representative in China from December 1945 to January 1947. For documentation on the Marshall Mission to China, see *Foreign Relations*, 1945, vol. VII, pp. 745 ff. and *ibid.*, 1946, volumes IX and X.

However, in the wake of the long, gruelling struggle against Japan, this renewed conflict has inflicted untold suffering upon the masses and prevented the Government from carrying out the plans of reconstruction which it had prepared during the war with Japan. The ravages of war followed by rapid deterioration of the economic life of the nation make it imperative that peace be restored as soon as possible.

As nations today are unavoidably interdependent and international peace and stability depends largely upon degree to which international cooperation can be achieved, it would be difficult for any nation to confine the effect of its own unsettled conditions to itself. The Chinese Government is, therefore, most anxious that her internal situation should not in any way become an impediment to the progress of world peace.

In consideration of the above facts, the President of the Republic of China, in his New Year message on January 1st, announced without hesitation his determination for the restoration of peace in the country. The decision thus proclaimed by the President has since received the general support of the people, who have through numerous messages and public statements echoed their prompt support for a peaceful settlement of the questions at issue between the Government and the Communists.

The US Government has on many occasions in the past demonstrated its friendly concern over the state of affairs in China and has cooperated with the Chinese Government for the promotion of international peace. The Chinese Government wishes hereby to assure the US Government of its sincere desire for a peaceful settlement with the Chinese Communist Party and particularly avail itself of this opportunity to ascertain the views of the US Government on this subject. The Chinese Government will welcome any suggestion by the US Government which may lead to an early restoration of peace in China. The Chinese Government further signifies its readiness, through the possible intermediary of the US Government, to initiate negotiations with the Chinese Communist Party with a view to attaining the end stated above.

Similar notes are being communicated to the French, the Soviet and the British Governments. An early reply from the US Government will be greatly appreciated."

Foreign Minister said he was delivering identical notes to other three Ambassadors this afternoon and he hoped we would treat this approach with greatest secrecy. I made no comment on substance of note and said that I would transmit it promptly to my Government. At 7 this evening I am having conference with British and French Ambassadors [49] on this Chinese approach and will report subsequently their views.

Sent Department 61, repeated London, Paris, Moscow unnumbered.

STUART

---

[49] Sir Ralph Stevenson and Jacques Meyrier, respectively.

893.00/1–849

Memorandum of Conversation, by Mr. Cloyce K. Huston, Counselor of Mission, Office of United States Political Adviser in Japan [50]

Tokyo, January 8, 1949.

Mr. Chakravarty, Chief of the Indian Mission here, discussed at length certain issues involved in the prospects of early communist domination of China in my conversation with him yesterday. He said it seemed clear to him that the Nationalist cause was now hopeless, that anything like an honest coalition would be unacceptable to the communist leaders, and that the American policy of extending aid to Generalissimo Chiang Kai Shek had definitely failed. He believed that the situation was not necessarily desperate, however, and found one line of thinking which gave him hope: he did not believe Soviet Russia would find communist China a willing servant of Moscow nor that the Soviet Government would be happy to have a vast and potentially powerful but non-compliant state, even though communist, as an eastern neighbor. Neither did Mr. Chakravarty agree with those who say that the Chinese communist is not a genuine communist. He felt certain that the Chinese communists were sincere adherents to communist principles and philosophy, even though he expected them to manifest strong political independence from Moscow; he was even more sure that they would always remain primarily Chinese, citing particularly in support of this argument the strong force of Chinese culture, which has its roots in China itself.

Mr. Chakravarty recalled that, just prior to his leaving Nanking for Tokyo late last spring, he had had a conversation with the Soviet Ambassador [51] there, formerly Soviet Military Attaché in China for a number of years. When Mr. Chakravarty remarked that he supposed that it would be a source of gratification to Soviet Russia to see the emergence of a communist China, the Soviet Ambassador replied that he saw no reason why his Government should interfere in the Chinese situation, saying "let them fight it out themselves" and going on to admit that a huge communist state on Soviet Russia's eastern frontier would create serious problems for his Government. The Soviet Ambassador implied that because of its vast extent and huge population China would prove to be "indigestible" even to the communist appetite, and concluded his remarks by saying: "let the Americans pour all the money they wish into China—it will only make them weaker".

---

[50] Copy transmitted to the Department by the acting Political Adviser in Japan (Sebald) in his despatch No. 18, January 8; received January 25.
[51] Maj. Gen. N. V. Roschin.

Mr. Chakravarty then went on to say that Soviet Russia was well content to have a number of small states, communist or not, on its eastern periphery, as they would constitute convenient buffers and offer no threat, but that a communist state of the magnitude and importance of China would not be an unmitigated blessing in any sense; it would undoubtedly not [sic] develop the same propensities for dissension and independence as had Yugoslavia, but on a vastly greater scale, and the Soviet Union would be forced as a result to maintain large military forces in the East. Mr. Chakravarty did not pretend to see the future too clearly, but concluded that the foregoing line of thinking gave him some hope that present communist successes in China would not necessarily serve to further Russian expansion but indeed might ultimately work to weaken the Soviet position in the East.

CLOYCE K. HUSTON

893.00/1–949 : Telegram

The Ambassador in China (Stuart) to the Secretary of State

NANKING, January 9, 1949—2 p. m.
[Received January 9—8 :51 a. m.]

62. At suggestion of my French colleague I met with him and British Ambassador last evening to discuss the Chinese approach to the four powers for restoration of peace in China (mytel 61, January 8). Both my colleagues said that they had made no comment to Foreign Minister other than to agree to transmit the substance of note promptly to their Governments.

During the course of our discussions last evening it became apparent that we were all agreed on following points:

1. That this is an effort by Chinese Government to play for time at this critical period;

2. That it is also effort to avoid loss of face by requesting others to perform unpleasant task of approaching Communists; that if Government were sincerely desirous of getting in touch with Communists, it could do so without outside assistance;

3. No possible chance of successful mediation unless all four powers willing act in concert and it is most unlikely that USSR would agree to participate;

4. Even if USSR agreed, it is doubtful its participation would be in good faith and thus ineffective on CCP.

We further agreed that there was nothing that we could do here other than transmit note to our respective Governments and await their instructions.

Department in its discretion please pass London and Paris.

STUART

893.00/1–1049 : Telegram

The Ambassador in China (Stuart) to the Secretary of State

NANKING, January 10, 1949—4 p. m.
[Received January 10—7:36 a. m.]

64. Perhaps we are unduly suspicious but there is possibility which should not be overlooked that prior understanding between Chinese Government and Soviet Embassy already exists re Saturday's approach for mediation (see Embtels 61, Jan. 8, and 62, Jan. 9). Should Soviets already have indicated willingness to mediate with CCP at Chinese Government request, it is obvious Chinese would have approached all four as they have done. Department will have noted that Chinese Government note does not suggest joint mediation but speaks only of "intermediary of the US Government". Since USSR received identical note, it would not be inappropriate for them to proceed on unilateral basis in mediating role should that for any reason seem expedient. It may, therefore, be desirable for our Embassy Moscow approach Soviet Foreign Office promptly on its reaction and feasibility of joint approach in attempt to forestall possible unilateral action by USSR with accompanying prestige attaching to any successful move to end hostilities here.

Department please pass Moscow in its discretion.

STUART

893.00/1–1049

Memorandum by the Director of the Policy Planning Staff (Kennan) [52]

[WASHINGTON,] January 10, 1949.

The concern of this Government for the re-establishment of peace and order in China is beyond question. (Record)

In the present instance, the initiative for disorder and bloodshed has clearly come from the Chinese communists, who are attacking the legitimate and recognized government of China. It is primarily to the communists that appeals for a cessation of hostilities would have to be addressed.

We have no reason to expect that the communists would be amenable to any appeals based on humanitarian considerations or on the obvious need of the Chinese people for the restoration of peace and order. We have also no reason to believe that the Chinese communist leaders would be inclined to pay serious heed to the views of the United States people, whose motives and aspirations they have been

---

[52] Copies sent to the Director of the Office of Far Eastern Affairs (Butterworth) and the Counselor of the Department (Bohlen).

maliciously maligning and distorting for years in their press and radio.

We recall that on other occasions, when this Government has endeavored to mediate, jointly with the Soviet Government, between communist parties and other political groupings of the same country, the only result was that these efforts were exploited by the communist side as one more stepping-stone on the road to the establishment of communist totalitarian dictatorship.

For these reasons, we doubt that any useful purpose would be served by a four-power effort at mediation.

893.00/1–1049

Memorandum by the Director of the Office of Far Eastern Affairs (Butterworth) to the Acting Secretary of State

[WASHINGTON,] January 10, 1949.

Subject: Chinese Government Proposal That the U.S. Government Act as an Intermediary in Initiating Negotiations With the Chinese Communist Party

Discussion:

Ambassador Stuart, in his telegram No. 61 of January 8, quotes an *aide-mémoire* from the Chinese Government proposing that the U.S. Government act as an intermediary in initiating negotiations with the Chinese Communist Party for the purpose of restoring peace in China. The *aide-mémoire* states that similar notes have been sent to the British, French and Soviet Ambassadors at Nanking. In his telegram No. 62 of January 9 the Ambassador reports his discussion of the matter with his British and French colleagues and their agreement on the following points:

1. The proposal represents a Chinese Government effort to play for time at this critical period.
2. It is an effort to avoid loss of face by requesting foreign powers to approach the Communists, an approach the Chinese Government could make if it so desired.
3. Mediation could not possibly succeed unless all four powers were willing to act in concert and it is most unlikely that the USSR would agree to participate.
4. Even if the USSR agreed to participate, its good faith would be doubtful and it would thus be ineffective in relation to the Chinese Communist Party.

In his telegram No. 64 of January 10, the Ambassador questions point 3 above and indicates the possibility that there may have been prior understanding between the Chinese Government and the Soviet Embassy for the proposal, the wording making it possible for the USSR to act as an intermediary on a unilateral basis. The Ambassador suggests that we might approach the USSR regarding the feasibility of a joint approach in an attempt to forestall possible unilateral action by the USSR with the accompanying prestige attaching to a successful move to end hostilities.

Various factors should be considered in connection with possible U.S. participation in an intermediary role:

1. The U.S. would be placed in the position of responsibility for seeking to form a coalition government with Chinese Communist participation, which would inevitably mean Communist domination. This would have extremely undesirable repercussions, particularly in France and Italy, as well as Japan and other areas of the Far East, and would affect the European Recovery Program and Western Union. It would also have unfavorable domestic reactions.

2. U.S. participation in an intermediary role would involve U.S. responsibility for whatever resulted from its action. The previous U.S. exercise of its good offices in China has resulted in criticism by Chinese Government officials who seek to place upon the U.S. a measure of responsibility for subsequent developments allegedly arising from the Chinese Government's negotiations with the Communists.

3. It is not certain that the USSR would refuse to act as an intermediary. If the three western powers were to refuse, the USSR might accept and utilize this action as propaganda material charging the western powers with "war mongering" and describing its action as evidence of its desire for peace. There would seem to be no possibility, however, that the three western powers could act in concert with the USSR as intermediaries. The USSR would obviously seek to obtain international sanction for Chinese Communist domination of China and, in view of the present strong military position of the Chinese Communists, would have in the background the threat of Communist military action as the decisive bargaining weapon in its hands.

4. The Chinese Government is undoubtedly playing for time and may be seeking to involve the western powers. Without Soviet participation there would be no chance of success, since the Chinese Communists in their present strong military position need not look with favor on negotiations and might even refuse to negotiate with the present Chinese Government.

The British Embassy has informed us that the matter will be taken up in the British Cabinet today and that the Foreign Office has indicated that it would like to act in general accord with the U.S. Government on the problem. The British Embassy also states that the British Government has approached the French Government in this regard.

Recommendations:

Attached is a suggested reply [53] to the Chinese Government's *aide-mémoire* for your approval and submission to the President. This affords us an opportunity to set the record clear with respect to General

---

[53] *Infra.*

Marshall's mission to China, an approach which cannot, of course, be made by the British and French Governments. The reply reviews the history of the previous U.S. good offices effort and concludes that no good purpose would be served by the U.S. Government's acting as an intermediary. It is suggested that the President's approval be obtained for the rejection of the Chinese proposal and the general tone of the reply, rather than the specific wording, in order to allow for such revision as may be necessary to meet the British desires in the matter, assuming that the British Government also declines the proposal.

893.00/1–849

Draft Prepared by the Chief of the Division of Chinese Affairs (Sprouse)[54]

AIDE-MÉMOIRE

[Here follow the first four paragraphs of this draft which are the same as those of the final text.]

The negotiations between the Chinese Government and the Chinese Communist Party subsequently broke down and the various agreements were not implemented. The United States Government, therefore, after having made every effort to bring peace to China, considered that it had no alternative to withdrawal from its position as an intermediary.

Since that time many Chinese Government officials have sought to place upon the United States a measure of responsibility for developments in China allegedly arising from the negotiations. There has been repeated criticism of the United States Government for what was an honest and sincere effort to assist the Chinese in bringing peace to China through implementation of the fundamental political agreements arising out of the Chinese Government's negotiations with the Chinese Communist Party immediately after the Japanese surrender.

In the light of the foregoing, it is not believed that any useful purpose would be served by the United States Government's attempting to act as an intermediary in initiating negotiations with the Chinese Communist Party. Although the United States Government has traditionally maintained close and friendly relations with the Government of the Republic of China and the people of the United States have always manifested a sympathetic interest in and genuine friendship for the people of China, the United States Government

---

[54] Initialed by Mr. Butterworth and "cleared in substance" with the Director of the Policy Planning Staff (Kennan). Notation added by Mr. Sprouse: "Read by Mr. Lovett to the President on January 10, 1949. The President approved, subject to the deletion of two sentences." For text as sent after revisions, see telegram No. 43, January 12, 7 p. m., to the Ambassador in China, p. 41.

holds the view that the solution of China's problems is one that must and can be reached only by the Chinese themselves.

WASHINGTON, [undated.]

893.00/1–1049 : Telegram

The Consul General at Shanghai (Cabot) to the Secretary of State

SHANGHAI, January 10, 1949.
[Received January 10—9 :30 p. m.]

74. *Tung Nan Jih Pao*, Kmt Southeast China organ, January 10 has January 9 Nanking despatch stating Communist Party has formally replied to Chiang's New Year peace message and offered resume peace talks under following 5 conditions:

1. Re-election of President and Vice President;
2. Revision of constitution;
3. Demarcation of areas held by Government and Communist forces;
4. Final reckoning for war criminals;
5. Formation coalition government in which Kuomintang have one-third seats, Communists one-third and other parties and groups one-third.

Sent Nanking 56; repeated Department 74.

CABOT

893.00/1–1049 : Telegram

The Consul General at Tientsin (Smyth) to the Secretary of State

TIENTSIN, January 10, 1949—4 p. m.
[Received January 11—5 :21 a. m.]

33. Local Government military have surprised everyone, including Military Command, by quite vigorous resistance thus far. While not showing any offensive spirit, they have shown considerable tenacity in defense. Communists have gradually closed in around city and in most sectors Government troops are now behind defense moat circling city. Communists reportedly only penetrated defense moat once, last night in western sector, but were driven back by machine gun fire. Resistance of Government troops may be due to the fact they are being well-fed with repeated cash bonuses for those on front line. (While doing fairly well against Communists, military treatment of populace is pretty bad.)

Comparatively few casualties reported in hospitals considering heavy fighting reported. However, this is not accurate gauge of factual casualties as Government forces have no organization to bring in wounded. Only those few wounded who can come in by themselves get coolies or rickshas to help reach hospitals.

Government forces have made prodigal use of mortar, artillery and small arms, and [it] seems doubtful whether present rate ammunition consumption can be kept up very long unless Government has large reserve stock here. Estimate at least 80% gunfire up to now from Government side.

Communists thus far obviously refraining from any general shelling of city. Some Communists shelling inside defense moat is known such as interdiction fire on race course air strip but this limited so far to times when planes attempted to operate (with exception few shells January 7). Other shells in central station area and western line district but it seems clear Communists have been trying to avoid any really destructive shelling of city. Also observers note many of Communists' shells which have fallen in city have fuses removed, indicating effort to limit destruction; no duds at airfield, however.

Communist operations against city so far seem to have been probing attacks attempting to find weak defense spot. Garrison Headquarters officer remarked yesterday Communists have found city defense system and defenders much stronger than expected and he expressed opinion Communists might possibly sit down around city and wait. for food to be exhausted. Believe Communists could take city if they made serious effort but they may not wish to sustain undue casualties or destroy parts of city by heavy shelling when waiting will accomplish same purpose. Mayor believes military food supplies sufficient for 3 months but Garrison Headquarters says not so much, civilian food supplies much less.

Since Government military retired to defense moat less than mile away and only open space between, our Consular houses definitely within Communist mortar and machine gun range. Houses nearly 3 miles from our office, as now impossible proceed to office at night, due strict curfew and tugger [trigger-] happy sentries, not to mention possibility interdiction by Communist gun fire or machine guns. Wellborn [55] and I spending nights in town where we can reach office, if necessary. Houses visited daily. No damage so far, but we will be lucky if houses come through present situation intact, particularly if Communists choose that area for attack.

Sent Department 33, repeated Nanking 31, Peiping 27, Shanghai 28.

SMYTH

---

[55] Alfred T. Wellborn, Consul at Tientsin.

893.00/1–1049 : Telegram

The Ambassador in France (Caffery) to the Secretary of State

PARIS, January 10, 1949—8 p. m.
[Received January 11—8:50 a. m.]

105. Chauvel [56] showed me today two telegrams from Nanking regarding the Chinese request for four-power good offices in China. The French Government is replying that it is asking the intentions of the other interested Governments. He says France will take no position at all until she hears from the other Governments and especially from US.

Sent Department 105, repeated London 25, Moscow as 10 and Nanking as 2.

CAFFERY

893.00/1–1149 : Telegram

The Consul General at Shanghai (Cabot) to the Secretary of State

SHANGHAI, January 11, 1949—10 a. m.
[Received January 11—12:19 a. m.]

82. Shanghai English language press reports Madam Sun Yat-sen statement that all rumors regarding her assuming any office or responsibility in Government [are] without foundation.

From sources close to Madam Sun we have reason believe press reports correct.

Sent Nanking 62, repeated Department.

CABOT

893.00/1–1149 : Telegram

The Ambassador in China (Stuart) to the Secretary of State

NANKING, January 11, 1949—noon.
[Received January 11—3:56 a. m.]

73. As possible indication French China policy is comment French Ambassador in discussing Chinese request for mediation (our 61, January 8, and 62, January 9) to effect that given repercussions Indochina of Communist regime in China, French interest required supporting any regime in China resisting Communism. This was true, he said, even though eventual collapse such resistance was inevitable as France would at least gain time.

Sent Department 73; repeated Paris 1.

STUART

---

[56] Jean Chauvel, Secretary General of the French Foreign Office.

893.00/1–1149 : Telegram

The Consul General at Shanghai (Cabot) to the Secretary of State

SHANGHAI, January 11, 1949.
[Received January 11—5:52 a. m.]

85. Vernacular press January 10 reports telegram appealing for peace sent to Generalissimo and Mao Tse-tung by All China Federation of Shipping Guilds signed by Tu Yueh-sheng, chairman.

Sent Nanking 67, repeated Department 85.

CABOT

893.00/1–1149 : Telegram

The Consul General at Peiping (Clubb) to the Secretary of State

PEIPING, January 11, 1949—2 p. m.
[Received January 12—12:47 p. m.]

25. Information received several quarters indicates conference delegates different parties excluding Kuomintang now in progress Shih-chiachuang. Previously mentioned Chang Tung-sun and three others, all of whom presumably Democratic League, are reported to now have left Peiping en route that point January 7.

Official US secretariat re matter opines general conference has as task unifying views of different groups in anticipation ultimate establish[ment] coalition government. He professed no information Li Chi-shen had arrived,[57] stated further Chu An-ping [58] (Shanghai 60, January 7 to Department [59]) was in town 10 days ago but present whereabouts unknown. (About week previously Hsu Ying, editor Peiping *Ta Kung Pao*, and other workers newspaper were held temporarily under unofficial house arrest on suspicion they knew whereabouts subject person.)

Same informant confirmed neither Fu nor Teng Pao-shan (vice commander NCBSH [60] who was earlier reported be takeover candidate should Fu renounce local duties and proceed Nanking) has yet proceeded Nanking or intends do so. He indicated present policy Fu's camp was to hold present position until changed situation Nanking might permit new departure North China, confirmed likewise fighting Peiping still only nature small clashes.

Informant was aware representatives Tientsin Peoples Political Council were making effort bring about truce Tientsin area but gave no indication either popular or official delegates had contact Commu-

---

[57] See footnote 34, p. 12.
[58] Editor of the banned *Observer Weekly*.
[59] Not printed.
[60] North China Bandit-Suppression Headquarters.

nists Peiping to same end. Note Shihchiachuang conference by all indications has no reference to question local truce.

Sent Department 25, Nanking 24, Shanghai 29, Tientsin 13.

CLUBB

893.00 Yunnan/1–1149 : Telegram

The Vice Consul at Kunming (Lutkins) to the Secretary of State

KUNMING, January 11, 1949.
[Received January 11—2:32 p.m.]

At a meeting held January 8, the Standing Committee of Yunnan Provincial Council decided (1) to telegraph Generalissimo and Mao Tze-tung requesting both sides to cease hostilities immediately and to invite representatives of different parties and groups to mediate; (2) to wire Ambassadors of Big Four requesting that they come forward and mediate; (3) organize movement to work for peace composed of representatives of all classes and groups.

Repeated to Shanghai and Nanking.

LUTKINS

893.00/1–1149

Memorandum of Conversation, by the Chief of the Division of Chinese Affairs (Sprouse)

[WASHINGTON,] January 11, 1949.

Subject: Chinese Proposal for Powers to Act as Intermediary

Mr. Daridan [61] called by appointment this afternoon in connection with the above-mentioned subject. He said that the French Government had not reached a decision regarding the Chinese proposal and was interested in learning the U.S. Government's attitude. I informed him that the question was under consideration but that no decision had yet been reached.

In answer to my inquiries, Mr. Daridan said that the French Government had indicated to its Embassy here that it would not unilaterally act as an intermediary. He also said that the French Government wished to concert its action in this matter with the British and U.S. Governments, and possibly the Soviet Government. Mr. Daridan pointed out that it was the French view that the United States was the nation in the strongest position in China with respect to such action and that the French Government would be likely to follow whatever course was decided upon by the U.S. Government.

I told Mr. Daridan that I would inform him as soon as possible of the reaction of the U.S. Government to the Chinese proposal. He said

---

[61] Jean Daridan, Counselor of the French Embassy in the United States.

that this would be helpful to the French Government in reaching its
decision.

_____

893.00/1–1149

The British Embassy to the Department of State

Mr. Bevin's [62] Views on the Chinese Approach for Intervention

These are my preliminary reactions. It is obvious that we cannot
delay our reply to the Chinese Government too long, if only because it
is going to be difficult to continue to deny that any approach by them
has been received.

On the whole I am inclined to think that intervention would be a
mistake. First because it is unlikely that such intervention would
materially alter the course of events and secondly because the failure
of the Western Powers to intervene successfully can only be expected
to react unfavourably upon their future relations with China.   I share
the view of Sir R. Stevenson that apart from the desire to gain time the
Chinese Government's approach is designed to put the blame upon
others for the situation which is likely to be created.   If we are correct
in assuming that mediation is unlikely to change the course of events
then the blame is likely to be placed on us for abandoning China to
the Communists.   Equally we should be held responsible for bringing
a regime into existence in China which sooner or later will be communist dominated.

My preliminary inclination would therefore be politely to decline
the Chinese request.   In so doing we might point to the fact that our
policy towards China is governed by the Moscow Declaration of 27th
December 1945,[63] in which we stated that we were in agreement as to
the need for a unified and democratic China under the National Government for broader participation by democratic elements in all
branches of the National Government and for a cessation of civil strife.
We also reaffirmed our adherence to the policy of non-intervention in
the internal affairs of China.   We might go on to say that we are
reluctant to intervene in the internal affairs of China since the future
of that country can after all only ultimately be determined by the
Chinese people themselves but we might express the hope for an early
termination of hostilities in order to relieve the suffering of the people.

If we should decide to reply to the Chinese on the lines of the foregoing paragraph we still have to consider what the Soviet Union will
be likely to do.   They might equally well abstain from intervention

_____

[62] Ernest Bevin, British Secretary of State for Foreign Affairs.
[63] For the communiqué on the Moscow Conference of Three Foreign Ministers,
December 27, 1945, see telegram 4284, December 27, 1945, 3 a. m., from Moscow,
Foreign Relations, 1945, vol. II, p. 815; or Department of State *Bulletin*, December 30, 1945, p. 1027.

since events are on the whole moving in their favour. If on the other hand they alone should decide to intervene then it is doubtful whether such intervention would in fact produce any different result. Too active an intervention by the Soviet Union might on the contrary tend eventually to antagonise the Chinese people. The Soviet Union will no doubt be waiting for us to put a foot wrong and on our present estimates we are more likely to do that if we intervene than if we do not.

When we and the Americans and the French have made up our minds I do not think we can escape the necessity for consultation with the Soviet Union and if we wait too long to do this we shall be open to the suspicion of having framed our attitude. To this extent therefore there is also some need for urgency.

I should be grateful to learn the views of the United States Government.

11 JANUARY, 1949.

893.00/1–1149 : Telegram

The Consul General at Tientsin (Smyth) to the Secretary of State

TIENTSIN, January 11, 1949—5 p. m.
[Received 11:30 p. m.]

39. Following account peace delegation (ourtel 28, Jan. 8 [64]) visit to Communist Headquarters obtained confidentially by Chinese our staff from reporter who got information from delegate.

Delegation returned here this morning having seen Lin Piao's Chief Staff, name unknown, at spot on Taching River in Chinghaihsien. Chief Staff said Communist offensive being stopped 24 hours beginning 6 p. m., January 10 to give Tientsin garrison commander Chen time consider following surrender terms: (1) disarming all Nationalist troops, (2) keep order in city and preserve warehouse stocks, (3) Communists guarantee safety Nationalist officers, dependents and property and option go Nationalist areas. Chief Staff said if resistance kept up, Communists had sufficient forces take city and would not hesitate level it if needed.

Delegates asked Chief Staff help them go to Peiping present terms to Fu Tso-yi but got reply Communist could not delay capture Tientsin.

Delegates now seeing Chen. Delegates supposed return to Communist lines before 6 p. m. today with Chen's reply.

Sent Department 39, repeated Nanking 38, Shanghai 33, Peiping 31.

SMYTH

---

[64] Not printed; four members of the Tientsin City Council undertook the mission.

893.00/1-1149 : Telegram

The Ambassador in France (Caffery) to the Secretary of State

PARIS, January 11, 1949—8 p. m.
[Received January 11—4:09 p. m.]

114. While French are sounding out Soviets as well as British and ourselves on Chinese mediation proposal (my 105, January 10), Foreign Office informs us approach to Soviets is perfunctory and consists only of having French Embassy Moscow ask Kremlin for indication of Soviet views. While Foreign Office does not expect favorable reply from Moscow in view of their reports that Nanking Government's approaches to Chinese Communists have gone without response except for sarcastic statements on Communist radio, French inclined to view that something should be done in slim hope of slowing up Red control of South China. (In this they are of course motivated by fear of effect on Indochina). Foreign Office also seems to expect negative reaction from US and British. (In this connection British Embassy has just shown us instructions from London to British Embassy Washington indicating British think it would be mistake to accept Chinese proposal.)

Sent Department 114, repeated London 28, Moscow 11, Nanking 32.

CAFFERY

893.9111 RR/1-1249 : Telegram

The Consul General at Shanghai (Cabot) to the Secretary of State

SHANGHAI, January 12, 1949—6 p. m.
[Received January 12—12:48 p. m.]

114. Re Contel 87, January 12 (repeated Department 109).[65] These press items together with other indications such as those reported in Contel 50, January 7 (repeated Department 63) and classified telegrams 28, January 6 (repeated Department as 36) and 39 January 7 (repeated Department as 50)[66] suggest vague pattern something as follows: Certain Nanking Government elements from factions which combined to elect Li Tsung-jen as Vice President and subsequently hoped to build a reformed regime uniting Nanking liberals with outside dissident elements such as Li Chi-shen's KmtRC, seem to be joining in hurried attempt led by the noisy C-C clique–Tu Yueh-sheng[67] combine to produce at Shanghai a conglomerate of all available elements of actual or professed neutral character, which could hold together long enough to pose as powerful third party ready and

---

[65] Not printed.
[66] Last two not printed.
[67] Shanghai political leader.

able to mediate between Nationalists and Communists. It would include leftists as bait to contact and interest Communists.

Without attempting premature analysis, we conjecture that this "movement" reflects among other things:

(1) Genuine peace objectives of all elements concerned;

(2) Desperate conviction of many that foreign mediation is by no means certain of obtainment and that internal mediating force must be somehow manufactured;

(3) Belief of former Government reformist enthusiasts that Li Chi-shen's departure to Communist territory ends all hope for establishing liberal anti-Communists' Government;

(4) Belief that Shanghai's internal atmosphere renders it best suited for peace talks;

(5) Purely selfish desire of C-C–Tu combine and other unscrupulous elements to involve US in protecting Shanghai to save their interests;

(6) Probable willingness of some local leftists join movement provided they can make political capital therefrom.

It is also probable that importance and scope of movement are being magnified by local Kmt press.

Sent Nanking 91, repeated Department.

CABOT

893.00/1–1249 : Telegram

The Chargé in the Soviet Union (Kohler) to the Secretary of State

Moscow, January 12, 1949—6 p. m.
[Received January 12—2 :49 p. m.]

86. Embassy does not expect Soviet Union react favorably Chinese mediation approach (Nanking 61, January 8). Action of CCP in naming Chiang and other Kmt leaders as war criminals, Tass denial press reports regarding possible Soviet mediation (Embtel 3, January 2 [68]) and attacks on "peace feelers" by Communist press outside Russia (Paris 85, January 7, to Department [68]) would seem accurately forecast Soviet attitude toward proposition now made by China.

Considerations motivating Soviet and CCP positions (which at least on this point Embassy assumes to be synonymous) undoubtedly include following:

(1) While coalition government remains for CCP as for other Communist parties classic objective, in present case CCP and Soviets probably see neither necessity nor desirability try achieve such objective through negotiations with present Kmt Government. On contrary, kind of coalition desired by CCP easily obtainable if present Kmt leadership—now branded war criminals—completely replaced.

---

[68] Not printed.

After all, Mao's stated objective is overthrow Kmt Government. (Nanking 85, November 21.[69])

(2) Soviets, believing time on their side, may see no advantage intervening now at Chiang Government request when it may expect CCP later establish government on own independent terms. Meanwhile CCP may more profitably concentrate consolidating territory now under control.

(3) Rejection negotiate present Kmt Government leaves Soviets and CCP completely free proceed deliberately to establishing own type "coalition" regime including such elements Li Chi-shen, other Kmt dissidents and representatives fellow-traveling parties.

(4) Both Soviets and CCP confident present Chinese Government possesses seeds own rapid decay and collapse. If such coalition, as suggested 3 above established, it would provide powerful attraction to any lingering or successor Kmt regime. Furthermore, Soviets and CCP undoubtedly confident that Western Powers can and will do nothing prevent such eventualities.

With regard question identity Stalin's [70] and Mao's policies, and plans for China, Embassy finds no evidence of divergence. As frequently reported by Nanking, CCP policy seems support Kremlin more openly than ever. Interestingly, Jap CP organ *Akahata* editorialized December 11 "Victory People's Liberation Army Is Victory CCP, Victory Marxism–Leninism".

However, foregoing by no means rules our [*out*] possibility Stalin may have misgivings about future docility headstrong Chinese offspring flushed with victory and sense own importance. Present silence Soviet press on China may indicate satisfactory agreement not yet worked out on nature and policies new Communist government for China. Unquestionably Soviets feel keenly overriding necessity prevent Tito-like defection China and therefore proceeding cautiously. Meanwhile, parties outside Soviet Union, without responsibility for future guidance China, exploit CCP victories to maximum, thus enhancing own prestige and the world Communist movement.

With regard to US reply to Chinese note, Embassy ventures only to comment that mediation by four powers offers little hope, that prospect of coalition government, regardless of Soviet attitude, is uninviting, and that best advice for China may be rally forces to maintain National Government within reduced territory on firmly established base so China, with broadened and reformed government including non-Kmt parties but no Communists.

Sent Department 86, repeated Nanking 6, Tokyo 4, London as 12, Paris as 17.

KOHLER

---

[69] Telegram No. 2273 to the Department; *Foreign Relations*, 1948, vol. VII, p. 593.
[70] Josif Vissarionovich Stalin, Soviet Prime Minister and President of the Council of Ministers of the Soviet Union.

893.00/1–1249

Memorandum by the Director of the Office of Far Eastern Affairs (Butterworth) to the Acting Secretary of State

[WASHINGTON,] January 12, 1949.

Attached is a document [71] handed me this afternoon by Mr. Graves, Counselor of the British Embassy, in which is quoted the British reply declining the Chinese proposal that the British Government act as an intermediary in initiating negotiations with the Chinese Communists.

The British Government indicates that it expects to notify the Soviet Government of its reply. I have informed Mr. Graves, after consultation with our Soviet experts, that we do not expect to inform the Soviets of our action in this matter. We are informing the French Embassy this afternoon that we are declining the Chinese proposal.

———————

893.00/1–1249

Memorandum of Conversation, by the Chief of the Division of Chinese Affairs (Sprouse)

[WASHINGTON,] January 12, 1949.

At my request, Mr. Daridan called this afternoon in connection with the Chinese proposal that foreign powers act as intermediaries in initiating negotiations with the Chinese Communists. I informed Mr. Daridan that, in the light of our past experience, we were declining the Chinese request. I further stated that we were informing the British Government of our action as well as the French Government, but that we were not informing the USSR, our reply to the Chinese *aide-mémoire* being based upon the assumption that the Chinese had approached each government unilaterally in this matter. I asked him if his Embassy had had any further indication of the French Government's attitude in this regard.

Mr. Daridan said that his Embassy had had no further word from the French Foreign Office beyond notification that the Foreign Office had received a note from the British Embassy at Paris setting forth the preliminary reactions of the British Government. He said that he did not anticipate that the French Government would accept the Chinese request in as much as it has already indicated to the Embassy that it would not act unilaterally as an intermediary. In reply to my question, Mr. Daridan said that the French Government had the impression that the Chinese request provided either for unilateral action by any one of the four powers or for joint action as intermedi-

———————

[71] Not printed.

aries. He explained that this impression grew out of a statement made orally to the French Ambassador at Nanking by the Chinese Foreign Minister at the time the latter delivered the *aide-mémoire*.

Mr. Daridan promised to let me know when his Embassy received information indicating the nature of the French Government's reply. I informed Mr. Daridan that my notification to him of our action was intended as notification to the French Government.

893.00/1–849 : Telegram

The Acting Secretary of State to the Ambassador in China (Stuart)

WASHINGTON, January 12, 1949—7 p. m.

43. Urtel 61 Jan. 8. Pls deliver Chi FonMin following *aide-mémoire* as US Govt reply to Chinese proposal:

"The United States Government has received and has given careful consideration to the *aide-mémoire* delivered by the Chinese Minister for Foreign Affairs to the United States Ambassador at Nanking on January 8, 1949.

It is noted in the *aide-mémoire* that the Chinese Government is most anxious that the internal situation in China should not in any way become an impediment to the progress of world peace. It is also noted that the Chinese Government took steps immediately following the Japanese surrender to initiate and carry on peace negotiations with the Chinese Communist Party.

It will be recalled that these negotiations in September and October 1945 resulted in agreement [72] for the convening of a Political Consultative Conference, to be composed of representatives of all political parties as well as non-party Chinese leaders, for the purpose of forming a constitutional government in which all Chinese parties and groups would be represented. It will also be recalled that subsequent to these negotiations clashes between the armed forces of the Chinese Government and of the Chinese Communist Party became increasingly widespread. It was at this juncture in December 1945 that the United States Government, motivated by the same anxiety as that expressed in the Chinese Government's *aide-mémoire* under acknowledgment with respect to the danger to world peace from the internal situation in China and desirous of doing everything within its power to assist in bringing peace to China, offered its good offices in the hope that a peaceful settlement of their differences could be achieved by the Chinese themselves along the lines of the agreement reached in September and October. In furtherance of that Chinese agreement and with the consent of the Chinese Government and the Chinese Communist Party, General Marshall, shortly after his arrival in China on December 21, exerted his good offices in assisting the Chinese Government and the Chinese Communist Party to reach an agreement for a cessa-

---

[72] For summary, see *United States Relations With China*, p. 577.

tion of hostilities [73] with the hope that discussions by the Chinese of their differences could be conducted in an atmosphere of peace.

Following the convening of the Political Consultative Conference and its approval of resolutions providing for the settlement of political differences and the establishment of a constitutional government to include all parties and groups in China, General Marshall again exerted his good offices in connection with the agreement reached for the reorganization of all Chinese armed forces and their amalgamation into a national army responsible to a civilian government.[74]

The negotiations between the Chinese Government and the Chinese Communist Party subsequently broke down and the various agreements were not implemented. The United States Government, therefore, after having made every effort to assist the Chinese in bringing peace to China through implementation of the fundamental political agreements arising out of the Chinese Government's negotiations with the Chinese Communist Party immediately after the Japanese surrender, considered that it had no alternative to withdrawal from its position as an intermediary.

In the light of the foregoing, it is not believed that any useful purpose would be served by the United States Government's attempting, in accordance with the Chinese Government's suggestion, to act as an intermediary in the present situation."

In handing *aide-mémoire* to FonMin you should confine your answers to any queries he puts to you to reiteration of pertinent part of Pres's message to Congress Feb 18 [75] and SecState's statement to House Forn Affairs Committee Feb 20.[76] Pres said it is and has been clear only ChiGovt itself can undertake vital measures necessary provide framework within which efforts toward peace and true economic recovery may be effective. SecState said it should be recognized for main part solution China's problems largely one for Chinese themselves. You should at the same time emphasize to FonMin manner in which United States Govt has been at pains over the years to maintain close and friendly relations with Govt of Repub of China and extent to which people of US have always manifested a sympathetic interest and genuine friendship for people of China.

Dept has been in touch with Brit and French Govts through their Embs here but has made and will make no approach to USSR. Accordingly you should avoid discussion with your Russian colleague. Brit Emb Nanking being instructed by Brit Govt to decline Chinese proposal and indications are that French Govt will take similar action. Brit Amb being instructed to deliver Brit *aide-mémoire* as soon as he learns that you have recd your instructions.

LOVETT

---

[73] January 10, 1946; *Foreign Relations*, 1946, vol. IX, p. 125.

[74] February 25, 1946; *ibid.*, p. 295.

[75] On proposed aid to China; Department of State *Bulletin*, February 29, 1948, p. 268.

[76] On China aid, delivered in executive session; *United States Relations With China*, p. 380.

893.00/1–1349 : Telegram

The Ambassador in China (Stuart) to the Secretary of State

NANKING, January 13, 1949—9 a. m.
[Received 1 :58 p. m.]

97. Reference Embtel 22 to Department, 13 to Shanghai, 2 to Taipei, January 4 and Embtel 77 to Department, 42 to Shanghai, 5 to Taipei, January 11.[77]

General evacuation of vital and valuable documents [of] various Government agencies now commencing. Various Ministries received instructions around January 10 to pack such documents at once for delivery to Ministry of Communications no later than January 13 for evacuation from Nanking. Government offices accordingly now mostly disrupted.

Ministry Industry and Commerce reportedly will soon evacuate 30 percent its personnel. Arrangements said underway permitting those so wishing to resign with 3 months' bonus.

Apparently recalling valuable services of NRC during war, Government has seemingly made more detailed plans this agency. Large portions NRC being shifted south, certain units going Canton, other Taiwan. Personnel having 5 years or more seniority may designate any place in China having NRC subsidiary to which they may be evacuated although they being encouraged stay with main units either in Canton, Taiwan or Nanking. Older bulky files shipped out 2 weeks ago; now more current and highly useful files being shipped.

Clearly level of efficiency Government here will decline as result and will become increasingly difficult transact official business in interim.

Sent Department 97, repeated Shanghai 41, Taipei 7, Canton 1.

STUART

893.00/1–1349 : Telegram

The Ambassador in China (Stuart) to the Secretary of State

NANKING, January 13, 1949—10 a. m.
[Received January 13—8 :27 a. m.]

98. French Ambassador called on our Soviet colleague yesterday concerning Chinese approach to Big Four for restoration peace in China (see Embtel 64, January 10). Soviet Ambassador said unofficially (apparently without instructions from Moscow) that USSR was not interested in any such proposal. While Roschin is not enjoying best of health, his indisposition is, according to my French colleague, not of such grave nature that it would have prevented him

---

[77] Neither printed; they described the reported removal of equipment of the National Resources Commission (NRC) from Nanking to Taiwan (893.00/1–449, 1–1149).

from calling at Foreign Office last Saturday with rest of us had he so desired.

Department please pass in its discretion to London, Paris and Moscow.

STUART

893.00/1–1349 : Telegram

The Consul General at Tientsin (Smyth) to the Secretary of State

TIENTSIN, January 13, 1949—2 p. m.
[Received 2:05 p. m.]

49. Chief Police Li Han-yuan told me last night he expected more indiscriminate Communist shelling of Tientsin. He believed Lin Piao angry over unexpected vigorous resistance which upset timetable. He thought Lin Piao would not agree General Chen's counter proposal (our telegram 41, January 12 [78]) to take troops out as unit via Tangku with rifles. He expressed opinion Tientsin could hold out another 2, possibly 3 weeks (mayor does not feel can hold out so long). Li said Government, military expected all-out Communist attack from east and west last night (this did not occur although heavy attack west gate repulsed).

Tientsin presents paradoxical situation of civil populace and press which has taken leadership among Chinese cities in advocating peace and garrison commander who has taken a so far successful, stubborn and bellicose attitude in face hopeless odds.

Sent Dept as 49, repeated Nanking 44, Shanghai 38, Peiping 35.

SMYTH

893.00/1–849 : Telegram

The Acting Secretary of State to the Ambassador in China (Stuart)

WASHINGTON, January 13, 1949—6 p. m.

48. Chi Amb called to see me today with view to finding out what this Govt's reaction would be to *aide-mémoire* (urtel 61 Jan 8). Beyond telling him that matter had recd careful consideration at highest levels he was given no info contents reply. He also sought ascertain whether this Govt was in consultation with other three Govts and was informed that US regarded *aide-mémoire* as being addressed individually to it as indeed was case. He was also given understand that you would deliver reply shortly.

Chi Amb also raised question that in event US would not act as intermediary whether it would issue statement indicating that ChiGovt sincerely desired peaceful settlement *et al.* As result further ques-

---

[78] Not printed.

tioning he stated Gimo convinced Chinese people wanted peace. He was then asked this being so was it desirable or appropriate for US Govt make statement interpreting will of Chinese people vis-à-vis their own Govt whereupon Chi Amb expressed opinion that if *démarche* to four powers did not result in mediation question of ChiGovt raising matter in SC [79] would arise. It was apparent other remarks Chi Amb that in his view Chi *démarche* was motivated by desire to produce situation whereby US would act with and on behalf ChiGovt vis-à-vis Russia and Chinese Communist Party.

LOVETT

893.00/1–1349 : Telegram

The Ambassador in France (Caffery) to the Secretary of State

PARIS, January 13, 1949—7 p. m.
[Received January 13—4 :40 p. m.]

156. Chauvel showed me Bonnet's [80] telegram repeating what Department had told him about our reply to Nanking. Bonnet remarked that Chinese Minister of Foreign Affairs had not spoken to our Ambassador at Nanking about "concerted actions" of four powers as he had to French Ambassador there. Chauvel indicated that it was Chinese reference to "concerted action" which had induced French to ask Soviet Government for their views. Up to present Foreign Office has received no reply from Moscow.

CAFFERY

893.00/1–1349 : Airgram

The Ambassador in China (Stuart) to the Secretary of State

NANKING, January 13, 1949.
[Received February 7—12 :01 a. m.]

A–12. We are concerned lest proclamations of People's Liberation Army which have been circulating during past month or more in Shanghai, Tsingtao, Peiping, and Tientsin be misconstrued as representing basic CCP policy. As reported in Emb despatch 520, December 29,[81] these proclamations all stem out of the proclamation issued just before capture of Tsinan last September and are part of CCP program of softening up major cities. In general these proclamations, which have so far been issued by ranking CCP military commanders, prescribe regulations to be followed by citizens in newly occupied cities. They contain threats against war criminals and dis-

---

[79] Security Council of the United Nations.
[80] Henri Bonnet, French Ambassador in the United States.
[81] *Foreign Relations*, 1948, vol. VII, p. 700.

orderly elements and promise good treatment to those who cooperate. Of particular interest to the US Government are promises of protection for foreign religious, business, and diplomatic establishments. Some promises are already being negated. For instance, we deduce from communication blockade of the American, British, and French ConGens, Mukden that they are being accorded a very poor form of protection. We also regard as poor form of protection CCP lip service to freedom of religion while simultaneously encouraging anti-religious propaganda in some areas.

As indicated above we regard these proclamations only as tactics. The basic theory or program of CCP is much more broad and uncompromising. In support of this we quote Mao Tze-tung himself. In his article for the Cominform journal last November commemorating the 31st anniversary of October Revolution, Mao gave in following order tasks of CCP: "To unite all revolutionary forces within whole country to drive out aggressive forces of American imperialism, overthrow reactionary rule of Kmt, and establish a unified democratic people's republic." [82]

STUART

893.00/1–1449 : Telegram

The Consul General at Tientsin (Smyth) to the Secretary of State

TIENTSIN, January 14, 1949—1 :30 p. m.
[Received January 14—8 :10 a. m.]

55. Reourtel 54, January 14, 11 a. m., to Dept,[83] repeated Nanking, Shanghai, Peiping. Shortly after sending our reftel, Communist shelling intensified spreading to other areas. A few minutes after noon shell hit either ammunition dump or gasoline dump in vicinity east railway station causing terrific explosion. Glass, doorways and windows our offices blown out. Electric power stopped temporarily putting out our radio until emergency generator put into commission.

No one injured our office; we are concentrated in hallway barricaded by piled-up rugs and away from windows. Our new USIS [84] offices next door to French Consulate hit by shell about 11 a. m., this time exploding. One Chinese girl employee cut in face by flying glass; taken to hospital by Vice Consul Yates,[85] acting director USIS, where wound pronounced not serious. Vice Consul Yates slightly cut by glass from same explosion.

---

[82] In telegram No. 106, January 13, the Ambassador quoted a Communist broadcast denunciation of American foreign policy (893.9111RR/1–1349).
[83] Not printed.
[84] United States Information Service.
[85] Sam L. Yates, Jr., Vice Consul at Tientsin.

At time writing this message, Communist shells are landing in vicinity Victoria Park and Municipal Building (ex-Gordon Hall). Also some are landing as we finish this message closer to our building. Several large fires burning in city.

No American casualties so far reported.

Sent Department 55, repeated Nanking 50, Peiping 42, Shanghai 45, Tsingtao 5.

SMYTH

893.01/1–1449 : Telegram

The Consul General at Shanghai (Cabot) to the Secretary of State

SHANGHAI, January 14, 1949—5 p. m.
[Received 7:59 p. m.]

127. Executive local airline saw Vice Minister Foreign Affairs [86] January 13 and in course his endeavors sell Vice Minister use of civil airlines for evacuation Government personnel, Nanking, was advised that large scale air movement of Government personnel to Taiwan from Assistant Minister level down was scheduled to be undertaken by CAF [87] on January 15.

Source also learned that CAF had moved from Nanking all motor vehicles which Air Force elected to keep; last LST left Nanking with this equipment on January 13. Source also quoted Vice Minister as saying he did not think that "cannon shots would be heard in Nanking for about 3 weeks".

Sent Department 127; repeated Nanking 99.

CABOT

893.00/1–1449 : Telegram

The Ambassador in China (Stuart) to the Secretary of State

NANKING, January 14, 1949—6 p. m.
[Received 10:47 p. m.]

113. I delivered our reply to Chinese request for mediation at 7 last evening (see Department's telegram 43, January 12, repeated London 140, Paris 103, Moscow 23). Foreign Minister and Vice Foreign Minister were present. Upon reading our *aide-mémoire*, their reaction was one of disappointment but not surprise. They asked if we had consulted with any of other governments and I replied that I was not in position to give them authoritative answer on this but I assumed there might well have been some informal discussions with British and French. In brief but general conversation that followed, I took occasion to emphasize US Government's continuing

[86] Tung Lin, Chinese Administrative Vice Minister for Foreign Affairs.
[87] Chinese Air Force.

friendship for and interest in welfare of Chinese people. I informed British Ambassador last night I had received Department's reply. He called on me this morning to tell me that he had instructions to reply to Chinese note in negative sense basing British position upon terms of Moscow Conference of 1945. I am informed that French Ambassador has not yet received his Government's reply.

Sent Department 113, repeated London 3, Paris 2, Moscow 1.

STUART

893.00/1–1449 : Telegram

The Consul General at Tientsin (Smyth) to the Secretary of State

TIENTSIN, January 14, 1949—10 :45 p. m.
[Received January 14—10 :02 p. m.]

61. Communist troops reported inside defense moat in western section of city.

Sent Department as 61; repeated Nanking 55, Shanghai 50, Peiping 47, Tsingtao 12.

SMYTH

893.00/1–1449 : Telegram

The Consul General at Peiping (Clubb) to the Secretary of State

PEIPING, January 14, 1949.
[Received January 14—11 :22 p. m.]

40. Communist North Shensi Chinese language broadcast approximately 1830 hours stated that subsequent to demand [by] Lin Piao and Political Commissioner Lo Jung-huan [that] Nationalist forces Peiping, Tientsin lay down arms, four delegates People's Political Council, Tientsin, proceeded 10th [to] Communist area, were received by Commander Li Ya-lou who set forth following propositions.

1. Communist army desired peaceful settlement Tientsin matter to avoid destruction which would be occasioned by fighting.

2. Nationalist army should voluntarily lay down arms whereupon their lives and property would be protected.

3. Communists would give 24-hour truce for reply.

4. If Tientsin garrison troops did not voluntarily lay down arms, Communist army would launch attack and commanding officers would bear responsibility for causing Tientsin incur war destructions and would be punished severely. Twenty-four-hour truce was extended after return delegates to Tientsin but to hour of reporting (this presumably prior to hour broadcast), reply unreceived, nor have Nationalist troops laid down arms. Item closed with statement that if no further indication from Nationalist side Communists would launch general attack January 14.

This picked up from regular speed broadcast subject check minor errors essentially correct.

Sent Tientsin direct. Sent Department 40, Nanking 38, Shanghai 37, Tientsin 23.

CLUBB

893.00/1–1449 : Telegram

The Consul General at Peiping (Clubb) to the Secretary of State

PEIPING, January 14, 1949.
[Received January 14—11:12 p. m.]

41. Having in mind possibility poor reception elsewhere (reception Peiping itself being poor today), report conditions set forth by Communist leader Mao Tse-tung today for undertaking peace talks with Nanking as reported Communist North Shensi Chinese language broadcast.

(1). Strict punishment war criminals.
(2). Abolition constitution.
(3). Abolition (Kuomintang?) legal system.
(4). Reorganization Nationalist troops according democratic principles.
(5). Confiscation "bureaucratic" capital.
(6). Reformation land system.
(7). Abolition treasonous treaties.
(8). Convocation PPC [PCC] [88] with nonparticipation "reactionary elements", establishment democratic coalition government, taking over all authority "Kuomintang reactionary government and all its strata [branches?]".

Sent Department 41, Nanking 39, Shanghai 38, Tientsin 24.

CLUBB

893.00/1–1549 : Telegram

The Consul General at Tientsin (Smyth) to the Secretary of State

TIENTSIN, January 15, 1949—1 p. m.
[Received January 15—2:16 a. m.]

68. With Communist occupation Tientsin rapidly being completed, question of possible National air bombing of Tientsin is seriously disturbing Americans and other foreign nationals as well as Chinese civilians in Tientsin. Such air bombing of this city would at this juncture serve no military purpose and could only be considered as inhuman act of a vindictive loser. Tientsin has suffered grievously during past few days and for humanitarian reasons it is earnestly

[88] Political Consultative Conference.

hoped that National authorities will refrain, or be persuaded to refrain, from adding unnecessary sorrow to already sorely tried city. Repeated to Nanking.

SMYTH

893.00/1–1549 : Telegram

The Consul General at Tientsin (Smyth) to the Secretary of State

TIENTSIN, January 15, 1949.
[Received January 15—2 :43 a. m.]

69. Communists now in occupation of large part of city including areas in which Consular and USIS offices located. Some shelling and small arms fire continuing in some parts. All members of staff safe. It would be appreciated if Department would telegraph this information to relatives of American staff listed in our telegram No. 485 of December 24[89] except families of Coffey and Hein who have left Tientsin. Consular offices not badly damaged. Damage consists only of smashed window panes and doorways which can be easily repaired. So far as we have been able to ascertain, all Americans in Tientsin are safe.

Sent Department 69, repeated Nanking 63, Peiping 54, Shanghai 57, Tsingtao 19.

SMYTH

893.00/1–1549 : Telegram

The Ambassador in France (Caffery) to the Secretary of State

PARIS [undated].
[Received January 15, 1949—3 :33 a. m.]

184. Chauvel tells me he has instructed French Ambassador in Nanking to give orally negative reply to Chinese.

CAFFERY

893.00/1–1549 : Telegram

The Ambassador in China (Stuart) to the Secretary of State

NANKING, January 15, 1949—2 p. m.
[Received January 15—1 :49 p. m.]

120. On evening 13 January, following delivery our *aide-mémoire*,[90] Generalissimo met with Premier,[91] Vice-Premier,[92] Shao Li-tze,[93]

---

[89] Not printed.
[90] See telegram No. 113, January 14, 6 p. m., p. 47.
[91] Sun Fo, president of the Executive Yuan and son of the late Sun Yat-sen.
[92] Wu Te-chen, concurrently Minister for Foreign Affairs.
[93] Kuomintang member and Chinese Ambassador in the Soviet Union, 1939–42.

Chang Chun,[94] Chang Chih-chung[95] and Chen Li-fu.[96] In view nature our communication, last three named were directed seek direct approach to Communists. Generalissimo's departure was also discussed. Indications suggest he may intend leave soon, going Foochow and Amoy and then Taiwan.

STUART

893.9111 RR/1–1549 : Telegram

The Ambassador in China (Stuart) to the Secretary of State

NANKING, January 15, 1949—3 p. m.
[Received January 16—5:46 a. m.]

121. CCP[97] North Shensi broadcast January 13 is much more than comment on General Marshall's resignation[98] (Embtel 106, January 3 [*13*][99]). It is also statement of foreign policy. Once again it reaffirms fact CCP policy makers view outside world through Bolshevik rather than Chinese eyes.

Not Chinese and hardly national interests of Chinese people are served by such distorted and vitriolic references to Marshall as that he "resigned in disgrace", that he is "two-faced", that his "treacherous scheme" was a vicious imperialist policy toward China and that he is "wolf in sheep's clothing". That is language and logic of Cominform.

We have noted with little surprise CCP theses that "the Marshall Plan, which conducted aggression against Europe and war preparations under name of assistance, not only met with sterner action at hands of all new democratic countries but also met with firm opposition of broad masses of people in Western Europe. At present, a united front against Marshall Plan is daily growing and strengthening throughout all Europe".

Sent Department 121, repeated Shanghai 58, Moscow 2.

STUART

---

[94] Military and Political Affairs Director for Southwest China.
[95] Military and Political Affairs Director for Northwest China and Government representative during the 1946 negotiations with the Chinese Communist Party.
[96] Chinese Minister without Portfolio and coleader of the so-called C-C clique in the Kuomintang.
[97] Chinese Communist Party.
[98] For exchange of letters between General Marshall and President Truman, January 3–7, see Department of State *Bulletin*, January 16, 1949, p. 86. On January 21 the oath of office as Secretary of State was taken by Dean G. Acheson; see *ibid.*, January 30, 1949, p. 150.
[99] Not printed; it quoted an earlier broadcast denouncing General Marshall and American foreign policy (893.9111 RR/1–1349).

893.00/1-1549 : Telegram

The Ambassador in China (Stuart) to the Secretary of State

NANKING, January 15, 1949—3 p. m.
[Received January 16—1:59 a. m.]

122. According to North Shensi broadcast January 13, General Tu Yu-ming[1] "will not escape punishment of revolutionary law" and "will receive just and severe retribution for his crimes in general and for repeatedly using poison gas in defiance of PLA[2] orders in particular". The broadcast recalled that Tu was listed among the 43 war criminals announced Xmas Day and that "his punishment would have been mitigated if he had ordered his troops to surrender immediately, did not damage equipment and did not use poison gas". The broadcast stated that unless Fu Tso-yi and other commanders in Peiping and Tientsin mend their ways they will be subjected to same retribution. US Military Attaché[3] has expressed belief CCP charge of Nationalist use of poison gas is not true.

Sent Department; pouched Shanghai.

STUART

893.00/1-1549 : Telegram

The Consul General at Peiping (Clubb) to the Secretary of State

PEIPING, January 15, 1949.
[Received January 16—12:07 p. m.]

43. Peace movement Peiping continues develop. Press reports Political Council 7 provinces and municipalities North China yesterday telegraphed President Chiang expressing hope that on basis principle established his New Year's Day message, he would cause early cessation hostilities and realization peace.

Shansi People's Political Council telegraphed Shanghai municipal PPC indicating sympathy with latter's proposal there should be established peace promotion society Shanghai. Various people's organization[s] Taiyuan, moreover, met January 13 and decided:

1. Telegraph whole country supporting President's New Year's Day message.

2. Telegraph Communist leader, Mao Tze-tung, promptly put down arms and discuss sincerely with Government matter peace.

3. Support Shanghai project organization peace promotion society. *Ping Jih Pao* reports Peiping mothers demand cessation hostilities North China. *Ping Ming Jih Pao* reports Li Yu-ying[4] (correct read-

---

[1] Captured by Chinese Communists on January 10.
[2] People's Liberation Army (Communist).
[3] Brig. Gen. Robert H. Soule.
[4] Adviser to Generalissimo Chiang Kai-shek.

ing [*sic*] see Contel 41, January 14) returned Nanking yesterday by CAF plane and that persons close to him reported that it was to be expected that upon return he would at least report to Vice President peace atmosphere Peiping.

CLUBB

893.00/1–1749 : Telegram

The Consul General at Peiping (Clubb) to the Secretary of State

PEIPING, January 17, 1949.
[Received January 16—10:38 p. m.]

48. Press today reports North China People's Peace Promotion Society yesterday dispatched telegrams President Chiang and Mao Tse-tung, requesting both sides cease hostilities and consult re peace early date and that same society proposes dispatch peace delegation persons [to] Hsiangshan (approximately 15 miles west of Peiping) to meet Communist leader Yeh Chien-ying for purpose discussion (per *Hsin Sheng Pao*) : (1) Immediate cessation artillery fire [*hostilities?*], General Fu Tso-yi having already agreed on behalf Nationalist forces not sortie or attack and (2) exchange commodities, with coal and grain to enter town and tobacco and cloth to go out.

Information lists among delegation ex-Mayor Ho Ssu-yuan, old-time publicist Liang Chiu-shui, Chou Ping-lin (head of college law, Peita University), representatives of Peiping Municipal Women's Society, Hopeh Chamber of Commerce, Postal Workers Union, general labor union, Peiping Municipal Chamber of Commerce and Pinghan railway labor union. Per schedule indicated, press delegation was to meet at Peiping Municipal Council 9 a. m., next proceed General Fu Tso-yi with request both sides cease fighting and depart from town in afternoon. Shell which struck ex-Mayor Ho's residence 3 a. m. this morning killed his daughter and injured him and his wife.

Sent Department 48, Nanking 47, Shanghai 44.

CLUBB

893.00/1–1749 : Telegram

The Consul General at Shanghai (Cabot) to the Secretary of State

SHANGHAI, January 17, 1949.
[Received January 17—2:41 a. m.]

140. Initial Shanghai reaction to Communist peace terms as reported *China Press* January 16, Pan Kung-chan, Chairman City Council, states CCP terms better than no response at all and calls

for immediate 2 months' cease-fire with both sides sending delegates Nanking and Shanghai for peace talks.

Sent Department 140; repeated Nanking 110.

CABOT

893.00/1–1749 : Telegram

The Consul General at Tientsin (Smyth) to the Secretary of State

TIENTSIN, January 17, 1949.
[Received January 17—5 :58 a. m.]

75. Consensus of opinion of Americans and other foreigners here is that the Communist attack on and occupation of Tientsin January 14 and 15 was a very well planned and executed operation and was carried out under the circumstances with a minimum of damage to the city. Earlier press reports of damage to the city were somewhat exaggerated. Damage to city seems to have been limited due to fact that Communists apparently used light artillery against places such as municipal government building (ex-Gordon Hall in Victoria Park) in vicinity of which are located American and British Consulates, banks, apartment houses, et cetera. As result of the use of lighter artillery, actual property damage in this area has been very small. Chief damage is broken window glass and much of this was due to concussion from explosion of Nationalist ammunition dump some distance away. Foreigners have freedom of movement. A Communist official had stated that all foreigners who comply with the law will be given full protection both as regards their persons and property. Americans and other foreigners have been impressed with the discipline and generally exemplary conduct of the occupying troops.

Sent Department 75, repeated Nanking 68, Peiping 57, Shanghai 60.

SMYTH

893.00/1–1549 : Telegram

The Acting Secretary of State to the Ambassador in China (Stuart)

WASHINGTON, January 17, 1949—7 p. m.

61. Re Tientsin's 68 Jan 15 rptd Nanking concerning possible bombing Tientsin, Emb authorized its discretion make approach similar that authorized Deptel 1519 Nov. 1.[5]

LOVETT

---

[5] *Foreign Relations,* 1948, vol. VII, p. 825.

893.00/1–1849 : Telegram

The Chargé in the Soviet Union (Kohler) to the Secretary of State

Moscow, January 18, 1949.
[Received January 18—5 :36 a. m.]

123. Soviet press January 18 carries following Foreign Office communiqué:

"On January 8 Minister Foreign Affairs, China, transmitted to Embassy USSR in China memorandum containing request from Chinese Government that Soviet Government act as mediator in peace talks between Chinese Government and Chinese CP. Soviet Ambassador was advised that Chinese Government had made similar proposal to Governments USA, Great Britain and France.

"On January 17 Deputy Minister Foreign Affairs USSR, Comrade Vyshinsky, A. Ya., received Ambassador of China in USSR, Mr. Foo Ping-sheung; and handed him reply Soviet Government in which was pointed out that Soviet Government, unalterably supporting principle non-intervention in internal affairs other countries, does not consider it appropriate take upon itself mediation mentioned in cited memorandum.

"In reply of Soviet Government it is noted that restoration unity China as democratic and peace-loving state is affair of Chinese people itself and that this unity could be attained most quickly by means of direct talks of the parties without foreign interference representing internal forces of China."

Soviet press January 18 also prints brief Nanking Tass dispatch referring press accounts that Chinese Government requests Britain, US, USSR, France act as mediators and noting reports that Britain and US refused.

Sent Department 123, passed Nanking 9.

KOHLER

893.00/1–1849 : Telegram

The Consul General at Peiping (Clubb) to the Secretary of State

PEIPING, January 18, 1949—6 p. m.
[Received 8 :29 p. m.]

61. Re Contel 54, January 18.[6] I am reliably informed peace delegation comprising 11 persons including ex-mayor Ho Ssu-yuan departed on mission from Peiping 3 :30 p. m. today.

Information received by USIS director about same time was that General Fu Tso-yi had dispatched his own delegate one-half hour previously.

Sent Department 61, repeated Nanking 57, Shanghai 57.

CLUBB

[6] Not printed.

893.00/1–1949 : Telegram

The Consul General at Shanghai (Cabot) to the Secretary of State

SHANGHAI, January 19, 1949.
[Received January 19—4:50 a. m.]

169. In response to telegrams from Shanghai City Council and other local organizations calling for convening of All-China Peace Promotion Conference in Shanghai around February 10, 12 public bodies have sent favorable replies in past few days, according to recent vernacular press, including Chekiang, Kiangsi and Kiangsu Provinces, Councils All-China Federation Chambers of Commerce, All-China Federation of Medical Doctors Association, Provisional Shantung Province Council, Hankow and Chungking city councils. Shanghai city council sent another telegram January 18 urging public bodies immediately publicize names of delegates so that conference can convene on schedule and work out peace plan based on General-issimo's five principles [7] and CCP's eight terms.

Shanghai Self-help and National Salvation Association sent similar telegram. Young China Party Central Committee issues statement January 18 asking Kmt and CCP issue immediate cease-fire orders and send delegates discuss peace terms together with third parties. *Ta Kung Pao* January 18 describes dinner at which more than 70 Legislative Yuan members now in Shanghai discuss peace proposals.

Sent Nanking 132; repeated Department 169.

CABOT

893.00B/1–1949 : Telegram

The Consul General at Tientsin (Smyth) to the Secretary of State

TIENTSIN, January 19, 1949—noon.
[Received January 19—6:31 a. m.]

86. Communist Army, as we saw it operate in taking Tientsin, is far superior to any National Government units we have ever seen. It is a highly effective military machine and its morale and discipline are striking compared to National Army. We do not believe National Government has the slightest chance of resisting, not to mention defeating Communist Army if other Communist units are anything like ones we have seen here. Its equipment (largely American in units which took Tientsin) is first rate and Communists know how to use it. Their strategy and tactics here were excellent. They did not waste ammunition except during actual Communist attack January 14, 15, Government artillery fired far more than Communists.

---

[7] See the New Year message of President Chiang Kai-shek, *United States Relations With China*, p. 920.

Communists, as we observed them, are determined to conquer China and seem fully capable of doing so. Viewed from here, with first-hand knowledge of Communist military superiority, the present discussions in Nanking as to what Communists' terms Government will accept seem pathetically unrealistic. At Tientsin Communists showed a complete refusal to compromise and also demonstrated what happens when their terms are not accepted.

SMYTH

893.00/1–1949 : Telegram

The Ambassador in China (Stuart) to the Secretary of State

NANKING, January 19, 1949.
[Received January 20—1:36 a. m.]

147. Official Kmt organ Nanking reported on January 19 that Government is collecting opinions from all circles and leaders of local governments regarding Mao Tze-tung's eight-point peace offer before final decision is made. Few local tabloids allege that Government's attitude changed from viewpoint that Communist and Government terms irreconcilable to belief that all Communist terms, except one concerning war criminals, are negotiable.

Evidence that further pressure being exerted on Generalissimo revealed by press reports that Carsun Chang paid third visit to President urging him to take vacation; peace appeal by National Assembly delegates to Generalissimo and Mao Tze-tung; statement by Nanking professors urging Government to send envoys to negotiate, and telegram to Mao Tze-tung by officers of women's leagues in Nanking.

Sent Department 147, repeated Shanghai 77.

STUART

893.00/1–2049 : Telegram

The Ambassador in China (Stuart) to the Secretary of State

NANKING, January 20, 1949—11 a. m.
[Received January 20—3:51 a. m.]

152. In January 19 interview with officer of Embassy, Naval Attaché and Assistant Military Attaché, Kan Chieh-hou [8] stated that Generalissimo has issued instructions [to] police to keep Vice President under surveillance and prevent his leaving Nanking. Vice President plans stay here long as possible in hope Generalissimo will respond popular pressure and resign, but admits this very

---

[8] Secretary to Vice President Li Tsung-jen.

forlorn hope. Expects that he will be forced leave capital with Generalissimo, but has plans for flight to Hankow or Kwangsi join Pai Chung-hsi.[9] Plan involves escape to Wuhu, where Kwangsi military unit stationed.

Kan also stated Pai Chung-hsi now in process forming bloc including northwestern Moslem leaders, Sikang, Szechuan, Yunnan, and Kwangtung. Exploratory conversations have been held with leaders these provinces, but apparently no firm agreement exists. Vice President has advised Pai open negotiations with Communists soon as possible and Pai has intention so doing. Both Pai and Vice President believe this action will result in solid adherence abovementioned leaders to bloc since most of them already seeking means cast off affiliations Nanking. As regards Kwangtung, Kan said Generalissimo controls only small segment of province with balance divided between Chen Chi-tang,[10] Li Chi-shen, Chang Fa-kwei,[11] and Yu Han-mou.[12] Latter, controlling strategically important Kukong area, more loyal to Vice President than to Generalissimo and could be expected join Pai at proper time. Also, Kan spoke as though Pai already sure of Kwangchow-wan and Luichow Peninsula.

Kan expressed believe [belief] negotiations with Communists possible on basis terms offered Mao Tse-tung January 14 statement. Said Vice President favors making offer on basis accepting Mao's points in principle while negotiating over details with both sides agreeing cease-fire and Li Chi-shen serving as mediator. Says this program accepted by peace advocated [advocates] in Government, but adamantly opposed by Generalissimo and C-C clique. Local Soviet Embassy was asked if peace possible through such program and replied in affirmative.

Sent Department 152, pouched Consuls China.

STUART

893.00/1–2049 : Telegram

The Ambassador in China (Stuart) to the Secretary of State

NANKING, January 20, 1949.
[Received January 20—7:05 a. m.]

160. Executive Yuan, at its regular meeting on January 19, discussed at length national situation and issued following statement:

---

[9] Military and Political Affairs Director for Central China.
[10] Governor of Hainan Island.
[11] Former Director of Generalissimo Chiang Kai-shek's Headquarters at Canton.
[12] Military and Political Affairs Director for South China.

"Government, in deference to general wishes of people for early realization of peace, hereby makes known its desire for both Government and Communist forces to cease fire unconditionally and immediately and for both sides to appoint delegates to start peace negotiations."

Nanking's official Kmt organ editorially commented that move indicated Government's sincere desire for peace and hoped Communist Party would adopt same attitude and cease fighting unconditionally. Editorial pointed out, however, time not yet ripe for discussion concrete peace terms since primary need of people is cessation of hostilities. People were urged to decide whether CP sincerely desirous of peace by whether or not Government proposal is accepted. In conclusion, paper warned people not to relax in preparing for continuation war or Communists would be provided with opportunity achieving their ends without fighting.

Sent Department 160, repeated Shanghai 82.

STUART

893.00/1–2049 : Telegram

The Consul General at Peiping (Clubb) to the Secretary of State

PEIPING, January 20, 1949—5 p. m.
[Received January 22—12:25 p. m.]

94. Cheng Ting-feng, Commander 94th Division, and number other important officials including BIS [13] men departed Peiping approximately 4:30 p. m. by plane, Cheng stating his departure removed last obstacle turnover Peiping.

Foreign Office official informed me (presumably after attending Fu Tso-yi [14] meeting, Contel 41 [15]) that political turnover occurred 10 a. m. this morning, that Fu remains temporarily in charge Peiping, that troops will be removed from Peiping gradually beginning tomorrow. Last information in accordance with statement Gen. Cheng that political agreement effective today, military agreement tomorrow.

Cavalry division by report proceeded Fengtai and 271st and the 73rd Divisions 101st Army to Huangtsun, both south Peiping today.

Communist Political Commission reportedly already present in town.

Sent Department 94, Nanking 89, Shanghai 83.

CLUBB

---

[13] Chinese Bureau of Investigation and Statistics (Security).
[14] Fu Tso-yi, Commander in Chief of Rebellion Suppression Forces in North China.
[15] January 14, p. 49.

761.93/1–2049 : Telegram

The Chargé in the Soviet Union (Kohler) to the Secretary of State

Moscow, January 20, 1949—10 p. m.
[Received January 20—4:52 p. m.]

151. In our view rapid sweep events China outpaced Soviet policy and compelled Kremlin quickly review and decide, probably in consultation CCP, their immediate policy toward Chinese conflict.

While Soviet mediation intimations made during past year, particularly by Ambassador Roschin, Nanking, may have been pure smoke screen, consider more probable Kremlin misjudged military capacities CCP and weaknesses Kmt Government and believed at the time political settlement would be advantageous. However, capture Mukden and brilliant successes CCP armies, coupled with publicly stated intransigent attitude Mao toward Kmt Government, must have given Kremlin pause for thought.

Embassy believes plausible that, either on initiative of Soviets who found it necessary take decision on expected mediation request by Chinese Central Government or on initiative Mao himself, who feared Soviets might favorably consider such proposal, a meeting between Soviet and CCP leaders may have taken place in Moscow to determine and coordinate policies.

Time table recent events lends credence this hypothesis:

January 2, after weeks rumors and premature news reports, Tass denied USSR had been approached or was considering mediating Sino conflict.

January 8 Chinese Government delivered notes Nanking.

January 9 to approximately 15, some distinguished foreign notable was undoubtedly present Moscow (Embtels 85, January 12 and 105, January 15 [16]).

January 15 Mao announced peace terms (not published Moscow until January 19).

January 17 negative Soviet reply handed Chinese Ambassador.

Meanwhile French Ambassador asked see Vyshinsky on matter January 11, was stalled to January 18, then informed announced decision reached only "late last night"—obviously deliberately false statement, since reply handed Chinese Ambassador previous afternoon.

From above Embassy believes Mao or emissary may possibly have been Moscow and Soviet–CCP agreement reached here. While hypothesis speculative, Department may have other information to deny or support.

Sent Department 151, repeated Nanking 11.

KOHLER

---

[16] Neither printed. The former reported: "Pure speculation based process elimination and international situation suggests possibility Polish Government or Chinese Communist delegation." (861.00/1–1249)

893.00B/1-2049

The Consul General at Shanghai (Cabot) to the Ambassador in China (Stuart)[17]

No. 9   SHANGHAI, January 20, 1949.

SIR: I have the honor to enclose and comment on a memorandum by Consul R. W. Rinden [18] summarizing views in regard to Chinese Communist thinking which were recently expressed, during a private discussion of that subject, by a group of Americans and British who have lived for considerable time in "Red China" in connection with medical relief and other philanthropic activities.

The Consulate General concurs in Mr. Rinden's opinion that the character and experience of these men invest their observations with especial value. So much of the material on the Chinese Communists represents hearsay, professional propaganda, emotional coloring, or, at best, honest but superficial information—covering, for example, a brief tour in Red territory, or statements obtained hurriedly and formally from members of a Communist community with which nothing approaching relations of mutual confidence have been previously developed. The observations recorded in Mr. Rinden's memorandum are those of a group of intelligent Americans and British whose organizational background, principles and strict devotion to impartial humanitarian work ensure a high degree of objectivity. These men have closely associated and dealt with the people and leaders in Communist sections over a considerable period. Through such association and through scrupulous disassociation from politics and from religious proselyting, they seem to have gained the confidence of their Communist communities. Accordingly, they have had real opportunity to study the thinking and ideological inspiration of rank and file members of the Chinese Communist administrative system—not those who make policy, it is true, but those upon whom the regime depends to have policy carried out.

Communist Plans for Shanghai. Of particular interest from the local standpoint is the group's understanding that the Chinese Communists, mindful of the unfortunate consequences which their delay in entering Tsinan had for that city, are now "actively and systematically" preparing for a quick take-over of Shanghai when the time comes for occupation of this port. The Communists, in the group's opinion, will do their utmost to protect American as well as other lives and property; though the group feels that the presence here of American marines would seriously exacerbate relations between Americans and the Chinese Communists.

---

[17] Copy transmitted to the Department without covering despatch; received February 8.
[18] Not printed.

Russian-Marxist versus Western Influence on Chinese Communists. The point of greatest general interest brought out in the memorandum is the group's analysis of the extent of Russian, Marxist and anti-Western ideological influence on the Chinese Communists. To say that Marxist and "party line" indoctrination is general among the Chinese Communists is to paint but half the picture, in the group's opinion. Many of the young Communist leaders, through prior attendance at colleges such as Yenching and Ch'ing Hua, are at the same time well grounded in western economic and political theory. They have found it possible to combine Marxist and "capitalist" interpretations and they are more influenced by the latter interpretation. They are much concerned over the need for trade between their regime and America and Britain. It is this type of Chinese Communist who, the group points out, conducts, and is likely to conduct, actual relations with Westerners.

Comment: These observations acquire additional significance when it is considered that they apply to men belonging to the small Party core of Communist-administered China—to those upon whom the regime must depend to preserve its Marxian character through the coming period of enforced rapid expansion when great numbers of unindoctrinated personnel must be suddenly enlisted to keep in motion the complex machinery of government and economic life in the great urban centers and the vast countryside of conquered Kuomintang China. Because of China's exceptional dearth of educated men, most of this new personnel accepted for administrative, economic and technical posts must inevitably be men from Kuomintang China, whose average orientation, as between Russia and the Western democracies, will of course be even more strongly toward the West than is that of the Western-educated Communist leaders described by the group. In a country of the type of Germany, such a situation could perhaps be quickly corrected by purges and replacements. In China, where educated men are produced in a trickle, it will take many years.

That the supreme Chinese Communist leadership may pledge China's subservience to Marx and Moscow is one question—possibly already decided. Whether, how soon and how effectively such a pledge can be fulfilled in a country of the character and dimensions of China is quite another question, which may well take decades to determine. The fact that the carrying out of Communist China's political and economic policies will for long have to be entrusted largely to men who are oriented more along Western democratic lines than along Soviet lines is but one of many difficulties in Moscow's path.

Another important "headache" will be the disbanding and the compelling or retaining the loyalty of various ambitious field commanders and enormous numbers of other military officers of Kuomintang or regional backgrounds, who have staffed not only Nanking's forces, but also many of those on the Communist side, and whose permanent career interests could hardly be satisfied with what a Moscow-dominated Marxist regime would have to offer.

Equally important, also, would seem, for example, such factors as:

The indispensability of economic and technical relations with the West to ensure the revival of China's national economy which the Communists must achieve if they are to escape the fate of the Nanking Government;

The universal Chinese admiration of American products (including the prized and widely advertised arms of the "American equipped" Communist divisions);

Deep-rooted friendship for the United States in many segments of the Chinese population;

Popular antipathy to alien control based on extreme racial and cultural divergence and on rising nationalism;

The immemorial Chinese practice of playing off one foreign power against another;

Pride of the Chinese Communists in their self-made, self-reliant record, as compared with the Russian mothering received by European Communists.

These remarks are not intended as an effort to minimize the threat which the Communists' military conquest of China poses for the United States and for the democratic cause. They are made, rather, in the thought that political observers are currently tending to over-stress the significance of what they conjecture will be the attitudes or cleavages in attitudes of Mao Tze-tung and a few other top Chinese Communist leaders toward control by Moscow—apparently forgetting that the successful Sovietizing of China depends a great deal on circumstances and forces beyond the fiat of Mao or of any other leader.

The extent to which Moscow will succeed in dominating China must depend on the extent to which it is able to overcome the combination of various unfavorable factors peculiar to the complex China scene. This combination is different and apparently more formidable than any which Moscow has yet surmounted elsewhere. It follows that, from the American standpoint, the opportunities and rewards for study and exploitation of factors helpful toward frustrating Moscow and salvaging something from the situation should be correspondingly greater than in the case of the Soviet satellite states of Europe.

While it is, of course, manifestly impossible to predict the future course of Chinese Communism, and while it is possible that there may evolve a harder core of Chinese Communism which will succeed in dominating the China stage, it is believed that factors such as those mentioned in this despatch and its enclosure will tend to counteract and will in any case delay the development of Communism along Russian lines. In this connection, reference may be made to Dairen's Report No. 10 of October 15, 1948, to the Department, "Notes on the Chinese Communist Movement Based on Information Provided by a Disillusioned Party Member".[19]

Respectfully yours,

JOHN M. CABOT

893.00 Yunnan/1–2049

The Consul General at Hong Kong (Hopper) to the Ambassador in China (Stuart)[20]

No. 3   HONG KONG, January 20, 1949.

SIR: I have the honor to enclose a copy of a memorandum prepared by Vice Consul R. M. Service,[19] describing an interview on January 19, 1949 with General Lung Yun, former governor of Yunnan. It will be recalled that General Lung arrived at Hong Kong on December 10, 1948 (reference this office's telegram no. 212, December 11, 3 p. m. to the Embassy, repeated to Canton), after escaping from Nanking by air.

Summary of Enclosure. Lung Yun said that he was convinced that the Generalissimo will not quit, although he has lost the respect and support of the people. Lung was encouraged by Washington's coolness toward the Nanking Government, and hoped that the United States will adhere to a "hand's off" policy until the present historical crisis is over, when China will welcome American friendship. He was interested in the American attitude toward Formosa, advocating self-rule on the island, and American cooperation to keep Chiang from making of it a final bastion of Kmt survival. He described Li Chi-shen's activity in north China as of the utmost significance to China's welfare, and predicted imminent convocation of the PCC. Lung said it was too late for south and west China leaders to form an alliance against Communism, as the Generalissimo had sacrificed too many troops and brought the CCP armies to the north bank of the Yangtze, and the Chinese people are war-weary. He said that Fu Tso-yi and Yen Hsi-shan[21] are entitled to make separate peace arrangements with the CCP, as Chiang did not give them promised support. Lung Yun said that he had come to Hong Kong for physical and spiritual relaxation, and that he had not yet formulated plans for the future. He avoided discussion of Yunnan and KmtRC[22] affairs. *End of Summary of Enclosure.*

---

[19] Not printed.
[20] Copy transmitted to the Department without covering despatch; received February 16.
[21] Marshal Yen was Governor of Shansi and Taiyuan Pacification Commissioner.
[22] Kuomintang Revolutionary Committee with headquarters at Hong Kong.

A source of uncertain reliability, describing a recent interview with Lung's secretary, said that differences between Lung and Lu Han, present governor of Yunnan, have not yet been resolved. This source said that Lung's half-brother will be obliged to come to a settlement with Lung, but that representatives of the two have not yet concluded their negotiations. Other sources have also said that delicate problems remain to be settled between the two Lo-los, but all are confident that Lung Yun will return to Yunnan when Central Government disintegration permits.

Respectfully yours,   GEORGE D. HOPPER

893.00/1–2149 : Telegram

The Ambassador in China (Stuart) to the Secretary of State

NANKING, January 21, 1949—11 a. m.
[Received January 22—3 :48 a. m.]

166. Our opinion that CCP Politburo is coldly determined to exact from Kmt Government something closely approximating unconditional surrender has not been altered by Mao Tse-tung's eight-point peace program of January 14.

If we hypothesize that Chinese Communist leaders are convinced Marxians of Leninist persuasion, we believe above judgment is logically tenable. Chinese Communists incidentally in all their theoretical writings stoutly proclaim their Bolshevik convictions. They have acquired from Lenin's Bolshevik party blueprint for revolutionary action which works. As long as it is pragmatically correct in China, they are not going to deviate radically from it. One cardinal tenet of Bolshevism is that proletarian revolution can be successfully completed only if state apparatus of bourgeois state is thoroughly smashed.

Consequently we interpret CCP list of 43 war criminals proclaimed on Xmas Day as initial step in total liquidation of Kmt Government. We explain fact that CCP has not announced openly its intentions to exact unconditional surrender from Kmt Government and then smash it as simply tactical silence due to likelihood that exhausted populace would not support such an extreme program.

Tide of Communist successes is flowing too rapidly for CCP to need content itself with anything less. Self-confidence of CCP is underlined in Mao's statement that "situation is extremely clear: PLA need only further deal some heavy blows at remaining Kmt troops and entire reactionary ruling machinery of Kmt will crumble into dust and extinction". Readiness to "carry revolution to very end" as stated in CCP New Year's Day message is reaffirmed in Mao's appeal to "all Comrade commanders and fighters of PLA" that "before Nanking reactionary government accepts and realizes genuine democratic peace, you must not slacken your battle efforts in the least.   You must firmly, thoroughly and completely wipe out any reactionaries who dare to resist".   Statements like these buttressing Mao's eight points give little support to hypothesis that CCP is willing to help bridge chasm separating CCP and Kmt.   Most immediate and irreconcilable divergence now is that Kmt wants armistice before beginning peace talks while CCP will not cease fire prior to Kmt capitulation to CCP peace terms.

Mao's long preamble, which indicts Kmt and American "reactionary" measures and applauds CCP "progressive" measures during past 30 months we look upon as designed more for consumption in CCP-occupied territory than in Nationalist China.   Communists now control population of over 200 million war-weary Chinese who have suffered much more than bulk of Nationals [*Nationalist*] population in southern China.   It must be not easy task for Mao to convince these people of necessity to continue war but he does all possible in his preamble by making peace contingent upon Nationals [*Nationalists*] accepting his terms.   Despite fact these terms essentially represent unconditional surrender which means further fighting, Mao still achieves his immediate purpose which is to give impression that CCP is as piously anxious as Kmt to end China's torment.   And in so doing he in no way is deflected from basic Bolshevik program of crushing Kmt state apparatus, beginning with war criminals and thereafter working on downward as far as seems necessary or expedient.

Following is our analysis of Mao's eight conditions:

1. Punishment of war criminals is merely borrowed refinement of ancient savagery as expressed in Roman phrase *vae victis*.   None of 43 persons listed is conceivably war criminal except by haughtily intolerant and bigoted CCP standard.   Many are men of high integrity and patriotic devotion.

2. It remains to be seen whether new CCP constitution will be any less "bogus" than that of Kmt to which incidentally CCP objects not so much on grounds of substance as on manner of its ratification.

3. Abolishment of Kmt's "legitimacy of traditional institutions" is rather vague but probably refers to formalized procedures of that party and its status as major party in China.

4. This doubtless refers to abolishment of Kmt armies as independent units and their eventual incorporation into PLA which, of course, is only army operated on "democratic principles" of CCP.

5 and 6. Confiscation of bureaucratic capital and agrarian reform represent socialistic trends in essential accord with both Three Principles [23] and Marxism.

7. Abrogation of "treaties of national betrayal" of course refers to American treaties and agreements entered into since V-J Day.

8. Convocation of a new PCC is most important condition from standpoint of American interests.   There is good ground to believe

---

[23] Sun Yat-sen's "Three People's Principles" (San Min Chu I).

that in 1946 CCP delegates sincerely wanted implementation of PCC resolutions,[24] sometimes to extent of themselves coming under suspicions of their Yenan comrades. At that time Generalissimo who then had power was more intransigent of two parties. Now that power has been transferred, it remains to be seen how intransigent CCP will itself be in "establishing without participation of reactionary elements a democratic-coalition government to take over power from Nanking Kmt reactionary government and its lower levels of government." A shadow of things to come was perhaps thrown by North Shensi broadcast of October 5 which announced that Tsinan military control committee had issued proclamation ordering "immediate dissolution of Kmt and all its open and secret Fascist organizations including the San Min Chu I Youth Corps and Secret Police". This order was directed not at "reactionary elements of Kmt" but at entire party membership in that city.

Sent Department, repeated Moscow 3, pouched Shanghai.

STUART

893.00/1–2149 : Telegram

The Ambassador in China (*Stuart*) *to the Secretary of State*

NANKING, January 21, 1949—5 p. m.
[Received January 22—12 :50 a. m.[25]]

179. Chen Li-fu, who had just returned from Generalissimo, tells us there has been no decision remove Government [to] Canton. Decision awaits outcome peace negotiations. Government is seeking direct contact with Communists so far unsuccessfully. Chen said he envisaged four possibilities :

(1) Cease-fire arrangement permitting Generalissimo and Government retain control south of Yangtze (he admitted this most unlikely) ;
(2) Retirement Generalissimo with Li Tsung-jen negotiating cease-fire which would permit Government under his leadership retain control south of Yangtze (this he also admitted unlikely) ;
(3) Generalissimo retiring and Li Tsung-jen seeking coalition government with Communists (while not ruling out this development, he felt it unlikely) ; and
(4) Continue the fight in Nanking and elsewhere to the bitter end from Taiwan (this he thought the most likely course).

Dr. Chen expressed considerable concern over recent evidences of desire of US for removal Generalissimo. He cited this connection :
(1) Drastic reduction and impending withdrawal JUSMAG ;[26]
(2) Our refusal to accede Chinese request for intervention, pointing out that we had not even bothered to consult Soviets before refusing ;

---

[24] January 31, 1946; see *United States Relations With China,* pp. 610–621.
[25] Text printed from corrected copy received January 24, 2 :50 a. m.
[26] Joint U.S. Military Advisory Group.

and (3) Bloom's [27] public demand for removal Generalissimo.[28] He could not understand why, if we supported resistance to Communism in China, we undermined publicly those forces resisting Communism in China, thus giving comfort to the enemy.   He asked in this regard whether it was true, as Generalissimo had been informed, that we would refuse to give any ECA [29] aid to areas under Communist control or to a government with Communist participation. He could not understand why we suppressed such information and publicized things detrimental to Chiang regime.

We explained that:

(1) Original conception JUSMAG was unrealistic in present situation China; that JUSMAG was not being withdrawn, but merely reduced to size more commensurate with present needs, and that it would not be withdrawn so long as Chinese Government remained Nanking and desired its presence;

(2) While we could not speak for our Government we felt confident one of basic reasons for refusal join with Soviets in intervention in China arose out of our most unhappy experience with Soviet cooperation in Germany; that to join with Soviets in intervention in China would give them legitimate and legal basis for obstructing and sabotaging every effort toward improving conditions Chinese people which would be neither in interests of China nor of US;

(3) While we were not aware of the background of Bloom's statement nor of his reasons therefor, we could assure Dr. Chen that in every instance here we had pointed out to Washington that proposed action might be detrimental to National Government and tend to undermine its authority, action proposed had not been taken. Speaking personally therefore, we said we felt confident that had Department had prior notice of Bloom's statement and ability to dissuade him from making it, statement would not have been made.

Dr. Chen felt that maybe it was too late for US to intervene effectively in China unless we were willing to come in and practically take over, yet he hoped we would not "wash our hands" of China. If we did not desire a Communist regime in China dominated and directed from Moscow he felt we should support any elements in China resisting Communism and hoped we would do so. We replied that while we could not commit Congress, we felt sure that policy of US was based on resistance to Moscow-dominated Communism in whatever area might be threatened by such domination; that while we could not promise any specific assistance to forces in China resisting Communism, he could always be sure of American sympathy for such action and of such support as might be feasible.

---

[27] Sol Bloom, Chairman of the House Committee on Foreign Affairs.

[28] For reported statement of January 17, see *Congressional Record*, Appendix, vol. 95, pt. 12, p. A272.

[29] Economic Cooperation Administration.

Obviously Dr. Chen, and we believe he represents the position of that small group including Dr. Hu Shih [30] who continue to favor no compromise with Communists and who believe that without Generalissimo resistance forces will disintegrate and collapse, is seeking some promises of support from US. We carefully refrained from making any promises, yet sought to encourage continued resistance to Communist domination of China, making it abundantly clear that decision as to ways and means and as to personalities who would lead or not lead rested solely with Chinese.

As indicative of "confusion confounded" which characterizes present China scene is fact that Vice Prime Minister and concurrently Foreign Minister Wu Teh-chen told Australian Ambassador at same time we were talking to Chen Li-fu that Government was moving to Canton, move to be completed by February 1 and that no limitation would be placed either on transportation or housing for personnel, archives and baggage of diplomatic missions. At same time member Legislative Yuan informed us that Yuan would meet in Nanking February 1 with assured quorum and with avowed purpose of discussing peace.

STUART

893.001 Chiang Kai-shek/1–2149 : Telegram

The Ambassador in China (Stuart) to the Secretary of State

NANKING, January 21, 1949.
[Received January 21—8:53 a. m.]

181. Government Information Office 1600 hours local time 21 January announced Generalissimo has left capital for Fenghua and that, in accordance with constitutional procedure, Vice President will exercise power in his absence.[31]

STUART

---

[30] Chinese Minister of Education and Chancellor of National Peking University.
[31] Maj. Gen. David G. Barr, Director of the Joint U.S. Military Advisory Group, China, in his report on operational advice given the Generalissimo on a strictly personal and secret basis as instructed by the Secretary of State (copy transmitted to the Department on April 14 by the Department of the Army), reported as follows concerning a last interview with the Generalissimo: "At a meeting with the Generalissimo on 22 [21?] January 1949, which proved to be the last, the following matters were discussed: (1) The Generalissimo said that he had asked me to come that afternoon in order that he could inform me personally that he had decided to retire from the Presidency temporarily and would leave Nanking immediately. During his temporary retirement, he said General Li Tsung-jen, the Vice President, would act on his behalf. He said that this would be the third time that he had had to retire or resign temporarily and stated that the Chinese people had requested his return on the first two occasions and he was confident that he would be asked to return again soon. He said that he hoped that his temporary departure from Nanking would give ample opportunities to those who so strongly advocated peace, to negotiate with the Commu-

Footnote continued on following page.

893.00/1–2149 : Telegram

The Ambassador in China (Stuart) to the Secretary of State

NANKING, January 21, 1949—5 p. m.
[Received January 22—3 :54 a. m.]

183. In January 21 interview with Military and Naval Attachés and officer of Embassy, General Sun Lien-chun,[32] director training Chinese ground forces,[33] stated that American arms now reaching China are being scattered in haphazardly fashion among various units and are not being issued en bloc to units trained in their employment. General Sun also expressed doubt over capability Government armies prevent Yangtze crossing by Communists due shortage troops and adequate commanders.

Sent Department; pouched Taipei, Shanghai; Canton, Hong Kong.

STUART

893.00/1–2149 : Telegram

The Chargé in the Soviet Union (Kohler) to the Secretary of State

MOSCOW, January 21, 1949—8 p. m.
[Received January 21—2 :42 p. m.]

158. Consistent recent Soviet "no-comment" policy China, following passage deleted by censor from New York *Herald Tribune* correspondent despatch on publication Mao Tse-tung peace terms:

"One opinion voiced here is that Communist revolution China is greatest event Twentieth Century after Russian revolution and defeat Germany two world wars.

From Soviet point of view Chinese revolution constitutes continuation and extension Bolshevik revolution Russia. It cited in support Soviet contention widely circulated on occasion 31st anniversary Bol-

---

Footnote continued from preceding page.

nists, but he expressed doubt that the Communists would listen to their appeals. (2) The Generalissimo again expressed deep regret that my ability could not be fully utilized by the Chinese Government during my year's service in China due to the abnormal conditions and the low intelligence standard of the Chinese military personnel. He said that if he returned to assume the responsibility of the Chinese Government again, he would like for me to return to assist him and China and sincerely hoped that I would consent to come. I told him that it had been a distinct honor and privilege to serve China and the Generalissimo. I said that I regretted that so little had been accomplished by my mission, the activities of which were necessarily limited by the United States Government policy. I said that I had learned to love the Chinese and that I admired tremendously the Generalissimo's fortitude and determination which had been displayed during my year's stay in China. I said that I too hoped that I could return to serve China again." General Barr left Nanking on January 24 (893.20 Mission/4–1449). For quotations of excerpts of his operational report, see *United States Relations With China*, pp. 325–338.

[32] Personal Chief of Staff to the President, 1948–49. General Sun Li-jen had been Deputy Commander in Chief of Chinese ground forces and Commander in Chief of Army Training Headquarters.

[33] On Formosa.

shevik revolution last November that Communist forces at home and abroad steadily becoming stronger while capitalist countries growing weaker. At that time Molotov [34] in anniversary speech Bolshoi Theatre said 'pillars imperialism steadily crumbling'. On same occasion previous year he said 'we live in age when all roads lead to Communism'."

After statement that Mao's terms "clearly reflect his adherence Communist ideology and views," censors suppressed following phrase "currently espoused by Communists different parts world". Censor also suppressed word "everywhere" following statement that "Mao's program confirms thinking Communists".

Sent Department 158; repeated Nanking as 12.

KOHLER

893.00/1–2249 : Telegram

The Consul General at Peiping (Clubb) to the Secretary of State

PEIPING, January 22, 1949—11 a. m.
[Received January 22—5 :08 a. m.]

84. Foreign Office official last night gave me purported Communist terms for North China:

1. War criminal label will be removed from Fu [35] if he surrenders Peiping intact;

2. Life, property families of self and subordinates would then be protected;

3. Local troops (including, informer thought, Central Government troops) would on surrender be removed from Peiping (Paoting?), reorganized and sent location to be agreed upon jointly by both sides.

Indications were from this information Fu had no concrete assurances re future character and disposition those troops or he would enjoy any authority under Communists. Informant suggested Fu might be found still in command Peiping but it seems unlikely.

Communist rejection January 21 Executive Yuan proposals cessation hostilities and Gimo retirement presumably introduce new elements into thinking Fu's camp which undoubtedly yearns over-all settlement. Same informer, however, stated time Peiping was short. This fits other indications (Sollenberger [36] got rumor last night [that] today Communist ultimatum deadline Peiping) seems probably local settlement be forced on Peiping prior over-all settlement. Information given Sollenberger today by power company official [that] agreement completed except disposition 13th and 16th Armies.

[34] V. M. Molotov, then Soviet Minister for Foreign Affairs.
[35] General Fu Tso-yi.
[36] Howard Sollenberger, Director of the Peiping Language School.

Official stated brief recent interruption current was truly due technical difficulties Peiping receives 2,000–6,000 KW, that they received Communists' instructions re procedure during takeover.

Important Government officials including at least two high ranking BIS leaders have departed Peiping and Minister of War, Hsu Yung-chang, reported arrived 20th and departed Peiping 21st.

Foreign Office representative states been determined explosion ex-Mayor Ho house caused by bomb, not artillery shell.

Sent Department 84; Nanking 74; Shanghai 73.

CLUBB

893.00/1–2249 : Telegram

The Consul General at Peiping (Clubb) to the Secretary of State

PEIPING, January 22, 1949.
[Received January 22—1 :08 a. m.]

85. Certain units Nationalist forces have begun to move out Peiping in implementation reputed turnover arrangement.

Sent Department, Nanking 75, Shanghai 74, Tientsin 27.

CLUBB

893.001 Chiang Kai-shek/1–2249 : Telegram

The Ambassador in China (Stuart) to the Secretary of State

NANKING, January 22, 1949—noon.
[Received January 22—4 :49 a. m.]

186. Generalissimo was accompanied to airport yesterday afternoon by Vice-President. Immediately after latter's return to his offices, his secretary, Kan Chieh-hou, called on me to report developments and to ask our support of new Acting Chief of State. After reviewing difficulties facing Li Tsung-jen in his new and somewhat ambiguous position, he asked if President or US Government could not make statement or send message indicating its approval and support of Li Tsung-jen in his new responsibilities. I made no comment other than to say I would refer request to my Government.

After careful consideration, we here have reached conclusion that US Government should say nothing at this point. Finality of Generalissimo's withdrawal from authority doubtful, legal position of Li Tsung-jen and scope of his authority not yet clear. We have refused constantly over past several months to make any kind of statement in support of Chinese Government under Generalissimo and anything we might say now in favor of Li would most certainly be considered partisan and unwarranted interference in Chinese domestic politics.

Sent Department; repeated Shanghai 91.

STUART

893.001 Chiang Kai-shek/1–2249 : Telegram

The Ambassador in China (Stuart) to the Secretary of State

NANKING, January 22, 1949—1 p. m.
[Received 2:31 p. m.]

193. From Generalissimo's farewell statement it may be assumed that mandate of Vice-President is based upon and limited by article 49 of the Chinese Constitution which reads in translation "should the President for any reason be unable to attend to his duties, the Vice-President shall perform the functions of his office in his place". (See Embtels 194 and 195, January 22, immediately following.)

The Constitution does not further elucidate with regard to relationship of President and Vice-President under conditions stated. However, two things seem clear from provisions of article 49. One is that Vice-President succeeds to all powers previously exercised by the President ("shall perform the functions of his office"). The other is that the President has not permanently abdicated, for the Vice-President performs the functions of his office "in his place". (This might also be rendered "on his behalf".) This means that the President can legally return at any time to take back his power from Vice-President and again "attend to his duties".

STUART

893.001 Chiang Kai-shek/1–2249 : Telegram

The Ambassador in China (Stuart) to the Secretary of State

NANKING, January 22, 1949.
[Received January 22—3:02 p. m.]

194. Following is Central News Agency's English translation of text of Vice-President Li Tsung-jen's message:

"In consideration of the difficulties confronting the nation and the hardships suffered by the people and with a view to promoting the early realization of peace, President Chiang Kai-shek has decided to retire from office. In accordance with article 49 of the Constitution I as Vice-President shall exercise the duties and powers of the President.

"It is with great diffidence that I accept such heavy responsibilities. I have worked for more than 20 years for the consummation of the revolution under the leadership of the President. In those years, I have gained an intimate knowledge of the great care the President exercised in performing the duties of his high offices and the emphasis he always placed upon the welfare of the nation and the people. In matters relating to his personal position, he has always exercised great prudence and shown extreme sincerity. Once a decision is made, he never changes his mind.

"In the circumstances, I have found it impossible to decline the performance of the duties thus entrusted to me. I can only do my best to serve the country with loyalty, hoping to maintain the continuity of the affairs of state and to complete the President's mission in bringing about the salvation of the nation and the people.

"It is my hope that all the people of the nation will extend to me their sincere cooperation, that all civil and military officials will remain at their respective posts and that one and all will, in accordance with the policies of peace and reconstruction, exert their concerted effort for the attainment of democracy and freedom."

STUART

893.001 Chiang Kai-shek/1–2249 : Telegram

The Ambassador in China (Stuart) to the Secretary of State

NANKING, January 22, 1949.
[Received January 22—3 : 58 p. m.]

195. Following Central News Agency's English translation of text of President Chiang Kai-shek's statement issued shortly before his departure from the capital this afternoon (January 21):

"Since I issued my New Year message urging the restoration of peace, the entire nation with one accord has echoed its unreserved support. However, although more than 2 weeks have now elapsed, warfare has not yet drawn to a close and the ultimate aim of achieving peace has not been realized. Consequently, an end to the people's sufferings is still not in sight.

With the hope that the hostilities may be brought to an end and the people's sufferings relieved, I have decided to retire. As from January the 21st, Vice-President Li Tsung-jen will exercise the duties and powers of the President in accordance with article 49 of the Constitution which provides that 'in the event the President is for any reason unable to perform his functions, his duties and powers shall be exercised by the Vice-President'.

I hope the entire nation, including both the military and civilian populations, as well as the various Government departments and agencies, will unreservedly and with one heart support Vice-President Li in order that a lasting peace may be achieved.

I have devoted my entire life to the work of the people's revolution, observing strictly the Three Principles of the People.[37] From the 15th year of the Republic when we set out from Canton to the northern punitive expedition [38] to the one when national unity was achieved,[39] I never for a moment failed to consider it my sacred duty

---

[37] The teachings of Sun Yat-sen.
[38] 1926.
[39] 1928.

to implement the principle of nationalism, give effect to the principle of democracy and improve the livelihood of the people.

At the same time I have also always realized that it is absolutely necessary to secure peace for the country before a sound foundation can be laid for the improvement of the nation's political and economic life. That is why for more than 20 years, while I was sometimes forced to resort to military measures in dealing with domestic affairs, I have always been prepared to make personal sacrifices and concessions. The only exception was the war of resistance against Japanese aggression, in which case I was determined to fight to the bitter end. This is a record well borne out by facts.

My earnest prayers will have been answered if the Communist Party henceforth comes to a full realization of the grave situation confronting the country, orders a cease-fire and agrees to commence peace talks with the Government. Thus the people will be spared their intense suffering, the spiritual and material resources of the nation preserved, and its territorial integrity and political sovereignty maintained. Thus, also, the continuity of the nation's history, culture and social order will be perpetuated and the people's livelihood and freedom safeguarded."

STUART

893.00/1–2249 : Telegram

The Consul General at Peiping (Clubb) to the Secretary of State

PEIPING, January 22, 1949.
[Received January 22—8:46 p. m.]

97. ReContel 93, January 22.[40]   At press conference there was read in Chinese statement of which following is translation supplied foreign pressmen by NCBSH liaison officer (slightly smoothed and condensed) :

For purpose shortening war, realizing public desire for peace, protecting industrial and commercial enterprises, and preserving cultural works, monuments, and antiquities, and lest vitality of country suffer further damage, and to bring forth early realization nationwide through peace, both parties after being consulted, agreed to publication following points (details regarding military problems being partly omitted).

1. Effective 10 a. m., January 22, both sides shall cease fighting.

2. During transitional period Joint Administrative Office (this translation checked with original Chinese) shall be established by representatives both sides. This Joint Administrative Office shall be charged with responsibility handling all military and political affairs.

3. Troops stationed inside city shall be unit—including army groups (translation here believed corrupt) beginning January 22, move out of city with their designation and organization [*sic*]. Above mentioned troops moving out of city shall be reorganized within about 1 month after arrival at designated location.

---

[40] Not printed.

4. Maintenance of order inside city in addition to regular police units and warehouse guards [*gendarmerie?*], necessary number of troops shall be retained as may be required inside city to assist in maintenance social order.

5. Political administrations stationed inside Peiping and all central [Government?] and local enterprises whether publicly operated or publicly utilized—banks, warehouses and cultural organizations and schools, etc.—shall maintain *status quo*. No damage or loss shall be permitted occur such organizations. Above-mentioned organizations, while maintaining *status quo*, shall await over-all settlement by Joint Administrative Office two parties. All personnel such organizations shall be assured personal safety.

6. Hopei provincial government and its subordinate organizations shall maintain their *status quo*, and no damage or loss shall occur such organizations. Those organizations, while maintaining *status quo*, shall await over-all settlement to be carried out by Joint Administrative Office. All personnel such organizations shall be assured personal safety.

7. Gold yuan currency shall be allowed circulate as usual pending issuance specific regulations re exchange to be later promulgated.

8. Construction all military fortifications shall accordingly be stopped.

9. Safety lives and property all foreign consulates and their diplomatic officials as well as foreign residents living Peiping shall be assured.

10. Postal and telegraph services shall maintain their routine connection with outside places.

11. All local newspapers may carry on publication as usual. These shall be subject to re-registration and examination to be later enforced.

12. Protection relics and antiquities of civilization as well as freedom of worship of all religions and their safety [*safety religious believers?*] shall be assured.

13. People all walks of life are requested carry on their lives as usual and no public panic shall be created.

Additional information indicates Joint Administrative Office is temporary in character and that Nationalist and Communist members will participate in equal number. Fu Tso-yi speech, which by report was delayed until 1600 hours, reputedly made reference Generalisimo's retirement. Meeting was attended by chief leaders local military and civil organs numbering something over 20 persons. Point covered in speech indicated that "in principle" Communist troops would not enter city (this presumably applying primarily transitional period).

General Yen who read statement in Chinese said Fu Tso-yi is still in Peiping. Asked whether he would remain there, he stated this unknown. Agreement reputedly applicable North China, but General Yen stated inapplicable Chahar and Suiyuan.

Sent Department 97, Nanking 87, Shanghai 86.

CLUBB

893.00/1–2349 : Telegram

The Consul General at Peiping (Clubb) to the Secretary of State

PEIPING, January 23, 1949.
[Received January 22—11 :57 p. m.]

103. ReEmbtel 24, January 23.[41] Political turnover completed presumably effective 10 a. m. January 22 (see Contel 87, January 22 [42]).

Ping Ming Jih Pao reports today Nationalist forces occupying Peiping yesterday were removing from city in direction Huangtsun to south and Huangszu (Yellow Temple) to north, that movement continues today, that it is understood all will have been removed tomorrow, January 24, for stationing outside city.

Sent Nanking 93, repeated Department 103, Shanghai 92.

CLUBB

II. EFFORTS OF ACTING PRESIDENT LI TSUNG-JEN TO ORGANIZE PEACE TALKS, AND NEGATIVE ATTITUDE OF CHINESE COMMUNISTS; UNOFFICIAL PEACE DELEGATIONS FROM NANKING AND SHANGHAI; MOVE OF EXECUTIVE YUAN FROM NANKING TO CANTON; FRICTION BETWEEN ACTING PRESIDENT LI AND PREMIER SUN FO; FALL OF SUN FO CABINET (JANUARY 23-MARCH 14)

893.00/1–2349 : Telegram

The Ambassador in China (Stuart) to the Secretary of State

NANKING, January 23, 1949.
[Received January 23—5 :10 a. m.]

196. Following delegation selected to talk peace with Communists: Chang Chih-chung,[43] Shao Li-tzu,[44] Huang Shao-hsiung,[45] Chung Tien-hsin,[46] Peng Chao-hsien.[47] This group will broadcast their intentions to Communists probably today, January 23, and ask where and when conference can be arranged.

STUART

893.00/1–2349 : Telegram

The Ambassador in China (Stuart) to the Secretary of State

NANKING, January 23, 1949—11 a. m.
[Received January 23—5 :30 a. m.]

197. Representative of Acting President Li Tsung-jen called on me this afternoon (January 22) to explain in futher detail reasons for

---

[41] Not found in Department of State files.
[42] Telegram No. 97 to the Department, *supra.*
[43] Military and Political Affairs Director for Northwest China and Government representative during 1946 negotiations with the Chinese Communist Party.
[44] Member of the Kuomintang Central Executive Committee ; Chinese Ambassador in the Soviet Union, 1939–42.
[45] Member of the Chinese Legislative Yuan.
[46] Chinese Minister for Water Conservancy.
[47] Chinese Minister of Interior.

Li's request of yesterday for American supporting statement (see Embtel 186, January 22). He said that Li had been in touch with the Soviet Embassy through an intermediary and had worked out a tentative three-point draft agreement between China and the USSR which the Soviet Ambassador [48] had taken with him to Moscow earlier this week. Points are: (1) Strict Chinese neutrality in any future international conflict; (2) eliminate American influence as much as possible from China; (3) establish a basis of real cooperation between USSR and China.

According to our informant, Li has already agreed to these points in principle although how he intends to implement them even if agreed to in Moscow not clear. Li's representative said that Acting President felt that a statement of support from the US at this time would strengthen his position in Moscow during the period of Roschin's visit there. I, of course, made no comment.

Sent Department 197, repeated Moscow 7.

STUART

893.00/1–2449 : Telegram

The Consul General at Shanghai (Cabot) to the Secretary of State

SHANGHAI, January 24, 1949.
[Received January 24—6 :30 a. m.]

235. Press 24th reports arrival Shanghai on 23rd Li Tsung-jen's personal adviser Kan Chieh-hou to persuade "third party" leaders to go to Nanking to assist Govt in revising [*reviving?*] peace talks with Communists, and that Chang Chih-chung and Shao Li-tse are expected to arrive today on similar mission.

Tribune reports Kan has seen Mme. Sun Yat-sen [49] and delivered letter from Li requesting her support but that she had declined invitation to act as official mediator. Kan also scheduled to call on Democratic League leaders Chang Lan, Huang Yen-pei and Lo Lung-chi and upon Carsun Chang, chairman Democratic Socialists.

Sent Nanking 177, repeated to Department 235.

CABOT

893.00/1–2449 : Telegram

The Consul General at Shanghai (Cabot) to the Secretary of State

SHANGHAI, January 24, 1949—4 p. m.
[Received January 24—7 :08 a. m.]

238. Mayor K. C. Wu called on me yesterday at his request with obvious purpose of sounding me out as to what American aid policy

---

[43] N. V. Roschin.
[49] Sister of T. V. Soong, Madame H. H. Kung, and Madame Chiang Kai-shek; widow of the founder of the Kuomintang and the Chinese Republic.

would be in the event that peace negotiations broke down because Communists insist on too harsh conditions. He repeated many arguments in favor of continued aid to Nationalists under those circumstances.

I replied in effect that I did not know and could not in any case answer such hypothetical question. I said that in my opinion our policy would depend in considerable part upon effectiveness of Government continuing resistance and degree of popular support it enjoyed among Chinese people.

Query may conceivably have some significance in reflecting Generalissimo's future plans in view of Wu's close friendship with him.

Sent Department, repeated Nanking 181.

CABOT

893.00/1–2549 : Telegram

The Ambassador in China (Stuart) to the Secretary of State

NANKING, January 25, 1949—11 a. m.
[Received January 25—5 :55 a. m.]

203. Supreme Headquarters report 7 of 8 Communist columns within 15- to 20-mile radius Pukow, moving toward that city. Only one inferior Nationalist Army remains on north bank Yangtze in Pukow vicinity and this army not expected fight. Within past 2 days 2 Nationalist Armies have crossed river moving through Nanking to undisclosed destination. Present composition Nanking Garrison unknown but it is believed that Generalissimo's elite guard has departed for Shanghai for onward movement elsewhere.

On political front Li Tsung-jen trying form bloc anti-Generalissimo elements and opportunists. It is reported that as enticement he and supporters are claiming American support on condition he form effective government. At same time, we understand he is attempting try secure Soviet intervention prevent Communists crossing Yangtze, informing Soviets that America will intervene substantially should crossing take place and also telling them that China will be neutral in event Soviet-American war.

On peace front Li is prepared accept Mao Tse-tung's[50] eight points[51] in principle and negotiate on details with negotiations prefaced by cease fire mission. Although negotiators chosen, no formal approach to Communists yet made. Up to present Communist radio tends scorn Li's peace attempts, labeling Generalissimo's retirement and Li's moves as "American plot."

---

[50] Chairman of the Central Committee of the Chinese Communist Party.
[51] See telegram No. 41, January 14, from the Consul General at Peiping, p. 49.

While Communist military intentions unknown, it would appear likely they have capability to take the capital within coming week. On basis present information, it is difficult foretell whether they have intention exercising this capability.   In any event, should they choose accept Government's offer negotiate, their presence in overwhelming force on north bank river close proximity Nanking will give them bargaining position for [*far*] above that which Li can obtain through present political maneuverings.   Indeed, there is little prospect Li can do other than accept Communist terms, however onerous, or move [to] Kwangsi.

Either these eventualities, we believe Generalissimo can be expected re-enter scene.   Through his departure, he effectively cut his loss—military and political—in lower Yangtze valley.   With secure well-defended base on Taiwan and relieved of responsibilities for forthcoming military debacle for surrender Government forces Nanking–Shanghai area, if negotiations succeed, which only possible if Government accepts Communist dictated terms, he can reject agreement as "national betrayal" and continue resistance from Taiwan and such areas on mainland where he may retain control.   If negotiations fail, and Li thus discredited, Generalissimo can then come forth attempt rally and lead all resistance forces.

In conclusion, it would appear that Communist control lower Yangtze valley, whether by military or political means, shortly forthcoming.   However, resistance will undoubtedly continue elsewhere China under Generalissimo's leadership.

Although Communists have military means occupy South China, this may prove time-consuming operation, especially since Generalissimo's military [re]sources probably commensurate with limited task holding Taiwan–Foochow–Amoy triangle, and delaying Communist advance into Kwangtung.

STUART

893.00/1–2549 : Telegram

The Ambassador in China (Stuart) to the Secretary of State

NANKING, January 25, 1949.
[Received January 25—9 :49 a. m.]

205. Following is summary North Shensi broadcast January 23:

Fifty-five so-called democratic figures headed by Marshal Li Chi-shen [52] have arrived in liberated areas and issued statement on current situation on January 22.   "Statement advocates relentless smashing of hypocritical peace offensive launched by Chiang Kai-shek and Ameri-

---

[52] Chairman of the Kuomintang Revolutionary Committee (KmtRC).

can imperialists and supports eight peace terms raised by Chairman Mao Tse-tung of CCP [53] in his January 14 statement."

Following is summary of statement entitled "Our Opinion on Current Situation":

"We have now successively arrived in liberated areas" and "we wish, united under the leadership of CCP, to exert our full efforts in course of people's liberation war to work together for swift success of Chinese people's democratic revolution, and early realization of independent, free, peaceful and happy new China."

We are greatly impressed by "atmosphere of democracy and freedom and vibrant, forward-moving spirit" in liberated areas and particularly by examples set by members of CCP.

During past 3 months people's liberation army has wiped out over one million Kmt [54] troops, liberated all Manchuria and nearly all North and Central China. Military offensives now point to south of Yangtze. "Beyond doubt, China will obtain full liberation in 1949."

Since reactionary Kmt bloc under wing of American imperialism is about to crumble into dust, it is changing its tricks and attempting to carry out political plots to drag out its existence. "As far back as when troops of Chiang Kai-shek began to collapse on northern front, American imperialism had launched its conspiratorial activities, employing venomous, double-edged scheme of disrupting Chinese revolution. On one hand they scheme to foment opposition within revolutionary camp, hoping to block or slow down revolutionary advance. On other hand, they incite reactionary Nanking bloc to launch peace offensive so as to win time for remnants of counter-revolutionary forces to make final desperate struggle south of Yangtze or in border provinces. We should be on guard against this."

"Today we must vigorously declare our belief: We hold that revolution must be carried through to very end. There is no possibility for compromise or conciliation between revolution and counter-revolution. We should bear well in mind bitter lessons of repeated defeat since 1911 revolution. Chinese people's revolution is today directed against imperialism, feudalism and bureaucratic capitalism. These are greatest enemies obstructing realization of independence, democracy, freedom and happiness for China. If they are not thoroughly swept away, no genuine peace in fact as well as aim can be realized."

"Therefore, we must relentlessly smash hypocritical peace offensive instigated by Chiang Kai-shek and American imperialism. Even more, we must raise our vigilance within our people's democratic camp, in our ranks order march in step, strengthen our solidarity to prevent infiltration counter-revolutionary forces. People's democratic dictatorship should embrace representatives of broadest strata of people, but cannot include germs of counter-revolution. It should bring full freedom to greatest majority of people, but cannot give handful of reactionaries freedom to oppose people. Therefore, we firmly believe that people throughout entire country who are really striving for democratic revolution should exert their efforts together so that there

---

[53] Chinese Communist Party.
[54] Kuomintang (Nationalist Party).

is no room for opposition foothold within people's democratic camp or for existence of so-called middle road." Peace offensive contained in Chiang Kai-shek's New Year's Day broadcast is simply a fraud. With his conditions, regime of Chiang Kai-shek dynasty headed by four families would rule in unbroken line for generations. However, we believe that our Chinese people will surely not be cheated by reactionary plots of Chiang Kai-shek and Americans. Chiang's peace offensive should be dealt with without compassion. "If anyone today slovenly gives in by indulging enemy so that great revolutionary case collapses on threshold of victory, he becomes a criminal against Chinese revolution and against nation."

"But we are very happy and elated in having read recent statement on current situation issued by Mao Tse-tung to carry revolution through to very end and shatter peace offensive. He keenly, firmly, comprehensively and sternly exposed plots of Chiang Kai-shek–American bloc and raised eight conditions for genuine people's democratic peace. We thoroughly support these eight conditions. Beyond all doubt common will of people of whole country is reflected here."

"Let us repeat these conditions in another form:

"We [War?] criminals must be tried and punished; bogus constitution and bogus legitimacy of traditional institutions must be abolished; all reactionary armies must be remolded in accordance with democratic principles; bureaucratic capital must be confiscated; agrarian system must be reformed; treaties of national betrayal must be annulled; all power of reactionary Nanking Government and all its levels of government must be taken over; new political consultative conference soon to be convoked and democratic coalition government soon to be established must refuse participation by reactionary elements.

"To sum up: People's revolution must be carried to very end. Day on which revolution is carried to very end is day of advent of genuine peace and complete liberation. Strength of liberated people is matchless. Look at our friend and neighbor, Soviet Union; after only 32 years of construction it has become strongest fortress of peace in whole world. We people of China are double people of Soviet Union in number and have in addition favorable conditions. We dare to believe that after we have smashed reactionary government we can in shorter time construct peaceful, democratic free new China. Bright perspective lies before us. We should exert our efforts in unison.["]

Sent Department 205, repeated Shanghai 96, Moscow.

STUART

893.00/1–2549 : Telegram

The Ambassador in China (Stuart) to the Secretary of State

NANKING, January 25, 1949—1 p. m.
[Received 2 :02 p. m.]

208. Govt under new Chief of State is doing utmost to secure peace. Present Cabinet claims following 5 points already to its credit toward this goal:

1. New Year's message of Gimo
2. Approach to Big Four for mediation [55]
3. Executive Yuan approval of cease-fire proposal [56]
4. Resignation Gimo
5. Appointment of peace delegation to represent Govt

Both Acting President and Foreign Minister,[57] however, have sent word to me that despite their all-out efforts for peace, Govt would not surrender; that if Communists finally prove intractable new President would withdraw with all remaining armed forces to South China and continue resistance from there. Foreign Minister together with Shao Li-tze and Chang Chih-chung have sent urgent request to me that US Govt issue some sort of statement reaffirming its traditional policy of national sovereignty and administrative and territorial integrity of China as an American desire for unity, peace, economic recovery and political democracy in China. They felt statement along these general lines would reassure "liberals in both Kmt and CCP". They further expressed hope that any public statement would avoid expression of refusal to deal with any form of coalition in which CCP was dominant.

Sent Dept 208, repeated Shanghai 99.

STUART

711.93/1–2549 : Telegram

The Ambassador in China (Stuart) to the Secretary of State

NANKING, January 25, 1949—4 p. m.
[Received 9 :52 p. m.]

211. It would seem inevitable that you will be questioned about changes Chinese Government at your first press conference. In such event we feel extreme caution must be exercised if we are to avoid accusation partisanship. We have resolutely refused several requests for official statements in support of Chiang regime and anything said now would be scrutinized most carefully for signs of support of Li Tsung-jen.

New Chief of State is angling in Moscow for Soviet support and has reportedly agreed to negotiate with Communists on basis of Mao Tse-tung's 8-point program one of which is abrogation treaties with US. New Head of State may succeed in his efforts to secure peace at almost any price, but this is hardly a program which we should encourage by support publicly.

If, therefore, you are impelled by circumstances to reply to press queries on subject, we suggest you stress that there has been no change

---

[55] See telegram No. 61, January 8, 7 p.m., p. 22.
[56] See telegram No. 160, January 20, p. 58.
[57] Wu Te-chen.

in American policy toward China; that we continue to advocate the Open Door Policy and to desire the independence and territorial integrity of a China wherein free institutions and individual liberties will be recognized.

STUART

893.00/1–2549 : Telegram

The Ambassador in China (Stuart) to the Secretary of State

NANKING, January 25, 1949.
[Received January 26—1 : 05 a. m.]

215. Acting President Li Tsung-jen reported by all Nanking vernacular papers January 25 to have issued following 7-point program to back up statement that all obstacles to democracy and freedom will be removed:

1. Conversion of all Bandit-Suppression Headquarters into headquarters of regional military commanders;
2. Abolition nation-wide martial law (except in areas near front lines);
3. Abolition Bandit-Suppression Corps;
4. Release of political prisoners;
5. Revival all banned newspapers and magazines;
6. Abolition all special courts; and
7. Cessation all activities special service men.

Reports on a decision to enforce 7-point program vary. Several organs report decision approved by Kmt Central Political Council, others claim Acting President merely mentioned decision to Council, while few claim Li Tsung-jen issued direct orders to Executive Yuan to enforce program.

In this connection, press featured report that Li ordered release young Marshal Chang Hsueh-liang [58] and Yang Hu-cheng [59] and played up brief speech by action service [*sic*] in which he pointed out present situation due more to Kmt weakness than to Communist superiority. Catholic organ stated Vice President claimed he would persevere toward peace, but, if Communists will not talk peace, he has "other schemes".

Repeated Shanghai 102.

STUART

---

[58] Former ruler of Manchuria and leader of the Sian coup by which Generalissimo Chiang Kai-shek was held prisoner in December 1936; see *Foreign Relations*, 1936, vol. IV, pp. 414–455, *passim*.
[59] Pacification Commissioner for Shensi at the time of the Sian coup.

761.93/1–2549 : Telegram

The Chargé in the Soviet Union (Kohler) to the Secretary of State

Moscow, January 25, 1949—5 p. m.
[Received January 26—6:07 a. m.]

186. Only ray hope which Chinese Ambassador [60] can find in present situation is difficulty CCP will face in bringing all China under control central Communist government and resultant opportunities for resistance certain provinces such as Szechuan, Kwangtung, Kwangsi and maintenance semblance independence which might later develop strength aimed to oust CCP.

Ambassador instructed see Molotov [61] January 8 was kept waiting until 12th. Foo stated confidentially he had been instructed make additional oral proposal for unilateral mediation by USSR.

Ambassador believes Soviets and CCP have been in consultation regarding terms and mediation proposal (Embtel 151, January 20).

Sent Department, repeated Nanking 14.

KOHLER

893.00/1–2349 : Telegram

The Secretary of State to the Ambassador in China (Stuart)

WASHINGTON, January 25, 1949—7 p. m.

94. Urtels 186 Jan 22 and 197 Jan 23. Dept considers incredible Li Tsung-jen seek US statement indicating support for purpose strengthening his position while at same time arranging tentative agreement with USSR calling for elimination US influence from China. If opportunity presents itself, you should express to Li's representative views along foregoing lines.

Dept agrees conclusions urtel 186.

ACHESON

893.00/1–2649 : Telegram

The Ambassador in China (Stuart) to the Secretary of State

NANKING, January 26, 1949—1 p. m.
[Received January 27—1:32 a. m.]

219. In line with Pai Chung-hsi's [62] recent refusal send favored Kwangsi troops for defense Nanking and rejection Generalissimo's request to confer in Nanking, Hankow ConGentel No. 8, January

---

[60] Foo Ping-sheung.
[61] V. M. Molotov, Soviet Minister for Foreign Affairs.
[62] Military and Political Affairs Director for Central China.

17 [63] offers following: Pai privately stated inability hold Hankow with intention withdraw if Communists reinforce Central China. Further believes his strength unable hold even Yangtze line. Consulate General observed January 15–16 military trainloads vehicles, horses, office equipment, furniture, et cetera en route Kweilin but no troops nor ordnance. Artillery ordnance and troops, however, continue cross river apparently for rapid Kwangsi retreat when time ripe.

Sent Department, Canton 9, pouched Shanghai.

STUART

893.00/1–2649 : Telegram

The Ambassador in China (Stuart) to the Secretary of State

NANKING, January 26, 1949—2 p. m.
[Received January 27—12:25 a. m.]

221. Communist radio January 25 broadcast reply Government proposal send delegation to negotiate peace. Communists accepted proposal, but hedged acceptance with conditions leaving Government no scope for bargaining. Communist spokesman stated "Government long ago unable represent people of China. Only Democratic Coalition Government to be created by new political consultative conference, which will soon be convened without participation reactionary elements, can be qualified represent people China. Therefore, our permitting reactionary Kmt Government send representatives negotiate is not recognition any qualification that Government represent people of China, but because that Government still has in its hands portion military force". Spokesman then said Government must realize its retaining [*remaining?*] military forces inferior to those of Communists, said Government must accept Mao Tse-tung's eight conditions and pointed to Peiping settlement as model which negotiations should follow.

From above, it would appear to us that Communists have coldly reaffirmed their decision to reject Government's attempt enter new coalition as intact bloc and that they will decide which members Kmt, if any, acceptable to new regime as individuals. It also appears clear that Communists are demanding surrender remaining Kmt armies in order that they may be "nationalized". It has been Li Tsung-jen's intention negotiate peace only if Communists willing offer equitable terms. In light this broadcast it would seem that Li has to choose between complete capitulation and continued resistance. We believe that he will choose latter course, basing his resistance in South and Southwest China.

STUART

---

[63] Apparently not sent to the Department of State.

893.00/1–2649 : Telegram

The Ambassador in China (Stuart) to the Secretary of State

NANKING, January 26, 1949—2 p. m.
[Received January 27—2 :54 a. m.]

226. In rejecting Peng Chao-hsien as Nationalist representative to proposed Kmt–CCP peace negotiations and terming him war criminal, North Shensi broadcast January 25 made its first addition to list of 43 war criminals announced Christmas Day.

Despite numerous current rumors, to our knowledge no names have yet been officially removed from initial war criminal list except possibly that of Fu Tso-yi [64] who has "partly atoned for his crimes". On the contrary, January 25 broadcast reaffirmed intention to expand list.

STUART

893.00/1–2749 : Telegram

The Consul General at Peiping (Clubb) to the Secretary of State

PEIPING, January 27, 1949—8 a. m.
[Received 6 :57 p. m.]

128. Re Contel 94, January 22 [20]. Old-time police official who recently met Communist delegates informed that on January 22 before making address to local officials Fu met with Yeh Chien-ying [65] in final conference before agreement. At meeting Yeh requested Fu hand over National Generals Shih Chueh and Li Wen but Fu refused and Yeh acquiesced.

Per this information, joint administrative organ already formed, personnel designated. Also public utility organs and administrative post as well. Holding up formal announcement question arranging for semblance proper authority in present circumstances for resignation Mayor Liu, appointment Yeh. Source said visit to Peiping of Li Tsung-jen delegate (telegram 116, January 24 [66]) related partly present problem. Also says Li agreed local settlement, that liaison officers are being dispatched from Nanking elsewhere for coordination moves leading first local to end overall settlement shall finally be one of pattern and that Yen Hsi-shan [67] is also in picture. He reports psychological difficulty as Yen regards Yeh as mere youngster and recent telegram from Fu to Yen remained unanswered [be]cause Yen senior relationship position to Fu.

---

[64] Commander in Chief of Rebellion Suppression Forces in North China.
[65] Communist Chief of Staff, mayor-designate of Peiping.
[66] Not printed.
[67] Commander, Taiyuan Pacification Commission Headquarters.

Re Fu's future, informant says Fu's sole request was for return troops Suiyuan (home of most) and their disbandment whereupon Fu intends retire. Believe reserve should be exercised on reaching conclusions re Fu's intentions.

Informant stated Communists recognize problems are (1) lack administrative personnel, (2) economic and (3) winning support of people. For source, Yeh Chien-ying, after above conference, returned headquarters Hsiangshan in west hills. This source emphasized both Nationalists and Communists aware high desirability extending full protection to foreigners and said Communists showed real interest also in developing foreign trade.

Sent Department 128; repeated Nanking 109, Shanghai 106.

CLUBB

893.00/1–2749 : Telegram

The Ambassador in China (Stuart) to the Secretary of State

NANKING, January 27, 1949—11 a. m.
[Received January 28—10 :33 a. m.]

237. Most thought-provoking is last paragraph Moscow's telegram 158, January 21 to Department which recounts how Soviet censor suppressed word "everywhere" following statement in NY *Herald Tribune* correspondent despatch that "Mao's program confirms thinking Communists".

From material reaching us, it seems apparent that Communists now Yugoslavia, France, Poland, and elsewhere except in USSR are greatly elated by CCP victories. Soviets are only Communists whose enthusiasm is lagging.

We cannot put our finger on any pat reason for lukewarm attitude of Soviets. Certainly it cannot be accounted for by theoretical writings of CCP which during past few months have been more than fervid in their protestations of loyalty to "first land of Socialism".

If lukewarm attitude is to be interpreted other than as maneuver in itself Soviet peace offensive or as error of censor, we would suggest as possible explanations:

(1) High level discussions between Soviet and Chinese CP's concerning policy in Southeast Asia, and particularly Manchuria, are running into snags;

(2) Kremlin planners, as Communists, are less enthusiastic over their little Chinese brothers than they are concerned, as Russians, over possible emergence of relatively strong and well-integrated Chinese state at their backdoor and

(3) Their misadventure in China during '20's, has conditioned Stalin [68] and few surviving old Bolsheviks to view all Chinese with profound distrust.

At this time it may be useful to record our impression that local Soviet Embassy personnel are far from enthusiastic about China, Chinese and even Chinese communism. Their opinion of Chinese seems to verge on contempt, an attitude which easily manifested itself to American officials in Vladivostok where Chinese colony was quite important before its liquidation in 1936. Soviet thinking was neatly epitomized recently by Soviet Military Attaché who told us he thought Chinese civil war is not "a genuine war" and that it does not even remotely resemble war allies recently fought in Europe.

Sent Department 237, pouched Shanghai, repeated Moscow 10.

STUART

893.00/1–2749 : Telegram

The Ambassador in China (Stuart) to the Secretary of State

NANKING, January 27, 1949—noon.
[Received January 27—10 :38 a. m.]

239. Minister-Counselor [69] was approached today by Dr. Han Li-wu, former Vice Minister Education, regarding possible military assistance for group of staunch liberals which would endeavor provide leadership for vigorous resistance to communism, using Kwangtung, Fukien and Taiwan as base. He spoke of declaring that area independent of any Communist government which might be formed and recognized by foreign powers. The group would like to see Generalissimo stay in retirement as they feel he would handicap their activities. He mentioned as among the leaders of movement Dr. Hu Shih,[70] Li Wei-kuo, former Secretary-General Executive Yuan and secretary to Generalissimo, General Sun Li-jen, American-trained, most efficient Chinese Army officer now in command training on Taiwan, Admiral Chou Hsien-chang, Chief of Staff Chinese Navy, and Wang Shih-chieh, just resigned Minister Foreign Affairs. The group was still seeking reliable leadership within Air Force and it would of course be necessary to obtain support General Chen Cheng, Governor Taiwan. Both would be difficult but if he could have assurances of American aid, task might be made easier.

---

[68] Josif Vissarionovich Stalin, Soviet Prime Minister and Chairman of the Council of Ministers of the Soviet Union.

[69] Lewis Clark.

[70] Former Chancellor of National Peking University and Chinese Ambassador in the United States, 1938–42.

He was informed by Minister-Counselor that we could make no promise of aid and that we could not commit the Congress of the US, but that he could be assured that American people did not desire to see China controlled by a Moscow-dominated Communist regime and that any Chinese elements of resistance to such a regime could be confident of the sympathy of the American people. Also, sympathizing with such resistance, the American people could be counted upon to do what was feasible to assist. We pointed out, however, that an overwhelming amount of war matériel had been lost in recent months to the Communists, that American resources were limited, and that we had commitments in other parts of the world.

The integrity of the persons allegedly involved in this movement is beyond question and it may be well for us to give them some form of encouragement. We cannot stress too strongly, of course, need for utmost secrecy if their lives are not to be in jeopardy.

STUART

893.002/1–2749 : Telegram

The Ambassador in China (Stuart) to the Secretary of State

NANKING, January 27, 1949—4 p. m.
[Received January 27—6 :37 a. m.]

242. Following a Cabinet meeting last night, Acting President agreed to follow government to Canton (see mytel 27 [*217*], January 26, noon [71]). Apparently he had not approved of Government's decision move capital and had made no decision about his own future movements.

Conclusive argument which finally convinced him was Communists were relentlessly marching against Nanking and that if he were taken prisoner his usefulness would be ended.

Only 40 officials left in Foreign Office today. Vice Minister Tung Lin leaving tomorrow. He reports Foreign Minister will give reception for Diplomatic Corps Canton February 5.

Sent Department; repeated Canton 11, Shanghai 110.

STUART

893.00/1–2749 : Telegram

The Consul General at Shanghai (Cabot) to the Secretary of State

SHANGHAI, January 27, 1949—7 p. m.
[Received January 27—10 :57 a. m.]

271. Heavy troop movements in area and mass exodus Government personnel from Nanking causing serious disruption service on Nan-

---

[71] *Post*, p. 663.

king–Shanghai and Shanghai–Hangchow–Ningpo railways. In past few days trains vastly overcrowded, running many hours late. Many of regularly scheduled passenger trains have been taken off run with military take-over facilities. Railway administration officials admit inability handle situation which is described as one of complete and unparalleled confusion and disorder. Terminals jammed, resulting in many accidents daily. Director Mint here has told Consulate General officer [that] 1,200 Ministry Finance employees passing through Shanghai en route Foochow.

Recent calm, which has pervaded Shanghai, now giving place to increasing nervousness over possibility of all-out defense attempt or of looting, disintegrating soldiery. Although armed deserters and stragglers on increase, garrison said to be making determined effort round up such elements. City remains at least superficially quiet with no immediate cause for alarm.

Sent Nanking 212, repeated Department 271.

CABOT

893.00/1–2849 : Telegram

The Consul General at Shanghai (Cabot) to the Secretary of State

SHANGHAI, January 28, 1949—9 a. m.
[Received 10:22 a. m.]

280. In conference today with Admiral Badger,[72] Mayor Lapham,[73] General Barr [74] and Admiral Crawford,[75] Wu [76] made following major points:

(1) He would turn over to us any official files in Shanghai for removal or photostating. I expressed interest in intelligence files. I would appreciate most urgent instructions re this.

(2) Wu asked Barr to discuss with SCAP [77] possibility of reestablishing trade between Japan and Taiwan, stating that Taiwan was planned as a last National bastion.

(3) Wu asked that Lapham divert as much ECA aid as possible to Taiwan.

(4) He said that 2,000,000 ounces of gold had already been shipped to Taiwan and that he was asking transfer of 500,000 more ounces of 800,000 remaining in Shanghai.

(5) He indicated that Chinese Air Force and Navy would withdraw to Taiwan to prevent a Commie invasion.

---

[72] Adm. Oscar C. Badger, Commander, U.S. Naval Forces in Western Pacific.
[73] Roger D. Lapham, Chief of China Mission, Economic Cooperation Administration (ECA) ; formerly Mayor of San Francisco.
[74] Maj. Gen. David G. Barr, Director of the Joint United States Military Advisory Group (JUSMAG).
[75] Rear Adm. George C. Crawford, Commander, Amphibious Group Three.
[76] K. C. Wu, Mayor of Shanghai.
[77] Supreme Commander, Allied Powers in Japan (Gen. Douglas MacArthur).

(6) He estimated that the Commies would take Shanghai in from 4 weeks to 3 months.

(7) In answer to questions, he said he did not expect serious unrest in Shanghai on flight of Li Tsung-jen or fall of Nanking. He felt unrest would start when Commies were at Soochow. He pointed out that police had received double pay last month and that he was arranging another large bonus this month. He added that with 150,000 Nationalist soldiers in Shanghai no one division would dare to mutiny for fear of being crushed by local divisions. General Barr expressed serious doubts: (1) that Shanghai could be held for more than 2 weeks if Commies really tried to take it in that time; (2) that Taiwan could be held with Air Force and Navy in present state of inefficiency.

In answer to Barr's question, Wu stated they felt reasonably confident of the loyalty of Air Force and Navy. He admitted that there was considerable Commie agitation among crews of merchant ships and agreed that disparities between Army and Air Force pay must be lessened. He felt that use of gold reserves would mitigate discontent in Taiwan resulting from inflation.

Mayor Wu asked what our plans were re protection of Americans in Shanghai. We explained our emergency evacuation plan briefly and asked whether he would agree to stationing of small Marine contingents at points specified in plan. Wu readily assented and suggested that undated letters be now exchanged in order that authority might exist if confusion should prevent us from obtaining it later. Unless Department instructs to contrary, I shall exchange such letters next week. Badger and I were careful to make it very clear that we could act only with scrupulous respect for Chinese sovereignty and for wishes of Nationalist authorities.

Sent Department 280, repeated Nanking 217.

Савот

893.00/1–2849 : Telegram

The Ambassador in China (Stuart) to the Secretary of State

Nanking, January 28, 1949—noon.
[Received January 29—5:55 a. m.]

254. North Shensi broadcast January 27 undermined still further possibility of negotiated peace by claiming that Mao's eight peace terms have indisputably become "sole policy for dealing with National affairs" and by suggesting that Li Tsung-jen government can best prove its sincere desire for peace by complying with first peace term, that is, immediate detention for trial by People's Government

of principal war criminals including Generalissimo, T. V. Soong,[78] Chen Li fu,[79] Ho Ying-chin,[80] et cetera.

We would observe that this broadcast strengthens evidence that (see Embtel 166, January 21) CCP does not desire negotiated peace at this stage, is striving for unconditional surrender of National Government, and is aiming completely to smash Kmt state apparatus.

Sent Department, pouched Shanghai, passed Moscow 11.

STUART

893.00/1–2849 : Telegram

The Ambassador in China (Stuart) to the Secretary of State

NANKING, January 28, 1949—noon.
[Received January 30—3:06 a. m.]

255. On January 27, officer of Embassy and Naval Attaché interviewed Kan Chieh-hou, just returned from Shanghai following series conferences with minority party leaders on behalf Li Tsung-jen. Kan said that, while these leaders not directly representing CCP, they are in sufficiently close touch with Communists that they can accurately report and interpret Communist policy. Leaders told him Communists have three peace requirements. First is no "middle road"; all political groups and factions must adopt same attitude toward CCP as KmtRC and Democratic League. Second is no further American influence in Chinese affairs, no further dealings with Americans including no acceptance American aid by any group. Third is no negotiations with any group on basis its possession military or territorial resources; negotiation only with individuals on basis past political performance and present political record. On basis above, Kan and President both convinced no agreement with Communists possible.

Despite Communist intransigence, Li intends attempt negotiate. Already has two delegates Peiping who made initial contact with Communists January 26. No report received on result contact. On 27th or 28th, plans send telegram Mao Tse-tung reaffirming sincere desire for peace in denying that he is creature of Americans and pointing out that, while Communists have claimed desire negotiate, their terms have been couched as ultimatum. As follow-up, Li then plans send Shao Li-tze and Chang Chih-chung [to] Peiping with instruc-

---

[78] Brother-in-law of Generalissimo Chiang Kai-shek and former President of the Chinese Executive Yuan and Minister of Finance.
[79] Chinese Minister without Portfolio and coleader of the C-C clique of the Kuomintang (Nationalist Party).
[80] Former Chinese Minister of National Defense.

tions wait until Communists receive them for purposes negotiation. Purpose of above is to show clearly onus for continuing war lies with Communists, thus gaining popular support for Nationalists. Also hopes pressure public opinion and Communist hope that they can get Government surrender through negotiations may make Communists delay crossing Yangtze. Li convinced no possibility get fair agreement from Communists, but hopes use this technique stall for time.

Government would like defend Yangtze line but lacks required forces. Tang En-po [82] deploying to defend Nanking–Shanghai Railroad over which he will withdraw when seriously threatened. Liu Ju-ming,[83] with very inferior forces, will try prevent crossing between Wuhu and Nanking. Pai Chung-hsi will retreat to Wuchang when threatened. After Communist crossing, Government hopes establish defense line along Chientang River into northern Kiangsi and Hunan with Kiangsi-Hunan sector under Pai Chung-hsi. Government will hold this line longest possible, hoping for American assistance. This aid must include military mission. No question interference with China's sovereign rights exists. American troops welcomed as would be American participation protection Taiwan.

We are in general agreement with contention that any agreement Government may reach with Communists will be at price of whatever resources it might have to preserve itself as entity in coalition government. Communists appear determined eradicate once and for all any political grouping which might conceivably form nucleus resistance their political and military control over entire country.

We think it highly unlikely Li's maneuvers will delay Communist attempt cross Yangtze. Also, it is doubtful if they will succeed in rousing any considerable degree popular support for Government. However, they will establish clearly total character Communist aims, and should to some extent succeed in firming up resistance sentiment [of] south and southwest China leaders.

Sent Department, pouched Consulates.

STUART

893.002/1–2849 : Telegram

The Ambassador in China (Stuart) to the Secretary of State

NANKING, January 28, 1949—3 p. m.
[Received January 29—6 :33 a. m.]

260. Premier [84] and Foreign Minister have already left Nanking probably en route Canton. Despite statement by Vice Foreign

---

[82] Head of the newly established Nanking–Shanghai–Hangchow garrison command.
[83] Deputy Commander in Chief, Rebellion Suppression Forces, Hsuchow area.
[84] Sun Fo.

Minister that they have gone to Shanghai for special purpose and are returning Nanking, their houses are both entirely closed and empty. Repeated Shanghai 116, Canton 13.

STUART

893.00/1–2849 : Telegram

The Ambassador in China (Stuart) to the Secretary of State

NANKING, January 28, 1949—6 p. m.
[Received January 30—2 :10 a. m.]

264. ReEmbtel 205, January 25, repeated Moscow 8. We do not doubt that CCP regards as important achievement statement of 55 members of minority parties and other left-wing organizations broadcast by North Shensi Radio January 23. By thus captivating these fellow-travelers, CCP must have greatly reduced apprehension that, following collapse of Kmt, Chinese public opinion might polarize around some left-wing political body other than CCP. Importance of neutralizing and then crushing competitive left-wing parties is, of course, emphasized in all of Lenin writings. That CCP takes this lesson to heart was manifested in North Shensi Radio broadcast of October 30, which went so far as to assert that US Government espionage organizations in China had set for themselves task of to "strive to reach an understanding with elements with leftist leanings in Socialist parties, develop anti-Communist activities in trade unions and peasant organizations, and stir up discord between leftist leaders and destroy their prestige".

In addition to labor leaders, so far we have recognized among signatories leaders of following parties: KmtRC, Democratic League, Che Kung Tung, Association for Promotion of Democratic Rule in China, Democratic Party of Chinese Farmers and Laborers, and National Salvation Association of Chinese People.

Essentially statement is nothing less than repetition, in slight paraphrase, of all important CCP pronouncements during past few months. Thoughts were excerpted from Mao Tse-tung's article on October Revolution, Liu Shao-chi's [85] article on "Nationalism and Internationalism", CCP New Year's Day message, Mao Tse-tung's eight point peace program of January 15 [14], etc. This statement makes no original contribution to announced CCP platform. On the contrary it endorses such CCP dogma as that there is no middle road between Communists and Kmt, revolution must be carried to very end, all Chinese left-wing parties are united under leadership of CCP, and Mao Tse-tung's eight points. We regard as strong evidence that Li Chi-shen and his KmtRC have become puppets of CCP [the] fact

---

[85] Vice-Chairman of the Central Committee of the Chinese Communist Party.

that statement does not make one single effort to entice liberal elements from Kmt over to KmtRC.

Slightly unfavorable side are facts that statement fails to reaffirm CCP refusal to order cease-fire prior to beginning peace negotiations and that only slight reference is made to Soviet Union with somewhat dubious compliment that signers believe they can establish peaceful, democratic and free-speaking China in shorter time than this was accomplished in USSR.

So thoroughly abject is statement that we can only conclude any "democratic coalition government" formed largely with participation of these 55 signatories would be so completely dominated by CCP as to render inapplicable adjectives "democratic" and "coalition".

Sent Department, repeated Moscow 13, pouched Nanking [*Shanghai?*].

STUART

893.00/1–2949 : Telegram

The Ambassador in China (Stuart) to the Secretary of State

NANKING, January 29, 1949—4 p. m.
[Received January 30—11:01 a. m.]

270. North Shensi broadcasts January 28 pounded home harder than ever new [*now?*] customary themes that peace can be negotiated solely on basis of Mao's eight peace points, punish war criminals, Nationalist peace proposals are "false peace conspiracy of American imperialism and Kmt reactionaries", etc. Article was signed by Central Committee of CCP and was in form of 41 slogans which, incidentally, follow pattern not only of slogans announced by CCP last May Day but also ape principal Soviet method of selling ideas to public. We would observe that continual emphasis on these themes, culminating in their presentation as slogans, means they are now basic dogmas from which, in Communist eyes, no departure is possible. They are stronger than isolated statements of official spokesmen or even of Mao Tse-tung.

Despite harshness of slogans, we note that they do not: (1) shut out possibility of peace talks, (2) insist on peace talks preceding cease-fire orders, and (3) add to terms or their severity. On other hand, slogans fail to promise favorable treatment to foreigners and small entrepreneurs as other recent statements have done.

Sent Department 270, pouched Shanghai.

STUART

893.00/2–149

The Consul General at Hankow (Callanan) to the Secretary of State

HANKOW, February 1, 1949—2 p. m.
[Received February 1—3:35 a. m.]

17. Pai will not sacrifice his Army defend Wuhan. Communists can take over any time they decide attack in force. Pai has denied separate peace (re Shanghai's 290, January 28 [86]) but admits privately Huang commissioned [to] contact Li Chi-shen group. Pai also has representatives in Peiping but expects close cooperation with Li Tsung-jen (remytel 15, January 30 [86]).

Military movements across river to Wuchang now greatly accelerated. Local populace jittery due outbreak looting and absence police. Most stores closed as silver dollar at GY [87] 2,000.

Sent Department, repeated Nanking 17, Shanghai 13.

CALLANAN

893.00/2–149 : Telegram

The Consul General at Shanghai (Cabot) to the Secretary of State

SHANGHAI, February 1, 1949.
[Received February 2—2:41 a. m.]

340. Local press, 1st, reports Li Tsung-jen accompanied by Shao Li-tze and Wu Yao-huan paid brief visit Shanghai yesterday where he conferred with Sun Fo, Wu Teh-chen and other cabinet members reportedly on matter of statement released last evening upon his return Nanking rejecting Communist demands for detention "war criminals" as condition to opening peace talks. As Li did not see any minority party leaders, his visit interpreted by press as bid for support "nonpartisan leaders".

At luncheon attended by small number of such leaders (civic, business and cultural) he is said to have appointed as his personal representatives delegation led by Chang Chih-chung. Li stated to have called on Madam Sun Yat-sen and Gen. Ho Ying-chin. One report surmising latter offered position Minister Defense. Li said to have announced determination remain Nanking.

Sent Nanking 259; repeated Department 340.

CABOT

---

[86] Not printed.
[87] Gold Yuan.

893.00/2–149 : Telegram

The Consul General at Peiping (Clubb) to the Secretary of State

PEIPING, February 1, 1949—6 p. m.
[Received February 2—3 :02 a. m.[88]]

161. Additional Communist forces entered city today, particularly from south, bringing total to minimum 25,000. Communist troops today chiefly engaged in relieving 104th Army of garrison duties. Some Communist troops bear arm bands designating them Peiping garrison. Troops well armed, well disciplined. Have been kept [in] quarters except on duty. Some Nationalist forces still in town, some moving out today.

Foreign Office representative states his office bureau and municipal government functioning as usual for time being. He confirmed discipline [and that?] supervisory commission and North China Bandit Suppression Headquarters both terminated effective c.o.b. January 31. Other information indicates Communist functionaries began take over procedure in some administration offices today. Foreign Office source said he believed joint administration office operating today as scheduled but with formal ceremony. Newsmen have been unable find either actual office directory [or?] Yeh Chien-ying.[89] Chinese report indicates leading Communists arrived Peiping only today.

Today was featured by some parades students and labor guilds. Some Communists gave pantomime performances (including representative Uncle Sam supporting badly lamed Gimo) and distributed propaganda and sang songs. No evidence noted of violent anti-American propaganda. No Communist posters yet discovered. Yenching and Tsinghua students still absent.

Sent Department 161, Nanking 135, Shanghai 133.

CLUBB

893.00/2–149 : Telegram

The Ambassador in China (Stuart) to the Secretary of State

NANKING, February 1, 1949—6 p. m.
[Received February 3—4 :33 a. m.]

287. Following is report of conversation in Peiping between C. C. Huang, representative of Li Tsung-jen, and Yeh Chien-ying, member of CCP Central Committee and mayor-designate of Peiping:

1. CP is ready to consider liaison with whom it will deal in peace negotiations.

2. CP wants real and permanent peace. It is essential therefore to liquidate present feudal sticklers of oligarchy. By this is meant "four

---

[88] Text printed from corrected copy received February 3, 2:20 a. m.
[89] Communist leader.

families". It has been suspicious that Generalissimo and Li have been playing double game but Huang's explanation helped to clear this up.

3. CP is anxious to establish radio communication between Nanking and Peiping.

CP is favorably disposed to Kwangsi leaders because of their previous record in improvement of people's welfare in their home province, in contrast, for instance, with more bureaucratic Chekiang group.

Yeh inquired whether US was backing Li and if so for what reason and whether another world war was imminent et cetera. Huang, who had studied in US and was there last year on special mission, described in some detail American desire for peace and unity in China as exemplified in Marshall Mission, failure of which was not its fault but due mainly to obduracy of Generalissimo.

Yeh concluded interview by giving assurance that he was speaking for Lin Piao and Nieh Jung-chen [90] as well as himself and that it would all be reported to the Central Committee of CCP.

Sent Department, pouched Shanghai.

STUART

893.00/2–149 : Telegram

The Ambassador in China (Stuart) to the Secretary of State

NANKING, February 1, 1949.
[Received February 1—9 :50 a. m.]

288. Lead article in vernacular press February 1 is Government spokesman's rebuttal Communist broadcast January 28 in which Communists voiced opposition to acquittal of Okamura,[91] demanded arrest so-called war criminals and objected to Government's attitude toward regional peace for Peiping. Spokesman rejected Communist demand that punishment Okamura be made condition for peace talks, pointing out that this is a judicial case with no bearing whatsoever on peace talks. If Communists keep raising new questions, it will be impossible for two parties ever to bring their viewpoints closer together. As to arresting war criminals, spokesman regarded this as problem to be solved at conference table and said there is no reason to demand execution of any terms before conference even convenes. This will only cause people to doubt that Communists sincerely wish peace. Third Communist charge impossible to answer as no concrete facts given.

---

[90] Chinese Communist military commanders.
[91] Lt. Gen. Yasutsugu Okamura, wartime Commander in Chief of Japanese armies in China.

Spokesman continued both Government and Communists should realize that peace is unanimous desire of nation's people. He pointed out Government not unable to fight but unwilling to fight, and warned that Communist military successes during past few months cannot determine final victory of [or] defeat. Government hopes Communists will with highest sincerity hasten early convening of peace conference, spokesman concluded. Moderate tone of Government statement contrasted sharply with sarcastic Communist broadcast to which it was reply.

STUART

893.00/2–149 : Telegram

The Ambassador in China (Stuart) to the Secretary of State

NANKING, February 1, 1949—10 p. m.
[Received February 3—3 :15 a. m.]

292. North Shensi broadcasts January 29 and 30 use some new sledge hammers in effort to drive home alleged justice of CCP peace conditions.

In new tactic, former broadcast claimed that acquittal of Japanese war criminal, General Okamura, former Commander in Chief of Japanese Expeditionary Army in China, in Shanghai on January 26 "scheme to use hypocritical peace negotiations as cover for regrouping Kmt forces and war preparations, including plot to bring Japanese reactionaries to China to join Nationalist Government in fighting Chinese people". Broadcast ordered Nationalist Government to rearrest Okamura and deliver him to PLA [92] at time and place to be designated. This demand will presumably be unacceptable to Nationalist Government, if only as point of honor, and may in any event be impossible of fulfillment as press February 1 reports Okamura already departed China en route Japan. While new demand is primarily tailored to influence Chinese public opinion and to embarrass Kmt, it also reflects deep-rooted CCP suspicions of Japanese and American policy in Japan.

Broadcast January 29 also referred to CCP correctness and success in "settling Peiping question peacefully in conformity with Mao's eight terms" and pointed out that "this not only prepares site for peace negotiations, but furthermore sets example for settling peace question of Nanking, Shanghai, Hankow, Taiyuan, Kunming, Canton, Lanchow, Tihwa, Clean [sic], Hainan, et cetera". Parenthetically, broadcast made no effort to explain contradiction between CCP offer to negotiate peace with Nationalist Government on basis of Mao's eight points and its strong implication that peace will be negotiated on in-

---

[92] People's Liberation Army (Communist).

dividual and regional basis with several commanders. Finally, broadcast repeated demand that Nationalist Government arrest 43 war criminals including particularly Chiang Kai-shek as well as Soong, Chen Cheng,[93] Ho Ying-chin, Chen brothers,[94] K. C. Wu, Wang Shih-chieh,[95] Tang En-po, and six others.

Broadcast January 30 related how 34 "democratic orators" including Li Chi-shen, Shen Chun-ju,[96] Ma Hsu-lun,[97] Kuo Mo-jo,[98] Madame Feng Yu-hsiang[99] and Tsai Ting-kai[1] attacked Kmt false peace plots and fully supported Mao's eight-point peace terms" at mass meeting January 26 in North China. Typical of approval of CCP policy by these persons was statement of novelist Mao Tun that "unless we obtain eight-point peace terms raised by CCP, PLA should fight all way to Hainan Island".

We would observe that no North Shensi broadcast to date has yet contained slightest hint of any relaxation in CCP peace terms. On contrary, with every attack peace terms become more firmly set. Principal significance of these broadcasts therefore resides in fact that they are part of great Kmt–CCP publicity and propaganda campaign now being waged for purpose of influencing public opinion of this weary and devastated country as respects which side is responsible for refusing to call halt to civil war.

Sent Department, repeated Embassy Canton 7, pouched Shanghai.

STUART

893.00/2–249 : Telegram

The Chargé in the United Kingdom (Holmes) to the Secretary of State

LONDON, February 2, 1949—1 p. m.
[Received 2 :07 p. m.]

388. Depintel January 24, 4 a. m.[2]

1. British Foreign Office has received no information re alleged draft agreement[3] and is of opinion it is just something formulated by Li Tsung-jen which Soviet Ambassador has agreed take Moscow.

---

[93] Governor of Taiwan.
[94] Chen Li-fu and Chen Kuo-fu, leaders of the C-C clique in the Kuomintang.
[95] Recently resigned Minister for Foreign Affairs.
[96] Democratic League member.
[97] Revolutionary pacifist.
[98] Poet and writer.
[99] Widow of Marshal Feng Yu-hsiang, who died in 1948 en route to Odessa aboard a Soviet ship.
[1] General and member of Kuomintang Revolutionary Committee.
[2] Not printed.
[3] See telegram No. 197, January 23, 11 a. m., from the Ambassador in China, p. 77.

2. Dening [4] believes alleged agreement to be typical Chinese double-cross in that (a) hope perhaps exists that report of agreement will frighten US into intervention, after which agreement can be disclaimed, and (b) Li going behind backs of Chinese Communists, dickering with USSR and hoping Cominform will instruct Chinese Communists make peace with Li, thus saving something of Kmt regime.

3. Dening does not believe maneuver will succeed because Chinese Communists in dominant military position and USSR can, therefore, deal direct with them instead going through remnants Kmt Government.

HOLMES

893.00/2–249 : Telegram

The Chargé in the Soviet Union (Kohler) to the Secretary of State

Moscow, February 2, 1949—2 p. m.
[Received February 2—11:21 a. m.]

260. Chinese Ambassador [5] informed me last night he was encouraged by most recent developments China. His Government had informed him new conditions would be rejected and Mao's eight points were accepted only as basis for negotiation and it was hoped Government could be established in south to continue resistance.

Ambassador said events had now made clear to all impossibility agreement with CCP and that if only disintegration Government and army could be stopped prospects not hopeless.

Ambassador said he realized US could not give positive support Chiang and that such was not needed. However, situation would be greatly helped if US would issue statement indicating interest in continued resistance to Communist aggression by appropriate patriotic Chinese elements. Such statement encouraging new leaders to organize government and continue resistance would have important effect on Chinese morale and contribute substantially to achievement basis [for] resistance.

I told Ambassador I would pass his views on [to] my Government.
Sent Department 260, repeated Nanking 22.

KOHLER

---

[4] Maberly E. Dening, British Assistant Under-Secretary of State for Foreign Affairs (Far East).
[5] Foo Ping-sheung.

893.00/2–249 : Telegram

The Consul General at Shanghai (Cabot) to the Secretary of State

SHANGHAI, February 2, 1949.
[Received February 3—1 :36 a. m.]

351. President Li's order to Executive Yuan that it move back to Nanking from Canton is highlighted by all Chinese papers. The Government, by this act, demonstrated its sincerity in seeking peace with Communist[s]. Presidents of Control Yuan and Legislative Yuan also telegraphed Premier Sun Fo, requesting his return to Nanking. Premier Sun flew to Nanking yesterday and it is expected he will remain there for time being. Legislative Yuan has decided to hold its forthcoming session in the capital.

Nanking peace delegation representing various civic bodies in the capital left for Peiping. While in Shanghai, the five-man peace delegation appointed by President Li held an important meeting yesterday to discuss how to carry out their mission. Reported that as soon as the Government decides its peace policy, the group will leave for Peiping. Shao Li-tze now here scheduled return Nanking today, and reportedly will fly to Peiping within few days.

Lanchow yesterday, General Chang Chih-chung told press that peace with Communists is still hopeful. There will be many difficulties, but must wait calmly for their solution. Communists taking over Peiping featured by all papers.

Chang Kan Army group has taken over the garrison duty of Pukow and Puchen, while General Li Yen-nien's men have moved to south bank of Yangtze. Emergency measures promulgated in Wuhan.

[Here follows section on other news unrelated to these particular subjects.]

CABOT

893.00/2–349 : Telegram

The Consul General at Shanghai (Cabot) to the Secretary of State

SHANGHAI, February 3, 1949.
[Received February 2—10 :25 p. m.]

359. Following news appears Shanghai press 2nd on Li Tsung-jen's unofficial peace delegation local nonpartisan leaders appointed 31st (ReContel to Nanking 259, February 1, to Department 340).

Chang Shih-chao [6] on 1st denied reports circulating city that mission of delegation will be seek separate peace for Shanghai which he described as premature in view absence immediate military threat. Chang stated delegation would visit Peiping shortly under instruc-

---

[6] Member of the National Policy Advisory Committee.

tions "to observe conditions, talk with officials there and report to President," and that it was not empowered to make decisions or to act in capacity similar to official peace delegations.

Secret meeting of delegates presided over by W. W. Yen [7] leads press to speculate whether all delegates agreeable accept mission.

Sent Nanking 272; repeated to Department 359.

CABOT

893.00/2–349 : Telegram

The Ambassador in China (Stuart) to the Secretary of State

NANKING, February 3, 1949—2 p. m.
[Received February 3—6 :52 a. m.]

302. CCP political agent for Shanghai–Nanking area (named Chang) on February 1 called on President Li and had 2-hour conversation. He stated Mao Tse-tung and his closest associates are puzzled by following happenings: Military gains are suprisingly ahead of timing; Generalissimo's New Year message and retirement; Li's vigorous peace offensive; readiness of Kmt and Soviet to sign Sinkiang pact; [8] removal Soviet Ambassador to Canton. Chang hinted he fears Russia is playing game to prevent peace. Mao is said ready for negotiated peace but strongly opposed by younger members CCP. Military leaders like Liu Po-chang and Peng Te-huai strongly advocating carrying fighting through to bitter end. Li also sensed from Chang's comments there is tension between Chen Yi [9] and Liu. They are as one however in opposing departure Lin Piao from North China on ground this would open way for Russian control from northeast to that region. Li stressed he was not opposed to CCP as such so much as to Russian expansionism and loss national independence and democratic rights.

Sent Department, repeated Canton 12.

STUART

893.00/2–349 : Telegram

The Consul General at Peiping (Clubb) to the Secretary of State

PEIPING, February 3, 1949—5 p. m.
[Received February 4—9 :08 a. m.]

178. In celebration "liberation" Peiping there was today held long military parade. Parade motorized large degree (many American trucks, much American equipment), cavalry, infantry, also featured.

Large numbers Chinese students present including apparently good number from Yenching [and] Tsinghua. Students' attempt to get on bandwagon not attended by outstanding success but they were present.

Some slogans pasted up by demonstrators bearing anti-American characters. But demonstration on whole not directly or violently anti-American. In course speeches given Peita University February 1 by local professors, likewise only one was strongly anti-American in content. Press generally still exercises restraint this regard but *People's Daily News* has anti-American slant.

104th Army by report has removed from town. Press reports to contrary notwithstanding, Fu Tso-yi reliably reported still in town (west suburbs).

Communist administrators yesterday took over light and water plants.

Sent Department 178, repeated Nanking 150, Shanghai 152.

CLUBB

893.00/2–349 : Telegram

The Chargé in the Soviet Union (Kohler) to the Secretary of State

Moscow, February 3, 1949—7 p. m.
[Received February 3—3 :35 p. m.]

279. February numbers *Literary Gazette* and *New Times* contain first recent Soviet editorial comment Chinese situation and furnish clear evidence present solid alignment Kremlin with CCP. Themes emphasized these articles identical those recently emanating from CCP, i.e., designation Gimo war criminal number one, Gimo's retirement merely manoeuvre designed win time, Kmt bastion being prepared South China, Kmt stooge to US, etc. Similarity wording two articles also leads conclusion Kremlin line Chinese situation finally issued and recent evasion this topic now ended.

Highlights *Literary Gazette* article: Gimo, war criminal number one, decided withdraw temporarily in order help Kmt peace talk possibilities and gain breathing spell; victory democratic forces means not only defeat Kmt reaction but simultaneously bankruptcy Wall Street's war-strategic aggressive plans; Chinese Communists most loyal, consistent, selfless strugglers for peace, democratic rights, real independence and freedom; can be no doubt Chinese people will carry to finish great cause full liberation country from reactionary dictatorship Chiang and American colonizers.

In addition, *Literary Gazette* cartoon depicts battered, bedraggled Gimo and unconsolable US Army officer mourning American 6 billion dollar loss in supporting Chiang. Cartoon clinches point, hit hard both articles, that US and Kmt one and same, that Kmt's loss also Wall Street's loss.

Sent Department 279, repeated Nanking 23.

KOHLER

893.00/2–449 : Telegram

The Minister-Counselor of Embassy in China (Clark) to the Secretary of State

CANTON, February 4, 1949—noon.
[Received February 4—11:17 a. m.]

Cantel 10. Chen Tai-chu, head American Section, Foreign Office, feels peace negotiations will fail. Li Tsung-jen, he said, is making honest effort secure reasonable peace, even disregarding all-important question of "face" and that when it became abundantly clear to the public that Communists would not grant reasonable peace terms but would demand surrender there would be an effort toward continued resistance. He did not know whether Li Tsung-jen would come to Canton or go to Kweilin or whether Generalissimo might re-emerge at that time and assume leadership. It was going to be however a most critical time in history of China as offering last opportunity rally resistance on mainland.

He did not think resistance could be effective under Generalissimo or under Li and quickly discarded such names as Hu Shih and K. C. Wu as being too western. A leader was needed, he said, who could inspire confidence in the masses of Chinese people who know nothing of western culture, yet the leader must himself have knowledge of the Occident. China undoubtedly had such a person and he might emerge when peace negotiations fail if there were indication of support from US.

I told him that he as others with whom I had spoken lately put the cart before the horse. Our Congress had voted many millions for an ECA [10] program contemplated to give China a breathing spell and an opportunity to help itself and the results had been most disheartening. With this experience he could not expect, I said, to have the US once again promise assistance to resistance elements which were not already organized. If those wishing to continue resistance were to organize and give even slight hope of effectiveness, I said, such elements could be sure of the sympathy of the American people. Without sympathy of the American people I added that they could [not?] be equally sure of such assistance as might be feasible. I pointed out, however, our commitments in other parts of the world and

---

[10] Economic Cooperation Administration.

the fact that our resources are limited. Dr. Chen agreed that this might be true, but said potential resistance elements in China were discouraged by public pronouncements of American officials such as Hoffman's [11] Shanghai press conference and the failure of Chinese efforts to obtain a restatement of our policy. They drew the conclusion that the US was indifferent toward the present regime and was prepared to deal with the Communists and recognize any government they set up. If we really do not want to see Communist government in China, we should say so publicly, he said, and announce the conditions on which we would continue aid to China. If we could find it possible to issue such a statement or in some way express publicly our hope for continued resistance in China to Communist encroachments and time the action with the breakdown in peace negotiations, Chen thought potential elements of resistance would be encouraged and the possibility of successful resistance enhanced.

Sent Department 10, repeated Nanking 10, Shanghai 7, pouched Tsingtao, Hankow, Kunming, Chungking.

CLARK

893.01/2–549 : Telegram

The Minister-Counselor of Embassy in China (Clark) to the Secretary of State

CANTON, February 5, 1949—5 p. m.
[Received February 6—9 :20 p. m.]

Cantel 12. As promised, Foreign Office started in business in Canton morning February 5 though we question from the obvious turmoil whether any business was transacted. Symbolically perhaps, Foreign Office is housed in two buildings on Shameen separated only by Soviet Embassy.

Prime Minister Sun Fo and Vice Prime Minister and Foreign Minister Wu Te-chen arrived by plane 4th and were met by local celebrities including Kwangtung Governor Hsueh Yueh who has announced his support of Acting President and who told me Li Tsung-jen would be in Canton shortly. Press indicates rift in Government may result effort retain Legislative and Control Yuans Nanking with Acting President, while Cabinet under Sun Fo will function Canton.

Considerable foreign diplomatic representation has already arrived. Soviet Ambassador is here with his Counselor and 30-odd members of his staff. The British have their Chinese Counselor and First Secretary, Assistant Military Attaché; and supporting staff; Australia has its First Secretary; India First Secretary; French have Counselor and Assistant Military Attaché; Italians have Counselor;

---

[11] Paul G. Hoffman, Administrator of the Economic Cooperation Administration.

Burma First Secretary; Czechoslovakia the Chargé; Netherlands Counselor and two others, Apostolic Internuncio his First Secretary. Due to arrive today are Counselor [of] Iran; Second Secretary [of] Turkey; First Secretary, Portugal; Chargé, Mexico; Commercial Counselor and others of Korea. There is still evidence of considerable chaos and I doubt that business can be done effectively with Government before middle or end next week.

CLARK

893.00/2–549

The Ambassador in China (Stuart) to the Secretary of State

No. 44　　　　　　　　　　　　　　　NANKING, February 5, 1949.
[Received February 18.]

SIR: I have the honor to comment on some of the deeper implications of the catastrophic events in China which are happening so rapidly that we have been reporting them almost entirely by telegraph.

What we have been observing since V–J Day, and especially during the latter half of last year, is in a sense the decay of the ancient Chinese system of Government. The original urge of the Kuomintang was chiefly anti-dynastic—as had been true of the earlier Taiping Rebellion—and, although it included democratic ideas and modern reforms, these were weakened or lost in a reversal to traditional practises. In the case of Chiang Kai-shek himself there is no need to question his personal probity nor his patriotic motives, but his concepts and methods were undemocratic. There were also many in the Government of high integrity and liberal views. But the system permitted and even fostered the evils which caused its downfall. It had become so corrupt and inefficient, and had so completely lost all popular support, that there was but little hope of orderly reforms arising from within, and revolutionary outbreaks might have been expected even had there been no Communist Movement.

This had its genesis in China independent of the Kuomintang and had already attained sizeable proportions before that Party had come into power. It would doubtless have gained adherents, as in other countries, regardless of the failings of the Kuomintang. But these were effectively exploited by the Chinese Communist Party and have been an important element in its success. This is the reason why so many of the more idealistic students have been attracted to it. It will therefore serve as a catalyst in ridding China once and for all of the scholar-official privileged caste. Whether in doing so it will enforce a worse form of totalitarian despotism is now the question.

American antipathy to the evils apparently inherent in the Communist State has led us to outspoken sympathy with and generous assistance to the Chiang Government. But to the leader of that Government and his most ardent followers Chinese Communism was at the outset more in the nature of one more rival faction to be subdued by force—like the warlords—than a social upheaval to be neutralized by political and economic reforms. Through all the following years this factional antagonism has been intensified by personal animosities. The American policy has been sorely misunderstood as seeming to be on the side of the present-day equivalent of the rascally and reactionary mandarins of a bygone age instead of with the pioneers of a new and nobler social order. This may seem naive to us or even disingenuous, but an attempt to see it through their eyes will help to explain not only the virulence of Communist anti-American propaganda but the embittered criticism of our policy prevailing among almost all of the younger and perhaps a majority of the older non-partisan intellectuals.

There is a poignant irony in all of this. We came into existence as a nation through a revolutionary struggle for freedom and have led the world as the defenders of political democracy and of basic human rights. Nowhere has this been more heartily acclaimed than in China. Nowhere have we given more unstinted moral inspiration and material assistance. Yet now we are being blamed by anti-Communist leaders for not coming more vigorously to their rescue, as we did against the Japanese, and by all others for strengthening a decadent feudalistic regime and by thus meddling in China's internal affairs lengthening a devastating civil war. Our motives are also impugned as being directed against the Soviet Union rather than for the welfare of the Chinese people.

None the less we have very great assets for the impending struggle. There is an immense reservoir of good will for us among the Chinese people. We have done much through our cultural activities in China and from what they themselves have learned of our way of life to reinforce the teachings of their revered sages as to human relationships and social justice. This heritage will not fit them for meekly enduring intolerant regimentation. As they come into power the Communists will probably perpetrate their customary excesses and this will tend to alienate those not yet sufficiently indoctrinated. There will for some time be large areas on the periphery of this country where we can continue to exert our influence. The President's Inaugural Address will have a profound effect as a declaration of the high-principled, dynamic foreign policy of the present Administration.

Acting President Li is making a brave effort to secure a negotiated peace and is thus far revealing a commendable patience and indifference to personal consequences. He is keeping the public fully informed and is pressing for an early settlement on behalf of the suffering people. There is a fair probability that he will be successful because of the popular desire for peace and the weakness of the Government. He hopes to make his case unmistakably clear before the Nation and the world as to whether or not Chinese Communism will agree to a reasonable peace and a truly democratic form of government. If not, he and Pai Chung-hsi will return to their native province and rally all those areas not yet subjugated in a new form of resistance depending primarily on popular support.

In any case we may expect a period of harshly dictatorial and discriminatory treatment of foreigners, especially of Americans. The Embassy is attempting to tabulate a factual record of this nature. Thus far the indications are far from reassuring—in Tsinan, Mukden, Tientsin, with ominous overtones from Peiping. Some allowance must be made of course for confusion and excessive self-assertion at the outset and for the period of nonrecognition. It will be useful to converse with the leaders when that becomes feasible and to ascertain as best we can what are their real intentions.

Meanwhile I venture to suggest an attitude of quiet and watchful reserve, with preparation for expansion of USIS[12] and emphasis on the spreading of stimulating ideas and practical information rather than on money or military power. These latter may be needed later. Continuation of E. C. A. might well be kept in abeyance until they raise the issue. One possible exception might be the Joint Commission on Rural Reconstruction in provinces not yet "liberated" where it can have immense value, both in directly improving the people's livelihood and in educating them for democratic citizenship.

The Acting President has committed himself to long-needed governmental reforms. He should, as he is able, carry these out and make it known. If Communist administration is as oppressive as we have reason to fear it may be, it can be confidently expected that a spirit of revolt will sooner or later find concrete expression and if this is under a leadership which has popular support we can give it our unreserved assistance. Until then we can deal with the new authorities on a basis flexible and friendly but also very firm, in the assurance that our cause is right and will in time be proven so to a people as intelligent and as sympathetic to our history and principles as are the Chinese.

Respectfully yours,   J. LEIGHTON STUART

---

[12] United States Information Service.

893.01/2–749 : Telegram

The Minister-Counselor of Embassy in China (Clark) to the Secretary of State

CANTON, February 7, 1949—noon.
[Received February 7—6:53 a. m.]

Cantel 15. On February 6 at what he termed his first press conference as Premier, Sun Fo recalled his Cabinet created to secure "honorable peace" and insisted that did not mean surrender or submission. The Government had moved to Canton to avoid threat of hostilities; Nanking remained the capital. Removal to Canton as a place for Government to function did not affect peace move. Cabinet would meet February 7, he said, as all Ministers and Ministers without Portfolio are here. He denied emphatically there was any friction or misunderstanding between President and his Cabinet. Li might come here for a visit, he said, and members of Cabinet had been asked orally to visit Nanking and Shanghai for frequent contact.

Notwithstanding our information, Canton tends confirm reports visit Control Yuan and Legislative Yuan Presidents to Canton is primarily, if not solely, to try to heal breach between Cabinet and Acting President Li.

Although Government is physically here, little, if any, business is being done and it is difficult to contact reliable sources of information. Archives are still being unpacked in the Ministries we have located, but neither the Ministers nor their ranking subordinates are available.

Sent Department repeated Nanking 15, Shanghai 9.

CLARK

893.00/2–749 : Telegram

The Consul General at Shanghai (Cabot) to the Secretary of State

SHANGHAI, February 7, 1949.
[Received February 7—8:26 a. m.]

414. Following are latest developments re unofficial peace delegation composed non-partisan Shanghai leaders as reported local press 5th, 6th, 7th—delegation has been expanded by one member. K. P. Chen and Leng Yu-chiu have withdrawn from delegation for "personal" reasons and have been replaced by P. P. Hou, northern industrialist, Henry Ling, President University Shanghai, and Y. H. Ou, President Great China University. Mission to depart for Peiping "within day or two"[13] upon return from Nanking [of] Kan Chien-

---

[13] Departure of the mission was delayed until February 13; see telegram No. 527, February 14, from the Consul General at Shanghai, p. 127.

hou, personal representative Li Tsung-jen with final instructions for delegation. Latest report is that Chang Chih-chung will arrive Shanghai from Lanchow to join in and Shao Li-tze who will accompany delegation to Peiping as Li's "private representatives" serving delegation in "reference" capacity.

Arrangements completed with Communists for reception of delegation whereby press will be excluded and secrecy will attend all conversations. Kan emphasizing that delegation is unofficial in character "to knock at door of peace", although Govt has no objection Communists' negotiating peace terms with them. Delegation will seek Communist agreement on time, place for peace talks and cessation military activities before and during negotiations. Kan reportedly stated he believed Communists' demand for arrest Nationalist "war criminals" being exploited only for "publicity and propaganda".

Sent Nanking 302, repeated Department 414, via pouch to Canton 9.

CABOT

893.00/2–749 : Telegram

The Consul General at Hankow (Callanan) to the Secretary of State

HANKOW, February 7, 1949—5 p. m.
[Received February 8—5:08 a. m.]

27. In private conversation with AMA [14] Pai Chung-hsi explained Communist withdrawal (remytel 21, February 3 [15]) in terms their need sort enormous war booty, absorb Nationalist war prisoners and decide next move. He does not expect Communist attack near future.

Pai expressed great bitterness toward Generalissimo accusing him worst military blunders in history but confident Generalissimo out for good. Meanwhile, widely circulated rumors here of Communist atrocities and allout US aid can be directly traced to Generalissimo faction who attempting sabotage peace efforts. Pai in continuing effort eliminate Generalissimo's influence is reinforcing Hankow area and Sinyang with Kwangsi troops. With removal Mayor Hsu, only major Generalissimo official left is garrison commander Chen Mingjen who slated go soon. Thus Pai attempting strengthen Li Tsungjen's hand in peace talks by preventing possibility Generalissimo double cross in Central China.

Despite Pai's previous statement to AMA re indefensibility Wuhan (remytel to Embassy 8, January 17 [15]), Pai now says will attempt hold it. In view his admission only 2 months' ammunition supply here and other arms shortages, plus fact of continued monopolization by military of all southbound freight space, this statement must be in-

---

[14] Assistant Military Attaché in China.
[15] Not printed.

terpreted as designed strengthen Pai's plea US aid which he made to AMA. Vague feelers on possibility US aid recently made by civilian advisor of Pai to Consul General but not reported pending more concrete suggestions. Pai claims backing of Kwangtung (see mytel 15, January 30 [16]), Hunan, Kiangsi, southwest and northwest as well as three provinces under his control. Mongolian representative Prince Teh and Ma Hung-kwei representative recently in Hankow and Kwangtung representative en route. Pai proceeding Nanking shortly where he will confer Li and Ho Ying-chin.

Though Pai not optimistic peace prospects due Communist unreasonableness, peace offensive continuing as PPC [17] delegates five central China provinces and Kwangsi opened peace conference Wuchang yesterday. Li and Pai peace efforts good propaganda as local Chinese opinion increasingly blaming Communists for continuation war by adopting uncompromising attitude.

Conclusion: Pai backing Li to hilt in struggle eliminate Generalissimo's influence from Nationalist China, present united front to Communist and seek reasonable peace. But continued cross river and southward movement military supplies indicate Pai will abandon Central China rather than make last ditch stand if Communist pressure too great.

Sent Department, repeated Nanking 24, Canton 2.

CALLANAN

893.00/2–849 : Telegram

The Ambassador in China (Stuart) to the Secretary of State

NANKING, February 8, 1949—10 a. m.
[Received 4 :49 p. m.]

336. 1. February 6 General Tsai Wen-chih [18] called on behalf of Generals Ho Ying-chin and Ku Chu-tung [19] to give me following information and to ask if there were any way in which USA could dissuade Gimo from his "present stupidly disastrous course". Gimo continues to direct military affairs himself, ignoring completely Ministry National Defense. He is working entirely through three fellow-provincials, Lin Wei,[20] Tang En-po,[21] Chou Chih-jou.[22] He intends to abandon Nanking and defend Shanghai. Failing in this, he would aim to defend Fukien province on east and Hengyang (southern

---

[16] Not printed.
[17] Presumably People's Political Councils.
[18] Chief of Operations of Yangtze Defense Armies.
[19] Chief of the Chinese General Staff.
[20] Deputy Military and Political Affairs Director for Southwest China.
[21] Deputy Military and Political Affairs Director for Southeast China.
[22] Commander in Chief of the Chinese Air Force.

Hunan) on west.   But latter, once taken by Communists, would enable them to reach Canton.

Tsai is now serving as chief of operations and has been working on plans for defense of Yangtze, which he feels certain would succeed. Communists plan to cross river at Wuhu and Chinkiang.   There are some 600,000 National troops along Shanghai–Nanking railway which could be used to divide and defeat Communists with help of Air Force and Navy.   Quite possibly these could all be so deployed as to prevent Communists from attempting to cross at least for few months.   But Gimo is drawing away best units from Nanking area, leaving Acting President unprotected and foiling his peace efforts, apparently with this deliberate intention.   Strategically abandonment of Nanking is thoroughly unsound.   It is almost inviting Communists to cross river, and once having accomplished this it would be impracticable from military standpoint to hold Shanghai.   Tsai denounced Gimo both for scuttling Li's efforts and for faulty military tactics.

Significant thing in above report is that it comes from two of staunchest military associates of Gimo for many years, through one of his most loyal and well-trained younger officers.   Tsai used very strong language in denouncing Gimo.   Appeal to US is sort of desperate attempt to avert consequences of what they regard as folly of Gimo before too late.

It was curious coincidence that on same afternoon Acting President, who of course knew nothing of Tsai's visit, sent message to effect that he is quite embarrassed by various military officers close to Gimo coming to him to complain about orders that Gimo continues to give them.   Thus Chou Chih-jou told him that Gimo telephones him almost daily about what CAF [23] should be doing, although much of this could not or should not be done.   Chou owes his advancement to Gimo and has no other recourse than to resign if he does not go on obeying these instructions.   But if he resigned his successor would face same problem.   Similarly Tang En-po describes himself as in similar predicament.   Li added that Gimo is in position of energetic man without enough now to occupy his time.

I am, of course, taking no action with respect to these pleas, except to report them.

Sent Department 336; repeated Shanghai 149; OffEmb Canton 22.

STUART

---

[23] Chinese Air Force.

893.00/2–849 : Telegram

The Consul General at Shanghai (Cabot) to the Secretary of State

SHANGHAI, February 8, 1949—4 p. m.
[Received February 8—7:17 a. m.]

428. Communist broadcast last night curtly excluding Kan Chieh-hou from Peiping conversations and declaring they have no intention engage peace talks at present (Contel 311, February 8, repeated Department as 424 [24]) leads Consul General conclude real purpose of their acceptance Li's delegation Shanghai non-partisan leaders is to impress group that Communists are determined on local peace for Shanghai area. Li Tsung-jen, Kan Chieh-hou and Shao Li-tze arrived Shanghai early this morning and are reportedly discussing with Yen advisability mission proceeding Peiping in light new developments.

F. C. Yen told officer Consulate General this morning his cousin W. W. Yen, whom he had seen previous evening, frankly admitted most mission could hope achieve was establishment of channel for future exchange views.

Press this morning reports General Huang Shao-hsiung has arrived Shanghai from Nanking and yesterday called on W. W. Yen and Huang Chi-han, recently returned from Peiping where he is said to have seen Communist leaders in behalf Li Tsung-jen. *Central News* states Huang Chi-han may be asked accompany Shanghai Delegation to Peiping.

Of interest in connection with these developments and with recent Communist radio emphasis on desirability local peace settlements is fact that latest propaganda leaflets of apparent Communist origin now being circularized in Shanghai concentrate on urgent need for Shanghai leaders to refuse support further fighting, to punish local warmongers and to cooperate in hastening local Shanghai peace.

Sent Nanking 314, repeated Dept, pouched Canton 25.

CABOT

893.00/2–849 : Telegram

The Ambassador in China (Stuart) to the Secretary of State

NANKING, February 8, 1949.
[Received February 8—6:13 p. m.]

342. According to February 6 North Shensi broadcast, "active preparations are now under way to convoke provisional congress of

---

[24] Not printed.

people's representatives of liberated central plains area between Yangtze and Yellow Rivers at which provisional people's democratic government for whole area will be established and administrative program for this government worked out. Preparations follow December proposal from central plains bureau of Central Committee of CCP." [25]

"Proposal states new people's government must be established on broad basis of people's democracy. Government should include broad democratic elements, from workers, peasants, urban poor, independent laborers, intelligentsia, professional people as well as liberal *bourgeoisie*, enlightened gentry and minority nationalities. CP members working in government should cooperate democratically with non-Communists on basis of revolutionary program."

People's representative congress is to be supreme government organ of power. It is to elect government council and work out administrative program. In view of wartime conditions and lack of time for preparations, government will be provisional one to be perfected gradually as time goes on."

Central plains liberated area is spread over five provinces of Honan, Hupeh, Shensi, Anhwei and Kiangsu.

Sent Department 342, pouched Shanghai and Embassy Canton.

STUART

893.00/2–849 : Telegram

The Ambassador in China (Stuart) to the Secretary of State

NANKING, February 8, 1949.
[Received February 8—3 :31 p. m.]

343. North Shensi radio February 7 broadcast statement of spokesman for CCP to effect that Kan Chieh-hou, personal adviser of Li Tsung-jen, would be *persona non grata* were he to proceed to Peiping for peace discussions. Statement continued that General Yeh Chien-ying, Mayor of Peiping, would receive Yen Hui-ching,[25a] Chang Shih-chao and others of Shanghai (Civic Peace Mission) if they visit Peiping in "private capacity and have something to discuss about national affairs" but reiterated that "CCP announced long ago that preparatory work for peace negotiations had not yet been completed and there is no way to talk at present time. We are not prepared to receive persons from any quarter for time being."

Sent Dept 343, repeated Emb Canton 28, Shanghai 151.

STUART

---

[25] Chinese Communist Party.
[25a] W. W. Yen.

893.00/2–849 : Telegram

The Ambassador in China (Stuart) to the Secretary of State

NANKING, February 8, 1949—6 p. m.
[Received February 9—12:35 a. m.]

350. Reference Office Embassy Canton telegram 10, February 4. At dinner February 4 Foreign Office Vice Minister George Yeh likewise felt peace negotiations doomed. Present exit civic groups from Nanking and Shanghai to Peiping as peace emissaries Yeh claims as feelers for possible future "official" delegation. Has serious doubts if any will succeed, as Communists in position where negotiations short of unconditional surrender undesirable.

Yeh felt Communist delay at Yangtze due greatly future administrative problems Nanking and Shanghai which probably not fully planned as timetable 6 months ahead of schedule. Expects at least 1 month before take-over.

Repeated Office Embassy Canton 34, Shanghai 158, pouched Tsingtao, Hankow, Kunming, Chungking.

STUART

893.01/2–849 : Telegram

The Minister-Counselor of Embassy in China (Clark) to the Secretary of State

CANTON, February 8, 1949—6 p. m.
[Received February 9—1:33 a. m.]

[Cantel] 22. Foreign Minister assured me today that neither his assumption of office nor move of Government to Canton meant any change whatever in China's foreign policy.

He said full Cabinet was already here as were presidents of Legislative and Control Yuans [26] and that Government is in fact functioning in Canton. Acting President Li would likely visit Canton in next few days, but would return north and remain there so long as peace negotiations continued. Should peace negotiations fail and Foreign Minister expressed his belief they would fail, the fight would be resumed. Although he, Prime Minister and other ranking officers of Government might visit Nanking should occasion arise, he stressed that Government is functioning in Canton only and he assured me there would be on hand in Canton at all times an Executive Yuan capable of making decisions. We must have patience, however, he said, until the various Ministries are housed and their records in order.

---

[26] Tung Kwan-hsien and Yu Yu-jen, respectively.

Wu Tieh-cheng thinks it will take Communists at least 3 months to prepare Yangtze crossing. He says Yangtze will be defended and that, if Air Force and Navy will cooperate with land forces, crossing can be prevented.

Repeated Nanking 20.

CLARK

893.00/2–949 : Telegram

The Minister-Counselor of Embassy in China (Clark) to the Secretary of State

CANTON, February 9, 1949—4 p. m.
[Received February 9—7 :13 a. m.]

TelCan [*Cantel*] 25. Chen Tai-chu has again approached me with respect to encouragement of potential resistant elements when peace talks have failed (mytel 10, February 4, repeated Nanking 10, Shanghai 7). He said it would be most helpful if I could meet informally with various groups in Canton who were laboring under impression we are disinterested in continued resistance and perfectly prepared to recognize Communist regime and talk to those groups along the line of my conversations with him. If US Government could not make public statement at this stage, my remarks, which would inevitably reach the press and be attributed to me, would be helpful. I told him I would have to think the matter over.

If the arguments I used in previous conversation with Chen and as used in my conversation with Chen Li-fu shortly before leaving Nanking and reported to Department conform with thinking in Washington, such informal meetings as those suggested might prove beneficial to our interests. There are undoubtedly many liberal Chinese who desperately do not want to come under Communist regime, but who see no alternative unless assistance is to be forthcoming from US. I have insisted that, although I could of course not commit the Congress, I found it difficult to believe further assistance would be forthcoming until there was some tangible resistant movement giving signs of effectiveness and to which help from US might bring success. Chen Tai-chu believes the discussions he has suggested might encourage potential resistant elements sufficiently that active measures would be undertaken to find a leader or leaders capable of reviving the will to resistance in free China.

I should appreciate urgently the Department's instructions.

Sent Department, repeated Nanking 25, Shanghai 14.

CLARK

893.01/2–1049 : Telegram

The Minister-Counselor of Embassy in China (Clark) to the Secretary of State

CANTON, February 10, 1949—6 p. m.
[Received February 12—12 :34 a. m.]

Cantel 28.   From our conversations in Canton, we gather following picture present situation :

Despite current official denials, rift between Acting President and Premier is established fact.   On surface cause is rooted in differences of opinion as to desirability of moving entire National Government to Canton.   Those familiar with current Chinese politics feel, however, that conflict springs from traditional antagonism between Kwangsi and Kwangtung cliques which goes back much further than race for Vice Presidency between Li Tsung-jen and Sun Fo.   Retirement Generalissimo which for time being promoted Li to post of Acting President seems to have deepened this antagonism.   Thus, followers of Sun Fo, including members of C–C clique, seek keep alive their allegiance to Generalissimo.   Credible reports insist that most Cabinet and top ranking Kmt members secretly visited Fenghua to see Generalissimo before coming to Canton.

Li Tsung-jen, seeking to save situation and augment his prestige by continuous peace offers, wants symbol of Government remain Nanking. Refugee government Canton would, he believes, psychologically cease to represent entire National territories.   Being located within sphere of influence of Cantonese generals and politicians, Li would become less than figurehead were he to reside in Canton as head of National Government.   His stand to maintain symbol of Government in Nanking is supported by large number legislators, some of the National Assembly delegates and many members of the Control Yuan.

Tung Kwan-hsien, President Legislative Yuan, and Yu Yu-jen, President Control Yuan, are in Canton for purpose of pouring oil on troubled waters.   They came at instance Li.   Tung tells us they had agreed with Sun Fo that latter would go Nanking with Vice Premier Wu Tieh-cheng when Legislative Yuan meets there, if not before.   It has been tentatively agreed, he says, that Sun Fo would make formal appearance before Legislative Yuan, but that Wu Tieh-cheng, who commands majority support of legislators, would handle interpellations.   This would prevent, they hoped, embarrassment to Sun Fo who would probably be subject to sharp attacks by legislators because of Cabinet ineptitude and reported scandals which Sun Fo and some of his Cabinet members are alleged to have committed since they came to office.   Sun's visit to Nanking would, it has been agreed, be reciprocated by an inspection tour to the south by Li Tsung-jen.

Should Sun Fo fail go Nanking, Cabinet may be censored by Legislative Yuan with possibility overthrow.   Sun fears this, as does Li. Should Government in fact fall, Wu Tieh-cheng appears favorite candidate Premiership.

.   .   .   .

Appoinment Chang Fa-kwei as Commander in Chief National Army, announced February 9 by Executive Yuan, is widely considered as move to retard present tendency toward fragmentation.   Foreign Minister more or less confirmed this to me.   Chang is said to get along with all military leaders involved and he plans to make trip visiting each and endeavoring to bring all into line toward further resistance when peace talks fail.

Sent Department, repeated Nanking 28, Shanghai 17.

CLARK

893.00/2–949 : Telegram

The Secretary of State to the Consul General at Canton (Ludden)

WASHINGTON, February 10, 1949—7 p. m.

44. TelCan 9. Urtel 25 Feb 9.   Approach described reftel similar in nature to other feelers during recent weeks and appears be part and parcel pol[itical] jockeying for advantage by various groups. In light Gen. Barr's estimate, with which you familiar, that in absence unlimited US aid, including immediate use US armed forces, Chi Govt cannot maintain foothold south China against determined Comm advance, seems unrealistic believe either public US Govt statement or even statements attributed to you could serve any useful purpose.   If resistance Comm advance to be effective, must obviously be based upon genuine Chinese effort and not upon issuance statements from outside China.   In any event, you will recall President's reply Gimo message which dealt with this question.[27]

In view continued implementation China Aid Act,[28] difficult understand impression conveyed to you US disinterested in contd resistance and perfectly prepared recognize Comm regime.

ACHESON

---

[27] See Department telegrams of November 12, 8 and 7 p. m., quoting this exchange, *Foreign Relations,* 1948, vol. VIII, pp. 201 and 202, respectively.

[28] Approved April 3, 1948 ; 62 Stat. 158.

893.01/2–1049 : Airgram

The Consul General at Shanghai (Cabot) to the Ambassador in China (Stuart)

SHANGHAI, February 10, 1949.
[Received February 17—5 :06 p. m.]

A–26. Remytel [to] Nanking 297, February 7 (repeated [to] Department 407,[29] via pouch to Canton) concerning protests by members of the Legislative Yuan in Shanghai against the removal of the Central Government from Nanking to Canton.

Further evidence of popular indignation at the "flight" of the Sun Fo Cabinet to Canton and apparent increasing public support of Acting President Li Tsung-jen may be found in an article printed by the *Ta Kung Pao* of February 6, which describes a meeting in Shanghai of the resident committee of the Provisional Kiangsu Provincial Council under the chairmanship of Pan Shu-sen at which the following resolutions were passed : 1) The Central Government should be requested to appoint a capable man to replace General Ting Chih-pan as Governor of Kiangsu, as the latter had not accomplished anything in the short time that he had held the post.   (Comment : Ting was appointed Governor in September, 1948, is a graduate of the first class of Whampoa Military Academy and is believed to be very close to the Generalissimo.)   2) Pang Tien-tsai, Lin Shao-chu and Kuang Sen-san should be appointed delegates to the peace promotion conferences to be held in Shanghai and Hupeh.   3) A telegram should be sent to Acting President Li Tsung-jen pledging full support.   4) A telegraphic request should be made of Premier Sun Fo and top officials of all Central Government agencies now in Canton to either return to Nanking or resign their posts.   5) The Government should be requested to dissolve all rebellion suppression organs in order to facilitate the progress of the peace talks.   6) The Government should order the cessation of conscription.   7) The Ministry of National Defense and the Shanghai–Woosung garrison should immediately issue orders to improve Army discipline.

CABOT

---

[29] Not printed.

893.01/2–1149 : Telegram

The Minister-Counselor of Embassy in China (Clark) to the Secretary of State

CANTON, February 11, 1949—5 p. m.
[Received February 12—12:34 a. m.]

TelCan [Cantel] 32. Chiang Monlin[30] confirms rift between Sun Fo and Li Tsung-jen and fact that Wu Tieh-cheng is endeavoring mediate. Although bitterness aroused by vice presidential campaign is undoubtedly element in rift, he says basic cause is constitutional; that duties and authority of a President and Premier so overlap as to make conflict inevitable. When he was Secretary-General of Executive Yuan, he said his principal task was trying to avoid conflict and T. V. Soong had admitted to him that without his mediation conflict of authority would have been even worse than it was.

Chiang says trend toward fragmentation and regional autonomy is strong and he does not think Chang Fa-kwei[31] can do anything to prevent it. He admits that regional autonomy would play into Communist hands but does not believe Communists will take active measures in near future to conquer peripheral areas. He estimates we will be at least a year in Canton and that it may be many years before Communists will seek to assert authority over northwest, west and southwest. He feels however that Communist domination of China is an eventual certainty for the reason that "he who controls Manchuria and North China controls all China".

He confirms that Generalissimo is still running things to the detriment of the interests of the Chinese people. If Generalissimo could be persuaded to retire in fact, much needed leadership might emerge. He recalled that Generalissimo himself had emerged from comparative obscurity and someone else might come forward now if Generalissimo's stultifying hand were not so evident. He could not name any name at the moment but said leader must be military, must not be open to criticism of being influenced by western civilization; and must be inspired.

The Kmt had failed, he said, for two prime reasons: (1) had permitted inflation and (2) it had failed to institute land reform. Any new leadership to attract support and succeed would have to give evidence that it could stop inflation and was instituting land reform. He came back again, however, to his basic belief that China was doomed eventually to Communist domination.

He said he did not believe Sun Fo would go to Nanking though he might visit Shanghai. Premier told me himself last night that ques-

---

[30] Chairman of the Chinese Rehabilitation Commission and of the Joint Commission for Rural Reconstruction.
[31] Commander in Chief of the National Army

tion of his trip north was far from settled. Chiang felt confident, however, that when Nanking fell, Li would come to Canton and not to Kweilin.

Repeated Nanking 33, Shanghai 19, pouched Hankow, Kunming, Chungking, Tsingtao.

CLARK

893.00/2–1149

Memorandum by Brigadier General Marshall S. Carter, Special Assistant to the Secretary of State, to the Assistant Director of the Executive Secretariat (Smith)

[Extracts]

[WASHINGTON,] February 11, 1949.

At 5:30 last night, Congressman Brooks Hays (Democrat) of Arkansas, called the Secretary. He said he wanted to brief the Secretary on a letter that some 54 Republican Members of Congress had written to the President about our China policy.[32] He said he did not suppose the letter had yet reached the Secretary. The Secretary said that he was aware of such a letter.

.   .   .   .

After the telephone call, the Secretary asked me to inform Butterworth [33] that a thorough study of this should be made on an urgent basis, so that action by the Department could be taken within the next 24 to 36 hours. (See my previous memorandum accompanying original of the letter sent to S/S yesterday [34]). The Secretary wondered if this might not be the time to give a direct answer to the letter. We have been holding the rug under the Nationalist Government, which has prevented us from really telling the story. He referred to General Marshall's [35] testimony in closed session before the House Foreign Affairs Committee,[36] which he thought was a masterful presentation of the matter. He thought that a re-draft of this was what really should go to the Congressmen, but that such action would definitely pull the rug out from under the Nationalist Government and probably leave us in a worse hole than ever as regards long-range benefits in China and the stopping of Communist take-over. I pointed

---

[32] For letter from 51 Republican Congressmen to President Truman, dated February 7, see *Congressional Record*, vol. 95, pt. 2, p. 1950. Separate letter from Rep. J. K. Javits, of New York, not printed. Both letters handed by President Truman to the Secretary of State on February 10.

[33] W. Walton Butterworth, Director of the Office of Far Eastern Affairs.

[34] Dated February 10, not printed.

[35] General of the Army George C. Marshall, Secretary of State, January 1947–49.

[36] For text of statement on February 20, 1948, see Department of State, *United States Relations With China* (Washington, Government Printing Office, 1949), p. 380. For public statement on same day, see *ibid.*, p. 983.

out that with the Generalissimo absconded, the Cabinet having moved to Canton, and Li-Sun-Jen [37] living in solitary splendor in Nanking attempting to negotiate a compromise with the Communists, it looked to me like the rug had already pretty well slipped on all four corners and in the middle. The Secretary agreed, but pointed out that pulling the rug now without some other hook on which to hang our hat would appear to leave the Communists in complete ascendency.

I got hold of Butterworth right away and talked to him substantially along the foregoing lines.

Please take appropriate follow-up action accordingly.

M[ARSHALL] S. CARTER

893.00/2–1249 : Telegram

The Consul at Tsingtao (Strong) to the Secretary of State

TSINGTAO, February 12, 1949—11 a. m.
[Received 11 :04 p. m.]

78. Appears to be increasing feeling here Communists not attempt take over civil administration for 2 or 3 months despite Nationalist withdrawal. Mayor, other leaders, feel Communists not wish extend control large cities until Peiping–Tientsin digested. Thus expect interim regime and later quiet turnover.

Mayor informed me he plans remain here until relieved; has told friends he will not leave for at least 1 month. Promise keep civil administration intact; says although some subordinates will leave with him, many are remaining. Believes only portion Nationalist troops being withdrawn.

Nationalist troops are key to future developments. If all withdrawn, believe negotiated turnover will occur shortly thereafter. If portion remain, Communists not strong enough take over. If portion of Nationalist troops which may remain join Communists, latter may be strong enough force negotiate take over. In any event, violence not expected.

Sent Nanking 70; repeated Office Embassy Canton 4, Department 78.

STRONG

893.00/2–1349 : Telegram

The Ambassador in China (Stuart) to the Secretary of State

NANKING, February 13, 1949.
[Received February 17—2 :56 a. m.]

383. *Chung Yang Jih Pao* February 12 carries interview with Wu Yu-hou, Secretary Nanking Peace Delegation which returned Nan-

---

[37] Li Tsung-jen, Acting President of the Republic of China.

king February 11. Wu says delegation brought back Communist views which are "more concrete and a step forward" from Mao's eight points, but contents cannot be revealed at this time. When reporter asked specifically regarding points 1 and 4, Wu smiled broadly and said, "there is hope for peace".

Wu says delay of party in Tsingtao due Yeh Chien-ying's having to refer names of delegates to CCP central authorities for approval and 2-day delay Peiping before conferring with Communist authorities also because Yeh awaiting instructions. Party warned not to have contact with outsiders in order prevent reporters issuing confused reports which would hinder peace talks.

Wu reports party had conversations with Yeh Chien-ying, Hsu Ping, Jung Tsu-ho (Nieh Jung-chen's political commissioner) and Tao Chu (Lin Piao's political commissioner) and that in addition he responded to private invitations to visit Lin Piao and Nieh Jung-chen. Wu quotes Yeh as affirming CCP's sincerity in wanting peace, citing as evidence sincerity, their sufferings in civil war, Mao's trip to Chungking and CCP's participation in Political Consultative Conference. Asserting Communists having difficulty taking over cities, Wu quotes Yeh as saying, "we entered Peiping like beggars, eyes wide with wonder. Having been used to wearing straw sandals, our newly-donned leather shoes still feel uncomfortable".

According to Wu, Communists have made few changes in Peiping government organs because of lack trained personnel. Proof of their low standards for political workers, he says, is fact that even primary school graduates can enter Peiping universities run by Communists for purpose training political corps. Wu asserts attitude of people in general towards Communists is reserved.

Sent Department 383; repeated American Embassy Canton 57, Peiping 49, Shanghai 176.

STUART

893.00/2–1449 : Telegram

The Ambassador in China (Stuart) to the Secretary of State

NANKING, February 14, 1949—noon.
[Received February 14—6:18 a. m.]

385. As Department of course aware, CCP announcements repeatedly claim Nationalist peace offensive simply maneuver to gain breathing spell rebuild Nationalist forces for further resistance. Actually, Communists are themselves now giving Nationalists breathing spell by their failure to press attack. However, our military attachés believe this respite, which has already lasted several weeks and may

last additional 1 to 3 months, will not be of much benefit to Nationalists since crucial problem of re-equipping new armies remains unsolved.

Sent Department, repeated Shanghai 177, AmEmbassy Canton 58.

STUART

893.00/2–1449 : Telegram

The Minister-Counselor of Embassy in China (Clark) to the Secretary of State

CANTON, February 14, 1949—3 p. m.
[Received February 14—3 :32 a. m.]

[Cantel] 40.   Premier Sun Fo, in statement in English to foreign press February 11, invited UN [38] mediation along lines suggested by Evatt,[39] "providing, of course, that the other side would be willing to accept the good offices of the UN". Sun mentioned Chinese Government's notes to Great Britain, France, USSR and US asking them to serve as intermediaries and then, in reference to attempts at direct negotiation being made by Li Tsung-jen, stated that "direct approaches may prove impossible. Under such circumstances, UN mediation may be only practical way to bring about a settlement of internal war in China".

In thus speaking of UN mediation as virtual last resort, Sun seems to indicate that portion of Chinese Government he heads has already abandoned idea of any compromise with the Communists (although portion of Government remaining Nanking is still actively trying to achieve such compromise) and is in effect making this appeal to UN as final gesture toward peace before declaring all attempts at settlement with Reds have proven fruitless. This, of course, would be prelude to call for irreconcilables to begin final all-out resistance from south, west and Taiwan.

Unusually reliable source states that Sun Fo issued this request for UN mediation without consulting either Acting President or members of his own Cabinet. In any event, this statement is further outward sign of deep inward policy split between portion of Government which moved south and portion which remained Nanking, and will undoubtedly place another stumbling block in path of Li Tsung-jen's peace mission to Communists.

Sent Department.   Repeated Nanking 41, Shanghai 20.

CLARK

---

[38] United Nations.
[39] Herbert V. Evatt, head of the Australian delegation to the United Nations General Assembly (UNGA).

893.00/2–1449 : Telegram

The Consul General at Shanghai (Cabot) to the Secretary of State

SHANGHAI, February 14, 1949.
[Received February 14—9:29 p. m.]

527. Departure for Peiping morning 13th of three-man Shanghai Peace Delegation reported local press 14th as follows:

Headed by W. W. Yen, mission composed Chang Shih-chao, jurist and one time Premier defunct Peking government, and Kiang Yung, jurist and former Minister Justice defunct Peking government. Accompanying delegation were: Shao Li-tze, former Ambassador Moscow who is acting in private capacity and not as member Nationalist official Peace Delegation, Dr. Kung An-ching, Yen's secretary-general mission, Huang Chi-han and Liu Chung-hua, "unofficial" representatives Li Tsung-jen, both of whom have recently returned from Peiping.

Huang and Liu will liaison between mission and Communists. Yen accompanied by physician and Shao by two secretaries, Chang Feng-hui of Fuhtan University and Chin Shan. Latter will act behalf local shipping interests on question reopening shipping with north. Kiang Yung stated he would approach Communists on behalf post administration urging early resumption mail service between Communist and Nationalist areas. Chang Shih-chao again emphasized mission not empowered negotiation peace but would exchange views on conditions for holding talks. Press hinted at blueprint government peace formula in possession Kung An-ching.

Mission to call on Mayor Yen Chien-ying and possibly General Lin Piao and Tientsin–Peiping garrison commander Nieh Jung-chen. Chou En-lai [40] again mentioned in press as possibly willing confer with delegates at Shihchia-chuang.

Sent Nanking 367, repeated Department 527; Peiping 39; via pouch to Canton.

CABOT

893.00/2–1449 : Telegram

The Minister-Counselor of Embassy in China (Clark) to the Secretary of State

CANTON, February 14, 1949—3 p. m.
[Received February 15—4:23 a. m.]

[Cantel] 43. Obviously I did not make myself clear in Mytel 25, February 9 (TelCan 9, February 10). In my conversations for some

---

[40] Member of the Central Committee of the Chinese Communist Party.

time, the important ones having been reported to Department, I have taken the position that Chinese had no further claim on American assistance until there was evident not only the will to resist Communist advance, but also possibility of success; that main effort had to be Chinese; that all we possibly could do was to help. I have gone on to say that US was supporting resistance to communism throughout the world and that we would be unhappy with a Communist-controlled China. My Chinese friends could be sure, therefore, of sympathy in the US for any evidence continuing resistance communism in China. I have pointed out that resources of US are limited and that we have commitments in other parts of the world where our aid is being put to good use. I have said that nevertheless if there were a genuine Chinese effort to resist communism in China which gave promise of success, its leaders might reasonably expect such assistance from us as was feasible; that we didn't want to see a Moscow-dominated Communist regime in China, and would do what we could to prevent it. I am, of course, familiar with General Barr's estimate and bear that in mind. I know also of the unlikelihood that we could ever replace the military equipment which has passed from Nationalists' into Communists' hands. I have mentioned this and remarked that with the overall shortage of military equipment we could not be expected to supply more to China until there was evidence that it would be properly used.

In talking thus, I have been motivated by my understanding that US interests would be served by maintenance of friendly government in China and one whose vote on Security Council and other international organizations would be cast for the principles for which we stand rather than those of Moscow. If my reasoning is correct, any encouragement we can give to those elements still wishing to resist communism in China should be in our interests. Chen's idea was merely that such encouragement would be more effective if publication were permitted than if my arguments were kept "top secret". If my reasoning is incorrect, I should certainly be informed.

CLARK

893.01/2–1449 : Telegram

The Minister-Counselor of Embassy in China (Clark) to the Secretary of State

CANTON, February 14, 1949—4 p. m.
[Received 9 :47 p. m.]

[Cantel] 44. Li Wei-kuo, currently Secretary-General Central Political Council Kmt, reminds me that Generalissimo is still supreme head of Kmt and that as such he cannot be disregarded. He finds it difficult to believe that Generalissimo is interfering in present situation other than with idea of assisting Li Tsung-jen. Generalissimo has told his intimates who visited Fenghua that under no considerations would he return to active public life during next 5 years. Li believes Generalissimo sincere in his intention withdraw public life and give Li Tsung-jen opportunity make peace or carry on struggle.

He thinks Acting President has grown in stature with responsibility; has shown remarkable ability follow middle of road so dear to Chinese, and shows some signs that he may become the leader needed to rally continued resistance. He has refused Sun Fo's suggestion that he bring Kwangsi elements into Cabinet and he has recognized Generalissimo's authority as head Kmt. He says Li realizes peace is impossible on reasonable terms; that he is merely taking every step open to him to secure a reasonable peace with idea that when he inevitably renews resistance he will have a better chance of rallying support of the war-weary. What is needed, according to Li Wei-kuo, is someone to bridge the gap between Generalissimo and Li Tsung-jen and to check trend toward regional autonomy. In 2 months he thinks situation will clarify. He realizes that China must give clear evidence of intention to continue resistance to communism and of ability to do so before further aid should be expected from US.

He points out that Premier is responsible to Legislative Yuan but not to President. Sun Fo might correctly refuse visit Nanking at behest Li but he should report to Legislative Yuan should that Yuan meet in Nanking. Ill-will between Sun and Li arising out of Vice Presidential election is deep, he says, and may dissuade Sun from proceeding Nanking. Sun is supported in this by his physicians who say his blood pressure has so risen in recent months the trip would be dangerous to his health. If Sun does not go out and Legislative Yuan meets Nanking, as seems likely, it may give vote non-confidence in Sun and Wu Tieh-chen may become Premier. Li feels this would be promising development as Sun Fo was "born with silver spoon in his mouth" and his followers are most corrupt and self-seeking, while Wu Tieh-cheng is self-made man whose sole purpose, at the moment anyway, is to secure continued and effective resistance to communism. Also with President a Kwangsi man, Premier must be from Kwangtung, as is Wu. Furthermore, Wu has confidence of Generalissimo and of Li Tsung-jen and could, he believes, bridge gap between the two.

As seat of Government is Canton, future military operation will be based on Kwangtung. Li says it is necessary to have Kwangtung generals in control here. Appointment Chang Fa-kwei as commander ground forces was made in this sense. (Incidentally Li insists Chang's appointment was made without prior consultation with Generalissimo, something unheard of in the past). Chang Fa-kwei does not however have the ability, he believes, to check the trend toward regionalism and bring the military leaders back into the fold. He anticipates, therefore, that should Wu become premier Ho Ying-chin will be called back as Minister National Defense. Ho is on good terms with all military leaders and has confidence of Generalissimo. Wu and Ho together might have some chance of success. Incidentally, Li Wei-kuo has been offered job as representative China FEC [41] and may accept.

Sent Department 44, repeated Nanking 42, Shanghai 2.

CLARK

───────────

893.00/2–1449 : Telegram

The Consul General at Hankow (Callanan) to the Secretary of State

HANKOW, February 14, 1949—5 p. m.
[Received February 15—5:35 a. m.]

38. Following more approaches last few days by persons connected with Pai to Consul General and AMA regarding possibility US aid (mytel 27, February 7), Pai's aide called on AMA urgently last night, stating Pai and Li position deteriorating rapidly due lack funds (remytel 32, February 9 [42]) and troops and requesting US Government immediately issue statement favorable to Li government. Today Pai personally reiterated plea for statement of US support asking AMA pass on to Ambassador Stuart.

Pai admitted showdown with Generalissimo faction must occur very soon but maintains Generalissimo cannot possibly come back. He continues claim support Kwangtung and other areas mentioned mytel 27. Also feels Li and Sun Fo differences relatively minor and can be ironed out, thus, uniting Nationalist China. He again stressed hopelessness of defending Yangtze line under present conditions, urging immediate US financial aid to stabilize currency and thus win support people. Also stressed need military aid.

Pai plans proceed Nanking shortly meet with Li and Ho Ying-chin try consolidate power Li government. Therefore, desperately needs US Government nod of approval soonest in order convince waiverers [that] his group firmly in saddle. Indications US willingness extend financial assistance of particular import. Judging by urgency recent appeals here Nationalist position truly critical and lack of response US Government may result complete breakdown.

Sent Department 38; repeated Nanking 31, Embassy Canton 7.

CALLANAN

───────────

[41] Far Eastern Commission in Washington.
[42] Not printed.

893.01/2–1549 : Telegram

The Consul General at Shanghai (Cabot) to the Secretary of State

SHANGHAI, February 15, 1949.
[Received February 15—5:55 a. m.]

548. Legislators and Control Yuan members in Shanghai continue resist Government evacuation capital. Vernacular papers 14th report Sun Fo was accused of desertion of Chief Executive in resolution unanimously passed at meeting Legislatures here which called for return Executive Yuan, Nanking. Majority Control Yuan members Shanghai again voiced opposition removal Yuan at meeting 13th presided over by Yu Yu-jen. Thirty members said to have entrained that evening for Nanking to attend monthly meeting Yuan under President.

Sent Nanking 378, repeated Department 548, via pouch to Canton.

CABOT

893.00/2–1549 : Telegram

The Ambassador in China (Stuart) to the Secretary of State

NANKING, February 15, 1949—2 p. m.
[Received February 15—10:46 a. m.]

398. Re Moscow telegram February 2, sent Department 259, repeated Nanking 21.[43] Increased Soviet press emphasis on contributions to Communist war effort of Chinese working class, as distinct from peasantry, which was so neatly picked up by Embassy Moscow, finds strong parallel in recent North Shensi broadcasts and CCP publications from Hong Kong.

This change in local emphasis is not very great and dates, generally, from about last October. We think it is explicable largely in terms of new conditions Communists face as result of their capture of numerous large cities, beginning with Tsinan last September. Also, same problems Communists are finding in dealing with urban populations will, according to their announced timetable, confront them this year in all remainder of China, most particularly in Shanghai and Hankow industrial areas. Presumably, therefore, Communists' propaganda organs are now attempting to mold public opinion in such way as to obtain maximum support for CCP from its newly acquired urban proletariat.

Sent Department 398, pouched Shanghai, Canton, repeated Moscow 16.

STUART

---

[43] Not printed.

893.00/2–1449

Memorandum by the Secretary of State of a Conversation With the President on February 14 at 12:30 p.m.[44]

[WASHINGTON,] February 15, 1949.

We discussed the letter from the Republican Members of the House to the President on the subject of China.[45] I said that there seemed to be three possible courses: One was to make a noncommittal reply, which would probably result in the publication of the correspondence and the charge that the Administration had no policy in China; the second course was to make a vigorous reply setting forth the facts. This inevitably would harm the Chinese Government. A third possible course was for me to get in touch with the signers of the letter and try to have an off-the-record and very frank discussion with them in the hope that that might serve in place of a written reply.

The President thought that the third course should be tried out. He also hoped to acknowledge the letter and, if possible, in the acknowledgment to say that he had asked me to talk with them. This necessitated some exploration by me first. This should be promptly pushed.

D[EAN] ACHESON

———————————

893.00/2–749

The Secretary of State to Representative Robert Hale, of Maine

WASHINGTON, February 15, 1949.

MY DEAR MR. HALE: The President has shown me your letter of February 7, 1949, which you and a number of your colleagues in the House of Representatives addressed to him with respect to the Chinese situation.[46] He has asked me to say that he has given it careful consideration and has suggested to me that I might seek an opportunity to meet with you and the other members of the Congress who share our concern over the course of developments in China and discuss this situation in the light of the information at hand. You will, of course, appreciate that such a discussion would be of a confidential nature.

———————————

[44] Memorandum sent to Mr. Butterworth "for action", and to other officers of the Department.
[45] See footnote 32, p. 123.
[46] See *ibid.*

I suggest as a time Monday, February 21, at 10:30 a. m. and I leave to you whether the meeting place should be in the Department of State or at the Capitol if you care to arrange it there. Would you be so good as to communicate the foregoing to the co-signers of your letter and let me know what will suit your convenience and theirs? [47]

Sincerely yours,   DEAN ACHESON

893.002/2–1549 : Telegram

The Minister-Counselor of Embassy in China (Clark) to the Secretary of State

CANTON, February 15, 1949.
[Received February 16—2:20 a. m.]

[Cantel] 45. Survey shows following Ministries, with responsible head indicated, are established Canton. Each, of course, has supporting staffs and all are still in midst of unpacking and assembling archives:

Executive Yuan—President, Sun Fo; Justice—Acting Minister, Chao Sen; Communications—Vice Minister, Lin Hung-hsiung; Agriculture and Forestry—representative, Hsu Chi-wu; Education—Acting Minister, Chen Yueh-ping; Social Affairs—Vice Minister, Huang Pei-tu; Land Administration—Minister, Wu Shang-ying; Industry and Commerce—Minister, Liu Wei-chi; Finance—Minister, Hsu Kan; National Resources Commission—representative, Li Pan-lin; Food—Minister, Kwan Chi-yu; Budget Statistics and Accounts—Minister, Poun Sung-chow; Mongolian and Tibetan Affairs Commission—representative, Chow Kuan-tien; Interior—Minister, Hung Lan-you; Overseas Chinese, Foreign Affairs—Minister, Wu Teh-chen; Legislative Yuan—Vice President, Liu Chien-chun (Tung Kwan-hsien was here but has returned north). Outside Canton, Examination Yuan has moved to Wuchow, Kwangsi; Judicial Yuan to Chungshan, Kwangtung. Also due to shortage housing accommodations within city limits Canton, some Ministries of more or less technical nature, such as Water Conservancy, will eventually move their offices to Shaokwan, a railway town in northern Kwangtung, seat Kwangtung Provincial Government during Japanese war.

Sent Department, Nanking 44.

CLARK

---

[47] The meeting took place on February 24 in the hearing room of the House Ways and Means Committee and was confidential.

893.00/2–1549

Memorandum of Conversation, by the Secretary of State

[WASHINGTON,] February 15, 1949.

Participants: Dr. V. K. Wellington Koo, Chinese Ambassador
The Secretary of State—Mr. Acheson
Mr. W. W. Butterworth, Director for Far Eastern
Affairs

The Chinese Ambassador called at his request and after the usual courtesies indicated that he had come to see me about three matters.

He gave a brief résumé of the situation in China with particular reference to the attempts of the Acting President to find a basis of negotiations with the Chinese Communist Party. He indicated that his Government wished to obtain the reaction of this Government and other friendly governments to the situation with which China was faced. He referred to the Chinese Government's previously expressed desires to have issued by the U.S. a sympathetic statement of support and the despatch to China of a high military personage with staff. We discussed the situation at some length, I emphasizing the friendly interest and concern and benevolent policy which the U.S. had consistently pursued for over a century and he with no little persistence seeking to obtain some statement of commitment by me on behalf of this Government.

[Here follows the next paragraph on ECA aid to China; for text, see volume IX, page 624. The last paragraph, on United States policy in Japan, is not printed.]

D[EAN] A[CHESON]

893.00/2–1649 : Telegram

The Ambassador in China (Stuart) to the Secretary of State

NANKING, February 16, 1949—1 p. m.
[Received 2:43 p. m.]

405. Conversation between Embassy officer and Wu Yu-hou, Secretary Nanking peace delegation, confirms opinion other observers here that mission obtained no important commitment from Communists. Wu specifically denied UP story that Communists promised to initiate peace talks with Government within month and not attack Yangtze defenses before or during talks. He said Communists merely cited fact they had not crossed Yangtze as evidence their sincere desire for peace. Later in discussion, in response to query as to when peace talks might be held, Communists replied not until complete liberation of Peiping which would take about a month. UP story apparently based on these two unrelated statements.

Delegation composed principally of national political university professors represented two small local organizations of which they themselves are leading members. They were obviously well treated by Communists and returned convinced of Communists' sincere desire for peace negotiations. Our impression after conversation with Wu was that delegation had done most of the talking while Communists replied noncommittally and merely promised pass views of delegation on to higher authorities. Perusal of conflicting press statements re delegation (see Embtels 383, February 13 and 404, February 16 [48]) also bears out conclusion that they failed to get any commitment of real value from Communists. Fact silence of Chiu Chih-chung, leader of delegation, in contrast to volubility of Wu, and fact that Chiu did not accompany Wu to Shanghai tend to confirm press reports of split in delegation. (See Shanghai's 513, February 14 to Department [49]).

Sent Department 405, repeated Canton 70, Shanghai 189.

STUART

893.01/2–1849 : Telegram

The Minister-Counselor of Embassy in China (Clark) to the Secretary of State

CANTON, February 18, 1949—4 p. m.
[Received 11 :14 p. m.]

[Cantel] 62. In interview with AP evening February 16, Sun Fo stated categorically he had not tendered resignation and had no intention resigning. Answering questions regarding his attitude toward demands of Control Yuan and portion of Legislative Yuan that he return Nanking explain his recent actions in moving Cabinet [to] Canton, he replied that he did not intend return Nanking "immediately". Sun added (off record) he believed things would soon become so "hot" around Nanking that portion Government remaining there would be forced move Canton and that following such move he would, of course, be prepared answer his questioners.

CLARK

893.01/2–1849 : Telegram

The Ambassador in China (Stuart) to the Secretary of State

NANKING, February 18, 1949—4 p. m.
[Received February 18—8 :16 a. m.]

417. Acting President told me he is summoning Sun Li-jen [50] here with view appointing him Governor of Taiwan and making that island

---
[48] Neither printed.
[49] Not printed.
[50] Director of training of Chinese ground forces on Formosa (Taiwan).

basis for Chinese-American constructive cooperation. Ch'en Ch'eng wants to resign [51] but Gimo preventing him. This one of many ways Gimo hindering Li's efforts.

Li intends appoint Shao Li-tze [52] premier if Sun Fo finally refused come Nanking. Should Shao be unwilling, will ask Ho Ying-chin be concurrently premier and Minister of National Defense. Reasons for choice of Ho is latter's ability persuade Whampoa [53] clique support Li and perhaps influence Gimo.

Shao Li-tze telephoned Li peace talks [54] began on morning February 16 and will continue several days with no public announcements. Shao feels rather optimistic. Li feels there one-third chance satisfactory results.

Sent Department 417, repeated AmEmb Canton 81, pouched Taipei.

STUART

893.50 Recovery/2–1949 : Telegram

The Ambassador in China (Stuart) to the Secretary of State

NANKING, February 19, 1949—5 p. m.
[Received February 20—2:04 a. m.]

427. Yen Hsi-shan [55] has been in Shanghai and Nanking for past few days to obtain assistance from Nationalist Government and ECA for his beleaguered city of Taiyuan. He has suggested to Chinese Navy that it transport one million gallons aviation gasoline Tsingtao in order that his airlift from that port may be continued. He has also approached ECA for direct assistance, including an air lift and food supplies Taiyuan. He called on me February 17 to press his appeal to ECA for food. I felt unable to give him any encouragement, believing this operation one for Chinese Government and not ECA.

Sent Department; repeated Shanghai 199, AmEmb Canton 88.

STUART

893.00/2–1949 : Airgram

The Ambassador in China (Stuart) to the Secretary of State

NANKING, February 19, 1949.
[Received March 4—2:18 p. m.]

A–46. Among the material on my desk this morning were two contrasting items. One was a USIS report from Washington, the tenor of which is apparent from the following excerpts:

---

[51] As Governor of Taiwan.
[52] Member of the Kuomintang.
[53] Whampoa Military Academy.
[54] By a Shanghai civic delegation headed by former Premier W. W. Yen.
[55] Taiyuan Pacification Commissioner and Governor of Shansi.

"Fifty-one Republican members of the U.S. House of Representatives have asked for a report on the Chinese situation by a commission of top-level military, economic and political advisers, asserting that a Communist victory in that country would be a 'monumental and historic' defeat for the United States and a grave threat to national security.

"In a letter to President Truman [56] made public tonight, they recommend establishment of the commission and also pose seven specific questions aimed at clarification of U.S. policy toward China.[57]

.   .   .   .

"The letter sharply criticizes the U.S. postwar policy on China, saying it has sought a coalition between Nationalists and the Communists, which it says now has 'proved to be disastrous'. It points to the 'dramatic demonstration' of the danger of such a policy as shown in Czechoslovakia, which through its coalition government 'was drawn behind the iron curtain'.

"The letter further states that Chinese Communists seem on the verge of a victory which, in opinion of signers, would constitute not only a grave threat to the United States but a 'defeat for the forces of freedom'."

The other was a copy of a letter to Mr. Roger D. Lapham [58] from which the following paragraphs are quoted:

"We, as a group of individual Christian citizens of Shanghai, with absolutely no political axe to grind, with no ulterior selfish ambitions, with nothing but pure Christian love for the millions of our suffering fellow-men, for whose welfare we have labored for years and will continue to strain our effort, have been watching the recent events with great anxiety and concern. We realize very keenly the critical, fluid nature of the present situation, and the great bearing on future developments of what is being done at the present juncture. We feel the urgent necessity of calling your attention to the following crucial points to which, we hope, you will give your serious and careful consideration.

"1. The strong bonds of cordial relationship between the Chinese and the American people, built up through the record of the past decades, are still strong as ever. We would like to see these bonds further strengthened by appropriate actions on the part of the American Government.

"2. We would strongly oppose any further military aid to any of the armies in China, and especially the proposed revival of the Flying Tigers. The whole nation is weary of war and at the point of exhaustion. Any attempt to prolong and intensify the present bloodshed and suffering on the part of an outside power will most certainly estrange the feelings of the people towards that power.

"3. We hope that the American Government will not entertain any preconceived judgments regarding the present developments

---

[56] For text of letter dated February 7, see *Congressional Record*, vol. 95, pt. 2, March 7, 1949, p. 1950.

[57] The following omission indicated in the source text.

[58] Chief of China Mission, Economic Cooperation Administration.

in China, but that it will maintain an open-minded attitude, and keep close contact with the constructive forces among the people of China, and hold its policy open for revision in the light of the changing situations.

"4. We urge the continuance of the ECA aid to the people of China for economic recovery and rural reconstruction in all parts of the country, irrespective of the political circumstances. We hope that in so far as possible or necessary, such aid may be administered through private agencies in which there is able and honest leadership."

The Republican Congressmen may be influenced in part by political considerations and the Chinese Christians by their special point of view. But they both illustrate how those who are equally anticommunist may disagree as to the solution. Various other evidences could be given of the haunting perplexity in determining on a wise and effective policy, consistent also with our own basic principles and global policies. Whatever recriminations may be indulged in as to the past the matter of practical interest to all is what to do about the situation now confronting us.

The assumption underlying the Congressmen's criticisms is that the victory of Communism in China would be a threat to American security. This is unquestionably true and makes it imperative that we make no mistakes in trying to prevent this. Their implied inference is that this could be done by voting enough money and military aid to the present National Government. This is emphatically erroneous. The basic mistake would be in doing this, for our own national interest and contrary to the clearly indicated will of the Chinese people. The Chiang Government has entirely failed to hold the overwhelming popular support it had at V–J Day, despite very considerable aid from us which is still not exhausted. If we supply more such aid and do nothing else we would merely inflame the anti-American imperialism sentiment to the great advantage alike of the Communists and of the less admirable elements of a rapidly disintegrating Government.

Fortunately there is much else that we can do to prevent the catastrophe which we all fear. This should be primarily along two lines. One is a publicity campaign exposing the evils of Communism and awakening thinking Chinese to this threat to national independence and individual human rights. The other is constructive assistance to the Chinese people through reforms in the Government, national and provincial, as recommended by us; by continuation of ECA at least in JCRR; [59] by special attention to Formosa; and by similar

---

[59] Joint Commission for Rural Reconstruction.

efforts to promote the welfare of the common people in ways that can be widely publicized. These should help to arouse a determined will among them to oppose the Communist menace under a new leadership which we could back up with all-out material and military aid.

STUART

893.00/2–2049 : Telegram

The Ambassador in China (Stuart) to the Secretary of State

NANKING, February 20, 1949—9 a. m.
[Received February 19—11:49 p. m.]

429. Department may care to take measures publicly or otherwise for refuting mistaken impressions created by press accounts of forthcoming large-scale American military aid, such as those reported in Embtel 420, February 18, repeated Embassy Canton 84, and Tokyo 21, and Shanghai's 586, February 17 to Department, repeated Tokyo 49, Nanking 398.[60] These reports, which were prominently published in vernacular and English language press China, have effect of inciting Generalissimo and his irreconcilables to retake leadership now in renewed resistance movement. He is already being influenced, I hear, by arguments of his indispensability from small group die-hard supporters whose motives are not entirely disinterested.

Meanwhile Generalissimo is interfering in military affairs, thus hampering rather than helping Yangtze defense. (See my 336, February 8 to Department, repeated Shanghai 149, Canton Embassy 22.) Li Tsung-jen may eventually be sufficiently thwarted by these factors to feel forced to retire south, prematurely abandoning peace efforts. Only hope for public support for renewed resistance against Communists lies in convincing Chinese people that CCP does not desire peace on any tolerable basis. Li is presently endeavoring to put this to thoroughgoing test. US can, I feel, help most at this stage by avoidance public debate and objective appraisal of coming developments. Tone of Secretary's recent statements on China [61] have been very useful in this regard.

Sent Department; repeated AmEmb Canton 89, Shanghai 200, Tokyo 22.

STUART

---

[60] Neither printed.
[61] On February 9 at a press conference Mr. Acheson stated that "our constant attitude is one of sympathy for not only the Chinese people but for the difficulties of the Government, and our whole attitude is one of sympathy for the Chinese situation." Department of State, *Press Releases*, vol. xx (1949).

711.93/2–2149: Telegram

The Minister-Counselor of Embassy in China (Clark) to the Secretary of State

CANTON, February 21, 1949—3 p. m.
[Received February 22—2:50 a. m.]

Cantel 66.   Chen Li-fu, who came Canton represent Generalissimo at funeral Tai Chi-tao,[62] asked me to call and I did so.   Tai Chi-tao, he says, died of overdose sleeping tablets.   Chen does not think it was suicide.

Chen was interested in knowing progress negotiations North Atlantic Pact (I told him we were sanguine such a pact would be negotiated) and inquired whether something similar couldn't be arranged for Pacific.   (I explained that the situation was different.)   He then came to real reason for wanting see me which was to inquire whether our China policy remained unchanged.   I assured him it did and in answer to his further queries reiterated our disappointment at failure of China to take advantage of aid previously given and expressed doubt that Congress would vote material additional aid unless there was good reason to believe aid would be put to useful purpose. Covering much of the old ground, I let him understand that main task was China's and all we could possibly do with best of good will was to help.   He seemed to appreciate justice of my argument and went on to query reason behind obvious British attempt to be neutral in China when Southeast Asia was so disturbed and would be more so with a Communist-dominated China.

Admitting that peace negotiations were a farce, he asked how long they should be continued.   That decision, I replied, was one solely for Chinese determination.

Chen said he had seen wire from peace mission in north to Acting President reporting friendly reception, yet mere promise to pass on Li's proposals to higher authority.   Chen said sole purpose of peace delegation was to persuade Communists fix place and date for negotiations.   Li, of course, had agreed to Mao Tse-tung's eight points as basis for such negotiations.   Shao Li-tze has been to Shihchiachuang and seen Mao Tse-tung, Chen believed, but no report from him has come through.

Chen says there is no real disagreement between Li Tsung-jen and Sun Fo.   What has happened, he says, is that Li was left in Nanking with no Cabinet to advise him or to act upon the innumerable requests he has been receiving which require Cabinet action.   If the Executive

---

[62] Former President of the Chinese Examination Yuan.

Yuan or the key Ministers thereof could divide their time between Nanking and Canton at this stage, this situation would be remedied. Li feels he must remain in Nanking so long as efforts to negotiate peace continue, yet admits Canton is most logical place at moment for Executive Yuan to function. He hopes by some division of their time, the key Ministries can function in both places.

As background for movement Government Canton, Chen stated without qualification that Legislative Yuan, in informal meeting attended by more than a quorum on January 25 in Nanking, voted move Canton. It was only the next day, January 26, that Executive Yuan with Li Tsung-jen present at discussion and agreeing, decided that Government should move Canton. These decisions were taken under imminent Communist attack on Nanking. When Communists suddenly halted and attack no longer seemed imminent, Legislative Yuan members became reluctant leave Nanking and move Canton where housing is inadequate and cost of living many times greater than in Nanking. They realize that eventually they will have to repair to Canton, but wish stay Nanking long as possible, hoping against hope that Communists will not attack.

Chen is convinced Generalissimo will not return to power in near future. He sees few people in Fenghua and, according to Chen, is not interfering with Li's activities. Chen, who is of course loyal Generalissimo supporter, insists that when peace negotiations have failed, every one must rally behind Li as the leader. Two things are essential, he said: (1) "We non-Communists must stick together", (2) "We must find some way to continue the cooperation at present existing between Li Tsung-jen and Sun Fo".

Sent Department, repeated Nanking 64, Shanghai 38.

CLARK

893.00/2–1449 : Telegram

The Secretary of State to the Consul General at Canton (Ludden)

WASHINGTON, February 21, 1949—4 p. m.

75. TelCan 25 [for Clark]. Reasoning urtel 43 Feb 14 correct and emergence Chi elements willing and having capability effectively resist communism in China would be in US interest. You will realize US has given both encouragement and material aid to Chi Govt in hope it would be able effectively maintain itself and provide barrier spread communism in China. Moreover no other group or combination groups known to exist which give indication attainment any greater degree success in resisting communism. Present state affairs

has come about in spite such encouragement and aid. It is difficult see how at this stage any action on part US Govt can in itself produce Chi leadership and spirit necessary meet Comm menace. Chi leadership and spirit must have roots in China if they are to become reality and be effective. US interest in China amply clear in extension aid but to state publicly US will continue support any groups China who willing resist communism would be unrealistic, particularly if such resistance groups opposing communism so bankrupt their actions must await public statement US intentions. Furthermore in view known unreliability Chi press any statement allowed to leak to press would inevitably be distorted to serve interests those jockeying for pol[itical] position.

ACHESON

893.001 Chiang Kai-shek/2–2149 : Telegram

The Ambassador in China (Stuart) to the Secretary of State

NANKING, February 21, 1949—7 p. m.
[Received February 22—4:29 a. m.]

440. Yesterday Ho Ying-chin asked me if it would be at all possible for American Government to invite Generalissimo to visit that country. He went on to say that USA had done so much for China in many ways but that at present this one thing would do more for national welfare than anything else. Generalissimo is at present hampering Acting President's peace negotiations and various reform measures. He is doing same in military affairs. General Ho feels that if he had 3 months with full authority he could so improve these that it would be quite difficult for Communists to cross Yangtze. He states desire to have Generalissimo leave country is becoming stronger even among his closest associates. General Ho has known him over 30 years and says he cannot understand his present behavior. Even members of C–C clique share in this sentiment. Chang Tao-fan [63] recently went to his home and advised him to make a trip, first to Europe, then to States, so he could observe life in other countries. Generalissimo became very angry and ordered him out of room. Another C–C man, Hung Lan-yu (former Secretary of National Assembly), had somewhat similar experience. General Ho argues that whether there will be peace or continued war, issues will be greatly simplified if Generalissimo could be persuaded to leave country.

STUART

---

[63] Former Chinese Minister of Information.

893.00/2–2249 : Telegram

The Minister-Counselor of Embassy in China (Clark) to the Secretary of State

CANTON, February 22, 1949—11 a. m.
[Received February 22—4 :14 a. m.]

Cantel 70. Acting President Li [64] tells me peace negotiations are proceeding normally, as in light of the overwhelming desire for peace, Communists do not dare refuse negotiate. He anticipates, however, that when terms of peace are discussed, Communists will demand practical surrender which would be unacceptable. They have insisted in talks in Peiping that all relations, cultural and material, must be severed with US, demanding prosecution of war criminals and incorporation all military forces into Communist Army. Li said he would accept any reasonable peace, but would not surrender.

It must be made abundantly clear at that time to the Chinese public and to the world that [it] is Communist intransigence which prevents peace. Li will hope at that time to rally resistance behind him and revive will to fight. He says he has received telegrams strongly supporting his program from the five Ma's [65] and from the Governors of Szechuan, Yunnan and Kweichow. Also since his arrival in Canton he believes Kwangtung generals are solidly behind his program. All realize Communist strategy in trying to separate regional areas and are aware of necessity of sticking together. Li realizes the need for new blood in Cabinet if he is going to revive will to resist and said that either at time breakdown negotiations or earlier he would bring younger and more active men into the Government.

When that time came the US must realize, he said, that the war in China would have become an international issue as a Communist-dominated China would have serious repercussions in Southeast Asia and the Pacific. He would hope for aid from the US and he mentioned a $200,000,000 silver loan which he said had been discussed in detail by Finance Minister with Merchant [66] and Parker.[67]

Li said Generalissimo did, in fact, continue to interfere in many ways and said: "That problem will have to be handled with care". He claims that leaders in increasing numbers are endeavoring persuade Generalissimo step entirely out of picture and give him, Li, free hand. Li is flying Kweilin today, thence to Changsha, Hankow, and back Nanking. He will be joined in Nanking in few days by certain

---

[64] In telegram Cantel 65, February 20, 2 p. m., the Minister-Counselor of Embassy reported Acting President Li's arrival at Canton on an inspection trip.
[65] Mohammedan leaders in northwestern provinces of Ningsia, Tsinghai, and Sinkiang.
[66] Livingston T. Merchant, Counselor of Embassy on special detail to Taiwan.
[67] Paul Parker, Acting Treasury Attaché in China.

members of Cabinet, including Vice Premier Wu Tieh-cheng. It is still uncertain whether Sun Fo will go, although Kan Chieh-hou, Li's advisor, told me positively Sun Fo impressed by generosity Li's visit Canton, had agreed go north.

Sent Department; repeated Nanking 67, Shanghai 40.

CLARK

893.01/2–2349 : Telegram

The Ambassador in China (Stuart) to the Secretary of State

NANKING, February 23, 1949—11 a. m.
[Received February 23—5 :11 a. m.]

450. In struggle for power between Li Tsung-jen and "Canton faction" headed by Sun Fo, Li in fundamentally weak position because he does not control larger portion army, lacks financial resources and does not command allegiance of that considerable portion Kmt bureaucracy controlled by Generalissimo and C–C politicians. This fundamental weakness has been frankly acknowledged, and probably somewhat exaggerated, by Pai's headquarters in statements to American Consulate, Hankow, appealing for US aid.

However, he has made some preparations recently in mobilizing popular support for his peace program. Most important single evidence [of] this is decision Legislative Yuan meet in Nanking rather than Canton. This is, of course, in direct defiance Premier's publicly expressed wishes. At Yuan session, Sun Fo is certain to be violently denounced, both for his sponsorship of Government move south and for speculations he is alleged to have committed. Significant indication feeling many legislators was press report that legislators resident Shanghai had passed resolution accusing Sun Fo "deserting" Acting President [and] calling for return of Executive Yuan to Nanking.

Further tangible demonstrations that Li is making progress are meeting Control Yuan here and their resolution to support him, announcement that Executive Yuan joint office will soon open Nanking, and arrival Ho Ying-chin in capital. Li also has backing important newspapers in Shanghai and Nanking, which praise his twin program peace and reform while condemning Kmt for ineptitude and corruption and censuring Sun Fo cabinet for "running away". Insofar as can be determined, support Li is growing among banking and business circles in Shanghai and Nanking and among that large but inarticulate section population who disregard larger issues and are principally interested in keeping destruction of war from their homes.

Li's present position is similar in some ways to that he occupied while campaigning for Vice President. At that time he became symbol of revolt against arbitrary dictation by Generalissimo and party and succeeded in uniting behind him all dissident (and often mutually incompatible) factions for purpose his election. He has again become symbol, this time symbol of yearning for peace that pervades this war-weary country. So long as his peace efforts make perceptible progress, or even succeed in delaying (or seeming to delay) Communist assault on Yangtze, he should be able maintain and utilize for his support this mobilized public opinion.

Li is aware basic weaknesses his position, but is astutely capitalizing on support those who see him as chief hope for peace, in order either heal breach between himself and Canton group, or at least win over to his side as many as possible of powerful leaders Kmt. He is also endeavoring to bolster his position in concrete ways by making overtures for US aid and planning economic and political reform. Extent to which he succeeds in these efforts will determine his strength either as negotiator with Communists or subsequently as leader of resistance should Communists renew attack.

Sent Department; repeated Embassy Canton 96.

STUART

893.01/2–2349 : Telegram

The Consul General at Peiping (Clubb) to the Secretary of State

PEIPING, February 23, 1949.
[Received February 23—6 :56 a. m.]

279. Official *Jen Min Jih Pao* yesterday announced that "highest administrative organization North China liberated areas, the North China People's Government", had removed to Peiping and formally began functioning here February 20.

Shih Chieh Jih Pao today reports Chairman Tung Pi-wu and heads various organizations that government have all in seriatim arrived Peiping.

Sent Department 279, Nanking 211, Shanghai 232.

CLUBB

893.00/2–2349 : Telegram

The Minister-Counselor of Embassy in China (Clark) to the Secretary of State

CANTON, February 23, 1949—2 p. m.
[Received 9 :58 p. m.]

Cantel 71. Recently we characterized the Chinese situation as "confusion worse confounded". It is still that; or is it Gilbert and Sullivan? We have the Communists pretending desire peace, yet offering peace only on terms (surrender) known to be unacceptable to National Government. We have Li Tsung-jen, Acting President, admitting that peace is impossible yet going to great extremes publicly to demonstrate his desire for peace on any "reasonable" terms, the while he is hampered by tendency toward regionalism and *sauve qui peut*, and by Generalissimo behind scenes interfering and directing things himself. We have Generalissimo relinquishing his authority as Chief of State with a flourish and retiring to his mountain retreat at Fenghua, yet retaining the director generalship of Kmt which gives him supreme authority and a right to meddle. The present government was appointed by him and its members are his friends. His henchmen hold the strategic military positions. He bowed to will of the articulate and retired so that Li could negotiate peace, yet it seems evident he is confident Li would fail and that conditions would develop calling him back to power.

Regardless, however, of what is in Generalissimo's mind, his henchmen are not yet ready to die as "war criminals" and are determined that Li will not, in a moment of weakness, accept clemency for himself at their expense. They scrutinize his every move and are determined to carry on resistance to communism as long as possible. Seeing no other likely leader, they are in effect marking time until Li's failure and what they believe to be the inevitable re-emergence of Generalissimo. They realize the ineffectiveness of Generalissimo's leadership in recent years, but he was the "proven" leader during those dire days of Japanese aggression and maybe he can do it again.

It is a black picture and one that gives little hope. Barring an act of God which would prevent reappearance of Generalissimo on scene, situation does in fact look hopeless. With Communist control of Manchuria and North China, generally considered as essential to domination all China, they are flushed with victory and adequately supplied with weapons of war. Opposed to them are reactionaries of the Kmt and the feudalistic leaders in southwest and northwest, whose armies are ill-equipped and uninspired.

Should Generalissimo reenter upon scene, as seems possible, we may expect an accentuation of the trend toward regionalism, with Generalissimo retiring eventually to the Foochow–Amoy–Taiwan triangle, leaving the leaders in the periphery to make their best terms with Communists. The Communists absorbed as they are with problems acquired through their capture of large areas and urban centers, may well permit degree of autonomy in such areas until such time as they feel strong enough to bring them under control. This would certainly take months; more likely years.

If, on the other hand, Generalissimo does not reenter scene, there is still an ever so slight possibility that resistance forces may get together under leadership of Li Tsung-jen.   Li is not the ideal leader but no other appears available.   He is giving remarkable demonstration of courage and willingness to disregard matters of prestige or sectional rivalry in interest of the State as a whole and he has grown greatly in stature since his assumption of Presidency.   He is here in Canton now trying to bridge difference between the Kwangtung and Kwangsi cliques and to pull resistance elements together.   His staunch supporter Pai Chung-hsi, probably the most influential Muslim in China outside northwest, has his armies still intact and encamped on route Communists must follow to reach south.   His influence would be great in northwest where, I am told, Chang Chih-chung has found the five Ma's determined to resist communism, or in their own words to "liberate ourselves".   I am told also that Chang Chun has had considerable success in rallying resistance elements in Szechuan and that Lu Han in Yunnan may be expected cooperate.   Li Tsung-jen seems to confirm this.   (Mytel Cantel 70, February 22 to Department, repeated Nanking 67, Shanghai 40).

The Communists defeated the National troops not by superior military forces or equipment, but by leadership and superior psychological approach.   In spite of the diabolical efficiency of Communist propaganda, there remain large elements in country aware of Communist treachery and seeking desperately for means to continue resistance.   They have been thoroughly disheartened by ineffectiveness of Generalissimo and Kmt and have no further will to resist unless inspired from elsewhere.

It is just barely possible under these circumstances that Li Tsung-jen, supported by Pai, may provide that leadership if he can bring the Kwangtung generals into line.   He has demonstrated considerable ability since he came to power and, if Generalissimo will leave him alone, results might be forthcoming.   If, as seems likely, Communist military progress has outdistanced their political planning it may take them some time to digest the areas already under their control and after they have taken the Yangtze urban centers they may well be prepared to tolerate for some time considerable autonomy in the peripheral areas.   It is during that time we should watch carefully for some tangible evidence of leadership and will to resist of a character giving promise of success.   Should Li prove to be such a leader, we should encourage him and offer him such support as proves feasible.   Even should he fail, we might at least delay complete domination Chinese by Communists and make their task more difficult in the interim.

Sent Department Cantel 71; repeated Nanking 68, Shanghai 41.

CLARK

893.00/2–2349 : Telegram

The Minister-Counselor of Embassy in China (Clark) to the Secretary of State

CANTON, February 23, 1949.
[Received February 23—5 :24 a. m.]

Cantel 74. Press report Acting President Li speaking to National Assembly delegates Canton stated that Government will not abandon peace efforts until peace becomes absolutely impossible and added, categorically, that should Communists begin attack Yangtze, peace would be considered impossible.

Sent Department Cantel 74, repeated Nanking 70, Shanghai 2.

CLARK

893.001/2–2349

The Ambassador in China (Stuart) to the Secretary of State

No. 54   NANKING, February 23, 1949.
[Received March 4.]

SIR: I have the honor to transmit a translation [68] of a speech broadcast February 15, 1949, by Acting President Li Tsung-jen. It acknowledges in the frankest terms that the Chinese Government's civil and military bureaucracy has deteriorated to a perilous state and that only the inculcation of a new spirit of public service and the elimination of worthless and corrupt officials can restore the people's faith in the Government and provide a base for reconstruction. Promising to give the problem of reform his closest attention, the Acting President urges officials of all ranks, and particularly the supervisory organs, to be diligent in carrying out reform.

The Acting President's statement, although somewhat more concrete and self-critical than similar statements in the past, still bears the stamp of "reform by exhortation" which has long characterized the utterances of National Government officials and has proved so ineffective in accomplishing the desired results. It is extremely doubtful that Li Tsung-jen has the power or temperament to act with the ruthlessness that would be necessary to effect a thorough cleaning out of the Government ranks.

Respectfully yours,

For the Ambassador:
JOHN WESLEY JONES
Counselor of Embassy

---

[68] Not printed.

893.00/2–2449 : Telegram

The Ambassador in China (Stuart) to the Secretary of State

NANKING, February 24, 1949.
[Received February 24—5:40 a. m.]

456. Nanking vernacular February 22 reports important meeting to be held this week presided by Li Tsung-jen, who has invited Chang Chun,[69] Hunan Governor Cheng Chien, Chang Chih-chung, Pai Chung-hsi, Chung Tien-hsin and Peng Chao-hsien. Last three reported already in Nanking while February 23 press prominently reports Chang Chih-chung arrival Nanking.

Sent Department; repeated AmEmb Canton 98, Shanghai 212.

STUART

893.00/2–2449 : Telegram

The Minister-Counselor of Embassy in China (Clark) to the Secretary of State

CANTON, February 24, 1949—4 p. m.
[Received February 25—12:02 a. m.]

Cantel 78. In contrast to Li Tsung-jen, whom I found exuding confidence and giving an impression of action (mytel 70, repeated Nanking 67, Shanghai 40, February 22), I found Sun Fo today disheartened and I suspect disgruntled by trend of events. Li seems to have accomplished much by his visit Canton. Sun Fo did not want go Nanking yet he was maneuvered into position where promise to do so was extracted from him and now against his better judgment he is afraid he is going to have to go north.

Sun could not confirm press reports quoting Li as saying that peace negotiations would be deemed to have failed if Communists attempted crossing Yangtze and said with some bitterness that there was still no agreement within Government circles on "acceptable" terms of peace. Li Tsung-jen had been thinking, he said, first, of a territorial arrangement, leaving Communists in control of areas they occupy, with an agreement to cease fighting; or, secondly, although Sun said it was too early for this phase, federation of the various regions, including those occupied by Communists. There had been no agreement with Li on this subject, however, so the Government was not in a position to negotiate even if Communists were willing. He said visit of Shao Li-tse to Shihchiachuang to see Mao Tse-tung had been postponed and Shao might likely return Nanking next few days. Wu Tieh-cheng had left [for] Nanking today and he, Sun, might himself be leaving in few days. With considerable embarrassment, Sun Fo ad-

---

[69] Administrator of Political and Military Affairs for Southwest China.

mitted he had authorized member his Cabinet, through mutual friend, to approach Communists Hong Kong regarding peace proposal (mytel 64, repeated Nanking 61, Shanghai 36, February 19 [70]). He insisted, however, that initiative was not his and that he was not sanguine of success of approach through Hong Kong.

If he should go to Nanking (in each case he used the conditional when speaking of Nanking), he would plan devote most of his time to military reform. Hsu Kan, Finance Minister, had spent hours, he said, trying to persuade military leaders to reduce standing army below present 5,000,000. Best he could obtain was agreement on 4,200,-000. Dr. Sun thought this figure much too high and insisted army would be much more efficient if reduced to 2,700,000 or 3,000,000 and streamlined. Under financial reforms which Hsu Kan would announce today, it should be possible to pay 3,000,000 soldiers, say, 10 silver dollars monthly, and with silver in their pockets and improved training, Sun thought will to fight could be revived. He had discussed this with Ho Ying-chin and he had agreed to come back into government as National Defense Minister at appropriate time.

Dr. Sun still does not admit defeat in respect of Legislative Yuan although he admitted likelihood success efforts President Tung Kwan-hsien to hold first meetings Nanking, the Legislative Yuan itself then voting to move later to Canton. Nanking, he said, being under constant threat, was no place to meet and it was highly possible, there might still be rival meeting Canton organized by legislators from southwest and Taiwan who supported Kwangtung members desiring meeting here. He spoke with feeling on the subject and with obvious resentment over developments.

Sent Department, repeated Nanking 74, Shanghai 47.

CLARK

893.00/2–2449 : Telegram

The Minister-Counselor of Embassy in China (Clark) to the Secretary of State

CANTON, February 24, 1949—5 p. m.
[Received 9 :58 p. m.]

Cantel 80. Director American Section Foreign Office tells me Government is convinced there exists real difference of opinion in Communist circles regarding desirability negotiating reasonable peace or continuing military operations. He believes it will take considerable time for Communists reach definite decision and that peace negotiations may continue for another 6 months to 1 year. He inquired what effect I thought such situation would have on considera-

---

[70] Not printed.

tion further US aid China. I replied that I could not presume to speak for Congress, but that I imagined uncertainty resulting from continued peace negotiations would make the decision of Congress more difficult.

Sent Department; repeated Nanking 76, Shanghai 48.

CLARK

893.00/2–2549 : Telegram

The Ambassador in China (Stuart) to the Secretary of State

NANKING, February 25, 1949.
[Received February 26—6:52 a. m.]

472. Following broadcast February 24 North Shensi station under Shihchiachuang dateline:

"Chairman Mao Tze-tung and General Chou En-lai received Yen Hui-ching, Shao Li-tze, Chang Shih-chao and Chiang Yung, who visited Peiping in private capacity, in Shihchiachuang on February 22. Opinions on peace talk, restoration of navigation and mail service were widely exchanged. Four visitors flew back to Peiping on February 24."

These are three members of "Shanghai peace mission" plus Shao Li-tze who traveled to Peiping in capacity of "unofficial delegate".

Sent Department, repeated AmEmb Canton 107, Shanghai 221.

STUART

893.00/2–2649 : Telegram

The Consul General at Peiping (Clubb) to the Secretary of State

PEIPING, February 26, 1949.
[Received February 26—10:36 p. m.]

313. ReContel 298, February 25.[71] *Jen Min Jih Pao* reports arrival Peiping yesterday from Mukden of 35 democratic leaders from all parts country who had gathered Manchuria including Li Chi-shen, Shen Chun-ju, Tan Ping-shan, Ma Hsu-lun, Chang Pe-chung, Kuo Mo-jo, Peng Tse-min.[72] They were accompanied on trip by chairman Shensi–Kansu–Ningsia border government Lin Po-chu, vice chairman Northeast Administrative Committee Kao Chung-min and playwright Tien Han.

They were met here by Lin Piao, Lo Jung-huan, Nieh Jung-chen, Tung Pi-wu, Po Yi-po, Yeh Chien-ying [73] and CCP Peiping Municipal Committee Secretary Peng Chen as well as by some hundred other persons comprising democratic leaders, both those coming from

---

[71] Not printed.
[72] Representing various groups cooperating with the Communists.
[73] Communist military or civilian officials.

Shihchiachuang and those of Peiping itself, and representatives of various local people's, students' and workers' organizations.

Both Mao Tse-tung and Chou En-lai unmentioned in press account first popular report [which?] presumed mistaken.

Sent Department 313, Nanking 224, Canton 9, Shanghai 246.

CLUBB

893.00/2–2649 : Telegram

The Consul General at Hankow (Callanan) to the Secretary of State

[Extract]

HANKOW, February 26, 1949—5 p. m.
[Received February 28—7 :37 a. m.]

57. Ma Chieh-lien, Chief Foreign Affairs, Pai's headquarters, conversing with Martin [74] stated his belief Li-Pai group will make terms with Communists if latter agree give Kwangsi clique prominent place coalition government, retain control Kwangsi troops and allow free hand south of Yangtze. He convinced important split Communist ranks with Mao Tse-tung being amenable make terms with Li government. Quotes returned Pai delegates from Communist territory as saying, while Communist Army superior Nationalists, because unified, Communist civil administration weak and not as revolutionary as touted.

Ma continues pessimistic regarding unity Nationalist China (mytel 44, February 16 [75]) readily discounting Pai statement to Ma that he has Kwangtung backing (mytel 38, February 14). Ma claims T. V. Soong now remitting money through Bank of Canton for expenses Hsueh Yueh's [76] troops who would combat any incursion from Kwangsi. In Hunan, Cheng Chien continues to be uncooperative with Li government and play lone hand. His refusal accept Li's invitation accompany him Changsha to Hankow is indicative. Generalissimo and company continued control of purse strings and thus of air force and various generals and politicians still seriously hampering Li government. Illustrative local incident was refusal of CAF allow chartered plane land Hankow military airport take Hupeh Legislative Yuan members to Nanking. Continued frustrations Li government may hasten settlement above terms, leaving Generalissimo group holding bag.

•   •   •   •   •   •   •

Sent Department 57, repeated Nanking 47, Canton 18.

CALLANAN

---

[74] Edwin W. Martin, Vice Consul at Hankow.
[75] Not printed.
[76] Governor of Kwangtung.

893.00/2–2849 : Telegram

The Consul General at Shanghai (Cabot) to the Secretary of State

SHANGHAI, February 28, 1949.
[Received February 28—6 a. m.]

695. H. H. Kung's [77] *China Press*, 28th, inspired by news accompanying return Yen's mission of imminency peace negotiations and Communists' willingness cease military activity during period, exhibits unprecedented degree anxiety lest talks fail and hostilities be resumed. Paper sees as greatest menace peace South China faction, led by Sun Fo, which with hopes for increased American aid might hold out for greater concessions from Communists than they are prepared to grant. It declares this viewpoint must not be permitted interfere with smooth progress talks.

"Time for American aid so definitely over—for time being aid to any one party would simply make other more determined continue conflict while aid to both would prolong war indefinitely—even if United States does make such an offer of help at present it would be better take rain check on it than to accept."

Sent Department 695, repeated Nanking unnumbered, via pouch to Canton.

CABOT

893.00/2–2849 : Telegram

The Ambassador in China (Stuart) to the Secretary of State

NANKING, February 28, 1949—4 p. m.
[Received February 28—8 :29 a. m.]

486. Reliably informed Sun Fo arriving here this afternoon following receipt of message from Generalissimo "ordering" him Nanking. Sent Department 486, repeated Canton 113, Shanghai 226.

STUART

893.00/2–2849 : Telegram

The Consul General at Shanghai (Cabot) to the Secretary of State

SHANGHAI, February 28, 1949—5 p. m.
[Received February 28—6 :21 a. m.]

696. From editorial 28th (reContel 695, February 28) advising against acceptance further American aid until peace achieved, it appears *China Press* (H. H. Kung) has committed *volte-face* from former position on American assistance Nationalist Government.

---

[77] Brother-in-law of Madame Chiang Kai-shek; former Chinese Minister of Finance.

Paper has recently aligned itself with Li Tsung-jen in factional split in Government and has given him and his peace program its staunch and unqualified support, evincing marked degree its distrust Sun Fo. There exists nevertheless possibility editorial summarized Reftel not in entire accord paper's policy as American editor, N. F. Allman (well-known for uncompromising support Generalissimo and program all-out Chinese), has been absent from Shanghai number days.

Sent Department 696; repeated Nanking 448, pouched Canton.

CABOT

893.00/2–2849 : Telegram

The Ambassador in China (Stuart) to the Secretary of State

NANKING, February 28, 1949—5 p. m.
[Received February 28—8 :49 a. m.]

488. Foreign Minister today gave me following report on W. W. Yen peace delegation:

CCP spokesmen assured delegation they really want peace settlement but it may be some time before place and persons determined because agreements must first be reached within CCP and with other groups such as KmtRC.[78] Delegation members received impression internal disagreements within CCP are rather acute, but they could not discover lines of cleavage. Shao Li-tze felt Chou En-lai was more broadminded than others but lacked influence he ought to have and tried to avoid thorough discussion. After their 40-minute conversation Chou insisted on postponement of further talk, evidently fearful saying too much.

It was agreed there should be restoration of five lines communications: shipping, mail, postal remittances, wireless and aviation with some reservations. It was also understood PLA would not undertake offensive military action this period.

Sent Department; repeated AmEmbassy Canton 116, Shanghai 227.

STUART

893.001/2–2849 : Telegram

The Ambassador in China (Stuart) to the Secretary of State

NANKING, February 28, 1949.
[Received February 28—11 :38 p. m.]

489. Acting President Li Tsung-jen requests following message be transmitted to President:

"Since assuming office as Acting President, I have had in mind a message to you expressing the hope that the historic friendship be-

---

[78] Kuomintang Revolutionary Committee.

tween our countries may be maintained, and assuring you of my appreciation for all that has been done for China under your administration."

Sent Department 489, repeated AmEmbassy Canton 117.

STUART

893.00/3–149 : Telegram

The Minister-Counselor of Embassy in China (Clark) to the Secretary of State

CANTON, March 1, 1949.
[Received March 1—3 :40 a. m.]

Cantel 88. Local press reports Sun Fo, accompanied by Minister Land Administration Wu Shang-yin and Acting Minister Education Chen Hsueh-ping, left Canton for Nanking by plane February 28. Sun is reported to have told reporters at the airfield that Executive Yuan will remain in Canton for the time being and that he would return here himself in about 1 week after personally reporting to Legislative Yuan and attending meetings Nanking. Remainder statement was to effect he would make personal effort to see that Government peace drive bore fruit as desired by the people. Press also reports Chang Fa-kwei, accompanied by Yu Han-mou,[79] left for Shaokwan (northern Kwangtung) to assume post Commander in Chief ground forces Nationalist armies.

Sent Department; repeated Nanking 83, Shanghai 54.

CLARK

893.00/3–149 : Telegram

The Ambassador in China (Stuart) to the Secretary of State

NANKING, March 1, 1949—10 a. m.
[Received March 1—4 :35 a. m.]

493. In conversation February 25 Vice Foreign Minister George Yeh ventured peace negotiations result Shihchiachuang meeting might very well last 6 months and felt certain Communists would not attempt Yangtze crossing during that period. Further stated that he came Nanking express purpose answering questions which might arise during legislators' convention. Contrary to report Yeh returned Nanking maintain branch of Foreign Office, tone of conversation lead us believe he would return Canton following conclusion above meeting.

Sent Department, repeated AmEmb Canton 120.

STUART

---

[79] Formerly Commander in Chief of Chinese Army; Military and Political Affairs Director for South China.

893.00/3–149 : Telegram

The Ambassador in China (Stuart) to the Secretary of State

NANKING, March 1, 1949.
[Received March 1—1:11 a. m.]

495. Vernacular press reports return to Nanking February 27 of Shanghai peace mission and carries following written statement released by mission:

"We have paid 2-week visit to Peiping in private capacity. During visit we talked with Communist leaders Yeh Chien-ying, Lin Piao, Nieh Jung-chen, Tung Pi-wu, Lo Jung-yuan and Po I-po, both individually and together. We were also invited to Shihchiachuang and there exchanged great variety of views on peace negotiations with Communist Chairman Mao Tze-tung and General Chou En-lai. We ended trip and returned south with conviction that although numerous difficulties still exist there is great hope for peace, and we shall return to Shanghai after reporting to Acting President Li Tsung-jen. While in Peiping and Shihchiachuang, we reached agreement in principle with Communist leaders in regard to opening of transportation and postal service between north and south. We expressed our thanks to Communist leaders for their hospitality toward us while [we] were in the two cities."

Statement signed by W. W. Yen, Kiang Yung, Chang Shih-chao, Shao Li-tzu.

Sent Department, repeated AmEmb Canton 122.

STUART

893.00/3–149 : Telegram

The Ambassador in China (Stuart) to the Secretary of State

NANKING, March 1, 1949.
[Received March 2—1:21 a. m.]

501. *Yi Shih Pao* March 1 carries statement on current situation by 50 Nanking professors headed by Liu Pu-tung, prominent legislator, and Ni Ching-yuan, Dean of College of Liberal Arts, Nanking. Statement makes following points:

1. Since people all demand peace, they are dissatisfied with Government leaders who are inconsistent and waver between peace and war.
2. To demonstrate peace sincerity both sides must stop war preparation. Today only small number of privileged people such as warlords and bureaucrats do not want peace.
3. China needs thorough social reform and the evil influences of feudalism, imperialism and bureaucratic capitalism must be uprooted.
4. Interference by any friendly nation in China's domestic affairs or proffer of military aid to prolong China's civil war should be resolutely opposed.

Sent Department; repeated AmEmb Canton 126.

STUART

893.00/3–249 : Telegram

The Consul General at Peiping (Clubb) to the Secretary of State

PEIPING, March 2, 1949—4 p. m.
[Received 10:45 p. m.]

339. ReContel 260, February 19, second paragraph.[80] Following are two natural points view re results of Yen mission: 1, peace possible; 2, peace improbable. Ex-Mayor Ho Ssu-yuan expresses first point view contending difficulties now experienced by Communists likely turn them to peaceful path. He points out peace talks and acceptance by Nanking of eight points first offered by Communists as peace condition have developed on Communist side as well as on national peace psychology, that anticipation and desire peace now growing among Communist troops as well general population. On economic side he points out absence integrated economic plans, coupled with popular disappointments regarding situation existing after Communists occupied Peiping, Tientsin, has made difficulties such as to give Communists pause. As examples he pointed out that 70,000 dock workers Tientsin now lie idle; that whereas before Peiping was allocated approximately 700,000 bags flour monthly none is now coming in; that monetary problems are unsolved.

Ho said March 1 that Yen mission came for exchange views; that mission desired discover whether Communists were prepared make any concessions (for unless they made concession, particularly re point one, there was no hope); that they took back no formal proposals but undoubtedly would discuss matters Nanking. He believed there would be further exchange views with Nanking delegates perhaps coming to Peiping; that in meantime PCC meeting scheduled be called here in March would be postponed pending developments other lines. If expressing March 1 general belief peace possible, be it noted that he seemed less hopeful than last week when he opined he might himself go south with peace delegation to assist (he may have desired escape).

Typifying second line thought is contention old time police official that peace most improbable. He explains this mission received because it would have been impolite refuse proffered visit prominent leader statesmen like Yen and Shao Li-tzu, that Communists experienced no loss in letting them come but would not have profited by keeping them away. He holds that there is no common ground for compromise between such unlike groups. Another Chinese commenting along same lines expressed belief Communists "would endeavor cheat Li Tsung-jen just like they cheated Fu Tso-yi".

[80] Not printed; it reported administrative difficulties experienced by Communists in Peiping (893.00/2–1949).

Invite attention to parallels between present situation and that prevailing 1927 when Communists proposed stop Hankow instead of proceeding Shanghai with risk revolution. All Communist ideology is directed toward avoidance compromise basic revolutionary aims. It seems highly improbable Communists could reach agreement with Nanking Government on anything above surrender level and avoid political compromise of aims they presently hold or even that they could accept total surrender Nanking and take responsibility for South China without compromise basic economic principles. It would seem more likely that they desire now stop military advance long enough consolidate present gains with military government period continuing in meantime North China and this area effectively autonomous in respect to Manchuria; that in due course by plan "breakdown negotiations with Nanking" would be announced at PCC held Peiping; that subsequently there would be set up coalition government exclusive Nanking elements but including Li Chi-shen groups for window dressing but with Communists effectively in control; and that Communists' aim at achieving ultimate political military control all China proper only after 1950 or later. Tung Pi-wu incidentally was quoted as stating in speech before cultural leaders February 20 (Contel 274, February 21[81]) that people should not expect achievement revolutionary aims too soon; that it would probably be 5 years before changes were perceptible; and that in order to achieve present aims of revolution 30 years would be requisite. Primary objective Communists by all logic must be presumed to be maintenance integrity their political line and all Soviet force, whether persuasive or organizational, could be expected support that line. Major Communist concerns for present, therefore, are presumably (1) consolidation of gains and (2) prevention consolidation Nationalist regime with or without outside help. Granted difficulties facing them in present circumstances their aim logically cannot be peace which would in actuality increase political dangers for them. They would in latter case cease be Communists.

Sent Department, repeated Nanking and Canton.

CLUBB

893.00/3–249 : Telegram

The Minister-Counselor of Embassy in China (Clark) to the Secretary of State

CANTON, March 2, 1949—5 p. m.
[Received March 3—1 :55 a. m.]

Cantel 92. Chen Tai-chu, Director American Section Foreign Office, again expressed to me today his belief peace negotiations might

---

[81] Not printed.

last for long time and might be successful (my 80, February 24, repeated Nanking 76, Shanghai 48). He remains convinced that there exists in Communist ranks serious difference of opinion between those who believe in desirability granting Nationalists reasonable peace and then attaining control through pattern set Eastern Europe, and those who insist on continuance military operations.

I am becoming convinced there may be something in what he says. Communists are not exercising their military capabilities. They have not attempted cross Yangtze, nor have they attacked Nanking or even shown their disrespect for that city by shelling it. They have permitted continuation of peace campaign during period prolonged military inactivity. The longer troops remain inactive, the more difficult it becomes to renew battle. This is true of Communists equally with Nationalists. Also strategy Acting President Li has been most successful in placing onus on Communists should fighting be renewed. Li has demonstrated most clearly that he is willing to go to almost any extreme regardless of his own prestige to attain reasonable peace. Communists realize war weariness of people exists in Communist areas as well as in those occupied by Nationalists. Therefore, after prolonged negotiations, during which resumption of postal, telegraph and transport facilities will take place, psychological situation will be reached where it seems unlikely fighting can be resumed. We know that Li Tsung-jen seeks: (1) Territorial arrangement which would give him opportunity demonstrate superiority democratic processes, or failing that (2) federation leaving considerable regional autonomy, thus also providing opportunity demonstrate superiority democratic processes; or (3) coalition in which Kmt and other elements would participate as group; and finally, failing even this, resumption of hostilities.

It is difficult to believe Communists would accept either territorial or federal arrangement, but it is entirely possible they may accept coalition even though in its early stages Kmt and others enter as units possibly after purging certain principal "war criminals". Such an arrangement should be attractive to Communists. They would take over functioning Nationalist and Provincial Government machinery. They would assume control of Nationalist Government already recognized internationally and would, in fact, assure eventual attainment their aims without that renewal of hostilities so dreaded by war-weary people. I do not believe, therefore, that we can rule out possibility Communists may change tactics and permit Li's peace negotiations to succeed. Should Sun Fo fail and be replaced by Shao Li-tze, possibility such development would increase.

I believe we could expect the Western leaders to go along with Li provided certain amount regional autonomy was recognized. Only fly in ointment is, of course, Generalissimo. He is most certainly one of "war criminals" and Li cannot deliver him over to Communists. He is still power to be reckoned with and should he see Li's peace efforts succeeding, he might re-emerge in defense of "democratic principles" and assume defense of his prepared bastion in the Foochow–Amoy–Taiwan triangle.

Sent Department; repeated Nanking 89, Shanghai 58, Moscow 4.

CLARK

893.00/3–249 : Telegram

The Minister-Counselor of Embassy in China (Clark) to the Secretary of State

CANTON, March 2, 1949—5 p. m.
[Received March 2—7 :06 a. m.]

Cantel 93.   Dr. Ku Yu-shui, Chancellor of National Political University Nanking, says that peace negotiators returned from north, with whom he has talked, all indicate disagreement among Communist leaders re continuing hostilities.   Mao Tze-tung is reported to favor cessation hostilities and coalition government.   Chen Yi, Liu Po-cheng and Lin Piao favor continuing military operations although Chen Yi is reported reluctant assume command Yangtze crossing operation, believing Lin Piao, who did not encounter serious opposition, should come south and reinforce him.   Li Li-san is reported to favor a "drag-the-feet" policy based on his belief that Moscow has not made up its mind whether best interests Communism lie in crossing Yangtze or permitting coalition.   He therefore favors stalling along with peace negotiations, at same time slowing down military operations sufficient give Moscow time make up its mind.   Source is, of course, loyal member Kmt and what he says should be considered in light of that fact.

From purely military standpoint he says Communists are experiencing difficulty.   It requires 300,000 troops keep Yen Hsi-shan contained Taiyuan and another 300,000 to assure stability Peiping area where Fu Tso-yi's troops have not been disbanded or reincorporated. His information is that although Fu and his generals have been relieved of command, the troops themselves and junior officers are refusing relinquish arms on basis they are professional soldiers and were promised incorporation, together with their arms, into Communists' forces.   Dr. Ku says Communists do not dare disarm them with violence for fear repercussions other Nationalist armies which Communists hope will accept "Peiping peace".

Sent Dept, repeated Nanking 88, Shanghai 57, pouched Peiping.

CLARK

893.00/3–249 : Telegram

The Ambassador in China (Stuart) to the Secretary of State

NANKING, March 2, 1949—11 p. m.
[Received March 3—2:19 a. m.]

507. Following is substance my conversation February 28 and March 1 with Li Tsung-jen, W. W. Yen, Shao Li-tze and Chang Chih-chung concerning findings of "Shanghai peace mission":

(1) Yen and Shao both think prospects for peace are very good although there will be many difficulties. They think CCP really does want peace. However, on other hand Mao Tze-tung and Chou En-lai both informed them that before genuine peace negotiations can be initiated it will be necessary call secret convention CCP leaders for purposes of (*a*) To win over extreme Leftist element within CCP in support of peace and (*b*) To determine place and personnel for eventual peace negotiations. As respects size of two delegations, CCP proposes there be four delegates on each side subject to later increase by mutual agreement. CCP also proposes future government of China eventually be composed in three equal parts of CCP, Kmt and non-partisans. In response to Shao's question to Mao and Chou whether it would be possible for CCP to issue cease-fire order without delay for purpose of creating favorable atmosphere, Chou replied that this was impossible because of internal disagreements within CCP but that they were acting as though such order had been given.

(2) Mao and Chou evidenced little spirit of compromise re CCP eight conditions. They were adamant in demanding punishment for "four families" and emphasized condition calling for nationalization all troops within China. However they did not push for land reform south of Yangtze along lines employed north of river, apparently recognizing importance of variations in land tenure practice.

(3) Peace delegates actually did carry to Li letter from Mao stating that CCP is aware of difficulties which confront former.

(4) Li informed me that he is personally much concerned over intensity CCP anti-Americanism as reported to him by Yen and Shao. These latter both talked earnestly with Mao and Chou but did not believe that they had reduced bitterness of Mao and Chou over military aid given Kmt by US. Li expressed view to me that it might be helpful if US could at this juncture make public statement clarifying its position.

(5) Finally CCP leaders assured Shao and Yen that they have no intention to interfere with private enterprise and "small capital" in Shanghai.

(6) Yen and Shao, it seems to us, demonstrated degree of naivete in some questions they put to Communist leaders. Replying to Yen's question re CCP policy on religious freedom, General Yeh Chien-ying replied: "Communists do not like religion but could not object to any one accepting it as long as he did not try to force it on others". As respects Communist attitude toward foreign church colleges, Chou spoke critically of St. John's University as "bourgeois and reac-

tionary" though National delegates inferred mission colleges were not objected to as such. In reply to question concerning CCP attitude toward Soviet violations of Yalta agreement [82] particularly at Dairen and Port Arthur, Chou blandly passed blame to US by replying that these Soviet acts were necessitated solely by American unilateral action in Japan and American postponement of final Japanese peace treaty. Chou replied to Yen's question whether CCP is really of Russian or Chinese character by saying that of course CCP is Chinese but that because of common beliefs and purposes there is naturally close sympathy between Soviet and Chinese Communists.

Sent Department; repeated Shanghai 234, Canton 131, passed Peiping 73.

STUART

893.9111RR/3–449 : Telegram

The Consul General at Shanghai (Cabot) to the Secretary of State

[Extract]

SHANGHAI, March 4, 1949.
[Received March 4—3:40 a. m.]

742. Shanghai press summary March 4. Sun Fo's statement yesterday that peace talks will be held after March 15 is top news. Li Tsung-jen appointed a 10-man committee to draft a peace formula, and Government will talk peace with Communists on equal footing. Both sides will appoint equal number of delegates, but number of delegates is not yet decided and delegates have yet to be named.

Sun Fo also announced that Government was trying to implement following reforms: Discontinue conscription, reduce size of army, stop food requisitioning, define governmental powers of central and local governments and institute land reform. He emphatically stated that press office and Executive Yuan are unanimous in opinions regarding peace.

Regarding UN mediation in China's internal disputes, Sun explained that war in China is a civil war, not an international war, and it is not function of UN to intervene other nations' affairs. Since the Communists oppose UN mediation and since they have agreed to start peace talks, the Government will negotiate directly with Communists.

Members of 10-man committee working on a peace formula agreed on following points: Constitution may be revised according to former PCC agreement. "War criminal" issue should be reconsidered by Communists. If necessary, National Assembly and Legislative Yuan may be dissolved. Reorganization of army should be carried out on equitable and rational basis.

---

[82] Signed February 11, 1945; *Foreign Relations*, The Conferences at Malta and Yalta, 1945, p. 984.

Ta Kung Pao and *Sin Wen Pao* report Gen. Chang Chi-chung left Nanking yesterday for a "certain place" and will stay there for few days.

Premier Sun entertained Legislative Yuan members yesterday and asked their support. Legislative Yuan members in Nanking met yesterday and discussed problems of political reform. Most of them expressed dissatisfaction with Sun Cabinet.

.   .   .   .   .   .

CABOT

893.00/3–649 : Telegram

The Ambassador in China (Stuart) to the Secretary of State

NANKING, March 6, 1949—3 p. m.
[Received March 7—12:43 a. m.]

525. Foreign Minister who is presently in Nanking asked me to call on him afternoon March 3. Our conversation was general and there was apparently no specific reason for his summons.

He said that Lapham (ECA Chief) had not been responsive to Chinese request for silver loan (Shanghai's telegram 682, February 26 to Department, repeated Nanking 444, Canton 98 [83]). I pointed out that ECA had no authority such matters and added it was improbable that Congress would feel itself in position to make loan to China in light current circumstances.

Wu Tieh-cheng then asked what were our anxieties re China and Chinese Government. I replied that these were two: (1) disunity within Government and (2) lack of public support for Government. In response to his question if I referred to differences between Nanking and Canton group, I replied that this interpretation was inevitable but that there was also considerable confusion respect to relations between retired President and Acting President, that American public did not understand what actual relationship between these two was. After exhausting usual "official" explanations, Foreign Minister frankly admitted that it is difficult for man who had held power so long suddenly become inactive. He continued that there had been some very serious discussions recently and that Government leaders were determined to start new system centering authority in Cabinet which would from now on be responsible with President being relegated to his "constitutional" status. Generalissimo would thus become "elder statesman" consulted on occasion but restrained from giving orders. To make move less pointed, it is proposed that several other of older Kuomintang leaders would be similarly treated. I expressed

---

[83] Vol. IX, p. 742.

hope there would be some success in putting these measures into effect.

Sent Department; repeated Canton 138.

STUART

893.00/3–749 : Telegram

The Ambassador in China (Stuart) to the Secretary of State

NANKING, March 7, 1949.
[Received March 8—1:17 a. m.]

528. Nanking vernacular press March 7 reports Government efforts draft peace formula with several meetings of 10-man committee and formation of following subcommittees:

Military Subcommittee: Chang Chih-chung, Ho Ying-chin, Liu Fei; Political Subcommittee: Chang Chun, Shao Li-tse, Wu Chung-hsin (study revision of existing constitution); Foreign Affairs Subcommittee: Sun Fo, Wu Tieh-cheng, Chu Chia-hua (study question of "traitorous treaties").

Ho Ping Jih Pao states army reorganization will be greatest obstacle in peace draft with no decision reached on which of following principles to adopt:

(1) Government and Communist each have own army; (2) overall reorganization at PCC; (3) reorganization after Peiping pattern.

Tabloid *Chung Kuo Jih Pao* states draft ready within 10 days, while Catholic organ *Yi Shih Pao* carries "unconfirmed report" committee has made following resolutions:

(1) Existing constitution may be modified or even radically changed if Communists insist; (2) Communists should reconsider demands, particularly regarding punishment war criminals as preliminary condition to peace talks; (3) new elements might be allowed participate in National Assembly and Legislative Yuan; (4) drafting overall army reorganization.

Sent Department; repeated Shanghai 243, Canton 139.

STUART

893.00/3–749

The Consul at Tsingtao (Strong) to the Ambassador in China (Stuart) [84]

[Extracts]

No. 3   TSINGTAO, March 7, 1949.

SIR: I have the honor to transmit the monthly political and military summary for the Tsingtao consular district for February 1949. The initial portion of this report is an introductory summary.

---

[84] Copy transmitted to the Department without covering despatch; received April 5.

INTRODUCTORY SUMMARY

Mid-February saw an almost complete about-face in the political and military prospects for Tsingtao. Instead of withdrawing as planned, the Nationalist troops were ordered to remain. In turn, the American Naval forces which were in the main to move out, leaving only a small rearguard, extended their stay. Thus the timing for a communist takeover of Tsingtao and its environs again has been revised; current prospects lead to the estimate of several months of relative stability before possible assumption of control by the communist regime. The reinvigoration of the Taiyuan airlift from Tsingtao; the apparent intention of the communists not to attack the Yangtze line during peace negotiations, thus freeing Nationalist forces for holding Tsingtao; the probability that the negotiations will continue for some time; and the logical desire of the Nationalist Government to hold as many points as possible in North China for prestige and bargaining purposes, all lead to this conclusion. Thus Tsingtao, which was to have been lopped off the body of Nationalist China as a useless appendage, has been brought into the national scene and its fate is now dependent on the momentous events of the next few months.

. . . .

Only the generous contributions of ECA to Tsingtao in terms of food and coal have kept Tsingtao afloat. The presence of the United States Naval Forces at Tsingtao is viewed as evidence of Nationalist intention to hold the city, and its withdrawal would initially be interpreted as the preliminary to departure of the Nationalist troops. Whereas in the past the U.S. Navy was regarded as the real protective force for Tsingtao, it is now recognized that the communists have no intention of posing a military threat to Tsingtao. Thus Chinese residents tend to gauge the intentions of the Nationalist Government toward Tsingtao by the activities of the U.S. Naval Forces. During the absence of Admiral Badger with his flagship for twelve days [this] had no visible effect on internal stability.

Evacuation of foreigners from Tsingtao was to all intents and purposes completed during the month. Somewhat over eight hundred non-Asiatics remain of whom over one-half are Soviet citizens. It is anticipated that the foreign community will hereafter remain stable.

The tension which pervaded Tsingtao in January and early February has almost entirely been eliminated. However with trade at low ebb and inflation rampant, Tsingtao's citizens are anxious to have their fate settled in one way or another in order that a return to more normal business and living conditions may improve their lot. (End of Introductory Summary)

[Here follows detailed report.]

Respectfully yours,

ROBERT C. STRONG

893.00/3–749

The Consul General at Shanghai (Cabot) to the Ambassador in China (Stuart)[85]

No. 26   SHANGHAI, March 7, 1949.

SIR: I have the honor to submit the following attempted estimate of the accomplishments of the Shanghai nonpartisan peace delegation to Peiping in the light of (1) careful scrutiny of local press news and editorial comment; (2) accounts given to officers of the Consulate General, by two persons close to Dr. W. W. Yen (his cousin, F. C. Yen, and Dr. James Pott of St. John's University) of observations which Dr. W. W. Yen made, separately, to them following the completion of his mission; and (3) recent known developments at Shanghai.

[Here follows detailed report respecting "an overall peace settlement", The Shanghai–Nanking area, and "restoration of communications".]

In the light of this background and of the before-mentioned clues as to the general tenor of the Shanghai delegation's talks with the Communists, it seems only logical to surmise that the mission's main efforts were concerned with peace and prosperity for Shanghai. The delegates presumably pledged themselves to the task of preserving the city's rich installations and resources against loss through removals, sabotage, plunder and resort to armed defense; and sought assurances from the Communists that, in return for such cooperation, the Communists would refrain from any precipitate forcible action against the city and would adopt tolerant policies toward private vested interests and business activities. That the delegates' promises may have gone beyond those of which Li Tsung-jen is aware, and approves, and included commitments looking to cooperation with Communists' plans for establishing their control or influence over the city even though a breakdown of Li's peace talks should force him to revert to war and armed defense of the Yangtze line is only conjectural, but entirely possible (despite Li's rapidly growing popularity in this area).

Whatever the delegates' promises were, it is clear that they were sufficient to elicit the desired assurances from the Communists to a degree which the delegates found encouraging. (According to a well-placed and generally reliable Chinese source, the Communists impressed the delegates with being less anxious to expedite establishment of complete physical control of the city than they were interested in effecting an early extension of their influence to certain key administrative and economic organs.) The return of the mission to

---

[85] Copy transmitted to the Department without covering despatch; received March 21.

Shanghai has brought a marked surge of optimism throughout the city, and such optimism is obviously more a matter of eased selfish apprehensions as to the future of Shanghai than it is one of hopefulness over the prospects of the Central Government's overall peace overtures. It is an optimism which chiefly reflects the relief of Shanghai propertied circles and their apparent confidence that the Communists (1) are in no hurry to take Shanghai; (2) will not seize it by force; and (3) will use moderation toward private property and enterprise. There are already indications that this optimism is swelling the movement back to Shanghai of wealthy Chinese who fled to Hongkong and elsewhere.

Respectfully yours, JOHN M. CABOT

893.00B/3–949 : Telegram

The Ambassador in China (Stuart) to the Secretary of State

NANKING, March 9, 1949—noon.
[Received March 9—3 :38 a. m.]

542. Acting President sent me following information from source he considers thoroughly reliable:

1. Zhukov,[86] with small staff Russian officers, has for some months been directing CCP military strategy.

2. CCP intends cross Yangtze at Wuhan rather than farther east. It regards Pai Chung-hsi as more dangerous than Generalissimo because his strategy less rigid and can be more easily directed in interest of American imperialism.

3. Politbureau has sent emissary to Manchuria to organize that area and North Korea into single bloc and make this base for further penetration of Japan.

I subsequently learned source was Li Ming-yang, who has just returned from mission to Communist General Chen Yi on behalf of Acting President.

Sent Department; repeated Canton 144, passed Moscow.

STUART

893.01/3–949 : Telegram

The Ambassador in China (Stuart) to the Secretary of State

NANKING, March 9, 1949.
[Received March 9—10 :56 p. m.]

548. Vernacular press March 9 reports Legislative Yuan yesterday passed resolution requesting Premier, heads of important Ministries

---

[86] Marshal G. K. Zhukov, Soviet Deputy Minister of Armed Forces and head of ground forces.

and Commissions and Ministers without Portfolio to return Nanking and manage political affairs from here during period of peace talks.

Sent Department 548; repeated Embassy Canton unnumbered.

STUART

893.001 Chiang Kai-shek/3–1049 : Telegram

The Minister-Counselor of Embassy in China (Clark) to the Secretary of State

CANTON, March 10, 1949.
[Received March 10—2:49 a. m.]

Cantel 122.   Tao Hsi-sheng, Vice Minister of Kmt Department of Publicity and former personal secretary to Generalissimo, answered questions at press conference Tuesday regarding present position Generalissimo.   Said Chiang will not resume direction of Government and has not been exercising any presidential authority since his retirement; said Chiang did not intend going Nanking, Canton or Taiwan, or Fukien; peace or war will be decided by Acting President Li and his Cabinet.   Tao, however, qualified this estimate, stating that as head of Kmt, Generalissimo still had right to lead and Kmt members "full right to listen to his orders without interference from any quarter".

Tao declared Generalissimo has also stopped exercising his powers as Commander-in-Chief, these powers now being exercised by Acting President Li, but added that Armed Forces are "spiritually behind" Generalissimo.   Tao said differences between Acting President Li and Sun Fo caused by Li's having acted unconstitutionally without Cabinet approval on peace talks.   Said Li's orders for release of Chang Hsiao-liang, Yang Hu-cheng [87] not carried out because of failure to obtain Cabinet approval.   Tao declared if Communist desire for peace sincere, will be possible merge troops both sides into a national army.

Sent Department; repeated Nanking 104, Shanghai 71.

CLARK

893.01/3–1049 : Telegram

The Minister-Counselor of Embassy in China (Clark) to the Secretary of State

CANTON, March 10, 1949—8 a. m.
[Received March 10—12:38 a. m.]

Cantel 123.   Despite resolution Legislative Yuan demanding return Nanking [of] Executive Yuan, Tung Lin, Vice Foreign Minister

---

[87] Marshal Chang Hsueh-liang and General Yang Hu-cheng were leaders of the Sian coup of December 1936, and were subsequently detained.

in charge Foreign Office Canton, doubts feasibility return Government Nanking this stage. He says conditions motivating removal Canton still exist Nanking, if anything in more aggravated form, and it would be folly return until removal Communist threat. He conceives possibility that few ranking members various Ministries might return Nanking so long as peace negotiations continue, but bulk Government will remain Canton.

He admitted that with Premier, Deputy Premier and Secretary General Executive Yuan all in Nanking, no Cabinet action was possible Canton and when I reminded him of promise Deputy Premier that Executive Yuan would at all times be functioning Canton to handle our title deed and other problems, Tung Lin said he would remind Wu Tieh-cheng this promise and suggest remedial action be taken pending formation new government.

Sent Department; repeated Nanking 105, Shanghai 72.

CLARK

893.002/3–1049 : Telegram

The Consul General at Shanghai (Cabot) to the Secretary of State

SHANGHAI, March 10, 1949.
[Received March 10—6:07 a. m.]

833. Recurrent theme in editorials on unlamented demise of Sun Fo Cabinet is added stature gained by President Li through recent developments.

Shanghai Evening Post March 9 says: "President Li's dogged refusal to be defeated by shifty tricks, concealed political manipulations and 57 varieties and degrees of desertion, have won general respect and a certain real admiration".

According to the MOI [88] organ, *China Daily Tribune*, March 10 editorial, "The reputation of Acting President Li, staying manfully in Nanking to grapple with the acute problems which are now confronting the nation has received a fillip. His prestige has been enhanced and we must express the hope that a premier will be found who will stand by his side in the effort to obtain that peace which the whole nation desires.["]

A continuing spate of editorials in vernacular press belabors disappointing performance of Sun and his Cabinet.

Sent Department, repeated Nanking and Canton unnumbered.

CABOT

---

[88] Ministry of Information.

893.00B/3–1049 : Telegram

The Consul General at Tientsin (Smyth) to the Secretary of State

TIENTSIN, March 10, 1949—10 a. m.[89]
[Received March 13—3 :29 a. m.]

130.[90] Following observations on local reaction to Communist occupation may be of interest: There was among local Chinese populace a certain air of exhilaration for first 3 or 4 days after "liberation" January 15, partly because trying days of attack on city were over, partly because of demise of a hated regime and partly because of excellent initial impression made by "liberators" on populace. This soon gave way to a period of reserved watchful waiting. This lasted about 2 weeks since it has been apparent that populace has genuine doubts that problems of a big city [will benefit?] and especially doubt that it can be beneficial to a city whose life depends upon import-export trade. There is a cautious but discernible resistance to Communist propaganda, originally designed for rural consumption and not altered sufficiently to avoid insult to a good portion of comparatively better educated urban mentality. While there is approval of unexpected leniency and toleration of Communist attitude in some matters compared to what has been feared, there is resentment that everyone is expected to fall in line. We have been surprised especially recently at freedom with which Chinese express their real feelings. Vice Consul Jenkins [91] reports there are many jokes about the new regime which are repeated in groups with minimum of caution.

Jenkins states a farmer with whom he talked in local market said things were better for him now that trade was restored with Tientsin and that it was a refreshing novelty not to have to pay heavy squeeze to bring his produce into city. He maintained, however, that people of his community did not like Communists; he said Communist officials ate and dressed better than country people and that general controls and restrictions were much more oppressive in rural areas than in city up to now. He said "listening committees" were highly organized everywhere and that independent Chinese farmers were both intimidated and irked.

Jenkins reports there is open fun made of newspaper statements that great masses of city population have spontaneously and joyously celebrated liberation of Tientsin and Peiping in impressive parades and ceremonies. Of newspaper itself (until recently only one official Communist paper published), more educated Chinese say it is journalistically poor and propaganda [is] juvenile. Former *Ta Kung Pao*

---

[89] Printed from corrected copy dated March 15, 1949, 11 :55 a. m.
[90] By a correction dated July 13, 1949, this was changed to read "No. 130."
[91] Alfred leSesne Jenkins.

now allowed to publish as "progressive daily" after apology for former sins; its news articles follow party line and editorials seem juvenile in argument except to uneducated. However, possible effect of constant bombardment of populace by same propaganda lines, whether juvenile or mature, should not be underestimated.

Laborers do not seem over-pleased with situation. They expected great things from Communists but, although they are supported as against employers, the general business situation is bad and lot of laborers has not notably improved. Workers in transportation and public utilities seem displeased over new low wages.

One matter which causes increasing resentment among Chinese is practice of Communist military and also civil personnel of billeting in homes. A great many Chinese have Communist soldiers billeted with them. Also resented is freedom with which Communist soldiers enter houses to look around and practice of "borrowing" anything from kitchenware to rugs and furniture. These same practices are also much resented by foreigners. Many Soviets, some British and other foreigners have soldiers billeted on them and "borrowing" has been a universal plague.

Although Communists announced that property of law abiding foreigners and Chinese would be protected they show little hesitation in taking what they wish. On March 7 Communist troops moved into billet in a large Butterfield [and] Swire [92] warehouse and paid no attention to protests. Due to Communist policy of not recognizing Consulates, foreigners have no recourse except to their own individual efforts. A number of foreign businessmen who have appealed to authorities for police protection against threats by unruly laborers have been put off and left to their devices. So far foreigners have suffered no physical harm but have been inconvenienced and worried by lack of security. Also red tape attending business and daily living, and prolonged delays of officials in acting on applications for numerous permits now required, are irksome and demoralizing. Majority of foreigners are getting fed up with conditions and if conditions do not improve in next few months it is expected that many will endeavor to depart.

Chinese who say present regime cannot last long are, we feel, not making a realistic appraisal of situation and are not taking into consideration the effects of controlled propaganda, the lack of a substitute government which might be supported, and the possibility that Communists will learn enough through their mistakes and deficiencies to gradually improve. One of chief dangers to Communists at present in Tientsin, aside from problem of getting foreign trade going, is absorption of former Kuomintang elements within their military

---

[92] British commercial firm.

and civil organizations. This danger would seem to arise not so much from possibility of shift in political affiliation back to Kmt as from inveterate habits of corruption which might prove contagious to newcomers. Reliable reports during last 2 weeks indicate that some Communist officials are taking squeeze duties; not yet possible to know how general this will become. At least it is a break from their former austere incorruptibility.

Most important question now facing Communists is whether they will prove to be more Chinese than Communist. This question has been discussed with a number of Americans and other foreigners during last few days and consensus is that they will prove to be more Chinese. Oldest American businessman in Tientsin, resident there for many years, is firm in his conviction on this point; he says he is betting his business on this conviction but will not venture prediction on how much time will take. He intends to remain 6 months or so to see how things develop.

As OTP with Department is our only code, we assume Department will relay our telegram to Embassy and interested Consulates.

SMYTH

893.00/3–1049 : Telegram

The Consul General at Peiping (Clubb) to the Secretary of State

PEIPING, March 10, 1949—3 p. m.
[Received March 10—3 :56 a. m.]

380. Re Nanking's 507 to Department March 3[2]. Offer observations that seem merited re Yen–Shao [93] attitude.

Re 1. Mao Tse-tung and Chou En-lai, being disciplined leaders who have contributed in large measure to present political integration and cohesion Chinese Communist movement, would probably neither have discussions nor make commitments Kmt peace delegation without reporting fully to Communist colleagues to whom Mao–Chou much closer than to persons in opposing camp.

Re proposed composition future Chinese Government, believe on basis Communist words and acts to date that by Kmt they mean KmtRC, not present Nanking leaders. Note insignificant role presently played by Li Chi-shen *et al.*, reduced to occasional statements support Mao's eight points while cooling heels waiting convocation PPC [*PPCC?* [94]] or similar political conference.

As noted Contel 339, March 2, indications are Communists now wish military breathing spell, a temporary cease-fire, to enable them consolidate tremendous and unwieldy gains. Initiative remains theirs but action not taken for other than own benefit.

---

[93] Dr. W. W. Yen and Shao Li-tze.
[94] "People's Political Consultative Conference."

Re 2, note peace settlement on basis Mao's eight points or effected piecemeal on Peiping pattern, two alternatives offered currently by Communists, is in fact surrender and would not result in any coalition incorporating balance power.

Believe Communists intend next [to] form nation-wide political control Chinese by Communists, that they are now unready shoulder political-economic tasks involved extending rule south Yangtze, that they prefer wait until they have adequate strength rather than endanger revolution by premature advance if waiting feasible. Military and political debility Nationalists' camp makes delay feasible. While believing in possibility coalition, I believe further that form coalition envisaged by Yen, Li Tsung-jen and Nanking leaders differs substantially from that conceived by Communists, Communists may plan forming North China interim coalition government including some KmtRC elements who would be captives of Communist machine, control which government would by plan eventually be extended all China, and coalition which possibly may be forced upon them by circumstance, Contel 363 [95] would be some time in evolving and would logically be combine from which extremist elements both right and left had been eliminated.

Repeated Nanking, Canton, Shanghai.

CLUBB

893.001/2–2849 : Telegram

The Secretary of State to the Ambassador in China (Stuart)

WASHINGTON, March 10, 1949—7 p. m.

324. Urtel 489, Feb. 28. Deliver following from President to Acting President Li Tsung-jen in reply to message

"I wish to express my sincere appreciation of your kind message of February 28 and to assure you of my very real desire to see a continuation of the traditional and close ties of friendship which have existed between the peoples and Governments of our two countries."

ACHESON

893.00B/3–1049

The Ambassador in China (Stuart) to the Secretary of State

No. 62   NANKING, March 10, 1949.
[Received March 28.]

SIR: I have the honor to request that I be authorized to discuss with top Communist leaders the points at issue between the United States of America and the Chinese Communist Party in the hope that this

---

[95] March 8, not printed.

would help toward a better mutual understanding. When and how such interviews could be arranged would necessarily be left to my discretion.

The Chinese Communist Party has revealed an increasingly anti-American sentiment. As its control spreads over the more important coastal provinces and further inland this will find concrete expression in many forms more harmful to us than their incessant vituperative broadcasts. Some of their anti-imperialism phraseology may be nothing more than the Party line inspired by the Kremlin. But a factor is unquestionably our military and other assistance to the National Government. The indignation over this is heartily shared by most of the intellectuals whether or not they are in sympathy with Communism. This is partly because they have lost all respect for their Government and partly because they believe that it is our aid alone which has enabled it to carry on the detested civil war. The Chinese Communist Party's animosity to us is greatly intensified by their suspicious attitude to all who are not of their own persuasion. It may be that there is something in Communist ideology which develops suspicion. It is also a distinctive Chinese characteristic. In any case I have never known anything else to compare with the suspicions of Chinese Communists. This colors all of their dealings with outsiders. They see the worst therefore in American behavior as this concerns China. Making full allowance for propagandist aims I am convinced that in their abuse of us there is a substantial residuum of genuine misapprehension. If this could be removed or to some extent reduced it would prepare the way for a settlement of the remaining problems. Or in a more hopeful vein, if American democratic influences could continue to pervade a communist dominated China and to modify its intolerance, the advantages for stability in Eastern Asia and elsewhere would be enormous.

I should like to approach the Chinese Communists not only as an official representative of the American Government but as one who through long residence here is known to have consistently stood for Chinese national independence and democratic progress as well as for closer American-Chinese relations primarily because of the benefits these would bring to the Chinese people. However much they might incline to discredit me as having in recent years become identified with what they denounce as bellicose American imperialism, I should expect that my previous activities and my personal acquaintance with many of them would not be entirely disregarded.

I should begin by reminding them of the long history of American good will for China as shown both by our Government and by private philanthropy or personal service, extending down to the statements issued by President Truman in December 1945 [96] and 1946 [97] and the intentions of the Marshall Mission.[98]   They cannot explain this away as wholly due to enlightened self-interest or to even baser motives, nor can the American nation have completely changed its character since then.   What has happened, however, is an extremely disconcerting experience in our dealings with the Soviet Union and our observation of the techniques and objectives of the Communist Party in other countries.   It is an ineluctable inference that these apply also to the Chinese Communist Party.   If they have suspicions of us we also have our suspicions.   These envisage the attempt to establish a totalitarian state in China, on the Russian model, in which all free intercourse of thought and action, of information and belief, will be banned and the usual coercive methods will be employed to enforce uniformity in harmony with communist ideology.   The American Government recognizes fully the right of the Chinese people to adopt any form of government they choose but is well aware that under this system there could be no untrammeled opportunity to express their genuine opinion.   So far from bringing "liberation" and "new democracy" it seems to us to be a more subtle and sinister form of despotism, the last phase of outmoded domination of the whole by a highly organized minority.   If it succeeds in China this would greatly strengthen the movement toward "one world" through violent revolution as advocated by orthodox exponents of communist strategy.   Or if, as is perhaps more probable, there would be continuing resistance the resultant disorders might also seem to constitute a threat to our own national security and to world peace.   My Government might therefore feel called upon to assist any nucleus of organized opposition first in arousing the Chinese people to the danger of their national sovereignty and personal liberties and then in using all possible means for their self-protection.   If this were undertaken at all I had reason to believe that we would use every available resource we possessed to restore real liberation to the Chinese people.   But the cost in human suffering and economic destruction would be enormous.   Under these circumstances it would be immensely to the advantage of all concerned to endeavor to clear away mutual suspicions or misunderstandings and to cooperate for the common good.   American public opinion would only be satisfied by convincing evidence of the basic freedoms and of a constructive, friendly foreign policy.   My deep interest in the welfare of the Chinese people, more especially of the students, and my appreciation of any truly demo-

---

[96] December 15, 1945 ; Department of State *Bulletin*, December 16, 1945, p. 945.
[97] December 18, 1946 ; *ibid.*, December 29, 1946, p. 1179.
[98] For documentation concerning the Marshall Mission, see *Foreign Relations*, 1945, vol. VII, pp. 745 ff. and *ibid.*, 1946, volumes IX and X.

cratic and progressive political program inspire me to make this final effort to serve a nation I have learned to love. In doing so I am confident also that the American people as a whole desire only China's independence, peace, economic recovery and open democracy, with no ulterior designs.

The above paragraph contains the substance of what I have in mind, but not as an official message to be delivered, still less as in any sense an ultimatum or threat. I should hope to convey these sentiments in friendly discussions. If these prove to be promising they can be implemented in some more specific form. If, on the other hand, my definite impression is unfavorable I fear that any hope of a viable solution through peaceful negotiations had better be abandoned. Careful thought could meanwhile be given to what course we should in this event adopt.

My matured opinion is that we can do most to combat Communism in China by the twin advocacy of nationalism and the basic freedoms. The former still wins the quickest response from politically conscious Chinese, including perhaps the majority of Communists, and is in any case one that the Chinese Communist Party cannot ignore in view of the prevalent fear of Russia. It is one on which our own history and our consistent China policy stand us in good stead. Among the freedoms that of publication is probably the most important. Chinese love to read and have keen intellectual curiosity. The Chinese Communist Party rely greatly on their own controlled publicity but have committed themselves to freedom of the press. Their denial of this will make them very unpopular and any attempts to disguise their control can be easily exposed. We shall be true to ourselves by emphasizing these two features and can thus accentuate the contrast with reactionary suppressive tactics. The meaning of this will not be lost in other Asiatic countries. Nor will the fact that we are not relying merely on our wealth and power. These can be reserved for later use if necessary. With free exchange of ideas and information we need have no fear of undue Russian influence in China.

Since General Marshall's departure from China over two years ago there has been steady deterioration both in the position of the National Government and in American prestige. It has distressed me to have been able to do so little to arrest these unfortunate trends. But I should find deep satisfaction in attempting this final service to my country and to the cause of liberalism in China. It may be naively visionary to imagine that I or any one else can influence the Chinese Communist Party to a more broadly tolerant policy. But in view of the fateful issues at stake it is abundantly worth the effort and will at the lowest justify us the more in any sterner measures we may feel called upon to take.

In view of the possibility of an early opportunity for such a conference I should appreciate an airgram in reply as soon as convenient.

Respectfully yours,   J. LEIGHTON STUART

893.00/3–1149 : Telegram

The Minister-Counselor of Embassy in China (Clark) to the Secretary of State

CANTON, March 11, 1949—11 a. m.
[Received March [11 ?]—3 :19 a. m.]

Cantel 128. In Cantel 71, February 23, I suggested possibility Li Tsung-jen might develop leadership necessary continue effective resistance [to] Communists. In Cantel 93, March 2, I warned against possibility Communists might agree reasonable peace and dominate Government thru eastern European pattern.

There is still third possibility which seems to me we should not overlook. Canton is far removed from theater of action, yet I get distinct impression that Communists are dallying with Li while making preparations cross Yangtze. We should not rule out possibility that Li may permit himself, much as Fu Tso-yi did in Peiping, to be manoeuvred into a position where he would wake up one morning and find he had no recourse but to surrender himself and his government. With completion [of] preparations [to] cross Yangtze which Communists continue, it seems entirely possible that with little, if any, advance warning they could isolate Nanking in such manner as to make departure of any considerable part of Government hazardous, if not impossible. Communists certainly have or can readily develop this capability. Whether they will exercise it may be arguable but should Government show unacceptable degree of independence in course forthcoming negotiations it would undoubtedly face this threat.

There seems the third possibility, therefore, that Li and his government may become at some stage unwillingly isolated [at] Nanking and at mercy [of] Communists. In such event we may expect Gimo re-emerge if he has not done so before and resume functions as President. Article of Constitution under which he vacated office seems to permit such action and he would have strong claim to legitimacy. In any event, I think we should be prepared for possibility such developments.

Sent Department, repeated Nanking 110, Shanghai 76.

CLARK

893.00/3–1149 : Telegram

The Minister-Counselor of Embassy in China (Clark) to the Secretary of State

CANTON, March 11, 1949—11 a. m.
[Received March 11—2 :17 a. m.]

Cantel 129. Chiang Monlin [99] believes Canton generals will co-operate with Ho Ying-chin if Ho accepts Premiership. Whoever forms new Govt, Chiang believes that although Ministries will remain Canton, head of each Ministry and an assistant or two will likely establish themselves Nanking so long as peace negotiations continue.

Although circumstances our conversation did not permit going into detail, Chiang insists that for many reasons Communists will not cross Yangtze. He expects peace negotiations to last several months, yet does not rule out possibility Communists will accept territorial arrangement as he is convinced Communists desire some compromise. This may be wishful thinking on his part, but Chiang is high in Kmt circles.

Sent Dept., repeated Nanking 11, Shanghai 77.

CLARK

893.001 Chiang Kai-shek/3–1249 : Telegram

The Ambassador in China (Stuart) to the Secretary of State

NANKING, March 12, 1949—1 p. m.
[Received March 12—4 :08 a. m.]

558. Chang Chih-chung and Wu Chung-hsin [1] returned from Fenghua yesterday. Had four conversations with Generalissimo. After usual polite preliminaries, Chang broached subject [of] Generalissimo's exit China suggesting trip abroad as beneficial. Reaction violent and suspicious. Said if he wanted go abroad would make decision on own initiative and not by dictation from others. Asked if Chang had been sent Fenghua by Li Tsung-jen or Pai Chung-hsi. Subject discussed subsequent conversations but Generalissimo did not mellow, change his position. Last word was [he] intended stay Fenghua.

Sent Dept., repeated Shanghai 260, AmEmb Canton 157.

STUART

---

[99] Chairman of the Joint Commission for Rural Reconstruction.
[1] The latter was formerly Secretary General of the President's office.

893.001 Chiang Kai-shek/3–1449 : Telegram

The Ambassador in China (Stuart) to the Secretary of State

NANKING, March 14, 1949—noon.
Received March 14—4:36 a. m.

562. Following return Chang Chih-chung and Wu Chung-hsin from Fenghua, lengthy conference was held with Acting President Friday evening in effort present [*prevent?*] impasse caused by Generalissimo's continued residence and activity in China. (See mytel 558, repeated Embassy Canton 157, March 12.) It was finally decided to telephone and talk to him directly, Chang Chih-chung speaking first, followed by Li Tsung-jen. Generalissimo replied he had decided to go abroad but that time and place would be of his own choosing. He expressed resentment at press reports, particularly American, that pressure was being put on him to leave China. Despite Generalissimo's truculent mood, Acting President is encouraged believe his assurances mean he will go abroad in near future. He hopes there will be as little publicity as possible prior to Generalissimo's departure and enjoined on me greatest caution and secrecy with respect this new development.

Sent Department, repeated AmEmb Canton 159.

STUART

893.9111 RR/3–1449 : Telegram

The Consul General at Shanghai (Cabot) to the Secretary of State

SHANGHAI, March 14, 1949.
[Received March 14—5:22 a. m.]

870. *China Press* March 14 carried Sun Fo statement on arrival Shanghai from Nanking last Saturday [2] that China should take neutral stand in event of third world war and be neither anti-US nor anti-USSR. Sun predicted Communists would join Soviet bloc when in control China. Also declared that China's failure obtain satisfactory results from past foreign policy due to deterioration in relations among wartime allies which affected Chinese situation. According to Sun, China was not responsible for this state of affairs, and there had been "no big mistakes in China's foreign policy".

Sent Department, repeated Nanking 516, Canton 155.

CABOT

---

[2] March 12.

893.002/3–1449 : Telegram

The Ambassador in China (Stuart) to the Secretary of State

NANKING, March 14, 1949—2 p. m.
[Received March 14—6 :32 a. m.]

566. Communist broadcast March 11 implied that Sun Fo's resignation was result of acting President's conversation with Admirals Badger and Pownall [3] and me last week end. Actually the three of us dined with Li Tsung-jen night March 6. Occasion was purely social except for brief conference before dinner between Badger and Li in which the former outlined present and future plans for US Navy Tsingtao. So far as I remember there was no mention of Sun Fo during entire evening.

Sent Department 566, repeated Canton 162, Shanghai 262, pouched Tsingtao.

STUART

III. FORMATION OF HO YING-CHIN CABINET; COLLAPSE OF PEACE TALKS BETWEEN THE CHINESE GOVERNMENT AND THE CHINESE COMMUNISTS AT PEIPING (MARCH 15–APRIL 22)

893.00/3–1549 : Telegram

The Ambassador in China (Stuart) to the Secretary of State

NANKING, March 15, 1949.
[Received March 15—5 :58 a. m.]

574. Vernacular press March 13 reports Legislative Yuan confirmation Ho Ying-chin [4] as Premier by vote 209 to 30. Kmt [5] Central Executive Committee members in Nanking favor Ho and Acting President [6] has cabled Kmt Central Headquarters in Canton requesting its approval, according to press.

Also reported is opening annual session Control Yuan at Nanking March 12.

Sent Department, repeated AmEmb Canton, unnumbered.

STUART

893.00/3–1549 : Telegram

The Consul General at Peiping (Clubb) to the Secretary of State

PEIPING, March 15, 1949—1 p. m.
[Received March 15—5 :41 a. m.]

[To Nanking :] Re Embtel 74, March 3.[7] Embassy will appreciate from recent Peiping telegrams that it is believed here coalition gov-

---

[3] Rear Adm. Charles A. Pownall, Commander, U.S. Naval Forces, Mariannas.
[4] Former Chinese Minister of National Defense.
[5] Kuomintang (Nationalist Party).
[6] General Li Tsung-jen.
[7] Not found in Department of State files.

ernment envisaged by Communists is one from which Nanking elements would be largely if not quite excluded and that present probabilities are Communists plan such government be established Peiping with actual authority over North China and Manchuria only but pretensions to authority for all China, that such organ would be set up after (1) announced breakdown peace negotiations and (2) holding peace conference Peiping in which Li Chi-shen [8] group participated. Li *et al.* would presumably be given government post, nominal authority as "liberal" front.

Above reasoning based on deductions both Communist propaganda and published statements both Li Chi-shen group and Peiping press. Likewise in line such Soviet thinking on subject as has been noted which seems to envisage political agreement of sorts on coalition basis but which presumably does not follow 1927 Borodin [9] thought groove which led Stalin [10] to defeat in China.

Manchuria because of presumed Soviet political advance that area constitutes uncertain factor and I feel that there is even possibility set up CCP [11] over-all organ may be delayed, leaving present "North China People's Govt" to carry on until further southward advance makes feasible establishment government for China proper. This would leave Manchuria in different status perhaps with interim geographical changes due to setting up "Inner Mongolian People's Republic" or adherence Chinese outer province to north or east. This paragraph highly speculative.

Sent Nanking 258, repeated Department, Shanghai, Embassy Canton unnumbered.

[CLUBB]

893.9111RR/3–1649 : Telegram

The Ambassador in China (Stuart) to the Secretary of State

NANKING, March 16, 1949.
[Received March 16—11:25 p. m.]

584. Vernacular press reports Ho Ying-chin in press conference March 15 declared peace talks would commence shortly and new Cabinet would seek humane and reasonable peace. On question foreign aid, Ho asserted any aid, whether from Britain, US, or Russia, would be acceptable to help avert economic crisis. Queried on Cabinet, Ho disclosed that W. W. Yen and Chiang Yung declined to

---

[8] Leader of Kuomintang Revolutionary Committee (KmtRC).
[9] Soviet Communist adviser to the Hankow government, 1926–27; known as Michael (Mikhail Markovich) Borodin.
[10] Josif Vissarionovich Stalin, in 1927 Secretary-General of the Soviet Communist Party; since 1946 Soviet Prime Minister and Chairman of the Council of Ministers of the Soviet Union.
[11] Chinese Communist Party.

participate, while Chang Shih-chao [12] might consider joining, Young China Party is ready to take part, and Democratic Socialists have not yet decided. He added that Chang Chih-chung [13] consented to be Minister without Portfolio, Shao Li-tzu [14] is interested in being peace delegate and Wu Chung-hsin [15] is still considering. Cabinet list has not been prepared, Ho said, because Legislative Yuan still working on simplification of Government structure. Ho also revealed there will be changes in Government's peace delegates.

Sent Department 584, repeated American Embassy Canton unnumbered.

STUART

893.50 Recovery/3–1649

The Ambassador in China (Stuart) to the Secretary of State

NANKING, March 16, 1949.
[Received April 18.]

SIR: I have the honor to refer to your letter of November 29, enclosing a Policy Statement on China of September [27,] 1948.[16] This statement on China is basically an excellent outline of American policy. Section (A), giving our objectives in China, is a sound and succinct expression of our long-term aims and requires no changes. However, Section (B)–1, dealing with policy issues, requires redrafting to take into consideration the momentous changes which have occurred in China during the past six months.

Despite our China Aid Program, intended to afford the Chinese Government a breathing spell during which it would have the opportunity to initiate the reforms essential to a long-range solution of its problems, the Chinese Communists have succeeded in occupying new and important areas, have destroyed a substantial part of the military forces remaining to the National Government and have forced the Government to sue for peace. The hoped-for reforms have not been instituted and economic conditions continue deteriorating at an accelerated rate. A feeling of extreme discouragement and defeatism pervades Nationalist China.

In the face of these developments we have been forced to withdraw our entire Military Advisory Group from China. The time is drawing near when the funds made available under the China Aid Act of 1948 [17] will be exhausted, and the question must be considered urgently whether a continuance of some form of aid to the Chinese

---

[12] Three members of unofficial Shanghai peace delegation to Peiping.
[13] Proposed head of Government peace delegation.
[14] Government representative on Shanghai peace delegation.
[15] Secretary General of the Presidents' Office.
[16] *Foreign Relations*, 1948, vol. VII, p. 612.
[17] Approved April 3, 1948; 62 Stat. 158.

Government will further our objectives in China. The arguments against all-out aid advanced on page 2 of the Policy Statement, apply more strongly than ever in the light of uninterrupted military defeats suffered by Nationalist forces in recent months. The continuation of some kind of a limited aid program, however, perhaps exclusive of the military feature, is undoubtedly needed to strengthen the position of the Acting President in his negotiations with the Communists during the present armistice phase.

The situation in China is extremely fluid, so much so that it could change radically during the time required for Congress to consider and act on a new China aid program. It is also extraordinarily difficult to predict just what direction such a change might take. The present preliminary peace negotiations might continue for months, accompanied by significant political and economic developments within the territories controlled by the two contending parties. On the other hand, negotiations might be broken off at an early date and fighting resumed, with the Communists endeavoring to continue to devour the country piecemeal in a series of regional settlements. A third alternative is some sort of peace settlement, probably resulting in a coalition government, within a relatively short period of time. The uncertainty as to which alternative—or what combination of these alternatives—will prevail in the immediate future makes it difficult to draw up an aid program which would have any assurance of influencing the situation in our favor. Therefore, it would appear that the only feasible policy for the present is a flexible aid program designed to take every advantage of a fluid situation. In magnitude it need not be more than a relatively modest appropriation sufficient to continue supplying certain basic commodities such as cotton, petroleum, fertilizer and rice in order to retard economic deterioration in Nationalist China, conserve the Government's foreign exchange and strengthen the Government's hand in peace negotiations or in a threat of continued resistance. This aid might also include continuation of JCRR [18] in areas open to it. United States Government representatives in China should continue to urge upon the Nationalist Government the institution of the basic reforms essential for its continued existence. Should progress be made along this line and as a result of this and other factors a political group arise showing promise of providing dynamic and progressive leadership in resistance to Communism, we could revive and expand our aid program.

Section B(2), dealing with economic issues, is a good statement, but out of date in certain respects. The Treaty of Friendship, Commerce and Navigation [19] has now gone into effect with the exchange

---

[18] Joint Commission for Rural Reconstruction.
[19] Signed at Nanking, November 4, 1946; for text, see Department of State Treaties and Other International Acts Series No. 1871, or 63 Stat. (pt. 2) 1299.

of ratifications and concurrent exchange of notes.[20]   This fact requires wholesale redrafting of the third and fourth paragraphs of this Section.

With respect to the sixth paragraph of this Section on the subject of opening river ports to foreign shipping, there should be a revision to show that the Chinese Government has agreed in principle to the admission to inland ports of foreign vessels carrying United States aid goods with the proviso that individual ships must be cleared as a matter of form with the Executive Yuan.   The fact is that there are no such cargoes in sight for the inland ports which renders the whole question academic.   Moreover, this paragraph and the succeeding one should be modified somewhat in reflection of the fact that at the present low level of foreign trade, China has sufficient ocean and river shipping to handle such cargoes as are available for movement.   On economic grounds of advantage either to us or to China, the opening of the river ports, at least under present conditions, no longer seems a sufficiently important objective to waste much political ammunition on.

Under Section (C), on relations with other states, it might be well to insert a paragraph referring to the current negotiations between China and the USSR regarding special rights for the latter in Sinkiang [21] and mentioning that we have informally expressed to the Chinese Government our interest in the proposed agreement with respect to our rights under the Treaty of Friendship.

Respectfully yours,   J. LEIGHTON STUART

893.00/3–1749 : Telegram

The Minister-Counselor of Embassy in China (Clark) to the Secretary of State

CANTON, March 17, 1949—5 p. m.
[Received 10 p. m.]

Cantel 142.   Wu Tieh-cheng [22] just returned from Nanking told me today of his refusal agree become member Ho Ying-chin Cabinet until he had reached satisfactory assurances regarding foreign policy and peace.   General Ho had been unable satisfy him on these counts. Wu insisted that foreign policy remain unchanged; that is, friendly toward US, and that peace be conditioned on possibility survival anti-Communist forces.

Wu said principal problems for Cabinet resolution were: (1) Military reorganization and (2) economic reform.   Li Tsung-jen had

---

[20] See *Foreign Relations*, 1948, Vol. VIII, pp. 752 ff.
[21] For documentation on this subject, see vol. IX, pp. 1037 ff.
[22] Vice President of the Chinese Executive Yuan and concurrently Minister for Foreign Affairs in the Sun Fo Cabinet.

called to Nanking military leaders from various regions China to discuss problem military reorganization and had found all in agreement necessity reduction number military personnel and need for reorientation military effort. On second point there was wide disagreement on approach. Hsu Kan, Finance Minister under Sun Fo,[23] had bungled financial reform in that he had extended real hope US Government 100 million ounces silver loan. On basis Hsu Kan's assurances, Cabinet had approved, Wu said, new financial measures which were obviously doomed to failure if no loan was forthcoming from US. Too late Cabinet realized Hsu Kan was speaking without authority and that silver loan from US could be authorized only by Congressional action.

Wu Tieh-cheng took advantage this opportunity to remark on what he termed inconsistencies between US policy Europe where we were devoting billions toward containing communism, and our policy in respect of China where we seem unwilling to devote any real effort toward curbing Communist expansion. This I refuted, pointing out obvious returns our investment Europe as opposed to obvious lack of returns our investment so far this theater, stressing that before China could expect interest American people in investing further in survival resistance communism China, there must be evidence money thus invested had possibility assisting in attainment ends desired.

In answer to my inquiry as to when peace negotiations might be considered as ended, General Wu said that as result his conversations Nanking he was convinced Communist strategy envisaged lulling Nationalists into sense security until Communists ready to strike. As we [Wu?] saw it, Communists would continue reorganize, reequip their military forces and re-deploy them until such time as they had occupied north bank Yangtze in Wuhan area, Wuhu and Chikiang and were prepared at moment's notice cross Yangtze. They would then, he thought, clarify their attitude toward peace negotiations by appointing delegates, stipulating time and place for meeting, and stating conditions under which they would agree to peace under circumstances which would make it obvious that Nationalist Government would accept these terms—an ultimatum—or continue the battle under terms which would obviously be favorable to Communists. General Wu said that, although Communists had so far restrained from crossing Yangtze by military action, their political propaganda was obviously already having its effect on the south bank.

General Ho Ying-chin, according to Wu Tieh-cheng, is having great difficulty forming Cabinet. Many who have been offered office

---

[23] President of the Chinese Executive Yuan, until March 1949; son of the late Sun Yat-sen.

are reluctant to accept responsibility under uncertainties present situation. Wu was offered Deputy Premiership plus Foreign Office under condition that he would be responsible for all administration Executive Yuan, but he refused. Others likewise were having difficulty making up their minds. Generalissimo [24] himself, Wu is convinced, would support Li Tsung-jen in any reasonable conditional peace he might negotiate and likewise would support him should Li decide renewal hostilities necessary. Generalissimo, he said, was much worried over situation and wanted to do the right thing, but did not know what the right thing was. Generalissimo, he said, was typical other leaders at this time, each wanting to do that which was in best interests of China, but at loss to know Communist aims. Each felt Communists were bluffing and that in spite of *intransigeant* attitude assumed over radio broadcast last minute arrangement might be possible. This might be wishful thinking, yet it was a phenomenon to be dealt with nevertheless.

Wu felt he had failed in organizing his supporters in current Legislative Yuan meetings Nanking: Sun Fo had gone and would not return, yet Wu felt change might have been made easier had he had better control Legislative Yuan members. There had, he said, been around 300 members present Nanking when Legislative Yuan convened, most of whom came from Nanking–Shanghai area. Nevertheless, the uncertainties of situation Nanking and of intentions Communists had resulted in gradual diminution number of Legislative Yuan members present Nanking. He anticipates that by next week there will be less than quorum present Nanking despite fact recess should not take place until May. In other words, he anticipates this session Legislative Yuan will die natural death.

General Wu envisages that under new Government, although seat of Government will remain Canton, principal Ministers, such as Finance, Defense and Interior, will spend most, if not all, their time Nanking. Unimportant Ministries still remain full time Canton and others such as Foreign Office will divide their time between Canton and Nanking. Given uncertainties situation, he feels such division of duties and responsibilities is unavoidable and must be put up with until such time as Communists have declared themselves.

All in all, he leaves impression initiative remains with Communists and Government will take no effective counteraction until Communist ultimatum which is expected when their forces are prepared cross Yangtze. Given effectiveness political, or should we say psychological, campaign Communists, we can expect little, if any, military resistance south Yangtze at that time. This seems further evidence of the complete bankruptcy Kmt leadership and of the inevitability that Com-

---

[24] Chiang Kai-shek, who retired as President on January 21, 1949.

munist interests will determine timetable of events in foreseeable future.

Repeated Nanking 122, Shanghai 87, pouched Kunming, Peiping, Hankow.

CLARK

893.00/3–1849 : Telegram

The Ambassador in China (Stuart) to the Secretary of State

NANKING, March 18, 1949—9 a. m.
[Received 9:10 a. m.]

595. Ten-man peace committee has not functioned since Sun Fo resignation by which time it had prepared first draft of peace formula. Reported Act[ing] President will authorize Premier Ho Ying-chin select new committee which now depleted by departure Sun Fo, Wu Tieh-cheng, Chang Chun [25] and resignation Chung Tien-hsin.

Peng Chao-hsien (C–C clique [26]) and Chung Tien-hsin (Sun Fo adherent) resigned as peace delegates for forthcoming peace negotiations, leaving Chang Chih-chung, Wu Chung-hsin and Shao Li-tze. Rumored W. W. Yen, Chang Shih-chao and Chiang Yung (Shanghai peace delegates) are favorites to succeed Huang and Chung.

In telephone conversation from Peiping, Li Tsung-jen emissary Huang Chi-han reportedly informed Li [that] Communists will name peace delegation, set time and designate place for opening of peace negotiations before March 20.

Sent Department 595, repeated Shanghai 272, Canton 169, Peiping 88.

STUART

893.20/3–1849

Memorandum by the Director of the Office of Far Eastern Affairs (Butterworth) to the Secretary of State

[WASHINGTON,] March 18, 1949.

CHINESE COMMUNIST MILITARY TIMETABLE

The Military Attaché at Nanking [27] has submitted an estimate of the military situation in a telegram dated March 9,[28] the substance of which follows:

This estimate is based on the assumption that peace negotiations will fail. Within 30 days thereafter, but not before May 30, the

---

[25] Military and Political Affairs Director for Southwest China.
[26] Kuomintang group led by two brothers, Chen Li-fu and Chen Kuo-fu.
[27] Brig. Gen. Robert H. Soule.
[28] Not found in Department of State files.

Communists will cross the Yangtze in the vicinity of Nanking, with Hangchow and Shanghai falling shortly thereafter, and in the vicinity of Hankow from whence they will push up the river to Chungking. These objectives can all be accomplished in four months.

The second phase will begin about November 1 with a two-pronged drive on Canton via the Canton–Hankow railroad and via the coastal provinces. This operation will be completed by the end of the year and will fulfill Mao's statement that the civil war would be won in a year.

<hr>

893.00/3–1849 : Telegram

The Minister-Counselor of Embassy in China (Clark) to the Secretary of State

CANTON, March 18, 1949—5 p. m.
[Received—11:36 p. m.]

Cantel 149. Chang Chun is returning Szechuan tomorrow. He is resisting pressure Ho Ying-chin to remain Cabinet without Portfolio, but says if Ho insists sufficiently he will accept although he plans spend little, if any, time Nanking.

He agrees with thesis that Communists plan complete preparations cross Yangtze, then offer peace terms which he anticipates will be "Peiping peace" and therefore unacceptable. He is confident no leaders south Yangtze will accept "Peiping peace". As "reasonable" peace which he would accept and which he is confident would be accepted by Li Tsung-jen and other leaders, he suggested: (1) Democratic government, (2) Socialist form of economy, (3) nationalized army, (4) freedom of the individual, (5) equality. He does not believe Communists will agree such peace and that resumption of hostilities is inevitable. Speaking for the southwest only, he said "we will defend ourselves". Equally, however, he felt confident other leaders south Yangtze would continue resistance.

Sent Department, repeated Nanking 127, Shanghai 91, pouched Kunming, Chungking, Peiping, Hankow.

CLARK

<hr>

893.00/3–1849 : Telegram

The Consul General at Shanghai (Cabot) to the Secretary of State

SHANGHAI, March 18, 1949—6 p. m.
[Received March 18—9:25 a. m.]

938. *Shanghai Evening Post* March 18 reports K. C. Wu's determination to resign as Mayor Shanghai. Although Wu has attempted resign on many previous occasions, Generalissimo never accepted and

always managed persuade him to remain on duty. This time it is believed Wu serious with following factors bearing on decision.

(1) Increased control over all aspects of Shanghai life by Tang En-po [29] and military authorities and accompanying diminution Wu's influence;

(2) Recent resignation of keymen in Wu's "Cabinet" including Commissioners of Social Affairs, Education, Land and Police, which make it increasingly difficult keep city's labor front tranquil, retain city's financial solvency and solve problems connection with feeding of city, threatened student demonstrations, et cetera.

(3) Wu's recurrent attack of malaria which has affected his health and vitality.

Believe it still possible Generalissimo's well-known desire retain Wu as mayor may again prevail. If not, last vestige of real civilian authority here may be said to have vanished.

Sent Nanking 548, repeated Department, Canton 176.

CABOT

893.00/3–2049 : Telegram

The Ambassador in China (Stuart) to the Secretary of State

NANKING, March 20, 1949—1 p. m.
[Received March 20—12:44 a. m.]

611. Acting President went Shanghai March 18 for purpose: (1) Persuading K. C. Wu to remain on job (Wu exasperated by strong arm tactics new police chief Mao Shen and has threatened resign ostensibly on grounds ill health), and (2) overcome reluctance of certain liberals, such as O. K. Yui,[30] to enter Ho Cabinet.

Sent Department, repeated Canton 178, Shanghai 218.

STUART

893.101/3–2149 : Telegram

The Consul General at Shanghai (Cabot) to the Secretary of State

SHANGHAI, March 21, 1949—noon.
[Received March 21—12:36 a. m.]

944. Reliably informed Mayor Wu has in fact presented resignation and Government has refused to accept it. Mayor is, however, insisting it be accepted.

Sent Nanking 554, repeated Department.

CABOT

---

[29] Chinese general commanding in the Shanghai area.
[30] Governor of the Central Bank of China.

893.00/3–2249 : Telegram

The Consul General at Shanghai (Cabot) to the Secretary of State

SHANGHAI, March 22, 1949.
[Received March 22—3 :37 a. m.]

965. Local press 21 and 22 features story on bombing of *Chungking* [31] at Hulutao by Nationalist planes [March] 18 and 19, publishing today's issue official AF photo showing ship, alleged to be *Chungking*, lying on side.

Sent Nanking 566; repeated Department 965, Canton 189.

CABOT

893.00/3–2249 : Telegram

The Minister-Counselor of Embassy in China (Clark) to the Secretary of State

CANTON, March 22, 1949—1 p. m.
[Received March 22—5 :13 a. m.]

Cantel 153.   Proposed response Connally's [32] request comments McCarran Bill [33] Depintel March 17 [34] seems most appropriate.   As I analyze situation at moment, we may expect Communists continue deployment troops north bank Yangtze and when they are ready attempt crossing we may anticipate announcement willingness negotiate peace on terms they will stipulate and which may be expected to be reiteration Mao Tse-tung's eight points. [35]   Their announced willingness negotiate will likely be in form ultimatum threatening crossing Yangtze if terms not accepted within time limit.   It is unlikely terms will be acceptable to Kmt leaders although they will appear reasonable to war-weary Chinese masses.

Even though rumors of Communist morale difficulties may have foundation, it may be anticipated Communist troops will fight.   On the contrary, however, there appears little likelihood Nationalist troops can be reinspired with will to resist.   Chang Chun may, as he claims, be able rally forces southwest to defend themselves, but it will unlikely be defense of character long to delay Communists once they have determined on advance.   There is even some thought that with breakdown peace negotiations, process regional fragmentation will be accelerated, with each area seeking fend for itself, thus making

---

[31] Chinese cruiser which deserted to Communists.
[32] Senator Tom Connally, Chairman of the Senate Foreign Relations Committee.
[33] Senator Pat McCarran, Chairman of the Senate Judiciary Committee; for documentation on his bill, see vol. IX, pp. 599 ff.
[34] Not printed.
[35] Mao Tse-tung, Chairman of the Central Executive Committee of the Chinese Communist Party; for the eight points, see telegram No. 41, January 14, from the Consul General at Peiping, p. 49.

more easy Communist task.   Dissident Kwangtung Legislative Yuan members remaining Canton demanding "defense of constitution" are an indication this trend.

As I see it, when Communists have deployed their troops and issued their ultimatum and had it rejected, they may be expected cross Yangtze, meeting little resistance and occupying urban centers Yangtze Valley.   They will then have the capability of continuing their advance in southwest or south, overcoming without too much difficulty any regional resistance they may encounter.   Whether they will proceed to the task immediately or delay for months or years rests solely for their determination.

In previous telegram, Cantel 71, February 23, repeated Nanking 68, Shanghai 41, I suggested possibility Li Tsung-jen might supply effective leadership.   I am now less inclined to that view.   He has increased tremendously, in stature; has greatly increased his following, yet the centripetal forces in Free China remain too strong for him to overcome.   The deep-seated Chinese characteristic of family solidarity is too strong and we are witnessing a frantic search by each individual leader to save himself and his family first, then maybe his province, with little if any thought to the principles involved or the nation.   Also, if, as alleged, cruiser *Chungking* has been put out of action by CAF [36] we may still see Gimo re-emerge in his Foochow–Amoy–Taiwan triangle.

I have been chided of late by many Chinese officials from the Vice Premier and Foreign Minister [37] down for what they term our "wait and see" policy in respect of China.   I have responded that unlike the British who are obviously seeking to follow a "neutral" policy in China, we are like the pugilist who is sparring for time and awaiting an opening for a telling blow, refraining in the meantime from wasting his strength on a haymaker.   I have put forward the arguments outlined Depintel March 17 and have stressed need for Chinese demonstrate possibility effective resistance Communist expansion before expecting US make further investments National China.   In each case I have been given impression of utter inability China cope unaided with situation.   In other words, sole means of turning tide in China would, as Department suggests, require use of "large US forces in actual combat, contrary our traditional policy and national interests".

Sent Department, repeated Nanking 132, Shanghai 95, pouched Chungking, Peiping, Hankow.

                                                                                CLARK

[36] Chinese Air Force.
[37] Wu Te-chen, who had resigned. The new Chinese Minister for Foreign Affairs had not yet left his post as Chinese Ambassador in the Soviet Union; pending the assumption of duties by Foo Ping-sheung, Vice Minister George Yeh was named Acting Minister on April 5.

893.002/3–2249 : Telegram

The Ambassador in China (Stuart) to the Secretary of State

NANKING, March 22, 1949.
[Received March 22—7 :28 a. m.]

615. Acting President announced personnel new Cabinet March 21. *Chung Yang Jih Pao* lists membership as follows:

Vice-Premier: Chia Ching-te.
Ministers without Portfolio: Chang Chih-chung, Chang Chun, Chu Chia-hua, Mo Te-hui, Ho Yao-tsu.
Secretary-General: Huang Chao-ku.
Deputy Secretary-General: Ni Chiung-sheng.
Minister of Interior: Li Han-hun.
Foreign Affairs: Fu Ping-chang.[38]
Economy: Sun Yueh-chi.
Finance: Liu Kung-yun.[39]
Education: Han Li-wu.
National Defense: Hsu Yung-chang.
Communications: Tuan Mu-chieh.[40]
Justice: Chang Chih-pen.
Mongolian and Tibetan Affairs Commission: Pai Yun-ti.
Overseas Chinese Affairs Commission: Tai Kuei-shang.
Bureau of Audit: Pang Sung-chou.

Acting President simultaneously promulgated revised organic law of Executive Yuan, reducing number of Ministries to those listed above, in accordance with measure previously passed by Legislative Yuan.

Repeated AmEmb Canton and Shanghai unnumbered.

STUART

893.00/3–2249 : Telegram

The Ambassador in China (Stuart) to the Secretary of State

NANKING, March 22, 1949—7 p. m.
[Received March 23—3 :10 p. m.]

628. Following our study of such CCP pronouncements as Mao Tse-tung's article commemorating October revolution and Liu Shao-chi's [41] article on "nationalism and internationalism" last November, we had concluded as reported that time that CCP, at least verbally, had left undone little to subordinate Chinese national interests to those of USSR. However, with North Shensi broadcast March 18 (repeated March 19 for emphasis) CCP advanced its satellite foreign policy still further by announcing "Chinese people cannot but regard

---

[38] Foo Ping-sheung, Chinese Ambassador in the Soviet Union.
[39] Known also as S. Y. Liu.
[40] Known also as Tuan Mu-kai (or Joseph K. Twammoh).
[41] Vice Chairman of the Central Committee of the Chinese Communist Party.

leaders of war provocateurs, American imperialist bellicose elements, as their mortal foes and cannot but regard leaders of world anti-imperialist front, great socialist state, Soviet Union, as their comrades in arms, from first to last".

Whole tone of broadcast is that CCP wholeheartedly and optimistically backs Soviet "struggle for peace" but that if worst comes to worst, CCP will enter war alongside USSR. At risk of reading falsely between lines, we do note, however, that (1) CCP commitment to fight could have been more clearly and irrevocably expressed than it was, and (2) it is conditioned upon USSR accepting "strong and independent China as good friend and ally". We do not derive much cheer from these observations, however, since (1) CCP commitment is no more indirect than statements of Thorez and Togliatti,[42] serving similar purpose; and (2) Soviets—particularly after their lesson in Yugoslavia—will doubtless display sufficient vision and tolerance in their foreign policy to avoid offending sensibilities of Chinese Communists, at least at present stage of history. Because of this as well as timing of broadcast, our convictions are strengthened that Chinese Communists are wittingly or unwittingly tools of Soviet expansion and as such are constitutionally incapable of objective international attitude toward US.

This reaffirmation of loyalty to USSR and world Communism on three important grounds seems far more Communist than Chinese. First, except for one passing reference to "Kmt reactionary government", principal enemy of CCP, US was sole target of attack. Second, it so debases Chinese national interests as to rationalize Soviet occupation of Dairen and Port Arthur as "severe blows to imperialist aggression in Far East and far-reaching guarantees of interest of Chinese people against aggression". Third, its timing with North Atlantic treaty,[43] which is certainly not of immediate consequence to China's struggle, betrays same kind of loyalty to Moscow and disregard of Chinese interest that prompted Mao Tse-tung in 1942 to urge concentration of united nations' efforts against Germany rather than Japan.

We fear this broadcast indicates Chinese Communists may be falling into same web of self-deception that cost Nazis and Fascists so dearly and which is now attracting Communists everywhere, namely that America is weak. Chinese Communists have long inveighed against our principles and good intentions. But now, for first time, they raise question of our power, saying "Chinese people see in American imperialism a paper tiger" and that "if only peace-loving forces unite

---

[42] Maurice Thorez and Palmiro Togliatti, leaders of the French and Italian Communist Parties, respectively.
[43] Signed at Washington, April 4, 1949; for text, see Department of State Treaties and Other International Acts Series No. 1964, or 63 Stat. (pt. 2) 2241.

in struggle and do not commit misjudging, American imperialism is sure to be vanquished". If CCP-controlled press and theoreticians succeed in cultivating this auto-intoxication, it will prove one more obstacle to CCP objective appraisal of international scene and China's proper place therein.

We consider this broadcast major statement of public policy, albeit described as "New China News Agency editorial". It is most disturbing in its implications for US and ominous for our continuing efforts to reach *modus vivendi* with Communists.

Sent Department 628; repeated Canton 181; Shanghai 286; Moscow 22.

STUART

893.002/3–2349 : Telegram

The Minister-Counselor of Embassy in China (Clark) to the Secretary of State

CANTON, March 23, 1949—10 a. m.
[Received March 23—5:42 a. m.]

Cantel 161. Chen Tai-chu, director American Department Foreign Office, who knows well Foreign Minister-designate Fu Ping-chang, assures me that Fu is if anything anti-Soviet and that his designation as Foreign Minister cannot mean any reorientation of Chinese foreign policy. He admitted, however, that General Ho Ying-chin, in appointing Fu, may have done so with idea that is [*in*] some way such an appointment would improve his position in respect Communists and of Soviet Union. Incidentally, he said Fu's appointment had aroused opposition in Supreme Council Kmt and it might yet be withdrawn. It would be few days before final decision would be reached.

He admitted possibility absence C–C clique member might represent effort improve possibility negotiations with Communists though he said composition Cabinet had been determined by realization peace increasingly unlikely and that principal task Government would be reorganization military for renewal hostilities although of course political and economic factors were also strongly involved.

Sent Department, repeated Nanking 143, Shanghai 102.

CLARK

893.00/3–2349 : Telegram

The Ambassador in China (Stuart) to the Secretary of State

NANKING, March 23, 1949—3 p. m.
[Received March 23—7:08 a. m.]

635. Acting President sent for me morning March 22 to submit following proposal for my Government's comment. Li Tsung-jen

contemplates journey to Moscow to discuss Chinese situation with Soviet leaders as further step in Nationalist Government's program to reach peaceful solution of civil war. He considers such approach in nature of trial balloon; if Soviet response is negative, he will be convinced that Chinese Communists have no intention to negotiate peace and Nationalist Government can make its plans accordingly. If on other hand invitation to visit Moscow is forthcoming, Acting President will feel encouraged for prospects of peaceful settlement and will attempt persuade Soviet leaders to act as restraining influence on Chinese Communists in anticipated negotiations. Following trip to USSR he may consider it desirable to visit Washington and London as well. President Li added that before making any approach to Russians he would like to have US Government's reaction.

In conversation that followed I pointed out that Soviets would undoubtedly disclaim any connection with or influence over CCP, that they would reiterate their passionate love of peace, their recent efforts in this direction, the negative response of the US, and their own record of non-interference in Chinese affairs as opposed to US position. On positive side I opined that appeal to Moscow would dramatize Russia's connection with CCP; would probably embarrass CCP thereby and would be further evidence to Chinese people of Nationalist Government's continuing serious efforts at peace.

Acting President covets US advice in this contemplated move because of our larger experience in dealing with USSR and Communists and because of close relations, similar international policies our two countries.

I told him I would convey his request for advice promptly and will await Department's instruction.

Sent Department; repeated AmEmb Canton for eyes only Clark 185, Shanghai for eyes only Cabot 291.

STUART

893.00/3–2349

The Consul General at Shanghai (Cabot) to the Ambassador in China (Stuart) [44]

[Extracts]

No. 49   SHANGHAI, March 23, 1949.

SIR: I have the honor to submit the following résumé of the more interesting observations made by Yeh Tu-yi and P'eng Wen-ying, members of the Democratic League group which has remained at Shanghai, in the course of general conversation with officers of the Consulate General at an informal dinner party on March 20:

.   .   .   .

---

[44] Copy transmitted to the Department without covering despatch; received April 5.

To explain why the Democratic Leaguers made common cause with the Communists, Mr. P'eng said that the former's prime desideratum was the civil war's speedy conclusion and the end of the Chinese people's intolerable suffering. As the Nationalists' consistent defeats show they cannot win the war, for the Democratic League to support them would serve only to help defer their inevitable defeat. On the other hand, in view of the Communists' demonstrated military prowess, to join with them is to speed the conclusion of hostilities—in turn, releasing the Chinese *lao pai hsing* (common people) from their present agony and providing a basis for economic recovery. It was such reasoning which caused the Democratic League to commit its fortunes, for better or worse, to cooperation with the Chinese Communist Party.

P'eng also expressed his fervent hope that the United States would cease assisting the Kuomintang, not only because such continued support would needlessly prolong the war and intensify Communist hatred of the United States but also because it would tend to destroy the pro-American sentiment of Democratic Leaguers, who now must go along with the Communists. If America continues to supply the Communists' enemies, he declared it would be impossible for Democratic Leaguers (and other pro-American elements in the Communist fold) to give a sympathetic interpretation of United States policy. Explaining that many of the Chinese Communists' inexplicable actions are due to their ignorance, provincialism and suspicion, he averred that because so many Democratic League members are American-returned students and well-acquainted with Western thought and methods, they could do much to help improve relations between Americans and the Chinese Communists—if not estopped by the bitterness engendered by continuing United States assistance to the Kuomintang.

Repeating the general line of thought expressed by them in previous talks with an officer of the Consulate General, Yeh and P'eng deplored the press publicized speculation on the question of Mao Tsetung's becoming a second Tito;[45] pointed out that this rendered it all the more difficult for Mao to make any conciliatory move toward the Western democracies; and said that, while Mao could of course not undertake at this stage any open or definite repudiation of Moscow, he might, granted favorable circumstances and a reasonable attitude on the part of the democracies, be willing and able to orient Chinese Communist policies unobstrusively toward a gradual improvement of relations with the latter.

It is the impression of the Consulate General—on the basis of the conversation under reference and previous once [*ones*]—that these

---

[45] Marshal Josip Broz Tito, head of the Yugoslav Communist Party and State, who defected from Moscow leadership in June 1948.

Democratic League members, confronted with a distasteful choice between the Nationalists and the Communists, chose the latter (not without misgivings)—as the lesser of two evils. Once having taken this irrevocable step, however, they are compelled to gloss over the mistakes and faults of the Chinese Communists—not necessarily at the cost of (but certainly with obvious strain on) their own intellectual integrity. The fact that many Democratic Leaguers were educated in the United States, sincerely like Americans and American ways, and eager for friendly relations between the United States and China and, at the same time, realize that the Chinese Communist attitude towards the West is, in many cases, ignorant, stupid, and suspicious, makes their role of Communist apologists an especially difficult one. Their anxious desire for improved relations between America and the Chinese Communists cannot be disassociated from the assuagement such a development would give their intellectual conflicts.

Respectfully yours,   JOHN M. CABOT

893.00/3–2449 : Telegram

The Minister-Counselor of Embassy in China (Clark) to the Secretary of State

CANTON, March 24, 1949—4 p. m.
[Received March 24—6:07 a. m.]

Cantel 165. Tending to confirm my belief likelihood Communist ultimatum on peace (my Cantel 153, March 22, repeated Nanking 132, Shanghai 95) is North Shensi broadcast March 23 which, after castigating Generalissimo, Li Tsung-jen, Ho Ying-chin and others as reactionaries organizing for war, continues: "Will Li Tsung-jen and his Ho Ying-chin Cabinet really accept and carry out the eight-point peace terms of the Communist Party and realize peace which the people need, thus giving themselves a chance to atone for their crimes? Or will they keep on utilizing the so-called 'reasonable, just and general peace' in order to pressure counter-revolutionary forces and cover up their plot of continuing the war? This will be proved in the very near future when peace negotiations are conducted."

Sent Department, repeated Nanking 148, Shanghai 106.

CLARK

893.101/3–2449 : Telegram

The Consul General at Shanghai (Cabot) to the Secretary of State

SHANGHAI, March 24, 1949—4 p. m.
[Received March 24—4:44 a. m.]

986. Mayor Wu's resignation, although submitted, not yet accepted as local papers report Premier Ho's return of resignation with note

saying "please stay". Past few days have seen storm of protests in newspapers against Wu decision, as well as petitions by various public and private organizations urging him to remain at post. Generally accepted Wu has done fine job in past reconciling groups which control Shanghai and maintaining order. Feared that his withdrawal will exacerbate relations between military authorities (who favor continued resistance to Communists) and "civic leaders" such as Tu Yueh-sheng (who have been striving reopen normal trade relations with North China) with possible disastrous effect on city stability. Recent press comment hints that in spite Wu's stated firm resolve to quit, he may be prevailed upon to retain post if allowed take vacation to recover "spiritual and physical" health. During absence city would be run by new Secretary-General Chen Liang. In past similar situations, Wu has agreed withdraw previous resignations in return for increased power vis-à-vis garrison commander, police commissioner and others vying for control city. Believed questionable whether he can squeeze significant concessions out of this situation as Tang En-po military control probably too firmly established under martial law status of city.

Sent Nanking 581; repeated Department 986 OffEmb, Canton 198.

CABOT

893.00/3–2349 : Telegram

The Secretary of State to the Ambassador in China (Stuart)

WASHINGTON, March 24, 1949—7 p. m.

390. Proposal contained urtel 635 Mar 23 inevitably recalls recent Chi Govt request for four-power mediation particularly with USSR taking lead.

You are authorized inform Acting Pres [that] US Govt while sympathetic his difficulties is of opinion matter one on which this Govt not in position offer advice; decision must be Chi responsibility.

If Li again brings up subject possible visit US you should say US Govt would naturally accord him every courtesy. At same time you should ensure that he understands that his visit would not result in any augmented US aid and therefore he would be assuming responsibility for any political consequences that might result from his returning to China without material results from his visit.

For your info sentiment in Congress this year even more than last year highlights difference between apparent strength advocacy large scale aid program China and actual support therefor. You will recall Administration's proposal for $570 million last year was cut down by Congress to $400 million and today's Executive Session Senate For[eig]n Relations Committ on ECA request for authority to use funds unexpended Apr 3 clearly indicates so far as that key body concerned no real enthusiasm even thus to act.

Dept concurs in general views expressed first sentence second para reference tel and doubts Li visit Moscow would have beneficial result.

ACHESON

893.9111RR/3–2549 : Telegram

The Consul General at Shanghai (Cabot) to the Secretary of State

[Extract]

SHANGHAI, March 25, 1949.
[Received March 25—2 :22 a. m.]

992. Shanghai vernacular press summary March 25. All papers feature first meeting of new Cabinet. Addressing Cabinet, Premier Ho declared Government would strive to win peace, carry out military and political reforms and stabilize people's livelihood. Government appointed Shao Li-tse, Chang Chih-chung, Huang Shao-hsiung, Tsang Chih-chao and Li Cheng as peace delegates and urges Communists immediately appoint peace delegates. Reported that Tsang Chih-chao accepted appointment and left Shanghai for Nanking.

. . . .

CABOT

893.002/3–2549 : Telegram

The Minister-Counselor of Embassy in China (Clark) to the Secretary of State

CANTON, March 25, 1949—3 p. m.
[Received March 26—3 :03 a. m.]

Cantel 169. New Cabinet seems to represent effort Li Tsung-jen and Ho Ying-chin to combine all aspects anti-Communist elements in supreme court [*final?*] effort obtain acceptable peace. Its principal feature appears to be absence C–C clique and others heretofore closely identified with and controlled by Generalissimo. This appears indication Cabinet will probably cooperate with Acting President and implement his policies to extent possible. However, its capability is limited by fact that Generalissimo and his associates still have great influence. Li in fact is on trial. Despite military influences Ho Ying-chin, Generalissimo can be expected continue control and does in fact control large segment army, navy and air force. Also, control secret police will almost certainly continue in Generalissimo. Finally, it is unlikely new government will gain control principal national reserves precious metals and foreign currency. These factors, taken in conjunction with pervasive and persistent developments toward regionalism, must inevitably restrict scope operation new Cabinet and greatly hamper its effectiveness. Unless these difficulties are overcome, for which there appears little hope, Nanking will have very weak bargaining position in peace talks with Communists, who may, and probably will, raise issue that Li Tsung-jen's government has little or no ability to commit non-Communist[s]. On peace issue, we believe new Cabinet will follow line taken by Acting President. In fact, there is evidence Li fails keep Cabinet informed all phases his activities toward peace. He has told us, and we are inclined to believe, that he will only agree to terms offering some guarantee his political survival, presumably either through inclusion himself heading bloc his followers in coalition, or formation coalition along regional lines with semi-independent south and southwest. We believe that Li will try secure such settlement by any means possible, including, if necessary, Soviet mediation. Wu Tieh-cheng's refusal join Cabinet appears based on his failure get from Li or Ho Ying-chin clear-cut statement on foreign policy or peace terms. From this and other considerations, we are inclined to believe that Li may be willing seek *rapprochement* with Soviets if feasible and necessary maintain himself in authority. Whether he would succeed in so doing is doubtful, but it is not unlikely that he may make attempt. Appointment Fu Ping-chang, who though reputedly not pro-Soviet has wide acquaintance Soviet officials, was probably made with view facilitating some such course action.

In final analysis, Generalissimo continues hold balance power in non-Communist China and is most unlikely commit his influence unconditionally in support Li. We are inclined believe Wu Tieh-cheng's statement that Generalissimo solely motivated by interest Chinese people (my Cantel 142, March 17, repeated Nanking 122, Shanghai 87), yet it is Generalissimo himself who will determine what Generalissimo deems in interest Chinese people. Formation new Cabinet reduced and almost entirely eliminated Generalissimo's formal influence in structure Government and to this extent improved position of Acting President. However, Generalissimo retains *de facto* and to some extent *de jure* power intervene in national affairs when and as he sees fit.

Initiative remains with Communists and they give no indication of willingness to accept anything other than practically surrender to which Li and his associates insist they will not agree.

Principal interest, therefore, is in Communist intentions and timetable. Their North Shensi broadcast of March 23 (my 165, March 24, repeated Nanking 148, Shanghai 106) is one of many indications that Communists intend conquer all China before ceasing military operations. It remains therefore only to determine when present temporary lull will end and hostilities on major scale will be resumed. In this situation, current change in Cabinet can have but little real political significance.

Sent Department, repeated Nanking 152, Shanghai 111. Pouched Peiping, Hankow, Kunming, Chungking.

CLARK

893.002/3–2549 : Telegram

The Minister-Counselor of Embassy in China (Clark) to the Secretary of State

CANTON, March 25, 1949—5 p. m.
[Received 9:58 p. m.]

Cantel 171. Acting Foreign Minister Tung Lin tells me he has urged Fu Ping-chang return China assume post Foreign Minister, so far without results. Dr. Tung said that not only did Fu seem unwilling accept post, but Central Executive Committee Kmt as well as members Legislative Yuan Canton are opposed appointment. He thought it highly probable therefore another Foreign Minister would eventually be appointed. Principal objection Fu seems to be that, notwithstanding his personal sentiments, his appointment will generally [be] considered as indication trend China foreign policy away from US toward Soviet Union. Realizing assumption office Fu unlikely influence Soviet or Chinese Communist policy, those opposing appointment feel have everthing to lose and nothing to gain.

Sent Department Cantel 171, repeated Nanking 155, Shanghai 114, Moscow 6.

CLARK

893.00B/3–2649 : Telegram

The Consul General at Peiping (Clubb) to the Secretary of State

PEIPING, March 26, 1949.
[Received March 26—2:09 a. m.]

486. North China Agency despatch March 25 announces the removal to Peiping on the same date of the Central Executive Headquarters of the Chinese Communist Party and the General Headquarters of the People's Liberation Army. Per same source, Chairman CEC CCP [46] Mao Tze-tung and Commander-in-Chief PLA [47] Chu Teh together with other CEC leaders Liu Shao-chi and Lin Po-chu all arrived Peiping approximately 1600 hours yesterday.

---

[46] Central Committee of the Chinese Communist Party.
[47] People's Liberation Army (Communist).

North Shensi Hsin Hua radio station announces its removal Peiping effective same date. Former Peiping Hsin Hua station becomes "Peiping People's Radio Station".

Sent Department, repeated Nanking 310, Canton 34, Shanghai 349.

CLUBB

893.9111RR/3–2649 : Telegram

The Consul General at Peiping (Clubb) to the Secretary of State

PEIPING, March 26, 1949.
[Received March 26—1:35 a. m.]

491. Peiping *Chieh Fang Pao* today carries item regarding revolted Nationalist cruiser *Chungking* [48] in course of which it states "American imperialists and Kmt's reactionary treason of Government in order prevent Chinese people establish their own national defenses on sea, on 17th, 18th, 19th and 20th of present month continuously flew over Hulutao and bombed with many American national flag B–29 type heavy bombers and on 19th finally succeeded in bombing that ship and on 20th sank it".

Same item continues: "in order to prevent that ship's moving, American Navy on 19th dispatched three submarines to sea (in vicinity) Hulutao. *Chungking* affair once more discloses evil of American imperialists' military intervention in Chinese civil war and causes Chinese people and peace-loving states of whole world once more clearly to recognize ugly face of American imperialists".

Ta Chung Jih Pao, today, regarding same matter asserts, "American Navy on 19th launched an attack on that ship from Tsingtao".

Sent Department 491, Nanking 311, OffEmb Canton Shanghai 350, Tsingtao.

CLUBB

893.002/3–2649 : Telegram

The Minister-Counselor of Embassy in China (Clark) to the Secretary of State

CANTON, March 26, 1949—3 p. m.
[Received March 27—4:14 a. m.]

Cantel 173. Sun Fo said that, in appointing Fu Ping-chang FonMin, Li Tsung-jen and Ho Ying-chin had some idea of pleasing Soviets and Communists. (According press, Fu has declined appointment and Ho has asked George Yeh to serve temporarily.) Dr. Sun said he was afraid Li Tsung-jen was rapidly letting himself be

---

[48] See telegram No. 965, March 22, from the Consul General at Shanghai, p. 190.

maneuvered into position where he is going to have no alternative to surrender. Communist broadcast of March 23 (Cantel 165, March 24, repeated Nanking 148, Shanghai 106) indicates he thought that Communists would require earnest of Li's good intentions and ability to carry out Mao Tse-tung's eight points as preliminary to real peace negotiations. "Produce the Generalissimo in chains and we will believe you can speak with authority and implement your undertakings." Not being able to do this, Li will seek some other means of satisfying the unbelievably overwhelming sentiment in Nanking and Shanghai for "peace at any price". This sentiment controls the thinking not only of the masses but also of Legislative and Control Yuans and many elements of Government.

Given this picture, Dr. Sun seems to think Li government, as at present constituted, will agree to "honorable surrender" much as did Fu Tso-yi.[49] At this stage he inquired, rather revealingly I thought, whether US aid would continue to a government that might result from such action even though it might be expected to be dominated by Communists. He also inquired re US attitude should Government split at that time and one element determine to continue resistance. Would we aid such resisting government? To this I replied that my Government would have to consider the situation as it existed at the time. I felt safe in saying, however, that my Govt would be unhappy to see a Communist-dominated government in China or even a coalition with Communist participation and that we would not grant aid to any such government. Given this fact, if the resisting element had supportable claim to legitimacy, that fact would increase its possibility of receiving the continued recognition of US and such aid as might be found in light then existing world conditions feasible. In this connection I mentioned the President's reply[50] to Generalissimo's message[51] which Dr. Sun had seen and understood.

Dr. Sun then remarked that, although constitution is silent on subject, intention was that, when President was unable to function and Vice President assumed office under Article 49 as Acting President, President could resume his office when the disability had been removed. No irrevocable retirement from office took place, he said, until resignation had been submitted to National Assembly and accepted. Generalissimo had not taken such action.

It seems obvious to me from this conversation that Dr. Sun and his followers anticipate that Li will be led to surrender any day and hope at that time to persuade Generalissimo to resume office as President

---

[49] General Fu remained in Peiping upon its occupation by Communist forces in January 1949.
[50] See telegram No. 1608, November 12, 1948, 7 p. m., *Foreign Relations*, 1948, vol. VIII, p. 202.
[51] See telegram No. Telmar 155, November 12, 1948, 8 p. m., to the Secretary of State, at Paris, *ibid.*, p. 201.

and carry on struggle. Dr. Sun, of course, is biased on subject of Li and his belief that Li may surrender may have elements of wishful thinking. Also, there is some evidence in Canton that Kwangtung clique plans split with Li government at appropriate time and establish here Legislative Yuan and Government. They can command quorum at any time. On other hand, Li Tsung-jen certainly assured me when in Canton last month (Cantel 70, February 22, repeated Nanking 67, Shanghai 40) that he would continue the fight if, as he then seemed to anticipate, reasonable peace were found impossible. Whether, in the face of overwhelming sentiment for peace, he can revive the will to fight is another question. That the fragmentation process continues seems certain.

Sent Department Cantel 173. Repeated Nanking 157, Shanghai 117. Pouched Kunming, Chungking, Hankow and Peiping.

CLARK

893.00/3–2749 : Telegram

The Consul General at Peiping (Clubb) to the Secretary of State

PEIPING, March 27, 1949.
[Received March 27—3 :44 a. m.]

493. Peiping Hsin Hua radio station last night 1800 hours broadcast following, basic text of which is published all local papers today:

"Radio station of Nanking Kuomintang reactionary government please note. This station by order is now broadcasting to you an important notification. Please note and receive message as follows:

"As regards matter of undertaking peace negotiations with Nanking Kuomintang reactionary government, Chinese Communist Party Central Committee today decided:

"(1) Time of beginning negotiations, April 1;

"(2) Place of negotiations, Peiping;

"(3) Chou En-lai,[52] Lin Po-chu,[53] Lin Piao,[54] Yeh Chien-ying,[55] Li Wei-han [56] designated as delegates, with Chou En-lai to be chief delegate, (to meet) with Nanking delegation using Chairman Mao Tse-tung's January 14 statement regarding political situation, and eight points proposed by him, as basis for bilateral negotiations;

"(4) Above-mentioned points to be notified through radio station same day to Nanking Kuomintang reactionary government, (which should) according above-stipulated time and place dispatch its delegation bearing all requisite material needed for eight points in order facilitate undertaking negotiations."

---

[52] Member of Central Committee of the Chinese Communist Party and its representative at the Chinese capital during the 1946 negotiations.
[53] Also known as Lin Tsu-han, Communist official.
[54] Communist military commander in North China.
[55] Communist mayor of Peiping, formerly Chief of Staff.
[56] Communist representative in Chungking during early 1946.

Above version from *Ta Chung Jih Pao*.
Sent Department; Nanking 315, OffEmb Canton, Shanghai 352.

CLUBB

893.00/3–2849 : Telegram

The Consul General at Canton (Ludden) to the Secretary of State

CANTON, March 28, 1949—3 p. m.
[Received March 28—4:33 a. m.]

73. Refmytel 43 to Embassy, repeated Department 71, March 27, 1 p. m.[57] As in previous conversations Soong's [58] central theme was inevitability US–Soviet war which now approaching apace following conclusion Atlantic Pact.

Soong characterized himself as one of very few Chinese who has never had illusions re power aims and Soviet orientation Chinese Communists. He classed as fools those who pursue the illusion Mao may become another Tito. According Soong, further illusion shared by many is possible split in CCP. This he considers highly unlikely because of current rapid infiltration Soviet-trained cadres at all levels CCP. Soong believes some rivalry exists between senior Communist military leaders but this normal in any army and not serious.

Soong convinced no peace possible with Communists except on their terms. He recalled 1945 conversations with Stalin re communism in which latter quoted "those who are not with us are against us". More recently Lin Piao told W. W. Yen at Peiping that National Government had choice of two peace settlements, that of Tientsin or that of Peiping, i.e., peace by defeat or peace by capitulation. Soong advocates continuance military struggle against advance Communists China and argues too much has already been allowed go by default. He stated will to resist in National forces can be restored by adequate pay as exemplified at Hsuchow.

Soong foresees geographic split as only outcome present situation and, in spite present Communist military predominance, he believes South China and Taiwan can hold out against further Communist advance. He professes to find in Kwangtung definite will to resist and same spirit can be developed Fukien, Kiangsi, Hunan and Kwangsi. He considers Yunnan and Kweichow unimportant; with regard Szechuan he considers Chang Chun a weakling fence sitter who will probably capitulate at first Communist threat.

According Soong, he came Canton March 25 at request Governor and Pacification Commander to confer with regard recruitment,

---

[57] Not printed.
[58] T. V. Soong, former President of the Chinese Executive Yuan and Minister of Finance; brother-in-law of Generalissimo Chiang Kai-shek.

training, disposition anti-Communist forces. Time is now important because Soong considers likely military development will become [be Comm.] advance to west and south avoiding lower Yangtze valley for time being.

Soong said he has had occasion communicate several times with Generalissimo but no indication from these contacts that Generalissimo contemplating emerging from retirement "at present".

In spite Soong's brave front and confidence in continued resistance South China on the eve of his own physical removal from China, must observe that there are no indications locally of economic, political or military strength that can offer effective resistance incursion Communists this area if their timetables so envisage.

Sent Nanking 44, repeated Department.

LUDDEN

893.00/3-2849 : Telegram

The Consul General at Shanghai (Cabot) to the Secretary of State

SHANGHAI, March 28, 1949—3 p. m.
[Received March 28—5 :26 a. m.]

1011. Yesterday Pan Pei-ying, novelist and calligrapher who accompanied Kiang Lung on Shanghai peace mission to Peiping and who will accompany Chang Shih-chao on National peace delegation leaving for Peiping March 31, told two officers this ConGen that members peace delegation must consult with Generalissimo before flying Peiping. (ConGen notes, however, this denied in March 28 press.) Pan stated that composition Communists' peace delegation was encouraging, as all Communist factions were represented with emphasis on moderate elements (Chou En-lai and Yeh Chien-ying). Pan stated conviction based on his previous Peiping trip that high Communist leaders want peace but may have trouble convincing military and lower echelon Communists who perhaps thirst for revenge. Pan appeared anxious to make point that US should not grant military aid to China at this time, but felt that extension of economic aid O.K.

General tenor of Pan's remarks is in line with similar statements made us by Chinese all types and various other evidence indicating that overwhelming majority Chinese in this area desire peace and hope that peace talks will not be endangered by any promise of American military aid to "Kuomintang" regime while peace talks in process.

Sent Nanking 596. Repeated Department 1011, Embassy Canton 212.

CABOT

893.001/3-2849 : Telegram

The Ambassador in China (Stuart) to the Secretary of State

NANKING, March 28, 1949—3 p. m.
[Received March 28—7 :28 a. m.]

663. We fear we may have failed emphasize sufficiently remarkable political job accomplished by Li Tsung-jen in few months of his accession to nominal authority. At time of his inauguration he had everything against him. Li succeeded an autocrat who did not resign but merely withdrew from public life—leaving manifestations of his continuing power everywhere. Li inherited an administration of a country in bankruptcy; an armed force, in defeat. The outlook could hardly have been darker. Yet within period of slightly more than 2 months he has won the respect, admiration of majority politically articulate Chinese by his vigorous pursual of things nearest their hearts—peace. He put Communists on defensive in political propaganda field by his unrelenting efforts for peace. He has succeeded in primary objective of his peace offensive—Communist agreement to open formal negotiations. He has ridded himself of despicable Sun Fo and last Generalissimo-appointed Cabinet. He has won his battle to keep Executive, Legislative and Control Yuans in Nanking. He has confirmed loyalty too of Pai Chung-hsi [59] and his still intact armies. He has secured the services and consequently support of Ho Ying-chin as his Premier whose authority and prestige among Nationalist generals is second only to Generalissimo's. With all this Li has avoided break with Generalissimo and secured his assurances, albeit vague, that he will go abroad in due course. All this signifies quiet achievement of position of leadership in China which may prove formidable to opposition either Communist or Generalissimo C–C clique.

Meanwhile economical deterioration had accelerated. Rate of increase in GY [60] issue during recent week has been attended by rise velocity. Situation now resembles period last June–July with little likelihood any new "reform" can take hold even if intelligently, comprehensively formulated, of which latter no sign as yet. Impending end ECA [61] commodity imports, coupled with Chinese unwillingness or inability to use gold for purchase consumer's imports, unhappily seems to augur further well-greased economic slide.

Li Tsung-jen is patriotic Chinese who can be counted on to make every effort to develop that part of China under his control into con-

[59] Military and Political Affairs Director for Central China.
[60] Gold Yuan.
[61] Economic Cooperation Administration.

structive positive force in Far East. He wants to maintain China's friendly cooperative policy with the West. We believe his present intentions are to resist unreasonable Communist demand in Peiping, hold out for reasonable settlement and if necessary resume armed resistance eventually. His usefulness to cause of world peace as effective instrument for containment of communism in Far East should not be underestimated. For these reasons we have believed that continuation economic support justified at least during negotiation period. If, on other hand, we cannot hold out hopes of maintaining economical aid for next several months on present scale, Li's position will be seriously jeopardized. In such event we should be prepared for early capitulation his delegates to overwhelming Communist demands at peace table, thus eliminating any prospect of renewed resistance on national scale to Communist encroachment.

Sent Department 663, repeated OffEmb Canton 198, Shanghai 304.

STUART

893.00/3-2949 : Telegram

The Consul General at Shanghai (Cabot) to the Secretary of State

SHANGHAI, March 29, 1949.
[Received March 29—9:49 a. m.]

1025. *China Daily Tribune* March 29 carries Democratic-Socialist Party statement its position on national situation and civil war which includes six main points:

1. Question of validity of constitution should be put aside for time being, with proposals for changes being introduced later.
2. People's basic freedoms must be guaranteed.
3. There should be number of political parties so that benefits of inter-party criticism can be realized and tradition of peaceful Government changes established.
4. Military forces should be nationalized to eliminate warlordism.
5. Economic Socialism, aimed at equalization of wealth, should be brought about through "enactment of laws in accordance with popular will".
6. Responsibility for past political maneuvers should not be traced, but criminal cases should be prosecuted according to process of law.

Full statement follows air mail.[62]

Sent Nanking 601, repeated Department 1025, Canton Embassy 217.

CABOT

---

[62] Not printed.

893.002/3–3049 : Telegram

The Chargé in the Soviet Union (Kohler) to the Secretary of State

Moscow, March 30, 1949—1 p. m.
[Received March 30—6 :49 a. m.]

786. Chinese Ambassador Foo informs me that after extensive telegraphic exchanges with his political friends in China, he feels obliged to accept proffered position Foreign Minister in Ho Cabinet (Embtel 729, March 22 [63]). He intends communicate decision today and leave in near future. Ambassador explained his initial unsuccessful attempt refuse as due fear his nomination would be regarded as indicating pro-Soviet change in China's foreign policy. He was at pains to assure me there would be no such change.

Repeated Nanking 34, Canton 3.

KOHLER

893.00/3–3049 : Telegram

The Ambassador in China (Stuart) to the Secretary of State

NANKING, March 30, 1949.
[Received March 30—7 :28 a. m.]

673. Executive Yuan session March 29 named General Liu Fei as sixth member Nationalist delegation.[64] Nanking vernacular March 29 reports appointment legislator Lu Yu-wen as Secretary General of Nationalist peace delegation and Chang Chih-chung announcement to legislators that no peace program had been drafted or would be brought to Peiping.

Sent Department, repeated Shanghai 311, EmbOff Canton unnumbered.

STUART

893.00/3–3049

Memorandum by the Deputy Director of the Office of Far Eastern Affairs (Allison) to the Secretary of State

[WASHINGTON,] March 30, 1949.

In his telegram No. 633 [*663*] of March 28 Ambassador Stuart has given a well-founded picture of the accomplishments of the Acting President in the face of great difficulties. He has also presented justification for the continuation of economic support during the

---

[63] Not printed.
[64] For names of the other five delegates, see telegram No. 992, March 25, from the Consul General at Shanghai, p. 199.

period of the impending negotiations between the National Government and the Chinese Communists.

Related to this description of the Acting President's accomplishments is one given by the Embassy Office at Canton in its telegram No. 169 of March 25, describing the still influential position of Generalissimo Chiang Kai-shek as follows: The Generalissimo can be expected to continue to control, and in fact does control, a large segment of the army, navy and air force and he will almost certainly continue to control the secret police. It is unlikely that the Acting President and his group will gain control of the principal reserves of gold and silver and foreign currency. These factors, together with the development toward regionalism, will greatly hamper the effectiveness of the Acting President and his new cabinet and unless these difficulties are overcome, for which there appears little hope, the Acting President will have a very weak bargaining position vis-à-vis the Communists. In the final analysis, the Generalissimo continues to hold the balance of power in non-Communist China and is most unlikely to commit his influence unconditionally in support of Li Tsung-jen.

Congressional action to extend the authority of the China Aid Act of 1948,[65] as requested by ECA and the Department, would enable for a short time continuation of U.S. economic support to the Chinese Government. However, the effect of such Congressional action and subsequent economic aid is likely to be modified by the limited character of the action and the possibility that about half of the funds available will be used for Taiwan industry and for the Rural Reconstruction program in south China, with a resulting sharp curtailment of cotton and petroleum deliveries to the Shanghai–Nanking area. This undoubtedly will be interpreted in China as a gradual liquidation of the ECA program.

Nevertheless, Canton's comments tend to confirm the probability that the bargaining position of the Acting President will be affected much more by internal developments in China than by the existence and prospect of continuing U.S. economic support. Certainly, the importation of necessarily modest quantities of U.S. financed goods can have only marginal effect on the outcome of political negotiations as compared with the importance of the known relative military capabilities of the Chinese Communist and National Government forces.

---

[65] Approved April 3, 1948; 62 Stat. 158.

893.00/3–3049 : Telegram

*The Minister-Counselor of Embassy in China (Clark) to the
Secretary of State*

CANTON, March 30, 1949—3 p. m.
[Received 9 :47 p. m.]

Cantel 179. While agreeing on increased stature Li Tsung-jen, am inclined disagree final sentence Nanking's 663, March 28, repeated Canton 198, Shanghai 304.

Li's weakness vis-à-vis terms in forthcoming peace negotiations, it seems to me, lies less in economic field than in political. As Sun Fo suggested (Cantel 173, March 26, repeated Nanking 157, Shanghai 117), Communists are likely demand acceptable evidence Li has authority to commit non-Communist China. Communists must know of Generalissimo's machinations. They must realize that peace with Li does not end all resistance to their expansion in China. He cannot commit in advance or control the five Ma's [66] in the northwest or the feudalistic overlords in the southwest any more than he can the Generalissimo. Why then offer him other than his choice of "Peiping" or "Tientsin" peace? Their broadcasts seem to indicate that to be their intention.

I agree that continued economic aid is desirable, but would justify its continuance on need to maintain order behind Government lines rather than on strengthening Li's hands in his negotiations which, I am convinced, are doomed in advance to failure unless he accepts "reasonable surrender".

Sent Department Cantel 179; repeated Nanking 162, Shanghai 120.

CLARK

893.00B/3–3049

The Ambassador in China (Stuart) to the Secretary of State

No. 70   NANKING, March 30, 1949.
[Received April 25.]

The Ambassador has the honor to transmit a copy of a memorandum prepared by Mr. Josiah W. Bennett, Director of the Nanking Branch of USIS,[67] on the subject of Chinese Communist anti-American propaganda.

This carefully written and well-documented memorandum places the propaganda on two levels, the strategic and the tactical. On the much more important strategic level, the propaganda reflects and

---

[66] Mohammedan leaders in the northwestern provinces of Ningsia, Tsinghai, and Sinkiang.
[67] United States Information Service.

supports the views of International Communism, i.e., the Soviet Union. On the tactical level, it serves nicely to ridicule the National Government as an instrument of American "imperialism" and to divert attention from charges that the Chinese Communists are themselves instruments of Soviet foreign policy. The memorandum contends that the real motivation of the anti-American propaganda of the Chinese Communists stems not from the present civil war in China but rather from the global struggle between the United States and the Soviet Union.

[Enclosure]

Memorandum by the Director of the Nanking Branch of the U.S.I.S. (Bennett) to the Acting Director of the U.S.I.S. in China (Conners)

Subject: The Nature of Chinese Communist Anti-American Propaganda

Chinese Communist propaganda against the United States, like Communist propaganda in other countries, may be said to operate on two levels, the strategic and the tactical.

Strategically, Communist propaganda reflects the world view of Communist leadership and is not a function of the situation in any particular country. This world view is embedded in Marxist theory and the various footnotes to this theory which have been authorized by Moscow. Being subscribed to by all party members, it necessarily governs the thinking of Communist propaganda organs. It may be regarded as a "basic directive" by which Communist propaganda policy, which is but one facet of over-all Communist policy, is guided.

The present Communist world view characterizes the United States as an international bogey man, enemy of all that is progressive and democratic. After the Second World War, which for the Western World was an imperialist war (only the USSR fought a patriotic war), the center of gravity of world capitalism moved to the United States. American "monopoly capital" assumed the role of a gigantic cabal, directing by unseen and insidious methods all capitalist enterprises the world over. Thus America, holding no colonies of its own, is represented as the world's greatest colonial power, by virtue of the fact that it is assumed to have swallowed up the home governments of the colonial powers of Europe. Further, the evil spirit of Fascism (a word which Communist propaganda has sedulously sought to keep alive) is represented as having found home in the congenially "reactionary" atmosphere of Washington and Wall Street. Thus, as the world situation now stands, all that Communism finds most hateful and vile, is now concentrated in purest essence in the United States.

These imputations are naturally enraging to Americans, who have just concluded a bloody and costly war against Fascism and the policy of whose government is to work for the orderly liquidation of the colonial system throughout the world. But Communists regard them as "objective" truth—not verifiable truth, but truth as revealed by infallible theory. The United States must be fostering the revival of Fascist militarism in Germany and Japan, not because there is evidence to that effect but because the United States is a capitalist power and that is how a capitalist power must act. Likewise, in colonial areas, the United States must be the master mind behind all attempts to keep native peoples in bondage, because it is the world's greatest capitalist power and that is the way a great capitalist power behaves. Communist theory has cast America in the role of evil genius of world reaction and would have her play out her part to the end.

The Chinese Communist Party apparently subscribes to this general view of the United States. American "imperialism" is constantly portrayed as successor to Japanese imperialism in China. The National Government of China is represented as a "semi-colonial" government of the United States. The United States is accused of deliberately fostering the revival of Japanese militarism. The Marshall Plan is condemned, and the Soviet Union applauded for its opposition thereto. But, more than this, Chinese Communist leaders have made explicit and detailed statements in which the Communist view of the United States is affirmed in detail. Early in November, when Chinese Communist armies were winning control of Manchuria, the Communist North Shensi Radio broadcast such a statement by Mao Tse-tung, Chairman of the Chinese Communist Party:

After the victory of the Second World War, American imperialism and its running dogs in various countries replaced Fascist Germany, Italy and Japan and are frenziedly preparing a new world war menacing the whole world. They reflect the extreme rottenness of the capitalist world and its panic in the face of impending extinction. This enemy still has its strength. Hence all revolutionary forces within every country must unite with each other. They must organize an anti-imperialist united front headed by the Soviet Union and pursue a correct policy. Otherwise, there can be no victory. (North Shensi Radio, November 7, 1948)

Here Mao declares the United States an enemy, not because of its policy in China, but because of its position as the world's most powerful capitalist power. The United States is the enemy because its very existence as a free nation is the greatest obstacle in the path of Communist world revolution.

A similar statement by Liu Shao-ch'i, well-known Chinese Communist theoretician, was publicized by the North Shensi Radio at about the same time. In a long article on the world situation, Liu analyzes the position of the United States as follows:

On the other hand, a population of 1,300,000,000 among all the nations of the world (excluding the United States of America) is either directly or indirectly under the rule of a single America, while imperialist reactionaries of Great Britain, France, the Netherlands and other countries have in reality become national traitors and accomplices of American imperialism. The United States of America has a population of only 140,000,000 and riding on their backs are only the eight well-known financial groups of Morgan, Rockefeller, Dupont, Mellon, etc., with a handful of representatives of their reactionary movements—only about 1,000 persons. (North Shensi Radio November 10, 1948)

By representing Great Britain, France and the Netherlands as captives of American imperialism, Liu completes the logical train which enables Communists to attack the United States as enemy of all movements of national liberation in Asia.

Like the whole of which it is a part, Chinese Communist propaganda is therefore forced by theoretical necessity to be profoundly anti-American. It is not within the power of the United States to escape this onus, except by the wholly unthinkable expedient of itself joining the Communist camp. So long as we choose to believe in and defend our democratic way of life, we shall continue to be the target of virulent propaganda from all true-believing Communist parties, including the Chinese.

The tactical employment of Communist strategic propaganda has greatly aided the Chinese Communist party in its struggle against the National Govt. By painting that government as a "semi-colonial" pawn of American "imperialism" Chinese Communist propagandists are enabled to represent their own war of rebellion as a great patriotic struggle against foreign "aggression." By the same token this line has helped them divert attention from their own role as instruments of Soviet Russian policy in China. All available local color is utilized to reinforce the concept of Americans as "imperialists," "aggressors", "exploiters", "reactionaries", and "warmongers." Every incident, every word is seized upon and twisted into an anti-American shape. Misdemeanors—real and fancied—of Americans in China become "atrocities." Dealings of our diplomatic representatives with the Government of China become "conspiracies", while treaties and agreements become "treaties of national betrayal." American military advisers "participate" and "intervene" in China's civil strife. American arms and "American trained and equipped" troops "slaughter" innocent Chinese. And so on.

Meanwhile the thesis that the National Government is but an American "stooge" is pushed both *ad absurdum* and *ad nauseam*. Chiang Kai-shek is accused of shipping phosphorus and salt to Japan "on MacArthur's orders" (North Shensi Radio, November 13, 1948). Okamura [68] was returned to Japan "at the orders of American imperialism". (North Shensi Radio, February 5, 1949). Pai Chung-hsi and Fu Tso-i [69] were promoted "on American instructions" (North Shensi Radio, November 1, 1948). Chiang Kai-shek's retirement and Li Tsung-jen's assumption of office was "at the prompting of the American Government" (North Shensi Radio, January 23, 1949). The peace movement of the Nationalist Government is "nothing but a huge fraud instigated by American imperialism." (North Shensi Radio, January 31, 1949). In other words, whatever the Chinese Government may do, whether it wages war or sues for peace, it does at the behest of American "imperialism."

The conclusion I think is clear. This anti-American propaganda on the tactical level was not dictated by the actual workings of American policy in China so much as by the propaganda strategy prescribed by the Communist canon for all loyal Communist parties. If American support of the Chinese Government had ceased abruptly on V–J Day, if a policy of the severest neutrality had been adopted at that time, Chinese Communist propaganda would in all likelihood still have been intensely anti-American. There would still be American machinations in Nanking to denounce. (That they bore no visible fruit would not be a serious hindrance). Events in Japan, Korea, and Southeast Asia would have provided limitless stores of ammunition if material were not ready to hand in China itself. For Chinese Communism sees itself as part of the Communist world revolution. Whatever the particulars of the situation in a given country, the ultimate villain in the piece, from the Communist point of view, is always the United States, the only source of strength in the non-Communist world.

Should the Chinese Communists succeed in their struggle to replace the present Government of China, we can expect Communist anti-American propaganda to continue, with only the emphasis changed. Domestically, nonconformists and deviationists may well be accused of intrigue with American "imperialism". American "imperialism", which already has been accused of organizing "disruptive plots" to split the Communist Party (North Shensi Radio, February 4, 1949), will doubtless be credited with various nefarious schemes to debase the purity of the revolutionary movement. But the most important change will probably be an increased emphasis on events in other parts of Asia. Already Chinese Communist propaganda has begun to take a brotherly interest in the activities of other Asiatic countries and Asiatic Communist parties in Japan, Korea, French Indo-China,

---

[68] Japanese Commander in Chief in China, 1944–45.
[69] General Fu remained in Peiping upon its occupation by Communist forces in January 1949.

Malaya and Indonesia. With the battle of China effectively won, the Chinese Communist propaganda front will probably be extended to all such areas in the hope of eventually securing all of East Asia for the world revolution. Here too strategic considerations will mark the United States as the primary object of attack.

893.00/3–3149 : Telegram

The Ambassador in China (Stuart) to the Secretary of State

NANKING, March 31, 1949—noon.
[Received March 31—2:01 a. m.]

677. Nationalist peace delegation head Chang Chih-chung flew to Chikow for conference with Gimo March 29 and expected return momentarily. Chang went with knowledge and consent of Acting President and Premier Ho not, we believe, to receive instructions from Gimo prior departure to Peiping, but rather to inform Gimo mission's plans, tactics, etc., probably in effort persuade him remain silent during negotiations as best service to Acting President.

Sent Department, repeated Shanghai 313, OffEmb Canton 205.

STUART

893.00/3–3149 : Telegram

The Consul General at Peiping (Clubb) to the Secretary of State

PEIPING, March 31, 1949.
[Received March 31—6:20 a. m.]

525. ReContel 502, March 28.[70] *Ta Chung Jih Pao* and other papers today carried following item entitled in reference paper "American Imperialism Acknowledges by Silence Crime of Bombing *Chungking* Was Done by It".

"According to New China News Agency despatch, after Agency's publication true facts of bombing of cruiser *Chungking* (which revolted against Kuomintang reactionary government) by American imperialists, who directly participated in the Kuomintang counter revolutionary civil war, American imperialists were unable deny and consequently did not dare make statement, and therefore issued two ambiguous news items through American imperialist news agency, Associated Press.

Two items, however, did not dare deny that *Chungking* was bombed by American-flag B–29 type (bomber), which is to say American imperialism acknowledges by silence its crime. The Chinese people will always remember *Chungking* incident: The foul crime that American imperialism directly participated in counter revolutionary civil war of Kuomintang reactionary clique and bombed Chinese people's

---

[70] Not printed.

naval warship, damaged coastal defense power of Chinese people and encroached upon sovereign air and sea rights of China.["]

Sent Department 525; repeated Nanking 330, Canton 36, Shanghai 366, Tsingtao.

CLUBB

893.00/3–3149 : Telegram

The Consul General at Peiping (Clubb) to the Secretary of State

PEIPING, March 31, 1949—3 p. m.
[Received March 31—4:26 a. m.]

526. ReContel 525, March 31. Recommend categorical firm denial allegation New China Agency despite fact identification bombers as American flag B–29 type ambiguous.

Repeated Nanking and Shanghai.

CLUBB

893.00/3–3149 : Telegram

The Ambassador in China (Stuart) to the Secretary of State

NANKING, March 31, 1949.
[Received March 31—6:37 a. m.]

685. Vernacular press March 26 reported Executive Yuan Council at first session March 24 decided retain its Chiefs of Ministries and Political Vice Ministers in Nanking, while retaining administrative units and Administrative Vice Ministers in Canton.

Sent Department 685; repeated Shanghai 315, Canton unnumbered.

STUART

893.00/4–149 : Telegram

The Minister-Counselor of Embassy in China (Clark) to the Secretary of State

CANTON, April 1, 1949—11 a. m.
[Received April 2—1:55 a. m.]

Cantel 181. Soviet Ambassador [71] sought me out at reception yesterday and in line present Soviet tactics was most cordial. His conversation seemed obviously directed toward lulling me into sense security and persuading me (1) that peace efforts Li Tsung-jen would fail because Li spoke only for himself and Pai Chung-hsi, but that

---

[71] N. V. Roschin.

nevertheless (2) when Communists finally took over they would be "riding a tiger" and confronted with situations impossible of solution.

In response to my inquiry whether he would return Nanking now that Ho Ying-chin Cabinet seemed to be establishing itself there, he said Nanking in effect only puppet; neither Li nor Ho could make any major decision without first consulting Central Executive Committee of Kmt which is in Canton and Generalissimo who is at Chikow. Had not Wu Tieh-cheng publicly upheld right of CEC to approve composition cabinet and peace proposals and had not Chang Chih-chung gone Chikow to see Generalissimo before proceeding Peiping head peace delegation? Even at that he did not see how "other side" could take seriously and [any?] promises Li's delegation might make as he certainly was not authorized to commit Ma brothers, Szechuan leaders or Lu Han in Yunnan. There was also considerable doubt in his mind whether the "Canton boys" would agree to any solution Li was able to work out.

He spoke at length on subject of traditional independence northwest leaders, of secret societies in Szechuan, of self assertion Chinese when suppressed too severely by their overlords, as witness recent uprisings Hunan and Yunnan and obviously sought magnify difficulty ruling China and leave impression that we should not worry too much about trend events as history indicated that no one could, in final analysis, control clannish Chinese. "Other side" therefore could not succeed any more than had Kmt.

Sent Department, repeated Nanking 167, Shanghai 122, Moscow 7.

CLARK

893.00/4–149 : Telegram

The Minister-Counselor of Embassy in China (Clark) to the Secretary of State

CANTON, April 1, 1949—4 p. m.
[Received 8 :34 p. m.]

Cantel 185. Allow such clearly calculated accusations re *Chungking* as those contained Peiping 525, March 31 to Department, repeated Nanking 300, Canton 36, go unnoticed would appear most dangerous. It is difficult know how answer effectively, but suggest desirability Ambassador take notice allegation and [answer?] it clearly in hope refutation will reach some ears.

Sent Nanking 171, repeated Department.

CLARK

893.00/4–149 : Telegram

The Ambassador in China (Stuart) to the Secretary of State

NANKING, April 1, 1949—5 p. m.
[Received 11 :02 p. m.]

687. Embassy concurs with Peiping telegram 526, March 31 sent Department re denial American participation in sinking *Chungking* and is prepared issue appropriate denial if Department so instructs.

Sent Department 687, repeated Shanghai 317.

STUART

893.00/4–149 : Telegram

The Consul General at Canton (Ludden) to the Secretary of State

CANTON, April 1, 1949—5 p. m.
[Received April 2—2 :06 a. m.]

75. Reference Embcirtel March 24, received March 30.[72] Canton pacification headquarters estimates approximately 37,000 Communist guerrillas Kwangtung. AMA [73] and I consider this figure small; total probably in neighborhood 55,000. In assessing so-called Communist strength South China consideration must be given long history banditry, piracy, main trade routes southeast Kwangtung, major food deficit area China, thus banditry for economic reasons common phenomenon probably accounting for major portion above estimate. In recent times organized lawlessness for profit, particularly along smuggling routes in delta, along East River and Bias Bay area, accounts for additional sizeable group. Third grouping developed since V–J Day and steadily increasing in direct ratio loss prestige National Government is composed individuals in opposition policies Government and, though believed numerically inferior compared first two groups, it is composed more intelligent, literate elements and is very probable main target Communist blandishments.

No question but that Communists endeavoring infiltrate bandit and dissident groups using Hong Kong as financial and propaganda base. Communist organization rural areas not thus far evident and not important with exception Hainan Island where regular Communist organizations similar former North China border region governments, function and control 80% of island by day and 100% of island by

---

[72] Not found in Department of State files: it probably was an Embassy instruction pursuant to telegram No. 356, March 17 (not printed), asking for report to the Department of extent of Communist infiltration in South and Southwest China through bandit activities or otherwise.

[73] Assistant Military Attaché.

night (see Canton voluntary report 1, January 11, 1949,[74] political conditions Hainan Island).

In considering total strength figure mentioned above, following points are important: (1) Ratio of men to serviceable weapons approximately 2 to 1; (2) training standards low to nonexistent; (3) discipline is by consent; (4) ability to stand determined assault poor. In summary, bandits, dissidence and/or Communists Kwangtung, except Hainan, composed heterogeneous small groups without cohesion. Many, possibly the majority, of these groups have of late assumed titles such as "People's Liberation Army", "People's Self Defence Unit", "People's anti-Collection Column", "Democratic Joint Army", but in the main their methods and operations continue as in the past to be those of gangsters, as little tinged by any political ideology as the operations of gangsters anywhere.

At present time there is no reason to doubt capability available national and provincial forces continue maintain reasonable level public security this area provided there is no major incursion southeast China regular Communist forces. Of late there has been a rash of highly irresponsible news reporting of increased "Communist" military strength this region. Of this we see no real evidence but insofar as economic conditions continue deteriorate unrest throughout southeast generally may be anticipated, with consequent increase Communist efforts take advantage thereof.

With regard Kwangsi, reliable information is to effect far better conditions stability [prevail than?] in Kwangtung. There is little if any banditry of [or?] dissidence; a generally healthy political situation prevails and the popular provincial administration is well in control of situation. Possible exception to foregoing is in Shih Wan Ta Shan region (22 north 108 east), notorious bandit stronghold from whence, according French reports of doubtful reliability, Chinese Communists are aiding Vietnam rebels.

AMA currently preparing detailed study Communist strength southeast.

Sent Nanking 46, repeated Department.

LUDDEN

893.00/4–149 : Telegram

The Consul General at Peiping (Clubb) to the Secretary of State

[Extract]

PEIPING, April 1, 1949.
[Received April 2—5 :38 a. m.]

541. ReContel 525, March 31. *Hsin Min Pao* today carried following item regarding cruiser *Chungking:*

---

[74] Not printed.

"Under leadership Commander Teng Chao-hsiang, warship *Chungking*, largest cruiser of Kuomintang reactionary navy, revolted February 25 and joined battle camp of People's forces. But Chiang Kai-shek, public enemy of the people, in collusion with the most fiendish and wicked American imperialist clique, who have determined to be enemy of Chinese people, sent air planes to Hulutao to bomb and sink cruiser *Chungking* on 4 consecutive days, March 17, 18, 19 and 20.

Upon hearing news all Chinese without exception were infuriated. They recognize that diabolical mien of American imperialists, the masters of bandit Chiang Kai-shek, has now been quite exposed; the following is letter written by group of primary school students:

. . . .

Sent Department 541, Nanking 334, Office Embassy Canton, Shanghai 374, Tsingtao, by mail to Tientsin.

CLUBB

893.00/4–149 : Telegram

The Consul General at Peiping (Clubb) to the Secretary of State

PEIPING, April 1, 1949.
[Received April 2—6 :16 a. m.]

546. *Jen Min Jih Pao* today reports arrival Peiping yesterday 19 persons of Nanking peace delegation, including Chang Chih-chung, Shao Li-tzu, Chang Shih-chao, Huang Shao-hsiung, Li Cheng and Liu Fei. Delegation was preceded March 31 by secretariat of 10 persons headed by Lu Yu-wen.

Same paper reports CC of CCP [75] has further designated Nieh Jung-chen as member CCP delegation, and Chi Yen-ming as Secretary General.

Sent Department, Nanking 337, OffEmb Canton 39, Shanghai 378, by mail to Tientsin.

CLUBB

893.00/4–149 : Airgram

The Consul General at Hankow (Callanan) to the Secretary of State

HANKOW, April 1, 1949.
[Received May 3—11 :19 a. m.]

A–0015. The Central China military front, quiescent for several months, was the scene of renewed activity on the part of the Communists during the past month. While prevailing opinion in both military and civilian quarters is still that the Communists will not launch a direct attack on the Wuhan area in the near future, recent moves on their part indicate that further isolation of Wuhan is in

---

[75] Central Executive Committee of the Chinese Communist Party.

the making. The focal point of the current Communist attack is Anking, the fall of which would effectively block further river communication with Nanking and Shanghai. In fact, river traffic has already been interrupted as the Communists now occupy "Christmas island", which lies astride the main navigation channel about eight miles upstream from Anking. On March 30, the last commercial steamer to pass this island, the San Peh Company's *Ta Ch'ing*, was fired upon and two persons aboard were killed and eight injured. According to an executive of this company, the Communists already occupy the north bank of the Yangtze in two hsien just above Anking. All vessels which had left Hankow for destinations beyond Anking have been halted at Kiukiang.

.   .   .   .

CALLANAN

893.00/4–249 : Telegram

The Minister-Counselor of Embassy in China (Clark) to the Secretary of State

CANTON, April 2, 1949—noon.
[Received 11:46 p. m.]

Cantel 188. Wu Tieh-cheng confirmed press report CEC action regarding directive peace delegate (Cantel 186, April 2,[76] repeated Nanking 172, Shanghai 125). A small secret subcommittee of CEC on which Wu may serve is to be established in Nanking to remain in daily contact with negotiators and see that no agreement is reached that is unsatisfactory to CEC. It will also be responsibility this secret subcommittee to assure that all points of agreement with Communists have support various regional elements now Communist China.

Wu is not sanguine success peace negotiations. He says that [when] Shao Li-tse and W. W. Yen were in Shihchiachuang, Chou En-lai rejected summarily any suggestions either of territorial arrangement or federation, insisting unwaveringly on coalition to be composed third Communists, third Kmt purged of reactionary element, and third others who would of course be Communist fellow-travellers. Such proposal, Wu said, would of course be unacceptable.

In strictest confidence he said Li Tsung-jen in last few days had asked Roschin, Soviet Ambassador, come Nanking with idea he could be of assistance in peace negotiations. Wu said he believes (and he implied and other leaders agreed) that with signing of North Atlantic

---

[76] Not printed.

Pact,[77] Soviets would prevent Communists from crossing Yangtze if they did, in fact, control Communist action. Soviets would not wish, he said, to risk conflict with North Atlantic powers which might arise out of possible Chinese Communist action in southeast Asia. How they reached that conclusion was unexplained, but he came back to point twice so idea must be in their minds. It may also have something to do with desire that Roschin return Nanking although invitation may be merely another of Li's efforts to convince everyone his sincere desire for peace.

Wu says negotiators are not taking counter-proposals to Mao's eight points, but will be guided by CEC directives. He does not anticipate that Communists will agree with Nationalists' demand for cease-fire during negotiations, but that fact of itself should not result in failure negotiations. He expects negotiations to break down over character coalition and reorganization military force, on both of which he said positions appear irreconcilable. He anticipates Communists will insist on assured control of vote, which would mean death warrant of those continuing oppose communism and would be therefore unacceptable Nationalist negotiators.

Wu insists that seat of Government remains Canton where all work will be done and that galaxy of Ministers and Political Vice Ministers in Nanking is only window dressing to impress Communists and people of sincerity Government in search of peace.

Sent Department; repeated Nanking 174, Shanghai 127, pouched Kunming, Chungking, Hankow, Peiping.

CLARK

893.00/4–349 : Telegram

The Ambassador in China (Stuart) to the Secretary of State

NANKING, April 3, 1949—11 a. m.
[Received April 3—6:04 a. m.]

696. ReEmbtel 693, April 1.[78] Following are some comments made to me yesterday and today by prominent Nationalists re prospects for Peiping peace negotiations:

Chang Chih-chung, head peace delegation, displayed optimism eve his departure Peiping. He intends request Commies to agree Chinese foreign policy should be neither pro-American nor pro-Soviet but should rather treat both nations same way. Chang claimed should Commies refuse proposal he would resign as peace delegate.

Shao Li-tze intends to do his best to restrain war-minded elements

---

[77] Signed at Washington, April 4, 1949; for text, see Department of State Treaties and Other International Acts Series No. 1964, or 63 Stat. (pt. 2) 2241.
[78] Not printed.

in Kmt and as delegate to persuade CCP to broaden its position. He has no illusions re prejudice and suspicions on both sides and feels his own responsibility very keenly.

Carsun Chang [79] supports Li Tsung-jen in his peace efforts but is very critical of Generalissimo. If peace talks fail, he proposes go abroad carry on literary activities against Commies, since he believes to do so in China would be almost impossible.

Li Huang, acting head Young China Party, informed me his party disposed to support Acting President in present policy, but is critical of many things about Government conduct of affairs in recent months. He confirmed what Carsun Chang had told me, namely, that plans are being considered unify Young China Party and Democratic Socialist Party as beginning more solidarity among non-Commie groups.

Sent Department, repeated Shanghai 324, OffEmb Canton 217.

STUART

893.00/4-449 : Telegram

The Ambassador in China (Stuart) to the Secretary of State

NANKING, April 4, 1949—noon.
[Received 11:37 p. m.[80]]

698. I do not believe there is serious disagreement between our views expressed in Embtel 663, March 28 to Department (repeated AmEmb Canton 198, Shanghai 304) and those of Embassy Canton set forth Cantel 179, March 30 (repeated Nanking 162, Shanghai 120). We too remain unconvinced that present peace talks can reach happy conclusion nor do we suggest continuing economic aid to Acting President and Government for purpose of bringing negotiations Peiping to successful conclusion. Rather we feel economic aspects China aid program should continue available to Li government to give him and his delegates [to] Peiping backbone to resist overwhelming Communist demands at peace table. Time is important for Nationalist Government and for anti-Communist cause. Longer they can resist in Peiping, longer they can spin out peace talks, better chance Li will have resisting eventually at Yangtze both militarily and politically. It apparent if Nationalist delegations unable resist at peace table there will be nothing left on national scale to resist militarily later. Nationalist delegation, without hope continued US economic assistance and steadily worsening economic-financial situation in their rear, cannot be expected resist with conviction or for period time tough, confident Communist delegation presently facing them Peiping. For these reasons we support and urge on Department continuation

---

[79] Also known as Chang Chun-mai, leader of Democratic Socialist Party.
[80] Text printed from corrected copy received April 6, 11:30 a. m.

present level economic assistance to Acting President Li and his government during this, perhaps decisive, phase of continuing Chinese resistance to Communism. In this connection I am disturbed by implications last sentence Deptel 410, March 30.[81]

Any funds reauthorized by Congress should, I feel, be used to continue program on present impartial basis for all free China with no obvious emphasis on any one aspect or region. Political benefits in keeping alive present Nationalist Government as long as possible seem to me to outweigh any other considerations. If Li's Cabinet should collapse as indications are it will next few weeks, unless there is both fiscal, moral support, question must be faced whether projects planned for other parts China will be politically worthwhile or even possible.

Sent Department 698; repeated Canton, Taipei.

STUART

893.00/3–3149 : Telegram

The Secretary of State to the Ambassador in China (Stuart)

WASHINGTON, April 4, 1949—2 p. m.

426. Re Peiping's 525 and 526, Mar 31. Emb authorized in its discretion coordinate with MA,[82] NA[83] and ComNavWesPac[84] in issuing categorical denial Commie charges US bombing cruiser *Chungking*. Emphasis shld be made on ridiculous nature of charges and official statements Chinese air force describing action. Rpt text any statement to Dept for use on VOA.[85]

ACHESON

893.00/4–449 : Telegram

The Ambassador in China (Stuart) to the Secretary of State

NANKING, April 4, 1949.
[Received April 4—10:59 p. m.]

700. Widely reported Nanking vernacular press April 2 is following translation initial written statement by Nationalist peace delegation issued immediately prior departure to Peiping April 1:

"While leaving for Peiping to open peace talks with Communists according to the Government's instructions, we are aware of heaviness of responsibilities and feel as if we are approaching the edge of an abyss or walking on thin ice. We also know that during peace negotiations there will arise many difficulties but we believe that if both sides place interests of the nation and people's welfare above all and peace talks are carried on in spirit of mutual trust and understanding

---

[81] Vol. IX, p. 752.
[82] Military Attaché.
[83] Naval Attaché.
[84] Commander, U.S. Naval Forces, Western Pacific.
[85] Voice of America.

any difficulty can be overcome. We will follow carefully Government's instructions and talk with Communists with greatest sincerity and hope an agreement can be reached so that true and lasting peace may be realized at an early date and the enthusiastic hope of the people satisfied. It is our hope that peace-loving people in various circles will give us from time to time their advice, guidance and support."

Sent Department 700; repeated Shanghai 328, OffEmb Canton unnumbered.

STUART

893.00/4–449 : Telegram

The Ambassador in China (Stuart) to the Secretary of State

NANKING, April 4, 1949—4 p. m.
[Received April 5—12:21 a. m.]

701. Two features which emerge from still somewhat confused picture student 1-day peace strike and riots Nanking April 1 are that to considerable extent demonstration was Communist-instigated and Government has acted with commendable restraint.

Participating students numbered at least 5000 and came from all Nanking Universities and Colleges, particularly National Central University. Slogans represented curious mixture student desires and Communist themes. Among former were demands for free food, lodging and tuition and end conscription and requisitioning. Among latter were demands cessation American aid and slogans calling against "false peace" and "legitimacy of Kmt institution". In general, it cannot be said demonstration was strongly anti-American. Number students were disenchanted by radical views organizers. Fine hand Communists demonstrated also by fact that workmen from schools paraded alongside students. Given Communist inspiration whole operation, it is therefore rather remarkable that more anti-Americanism was not shown.

Main parade occurred during morning, was orderly and without police interference. It was in afternoon that trouble commenced. After disbanding, two groups became consecutively involved in brawls with wounded and ex-POW National soldiers angered at students dancing Yangko and plastering anti-Government posters around streets. There is no reason believe special agents Garrison Command incited soldiers to violence.

Unconfirmable reports indicate about 100 students injured, perhaps 12 seriously, and 2 or 3 have since died. Soldier casualties were around 50.

While too much importance should not be attached this unfortunate incident, Communists will doubtless capitalize on it maximum extent.

Their Peiping broadcast April 2 picked it up promptly, claiming in injured tones that students had been brutally beaten by Kmt troops and secret police. National Government attempt forestall this has been quick. On April 1, for that night alone, curfew was advanced from midnight to 10 p. m. Garrison Command issued press release same evening and reaffirmed previous order against demonstrations, which had been given same morning under authority martial law. Government will pay hospital bills of students. Executive Yuan has ordered Minister of Education and Garrison Command locate responsibility for incident and settle it.

Sent Department, repeated OffEmb Canton 220, Shanghai 329.

STUART

893.01/4–449 : Telegram

The Ambassador in China (Stuart) to the Secretary of State

NANKING, April 4, 1949.
[Received April 4—11 :05 p. m.]

702. Official Kmt organ *Chung Yang Jih Pao* April 4 quotes Government spokesman re Executive Yuan status as follows:

"The Government spokesman said: 'Since formation of new Cabinet, heads of Ministries and commissions have gathered in Nanking, and this has led some people to think that Government has returned to Nanking. Actually, the seat of Government at present is still at Canton. Heads of Ministries and commissions are only in Nanking temporarily to assist Premier Ho Ying-chin in carrying out political functions. All routine administrative functions are still performed at Canton. This policy was decided by Sun Cabinet, and Premier Ho has not altered this decision.' "

It is learned, paper continues, that an "Executive Yuan Nanking office" is to be established at OMEA [86] premises for handling affairs which must be settled in Nanking.

Sent Department 702, repeated OffEmb Canton and Shanghai unnumbered.

STUART

893.00/4–449 : Telegram

The Ambassador in China (Stuart) to the Secretary of State

NANKING, April 4, 1949.
[Received April 4—10 :56 p. m.]

703. Kmt Army organ *Ho Ping Jih Pao* and other vernacular papers today report that, in order to unify views on peace within

---

[86] Officers Moral Endeavor Association.

Kmt, special committee has been set up which will serve as party clearing house for all opinions. Committee members include Sun Fo, Chang Chun, Yu Yu-jen, Chu Cheng, Wu Chung-hsin, Wu Te-chen, Chen Li-fu, Chu Chia-hua, Hung Lan-yu and Chen Yen-feng. Committee periodically will submit reports to Kmt chairman Chiang Kai-shek. Tabloid *Chung Kuo Jih Pao* adds that meeting of above committee will be called by Acting President Li.

Sent Department 703; repeated Shanghai 330, OffEmb Canton unnumbered.

STUART

893.00/4–549 : Telegram

The Ambassador in China (Stuart) to the Secretary of State

NANKING, April 5, 1949.
[Received April 4—10:46 p. m.]

699. North Shensi broadcast April 1 announces appointment Nieh Jung-chen sixth Communist peace delegate and Chi Yi-ming Secretary General Communist delegation.

Sent Department 699, repeated Shanghai 327, OffEmb Canton unnumbered.

STUART

893.00/4–549 : Telegram

The Ambassador in China (Stuart) to the Secretary of State

NANKING, April 5, 1949—3 p. m.
[Received April 5—6:39 a. m.]

707. Acting President discouraged over prospects peace. When I saw him and his advisor, Kan Chieh-hou, over week end they gave me various reasons why they thought peace talks would fail. They have evidence from captured Communist forces containing orders cross Yangtze before water rises. Furthermore there have been repeated proposals from CCP military commanders that their forces be allowed occupy cities Nanking, Shanghai regardless progress, outcome peace talks. As additional evidence Communist intention pursue military conquest China, Kan cited behavior Soviet Ambassador in following terms. When Acting President visited Canton late February he sent word to Roschin asking him remain behind for conference following diplomatic reception which Li held in southern provisional capital. Roschin replied that it would be difficult for him linger, that they would lack privacy and that in any event there was nothing to be discussed between them. Li sent his advisor second time to Roschin suggesting another time. Soviet Ambassador again

demurred and Kan reminded him this was official request from Head of State to Soviet Representative. Interview, when it finally occurred, was entirely unsatisfactory, Ambassador apparently deliberately using up allotted time by talking steadily of discomforts himself and staff in Canton and delays signing Sinkiang pact.[87] President finally terminated interview without having been permitted opportunity discuss Sino-Soviet relations. Recently Li Tsung-jen has sent suggestion through Chinese Foreign Office to Soviet Ambassador that, since Acting President and Cabinet are remaining Nanking, Roschin should return here. Suggestion has been repeated but no reply has been received from Roschin to date. (See Cantel 188, April 2, repeated Nanking 174.)

Both Li and Kan interpret this attitude as indication that CCP has intention continue its military activities south of Yangtze with Soviet knowledge and approval.

Both President and Premier have assured me that if Communist forces cross Yangtze during peace talks Nationalist delegation now Peiping will be promptly recalled.

Sent Department, repeated OffEmb Canton 222, Shanghai 333.

STUART

893.00/4–649 : Telegram

The Ambassador in China (Stuart) to the Secretary of State

NANKING, April 6, 1949—6 p. m.
[Received April 6—8:23 a. m.]

716. Li Tsung-jen sent me following report by his advisor Kan Chieh-hou. Emissary from Peiping arrived last night with message for Acting President which latter interprets is in nature of ultimatum from Communists. It is desired that some high-ranking person proceed at once to Peiping to represent Nationalist Government on Army Reorganization Committee. It is expected by Communist[s] that Acting President himself will proceed to Peiping as this representative. If so, Mao will act as chairman and Li Tsung-jen as vice chairman of committee. If Li will not go, Ho Ying-chin is suggested. Formal conversation of Army Reorganization Committee will begin April 9 and terminate 12th. Talks must be concluded by latter date. There will be no crossing of Yangtze before 12th unless peace talks break down. Communist forces will cross Yangtze whether there is peace or war. Failure to send representative or to reach agreement by specified date will cause Communists to cross river promptly.

It is further stipulated that CCP will have majority of one on Army Reorganization Committee. In addition to President and

---

[87] For documentation concerning Sinkiang, see vol. IX, pp. 1037 ff.

Premier it would be desirable to have heads of three Yuans, Chu Cheng, Tung Kuan-hsien and Yu Yu-jen. Committee would designate location for Government troops by divisions (no two divisions stationed together). Training of Nationalist divisions will begin immediately. After Communist forces have crossed Yangtze, they will take over administration of all municipalities and control of all local militia and police.

Following convocation of Army Reorganization Committee, Political Consultative Conference based on one held under General Marshall will be resumed. Kmt will not be accepted as such, KmtRC [88] taking its place. Individual Kmt members may join latter group; minor parties to be ignored.

Re war criminals, no leniency for Generalissimo, Chen brothers and Chen Cheng,[89] (T. V. Soong and H. H. Kung [90] were not mentioned possibly because they are both outside Chinese jurisdiction). All others on war criminal list may redeem themselves by doing something to assist new order such as ceasing resistance, et cetera.

While messenger was non-Communist and member of KmtRC, Acting President regards him as emissary in fact for CCP.

Department please pass Peiping in its discretion.

Sent Department 716, repeated OffEmb Canton 228, Shanghai 342.

STUART

893.00B/4–649 : Airgram

The Secretary of State to the Ambassador in China (Stuart)

WASHINGTON, April 6, 1949.

A–33. Urdesp 62, March 10. Department has given careful consideration to proposal set forth in urdesp 62 and particularly to nature of approach you would expect to make to Communist leaders as described on page 2 of this despatch. You are hereby authorized to discuss with the top Chinese Communist leaders the points described in urdesp except as set forth hereunder.

Department notes your statement: "My Government might therefore feel called upon to assist any nucleus of organized opposition first in arousing the Chinese people to the danger of their national sovereignty and personal liberties and then in using all possible means for their self-protection. If this were undertaken at all I had reason to believe that we would use every available resource we possessed to restore real liberation to the Chinese people." While you state that your approach would not in any sense represent an ultimatum

---

[88] Kuomintang Revolutionary Committee.
[89] Governor of Taiwan.
[90] Former Chinese Ministers of Finance and brothers-in-law of Generalissimo Chiang Kai-shek.

or threat, it would be difficult to avoid an interpretation of the two above-quoted sentences as a threat of possible U.S. action under certain circumstances. Even more pertinent in this connection is the strong unlikelihood that the U.S. could or would "use every available resource we possessed to restore real liberation to the Chinese people". Should there be continuing resistance and resultant disorder following a breakdown of peace negotiations, the U.S. would, of course, have to examine the situation with a view to deciding what course it might adopt. However, given the current situation and the estimates of the relative military capabilities of the National Government and the Chinese Communists, there is little ground for assuming that the U.S. Government would at this juncture embark upon a program of all-out military and economic aid for China.

In the light of the foregoing, it is desired that this portion of your proposed manner of approach be changed to read along the following lines: "Should this situation appear to constitute a threat to the national security and interests of the United States, the U.S. Government would have to re-examine the situation in China with a view to adopting a course of action calculated best to serve the interests of the American people and world peace."

While the Department agrees with your view that it may be visionary to imagine that the Chinese Communists can be influenced toward a more broadly tolerant policy, it also agrees with your statement that because of the important issues at stake such an approach is worth the effort. In the event that your approach achieves no results, it might be desirable to give full publicity to the nature of the discussion with the Chinese Communists and the Communist rejection of the overtures. However, every care should be taken to avoid any publicity regarding your approach to the Chinese Communist leaders and the nature of such an approach. The question of giving publicity to the proposed discussions should be referred with your recommendations to the Department for decision. In any telegraphic reports you may submit in regard to this matter, you should classify them as eyes only for the Secretary.

ACHESON

893.00/4–649 : Telegram

The Consul General at Peiping (Clubb) to the Secretary of State

PEIPING, April 6, 1949.
[Received April 7—1:10 a. m.]

570. Having reference to an instruction reputedly issued March 31 by MOI [91] Nanking regarding propaganda, all papers today carry

---

[91] Chinese Ministry of Information.

New China News Agency editorial entitled "We Demand Nanking Government Surrender to the People". High points as follows:

It was stated by Mao Tze-tung in his reply to telegram from Fu Tso-yi that Communists welcome all civil and military officials of Kmt Government who pursued past policy of counter-revolutionary civil war, if only such officials discriminate between right and wrong and express repentance deeds in order to further progress liberation of people and peaceful solution domestic problems.

If responsible and important party administrative and military personnel fail to act in that manner, they will be unable to avoid trial and punishment by the people. Fu Tso-yi in his telegram April 1 chose that line but many major Nanking Kmt personnel have not acted likewise but contrariwise advocated "equal and glorious peace". Substance of such advocacy is disclosed in MOI order under reference.

Demand by those elements for "equal and glorious peace" shows refusal assume responsibility for civil war, refusal to hand over government to the people, desire preserve reactionary forces in order make comeback in future. They even demand restoration position existing at time defunct PCC [92] of January, 1946, demand unconditional cease fire, demand that People's Liberation Army shall not cross Yangtze to liberate 200,000,000 oppressed fellow-countrymen in south; in short they pretend they are not group of war criminals, that they have not been finally defeated and demand that they be placed on equal footing with Chinese revolutionary people and people's leader, the CCP, who have been struggling for independence, democracy and peace.

"No equality should be tolerated between the reactionary and treasonous war criminals and the revolutionary people." During 44 months since Japanese surrender Kmt reactionary and treasonous government, with support American imperialism, rejected many times the people's demand for peace, destroyed the agreements signed with CCP and other democratic parties to start civil war which resulted in human catastrophe unprecedented in history civil war in China— as stated by Li Tsung-jen.

Unexpectedly the Chinese people and CCP propose that they may expiate their crime through merit under conditions of the eight terms of peace. War criminals cannot demand that so-called glory from the revolutionary people. For them to take some glorious action would be for them to surrender to the people. Kmt party administrative and military personnel must understand that if they are unwilling to take initiative and surrender to the people, unwilling to confess their counter-revolutionary sins, unwilling to hand over counter-revolutionary arms in both military and political fields, there would not be true peace between them and the people. "In China today there is only one

---

[92] Political Consultative Conference.

kind of peace and that is a peace whereby counter-revolutionary elements effect basic surrender to revolutionary forces of the people."
This is political prerequisite to acceptance of the eight terms of peace
which must be fulfilled strictly. Such surrender would be advantageous to the people and the fatherland and Kmt personnel could
then expect pardon by the people and the fatherland. "They would
be able thus get much more glory than they would be able to obtain
by refusing to surrender to the people and continuing meaningless
struggle, only to be eventually arrested one by one and tried and
punished."

Sent Department, Nanking 349, OffEmb Canton 41, Shanghai 391,
By mail to Tientsin.

CLUBB

893.00/4–749 : Telegram

The Ambassador in China (Stuart) to the Secretary of State

NANKING, April 7, 1949—9 a. m.
[Received April 7—3 :50 a. m.]

719. Alacrity with which Communist propaganda has seized upon
Nanking student riot April 1 as excuse with which further to darken
prospects of peace negotiations lends important substance to belief
expressed in Embtel 701, April 4 that incident was instigated by
Communists. Their April 2 broadcast from Peiping played up subject even before facts were clearly known in Nanking. But it was
their April 4 broadcast which carried their "righteous indignation"
to such extreme as to leave no doubt regarding its hypocritical nature
and fact that Communists are engaged in substituting for real reasons
ostensible reasons to break off peace negotiations at first opportunity.

It seems to us that Communist propaganda has become so violent
as to be explicable only on grounds that Communists are attempting
to conceal their complicity in student tragedy while simultaneously
using it as weapon with which further to intimidate Nationalist
Government into practically unconditional surrender or, failing this,
as excuse to continue their drive to smash opposition. Only by these
postulates can we explain such Communist conclusions as: "(Nanking
massacre) again tells Chinese people that if it wants to fight for
existence, freedom and peace, it must resolutely, thoroughly, and completely sweep away this pack of man-eating (Kmt war criminal)
wild beasts." "The effective way of exterminating Chiang Kai-shek
reactionary bloc is none other than to rely on PLA to capture them
alive one by one." "Nanking massacre clearly shows that no revision
must be permitted with regard to all eight terms, above all first term
dealing with punishment of war criminals." "The Nanking reaction-

ary government has very seriously undermined premise for peace negotiations and blocked road to peace with blood and corpses of revolutionary youths." "PLA is preparing to cross south of Yangtze to sweep away all murderers." "Day is not far when patriotic peoples sacrificed in Nanking and other massacres will be avenged, and people south of Yangtze and throughout country liberated."

By way of counterbalance to breast beating of Communists we would like to reaffirm our other conclusion expressed in Embassy's reference telegram that Government has handled incident with commendable restraint, both before and after its occurrence.

Sent Department; repeated Shanghai 343, Embassy Canton 230.

STUART

893.00/4–849 : Telegram

The Minister-Counselor of Embassy in China (Clark) to the Secretary of State

CANTON, April 8, 1949—4 p. m.
[Received April 9—9 :23 a. m.]

Cantel 199.   April 7 joint session Central Executive Committee and Central Political Council Canton was attended by more than 30 party notables, including Sun Fo, Chen Li-fu,[93] Wu Teh-chen, Yu Han-mou,[94] Hsueh Yueh,[95] Chen Chi-tang,[96] Pang Kung-tzu [97] and Chiang Monlin.[98]

We are reliably informed by member of CEC who recently arrived from Taiwan to attend these meetings and who is known to represent Chen Cheng that Premier Ho reported at length on military situation, stating that Red strength along Yangtze had increased to point where crossing could be expected very soon. Ho said Government had no hope arranging cease-fire and that he personally believed there was no chance reasonable peace settlement.

George Yeh then presented summary of aims China's foreign policy, stating that status Taiwan was most vital question at present. Yeh indicated that since US is thought to consider Taiwan an essential link in its Western Pacific defense chain, there was little likelihood that it would be allowed to fall to Reds.

Premier then asked for advice of members present and suggested that joint session might wish reach some conclusion for transmission

---

[93] Coleader with his brother, Chen Kuo-fu, of the C–C clique (Kuomintang).
[94] Formerly Commander in Chief of the Chinese Army; Military and Political Affairs Director for South China.
[95] Governor of Kwangtung.
[96] Administrator of Hainan Island.
[97] Pang Sung-chou was a Chinese official in fiscal operations.
[98] Chairman of the Joint Commission for Rural Reconstruction.

to Cabinet on his return Nanking. Session reached no conclusion and adjourned until morning 8th.

Source stated Premier made no mention of Red emissary now Nanking (Nanking's 716, to Department [99]), although everyone Canton knows Ho was closeted with Li Tsung-jen for entire evening after emissary arrived. However, this phase peace negotiations will doubtless be discussed today's session on which Embassy expects to obtain a full report.

At April 7 reception for Canton foreign Diplomatic Corps, Premier and Foreign Minister obviously preoccupied with own concerns and limited conversations with guests to banal generalities. Premier made obvious point of conversing at length and privately with American and Soviet representatives.

Sent Department Cantel 199, repeated Nanking 182, Shanghai 132.

CLARK

893.00/4–949 : Telegram

The Minister-Counselor of Embassy in China (Clark) to the Secretary of State

CANTON, April 9, 1949—2 p. m.
[Received April 11—4 :41 a. m.]

Cantel 204. In April 8 meeting Canton Central Executive Committee Kuomintang members present voted full support for Li Tsung-jen. Question of return Generalissimo to lead opposition to Communists was not raised. Resolution passed that peace negotiations should end when and if Communists cross Yangtze. Participation in coalition with Communists was rejected and territorial settlement with Yangtze as dividing line was approved. Premier returned to Nanking to report above to Acting President.

Sent Department, repeated Nanking 184, Shanghai 134.

CLARK

893.00/4–1049 : Telegram

The Ambassador in China (Stuart) to the Secretary o, State

NANKING, April 10, 1949—noon.
[Received April 10—4 :22 a. m.]

740. Generalissimo has volunteered to two recent visitors information that he will not come back public life to lead renewed resistance if peace talks fail. He is reported to have said that he will support Li in peace or in war, only condition being that Li does not sell out to Communists in peace negotiations. Generalissimo added that he

[99] April 6, p. 229.

was prepared to resist pressure from his supporters to stage come-back. Our two informants are General Yen Hsi-shan [1] and General Sun Li-jen [2] who visited Chikow separately but who both brought back reports in above sense. General Sun went on to express his personal conviction that Generalissimo meant what he said.

Sent Department 740, repeated OffEmb Canton 237, AmConGen Shanghai 354, pouched Taipei.

STUART

893.00/4–1149 : Telegram

The Ambassador in China (Stuart) to the Secretary of State

NANKING, April 11, 1949.
[Received April 11—3 :13 a. m.]

742. Translation text of Acting President's telegram April 7 to Mao Tse-tung appearing in official Kmt organ *Chung Yang Jih Pao* April 9 follows:

"Since I assumed charge of the Government, I have been braving all difficulties in my determination to seek peace and my sincerity must have been fully recognized by your party as well as other demo-cratic leaders.

"Peace talks have now been initiated. The Government delegates have arrived in Peiping in response to your invitation. Peace discus-sions are also to be conducted on basis of eight conditions which your party has brought up.

"At this juncture, I am fully cognizant of the horrors brought about by the war, the sufferings of our people, and mistakes which have been unavoidable in course of human history. For this reason I am led to a feeling of anxiety over difficulties which may be encountered in course of peace talks.

"Upholding view that I should be the first to suffer from hunger and cold, I now take it upon myself to make a further manifestation of my desire, I am personally prepared to undergo the severest punish-ment, even to extent of being thrown into cauldron of boiling water for past mistakes which the Government might have committed, and which might constitute an impediment to progress of peace talks such as the questions involving war criminals.

"As to fundamental policies for future of our nation, Government is prepared to carry out fully the immortal teachings of the late Dr. Sun Yat-sen, by cooperating with your party and taking up jointly with all democratic elements the task of building a new China.

"Moreover, at the present moment when the international situation is fraught with such uncertainties, there is a greater call for coopera-tion between the Kuomintang and the Communist Party. If both of us will fully uphold this basic principle, all other issues will prove easy of solution.

---

[1] Governor of Shansi.
[2] Deputy Director of Military and Political Affairs for Southeast China.

"I have personally no other wish but that the war will end and be replaced by peace, and that the people will be delivered from their present sufferings.   My intentions are open to the closest scrutiny.   I hope you will appreciate my well-meant intentions."

Sent Department, repeated Shanghai and OffEmb Canton unnumbered.

STUART

893.00/4–1149 : Telegram

The Ambassador in China (Stuart) to the Secretary of State

NANKING, April 11, 1949—10 a. m.
[Received April 11—3 :26 a. m.]

743. See Embassy's Presstel April 11.[3]   Mao's reply, April [11?] broadcast Peiping radio, to Acting President's message on peace negotiations has lessened tension here somewhat.   It is interpreted in Chinese official circles as polite, conciliatory and step toward getting formal negotiations back on track following brutal feeler of "ultimatum".   Li Tsung-jen described latter as Chinese merchant's asking price, which he said he would counter with customer's usual first offer.

Sent Department; repeated Embassy Canton 239, Shanghai 356.

STUART

893.00/4–1149 : Telegram

The Ambassador in China (Stuart) to the Secretary of State

NANKING, April 11, 1949—11 a. m.
[Received April 11—3 :23 a. m.]

744. Ho Ying-chin's visit Canton considered here beneficial and to have contributed measurably to better understanding, cooperation between Nanking Government and Canton Kmt factions.   Premier and President Legislative Yuan[4] inform us they brought back following four conditions as Canton requirements for acceptable peace:

(1) Peace terms must protect welfare of Chinese people, economic, human rights, etc.
(2) They should preserve Chinese cultural tradition.
(3) They should be in accord with principles of UN.
(4) Cease-fire order is necessary to prove sincerity of CCP and this must mean no crossing of Yangtze.

Ho and Tung Kuan-hsien find conditions much more moderate than might have been expected from extreme right-wing of party and are

---

[3] *Supra.*
[4] Tung Kuan-hsien.

accordingly encouraged at prospects unity between Nanking and Canton in Government's continuing peace efforts.

Sent Department; repeated Embassy Canton 240, Shanghai 357.

STUART

893.00/4–1349 : Telegram

The Consul General at Shanghai (Cabot) to the Secretary of State

SHANGHAI, April 13, 1949.
[Received April 13—5 :58 a. m.]

1180. Local English-language press 12th carried AP despatch datelined Hong Kong 11 (possibly not yet seen by Department), reporting statement that day by Lung Yun [5] to press conference calling on Li Tsung-jen to accept Mao's eight-point peace terms.

Lung is quoted as saying no shame involved in surrender and advising Li against accepting advice from "behind the scenes" manipulators, warning Li that, in event Nationalist Government attempts hold Yunnan, he, Lung, would "join with the people to overthrow the forces of reaction". He, Lung, said he would prefer Communists in power in Yunnan to present regime.

Lung further quoted as asserting that Communists and "democratic elements" are fighting for peace, elimination of oppression, imperialism and feudalism, that Communists are following Sun Yat-sen's principles, and that opposing them is Chiang Kai-shek who wants "perpetuate himself in power and continue to suppress the people", but whose prospects for success are nil. Lung accused Chiang of attempting run peace negotiations from Chikow. According to article, "Lung turned down Li's offer of a responsible position in the Yunnan government, saying he was afraid of Chiang Kai-shek's agents in Yunnan".

"Questioned about the possibility of China's joining in any Pacific pact comparable to the Atlantic Pact, Lung said China would stand alone rather than join the Western Allies."

Sent Department 1180, repeated Nanking 676, Canton 259, Kunming 21, via pouch to Hong Kong.

CABOT

893.00/4–1449 : Telegram

The Consul General at Peiping (Clubb) to the Secretary of State

PEIPING, April 14, 1949.
[Received April 14—4 :32 a. m.]

614. Press today carries following New China News Agency item datelined Peiping April 13 :

---

[5] Governor of Yunnan, 1927–45.

"Discussions Chinese Communist Party terms on basis (Mao Tsetung's) eight points have been carried on through 12 days. During these 12 days two sides informally exchanged opinions respecting all types problems. As from today there was entry upon stage formal negotiations."

Sent Department 614; repeated Nanking 385, OffEmb Canton 53, Shanghai 417, by mail Tientsin.

CLUBB

893.00/4–1449 : Telegram

The Minister-Counselor of Embassy in China (Clark) to the Secretary of State

CANTON, April 14, 1949—3 p. m.
[Received 8 :54 p. m.]

Cantel 211. . . . Source is informed . . . that Provincial Governor Hsueh Yueh [6] convened policy-making meeting Cantonese military political leaders after return Premier Ho to Nanking. Meeting decided to oppose any settlement between Communists and Nanking Government which involves "surrender", to oppose settlement involving coalition which would bring Communists into Kwangtung Provincial and local governments, to support settlement on territorial basis keeping Communists militarily and politically out of South China and to seek ways and means improve local military position so as to prevent Communist invasion South China. Sense of these decisions generally supported by Cantonese members Legislative Yuan and National Assembly, who are much dissatisfied with Premier's report on situation made during his recent visit here and are fearful Acting President and Premier will seek commit Nationalist Government to settlement involving too great concessions to Communists.

Informant was positive in statements and from above as well as from general tenor his comments it would appear that united efforts for peace between Cantonese factions and present Government may not be as complete as claimed by Premier and reported in Nanking's 744 of 11 April to Department.

Sent Department Cantel 211; repeated Nanking 186, Shanghai 136.

CLARK

---

[6] Governor of Kwangtung.

893.00/4–1449 : Telegram

The Minister-Counselor of Embassy in China (Clark) to the Secretary of State

CANTON, April 14, 1949—3 p. m.
[Received 11 :37 p. m.]

Cantel 212. Hsueh Yueh confirms that he and Kuangtung legislators will not accept coalition either nationally or provincially, Cantel 211, repeated Nanking 186, Shanghai 136, April 14, 3 p. m. They retain deep suspicion that Li Tsung-jen may be led sell out [to] Communists and Hsueh Yueh says he has received direct word from Peiping that Li Chi-shen, Fu Tso-yi and others who have succumbed to Communist propaganda are much restricted in their activities and are unhappy.

Sent Department; repeated Nanking 187, Shanghai 137.

CLARK

893.01/4–1549 : Telegram

The Minister-Counselor of Embassy in China (Clark) to the Secretary of State

CANTON, April 15, 1949—9 a. m.
[Received April 15—1 :12 a. m.]

Cantel 214. Chen Tai-chu, director American Section Foreign Office, but long associated Soviet affairs, expressed opinion that action Vishinsky [8] in leaving sickbed to permit Chinese Ambassador, Moscow, pay farewell call before assuming functions Minister Foreign Affairs, was to give public support to Nationalist Government as opposed Communist. He feels likewise that principal reasons Soviet Ambassador China and entire staff came Canton when Government moved was to support Nationalist Government. He is convinced Soviets fear emergence nationalism among Chinese Communists with possible resulting independence Soviet direction. For same reasons he believes Soviets would be reluctant see extension Communist domination over all China, at least at this stage.

Sent Department; repeated Nanking 189, Shanghai 139.

CLARK

893.00/4–1549 : Telegram

The Ambassador in China (Stuart) to the Secretary of State

NANKING, April 15, 1949—11 a. m.
[Received April 15—2 :54 a. m.]

768. Acting President has sent another appeal to me for assistance. He asked if it would not be possible for US Government make some

---

[8] A. Ya. Vyshinsky, Soviet Deputy Minister for Foreign Affairs.

kind of statement deterring Communists from crossing Yangtze. What he has in mind is apparently statement by the President or Secretary to the effect that Communist crossing of Yangtze would be considered threat to security of US and that should such military operation be undertaken US would have to give consideration to appropriate measures to be taken. Statement in a press conference in reply to pertinent question might prove most suitable method or some interested Senator such as Connally [9] might give his views on implications of Communists coming south of river.

I have every sympathy with Acting President in his efforts contain Communists north of Yangtze. His appeal is further evidence of desperate position of Nationalist Government vis-à-vis Communists and small confidence he places in peace negotiations Peiping. Any statement of sympathy from US at this time would encourage him enormously. I am not, however, able to support Li's request unless US Government prepared to back up such statement by some kind effective assistance. Since Acting President's request requires reply, I would be grateful for Department's instructions.

Repeated American Embassy Canton 252, Shanghai 376.

STUART

893.00/4–1549 : Telegram

The Vice Consul at Chungking (McGeary) to the Secretary of State

CHUNGKING, April 15, 1949—5 p. m.
[Received 11:02 p. m.]

40. Chang Tu-lun, Secretary General Political Commission [of] Southwest Military Political Administration, former mayor Chungking, former governor Hupeh, states if peace talks fail Chang Chun will return from Nanking with full powers for control of southwest. This would mean full autonomy with only nominal ties to Li and Ho government.

Chang Tu-lun insists leaders this area will resist Communists (contrary to other information we have reported) but admits available forces inadequate if Communists place major emphasis on conquest Szech[uan]. He discounts likelihood troop defections but admits students, peasants and labor elements might create serious trouble in event Communist attack.

He states present Sikang unrest will not result in removal of Liu Wen-hui [10] but increased powers for Chang Chun might be followed by replacement top officials if they cannot or do not produce although

---

[9] Senator Tom Connally, of Texas, Chairman of the Senate Foreign Relations Committee.
[10] Governor of Sikang.

main effort will be to obtain capable second and middle rank officials. Despatch follows.[11]

Sent Nanking 68, repeated Canton 17, Department 40.

McGeary

893.00/4–1649 : Telegram

The Ambassador in China (Stuart) to the Secretary of State

NANKING, April 16, 1949—11 a. m.
[Received April 16—3 :16 a. m.]

771. Before expiration of Communist "ultimatum" (see my 716 to Department April 6, repeated Canton 228, Shanghai 342) on April 12, two things happened which influenced their subsequent action:

(1) Li Tsung-jen sent humble, politically astute message to Mao Tse-tung; (2) local press published story of ultimatum with fair degree accuracy. These developments, according to Li's advisor Kan, gave Communists cause [*pause*] and nothing more has been heard about ultimatum or deadline in those precise terms. In fact during this period Mao dispatched his polite, conciliatory message (see my 743 to Department April 11, repeated Canton 239, Shanghai 356) and in discussions in Peiping is reported to have replied to Nationalist delegates' remonstrances that crossing of Yangtze by Communist troops would be natural consequence of coalition government at which time Communist troops should be able to come south and Nationalist troops move north.

April 14, however, Communists reverted to sterner position with demand made through Nationalist delegation Peiping that as token Nationalist Government good faith Communist military force be allowed now to establish bridgeheads on south bank Yangtze at two points: (1) Kiangyin (first fortified point on Yangtze upstream from Moluh); (2) nine districts (hsien) opposite Anking. Government instructed its delegate Peiping to reply this demand not acceptable.

Communists have repeated on several occasions and constantly revert to proposal for peaceful crossing of Yangtze. It would seem to indicate no great confidence in their own ability to force crossing. While there is no time limit on this most recent demand, Nationalist Government continues to be apprehensive of resumption military offensive from day-to-day. Government feels Communists have not settled down serious discussion eight points pending efforts induce Government permit peaceful crossing of river.

There have been, however, some discussions between Nationalist and Communist delegates on first of Mao's eight points, that is, war

[11] Not printed.

criminals. Position Nationalist delegates took was that it was unfortunate to insist on designation of various Chinese leaders as war criminals in civil struggle. Mao Tse-tung is reported to have replied that names could be eliminated from agreement with clause merely stating that those guilty of war crimes would be punished. This was received in local government circles as important conclusion on part of Communists and possible useful formula for point one.

Sent Department 771; repeated Embassy Canton 255, Shanghai 379, Peiping 126.

STUART

893.00/4–1649 : Telegram

The Ambassador in China (Stuart) to the Secretary of State

NANKING, April 16, 1949—noon.
[Received April 16—3 :08 a. m.]

772. Acting President has invited me to conference Monday afternoon with my British, French, Italian colleagues. He wants to discuss current Chinese situation with us all and asked that meeting be kept confidential as possible.

Sent Department; repeated OffEmb Canton 256.

STUART

893.00/4–1649 : Telegram

The Ambassador in China (Stuart) to the Secretary of State

NANKING, April 16, 1949—6 p. m.
[Received April 16—9 :44 a. m.]

777. At request of Ma Hung-kwei [12] I met and talked to him yesterday in house of mutual friend (see my 758 to Dept April 13,[13] repeated Canton 247). He is here to discuss with Acting President and others his plan for northern federation, either within framework of Nationalist China or independently to continue resistance to Communists. His plan would include provinces of Suiyuan, Ningsia, Kansu, as much of Sinkiang as possible and parts of Shensi and Shansi. He says that for geographical reasons it will be difficult for Communists to infiltrate with any degree of effectiveness in this area.

He asked about possibilities of American advisors for region. He said that during time army advisory group was here he had asked Generalissimo many times for their assistance in advisory capacity without success. He also mentioned US experts in irrigation, agriculture, engineering as desirable, necessary for his future plans for

[12] Governor of Ningsia.
[13] Not printed.

relatively autonomous North Central China. He expressed desire to visit US ostensibly for medical treatment, where he would seek support for his plan from rich overseas Chinese and would, of course, like to talk to interested officials in Washington.

It has occurred to me that ECA might as preliminary response to this appeal take more active interest in that area sending more of its people into northern provinces to make surveys and report on possibilities future US assistance.

Sent Department 777, repeated OffEmb Canton 260.

STUART

893.01/4–1849 : Telegram

The Ambassador in China (Stuart) to the Secretary of State

NANKING, April 18, 1949—noon.
[Received April 18—7:21 a. m.]

782. At request Acting President, I arranged meeting for him with British, French, Australian Ambassadors my house last evening. He came accompanied only by his advisor-interpreter Kan Chieh-hou. (See my 772 to Department April 16, repeated Canton 256.)

Acting President informed me and my colleagues that Huang Shao-hsiung had returned from Peiping with written draft agreement. Draft had been prepared by CCP and given to Nationalist delegates in early stage of discussions. After days of arguing Nationalist delegates have succeeded in achieving slight drafting changes but nothing of substance and they emphasize to their Government here that this present draft must be accepted as no more changes possible. CCP has given Government until April 20 to accept or reject draft. If not accepted by deadline, CCP will break off peace negotiations. Li Tsung-jen has replied that since some Government leaders are in Shanghai and since document will require study by full Cabinet, he will require 2 or 3 more days which in any event will not carry deadline beyond 23d.

Dr. Kan then read out in English résumé of most important points of draft agreement.

Begin Résumé. Preamble points out mistakes made by Nanking Government, that it has lost confidence of people, that its armed forces are defeated, reviews efforts for peace since January 1 ending in appointment of plenipotentiaries by two opposing forces, says they agree Nanking Government has full responsibility for mistaken policies of war and agree to following terms:

(1) War criminals responsible for initiating and carrying out civil war shall be punished; however, leniency will be shown if they per-

form useful service to CCP and assist in liberation of remainder of China by peaceful means. The case of Japanese war criminal Okamura and 260 other Japanese war criminals shall be left open to be dealt with finally by new democratic coalition government.

(2) Present constitution to be abolished. New PCC and democratic coalition government will formulate new statute.

(3) Legal status of Nanking Government shall be denounced.

(4) All armed forces shall be reorganized into regular People's Liberation Army. Reorganization shall be carried out by National Reorganization Committee which shall have Communist as chairman and Nationalist as vice chairman and on which Communists shall have one extra member. Reorganization divided into two periods:

(a) Nationalist forces in areas held by People's Liberation Army shall turn over peacefully and thence move to designated places; military establishments, military matériel likewise turned over.

(b) Ground, naval, air force shall be reorganized into regular PLA after their move to designated places and according to PLA system. Nanking Government undertakes preserve, protect military establishment matériel where PLA has not yet arrived. (Military reorganization committee affects only Nationalist Army and not PLA which remains under jurisdiction People's Revolutionary Military Committee Peiping.)

(5) Properties such as banks, mines, vessels, business firms acquired through political power or by wealthy families be confiscated as well as all enterprises financed by wealthy officials.

(6) Following arrival of PLA there shall be general reduction rents, interest rates and redistribution of land.

(7) Nanking Government shall turn over to democratic coalition government all treaties and agreements concluded as well as open and secret despatches and documents. Democratic coalition government will denounce or revise treaties which betray or are detrimental to interests of Chinese people.

(8) Until establishment of democratic coalition government, Nanking Government will function in consultation with people's revolutionary military committee. It will help PLA in taking over various areas under Nationalist Government control including local government. Nanking Government will preserve peace and order; preserve all mines, banks, ships, airplanes, warehouses, communications, antiques, gold, silver, bullion, foreign exchange and turn them over to democratic coalition government after latter's establishment. When this has finally been accomplished, Nanking Government will then declare its own demise. *End of Résumé.*

Huang Shao-hsiung also brought oral message to effect that when PLA crosses Yangtze under terms of above agreement it shall be understood that they will promptly occupy and control six Yangtze basin provinces of Honan, Hupeh, Kiangsi, Anhwei, Kiangsu and Chekiang. Also Nationalist Government shall provide for Communist occupation promptly of Lungwing [*sic*], an area between provinces of Shensi and Kansu.

Acting President told us he felt sure terms would be unacceptable to his Government. He said he had worked hard for peace, his delegation had spent days in Peiping defending Nationalist position, but now with this reply he was convinced peaceful settlement could not be reached with Communists. He went on to say that some members of Government might feel that these terms should be accepted because China's war-time allies and powers friendly to her had indicated no willingness to come to her assistance, not even with moral support; that chances of successful resistance to Communists under these circumstances were slight. Li then said he would be grateful for our comments and advice on what he should do.

British Ambassador [14] acted as spokesman by earlier agreement among us (I felt this good opportunity for Li to hear views of someone other than US Ambassador). Stevenson said that we all appreciated confidence Acting President had shown by informing contents this secret document and expressed our great admiration for the steadfast purpose and calm patience Li Tsung-jen had shown during past several months. British Ambassador continued that he was sure in face of this record that Li would do what was best for Chinese people. As far as British Government was concerned he said they stood by Moscow Declaration of 1945 [15] pledging complete non-interference in Chinese internal affairs. Consequently while we had great sympathy with Li and present heavy responsibility and would like to help him, there was in fact nothing that his Government could do. We all said we agreed with Stevenson. Australian pointed out it was Chinese problem which must be settled by Chinese themselves. I added that President must not give up hope and [must] do what he thought was right. Li was obviously disheartened, chilled by our reserved, somewhat formal attitudes. He agreed that while it was true that this was Chinese problem in one sense, his opponent Mao Tse-tung did not believe so, referring to Mao's recent statement that in event of war between "the imperialists" and USSR, Communist China would fight with Russians.

I received impression that Government will not accept CCP terms despite noncommittal attitude of my colleagues last night and recent indications no more substantial US aid.

Sent Department, repeated OffEmb Canton 261 eyes only Clark, Shanghai 384 eyes only Cabot.

STUART

---

[14] Sir Ralph Stevenson.
[15] December 27, 1945; Department of State *Bulletin*, December 30, 1945, p. 1027.

893.00/4–1849 : Telegram

The Ambassador in China (Stuart) to the Secretary of State

NANKING, April 18, 1949—5 p. m.
[Received April 19—5 :15 a. m.]

784. General Pai Chung-hsi called on me this morning to report that Acting President, in view of latest Communist demands (see my 782 to Department, April 18, reported Canton 261, Shanghai 384), will propose to Gimo that, peace being impossible, he should either resume full responsibilities of Presidency including military affairs or leave China, turning over all authority, national resources to Li Tsung-jen. By such steps Acting President will seek to force Gimo to end by clear cut decision present state of confusion which latter himself has [brought about?]. Elaboration of this plan calls for suggestion that Gimo go abroad on mission of arousing peoples of Southeast Asia to dangers of Communism as manifested in China. He could continue on such mission to India, Europe and possibly US. Should Gimo act on this suggestion, Acting President intends replacing Wellington Koo [16] by Kan Chieh-hou [17] in Washington.

Sent Department, repeated OffEmb Canton 263, Shanghai 390.

STUART

893.00/4–1949 : Telegram

The Minister-Counselor of Embassy in China (Clark) to the Secretary of State

CANTON, April 19, 1949—9 a. m.
[Received April 19—6 :38 a. m.]

Cantel 232. Sources termed by Canton British ConGen as "very reliable" state Communists relaxing demands in Peiping negotiations to point where settlement with Li Tsung-jen representatives becoming possible. Communists reportedly agreeing to coalition government to be formed by PCC in which Ministers of Defense, Foreign Affairs, and Interior go to Communists with balance to other groups. Li and followers to have place in this government. Source also reported that Gimo and followers and Cantonese would not accept such an agreement, but would continue resistance. In discussing this report with us, British ConGen stated belief Communists probably willing modify original demands if Li and followers would agree re-orient foreign policy in pro-Soviet, anti-Western Power direction, and that this was probably one of principal Communist requirements in present situation.

---

[16] V. K. Wellington Koo, Chinese Ambassador in the United States.
[17] Personal adviser to Acting President Li Tsung-jen.

While Communists have not up to present given any overt indication abandon stringent interpretation eight points of Mao Tse-tung as basis peace, if they have become convinced of their ability form coalition which they can dominate and if they convinced that following formation coalition there will not remain any residual political entity able to serve as effective base for counter revolution, it is conceivable that they would make concessions which would entice Acting President and followers into coalition and so facilitate crossing Yangtze and penetration South China. Account of British ConGen is borne out by Cantel 212, dated April 14 and also by Shanghai's 687 to Embassy, repeated to Department as 1206 dated 15 April.[18] Despatch quoted in latter presumably by Ravenholt who has excellent sources Nanking and who is careful reporter.

Also, we consider ConGen's appraisal Communist foreign policy requirements in this situation as probably valid. Sino-Communists' alignment with USSR on international questions has been complete. Sino-Communists have spared no efforts alienate United States even though by conciliation American opinion so as to permit receipt American economic aid they could immeasurably facilitate achievement their social and economic aims. This propensity place requirements international Communism and Soviet aggrandizement before needs their own people would argue their decision relax prosecution domestic political revolution toward logical goal if by so doing they could commit large non-Communist grouping to anti-American front. It is true that Li has given no indication adoption such course. However, it must be clear to him that he has little or no hope creating effective resistance movement which would make it possible for us help him. In this situation, were rejection of *rapprochement* with Western Powers to gain him even slight hope political survival, he might well choose adopt such course. Our response Acting President request for financial support, Embtel 709 of 6 April,[19] and more recent request for American statement re Yangtze crossing, Embtel 768 of April 15, may well help him make up his mind this point.

Sent Department, repeated Nanking 200, Shanghai 148.

CLARK

893.00/4–1949 : Telegram

The Minister-Counselor of Embassy in China (Clark) to the Secretary of State

CANTON, April 19, 1949—11 a. m.
[Received April 19—6:10 a. m.]

Cantel 233. We agree on desirability encouraging Ma Hung-kwei (Nanking 777, April 16). Recent reports suggest that Mohammedan

---

[18] Latter not printed.
[19] Vol. IX, p. 753.

leaders Northwest are taking all possible action necessary keep Communists from their territories.   Besides recruiting and redisposing forces and spending own funds [to] arm them, Ma brothers are sinking ancient differences with Mongolians in attempt create united anti-Communist front.   Given resources [of] parties concerned, scale effort necessarily small, but honest attempt apparently being made to firm up effective resistance movement virtually unparalleled elsewhere in country.   If such resistance carried out, given difficulties terrain, temper and fighting qualities Muslim and Mongolian troops and probable preoccupation of Communists elsewhere, movement might well prove source considerable embarrassment to Communists.

As Nanking suggests, ECA technical advisors might be made vehicle this encouragement.   ECA currently has mission in area and by strengthening it with personnel covertly detailed for specific purpose advising Northwestern provincial administrations, Ma and followers would doubtless be considerably heartened.   If carefully carried out, such action should be inconspicuous and not involve US in embarrassing commitments.   On other hand, flat refusal Ma request might alienate him to detriment our interests.

Sent Department Cantel 233; repeated Nanking 202.

CLARK

893.00/4–1949 : Telegram

The Minister-Counselor of Embassy in China (Clark) to the Secretary of State

CANTON, April 19, 1949—noon.
[Received April 19—3:41 a. m.]

Cantel 234.   George Yeh, Acting Foreign Minister, says press reports Communist peace terms founded [*unfounded?*]; that they are of course unacceptable, and that in this connection he returning Nanking April 22, but expects be back Canton within "short time". Tung Lin, other Vice Minister, will return Canton prior departure Yeh.

Sent Department Cantel 234; repeated Nanking 203, Shanghai 150.

CLARK

893.00/4–1949 : Telegram

The Chargé in the Soviet Union (Kohler) to the Secretary of State

Moscow, April 19, 1949—7 p. m.
[Received April 19—3:14 p. m.]

971. Not only content, but space accorded it by *Pravda* suggest significance statement by Jen Pi-shih at CCP Youth Congress

(Embtel 949, April 18 [20]). This seems to Embassy on basis information reaching us to be most important CCP policy statement to be issued in many months. Embassy will not undertake analysis which Nanking much more capable doing. We only desire point out that statement seems to us be clear effort publicly serve notice that CCP on straight narrow orthodox Moscow path and quash rumors possibility Titoist [21] deviations. Emphasis on industrialization and statement center of gravity moved from countryside to city has ring of pledge of faith to Cominform and final determination and proclamation of line already hinted (Embtel 259, February 2 [20]).

Embassy believes China problem at top Politburo agenda; in fact reliable source reports Molotov [22] now primarily concerned China (A–390, April 18 [20]). Lack editorial comment on Chinese problem probably due its restriction as subject too hot for any but highest level to handle. Kremlin obviously cannot risk loss of fruits greatest victory since Russian revolution and therefore we can be sure best talent [and] maximum energy being concentrated to steer Chinese developments in way Moscow desires and to guarantee no deviation or heresy will occur.

Permanent identity Mao's and Kremlin's policies is of course great question. Mao enjoys personal prestige and adulation not permitted leaders most other parties.

Embassy notes that CCP has not yet descended to degree of abject Stalin-worship followed most other Communist regimes; seems interesting that Jen Pi-shih cites Mao's leadership as one reason Chinese economy will be built more quickly than Soviet economy after October revolution, and neglects mention Stalin or Lenin. However, all indications point to present Stalin–Mao solidarity and uncertainties of CCP–USSR relations are uncertainties of future and not of present.

We believe that meanwhile Soviets encourage propaganda that Chinese cannot be easily absorbed (Cantel 181, April 1 to Department) and are even pleased at dissemination in West of idea Mao will turn Tito. If Western vigilance can thus be weakened, Moscow benefits. For this reason, we think unfortunate that US public opinion should be led to accept comfortable feeling Mao rebel at heart. Healthier attitude would be public assumption no rift is possible.

Facing discouraging Chinese situation, seems to us we must work as hard to develop Soviet–CCP rift as Molotov must be working to

---

[20] Not printed.
[21] Marshal Josip Broz Tito, head of the Yugoslav Communist Party and State, defected from Moscow leadership in June 1948.
[22] V. M. Molotov, Soviet Minister for Foreign Affairs.

prevent it. With full realization optimism not justified, we must explore every way and means to break the Moscow hold on China.

Sent Department 971, repeated Nanking 43, Canton 11.

KOHLER

893.00/4–1949 : Telegram

The Ambassador in China (Stuart) to the Secretary of State

NANKING, April 19, 1949.
[Received April 20—1:29 a. m.]

795. Vernacular press April 19 carries statement on peace talks released by Kmt Central Executive Committee. Summary follows: In order counteract malicious rumors which are hindering peace talks, party is reiterating viewpoint it has consistently maintained. First point to be understood is that Acting President Li and Premier Ho are conducting peace talks with full support of people and party. Thus, Kmt Central Standing Committee on April 7 passed following resolution concerning peace talks:

(1) To demonstrate sincerity, both sides should issue immediate cease-fire order. Communist crossing of river during talks would demonstrate their lack of sincerity and Government would have to recall its peace delegates and declare Communists responsible for rupture of negotiations.

(2) Foreign policy should be designed to preserve world peace in accordance with UN Charter [23] and to maintain spirit of national independence.

(3) In order preserve people's free way of life, policy of violence should cease and people's freedoms and their lives and property should be legally protected.

(4) Armies of both sides should be reorganized under conditions of equality in areas they now occupy. April 14 Kmt CSC passed following additional resolution:

(5) Prior to revision of constitution and setting up of new government, areas of control for each side should be demarcated.

Kmt has always worked solely for realization of San Min Chu I [24] and has no intention of monopolizing power. However, it can never permit changing name of Chinese Republic, depriving people of basic rights guaranteed them by the constitution, impairing of China's sovereignty and independence or effecting of social reforms by violent means.

Sent Department 795; repeated OffEmb Canton and Shanghai unnumbered.

STUART

---

[23] Signed at San Francisco, June 26, 1945; for text, see Department of State Treaty Series No. 993, or 59 Stat. (pt. 2) 1031.
[24] Three People's Principles formulated by the late Sun Yat-sen.

893.00/4–1949 : Airgram

The Ambassador in China (Stuart) to the Secretary of State

NANKING, April 19, 1949.
[Received May 18—12 :49 p. m.]

A–84. Beginning faintly in the New Year message of Chiang Kai-shek but becoming more positive and with an appealingly ironic note after Li Tsung-jen took over, the Government has done everything within reason to secure a negotiated peace. Li risked inner solidarity within the Kmt by accepting the extremely harsh Eight Points of Mao Tse-tung as a basis for discussion and sent a well-chosen delegation to the place designated by the CCP. Beginning April 1 these delegates held informal discussions with Mao and others, but the net result of the 2 weeks thus occupied was to soften a few phrases in a lengthy "Agreement" prepared in advance which the Government leaders were required to sign without further alteration. Meanwhile two specific demands were made for crossing the Yangtze at certain points and yielding other vital concessions before formal talks had even begun. These were contrary to the whole spirit of the mutually accepted terms for a conference. But on April 16 one of Li's special representatives in Peiping flew back with the document which had been the sole basis for discussion on the part of the CCP. All the other procedure had therefore been irrelevant.

This document is valuable for a study of Communist theory and practice in general with special reference to that of the CCP. These latter were given every inducement to be reasonable by the tact, patience and humility with which Li approached them after the retirement of the Gimo and the withdrawal of the more timid or reactionary Kmt members to Canton, and even more by the longing of the Chinese people for peace. Allowance should be made for the deeply suspicious Communist attitude as well as for the quite natural intoxication of success. But this document represents careful premeditation among their most highly-trained and experienced makers of policy. It is therefore a revelation of their spirit and intentions. It forces all who have opposed or disagreed with them to make public confession of error and a cringing apology coupled with evidential deeds or to be denounced and treated as war criminals. In this and in all other ways it is implacable, uncompromising, relentless. This, together with their iron discipline and close-knit organization, is almost a new phenomenon in China. Before its onslaught almost all resistance will evaporate or be driven to peripheral regions where it can be systematically eradicated. Opportunists will join the movement. There will be every temptation to show an excess of zeal by intemperate or even sadistic acts. Cautiously, perhaps at first, cultural and religious activities will be controlled or rendered innocuous. This means that missionaries will be so hampered or harassed that they will by degrees abandon the futile struggle, with possible exceptions which will be fully advertised. The same will hold true of foreign commercial interests after those useful to the Communists will have been sufficiently exploited.

It may be safely assumed that having overrun China the CCP will engage in their usual subversive and quite possibly militant attacks against Hong Kong, Macao, Indo-China and other regions of South-east Asia. It would be splendidly foresighted statesmanship for the Western powers to anticipate this by concerted and calmly calculated plans to end all colonial claims over these regions and to prepare their peoples for real independence.

This would be essential before any united policy by such nations as are now included in the North Atlantic Pact could be formulated for Eastern Asia. Japan and South Korea will before long feel the effects of a Communist-controlled China. A program led by the United States, daring in its self-abnegation and defiant in its reliance on ideological weapons, would be startling evidence of our spiritual emphasis as against military or material, and would probably prove very disconcerting to Communist strategists. The dominant note in our propaganda should be anti-aggression rather than freedom, democracy or even economic aid. The heart of the Soviet-led Communist Party issue would seem to be the "historical necessity" of conflict between the capitalist and "socialist" countries and the aggressive urge among all who hold this belief. By concentrating on this threat to world peace and to stability within each country we have a message dramatic and convincing, exposing those who join in this aggression or interference within each country as being the real imperialists.

This intolerance, this arrogant belief that they alone are right and the attempt to force confessions to this effect from others, will in the end be their undoing. It might have been hoped that with their Chinese heritage they would be less drastic. There might thus have been a blend of their reforming zeal with progressive elements in the Kmt and liberal non-partisan strains. But they have chosen to follow the orthodox pattern in step with their Soviet exemplar. This extremist bigotry and their genuine social idealism will continue to give them a dynamic energy, but—especially in a Chinese milieu—it will probably arouse a resentment which if stimulated by world opinion and other forms of assistance may restore China to a more normal political evolution.

STUART

893.00/4–2049 : Telegram

The Minister-Counselor of Embassy in China (Clark) to the Secretary of State

CANTON, April 20, 1949—9 a. m.
[Received April 20—6 :16 a. m.]

Cantel 241. George Yeh, Acting Foreign Minister, said that when Li Tsung-jen at Canton he was accused at meeting CEC of having eventual intention to sell out to Communists. Li had insisted he was no coward; had no intention of surrendering, and pled with those present not to prejudge him but to await his actions. Yeh is convinced Li will not accept Communist ultimatum and that fighting will be resumed, but he anticipates reshuffle in Cabinet. Of prime importance is to obtain leader who can hold military together in some semblance unified command and Ho Ying-chin seems only one available. Yeh said there has been talk of making Ho Supreme Commander in Chief, but Ho continues refuse. Yeh thinks, therefore, Ho will remain Premier and may assume tasks if suitable Commander in Chief unfound.

Sent Department Cantel 241; repeated Nanking 206, Shanghai 159.

CLARK

893.00/4–2049 : Telegram

The Ambassador in China (Stuart) to the Secretary of State

NANKING, April 20, 1949—noon.
[Received April 20—2 :16 a. m.]

799. Re my 784, April 18, repeated OffEmb Canton 263, Shanghai 390. Reliably informed Wu Chung-hsin, liaison between Generalissimo and Acting President, carried Communist peace proposals to Generalissimo April 17. Chang Chun known to have gone Chikow April 18. Same source informs us his mission twofold:

(1) Deliver message from Acting President to Generalissimo which states he (Li) has been unsuccessful in peace negotiations and, if Generalissimo so wishes, he should come out of retirement to lead continent [continued?] resistance. Otherwise Generalissimo should turn over full authority to Li.

(2) Attempt to convince Generalissimo that strategically speaking the defense of Yangtze is far superior to his proposed Shanghai, Hangchow, Nanchang line and in fact absolutely necessary if Communist penetration into South China is to be prevented. Wu returned Nanking April 18; Chang due 19th. Will report results visit soonest.

Sent Department, repeated Shanghai 399, OffEmb Canton 268.

STUART

893.00/4–2049 : Telegram

The Ambassador in China (Stuart) to the Secretary of State

NANKING, April 20, 1949—5 p. m.
[Received April 20—8 :16 a. m.]

805. Nationalist Government has asked for extension of time to April 25 to consider CCP draft peace agreement. Although today is Communist deadline, no reply has been received. Among themselves Nationalist Government have decided to reject agreement and to continue resistance to end. Understand present plan is to publish all delegation proceedings and related documents for people's information and at that time state publicly unable accept terms.

Chang Chun and Wu Chung-hsin have returned from Chikow. (See Embtel 799 to Department, April 20, repeated Canton 268, Shanghai 399). Their news is on the whole encouraging. Generalissimo's wavering confidence in Li greatly strengthened by Acting President's firm prompt decision to reject Communist terms and he sent word to Ho Ying-chin to support Li strongly in will to resist. He has also, according to our reports, rejected suggestion return public life lead resistance himself. Government leaders all united in decision to continue resistance and are presently working out plans unified command with Generalissimo's approval, which may include President Li, Premier Ho and General Pai Chung-hsi.

Sent Department 805, repeated OffEmb Canton 272, Shanghai 403.

STUART

___

893.00/4–2049 : Telegram

The Ambassador in China (Stuart) to the Secretary of State

NANKING, April 20, 1949—5 p. m.
[Received April 20—5 :59 a. m.]

807. National Government has sent message Communists rejecting draft peace agreement but requesting cease-fire order so discussions aimed at achieving acceptable settlement may continue. Message expected be delivered Communist in Peiping around 6 p. m.

Meanwhile Communists have informed National peace delegation Peiping that if negative answer or no answer is received to their proposals today they will consider negotiations broken off and will begin crossing river. This message signifies rejection National Government request for extension time limit to April 25.

Executive Yuan decided today to take steps for immediate removal remaining National Government's Ministries, Bureaus and offices from Nanking.

Sent Department, repeated OffEmb Canton 273, Shanghai 405.

STUART

893.00B/4–2049

The Consul General at Shanghai (Cabot) to the Ambassador in China (Stuart) [26]

No. 68   SHANGHAI, April 20, 1949.

SIR: I have read with great interest the Embassy's despatch No. 70, March 30, enclosing an interesting memorandum prepared by Mr. Bennett on the subject of Chinese Communist anti-American propaganda. While Mr. Bennett's analysis of this propaganda may well, and probably does, give the correct explanation, I feel that another explanation is possible and that it should not be fully discarded.

Totalitarian propaganda always requires a whipping boy. With Nazism it was the Jews; with Communism it is monopoly capitalism and its allegedly resultant imperialism. The downfall of Japan deprived the Chinese Communists of their favored whipping boy. The void was the more embarrassing because Chinese nationalism had a peculiarly strong antipathy for foreign imperialism and the most obvious imperialism against which it might turn was that of Soviet Russia. Alleged American imperialism was obviously the most satisfactory substitute and was therefore picked for attack. It may be said that Kuomintang propaganda showed its utter ineptitude by not only failing to counterattack on the issue of Soviet imperialism but also playing into the hands of Communist propaganda: (a) by soft pedaling attacks on Soviet Russia; and (b) by itself making forays into the field of anti-American and anti-British propaganda. It may be argued that the United States also played into the hands of Communist propaganda by various of its actions here after the renewal of the civil war, for example, by the maintenance of Marines and of the Advisory Groups in China.

It is obvious that Chinese Communist propaganda derives much of its inspiration and tactics from world Communism. It is nevertheless probable, in my opinion, that in considerable measure the propaganda is a reflection of what Chinese Communists sincerely feel. It would not be surprising, for example, if most Chinese Communists were very resentful of the aid which the United States has given to the Nationalist Government and if many of them honestly believed that this aid was given for imperialistic motives. The charge that the Nationalist Government is subservient to the United States is equally convenient from the Chinese Communist and the Soviet viewpoint.

It is impossible, however, to explain—especially with reference to their timing—the recent Chinese Communist declarations of solidarity with Soviet Russia in the event of an aggressive war against the latter,

---

[26] Copy transmitted to the Department without covering despatch; received May 3.

and Chinese Communist denunciation of the Atlantic Pact as dictated by what the Chinese Communists would logically feel to be in their own immediate interests. Clearly they reflect a Soviet Russian rather than a Chinese Communist inspiration. The most plausible explanation is that they were made because the Kremlin demanded it—either by explicit directive or by indications so unmistakable as to be tantamount thereto. It is a very cogent argument that the Chinese Communists would not gratuitously take such a strong stand in a matter not vitally affecting their interests unless they were acting in accordance with orders from the Kremlin, which presumably does feel that its vital interests are at stake.

I think nevertheless that there may be another explanation. All over the world, and particularly in the United States, there has been a great deal of public speculation as to whether the Chinese Communist movement is headed for "Titoism", more especially since Mao Tze-tung has on past occasions not followed faithfully the Communist party line as dictated by the Kremlin. He must feel that the Kremlin does not altogether trust him, and the same is believed to apply to many of the other Chinese Communist leaders. Obviously at this particular moment, the Chinese Communists must be embarrassed by all this speculation, and must be seriously concerned at its corrosive effects on the abnormally suspicious minds of the Soviet Politburo. Lip service is the cheapest kind of service to give Soviet Russia to reassure the latter of the loyalty of the Chinese Communists. It seems to me quite possible therefore that the notable vehemence in recent weeks of the Communist anti-American propaganda may well stem from a desire to reassure and placate Soviet Russia rather than from any increased spleen at the United States, and that it should not necessarily be taken as proving that the Chinese Communists are, and will remain, completely subservient to the Kremlin's orders, as has been so widely assumed. If it is assumed that some, but not all, Chinese Communist leaders take orders from Moscow, the same line of thought suggests that those not subservient to Moscow might for reasons of prudence and harmony go along with those that are in giving lip service to the party line dictated by the Soviets. In other words, the rule that nothing a Communist says is to be believed cuts both ways; the recent spate of Communist anti-American propaganda strongly suggests that the Chinese Communists are in fact subservient to Moscow, but we should not uncritically overlook the other possibility that some Chinese Communist leaders have mouthed this propaganda with tongue in cheek to conceal their intention to be eventually masters in their own house.

Respectfully yours,   JOHN M. CABOT

893.00/4–2149 : Telegram

The Minister-Counselor of Embassy in China (Clark) to the Secretary of State

CANTON, April 21, 1949—3 p. m.
[Received April 21—8 :34 a. m.]

Cantel 247. Chen Li-fu says decision last night Canton of CEC and that of Government Nanking to reject Communist terms were both unanimous. He is sanguine that bickering between various elements Kmt has terminated and that party will rally as unit for renewed resistance. He envisages complete removal Government [to] Canton, leaving CinC Armed Forces with headquarters Nanking. He is confident Air Forces and Navy will cooperate with Ground Forces and that Yangtze crossing on any important scale can be delayed months if not prevented. So far as he is aware, Generalissimo continues willingness send complete support Li Tsung-jen with no present intention resuming authority himself.

With closing ranks Kmt, Chen is sanguine effective resistance Communist advance, yet desperately wants assurances further US aid. After reviewing unhappy results our past efforts help China and our failure largely because China refused help itself, I cautioned him not to count upon further US aid unless and until Government had first demonstrated its ability with broadened basis rally support in territory it still controls for further and effective resistance on scale giving promise of ability eventually retake offensive. I mentioned our axiom "God helps him who helps himself", of which there is Chinese equivalent, and said American people could not be expected invest any more money in Kmt regime until it gave promise of offering effective alternative to Communism. Chen tried unsuccessfully to pin me down as to what would be considered effective resistance, but obviously his back was to the wall and he, like others in his position, is determined upon desperate measures to avoid the almost inevitable Communist domination of all China. Now that those who thought peace possible have been disillusioned he is sanguine Kmt with united ranks will be able rally sufficient support to prolong struggle until US can be persuaded once again intervene. Should that time come he hopes we will lay our cards frankly on the table and demand a definite *quid pro quo* for anything we give. That is the only way, he said, we could assure accomplishment ends we desire.

Sent Department Cantel 247, repeated Nanking 209, Shanghai 159.

CLARK

893.01/4–1849 : Telegram

The Secretary of State to the Ambassador in China (Stuart)

WASHINGTON, April 21, 1949—7 p. m.

501. Urtel 768 April 15. Act Pres request reftel appears be over-lapped by meeting described urtel 782 Apr 18 and overtaken by events. Dept concurs views expressed by you and ur colleagues.

As you aware only Congressional authority presently existing for aiding Chi Govt is legislation extending availability residual China Aid Act[27] funds. Dept's views this subject set forth in SecState letter to Sen Connally Mar 15[28] re McCarran proposal. For ur info, text letter to Sen Connally not released by Dept which wished to avoid possible adverse effect on Chi Govt and Li's position in negotiations with Commies. Copy letter forwarded by member Senate Fon Rel Committee without Committee's clearance to con-stituent who made letter available to press.

ACHESON

893.00/4–2149 : Telegram

The Consul General at Peiping (Clubb) to the Secretary of State

PEIPING, April 21, 1949.
[Received April 21—11 : 23 p. m.]

678. Extra just issued by *Jen Min Jih Pao* gives text Hsin Hua News Agency item dateline Peiping April 21 under headline "Nanking Kmt Government rejects domestic peace agreement. Chairman Mao [and] Commander in Chief Chu ordered whole army decisively thor-oughly clean up whole outfit, annihilate enemy *in toto*, capture all evil unrepentant war criminals, especially taking care to apprehend bandit leader Chiang Kai-shek. After great armies surround Nanking, Li Tsung-jen government will be given final opportunity to sign". Text as follows:

"Chairman Mao Tse-tung [and] Commander in Chief Chu Teh today issued order to People's Liberation Army as follows:

"Chinese People's Liberation Army first field army, comrades Peng Teh-huai, Chang Tsung-hsun, Chao Shou-shan; Chinese PLA sec-ond field army comrades Liu Po-cheng, Teng Hsiao-ping, Chang Chi-chun; Chinese PLA third field army comrades Chen Yi, Yao Shu-shih, Li Yu-lin; Chinese PLA fourth army comrades Lin Piao, Lo Jung-huan; Taiyuan front PLA comrades Hsu Hsiang-chien, Chou Shih-ti, Lo Jui-ching; whole body commanding officers and fighting men of all field armies; PLA comrades of all guerila areas in south:

"Projected domestic peace agreement coming from long period ne-gotiation between Chinese Communist Party delegation and Nanking

---

[27] Approved April 3, 1948 ; 62 Stat. 158.
[28] Vol. IX, p. 607.

Kmt delegation has been rejected by Nanking Kmt Government. Responsible officials of Nanking Kmt Government reject this domestic peace agreement because they still follow American imperialists and Kmt bandit commander Chiang Kai-shek's orders with aim preventing advance matter Chinese people's liberation with aim preventing use of peaceful methods for settling domestic problems.

"Projected domestic peace agreement comprising 8 articles and 24 clauses coming from negotiations between two sides showed generous handling of question war criminals and generous handling in respect to officers and troops Kmt armies and workers of Kmt Government and satisfactorily resolved all other problems, not without regard to interest of race and interest of people. Rejection of this agreement then shows Kmt reactionary clique has decided to launch their anti-revolutionary struggle to the end. Rejection of this agreement then shows Kmt reactionary clique in proposing January 1 of this year peace negotiations planned no more than to check PLA from advancing forward in order facilitate reactionary clique obtaining breathing spell and afterwards come rolling back in new advance to annihilate revolutionary influence. Rejection of this agreement then show[s] Nanking Li Tsung-jen government in stating they accepted 8 piece [peace] points of CCP as basis for negotiations was entirely false because if they recognize punishment of war criminals and use of democratic principles for reorganization of all Kmt reactionary troops and take over of all authority of Nanking Government and all appertaining to governmental strata, and all other basic articles, it is without reason to reject all these concrete procedures based upon the several basic points and moreover most generous. In these circumstances we order you:

"(1) Bravely to advance and strongly, definitively, cleanly to wipe out entirely all that Kmt reactionary clique which dares to resist inside Chinese territory, to liberate people of whole country, to protect sovereign independence and integrity of Chinese territory.

"(2) Bravely to advance, capture all evil and unrepentant war criminals without regard to where they flee and all must be captured and brought to account and punishment in accordance with law [and] special care should be taken to apprehend bandit leader Chiang Kai-shek.

"(3) To proclaim the final revised text of domestic peace agreement toward any Kmt local government and local military organs. As regards all who desire to stop warfare and use peaceful methods of settlement, you may in general accord with this final revised text at once sign with them a local agreement.

"(4) After PLA has surrounded Nanking in [if?] Nanking Li Tsung-jen government has not dispersed and desires sign domestic peace agreement, we are willing once more to give that government opportunity to sign.

"Chinese People's Revolutionary Military Affairs Committee Chairman Mao Tse-tung, Chinese People's Liberation Army Commander in Chief Chu Teh, April 21, 1949."

To note: An extra states that final revised text of peace negotiation will be published tomorrow in total.

Sent Department 678, Nanking 426, OffEmb Canton, Shanghai 465. By mail to Tientsin.

CLUBB

893.00/5–1049

Memorandum of Conversation, by Ambassador Francis B. Sayre, of the United States Delegation to the General Assembly of the United Nations [29]

[NEW YORK,] April 21, 1949.

I lunched alone with Dr. Wellington Koo [30] and talked with him confidentially and very informally about the general world situation. We both agreed that as a result of the Atlantic Pact the chances are strong that the Soviet Government will not make an armed attack or seek to advance through Western Europe. Doubtless the result of the Atlantic Pact will be to intensify the Soviet efforts in the Far East.

Dr. Wellington Koo stressed what has often been said before—that from the world point of view it is just as necessary, if not more so, to block further Soviet advance in the Far East as in the West. He said that in his opinion until the Soviet Government had succeeded in effectively closing the frontier in China to prevent American troops from entering the Soviet back door through China, the Soviet Government could not undertake a strong advance through the West. In his opinion, therefore, the Soviet Government is even more vitally concerned at the present, as one of the preliminary steps in seeking world domination, in effectively sewing up the position in the Far East and thus preventing a backdoor attack than in temporary victories in the West.

Dr. Wellington Koo went on to say that the Chinese people for many years had felt the friendship of America and believed in the friendly concern of the people of America for the people of China. He said that it was a matter of keen regret to him that due to recent events the Chinese people were now beginning to feel that America's friendship for them was only superficial and they were coming to believe that the present American attitude is to leave the Chinese people to their own fate.

I asked Dr. Wellington Koo what was in his mind as to the most constructive program which the United States might follow in the face of the present exceedingly difficult conditions. He replied that in his opinion the first constructive step which the United States should take would be the issue of a statement by the President or the Secretary of State making clear that the American people still feel a

---

[29] Submitted to the Secretary of State on May 10 by Mr. Butterworth.
[30] Chinese Ambassador in the United States.

vital friendship for the Chinese people and view with deep concern their present plight. He said that this would put new heart into the Chinese people who are at present discouraged and disheartened. He said that the effect of this would of course last only a few months and he hoped that the second step would be the sending by the United States of a mission to China to explore possible avenues and methods of getting technical help to China to buttress her defenses against increasing Soviet infiltration and advance. He said that the conditions in China and in the world had so vitally changed since the visit of the Marshall Mission [31] that the time called for a new appraisal of the situation and a new exploration of constructive means by which the American people could give assistance to the Chinese.

He went on to describe methods of Soviet infiltration. He said that so-called "people's courts" would be set up by the Soviets to arrest and try landlords of a district. In these "people's courts" accusation by the peasants against landholders would be heard and the landholders systematically liquidated either by shooting or deportation. The peasants would then be told that the land was now theirs under the progressive and friendly Communist rule. The peasants would also be informed that in place of the 50% of the produce of the land which was formerly taken by the Chinese Government for taxes, the new landholders would be asked to contribute only 30%. Several months of this "honeymoon" would continue. After the expiration of several months, the new landholders would be told that increased funds were necessary to finance and support the Communist soldiers who were fighting to protect them from the return of the former landlords. An additional 10% of the produce from the land would therefore be added to the fixed 30%. In another month or two, a fresh requisition of an additional 10% would be asked, perhaps for the building of hospitals for the soldiers; and so it would go on with increases of 10% until some 70% of the produce of the land would be required to be paid by the new landholders to the Communist Government. By then, the Chinese peasants would be in the tight grip of Communist rule with all hope gone of overthrowing their new rulers.

Dr. Wellington Koo said that this infiltration and penetration of Soviet rule had by this time engulfed Inner Mongolia and was proceeding fast in Manchuria and in other parts of northern China.

He concluded by again telling of the present disheartened feelings of the Chinese people and expressing the strong hope that the United States Government would put new heart into them by a public state-

---

[31] For documentation, see *Foreign Relations*, 1945, vol. VII, pp. 745 ff., and *ibid.*, 1946, volumes IX and X.

ment, followed in a few months by the sending of a new United States mission to China to explore possible avenues of help and assistance.

893.00/4–2249 : Telegram

The Ambassador in China (Stuart) to the Secretary of State

NANKING, April 22, 1949.
[Received April 22—2 :24 a. m.]

811. Government today released text message sent by Li and Ho April 22 to Government peace delegation Peiping for forwarding to Communists. Summary follows:

In our efforts to lay foundation of durable peace we have been guided solely by people's earnest desire for peace and have considered nothing but basic interests of people. We have compromised, and stood up against ridicule but have spared no pains to seek peace. Our sincerity should be known to entire nation.

However, fundamental spirit of Communist-proposed peace agreement is tantamount to disposal of conquered by conqueror. Even if Government were willing to humiliate self and sign document, it is suspected that narrow-minded attitude and oppressive spirit pervading it would infuriate army and people and goad them into action. In such event, Government would be powerless to guarantee its enforcement.

On reorganization of troops, agreement proposes all Government armed forces should be amalgamated into People's Liberation Army and hand over to this army all military equipment. This would mean total elimination of National Army. Politically, although Government would be allowed to administer affairs of state pending establishment of a coalition government it could do so only at beck and call of Communist Military Headquarters. Regarding PCC, Government could only participate insofar as Communists found its implementation of proposed peace agreement "satisfactory" and its participation in coalition government would also be dependent upon Communists' recommendation.

Above are only few instances. Entire so-called peace agreement is nothing more than Government acquiescence in Communist conquest of China. If Communist troops and civilian personnel continue to penetrate Government territory, resistance by National Army and people will be inevitable. Bloodshed and fighting will take place in every city and village. Suffering of people will be immeasurably deepened and loss to nation increased. If we truly recognize peace as being earnest desire of all people and are equally sincere in our efforts to seek it, we must give up all ideas of hostility and retaliation and find reasonable and effective means to stop civil strife. Government, therefore, hopes Communists, out of respect to people's interests, will change motivating spirit of agreement and reconsider its contents. In order create atmosphere favorable to progress of peace talks, it is sincere desire of Government for early conclusion of temporary truce agreement. Your reply awaited.

Sent Department, repeated Shanghai 407, OffEmb Canton 274.

STUART

IV. CHINESE COMMUNIST CROSSING OF THE YANGTZE; FALL OF NANKING, HANKOW, SHANGHAI, TAIYUAN; MOUNTING POLITICAL CONFUSION IN NATIONALIST CHINA (APRIL 22–MAY 31)

893.00/4–2249 : Telegram

The Consul General at Shanghai (Cabot) to the Secretary of State

SHANGHAI, April 22, 1949.
[Received April 22—5 : 27 a. m.]

1304. Evening vernacular papers report announcement by Shanghai-Woosung Garrison Headquarters of "state of siege" in Shanghai and return to 11 o'clock curfew as from night of 21st–22nd.

Sent Nanking 752, repeated Department, Canton 308.

CABOT

893.00/4–2249 : Telegram

The Ambassador in China (Stuart) to the Secretary of State

NANKING, April 22, 1949.
[Received April 22—7 : 51 a. m.]

826. Communist broadcast April 22 announces river crossing starting midnight April 20, smashing Yangtze defense line, built by Kmt [32] reactionaries during past 3½ months, like hacking away a lot of dead wood. Enemy troops had no will to fight and fell back in utter confusion. In less than 24 hours 300,000 PLA [33] men completed crossing and wrested away wide areas of south bank including Fanchang, Nanling, Tsingyang, Tikang and other cities, broadcast states.

Sent Department 826, repeated Shanghai and OffEmb Canton unnumbered.

STUART

893.00/4–2249 : Telegram

The Minister-Counselor of Embassy in China (Clark) to the Secretary of State

CANTON, April 22, 1949—3 p. m.
[Received April 22—8 : 20 a. m.]

Cantel 251. Wu Tieh-cheng,[34] just returned from Nanking via Chikow where he saw Generalissimo,[35] tells me Generalissimo and Act-

---

[32] Kuomintang (Nationalist Party).
[33] People's Liberation Army (Communist).
[34] Former Vice President of the Chinese Executive Yuan and Minister for Foreign Affairs.
[35] Chiang Kai-shek, who retired as President on January 21, 1949.

ing President [36] lunching together today Hangchow to plan future. He insists Generalissimo continues support Li fullest. Among decisions to be reached Hangchow is that of selecting over-all military Commander in Chief. Wu thinks Ho Ying-chin [37] will be selected, possibly with Pai Chung-hsi [38] as deputy.

Wu says harshness Communist terms has united all forces opposing Communists and has renewed and strengthened will to resist. "We will stop them everywhere," he said.

All government organs not already [in] Canton, including Cabinet and Legislative Yuan, will move here immediately. Acting President expected possibly next week.

Despite forceful manner in which Wu expressed determination stop Communists, he admitted they had already crossed Yangtze in two places—one west of Wuhu, the other up river from Chinkiang, at both of which places serious fighting, he said, is now taking place.

Repeated Nanking 210, Shanghai 161.

CLARK

893.00/4–2349 : Telegram

The Ambassador in China (Stuart) to the Secretary of State

NANKING, April 23, 1949.
[Received April 22—11 : 23 p. m.]

830. Practically all top government officials left Nanking yesterday. During night there was heavy firing across river and city government and police have now evacuated, bulk of troops have been withdrawn and mobs are looting mayor's house and police station. Some Communists crossed river during night and either they or local Communists now control Hsiakwan and railway station. No fighting in city.

Sent Department 830, repeated AmEmb Canton 282, Shanghai 417.

STUART

893.00/4–2349 : Telegram

The Minister-Counselor of Embassy in China (Clark) to the Secretary of State

CANTON, April 23, 1949.
[Received April 23—7 : 39 a. m.]

Cantel 258. Kmt CC [39] statement April 20 declaring stand Communist peace terms, full text released local press April 21. English

---

[36] General Li Tsung-jen.
[37] President of the Chinese Executive Yuan (premier).
[38] Military and Political Affairs Director for Central China.
[39] Kuomintang Central Executive Committee.

translation supplied Central News. Gist: Rejects Communist terms as demand unconditional surrender. Move [to] enslave people, install Communist dictatorship, make China another Czechoslovakia. Calls upon Communists issue cease-fire, allow negotiations continue. Emphasizes Communist unjustified attempt pin full responsibility civil war on Kmt, reviews history Communist–Kmt relations, placing full blame on Communists.

"If CCP [40] had not unreasonably pinned war guilt on Central Government, this party for sake of bringing hostilities to end quite willing let by-gones be by-gones. However, since CCP had so twisted facts in order blind entire world, this party . . . [41] cannot possibly accept Communist charges . . ."

Communist terms

"no more than tyrannical judgment imposed on people and nation. Their ultimate aim [to] set up one-party dictatorship under CCP. They not only seek wipe out from record this party's effort at propagating democratic constitutionalism, but they also give not slightest consideration to people's present demand for peace and for their personal liberty and security. . . . CCP virtually seeks knock entire Chinese nation and Chinese people behind iron curtain, making them counterpart of Poland and Czechoslovakia."

Then says peace agreement must be based on principles enunciated by Kmt April 18 (see ourtel April 19 [42]). In calling for Communist cease-fire order, cites government compliance with Communist request January 1946 for immediate truce before convening of PCC.[43]

First part statement devoted lengthy review history Nationalist-Communist relations since 1928, stating party's case, CCP not Kmt responsible civil war. "For past 20 years damage sustained by our people as result Communist rebellion and betrayal in no wise less than that sustained by people as result of Jap invasion. In fact it might exceed latter in severity." Contends that "since government first proposed restoration of peace to nation" (Generalissimo's New Year statement) has been willing ignore question responsibility civil war.

Contends that during period 1928 (after "national unity" was effected) to 1937 national "rehabilitation" not achieved because "Communist Party repeatedly initiated rebellious activities and destroyed this unity. . . ."

---

[40] Chinese Communist Party.
[41] Omissions indicated in the source text.
[42] Not printed.
[43] Political Consultative Conference.

Then quotes in full CCP statement 1937 [44] (after Marco Polo bridge [45]), stating CCP agreed (1) adhere Sun's Three People's Principles, (2) abandon "terroristic activities and communication movements to overthrow political power of Kmt and suspend policy of forcibly confiscating private land", (3) "abolish Soviet regime and put into effect democratic rule", (4) abolish designation "Red Army" to be "renamed people's revolutionary army, placed directly under command national military council of National Government."

Then alleges during anti-Jap war Communists "broke their promise", "created disturbances everywhere" and "launched military offensives". "If it had not been for government's utmost patience and broadmindedness military situation. . . . would have almost been rendered untenable and very life of nation terminated".

In post-war period, states Kmt "took lead proposing peaceful settlement," convened PCC, National Assembly, drafted constitution. "However, CCP. . . . continued seize power through military means. . . . brought about widespread unrest throughout nation", destroyed fruits of victory over Japanese.

Sent Department 258, repeated Nanking unnumbered, Shanghai 165.

CLARK

893.00/4–2349 : Telegram

The Ambassador in China (Stuart) to the Secretary of State

NANKING, April 23, 1949.
[Received April 23—9:44 a. m.]

835. Army formerly defending Pukow has been withdrawing across river with little opposition and is now streaming through city in reasonable orderly retreat south. Local authority has completely disappeared and looting, which began with unoccupied houses and government offices, has now spread to rice and flour shops and appears to be increasing. Scattered shots are heard occasionally but no fighting taking place in city. Earlier report that Communists had taken over Hsiakwan area and railroad station premature, but local Communists believe well-organized and in position to take over as soon as Nationalist army completely withdrawn from city. Several fires burning Hsiakwan following explosions. Nationalist troops reliably reported to have blown up railroad station.

Sent Department; repeated AmEmbassy Canton 285, Shanghai 422.

STUART

---

[44] For Communist "Manifesto on Unity" of September 22, 1937, see Department of State, *United States Relations With China* (Washington, Government Printing Office, 1949), p. 523.
[45] For documentation on clash of July 7, 1937, see *Foreign Relations*, 1937, vol. III, pp. 128 ff.

893.00/4–2349 : Telegram

The Ambassador in China (Stuart) to the Secretary of State

NANKING, April 23, 1949—4 p. m.
[Received April 23—6 : 43 a. m.[46]]

836. Acting President, Premier and few remaining officials Ministry National Defense fled Nanking this morning for Shanghai whence they will soon proceed Canton. Sino–3 [47] last night admitted hopelessness stemming flow of Communist troops across river and said all armies deployed for Yangtze defense have been ordered withdraw south to Chientang river line. Sino–3 says Shanghai will not be defended except in possible rear guard action and all effort will be concentrated on withdrawing armies intact for further resistance on new line. Ridiculously easy Communist crossing of Yangtze made possible by defections at key points, disagreements in High Command and failure airforce give effective support.

Sent Department, repeated OffEmb Canton 286, Shanghai 423.

STUART

893.00/4–2349 : Telegram

The Ambassador in China (Stuart) to the Secretary of State

NANKING, April 23, 1949—7 p. m.
[Received 11 : 15 p. m.]

843. Posters have appeared in city naming Ma Ching-yuan as chairman People's Peace Preservation Committee for Nanking and Wu Yi-fang, President Ginling College, as vice-chairman. Dr. Wu said matter complete mystery to her as she had never been approached this regard. Ma, National Assembly delegate from North China, she knows only slightly and does not know what his connections may be.

Dr. Wu says Chamber of Commerce sending representatives across river to welcome Communists who are expected to take over city tomorrow morning.

Meeting of civic leaders now being held to organize patrols in order maintain public order during night, another reliable source reports.

Repeated OffEmb Canton 291, Shanghai 430.

STUART

---

[46] Text printed from corrected copy received April 23, 10 a. m.
[47] Probably a spokesman for the Operations Staff of the Chinese High Command.

893.00/4–2349 : Telegram

The Ambassador in China (Stuart) to the Secretary of State

NANKING, April 23, 1949.
[Received April 23—9 : 39 a. m.]

847. Posters now displayed throughout city stating Communists will take over administration city 7 a. m. tomorrow. Mob looting continues. City power still functioning. At least four ammunition dumps blown north and outside city.

Sent Department; repeated Shanghai 433, Embassy Canton 293.

STUART

893.00/4–2349 : Telegram

The Ambassador in China (Stuart) to the Secretary of State

NANKING, April 24, 1949.
[Received April 23—5 : 24 p. m.]

848. Embassy informed Communist troops began entering city by Northwest gate at approximately 5 a. m. 24th. Desultory shots exchanged during night in streets between emergency police force and marauders have virtually ceased. No disorders in neighborhood Embassy compounds. No American nationals have applied to Embassy for permission move [into] Chancery compound, despite notice circulated 23d. Embassy personnel and offices secure.

Sent Department 848, repeated Shanghai 434, American Embassy Canton 294.

STUART

893.00/4–2449 : Telegram

The Consul General at Shanghai (Cabot) to the Secretary of State

SHANGHAI, April 24, 1949—2 p. m.
[Received April 24—4 : 45 a. m.]

1321. Shanghai main city still quiet. Refugees now pouring into suburbs especially Hungjao where roads heavily jammed outside wooden wall (near Hangchow relay). Troops preventing their entrance city proper with roadblocks.

Soochow occupied by Communists early this morning, according information received by Assistant Military Attaché. Local papers have not yet admitted this though one reports Nationalist troops evacuating Soochow southward. *Sin Wen Pao* 24th reports battalion Communist troops entered Wusih late last night. Trains from Shanghai said running only as far as Quinsan.

Pursuant to emergency order by Garrison Headquarters, River Police have cleared Soochow Creek of river craft forcing thousands junks, etc., into Whangpoo and beyond. Purpose unclear. American resident Pootung has just reported two Chinese gunboats and one LSM all apparently readied for action are coming up Whangpoo toward Shanghai, also large floating crane. Same source says 1500 drums fuel oil being moved Shanghaiward from Pootung installations. These developments suggest Nationalist military leaders still contemplate offering battle. This also seems confirmed by reliable information received by Assistant Military Attaché that movement of Nationalist troops from Hangchow north toward Shanghai now under way, though this may likely be for purpose providing stronger cover for retreat from Shanghai. Meanwhile, AP despatch cited in local press asserts Reds advancing unopposed from Kiangyin area towards Shanghai.

Vernacular press reports Shanghai Kmt Chief Fang Chih arrived Taiwan. *China Press* reports yesterday meeting of 150 Legislative Yuan members now at Shanghai reached decision that their group will leave Shanghai within 3 days for Taiwan, Canton and Kweilin. Hong Kong 23d Reuters despatch reports heavy air arrivals Hong Kong and Canton of rich Shanghai merchants with service between Shanghai and Canton said increased to 30 planes daily.

Sent Department, repeated Nanking 763, Canton 315.

CABOT

893.00/4–2549 : Telegram

The Ambassador in China (Stuart) to the Secretary of State

NANKING, April 25, 1949.
[Received April 25—1:07 p. m.]

861. *Yi Shih Pao*, April 25, reports following proclamation issued April 24 by China PLA East China Area HQ, Political Section:

"This army is ordered to eradicate Chiang bandits in the East China area and to liberate East China, and makes the following bindings with the newly liberated cities and peoples in the East China area:

(1) This army protects freedom and democracy, life and property of all classes of people in the cities. It is hoped that entire body of city populace will strictly observe good order and not to believe in rumors so as to frighten themselves.

(2) This army protects civilian industries and private capital. All private factories, enterprises, companies, banks, shops, godowns and storages will be protected. It is hoped that business will be carried on as usual.

(3) All Chiang bandit-operated factories, enterprises, banks, corporations, godowns and storages must await investigation and disposal. If found to be actually bureaucratic capital, concerns shall be taken over by democratic government. If it is found that such concerns actually contain a portion of civilian capital, ownership will be recognized, and the owners will enjoy right to run these concerns jointly with democratic government. It is hoped that employees serving in bureaucratic capital enterprises shall all keep on working in their posts and assume responsibility of safeguarding assets, documents, charts and drawings, accounts and files to await take-over. Those who render meritorious service in safeguarding things will be rewarded and those who stage sabotage and inflict damages shall be punished. The democratic government will employ and give salary and wages to law-abiding employees.

(4) This army will protect directors, general managers, factory directors, staff members, technicians, workers, school masters, professors, faculty members, students, hospital and museum directors, archbishops and priests, [employees?] of water works, power company, telephone, postal and telecommunication, highway, shipping, harbor, universities, middle schools, primary schools, people's educational institutions, libraries, custodian offices of cultural and ancient relics, hospitals, churches, charity organizations, amusement centers and gymnasiums. They shall not be infringed upon, and it is hoped that they shall carry on their functions and classes as usual.

(5) With exception of principal war criminals, all civilian administrators, police and *chu, shan, cheng* and *pao* chiefs of Kuomintang, provincial, municipal, hsien and other governments will not be arrested and treated as captives if they do not give armed resistance to this army. They should be law abiding and obey the orders of this army and the democratic government and assume responsibility of safeguarding assets and files of their respective organizations. They shall not destroy or hide (such assets and files) but await take-over and disposal. If they are not reactionary in their ways and are not guilty of serious malpractices, they shall be graded and re-employed.

(6) All Embassies, legations and consulates and the life and property of all foreign residents shall be protected if they will observe the orders of the democratic government, will not act as spies of the enemy, keep war criminals in hiding nor inflict any sort of damage.

(7) Whether before or after this army enters the city, all citizens and people of all circles are responsible for maintaining order in the entire city so as to avoid damages. Those who render meritorious service in safeguarding things shall be awarded, and those who inflict or plan damage shall be punished.

This army is strictly disciplined and will buy and sell legitimately. Not a needle nor a thread will be taken from the people. It is hoped that the entire populace will carry on with their business in peace and not frighten themselves. The above is notified for public observance.

Signed: Commanding Officer Chen Yi, Deputy Commanding Officer Chang Yun-yi, Political Commissar Yao Shu-shih, director Shu Tung."

Sent Department 861, repeated Embassy Canton 304, Shanghai 443, Peiping 135.

STUART

893.00/4–2549 : Telegram

The Ambassador in China (Stuart) to the Secretary of State

NANKING, April 25, 1949.
[Received April 25—11 : 03 a. m.]

863. *Min Chu Jih Pao* reports meeting of Nanking Provisional Peace Preservation Committee night of April 23: Hu Yi-min and Hu Yi-hung, representatives of East China Bureau of CPLA, made following statement to committee:

(1) CPLA will protect people's properties and confiscate bureaucratic capital;

(2) After entry of liberated army into city, factories should begin operation as quickly as possible, schools should re-open at early date and shops carry on business;

(3) *Pao* and *chia* chiefs are expected to see that residents within their respective areas do not participate in looting;

(4) The Peace Preservation Committee is expected to:

(*a*) Maintain local order.
(*b*) Prepare to welcome the PLA.

Committee issued regulations governing maintenance of social order as follows:

(1) Comrades in the former Nanking police force are to voluntarily gather together at the Police Commission this morning. After obtaining letters from the Commission they are to report at the Peace Preservation Committee and await assignment of duty. Otherwise, they shall be treated as stray bands of soldiers.

(2) Former Nanking People's Self-preservation Groups and Protective Corps are to be established immediately and shall be responsible for maintenance of social order under the direction of the Police Commission.

(3) All former *chu* and *pao* chiefs shall be responsible in leading and assisting in maintenance of social order in their respective *chu* and *pao*. *Chu* and *pao* chiefs shall be rated in accordance with their accomplishments in maintenance of social order.

(4) Those who gather in a crowd, arm themselves and stage looting shall be killed on the spot.

Sent Department, repeated Canton and Shanghai.

STUART

893.01/4–2549 : Telegram

The Minister-Counselor of Embassy in China (Clark) to the Secretary of State

CANTON, April 25, 1949—4 p. m.
[Received 10:27 p. m.]

Cantel 266. Chu Chang-wei,[48] who occupies with Li Tsung-jen position similar to that of Kan Chieh-hou,[49] is in Canton as representative Li, sounding out Kwangtung generals as to whether they want Li to remain in authority or want Generalissimo return. He tells me that at meeting between Generalissimo and Li at Hangchow, Generalissimo suggested reconstitution national war committee with Generalissimo as chairman, Li Tsung-jen and Sun Fo[50] vice chairmen. Li had refused agree such action, according Chu, insisting that either Generalissimo resume presidency or let him (Li) continue with full authority unhampered by intervention Generalissimo. Chu confirmed that Generalissimo had blocked Li's efforts resist Communists' crossing Yangtze, Generalissimo being stubbornly convinced defense could be better prepared on Chientang line. Li is bitter, he says, at Generalissimo's obstruction from behind scenes and unless he can obtain full authority and removal abroad [of] Generalissimo, he will retire to Kwangsi and fight from there. If Kwangtung generals side with Li, one of them—either Hsueh Yueh[51] or Yu Han-mou,[52] will return with Chu to Kweilin. Chu is bringing me tomorrow personal letter from Li Tsung-jen who apparently desires our advice. Will report further when letter arrives.

Sent Department Cantel 266, repeated Nanking 220, Shanghai 171.

CLARK

893.00/4–2549 : Telegram

The Consul General at Shanghai (Cabot) to the Secretary of State

SHANGHAI, April 25, 1949—7 p. m.
[Received 7:04 p. m.]

1349. After morning of wild rumors (possibly spread by Communists to hasten National collapse) which indicated Soochow, Kashing, Chiating and Nanhsiang had all fallen, with seizure of Shanghai imminent, it became known all 4 places still in Nationalist hands and Communist advance appeared [to] have lost initial momentum. Phone call from American missionary in Soochow indicated Soochow still standing as of 1300 today, with Communist entrance expected soon.

---

[43] Political adviser to Acting President Li.
[49] Secretary and adviser to Acting President Li.
[50] Former President of the Chinese Executive Yuan.
[51] Governor of Kwangtung.
[52] Military and Political Affairs Director for South China.

Farthest known point of Communist advance is town 7 miles west of Soochow, Kashing still in Nationalists' hands, with rumored arrest of *North China Daily News* editor for printing story of its fall this morning. Reportedly Government troops repulsed attempted new Communist crossing at Hupu, east of Kiangyin. If true, this is first known effective resistance offered by National Government troops this area. Generally believed most Government troops retreated from moment of first Communist crossing.

Military authorities were still stoutly maintaining Shanghai will be defended but apparently pressure being exerted by "civil and industrial leaders" and probably underground elements to change this resolve. Rumors [that] Tang En-po [53] will withdraw without fighting are widespread. However, in countryside outside city limits, active preparation for defense continues. In Hungjao area servants have been pressed into labor service, trees and grave mounds being leveled, blockades erected, ditches dug and guns placed in pillboxes—perhaps on theory if soldiers kept busy, [they] won't have time to think of running away.

Estimates of when Communists will enter Shanghai vary. Latest reports indicate Communists possibly aiming for capture Hangchow first. Reliably reported Ministry National Defense which now has headquarters in New Asia Hotel expects to remove its last planeload of personnel from Shanghai April 27. This is possible indication Communists not expected until several days later.

According some reports, Tu Yueh-sheng [54] left Shanghai for Hong Kong 2 days ago. However, another source equally reliable indicates his departure was prevented by return of severe asthma condition. Yang Hu and other "city fathers" remain Shanghai with rumor current of active negotiations on their part with Communists. Pan Kung-chan [55] reported packed and ready to leave at moment's notice.

Sent Department 1349, repeated Nanking 780, OffEmb Canton 329.

CABOT

893.01/4–2549 : Telegram

The Minister-Counselor of Embassy in China (Clark) to the Secretary of State

CANTON, April 25, 1949.
[Received April 25—10 : 55 p. m.]

Cantel 268. Both Canton airfields crowded last 2 days with more than half top government officials already here from Shanghai and more due today.

---

[53] Garrison commander of the Shanghai area.
[54] Shanghai banker-industrialist.
[55] Chairman of the Shanghai City Council.

Premier Ho Ying-chin arrived yesterday accompanied by Executive Yuan Vice President Chia Chin-teh and Secretary General Huang Shao-ku. Minister Interior Li Han-hun, Minister Commerce Tuan Mu-chieh and heads several minor ministries now here with Minister Education Han Li-wu expected today.

Legislative Yuan now has quorum, with Vice President Liu Chien-chun in charge. President Tung Kwan-hsien still Shanghai but expected soon and legislators are awaiting his arrival or instructions before beginning formal sessions. Of 180 members now here, 60 remained Canton during entire peace negotiations, remainder having arrived on US [apparent omission] week-end from Shanghai and Taiwan. Over 100 legislators still in Shanghai awaiting transportation.

Control Yuan President Yu Yu-jen expected today. Vice President Liu Chieh and other senior Yuan officials already Canton.

Arrival Wong Wen-hao [56] and Yen Hsi-shan [57] reported but not confirmed.

Sent Department Cantel 268, repeated Nanking 222, Shanghai 172.

CLARK

893.00/4–2649 : Telegram

The Consul General at Hankow (Callanan) to the Secretary of State

HANKOW, April 26, 1949—11 a. m.
[Received April 26—6 : 12 a. m.]

122. Pai's headquarters will set up command headquarters Wuchang shortly but do not expect to move to Changsha near future. Mytel 116, April 22 [58] and previous. Headquarters source told Martin [59] this morning Pai will not abandon Wuhan until forced to as Pai desires important tax revenue here support his armies. Headquarters sees Commies concentrating attacks on Generalissimo territory next few weeks so unlike[ly] bother Pai. Even mention possibility renewing peace talks when Generalissimo's armies defeated. Comment: Pai's headquarters appear display remarkable indifference disaster in east China which may indicate Pai and Li even now will not cooperate with Generalissimo and Kwangtung factions.

Sent Department 122, repeated Nanking 87, AmEmbassy Canton 44.

CALLANAN

---

[56] Secretary-General of the President's office.
[57] Governor of Shansi.
[58] Not printed.
[59] Edwin W. Martin, Vice Consul at Hankow.

893.00/4–2649 : Telegram

The Minister-Counselor of Embassy in China (Clark) to the Secretary of State

CANTON, April 26, 1949.
[Received April 26—5 : 24 p. m.]

Cantel 270. Cabinet Secretary-General Huang Shao-ku statement to press on behalf Premier Ho upon their arrival Canton April 24:

Shanghai will be defended, neither acting Premier [*President*] nor Ho will resign, government will never again try talk peace with Communists. Denied report Central China HQ had moved from Hankow to Changsha, said government would establish 2nd line of defense, would not specify where, refused comment on evacuation for diplomats from Nanking to Canton.

Referred reports Kmt Secretary whether Generalissimo come Canton lead Kmt. Other Kmt officials, Generalissimo will remain as head of party, with Li and Ho keeping present positions.

Local press, April 24, and UP carried story Kmt officials requested Generalissimo and Li, said to be in Kweilin, temporarily come Canton lead anti-Communist war. Other arrivals Canton as reported local press, UP, Executive Yuan V.P., Chia King-teh; Communications Minister, Pun Mu-chieh, V. Minister Finance, Leung Yung-min.

CLARK

893.01/4–2649 : Telegram

The Minister-Counselor of Embassy in China (Clark) to the Secretary of State

CANTON, April 26, 1949—2 p. m.
[Received 4 : 56 p. m.]

Cantel 278. Chu Chang-wei called again today (Cantel 266, April 25; repeated Nanking 220; Shanghai 171), and handed me letter from Li Tsung-jen, translation of which is quoted below, and requested I communicate it to my Government.

Chu was emphatic in his statement that Li Tsung-jen is going to have show-down with Gimo. There must be house-cleaning of Government and Party, particularly removal C–C clique [60] elements in Kwangtung and recognition by Gimo and his followers of supreme authority Li Tsung-jen, or Li would remain Kweilin and from there direct defense southwest. He says Li has support military leaders Hunan, Kweichow, Yunnan, Szechuan and Sikang and that local mili-

---

[60] Group within the Kuomintang led by the Chen brothers, Li-fu and Kuo-fu.

tary leaders, not Chang Chun,[61] were ones to speak with authority these provinces.

Chu said he was making favorable progress in his discussion and hoped for full statement of support of ECA [Li?] by Kwangtung generals. In any event, decision would be taken in immediate future. In meantime President Li, and he stressed word "President", requested that remaining ECA [62] funds be not obligated without his (Li's) prior approval. He is particularly anxious no ECA funds be used in Taiwan or other area under Gimo's influence.

Chu said Li had requested President's Control and Legislative Yuans visit him Kweilin and he thought both would do so before coming Canton. Chu has promised keep me informed progress his negotiations Canton.

Text letter follows:

"My dear Minister Clark: The peace negotiations between the Chinese Government and the Chinese Communists for which I tried my utmost during the past 3 months have finally broken down due to refusal by the Chinese Communists to change their scheme to conquer entire China by military might. Now the Communist troops have already crossed the Yangtze to threaten Nanking and Shanghai, and their bloodthirsty designs are entirely uncovered. For the purpose of saving the people from rule by brutal force, the Government has decided to defend the southwest and to resist to the last ditch. If the growth of power of the Chinese Communists cannot be checked, it is not only that democracy in China will be destroyed at its root but that world peace will also be endangered. Acting upon our own responsibility, we must forever be determined to fight against this antidemocratic force.

"As Your Excellency no doubt must be concerned with the present situation in China, I therefore have specially designated Mr. Chu Chang-wei to come on my behalf to convey to you my humble views. Your understanding is solicited.

With highest regards, Respectfully yours, Li Tsung-jen (signed)."

Sent Department Cantel 276 [278]; repeated Nanking 225; Shanghai 176.

CLARK

893.00/4–2649 : Telegram

The Ambassador in China (Stuart) to the Secretary of State

NANKING, April 26, 1949—3 p. m.
[Received 10 : 09 p. m.]

875. A message has reached me indirectly from Chinese colleague of many years on Yenching [63] faculty, teacher of philosophy who has

---

[61] Military and Political Affairs Director for Southwest China.
[62] Economic Cooperation Administration.
[63] University at Peiping where Ambassador Stuart had been President until 1946.

more recently been drawn into political activities with his close friend Carsun Chang [64] in order to help bring peace to his distracted country. He has been mediating with high hopes between Kmt and CCP in Peiping and has been in close touch with latter since their occupation of city. That has enabled him to learn something of their real policies and he is apparently bitterly disillusioned. He is convinced CCP, in thorough understanding with Kremlin, are aiming at world revolution and that to this end will try to eliminate foreigners from China and to prepare this country for its part, on Moscow theory that war is inevitable and should not be postponed until USA is prepared. (This last does not seem to fit in with evidence from other sources that Russia is not ready yet for hostilities.)

In any case, taking this message as sort of "text," its basic ideas are in accord with other impressions I have recently been receiving.[65] Among these are truculent tone and terms of lengthy ultimatum brought to Nanking on April 16; utterly indefensible and deliberate bombardment of British warships on April 20 and 21; treatment of foreign consular officers in northern cities, notably American Consul General, Mukden; unstinted praise of USSR and its peaceful aims; and general harmony between Soviet and CCP propaganda. More especially does vitriolic abuse of USA, repetitious and often seemingly irrelevant, seem to have in view something more than resentment over our past aid to Kmt or attempt to deter us from continuing this. It seems to be in line with the Soviet acceptance of contention that we are chief bulwark of capitalism and must therefore be overthrown. These are among outstanding indications of what I am reluctantly coming to believe is correct description of CCP policy. We have suffered in past from our unwillingness to recognize intensity of conviction or of ambition in lust for world dominion. I had to overcome all my own instincts and presuppositions before I finally admitted to myself that Japanese had this illusory dream. I find myself passing through somewhat similar process in observing CCP. In their case we are fully aware of "historical necessity" for this in their fanatical[ly] believed dogmas. There is at any rate enough of a probability for such program as already actually entered upon by CCP for us to consider concrete details of our own policy in its light. It is after all no more than speeding up of their openly avowed objectives, made possible by unexpectedly swift weakening of Kmt capacity to retard their advance.

Sent Department 875, repeated Shanghai 455, OffEmb Canton 313.

STUART

---

[64] Leader of Democratic Socialist Party.

[65] For documentation on problems of United States Consulates in areas occupied by the Communists, see pp. 933 ff.

893.00/4-2649 : Telegram

The Consul General at Shanghai (Cabot) to the Secretary of State

SHANGHAI, April 26, 1949.
[Received April 28—10 : 21 a. m.]

1355. According to local papers April 26 Shanghai–Woosung garrison apparently making strenuous efforts thin out population Shanghai. Following decisions made at garrison meeting April 25 : No residents, military or civilian, will be allowed reenter Shanghai after leaving it without resident certificates or official identification certificates effective immediately. No new resident certificates will be issued Shanghai; persons in Shanghai without resident or official identification certificates should immediately leave city voluntarily or they will be marched out; persons resisting while being marched out will be shot on spot.

Further stringent measures passed by garrison govern ship movements this area with special permits required before ships allowed enter or leave harbor, load or unload cargo or passengers. Ships failing observe rules will be fired on by garrison and, if possible, sunk.

According *China Daily Tribune* April 26, as war-time measure, municipal police sets up new Peace Preservation Department headed by Lt. General Huang Ping-yen of Nanking-Shanghai-Hangchow Hdqs. staff and political department. "Speedy Action Squad" also established, headed by Tsung Min, chief first section supervisory department of police bureau.

Sent Department 1355, repeated Nanking 784, Canton 333.

CABOT

893.00/4-2749 : Telegram

The Minister-Counselor of Embassy in China (Clark) to the Secretary of State

CANTON, April 27, 1949.
[Received April 27—5 : 07 a. m.]

Cantel 281. Air traffic into Canton continues heavy, with 59 arrivals and 53 departures April 25, setting record for commercial field. Press reports traffic Hong Kong airport same day with slightly smaller number planes arriving and departing. Pilots arriving from Shanghai state crews are sleeping at airport between flights. Yen Hsi-shan, Yu Yu-jen [66] and Tung Kwan-hsien [67] have arrived and all major government organs except Acting President's Office are now established

---

[66] President of the Control Yuan.
[67] President of the Legislative Yuan.

Canton. Legislative Yuan has 210 members here and May 3 has been set as tentative date beginning formal meetings.

Sent Department, Nanking 226, Shanghai 177.

CLARK

893.00/4–2749 : Telegram

The Minister-Counselor of Embassy in China (Clark) to the Secretary of State

CANTON, April 27, 1949—11 a. m.
[Received April 27—5 : 15 a. m.]

Cantel 282. Vernacular press reports CEC [68] decided April 25 send Wu Teh-chen and Li Wen-fan [69] [to] Kweilin ask Li Tsung-jen come Canton. Member CEC has informed Embassy confidentially that CEC knew at time this decision made that Li did not wish to receive such a delegation since Li had previously informed CEC that he was coming Canton later, but at his own convenience, after he had had rest Kweilin. Li's message suggested politely that he wished spare delegation inconvenience unnecessary trip.

Li's adviser, Chu Chang-wei, states delegation has not left Canton and that he had informed Wu Teh-chen that trip would be complete waste time as Li will not be at home to anyone next few days.

CEC move ostensibly designed as gesture support designed virtually force him come Canton. Li apparently determined remain Kweilin in attempt force issue with Generalissimo. (Reference Cantel 266, April 25.)

Sent Department Cantel 282, repeated Nanking 227, Shanghai 178.

CLARK

893.00/4–2749 : Telegram

The Minister-Counselor of Embassy in China (Clark) to the Secretary of State

CANTON, April 27, 1949—4 p. m.
[Received April 28—7 : 49 a. m.]

Cantel 287. Presence Canton Chu Chang-wei (Cantel 266, April 25 and 278, April 26) as well as information coming from other sources indicates strong probability that Li Tsung-jen has found his position untenable and is really determined upon showdown with Gimo.

Since taking office as Acting President, Li has had constant failure obtain respect his authority with resulting frustration largely through

---

[68] Central Executive Committee of the Kuomintang.
[69] Member of the National Policy Advisory Committee and former Vice President of the Chinese Judicial Yuan.

interference Gimo. Thru his control Kmt, armed forces, Nationalist treasury, secret police and persons remaining in office who are personal followers, Gimo has exerted his authority [garble] and can continue do so despite anything Li can do. Either, therefore, Gimo must be removed irrevocably from scene or Li must make other plans. He cannot be expected continue in present untenable position.

Gimo's response to Li's efforts at Hangchow was offer of compromise wherein both ostensibly shared power, altho in reality Li's position remained unchanged. Li has rejected proposal and is currently attempting secure adherence Kwangtung generals and get promise support from US.

Li's plans envisage rallying and organizing bloc, comprising northwest, southwest and south China, to continue civil war and seek material aid from US. On other hand, Gimo's policy involves concentration all possible resources Taiwan for prolonged defense island in hope that he may hold it until war between Soviet Union and US saves him. Thus he is unwilling risk any considerable portion his resources for military adventures on mainland. Under these conditions it is virtually certain he will refuse accede Li's demands, and open break between Li and Gimo may be confidently expected.

Without resources controlled by Gimo, Li lacks means for prolonged resistance. Altho he claims support various provincial leaders west and south China, it is highly doubtful that this would include any substantial military effort on part those concerned. They are largely interested in maintaining their own position and even if Li could offer prospect large US aid it is unlikely they would come positively to his assistance. When Li fully realizes that no US aid is forthcoming, that he cannot rely on positive assistance from his southwestern would-be allies, and that his sole remaining source of strength is armies Pai Chung-hsi, he will very likely remain Kwangsi and make whatever arrangement with Communists may be possible. Communists might conceivably by-pass Kwangsi and leave Li in peace for quite some time.

Factors outlined above give impetus to already strong trend toward regionalism, and so defeat attempt on part any Nationalist leaders [to] firm up organized resistance. Thus, further Communist advance into South China likely follow pattern series local settlements, with little military activity involved. It may well be that, convinced effective resistance an impracticality, and seeking most favorable possible terms, Li and Pai will agree lend their forces to facilitate Communist take-over of South. There is certainly no friendship or trust at present between Li and the Canton generals. In any event, day is obviously not far off when anti-Communist China will be so fragmented politically that Nationalist Govt will cease to exist as Nationalist force and will become little more than another regional authority. At that time we will have to scrutinize situation carefully in effort to determine whether continued recognition will make us look ridiculous in eyes of the world.

Sent Department, repeated Shanghai 180, Nanking 228.

CLARK

893.00/4–2749 : Telegram

The Minister-Counselor of Embassy in China (Clark) to the Secretary of State

CANTON, April 27, 1949—5 p. m.
[Received April 27—3 : 28 p. m.]

Cantel 288. Chu Chang-wei called again today, Cantel 276 [*278*], April 26, repeated Nanking 225, Shanghai 176, this time accompanied by Kan Chieh-hou. Kan is proceeding immediately to US in guise adviser Foreign Office but in fact special representative Li Tsung-jen, bearing letter of Li to President.[70]

Both Chu and Kan expressed complete confidence support Kwangtung Generals Chang Fa-kwei,[71] Hsueh Yueh, Yu Han-mou, as well as of Ho Ying-chin, in struggle with Generalissimo. Chang Chun, they insist, is also with them.

Plan is to reorganize armed services and government offices by removal incompetents, replacing them by vigorous young men of ability, and rearming and streamlining armed services as well as government offices. One of most difficult tasks this regard, but one they insist they will tackle immediately, is removal Chen Cheng from governorship Taiwan; and his replacement by more capable man. They feel sure such is Sun Li-jen who commands troops Taiwan and are sanguine they can unseat Chen Cheng. Should they succeed, they anticipate Chen will be left in Fukien supported only by troops of Tang En-po actuated from Shanghai.

By rejuvenation armed forces and government administration, they hope revive fighting spirit and produce victories and reforms which will enable Kan Chieh-hou persuade US grant government further aid.

Sent Department Cantel 288; repeated Shanghai 182, Nanking 229.

CLARK

---

[70] Dated May 5 ; see vol. IX, p. 699.
[71] Commander of the Chinese Ground Forces.

893.00/4–2849 : Telegram

The Minister-Counselor of Embassy in China (Clark) to the Secretary of State

CANTON, April 28, 1949—4 p. m.
[Received April 29—5 : 55 a. m.[72]]

Cantel 291. Process disintegration anti-Communist elements China continues. Tung Kwang-hsien, president Legislative Yuan, is leaving Canton today with family "for trip abroad". He admits to me that he has set date for opening Legislative Yuan May 6, but C–C Clique will that time control Legislative Yuan and would likely unseat him even though he remained Canton. He confirms press report Kmt idea of creating supreme policy-making body, "special war committee", its membership to include Li Tsung-jen, Sun Fo, Wu Tieh-chen, Chen Li-fu [73] and president[s] of five yuans. This body would work in close cooperation with Gimo as director general Kmt and Legislative and Control Yuans would be suppressed for duration "war".

Tung Kwang-hsien thinks situation hopeless. Although anti-Communists, confronted as they are with harsh Communist peace terms, should unite in resistance, he sees each individual looking at matter solely with his personal interests in view, with result there is increased fragmentation rather than unity. He is convinced Li Tsung-jen will not be fooled by any such special war committee as that C–C Clique envisages. Tung believes Li means business and that if he cannot obtain recognition his authority all anti-Communist China, including Taiwan, he will either retire Kwangsi or go abroad. Tung does not believe Li will accept to go down in history as leading armies doomed to certain defeat as will most certainly be case if he is unable obtain full recognition his authority. He agrees Gimo will under no circumstances voluntarily release authority. He sees therefore only further fragmentation and eventual Communist domination.

Tung confirms Li's unsuccessful efforts defend Yangtze, citing as example his inability enforce his authority defense Tikiang where Communists crossed Yangtze in first instance. He said that Li, knowing threat, asked Tang En-po for three divisions to counter it. Tang refused under Gimo's orders, but finally sent one division Tikiang and that division immediately defected to Communists. With some feeling he gave me details of Li's inability even to pick police commissioner Nanking because of Gimo's obstruction.

Tung is not so certain of support Kwangtung generals of Li. Li, he thinks, can count on support Chang Fa-kwei. Hsueh Yueh has inti-

---

[72] Text printed from corrected copy received May 1, 9 : 45 a. m.
[73] Wu had been Vice President of the Chinese Executive Yuan ; Chen, leader of the C–C clique, was Chinese Minister without Portfolio.

mate relations with Chen Cheng, governor Taiwan, ardent supporter Gimo, and may hesitate render unqualified support Li. Yu Han-mou, he says, feels strongly on neither one side or other and will go with tide. Ho Ying-chin is a weakling who agrees with the man with whom he is talking.

As pointed out Cantel 287, April 27, repeated Nanking 228, Shanghai 180, it seems to me that spirit of *sauve qui peut* so permeates thinking of leaders anti-Communist China and that it is so certain Gimo will not irrevocably relinquish his authority we can expect the further fragmentation Tung Kwang-hsien forces and collapse of organized resistance earlier than we had hitherto thought. As I gather that despite public announcements to contrary Li will not come Canton unless he is assured authority he demands, I plan, weather permitting in next day or so, fly Kweilin see Li in effort obtain direct from him confirmation reports his emissaries Canton. Tung tells me Ho Ying-chin flying Kweilin today. If, as anticipated, Ho's visit unsuccessful, Li's decision should have been taken when I arrive and pattern immediate future events determined.

Sent Department; repeated Nanking 230, Shanghai 13.

                                                        CLARK

893.00/4–2849 : Telegram

The Consul General at Shanghai (Cabot) to the Secretary of State

                                        SHANGHAI, April 28, 1949.
                                        [Received April 29—2 : 49 p. m.]

1430. *China Daily Tribune* April 28 publishes Central News version Gimo statement under Chikow, April 28 dateline. In first public statement since retirement January 21, Chiang urged all Chinese join struggle free country from Communist tyranny by recovery determination and courage which characterized war against Jap aggression. Charged Communists seeking enslavement of China people to cause of international Communism as military base and source manpower for Communist world domination. Said China not alone in struggle. Called for popular support government in effort effect drastic political, military, and economic reforms. Promised full support Li Tsung-jen. Stated Communist rejection peaceful settlement and crossing Yangtze repetition Jap political and military errors. Communists have reached peaks and crossing Yangtze will bring military, political, and economic problems which will result their inevitable downfall. Prophesied final victory within 3 years. Reviewed government's attempts peaceful settlement with Communists after Jap war. Communist actions finally forced government take military measures. Political and military shortcomings, misapprehension Communist intentions among Chinese and foreign public, Communist fifth column China and abroad contribute to failure government's efforts conclude war successfully. After own retirement, Li Tsung-jen repeatedly made concessions toward peaceful settlement but Communists openly announced intentions fight with Soviet Union in third world war, presented ultimatum, and launched general offensive. Communists have openly confessed desire carry out class warfare and world revolution. Outcome struggle will determine Chinese mode [of] life for generations. Stated Mao Tse-tung [74] more dangerous traitor than Wang Ching-wei.[75] Wang was Jap tool because he was weakling. Mao seeks enslave and destroy own nation to fulfill aggressive designs for power.

Sent Department 1430, repeated Nanking 817, Canton 365.

CABOT

893.00/4–2949 : Telegram

The Minister-Counselor of Embassy in China (Clark) to the Secretary of State

CANTON, April 29, 1949—10 a. m.
[Received 6 : 18 p. m.]

Cantel 294. Jockeying for position in anti-Communist China continues. Chu Chang-wei tells me Ho Ying-chin did not visit Kweilin yesterday (Cantel 291, April 28, repeated Nanking 230, Shanghai 183), as Li had sent word his visit would serve no useful purpose and had renewed his promise come Canton in near future. Chang Fa-kwei is, however, proceeding Kweilin today carrying unqualified assurances of support to Li from himself, Hsueh Yueh and Yu Han-mou.

Conceding that control Taiwan resources necessary to success Li's efforts, Chu says plans envisage approach to Chen Cheng, Governor Taiwan, through Hsueh Yueh, Governor Kwangtung, in effort persuade Chen that best interests himself and China lie in full support Li rather than Generalissimo. Only if persuasion fails do they plan more forceful measures remove Chen. I gather they have not yet even approached Sun Li-jen [76] although they feel confident his support. Despite information other sources to contrary, they insist Sun has control sufficient military forces Taiwan to remove Chen.

Sent Department Cantel 294, repeated Nanking 231. Shanghai 184.

CLARK

---

[74] Chairman of the Central Committee of the Chinese Communist Party.
[75] Head of Japanese-sponsored regime at Nanking, 1940–1944.
[76] Commander in Chief of the Taiwan Defense Headquarters and deputy director of Military and Poltical Affairs for Southeast China.

893.00/4–2949 : Telegram

The Minister-Counselor of Embassy in China (Clark) to the Secretary of State

CANTON, April 29, 1949—4 p. m.
[Received April 30—4:06 a. m.]

Cantel 299. George Yeh, acting FonMin, sent for me today. He is worried over reports appearing in American press indicating government abandoned Diplomatic Corps Nanking to its fate and in hurried withdrawal left large quantities ammunition, military equipment to fall into Communist hands. He asked me to report facts as follows:

Evacuation Nanking had been precipitated by defection April 19 Commanders [at] Kiangyin and Tikiang which placed Nanking in untenable position. Government had determined upon withdrawal, and an orderly withdrawal was in progress, when he (Yeh) arrived Nanking April 21 and he had immediately arranged CAF [77] transportation for Diplomatic Corps and urgently requested withdrawal, speaking personally to American, French and Canadian Ambassadors. Further and more urgent suggestion Diplomatic Corps leave was made on 22d. Also Yeh had himself arranged, in cooperation Mayor Nanking, to leave 300 police specially designated to protect Diplomatic Corps area. Unfortunately rumors resulted in these police throwing away their arms and uniforms and submerging into community. He asked with simulated sincerity as to welfare Ambassador Stuart and was most regretful any indignities to which he had been subjected through lack of protection by municipal police.[78]

Yeh said government had determined to defend Shanghai, not in city, but in outlying districts and that defense would be fully supported by CAF.

Fu Ping-chang [79] has still not accepted appointment FonMin and Yeh says no one is willing accept appointment these days until military have produced a victory.

Sent Department, repeated Nanking 235, Shanghai 187.

CLARK

893.001 Chiang Kai-shek/4–2949 : Telegram

The Minister-Counselor of Embassy in China (Clark) to the Secretary of State

CANTON, April 29, 1949—7 p. m.
[Received April 30—1:46 p. m.]

Cantel 301. When Sun Fo received me today in his heavily guarded Tungshan residence, he obviously had jitters and was most uncommu-

[77] Chinese Air Force.
[78] For further documentation on the Ambassador's experiences after occupation of Nanking by the Chinese Communists, see pp. 723 ff.
[79] Foo Ping-sheung, Chinese Ambassador in the Soviet Union.

nicative. He confirmed, however, Gimo's proposal at Hangchow to Li Tsung-jen for creation supreme policy committee which Gimo would head and which would be superior to Cabinet. Sun tried to leave me with impression Li had agreed and insisted creation some such organ capable quick action was needed. Its creation would not affect Legislative and Control Yuans, he said. He was obviously depressed as well as jittery and insisted without conviction that Shanghai would be defended.

Sent Department Cantel 301, repeated Nanking 236, Shanghai 189.

CLARK

893.001 Chiang Kai-shek/5–149 : Telegram

The Minister-Counselor of Embassy in China (Clark) to the Secretary of State

CANTON, May 1, 1949—4 p. m.
[Received May 5—11 : 49 a. m.[80]]

Cantel 303. After more than 4 hours with Acting President Li in Kweilin yesterday, I am convinced he means business; is determined upon showdown with Generalissimo, and is hopeful of success. Chang Fa-kwei and representative [of] Ho Ying-chin were Kweilin while I was there and Li said that they brought assurances of agreement among Canton generals and Ho on need remove Generalissimo irretrievably from scene. Without Generalissimo, C–C Clique would disappear and Li's authority could be made effective.

Problem of how remove Generalissimo is one occupying negotiations at moment. Generalissimo wants resume power, Li said, but feels he cannot do so except at Canton, seat of government, and that he cannot come Canton unless Li also present. Li, therefore, is not coming Canton until he has, to him, convincing assurances that he can control situation and Generalissimo cannot stage come-back. Among the assurances he is seeking of Canton generals and Ho is one that they will not permit Generalissimo come Canton under any circumstances.

Li says Generalissimo is en route Amoy. As he cannot from there resume presidency nor position of commander in chief, Generalissimo plans endeavor exert his authority through party. It was with this idea in view that Generalissimo suggested at Hangchow the 11-man policy committee (apropos this policy committee, Chu Chang-wei said he told Chen Li-fu: "You can tell Generalissimo he may think he can play role Empress Dowager, but he can be sure Li will never be his 'Kuang Hsu' "[81]). Li said he refused flatly have anything do with such policy committee. Party's influence in executive branch government,

---

[80] Garbled text received May 3, 10 : 30 a. m.
[81] Kuang-hsu reign, 1889–1908, during which the Emperor's widowed aunt wielded power "from behind the curtain" as virtual regent.

he said, should be exercised solely through Legislative Yuan. Li thinks he can get control Taiwan; he will not only have spoiled General-issimo's plan to make last stand there, thus increasing likelihood Generalissimo may be prevailed upon go abroad, but will also assure to himself the vast resources Generalissimo has concentrated on island. With those resources, Li thinks he can make resistance on scale that will convince Congress further investment China warranted. He expressed firm determination root out all incompetents in armed forces and government and replace them by qualified young men and he expressed hope that when he had done so we would assist him with advisors in fields where qualified Chinese talent was unavailable. He is fully aware that he must demonstrate ability offer alternative to Communism before he can expect any further aid, but he hopes by stemming tide of Communist advance and holding fast, we may be led reconsider our position.

Taiwan being key to problem, Chen Cheng becomes all-important. Li is determined that he shall be removed as Governor Taiwan and replaced by a Li man so as to remove Taiwan as possibility refuge Generalissimo, as well as to obtain control of resources there. With full prestige of Li, supported by Canton generals and Ho Ying-chin, Li hopes Chen Cheng will see reason and accept transfer. On other hand, he might not. Li is very interested, therefore, in obtaining some form of US support of his action. He suggested a statement from us which I immediately said would be inconceivable. He then stated as a fact that when Generalissimo was considering retiring, he had first planned retire Taiwan. Governor had mentioned possibility to our Consul General who had remarked casually that legal status Taiwan would not be determined until Japanese [peace] treaty was signed. This casual remark, according to Li, was reported to Generalissimo with result Generalissimo decided he could not retire to place where sovereignty China might be questioned, and thus went Fenghwa instead. Li wondered whether our Consul General there could not be authorized at time Chen Cheng is transferred to remark casually to Chen that he assumed he would be obeying his instructions as in interest of his country. I changed subject without comment, but the idea may have merit. Although Li would not admit possibility miscarriage his plans, he left me with impression of conviction that without him and his supporters C–C clique and Generalissimo would be unable form even façade of government.

Sent Department Cantel 303, repeated Nanking 238, Shanghai 191.

CLARK

893.00/5–349 : Telegram

*The Minister-Counselor of Embassy in China (Clark) to the
Secretary of State*

CANTON, May 3, 1949—5 p. m.
[Received 8 : 18 p. m.]

Cantel 313. Li Han-hun, Minister Interior, is among those believing
anti-Communist forces China can still rally if properly led and offer
effective resistance Communists. Reactionary Kmt must go, he says,
but liberals in Kmt and outside are getting together with strength increasing daily and he is convinced will soon offer alternative to Communism. He supports efforts get Li Tsung-jen come Canton, yet realizes Li must have authority he demands. He also tends to confirm
rumors that Chen Cheng, Governor Taiwan, is expected Canton
shortly.

He expressed hope that Ambassador Stuart when he reaches US
will explain to American people actual situation China. He hopes also
that Kan Chieh-hou, Li Tsung-jen's prospective representative, will
also be able convince American people need review situation when
evidence provided effective resistance Communism.

Sent Department; repeated Nanking 242, Shanghai 195.

CLARK

893.00/5–449 : Telegram

The Consul at Tsingtao (Strong) to the Secretary of State

TSINGTAO, May 4, 1949—5 p. m.
[Received May 4—2 :41 p. m.]

173. Local military and economic situation steadily deteriorating.
Nationalist lines withdrawn to inner defenses near airfields with few
lightly-held points in forward areas. Several engagements in increasing size occurred during past week involving up to 600 Communists.
Estimated 35,000 Nationalist troops of which 6,000 PPC's [82] worthless, 7,000 of Thirty-two Army largely unreliable (4,000 desertions
recently), 22,000 Fifty Army of questionable morale. Despite fact
silver brought here 3 weeks ago for purpose, troops unpaid for some
time. Chinese commander states food for troops will last only until
May 20.

Seven B–24's bombed airfields Mukden from Tsingtao May 3 and 4,
claiming several aircraft destroyed on ground and hits on hangars.

Textile mills closed 2 weeks ago, business virtually at standstill,
acute money shortage, thousands of government workers unpaid for
long period believed near strike. Four thousand military police in city

---

[82] Peace Preservation Corps.

to maintain order, principally in industrial area in northern part of city. Coal supply for 1 week only but hopeful 7,000 tons Japanese coal within 10 days. Small shipments US cotton due later in May. Governor Chin Teh-chun understand still attempting obtain funds Shanghai for government operations here.

Gen Liu An-chi visiting Generalissimo's headquarters today at latter's urgent request to discuss Tsingtao. Liu understood to believe he will be ordered out though decision may hang on what they think US Navy plans.

Current estimates give Tsingtao from 2 to 6 weeks before "liberation."

Sent Nanking 135; OffEmb Canton 42; Department 173.

STRONG

893.00/5–449 : Telegram

The Consul General at Shanghai (Cabot) to the Secretary of State

SHANGHAI, May 4, 1949—6 p. m.
[Received May 5—2 : 32 a. m.[83]]

1506. While conflicting opinions and uncertain factors preclude predicting, our best information would indicate a probable shaping of events since breakdown peace negotiations along following general lines:

Li Tsung-jen's plan hold Yangtze was ruined by (a) disregard of his powers by Tang En-po's forces and (b) a progressive defecting of other Yangtze defense units which his lack of authority had rendered him powerless to combat (and which, through the resultant Tikiang and Kiangyin defections, forced his premature abandonment of Nanking, according to some sources). Thus convinced of utter futility of attempting lead anti-Communist resistance unless invested with full leadership, Li flew Chikow with Ho Ying-chin and demanded that Generalissimo either himself resume active military leadership and responsibility or give Li complete control Nationalist armies and resources. Generalissimo has done neither. While publicity [*publicly?*] professing full support of Li, he continues direct affairs and by way of added insult has advertised Ho rather than Li as chief Nationalist leader. Hence Li's return to Kwangsi.

Generalissimo meanwhile has come Shanghai and still remains here—press reports to contrary, accenting his presence by recent dramatic speech declaring determination continue implacable fight against international Communism. Weight evidence suggests he seriously

---

[83] Text printed from corrected copy received May 8, 11 : 30 p. m.

hopes and prepares to have Nationalists hold Shanghai long enough to:

(1) Permit southward withdrawal Nationalist troops to Shanghai–Hangchow line and strengthen Ningpo–Hangchow–Nanchang defense system for protection Generalissimo's Fukien base. Late information indicates this objective already impossible.

(2) Complete southward evacuation from Shanghai by sea all of most valuable remaining troops, military equipment and general materiel. While no heavy troop evacuations yet confirmed, this conclusion supported by logic and fragmentary evidence including departure certain specialized units and Generalissimo's evident preoccupation with assembling large fleet ships to prepare getaway.

(3) Impress America, Britain with ability stage gallant defence city. Believed reliable sources state that on April 26 Generalissimo told Army Commanders American China policy could be expected change basically in 1 or 2 months and that Tang must hold city minimum 1 month. Tang reportedly declared would hold 3 months or suicide. Generalissimo also said giving pep talks to officers down to battalion commanders, promising World War III in 6 months.

(4) In line with 2 and 3, suppress or at least delay action by Shanghai elements toward arranging peaceful turnover city in "going" and intact state to Communist. Aside from heavy shipments moveable physical assets, Generalissimo is known to be trying force evacuation of many professional persons against their desires, including entire bank staffs and also persons who he has reason believe will be key participants in peaceful turnover movement. Thus Tu Yueh-sheng's departure for Hong Kong May 1 said forced by Generalissimo, who also said pressing Yang Hu to leave. Yang said feigning prepare leave but determined remain. Some allege that Generalissimo or his Military BIS [84] supporters may take further step of ordering a scorched earth destruction or even physical attacks on foreigners (with intention incriminate Communists and involve foreign powers).

Powerful Shanghai interests deeming military defense city hopeless and anxious minimize destruction and make best of inevitable Communist occupation are seeking complete secret arrangements with Communists looking to early takeover city by intermediate regime made up of various local groups (Chambers Commerce, guilds, etc.) and backed by Yang Hu–Tu Yueh-sheng Green-Red Gangs organization, which would shortly hand over to Communist Government (see previous ConGentels). This plan envisages prior neutralization of at least part Nationalist troops and police through propaganda or bribery and special steps to protect vital properties and (allegedly) foreign lives. Underground representatives having approached ConGen claim that Communist cooperation already assured and that foreign, especially American, cooperation most important from standpoint of food supplies and winning public confidence in regime. Believe that, although these representatives probably exaggerate progress of their

[84] Bureau of Investigation and Statistics (Security).

project toward winning Communist approval, something on general pattern of project is likely materialize.

Despite swift thrust of some units along Wusih–Soochow and Wusih–Kashing approaches to Shanghai, Communist main efforts appear thus far directed toward liquidating Nationalist armies west of Taihu Lake with view opening up Nationalist Hangchow–Nanchang defense line preparations to easy destruction and isolating Shanghai from Hangchow; and Communist operations nearest Shanghai seem still in nature probings by light forces. Observers feel that as soon as sizeable force is readied for task, Communists can take Shanghai in short order; but that entirely possible they may deliberately delay occupation for considerations such as (1) food shortage and inability take over task of feeding population and factories, (2) unreadiness with respect administrative personnel, or (3) extreme anxiety to avoid destruction of city installations and consequent tendency to delay occupation pending further progress of secret arrangements to ensure peaceful turnover with adequate precautions for protection of city assets. Believe especial importance to last factor, which probably explains why, despite Communists' undoubted ability to stir up major internal troubles through their infiltration of police and other key organs and their reliably reported armed underground forces within Shanghai, city remains surprisingly quiet considering the very precarious labor situation. Same factor might also cause Communists to avoid pressing Generalissimo withdrawal too closely for fear it might precipitate his resort to scorched earth tactics before Communists have completed secret arrangements to combat such action. Course and timing of events remain unpredictable in view various uncertain factors such as: Extent to which silver dollars can make Nationalists fight; availability of dollars; Generalissimo's real intentions; Communists' planning regarding Shanghai; extent to which Communists have actually committed selves to any local peace group; dependability of police (already known to include many Communists and Green-Red Gangs said to be taking action suggesting possible intention to cooperate eventually with peace planners); and the chances of serious misbehaviour by Nationalist troops or labor riots (from purely economic causes) which might force events and alter whole picture.

While risking no prediction we hazard guess that mounting labor tension is momentarily more menacing than politico-military potentialities and that, barring internal disorders serious enough to force Communist hand prematurely, city may well continue under reasonably orderly Nationalist control for at least week with fair possibility that no drastic change will eventuate for month or more.

One possibility to be kept in mind is that Communists, in hopes of maintenance ECA aid, may attempt effect changeover from local emergency regime to Communist dominated government in gradual manner with view to having their domination so camouflaged by local-coalition appearance during initial period that government could be declared still non-Communist.

CABOT

893.00/5–549 : Telegram

The Minister-Counselor of Embassy in China (Clark) to the Secretary of State

CANTON, May 5, 1949—6 p. m.
[Received May 5—4 : 30 p. m.]

Cantel 320. As indicative of complete bankruptcy of leadership anti-Communist China at moment is fact that Legislative Yuan is reconvening May 6 without its president [85] who has fled Hong Kong with family in realization hopelessness situation. Li Tsung-jen sits in Kweilin successfully discouraging visits from such as Ho Ying-chin and Wu Tieh-cheng on basis he can be influenced by deeds not words, yet finally acquiescing in visit mission headed by Yen Hsi-shan whom C–C clique is seeking to use as window dressing and telling all and sundry without qualification that he has learned his lesson and refuses again to accept responsibility without full authority. He is reported to have put it baldly to Yen that he would not be "puppet" of Generalissimo.

Generalissimo hovers in background somewhere between Fenghua and Amoy (reports have him in Taiwan) presenting real and insurmountable obstacle to rallying of forces of resistance behind Li Tsung-jen. He has accumulated his treasure and his armed forces on Taiwan and is determined to conserve those for last-ditch stand on Foochow–Amoy–Taiwan triangle in hope he can survive until what he conceives to be the inevitable war between USSR and US out of which in some way he will re-emerge as ruler of all China. He seems oblivious to fundamental fact that after defeat international Communism directed from Moscow, US would have no interest in reestablishing his authority China.

In between these extremes, C–C clique and Canton generals seeking desperately find some means overcoming what is in effect an insurmountable obstacle of complete collaboration between Generalissimo and Li Tsung-jen in their present moods. Canton generals are in quandary. They have no resources protect themselves and Li promises protection only if they will produce Taiwan resources accumulated by Generalissimo which they cannot do and Generalissimo is not

---

[85] Tung Kwan-hsien.

interested in defending Kwangtung. As a result, they are wringing their hands and at loss to know what to do.

Result is that Nationalist Government, in its death throes, is without leadership. Principal Government leaders are attending conferences all day long fruitlessly seeking the impossible, while their subordinates sit with their feet on desks reading newspapers and wondering how life will be under Communists or on Taiwan. It seems to me that what little possibility may have existed that anti-Communist forces could be unified and rallied to effective resistance to Communism is fast disappearing if it has not already done so. Communists are grimly setting about their tasks of occupying rest of China while anti-Communist leaders, incapable of viewing problem from other than basis their selfish personal interests, are going around in circles accomplishing nothing. Suspicion is so deep-seated and differences between Li Tsung-jen and Generalissimo so absolutely irreconcilable that, barring miracle, we may see early disappearance any Nationalist Government worthy of the name.

Sent Department Cantel 320; repeated Nanking 248; Shanghai 202.

CLARK

893.00/5–649 : Telegram

The Minister-Counselor of Embassy in China (Clark) to the Secretary of State

CANTON, May 6, 1949—3 p. m.
[Received May 6—2 : 10 p. m.]

Cantel 323. Returned from Kweilin where he went heading C–C delegation seeking return Canton Li Tsung-jen, Marshal Yen Hsi-shan tells us Li continues refuse come Canton until assured free hand running government. In addition to control over finances and economic planning, Yen says military strategy is one of main points of conflict between Li and Generalissimo, claiming Generalissimo wants defend coast while Li favors withdrawal into interior.

Repeated Nanking 249, Shanghai 205.

CLARK

893.01/5–649 : Telegram

The Minister-Counselor of Embassy in China (Clark) to the Secretary of State

CANTON, May 6, 1949.
[Received May 6—4 : 13 p. m.]

Cantel 331. Reuter despatch, datelined Canton May 5, states letter Li to Generalissimo brought back from Kweilin by Li Wen-fan [86] contains following terms:

---

[86] Former Vice President of the Chinese Judicial Yuan.

1. Economically, all national property including gold, silver bars and foreign currency transferred Taiwan 2 months ago be placed disposal of Li.
2. Politically, government organs Canton go under control of Li.
3. Militarily, all troops Central [and] South China go under command of Li.

Sent Department Cantel 331, Nanking 253, Shanghai 211.

CLARK

893.00/5–749 : Telegram

The Consul General at Shanghai (Cabot) to the Secretary of State

SHANGHAI, May 7, 1949—3 p. m.
[Received May 8—3 : 33 a. m.]

1549. While Generalissimo's intentions re staging real fighting for Shanghai remain unknown, it seems increasingly clear that his immediate objectives include at least (1) fleecing of city of last available dollar and (2) greatest possible removal of transportable equipment and other assets as well as personnel useful to Communists. Latest economic financial measures which Tang's garrison command striving ruthlessly enforce seem designed to bring quick profits and hard money to Nationalist military authorities which they can ship or take from Shanghai; and behavior Tang's forces and other evidence strongly suggests build-up for bigger shake-downs of city. Personnel whom, according several good sources, Generalissimo has ordered to leave city include particularly economic specialists and "big city bosses" whose huge local investments and widely ramified power make them natural organizers for peaceful turnover. Those of first category who have already left Shanghai include virtually all top financiers such as Chang Kia-ngao, K. P. Chen, Li Ming, Hsi Teh-mou, *et al.* In second category there have departed not only Tu Yueh-sheng but also number of his chief lieutenants as well as Chien Yung-ming.[87]

While some of these economic and civic leaders have probably left by desire, others understood to have only gone under pressure. Middle-ranking personnel also affected with many hundred bankers, et cetera ordered leave and majority attempting evade compliance. Important bosses still left but under pressure to leave include Yang Hu, Wang Hsiao-lai [88] and other Chamber Commerce leaders. Generalissimo's special pressure on city bosses together with reliable reports that W. W. Yen,[89] who is generally regarded as most likely front for an interim regime, is being pressed to leave (and feigning hospitalization in order to stay) seems indicate that Generalissimo determined prevent peace-

---

[87] Chairman of board of directors, Bank of Communications.
[88] Chairman of Chinese National Federation of Chambers of Commerce.
[89] Leader of Shanghai peace delegation to Peiping in February.

ful turn-over of intact city to Communists. These and other ruthless measures being enforced by Tang under undoubted order of Generalissimo, as dispersal of part populace to countryside, increasing resort to terrorism (arbitrary arrests, executions, et cetera), seizures and forced evacuations of private properties and leveling of buildings—all indicating utter disregard for Shanghai populace and defiant rejection of any thought of retaining loophole for settlement with Communists on other than battle basis—seem to constitute strong evidence that Generalissimo really does intend fight at least until city's stripping been completed. Hectic preparations and Generalissimo's attempts to bolster troops' failing morale with rash promises of American aid and third world war (see reftel) would also seem justify such conclusion. There is nevertheless possibility that instead of an intention to stage serious fight all these manifestations represent gigantic bluff with double purpose of (*a*) inducing Communists to delay their advance on city—thus giving Generalissimo more time for rehabilitation work—and (*b*) frightening Shanghai populace into generous response to last big shake-down which Nationalists may demand as price for withdrawal without fight. As indicated, however, Generalissimo's intention leave city emptied if not a wreck (if reported intentions to carry out demolitions are correct) is certainly no bluff.

See my next numbered telegram.[90]

Sent Nanking 864; repeated Department, OffEmb Canton 417.

CABOT

893.50/5–749 : Telegram

The Consul General at Shanghai (Cabot) to the Secretary of State

SHANGHAI, May 7, 1949—3 p. m.
[Received May 7—8 : 20 a. m.]

1550. Economic situation in Shanghai continues grave with no evident signs of improvement regardless of military developments. Cash shortage slightly eased with Central Bank paying out only 25–35 percent overnight deposits in cashier's checks not in DP [*GY*] [91] or silver. Nevertheless business is steadily falling off with many firms operating at deficit, factory production dropping and unemployment increasing. Tendency accentuated by departure many Chinese industrial and business leaders. Public clamor has resulted in reduction of utility rates by 70 percent at which level utilities cannot even pay for fuel—yet at higher levels rates are ruinous to consumers.

Psychologically even conservative business men are now longing for Commie entry. They naturally consider it inevitable, do not want

---

[90] *Infra.*
[91] Gold yuan.

Shanghai made a battleground and think nothing could be worse than present situation.

It seems to us probable that situation will get worse rather than better in immediate future. We doubt continuing disintegration can be prevented so long as Shanghai remains in Nationalist hands. Entry of Commies even if peaceful is likely to cause further drop in business which will probably be even more serious in event of violent entry or important demolitions. After Commie entry it seems inevitable they will have grave problems to secure needed supplies of food, cotton and oil. It is possible they can get food and cotton in China but fuel oil essential to run utilities can only be secured from abroad and if it is not secured promptly a major catastrophe seems unavoidable. Moreover there is widespread conviction particularly among British that Generalissimo wants Shanghai laid waste and that he will destroy utilities and industries in order to (1) punish Shanghai which he has allegedly always hated, (2) give impression abroad of heroic resistance to Communism, (3) leave insoluble problem for Commies, (4) get even with foreigners for not helping him in his hour of need, (5) create a sort of Hitlerian Götterdämmerung.

I feel that Dept should earnestly consider following questions: (1) Should we take any action to prevent fighting within Shanghai; (2) should I be instructed to make firm representations on demolitions (our position re American utilities seems particularly strong); (3) should we take any constructive action to assure Shanghai of essential supplies particularly oil after takeover; (4) if Shanghai should be reduced to complete chaos by fighting, demolitions, economic prostration, power failure or epidemics, should we not be prepared as far as possible to remove Americans from Shanghai area even after takeover.

Re (1), I realize this is very delicate matter, yet on other hand strong humanitarian considerations favor action. Re (3), quite apart from problem of scheduling incoming shipments I think it unlikely Commies will have foreign exchange available for payments or adequate goods for sale or barter. Only other alternative would appear to be some credit arrangements which might perhaps be obtainable privately with our acquiescence. Despite strong objections to this we should also consider whether our interests would be advanced by chaos and suffering in Shanghai and whether we might not profit by agreeing to credit on strict conditions.

I should appreciate Dept's views on above points. Dept may wish to discuss them with British. If Dept feels any action warranted, it might in view of great British interest be able to secure more British cooperation in other matters notably controls on exports to Commie China (see my immediately preceding telegram).

Sent Dept 1550, repeated Nanking 865, Canton 418.

CABOT

893.00/5–849 : Telegram

The Consul General at Shanghai (Cabot) to the Secretary of State

SHANGHAI, May 8, 1949—11 a. m.
[Received May 8—2 : 59 a. m.]

1551. General Tang En-po informs me that three Communist armies are now advancing on Shanghai, on Changshu–Soochow front, two more have turned back from Hangchow towards Kashing and about three more seem to be getting into line for attack on Shanghai. Tang expects attack to come from southwest aimed at Pootung sector which is fortified but not as heavily as elsewhere. He denies reports that reinforcements have been brought from Taiwan.

Tang says no fighting as yet on Pai Chung-hsi's front. He at one moment insinuates Pai has made a deal, at next claims he is still loyal to Nationalists. Tang openly avows his loyalty to Generalissimo.

Tang also states that Communists are divided into Chinese and international factions and claims there is friction between Chinese Communists and Soviets.

Tang admits that maintenance of order in Shanghai is going to be difficult and by inference that he cannot hold Shanghai.

Tang says cannonading heard near Woosung May 6 was practice.

Sent Department, repeated Nanking 867, Canton 419, ComNav-WesPac.[92]

CABOT

893.00/5–949 : Telegram

The Consul General at Shanghai (Cabot) to the Secretary of State

SHANGHAI, May 9, 1949—4 p. m.
[Received May 11—12 : 37 p. m.]

1565. Editor *Sin Wen Pao* told me yesterday that there would be no strong defense of Shanghai. He said that Generalissimo had left Friday and had ordered release arrested students on departing; that General Tang En-po would stay in Shanghai with his forces about 10 days more during which he would thoroughly clean out city while his best forces hold Woosung and would then depart on ships already held for this purpose. He said Generalissimo's plans were to hold Taiwan and

---

[92] Commander, U.S. Naval Forces, Western Pacific.

Fukien triangle, waiting World War III, and that no military show-down would be risked until that point reached. He pointed out that requisitioning of trucks and cars which started today is necessary because forces in Shanghai have already shipped so much of their equipment out and claims that, contrary to reports, troops are being taken from Shanghai rather than brought in.

Editor also said that W. W. Yen will definitely head an interim government and that police with exception of few top men would, unlike those in Nanking, remain on job under orders of committee headed by Yen in order to maintain order. He said Yen already in touch with Communists.

Despite being known as C–C stalwart, editor expressed complete disillusionment with Kmt and he is determined to stay here and make best possible terms with Communists. I think that his version which is that generally favored in other well-informed sources is probably the correct one and that British (third paragraph mytel 1550, May 7, 3 p. m.) are mistaken. Nevertheless, I feel need for policy determinations on points raised in reference telegram. Even if Nationalists have no intention of making a real stand in Shanghai, it should do us no harm if Chinese and British know we made representations against fighting and demolition in Shanghai. Even for Nationalists, it might serve as a face-saver.

Sent Department, repeated Nanking 870, Canton 41.

CABOT

893.00/5–949 : Telegram

The Minister-Counselor of Embassy in China (Clark) to the Secretary of State

CANTON, May 9, 1949—7 p. m.
[Received May 11—1:17 p. m.]

Cantel 338. As result exchange letters with Generalissimo, Li Tsung-jen has come Canton. I do not believe, however, that his presence Canton materially changes picture portrayed Cantel 320, May 5, repeated Nanking 248, Shanghai 202, but represents merely further jockeying for position. Tung Kwan-hsien, President Legislative Yuan and Li's supporter, informs us that introductory part of Li's letter to Generalissimo pointed out that, although Communists were harsh in their peace terms, responsibility present situation really rested on government. Li went on to propose that he would go abroad to solicit foreign aid while Generalissimo would again assume control of government. Finally Li stated that if Generalissimo insisted on staying in retirement he must have satisfactory assurances on following:

1. Li must have full authority direct government administration;
2. Nationalist Defense Ministry must have full control all government troops;
3. Gold, silver and foreign exchange reserve now Taiwan must be placed at government disposal;
4. All military equipment stored Taiwan must be placed at government disposal;
5. Kmt must not interfere with operation of constitutional government by devices such as proposed super-policy organ;
6. Generalissimo must go abroad and solicit foreign aid.

Li concluded by saying that unless satisfactory assurances were forthcoming he would remain Kweilin.

Generalissimo's answers which reached Canton Friday are:

1. As Acting President, Li can exercise all his constitutional powers;
2. That Generalissimo did not himself set any precedent for field commanders to destroy government orders; that he cannot guarantee that all government orders will be obyed by commanders, even if he himself were in command, and advised Li to try to restore discipline;
3. That since all gold, silver and foreign exchange belonged to the government, Li of course can make use of them;
4. That all military equipment would be at disposal of government;
5. That he would cause no interference by the party;
6. That since China has not yet been conquered by any foreign country, he (Generalissimo) should still enjoy freedom to live where he wills.

Although I shall inquire more deeply and report further, these moves seem, on their face, largely for the record. Li tried put Generalissimo on spot by requesting in writing the assurances he was demanding of respect for his authority. Generalissimo could not afford to do other than assure Li of his complete innocence of past crimes or future intention to interfere in any way. Nevertheless, given the character of his responses, Li felt it necessary come Canton, resume authority and ascertain whether Generalissimo will in fact behave. My best judgment is that he won't and that these maneuvers merely delay disintegration and that eventually Li will be led publicly to denounce Generalissimo and his machinations.

Repeated Nanking 260.

CLARK

893.00/5–1049 : Telegram

The Consul General at Hankow (Callanan) to the Secretary of State

HANKOW, May 10, 1949—2 p. m.
[Received May 13—11 : 38 a. m.]

133. Pai summoned Consuls meeting yesterday. He said acceptance Communist demands unthinkable and war must go on. He said war approaching Wuhan and assured he would protect foreign lives, property while he was in control.

He invited questions and British Consul General asked re British floating equipment on Yangtze. He asserted civilian installations equipment would not be destroyed but military equipment whether Chinese or foreign owned would be treated according military necessity. He said categorically power stations, water works and dykes would not be damaged.

To my query whether fighting was to be expected Wuhan cities, he declined answer on grounds military secrets.

He offered assist foreigners re rail reservations southward, this due military requisition all trains immediate future.

Comment: Consider meeting was Pai's way saying goodbye to Consuls. We have it clearly thru AMA [93] Captain McAllister past few days and from earlier general reports that Pai will not fight in Wuhan. Events on line east–west through Nanchang will dictate timing his withdrawal. At same time General Lu Tao-yuan, Wuhan defense commander, will remain fight rear guard action and may indulge demolitions with or without Pai's consent.

Reliably reported security committee has and will maintain organized police during interregnum. Pai's headquarters departing today leaving only command post Wuchang.

Sent Department 133, Nanking 98, AmEmbassy Canton 55.

CALLANAN

893.00/5–1049 : Telegram

The Minister-Counselor of Embassy in China (Clark) to the Secretary of State

CANTON, May 10, 1949—6 p. m.
[Received May 11—1 : 13 a. m.]

Cantel 343. Han Li-wu, Minister Education, confirms that mutual suspicion continues hamper efforts unify forces resistance Communism. Generalissimo, he says, fears place complete trust Li Tsung-jen until he has demonstrated greater determination fight to finish. He thinks Generalissimo must have communed deeply with himself before

[93] Assistant Military Attaché.

sending response to Li, yet having sent response he believes Generalissimo will keep his word. He admits, on other hand, justice in Li's insistence on full authority if he is to retain responsibility. He agrees Li is following correct policy in taking Generalissimo at his word, coming Canton and acting on assumption his authority will be respected. In some way, Han hopes that this vicious circle of mistrust can be broken and all resistance forces unified behind Li Tsung-jen.

Sent Department Cantel 343; repeated Nanking 264, Shanghai 223.

CLARK

893.50/5–1049 : Telegram

The Ambassador in China (Stuart) to the Secretary of State

NANKING, May 10, 1949—7 p. m.
[Received May 11—1 : 45 a. m.]

989. [To Shanghai:] I met with my French and British colleagues, latter's request, this morning to discuss present, future situation Shanghai and possible courses action by you and your colleagues to mitigate effects all-out defense of city. (Reurtel 1550 to Department May 7, repeated Nanking 865, Canton 418.) We decided to recommend to you and British, French ConGens that you suggest to your respective Chambers of Commerce that they participate in and support any move of non-political nature by local Chinese (presumably Chinese Chamber of Commerce) vis-à-vis military authorities to preserve physical plant of city, principally utilities and industries, from deliberate destruction. It was felt that any approach should be Chinese-led although appropriately supported by local foreign interests.

We further agreed that should this appeal of Chinese and foreign interests materialize and prove successful, the foreign governments might possibly endorse action taken by local bodies.

Since French Ambassador experiencing some difficulty communicating with his ConGen Shanghai, please inform your French colleague substance of above in which Meyrier concurs. Your British colleague receiving similar message direct from Stevenson.

Re first consideration urtel under reference, you will remember question joint foreign intervention in somewhat different terms was considered by Department early December and was discouraged at that time. Second consideration is covered by above recommendations. Re third consideration, I can not believe our best interests would be served by gratuitous stocking of supplies, including oil, preparatory to Communist takeover or extending credit for their subsequent acquisition. We have recommended against any additional aid to Nationalist defenders of Shanghai (see Embtel 493, May 3, repeated Department 926 [94] Canton 346) and could scarcely justify, on political grounds at least, similar assistance to their enemies.

I want to take this opportunity to assure you and American community Shanghai of my lively sympathy your predicament and full appreciation heavy responsibility for protection American lives and interests which rests upon you.

Sent Shanghai 550, repeated Department, OffEmb Canton 393.

STUART

893.01/5–1149 : Telegram

The Ambassador in China (Stuart) to the Secretary of State

NANKING, May 11, 1949.
[Received May 11—1 : 18 a. m.]

996. Nanking *Hsin Hua Jih Pao* May 10 carries exclusive announcement of formation of new Nanking municipal government. Chinese People's Revolutionary Military Council appointed Liu Po-cheng as Mayor, Ko Ching-shih and Chang Lin-chih as Deputy Mayors.

Sent Department 996; repeated Shanghai 554, Peiping 153, Embassy Canton 396.

STUART

893.00/5–1149 : Telegram

The Consul at Tsingtao (Strong) to the Secretary of State

TSINGTAO, May 11, 1949—3 p. m.
[Received May 11—6 : 58 a. m.]

185. Following battle night May 6–7 in which they were defeated, Communists began withdrawal from perimeter. Main body now stated some 40 miles due north Tsingtao.

Source close to Liu An-chi states during confab at Shanghai last week Generalissimo authorized Liu withdraw forces from Tsingtao and choose own timing in order avoid losses.

Morale of Nationalist soldiers somewhat elevated by victory over Communists and by payment to portion of Army and to all wounded silver dollars in amounts varying from 4 to private to 50 to colonel.

Sent Nanking 144, OffEmb Canton 49, Department 185.

STRONG

---

[94] Vol. IX, p. 641.

893.24/5–1149

Memorandum of Conversation, by the Secretary of State

[WASHINGTON,] May 11, 1949.

The Chinese Ambassador [95] called to see me at his request. He said that in the first place he wished to call attention to the fact that the peace negotiations about which he had commented on his previous visit had broken down and that his Government had decided to resist the Chinese Communist onslaught. It was painful to see him try to make the case that the Chinese Nationalist armies were effectively resisting and that therefore the United States should now take some additional action in support of the Nationalist Government, he being as aware as I that in the past three weeks the Chinese Communist armies have crossed unimpeded the Yangtze River and established a 400-mile beachhead along its bank penetrating at some places as deep as 200 miles and enveloping Shanghai. He did ask for some general statement which would have the effect of improving the morale of the troops and the people within Nationalist areas, though he did so in a *pro forma* way as if only because he felt bound by his instructions. I said I would be glad to consider the matter. He went on to inquire about silver and was informed that the Department had today authorized the Treasury Department to proceed with the arrangements to mint silver coins for the Chinese Government with silver supplied by the latter and at cost. In response to his queries he was also informed of this Government's decision that it could not lend the Chinese Government silver for this purpose nor could the ECA use the funds, as he suggested, derived from the sale of cotton diverted from Shanghai, which amount he set at $16 million, to purchase silver in Mexico or India.

Dr. Koo also suggested that it would be helpful if I would find occasion to mention that the ERP,[96] the Atlantic Pact and the meeting of the Council of Foreign Ministers did not indicate diminution of interest in Asian affairs on the part of the United States. I thanked him for this suggestion and pointed out that the President had made a reference of this kind and that on at least three occasions I had done likewise, but that I agreed that every effort should be made to keep this attitude, which in fact was the attitude of the U.S. Government, to the forefront of people's minds.

Dr. Koo inquired as to Ambassador Stuart's plans and suggested the desirability of his proceeding to Canton before returning to the U.S. His attention was drawn to the press announcement about Dr. Stuart's return for consultation which pointed out that he was only to depart after he had satisfied himself as to the safety of American citizens in

---

[95] V. K. Wellington Koo.
[96] European Recovery Program.

the lower Yangtze Valley and that this phrase was designed to convey the thought that he would not be returning until the situation in Shanghai had resolved itself. In this general connection, I made mention of the fact that Mr. Lewis Clark our Minister was in Canton and in contact with Dr. Koo's Government.

The Chinese Ambassador then referred to the assurances which General Marshall [97] had given him prior to the General's departure for the London meeting last year to the effect that China would not be discussed at that meeting and inquired whether Far Eastern affairs were on the agenda for the meeting of the Council of Foreign Ministers in Paris. I told him that they were not and that the suggestion was new to me that China might be on the agenda. The Chinese Ambassador asked if the questions directly affecting China came up whether China would be notified and consulted and I replied that I felt it proper and right that it should. The Chinese Ambassador expressed appreciation and satisfaction and took his leave after telling me that Dr. Hu Shih [98] had arrived in this country and wanted me to know that he had come on a private visit and not with any official character. I said that Dr. Hu Shih was an old friend and I looked forward to seeing him.

D[EAN] A[CHESON]

893.00B/5–1149 : Telegram

The Consul General at Peiping (Clubb) to the Secretary of State

PEIPING, May 11, 1949—5 p. m.
[Received May 14—5 : 22 a. m.]

808. [To Nanking:] ReEmbtel 76, March 5,[99] Contels 257, March 12, and 476, May 2 [4].[1] Following is report on Communist administrative take over process and personnel.

Takeover Peiping was conducted efficiently and in good order without dislocation or sabotage. Personnel old regime generally remained at posts. Immediately prior to occupation responsible persons some establishments reputedly received Communist orders assume responsibility for protection interests and equipment of unit. Many sympathizers apparently had established contact with Communists before occupation and had undertaken duties guarding against Kmt sabotage. On takeover military committee assigned various administrative units representatives who took charge and maintained liaison with control organ. Management original administrative system generally left unchanged excepting where duplication and overlapping functions

---

[97] General of the Army George C. Marshall, Secretary of State, January 1947–49.
[98] Chinese Ambassador in the United States, 1938–1942.
[99] Not found in Department of State files.
[1] Latter two telegrams not printed.

patently require adjustment. Transportation, communications and productive enterprises get top priority. In initial stage PLA seems to have been in main successful.

General[ly,] Communists appear be making real efforts win over intelligentsia and all useful personnel except those politically closely connected with Nationalists. Selection made in part through use meetings at which vigorous progressive elements are spotted. Few cadres are assigned each section with joint duties of supervision and study. Absorption selected elements to those cadres reliable personnel corps built up, labor movement vigorously pushed. Workers being considered basic material for future operations. All old personnel undergo re-education process during which unsatisfactory elements sifted out during process. New cadres generally unacquainted with new function expected learn on spot. Indications are that supervisory personnel for local trade, banking and communications just adequate, but for engineering and technical work inadequate. In latter categories workers old staffs receive higher pay and are encouraged remain at posts. New cadres reported be generally politically sound Communists, disciplined, active and incorrupt. Their present weakness is inexperience and incompetence in respect handling modern affairs. In old staff middle and lower groups workers in organizations where preoccupation salaries are paid have to date been generally content and adaptable. There is reported some apparent improvement morale due education and example new cadres in respect living conditions. This situation in administrative branches is in contrast with grumbling heard among laboring and merchant classes in town due slowness trade and rising cost living. Bureaucrats can likewise be expected suffer and perhaps show disaffection, if price rises continue. Communists show readiness experiment and learn and willingness make changes where dictated by circumstances. They have proven themselves capable Peiping take over city administration and public enterprises and operate them with reasonable competence, in first stages.

This accomplishment balanced by remarkable Communist ignorance shown in respect problems economy on national and international scale, in agriculture, industry, commerce. Presumed Communist intelligence at top is hampered, sometimes blocked by ignorance and fanaticism at lower levels. Bureaucracy and lack coordination seriously slows up progress, hardly halts deterioration. Open question whether Communists will be able overcome problems facing them in large spheres national and international effort particularly in respect problems population and food supply, restoration industry, development foreign trade.

Sent Nanking 521, repeated Department, OffEmb Canton 105, Shanghai 536.

CLUBB

893.01/5–1149 : Telegram

The Minister-Counselor of Embassy in China (Clark) to the Secretary of State

CANTON, May 11, 1949—6 p. m.
[Received May 12—2:59 p. m.]

Cantel 360. Chu Chang-wei, Li Tsung-jen's political advisor, has clarified exchange messages between Li and Generalissimo and Li's resulting plans. Li's message to Generalissimo was not letter, but was in form notes of conversation with delegation sent from Canton headed by Yen Hsi-shan. These notes were sent by CEC to Generalissimo who replied in letter to Ho Ying-chin. With letter to Ho as written evidence [of] Generalissimo's intention, Li felt his proper course was come Canton on assumption Generalissimo acting good faith.

Cabinet will be reorganized next few days with either Chu Cheng, President Judicial Yuan, or Yen Hsi-shan likely premier. Ho Ying-chin will continue as Minister National Defense, assisted by Pai Chung-hsi who has agreed serve Chief of Staff.

First move after reorganization will be direct Chen Cheng ship treasure from Taiwan to Canton. Should he refuse, he will be removed as Governor Taiwan and replaced by another. Even should treasure be shipped, eventual removal Chen Cheng is contemplated. At time removal Chen, Li renews his request we take some action strengthening his hand. If we are unwilling make public statement, he hopes Consul [at] Taipei can be instructed along lines suggested Cantel 303, May 1, repeated Nanking 238, Shanghai 191. They believe some such informal *démarche* by Consul [at] Taipei will have desired effect on Chen Cheng.

Would appreciate Department's reaction this suggestion. Li seems determined upon action in any event, but is desperately hoping that, in some way, he will have at least our moral support.

Sent Department Cantel 360, repeated Nanking 270, Shanghai 229.

CLARK

893.00/5–1149

The Consul General at Shanghai (Cabot) to the Director of the Office of Far Eastern Affairs (Butterworth)

SHANGHAI, May 11, 1949.
[Received June 6.]

DEAR WALT: My telegram No. 1389 of April 27 [2] seems to have drawn quite a lot of rebuttal. Since I don't like to argue with the Embassy in official telegrams on policy matters, I think that my com-

---

[2] Vol. IX, p. 1251.

ments on Nanking's No. 921 of May 3 [3] and Canton's No. 296 of April 29 [4] can best be forwarded to you in this letter.

Lewis Clark seems to have completely overlooked the real purpose of my message, which was to warn the Commies that they might upset their own applecart if they continued to behave obstreperously, rather than to come around to them hat in hand. Obviously, the warning would be effective only insofar as it indicated the Commies had something to lose by not heeding it. There would, then, be no question of having an overture rejected.

With regard to Lewis' point about the Commies' need for commodities, I have often emphasized this point in my telegrams, as you know; nevertheless, if we have no means of holding up essential imports, such as oil—and that is the purport of the messages which the Department has been sending out—then I foresee here another situation developing much as that in Tientsin has developed. If we cannot take effective measures, there is no use pretending that we can, or threatening that we will; but we certainly will not be in the driver's seat in this matter according to anything that I have seen.

Lewis also rebuts my introductory remark about non-intervention in the civil war. Here again I do not see that the course I proposed would leave us open to any demands. My suggestion would merely call their attention to what has been happening in recent months and what might happen in the immediate future. I did wonder whether such a statement would be advisable in that it would give the Commies reassurances which they might be only too glad to have. The publication of Acheson's letter,[5] though not intended by the Department, pretty well shows our intention to withdraw further aid rather than to intensify it, so I scarcely see how my suggested statement would alter the position.

I do not quite understand Lewis' point about the withdrawal of Consular personnel, since I did not suggest this. I did, at one time, suggest that there would probably be a substantial falling off of work in this Consulate General when the Commies enter Shanghai, and I asked authority to put some of the staff aboard U.S. warships at the last moment before the Commies took over. Although I still think that there will be a falling off in the work here when the Commies take over, the staff has now been stripped down by a third, and there seems less reason to fear that we will be immobilized here, so that I see no reason for acting on this suggestion any more, even if the Department had approved it and the Navy were still in the Whangpoo.

Much the same comments apply to Nanking's telegram. With regard to the argument that we can afford to wait, the fact is that, as to recog-

[3] Vol. IX, p. 14.
[4] *Ibid.*, p. 934.
[5] See letter of March 15 to Senator Tom Connally of Texas, *ibid.*, p. 607.

nition, the British have not waited, but have already spoken of establishing "friendly relations". We ourselves seem to have spoken of "working contacts" which means nothing unless it is a hint that we are planning to move toward some sort of recognition, since clearly under the present circumstances, we would like to establish working contacts and can't.

As for the united front, I have been advocating that ever since last Fall. Since it now appears that the British will not fully coöperate with us in establishing and utilizing trade controls, it seems to me pretty clear that the united front idea is out the window. Maybe we think we can afford to wait, and maybe it would be to our advantage to wait even if others get in ahead of us, but I do not think that we should be under any illusions that others are going to wait indefinitely for us to climb on the bandwagon they are already fashioning.

I gather from the two above quoted statements which seem to have originated from official sources, there may have been quite a bit of talking between Washington and London, and perhaps Paris, with regard to this whole matter. I hope that information regarding any such talks will be forwarded to us at an early date. I find that when we, in the field, know the precise contingencies which the U.S. is facing, we generally are in close agreement with the Department as to what should be done. Whether we like it or not, it is pretty clear that we will have to face the question of recognition at no distant date, since Lewis' telegrams make it evident that we cannot anticipate that any real National authority will survive for very long.

I have just received your letter of May 6 [6] about my leave, and I quite agree with your comments, much as I hate to do so. There is an ever persistent rumour that the Commies have announced over their radio that they will not take Shanghai for some time—by latest account, July 1. I should not suggest that I hope it is sooner than that for fear that Styles Bridges [7] might try to investigate me—and shall hope to survive until then. (At least the picture of my running is different from that of quite a number of Shanghailanders!)

The situation in Shanghai is going from bad to worse. Nationalists still here are carrying on a gigantic and sickening racket to strip the town clean before they hand it over. Tang En-po's terrorism strips the last pretense of "democracy" from the Nationalists façade. Even in Yugoslavia I never saw anything quite so crude and arbitrary as the recent wave of executions. The currency manipulations and the many extortions which have been leveled against Shanghai are another part of the picture. As a result of these and other factors, Shanghai is rapidly sinking into economic prostration. A good way to gauge this is the precipitous fall in the demand for electric power; until March

---

[6] Not found in Department of State files.
[7] Senator from New Hampshire.

the Shanghai Power Company was maintaining its maximum potential output of approximately 165,000 KW without satisfying the demand, and it was still 145,000 KW on April 30. Today it has dropped to 120,000 KW. Another example is furnished by the horde of street hawkers selling all sorts of goods along the principal thoroughfare. Factories, unable to pay wages in cash, have given their own employees products to sell, and these pathetic people are trying to get enough cash to buy food. Since everyone else is short of cash and the goods are often not the kind which meet a popular demand, I am afraid they are not having much success. The Nationalist regime is certainly taking pains to assure itself of universal and permanent execration while it is on its way out.

Incidentally, if there is any need for me to uphold the Department's course before the Congressional Committee when I return to the U.S., I should not in the least mind doing so. With my impeccable, cold roast Boston background and my numerous public attacks on Communism, I scarcely feel that I will be suspected of any leanings in that direction.

The heat is on in Shanghai in more ways than one. Yours for a cool day on the North shore, with every good wish,

Very sincerely,

JACK

893.00/5–1249 : Telegram

The Consul General at Shanghai (Cabot) to the Secretary of State

SHANGHAI, May 12, 1949.
[Received May 12—8 : 05 p. m.]

1619. *China Daily Tribune*, Shanghai, May 12, states political council garrison headquarters ordered all Central Government organizations now functioning Shanghai evacuate city within 2 weeks and instructed Central Bank if Central Government offices remain past designated date, bank must no longer provide money such organizations.

Council also instructed Central Bank to pay only for military supplies bought Shanghai and used for defense Shanghai; to pay for military supplies for Tsingtao only with special permission General Tang En-po; to loan no money any organization not related military affairs; to regulate remittances from and to other National Government ports.

Sent Department 1619; repeated Nanking as 890, Canton as 441.

CABOT

893.00/5–1249 : Telegram

The Minister-Counselor of Embassy in China (Clark) to the Secretary of State

CANTON, May 12, 1949—4 p. m.
[Received May 14—7 : 27 a. m.]

Cantel 367. . . . Source is informed . . . that Liu Po-cheng has concentrated 9 field armies in Nanfeng area, eastern central Kiangsi Province. Nationalists believe part of this force will take Amoy and balance move against Canton. No Nationalist troops with any considerable battle experience or reliability are at present south of this concentration.

We estimate Communists have capability take Canton within 4 weeks and believe they will probably decide exercise this capability in order separate Taiwan and Fukien Nationalists from south and west China, so preventing united action Generalissimo and Li Tsung-jen.

Repeated Nanking 275, Shanghai 232.

CLARK

893.00/5–1249 : Telegram

The Consul General at Shanghai (Cabot) to the Secretary of State

SHANGHAI, May 12, 1949—5 p. m.
[Received 8 : 37 p. m.]

1620. Lo Lung-chi and Chang Lan [8] being held in single room at Hungjao Hospital together with one garrison guard who present at all times (remytel to Department 1594, May 10 [9]). Visitors not allowed.

Lo and Chang both known to be in good health, well treated except for rather abusive, rude, verbal handling on night of arrest.

American correspondents have unsuccessfully sought admittance Lo's room. All press releases concerning arrest killed by censorship.

ConGen informed by member Democratic League close to Lo that Lo and probably Chang, fearing drastic measures by military authorities against leftist leaders still in Shanghai, were planning quick getaway to North China in morning before arrest. Believed possible arrests were timed primarily to prevent their departure. However, seems probable that they are also part of planned larger roundup of leftists and Communist sympathizers. Peng Wen-yi, chairman Shanghai branch Democratic League, informed officers ConGen he had narrowly escaped arrest Tuesday night by hiding on roof while police searched friend's flat where he had taken refuge after hearing of Lo's detention. Yeh Tu-yi in hiding for fear arrest. Fear also expressed over safety Miss Pu Hsi-hsiu, journalist and fiancée of Lo, who released

---

[8] Leaders of the Democratic League.
[9] Not printed.

several months ago from 70-day jail term in Nanking. Chang, Miss Pu and other members League fear military authorities have "black list" of leftist leaders whom they wish detain for hostage purposes. They anxious that acting President Li Tsung-jen be prevailed upon to act their behalf though aware unlikelihood that he has sufficient influence this area and express hope that in view censorship of news our Embassy Canton might find opportunity to inform Li re perilous situation of Democratic Leaguers and similar groups. They say even Tang En-po powerless as their fate lies in hands three persons: Mao Sen [10] who takes orders direct from Generalissimo, Chiang Ching-kuo, Generalissimo's eldest son who they say once again in Shanghai, or Generalissimo himself.

Sent Department 1620, repeated Nanking 891, Embassy Canton 442. Passed Peiping 148, and Hong Kong 91.

CABOT

893.00B/5–1249

The Consul General at Peiping (Clubb) to the Secretary of State

PEIPING, May 12, 1949—5 p. m.
[Received May 13—7:28 a. m.]

825. ReContel 808, May 11. As distinct from initial successes administrative field, Commies are encountering difficulties as regards carrying out economic policies Peiping. Basically many local entrepreneurs are also landowners and with full knowledge what happened countryside and towns Manchuria have little faith in declared objectives new democracy economy. Many took action in advance of event as shown by flight capital and removal southward business activities beginning last year. All remaining adopted policies curtailment or liquidation, preferring reduce risks and wait see before making new positive commitments. Result is general trade inactivity.

Communists attack such fears and skepticism through meetings with entrepreneurs and workers for mutual explanations. That is purpose symposia reported currently by ConGen. Peng Chen is one main CCP leaders charged with task soothing fears and interpreting CCP policy "benefits to both labor capital" in such manner as to remove skepticism. Pertinent reports indicate full sympathy and "understanding" entrepreneurs still far from achievement. If private entrepreneurs still do not show open hostility, there is nevertheless large measure pessimism and peaceful non-cooperation on their part.

Long years experience local population under many different rulers has given both petty capitalists and labor deep fund common sense and practical sophistication. CCP [garble] Peiping will be able obtain

---

[10] Shanghai police commissioner.

full sympathy population only insofar as Communists can show results in terms people understand.

Sent Department; repeated Nanking 524, OffEmb Canton 111, Shanghai 550.

CLUBB

893.50/5–749 : Telegram

The Secretary of State to the Consul General at Shanghai (Cabot)

WASHINGTON, May 12, 1949—7 p. m.

918. Urtel 1550, May 7. Dept appreciative comprehensive timely coverage and thorough analysis Shanghai developments provided by ConGen and fully cognizant potentially explosive situation now existing. However, US Govt cannot take any official action which wld have effect directly assisting Chi Commies in efforts occupy all China intact and accelerating complete disintegration anti-Commie resistance. US Govt has consistently followed policy China of avoiding representations this character which might constitute involvement civil strife, but is nevertheless desirous take all appropriate steps protect Amer lives and properties. Dept wld have no objection, therefore, to procedure outlined first par Nanking's 989, May 10, rptd Shanghai 550 in order reduce insofar as possible deleterious effects on American interests which any determined efforts defend city might have.

Re problem possible large scale demolitions, Dept of opinion extreme care must be exercised avoid premature discussions this question with Chi officials. Having in mind analysis in third par reftel, undue concern or veiled threats by US re demolition Amer properties might result opposite effect than that desired. When you are convinced such demolition imminent, therefore, you are authorized in ur discretion make appropriate representations highest mil and civ authorities urging protection Amer properties.

Re point (3), specific Congressional prohibition against using ECA funds in areas under Commie domination clearly precludes excess stockpiling Shanghai. However decision maintain 30-day level essential supplies for present wld appear somewhat mitigate this problem. Dept cannot imagine private capital undertaking credit hazards under present circumstances and conditions China.

Re (4), although official participation and assistance in evacuation Amers from Shanghai area considered completed, Dept wld of course make every effort reestablish evacuation facilities, both commercial and govt, for removal Amers from Shanghai shld conditions following takeover so warrant. With pattern defections, absence determined resistance and failure carry out demolitions established in all cities lost to Commies from Changchun to Nanking, however, wld appear unlikely trend will be reversed Shanghai where eventual defeat Nationalists inevitable and escape virtually impossible.

ACHESON

893.50/5–1349 : Telegram

The Consul General at Shanghai (Cabot) to the Secretary of State

SHANGHAI, May 13, 1949—5 p. m.
[Received May 14—9:05 a. m.]

1639. [To Nanking:] Reurtel 550, May 10, repeated Department 989. Question of securing Chinese leadership to confront various aspects difficult circumstances now facing Shanghai has been repeatedly discussed by foreign officials and business leaders and on several occasions Chinese have been approached. Most of Chinese of sufficient importance to give weight to representations have left Shanghai and those left are far too frightened to take any initiative. We must, therefore, face stark alternative of taking initiative ourselves or letting matters take their course. Despite possible catastrophic results of latter, I realize former may, nevertheless, be even more undesirable. We must not, however, think we can evade issue or avoid being blamed for whatever happens in Shanghai. It seems to me clear that whatever we do or do not do, both Nationalists and Communists will try place on us responsibility for anything which goes wrong. Moreover, entire western interest in Shanghai is perhaps at stake. Under circumstances, much as I hesitate to recommend action, still believe some action at least to prevent demolition of utilities and industries (second query mytel 1550, May 7) desirable.

Re my third query, I do not advocate stockpiling in Shanghai beyond 30-day period already recommended and agreed as being minimum in which Communists can arrange for own supplies to reach Shanghai. My question is whether we should take any action whatsoever beyond that point to help Communists get supplies on commercial basis. My thought is that foreign interests here might cooperate to this end if they knew we had no objections. If Communists are as short of foreign exchange as they seem to be and Shanghai stripped as clean of assets as now seems probable, I do not see how the Communists can possibly arrange without some cooperation to secure supplies necessary to keep Shanghai running. It may boil down to issue of either extending private credit or seeing highly integrated economy of Shanghai, unique in China, utterly collapse with disquieting consequences. Should oil, food, cotton, et cetera, be unobtainable, I would expect Shanghai to be reduced to utter chaos and to become uninhabitable for westerners. If we expect collapse in Shanghai and either think Communists will thereby be embarrassed or at least intend to do nothing effective to prevent it, I believe we should have candor so to inform our citizens and perhaps those of other friendly nations. Under such circumstances, we feel that there would be no point to encouraging Americans even in vital positions to stay here but rather that we should urge them to leave now while they still easily can.

I realize this may be unduly pessimistic view to take of situation and yet, with facts as they appear, I think my conclusions are inescapable. Shanghai is in vastly more vulnerable position than Tientsin and even without demolitions has been reduced already to a worse economic plight than that of Tientsin before takeover. Economic prostration is increasing every day with numerous problems (such as adequate supply of currency, distribution of factory production, maintenance of employment and just utility rates) apparently insoluble under present circumstances. Tientsin experience indicates situation will for some time get worse after Communist occupation.

I see no reason to feel situation will correct itself in foreseeable future and that we should therefore either take constructive remedial action before crisis or should not delude ourselves that we can save any considerable part of our position and our assets at stake here.

Sent Nanking 907, repeated Department, EmbOff Canton 452.

CABOT

893.00/5–1449 : Telegram

The Minister-Counselor of Embassy in China (Clark) to the Secretary of State

CANTON, May 14, 1949—11 a. m.
[Received May 15—3 : 55 a. m.]

Cantel 378. . . . Source in touch with Li Tsung-jen supporters in Legislative Yuan reports this group in process organization anti-Communist movement to continue resistance after Communists control entire country. Organization will have overt phase with headquarters outside China, initially Hong Kong, similar old KmtRC.[12] Overt phase will take form political party and will carry out propaganda work in foreign countries, organize overseas Chinese and raise funds from these and other sources. Party will also have underground phase, existence and character of which known only to small group, for purpose clandestine operations China proper.

Li Tsung-jen aware general plans of group and approves them. When unable remain longer China proper he may assume leadership. Nucleus group going Hong Kong shortly open offices publish magazine. Plans send mission to US shortly with aim acquainting American

---

[12] Kuomintang Revolutionary Committee, headed by Marshal Li Chi-shen.

officials and public their existence and aims. Similar missions planned for Southeast Asia.

Basic aim of organization is attempt to further and exploit factionalism latent in Sino Communist Party so as to break down present pro-Soviet orientation and permit change toward multi-party government which would allow them exercise political influence. They appear aware difficulties this task but say they must make attempt. While status progress of group in organizing is unknown, fuller details will be obtained later. At present initial preparations underground have been made with certain group members staying behind Nanking and Shanghai.

So far as we are aware, there is no other organization with comparably advanced plans for independent political action within Communist-dominated China. If properly led, organization described above has considerable potentialities as resistance movement. Persons attached to it are reputable, well-known liberals who should be able develop considerable following both within China and among overseas Chinese. We intend continue maintain contact with them and report significant developments to Department. Meanwhile we would appreciate any suggestions Department may care to make along lines possibility utilizing their underground for propaganda and similar activities.

CLARK

_____

893.01/5-1449 : Telegram

The Minister-Counselor of Embassy in China (Clark) to the Secretary of State

CANTON, May 14, 1949—noon.
[Received May 15—10: 49 p. m.]

Cantel 379. Feel we must wait event before determining who should follow Nationalist Government in move from Canton (telCan 160, May 11 [*10*],[13] repeated Nanking 570, Shanghai 895). As I see picture at moment, Generalissimo is not acting in good faith and resources Taiwan will not be subject authority Li Tsung-jen. Also, I do not believe Generalissimo plans resume authority this stage.

Canton appears at mercy Communists whenever they choose exercise capabilities occupying city. The protestations of all and sundry, including highest government leaders with whom I have talked of determination fight to finish do not carry conviction. Underlying everything they say is evidence fundamental belief eventual Communist occupation all China. Even Li Tsung-jen's supporters are

_____

[13] *Post*, p. 687.

planning for a future envisaging Communist China. (Cantel 378, May 14, 11 a. m.)

When final break with Generalissimo comes, whether it is published or not, Li appears to have three alternatives: (1) remove capital elsewhere on mainland—Chungking is prominently mentioned—and continue battle; or (2) withdraw to Kwangsi with support by Pai Chunghsi's Army, hoping Communists will by-pass province and eventually permit conclusion "Peiping peace" on terms acceptable to Li; (3) go abroad and endeavor rally overseas Chinese and others to support by clandestine as well as by overt measures elements remaining in China in resistance to Communism.

There is much talk at moment that first course will be followed and that resistance forces will be organized in northwest and southwest China. I have been asked by three separate cabinet members as to advisability maintaining capital on mainland as opposed moving Taiwan. I have, of course, insisted decision must be Chinese.

My best guess at moment is that in the event Li may pursue each of the three alternatives in turn. In other words, he may seek move government in first instance Chungking. Retaining Kwangsi as his own personal bastion, Pai Chung-hsi's headquarters are at Chuanhsien, Kwangsi, obviously indicating likelihood falling back on Kwangsi province. Should his position Szechwan prove untenable and should he be unable negotiate satisfactory "Peiping peace", Li could then go abroad. Since Li is aware insignificant role being played by Li Chi-shen and Fu Tso-yi,[14] he will [not] attempt to place himself in similar position. Likelihood is, therefore, that he will wind up abroad.

It seems certain that Canton will fall in a matter of weeks. My present guess is mid-June. It seems to me that the talk of rallying northwest and southwest behind a government removed to Chungking is largely wishful thinking. As I have previously reported the prime motivation in actions of all leaders with whom I have come in contact is self-interest. There are unimportant exceptions to that statement. I cannot conceive that leaders in the northwest or southwest can be prevailed upon to give other than lip service in support of any Li Tsung-jen government that might move from Canton. Li will be able to count on armies Pai Chung-hsi only and his government would represent and be supported by only those who could expect short shrift under Communists. People almost without exception want peace and are unaware of and uninterested in implications Communist China. Even among literate there is belief in the inevitability of Communist domination and determination endeavor temper its harshness. Any such government would not, of course, exercise any control over Tai-

---

[14] Chinese commander in north China who remained in Peiping after Communist occupation.

wan which Chen Cheng admits will be the haven for Generalissimo should he choose go there.

On balance, therefore, at this stage, I feel we would run risk of making ourselves ridiculous if we were to follow any government which might be set up elsewhere than Canton when Canton falls. On other hand, desirability maintaining friendly vote in UN and other international organs might warrant running risk. It seems to me to follow French suggestion of sending "officers of lesser rank" to follow government would be inadvisable. Either we support the government and I go along, or there is no need of sending anyone.

Sent Department Cantel 379, repeating Nanking 283, Shanghai 236.

CLARK

893.00/5–1449 : Telegram

The Consul General at Shanghai (Cabot) to the Secretary of State

SHANGHAI, May 14, 1949—2 p. m.
[Received May 14—8 : 39 a. m.]

1648. Warfare approaching Shanghai proper with clearly audible artillery increasing in intensity during past 2 days. According AMA who maintains contact with General Hu Hsing, Tang En-po's senior staff member, Nationalists have withdrawn from positions at Liuho and Taichang, which had become unconnected outposts of Nationalist resistance, to second defense line running from Lotien, Chiating through Chingpu to Pinghu on Chekiang–Kiangsu border. Communists on night May 12 made offensive stab north of Chiating to Yuehpuchen 5 kilos west of Paoshan where engaged by Nationalist troops. Fighting this area still going on with mounting vigor as Communists throwing additional troops reportedly totaling 30,000 into fray and Nationalists countering with roughly equal numbers. According Hu, some evidence Communist withdrawal this morning. According AMA, thrust seems to be Communist effort pinch off Paoshan and Woosung in order cut off possible Nationalist retreat from Shanghai by this route. Woosung reported by Chinese source already under range Communist artillery and another Chinese source rated B–2 states Nationalist navy starting withdraw from Whangpoo in anticipation early impassability Woosung Channel.

Remarks by Admiral Kuei, General Hu and other Nationalist military authorities have led AMA and ANA [15] believe that Nationalists expect eventually abandon Shanghai, retreat to south of Whangpoo by boat and by vehicle on road running along east bank of River and evacuate à la Dunkirk from banks of Yangtze which apparently ideal for this purpose. Belief supported by Nationalist gun emplacements

---

[15] Assistant Naval Attaché.

north of Shanghai which point southward toward city presumably to cover such retreat. If belief correct, absolutely essential Nationalists repel Communist thrust toward Paoshan as Communist success would jeopardize retreat and seriously threaten trap Nationalist forces in Shanghai. AMA believes Nationalists, barring defections, may successfully hold Communists this time with momentary stabilization situation west of Paoshan. However Communists, with superior forces, will probably probe farther south or elsewhere forcing Nationalists extend defense line until it becomes thin enough for Communists to break through in major push.

Reliably reported that Nationalist troops have evacuated Sungkiang, about 20 miles southwest of Shanghai, and trains no longer running there. No reports of Communist activity that area, however. Repeated Nanking 913.

CABOT

893.00/5–1549 : Telegram

The Ambassador in China (Stuart) to the Secretary of State

NANKING, May 15, 1949—9 a. m.
[Received May 15–12 : 34 a. m.]

1026. I received message dated May 5 from Acting President through Pai Chung-hsi's headquarters, Hankow. Following is English version :

"When Communists announced peace terms of 8 conditions, 24 articles they were so severe that acceptance would mean surrender Nationalist Government and converting armed forces into Communist armed force.

"Ambition of Communists is not only convert all China to Communism but also become member Third International and join fight against world peace.

"Nationalist Government receiving these conditions decided no alternative but continue resisting to bitter end in order safeguard independence [and] liberty of country and so hope protect peace of world.

"Resources remaining for use continued resistance are : 18 provinces and northwest with total population over 230,000,000; total armed force 3,000,000 plus.

"We will continue war until day we achieve liberty and democracy for peoples of China. We believe this decision will have support and sympathy those nations which believe in democracy and world peace.

"We especially look to you, the USA, for this support and sincerely hope you will change policy as regards Nationalist China and her conduct to this war against Communism.

"Besides appointing Dr. Kan Chieh-hou to go US to present case, we sincerely hope Ambassador will present our case to Congress before recess.

"We hope you will be able persuade Congress and Government to change attitude towards Nationalist China and adopted [*adopt?*] emergency measures to support us in our war."

I have merely acknowledged message through same channel, saying that it has received my sympathetic consideration.

STUART

893.03/5–1649 : Telegram

The Minister-Counselor of Embassy in China (Clark) to the Secretary of State

CANTON, May 16, 1949—noon.
[Received May 16—8 : 06 a. m.]

Cantel 387. Legislative Yuan at close discussion meeting Saturday May 14 decided vest complete government authority in Executive Yuan and for this purpose has asked Executive Yuan to submit emergency wartime powers bill to Legislative Yuan for approval at regular meeting Tuesday May 17. Legislative Yuan desires retain only power of review. If no hitch occurs, this *démarche* will legalize Legislative Yuan's long established status as debating society.

This move coincides with naming of committee of 9 to prepare for Legislative Yuan evacuation from Canton. It will be recalled that present (3d) session constitutionally ends May 31. There is no indication whatever that Legislative Yuan intends extend session beyond that date. On contrary, quite likely recess will be advanced to start from May 20.

In short, seems reasonable view above two developments as marking final demise of Legislative Yuan with little likelihood of reincarnation as effective political force at any future time or place.

Sent Dept Cantel 387, repeated Nanking 286, Shanghai 241.

CLARK

893.00/5–1649 : Telegram

The Consul General at Shanghai (Cabot) to the Secretary of State

SHANGHAI, May 16, 1949—1 p. m.
[Received May 16—8 : 15 a. m.]

1656. That Generalissimo feels no compunction but likely satisfaction in seeking make Shanghai battlefield and shambles regardless all but his own shortsighted interests is conviction most observers based on evidence such as :

Feverish defense preparations : Ruthless leveling wide belt villages and estates around city perimeter now being followed by fortifying roof tops and sandbagging main buildings and junction spots into very heart city with apparent expectation street fighting.

Other military signs such as selective retention in city all operable army tanks and air strafing of Communists at very low level rarely risked by Nationalist planes.

Anti-Communist parade with floats depicting Communist and Yellow Ox atrocities; exhortation of populace by speeches, hand bills to support "supreme military authority" unconquerable stand against "Red bandits", make Shanghai second Stalingrad, et cetera.

Desperate efforts bolster collapsing army morale with various rumors American aid, announcements of unprecedented privileges, free meals, entertainments, et cetera, to be given "our soldier heroes" and alleged hasty replacements undependable units with new divisions from Formosa.

Intense secret service activity directed by Generalissimo through his son Ching-kuo and BIS chiefs: Assignment special troops handle desertions and rebellion; and increasing terroristic suppression student, leftist, civil and business elements suspected as likely promoters peaceful turnover by wholesale arrests, man hunts, deportations and intimidation. Even Mme. Sun Yat-sen [16] said now in some danger arrest.

Attempted removal all government organs from city; arbitrary requisitioning of motor cars; heavy exporting of city's removable equipment and materials; and financial manipulations to syphon off all available wealth.

Persistently reported plans demolish utilities, dockyards, et cetera, upon final withdrawal Nationalist forces.

Generalissimo's apparent strategy making Woosung region his final defense area to permit full completion his stripping, demolition and evacuation programs.

Aside from vindictive punishment Shanghai leaders and groups whose non-cooperation has earned them his bitter hatred, Generalissimo's primary motives for apparent planning this senseless fighting and destruction appear to be:

1. Exploit Shanghai stage for limelighting melodramatic show last ditch defense of "international city" against world Communism in face overwhelming odds unaided by "ungrateful" America.

2. Crush all possibility of an orderly city turnover under circumstances propitious for development of mutually beneficial *modus vivendi* among Communists Shanghai Chinese and international interests; and force Communists to take city in ruined chaotic state with every possible liability and problem serving to complicate city's existence, exacerbate Communists relations with foreign interests, and increase tension between Moscow and western democracies.

3. Protect Generalissimo's operations "drama" "udder" "dynamite" and "Dunkirk" to last possible moment.

---

[16] Widow of the founder of the Kuomintang and of the Chinese Republic; sister of Mesdames Chiang Kai-shek and H. H. Kung and of T. V. Soong.

Meanwhile mounting Communist military pressure and close approach city leads many now believe final showdown may come any moment. Seems likely Communists will (1) press attacks at many points perimeter with view force Nationalists spread thin their inferior strength; (2) seek minimize destruction in city by avoiding heavy bombardment and taking city by infantry alone as far as possible; (3) close in on Nationalists' Woosung bastion with view cutting off of Generalissimo's evacuation. Generalissimo's need to retain Woosung area longest and general Communist pressure around city will probably force him attempt early withdrawal from city to Woosung or coast to escape trapping. Observers feel his forces will disintegrate rapidly under Communist attack and that Communists could smash his resistance in week or so if ready for determined effort. Prospects of imminent violence and disorders in city preceding, during and immediately following final battle are increasing in view of following factors:

(1) Progress of secret preparations for establishment of intermediate peace maintenance regime appears delayed as result of Generalissimo's energetic surveillance of movement's chief organizers, of his bellicose preparations—which lessen chances for early crumbling or voluntary abandonment of Nationalist resistance and, perhaps, of Communists' waning interest in project owing to its now dubious potentialities for effective action. [W. W.] Yen, following his recent creation of maintenance regime, has been hounded by Generalissimo to point forcing him retire to hospital confinement; and Chinese source who claims regular contact with Communists says Communists themselves disapproved of his relief body as method for formation peace regime. Other leading organizers (Yang Hu, Hu Chow-wen and Hsu Kuo-mou) said in imminent danger arrest.

(2) Generalissimo's reported intention to force municipal police to leave city with withdrawing troops, if carried out, could materially increase looting and lawless excesses, though known control of part police force by anti-Generalissimo groups and probably refusal of many police to leave posts (especially if adequately paid and fed) would undoubtedly nullify his efforts to some extent. Military has savagely threatened any police who defect.

(3) Events seem heading rapidly toward moment when commencement of attempted Nationalist evacuation of city will set stage for Generalissimo's reported demolition program; final looting by armed and unsated Nationalist soldiers ideally distributed for effective plundering of entire city; further pillaging by local riffraff. Communist underground and Yang Hu's police and plain-clothes agents are understood to be ready prevent some destruction but they can hardly hope to stop general looting (unless Yang's troops have been bought off to much greater extent than Consul General aware) and their very efforts will provoke fighting.

(4) Any further aggravation of food, fuel, currency and labor aspects of economic crisis is likely precipitate rioting with street fighting in which Communist underground may feel compelled to participate.

While these conjectures represent well-informed consensus, events may prove them unduly pessimistic. Possibility of reports being spread for ulterior motives should be always kept in mind. We have fortunately no concrete evidence support observers' general expectation Generalissimo's plans demolish utilities and demolitions thus far have all been outside city proper. Also source close to Yang Hu tells us this morning change-over will come soon without serious disorders—though unknown capabilities of Yang's organization suggest great caution re this assurance. All in all there remains little visible basis for optimism. Best hope is that events, perhaps spurred by massive defections, will move with sufficient rapidity to prevent destructive fighting in city or extensive demolitions. If Communists are welcome even by conservative business interests not to mention populace, it will not be surprising.

If any approach to Nationalist authorities to urge them abandon senseless fighting and destruction is to be made, need for action is urgent. Delicacy and probable inadvisability of attempting have Shanghai declared open city is realized, but feel we could properly insist to Nationalist military authorities there be no demolitions of essentially civilian installations—possibly taking parallel action with British and French—in view fact utilities are virtually all owned by interests of the three countries. I urge Department authorize representations this sense.

Sent Nanking 919, repeated Department, OffEmb Canton 461.

CABOT

893.00/5–1649 : Telegram

The Consul General at Shanghai (Cabot) to the Secretary of State

SHANGHAI, May 16, 1949—2 p. m.
[Received May 16—7:22 a. m.]

1657. Battle coming closer Shanghai on all sides with fires visible from tall buildings indicating fighting about 5 miles from center city. NWA and PAA [17] discontinuing flights today with last flight expected leave around noon. Principal reason for this is that homing tower south of city knocked out by Commies with resulting technical difficulties bringing planes in. Main Commie drive in Yuehpuchen area apparently halted momentarily, with Commies probing further south near Liuheng and Tazang.

Some fighting also going on in Chipao area south of Hungjao airport with villages going up in flames, some apparently by torch per Nationalist policy destruction to clear line of fire.

Although rumored that around 400,000 Commie troops in Shanghai

---

[17] Northwestern and Pan American Airlines, respectively.

area including 100,000 of Lin Piao's men, AMA states rumor doubtful and that so far Nationalists have been unable locate main body Commie forces. Commie drive in Yuehpu area is the only one of significant size and AMA feels probable that fighting elsewhere largely by local Commie forces now stirring up trouble preparatory to drive by regular Commie troops. In this connection, reportedly native Commie troops in Pootung area advancing from Fenghsien attacked Nanhuei and headed towards Chwangsha.

Sent Department 1657, repeated Nanking 920, OffEmb Canton 462.

CABOT

___

893.00/5–1749 : Telegram

The Minister-Counselor of Embassy in China (Clark) to the Secretary of State

CANTON, May 17, 1949—10 a. m.
[Received May 17—9 : 56 a. m.]

Cantel 390. Chen Li-fu says Li Tsung-jen is unconvincing in his protestations of determination resist Communism. His statement when he returned Canton left loophole further peace negotiations. Chen said Li should make unqualified public statement of determination fight to finish and C–C clique might believe him. Chen thinks neither Li nor Gimo can save situation alone and is making strenuous efforts bring them together. He is suggesting that Gimo come Canton as head party and that he with Li as head of government would determine policy, Li executing decisions. This of course just what Li has so far refused flatly to do.

Sent Department Cantel 390; repeated Nanking 287, Shanghai 243.

CLARK

___

893.50/5–1749 : Telegram

The Ambassador in China (Stuart) to the Secretary of State

NANKING, May 17, 1949—noon.
[Received May 17—2 : 47 a. m.]

1039. [To Shanghai:] I note Department in its telegram 918, May 12, repeated Nanking 578, Canton 165, has granted you authority under certain circumstances and in your discretion to "make appropriate representations highest military and civil authorities urging protection American properties". I am of course in full agreement in leaving such representations to your good judgment. I feel you should consider, however, Generalissimo's present frame of mind and probable reaction to appeal from foreign interests behalf public utilities which are legitimate targets all-out warfare.

We have greatest concern for you and your problems in these critical days (urtel 919, May 16, repeated Department 1656, Canton 461) and would like to be more helpful. I am keeping in close touch here with my British and French colleagues who, while agreeing with me there is little foreign representations can do to influence course of war in Shanghai, yet approve joint action in any approach you may decide to make.

Sent Shanghai 586, repeated Department, OffEmb Canton 427.

STUART

893.00/5–1749 : Telegram

The Minister-Counselor of Embassy in China (Clark) to the Secretary of State

CANTON, May 17, 1949—noon.
[Received May 17—10:29 a. m.]

Cantel 392. Tung Kwan-hsien, President Legislative Yuan, says: (1) that Li Tsung-jen has agreed that General Yen Hsi-shan, General Wu Chung-hsin, former Secretary General of Li, and Chu Chia-hua, former Minister of Education, can proceed Taiwan make arrangements for Generalissimo and Li get-together. Initiative move said rest with Yen Hsi-shan who believes that if two can get together, some solution differences may be found; and (2) that while Generalissimo emphasizes importance coastal towns, Li insists on holding interior provinces. C–C clique proposes make Chungking political center with Taiwan and Hainan Islands as arsenals. Should these ideas materialize, government may move [to] Chungking, according Tung, recalling Chungking has for some time been designated alternate capital.

Sent Department Cantel 392, repeated Nanking 289, Shanghai 248.

CLARK

893.00/5–1749

Memorandum by the Director of the Office of Far Eastern Affairs (Butterworth) to the Under Secretary of State (Webb)

[WASHINGTON,] May 17, 1949.

The most important aspect of the situation in Nationalist China is the continued failure of the leadership to unify its defense efforts. In the struggle between the Generalissimo and Acting President Li Tsung-jen, Li is demanding that the Generalissimo either resume office or give Li full control over the Government, all its armed forces and the gold, silver and foreign exchange now held by the Generalissimo. He also demands the Generalissimo's departure from China and a cessation of Kuomintang interference with the Government. While the

Generalissimo's reply gives an appearance of agreement to these demands, his activities indicate no real relinquishment of his power. The prospect is a Nationalist China divided between the Fukien-Formosa (southeast coast) area under the Generalissimo and parts of south and west China under Li and General Pai Chung-hsi (Government commander in central China). Telegrams from the Embassy and the Embassy Office at Canton (Tabs A and B [18]) indicate that Canton's fall is a matter of weeks and that there is little or no possibility of rallying the northwest and southwest areas behind a government removed to Chungking.

Economic deterioration continues. The Consul General at Shanghai reports (Tab C [19]) that the Generalissimo is stripping Shanghai of whatever assets, including technical personnel, that can be shipped out. ECA is endeavoring to provide a 30-day supply of foodstuffs and petroleum, based on its previous allocations, in order to ensure continued operations of public utilities and to lessen the possibility of serious disorder. It is persistently reported that the Generalissimo has ordered the demolition of utilities and important industries when his troops withdraw.

Increasing Communist difficulties are reflected in rising urban prices, poor prospects for coming harvests and shortages of goods. In their rapid military advance, now reaching into south China, the Communists are inheriting economic instability and the disruptions of the Kuomintang inflationary economy, highly aggravated in north China by their own food shortages. Communist efforts are handicapped by a dearth of technical and administrative personnel to administer urban areas and by lack of foreign exchange to enable them to import essential materials. As evidenced by their propaganda, they are bitterly hostile to the U.S. and reflect the usual Communist attitude toward U.S. and British "imperialism", while ignoring Soviet actions.

The chief problems for the U.S. in this situation are:

1. *Recognition of a "Chinese Communist Government"*.[20] In the absence of any unified Communist government, this question has not yet arisen. In consultation with friendly governments, the U.S. Government is trying to maintain a common front on this question and forestall hasty action.

2. *Formosa*.[21] Under the Department's instructions, Mr. Merchant, Counselor of Embassy on special detail in Formosa, is proceeding to the U.S. for consultation. In the light of his recommendations, it may

---

[18] The former not printed; it was a weekly summary prepared jointly by the Embassy's political section, the Military Attaché, and the Naval Attaché at Nanking, No. 17, May 13 (893.00(W)/5–1349). For the latter, see Cantel 379, May 14, p. 316.

[19] See telegram No. 1656, May 16, p. 320.

[20] For further documentation on this subject, see vol. IX, pp. 1 ff.

[21] For further documentation on this subject, see *ibid.*, pp. 261 ff.

be desirable to seek revision of our present policy toward Formosa, as approved by NSC.[22]

3. *Withdrawal of U.S. Navy Forces at Tsingtao.*[23] Pursuant to Admiral Badger's [24] recommendation and with the concurrence of this Department, the Navy Department is authorizing Admiral Badger to withdraw his forces from Tsingtao about May 24, date of the withdrawal of Nationalist forces, or to withdraw his forces when Shanghai falls if the latter city should fall prior to May 24.

4. Pursuant to NSC 41[25] regarding trade with Communist areas, plans have been completed for the application of the R procedure to govern exports to China. SCAP [26] will apply similar controls over exports from Japan. The Department is seeking British cooperation in applying similar controls over British exports, but to date has had no reply from the British Government.

5. *Chinese Official Funds in the U.S.*[27] Discussions are being held with the Treasury Department regarding possible steps to prevent Chinese official funds in the U.S. from falling into the hands of the Chinese Communists or from being transferred to private accounts if the National Government should collapse. No decision has been reached.

6. *Removal of the National Government from Canton.* If the Government should leave Canton, the U.S. Government would have to decide whether a diplomatic officer should accompany it to a new location.

893.00/5–1749 : Telegram

The Minister-Counselor of Embassy in China (Clark) to the Secretary of State

[Received May 18—4 : 49 p. m.]
[Received May 18—4 : 49 p. m.]

Cantel 396. Li Tsung-jen appears to be making no progress in organized resistance and forces disintegration continue. Chu Chang-wei, advisor to Li Tsung-jen, tells me Generalissimo not abiding by his promises and that Li is meeting insurmountable obstacle from C–C clique and Sun Fo followers in his efforts mobilize resources for continued resistance. Chen Cheng, Governor Taiwan, is due Canton today and Li plans endeavor convince him expediency supporting Li.

Chu says standing committee Kmt did in fact vote to send delegation to Generalissimo in effort persuade him come Canton (he says Generalissimo is on gunboat Shanghai) but that Pai Chung-hsi was not, as reported, to head that delegation as neither he nor Li Tsung-jen had prior knowledge proposed action standing committee. Action was instigated by Sun Fo and C–C clique who, Chu says, continue mistrust

---

[22] National Security Council.
[23] For further documentation on this subject, see vol. IX, pp. 1191 ff.
[24] Adm. Oscar C. Badger, Commander, U.S. Naval Forces, Western Pacific.
[25] February 28, vol. IX, p. 826.
[26] Supreme Commander, Allied Powers in Japan (MacArthur).
[27] See also vol. IX, pp. 729 ff.

Li and ask protection Generalissimo. Chu went on to justify their anxiety by saying Li would purge government of all corrupt elements, including Sun Fo, Wu Tieh-cheng and Chen Li-fu, but that he would deal with incorrupt members of C–C clique in hopes of winning them over to liberalism. Ho Ying-chin, whom he continues characterize as weakling, must stay, he said, to bridge gap between Li and Generalissimo.

Li Tsung-jen being confronted with these obstacles to the exercise of his full authority hopes desperately that US can come out with some public statement indicating its support of him in preference other Chinese leaders. When I told Chu such statement was unthinkable as we could not take onus supporting any one faction as opposed to any other, he pled for a US statement in support of Nationalist Government so long as it maintained resistance to spread [of] Communism China. Even such statement in support government without mentioning Acting President, he thought, would strengthen Li's hands. He said some of Li's closest advisors were urging him to resign and Li might do so if he continued to meet frustration at hands Generalissimo adherents. I called attention to indications Congress might demand full public airing US policy China which would give ample evidence our sentiments toward present regime, but Chu insisted that I pass on these requests for statement at this time. I should appreciate instructions as to reply I should make.

Despite his plea for help with assurances of successful resistance if help given, Chu was sufficiently frank to agree with my analysis of the situation as follows: Generalissimo will not alter his plan make Taiwan his last bastion, with result that jockeying for position will continue in Canton until Communists arrive, at which time Li Tsung-jen will move west with part of government, the remainder seeking sanctuary under wing of Generalissimo on Taiwan as he might be expected re-emerge at that time resuming presidency. In agreeing with that analysis, he asked what our reaction would be and exhibited fear that we might recognize Generalissimo. I could only reply that we could not commit ourselves in advance on such problem which would be most difficult one.

Chu says troops from Tsingtao are being brought Kwangtung to defend east river area and that troops [of] Hu Tsung-nan and Chang Chih-chung from northwest are being moved into Szechwan to strengthen defenses that area. Should he have to leave Canton, Li plans make final stand based on Szechwan, Yunnan, Kweichow, Kwangsi and southern Hunan. Pai Chung-hsi is returning Canton next day or so to assume his functions, Chu said, as chief of staff.

Sent Department Cantel 396, repeated Nanking 293, Shanghai 247.

CLARK

893.50/5–1749 : Telegram

The Secretary of State to the Consul General at Shanghai (Cabot)

WASHINGTON, May 17, 1949—7 p. m.

971. Urtel 1656 May 16. Dept had assumed Deptel 918 May 12 furnished sufficient authorization for action suggested final para ref tel. Assuming you will keep in mind Embtel 1039 May 17 Dept authorizes you in your discretion approach Nationalist milit authorities re demolitions Amer properties, including utilities. If you consider desirable you authorized approach your Brit and French colleagues with view their taking parallel action.

ACHESON

893.00/5–1849 : Telegram

The Consul General at Shanghai (Cabot) to the Secretary of State

[Extracts]

SHANGHAI, May 18, 1949—1 p. m.
[Received May 19—1:51 p. m.]

1700. Signs now point increasing likelihood early Nationalist abandonment Shanghai defense:

1. According source close to Yang Hu, General L. S. Chou, head Political Section Nanking–Shanghai–Woosung Garrison and incidentally son-in-law of Yang, has just told Yang [that] Tang En-po now prepared withdraw troops in week (Chou previously quoted Tang as boasting would hold city 1 to 2 months); that Tang will shortly hit local merchants for final withdrawal bribe but in smaller sum than originally planned; that Tang has ordered troops refrain fighting in city proper; that he even agrees leave police and few regiments behind to keep order. Source also states that special service troops and demolition units have been withdrawn from [former] international settlement [and]concession areas. Source feels Generalissimo must have approved this changed attitude which source attributes to reluctant realization (a) impossibility resist Communists more than week or so and (b) unwisdom antagonize foreign interests by senseless fighting, destruction.

2. Mayor (strong Tang man) on May 16 confided to W. W. Yen his expectation early end battle and his readiness [garble] mayor to look after civilian populace. Asked Yen's advice how gain support Chinese and foreign population in order avoid appearance being traitor. He was advised first to get some authoritative Chinese civic body to ask

him stay and then seek foreign cooperation (remytel 1668 to Department May 16 ²⁸).

. . . .

Sent Nanking 940; repeated Department 1700, OffEmb Canton 480.

CABOT

893.00/5–1849 : Telegram

The Consul General at Shanghai (Cabot) to the Secretary of State

SHANGHAI, May 18, 1949.
[Received May 18—4: 50 p. m.]

1701. Following notice (abbreviated by Consulate General) has been widely distributed past few days among local foreign quarters:

To foreign nationals, foreign enterprises, and foreign public and private organizations: You hereby notified that according to No. 8 point of 8-point observance of General Headquarters of People's Liberation Army:
Protect lives and property of all foreign nationals. Hoped that all foreign nationals will remain posts and maintain order. All foreign nationals should abide by laws and regulations of People's Liberation Army and People's Government and must not indulge in espionage activities, oppose China [garble] independence and Chinese people's liberation cause, or shelter China's war criminals, counter-rev elements and other criminals. Otherwise, they will be punished accord laws of People's Liberation Army and People's Government.
Hence be it reassured:

(1) Under no circumstance should foreign nations [*nationals?*] assist war criminals, secret service agents and other enemies of Chinese people for latter's hiding or escape, and
(2) Under no circumstance should foreign nations [*nationals?*] receive, help transform, or help transfer movable and immovable property of war criminals, bureaucratic capitalists, secret service agents, or other enemies of the Chinese people. In order restore peace and order and build up people's democratic China, absolutely essential for Chinese people annihilate resolutely, thoroughly and completely all Kmt war criminals, bureaucratic capitalists, secret service agents and other counter-rev elements. Hoped that you will observe the 8-point observance without fail.

Signed: Publicity Department, Shanghai Office, People's Liberation Army of China.
Enclosure: English translation of the 8-point observance (refers to that issued April 25 by Mao Tze-tung and Chu Teh).

Sent Nanking 941, repeated Department 1701, to Canton 481.

CABOT

²⁸ Not printed.

893.00/5–1849 : Telegram

The Minister-Counselor of Embassy in China (Clark) to the Secretary of State

CANTON, May 18, 1949—5 p. m.
[Received May 16 [*18*]—4 : 17 p. m.]

Cantel 406. Long conversation with Wu Tieh-cheng strengthens my conviction that distrust is so deep-seated among leaders that unified resistance is impossibility. Wu and those who think like him have real fear that Li may leave them in lurch and make peace with Communists. Wu insists that Li has full authority dispose treasure Taiwan and fire anyone he chooses. He is indignant that Li demands Generalissimo go abroad before exercising authority he already has. In explanation Li's unwillingness force issue by exercising authority, Wu said he was convinced that Li, in typical Chinese fashion, was reluctant take action which would hurt someone else's feelings. (Fact of matter is, it seems to me, that Li knows his orders would not be obeyed and is unwilling risk loss of face which would inevitably result.)

Wu says China needs both Generalissimo and Li Tsung-jen. Three times, he said, Li had suggested that one or the other go abroad, but Generalissimo was adamant that he would remain China in retirement.

In their efforts to bring Generalissimo and Li together, Wu and his group are seeking public statement from Li couched in terms which would make later reconciliation with Communists impossible. They will insist that Generalissimo can function as head of party, with Li functioning as head of government, without friction. Li knows better.

Wu admits basic differences in strategy of Li and Generalissimo, with Li advocating defense mainland and Generalissimo defense southeast coast line and Taiwan. In effort reconcile these differences and assure defense of both, meeting of governors of provinces of southwest and Taiwan is taking place in Canton. Conference will study political, military and economic problems of defense. Wu expressed hope that out of conference would come plans resulting in halting Communist advance though he didn't say so with conviction.

Sent Department Cantel 406; repeated Nanking 298, Shanghai 251.

CLARK

893.00/5–1849 : Telegram

The Minister-Counselor of Embassy in China (Clark) to the Secretary of State

CANTON, May 18, 1949—5 p. m.
[Received 5 : 14 p. m.]

Cantel 408. Following summary of discussion by Parker [29] with H. J. Shen [30] at Shen's initiative is representative of general attitude

[29] Paul Parker, Acting Treasury Attaché in China.
[30] Head of the Central Trust of China.

552–963—78——22

of growing number liberals in China who are both anti-Communist and anti-Kmt. This particular group is of special importance as comprising the more capable financial personnel in China who have ability not known to be available to Communists and greatly needed by them.

Future of Central Bank is subject violent tug war between Generalissimo and Li factions. Former pressuring Finance Minister Liu remove bank to Taiwan while Li group fearful such move will deprive government last remaining foreign exchange assets. Actual control bank operations now in hands small group younger American trained economists headed by H. J. Shen (now head Central Trust). Shen advised flatly that except for transfer foreign exchange operations Hong Kong, Central Bank had no plans move and that Liu had told him last night bank would not go Taiwan while he remained governor.

Younger liberal economists have been meeting together last few days discuss their future plans. Although still undecided, have tentatively agreed they should begin dissociate selves from Kmt bureaucracy and not follow either Li or Generalissimo rump governments. Shen has long insisted they "hate" Kmt and served only because they felt position with government financial institutions best method serving Chinese people. Men in this group have generally high integrity and because considerably more honest than most Chinese Government officials are without extensive personal resources. They now feel present government incapable of giving any considerable further service to Chinese people and they are unwilling retreat any further. Are approaching decision that China will need intelligent trained men who have understanding and appreciation western ideas. Therefore they inclined remain and although not organized into an active underground, exercise whatever influence possible as a result recognition and prestige they gain through their professional ability and background.

Group probably would not have left Shanghai except fearful personal safety under Tang En-po during transition period. Shen seeking advice from close American friends and elder Chinese statesmen as K. P. Chen and Li Ming, who now Hong Kong. If they remain China, will attempt maintain outside contacts through Chen and Li.

Sent Department Cantel 408; repeated Nanking 301, Shanghai 253.

CLARK

893.00/5–1849 : Telegram

The Ambassador in China (Stuart) to the Secretary of State

NANKING, May 18, 1949—7 p. m.
[Received May 18—12:35 p. m.]

1060. Re Shanghai's 919, May 16, repeated Department 1656, EmbOff Canton 461. While public utilities, dock freight yards, et cetera, usually considered legitimate targets all-out warfare, we feel

Generalissimo would pull strategic blunder if he decides follow suspected demolition policy. With destruction power company, factories, shipping facilities by retreating Nationalist forces, Communists would have perfect alibi to present Shanghai populace for inability make city going concern blaming "treacherous Kmt forces" for deliberate destruction of "people's" enterprises. If, on other hand, Generalissimo were to complete removal military personnel equipment and city were turned over to Communists in more or less working order, burden would be squarely on Communists' shoulders with no scapegoat to turn to.

Economic-financial difficulties which over period of time are bound to make Shanghai almost insurmountable task for Communist authorities enumerated Shanghai's 1642, May 13, repeated Nanking 910.[31]

With above in mind, request Department's opinion feasibility EmbOff Canton approaching informally appropriate Generalissimo-controlled official, such as Wu Tieh-cheng, stressing our concern for protection American interests and pointing out benefit Nationalist cause would gain in long run when it became apparent that Communists were having difficulties operating Shanghai successfully even though they took over city intact.

Sent Department 1060, repeated EmbOff Canton 443, Shanghai 603.

STUART

893.00/5–1449 : Telegram

The Secretary of State to the Minister-Counselor of Embassy in China (Clark), at Canton

WASHINGTON, May 18, 1949—8 p. m.

TelCan 196. ReCantel 378, May 14. Dept considerably interested in organization described reftel and wld appreciate receiving further details with names individuals concerned and continuing reports their progress. Dept now looking into possibility action along lines you suggest and will inform you when thinking more advanced.

ACHESON

893.00/5–1849 : Telegram

The Secretary of State to the Minister-Counselor of Embassy in China (Clark), at Canton

WASHINGTON, May 18, 1949—8 p. m.

TelCan 198. Re Nanking's 1060 May 18 rptd EmbOff 443. You may in your discretion approach Wu Tieh-cheng or other suitable official and make available Emb's opinions as reflected reftel. Such approach

---

[31] Not printed; it reported activities of the British community.

should be made as if on your own initiative and reflecting only your own ideas this matter without indication that position constitutes US Govt attitude this regard.

ACHESON

893.00/5–1949 : Telegram

The Consul General at Shanghai (Cabot) to the Secretary of State

SHANGHAI, May 19, 1949—1 p. m.
[Received May 19—6 : 36 a. m.]

1722. Remytel 940, May 18, repeated Department 1700, Canton 480. Yang Hu source who has proven fairly reliable states that Generalissimo and son Ching-kuo, after moving to ex-French concession for 2-day stay (confirmed by another good source), left last night for Chusan Island. Source states that General L. S. Chou, Head Political Section of Nanking–Shanghai–Hangchow Garrison, told Yang Hu (his father-in-law) that Generalissimo quite pleased by "strong" Nationalist stand in Pootung; that Shanghai area fighting thus far has cost each side about 5% casualties (9,000 for Communists and 5,000 for Nationalists). Source says that Tang has not yet definitely agreed limit fighting to outside perimeter former settlement-concession areas but is still discussing matter with Yang Hu and W. W. Yen thru medium of General Chou.

Increasingly strong rumors that final payoff troops by local merchants being completed and that end Nationalist resistance may come this weekend.

Sent Nanking 957, repeated Department 1722, OffEmb Canton.

CABOT

893.00/5–1949 : Telegram

The Consul General at Shanghai (Cabot) to the Secretary of State

SHANGHAI, May 19, 1949—2 p. m.
[Received May 19—9 : 41 a. m.]

1724. At special Consular body meeting last night Swiss Consul General as Senior Consul proposed he be designated by Consular body to offer his services as intermediary to arrange local settlement of battle for Shanghai. Pursuant to Department's instructions (Deptel 918, May 12), I made it clear I could not associate myself with any such action. Further discussion having revealed obvious flaws in proposal, Consular body eventually authorized Swiss Consul General to explore possibilities with local authorities of preventing fighting within city in order prevent losses of foreign lives and property. Canadian Consul General and I, having made our position clear in the minutes, abstained from voting. All other Consular representatives agreed; no Russian representative present.

Repeated Nanking 958, OffEmb Canton 492.

CABOT

893.01/5–1949 : Telegram

The Consul General at Shanghai (Cabot) to the Secretary of State

SHANGHAI, May 19, 1949.
[Received May 19—11: 26 a. m.]

1728. *Ta Kung Pao* May 17 reports that Central Government, in view of strategic position of Chushan Archipelago, has decided set up Chushan-Chengszu Defense Headquarters with Wang Yung-lin as Commander having jurisdiction all Chushan and Chengszu islands; that "all" Chekiang Provincial Government employees and archives are being evacuated from Ningpo to Tinghai (largest island of Chushan group); that "all" personnel of Kiangsu and Shantung Provincial Governments also gathering at Archipelago; and that large numbers ships chartered by Nationalist Government assembling there.

Sent Nanking 959, repeated Department [1728] and Canton 494.

CABOT

893.00/5–1949 : Telegram

The Consul General at Shanghai (Cabot) to the Secretary of State

SHANGHAI, May 19, 1949.
[Received May 19—7: 11 p. m.]

1730. Past few days Communist-sponsored English language circulars have been appearing Shanghai and are being sent various US firms and organizations. Example is mimeographed sheet entitled *Shanghai People* published by "federation of the People's Organizations of Shanghai". Sheet states "American imperialists" and Chiang Kai-shek plotting to remove all possible materials from Shanghai, to arrest all leaders [of] people's organizations, democratic personage[s?] to destroy utility plants and factories, and to encourage looting and destruction during "liberation" Shanghai. To "smash" this plot is stated to be task of "Federation of People's Organizations" and purpose of the publication.

Publication volume 1, No. 1, May 10, carries article entitled "How Foreign Nationals Should Act Towards The Chinese" which stresses "imperialistic" sins of foreigners in past, spying, insidious activities of missionaries as secret agents imperialists, necessity of foreign nationals now "severing themselves clearly from Kmt reactionaries". Remainder of publication repeats news items from Communist broadcasts. Publication volume 1, No. 2, May 13, has feature article dealing with Shanghai arrests of professors and students, a protest against incident involving British warships on the Yangtze, a long list of slogans to be used in welcoming People's Army, and news items.

Sent Nanking 961; repeated Department 1730; Canton 495.

[CABOT]

893.00/5–1949 : Telegram

The Consul General at Hankow (Callanan) to the Secretary of State

HANKOW, May 19, 1949—5 p. m.
[Received May 20—11 : 06 a. m.]

152. Reviewing events past 5 days Wuhan cities, outstanding fact appears rapid acceleration Nationalist withdrawal in final stages. While retreat main body General Pai's forces with equipment, supplies was well organized and spread over several weeks, seems clear that rapidity Communist advance west and south from Nanchang area so seriously threatened rear Nationalist forces in Wuhan that they accelerated their timetable drastically. Defense command remaining ostensibly for rear guard action left Hankow early morning 16th, 6 days behind Pai's headquarters. First few hundred Communist troops appeared p. m. 16th obviously weary, followed by larger numbers during night. Most guesses that 4 to 5 thousand are here and probable that Communists unprepared have Wuhan drop in their laps so suddenly. Extensive damage done [by] Nationalists in blasting pontoons and river craft—operation which started about 13 hours on 15th and concluded about 9 hours on 16th—stands out as the serious development in abandoning area. Port is seriously crippled.

Formal entry not yet made Hankow. Parade announced in press for 19th postponed. Small business gradually reopening, city resuming normal appearance with small unobtrusive groups Communist soldiers in streets and sentries posted places formerly occupied by Nationalists. Civic organizations not yet in evidence.

Press reports Kiukiang occupied 17th but nothing reported from Changsha or south.

Only local mail is now accepted by post office and all plane, rail, river communications beyond immediate area severed.

No incident yet reported involving Americans and all are safe and well.

Sent Department 152; repeated Nanking 116, OffEmb Canton 71.

CALLANAN

893.00/5–1949 : Telegram

The Consul General at Shanghai (Cabot) to the Secretary of State

SHANGHAI, May 19, 1949—6 p. m.
[Received May 19—5:47 p. m.]

1732. Shanghai police commissioner Mao Sen convoked representatives foreign nationals 18 May to solicit cooperation for emergency. He envisaged attempted looting, robbery, internal Communist uprising and implied knowledge early Nationalist troop withdrawal with internal order city now his responsibility. Suggested blocking of family property to deter robbery and concentration foreign nationals facilitate police protection.

Foreign representatives agreed delegate police liaison to small group consisting representatives British, French, US, port, police and subcommittee food and fuel to meet daily police headquarters review problems, exchange information. No garrison representative present second meeting 19 May although requested by foreign representatives and promised by police.

Police proposed deputizing foreign nationals as auxiliary volunteers which unanimously but politely rejected. Concentration foreign nationals without prospect evacuation also rejected except for temporary emergency refuge. Liaison courier service for emergency breakdown communications being worked out.

Consulate General proposes cooperate fully with committee but will maintain present effective direct contact police and garrison through normal channels to protect US interest.

Sent Department 1732; repeated Canton 496.

CABOT

894A.01/5–2049 : Telegram

The Minister-Counselor of Embassy in China (Clark) to the Secretary of State

CANTON, May 20, 1949—10 a. m.
[Received May 21—7: 31 a. m.]

Cantel 431. Chen Cheng, Governor Taiwan, asked me tea yesterday and from conversation it was obvious purpose invitation was persuade me visit Taiwan and support his requests for aid.

Chen said he has had profitable conversation with Li Tsung-jen who had described conversation at meeting of governors yesterday as "most satisfactory". Chen said he had endeavored so far unsuccessfully to persuade Li to remove from his mind all thought of any possible future arrangement from Communists and issue statement of determination fight to finish. Li's response indicated, he said, firm conviction in desirability not closing all routes to peace. Chen went on to

FOREIGN RELATIONS, 1949, VOLUME VIII

say that all should stand together if Communists were to be successfully resisted and stated without qualification that if Li would agree
to fight to finish the resources of Taiwan would be placed at his
disposal. The inference was, if not, then Taiwan resources would not
be placed at his disposal. Although Chen said conference of governors
is accomplishing much in field coordination efforts various provinces,
he indicated that there would be no more pooling of resources but
that each would let another have any surplus on barter basis. He mentioned this connection deal between him and Chen Chi-tang, Governor
Hainan, to exchange rice for iron ore.

Sent Department, repeated Nanking 309, Shanghai 262.

CLARK

893.00/5–2049 : Telegram

*The Minister-Counselor of Embassy in China (Clark) to the Secretary
of State*

CANTON, May 20, 1949—7 p. m.
[Received May 21—5 : 39 a. m.]

Cantel 438. Han Li-wu, Minister Education, informs me Li Tsung-
jen has agreed in principle to further meeting with Generalissimo. He
confirms mutual distrust is seat present difficulties in efforts unify
resistance and believes further meetings should be helpful.

He says Ho Ying-chin will stay as Premier and is determined defend
Canton. If Canton should prove indefensible, Han says selected Cabinet, assisted by selected senior subordinates will move Chungking and
establish government. It is of course hoped that diplomatic missions
will accompany such move. No element of government, he says, will
move Taiwan.

Sent Department, repeated Nanking 312, Shanghai 264.

CLARK

893.00/5–2049 : Telegram

*The Minister-Counselor of Embassy in China (Clark) to the Secretary
of State*

CANTON, May 20, 1949—2 [7?] p. m.
[Received May 21—6 : 43 a. m.]

Cantel 439. Han Li-wu, Minister Education and liberal, expressing
determination resist comparable that of Churchill[32] at time Battle of
Britain, is still sanguine effective resistance Communist[s] possible and
is taking action on his own toward that end. Faced with ineffective
propaganda Minister Information, Han is using funds Minister Edu-

---

[32] Winston S. Churchill, British Prime Minister, 1940–1945.

cation in effort portray life under Communists North China and educate people need to resist. This will be done in lectures [by] prominent escapees from North and through "Free China" publication.

In effort solve costly refugee student problem, Han plans send some to Taiwan for military training to serve as junior officers and prior next semester he plans hold strict examinations and eliminate all but most qualified students. Others will go through military training either as communications technicians, drivers, or other similar specialists. Fourteen hundred students have already been picked for Taiwan to be trained under Sun Li-jen who has officer at Canton making arrangements.

If there were more like Han Li-wu, there might be hope for non-Communist China, but am afraid he is the exception. He inquired as to possibility obtaining qualified Americans to teach in technical schools for army training and we hedged by suggesting that graduates of the Ramgahr School should be available in China for that purpose.

CLARK

893.00/5–2149 : Telegram

The Consul at Taipei (Edgar) to the Secretary of State

TAIPEI, May 21, 1949—4 p. m.
[Received May 22—6 : 41 a. m.]

181. Persistent rumor in Taiwan that top level Kmt conference in preparation there. Local officials vacating residences for exalted guests. K. C. Wu [33] and Tao Hsi-sheng [34] there now. Generalissimo expected. Constant rumors Generalissimo already in Taiwan but best information says still Yangtze anchorage although quarters at Sun-Moon Lake and Taipei have been prepared.

Sent Department 181, repeated Canton 42, Shanghai 145.

EDGAR

893.00/5–2249 : Telegram

The Consul General at Shanghai (Cabot) to the Secretary of State

SHANGHAI, May 22, 1949—5 p. m.
[Received May 22—8 : 15 a. m.]

1775. Communist strategy still seems directed to moving pressure further south with resultant increased action last night against Nationalist lines in west (Nansiang), southwest (Hungjao) and south southeast (Lunghwa and return eastward across Whangpoo) which

[33] Former Mayor of Shanghai.
[34] Chinese Vice Minister of the Kuomintang Ministry of Information.

gained Communists full control Chipao and CAT [35] airfield to point mile or two east of field along Hungjao road. Nationalists still hold Lunghua field with CATC [36] and CNAC [37] planes taking on passengers, thereafter bringing ammunition to Kiangwan field. However, troops of 38th Army which took over defense Lunghua field from 75th Army reported busy looting cargoes and supplies at field. Nationalists seem still holding well Woosung and north Pootung areas and general military situation around city shows little surface change; but evidence growing Communist numerical superiority and Nationalist vulnerability to attack from southwest and east suggests that any considerable further delay in Communist capture city may be attributable less to Nationalist resistance than to Communist unreadiness take over.

Kiangnan dockyard destroyed by explosions about dawn today evidently deliberate demolition by Nationalists as expected, possibly hastened by Communist threat at immediate opposite Pootung shore. Well-connected source feels Nationalists no longer planning demolish utilities but still may blow factories. Destruction and removal government files in Kiangwan and city sectors under way.

Ex-settlement-concession areas continue superficially quiet, only noticeable change being extensive conscription civilian labor gangs in heart city which hitherto only reported in suburbs.

Generalissimo reported now at Kiangwan.

Sent Department 1775, repeated Nanking 978, EmbCanton 516.

CABOT

893.00/5–2349 : Telegram

The Minister-Counselor of Embassy in China (Clark) to the Secretary of State

CANTON, May 23, 1949—9 p. m.
[Received May 24—9:21 a. m.]

Cantel 457. There is much rejoicing Kmt reactionary circles and in fact generally over Li Tsung-jen's statement castigating Communists and declaring determination fight to finish. Kmt leaders with whom I have talked express assurance statement will be followed by meeting between Li and Generalissimo, probably this week; that bickering and jockeying for position are ended and there will henceforth be unity in resisting Communist advance.

Chen Li-fu was frank enough to admit, however, that basically statement had changed nothing. Generalissimo, he said, just did not trust Li to continue fight against Communists under all conditions and Li's statement would not alter situation. Chen hoped, however, that

---

[35] Civil Air Transport.
[36] Central Air Transport Corporation.
[37] China National Aviation Corporation.

meeting Li and Generalissimo would result some working arrangement where Generalissimo would be sufficiently close to operations to assure that Li did not conclude peace with Communists. Chen envisages creation some such policy committee as that previously suggested in which Generalissimo, as head Kmt, will form policy jointly with Li, leaving Li executive. Yen Hsi-shan, who seems to have made great impression both among Li's followers and in Kmt reactionary circles, is to be emissary between Li and Generalissimo. As indicated above, I cannot see how Li's statement changes picture. The distrust is too deep-seated to be removed by any mere statement. Li seems to be weakening, however, in his previous determination to refuse responsibility without full authority and it is conceivable that further meeting with Generalissimo may result in creation some such policy organ as that designated by Kmt reactionaries. Although such supreme policy committee might give appearance unity, am afraid selfish interests are too predominant to result in real unified action.

Repeated Nanking 317, Shanghai 270.

CLARK

893.00/5–2349 : Telegram

The Minister-Counselor of Embassy in China (Clark) to the Secretary of State

CANTON, May 23, 1949—9 p. m.
[Received May 24—12 : 02 p. m.]

Cantel 458. Took advantage conversation Chen Li-fu today to put forward on personal basis arguments advanced Nanking's 1060, May 18 to Department; repeated Shanghai 603, Canton 443, regarding demolition Shanghai. Chen agreed with reasoning and promised to do something about it although I gather from Shanghai's 1717 to Department May 18,[38] repeated Nanking 953, Canton 489, problem may already have been solved.

Sent Department Cantel 458, repeated Nanking 318, Shanghai 271.

CLARK

893.00/5–2449 : Telegram

The Ambassador in China (Stuart) to the Secretary of State

NANKING, May 24, 1949—2 p. m.
[Received May 24—7 : 39 a. m.]

1100. This is not first time Acting President has asked for statement of support (see Cantel 396, May 17, to Department, repeated Nanking 293, Shanghai 247). With all my sympathy for Li Tsung-jen and his determination to resist Communists, I cannot envisage any

---

[38] Not printed.

statement US Government could make this late date which would be effective in changing course of military events, which could avoid embroiling us further in Chinese political confusion.

Sent Department 1100, repeated AmEmb Canton 458, Shanghai 622.

STUART

893.00/5–2449 : Telegram

The Consul General at Shanghai (Cabot) to the Secretary of State

SHANGHAI, May 24, 1949—11 p. m.
[Received May 24—1 : 12 p. m.]

1815. Although there have been strong indications all day that turn-over at least in section of city south and west of Soochow creek is imminent, we have at 9 p. m. no authentic reports that Communists have broken into city. Possibly however turn-over to interim regime may precede Communist arrival as one good source informs us that provisional mayor and chief police have been appointed. General Hu Hsing, chief staff to Tang En-po, described situation this morning as "critical". Combined with facts reported Contel 1807 [39] and steady movement soldiers through city toward Woosung plus other significant signs, we believe this indicates that further fighting will primarily cover evacuation. There is some evidence that Communists are preparing apply real military pressure rather than merely encourage defection or withdrawal.

If this analysis correct, city is extraordinarily calm. Police remain on duty; most shops open though many shuttered; crowds lining streets as if awaiting parade; general air expectance. Light barbed wire road blocks ready at many intersections and sandbag pill boxes at numerous important points. No signs yet of looting or disorder though traffic at times a trifle strained. City proper as yet spared serious casualties or damage from artillery or machine gun fire.

Consul General taking extraordinary precautions to safeguard personnel, also to protect Glenline building from possible mob violence. At moment, however, we feel guardedly optimistic.

Repeated Nanking 989, OffEmb Canton 530.

CABOT

893.00/5–2549 : Telegram

The Consul General at Shanghai (Cabot) to the Secretary of State

SHANGHAI, May 25, 1949.
[Received May 24—11 : 22 p. m.]

1819. Officer in Hamilton House reports Communist soldiers have just reached municipal building. Report that interim mayor is T. K.

---

[39] May 24, not printed.

Chao and police commander Lo Ta-kung, confirmed by latter personally, but first edition of *Sin Wen Pao* carrying *Hsin Hua* (Communist) news indicates Hsu Hsu may take over from him and confirms Communist take-over municipality. Lo stated majority police remaining on job. Main police station evacuated last night.

Police stations, pillboxes and other points this side Soochow Creek reported flying white flags but AMA states troops of 37th Army (not Peace Preservation Corps) still holding positions around Consulate and possibly planning hold Garden Bridge which may mean fighting directly around Consulate. Have therefore instructed staff, except several who have already arrived here, not to come. Numerous eyewitness reports indicate take-over on whole peaceful but there was occasional random tank, machine gun and rifle fire from Communist units which entered city through former French concession between midnight and 3 a. m. Skirmish near former Navy Club in which one Nationalist tank knocked out. Sporadic rifle fire still reported various points; numerous people on streets but few vehicles. No reports looting or injury Americans.

Sent Department 1819; repeated Nanking 993, OffEmb Canton 534.

CABOT

893.00/5–2549 : Telegram

The Consul General at Shanghai (Cabot) to the Secretary of State

SHANGHAI, May 25, 1949—noon.
[Received May 25—2:29 a. m.]

1821. Various reports have reached Consulate of sharp skirmishes during night at points this side Soochow Creek. At moment Communists have taken French Bund and Nationalists have established holding position almost directly below Consulate to cover Garden Bridge. Other bridges reported barricaded. Frequent bursts machine gun and rifle fire in vicinity Consulate. We are checking with American organizations regarding safety Americans. All so far O.K. Most Americans remaining homes. Further sinkings of vessels in Whangpoo but some still afloat. Power Company still in Nationalist hands, plant operating with light load.

Sent Department 1821, Nanking 994, OffEmb Canton 535.

CABOT

893.00/5–2549 : Telegram

The Consul General at Shanghai (Cabot) to the Secretary of State

SHANGHAI, May 25, 1949.
[Received May 25—7:06 p. m.]

1828. *Shih Shih Hsin Pao*, 25 May, says Shanghai Security Council formed, W. W. Yen, chairman. Vice-chairmen, Hsu Chi-ching (chairman Shanghai Chamber Commerce), Fang Chiu-wei (associate of Chow I-chih, Kmt dissident group), Chiang Hao (city councillor). Other Council members to be announced due time. Office of Council located Ningpo Guild, Avenue Foch. Council organized jointly Shanghai City Council and prominent members local, trade, industrial and charity groups.

Public notice issued by Council says:

1. All administrative organs will function as usual.
2. Public utilities will continue operation.
3. All wharves and communication facilities must not be destroyed.
4. Stragglers who commit looting, rape, or arson will be severely punished.
5. Factories and markets will resume operations immediately.
6. Refugees will be cared for.

CABOT

893.00/5–2549 : Telegram

The Consul General at Shanghai (Cabot) to the Secretary of State

SHANGHAI, May 25, 1949—6 p. m.
[Received May 25—11 : 44 a. m.]

1829. Lo Ta-kung, provisional police commissioner, appears to be a "Yang Hu man" who was already in police force. Already contacted by Consulate General, he manifests desire cooperate and assist us. Confirmation of T. K. Chao's assumption acting mayor still lacking. Meanwhile Shanghai Security Council under W. W. Yen and members apparently representing civic, industrial, Yang Hu Green-Red Gang and KmtRC groups has been established and evidently assisting maintenance order, et cetera, ConGentel 1828, May 25.

Highly trustworthy American missionary reports information from policeman (long known personally to him) that friction has developed between local Communist underground (now operating openly) and incoming Communist authorities over question treatment police. Local Communists feeling grudge against police killed six which is said to have angered incoming Communist authorities who feel police should be given chance demostrate loyalty to new regime.

All information thus far indicates Communist soldiers well disciplined and behaved. Those thus far contacted are Shantung men.

Twenty-seven Chinese Air Force planes left Kiangwan southward this morning, including according to press General Chou Tse-jou. Presumably some of remaining Nationalist VIPs, such as Kmt C–C leaders Lei Chen, Fang Chih and Ku Chen-kang, on board.

To prevent what they considered danger of Nationalist abduction, Yang Hu agents yesterday "rescued" Democrat [League] leaders Lo

Lung-chi and Chang Lan from their hospital imprisonment by Nationalists and Lo phoned Consulate General to report their escape. Sent Department 1829, repeated Nanking 1000, Canton 542.

CABOT

893.00/5–2649 : Telegram

The Consul General at Shanghai (Cabot) to the Secretary of State

SHANGHAI, May 26, 1949.
[Received May 25—11 : 56 p. m.]

1832. Situation seems substantially unchanged since last night. Nationalists still hold position directly in front of Consulate and along north bank of Soochow Creek. Now being attacked by Communists with light arms, grenades and mortars. Firing in other nearby streets. Building still being struck by bullets and Cabot servant injured on head by flying glass from window. Consulate well stocked with food, has water, light, and telephone. Staff, of course, directed not to come to work; they report situation generally quiet in districts taken by Communists except for sporadic firing and occasional small skirmishes, evidently in streets where Communist control still being consolidated. Shelling duel across west part Soochow Creek visible last night.

Ta Kung Pao 26th carries following item:

"Liberation Army has not advanced towards the Soochow Creek. Bridges are still in Kmt hands. Nationalist troops who had gone to Woosung to embark have again returned to Hongkew because there are not enough ships. Communist troops have occupied North Station."

Liberation Army units in western district belong to 27th Army of Chen Yi's Third Field Army. Tram and bus services partially restored.

Sent Department, repeated Nanking 1003, Canton 544, ComNav-WesPac.

[CABOT]

893.00/5–2649 : Telegram

The Consul General at Shanghai (Cabot) to the Secretary of State

SHANGHAI, May 26, 1949.
[Received May 26—8 : 06 p. m.]

1847. Nationalist resistance in this area ceased about 6 p. m. Both sides Soochow Creek now appear completely under Communist control. Several members of staff have already returned to homes in different sections of former settlement and French concession while other staff members have arrived here from homes—all reporting no trouble. Festive demonstrations and parade of freshly arrived troops taking place on main streets. Curfew being ignored. No reports of any injury to Americans. Considerable firing still heard to north and east, however, evidently in northern Yangtzepoo where fighting said still in progress.

Sent Department 1847; repeated Nanking 1014; OffEmb Canton 556.

CABOT

893.00B/5–2649 : Telegram

The Minister-Counselor of Embassy in China (Clark) to the Secretary of State

CANTON, May 26, 1949—11 a. m.
[Received 11:41 p. m.]

Cantel 475. Penultimate paragraph Nanking's 1076, May 21, to Department,[40] repeated Shanghai 608, Canton 447, prompts me report that more than one Chinese student of situation has cautioned me not to underestimate Mao Tse-tung, saying Mao has no idea of emulating Tito, but aspires to be Asian Lenin. Careful scrutiny Communist propaganda will substantiate that there is paucity of mention of Marxist, Leninist or Stalinist doctrine, sole stress being on Mao Tse-tung. Possibility my cautioners may be correct would seem to have far-reaching implications.

Sent Nanking 326, repeated Department, Shanghai 279.

CLARK

893.00/5–2649 : Telegram

The Minister-Counselor of Embassy in China (Clark) to the Secretary of State

CANTON, May 26, 1949—11 a. m.
[Received May 27—10:28 a. m.]

Cantel 476. Illness Li Tsung-jen was not diplomatic. He still looks bad. Nevertheless he spent more than an hour today endeavoring convince me that if China goes Communist Southeast Asia, Japan, Philippines and Australia are doomed to militant Communism. One reason cited was revealing statement that during Peiping peace negotiations, Mao Tse-tung had sent word to Pai Chung-hsi that on termination hostilities, he (Pai) would have even more troops under his command than now, an obvious effort by Communists wean Li and Pai away from Kmt.

---

[40] Not printed.

Machinery has been set in motion for meeting Li and Generalissimo but nothing yet definitely fixed. Li's talk with Chen Cheng, Governor Taiwan, he said, was most satisfactory; that he and Chen agreed on necessity fighting Communism to finish. When I inquired whether as result his statement made under pressure from right wing Kmt he anticipated access Taiwan treasure, he laughingly said: "Making promises is one thing; carrying them out is another".

Li continues express determination defend Southwest China in which he hopes to include Kwangtung, but will at least include West River area. He still does not speak with conviction, however, and was bitter in his condemnation of Hu Tsung-nan for having withdrawn from Sian without battle and without instructions from Minister National Defense.[41]

Sent Department, repeated Nanking 327, Shanghai 280.

CLARK

893.01/5–2649 : Telegram

The Minister-Counselor of Embassy in China (Clark) to the Secretary of State

CANTON, May 26, 1949—5 p. m.
[Received May 27—3 : 07 a. m.]

Cantel 480. Chiang Monlin, very much of an elder statesman [of] Kmt himself, says elder statesmen still hope bring Li Tsung-jen and Generalissimo sufficiently close together that they will at least stop fighting each other. Li, he says, has agreed to further meeting with Generalissimo who remains reluctant.

Forces of disintegration seem to be moving almost irresistibly, he said, and admitted matters were not being improved by position Acting President [in] Canton with responsibility and insufficient authority. He admitted Tang En-po, for example, would not obey any instruction Li gave him, but hoped that if Li and Generalissimo could get closer together they would discontinue working at cross purposes.

Chiang stated categorically to me that Generalissimo has placed Taiwan gold completely at disposal government and recent visit S. Y. Liu to a "certain place" was to interview Generalissimo this regard and make arrangements using gold assets, which Chiang estimated at $260 million, in support new financial measures which will be instituted soonest. Chiang Monlin, giving evidence of fatalism which I am encountering more and more of late, said Communist doctrine is so diametrically opposed to fundamental of Chinese society and tradition as eventually to prove unworkable. He takes comfort in this belief,

---

[41] The Consul General at Peiping in his telegram No. 899, May 26, 5 p.m., reported the recent capture of Taiyuan, capital of Shansi, by Communist forces (893.00B/5–2649).

therefore, that Communism will not survive in China more than 30 or 40 years which, after all, is "nothing in our history".

Sent Department 480; repeated Nanking 330, Shanghai 280.

CLARK

893.00/5–1749 : Telegram

The Acting Secretary of State to the Minister-Counselor of Embassy in China (Clark), at Canton[42]

WASHINGTON, May 26, 1949—8 p. m.

TelCan 243. Ur 396 May 17. Dept approves ur response Chu's statement Li hopes US can make public statement indicating its support of him in preference other Chinese leaders.

With respect to US public statement in support Natl Govt, Dept concurs Emb view (Nanking tel 1100 May 24, rptd Emb Off Canton 458) that there is no statement US Govt could make this time which would be effective in changing course of military events or which could avoid embroiling us further in Chinese political confusion.

If Chu again approaches you in this regard, you shld inform him Dept has noted Li Tsung-jen's reported statement to UP correspondent Canton May 26 in which *inter alia* he expressed desire for indication US realizes import events in Asia. In this connection, you shld point out Secy stated press conference May 18 [43] conclusion North Atlantic Treaty does not mean lessening US interest in security other areas, as he has taken pains make clear on several occasions, and, referring to serious dangers to world peace existing in situation in Asia, said dangers in mind are those which revolve around present disturbed conditions in China.

If text Li statement not available Canton, Dept will transmit.

WEBB

893.00/5–2749 : Telegram

The Consul General at Shanghai (Cabot) to the Secretary of State

SHANGHAI, May 27, 1949.
[Received May 27—9 : 26 a. m.]

1864. Reliably reported that approximately 10,000 Nationalist troops in Yangtzepoo area have ceased fighting and details for their disposition being worked out. Riverside power plant vacated by Nationalist troops around 3 p. m., without damage.

Sent Department; repeated Nanking 1022, Canton 565.

CABOT

---

[42] Repeated as Nos. 642 and 1068 to the Ambassador at Nanking and the Consul General at Shanghai, respectively.
[43] Department of State *Bulletin*, May 29, 1949, p. 696.

893.00/5–2749

The Minister-Counselor of Embassy in China (Clark) to the
Secretary of State

No. 15   CANTON, May 27, 1949.
                                                [Received June 7.]

SIR: I have the honor to enclose a full translation [44] of a public statement made by Acting President Li Tsung-jen on May 21, 1949 and to summarize the main points of this proclamation as follows:

Li puts the entire blame for the failure of the Peiping peace talks on the Communists. He declares that the Communists are willing slaves of the Communist International, that they will try to destroy all non-Communist elements in China, and that they are bent upon the eradication of China's "best moral and cultural traditions". The Nationalist Government, on the other hand, is fighting for freedom, democracy, and independence.

Granting that the continuation of China's civil war will mean further hardships for the Chinese people, Li points out that failure to resist the Communists will mean slavery and even greater hardships. All efforts to settle the Communist problem by peaceful means having come to naught, Li says "we are compelled against our wishes to end war by war". Repeating the charge that the Chinese Communists will fight on the side of Russia in any future world war, Li ridicules the Communist accusations that the Nationalist Government has sold out to America. "My fellow countrymen," he states, "please try to think again which is more treasonable—to accept aid from the United States which treats us as equals, or to accept the leadership of, to be loyal to and to die for the Communist International by sacrificing our national independence and our people?"

In conclusion, Li admits the precariousness of the Nationalist situation but states that there is nothing to fear if the people "know the realities. . ."[45] and understand the intrigue of the Chinese Communists." Furthermore, he says, "the Government which I lead is now determined to resist the oppression of this brutal force and will not yield even if we have only one soldier left." At the same time political, economic, and military reforms are not to be blocked by obstacles of any sort. "With the solid support of the people, we will win the final victory."

Respectfully yours,   LEWIS CLARK

---

[44] Not printed.
[45] Omission indicated in the source text.

893.00/5–2849 : Telegram

The Ambassador in China (Stuart) to the Secretary of State

NANKING, May 28, 1949—1 p. m.
[Received May 28—5 : 42 a. m.]

1129. Following is report from Clubb [46] who has taken message to Chang Tung-sun [47] at Yenching. I asked Chang come here feeling confident he had information useful me take Washington.

"Communists still free to determine policy as respects domestic affairs and indications are that they are inclining to right. They are still, however, not in position part from USSR and take separate line foreign affairs. Of primary present significance in their respect foreign relations is Council Foreign Ministers now meeting Paris. If as result that meeting USSR retreats there can come about change in respect CCP foreign policy. If CFM on contrary breaks up this can be bad for Americans in China. Those personally who would assist re amelioration Sino-American relations must now be very careful in order preserve opportunity act effectively later. It is essential await outcome CFM meeting. If USSR retreats along lines indicated above, Chang would be in position go Nanking. If CFM, however, breaks up it could be anticipated war would occur within 6 months (approximately 10 characters garbled) useless.

Chang saw Chou En-lai yesterday and reported latter indicated receptive attitude re particular question trade with foreign nations. He said people like Mao Tse-tung, Liu Shao-chi and Chou were aware of need re forming trade and foreign relations but were not in position readily impose their concepts and judgments on lower strata in part which has been subjected education along different lines. He emphasized his belief that there was tendency toward adjustment position this respect as far as concerned Americans but said Communists acted very slowly.

Chang said that he had proposed to Chou that after occupation Shanghai he, Chang, should go to Shanghai to look things over. Chou had approved suggestion and Chang therefore proposed tentatively depart end June or beginning July. He modified what he had said previously to extent asking me tell you that if he went Shanghai he would then go Nanking see you. In view all circumstances, however, he considered it useless proceed prior to crystallization events at CFM meeting.["]

Sent Department, repeated OffEmb Canton 471, Shanghai 631.

STUART

---

[46] O. Edmund Clubb, Consul General at Peiping.
[47] Peiping leader of the Democratic League.

893.00/5–2849 : Telegram

The Minister-Counselor of Embassy in China (Clark) to the Secretary of State

CANTON, May 28, 1949—2 p. m.
[Received May 28—6 : 47 a. m.]

Cantel 490. Gather from Chu Chang-wei, political advisor Li Tsung-jen, that neither Li nor Gimo feels further meeting would serve useful purpose. Li nevertheless is unwilling lay himself open to charge lack cooperation and has with some reluctance acceded request Kmt elders and written letter Gimo inviting Gimo come Canton and alternatively offering visit Gimo Tainan [48] where Gimo now is. Letter was carried Tainan 27th by group, including Yen Hsi-shan, Yu Yu-jen, Chen Li-fu and Chi [Chu] Chia-hua. Group is due return Canton today.

Chu says Governor Chen Cheng has agreed, obviously with Gimo permission, that government can have access Taiwan treasure provided all expenses Nationalist Government on Taiwan are first reimbursed to Taiwan Provincial Government. Government is proceeding this basis and Ministry of Finance endeavoring implement his financial planning. Although Chu understands treasure that had been accumulated Amoy has already been made available and is being air-lifted southwest, he remains skeptical Taiwan treasure in any material amount will be made available.

Sent Department; repeated Nanking 337, Shanghai 290, Taipei 21.

CLARK

893.00/5–2849 : Telegram

The Consul General at Shanghai (Cabot) to the Secretary of State

SHANGHAI, May 28, 1949.
[Received May 28—8 : 19 a. m.]

1883. Shanghai almost normal today with pedestrian and pedicab traffic thick, public transportation running, but private autos still not plentiful. Banks, including Chase and National City, open several hours in morning. Street hawkers not operating. Shops reopening. Money changers out in limited numbers.

According press, big parade planned, so far celebration confined to small-scale demonstrations, trucks filled with singing students, et cetera, perhaps due inclement weather. Number slogans on walls increasing but that mostly general in character and moderate tone posters and other publicity media contain very little mention foreign nations.

---

[48] Southwest coast of Taiwan

Communist soldiers walking around more freely although some still on sentry duty at large banks and downtown street corners. American concerns open for business but as yet no business. No members of staff stopped today, and autos apparently unhindered.

Normal train service between Shanghai and Nanking expected resume shortly as first train from Nanking since liberation has arrived Shanghai. Press announces highway bus service to Soochow and Wusih will soon start. Although no official announcement, curfew apparently lifted. But night life not yet reestablished.

Textile mills resume operations with exception No. 5 cotton mill on Jessfield Road which has not recovered from damage sustained during fighting.

No more artillery or small arms fire. Long lines unarmed Nationalist soldiers marching under guard from Yangtzepoo area towards Shanghai suburbs. PLA still searching for Nationalist soldiers and local press reports uncovering of underground organization of Kmt special service agents.

Press censorship established today but not enforced as no censors yet on duty.

Sent Department 1883, repeated Nanking 1031, Canton.

CABOT

893.00/5–2849 : Telegram

The Consul at Tsingtao (Strong) to the Secretary of State

TSINGTAO, May 28, 1949—3 p. m.
[Received May 29—4 : 44 a. m.]

217. Despite telegram from Governor Chin Teh-chun [from] Canton May 27 to Municipal Council, stating Nationalist Government decided hold Tsingtao, evacuation Nationalist forces proceeding apace to be completed May 30 if on schedule; number of loaded ships sailed last night. Police authority boarding ship 29 with portion police force. Curfew 8 p. m. to 8 a. m. enforced from evening May 27. Few persons on street view fear male conscription. Prices skyrocketed May 27 after sinking to record lows morning May 26; reasons are closing majority shops and seizure godown stocks by military and police.

Consul General held meeting American citizens this morning to learn plans each organization, individual; offered sanctuary event serious disorders to women and children and others without property obligations. Have facilities billet, feed considerable number people within Consulate General which relatively secure.

Sent Nanking 162; repeated OffEmb Canton 68, Department 217.

STRONG

893.101/5–2849 : Telegram

The Consul at Tsingtao (Strong) to the Secretary of State

TSINGTAO, May 28, 1949.
[Received May 29—3 : 10 a. m.]

222. Acting Mayor informs Consulate General telegram received from Canton [that] new mayor to arrive Tsingtao within few days and Tsingtao to be held (remytel 165 to Nanking, 71 to Canton and 221 to Department [49]). Comment: Order probably not unrelated to move of Nationalist Government to Chungking. Delayed Nationalist evacuation expected to be of nuisance value only.

Sent Nanking 166; repeated OffEmb Canton 71, Department 222, info ComNavWesPac.

STRONG

893.001 Chiang Kai-shek/5–2949 : Telegram

The Minister-Counselor of Embassy in China (Clark) to the Secretary of State

CANTON, May 29, 1949—7 p. m.
[Received May 30—5 : 48 a. m.]

Cantel 496. Delegation that visited Generalissimo has returned Canton (Cantel 490,[50] repeated Nanking 337, Shanghai 290, Taipei 21). Am told Generalissimo unwilling come Canton unless there is overwhelming demand by people for his presence here and that likewise he felt Li had too many duties Canton to justify visit [to] Generalissimo, Taiwan. Delegation supposedly brings Generalissimo assurance availability Taiwan treasure after satisfaction demand Taiwan Provincial Government.

Sent Department; repeated Nanking 341, Shanghai 293, Taipei 22.

CLARK

893.002/5–3049 : Telegram

The Minister-Counselor of Embassy in China (Clark) to the Secretary of State

CANTON, May 30, 1949—2 p. m.
[Received May 30—5 : 49 a. m.]

Cantel 499. Can find no confirmation press reports Generalissimo plans visit Canton. On other hand, there is likelihood Li Tsung-jen will visit Generalissimo sometime prior removal capital Chungking.

[49] Not printed.
[50] May 28, p. 351.

Reshuffle Cabinet being discussed today with Chu Cheng, President Judicial Yuan, likely Premier. Subordinate personnel various ministries have been asked choose whether they desire accompany Government Chungking, remain Canton or proceed Taiwan. Because of transportation difficulties, movement of subordinate personnel has been authorized and starting. Although some may stop Chungking, seems likely vast majority will either remain Canton or go Taiwan. Likelihood increased therefore that when Government moves Chungking, will be façade only of ministers without adequate staff.

Have rumor that if Chu Cheng become[s] Premier, Wellington Koo will be appointed some position UN and replaced possibly by Quo Tai-chi.[51]

Sent Department, repeated Nanking 342, Shanghai 295.

CLARK

893.20/5–3149 : Telegram

The Ambassador in China (Stuart) to the Secretary of State

NANKING, May 31, 1949—5 p. m.
[Received 11:55 p. m.]

1159. Assume Department noticed in May 27 Peiping broadcast that "second-line troops of PLA in Manchuria will go into 6-month training program" in order "to lay initial foundation of modern army", according to Kao Kang, political commissar of northeast military area. "Task of this training program is to train fighters to be politically conscious and in use of modern weapons."

This is first reference to post-war military plans of CCP which [I] have seen. Significance of statement is underlined by fact that Kao Kang is member of CCP Politburo and reputedly associate of Li Li-san.

While accordance of high priority to military machine is of course characteristic of both Chinese and Communists, both stature of spokesman and fact that first listed task of training program is to make fighters "politically conscious" both seem to indicate that tone of program is more of Communist than Chinese inspiration. If program actually is motivated by Communist psychology, it can only mean that CCP intends to try to follow Soviet practice in maintaining large standing army equipped with modern weapons. Certainly US would not provide these weapons, and USSR has few to spare. Presumably therefore CCP would have to manufacture them itself with all the added sacrifices and difficulties this would mean to Mao's vaunted industrialization of China.

Sent Department, repeated Shanghai 635, OffEmb Canton 477.

STUART

---

[51] Chinese Minister for Foreign Affairs in 1941.

893.002/5–3149 : Telegram

The Minister-Counselor of Embassy in China (Clark) to the Secretary of State

CANTON, May 31, 1949—5 p. m.
[Received June 1—10 : 09 a. m.]

Cantel 509. Chu Chang-wei, political adviser to Li Tsung-jen, tells me Chu Cheng selection Premier was approved by Legislative Yuan today by vote 151 to 143. Opposition came from C–C clique who thought him too old (he is past 70), from Whampoa clique who resented removal Ho Ying-chin, and from some supporters Yen Hsi-shan who were against anyone other than Yen. Chu Cheng is now free form Cabinet which need not be submitted Legislative Yuan for approval. Latter adjourns today until September when it will meet, in theory at least, wherever government is located.

Chu thinks Ho Ying-chin will refuse accept any post new Cabinet and says S. Y. Liu will be replaced as Finance Minister by Hsu Kan. Selection Hsu Kan as Finance Minister was dictated by need have Szechuanese that position with likelihood government will move Szechuan. Monetary measures framed under Liu will be delayed in implementation few days yet; Liu will remain on standing committee Central Bank to assist.

Chu says Generalissimo will not come Canton nor will Li visit Generalissimo. Generalissimo, he says, is now at sea again, having visited Taiwan to receive delegation "old men". He thinks Generalissimo may be en route Amoy.

Neither treasure accumulated Amoy or Taiwan has yet been made available, according to Chu, although its availability has been promised. He confirms that in view transportation difficulty only minimum personnel will accompany government Chungking and that many will proceed elsewhere. It is those who will not go Chungking who are being permitted depart Canton this state [*date?*] for Taiwan. Chu would not suggest timetable but seemed convinced inevitability eventual removal capital to Chungking.

Sent Department 509, repeated Nanking 346, Shanghai 298.

CLARK

893.00B/5–3149 : Telegram

The Consul General at Shanghai (Cabot) to the Secretary of State

SHANGHAI, May 31, 1949—7 p. m.
[Received June 1—4 : 24 a. m.]

1917. I trust that I shall not be considered impertinent if I point out there seems to be strong tendency for us to swing from one extreme to other in our thinking re Chinese Communist orientation. When I arrived here I was seriously disturbed by a general tendency particularly among those with great experience in China but not in Communist countries to discount possibility that Chinese Communist could ever be truly Communist. Faithful adherence to Kremlin propaganda line suggested to me that close working links existed between Chinese and Soviet Communist parties.

Now that Communists have taken over several big cities there seems to be strong swing in other direction—a belief that all Communist activities in China are Soviet Punch and Judy show. Much is made of their toughness, their illiberalism, their virulent anti-American propaganda, their deviousness, suspicion and secrecy.

That Chinese Communists are guided by Communist ideology is axiomatic. Significant items to watch are not similarities and parroted propaganda but deviations and non-Marxist deeds. They have been tough but not half as tough as Soviet might have been. Any liberal who has been duped by Communist propaganda naturally swings to violent disillusionment when he finds out the truth (see Tientsin's to Department 356, May 26 [52]) ; surprising thing is Chinese Communists have not been more narrow and tyrannical. Virulent anti-American propaganda is natural in view of our aid to Nationals. Re vociferous Chinese Communist adherence to Soviet Russia this only to be expected in view widespread speculation re possible Titoism.

Interesting points to my mind are indications that Chinese Communists are not 100% subservient to Kremlin, that their party is not monolithic in basic thinking on such vital points as relations with west and that Soviets themselves are not too pleased with Chinese Communist successes.

To discuss last point only note:

1. Sino-Soviet treaty 1945 [53] was implied sellout of Chinese Communists.
2. Soviet Embassy was only one to go to Canton.
3. Vyshinsky got out of sick bed to see Ambassador Foo on departure to assume Foreign Ministry.
4. Sinkiang negotiations have been with collapsing National regime.
5. Relative failure of Soviets to help Chinese Communists as compared with Greek Communists.
6. Anna Louise Strong [54] deportation.
7. Reported absence of any glorification of Chinese Communist heroes in recent May 1 parade Moscow.
8. Closing of Soviet Consulate Peiping, Shanghai.

Evidence regarding other points too extensive, varied and controversial to discuss in one telegram; it ranges from such major points

---

[52] Not printed.
[53] Signed at Moscow, August 14, 1945 ; Department of State, *United States Relations With China* (Washington, Government Printing Office, 1949), p. 585, or United Nations Treaty Series, vol. x, p. 300.
[54] American writer visiting Chinese Communist areas and the Soviet Union.

as Chinese Communist insistence on protection foreign property to such trifling straws in wind as relative absence of pictures of Stalin.

Although far from conclusive above points give some plausibility to French ConGen's view that Soviets do not want strong united China because they know they cannot control such a China; that their whole game has been to weaken and divide China (note possible analogy to Soviet opposition to south Slav federation).

To my mind it is as yet far too early to say whether Chinese Communists are in fact subservient to Soviets or not. Deviations may be significant or may merely represent a temporary yielding to expediency. Test will probably come when Communists control entire country and have had some time to reveal policies.

Viewing situation in historical perspective it seems to me inherently improbable that Soviets can indefinitely exert control over China through Chinese Communists who have risen to power largely through own efforts and can scarcely be brought to heel by force. Vital question is whether break will come in 2 years or 200. Our own policies may profoundly influence this. I must reiterate that this telegram should not be taken as predicting an early break. I merely want to indicate it is still much too early to form a considered final judgment.

Sent Department, repeated Nanking 1048, Canton 590.

CABOT

V. THE QUESTION OF POSSIBLE AID TO THE NEW REGIME; MEETING AT PEIPING OF THE COMMUNIST-SPONSORED PREPARATORY COMMITTEE FOR THE NEW POLITICAL CONSULTATIVE CONFERENCE; CONTINUING FACTIONALISM IN NATIONALIST CHINA (JUNE 1–JULY 6)

893.00/6–149 : Telegram

The Consul General at Peiping (Clubb) to the Secretary of State

PEIPING, June 1, 1949—2 a. m.
[Received June 2—2 : 55 p. m.]

917. Following message given Assistant Military Attaché Barrett [55] May 31 by reliable intermediary, origin being Chou En-lai.[56] Chou desired message be transmitted highest American authorities on top secret level without his name being mentioned, said in fact that if it were attributed him he would positively disavow it. Essential there be no leak his name to outside channels. Chou approved transmittal via Barrett who gave message me to transmit, but wanted name unmentioned even to Barrett. Chou desired what he said be conveyed to British, expressed preference transmittal be through Department.

---

[55] Col. David D. Barrett.
[56] Member of the Central Committee of the Chinese Communist Party (CCP) and of its politburo.

There were few disagreements in CCP Party [*sic*] during agrarian stage revolution but with arrival at urban stage there have now developed disagreements of serious nature primarily re industrial-commercial policies and questions international relations. There is still no actual split within party but definite separation into liberal and radical wings, with Chou being of liberal, and Liu Shao-chi [57] of radical wing. Chou however said it would be as big mistake to base any policy toward China on idea there would develop major split in party as it was to attempt stop Communism in China by aiding Kmt [58] para-liberal group; feels that country is in such bad shape that most pressing need is reconstruction without regard political theories and that Mao Tse-tung [59] concepts regarding private capital should be effected. Group feels there should have been coalition with Kmt because of party lack necessary knowledge regarding reconstruction, did not favor coalition with elements Ho Ying-chin–Chen Li-fu [60] type but felt that without coalition reconstruction might be so delayed that party would lose support people. Realistic coalition advocated by group failed after big dispute involving most of higher figures in party with exception Mao (Chou was most careful in references to Mao). Coalition having failed, party must make most of bad job and obtain aid from outside. USSR cannot give aid which, therefore, must come from USA or possibly Britain. Chou favors getting help from USA and does not accord Soviet attitude regarding USA. Chou professedly sincere Communist but feels there has developed in USA economy something which is outside Marxist theories and that present American economic situation is, therefore, not susceptible Marxian interpretation. Therefore, Soviet attitude this respect wrong, feels American economy will continue without internal collapse or revolution and that there is no real bar to relations between USA and other governments, different political type. Unequivocally opposed to American aid to Kmt but feels this was given from mistaken motives altruism rather than American viciousness. Feels USA has genuine interest in Chinese people which could become basis friendly relations between two countries.

Chou, speaking for liberal group, felt China should speedily establish *de facto* working relations with foreign governments.

This question will be prime issue in struggle between two wings. Radicals wish alliance with USSR, sort now existing between US and Britain, while liberals regard Soviet international policy as "crazy". Chou feels USSR is risking war which it is unable fight successfully

---

[57] Vice Chairman of the Central Committee of the Chinese Communist Party.
[58] Kuomintang (Nationalist Party).
[59] Chairman of the Central Committee of the Chinese Communist Party.
[60] General Ho resigned May 31 as President of the Chinese Executive Yuan; Chen, Minister without Portfolio, was a leader of the C–C clique of the Kuomintang.

and that good working relations between China and USA would have definite softening effect on party attitude toward Western countries. Chou desires these relations because he feels China desperately needs that outside aid which USSR unable give. Feels China on brink complete economic and physical collapse, by "physical" meaning breakdown physical well-being of people.

Chou feels USA should aid China because: (1) China still not Communist and if Mao's policies are correctly implemented may not be so for long time; (2) democratic China would serve in international sphere as mediator between Western Powers and USSR; (3) China in chaos under any regime would be menace to peace Asia and world. Chou emphasized he spoke solely for certain people personally and not as member party, that he was not in position make formal or informal commitments or proposals. He hoped American authorities would recall wartime contacts with Communists and character and opinions of many whom they knew at that time. He hoped American authorities remembering this would believe there were genuine liberals in party who are concerned with everything connected with welfare Chinese people and "peace in our time" rather than doctrinaire theories. As spokesman for liberal wing he could say that when time came for Communist participation in international affairs his group would work within party for sensible solution impasse between USSR and west and would do its best make USSR discard policies leading to war.

In response particular questions Chou made following statements: There is bad personal feeling between Lin Piao and Peng Teh-huai [61] but without more significance than would be a dispute between MacArthur and Eisenhower.[62] Lin has complete confidence party leaders as shown by fact he was chosen to command Manchuria and will probably emerge eventually as China's top military leader. Liu Shao-chi has best party mind re propounding theories, is master of personnel organization but whether he is realist and capable of administering towns is one of points at issue between two wings. Laws prohibiting certain types business came largely from Liu. Liberals oppose such restrictions, believing them helpless, hopeless tinkering with economic system. When it was suggested Liu's ability as organizer personnel and party machinery might enable him become another Stalin,[63] Chou flushed, said nothing. Liberals oppose suppression press but in all his years as party member Chou has never been able get control propaganda section. Party has consequently frequently made fool of itself through propaganda, and propaganda is doing much harm because party itself is beginning believe it. Chou emphasized that despite

---

[61] Two leading Chinese Communist military commanders.
[62] Generals of the Army Douglas MacArthur, Supreme Commander, Allied Powers in Japan, and Dwight D. Eisenhower, former Chief of Staff, U.S. Army.
[63] Josif Vissarionovich Stalin, Soviet Prime Minister and Chairman of the Council of Ministers of the Soviet Union.

deficiencies, errors, disagreements, Communists had won military victory and in spite of same drawbacks would win future victory in reconstruction. Chou said Mao Tse-tung stands aside from party disputes using Chou, Liu Shao-chi and other liberals and radicals for specific purposes as he sees fit. Mao is genius in listening arguments various sides, then translating ideas into practical working policies.

Chou per source appeared very nervous and worried.

Comment follows.[64]

Sent Department 917; repeated Nanking 600, OffEmb Canton 138.

CLUBB

893.002/6–149 : Telegram

The Minister-Counselor of Embassy in China (Clark) to the Secretary of State

CANTON, June 1, 1949—7 p. m.
[Received June 2—3:45 a. m.]

Cantel 516. When Chu Chang-wei [65] informed me approval by Legislative Yuan appointment [of] Chu Cheng [66] as Premier, Cantel 509, May 31, repeated Nanking 346, Shanghai 298, he had lost sight of fact that positive majority those present is required for approval. There were 303 members present, 9 ballots declared void, thus giving Chu 1 short necessary majority. Opposition Chu Cheng was stronger than had been expected.

Chu now informs me that Li Tsung-jen is considering 3 courses action:

1. Reappointment Chu Cheng, risking second defeat;
2. Appointment Yen Hsi-shan [67] which he is reluctant to do because C–C clique is supporting Yen so strongly;
3. Choose another. He mentioned possibly Chu Chia-hua, former Minister Education, this regard. There is also possibility letting Acting Vice Premier carry on for time being. Legislative Yuan is remaining in session through June 3 this regard.

Sent Department repeated Nanking 352, Shanghai 303.

CLARK

893.00B/6–249 : Telegram

The Consul General at Shanghai (Cabot) to the Secretary of State

SHANGHAI, June 2, 1949—2 p. m.
[Received June 2—11:15 a. m.]

1951. Signs suggest Communists have adopted wary attitude toward involvement complex Shanghai politics—especially with respect en-

---

[64] Telegram No. 928, June 2, 6 p.m. p. 363.
[65] Political adviser to Acting President Li Tsung-jen.
[66] President of the Chinese Judicial Yuan.
[67] Former Governor of Shansi.

couragement ambitious local groups (including perhaps their own pre-established Communist underground) which seem vying to prove their "popular" character and facilities for helping Communists as partners and media in establishing new regime's control of city: Communist leaders seem accordingly have acted swiftly in making it quite clear that displays of helpfulness and democratic ebullience will be strictly as dictated by Communist high command:

1. Two rival "popular" bodies were formed about May 25 to maintain order and protect city in interval between Nationalist evacuation and Communist take-over: Shanghai Security Council organized jointly by Shanghai city council and leaders of "trade, industry and charity groups" and purportedly headed by W. W. Yen;[68] and People's Security Corps formed by Federation of People's Organizations of Shanghai (stressing workers and students). Former organization was disapproved by Communists and accordingly disowned by Yen and shortly folded up. Latter organization had Communist support but closed promptly May 28 after "accomplishing mission".
2. Reliably reported a statement prepared by Shanghai Democratic League leaders May 27 was suppressed by Communists.
3. "China Democratic Joint Army" manifesto of May 26 (ConGentel 1952, June 2[69]) which was published as if with approval of Chang Po-chung[70] as [was] subsequently denied by Chang. Significant manifesto played up achievements of CDJA as on par with PLA[71]—hardly likely to please Communists.
4. Text of May 28 joint announcement of democratic parties and groups in Shanghai (ConGentel 1952) gives every evidence of being result of Communist ultimatum insisting on dictatorship which other groups have ruefully accepted.
5. Reliable source states demand by Hsu Hsu, underground Communist member police force, to be made police commissioner was rejected by Chen Yi[72] (see also ConGentel 1829, May 25).
6. Well-informed source with Communist contacts states few days ago Mao Tse-tung wired Chen Yi instruct any Shanghai local elements throwing weight around should be promptly put in place.
7. One of Yang Hu's[73] chief assistants who has been in frequent contact with officer of Consulate General has changed attitude abruptly since Communist take-over. He had previously looked with certainty and relish to Yang's and his taking important posts in "coalition" regime. He now says Communists offered him one of city's deputy mayorships; that he turned it down though offering serve as informal advisor; and that while he might accept post if and when real coalition is established he is dubious this will materialize in view of new signs that Communists are veering from their "sensible decisions reached at Shihchiachuang".

---

[68] Head of Shanghai peace delegation to Peiping in February; former Chinese premier.
[69] Not printed.
[70] Known also as Chang Pai-chun, leader of the Chinese Peasants and Workers Democratic Party.
[71] Communist People's Liberation Army.
[72] Communist Mayor of Shanghai.
[73] A Shanghai leader.

Such slapping down and disillusionment fellow traveler and local groups is presumably common feature of victory flushed Communist take-overs. Believe, however, it may have more significance in Shanghai in view greater strength and apparently greater solidarity of "friendly" opposition forces resulting from size and political-social complexity of city and especially from circumstance that Yang Hu and his chief lieutenants are concurrently (1) members of KmtRC,[74] (2) fairly close friends of Democratic Leaguers and Chen Ming-shu's association of comrades of Three Principles and three (bosses of ancient "Green-Red Gang") secret societies. Liberal-Leftist intellectual groups are thus superimposed upon social substratum of considerable strength and political toughness. While thus constituted heterogeneous opposition is clearly much inferior in power, coordination and dynamic urge to Communists, it might nevertheless if treated too cavalierly by latter and with possible aid of stubborn Shanghai merchant guilds provide resistance to point where Communists might have to choose between compromise or drastic purge methods.

Communist action likely to be tempered for while by fact they owe debt of gratitude to Yang Hu for all-important role which his underground social organization—and to lesser extent KmtRC and Chen Ming-shu's organization[—]displayed in effecting easy turnover of city. Also, they need his help for present. His prospects for long political (if not physical) survival seem questionable, however.

Sent Department 1951, repeated Nanking 1065, Canton 606, Peiping 162.

CABOT

893.00/6-249 : Telegram

The Consul at Tsingtao (*Hawthorne*) *to the Secretary of State*

TSINGTAO, June 2, 1949.
[Received June 2—1 : 33 p. m.]

235. All vessels evacuating Kmt troops and police departed Kiaochow Bay June 020430 Z.[75] Some units outside city abandoned as well as about 2,000 officers and men on pier No. 5 Tsingtao. All expected surrender rather than seriously resist. Three hundred armed men of fire brigade patrolling streets to maintain order have proven ineffective and looting and lawlessness fairly widespread. Three Americans and one Englishman known to have been robbed on streets of wallets and jewelry by armed men in mufti.

---

[74] Kuomintang Revolutionary Committee, headed by Marshal Li Chi-shen at Peiping.
[75] June 2, 4 : 30 a. m.

Communist[s] have entered city from two sides and detachment Communist troops passed by undersigned while returning office after lunch. Fully expect peace and order will be restored before nightfall. Sent Nanking 173, repeated EmbOff Canton 81, Department 235.

HAWTHORNE

893.00/6-249 : Telegram

The Consul General at Peiping (Clubb) to the Secretary of State

PEIPING, June 2, 1949—6 p. m.
[Received June 3—4 : 21 a. m.]

928. ReContel 917, June 1. In absence definitive information, two alternative explanations available in logic for Chou En-lai *démarche :* (1) Chou and his group may be seriously at odds with so-called radical wing and may be straining toward Titoism,[76] or (2) Chou took action with full knowledge and accord party apparatus with political design which perhaps even would have approval USSR.

My belief in possibility development China Titoism has been expressed before. Events in Manchuria where there are new reports of Soviet troop movements (being reported today by AstAMilAt [77]) may have placed new strains on Communist credulity and camaraderie. Present move could reflect divergence opinion in high Communist councils greater than heretofore suspected by observers, when it would show Chou's fear of possibility party split near future and of possible purge elements non-sympathetic to Soviet line (Dairen's 160, May 27 [26] to Department [78]). Chou controls no troops and unless his views have support important military elements he and other potential Titos would assuredly lose out in any attempt palace coup. My own estimate of situation from data at hand is that it would be premature accept development Titoism this juncture before party rank and file have really appreciated gravity their economic and political predicament (Contel 898, May 25 [78]) and that particularly where development in any event still uncrystallized our action had best be based on realization that China and particularly Chinese Communists are always closer each [other] than to any foreigners and present move therefore very possibly had authoritative approval Chou's own camp.

Second alternative, that move is one of high Communist policy, finds logical basis in grave economic debility China and seems indicated in Chou's recommendation that US aid China. Aid as conceived by him must be economic rather than political in nature. China's

---

[76] Defection from Moscow party line of Marshal Josip Broz Tito, head of Yugoslav State and Communist Party, June 1948.
[77] Col. David D. Barrett, Assistant American Military Attaché.
[78] Not printed.

economic crisis still unarrived in full force but with partial crop failure present year, occupation Shanghai before foreign trade channels have been opened to give China access to food South Seas, extremely deteriorated condition industrial equipment, financial bankruptcy, and generally bad political relations with all countries but "China's great friend Russia", widespread famine by spring 1950 can be forecast high degree certainty (Contel 699, April 25 [79]).

In circumstances must conclude greater probability that Communist desire continue diet Soviet political bread but eke out diet with American economic cake. Until such time as there may be actual break with USSR Communists must be assumed remaining in Soviet political camp. It is probably already clear [to] both Soviets and Communists that USSR unable supply China economic needs, both may be reconciled to necessity China's having deal with USA to avoid calamitous economic collapse. China unable pay for food, raw materials and machinery it needs, both Communists and USSR probably now would be willing have USA resurrect something in nature ECA [80] and "beg" China to accept aid even as to grant foreign relations (Contel 869, May 20 [19?][79]). Chang Tsung-ping[81] in three different conversations unsolicitedly indicated belief Communists would eventually "be prepared accept American aid". Chou démarche must have had particular relationship inter alia anticipate grave food shortage facing nation within year. Communist China, aided [by] economic grants by USA while retaining close political ties with USSR, would be strengthened so that it could better aid USSR politically and militarily against USA in hypothetical future contingencies. That particular booby trap is easily avoided. For so long as Communist China is run for political benefit USSR let it pay on barrel head for what it receives, either in economic equivalent or in terms political concessions designed break up its alliance with USSR.

Chou asked no reply but believe one could well be given, along following lines: USA has long been friend Chinese nation and hopes remain so, it is ready even desire develop social, economic and political relations with China nation insofar as those relations may meet like aspirations from Chinese side; such relations however, as can be deduced from knowledge of American policies in international affairs, must be based on mutual understanding respect and cooperation, on reciprocity as well as egalitarianism, and it is hardly to be expected that where those elements are lacking, full fruits of intercourse can be obtained.

Sent Department, repeated Nanking 608, OffEmb Canton 143.

CLUBB

---

[79] Not printed.
[80] Economic Cooperation Administration.
[81] Son of Chang Tung-sun, Peiping leader of the Democratic League.

893.00B/6–349 : Telegram

The Consul at Tsingtao (Hawthorne) to the Secretary of State

TSINGTAO, June 3, 1949.
[Received June 3—12 : 23 a. m.]

238. CC[82] troops occupied Tsingtao afternoon June 2 local time and issued usual 7-point proclamation. Martial law enforced and law and order appear to have been restored. Local radio announced Ma Pao-shan as Mayor and Liu Yi-ping as Commander General.

Because joint consular representations or lack time, National troops did not damage utilities prior withdrawal.

Chinese police, paid by ConGen [to] guard U.S. Government prop-erties, disarmed and U.S. Government property No. 1 Kwangsi Road, used store ConGen's fuel, occupied and guards placed entrance ConGen prevented egress radio operators. No vehicular traffic without pass, source which as yet unknown but will lodge appropriate pro-tests when possible.

SS *President Taft* loaded with cotton for city granted permission enter harbor today through arrangements by consignees with new regime.

Forty-six Americans Tsingtao believed safe, well; Department please notify next kin including Mrs. Hawthorne. 915 Pierce Street, San Francisco.

This message by telephone from residence to office.

Sent Nanking 174, repeated OffEmb Canton 82, Department 238.

HAWTHORNE

893.002/6–349 : Telegram

The Minister-Counselor of Embassy in China (Clark) to the Secretary of State

CANTON, June 3, 1949—9 p. m.
[Received June 4—12 : 38 p. m.]

Cantel 529. Legislative Yuan approved Yen Hsi-shan as premier this morning by 254 to 56 with 10 ballots invalid. Entire process took only little over 1 hour including half-hour insipid pro-Yen speeches. Few scattered handclaps when results announced.

Easy majority favoring Yen probably accounted for by: (1) C–C Clique satisfied Yen definitely not hostile toward Gimo; [83] (2) Legis-

---

[81] Chinese Communist.
[83] Generalissimo Chiang Kai-Shek, who retired as President of the Republic of China on January 21, 1949.

lative Yuan anxiety recess for summer and board ships now awaiting take them Formosa. Interesting to note that Yen flew Formosa yesterday ostensibly to bury mother.

Sent Department Cantel 529; repeated Nanking 360; Shanghai 307.

CLARK

893.00 Manchuria/6–449 : Telegram

The Ambassador in China (Stuart) to the Secretary of State

NANKING, June 4, 1949—10 a. m.
[Received May [*June*] 4—4: 52 a. m.]

1194. Embassy thinking on Manchuria as follows:

Among potential sore spots between CCP [85] and USSR, far the tenderest is Manchuria. Soviet Union has now probably gained its minimal necessary strategic objectives that area, having presumably denied any enemy its use. That Soviet influence in area is strong is commonly accepted fact. That USSR has aleady established effective control over the area and is undertaking industrialization Manchuria, presumably with Chinese Communists' assent, becoming increasingly evident. This attested by indirect evidence such as CCP statement that Manchurian progress toward socialization will be much faster than that of rest of China.

From CCP viewpoint Manchuria is China's only developed industrial complex, only indigenous source of machines without which even minimum nation-wide industrial development impossible. But if Manchuria being developed and exploited, Russia's Far East too has desperate needs. Opposition might be expected to arise here, thus far they have not, presumably because CCP accepts USSR role of pre-eminence in industrialization of NE. Certainly USSR would not permit vast, heavy industrial area so near her borders without strong Russian control, which undoubtedly already contributing cause in treatment our Consuls [at] Mukden and Dairen.[86] When this control will become irksome, whether CCP will eventually resist further Soviet encroachment or resent that already accomplished (thus establishing conditions prerequisite Titoism), whether already too late extricate Manchuria from Soviet domination, are moot points. In light USSR past performance and CCP record subservience, prospects solutions favorable China and West are slight. Problem remains, however.

Sent Department, passed Peiping 194.

STUART

---

[85] Chinese Communist Party.
[86] For documentation, see pp. 933 ff. and pp. 860 ff., respectively.

893.00/6–449 : Telegram

The Consul General at Hankow (Callanan) to the Secretary of State

HANKOW, June 4, 1949—noon.
[Received June 4—4 : 57 a. m.]

171. Changsha reported evacuated by General Pai [87] June 2.
Sent Department, repeated Nanking 131, OffEmb Canton 78.

CALLANAN

893.00/6–249 : Telegram

The Acting Secretary of State to the Ambassador in China (Stuart)

WASHINGTON, June 4, 1949—6 p. m.

672. Dept assumes knowledge and distribution Peiping tels 917 and 928 Jun 2 (rptd Emb 600 and 608, OffEmb 138 and 143) being restricted to you and immediate top ranking members ur staff and desires every precaution be taken ensure even receipt message not be known except by such authorized personnel.

WEBB

893.01/6–549 : Telegram

The Minister-Counselor of Embassy in China (Clark) to the Secretary of State

CANTON, June 5, 1949—noon.
[Received June 6—10 : 16 p. m.]

Cantel 531. Choice Yen Hsi-shan, last surviving war lord, as premier, (Cantel 529, June 3 ; repeated Nanking 360, Shanghai 307) seems further evidence, if further evidence is needed, of complete bankruptcy Kmt leadership. His choice, I believe, was motivated by fact that having been holed up so long in Taiyuan he is neutral in clique bickering which has been going on, and forgetting his past ill deeds, his long stand against Communists in Taiyuan is looked upon in some way as evidence of capability that he can defeat Communists. Yen remains Taiwan and is expected return Canton early next week. Meanwhile Ho Ying-chin Cabinet continues to meet and go through motions of governing. It will be interesting to see composition of Yen's cabinet as it is most difficult these days find anyone willing serve. Sun Fo [88] and his

---

[87] Pai Chung-hsi, Military and Political Affairs Director for Central China.
[88] Former President of the Chinese Executive Yuan.

ilk are going abroad in various official capacities, Sun Fo to US to augment staff of Wellington Koo.[89]

Sent Department Cantel 531; repeated Nanking 361, Shanghai 308.

CLARK

893.00B/6–649 : Telegram

The Ambassador in China (Stuart) to the Secretary of State

NANKING, June 6, 1949—8 a. m.
[Received June 7—2 : 17 a. m.]

1212. Re Embassy Cantel 475, May 26. We wish it were true that "Mao has no idea of emulating Tito, but aspires to be Asian Lenin". We believe that from our point of view this development would be an even greater blessing than that of Titoism in China, for Russian arrogance and suspicion would make idea of Asian Lenin even more repulsive than that of Balkan Tito. Russians, by everything they have done since July 1920 (when at second Congress of Comintern they forced Bolshevik organization and principles on all Communist parties abroad), have demonstrated they have to lead world revolution themselves. They are constitutionally incapable of delegating responsibility in this great endeavor. Nothing would be better calculated to cause a split, if not war, between USSR and Communist China than Mao having temerity to set himself up as Asian Lenin [garble], although way is now almost wide open to CCP military-political penetration into Indochina, Burma, Malaya, Hong Kong, etc., we in Nanking have still found little evidence to support theory that Mao aspires independently to pull strings of revolution in Southeast Asia as Lenin pulled them in Russia. (That Mao may strive for Lenin's humanity, austerity, perseverance, wisdom, perceptivity is of course quite possible but these qualities are not germane to main issues of power and autonomy.) On the contrary, it seems to us that Mao's relation to USSR is that of brilliant disciplined if somewhat junior ally in "world anti-imperialist front" which Chinese Communists themselves almost invariably refer to as led by greatest Socialist state.

We question statement that "careful study Communist propaganda will substantiate that there is paucity of mention of Marxist, Leninist or Stalinist doctrine, sole stress being on Mao Tse-tung". Bookshops of Nanking now display many translations of Soviet pontiffs. To mention only few of many possible quotations, North Shensi broadcast March 21 featured article entitled "lesson from events in Indonesia", which recommended to Indonesians that they should learn,

---

[89] Chinese Ambassador in the United States.

as has CCP, to "combine universal truth of Marxism-Leninism with practical revolutionary activities of peoples of country". Jen Pi-shih, in addressing first All China Congress of new Democratic Youth League April 12, stated that "within league, education in Marxism-Leninism should be carried out systematically". Chu Teh [90] May 4 urged delegates to All China Youth Congress "to equip themselves with teachings of Marx, Lenin, Stalin, and Mao Tse-tung (in order named) so that they could play full part in development of country". Hsin Hua radio Mukden recently announced that "in order to promote internationalistic revolutionary spirit, show respect and admiration to revolutionary leaders, express friendship for Soviet Union and support Chinese leaders, propaganda department northeast CCP Central Committee has directed display of portraits Marx, Engels, Lenin and Stalin in order named from left to right in all public meeting places, government offices, factories, schools, et cetera".

Emphasis on industrialization and shifting of center of gravity of party work from rural to urban areas which was announced in March 1949 report of second plenary session of present CCP Central Committee we interpret not only as natural result of Communist capture of large cities but also as notice to world that Chinese Communists have grown up and want to wear long pants in Marxian society. This plus their closer relations with other Communist parties including those of Southeast Asia, their role at Paris, Praha World Congress for Peace, their support of WFTU,[91] their close adherence to propaganda line of USSR, however, are all conducted within framework of behavior demanded from Cominform countries. They betray not slightest trace of contumacy against Soviet leadership, but rather sympathetic unquestioning acceptance of it. Not only do Chinese Communists give enthusiastic lip service to Soviet Russia, they also give of themselves, as was reported in Embtel 1194, June 4, re CCP and Soviet plans for Manchurian industry.

All this attests to fact that of many forms of Marxism that which has taken root in China and thrived so well is Leninism. Chinese Communists have so mastered Leninist precepts of discipline and loyalty to world revolution that now, even at hour of their greatest glory, by neither word nor deed have they yet betrayed to world one single trace of deviation which might be expected foreshadow any unorthodox aspiration of Mao Tse-tung.

Sent Department 1262 [*1212*]; repeated OffEmb Canton 498, Shanghai 656, Moscow 36.

STUART

---

[90] Commander in Chief of Chinese Communist armies.
[91] World Federation of Trade Unions.

893.00B/6–649 : Telegram

The Minister-Counselor of Embassy in China (Clark) to the Secretary of State

CANTON, June 6, 1949—2 p. m.
[Received 3 : 24 p. m.]

Cantel 534. Believe we should be most suspicious Chou En-lai *démarche* (Peiping's 917, June 1, repeated Nanking 600, Canton 138). Move smacks much more of tactics than strategy. What more natural than Communists' endeavors convince us bickering exists in their ranks and that Soviet tie is not binding. How fatal for us to permit ourselves be enticed into assisting Communists in their desperate need only to discover too late that they wanted our help solely during interim and until they could get along without us. Believe Chou should be encouraged but that we should move warily.

Sent Department Cantel 534; repeated Nanking 362, Peiping 10.

CLARK

893.00/6–649 : Telegram

The Consul General at Shanghai (Cabot) to the Secretary of State

SHANGHAI, June 6, 1949—6 p. m.
[Received June 6—10 : 15 a. m.]

2010. Member Democratic League well known to Consul General attended meeting Shanghai cultural leaders June 6 and reported following highlights of several hours' speech by Mayor Chen Yi:

1. Chinese products formerly exported to SE Asia as matter "face" to give semblance of prosperity would be kept in China to meet needs Chinese people.

2. As USSR and "satellites" might not be able offer assistance to China for time being, aid from US and British would be accepted if presented on basis of equality with no strings detrimental to Chinese sovereignty attached. Source stressed this "aid" meant loan, technical assistance or help of Marshall Plan nature, as distinguished from ordinary trade, which naturally also desired by Communists.

3. Students who wanted substitute Russian for English language in educational institutions were cautioned that English language very important and should be studied by Chinese students as means achieving greater knowledge.

Of particular interest was source's comment that Chen's speech was for internal consumption Shanghai Communists and cultural workers and not for foreigners, which apparently [is] confirmed by routine report of meeting carried by *Chieh Fang Jih Pao* and *Ta Kung Pao* June 6 omitting above points.

Repeated Hong Kong 141, Peiping 165. Department pass Tientsin as 68.

CABOT

893.01/6–649 : Telegram

The Minister-Counselor of Embassy in China (Clark) to the Secretary of State

CANTON, June 6, 1949—7 p. m.
[Received June 7—5 : 29 a. m.]

Cantel 539. Tung Ling, Vice Minister Foreign Office, confirms reports heard elsewhere that Foreign Office and other organs government have been directed reduce personnel by two-thirds. This reduction will also be applied Chinese diplomatic and consular service abroad. Move is to reduce most government and make ministries more mobile. Preliminary arrangements removal government Chungking already undertaken, he says, but admits government unlikely remain Chungking for long. His thinking, like that I encounter with increasing frequency of late, is that although government must maintain foothold on mainland long as possible, it is inevitable last bastion will be Taiwan where he hopes stand can be maintained until US–Soviet war which he believes inevitable.

Sent Department; repeated Nanking 365, Shanghai 311.

CLARK

893.00/6–749 : Telegram

The Ambassador in China (Stuart) to the Secretary of State

NANKING, June 7, 1949—3 p. m.
[Received 6 : 30 p. m.]

1227. If further evidence were needed of completely subservient role being played by KmtRC, it is provided by latter's proclamation to Kmt members in South China summarized in NCNA [92] broadcast June 4. Full text printed in *Hsin Hua Jih Pao* June 5 is thoroughly Communist in viewpoint and phraseology and contains usual reference to weakness of US and British imperialism as contrasted with growing strength of socialist and new democratic countries headed by Soviet. Proclamation urges Kmt members in political and military posts to cooperate with PLA, but significantly omits invitation for them to join KmtRC.

As Kmt and its satellite parties have been dissolved in Communist China and Communists are unlikely permit large scale recruiting by so-called "democratic" parties, CCP will remain only party with mass base. This does not mean idea of coalition government has been abandoned. Widespread dissemination and vigorous official encouragement to study Mao Tse-tung's new democracy and on coalition govern-

---

[92] New China News Agency (Communist).

ment both of which envisage coalition, argue against this. However, since "democratic leaders" given place in coalition for window dressing will have little personal following and no party machine, political task of CP will from outset be simpler than in countries like Poland or Hungary.

Sent Department; repeated Shanghai 661, OffEmb Canton 506, Peiping 203.

STUART

893.00/6–749 : Telegram

The Ambassador in China (Stuart) to the Secretary of State

NANKING, June 7, 1949—4 p. m.
[Received June 7—7 : 24 a.m.]

1229. Commenting on Peiping's 917 to Department, it contains extremely important indication as to possible American policy. (With this in view I have been trying to keep in personal contact with Chou whenever practicable.) We must be careful not to over-play our chance while also taking full advantage of it. Nor should we overrate its significance. It implies no basic change in CCP theory or program. It is struggle for power between two men next in line after Mao, together with their respective emphases and experiences. Liu is wholly pro-Soviet and because of current anti-American sentiment has been gaining ascendency. Chou's message is call for help. He would never have taken this risk [omission indicated in the source text] sending one. It might begin by referring to our traditional policy of friendly good will for people of China in their struggles to attain independence and national sovereignty and in their need of economic betterment and technological progress; then continue that we would be as ready now as we have always been to assist toward these two interrelated objectives if basis of mutual self-respect and confidence could be reestablished between China and US; that atmosphere conducive to friendly cooperation cannot be created by such developments as present treatment our Consular officers in China, particularly Mukden; by constant anti-American propaganda which deliberately distorts our motives and deeds; by official stimulation of anti-western sentiment among the Chinese people through controlled press and radio, et cetera. Communication might close with statement that we sincerely welcome Chou's protestations of pro-western sentiment but that they cannot be expected to bear fruit until they have been translated into deeds capable of convincing people of US that continued American support of Chinese objectives is in mutual interest of both countries.

Department may feel it unwise at this stage to commit itself officially and prefer that I reply in somewhat personal tone. In any case

I shall have other suggestions as to how to follow up this lead if considered desirable.

We assume Clubb will develop better channel of reply on this subject than initial intermediary, Michael Keon, an Australian newspaperman employed by United Press.

Repeated Canton 507, Peiping 205.

STUART

893.00B/6-749 : Telegram

The Consul General at Hong Kong (Hopper) to the Secretary of State

HONG KONG, June 7, 1949—4 p. m.
[Received June 7—7:41 a. m.]

311. . . . Source reports . . . that Chiao Mu [93] now acting as informal unofficial Consul [at] Hong Kong for Communists. Chiao performs such functions as clearing travellers desiring go Shanghai and handling problems arising from foreign shipping. In conversation with source June 4, Chiao indicated strong desire Communists for US trade but stated if US adopted restrictive measures directed at Communist government, Communist reaction would be swift and strong. Chiao estimated Canton be taken by Communists at will and they would do so by July 1. Chiao volunteered Hong Kong question can only be settled on highest level and will be considered by Communists as integral factor in Communist–British relations.

Sent Department 311; repeated Shanghai 82, OffEmb Canton.

HOPPER

893.00/6-749 : Telegram

The Minister-Counselor of Embassy in China (Clark) to the Secretary of State

CANTON, June 7, 1949—6 p. m.
[Received June 8—3:34 p. m.]

Cantel 546. Tung Chi-ling, Vice Minister Economic Affairs, is extremely pessimistic. Personal opinion is situation hopeless. Unless Generalissimo and Li forget differences, pool resources and form some kind of united front, Nationalist Government is doomed.

Economically Nationalist China at present is in complete void, he said. Exports are at virtual standstill with little or no goods moving from interior to coast. If Canton falls, Nationalists will lose last port capable of maintaining any foreign trade. Troops reportedly refusing fight unless paid hard coin.

Tung has little confidence in proposed silver currency program, believing initial issue will disappear through hoarding. He said also

---

[93] Chinese Communist spokesman at Hong Kong.

government does not have funds maintain silver purchases abroad and that only US loan could finance program envisaged.

Steering conversation back [to] matters economic, Tung could only say that commerce was at standstill and Canton industry in doldrums. Apparently all thinking in government circles is paralyzed by situation and no plans of any kind appear evident. He seemed to derive some satisfaction that Nationalists still control several of richest provinces. On other hand, he deplored Generalissimo's "last bastion" policy in Taiwan and thought that island should divorce itself from mainland economy.

Lack of funds seems to be principal concern of Chinese Government offices. Tung said his own department was barely able to function or meet payrolls.

Tung certainly spoke frankly when he closed talk by saying: "Since we don't fight, appear to have no vigor to fight and are divided against ourselves, my opinion is we should quit".

Sent Department Cantel 546; repeated Nanking 370; Shanghai 316.

CLARK

893.00/6–849 : Telegram

The Consul General at Hong Kong (Hopper) to the Secretary of State

HONG KONG, June 8, 1949—1 p. m.
[Received June 8—9 a. m.]

317. On June 8 interview with officer Consulate General, Yeh Tu-yi, Democratic League official, stated his intention go Shanghai June 10, join Lo Lung-chi and Chang Lan,[94] proceed Peiping on invitation Mao Tse-tung. Purpose trip is prepare for PCC [95] which now planned for early August. Yeh said Democratic League hopes to be "bridge" between Chinese Communists and US and so change Communists' present anti-American orientation.

Sent Department 317, repeated Shanghai 83, Nanking 32, Peiping unnumbered.

HOPPER

893.00 Manchuria/6–949 : Telegram

The Ambassador in China (Stuart) to the Secretary of State

NANKING, June 9, 1949—noon.
[Received June 9—6 : 30 a. m.]

1246. ReEmbtel 1194, June 4. CCP press and radio have recently thrown new light on Soviet and CCP plans for Manchuria.

---

[94] Leaders of the Democratic League.
[95] Political Consultative Conference.

1. Industrialization China is going to be based on Manchurian industry. To quote from Peiping radio May 6, "although foundation of modern industry was laid in Manchuria by Japs, yet it was on colonial pattern in Jap imperialist system and not suitable for sovereign state and balanced economy. People's Government must not only restore factories and plants, but also build up modern industry on basis of independent self-supplying economy, thus laying firm foundation for industrialization of China".

2. Industrialization of Manchuria (which contained 70% all Chinese industry) will be pushed and perhaps aided substantially by USSR. To quote from somewhat ambiguous March 1949 report of second plenary session present CCP Central Committee, "because of victory of democratic revolution, establishment of people's democratic republic and leadership of CCP, in addition to aid of powerful anti-imperialist front headed by Soviet Union, tempo of economic construction in China will not be slow but possibly rather fast".

3. Current CCP propaganda line that corrupt Kmt (rather than USSR) is responsible for destruction Manchurian industry as well as continuing reports Soviet influence in Manchuria show how tide is running. For instance, Embtel 1152, May 31, to Department [96] reported CCP trying negotiate with USSR allow shipment soybeans and kaoliang into North China from Manchuria. Another recent Embassy telegram to Department reported statement Chinese Commie that CCP expects expansion Manchurian industry will be accomplished with Soviet aid and considers Manchuria as separate problem distinct from rest China, Peiping telegram 889, May 25, to Department,[97] reported opinion of informed Chinese that ultimate authority over American Consulate General personnel Mukden is exercised by Soviets. All these reports, while as yet unconfirmed, indicate Soviets have changed their minds about having strong Manchurian industrial complex on their border since their rape of area in 1945–46. Best explanation for reversal is that Soviets have now obtained sufficient interest in and control over Manchurian industry for them not be to be worried about its resurrection, but rather to be interested in its successful development.

4. Emergence CCP as rival authority in Dairen and opening Yingkow harbor to domestic and foreign shipping last April seem to point up that Soviets and CCP have reached fundamental agreements on Manchuria.

One important fact about administration and reconstruction area is that they are following Soviet pattern. All press and radio reports on subject attest how Chinese Commies have adopted as their own, in Manchuria more than anywhere else, such Soviet tools as: Planned economy, socialist competition, production quotas, heroes Chinese labor, high pressure enthusiasm in press, self-criticism, participation workers in factory management, use trade unions and workers' organizations as instruments state administration.

---

[96] Not printed; it speculated on possible political implications of agricultural distress in Communist-occupied North China (893.61/5–3149).
[97] Not printed.

CCP press emphasizes achievement already made in reconstruction Manchurian industry, particularly following branches: Railroads, coal, power, textiles, chemical plants, petroleum refining, steel, non-ferrous metals including gold and silver. While CCP publicity organs never mention Sino-Soviet joint enterprise companies, it is of course known that they administer at least railroads. Pride with which Chinese Commies announce their accomplishments Manchuria presumably reflects to some extent satisfaction with which they regard Soviet participation and advice. Political sympathy between two parties also promises that collaboration sincere.

It may be expected that, with their characteristic greed, Soviets will obtain large earnings from joint enterprise companies and possibly, in future, from control over Dairen entrepôt trade. Presumably these earnings will finance Soviet imports from China, thus materially reducing Soviet exports China with consequently deleterious effect Manchurian economy.

Sent Department 1246, repeated Shanghai 669, OffEmb Canton 516, Moscow 37. Department please pass Peiping in its discretion.[98]

STUART

893.00B/6–1049 : Telegram

The Consul General at Peiping (Clubb) to the Secretary of State

PEIPING, June 9, 1949—3 p. m.
[Received June 10—9:23 a. m.]

969. [To Nanking:] Re Contel 639, June 8.[99] Joseph Chang [1] called today [and] said he brought message from father requiring substantial correction information contained Conreftel. He said it had been decided by Communist[s] hold PCC in August and establish coalition central govt October 10. PPC [2] preparatory meeting will be convoked June 15. There are important changes proportions of delegations attending preparatory meeting. At that meeting Democratic League previously allocated 3, namely Shen Chun-ju, Chang Po-chun and Chou Hsin-min, now will have 7, additional members being Chang Lan, Lo Lung-chi, Chang Tung-sun himself and one other. Democratic League personalities will also represent other parties particularly as follows: Huang Yen-pei for national salvation society, Wu Han for Peiping-Tientsin professors, and Tseng Chao-lun for Peita [3] scientific workers. Democratic League will thus have total representation 10 or 12 persons at meeting. Preparatory meeting is to reach basic joint

---

[98] Notation : "Not relayed Peiping by Department".
[99] Notation : "Peiping's 639 to Nanking not repeated to Dept".
[1] Son of Professor Chang Tung-sun, Peiping leader of the Democratic League.
[2] People's Political Council.
[3] National Peking University.

agreement on practically all problems and formal meeting August would merely rubber stamp those decisions.

Per **Chang Tung-sun** interpretation, this sudden change reflects willingness compromise. Possible explanations he considers two: (1) it is now intended have real coalition govt and this represents Soviet retreat in Asia, or (2) Chou En-lai *et al*, have advance knowledge indicating Soviets propose yield CFM[4] meeting Paris. He is unsure exact significance but notes its sudden character and Roschin's[5] going directly to Paris and therefore proposes particularly you postpone departure pending clarification events.

Joseph Chang reported *inter alia* Chou in recent speech to professors said Chinese Communists would not go along line Titoism. Chang said this explanation seemed uncalled-for in circumstances and per his father might in fact indicate Communists were considering going along that line.

Venture repeat this directly Dept, Canton view current important interest.

Sent Nanking 644; repeated Dept 969, AmEmb Canton 155.

[CLUBB]

893.00B/6–949 : Telegram

The Ambassador in China (Stuart) to the Secretary of State

NANKING, June 9, 1949—7 p. m.
[Received June 9—10:29 a. m.]

1250. Philip Fugh[6] called on Huang Hua[7] at latter's request yesterday. Huang referred to Fugh's question at earlier conference : Whether CCP desired China be first Communized or first industrialized, since two apparently could not go along together. Huang said he could not answer this question; that CCP is anxious to have economic recovery for Chinese people; that this goal requires (1) end to civil war and (2) receipt of American aid which will be decisive. Fugh interpreted this to mean CCP, or at least so-called liberal wing (Huang is believed to be Chou En-lai man), places industrialization ahead of Communization. This is first time Huang has raised, albeit indirectly, question American economic assistance.

Huang continued that CCP could not follow isolationist policy in China's reconstruction and that CCP would require particularly American help. Fugh remonstrated that this was hardly consonant with CCP attitude of constant vituperation, with treatment of ConGen Ward and staff Mukden, with HMS *Amethyst* incident and subsequent

---

[4] Council of Foreign Ministers.
[5] Nikolay Vasilyevich Roschin, Soviet Ambassador to China.
[6] Personal secretary to Ambassador Stuart.
[7] Director of the alien affairs office of the Chinese Communist military control commission at Nanking.

misrepresentation thereof. Huang replied as soon as normal diplomatic relations established all such issues could be easily cleared up. He was forced to acknowledge, however, truth of Fugh's assertion that occurrences such as those listed would only make more difficult establishment of friendly relations.

Huang went through his usual routine of US assistance to Kmt and US underestimation of CCP strength. He did say, however, that USSR could not give China required assistance since Soviet expectations had not yet been realized.

Sent Department; repeated AmEmb Canton 517, Shanghai 671.

STUART

893.00/6–1049 : Telegram

The Consul General at Shanghai (Cabot) to the Secretary of State

SHANGHAI, June 10, 1949—11 a. m.
[Received June 10—5:37 a. m.]

2188. Respectfully reiterate to Department recommendation I made in Yugoslavia re great desirability legislation permitting executive take measures control immigrant remittances from US.

Number of Communist Governments derive from such remittances resources vital to execution of their programs. This pattern presumably to be followed in China. At moment we are seeking means convince Chinese Communists we have will and means curb their more obnoxious activities; it seems to me clear no field is more promising because less subject to retaliation than control immigrant remittances. Other western nations might join us in establishing control measures to give weight to their own representations.

Principal objection I foresee is that immigrants making remittances might demur. I feel this could be met by pointing out normal effect of control measures would be to ensure recipients received full value remittances, in Yugoslavia 80% in effect in Government.

We are confronted locally—and elsewhere in China, notably at Mukden—with unilateral action by Communists very detrimental to our interests. I do not feel we can afford overlook such golden opportunity for action on our part to show Communists unilateral action in China is two-edged sword. I do not suggest this legislation as basis for immediate sanctions but rather as means to ensure fair treatment for remitters in US and as warning to Communists we really have means to be disagreeable if they carry some of their present theories too far.[8]

Sent Department; repeated Nanking 1147, Embassy Canton 674.

CABOT

---

[8] The Department replied in telegram No. 1214, June 16, 7 p. m.: "Dept giving careful consideration urtel 2188 Jun 10 which involves complex legal questions as well as far-reaching policy implications."

893.00B/6–1049 : Telegram

The Ambassador in China (Stuart) to the Secretary of State [9]

NANKING, June 10, 1949—5 p. m.
[Received June 10—11 : 30 a. m.]

1258. Re Moscow telegram 63, June 7 to Department; [10] repeated Bucharest 20, Canton 29. Department will recall that summary Liu Shao-chi article "On Internationalism and Nationalism" appeared first on North Shensi broadcasts last November 9 and 10 and was extensively commented on by Embassy at time.[11]

It is interesting Soviets have not hitherto used article. Article is complete sellout to Soviet objectives and political theory. It was written by perhaps third ranking member of CCP Politburo. Its publication in *Pravda* shortly after Communist crossing of Yangtze and occupation Nanking, Shanghai suggests Soviets are becoming more prone to recognize CCP as full-fledged member of world Communist front. Embassy suggests it would be worthwhile to compare Soviet and original Chinese texts.

Sent Department 1258; repeated Canton 520, Bucharest 1, Moscow 39.

STUART

893.00/6–1149 : Telegram

The Consul General at Peiping (Clubb) to the Secretary of State

PEIPING, June 11, 1949—9 a. m.
[Received June 13—10 a. m.]

996. ReContels 917, June 1 and 969, June 9. Ex-Mayor Ho Ssu-yuan June 3 confirmed that there existed in CCP party leadership realization necessity veering toward USA and British for economic reasons particularly. Need trade with USA and other Pacific area countries for upkeep industrial plant and food supply. USSR unable supply with only one rail line from Europe, even if willing do so. Communist leaders were trying swing revolutionary thinking to right into nominal channels "new democracy" instead of Communism but were having difficulties due obduracy in lower Communist strata. No strain however now exists in party as consequence. Liu Shao-chi one of best thinkers in party and not radical in his approach economic matters.

---

[9] The Ambassador was away from Nanking June 11–16 on a trip to Shanghai; see telegram No. 1325, June 19, noon, p. 763. Telegrams from Nanking in this period were sent in his name.
[10] Sent as No. 1474, not printed.
[11] For summary, see telegram No. 2273, 2 p. m., November 21, 1948, from the Ambassador in China, *Foreign Relations,* 1948, vol. VII, p. 593.

Liu at least previously opposed Li Li-san [12] as shown in his brochure "report regarding party organization regulations" published 1945 (brief review will be sent by despatch). Ho attributed Communist delay in holding PCC to political and economic difficulties being experienced. (This conversation antedated report PCC scheduled for August, note Chang said decision advance date came suddenly.) He remarked Communist policies Shanghai were patently more liberal than even Peiping, Tientsin and constituted recognition necessity having relations with other countries than USSR.

Ho said party leaders were Nationalists instead of anti-Communists in their approach Chinese problems. Many of them appreciated significance Soviet political manipulations Manchuria and particularly Inner Mongolia [and] Sinkiang but it was impossible for them break with USSR present juncture. In event any split developed in party [either?] Chiang Kai-shek or Li Tsung-jen would stage come-back and revolution get setback. Leaders therefore felt under necessity continuing along present line at least until military control achieved over all China. Communists themselves however would be first to learn how profitless was dealing with USSR and one year hence would have much better appreciation hard facts than at present time. It was only necessary for USA to wait.

(I remarked Chinese trade was of relatively little consequence USA, that we could wait indefinitely on basis economic factors, but it seemed appear to me China itself was in position where waiting was impossible.)

Joseph Chang said June 9 that whereas it had previously been considered that split within Communist Party was possible present indications are that Mao Tse-tung, Chou En-lai and Liu Shao-chi were working together and had situation well in hand. Mentioning possibility Titoism, he said in response question Titoism China would possibly come about through shift to right of CCP apparatus as whole without split. ReContel 898, May 25,[13] this may be theoretically possible but since Titoism by definition means split with USSR such general shift could be only in form general Communist agreement regarding advisability abandoning Soviet camp in favor camp western democracies, and at same time Communist reconciliation to abandonment Manchuria to USSR. Latter move would itself however be something in nature split since Communists Manchuria must be considered already more under Soviet thumb than Communists China proper, and would presumably be found in Soviet camp if Titoism developed inside Wall.

---

[12] Vice President of the Communist All-China Federation of Labor.
[13] Not printed.

Per unconfirmed report, Tan Kah-kee [14] at meeting several days ago indicated Communists should modify political-economic positions if they desired support overseas Chinese.

Repeated Nanking 71, OffEmb Canton 169, Shanghai 665.

CLUBB

893.00B/6–1149 : Telegram

The Consul General at Shanghai (Cabot) to the Secretary of State

SHANGHAI, June 11, 1949—2 p. m.
[Received June 11—7:43 a. m.]

2215. While not of course to be taken as disproof theses that basic Chinese Communist attitude toward Moscow may be one of unquestioning subservience (Embtel 656 June 6, sent Dept 1212) or even as definitely establishing Communist propaganda policy in Shanghai (which may change overnight), it is nevertheless noteworthy fact that thus far in Shanghai outward evidence of Communist devotion to Moscow is conspicuous by its absence. Among the thousands of posters put up since liberation, there have been, far as we can ascertain, no displays pictures Lenin, Stalin, et al. except a few which were almost immediately removed. Moreover, references to Soviet inspiration and example in editorials, speeches, etc., have been rare and, when made, usually confined to old doctrinists Marx, Lenin, without mention present Soviet leadership.

Sent Dept, repeated Nanking 1167, OffEmb Canton 689.

CABOT

893.00B/6–1349 : Telegram

The Ambassador in China (Stuart) to the Secretary of State

NANKING, June 13, 1949—2 p. m.
[Received June 13—10:19 a. m.]

1274. Controlled press and radio of Communist China provide some substantiation of our surmise that sun of Chou En-lai is being eclipsed by that of Liu Shao-chi.

Only honor received by Chou during at least past year was appointment as chairman of CCP delegation to abortive peace discussions in Peiping last April. Press has not carried any speech delivered or article written by Chou. On May 10 press reported he addressed All China Youth League Congress in Peiping May 7 but, contrary to custom, it failed to publish text.

On other hand, Peiping radio reports of arrival of central committee of CCP and general headquarters of PLA at Peiping March 25 listed arrivals of Mao Tse-tung, Chu Teh, Liu Shao-chi, Chou En-lai, Jen

[14] Chinese visitor from Singapore.

Pi-shih and Lin Tzu-han in that order. Following Communist capture of Tientsin, Liu had important assignment as economic trouble shooter that area. He delivered report about May 5 to North China labor congress, and it was published. He, as "leader of Chinese labor movement", May 30 was elected honorary president of All China Federation of Labor. His biography was broadcast to world June 3 by Peiping radio English Morsecast. He received signal honor of having his article "On Internationalism and Nationalism" published in Cominform *Journal* and *Pravda* (re Embtel 1258, June 10).

Sent Dept 1274, repeated Shanghai 687, American Embassy Canton 527, Peiping 214, Moscow 41.

STUART

893.002/6–1349 : Telegram

The Minister-Counselor of Embassy in China (Clark) to the Secretary of State

CANTON, June 13, 1949.
[Received June 13—3 : 38 p. m.]

Cantel 579. Following complete list Yen Hsi-shan Cabinet announced Saturday June 11.

Vice President Executive Yuan—Chu Chia-hua.[15]
Secretary General Executive Yuan—Chia Ching-teh.[16]
Ministers,   National Defense—Yen Hsi-shan concurrently;
            Foreign Affairs—Hu Shih; [17]
            Interior—Li Han-hun; [18]
            Finance—Hsu Kan;
            Communications—Tuan Mu-chieh; [19]
            Economic Affairs—Liu Hang-shen; [20]
            Education—Han Li-wu; [21]
            Justice—Chang Shih-pen; [22]
Commissions—Mongolian-Tibetan Affairs—Kuan Chi-yu;[23]
            Overseas Chinese Affairs—Tai Kuei-sheng;[24]
Ministers without Portfolio: Chen Li-fu,
                 Chang Chun [25] (resigned June 12),
                 Wu Tieh-cheng,[26]

---

[15] Chinese Minister of Education, 1944–48.
[16] Vice President of the Chinese Examination Yuan, 1948–49.
[17] Chinese Ambassador to the United States, 1938–42.
[18] Governor of Kwangtung, 1938–45.
[19] Secretary-general of the Chinese Judicial Yuan.
[20] Former Chinese Vice Minister of Food.
[21] Chinese Vice Minister of Education.
[22] Grand Justice of the Chinese Judicial Yuan.
[23] Chinese Minister of Food.
[24] Chinese Vice Minister of the Kuomintang Board of Overseas Affairs.
[25] President of the Chinese Executive Yuan, 1947–48; Military and Political Affairs Director for Southwest China.
[26] Vice President of the Chinese Executive Yuan, 1948–49.

Huang Shao-ku,[27]
Hu Yung-chang,[28]
Wang   Shih-tien   (Young   China
Party).

Dept pass VOANY.[29]

Sent Dept Cantel 579, repeated Nanking 387, Shanghai 328.

CLARK

893.00/6-1449 : Telegram

*The Minister-Counselor of Embassy in China (Clark) to the Secretary
of State*

CANTON, June 14, 1949—4 p. m.
[Received June 15—4:14 a. m.]

Cantel 585. Chen Li-fu confirms organ "Emergency Committee of
CEC Kmt" which will replace former Central Political Committee
which has proven unwieldy. Generalissimo will [get?] Chairmanship
new committee and Li Tsung-jen will be Vice-Chairman. As Sun Fo
was Vice-Chairman Central Political Committee, he could not be
ignored, so position Second Vice-Chairman is created in case Sun Fo
desires serve. Chen insists Li Tsung-jen has at last agreed this setup
under which he acquiesces in Generalissimo's continued interference
functioning government. Chen says Generalissimo has promised come
Canton if there is real necessity his presence here. Chen does not think
Generalissimo will come Canton. Chen confirms that Hsu Kan, Minister Finance, has gone Taiwan endeavor obtain from Generalissimo
access to gold supply and likelihood is Hsu Kan will refuse serve if
unsuccessful. Appointment Hu Shih, he says, was announced without
any reply having been received from Dr. Hu to numerous telegrams
sent him offering him Foreign Office. Chen was not too sure how Yen
Hsi-shan and Li Tsung-jen were going to get along, but said: "We
first need unity, then a victory, and then we can get after the economic
problem."

He inquired regarding success mission Kan Chieh-hou [30] in manner
indicating he hoped mission would be failure. He demonstrated
throughout conversation quite clearly that rift between C–C clique and
Li Tsung-jen is still unbridgeable.

Sent Department, repeated Nanking 392, Shanghai 333.

[CLARK]

---

[27] Chinese Acting Minister of the Kuomintang Ministry of Information.
[28] Chinese Minister of National Defense.
[29] Voice of America, New York.
[30] Secretary and political adviser to Acting President Li Tsung-jen on mission
to the United States; for documentation, see vol. IX, pp. 699 ff.

893.00/6–249 : Telegram

The Acting Secretary of State to the Consul General at Peiping
(Clubb)

WASHINGTON, June 14, 1949—5 p. m.

367. Urtel 917 Jun 1. Dept very appreciative ur excellent interpretative comment on message in urtel 928 Jun 2. Dept willing authorize reply but does not consider use intermediary thru whom ur message transmitted provides sufficient guarantee against disclosure. If you are able to transmit reply either directly or thru completely reliable intermediary without danger disclosure, you are authorized make reply along lines set forth below. To guard against future distortion such message, you might prepare reply on plain paper without signature or designation source.

Begin message. US has traditionally maintained close and friendly relations with China and has thruout past 100 years Sino-US relations, particularly since end last century, taken lead in efforts obtain internatl respect for Chi territorial and administrative integrity to end that China might develop as stable, united and independent nation. Unique record US relations with China gives clear evidence US has no territorial designs on China and has sought no special privileges or rights which were not granted other fon nations; US has sought maintain relations on basis mutual benefit and respect. Basic US objectives and principles remain unchanged.

In present situation US hopes maintain friendly relations with China and continue social, economic and polit relations with that country insofar as these relations based upon principle mutual respect and understanding and principle equality and are to mutual benefit two nations. In absence these basic principles, it can hardly be expected that full benefit Sino-US relations can be attained.

In this connection, US Govt and people are naturally disturbed and seriously concerned over certain recent occurrences which represent significant departure from these principles and some of which, in fact, widely at variance with accepted internatl custom and practice: Repeated bitter propaganda misrepresenting US actions and motives in China and elsewhere in world; arbitrary restrictions on movement and denial communications ConGen Mukden and Commie failure reply to ConGen Peiping repeated representations this matter, including request withdraw ConGen and staff Mukden; and Commie failure take action release two US Marine flyers or reply ConGen Peiping representations this matter.[31]

While we welcome expressions friendly sentiments, he must realize that they cannot be expected bear fruit until they have been translated into deeds capable of convincing American people that Sino-US rela-

---

[31] On October 19, 1948, 2 American servicemen, William C. Smith, Chief Construction Electrician, U.S. Navy, and Elmer C. Bender, Master Sergeant, U.S. Marine Corps, members of the U.S. Naval Headquarters at Tsingtao, failed to return from a routine training flight. For their eventual release and homeward journey, see statement on May 19, 1950, by Acting Secretary of State Webb, Department of State *Bulletin,* May 29, 1950, p. 868.

tions can be placed upon solid basis mutual respect and understanding to benefit both nations. *End message.*

Dept has not communicated substance Peiping tel 917 to Brit and does not contemplate so doing unless names of intermediary and source are to be revealed.

WEBB

893.00B/6–1549 : Telegram

The Ambassador in China (Stuart) to the Secretary of State

NANKING, June 15, 1949—noon.
[Received June 15—8 :14 a. m.]

1288. Reference Shanghai telegram 1917, May 31 to Dept. We heartily concur with Shanghai observation that Communist activities in China are far from Soviet Punch and Judy show. That Soviets themselves realize this is indicated by Moscow telegram 971, April 19 to Dept which reported belief that China problem is at top of Politburo agenda, that Molotov [32] is primarily now concerned with China and that best talent, maximum energy is now being concentrated to steer Chinese developments along channels desired by Kremlin. We do not doubt that Soviets have courage and self-confidence to attempt this. They were not in least daunted by historic Polish hatred of all things Russian or by virile nationalism of Germany or by Balkan cockpit.

However, we would like to reaffirm our belief that top Chinese Communists are showing every evidence of trying to work closely with Soviet leaders. All hints of Soviet–CCP friction come from Soviet side. For any country to dovetail its foreign and domestic policies with those of USSR is one of thorniest tasks in field of international relations. USSR is hard taskmaster. But it seems to us that Chinese Communists have so far acquitted themselves exceedingly well. Maybe they will prove constitutionally incapable of being real Communists in Eastern European sense of word; perhaps they actually are rather naive immature Marxians, as some Cominform elements seem to believe; possibly their social, economic, racial characteristics will prove stronger than their hero worship of Soviet Union and devotion to world revolution. There are many good reasons to support those hypotheses which only time will prove. But at this stage Chinese Communists certainly deserve from Kremlin rating "excellent" for their recent successes and current endeavors.

Sent Department 1288, repeated Canton 537, Shanghai 699, Moscow 42.

STUART

---

[32] V. M. Molotov, Deputy Chairman of the Council of Ministers of the Soviet Union.

893.00/6–1649 : Telegram

The Consul at Tsingtao (Hawthorne) to the Secretary of State

TSINGTAO, June 16, 1949—11 a. m.
[Received June 16—3 : 18 a. m.]

269. Mass demonstration marking liberation held June 16 in orderly manner without incident, though Americans warned by Consulate General keep off streets far as possible. US Navy ridiculed by parader dressed as American sailor who carried bottle and feigned intoxication, but anti-foreign slogans conspicuously absent.

Consulate General still handicapped lack vehicle passes, issuance which delayed owing change in procedure before our applications processed.

Sent Department 269; repeated Nanking 193, Shanghai 110.

HAWTHORNE

893.00/6–1649 : Telegram

The Ambassador in China (Stuart) to the Secretary of State

NANKING, June 16, 1949—1 p. m.
[Received June 16—5 : 09 a. m.]

1300. [To Shanghai:] Reftel 2215 to Department.[33] Suggest you continue follow closely as possible whole range Communist printed material distributed Shanghai to determine whether, as compared other parts China, Communists there are playing down USSR inspiration and example. Such action, presumably out of deference to Western opinion, would seem to conflict with primary objective of properly indoctrinating China's large concentration of urban proletariat, group which Communists have stated they henceforth intend use as principal base for revolutionary activities of party. If in Shanghai propaganda Communists actually do minimize USSR connection, it would be interesting commentary on importance they attach to western opinion.

In Nanking fact that Communists look to Moscow for inspiration and example has been quite apparent in vernacular press. In addition to foreign news being almost exclusively from Tass and therefore faithfully presenting Kremlin view of world affairs, *Hsin Huo Jih Pao* in past month has published some 20 articles by Soviet writers ranging from Lenin's "Competition in Forming Organizations",

---

[33] June 11, 2 p.m., from the Consul General at Shanghai, p. 381.

Kalinin's [34] "How Youth Should Acquire Knowledge", and Zhdanov's [35] "Report on Current Situation" to articles on "order and discipline in Soviet factories" and "economical use of metals". *Hsin Hua* bookstore also carries considerable range of translations of Soviet political, economic and literary works as well as translations of Soviet political, economic and literary works as well as translations of American and English writers currently acceptable in USSR such as Steinbeck, Dickens and Jack London. We would be interested in learning of significant departures from this pattern in Shanghai.

Sent Shanghai 707; repeated Department, OffEmb Canton 541.

STUART

893.00/6–1649 : Telegram

The Consul General at Peiping (Clubb) to the Secretary of State

PEIPING, June 16, 1949.
[Received June 16—9 : 54 a. m.]

1022. *Kuang Ming Jih Pao* today reports that chairman [of] Democratic League Chang Lan and standing committee members Lo Lung-chi and Shih Liang are scheduled depart Shanghai en route Peiping June 18 and that after their arrival Peiping there can be determined date for holding 4th plenary conference now in process preparation. Per item it is moreover reported that within League headquarters temporary working committee there has been established 2 discussion organizations of temporary nature, one being political study group headed by Huang Yen-pei and Li Po-chiu, the other being League affairs study group headed by Chang Tung-sun and Chu Tu-nan.

Another item same paper reports that KmtRC Peiping branch preparatory commission at present time is preparing for convocation conference members to facilitate establishment branch society. Preparatory work and registration members are responsible 9 persons including Li Hsi-chiu, Yu Hsin-ching, Chen Shao-hsien. Same source reports Chen Ming-shu who is one of 5 members designated assume responsibility for KmtRC affairs Shanghai arrived Tsinan June 14 en route Peiping.

Repeated Nanking 700, OffEmb Canton Shanghai 683, to Tientsin by mail.

CLUBB

---

[34] The late M. I. Kalinin, President of the Presidium of the Supreme Council of the Soviet Union.
[35] The late Lt. Gen. A. A. Zhdanov, Secretary of the Central Executive Committee of the Communist Party of the Soviet Union at the time of his death in 1948.

893.00/6–1649

Memorandum by the Acting Secretary of State of a Conversation With the President

[WASHINGTON,] June 16, 1949.

CHOU EN-LAI "DÉMARCHE"

I brought the President up to date with respect to the Chou En-lai *Démarche* and read to him the pertinent sections of our reply.[36] He approved this course of action and directs us to be most careful not to indicate any softening toward the Communists but to insist on judging their intentions by their actions.

JAMES E. WEBB

893.002/6–1649 : Telegram

The Minister-Counselor of Embassy in China (Clark) to the Secretary of State

CANTON, June 16, 1949—5 p. m.
[Received June 17—10 : 09 a. m.]

Cantel 596. New Premier Yen Hsi-shan is old man, old even for his 67 years. After long conversation, would almost say he is in his dotage and it is to this man free China is entrusting its destiny.

Yen plans assume active role in administering affairs and hopes by his leadership to improve morale and by revising tactics along lines pursued so successfully by Communists 2 years ago to inspire Nationalist soldiers to fight. Also he plans a budget almost in balance, drawing only small sums each month from gold Hsu Kan is endeavoring obtain from Generalissimo. His talk was largely in vague generalities and didn't carry conviction. He wouldn't admit possibility government might move Chungking, saying "Cabinet will fight here to the last".

There is nothing to indicate that government under him will be any more efficient than its predecessor. Each Ministry is arranging deploy its forces in Taiwan, Chungking and Canton and in no Ministry, unless it is that of Education, is there any evidence of constructive thinking. The stultifying hand of Kmt leadership has the government in its grasp. No one seems capable of taking positive action and there is increasing evidence of fatalistic feeling that as course of events cannot be altered resistance is futile. I even sense a growing feeling of "why bother go Chungking?" Bulk ministerial personnel is going Taiwan now. I gather controlling element in decision government move Chungking rather than Taiwan is fear international repercussions

---

[36] See telegram No. 367, June 14, 5 p.m., p. 384.

should seat government be established other than on mainland and particularly on Taiwan, status of which might be subject to question. There seems feeling impatience with slowness of march of events and desire get on to next phase wherein some way God, US or Confucius will bring about dawn of better day.

This connection, am becoming increasingly suspicious that Li Tsung-jen is in contact with Communists. Chu Chang-wei has been for some days in Hong Kong consulting Huang Shao-hsiung, member abortive peace delegation, who is reported on reliable authority to have recommended that time Li make his own peace with Communists. Press carries report which I am investigating that Liu Fei, former Vice Minister National Defense, and also at peace conference, paid secret visit Canton to see Li Tsung-jen this connection. Shall follow this matter further, of course, but deployment Pai Chung-hsi's troops and his unhappy state of mind when he last visited Canton tend confirm my suspicion.

Sent Department Cantel 596, repeated Nanking 398, Shanghai 341.

CLARK

893.00/6–1749 : Telegram

The Consul General at Peiping (Clubb) to the Secretary of State

PEIPING, June 17, 1949—5 p. m.
[Received June 17—6 : 42 a. m.]

1031. ReDeptel 367, June 14. I agree in undesirability committing reply to original channel as direct transmitting agency. Believe further, however, undesirable endeavor use new channel since this would merely broaden possibilities leakage.

After consultation with Barrett, believe best procedure would be inform Keon it is desired make reply but by direct contact either Barrett or myself with either Chou En-lai or his secretary (who made arrangements for first interview with Keon) with Chou himself to stipulate what channel he would prefer for safe reply.

Note this would (1) avoid any compromise Chou by insecurity new channel, (2) leave up to his own judgment in first instance matter of security reply (any counter-proposition from Chou would of course have to be acceptable to us to get our compliance), (3) incidentally check Chou's willingness accept such communication, and (4) provide practical check at same time on first communication. By this procedure be it noted there would be avoided any further diffusion of matter.

Please instruct.

CLUBB

893.00/6–1949 : Telegram

*The Minister-Counselor of Embassy in China (Clark) to the
Secretary of State*

CANTON, June 19, 1949—3 p. m.
[Received June 20—12:25 a. m.]

Cantel 613. Chu Chang-wei confirms agreement Li Tsung-jen to creation "policy committee" of Kmt. Li became convinced, he says, that Generalissimo would not come Canton and that he (Li) could control situation better through small policy committee with him as acting chairman than he could through existing political committee and standing committee of Kmt, in neither of which does Li have chairmanship and both of which are packed with articulate reactionary Kmt. Li plans use this policy committee as channel his control government activities. As indicative inertia present day Canton is fact that committee, although agreed to over 2 weeks ago, is still not organized and does not function.

Chu says Hu Shih has turned down offer be Minister FonAffs and that Chang Chun has refused position Minister without Portfolio. He says Li agreed appointment Yen Hsi-shan largely to please C–C clique.

Chu says Hsu Kan phoned from Taipei yesterday saying he would accept Finance Ministry and was returning Canton immediately. That indicates to Chu that Generalissimo has promised treasure. He shook his head, however, and said Pai Chung-hsi still had insufficient money pay his troops.

Chu confirms that Liu Fei visited Canton and saw Li Tsung-jen. He insists Liu Fei was not bearer proposals from Communists and that Li is not considering peace. Chu says Liu Fei and Huang Shao-hsiung with whom Chu had many conversations in Hong Kong are both most pessimistic over situation and he admits that they advocate peace. In spite of Chu's protest to contrary and his unqualified statement that Li and Pai Chung-hsi will fight to the last, there seems possibility Liu Fei did, in fact, bring Communist proposition. While Li may be unwilling consider peace this state he may think differently as disintegration continues and should that day arrive when he and Pai have their backs to the wall in Kwangsi they may be more susceptible to Communist offers.

Sent Department, repeated Nanking 411, Shanghai 349.

CLARK

893.00/6–2049 : Telegram

The Consul General at Shanghai (Cabot) to the Secretary of State

SHANGHAI, June 20, 1949—noon.
[Received 12:34 p. m.]

2354. Cheng Kang-chi, former head of local Foreign Office who stayed behind when Kmt forces evacuated Shanghai because of liberal sentiments and disgust with Kmt, has quoted to me several conversations with Communist officials indicating that Chinese Communists are far from pleased with Russian intrusions in Manchuria, Sinkiang, Port Arthur and Dairen. He said that people who took over wanted him to take job under new regime since they were so inexperienced in foreign affairs, but he felt he could not properly do so at once. Although he may have had ulterior purposes, I have always considered him intelligent, sincere pro-American and personally friendly.

Conversations indicate Chinese Communists are thinking very definitely in terms recovering full Chinese sovereignty where Soviets have acquired special rights; that they are waiting only until more urgent business is finished to press matter; that they have already raised question of Dairen and Port Arthur and have been rebuffed on ground that Kmt made arrangements with Soviets. He also quoted a fellow-travelling friend as reversing his defense of Soviet demands in Sinkiang after consulting Communist leader. He mentioned point we have from other sources that Chinese Communist leaders are by no means as fanatical and pro-Soviet as lower Communist echelons.

Two other interesting points:

(1) He said he was sure Chinese Communists do not want *de facto* recognition for fear it will delay *de jure* recognition.

(2) He quoted director of Shanghai Cultural and Educational Committee as ordering removal of poster attacking American imperialism because against party policy. Incidentally, he laughed at *Ta Kung Pao's* frantic and undignified efforts to curry favor.

I emphasized our open-mindedness and said that with moderation on both sides I was confident relations would improve. I pointed out, however, that vituperative propaganda parroting Kremlin line had been very damaging to any sentiment in US toward greater cooperation. I added that Communist attitude of cold-shouldering foreign representations might not only occasion misunderstandings but also prove prejudicial to Communist objectives. He said he had pointed this out also but that present impasse must be worked out gradually.

Sent Department 2354; repeated Nanking 1251; Canton 747.

CABOT

893.00B/6–2049 : Telegram

The Consul General at Peiping (Clubb) to the Secretary of State

PEIPING, June 20, 1949.
[Received June 22—8:34 p. m.]

1045. ReContel 1042, June 20.[37] NCNA English language service today carries full text Mao Tse-tung speech June 15 to meeting convoked for purpose establishing preparatory committee new PCC, highlights as follows:

Task of meeting is to accomplish all preparatory work necessary for swift convocation new PCC to form democratic coalition government so as to lead people throughout country to clean up remnant forces Kmt reactionaries, unify all China, carry out economic, cultural and national defense construction. Convocation new PCC was proposed to country generally by CCP May 1, 1948. It got general support democratic parties and groups and popular organizations and democratic personages, national minorities throughout the country and among overseas Chinese.

All considered that the rule of imperialism, feudalism, bureaucratic capitalism and Kmt reactionary clique had to be overthrown and there be convened PCC embracing representative democratic parties and groups, popular organizations, democratic personages, national minorities and overseas Chinese for establishment People's Democracy of China and election of democratic coalition government representing that republic. Only thus can China free itself from semi-colonial and semi-feudal fate and travel along road independence, freedom, peace, unity, strength and prosperity. That is common political basis for unified struggle by CCP and other groups and for unified struggle of people as whole. This political basis is held by all conscientious democratic parties or groups, people's organizations and personages as being correct direction for solution all China's problems. People's liberation war has lasted 3 years since its beginning July 1946. "This war was launched by the Kuomintang reactionaries with the help of foreign imperalism." Now PLA has marched to victory after victory (brief survey is given) and Kmt remnant forces remaining number only about one and half million men. It will not be long before those enemy remnants are cleaned up. This is victory of people throughout country and is also victory of peoples of world. Whole world, except for imperialists and reactionaries, are jubilant over great victory of Chinese people. Struggle of Chinese people against their enemies and struggle of people of world against their own enemies bear same meaning. People of China and people of world note fact that imperialists directed reactionaries China to oppose Chinese people brutally with counter-revolutionary war.

---

[37] Not printed.

"At this point, I think it necessary call people's attention to fact imperialists and their running dogs, the Chinese reactionaries, will not take their defeat in China lying down. They will still work in collusion each other and use all possible means oppose Chinese people. They will, for example, send their lackeys to bore into China, carry out work disintegration and disruption. This is inevitable and they will certainly not forget this work. They will, for instance, egg on Chinese reactionaries or may in addition even come out with own forces to blockade seaports of China. They will do this if it still possible do so. Furthermore, if they want to be adventuristic, sending part their armed forces encroach on China's frontiers not an impossibility. We must fully take all this into account. We must decidedly not, because of our victories, relax vigilance towards wild retaliatory plots of imperialistic elements and their running dogs.

Whoever relaxes such vigilance will be politically disarmed and placed in passive position. Under these circumstances, people throughout country must unite and smash firmly, thoroughly, cleanly, and completely all anti-popular conspiratorial schemes imperialists and their lackeys, the reactionaries in China. China must be independent, China must be liberated, the affairs of China must be decided on and dealt with by Chinese people themselves and not slightest intervention by any imperialist country is allowed.

Revolution of China is revolution by masses of people of entire nation. Except for imperialists, feudalists, bureaucratic bourgeoisie, Kuomintang reactionaries and their henchmen, all persons are our friends. We have broad and consolidated revolutionary united front which is so broad it includes working class, peasant class, petty bourgeoisie and national bourgeoisie, and which is so consolidated it has powerful will and inexhaustible capacity vanquish all enemies and conquer all difficulties. We are now in era in which imperialist system is heading towards complete collapse. Imperialists are bogged in inescapable crisis, and no matter how they still want continue oppose Chinese people, Chinese people have the means win final victory. At same time, we wish declare to whole world: We only oppose the imperialist system and its conspiratorial schemes against Chinese people. We are willing negotiate establishment of diplomatic relations with any foreign government on basis of principles equality, mutual benefits and mutual respecting of territorial sovereignty, provided it is willing sever relations with Chinese reactionaries and no longer helps or works in collusion with them and provided it adopts real and not hypocritical attitude amity towards China of the people. Chinese people willing carry out friendly cooperation with peoples all countries in world in restoring and developing international trading relations so as to favour development production and bringing about flourishing economy."

All conditions for convocation new PCC for formation democratic coalition government have matured. People throughout country look forward to convocation of conference and setting up of government. It is believed that work which has been begun can satisfy that hope and that before long, with formation democratic coalition government, its center of gravity for work will be: To clean up remnants reactionary clique and suppress their disruptive activities, to use all means and exert utmost efforts in rehabilitation and development economic work of the people and concurrently rehabilitating and developing people's cultural and educational work.

"Once destiny of China is in hands of people, Chinese people will see a China rising like sun from east and shining on earth with its brilliant rays and see her swiftly wash away dirt left behind by reactionary government, heal scars of war and build up new, strong and prosperous People's Democratic Republic of China which will be true to its name."

Sent Department 1045, repeated Nanking, Canton, Shanghai, Tientsin by mail.

CLUBB

893.00B/6–2249 : Telegram

The Ambassador in China (Stuart) to the Secretary of State

NANKING, June 22, 1949.
[Received June 22—6 : 02 a. m.]

1346. Local press June 20 reports Chang Lan, Shih Liang, Lo Lungchi, Wang Pao-chang, Kuo Chen-tao,[38] others arrived in Nanking June 19 on way to Peiping. Chang, Lo, Shih, press states, aside from attending preparatory committee of new PCC will also attend fourth plenary session of Democratic League.

Sent Department, repeated Peiping 231, Shanghai 739, OffEmb Canton unnumbered.

STUART

893.00/6–2249 : Telegram

The Consul General at Peiping (Clubb) to the Secretary of State

PEIPING, June 22, 1949—2 p. m.
[Received June 22—6 : 51 a. m.]

1058. ReDeptels 367, June 14 and 376, June 17.[39] In light speech Mao Tse-tung, Assistant AMilAt [40] Barrett recommended whole project of making reply should be discarded. He reported accordingly AMilAt Nanking.

---

[38] All Democratic League members; they reached Peiping on June 24.
[39] Latter not printed.
[40] American Military Attaché.

Matter was thoroughly discussed between us and point of Barrett's recommendation is clear: Such approach by Commie leader international problems by all outward indications holds little promise for *rapprochement* China, USA, with China seemingly tightly tied Soviet chariot. This impression is only strengthened by current Commie publicity re position Japan. Indications are in short Commies anticipate increasingly close political relations with the USSR and probably early recognition by USSR of any new Central Government.

I nevertheless concluded project should be carried out as originally formulated. This partly for reasons set forth Contel 1031, June 17. With particular reference to reaction indicated second paragraph, note further following points: (1) fact Mao is currently being referred to in American press as prospective Tito may have caused him use more violent verbiage than would otherwise have been case, (2) Chou's *démarche* may have been made with knowledge other influential circles CCP as suggested Contel 928, June 2, but without knowledge USSR Commies (now isolated except for USSR liaison), hoping better contacts with Anglo-American groups to give them more freedom movement, (3) if Chou approach represented will of important group, it should be exploited as perhaps opening door to other important developments, and (4) if Chou's approach was isolated or has now been cancelled out by group decision [no?] loss would be sustained by presenting so clear and firm statement of American policy as given in Depreftel. Mao Tse-tung speech makes present reply perhaps even more pertinent. Limited success achieved CFM conference Paris weakens Commie position Asia, as Europe. That weakness should be exploited. Whether Chou *démarche* offers some opportunity for exploitation position China for benefit USA can be determined only by trial. If optimism unwarranted, it is still desirable explore possibilities.

Barrett contacting intermediary for first step.

Sent Department, repeated Nanking 735.

CLUBB

893.00B/6–2249 : Telegram

The Ambassador in China (Stuart) to the Secretary of State

NANKING, June 22, 1949—4 p. m.
[Received June 23—9 : 40 a. m.]

1351. Mao's speech before Preparatory Committee of new PCC as carried in NCNA broadcast June 19 consists largely of same broad generalizations on nature of Chinese revolution which he used so successfully in his "New Democracy" to gain support of large numbers of non-Communist Chinese intellectuals. As immediate objective is establishment of "coalition" government, Mao does not emphasize leading role of CCP in revolution, but on contrary stresses that it is revolution by "masses of the people" and participated in by all "democratic parties and groups", even including "petty bourgeoisie" and "national bourgeoisie".

Mao's reference to their willingness to establish diplomatic relations with foreign countries, their desire for foreign trade and their anxiety re blockading of seaports, indicates one important reason for speeding up establishment of Central Government may be increasing economic pressure and their growing awareness of China's vital need of imports.

Of incidental interest were Mao's calling Nanking "capital of Kmt reactionaries", lending support to widely held opinion that Nanking will not be seat of new government. Name "People's Democratic Republic of China" used by Mao will probably be adopted as official designation for China under new government. This title as well as Mao's statement that one of tasks of new government will be to "unify all China" indicate that China may continue to be single republic rather than union of republics on Soviet pattern as has been suggested by some observers.

Sent Dept 1351, repeated EmbOff Canton 573.

STUART

893.00B/6–2349 : Telegram

The Ambassador in China (Stuart) to the Secretary of State

NANKING, June 23, 1949—9 p. m.
[Received June 24—7 : 52 a. m.]

1358. Although some observers believe election of Chou En-lai as first Vice Chairman standing committee of Preparatory Committee for new PCC implies Chou has strengthened his position vis-à-vis Liu Shao-chi who is not even appointed to standing committee, it seems to us quite reasonable that Chou should receive this position because of his experience at first PCC, his chairmanship of abortive CCP peace delegation and his general background, reputation as negotiator with non-Communists. Liu Shao-chi, on other hand, is qualified more as labor leader, theoretician, party organizer and to some extent as economic trouble shooter.

We are little impressed by parliamentarian façade for new PCC. Obviously entire conference will be controlled by CCP. Profession of CCP kinship for "democratic parties and groups" and non-participation of "reactionary parties and groups" are strongly reminiscent of Soviet idea of "party and non-party bloc". Communists decided which elements will be represented at PCC. Undoubtedly they allocated chairmanships and committee memberships. They even retain power of veto over delegates to new PCC by provision that although each unit represented may elect its own delegates, these delegates must also be approved by Preparatory Committee. As long as CCP maintains army of three million and has plans for recruitment and training of additional million, we may expect a military dictatorship of most authoritarian character. It is obvious that "democratic parties and groups" and "democratic personages" who have not even mass political following are helpless before such power and cannot be expected to develop or pursue policy different from that laid down by CCP. Certainly in all public statements made by various "democratic personages" now participating in Preparatory Committee there has been no deviation whatsoever from Communist line.

Sent Department 1358, repeated EmbOff Canton 577, Shanghai 749, Peiping 235.

STUART

893.00/6–2449 : Telegram

The Consul General at Peiping (Clubb) to the Secretary of State

PEIPING, June 24, 1949—5 p. m.
[Received June 24—7 : 27 a. m.]

1073. ReContel 1058, June 22. Intermediary today reported to Barrett and me that he June 22 approached contact man who had arranged first meeting with Chou En-lai, proposed arrangements for making reply in manner indicated. Contact took message, got in touch with intermediary later in day, showed obvious desire ascertain whether intermediary knew origin and content of message, wanted know why same channel unchosen for reply. Intermediary said he knew nothing of reply, would not have consented transmit it if he had been asked.

On following day contact saw intermediary again, covered same ground, was much stiffer ("Gestapo-like" in words intermediary) in attitude, stated Communist side unprepared accept reply that character by those means, and that Chou had no suggestion of any description make regarding means transmittal. Consented forward personal note from intermediary to Chou's secretary (who with translator had been present first meeting), but said it would make no difference. Informed intermediary finally that latter should not henceforth on his own initiative approach him regarding making contacts with Communist acquaintances. (Contact not well-known to intermediary, did not himself participate in original meeting with Chou.)

Intermediary expressed to us his chagrin, said willing assist in any other way possible, make approach by new channel if desired. I said it appeared to me that Communist side had given firm reply after due deliberation, if they were undesirous receiving reply of whatever character from American side I perceived no point asking him pursue matter further since it was not our intention Communist side accept such communication. Barrett agreed.

Comment follows.[41]

Repeated Nanking 746, Canton 188.

CLUBB

893.00/6–2749 : Telegram

The Consul General at Peiping (Clubb) to the Secretary of State

PEIPING, June 27, 1949—11 a. m.
[Received June 27—7 : 38 a. m.]

1080. ReContel 1073, June 24. Suggest re denouement following alternative explanations (listed in order believed of worth) :

1. Move was designed serve political purpose of causing USA view Communist leaders more sympathetically, and perhaps letting sympathy affect US attitude re trade or direct aid, but did not constitute sincere expression Communist policy views. Barrett thinks this unlikely in view Chou's character; I consider it most logical explanation on Chou's Communist practices (Contel 928, June 2), but concede motives could well have been as indicated next point.

2. Communist leadership or Chou group was willing send message for record, perhaps even willing receive reply by channel which could readily be disavowed or discredited, but unwilling have contact now which would commit them more officially and definitely. Aim: To achieve increased mobility vis-à-vis USSR (that is, it would have been budding Titoism). See Contel 1058, June 22.

3. Chou group sent out first message in temporary panic, now would disavow move. This unlikely. (Note here, however, that any suspicion in Chou group of leak would increase their wariness and aloofness, assuming them to be acting independently. Intermediary reported several days after first message that Chou's secretary meeting him on street had "looked through" him instead of giving nod recognition as usual.)

4. Move was soberly considered in first instance but reconsidered in light later developments. Note convocation PCC Preparatory Committee meeting, renewal anti-imperialist blasts from Mao Tse-tung, proposals re Japanese peace treaty (Contel 1071, June 23 [42]) and agitation re Formosa, might all reflect policy decisions which might have borne significance for Chou *démarche*. Decisions might have incorporated Soviet as well as Communist views, might have been accompanied by new Sino-Soviet agreement or understanding.

Believe offer of reply has served purpose of (1) testing willingness Chou's group continue with matter and (2) exploring field. Believe it would be undesirable try send message indirectly through present or other channels, for if Communists unprepared accept even direct contact, any such transmittal orally would satisfy no important

---

[41] See telegram No. 1080, June 27, 11 a. m., *infra*.
[42] Not printed.

American purpose and might give Communists possibility making capital propaganda use of material obtained in such uncertain way. Would propose therefore matter be dropped at present point.

Sent Department, repeated Nanking 753, OffEmb Canton 189.

CLUBB

893.00/6–2749 : Telegram

The Consul General at Hong Kong (Hopper) to the Secretary of State

HONG KONG, June 27, 1949—11 a. m.
[Received 11:27 a. m.]

380. [Member] . . . of Legislative Yuan group Li Tsung-jen supporters (mentioned Cantel 378, to Department [43]), in June 24 interview informed . . . source their intention meet with Huang Shaohsiung, Liu Fei and Tung Kuan-hsien about July 1 issue statement on behalf "progressive elements Kmt" offering political cooperation with Communists in forthcoming coalition Government. [Informant] stated group, which now calls itself China Democratic Association, reluctant embark on this course, but sees no other means effectively combat Communist monopoly political power. Also stated would like views American Government on this move and would also like American financial support since funds exhausted and badly need resources continue organizational work. Concluded that group would work for democratic China and preserve present anti-Communist pro-American orientation whether or not American aid received.

Evidence suggests this group may well prove rallying point all anti-Generalissimo and anti-C–C Clique elements of Kmt remaining Nationalist China, with leadership eventually in hands Li Tsung-jen. If so, and given increasingly strong possibility Li may feel forced make peace with Communists, this group would form nucleus his political machine and serve as counterpoint KmtRC of Li Chi-shen who would be his principal rival in coalition government. Presence Liu Fei in Democratic Association activities certainly suggests Communists interested in bargaining with group.

HOPPER

893.00/6–2749 : Telegram

The Chargé in the Soviet Union (Kohler) to the Secretary of State

MOSCOW, June 27, 1949—1 p. m.
[Received 6:54 p. m.]

1620. Not surprising to Embassy are reports from Chinese Communist sources of elements "veering toward US" and of Communist

---

[43] May 14, p. 315.

anxiety for US aid (Department info[rmation] airgrams, June 15, 8:05 and 8:35 a. m.[44]). Chinese Communists intelligent, hardheaded realists who can be expected exert selves utmost wangle trade concessions from west.

Chief Nanking Alien Affairs Office, Huang Hua, can be depended do particularly good job trying convince US "liberal" CCP attitude. Notable he and Chen Chia-kan (vice-president WFDY,[45] delegate Paris peace conference, etc.) seem be playing important role CCP regime. Training and experience as interpreters US observers section Yenan prepared them for present important diplomatic duties. However, whether either is more "liberal" than other Chinese may be open to doubt.

Embassy believes axiomatic that CCP unlikely be weaned away from Communist orthodoxy by west eagerness trade now. Communists may try for time get best of two possible worlds: Soviets and ours. Economic recovery can come quickest through US aid. Their willingness try US first does not however carry offer to change Communist principles. Real attitude clearly expressed Liu Shao-chi his November 1948 treatise "Nationalism and Internationalism" recently published *Pravda* (Embtel June 7 [46]). According *Pravda* version, he said "No oppressed people can receive real liberation and independence as result so-called 'aid' of imperialist countries. Therefore very mistaken and harmful cherish illusions to effect American imperialism sincerely wishes help Chinese people achieve real independence, peace and democracy."

Kremlin cannot afford lose China and, if CCP strategy get help from west fails, Soviets will certainly strain to aid China. Such effort, whether successful or not, would impose drain on Soviet economy perhaps serious enough weaken its activities among satellites. If unsuccessful, CCP may then take stock to consider how industrialization China is to be accomplished. Only at that moment, if we have previously maintained our firmness and have refrained from encouraging Chinese Communist regime, is there hope that Mao and company may toy with idea following independent path from Soviet teachers.

If this interpretation correct, China policy of west must be based not on China alone but upon our relationship with entire Soviet-dominated Communist world. Policy must be firm, patient and impervious to temptation. Above all valiant missionary effort will be required convince our west friends that long view is only view and that Mao is not for sale now.

Sent Department 1620; repeated Nanking 70, Paris 265, Canton 35, Canberra 11, London 156.

KOHLER

---

[44] Neither printed.
[45] Communist-sponsored World Federation of Democratic Youth.
[46] No. 1474, not printed.

893.001/6–2949 : Telegram

The Minister-Counselor of Embassy in China (Clark) to the Secretary of State

CANTON, June 29, 1949—10 a. m.
[Received June 30—6:17 a. m.]

Cantel 664. Li Tsung-jen confirmed to me that there is renewed activity get him and Generalissimo together. If Generalissimo does not come Canton, he, Li, accompanied by Yen Hsi-shan, will visit Generalissimo either Taiwan or Amoy in near future. Meeting is further effort bridge gap between them and resolve difficulty. Li said Hsu Kan had brought some treasure with him when he returned from Taiwan last time and was at present back in Taiwan for more. With wry face, he admitted, however, that Pai Chung-hsi was short of funds pay his armies. He still had not funds sufficient pay for rations, latter half June. In explanation delay Pai counter-offensive, he said Pai was busy reorganizing armies in which, he said, there are too many divisions and not enough troops.

Sent Department, repeated Nanking 443, Shanghai 379.

CLARK

893.00/6–3049 : Telegram

The Consul General at Peiping (Clubb) to the Secretary of State

PEIPING, June 30, 1949—5 p. m.
[Received July 1—5:25 p. m.]

1099. Alien employee . . . this office June 17 forwarded personal letter Li Li-san noting consular connections. Li's secretary Sun Fa June 18 made appointment and called same evening. Sun stated Li very busy but glad to receive letter and offered transmit anything . . . might have to tell Li. . . . said merely desired pay respects whereupon Sun promised let him know when appropriate time. (. . . formerly attached Executive Headquarters [47] [and] knew Li [in] Manchuria.)

In discussing economics Sun emphasized that hesitation entrepreneurs to invest was due lack understanding principle mutual benefit to labor and capital. Said much remained be done to remove doubts and bring confidence. Sun admitted military developments were too rapid for political work to keep abreast and that shortcomings inevitable. Said that economic potentialities were greater than apparent and things would look better when new democratic government began function. By present Communist policy only privileged classes comprising minority were hit, with majority to benefit in time.

---

[47] Established during mission of General of the Army George C. Marshall in China, 1946–1947.

Queried re bitter feelings toward Americans who had sent so much relief goods needed by people, Sun stated that what Americans had done in words and deeds to Communists was thousand times more antagonistic than otherwise. Distresses of civil war were designed in USA and made in China and could not be redeemed simply by shiploads relief supplies. Communists had been unusually big-hearted towards Americans, considering serious blunders latter had committed and suffering caused. They harbored no hatred for American citizens but certainly were unable forget US Government's China policy of supporting Kmt to destroy the Chinese people.

Sun denied Communists had received more than moral support from Soviets. Said it was entirely due to people's own efforts that present successes had been achieved. Re status Dairen, Port Arthur, Sun said it was people's task make China independent nation with maintenance of sovereign rights, that any nation dreaming of colonies in China territory would be disappointed, that any nation thinking China had to rely on it for national reconstruction would be mistaken. (Note Sun evaded direct answer.)

In conversation June 27 ex-mayor Ho Ssu-yuan said that he had learned from source near Li Chi-shen that Communists had anticipated they would shortly be able establish relations with USA but that they had discovered that American side would demand as condition for recognition Communist respect treaty obligation. He attributed to this Communist realization recent recrudescence anti-foreign statements. Believe purported explanation invalid. Communists presumably desire appear strongly anti-foreign to Chi while perhaps trying mollify foreigners themselves with "explanations" incidentally designed cause powers adjust policies to Communist benefit. I believe Communists are worried by course events particularly by (1) their political isolation and probably continued Soviet exploitation of it, (2) continued refusal Nationalists surrender [(]Contel 1091, June 28 to Department [48]), (3) lethargy foreign and domestic trade and probably growing appreciation immensity economic tasks before them, (4) failure "imperialists" be harried by PLA advance. . . . told me some time back Communists fully expected Nationalist Government accept Communist peace terms April, had actually made arrangements for signing ceremony. Ho Ssu-yuan reports growing conflict ambitions in camp "democrats" particularly, and Communists' uneasiness at possibilities for development something akin old warlords, with Communist military leaders set up in high authority different areas.

Dutch Consul reports well-connected Chinese official was quick to reject suggestion first stage foreign relations would be on *de facto* basis, stating that would be unsatisfactory Communist side, relations would have to be *de jure*.

---

[48] Not printed.

Sent Nanking 765; repeated Department 1099, OffEmb Canton 191, Shanghai 733.

[CLUBB]

893.00/7–149 : Telegram

The Minister-Counselor of Embassy in China (Clark) to the Secretary of State

CANTON, July 1, 1949—noon.
[Received July 2—2:26 p. m.]

Cantel 677. Survey present overall picture Nationalist China leads to inescapable conclusion situation continues normal pattern of deterioration and that nothing really effective is being done by present Kmt leadership to prevent eventual Communist control of all China. Generalissimo apparently has released just enough treasure to keep government alive to maintain resistance on mainland. Nevertheless, there is only continued planning, no action. Only really positive effort is by each clique or section seeking its own safe haven. Cabinet seems weak and incompetent. Four weeks premiership doddering Yen Hsishan was marred in initial stage by Yen's pitiful efforts to scrape together cabinet which is still incomplete because of inability to find Foreign Minister or Minister National Defense. Yen himself has had assume latter post in what he calls his "fighting cabinet". His "fighting cabinet", however, has nothing effective with which to fight. Its troops are undisciplined, untrained and unpaid and Generalissimo has the money. Finance Minister has been going back and forth to Taiwan seeking funds from Generalissimo, but has only partially succeeded. It seems fantastic, yet it is true, that even though Generalissimo is in "retirement", government can only function at his will. "Fighting cabinet" has thus far accomplished nothing except attempting clever move "close" Communist-held ports and decision to bomb Communists strategic-objectives. Even bombing and strafing of *Anchises*, interception of *Star of Suez*, and abduction of Yangtze pilots in advance of "closure" deadline, only further emphasizes disintegration and indicates Canton government has no real control even over its own instruments when stationed on Taiwan under influence Generalissimo. "Supreme policy" committee so ardently sought by C–C clique, and finally agreed to by Li when Yen cabinet was set up, is still to be organized. It was so important to so many, yet nothing has been done.

Process of fragmentation continues. Some time ago Sinkiang declared its practical autonomy from Nationalist Government and now Yunnan has done likewise. Outraged howls of protest greeted proposals send troops Yunnan and provincial government has ceased forward to Canton any revenue, even that from maritime customs. Kweichow has issued formal notice that retreating troops and other refugees would definitely not be admitted within its borders. Szechuan shows increasing restiveness under threat move government Chungking and each province, including even Kwangtung, is setting up its own currency. Taiwan, of course, offers shining example of inability "central government" exercise its influence. Li Tsung-jen has toyed with idea unseating Taiwan Governor Chen Cheng, but, failing, we gather, to obtain unqualified promise of support from Sun Li-jen, has given up idea. They say Sun is not sufficiently forceful.

Li and Generalissimo are no closer together. From hill top at Kaohsiung and with occasional sallies to Taichung and Taipei, Generalissimo continues call turns through never-ending series conferences and visits leading officials from mainland. Generalissimo has made it known through emissary that he stands ready come Canton "when needed" and there is strong pressure from right-wing Kmt circles that he do so. We gather there are many party matters of importance that Generalissimo alone can decide. Bickering seems to have developed and Generalissimo's presence needed restore order. Li Tsung-jen told us several days ago in this connection that decision had not yet been taken, but that, if Generalissimo did not come Canton, he and Yen would go interior [*instead?*] and see Generalissimo. Knowing well that differences between him and Generalissimo are unbridgeable, Li nevertheless seems determined avoid any basis charge he unwilling cooperate. This attitude of subservience to Generalissimo may please right-wing Kmt, but it is alienating others. Am told authoritatively, for example, that resignation Chang Fa-kwei as ground forces commander was due solely to his disgust with Li's continued willingness compromise with Generalissimo.

Defeatism and despair continue. Public statements promising "final victory", "defense of South China", "fight to death", etc., still abound, but sound more hollow than ever and Yen Hsi-shan is reported have taken same suicide oath—minus poison—as in Taiyuan. Central Government continues issue periodic statement denying any move to Chungking or Taipei, yet its organs have already begun move both places by bits and pieces under guise of "establishing regional offices". Locally Hainan Island is fast becoming "little" as troops evacuated mainly from Tsingtao pour in with mission of eradicating Communists and establishing base of operations for Kwangtung provincial government which will evacuate Canton "when situation warrants." It is possible some futile attempt hold Canton may be made, but present developments indicate more likely central government will split and move part to Chungking and part to Formosa and that Nationalist troops will scatter or defect in time avoid Communist fire. Prize illustration of general attitude toward setting up central government in Chungking found in figures of departing legislators: Of well over 200 who left Canton, about 150 proceeded Taiwan, less that 10 Chungking.

Li–Communist deal? We suspect there is more to Liu Fei's interview with Li in Canton and Chu Chang-wei's two recent visits to Hong Kong, where three former peace delegates including Huang Shao-hsiung and Chang Shih-chao now staying, than polite inquiries into conditions in Peiping, but we lack proof any deal is in prospect. Both Li and Chu deny emphatically that any thing is in air. It seems conceivable nevertheless that in extremity Li and Pai Chung-hsi might consider agreement giving them temporary peace and security in Kwangsi. Li insists that lesson of Fu Tso-yi [49] has been taken to heart, but who knows? Li has mentioned to us Communist offer Pai during peace negotiation of command even more troops than he now possesses and Pai may not forget this offer when his troops have withdrawn to the confines of Kwangsi. It would be in Chinese pattern to recognize the inevitable and make the best of it.

Sent Department Cantel 677, repeated Nanking 453, Shanghai 390.

CLARK

893.001 Chiang Kai-shek/7–549 : Telegram

The Minister-Counselor of Embassy in China (Clark) to the Secretary of State

CANTON, July 5, 1949—3 p. m.
[Received 10 : 53 p. m.]

Cantel 689. President Li Tsung-jen tells me no meeting with Generalissimo has yet been arranged. In view Li's previous statement that if Generalissimo did not come Canton he and Yen Hsi-shan would visit Generalissimo, it would seem Generalissimo is the reluctant bride.

Sent Dept Cantel 689, repeated Nanking 462, Shanghai 398.

CLARK

893.00/7–649 : Telegram

The Ambassador in China (Stuart) to the Secretary of State

NANKING, July 6, 1949—1 p. m.
[Received July 6—6 : 34 a. m.]

1443. We owe to Mao Tse-tung vote of thanks for his article "On People's Democratic Dictatorship" as an unprecedentedly clear exposition of just where top leadership of CCP stands. Here, etched in clean sharp lines, is plan of how "science of Marxism-Leninism" is to be applied to Chinese society. Here also is expert presentation from

---

[49] Chinese commanding general in North China who remained in Peiping upon its occupation by Communists.

Marxian point view of Chinese history last 28 years. In light of recent development in China, we see no reason to try to read between lines or to attribute to Mao any different standards and goals than he has himself set. It seems to us, rather, that Mao is merely dotting i's and crossing t's of his previous writings, of political theory formulated in his "new democracy" and solidarity with USSR expressed in many important CCP pronouncements since release last November of Liu Shao-chi's article "On Nationalism and Internationalism". Threat and rationalization of police power is only theme not previously covered in CCP writings.

Article is replete with faith in righteousness of CCP crusade. Its principal tones are of unswerving allegiance to doctrine of world revolution by violence, of devotion to USSR as center of revolutionary power, of destructive hatred of all opposing forces, of absolutism and irreconcilability Communist creed with any other political or social theory. What are to us horrors of bloody struggle are to Mao and his associates only necessary, desirable surgery on body politic of China.

In references to use of police power and other organs of state compulsion, article shows how strong is influence of Stalinism on political theory that guides CCP. It is excellent rationalization for existence of police state. Mao shares with Stalin conviction that "all mankind has to travel along road of eliminating classes, state authority and party" at some time in distant future, as well as conviction that at present time "task is to strengthen people's state apparatus, which refers mainly to people's army, people's police and people's courts". In name of "people" it intends to base its authority on same totalitarian techniques developed in Russia. Even labor camps are foreshadowed by threat that if members of reactionary classes "are unwilling to work, people's state police compel them to work".

Short of unconditional promise to side with USSR in any war (which CCP pronouncements have so far avoided), article could not have aligned CCP closer to USSR. Contrarywise, it could hardly have demonstrated greater hostility toward western democracies. Solidity of alignment is shown by Mao's claim that although China's economic problems are so great that she has so far taken "simply first step in 10,000-mile long march", nonetheless, it is "childish" to think of receiving genuine British or American aid, because "internationally CCP belongs to anti-imperialistic front headed by USSR and can only look for genuine friendly aid from that front".

Manner in which Mao emphasizes to Chinese both within and outside party his conviction that no compromise is possible with west shows realization that there are great numbers of people in China, particularly among educated classes, who are not convinced Communism is only road, who aspire to make China bridge between US and USSR, who are unwilling to make sacrifices necessary to industrialize China in face of hostile west. Much of speech is devoted to refuting such views dear to heart of western-oriented Chinese liberal as importance of western-styled democracy, ties with US and Britain, independence from USSR, etc.; there is more than hint that people who expound such views will be considered "lackeys of foreign imperialists" and will be suitably punished.

Certain other aspects of article are also of interest. Style shows interesting similarities to that of Stalin, in use of question and answers, in way paragraphs overlap for easy readability, in simplicity of presentation, in its tailoring for unlearned, untrained audience. Admission that "young comrades who have just joined party and have not read Marxism-Leninism may not understand truth" regarding goal of classless society implies that CCP membership is far from well-indoctrinated unified organization it claims to be. That socialization or collectivization of agriculture with all its attendant disruptions and sacrifices is coming to China is indicated by assertion that "without socialization of agriculture, there will be no complete and consolidated socialism"; Mao's plans for countryside obviously go far beyond simple agrarian reform. As respects domestic economy, Mao states that "our present policy is to restrict capitalism and not eliminate it", thus implying policy will change as soon as conditions permit. Only passing reference to importance of foreign trade to China as opposed to emphasis devoted to necessity for China's industrialization and autarchic independence from western world once more demonstrates extent to which Communist leadership is guided by political rather than economic considerations. This leadership shows little fear of American economic warfare seriously retarding its progress. There could be no better evidence to correctness of conclusions of our Embassy Moscow in its telegram 1620, June 27 to Department, that long view is only view US Government and its friends in west can take on China and "that Mao is not for sale now".

Sent Dept 1443, repeated Shanghai 803, OffEmb Canton 611, Moscow 47.

STUART

893.00/7–649 : Telegram

The Minister-Counselor of Embassy in China (Clark) to the Secretary of State

CANTON, July 6, 1949—1 p. m.
[Received July 6—8:05 a. m.]

Cantel 691. Wu Tieh-cheng, Minister without Portfolio, is considerably encouraged by recent developments. Gimo, he says, will visit Canton this week and his presence here will be occasion for issuance statement solidarity signed by civilian and military leaders headed by Gimo and Li Tsung-jen. He, like many others with whom I have talked of late, takes comfort and certain sense security from fact Communist advance has been held up past few weeks due serious floods Hunan–Kiangsi. They read all sorts of things into delay : Communists are handicapped by uprisings in Honan–Hupeh–Anhwei areas; their troops are having difficulty getting acclimated to South China, there being sickness and lack accustomed food. He does not expect resumption Communist offensive until September and says at that time Communists will meet real resistance.

Wu says government has enough treasure to support monetary program for one year (they admit deficit 30 million silver dollars per month which makes Wu's statement sound fantastic).

Meetings are taking place in Taipei at present, he said, to determine military strategy. Principals at moment are Gimo, Tang En-po and Chen Cheng. Two months ago, he said, decision had been taken not to defend Kwangtung. Now however outlook was so much brighter, firm decision had been taken to defend Kwangtung and southeast coast. It was still undecided whether Fukien and Kwangtung would be placed under one command, with Kwangsi, Kweichow and Yunnan under another, or all 5 provinces under single command. (He ignores fact that neither Yunnan nor Kweichow will have any dealings this government.) Reinforcements were already arriving Amoy, Swatow and forces around Canton would be strengthened, he said. He spoke with assurance and gave picture of confidence that government would be able offer alternative Communism which would encourage further US aid. This connection, he said Kan Chieh-hou (Li man, of course) had gone US too soon. He should have awaited demonstration here that Nationalist government offered alternative Communism. When that happened he, Wu, would like visit US seek aid and hoped then aid might be forthcoming.

Wu expressed conviction that at last Li Tsung-jen has removed from his thinking any possibility of accommodation with Communists. He, Wu, had seen Liu Fei when latter visited Canton and he confirmed what Li told me, that Liu did not bring Communist proposal. He did however bring condemnatory letter from Shao Li-tze [50] to Li and preached abject defeatism, using many arguments to persuade Li and other[s] that their cause was hopeless and that they had better recognize the inevitable and make peace while peace was still possible. Obviously, although Liu brought no Communist proposals, he did bring Communist threat of dire consequences of further resistance. Nevertheless, the lull has created recurrence confidence.

Sent Dept. Cantel 691, repeated Nanking 466, Shanghai 401.

CLARK

---

[50] Member of Kuomintang peace delegation to Peiping.

893.00B/7–649 : Telegram

The Ambassador in China (Stuart) to the Secretary of State

NANKING, July 6, 1949.
[Received July 6—3 : 34 p. m.]

1447. Official *Hsin Hua Jih Pao* June 29 announces propaganda material to be used in celebration of liberation Shanghai, Nanking, Hangchow July 1–7. Main points are:

(1) July 7 marks Chinese people's great struggle against Japanese imperialism. Chinese people, PLA, fighting shoulder to shoulder with Soviet-led allied forces, smashed Kmt schemings and won victory for people. Thus victory over Japan belongs to people, not to Kmt reactionaries.

(2) US fostering of Japan is part of US imperialists' scheme to conquer world, monopolize world's resources, markets, US indefinite postponement of Japanese peace treaty threatens peace for entire world.

(3) Liberation of Nanking, Shanghai, Hangchow not only victory of Chinese people but of world's people and made possible through correct leadership of CCP.

(4) Establishment of PCC marks beginning of new China.

Sent Department 1447; repeated Shanghai 805, Embassy Canton unnumbered.

STUART

893.00/7–649 : Telegram

The Consul at Canton (Scott) to the Secretary of State

CANTON, July 6, 1949—4 p. m.
[Received July 6—6 : 47 a. m.]

217. Remytel 147, June 3.[51] Millet[52] returned July 5 from Amoy, not visiting Foochow due closer approach Communists now reported Shuikow 53 miles up river from Foochow and Lienkong 27 miles northwest Pagoda anchorage.

Uncertain if these organized columns from north or local Communist guerrillas but fall Foochow now widely believed awaiting only Communist initiative.

Amoy building concrete pillboxes desultorily. Crack troops still there except gendarmes starting depart for Taiwan. Return of house said reserved Gimo recently offered to Customs Commissioner. Certain of troops now at Amoy noted last month at Foochow; garrison contains both good and poor troops. Li Liang-yung, Fukien Governor last year, now commands Amoy garrison and forts.

See my telegram 218, same date, for evacuation data.[51]

SCOTT

[51] Not printed.
[52] Charles S. Millet, Consul at Shanghai.

893.00B/7–649 : Telegram

The Ambassador in China (Stuart) to the Secretary of State

NANKING, July 6, 1949.
[Received July 6—4 : 27 p. m.]

1448. Re Embtel 1447, July 6. Local *Hsin Min Pao* July 2 reports meeting of propaganda department preparing for celebration July 7 of liberation Nanking, Shanghai, Hangchow. Shih Hsi-min, department deputy director, instructed members to strengthen anti-US imperialistic propaganda, demand early signing of Japanese peace treaty, stress this treaty must have concurrence of USSR and "the new China", Chiang bandit group having no right to participate.

Sent Department 1448; repeated Shanghai 806; Peiping 256.

STUART

VI. INCREASE OF ACTIVITIES OF GENERALISSIMO CHIANG KAI-SHEK (PRESS INTERVIEW, VISITS TO CANTON AND CHUNGKING, ESTAB-LISHMENT OF PERSONAL HEADQUARTERS ON FORMOSA); VISIT OF ACTING PRESIDENT LI TSUNG-JEN TO FORMOSA; CONTINUING COLLAPSE OF NATIONAL GOVERNMENT'S MILITARY POSITIONS; POLITICAL ACTIVITIES IN COMMUNIST-OCCUPIED CHINA (JULY 8–SEPTEMBER 23)

893.001 Chiang Kai-shek/7–849 : Telegram

The Consul at Taipei (Edgar) to the Secretary of State

TAIPEI, July 8, 1949—3 p. m.
[Received July 8—7 : 51 a. m.]

274. Chen Cheng [54] yesterday told Steele, *Herald Tribune*, [that] Generalissimo [55] will go Canton next week to develop solidarity on basis recent manifesto. May go inland after Canton. Chen stated past defeats not due lack armies or matériel but lack will to fight. Foresees resurgence national spirit through Generalissimo's efforts.

Sent Canton 117, repeated Secretary of State 274.

EDGAR

_____

893.00/7–849 : Telegram

The Minister-Counselor of Embassy in China (Clark) to the Secretary of State

CANTON, July 8, 1949—6 p. m.
[Received July 8—11 : 36 a. m.]

Cantel 703. Chu Chang-wei [56] tells me Li Tsung-jen finally wrote Generalissimo saying he planned inspection trip Fukien, Taiwan,

_____

[54] Governor of Taiwan (Formosa).
[55] Chiang Kai-shek, who retired as President of the Republic of China on January 21, 1949.
[56] Secretary and political adviser to Acting President Li Tsung-jen.

Hainan and would like see Generalissimo en route. Generalissimo had replied saying he planned come Canton immediate future and would hope see Li then. Chu expects Generalissimo arrive Canton almost any day. Advantage will be taken Generalissimo's presence Canton to ask to organize "supreme policy committee" so dear to hearts C–C clique.[57]

Chu evinced considerable perturbation over Generalissimo's Taiwan statement to press,[58] inquired what State Department reaction had been to Generalissimo's remarks, and what reaction might be if Generalissimo resumed office. In reply I mentioned Secretary's statement [59] re Generalissimo's statement and stressed our disinterest in who might lead resistance in China so long as resistance is effective. I said we could not conceivably voice any preference between factions or leaders in Free China and that our hope was all would pull together.

With some bitterness Chu mentioned military conference Taipei held under Generalissimo's auspices and said planning future strategy was task Ministry National Defense, not Generalissimo. Nevertheless Generalissimo was determined Tang En-po [60] would command resistance armies SE China including Chekiang, Fukien and Taiwan, and Chu seemed think nothing could be done about it. He said Li Tsung-jen is determined Pai Chung-hsi [61] shall become Minister National Defense but is meeting resistance from Yen Hsi-shan [62] who, Chu says, is afraid of Generalissimo.

Although Chu expressed unfamiliarity with financial program, he understood gold actually being shipped from Taiwan to support program. This connection he said his estimate total Generalissimo treasure-trove is US dollars 300 million.

Discussing visit US Dr. Kan Chieh-hou,[63] I gathered Kan's report of his conversation with the President was not as forceful as would appear to have been warranted by the memo of that conversation supplied me by the Department.[64] When I told Chu of my recollection of the conversation, he asked if I could give him copy of memo as he wished make sure Li Tsung-jen had accurate report of what is in President's mind. I promised endeavor obtain Department's authoriza-

---

[57] Led by Chen Li-fu, Chinese Minister without Portfolio.

[58] *Infra.*

[59] When asked at his press conference on July 6 about the interview, the Secretary of State stated that the United States recognized the Chinese Government, an aid statute was "on the books", and the United States through the Economic Cooperation Administration (ECA) had been giving all aid that could be effectively delivered to China "at the present time".

[60] Former commander of the Shanghai area; subsequently Pacification Commissioner for Fukien.

[61] Military and Political Affairs Director for Central China.

[62] President of the Chinese Executive Yuan and concurrently Minister of National Defense.

[63] For documentation on mission to the United States of the Acting President's political adviser, see vol. IX, pp. 699 ff.

[64] June 22, *ibid.*, p. 708.

tion comply his request. If Department agreeable supplying Li copy memo, please repeat it to me by cable as my copy has been burned.

Sent Department Cantel 703, repeated Nanking 473, Shanghai 406.

CLARK

893.001 Chiang Kai-shek/7–849

Press Interview by Generalissimo Chiang Kai-shek [65]

Generalissimo Chiang Kai-shek broke his long silence on Monday [66] to declare his continued "revolutionary leadership" of the Chinese people, to appeal to the United States for support against Communism and to accuse the Soviet Union as a treaty-breaker bent upon world dominion.

The 62-year-old generalissimo, who retired from the presidency of China last January 21, but who has retained and strengthened his leadership of the Kuomintang,[67] party of original Chinese revolution, received two correspondents in a joint interview which may portend his imminent return to active leadership.

Generalissimo Chiang, who seemed in the best of health and spirits, chatted with the correspondents in polite brevity and reserved nearly all of his statements for publication to written answers that [had] been prepared to questions submitted in advance.

The Generalissimo's answers included his firmest language for publication thus far on the relation of the Soviet Union to Chinese Communism. With a simple "yes" he answered the following question:

"Do you feel that if Communist forces in China are not now checked the Communist movement will spread throughout Asia? Do you believe that this spreading Communist movement is part of a plan by the Soviet Union to dominate the entire Far East in a campaign eventually to dominate the entire world?"

The Generalissimo also had been asked to what extent the Chinese Communists serve the aims and interests of the Soviet Union, and what he considered those to be in China, Asia and the world at large.

"I would advise all persons interested in this question to read a document called 'Theses of the Revolutionary Movement in the Colonies and Semi-Colonies' adopted at the sixth world congress of the Communist International on December 12, 1928.

"This is the blueprint of Communist revolutionary activities in all of Asia, now being realized step by step. Lenin [68] stated that the road

---

[65] By Clyde Farnsworth, Scripps-Howard correspondent; copy transmitted to the Department by the Consul at Taipei (Edgar) in his despatch No. 33, July 8; received July 18.

[66] July 4.

[67] Nationalist Party.

[68] Soviet Premier who died in 1924.

to conquest of Europe lies through Asia. This policy of the founder and teacher of international Communism is now being pursued by his faithful followers."

Another question:

"Is there any chance in your opinion that Chinese Communism can or will develop along separatist, nationalist lines, irresponsive to the main currents of the international Communist drive toward world revolution? Is Mao Tse-tung [69] a puppet or a free agent? Can he be 'another Tito'?" [70]

Answer: "By the very pronouncement of Chinese Communist leaders as well as by the history of their party, there is nothing to indicate whatsoever that the Communist party in China may break with the center of International Communism, the Cominform, as Marshal Tito of Yugoslavia apparently did.

"The Communist party in China has on many occasions placed on record its full support to the Cominform against Marshal Tito. By a resolution of the whole party, it approved the expulsion of Yugoslavia by the Cominform.

"The latest proof is to [be] found in published articles by Liu Shao-chi,[71] chief of the organization department, and often considered second in command in the Communist party in China. These articles denounced Tito as a 'Traitor who joined capitalist camp.'

"Further, in those articles, Liu Shao-chi called on the proletariat in all countries to unite and join forces with the Soviet Union and Eastern Europe 'to inflict defeat on the plans of the American imperialists.'

"Any suggestion that the Chinese Communists might break with Moscow is insidious propaganda designed to confuse. Many years ago the Communists used to say that the Communists [in] China were not real Communists at all, but merely 'agrarian reformers.' They succeeded in confusing and misleading many people, to their own distinct advantage.

"This talk of Chinese Communism possibly taking a Tito turn is just one more of their propaganda tricks deliberately designed to mislead, and will prove as false and unfounded as their previous efforts to confuse.

"Were Communists permitted to dominate China, her relations with the outside world would be the same as those of other countries now behind the Iron Curtain. They could not possibly be any different."

Question: "There has been recently a great growth of concern abroad over the trend of events in China, but with it also has grown a fatalistic

---

[69] Chairman of the Chinese Communist Party (CCP).
[70] Marshal Josip Broz Tito, head of the Yugoslav State and Communist Party.
[71] Chairman of Communist All-China Federation of Labor.

conviction among many that the situation in China already is beyond repair and that the Communist conquest of China and perhaps of all Asia must run its course. Is it already too late for the United States to help? Will it ever be too late?"

Answer: "The area and population now under Communist domination are less than the area and population under Japanese occupation after one year of the War of Resistance in 1938. That war, as you know, went on for seven more years with increasing intensity until victory was won.

"The erroneous impression that the present situation is beyond repair has been created by Communist propaganda in disseminating defeatism.

"It is my conviction that all struggles for human freedom and nation[al] independence, as against tyranny and foreign domination, must succeed. I do not believe that efforts—either our own efforts or the efforts of friendly countries—to save the situation in China will be too late.

"However, if timely help is not given in China's anti-Communist fight, the price to be paid by the democratic countries in the future will be beyond comprehension. When Communism cannot be checked in China, it will spread over the whole of Asia.

"Should that occur, another world war would be inevitable. Therefore in view of this and of the responsibility of the democratic countries toward all peace-loving peoples, I must point out that further loss of time in checking Communism in China is decidedly dangerous."

Question: "Have the Communists won or can they ever win the mass support of the Chinese people in the areas of their military control? Do you believe that the National Government commands popular support there or in areas still beyond Communist conquest? If the Communists do not have popular support what are the chief causes of the Government's setback?"

Answer: "A reign of terror is holding the people in submission in Communist-held areas. Instead of popular support, the hatred of the people for the Communists is increasing. The Communists themselves have openly admitted that peasant uprisings have occurred and recurred in all areas under their control.

"The people under Communist rule are all hoping for an early restoration of the authority of the National Government. It is a matter of record that a large number of teachers, students, peasants and persons in other walks of life have fled from the Communist areas into government areas despite the difficulties and danger attending such flights. With the exception of a small number of political opportunists, no one cares to live under the Communist regime.

"As regards the causes for the setback of the government, other than military, there are two: First, nonfulfillment by the U.S.S.R. of her obligations under the Sino-Soviet treaty of 1945 [72] which was based upon the Yalta agreement.[73] As you know, China made a great sacrifice by signing that treaty.

"In spite of this sacrifice on our part, the U.S.S.R. has not observed her treaty obligations. This has not only prevented restoration of Manchuria to China but has also enabled the Chinese communists to develop a tremendous military force there.

"The second cause is economic. After the sufferings and tribulations sustained by the people during eight years of war against aggression, the country has been further impoverished by the rebellion of the Communists, accompanied by destruction.

"As a result, all of the Chinese people, such as teachers, public servants and soldiers, have been compelled to live for many years below the subsistence line. Many political ills have arisen out of this deteriorating economic situation."

Question: "How can China win this new War of Resistance? What help does she require? Can the National Government survive without foreign help? Do you expect a third world war?"

Answer: "The first step, it seems to me, is for the United States to reactivate its policy of giving moral support to the Chinese government in its fight against communism. This fight against communism in China is not only a fight for Chinese freedom from the present Communist menace but it is a fight for the peace and security of the free world, which doubtless is the very principle pursued by the United States in other parts of the world.

"The present Communist menace to China is a legacy of the last world war. I take it that the United States with which we fought together and bled together in that war will not be indifferent to what is going on in China, a former ally.

"Nor by her assumption of world leadership in the fight against Communism will the United States exclude China from the scope of her aid. Otherwise the future of the fight by the democratic countries against Communism will be gloomy indeed and the calamity for mankind will be irretrievable."

Question: "Is there even the slightest possibility now of a negotiated peace with the Communists?"

Answer: "From our experience with dealing with Communists for 25 years we have learned that it is impossible for anyone to reach a

---

[72] Signed at Moscow, August 14, 1945; United Nations Treaty Series, vol. x, p. 300.
[73] Signed February 11, 1945; *Foreign Relations*, The Conferences at Malta and Yalta, 1945, p. 984.

settlement with Communists. On this question there is no difference of opinion among members of the Kuomintang or of the government.

"I shall do my utmost further to strengthen the solidarity of the Kuomintang for the fight against Communism."

Question: "How do you construe your own present or future role in this struggle for China? Under what conditions, if any, would you return to active leadership of the nation?"

Answer: "Since my succession to the revolutionary leadership of Dr. Sun Yat-sen upon his death,[74] I have dedicated my life to the cause of the freedom and independence of the Chinese people. In that role I shall continue to carry out this important trust.

"With world Communism threatening to conquer China and destroy her independence and historic civilization, I consider it my duty to do everything I can in rallying all the forces to fight against it.

"Regardless of whether I hold any political office, I cannot give up my revolutionary leadership. That is to say, as long as the independence of the nation and the freedom of the people are not achieved I cannot shirk my responsibility of carrying on the struggle."

The questions for the generalissimo went through a double translation. From English they had been translated into Chinese for him several days ago. He perused them last week when he was not busy with the round of military and other conferences for which he came to Taipeh on June 22.

Over the week-end, the generalissimo's answers were recast in English and typed copies of them were handed out Monday as he and his visitors chatted over five o'clock bowlsful of cold-almond-flavored beancurd.

Generalissimo Chiang received the two correspondents, both Americans, in a mountainside guest house of the Taiwan provincial government at Tsaoshan, about 10 miles from the valley capital, Taipeh.

He asked his visitors to convey his earnest best wishes to President Truman, and, as one of the correspondents was from Tokyo, he asked that his felicitations also be passed on to General MacArthur.[75]

From his own small house at Tsaoshan, Generalissimo Chiang motored to the press meeting about a quarter of a mile uphill. But it was a bright, pleasant afternoon and so when the meeting was over he walked home at the head of a covey of bodyguards.

He wore a sun helmet and carried a heavy cane which he could have done without, for the Generalissimo is very spry and often goes strolling for exercise. He was dressed in a high-collared olive drab "Chung Shan" suit, the semi-military garb popularized by Sun Yat-sen for Kuomintang members, but he wore no insignia of any kind.

---

[74] At Peking, March 12, 1925.
[75] General of the Army Douglas MacArthur, Supreme Commander, Allied Powers in Japan (SCAP).

893.00/7–949 : Telegram

The Ambassador in the Soviet Union (Kirk) to the Secretary of State

Moscow, July 9, 1949—2 p. m.
[Received July 9—10 a. m.]

1719. Embassy finds instructive compare Mao's anniversary article (Embtel 1689,[76] and Nanking 1443 to Dept [77]) with *Ta Kung Pao* correspondent 1944 report on 23d anniversary celebration Yenan. Mao at that time made no reference Soviet Union, in fact, his 1942 statement to party school was quoted to effect record theoretical front would be considered bad if Chinese Communists ignored Chinese problems "seeing nothing other than volumes Marx, Engels, Lenin, Stalin".[78] Mao 1944 emphasis was on postponement socialization and indefinite nature proletarian dictatorship which would be instituted after Socialist revolution only if people desired.

Five years later Mao has no need adorn Communist dictatorship. He has outdone Kremlin in starkness regime he depicts. For this reason believe we should encourage widest possible dissemination Mao's words.

Sent Dept 1719, repeated Nanking 75, Shanghai 16, Canton 40.

KIRK

893.00/7–949

The Minister-Counselor of Embassy in China (Clark) to the Secretary of State

No. 26   CANTON, July 9, 1949.
[Received July 25.]

SIR: I have the honor to enclose in translation the "Joint Anti-Communist and National Salvation Manifesto" issued at Canton on July 7, 1949, twelfth anniversary of the opening of the War of Resistance against Japan, by leaders of political parties, noted educators, and scholars in Nationalist China.

This Manifesto was released to the public at a special press conference held at the Executive Yuan on the afternoon of July 6. The press conference featured speeches by two Kuomintang leading lights and by the chiefs of the Young China and Democratic Socialist Parties discussing the significance of this statement of unity. The Manifesto was stated to have been signed personally by a huge number of national leaders, including the Gimo, Li Tsung-jen, Bishop Paul Yu Pin,[79] Hu Shih,[80] etc., etc.

---

[76] July 6, not printed.
[77] July 6, p. 405.
[78] Marshal Josif Vissarionovich Stalin, Soviet Prime Minister and Chairman of the Council of Ministers of the Soviet Union.
[79] Of the Roman Catholic Church in China.
[80] Chinese Ambassador to the United States, 1938–42; former Chancellor of National Peking University.

This translation was supplied by the Information Office of the Executive Yuan.

Respectfully yours,   LEWIS CLARK

[Enclosure]

Translation of "Joint Anti-Communist and National Salvation Manifesto" Issued July 7, 1949

As an expression of solidarity top-level officials of the Chinese Government, leaders of the different political parties, and noted educators and scholars issue the following joint anti-Communist and national salvation manifesto on the occasion of the 12th anniversary of July 7th.

Twelve years ago today, the Chinese Government and people in order to safeguard the existence of the nation and to preserve the peace of the world undertook to launch an all-out resistance against the Japanese aggressors. After a period of bitter struggle the war of resistance was finally won. Four years have elapsed. During this period if the communists had truly appreciated the difficult task of nation-building and the magnitude of the sacrifices the people had made, and if they had demonstrated their patriotism by not indulging themselves in armed rebellion and by accepting the Government's program of peace and reconstruction, the earnest desire of the people to live and carry on their pursuits in peace would have been realised, the policy of the Government for the mobilization of the nation's manpower for purposes of reconstruction would have been put into effect, and China would have become now a unified, peaceful and prosperous country, contributing her due share to the security of the world and the welfare of mankind. Unfortunately, the Chinese communists taking advantage of the opportunity offered by the war of resistance and the weakened state of the nation undertook to expand their armed forces and to disturb national peace, thereby bringing to nought the fruits of eight years of war of resistance, and making the plight of the country more serious than it was twelve years ago.

We know too well, under Communist domination the country can have no independence, the individuals can have no freedom, there can be no improvement in the livelihood of the people, and Chinese culture and civilization must face extinction. The danger which confronts the nation today is in truth the greatest that has ever faced the nation in its entire history. With the fall of the iron curtain on the 450,000,000 people which will inevitably follow the communist domination, the stability of the Far East and the peace of the world will no doubt be disturbed. In view of the gravity of the situation we must present a united front and dedicate ourselves to the fight for freedom against the communists to the bitter end. What will our lives matter and what is the good of party differences should the nation perish? Our efforts must therefore be relentless and unceasing until our territorial integrity is preserved, until our national independence is guaranteed, and until our political and economic rights are maintained.

It is greatly to be hoped that our people will sincerely and fully cooperate with the Government, pool their resources, revive their spirit of the war of resistance and in a determined effort to subdue the present unprecedented crisis and to consummate the task of national salvation and reconstruction, carry our national front to a successful end.

893.00B/7–949

The Consul General at Peiping (*Clubb*) *to the Secretary of State*

No. 85   PEIPING, July 9, 1949.
                                             [Received September 19.]

SIR: I have the honor to enclose for the information of the Department a copy (in translation) of an editorial [81] published in the *Jen Min Jih Pao* (People's Daily, Peiping) on July 3, 1949, under the title "Struggle for Further Consolidation of the Party in North China," setting forth certain data respecting the North China (section of the) Chinese Communist Party.

Summary of article:

The total membership of the North China Party is 1,520,000 of whom .03% joined the Party during the 1921–27 period, .66% during the period 1927–36, 39.31% in 1937–45, and a full 60% joined the Party during the War of Liberation (that is, in the post VJ–Day period). The members who joined the Party during the Revolutionary and Civil War periods constitute the backbone of the Party leadership. However, the membership acquired during the War of Liberation is considered "the new blood of the Party." The majority of the membership came from the peasantry but "due to their very low level of culture and understanding of Marxism and Leninism" they often cause deviations in the prosecution of Party policies.

The 68,000 Party branches in North China are scattered throughout 68% of the total 100,000 North China villages.

With the liberation of all North China, the center of gravity of Party leadership has shifted from the rural countryside to the towns, and from military affairs to reconstruction. There therefore arise the problems of uniting Party members of the working class with those of peasant background, of uniting work-farmer cadres and intelligentsia cadres, of unifying urban with village cadres as well as Party with non-Party cadres.

To meet the development and needs of the revolutionary situation, the North China Party in the last three years selected over 5,000 members of regional cadres, most of whom were sent to Manchuria, Central China and regions south of the Yangtze River to undertake activities. Part of that group undertook work in recently liberated towns and dis-

---

[81] Not printed.

tricts in North China. There has resulted a quantitative shortage and qualitative weakness of cadres, especially in the hsien echelon in the North China areas. Since cadres of that echelon constitute the liaison between Party sectors and hsien committees and are an important link in carrying Party policies down into the lower stratum Party organs, there is before the North China Party the task of selecting and cultivating a large number of cadres. *End of Summary.*

One of the outstanding phenomena in recent political developments in China has been the notable shortage of adequately trained personnel and the parallel effort of the Chinese Communist authorities to train new personnel to take the place of the old. In the interim, strong efforts have been made to keep old personnel at their posts. Experience in Manchuria has shown that this is to be considered in main a training period in which new personnel will be trained and—once trained— the old personnel tainted by former close Kuomintang associations will be ousted.

Apprehension respecting the future based upon knowledge of developments elsewhere under Communist control, constitutes one of the main obstacles to the efficient operation of Government organs under present circumstances. It is obvious it is deadly for all initiative. The Chinese Communists have been reported as believing that they can afford in long-term planning to disregard the welfare, livelihood and ideology of all elements of the population presently more than forty years of age, the ultimate aim being to effect their complete replacement by a fully indoctrinated new generation. It is evident that such a philosophy must work in due course a considerable hardship upon large numbers of the population. Even though limited in application (as does not seem necessarily to be the case) simply to the bureaucracy, it still creates obstacles to the effective operation of the Communist machinery at a time when the utmost in effectiveness is gravely needed. As is of course well-known—being remarked in all publications and speeches given under Communist auspices—the task of overcoming those difficulties has been placed on the shoulders of the Chinese Communist Party.

Respectfully yours,	O. EDMUND CLUBB

811.91293/7–1149 : Telegram

The Minister-Counselor of Embassy in China (Clark) to the Secretary of State

CANTON, July 11, 1949—1 p. m.
[Received July 11—7 : 57 a. m.]

Cantel 709. Re Generalissimo's press interview from Formosa, reliably informed by other American correspondents who also sought interview unsuccessfully that apparently special considerations resulted choice INS [82] Handelman and Scripps-Howard Farnsworth. Handelman came specially from Tokyo to attend. Others had been turned down only few days before grounds Generalissimo in retirement. Seems possible suggestion originated Stateside, possibly Madame,[83] for interview with attention paid propaganda value there in China aid cause.

CLARK

711.93/7–1149 : Telegram

The Minister-Counselor of Embassy in China (Clark) to the Secretary of State

CANTON, July 11, 1949—2 p. m.
[Received July 11—7 : 14 a. m.]

Cantel 710. Chinese Government press and radio increasingly critical US policy toward China. Seized Olive's arrest [84] for instance as peg to blame wrong policy result refusing withdraw diplomatic personnel from Nanking and seeking trade with Communists.

Chen Tai-chu, head American Section Foreign Office, indicated to us this and other similar press comment directly attributable Chinese fear upcoming Department White Paper [85] be published. Impression received during conversation that more same type criticism our policy probable until decision reached on publication White Paper.

CLARK

701.9311/7–1149 : Telegram

The Minister-Counselor of Embassy in China (Clark) to the Secretary of State

CANTON, July 11, 1949—7 p. m.
[Received July 12—12 : 35 p. m.]

Cantel 714. During past week, we received unusual number requests visas Foreign Office officials assigned various posts US and on investigation learn Foreign Office had agreed issue diplomatic or official passports and give choice of post assignment abroad to any their employees who could pay own way to post and support themselves there indefinitely without receiving any salary or allowances from Chinese Government.

As soon as this information obtained, I approached Vice Minister Tung who stated all these people accepting such assignments as patriotic duty in order save Chinese Government funds and that all would

---

[82] International News Service.
[83] Madame Chiang Kai-shek.
[84] William M. Olive, Vice Consul at Shanghai ; for documentation, see pp. 1199 ff..
[85] For further documentation on this subject, see vol. IX, pp. 1365 ff.

work full time post of assignment. He stated only 10 such appointments would be made posts US, of which 7 have already obtained visas.

I pointed out obvious effect such procedure on those his own Ministry who could not afford "assign themselves abroad" as well as hue and cry bound to arise when other government agencies learn Foreign Ministry is taking such advantage its special position. I went on say that this, coming on heels Sun Fo case,[86] was bound make US scrutinize requests diplomatic and official visas much more carefully and that if large number requests for visas continued we would be forced to go into each case in detail and probably obtain individual clearance from Department before issuing visas.

Persons who obtained appointments under this arrangement generally very mediocre calibre . . . Tung states, however, their services needed at posts and unless given assignment abroad might go over Communists.

Rush to secure assignments abroad may be taken indication extent Chinese Government officials believe their own recent statements that situation South China now stabilized and Canton safe for indefinite future. Manner which Foreign Office dealing out diplomatic passports and assignments abroad also indicates utter venality many those official Chinese who continue approach US for statement "moral support".

CLARK

893.001 Chiang Kai-shek/7–1149 : Telegram

The Minister-Counselor of Embassy in China (Clark) to the Secretary of State

CANTON, July 11, 1949—8 p. m.
[Received July 12—1 : 18 p. m.]

Cantel 715. It seems to me visit Generalissimo [to] Philippines [87] marks definite change from "retirement"; receiving innumerable callers seeking his counsel in traditional Chinese pattern of loyalty to individual rather than to government or other institution. There was no need for him to direct, his mere suggestion sufficed.

Publicly he was giving Li Tsung-jen opportunity demonstrate, first, his ability negotiate peace, which failed, and later his ability govern remainder country, which also has failed except to extent Generalissimo has been willing assist. Li has tried valiantly make a success as Acting President, but he has lacked the forcefulness and the means. His realization of his inability act without Generalissimo has manifested itself in his constant willingness compromise. He came Canton

---

[86] The former President of the Chinese Executive Yuan had planned to join the staff of the Chinese Ambassador in the United States.
[87] For further documentation on this subject, see vol. VII, Part 2, pp. 1115 ff.

from Kweilin against advice some of his supporters largely in hope move would influence Generalissimo toward full support government. Since his arrival Canton he has demeaned himself in various ways seeking better basis for cooperation with Generalissimo, most recent one being his acceptance of Kmt [88] Supreme Policy Committee which, with Generalissimo [as] chairman, puts ultimate authority for Government China in hands Generalissimo and not in those of Acting President.

I sense at moment considerable perturbation in Li Tsung-jen camp over recent activities Generalissimo and feel Generalissimo has definitely decided publicly to resume power. (Several have inquired of me what our reaction would be to such an event.) This feeling, I infer, is based at least to some extent on fact that after long period during which publicity was shunned and even Generalissimo's whereabouts were kept secret, he has suddenly held conference Taipei to decide future military strategy; has given press interview stating determination continue leadership resistance Communism; has gone to Philippines without a "by your leave" from the government; (the government was not even informed that he had accepted Quirino's [89] invitation); and the evidence that he plans at "his" convenience come Canton assist inauguration Supreme Policy Committee which he will head.

Nevertheless I find it difficult believe Generalissimo will return to presidency this stage. There is no need for him to do so. He already controls air force, navy, and all organized land forces except those of Pai Chung-hsi, of the Ma's,[90] and possibly those in Szechuan, and he controls the purse strings. The government with an admitted deficit of 30 million silver dollars monthly cannot survive long without his largesse, and through his position as head of the Kmt, operating through the new Supreme Policy Committee, he can prevent that government from taking any action which he disapproves.

Although Generalissimo may take this occasion resume presidency it appears more likely we are coming to phase where he will be more openly and actively in control without actually resuming presidency. Whether Li will tolerate such a situation is another question. His actions so far would lead one to believe that he will. Whether we like it or not, therefore, we are likely have Generalissimo once more fully in control. He is the only visible leader who has any chance whatsoever at this stage of reviving the will to resist the Communist advance in China and we are going to have make the best of it.

Sent Department Cantel 715; repeated Nanking 479, Shanghai 412.

CLARK

---

[88] Kuomintang (Nationalist Party).
[89] Elpidio Quirino, President of the Philippines.
[90] Surname of Mohammedan generals controlling Northwest China (Ma Chan-hsiang, Ma Hung-pin, Ma Hung-kwei, Ma Pu-ching, and Ma Pu-fang).

893.00/7–1249 : Telegram

The Ambassador in China (Stuart) to the Secretary of State

NANKING, July 12, 1949—10 a. m.
[Received July 13—12:01 a. m.]

1482. ReEmbtel 1443, July 6 to Department. In conversation with Huang Hua [91] July 2, Philip Fugh [92] asked him what he thought of Mao's July 1 article "on people's democratic dictatorship". Huang replied that he thought spirit and principles were about same as Mao's speech of June 15 to preparatory meeting for new PCC.[93] Fugh disagreed on ground that June speech had softer tone and indicated more liberal foreign policy than July article which clearly stated there is no middle ground and that CCP [94] is unreservedly on side of USSR. To this Huang responded that Mao could not but talk in that vein. Against Fugh's insistence that two pronouncements are contradictory, Huang reiterated that he was unable to add any more. To Fugh's observation that Mao's article implied China will hereafter have relations only with USSR, Huang protested that Mao had said nothing of kind.

We have impression that Huang is disappointed by Mao's July 1 article in its foreign policy implication. We believe that his sympathies are with the so-called liberal wing led by Chou En-lai [95] and that he had been highly encouraged, optimistic by Mao's speech last month to preparatory meeting PCC. Unequivocal statement foreign–domestic policy contained in Mao's later article implied decline of "liberal wing" (if indeed such exists) and victory for pro-Soviet reactionaries led by Liu Shao-chi. While our local director of aliens affairs could not but defend July 1 article, his defense was without enthusiasm. Nevertheless, he will fall into line and we may expect more cautious, less cooperative attitude toward our problems and occidentals generally.

Sent Department, repeated Embassy Canton 622, Shanghai 827.

STUART

───────────

893.00B/7–1249 : Telegram

The Consul General at Shanghai (Cabot) to the Secretary of State

SHANGHAI, July 12, 1949—4 p. m.
[Received July 12—10:29 a. m.]

2717. Persistency and extent Communists' efforts to woo Mme. Sun Yat-sen reveals importance they attach to winning her active identifi-

---

[91] Director of Communist alien affairs office of military control commission, Nanking.
[92] Chinese personal secretary of Ambassador Stuart.
[93] Political Consultative Conference.
[94] Chinese Communist Party.
[95] Member of the Central Committee of the Chinese Communist Party and its Politburo.

cation with their cause—not only as widow of Dr. Sun (thereby providing symbolic reaffirmation to public of Sun's "approval" of Communist principles and pro-Soviet orientation) but also as widely popular liberal-humanitarian in her own right, and finally as a Soong sister [96] whose very fact of blood connection with Kmt's four families [97] invests her support with enhanced value and with opportunity for impressive display of truth Communists' contention that their cause commands a loyalty transcending personal and family ties.

May be recalled that Li Tsung-jen in connection attempts strengthen his peace bargaining position tried vainly win some approving gesture from Mme. Sun. Later as Communist occupation Shanghai drew closer she was reported pressed by various apprehensive quarters for her patronage as protective leftist cover for their enterprises. [Possibility?] of Generalissimo's including her in group of prominent pro-Communist suspects whom he pressured into removing to Hong Kong from Shanghai before Communist occupation was also rumored. She steadfastly resisted these various pressures and was reliably reported to be determined avoid political involvements and devote herself solely to her humanitarian work Shanghai.

Immediately following Communist occupation Shanghai, Chen Yi [98] honored Mme. Sun by what understood to be his first official call. This was followed by three telegrams June 6 despatched to her by All-China Women's Federation leaders, including Mesdames Chou En-lai and Feng Yu-hsiang,[99] KmtRC Chairman Li Chi-shen [1] and Democratic League leaders respectively felicitating her on liberation Shanghai and approaching realization of common "freedom and democracy" goals and indicating high esteem for her and implied hope for renewal personal association with her at Peiping. Mme. Sun's reply was reportedly to effect that she appreciated felicitations but unable visit North China for present as recuperating from illness in Shanghai.

On June 25 Teng Ying-chao (Mme. Chou En-lai) arrived Shanghai for visit which was publicly explained as for purpose medical attention but which two reliable sources state was to persuade Mme. Sun proceed Peiping to join pre-PPC meetings. First reports indicated Mme. Sun adamantly sick [opposed?] to these overtures. Pressure continued, however. On July 1 she attended Communist Party anniversary gathering where she was accorded special honor and contributed a speech hailing Communist Party leadership which in view her "indisposition" was read for her by Mme. Chou. Same procedure repeated

---

[96] The three Soong sisters were Mesdames H. H. Kung, Sun Yat-sen, and Chiang Kai-shek; their most prominent brother was T. V. Soong.

[97] Chiang, Soong, Kung, and Chen.

[98] Communist mayor of Shanghai.

[99] Madame Feng was the widow of the "Christian General", Marshal Feng Yu-hsiang.

[1] Leader of the Kuomintang Revolutionary Committee (KmtRC).

at July 7 Lukouchiao anniversary [2] gathering where the speech read for her by Mme. Chou warned foreign imperialists to "get out of China". (See Contel 2713 [3] for texts.)

Close American friend of Mme. Sun says he suspects that second speech was prepared not by her but by others. He believes that while Communists would never venture to employ rough methods force her comply with their wishes they are applying such steady "friendly" pressure that she is gradually weakening in determination to avoid political involvements and may quite likely go north before long.

Sent Department 2717; repeated Nanking 1526, Canton operational; Department pass Peiping 202.

CABOT

893.001 Chiang Kai-shek/7–1249 : Telegram

The Minister-Counselor of Embassy in China (Clark) to the Secretary of State

CANTON, July 12, 1949—9 p. m.
[Received July 13—12 : 45 a. m.]

Cantel 721. Li Tsung-jen camp is much perturbed over activities Generalissimo and there is elation among reactionary elements Kmt at prospect Generalissimo may assume more openly active role. George Yeh, Acting Foreign Minister, tells me Generalissimo and party have arrived back Taiwan and that Generalissimo is expected Canton July 16. Invitation to Generalissimo was sent by Chinese Ambassador [in] Manila to Foreign Office which passed it on to Generalissimo without comment. Acceptance was direct and government here was uninformed until after Generalissimo and party were airborne. In fact many big shots went military airfield Canton immediately upon receipt information Generalissimo was in air in anticipation Generalissimo was coming Canton. They later pretended to save face that he flew over Canton and communicated with them from plane by radio.

High-handed manner in which Generalissimo has acted of late, and particularly in this case, seems to indicate his lack of respect for Li Tsung-jen and Yen Hsi-shan government and to make more difficult Li's efforts to cooperate. Am becoming increasingly convinced Generalissimo now plans use Li Tsung-jen as figurehead much as former President Lin Sen [4] was used, with full responsibility for functioning government resting in fact with Generalissimo. In other words, he feels

---

[2] Beginning of undeclared war between Japan and China, 1937.
[3] July 12, not printed.
[4] President of the National Government of the Republic of China, December 1931 to August 1943, when he died.

that Li has had his chance, has failed, and that the interests of the Chinese people once again require the firm hand of the Generalissimo.

Belief rampant in foreign press circles here Li will not accede to any such plan despite fact he planned supposed survey trip to several coastal cities, Hainan and Taiwan whose real purpose was to be meeting with Generalissimo whom he was seeking out in view failure Generalissimo come Canton. It is now rumored that Li plans delay trip only until Generalissimo's arrival; that he plans spend 1 day with him in conference, then leave Canton ostensibly survey trip but actually to save face since Generalissimo coming really to give orders. Also, now reported that Kweilin added to tour and Li will make that last stop. He may well remain there if Generalissimo's role too active. Endeavoring to check this story but since it ties in with Li's usual facesaving moves, may well prove true and offer it only as unverified rumor today.

Sent Department, repeated Nanking 481, Shanghai 414.

CLARK

893.00/7–1349 : Telegram

The Minister-Counselor of Embassy in China (Clark) to the Secretary of State

CANTON, July 13, 1949—4 p. m.
[Received July 13—9 : 29 a. m.]

Cantel 729. Hollington Tong,[5] who insists he did not come Canton in connection Gimo[6] visit, tells me purpose Gimo's coming here is try iron out differences which have arisen among various leaders Kmt and those between himself and Li Tsung-jen. Tong says Gimo hopes persuade Li remain President and that he, Gimo, will give Li full support in that office. Nevertheless as head Kmt and as "revolutionary leader" Gimo feels he has certain responsibilities to rally support for continued resistance Commie advance. Therefore, after completing business Canton, Gimo plans visit Chungking, Chengtu and possibly Lanchow. Tong says there are many differences among leaders those areas which Gimo hopes to remove. He anticipates Gimo will then return Taiwan to "retirement".

Sent Department Cantel 729, repeated Nanking 485, Shanghai 418.

CLARK

---

[5] Director of the information department of the Kuomintang leadership office.
[6] Generalissimo Chiang Kai-shek.

893.00 Yunnan/7–1349

The Vice Consul at Kunming (Lutkins) to the Secretary of State

[Extracts]

No. 56   KUNMING, July 13, 1949.
                                               [Received July 27.]

SIR: I have the honor to report concerning a two-hour interview which I had with Governor Lu Han on July 9, 1949, in the course of which the Governor expressed his views on the present situation.

Summary—The Governor was optimistic about the prospects of the Nationalist troops holding South China for a period of at least several months and believed that the Central Government and its military leaders had resolved to resist the Communists to the last. In the event that the Communists over-ran South China, he considered it probable that the Nationalist forces would withdraw westward and continue the struggle from Yunnan, Szechwan, and the North-West. If this proved true, Governor Lu continued, the Provincial Government could do nothing but comply despite its own desire to remain aloof from the fighting and the general opposition of the Yunnanese people to the utilization of the province by the Central Government as an anti-Communist base.

The Governor regarded the National and Provincial troops presently stationed in Yunnan as quite sufficient to deal with the local banditry problem. He minimized the importance of Communist activity in the province, attributing local unrest entirely to the economic distress of the people; the most important factor in this respect, in his opinion, had been the crushing burden of the land tax on the peasantry during the last fifteen years. He explained that excellent pacification results had already been obtained following the abolition by the Provincial Government in March of conscription and the collection of land tax in kind, and that a more equitable land tax system was now being devised.

The Governor quoted figures which showed that the Provincial budget was now seriously out of balance, largely because of high bandit-suppression costs and the necessity for the Provincial Government to advance funds for the upkeep of the Nationalist troops in the province. The budget deficit was temporarily being met by loans from the Yunnan People's Development Corporation, but it was hoped that the Provincial finances could be satisfactorily adjusted within a few months when the province had been completely pacified, a revised tax structure had been instituted, and the collection of this year's land tax had commenced.

. . . .

Respectfully yours,   LARUE R. LUTKINS

893.00/7–2749

The Vice Consul at Chungking (McGeary) to the Secretary of State

[Extract]

No. 48   CHUNGKING, [July 1949.[7]]
                                                       [Received July 27.]

SIR: I have the honor to submit for the information of the Department and the Embassy a report concerning recent military and political information obtained by the Consulate. Sources contributing to this information include Wang Lin-chi, Governor of Szechwan, Wang Chuan, representative in Chengtu of General Hu Tsung-nan, Chang Tu-lun, Secretary-General of the Political Commission of the Southwest Military and Political Administration, Ho Pei-hen, Commissioner of Reconstruction of the Szechwan provincial government and local press reports.

I

General Wang Chuan, who is one of several representatives Hu Tsung-nan maintains in Chengtu for liaison and supply duty, stated to a representative of the Consulate that General Hu has a total of 400,000 troops in Shensi and Kansu but that only about 100,000 of these were on active duty. He asserted that those on active duty were adequate to hold their present positions and ultimately launch attacks to regain control of Shensi province. He readily agreed that the assistance of troops from Kansu under the control of Ma Pu-fang was very helpful but stated that Ma's forces would probably not be available for any purpose but the defense of the Kansu perimeter. He repeatedly emphasized that Hu had no intention of remaining permanently on the defensive. He stated further that replacements of personnel and supplies and equipment for Hu's army must come from Szechwan and that if this province failed to do its part then whatever happened would not be General Hu's responsibility.

It is very doubtful that much in the way of equipment will be available from this area, although foodstuffs and man power are available and will probably be furnished in proportion to the extent that the Central Government maintains firm control over the province. It appears increasingly likely that such control will be maintained with little likelihood of successful challenge from the groups previously reported as desiring autonomy and freedom of action to make whatever arrangements might be dictated by expediency without reference to any loyalty to the Nationalists.

News reports today indicate that Paochi, Shensi, which is a point commanding roads leading westward into Kansu southward into

---

[7] Written July 12 or later.

Szechwan and eastward toward Sian the capital of Shensi, is again in Communist hands. On two previous occasions the Communists have captured Paochi but have been unable to hold it. The forces of Ma Pu-fang are unwilling to allow them to remain in possession of Paochi because of the threat thus posed to Kansu, while Hu Tsung-nan's forces are similarly unwilling to permit Paochi's occupation because of the threat posed to Szechwan. Previously it has been Mohammedan troops from Ma's command which have counter-attacked and thrust the Communists out of Paochi.

If the Communists were able to retain a firm hold on Paochi it is likely that Szechwan would be more menaced than Kansu since the defenses of Szechwan are less formidable than those of Kansu and the capture of Szechwan with its resources of manpower and food supply would be of far greater use to the Communists than the capture of Kansu.

.   .   .   .

Respectfully yours,   STANLEY A. McGEARY

711.93/8–1549

Memorandum by the Ambassador in China (Stuart)[8]

NANKING, July 14, 1949.

NOTES ON A FUTURE AMERICAN CHINA POLICY

1. This should be free from any illusions as to the nature of Chinese Communism. The CCP is thoroughly imbued with the Marxist-Leninist doctrines of the historical necessity of world revolution through violence, of promoting this through the cooperative efforts of the CPs in all countries in close allegiance to the USSR, and of the ultimate goal of a classless society in a completely communized world in which all capitalist or "imperialistic" governments will have been overthrown. Chinese Communist Party discipline and popular indoctrination have been to this end thorough and effective to a degree unknown heretofore in China.

2. Full account should be taken also of the passionately nationalistic element in all of CCP teaching and practice. With many of its more liberal leaders and educated followers this is perhaps the more powerful motive, the CCP and its technique being considered the best vehicle for ridding the nation of its semi-colonial backwardness and making it strong and self-reliant. Mao Tse-tung and his contempo-

---

[8] Memorandum transmitted by the Ambassador in person to the Department upon his arrival from China and mentioned on August 11 in a conversation with the Secretary of State; copy forwarded to the Secretary of State on August 15 by the Director of the Office of Far Eastern Affairs (Butterworth).

raries began their careers in the period of nascent nationalistic consciousness and most of them have never lost these convictions. The Kmt also owes its inception to the same impulse. It must be recognized that this is an essential element in the development of a modern Chinese state and will continue to exert a strong appeal, particularly to students and intellectuals. Unless converted wholly to the Soviet pattern of internationalism, such as preached by Liu Shao-ch'i, it need not work to our disadvantage. While protecting our national interests, we should seek to avoid placing ourselves in the position of apparently blind opposition to manifestations of Chinese nationalism and to emphasize our traditional role as champion of legitimate Chinese national aspirations, portraying Russia in its traditional role of suppressor of those aspirations.

3. A third factor is the social awakening of which the CCP is the most articulate and dynamic expression. This had already asserted itself in such movements as the Taiping Rebellion,[9] the Sun Yat-sen Revolution,[10] etc., to which the CCP claims it is in the succession, and in numerous less conspicuous processes. Disillusionment over the Kmt for having neglected this feature of its avowed program has been perhaps one of the most potent influences in sending idealists over to the CCP whose emphasis has been upon economic justice and amelioration for the masses rather than upon political liberty. It is imperative that we bear constantly in mind the fact that Chinese intellectuals and progressive forces have been hostile to our policy of aiding the Nationalist Government because they feel that thereby we sought to block Chinese national and social progress to our own selfish advantage. The failure of our aid program must in some measure be ascribed to this opinion so often expressed and so deeply felt by many Chinese intellectuals and progressives.

4. Whether any form of American military aid or other intervention would at any stage have altered the course of events for the better is now an academic question. Further American aid or intervention in the foreseeable future is impossible; is seems conceivable at the moment only if the ability of the Kmt or other non-Communist power to resist were miraculously to revivify, or if the Communists should so trample on American rights and interests as to bring American public opinion to demand action against them.

5. A situation has now emerged in China, analogous to that already reached in Europe, in which the conflict will be one of ideas and the consequences of these for human welfare. We Americans ought to welcome this comparison of ideologies, freed from most of the factitious features which have hitherto distorted the issue in China. Our leadership in world affairs is not merely a matter of dispensing money

---

[9] 1850–1865.
[10] 1911–1912.

and munitions. We have an experimental faith in the philosophy which underlies our political and economic institutions. Communists in China and elsewhere cannot be convinced by argument, still less by any reliance on their own brutal tactics of suppression. They too must learn by the empirical way. This may take a long time.

6. In the present circumstances, perhaps the nearest to an ideal solution of China's ills from the American standpoint would be a true coalition composed of one-third CCP, one-third KmtRC, and one-third "democratic elements" with each having equal authority and responsibility. That being out of the question, the next best would be the strengthening of the non-Communist democratic elements which will participate in the Communist-dominated coalition government. While we are not sanguine that they will be effective to any important degree, their strengthening and continuing struggle for independence as political parties within the coalition may tend to adulterate or modify extremist CCP doctrines or at least their current tactical application. Furthermore, the force of circumstances and the enormous inertia of Chinese society over a period of time may tend to debilitate the undeviating orthodoxy presently avowed by CCP leadership. Although the extent to which we can influence CCP members themselves is strictly limited in an anti-American police state, nevertheless we should be alert for opportunities where we might by pressure, education or personal contact strengthen the more liberal wing of the CCP against the uncompromising Stalinists. However, mere needling or ill-considered sanctions against Communist China may well result in strengthening the extremist wing of the CCP against the more moderate elements.

7. The essence of American concern over the course of events in China is not the volume of our trade, nor even the maintenance of our much larger cultural activities, but the threat to world peace. It is conceivable that a Marxian type of government may be established which permits a measure of continued commercial and cultural intercourse. Or our merchants and missionaries may alike be forced to leave the country. These considerations are of great importance to certain elements of the American people. But the aggressive quality in the CCP program is the paramount issue. That this is not mere doctrinaire orthodoxy may be seen in the current slogan involving our policy in Japan.

8. The outlook is not by any means as hopeless as might be assumed. In reply to the charge of the failure of our recent policy it might even be admitted that we are learning by trial and error and argued that this has not been entirely wasted. There is an immense reservoir of friendly feeling all over China toward the USA and it will take much insistent propaganda to obliterate this. There is also an instinctive fear of the USSR and dislike of Russians personally. The Chinese social

tradition is against excessive regimentation such as the CCP is compelled by its tenaciously held theories to enforce. It may well be that they will yield to their environment and become so diluted by this that we have nothing to fear or that they will continue true to form in which case they will inflame the innate resentment at such treatment which is already showing itself. There are also geographical and sociological factors—the long coastline, the distinctive Chinese cultural heritage, etc.—which will militate against the totalitarian methods of a police state. But the fundamental problem—as the CCP itself realizes—will be economic. This cannot be solved merely by arbitrary confiscation and division of land. Public opinion in China as to whether a government is good or bad is determined by the price of rice. China will be a significant laboratory for the application of peculiarly Russian terminology and techniques to a radically different civilization.

9. In facing this situation one of our two principal instruments is *publicity*. This is one which the CCP has from the outset employed most effectively. From village classes and political indoctrination of troops and workers to scholarly periodicals and worldwide broadcasts, it uses propaganda with unremitting zeal. This propaganda is unscrupulous and crassly one-sided, but also extremely intelligent and over a period of time probably effective. As Americans become aware of the crucial importance of this tool, we should strive to develop it to the point where the impact of our publicity on the people of China is greatly increased. We have the advantage of needing only to purvey the facts—chiefly about the USSR, our historic treatment of China, our efforts for world peace, etc. We have the further advantages of Chinese skepticism of the news available in Communist China today, Chinese eagerness to hear and willingness to believe news from the outside, and the moderate cost of an intensive use of radio, printed matter, etc.

The great obstacle to increasing our information activities within Communist China is, of course, the determination of the authorities to limit access to news to official sources. So long as it may be possible to do so, we should print in the Chinese language and distribute in large quantities throughout Nationalist China a wide variety of material supporting our point of view and refuting the distorted accusations of the CCP. Much of this material will eventually find its way across the lines. Furthermore, because of the expansionist nature of Communism, and our desire to contain it within the borders of China, we should immediately and substantially expand USIS activities in all Southeast Asian countries. In this area, where there are large Chinese minorities, we should put out huge quantities of printed material in the Chinese language. In this way we can not only work to counteract the CCP's efforts to use these minorities as fifth-columns in the countries where they reside, but also may be able to get a certain amount of the material into China proper. The CCP will not be able to seal the country off from its Chinese minorities abroad, nor will it be able to control their sources of information as it does for residents of China proper. In our propaganda in these areas we should particularly play up the aggressive activities of the USSR in China.

10. The second instrument we have is the powerful *economic* one. Foreign trade and economic assistance are far more important to urban and other modern segments of China's economy than in many countries, and Sino-American trade is vastly more significant to China than to the United States. Already apparent domestically are the effects of cessation of trade in the great port of Shanghai and the permanent stoppage of ECA [11] inward shipments of sorely needed relief and other supplies.

At the same time, however, we must never overlook the deep-seated doctrinal repugnance to the CCP of compromising political principle in exchange for economic assistance. To hurdle this our action must be properly timed, and it must be incisive. To adopt economic sanctions or retaliatory US tariff adjustments at present would be largely a wasted gesture because of the current stagnation of China's foreign trade. To show our willingness to trade with CCP-controlled areas (on a purely commercial basis), even to permit the initiation of such trade, and then decisively to control it at the time when the effect would be most telling would seem the wisest policy.

Our policy must be sufficiently thorough to counter the traditional Chinese tactic of playing off one interest or nationality against another. Additionally, it must be made transparently clear to the CCP just what particular *quid pro quo* we are seeking. The policy as a whole should also be remarkably flexible so that, clearly sighting our strategic objective, we can move tactically as the situation warrants. The success of our tactics would probably depend in large degree on American determination to make non-vital commercial and individual interests secondary to the broad objectives of national policy.

The use of the economic weapon should not be tied too closely to the question of diplomatic recognition, for we should remain free to employ it after as well as before any possible recognition. We must also guard against too obvious use of this weapon for political purposes, against seeming to be bluntly hostile or vindictive or in any sense imperialistic. There are many ways in which the Chinese people can be educated to the reciprocally beneficial nature of trade, the advantages of multilateral commercial intercourse in the modern world, and our readiness to continue our help if given the proper conditions. These are subjects in which the Chinese are apt pupils. Sooner or later the CCP must face up to the issue of either fanatically clinging to a foreign ideological theory or of satisfying as best it can

---

[11] Economic Cooperation Administration.

the economic necessities of a socially awakened and probably better informed, less docile people than the Russians.

11. In view of the widespread interest in the matter of the recognition of the Chinese government now forming, it may be advisable to prepare an educative campaign for the Chinese people as to what this involves. At the same time it would be well for us to prepare a series of trenchantly incisive questions to be put at the right time to the new coalition government. These questions would be concerned with such matters as the declared sympathy of the CCP with insurgent minorities in Southeast Asian countries and its implied intent to assist in the violent overthrow of the governments of these countries; assurances of equal treatment for foreign nationals and interests in China; the attitude of the new government toward basic human rights and freedoms; recognition of normal obligations imposed on a state by international law, etc. It would be desirable to develop these questions in consultation with other interested governments and possible in some relation to the United Nations.

12. An attitude of indifference or unconcern should be cultivated, letting it be transparently clear that China needs intercourse with other countries, especially the United States, more than they need commercial and other relations with China. We must understand, however, that the Communists, in their present mood, are fully prepared to do without anything they cannot get from the West on their own terms. They will not hesitate to force the Chinese people to undergo severe privation in order to attain their goal of a socialized China, free from Western influence. They are probably counting heavily on playing off one Western power against another in order to satisfy their vital needs. There is doubtless a point at which popular discontent and lack of progress in their industralization program, combined with friction with the USSR, may force the Communists to adopt a more reasonable attitude toward the West. We do not know what that point is. Consequently, we should not place undue hope in an early change in CCP policy. The chief virtues for us to exercise at present are perhaps patience, self-restraint and reserve—fortified by firmness of purpose.

J. L[EIGHTON] S[TUART]

893.00/7–1549 : Telegram

The Consul at Tsingtao (Hawthorne) to the Secretary of State [12]

TSINGTAO, July 15, 1949—3 p. m.
[Received 11 : 35 p.m.]

340. Establishment local people's court July 11 and completion takeover various government organs by Communists ushered in pe-

---

[12] Text printed from corrected copy received July 17, 6 a.m.

riod of uncertainty for all but Communist adherents of long standing and many people now fearful their lives. Lot of masses not only unimproved but all classes economically worse off than ever. Shantung Peninsula faced with famine owing lack rain and conscription young men. Taxes in interior even higher than imposed by Nationalist regime, excuse being necessity liberate all China. First hand report indicates economic conditions Tsinan deplorable.

Consequently people rapidly being disillusioned and anticipated underground resistance, so far unimportant, will grow. In fact believed only by Gestapo methods, to which Communists do not appear averse, can CCP hope retain power in Shantung.

Sent Department; repeated Nanking 227, Shanghai 139.

HAWTHORNE

893.00B/7–1649 : Telegram

The Consul General at Shanghai (Cabot) to the Secretary of State

SHANGHAI, July 16, 1949—8 a. m.
[Received July 16—2 : 28 a. m.]

2796. As I prepare leave China, I present for what they may be worth following thoughts re basic policy problem confronting US in China:

1. Essential question is whether Chinese Communists can operate independently of Kremlin. In Eastern Europe, except Yugoslavia, Communists cannot so operate, any leader who tries such course is promptly eliminated by orders from Kremlin. I am inclined think Kremlin does not have that power now in China. Despite friendly and close links with Soviets and despite ever more vociferous statements indicating Chinese Communists will slavishly follow Kremlin lead in international affairs, there is considerable evidence that even now Chinese Communists do not always see eye to eye with Kremlin and conceal this, if at all, only because they have easier and more important matters to attend to.

2. If Chinese Communists can make independent decisions, their eventual cooling off towards Soviets seem[s] probable. Even Chinese Communists cannot indefinitely gloss over gross evidence of Soviet imperialism on Chinese soil, their laughable attempts [to] explain them away show how much they irk even now, and as pressures from "Western imperialism" diminish, explanations will become even more absurd.

3. Chinese Communists are by no means monolithic bloc favored by Soviet theorists. We have ample evidence of fissures flowing from personalities, issues, regional differences, et cetera.

4. Our problem then is to prevent Soviets from getting firm control of Chinese government before natural forces cause it to split from

Soviets. Problem is formidable, because apart from core of Kremlin stooges among Chinese Communists who know what they want when others don't, there are undoubtedly many (as in Eastern Europe) who will unwittingly play Moscow's game till it is too late. Nevertheless, inherent factors are even more favorable to West here than they were in Yugoslavia because:

(a) Chinese Communists [are] even less beholden than Tito [to] Soviets for attainment present position.
(b) Chinese Communists less dependent on Soviets than Tito.
(c) Yugoslavs Slavic whereas China has own civilization with almost inescapable Western links.
(d) Russia historically and today imperialist threat to China, whereas traditionally friend and protector of Serbs.
(e) Despite Chinese Communist pronouncement, Chinese Communism today in practice resembles Soviet Communism scarcely more than Taiping dogma resembled Christianity. (However, these differences with Soviet Communism may well be deceiving.)

5. It is clear that a Communist-dominated regime is to control China and that there is no force now discernible which might challenge this control. If any regime more responsive to our viewpoint is to arise in future, it will probably stem from ranks now Communist rather than Nationalist.

6. Most serious threat Communists must now face is economic rather than military or political. Cumulative effects of over-population maladjustments, prolonged warring, Kmt corruption and incompetence, continuing inflationary factors and nationwide crop deficiency are being aggravated by blockade, continuance of civil war, and fact that Communists unlike Nationalists have no fat on which to draw. These factors coupled with Communist inexperience with urban economics, doctrinaire approach, long isolation and suspicion and hesitancy in accepting outside expert advice are swiftly forcing China's economy, with vortex at Shanghai, towards disaster. This may well force new authorities to take drastic action involving fundamental decisions of vital imports of [*importance to?*] foreigners.

7. In its foreign aspects, such new action line can hardly fail to be in one of two general directions (opposing urges towards each of which have already been discernible in Communist utterances and behaviour):

(a) That of gaining Western economic technical cooperation in solving crisis—which of course would necessitate exploratory friendly advances (presumably very cautious at start), readiness for compromise and moderation of intensely suspicious belligerent attitude towards foreigners.
(b) That of rejecting concept of cooperation with West as impossible and proceeding to uproot all Western activities and interests in China. Economic disadvantages this course might be partly counterbalanced by:

(1) Plundering of Western capital through labor excesses, wages and other impositions, hostage tactics and downright confiscation.

(2) Exploiting to full possibilities of turning popular resentment over economic distress against foreigners rather than authorities as scapegoats.

8. I have little doubt Chinese Communists would emotionally prefer follow second course. Nevertheless, it is clear their basic policy is to make substantial concessions to first course. Motives for this are probably varied and mixed; any Communists despite past Western arrogance and imperialism, and American aid to Nationalists, would doubtless genuinely welcome better relations with West; others consider them necessary on a hard-headed economic basis; and yet others probably want milk West of everything possible before deliberately squeezing Western activities in China dry. Difficulty is, however, that basic policy considerations are being overridden by inexorable contradictions in Communist doctrine (for example in attitude towards foreigners) and by insoluble problems (Shanghai economics). Considerable unrest and discontent is already evident in Communist-held areas which Communists obviously reluctant curb with too heavy hand. With economic situation deteriorating, their difficulties likely grow.

9. Under these circumstances, course ultimately followed by Chinese Communists may well depend in large measure on course adopted by West. In this connection, it is well to remember that Yugoslavia was definitely committed to Soviet economic bloc; China as yet does not seem to be. If Communist moderation and tentative pro-Western moves are met by rebuffs, further pressures, trade limitations, and vitriolic publicity (corresponding to Communist propaganda which has done such harm to their relations with West), then Communists are likely to reason that *modus vivendi* with West is impossible, and advocates of that course have likely to keep silent or be driven from power. Given Communist ideology and emotions, advocates of moderate policy must be in position to show positive results if they are to get anywhere. On other hand, too yielding a policy on part of West may convince Communists they can get what they want without making any real concessions; that Westerners will accept anything to make profits.

10. If West pursues a course of positive hostility to Chinese Communists, this may so undermine shaky economy of Communist-held areas that regime will eventually collapse. But if any such course is pursued we must realize not only that it implies end of Western activities in Communist-held areas and confiscation of Western property, but also that it will endanger life and freedom of every Westerner in these areas. We must also remember that real solidarity among Western nations under those circumstances is improbable.

11. In light of above considerations, I feel we should get all Americans we can out of Communist China as soon as possible. This should bring issue to head before situation has reached climax, should give Communist leaders pause and in long run will, I hope, diminish dangerous issues rather than increase them. Principal complication I see from policy standpoint is that British and French because less exposed and more heavily involved are willing to accept humiliations and dangers to greater extent than we.

12. There are of course other issues regarding which Communists will yammer even if we withdraw from China: Korea, Japan, Formosa, Hong Kong, French Indochina, et cetera. Nevertheless, the less pledges to fortune we have in China proper, the tougher we can be on those issues. Moreover, they should not have quite same appeal to populace, and we should therefore be in better position to mount a counteroffensive re Russian imperialism in China.

13. The fewer Americans and American interests on which Communists can exert pressure, the better position we shall be in to sit back and wait for Chinese Communists to come to us. Nothing I should imagine would suit our purposes better than to have Soviets sucked into Chinese [situation?] economically; catastrophic economic situation here would prove costly drain on Soviet economy, and Chinese Nationalism should make it thankless task.

14. To get out of China now may therefore paradoxically prove best means of accomplishing our fundamental purpose of causing a split between Soviets and Chinese Communists. It would be somewhat expensive and it might well result in permanent diminution of our influence in China. On other hand, it would give us better chance to sit with dignity on sidelines, not necessarily needling Communists, but denying them many things they want badly.

15. If Communist[s] want decent relations with West, proposal to withdraw Americans from China will show them they can have such relations only at reasonable price. If they do not, Americans should not be here.

16. In larger sense as I see it our ability to sit it out and make it clear to Communists they are losing far more than we through bad relations will be greatly strengthened if important business and missionary interests are not pressing for appeasement. By avoiding provocation yet making it clear Chinese Communists can't have what they want without meeting reasonable terms, Chinese should eventually come to realize Communists are authors of their misfortunes and even Communists may realize this too. In meantime I should imagine that Chinese Nationalist sentiment plus economic misery both deftly stimulated by propaganda might well produce change in Communist policies, splits among Communist leaders, or even successful revolt against Communists. Any of these developments would presumably

promote a China independent of Soviets in international affairs, which I conceive to be supreme aim of American policy in China.

Sent Department, repeated Nanking 1575, OffEmb Canton 888.

CABOT

893.001 Chiang Kai-shek/7–1749 : Telegram

The Minister-Counselor of Embassy in China (Clark) to the Secretary of State

CANTON, July 17, 1949—4 p. m.
[Received 9:47 p. m.]

Cantel 752. According Chu Chang-wei, political advisor Li Tsung-jen, Li still doesn't like Generalissimo visit Baguio, but is inclined let matter drop as water over dam. Chu says Generalissimo reports no military alliance contemplated primarily because he said some Philippine commitments US. Agreement, if possible, will be in political and economic fields with idea unifying and fortifying resistance Communist advance Far East. Wu Tieh-cheng's visit Japan is in this connection and he will go on to Korea.

Chu says differences between Li and Generalissimo remain, but that Li is determined do everything reasonable get together with Generalissimo in unified resistance. Li insists, however, that Pai Chung-hsi be appointed Minister National Defense, saying Yen Hsi-shan is too old and has too much else to do. George Yeh [13] will likely be appointed Foreign Minister.

Chu thinks Generalissimo may remain Canton [14] possibly week longer iron out many party difficulties. Supreme Policy Committee has definitely been agreed to and will hold its first meeting any day. It will replace Central Political Committee and Central Executive Committee as organ through which Kmt will control government. Chu says even though Generalissimo camp will have large representation, Li feels his ideas will receive more consideration in smaller body of which he is vice chairman than they have had or might be expected to receive in the larger CPC and CEC.

Am seeing Wang Shih-chieh [15] tonight and will report further.

Sent Department Cantel 752; repeated Nanking 498; Shanghai 427.

CLARK

---

[13] Vice Minister for Foreign Affairs.
[14] He arrived at Canton on July 14, 1949.
[15] Former Chinese Minister for Foreign Affairs.

893.00/7–1849 : Telegram

The Consul at Shanghai (McConaughy) to the Secretary of State

SHANGHAI, July 18, 1949—9 a. m.
[Received July 18—3 : 46 a. m.]

2808. Analysis various eyewitness accounts of victory parade celebrating Double Seventh Sino-Japanese War anniversary and "liberation" Shanghai appears justify following observations:

Official press estimate 1,300,000 marchers (300,000 PLA [16] troops and 1,000,000 workers) exaggerated by at least 50%. Claim to be largest parade in history Shanghai believed correct, however.

Owing fear Nationalist air attacks, main parade was held July 6 (instead July 7 as originally announced) at very short notice and in pouring rain. Despite these handicaps, show as whole (military display floats, singing, dramatic sketches, dances, etc.) was well organized and staged, drawing popular response which, while not boisterous, certainly exceeded usual reaction Kmt parades. Several observers noted genuine enthusiasm among poorer elements over their "First People's Army". In richer sections such enthusiasm lacking. Parade of workers (many of whom were ordered to march) and crowd's reaction thereto were relatively apathetic.

While anti-foreignism was manifested in form of slogans displayed and shouted and few floats (associating Uncle Sam with Kmt four families and Japanese), it was given only secondary emphasis. Noteworthy was fact that despite prolonged heavy concentration of paraders in Bund next ConGen and of fact that ConGen was then being picketed by ex-Navy employees,[17] there were no hostile demonstrations toward US.

As confirmed by Assistant Military Attaché, troops' equipment was over half American, including virtually all trucks, all (45) tanks and probally all artillery (105 Howitzers). Official *Chieh Fang Jih Pao* reported proudly:

"First regiment of corps was entirely equipped with American made Thompson guns. With 20 rocket guns taking lead, parading troops carried with them American-made light machine guns, heavy machine guns, anti-tank guns, trench mortars and stretchers. Second regiment of corps was entirely equipped with Japanese-made arms, while third regiment had American-made rifles, machine guns and artillery pieces."

Demonstrations as continued on July 7 included parades on smaller scale, dragon boat racing, mass meeting and opening of exhibition pictures, one series of which depicted "participation in world peace convention of Chinese liberationist delegates".

[McCONAUGHY]

---

[16] Communist People's Liberation Army.
[17] For further documentation on this subject, see pp. 1155 ff.

894A.00/7–1849 : Telegram

The Consul at Taipei (Edgar) to the Secretary of State

[Extract]

TAIPEI, July 18, 1949—9 p. m.
[Received July 18—12 : 29 a. m.]

292.

. . . .

Wu [18] asked if I could obtain confidential US reaction to program since success or failure depended ultimately on US assistance. He stated inner group of which he was one (and I suspect leader) was constantly working for improved internal conditions to supplant Chinese maladministration and corruption. Old timers like Sun Fo and Chen Li-fu [19] reluctant to get out but Wu believes extreme adversity will purify Government. Expects fall of Canton will shock Chinese into realization that old systems must be discarded. Foresees great organizational and membership changes thereafter. Has hope Foochow, Amoy, Swatow will be held.

Emphasizing confidence Wu said Generalissimo has changed point of view greatly in recent weeks. No longer angers at criticism of followers. At Tainan stop after Baguio Generalissimo and four advisers had blunt 3-hour discussion of politics, personalities, and military reorganization. Generalissimo for first time calmly admitted justness of criticism. Accepted recommendation to drop plan to appoint Sun Fo as Second Vice President of new Kmt Council and agreed to Premier ex-officio instead. Also agreed to defer to Li as Acting President and make every effort at conciliation in interests of solidarity. Wu says if Generalissimo keeps these two promises he will believe new course has been taken. Wu himself will accept no new official position until he is convinced of adoption of reform. Cited Shanghai departure as disagreement with Tang En-po. That debacle removes Tang as candidate for head of new Directorate General to be approved in Canton and established in Provincial Building Taipei. Lin Wei too subordinate. Chen Cheng most likely may continue governorship concurrently although considered incompetent as administrator and economist.

In matter of internal reform, Wu said those working here would be greatly aided if Secretary Acheson would call in Chinese Ambassador and have frank talk pointing out reasons for Department's "inaction" and stating confidentially what internal reforms should be made.[20]

---

[18] K. C. Wu, former Mayor of Shanghai.
[19] Latter was leader of the so-called C–C clique in the Kuomintang and Minister without Portfolio.
[20] In telegram No. 213, August 4, 2 p. m., the Department replied that it found this telegram "most interesting and helpful" but that after careful consideration it was decided not to call on the Chinese Ambassador to suggest reforms in view of the impending issuance of the White Paper on China.

Replying my citation Marshall statement,[21] Wu said it was bitter denunciation by frustrated man and like red flag to Generalissimo. Therefore I believe Wu's group wants proposed reforms list for guidance of Generalissimo.

During 2-hour talk, Wu repeatedly emphasized basic objectives both countries identical and highest US statesmanship needed. Cited F.D.R. offer of loan on fall of Canton and Hankow.[22] Urged adoption of Gilpatrick system of US-supervised relief distribution to insure proper use of US aid in future. Repeated belief fall of Canton will result in removal of worst elements and make bad men better. As previously reported this is not first time Wu has intimated great reforms after loss Canton and suggested new US attitude thereafter. I cannot estimate how important his group or movement is.

Sent Department, repeated Canton 127.

EDGAR

893.00/7–2049 : Telegram

The Consul General at Peiping (Clubb) to the Secretary of State[23]

PEIPING, July 19, 1949—9 a.m.
[Received July 20—9:02 a. m.]

1195. [To Nanking:] ReContel 844, July 18.[24] On invitation July 17 met with Lo Lung-chi, Chang Tung-sun, Chou Chin-wen and Joseph Chang.[25] In addition to information communicated Conreftel, Lo had following to say:

Position Mao difficult: As leader Communist Party he must maintain proper position vis-à-vis USSR. Mao, however, as a Chinese leader may talk one way and act another, would act in accordance with practical requirements situation. This should be kept in mind in reading Communist propaganda. I noted specific practical matters presently before us, said Americans would reach judgments on basis Communist actions. Lo next said difficulties experienced re such matters probably respected preoccupation Communist leaders with matters primary importance to neglect such matters as future small number foreign businessmen. He said talk of Mao's being potential Tito of course made

---

[21] For statement by General of the Army George C. Marshall, Special Representative of President Truman, on January 7, 1947, see Department of State, *United States Relations With China* (Washington, Government Printing Office, 1949), p. 686.
[22] See President Roosevelt's letter of October 26, 1938, to the President of the Chinese Executive Yuan (Kung), *Foreign Relations*, 1938, vol. III, p. 342. For announcement on December 15, 1938, of $25,000,000 credit by the Export-Import Bank of Washington to finance trade with China, see *ibid.*, p. 586.
[23] Repeated July 20, 11 a. m., to the Department.
[24] Not found in Department of State files.
[25] Members of the Democratic League; Joseph Chang was a son of Chang Tung-sun.

it harder for such development to occur, that an adept American policy such as Japan or Britain would have adopted would incorporate more indirect approach and achieve greater degree success. Held that Communists had good reason feel begrieved [*sic*] re USA by reason past American actions. I observed Marshall mission had undertaken mediation at invitation both parties to dispute. Lo said many mistakes made by mission. If USA, for instance, had opposed Chiang Kai-shek's dissolution of Democratic League, democratic groups would today be stronger. USA also should not have withdrawn ECA. I noted Communist action re ECA Tientsin, Peiping. Lo said Communists excuse those by saying they were confiscating Chinese Government food; that if USA had continued nevertheless send supplies there would have been no further Communist interference but of course USA would have had to send without conditions such as attached Nationals since Communists very sensitive re their high probity. Lo said at present there was Communist revival of anti-USA attitude due Generalissimo's trip Philippines which USA could have prevented. I noted Philippines was sovereign state and invited attention Acheson statement [26] in premises. Lo said first requisite for better relations was severance connections with Generalissimo and recognition Communist regime. I noted none existed. Lo said there would be but that then Communists would not sue for recognition, USA should come forward and offer. Joseph Chang observed that if USA offered recognition before USSR Communists would have to refuse, ruled down by Chang Tung-sun. Lo proposed support Democrats. Chou pointed out impracticability supporting under present circumstances (garble) would be done. Joseph Chang said support now would only irritate Communists. Chang Tung-sun said best chance for (garble) Chinese liberals was through discarding Generalissimo and enabling Li Tsung-jen continue on (garble) Lo held further course relations with Communist China depended upon policy USA. (Garble) traditional friendship USA for Chinese nation and opined that better relations would depend upon solution concrete problems at hand. As before cited outstanding cases. Lo stated that recent Chou speech re Chinese self-sufficiency was direct reply to Ambassador's argument vis-à-vis Chen Min-shu [27] to effect that USA not economically dependent on China, being designed show China likewise had no need rely on USA. Foreigners should remember Chinese peo-

---

[26] At his press conference on July 13 the Secretary of State was asked whether the Chiang–Quirino talks on a Pacific Pact had been brought to his attention. The Secretary replied that he had not yet read the "texts", although they had been received in the Department. Asked whether the United States was "any more amenable to a Pacific Pact" than in May, Secretary Acheson replied, "I think the attitude as stated by me in May still stands" (see Department of State *Bulletin*, May 29, 1949, p. 696).

[27] Shanghai Kuomintang Revolutionary Committee (KmtRC) leader; for further information on this Stuart–Chen conversation, see p. 771.

ple's capacity for endurance. Admitting that capacity, I observed that if China which had been undergoing deterioration for 10 war years desired get on road to construction it could best do so by making use of help from any and all quarters available.

Names not in any circumstances to be mentioned. Lo said Mao told him CCP was in no way committed in event war between USA and USSR [to] "come out immediately" and join USSR against USA, that statement (presumably that of April 3) which had attracted so much attention was by (garble) personalities, not official statement CCP. (Note here that version published official *Jen Min Jih Pao* April 4 born (garble) nature Mao Tse-tung in capacity chairman CCP).

Lo asked my opinion present world situation. I replied it was generally considered position one so-called "camp" (garble) become more consolidated, better integrated, stronger. Results [of?] Paris meeting was marked improvement. I asked whether local Chinese considered as reported by Chinese like Soviet press that Paris was victory for USSR. Chang but not Lo said none considered such was case. Lo said there was talk of war in year or two, asked opinion. I said Americans considered war not inevitable but recognized possibility, that lots of things could happen to alter course of events but that in any (garble) be ready for peace or war.

I said it seemed to me that Communist side should note our own present attitude was one of noninterference Chinese affairs, one of letting dust settle, that Communist propaganda directed against "American imperialist plots" of which most were either exaggerated or made out of whole cloth hardly served useful purpose, and that I thought Communists themselves would perhaps be well-advised let propaganda dust settle if it was desired work things out on practical basis.

I did not know before arrival at house Joseph Chang I was to meet Lo Lung-chi, had not sought or suggested such meeting. Believe Lo's attitude when discussing recent Sino-American and particularly such matters as Marshall Mission and ECA disclosed clearly close sympathy for Communist viewpoint. Believed probably meeting was held with foreknowledge Mao and that possibly Communists now have some feeling regret they refused accept Department's message (Contel 746, June 24 [28]) and desire in this indirect manner reopen door again, at least keep it ajar (see AstAMilAttel July 18). [29] Recommend no response whatsoever.

Sent Nanking 848, repeated Department 1195, OffEmb Canton 222, Shanghai 808.

[CLUBB]

---

[28] Same as telegram No. 1073 from Peiping, p. 397.
[29] Not found in Department of State files.

893.01/7–1949 : Telegram

The Minister-Counselor of Embassy in China (Clark) to the Secretary of State

CANTON, July 19, 1949—2 p. m.
[Received July 19—1:32 p. m.]

Cantel 776. Generalissimo looks well and was in good spirits when I saw him today. He has been preoccupied of late, he says, with reorganization of Kmt, plan for which was submitted party yesterday, and is not too familiar with military situation, he claims. He believes supreme policy committee will be much more efficient organ through which party can make its influence felt on government and he plans, he says, visiting Canton from time to time to chairman committee. In his absence, Li Tsung-jen will represent him in his capacity as vice-chairman. Li has agreed to stay on as Acting President and Generalissimo indicated that if their differences had not been resolved, a *modus operandi* had been evolved.

Took advantage conversation [to] say my piece on bombing and Generalissimo replied that we might have a case there, that he would consider problem further and at least make sure that only important strategic objectives were bombed.

Generalissimo has been impressed by revival [of] will to resist which he has noticed Canton and he plans "rally-resistance" trip to west, including Chungking, Chengtu and Lanchow when he leaves Canton, which he says will be "few days". Generalissimo confirms that here will be only unified "southeast command" under General Chen Cheng, concurrently Governor Taiwan. In addition Taiwan, command will include Kiangsu, Chekiang and Fukien. It will have assigned to it adequate air force and naval support, thus giving Chen command all forces that area.

Possibly indicative of Generalissimo's resentment that American and other ambassadors did not follow government Canton is fact that neither he nor Chen Chang-huan, Yenching graduate and once again Generalissimo's secretary, made no [any?] inquiry regarding welfare Dr. Stuart.

Sent Department Cantel 776; repeated Nanking 511, Shanghai 437, Taipei 67.

CLARK

893.01/7–2049 : Telegram

The Consul General at Taipei (Macdonald) to the Secretary of State

TAIPEI, July 20, 1949.
[Received July 20—5:07 a. m.]

300. Press carries announcement of creation of office of Generalissimo in Taipei under Chief Secretary Huang Shao-ku. Five sections:

Party and political sections under Ku Cheng-kang; foreign section under Wang Shih-chieh; finance section under O. K. Yui; military section under General Wang Tung-yuan; secretariat under Professor Chang Chi-yun.

Sent Department; repeated OffEmb Canton 130.

MACDONALD

893.00/7–2049 : Telegram

The Minister-Counselor of Embassy in China (Clark) to the Secretary of State

CANTON, July 20, 1949—10 a. m.
[Received 1 : 26 p. m.]

Cantel 783. Cheng Szu-yuan, advisor Li Tsung-jen and newly elected secretary Kmt Supreme Policy Committee, tells us so far real results Generalissimo's visit Canton, including two short talks with Li, precisely nil. Cheng quite pessimistic any understanding between Li and Generalissimo will ever be reached and thinks entirely possible Generalissimo may leave Canton in few days without having made any real attempt come to grips with differences between two. Cheng says questions of paramount importance now are military strategy and troop control. (He says control money and supplies secondary as Canton regime has enough get along for time being.) Li and Generalissimo military views remain diametrically opposed :

(1) Generalissimo insists on defense Taiwan and coastal areas; would feel no compunctions over abandonment interior. Li believes useless try hold Formosa and coast; thinks absolutely essential and eminently possible hold southwest and northwest hinterland.

(2) Generalissimo continues play off military commanders against each other and allots arms, money, supplies on basis friendship, personal loyalty and Whampoa connections. Li, according to Cheng, wants get complete control MND [30] and effect radical reorganization entire military setup. Specifically Li would assign or remove commanders and distribute arms, money, supplies on one criterion alone— who will and can fight Communists effectively. (Cheng incidentally suggests any future American aid must also be used this basis.) To carry out this program Li considers essential Pai Chung-hsi takeover MND and Chang Fa-kuei assume important post, probably Chief of Staff. Cheng says Li's desires latter regard firmly opposed by Generalissimo who wants keep his man Ku Chu-tung present job.[31] In passing, Cheng admits Li shows increasing lack determination stand up talk back to Generalissimo.

Sent Department Cantel 783, repeated Nanking 516, Shanghai 441, Taipei 69.

CLARK

---

[30] Ministry of National Defense.
[31] Chief of Chinese General Staff.

761.93/7–2049 : Telegram

The Ambassador in China (Stuart) to the Secretary of State

NANKING, July 20, 1949—5 p. m.
[Received July 20—10 : 44 a. m.]

1556. Assumed Department has seen summary of Chou En-lai's speech before meeting of sponsors of Sino-Soviet Friendship Association as broadcast by Peiping radio July 19. It contains several important revelations.

It is first speech of Chou which Communist propaganda organs have carried in many months. It may be tailored to bring Chou back into good graces of party leadership.

It goes far in closing reported gap between political thinking of Chou and that of Liu Shao-chi. Indeed speech is partly paraphrase of latter's famed article on "Nationalism and Internationalism" which appeared last November.[32] Speech appears to align Chou closer to pro-Soviet clique of CCP.

It endorses Sino-Soviet treaty of August 14, 1945,[33] by pointing out that treaty "wholly accorded with overall revolutionary interests of Chinese people".

It reveals that top CCP leadership expects that "US imperialism and Kmt reactionaries are scheming to blockade China economically" and that therefore "Chinese people must be fully prepared against a blockade of 8 to 10 years and must stand this new test".

Sent Department; repeated Shanghai 874, Moscow 49.

Department pass to Peiping 284.

STUART

893.00/7–2149

The Ambassador in China (Stuart) to the Secretary of State

No. 84   NANKING, July 21, 1949.
[Received August 11.]

SIR: I have the honor to transmit a translation[34] of an editorial entitled, "Strive Further to Strengthen the North China Party" from the *Jen Min Jih Pao* in Peiping, which was published in the Nanking *Hsin Hua Jih Pao* on July 5, 1949.

According to the editorial, the total membership of the North China section of the Chinese Communist Party is now 1,520,000. Of this number less than one percent were members of the party prior to the out-

---

[32] See telegram No. 2273, November 21, 1948, 2 p. m., from the Ambassador in China, *Foreign Relations*, 1948, vol. VII, p. 593.
[33] Signed at Moscow with the National Government of China ; United Nations Treaty Series, vol. X, p. 300.
[34] Not printed.

break of the Sino-Japanese War, and more than 60% of the present membership joined the party after V–J day. The editorial recognizes that an immediate problem facing the North China Party is the fact that such a large proportion of its members has been so recently recruited that their doctrination has necessarily been rather superficial. Furthermore, the party organizationally falls very short of the ideal, as branch headquarters have been established in only 68% of the 100,000 rural districts of North China. Nevertheless the North China Party has served as a very important recruiting ground for cadres to be sent to other areas. The editorial states that more than 50,000 rural cadres have been drafted during the past three years from the old liberated areas and assigned principally to Manchuria, Central China and south of the Yangtze.

The editorial considers that the principal problems facing the party are:

1. To raise the standard of knowledge of Marxism–Leninism and Mao Tse-tung ideology among party members;

2. To encourage the study of economics in order to be able to carry out successfully the industrial and commercial tasks f reconstruction;

3. To prevent sectarianism in the Party and eliminate the differences which exist between laborers and farmers, between urban and rural cadres, between laborer and farmer members and intellectual cadres, and between party and nonparty cadres;

4. To maintain close contact with the masses, consulting the views of the masses in all matters;

5. To solidify the alliance between the laborer and farmer and between the Communist Party and other democratic parties and persons;

6. To guard against sabotage by Kmt bandit groups;

7. To increase the party membership and set up new branch headquarters.

Comments:

The Chinese Communist Party is what is known as a "soft" party. It has an exceptionally small hard core of long-time party members. This means that the great mass of party members who must be relied upon to carry out day to day administrative activities have not had an opportunity to be thoroughly educated either with regard to the party line or to the particular job they have been assigned to handle. Nevertheless, because of the urgent need for more and more cadres to serve in newly occupied areas, the party must continue recruiting.

In order to overcome this general party weakness in political training and administrative skills the main reliance at this stage is being placed upon education and persuasion. It would seem that the party cannot at this point indulge in widespread purges or severe punishment of those who deviate from the party line. A further manifestation of the party's weakness, both quantitative and qualitative, is the strong emphasis on a united front with other "democratic" parties and persons. This is essential at this stage if the party is to cope successfully with the vast problems confronting it. The ignorance of economics, which the Communists frankly confess in the editorial, is doubtless one of the most potent factors compelling them to a policy of attracting and utilizing in relatively important positions, many who are not partv members.

It must not be inferred from the weaknesses exposed in this self-critical article that the Chinese Communist Party will not be able to overcome them. So long as there is no powerful, active, organized opposition, it may only be a question of time until the CCP is able to transform itself into a disciplined, monolithic party which can afford ruthlessly to purge deviationists and crush outside obstruction.

Respectfully yours,

For the Ambassador:
JOHN WESLEY JONES
Counselor of Embassy

893.00/6–2749 : Telegram

The Secretary of State to the Consul General at Hong Kong (Hopper)

WASHINGTON, July 22, 1949—5 p. m.

635. Reurtel 380, June 27, Dept has found this report of considerable interest as indicating possible alignments various Chi elements and hopes contacts can be continued and further info reported. As for direct questions raised by informants, if Amer source replies he might limit himself to expressing personal view that Amer Govt has continuously favored and long worked for emergence of united, stable and truly independent China; emphasis under present circumstances w[ou]ld be on genuine independence of regime, as prerequisite to eventual unity and representative govt.

It would obviously be inappropriate for this Govt to furnish financial support to parties or polit elements in another country.

ACHESON

893.00/7–2249 : Telegram

The Minister-Counselor of Embassy in China (Clark) to the Secretary of State

CANTON, July 22, 1949—5 p. m.
[Received 11 : 16 p. m.]

Cantel 800. Burden of more than 2-hour conversation Chen Li-fu today was which came first, the hen or egg, he maintaining that economic aid must come before military victory and I taking other side argument. He is much uplifted by what he considers success Generalissimo's visit Canton in which he claims to have played a large part and assures me that Kmt train is back on track, will be purged, streamlined and made efficiently functioning vehicle.

Chen insists that although all differences between Li Tsung-jen and Generalissimo were not removed, Li has been mollified—in other words, buttered up by Generalissimo—and is prepared go along with Generalissimo's plans in full spirit cooperation. As earnest this cooperation he said Li had been persuaded not to insist on Pai Chung-hsi as Minister National Defense. Generalissimo's line was that Pai's talents were needed in command his armies and that other commanders being unfamiliar Pai's capabilities might not trust his judgment as Minister National Defense.

Chen was much impressed by President's speech Chicago [35] and pleased with Secretary's statement re Far Eastern pact.[36] Although he repeated more than once that he had insisted to Generalissimo that Nationalist Government must itself demonstrate its ability do something before expecting aid from US, he kept coming back with expression hope we would in some way reconsider and provide at least stabilization loan or grant. It was on these occasions that the hen and egg question continually arose.

Sent Department, repeated Nanking 533, Shanghai 450, Taipei 75.

CLARK

893.01/7–2349 : Telegram

The Consul at Shanghai (McConaughy) to the Secretary of State

SHANGHAI, July 23, 1949—9 a. m.
[Received July 22—11 : 16 p. m.]

2901. *Sin Min Wan Pao* July 20 reports that "leftover personnel" of various sections of defunct Shanghai Municipal Government have completed month's re-education training. Article reports that as most these persons superfluous, People's Government for sake of economy and to enable each man to "develop his ability" has "allowed" portion of them to resign, giving them 1½ month's salaries each as separation allowance. The rest have been retained for service. According to article, those who resigned have either returned to home towns to engage in productive activities, taken new jobs or requested People's City Government to recommend them to Revolutionary College to continue studies.

Of possible interest in connection with above is unverified rumor that Peiping Government displeased with Mayor Chen Yi over large-

---

[35] Address entitled "Public Opinion and American Foreign Policy," delivered on July 19, 1949, at the Imperial Council Session of the Shrine of North America ; Department of State *Bulletin*, August 1, 1949, p. 145.
[36] Apparently statements by the Secretary of State at his press conference on July 13 ; see footnote 26, p. 444.

scale disorganization in Shanghai Government offices. Allegedly Peiping Government annoyed that more trained personnel not retained in their positions by Communists after Shanghai take-over; apparently lack experienced personnel may have contributed to deteriorating situation in city.

Sent Department; repeated Nanking 1631, OffEmb Canton 915. Department pass Peiping 220.

McConaughy

893.00/7–2349 : Telegram

The Consul at Shanghai (McConaughy) to the Secretary of State

SHANGHAI, July 23, 1949—1 p. m.
[Received July 23—5 : 27 a. m.]

2906. This editorial [37] is good example of now out-pouring vicious propaganda painting American Government as primarily responsible for continuance civil war, blockade and economic misery. (ReContel 2905) serious realities of blockade and air raids for Shanghai populace, American origin of blockading ships and strafing planes and known fact of Generalissimo's Manila visit (which has stirred local Chinese suspicions to fever pitch) make Shanghai public easily gullible to such propaganda and greatly increase its potentialities for inflaming sentiment to point endangering well-being, if not lives, of local Americans. Prominent Americans have privately expressed to us justifiable alarm over press articles of this character; and would, of course, welcome issuance public statements by American Government or other channel denying or explaining away charges and implications. Consulate General realizes that such statements would not be always practicable. It occurs to us however that, alternatively or supplementarily, Department upon receiving our report of outstandingly slanderous editorial such as that under reference might undertake supply us brief factual material regarding specific points (as for example Chennault,[38] Wu Te-chen's [39] heralded trip to Japan, developing American attitude toward blockade). We would find such material very helpful to use in our private talks with Chinese contacts, without quoting Department, as authoritative information to combat some of more serious false charges.

Sent Department; repeated Nanking 1634, OffEmb Canton 919.

McConaughy

---

[37] Telegram No. 2905, July 23, not printed, reported a Communist paper's denunciation of "American imperialism" (893.9111 RR/7–2349).
[38] Maj. Gen. Claire L. Chennault (ret.), Chairman of the Board of Civil Air Transport (in China).
[39] Former Vice President of the Chinese Executive Yuan and Minister for Foreign Affairs.

893.00/7–2349 : Telegram

*The Minister-Counselor of Embassy in China (Clark) to the
Secretary of State*

CANTON, July 23, 1949—3 p. m.
[Received July 23—6 : 22 a. m.]

Cantel 805. Conversation last night Cheng Szu-yuan repeated almost word for word contents Cantel 783, repeated Nanking 516, Shanghai 441, Taipei 69, July 19 [*20*], and said subsequent developments have confirmed his unhappy prediction Gimo would leave Canton without any real attempt settle differences with Li. Cheng characterized Gimo's tactics with one Chinese word "tuo", meaning combination of delay and evasion. Best example Gimo's facility in side-stepping issues was his promise bring up question Pai Chung-hsi appointment as Minister National Defense at "appropriate time" which never arrived.

In terms utter frustration over Li's position and bitter damnation Gimo's maneuvers, Cheng summed up situation as follows: Gimo has no intention effecting any real reform in govt or military leadership and steadfastly insists on maintaining his Formosan fortress even at expense abandoning entire mainland to Commies. Li still believes drastic reorganization National Defense Ministry and installation Pai as Minister imperative if tide ever to be turned against Commies. But Li depends on Gimo money dole. Thus the dilemma : If Li cannot reform, he loses; if he does try reform, Gimo cuts off dole and Li still loses.

Cheng continued : Gimo, viewing scene with cold-blooded calculation, feels certain Li bound to fail. This ultimate collapse of Li and loss entire China will leave Gimo sitting high and dry on Formosa, Li disposed of, waiting for outbreak third world war and end to Commie problem in China. While awaiting Li downfall and world war III, Gimo will busy himself fortifying his position on Formosa, keeping a deft hand in mainland affairs, and building up prestige abroad as great anti-Commie leader.

For story told from different angle, see Cantel 800, July 22, repeated Nanking 533, Shanghai 450, Taipei 75.

Sent Dept, repeated Nanking 535, Shanghai 453, Taipei 76.

CLARK

893.00/7–2449 : Telegram

*The Minister-Counselor of Embassy in China (Clark) to the
Secretary of State*

CANTON, July 24, 1949—10 p. m.
[Received July 28—7 : 42 p .m.]

Cantel 812. After long and rather frank talk with Chu Chang-wei, political advisor Li Tsung-jen and Secretary-General office President, gather that, although visit Generalissimo Canton did not settle everything, much good was accomplished. Chu says that as might be expected, direct talks between Li and Generalissimo proved beneficial, as did general discussion around table among Kmt leaders. Differences still exist, but there is better understanding of reasons therefor and less inclination continue bickering which, in large measure, was responsible for Generalissimo's visit. Generalissimo, for instance, agreed with Li on desirability appointing Pai Chung-hsi as Minister National Defense, yet was able persuade Li, [that] Pai's services more needed at present in command his armies and promised that the Generalissimo would suggest appointment Pai at proper time.

The "office of Director General Kmt" which Generalissimo has established Taiwan to assist him function as leader Kmt will, according Chu, have eight sections headed by luminaries Generalissimo regime on scale which (although Chu did not say so) indicates to me that Generalissimo plans much more active participation in government affairs. Chu says little real importance was attached to newly-created Supreme Policy Committee of Kmt and little use would be made of it. Li and Yen Hsi-shan would discuss matters and, by-passing committee, communicate direct with Generalissimo. Li realizes he cannot act without Generalissimo's approval and is reconciled full collaboration with him.

Chu says Li still plans his tour as Acting President and will in near future, accompanied by Chu Chia-hua, Vice Premier, and others, visit Amoy, Taiwan and Yunnan. Chu did not know whether Generalissimo would in fact visit Szechuan.

Almost giving impression he was "whistling in the dark", Chu said he felt Communist successes had reached "high water mark". As basis, however, for this statement he could only remark that they now controlled sufficiently large sector China; that realization would soon be borne in among them of the insoluble problems of government they have inherited.

In next breath he went on to say government anticipates strong drive by Communist armies: (1) Into Fukien and down to East River area; (2) a three-pronged attack on Kiangsi, Hunan front in effort annihilate Pai Chung-hsi's forces; and (3) a two-pronged attack on Szechuan in effort obtain rice crop. He insists Canton defenses are being strengthened and that Pai will fight to finish. He admitted, however, that there was no evidence of revived will to fight among National troops and of the need for such revived will to fight if resistance was to be successful.

Also belying his confidence that "high water mark" Communist successes had been reached was his admission that all was not well in

Szechuan or in Yunnan. He admitted that Chang Chun [40] had "prestige but no authority" in Szechuan and that Governor Wang [41] and other military leaders Szechuan were proving difficult to handle. Also, he said government had positive information that Governor Lu Han of Yunnan, using former Governor Lung Yun as intermediary, was discussing terms with Communists. Central government troops, however, still control situation in Yunnan and government is sending military officer there investigate situation.

On balance, I should say Generalissimo's visit has served as temporary stimulant only; that nothing fundamentally has changed; that nation lost will to resist is no better than it was; and that Communists continue capability occupying any part China they choose. There indications at moment of major Communist effort southeast China and probably Szechuan, Yunnan as well.

Sent Department Cantel 812, repeated Nanking 538, Shanghai 457, Taipei 77. By pouch to Chungking 38, Kunming 10.

CLARK

893.20/7–2549 : Telegram

The Minister-Counselor of Embassy in China (Clark) to the Secretary of State

CANTON, July 25, 1949—9 a. m.
[Received 9 : 49 p. m.]

Cantel 815. As further evidence bankruptcy present leadership and desperate situation government is decision Cabinet taken July 23, reported to me by Chu Chang-wei, approving creation "foreign legion" as vehicle for enlistment Americans, Japanese or others. Chu said Chennault already had large number volunteer airmen.

Believe lack of funds will prevent implementation idea but nevertheless told Chu he could be sure US Government would prevent, to the extent possible, enlistment Americans in proposed legion. I pointed out differences between war against Japan and present conflict which, despite its international aspects, is in fact civil war.

Sent Department; repeated Nanking 541, Shanghai 459, Taipei 78.

CLARK

---

[40] Military and Political Affairs Director for Southwest China and Minister without Portfolio.
[41] Wang Lin-chi.

893.01/7–2549 : Telegram

The Ambassador in China (Stuart) to the Secretary of State

NANKING, July 25, 1949—6 p. m.
[Received July 25—6 : 22 a. m.]

1609. In their conversation July 24, Huang Hua told Philip Fugh that he expects PLA will take Canton in not much more than 10 days and that PCC will convene promptly after that event. Huang added that coalition government is expected to be formed about 6 weeks after PCC convenes and that recognition of foreign governments would proceed normally without delay.

Sent Department; repeated OffEmb Canton 673. Department pass Peiping.

STUART

893.20/7–2549 : Airgram

The Minister-Counselor of Embassy in China (Clark) to the Secretary of State

CANTON, July 25, 1949.
[Received August 7—10 a. m.]

A–38. Reference Cantel 815, July 25, 1949, rptd Taipei 78. Some details concerning the organization of a Foreign Legion and Volunteer Air Force, first broached in the reference telegram, were recently made known to the Embassy by Yin Jen-chai, Secretary and Advisor to Premier Yen Hsi-shan.

According to Premier Yen's present plans, which Yin says have been discussed with, and heartily approved by, both Li Tsung-jen and the Gimo, the Foreign Legion would total 100,000 soldiers from all countries of the world. No plans regarding recruitment, budget, organization, etc., have yet been formed. When it was suggested to Yin that the goal might be a little high, he said that the Premier has received numerous offers of help from various and sundry people. He mentioned specifically that Stennes, Chiang's former chief bodyguard now in Germany, would probably help.

On the Air Force, Yen's proposals are more concrete. Present plans call for a total of 166 planes. Of the total, 150 would be fighter, bomber, observation, and other types which could be bought from the United States surplus at a total cost of $2,000,000 (U.S.). The other 16 planes would be transports which it is hoped Chennault would furnish free of charge. The total personnel of this Air Force would number roughly 1,300 foreigners (pilots, crew members, etc.) and 2,000 Chinese. Total operating costs for the Air Force are estimated at US$1,000,000 per month, for salaries, gasoline, parts, etc.

Both the Air Force and Foreign Legion would be directly responsible to the Supreme Policy Committee and would have only liaison connections with the Ministry of National Defense and CAF.[42]

Mr. Yin of course thought these two organizations would require some foreign financial support.

CLARK

893.00/7–2649 : Telegram

The Secretary of State to the Minister-Counselor of Embassy in China (Clark), at Canton

WASHINGTON, July 26, 1949—11 a. m.

TelCan 496. Pls give Dept ur best estimate of when Canton is likely to fall.

ACHESON

711.93/7–2649 : Telegram

The Ambassador in China (Stuart) to the Secretary of State

NANKING, July 26, 1949—3 p. m.
[Received July 26—10 : 45 a. m.]

1617. Embtel 1601, July 24 to Department.[43] While much of CCP hostility toward USA traces back to misunderstanding, ignorance and provinciality, we submit that much of its expression stems also from deliberate mendacity and policy. In support we cite new propaganda line being developed by Communist press to effect that USA is responsible for present blockade of Communist ports. As phrased by Peiping radio broadcast July 21, "with American imperialists pulling strings behind the scene, Kmt has imposed naval blockade from mouth of Yangtze to Shantung coast, bombed, strafed areas around Shanghai–Nanking and is now planning organize so-called international volunteers and special air force". Our whole record regarding Nationalist port closure and bombing shows this new propaganda line to be as unrealistic as Communist injunction contained in Embassy reference telegram to "encourage staff members voluntarily to ask for salary reductions".

It is significant that in local editorial reported reference telegram, "imperialists" are each time given pride of place over "Kmt reactionaries" in responsibility for economic blockade; furthermore, that economic blockade has been adroitly turned to support economic pol-

---

[42] Chinese Air Force.
[43] Not printed.

icy of autarchy for China which at least extreme elements of CCP undoubtedly desire.

Repeated Shanghai 906, Canton 676.

STUART

893.00/7–2649 : Telegram

The Minister-Counselor of Embassy in China (Clark) to the Secretary of State

CANTON, July 26, 1949—3 p. m.
[Received July 27—11 : 08 p. m.]

Cantel 826. For Strong.[44] Chu Chang-wei informs me Acting President Li Tsung-jen flew Hengyang this morning for conference Pai Chung-hsi. Li will then proceed Foochow, stay overnight, then go Taiwan.[45] Chu believes Li will omit Hainan from itinerary and will return Canton before proceeding contemplated visit Chungking.

Chu says government is more worried by situation Szechuan than by that Canton. He says Hu Tsung-nan's troops are falling back from Paochi down road to Szechuan plain and that general situation in that province is sour. He left me with decided impression that government may have to revise its plans and may not move Chungking; if it does so, move will be on such small scale as to make further evacuations simple matter.

Sent Department Cantel 826, repeated Nanking 553, Shanghai 463, Taipei 82, Chungking 70.

CLARK

761.93/7–2649 : Telegram

The Ambassador in China (Stuart) to the Secretary of State

NANKING, July 26, 1949—4 p. m.
[Received July 26—noon.]

1621. Re Moscow telegram 1810, July 21 to Department.[46] Cursory treatment given by Soviet press to establishment of Sino-Soviet Friendship Association as compared with fulsome publicity accorded it by CCP press suggests that Soviets are not much impressed by this friendly act of their Chinese comrades. Had Soviets wished to publish more material on this subject, it would have been readily available

---

[44] Robert C. Strong, First Secretary of Embassy in China, was on special detail at Chungking.

[45] The Military Attaché in China (Soule) on July 29 reported that Acting President Li had flown to Taiwan "presumably [to] continue with Chiang Kai-shek his unsuccessful discussions re resistance plan for mainland" (893.00(W)/7–2949).

[46] Not printed ; it reported Soviet press comment.

in form of Peiping radio broadcasts July 17 through 19 which Soviets certainly monitor. It is also interesting that Chou En-lai's speech, which was broadcast July 19, was not carried in Soviet press for, as we pointed out in Embtel 1556, July 20 to Department, that speech appeared to be important step in aligning Chou closer [to] more extreme pro-Soviet elements within CCP.

We do not at this stage have any explanation for Soviet coolness toward Sino-Soviet Friendship Association.

Repeated Shanghai 907, Moscow 53, Department pass Peiping 299.

STUART

893.00/7–2749 : Telegram

The Minister-Counselor of Embassy in China (Clark) to the Secretary of State

CANTON, July 27, 1949—10 p. m. [a. m.?]
[Received July 30—12:26 p. m.]

Cantel 829. Following through on thoughts reported Cantel 814, July 24,[47] repeated Nanking 540, Shanghai 458, I envisage course of events more or less as follows:

Pai Chung-hsi will conserve his strength and eventually resort to guerrilla tactics in mountainous regions Kwangsi. (Can find no evidence intention Pai put up real battle anywhere; his ammunition is low with no replacement in sight.) Szechuan and Yunnan will fall in comparatively near future, but northwest for some time may maintain autonomy under Ma's who will also eventually take to hills as guerrillas. (Despite excellent leadership and morale, Ma's troops have nothing with which fight prolonged battle.) There is already evidence guerrilla activities in Ta Pieh Shan area on Honan–Anwhei–Hupeh border. When Communists have driven Nationalists from mainland to fortress Taiwan, these will be only remaining areas resistance mainland China unless similar elements coalesce some other area. (Even though Kwangtung Provincial Government moves Hainan as planned, do not believe they can hold it for long.) To exacerbate Communist economic problems, Nationalist blockade of mainland will be continued from Taiwan, although we should not lose sight of possibility Communists may one day succeed occupying Taiwan through infiltration and similar tactics.

Communist theory, as I see it, is the negation of deep-seated Chinese tradition. In seeking disruption of family and regimentation, which is inevitable if Communists are to succeed in imposing their theories on country, they will arouse incalculable passions and resistance. As their measures increase in harshness, resentment and resistance will

---

[47] Vol. IX, p. 1272.

increase and the organized guerrilla forces of resistance in such places as Ta Pieh Shan and Kwangsi may be augmented. There may even come a time when from these forces of resistance there will arise a new leader or leaders capable of taking the offensive against Communism. If we have acted wisely in interim we may be able take advantage that development to serve our purposes.

It seems, therefore, that for some time to come China will be ruled by Communist regime or regimes unfriendly to US. Certainly Communist propaganda, including the statements of its leaders, indicate firm intention to vilify US, inflaming the people toward an active hatred of the US while friendship with the Soviet Union is being fostered by every means. Communist propaganda goes even so far as to proclaim that aid or advice from the western world would not be accepted even if proffered. To accept such aid or advice would be to pervert Communist purity, they say. China will accept, therefore, aid and technical advice only from her friends, the Soviets and Soviet satellites.

If this analysis is founded, could we not profit by Soviet tactics in Western Europe and endeavor manoeuvre Soviets into assuming responsibility for this morass that is China? Why not step aside, remain aloof except possibly for covert support to resistance elements, and let Communists go to Soviets for the aid and technical advice they must have if they are to realize any of their plans, or for that matter, if they are to prevent the port cities from sinking under the blockade into economic collapse and chaos. By holding aloof we would place full burden Communist difficulties on Communists themselves and remove basis their propaganda against American imperialism. At same time a Communist China foundering in morass of administrative inefficiency and economic want might dampen ardor fellow-travelers southeast Asia. If we take no initiative in trying to improve relations with Chinese Communists and if we strike a hard bargain in the case of any request they make of us, they will be forced to carry out their avowed policy and seek their aid from the Soviet Union. Any action along these lines would, of course, require that we bring into line other major trading nations.

There is reason to believe that the Soviets seek to exploit China, not assist her. Even so, everything I read indicates that should Soviets really come to assistance China they can do so only at expense their own economy. Either the Soviets seek to supply Communist China requirements and bog down in the morass or they embarrass Communist propaganda by their failure to do so. The net result may be chaos in China for a long time. Sometimes, however, I shudder at the thought that an unfriendly government might organize efficiently and regiment the tremendous manpower of this country and the longer we can delay the possibility of such a day should be beneficial.

Effect of 100 years of western Christianizing influence on Chinese people cannot be eradicated in a day and there should remain, although temporarily submerged, a good will toward the US that would assist us when the time comes to reassert ourselves positively in China. In the meantime, by continued recognition of Nationalist Government, even though confined to Taiwan, we would have retained friendly vote China in international councils.

Sent Department Cantel 829, repeated Nanking 555, Shanghai 465, Taipei 84.

CLARK

893.00/7–2749 : Telegram

The Minister-Counselor of Embassy in China (Clark) to the Secretary of State

CANTON, July 27, 1949—noon.
[Received July 27—1 : 36 a. m.]

Cantel 830. All information leads to belief Communists will encounter no real resistance in attacks toward Canton, TelCan 496, July 26. Pai Chung-hsi is short ammunition, is conserving it, and am convinced he will not put up real fight until mountains Kwangsi. Remaining troops between Communists and Canton have poor morale and leadership. Much defection, little fighting expected. Canton being reinforced by former Tsingtao garrison of ill-repute via Hainan. They expected defeat.

Best estimate Communist capabilities is they can take Canton 10 days. Our guess is mid-August.

Foreign Office admits that in light military developments Szechuan, government reviewing decision remove capital Chungking. Chu Chang-wei rules out Kweilin or Kweiyang as alternative seat government.

CLARK

893.01/7–2749 : Telegram

The Minister-Counselor of Embassy in China (Clark) to the Secretary of State

CANTON, July 27, 1949—2 p. m.
[Received July 28—11 : 35 a. m.]

Cantel 833. Communist threat Szechuan has led to review government plans move Chungking and cancellation is possibility. Most government organs (with notable exception Ministry National Defense) have sent families, files and some personnel Taiwan. Some ministries still talking sending few top personnel if capital goes

Chungking but none seriously considering setting up establishment any size there.

Foreign Minister has sent files and three senior officers Taiwan and Vice Minister has been there [to] look for housing and office space, while single junior officer Chungking does not even have office. Minister of Education has cancelled plans send advance party Chungking and instead Minister is making trip Taiwan this week. Similarly Minister of Communications, Minister of Finance and banking institutions no longer thinking moving even part their establishments Szechuan. Central News now has only skeleton staff Canton, with 200 trained personnel, radios and files having gone Taipei last week. Sole exception Ministry National Defense has moved several thousand personnel and dependents Chungking and has had average 15 chartered planes going there daily past week [with?] service and BIS [48] personnel who "not needed" Taiwan, with inference plain they are mouths which no one Taiwan wants take responsibility feeding.

Portion government unwilling go "Gimo's island", completely undecided where next stop will be. This evidenced by Yen Hsi-shan statement to President Legislative Yuan that he could give no indication where September meeting that group should take place until after August 15.

Sent Department, repeated Taipei 85. By pouch Chungking 72.

CLARK

893.00/7–2749 : Telegram

The Consul General at Hong Kong (Hopper) to the Secretary of State

HONG KONG, July 27, 1949—4 p. m.
[Received July 27—9 : 38 a. m.]

503. Appropriate parts Deptel 635 [49] passed to persons concerned who express agreement therewith, stressing their concern Department aware their existence and plans. See further Hong Kong telegram July 27, pouched Canton EmbOff for relay Department.[50]

HOPPER

---

[48] Chinese Bureau of Investigation and Statistics (security).
[49] July 22, p. 450.
[50] Not found in Department of State files.

893.001 Chiang Kai-shek/7–2849 : Telegram

The Consul General at Taipei (Macdonald) to the Secretary of State

TAIPEI, July 28, 1949—4 p. m.
[Received July 28—1 : 02 p. m.]

325. Reliably informed that Generalissimo will remain Taiwan only 1 week [to] complete organization new offices here, then proceed Chungking and Lanchow. Quirino [and] he may go Korea for Far East Union Conference middle August. New signatories to pact may subscribe only to principles or to one or more material commitments depending on each nation's desire.

Repeated Canton 137.

MACDONALD

893.01/7–2949 : Telegram

The Minister-Counselor of Embassy in China (Clark) to the Secretary of State

CANTON, July 29, 1949—11 a. m.
[Received 7 : 23 p. m.]

Cantel 847. Tung Ling, Vice Foreign Minister, tells me Cabinet still has under review question removal Chungking when Canton threatened. No decision has been reached but Tung expressed his conviction government would at least nominally move Chungking short period. He ruled out possibility removal capital any other location mainland when Chungking threatened and says government will go Taiwan that time.

Obviously the time-table move Chungking depends Communist military time-table. All evidence points fact Ma Pu-fang's [51] troops badly chewed up west Sian and that troops Hu Tsung-nan [52] are not fighting south Paochi. Communist troops which captured Ichang, Shasi have crossed river, captured Changteh and appear be moving westward. It seems only question time when Szechuan will fall. Communists have publicly announced intention capture Canton by August 15.

In view, therefore, what Tung Ling tells me it seems likely at least façade government will move Chungking early August. Fall of Hengyang is mentioned as signal for move.

Sent Department Cantel 847; repeated Nanking 562, Shanghai 468, Taipei 87.

CLARK

---

[51] Military and Political Affairs Director for Northwest China and Governor of Tsinghai.
[52] Pacification Commissioner for Shensi.

893.00/7–2949 : Telegram

The Vice Consul at Chungking (McGeary) to the Secretary of State

CHUNGKING, July 29, 1949—11 a. m.
[Received July 30—3 : 55 a. m.]

124. From Strong. Lt. General Wang Ling-yuen preparing leave here early August with 100 staff members technicians, 10 radio sets, etc., to organize resistance force in southwest Honan. Has received reports from that area stating 100,000 men have arms and twice as many more anxious join guerrilla forces. Reports claim Communists not directly control over 20 hsien southwest Honan where people have killed over 1,000 Communist political commissars and Communist soldiers sent to punish people for killings.

Wang plans organize armed group, then request ammunition and rifles by air drop. Expects disrupt Communist rear and coordinate with Nationalist activities at front. Eventually hopes begin recapture cities. Has been appointed head Military and Political Officer of Nationalist Government southwest Honan.

Nationalist official[s] here hope Wang's mission will disrupt Communists' plans, give morale to people under Nationalist Government and thus enable come-back which would entitle Nationalist Government to US aid. If Wang successful, believe other Nationalist generals and leaders will return to home areas organize similar movements.

Despite fact Wang requested secrecy when revealing plans, he produced calling cards printed with Honan titles. Also is taking large group and has several hundred other Honan refugees on waiting list. Such numbers bound to create discussion and general knowledge of plans, thus jeopardizing mission. Also probably unwise take back officials who ran away from Communists [in] view fact new local leadership will have arisen.

Sent Department, repeated Nanking 133, OffEmb Canton 74, [Strong].

MCGEARY

893.01/7–2949

The Minister-Counselor of Embassy in China (Clark) to the Secretary of State

No. 33   CANTON, July 29, 1949.
[Received August 11.]

SIR: I have the honor to enclose certain information regarding the present composition and future plans of the Ministry of Foreign Affairs.

In summary, it might be said that 15 of the 41 persons of the rank of Section Chief or above have left the Ministry without replacement since June 1. Adding resignations which will take place before the capital moves, it appears that less than half of the Officer personnel and an even smaller percentage of the clerical personnel who came here from Nanking will be with the Ministry at the next capital.

Although all foreign diplomatic offices in Canton were asked over a month ago to send advance parties to Chungking, the Ministry itself has sent only one minor official to that city. Three Senior Officers and all of the Ministry's important files have been sent to Taiwan. The Ministry had previously told half of its personnel that they would go to Chungking when the capital moved, with the other half to go to Taipei, but it now appears that plans to establish the next capital in Chungking have been virtually abandoned. Although final arrangements have not yet been made, it seems that the Ministry's next working address will be Taipei.

Despite disorganization resulting from poor working conditions, lack of adequate files, the losses of personnel cited above, and the lack of interest and ineptitude on the part of many of the personnel remaining, the Ministry of Foreign Affairs is generally considered the most efficient remaining portion of the Chinese Government. (End summary)

[Here follows detailed report on personnel, plans, and recent sojourn at Canton.]

Respectfully yours,   LEWIS CLARK

———————————

761.93/7–3049 : Telegram

The Consul General at Peiping (Clubb) to the Secretary of State

PEIPING, July 30, 1949.
[Received July 31—7 p. m.]

1269. Report of speech by Chou En-lai to sponsors meeting Sino-Soviet Friendship Association July 17 as carried by NCNA English language release July 20 was faithful translation. News report text as contained *Jen Min Jih Pao* July 17 excepting that Chinese text had final paragraph as follows:

"Finally Chou expressed gratitude to great revolutionary leader and teacher of world proletariat and depressed people, Lenin; expressed thanks to Sun Yat-sen who had advocated Kmt–CCP cooperation and effecting a policy of union with USSR; expressed thanks to leader and teacher people USSR and leader-teacher whole Marxist world, Stalin; expressed thanks to Chairman Mao Tse-tung who has led Chinese people in conduct new democracy revolution and has created strong foundation for advancement Sino-Soviet friendship."

Please confirm whether there has been monitored brief speech Commander-Chief Chu Teh, long speech Kuo Mo-jo [53] same occasion.

———
[53] Poet and writer.

Sent Nanking 900, Department 1269, OffEmb Canton, Shanghai 839.

CLUBB

893.00/7–3149 : Telegram

The Ambassador in China (Stuart) to the Secretary of State

NANKING, July 31, 1949.
[Received July 31—5 : 10 a. m.]

1666. *Hsin Hua Jih Pao* July 18 reprinted editorial from *Chang Chiang Jih Pao* commenting on Lin Piao's [54] recent announcement that in Central China main emphasis to be placed on rural areas rather than cities. Editorial confirms that new policy expected continue 3 or 4 years "until land reform completed and Sun Yat-sen's land-to-the-tiller policy realized". With regard to attitude CCP members, editorial pointedly remarks:

"We make no bones about fact that ever since announcement of the policy of Central Committee's second plenary session, and particularly at this time when rapid progress is being made in the war, certain problems have arisen in thought of our senior officers. Some of them think that, now that revolution has succeeded, they should start to enjoy fruits of labor. Consequently they prefer cities to countryside, and industrial work to rural work. Persons who entertain such thoughts may orally agree to go out into the country, but actually they are afraid of hardships. They will not do a good job even if they remain in the city.

"Another group of persons misinterpret sentiment plenary sessions placing of emphasis on cities. They flock to cities where there is little or no industry, leaving countryside to be exploited by ruffians, bandits and secret service agents. In accepting new policy of Central China Bureau, these two groups of people should reflect on causes of their erroneous thoughts and take action to correct them. Erroneous thoughts, if not corrected, will be detrimental to execution of new policy. At present, such bourgeois thoughts as fear of hardships, seeking of material enjoyment, pride and egotism, contempt for others, concern with position, and disobedience to organization are chief dangerous thoughts, which will resist the execution of new policy with all kinds of excuses. We call on Communist leading organs at different levels in Central China to pay attention to these dangerous thoughts and overcome them.

"Now that new policy of Central China Bureau has been announced, we hope Committee members and all revolutionary workers will enthusiastically put it into effect; and leading organs at different levels will follow new policy by setting a good example, and at same time mobilize and organize senior officers so as to insure success of new policy. Our slogan is: 'Go to rural areas!' 'Mix with masses of peasants!'"

STUART

---

[54] Communist military commander in North China.

893.00/8–149 : Telegram

The Consul General at Taipei (Macdonald) to the Secretary of State

TAIPEI, August 1, 1949—3 p. m.
[Received 8 : 04 p. m.]

341. According Wang Shih-chieh, coordination military activity and how forces can best be used was major topic discussions here last week between Acting President and Generalissimo.[55] Matters taken up in Canton also discussed. Wang said better spirit of cooperation prevailed.

Another matter of grave concern to Generalissimo taken up with Li, stated Wang, is question of Kmt party members and ex-government officials residing Hong Kong who are defeatists and establishing contact with Communists and encouraging defections. Generalissimo demanded drastic action be taken against them but only recourse open National Government is to expel them from party and public condemnation. Wang claims Hong Kong Government refuses cooperate with National Government and feels for own good colony such persons should be deported (actually turned over Chinese National authorities). He thinks Hong Kong Government might cooperate this and if requested by US and expressed desire State Department approach British this respect.

Wang asked when White Paper [56] being released. I replied in negative.

Sent Department 341, repeated OffEmb Canton 150.

MACDONALD

893.01/8–249 : Telegram

The Consul General at Taipei (Macdonald) to the Secretary of State

TAIPEI, August 2, 1949.
[Received August 3—8 : 05 p. m.]

344. Reference mytel 300, July 20. Generalissimo's headquarters inaugurated August 1st with following personnel: Huang Shao-ku, secretary-general; Wang Shih-chieh, advisor; Ku Cheng-kang, party and political section; Wang Tung-yuan, military section; Hollington Tong, information section; Tao Hsi-sheng, research section; Chang Chi-yun, secretariat; General Yu Chih-shih, chief administrative officer; and Chen Shun-keng, administrative section. Economic and security section chiefs not yet appointed.

Sent Department 344, repeated OffEmb Canton 153.

MACDONALD

---

[55] Acting President Li made his first visit to Taiwan July 27–August 1, 1949.
[56] Department of State, *United States Relations With China* (Washington, Government Printing Office, 1949). For further documentation on its release, see vol. IX, pp. 1365 ff.

893.01/8–249 : Telegram

The Consul General at Taipei (Macdonald) to the Secretary of State

TAIPEI, August 2, 1949—4 p. m.
[Received August 5—1 : 23 p. m.]

346. Information mytel 344, repeated to Canton 153 August 2, confirmed officially. Informant said however this organization should not be called headquarters but Gimo's private secretariat. It is also referred to as Tsungtsai's office (office of the Director General of the Kuomintang).

Sent Department 346, repeated Canton 155.

MACDONALD

893.00/8–249 : Telegram

The Consul General at Taipei (Macdonald) to the Secretary of State

TAIPEI, August 2, 1949—5 p. m.
[Received August 3—2 : 09 p. m.]

347. Refmytel 341, repeated Canton 150, August 1. K. C. Wu said Acting President's visit Taipei was principally to discuss with Gimo implementation of matters taken up during Canton conferences and prosecution war. Wu claims all friction between Gimo and Li eliminated and is substituted by complete solidarity of purpose to pursue struggle against Communism.

Gimo has absolutely no intention of coming out of retirement and resuming his position as President, according to Wu, since he now has confidence in Li and is prepared to give him all necessary backing. Wu stressed that people no longer have to fear lack of solidarity between Gimo and Li, then said he considers Gimo greatest man Asia has produced in modern times and again commented on how he has broadened and changed his outlook.

Sent Department 347, repeated OffEmb Canton 156.

MACDONALD

893.00/8–349 : Telegram

The Vice Consul at Chungking (McGeary) to the Secretary of State

CHUNGKING, August 3, 1949—noon.
[Received August 7—2 : 17 p. m.]

135. Following report 8-day trip Vice Consul [apparent garble] T. A. Wahl[57] to Lanchow where Chinese educators, government officials and foreigners interviewed :

---

[57] Theodore A. Wahl, Vice Consul at Chungking.

Reported Pingliang and Tienshui occupied or threatened by Communists as bases for pincer movement on Lanchow and NW. Recent reverses Shensi battle largely attributed failure Hu Tsung-nan hold sector. Some say Hu refused fight. Ma Hung-kwei troops also reported uncooperative and refuse to fight. Most private citizens feel Communist occupation inevitable although proper action and cooperation month ago could have secured NW. Some see only hope in Communists' voluntarily turning southward to Szechuan, but admit not probable since Communist known [know?] weakness caused by uncoordinated efforts defending army groups as well as political division Kansu and Moslem-Han Chinese feeling. Oil and other resources make NW valuable objective. Ma Pu-fang reportedly plans last minute retreat to west Tsinghai.

Appointment Ma Hung-kwei governor Kansu seemed surprise everyone. Most thought ill health would prevent return NW. None could explain apparent inconsistencies Ma Hung-kwei who tells intimates he wants retire, then goes Canton take initiative obtain governorship Kansu. Reported promises support his 60,000 troops important factor Ma Pu-fang acceptance directorship NW headquarters but these troops uncooperative in Shensi battles. Ma Hung-kwei long desired governorship native province Kansu but is unpopular there as result feudal and dictatorial rule Ninghsia province. Unpopularity increased result action troops in battle and unilateral turning over Ninghsia government his son. More dictatorial government and greater military organization expected in Kansu; also drastic changes provisional government officialdom.

Difficult obtain consistent views attitude Han Chinese toward Moslems. Ma Pu-fang apparently trying best eradicate past bad feeling by making donations to schools, giving entertainments and keeping troops in line. Most agree however that despite these efforts and respect for progressiveness Moslems, Han Chinese still hate and fear Moslems; some would prefer Communist dictatorship to Moslem rule. Many recall cruelty Moslem marauders in parts Kansu as late as mid-thirties. Kansu estimated 20 percent Moslem.

Main source Shui Tien-tung, dean Arts College, Lanchow University.

Sent Department 135, repeated OffEmb Canton 88, AmEmb Nanking 140.

McGeary

893.00/8–449 : Telegram

The Vice Consul at Chungking (McGeary) to the Secretary of State

CHUNGKING, August 4, 1949—9 a. m.
[Received August 8—5:50 p. m.]

137. From Strong. Nationalist military forces now beginning same measures here which alienated population Tsingtao (as example known to me).

Ministry National Defense has ordered SWMPA [58] raise one million silver dollars for construction defense works vicinity Chungking. Garrison headquarters to collect funds in cooperation with city government and will carry out work. City Council opposes measure on valid grounds defense should take place at border and defense works around city useless if Communists penetrate so far. Garrison making outright levies on banks, commercial houses, industries and landowners but all have so far avoided actual payment. Aside from futility of project, people have legitimate fear that, as at Tsingtao, it will turn into another boondoggle for private gain. Recent serious food price rises attributed in large [part?] to illegal conscription activities by various military units which are under declared strength; view fear Defense Commander that strength may be examined by Central Government before committed to combat near future, they obliged round up defenceless civilians to fill in ranks since cannot obtain men from legal conscription center. Effect has been to make farmers afraid enter city, thus creating scarcities. Garrison now using military police patrol city prevent such illegal activities. This measure plus fact silver and gold reserves exceed amount paper notes issued hoped bring price decline.

Repeated Nanking 141; OffEmb Canton 91. [Strong.]

McGEARY

893.00/8–449 : Telegram

The Vice Consul at Chungking (McGeary) to the Secretary of State

CHUNGKING, August 4, 1949—10 a. m.
[Received August 5—9:57 p. m.]

138. From Strong. Chairman of local Municipal Council, critic of Nationalist Government but not pro-Communist, states Chang Chun has no real authority and unable unify various military forces in Szechwan. Describes Governor Wang Lin-chi as competing directly with Chang for power, seeking retain all in his own hands. Ascribes failure attain unity to Generalissimo, who continues support Wang despite appointment Chang to supposed supreme position. Does not

[58] Southwest Military and Political Administration.

believe unity attainable either within Szechwan or between Ma Pu-fang, Hu Tsung-nan and Lo Kwan-wen.

As is case with Provincial Council, City Council bitter over failure Nationalist Government pay heed to attitude of "people's representatives" on numerous matters.

Sent Department 138, repeated Nanking 142, OffEmb Canton 92. [Strong.]

McGEARY

893.00/8–449 : Telegram

The Chargé in China (Clark) to the Secretary of State

CANTON, August 4, 1949—2 p. m.
[Received August 9—9 : 41 a. m.]

Cantel 872. Tried out on Malcolm MacDonald, High Commissioner for Southeast Asia, whom I encountered Hong Kong, ideas future policy re China outlined Cantel 829, July 27, repeated Nanking 585, Shanghai 465, Taipei 84. Malcolm thought it interesting approach which might prove profitable but would need lot of thinking through. If such policy were pursued and did in fact result chaotic condition China, Malcolm said situation would have salutary effect Southeast Asia, strengthening determination those wanting resist, putting heart into those hesitating and generally strengthening democratic elements. Prime British consideration at moment is Hong Kong and British business interests. He said Hong Kong community had been buoyed by British determination defend colony, but was extremely depressed over prospects trade with Communists. Feeling thus re Hong Kong was almost as strong, he said, as that Shanghai. Problem, as British saw it, was whether preferable treat Communists with friendship in hopes trade would be permitted over long term or whether that hope was futile and they should immediately take firm stand against Communists, make Hong Kong fortress, and try weather storm. In any event, Hong Kong would be defended, he said. If economic situation caused great unemployment, Chinese not British subjects would be deported.

Malcolm said he hoped Quirino–Chiang Pacific Pact would be "stillborn". It could not but fail under such parentage. He feels nevertheless there should be some broad concerted action countries Southeast Asia at proper time. He believes there is some hope this regard if trends French Indochina and Indonesia continue. His people Indochina say Bao Dai [59] is doing much better than had been expected. If he can continue political success and if French commander can get military reinforcements he has been led believe will be forth-

[59] Former Emperor of Annam; Chief of State of Vietnam since June 14, 1949.

coming from France and if they can have 9 months to 1 year before Communists attack across border from China, Malcolm believes Indochina can be saved. Indonesia seems definitely better, he says, and President's Point Four program might help there. In Burma anything can happen, but he believes that so long as Thakin Nu [60] is in control Communists would not get anywhere there. Although export rice had brought in sufficient current funds Thakin Nu had requested the rice loan from India, Pakistan, Ceylon and UK be held open, which has been done. Malcolm feels Nehru [61] is all-important in India. Change of Nehru from anti-West to realization Communism is bad had resulted in his agreement remain Commonwealth, but Malcolm thought Nehru still fascinated by Communism as intellectual theory. If Nehru got killed, Indian situation might develop badly, he says, as Patel [62] is no answer, being too old and essentially an organizer who does not hold imagination Indians as does Nehru. In his own Malaya, things are going really quite nicely, he said, and terrorists are being driven further and further into interior and will be eliminated.

Sent Department, repeated Nanking 578, Shanghai 478, Taipei 92, London 3. Pouched to Saigon 2, Rangoon 3, New Delhi unnumbered, Singapore unnumbered, Hong Kong 25.

CLARK

893.00/8–449 : Telegram

The Chargé in China (Clark) to the Secretary of State

CANTON, August 4, 1949—3 p. m.
[Received August 9—10 : 34 p. m.]

Cantel 875. Views and information from Cheng Szu-yuan, Li advisor and Assistant Secretary-General Kmt Supreme Policy Committee, as follows:

1. Li Tsung-jen trip to Formosa in nature formal return call. Nothing accomplished. Views Li and Generalissimo on military strategy divergent as ever. Generalissimo has sent, is sending more, Liu An-chi troops from Hainan to Canton, but these troops strictly for use around city, not on Kwangtung–Kiangsi border where Cheng says they are badly needed and might do some real good.

2. Communist forces afraid launch frontal attack on Pai Chung-hsi at Hengyang. Cheng believes Communists instead will try cut in north and south Hengyang for purposes (a) sucking Pai's troops into small encounters disadvantageous to Pai, and (b) cutting off Pai's route into Kwangsi. Cheng says Pai's position heavily dependent on support other Nationalist troops around Taiho–Kanchow and under Sung Hsi-lien in Western Hunan. Next few weeks will tell tale these things.

---

[60] Burmese Prime Minister.
[61] Jawaharlal Nehru, Indian Prime Minister.
[63] Sardar Vallabhbhai Patel, Indian Deputy Prime Minister.

3. Kmt Supreme Policy Committee held second regular meeting 3 days running August 1 through 3. No important decision. Only 7 of 12 members present, absentees in Hong Kong or Formosa. SPC did discuss question capital removal but decided government best stay Canton "for time being". Chungking not ruled out as next site, but everyone well aware Chungking may prove no more secure than Canton. Meantime "dispersal" minor employees and unimportant records will continue.

4. Cheng says Communist Chinese language broadcast Cheng Chien, former Governor Hunan, "capture" day or so ago, but former not sure whether latter actually captured or willingly went over. In any case, Cheng gave this background information: Pai Chung-hsi deposed Cheng Chien because latter strong advocate "local peace" with Communists. Cheng then went Shaoyang (Southern Hunan) from there back to town near Changsha from which he invited new Hunan Governor Chen Ming-jen come over discuss "local peace". Chen refused go, so Cheng apparently started back south and was "captured" around Hsiangtan.

Sent Department Cantel 875, repeated Nanking 581, Taipei 94.

CLARK

893.01/8–449 : Telegram

The Chargé in China (Clark) to the Secretary of State

CANTON, August 4, 1949—8 p. m.
[Received August 7—7 : 19 p. m.]

Cantel 876. Tung Ling, Vice Minister Foreign Office, confirms my impression fall Hengyang may be signal for removal government [from] Canton, Cantel 847, July 29. August 15 may be little early, but certainly expect action some time this month. Present government plans continue contemplate removal to Chungking, even if temporary and on infinitesimal scale.

Sent Department Cantel 876; repeated Chungking as 75.

CLARK

893.00/8–449 : Airgram

The Chargé in China (Clark) to the Secretary of State

CANTON, August 4, 1949.
[Received August 14—9 : 49 a. m.]

A–41. Mr. Yin Jen-chai, Secretary to Premier Yen Hsi-shan and one of the Embassy's most helpful sources, has provided this office with a confidential copy of the Premier's proposals for an overall solution to the manifold problems now facing the Central Government. These proposals have been drawn up in the form of a bill entitled: "A Bill to Remedy the Present Situation", an 8,000-character long product of several weeks' intensive effort on the part of Yen and his advisors.

Although the exact status of this Bill is not clear, it appears to have been accepted in principle by the Supreme Policy Committee of the Kmt at its first session held in Canton on July 20. Yen's advisors state that the Bill, the details of which have still not been completed, requires no further approval by any other organ of the Central Government and will be enforced by the various Governmental agencies as conditions develop.

The vagueness of the enforcement procedure is matched, with some few exceptions, by the vagueness of the Bill itself. On the whole, the Bill appears to be nothing more than another general statement of principles or overall plan for "averting the crisis" or "saving the situation", which have been the distinguishing handiwork of Central Government leaders in recent years of decadence and inaction. These plans to reform, to establish committees and commissions and councils, to reorganize, to regroup, to unite the nation, to improve morale, to stop inflation, to win over the common people, and so on ad infinitum, have been so numerous and so signally ineffective that it will be nothing short of a miracle if Yen's plan to remedy the situation ever takes concrete shape and is carried out.

Since Yen's Bill does not yet appear to be either law or a definitive statement of policy, its provisions will not be dealt with in detail here. Very briefly, the Bill consists of four parts:

The first part is a general introduction in which the Premier advances the thesis that Nationalist forces must adopt Communist guerrilla-type tactics of attacking where the enemy is weak or unprepared and overwhelming him by superiority in numbers. This type of mobile warfare would be maintained until a new force could be built up or until a change in the international situation brought foreign aid and cooperation.

The second part explains the different stages at which the Communists succeeded in developing their military might; to wit, during the recent war and taking advantage of Nationalist troops then engaged in fighting the Japanese.

The third part gives the Premier's estimate of the reasons for Communist successes; namely, their flexible policy of adapting their methods to the particular time and place, popular regimentation, mobile warfare, and liquidation of all classes to the point where everyone is dependent upon the CCP for livelihood and protection.

The fourth part contains the specific proposals on governmental finance and budget balancing, troop readjustments, total warfare, local government authority, foreign policy, education, and so on.

As stated above, even these "specific proposals" are for the most part quite vague. They will, however, be covered in detail in a subsequent report should developments make it worth while.

CLARK

893.00/8–549 : Telegram

The Chargé in China (Clark) to the Secretary of State

CANTON, August 5, 1949—noon.
[Received August 9—5 : 22 a. m.]

Cantel 881. Chu Chang-wei, political advisor to President, told me General Pai Chung-hsi position critical [as] result defection Hunan Governor Cheng Chien who tried make local peace and now gone over to Commies. Government hoping Hunan troops remain loyal [to] new Governor Chen Ming-jen, whom Pai appointed because once also commanded same troops. Also admitted ammunition situation growing serious and stated no ammunition forthcoming from Taiwan. Said Ma's needs for ammunition also not met.

CLARK

893.00/8–649 : Telegram

The Counselor of Embassy in China (Jones) to the Secretary of State

NANKING, August 6, 1949—4 p. m.
[Received August 7—1 : 57 a. m.]

1731. Following is translation of propaganda leaflet dropped by CAF during Nanking air raid August 1. This is first example we have seen of Nationalist attempt distribute effective propaganda.

"Fellow countrymen in bandit-occupied areas: Since arrival of Communist bandits, you have been living an incarcerated, miserable life. When we think of this, we are extremely perturbed and pained. Fellow countrymen, you have clearly seen true face of Communist bandits. Their hearts are more cruel than those of beasts. All they say is false, deceiving. They speak of democracy day and night, but actually there is not slightest degree of democracy in occupied areas. They praise 'the people' as they do gods, but in truth they treat them as beasts of burden. They send all able-bodied youths to the front to be used as cannon fodder, yet they say it is the youths themselves who want to 'join the army'. They force people to surrender their food, yet they claim it is the people themselves who are willing to 'contribute' their food stuffs. Similar deceitful practices are too numerous to list here. In any event you have seen enough already.

"Fellow countrymen, the Communist bandits do not love their country, much less the people. They are fighting for the Lao Mao Tze (ed. "old hairy ones", meaning USSR). They wish to give away our beloved country to foreigners, let our children of future generations serve as slaves of foreigners. How can we Chinese labor as beasts for those foreign devils? We must exterminate Communist bandits, good-for-nothing traitors for sake of independence of our nation, existence of our people, our own freedom, welfare of our future generations.

"Through desperation resulting from Communist oppression, fellow countrymen in Hupeh, Honan, northern Anhwei have already started fighting Communist bandits with knives, guns, etc., which has given them many headaches. Peiping workers, bitter against cheating of Communist bandits, burned over 50 tramcars in one night, set fire to laboratory of the Shihchungshan mines. Every patriotic fellow countryman should follow their example. To exterminate Communist bandits is to save nation and yourselves. If you do not exterminate them, they will exterminate you. If you cannot fight them now, do not cooperate with them. Never assist Communist bandits or collaborate with them in their traitorous intrigue. We will fight back soon, final victory will be ours. Sooner or later Communist bandits will fail, completely wiped out by us. Begin your struggle against them immediately. Destroy their factories, defense works; annihilate their troops; kill their village officers, special service men; blow up their ships, vehicles, bridges. They will collapse when our forces strike back. Arise, fellow countrymen in bandit-held areas. Fight on courageously for our fatherland and for yourselves. (Signed) Army, Navy, Air Force Revolutionary Comrades Society.["]

Sent Department, repeated OffEmb Canton 725, Shanghai 951.

JONES

893.00/8–649 : Telegram

The Chargé in China (Clark) to the Secretary of State

CANTON, August 6, 1949—1 p. m.
[Received August 9—8 :47 a. m.]

Cantel 886. Li Tsung-jen is a worried man and, I believe, is already planning for the day when he will lead a local area of resistance. He told me today that he planned give increased authority to local governments in the hope that will to resist would be revived. Difficulty was, he said, that local governments could not afford pay cost armies. He inquired this regard whether US would support autonomous areas continuing to resist Communism and admitted finally that he had himself, with Pai Chung-hsi and Ma Pu-fang in mind. In other words, when government is forced flee mainland, Li envisages that he will remain Kwangsi as leader resistance forces commanded by Pai Chung-hsi and he would like American aid. I replied that his question was at same time most easy and most difficult one to answer; that decision US Government would have to be made in light of circumstances existing that time, but he could be assured our desire assist anti-Communist forces wherever they showed signs of effectiveness. I added that accessibility to region occupied would be an element in problem, pointing out difficulty in supplying Ma Pu-fang in Northwest, even with best good will.

Gather from Li that his visit with Gimo, Taiwan, accomplished nothing. Li asked for more arms and ammunition for armies Pai Chung-hsi and Ma Pu-fang and was told by Gimo all available supplies had already been allocated. He asked for money for Pai's armies and was told that reserves must be conserved so as to last 2 years. He asked for political reform and removal grafting and incompetent officials, both military and civilian, and was told that action that field should not be taken precipitously and in any event presented certain problems. He insisted that Yen Hsi-shan was too old and too busy with other things to fill position Ministry National Defense in addition that Prime Minister and demanded appointment Pai Chung-hsi as Minister National Defense and was told idea was good one but moment was not opportune. In other words, Li admits that he has been stymied in all his efforts to get something for himself out of Gimo, yet he seems willing continue Acting President at least until government forced flee mainland.

Li seemed considerably perturbed over defection three Hunanese armies under Cheng Ming-jen and said it would greatly embarrass Pai Chung-hsi. I continue of impression Pai will not put up any serious battle until chased to hills of Kwangsi.

Sent Department; repeated Nanking 584, Shanghai 479, Taipei 97.

CLARK

893.00B/8–949 : Telegram

The Chargé in China (Clark) to the Secretary of State

CANTON, August 9, 1949—8 p. m.
[Received August 15—9 : 13 a. m.]

Cantel 912. Han Li-wu, Minister of Education, although denying that present phase is rapidly coming to end, agrees that next phase to problem will be battle for Chinese mind. Problem will be to reach disillusioned elements under Communist domination and inspire them, to hampering Communist activities and eventually to uprising in revolt against Communist regime. Reports have been coming to him, as they have to me, of widespread and growing disillusionment in Communist-dominated areas. It is fertile soil in which we should seek plant seeds of democracy. First issue of long-awaited periodical *Free China* is planned for this month and despite our information to contrary, Dr. Han believes Dr. Hu Shih will return by October to Taiwan to head up publication periodical and related activities under aegis Ministry of Education.

I told Dr. Han that it seemed to me obvious from Secretary's covering letter to President re White Paper [63] that we would desire to support in China any measures giving promise of enabling Chinese people create society they desire unhampered by foreign ideology or interference and I asked him give me memorandum outlining his plans. I said that, speaking personally, as I had not even reported subject to Department, let alone received its instructions, it seemed to me

---

[63] Department of State, *United States Relations With China* (Washington, Government Printing Office, 1949), p. III.

that if he could outline program giving possibility effective rallying of resistance within Communist-dominated China, we would desire to help. Although I will, of course, submit any memorandum he gives to me to Department for consideration, should appreciate Department's preliminary reaction line I have been taking.

Dr. Han, who, as I reported from Nanking, is one of the small group determined upon resistance unto death to Communism, refuses to admit possibility government will not remove Chungking should Canton be threatened and, to prove his case, is planning go there, takhis wife and family with him, despite the obvious objection his wife.

In an off moment, Dr. Han admitted Pai Chung-hsi is conservative, [anti?] Communistic and is unlikely make firm stand until he has become guerrilla in mountains Kwangsi.

He says Li Tsung-jen was advised when he assumed office Acting President that he should decide whether to try to be a Chiang Kai-shek or a Lin Sen.[64] He said Li had determined endeavor emulate Generalissimo, but had failed and now seems reconciled to role Lin Sen. He admitted Li had gotten brush-off from Generalissimo when last he visited Taiwan, but feels Yen Hsi-shan is being effective bridge between two and that Li will stay on role Lin Sen, even though government eventually move Taiwan. As indicative of individual bickering which is continuing, Dr. Han admitted reluctantly that Chu Chia-hua, who former Minister Education when Han was Vice-Minister and now Vice-Premier, has hampered his, Han's action, there being jealousy on part Chu and unwillingness see Han succeed where he, Chu, had failed.

As I have previously reported, Han Li-wu seems the one bright spot in present government. If there is any way we could help him in his battle for the Chinese mind, believe it would be beneficial to us and might have possibility eventual success.

Sent Department Cantel 912, repeated Nanking 601, Shanghai 486, Taipei 105.

CLARK

761.93/8-1049 : Telegram

The Consul at Shanghai (McConaughy) to the Secretary of State

SHANGHAI, August 10, 1949—7 p. m.
[Received August 10—10 : 59 a. m.]

3164. Three prominent American businessmen with close well-informed Chinese contacts have separately repeated to us information from Chinese sources whom they regard highly, all agreeing re main thesis re Soviet pressure on Mao Tze-tung.

---

[64] President of the National Government of the Republic of China, 1931–1943.

Stories all agree that Kremlin, strongly disapproving Mao's deviationist tendencies and unsatisfactory declarations subservience Moscow, forced Mao adopt strongly pro-Soviet line in his July 1st statement. (According one source, special Soviet emissary sent to Peiping for this purpose.) Mao, indignant but helpless in face powerful Soviet forces along border, has since sulked, refraining from public utterances (notably on Red Army Day August 1 when he would normally give one) and actually sick, according one report.

One source had it that Moscow much displeased over recent wide circulation and popularity of Mao's "New Democracy" (supposedly written under influence of later discredited Pletkhanov [65]) in Europe satellite countries.

In recent talk with officer ConGen, Han Ming voiced similar belief re Mao's July 1 speech being written under Soviet pressure; and said that Soviet pressure on Chinese Communists is reflected from top to bottom of Communist hierarchy, with every Communist watched by other Communists and afraid express anti-Soviet views.

While ConGen unable evaluate this information, it believes worth reporting as at least moderacy of newly issued Shanghai labor regulations and alleged basis hope for easier treatment Shanghai foreigners (ReContel 3007, August 3 [66]).

Another possible straw in wind and illustration of difficulty evaluating conflicting evidence re strength of Soviet hand in Shanghai is report which we attempting verify that Soviet Russian language paper (presumably *Novosti Dnya*) due financial reasons has applied for suspension and been refused by authorities.

As somewhat related to above may also be reported conviction here among some observers that blockade is having inevitable effect force Communists more into Soviet arms through dependence on Soviet economic help and that it may well have been factor in hastening recent Manchurian trade agreement.

Sent Department; repeated Nanking 1735, OffEmb Canton 981. Department pass Peiping 25.

McCONAUGHY

893.001 Chiang Kai-shek/8–1049 : Airgram

The Chargé in China (Clark) to the Secretary of State

CANTON, August 10, 1949.
[Received August 24—5 : 11 p. m.]

A–45. In a recent conversation with one of the FS Officers in Canton, Shih Chao-ying, Director of Information, Chinese Foreign Office, made certain revealing observations about Generalissimo Chiang.

---

[65] Perhaps G. V. Plekhanov, theoretician of Russian Marxism.
[66] Not printed.

One of the leading reasons for the failure of the Gimo's administration, Mr. Shih declared, was the fact that the former had been very badly advised on several vital questions. He mentioned particularly General Chiang's preoccupation with the imminence of a war between United States and the Soviet Union and attributed much of this bemusement to the bad advice of Wang Shih-chieh, former Foreign Minister and at present a member of the Gimo's retinue.

When in Nanking, as Director of Information, Mr. Shih always attended the weekly Wednesday meetings at which the Gimo reviewed general policy and current developments. On one occasion, General Chiang predicted that a USA–USSR war would break out within 18 months and on another occasion (at the time of the Presidential and Vice-Presidential elections in the spring of 1948) he became angry about something and asserted that within 1 year such a war would begin. From Mr. Shih's remarks, I inferred that the Gimo, because of his misconceptions on this subject, had taken ill-advised action (or had refrained from needed action) in other fields.

The Gimo, according to Mr. Shih, attributed the shortcomings of his Government, in large measure, to lack of discipline in the Kuomintang (the Gimo, as Director-General, and the Central Executive Committee would not enforce implementation of their decisions on the lower levels of Party leadership) and to inadequate preparation (especially in the case of local governmental units) for the introduction of democratic government.

However, disclaiming that he is a supporter of General Chiang and stating that he has never joined the Kuomintang, Mr. Shih believes that the Gimo, with all his failings, is still the only leader in the Kmt with great enough personal prestige and authority to silence its disputing factions. It seems that after the Gimo has spoken, further discussion is unnecessary.

CLARK

893.00/8–1149 : Telegram

The Consul General at Hong Kong (Hopper) to the Secretary of State

HONG KONG, August 11, 1949—10 a. m.
[Received August 11—9 : 52 a. m.]

531. . . . Source reports Communist military and political chief South China Fang appears to have departed for interior [to] contact forces now advancing from north. Yeh Chien-ying [67] reportedly commanding offensive directed against Canton, with Fang probably subordinated to him after fall that city which Communists expect take by 1 September. Communists wish expedite capture Canton

---

[67] Hitherto Communist mayor of Peiping.

[to] circumvent coastal blockade and also wish announce this prior or immediately after convocation PPC [68] Peiping. Meanwhile various important functionaries for new Canton administration assembling Hong Kong for entry their new posts.

Communists apparently unwilling negotiate peace Kwangsi leaders short of acceptance unconditional surrender. Their present campaign in south includes destruction Kwangsi armies and occupation both Kwangtung, Kwangsi. Thereafter plan move against Szechuan.

Some evidence suggests ships successfully running blockade from North China ports, possibly by bribing Nationalist guard ships. While total this traffic unknown, believed relatively small. Most British firms Hong Kong reportedly eager resume trade with North, and pressuring their government take necessary measures get trade started.

Extent Communist activity within Hong Kong difficult ascertain, but probably mainly along lines organizing among labor unions. While Communist propaganda organs active, Hong Kong Government and British authorities never attacked. Indications suggest Communists have no immediate intention [garble] or military move against Hong Kong.

Communists have taken over bulk of political and military organizations in Kwangtung formerly belonging Li Chi-sen.[69] Some former followers Li now appearing as CCP agents. Li believed not coming south after formation coalition government as once expected.

Sent OffEmb Canton 55, repeated Department 531, Nanking 41, Shanghai 114, Peiping unnumbered.

HOPPER

893.00B/8–1149 : Telegram

The Consul General at Peiping (Clubb) to the Secretary of State

PEIPING, August 11, 1949—noon.
[Received August 14—12 : 14 a. m.]

1346. Re Contel 1071, June 23.[70] Ex-Mayor Ho Su-yuan August 9 informed me PCC scheduled be convoked August 20. Joseph Chang shortly before said August 15, will last about 1 month. Ho said subject[s] conference agenda were now under discussion by Communists who had circularized other groups setting forth their position re government organization "for reference". Circular provided small space for noting down comments by other groups but opinions would hardly be opposed strongly by Democrats who continued as before squabble vigorously among selves. Those squabbles had irritated Com-

---
[68] People's Political Council. Probably this should be the PCC (Political Consultative Conference).
[69] Formerly head of the Kuomintang Revolutionary Committee at Hong Kong.
[70] Not printed.

munists who had placed spies on them. Definitive discussions were being held in closed-in Communist council, not public meetings. PCC date would be postponed only if there was failure reach decision on outstanding questions, it being expected government be set up October. Note confirmatory indications PCC will be rubber stamp conference.

Ho criticized BBC [71] report of differences opinion between Chou En-lai and Liu Shao-chi saying Liu is like Chou in fact to be considered highest in CCP in opposition [to] Li Li-san orientation. There are true differences of opinion within CCP respecting international orientation but it is not to be expected that there would be any split within CCP at this time. Ho opined further there was no change in Communist attitude vis-à-vis either USSR or USA.

Would comment that Communists presumably are presently concentrating attention on scheduled PCC and completion this stage military campaign and that question international orientation can therefore hardly be expected occupy much of their energies at present. Invite attention recent spate Communist reports showing high hopes for economic assistance from USSR particularly re industrialization and even foodstuffs (Shanghai's 3125, 5 a. m., August 9 to Department [72]). Express firm opinion that at present juncture adamant economic factors offer strong guarantees that Communism in China will remain weak and opine further that with such hopes re Soviet help Communists possibly now face winter of their discontent with USSR.

Sent Department 1346, repeated Nanking 966, OffEmb Canton 258, Shanghai 883.

CLUBB

893.00/8–1149 : Telegram

The Chargé in China (Clark) to the Secretary of State

CANTON, August 11, 1949—2 p. m.
[Received August 14—3 :39 a. m.]

Cantel 923. Ku Meng-yu called by appointment today obviously to sound out our reaction toward possibility creation third force China. Ku was Dean Peking University early 1920's; Kmt Minister Publicity during northern expedition; Minister Railways before World War II; Chancellor National Central University before VJ Day; resided in US number years during and after war; and returned China about year ago and was offered Premiership by Li Tsung-jen after fall Sun Fo Cabinet.

Ku inquired as to our reaction in event there developed third force China recruited from liberals in Kmt and outside which would cast

---

[71] British Broadcasting Company
[72] Not printed.

aside Generalissimo and reactionary elements, endeavoring present people's reforms and alternative both Kmt and Communists. He said Fu [*he?*] thought we and Britain allowed our interests suffer through legalistic approach such problems. He cited our support Yuan Shih-kai when he was legitimate President,[73] denying assistance to Sun Yat-sen when he really represented dynamic force which could have been directed along course in our interests. Ku said he was convinced that Sun Yat-sen turned to Soviets at that time [74] only because he had been denied support by US and Britain. He hoped that US would not permit diplomatic or legalistic niceties to lead US into continued support of a Generalissimo regime or a forthcoming Communist regime at the expense of liberal elements which might coalesce and offer resistance even though technically illegal to constituted authority in China.

I explained to Ku that our interest was not in an individual or in cliques, but in effective resistance to Communism in China. I said that, speaking personally as I was without instructions, I felt sure my Government would view with pleasure the emergence of any group or groups in China giving promise of effective resistance to Communism, would study situation created by emergence of such groups, and aid them to the extent found feasible under the circumstances existing at the time.

This was the assurance, I am convinced, that was sought by Ku Meng-yu and he will proceed with his plan. His reticence and his unwillingness to admit even in broad outline, however, what his real plan is made it impossible to ascertain exactly what he has in mind or whether his activities are known to Li Tsung-jen with whom he is most friendly.

Suspect we will encounter more like Ku Meng-yu seeking new means of resistance to Communism as realization becomes more widespread that present phase is reaching its conclusion.

Sent Dept. Cantel 923; repeated Nanking 609, Shanghai 489, Taipei 112.

CLARK

893.001 Chiang Kai-shek/8–1149 : Telegram

The Consul General at Taipei (Macdonald) to the Secretary of State

TAIPEI, August 11, 1949—3 p. m.
[Received August 12—3 : 57 p. m.]

375. Visited General Sun Li-jen [75] at his headquarters during official visit South Taiwan. He looked tired, despondent and holds little hope

---

[73] 1913–1916.
[74] 1923.
[75] Commanding General Taiwan Defense Headquarters and Deputy Director of Military and Political Affairs for Southeast China.

for Nationalist forces. He severely criticized Government, saying officials only interested security their positions. Numerous conferences have accomplished nothing, according him. He said Government is disintegrating due its own corruption and rottenness and Gimo is badly mistaken if he thinks he can hold it together through personal loyalty as leader. Sun claims Gimo made great mistake by not retiring entirely from political scene and any hope of Acting President and Gimo reaching complete agreement or solidarity and working together on major issues is pure figment of imagination.

He foresees total collapse of Nationalist armies, saying armed forces no longer have will to resist and that civilians have lost all confidence in President, Government. He remarked that it is so hopeless he can't see why they carry on. Sun impressed me as having taken just about as much as he can stand and about ready to give up but continues to do his duty out of sheer patriotism.

Sent Department 375, repeated Canton 176.

MACDONALD

893.01/8–1249 : Telegram

The Chargé in China (Clark) to the Secretary of State

CANTON, August 12, 1949—6 p. m.
[Received August 13—7 : 13 p. m.]

Cantel 932. Face [*Fact?*] Communist drives from Shansi and Hupeh. which appeared headed Szechuan last month, now turned northwest toward Lanchow and south into western Hunan, has led Chinese Government dust off plan for capital Chungking which had previously been virtually relegated ash can (Cantel 833, July 27, repeated Taipei 85, Chungking 72). Two thousand top officials who will remain Canton, after "dispersal" completed (see below), will be ready, as one pressman states, go airport "brief case in hand" (meaning all else has already left Canton) to follow Acting President and Premier [to] Chungking, where they will set up offices close enough airport to be able get out to Formosa when Szechuan is lost.

Figures Central Government dispersal commission indicate 12,000 persons, comprising 8,500 dependents and 3,500 unessential personnel, scheduled depart Canton between August 8 and 20 in final step reduce government to elite "brief case corps". Ten percent dispersees are going Formosa and represent those government definitely wishes retain, while 90 percent proceeding Chungking are, according one source, "not welcome Taiwan" as government unable even attempt provide quarters and food. Important files plus families and servants of top officials remaining Canton have already been sent Formosa. Thus all information present indicates that if capital moves Chungking it will be merely passed [*pause?*] in flight en route final resting place Formosa.

Sent Department Cantel 932; repeated Taipei 117, pouched Chungking 81.

CLARK

893.00/8–1249 : Telegram

The Consul General at Peiping (Clubb) to the Secretary of State

PEIPING, August 12, 1949.
[Received August 14—6 : 49 a. m.]

1351. *Kuang Ming Jih Pao* August 11 reporting on second day of conference representatives all circles Peiping stated Vice Chairman Chinese People's Revolutionary Military Affairs Committee Chou En-lai attended and made political report on subject "carry revolution through to end and construct new China".

Per this version, Chou [in] course report discussing Ambassador J. Leighton Stuart quoted World [*Peiping?*] Mayor Yeh Chien-ying, "this is an honest man who tells lies". Item continued, "true depicting of face this American Ambassador drew roar laughter from whole gathering".

Then (per item) Vice Chairman Chou Mun [*made?*] penetrating analysis American Ambassadors stationed China last few years, Hurley,[76] Marshall,[77] Wedemeyer [78] and J. Leighton Stuart. Vice Chairman Chou said these several Ambassadors could be divided into two types as that of Marshall and J. Leighton Stuart, who were accustomed in appearing with deceptive countenances falsely covered with affability. However, their objectives alike were none other than desiring maintain special privileges of American imperialism in China and to force Chinese people into fold (in sense "to subject to control" due PLA).

Sent Department; repeated OffEmb Canton, Nanking 970, Shanghai 887. Tientsin by mail.

CLUBB

---

[76] Maj. Gen. Patrick J. Hurley, Special Representative of President Roosevelt in China, August 1944; Ambassador, December 1944–November 1945.

[77] General of the Army George C. Marshall, Special Representative of President Truman in China, December 1945–January 1947.

[78] Lt. Gen. Albert C. Wedemeyer, Special Representative of President Truman in China, July–September 1947.

893.00/8-1349 : Telegram

The Consul at Shanghai (McConaughy) to the Secretary of State

SHANGHAI, August 13, 1949—2 p. m.
[Received August 13—8 : 14 a. m.]

3224. Re Hong Kong telegram 514 [*114?*], August 11.[79] Hong Kong Li Tsung-jen supporters scheme gain place in coalition government to fight Communists' power monopoly believed closely related to underground maneuverings of pro-Li Shanghai groups, including Yang Hu Green Gang, Kmt remnants and possibly even KmtRC leaders (long well-disposed to Li). Recall that such elements, plus many intellectuals and important banking and business quarters including several leaders such as Li Ming, played major role in bringing about election of Li as vice president and of pro-Li Kmt dissidents to Legislative Yuan. Bitterly anti-Generalissimo, same groups still strongly for Li, the more so in view disillusionment re Communist Shanghai policies. Member Green Gang recently made statements to officer Consulate General revealing (1) intense interest in Kwangsi faction's prospects for American aid and/or for political-military developments to force Communists make political settlement with Li and (2) inauguration regular secret contact between Shanghai and Li and his Hong Kong supporters. He also indicated sympathy with rural anti-Communist rebellions, such those of Red Spears (with whom Green Gang "has connections"), evidently feeling that any added difficulties harassing Communists will help force them compromise with Li.

While support which Li's Shanghai followers can give him is negligible in direct effect on military developments, it has some significance in increasing Communist difficulties keeping Shanghai popular support—a factor which might help influence Communists either toward compromise with Li, or more likely the opposite course (assuming Communists regard Li and allies as too undependable elements to permit survival).

Sent Department 3224, repeated Nanking 1759, Canton 1003, Department pass Peiping 259, Hong Kong 190.

McCONAUGHY

893.00/8-1449 : Telegram

The Chargé in China (Clark) to the Secretary of State

CANTON, August 14, 1949—4 p. m.
[Received August 15—3 : 53 a. m.]

Cantel 943. Reliable American newsman returned from Lanchow yesterday, states city still Nationalist hands but entire provincial

---

[79] Same as telegram No. 531 from Hong Kong, p. 480.

government already moved Tsining with schools, hospitals, etc., ordered move personnel and equipment there if they can obtain transportation. One inferior division reported detected [*defected?*] near Taihshu, after fall that city, but balance Ma Pu-fang's troops retreating through Lanchow toward Tsining in good order.

Appears all good troops being withdrawn to Tsining area, leaving Kansu Corridor unprotected, so that Reds can seize it virtually without a fight after capture Lanchow and thus completely separate areas held by Ma Pu-fang and Ma Hung-kwei. Source states all information he obtained Northwest indicates separation between Ma cousins already exists to large extent due "personality differences".

CLARK

893.00B/8–1549 : Telegram

The Counselor of Embassy in China (Jones) to the Secretary of State

NANKING, August 15, 1949—3 p. m.
[Received August 15—10 : 21 a. m.]

1794. Various indications that CCP considers USA number one enemy are of interest. Australian Ambassador while in Shanghai recently had conversation with educated, thoughtful leftist whom he described as fellow-traveler but not Communist. His informant said CCP hostility to USA implacable and based on three counts:

(1) US is still supply military aid to Kuomintang. He referred to recently announced $10,000,000 military aid program (possibly referring to OFLC's final report [80] including $12,000,000 worth combat material sold China. See Radio Bulletin 178, July 29).

(2) USA had instigated and was supporting Nationalist Government's blockade of Communist China ports. (This conviction strengthened by reported statement to press in Tokyo by Admiral Badger in early June re Nationalist Government mining of Yangtze mouth.[81])

(3) USA was obviously backing anti-Communist Pacific pact growing out of Chiang-Quirino talks.

Australian Ambassador received impression that while his informant was supposedly only repeating Communist viewpoint he was actually convinced himself by apparent reasonableness Communist position.

According to . . . source, Hong Kong report, Chiang Mu, Communist representative there, recently delivered tirade against USA basing accusations on practically identical charges those listed above with one addition: That US was making silver available to Nationalist Government. Canadian diplomatic secretary, recently Shanghai, when applying for return permit Nanking was "lectured" at length by

---

[80] Department of State, Office of the Foreign Liquidation Commissioner, *Report to Congress on Foreign Surplus Disposal*, July 1949.
[81] For further documentation, see vol. IX, pp. 1098 ff.

official Alien Affairs Office on iniquities American imperialism. Same Canadian in recent encounter with Communist soldier for violation restricted military area Nanking received profuse apology when soldier discovered that he was not American.

CCP reply to White Paper [82] (see Embtel 1785, August 14 to Department; [83] repeated Shanghai 990) is perhaps more vituperative than usual.

Constant violent Communist propaganda against USA is undoubtedly having its effects on minds and attitudes of Chinese, particularly those subject to any degree of indoctrination, such as civil military employees. Effects on local populace much less impressive and Americans are treated with same friendly curiosity by people as before.

Sent Department; repeated OffEmb Canton 756, Shanghai 994.

JONES

761.93/8–1549 : Telegram

The Counselor of Embassy in China (Jones) to the Secretary of State

NANKING, August 15, 1949—4 p. m.
[Received August 15—10 : 11 a. m.]

1796. Re Shanghai's 3164, August 10. We are inclined discount reports that strong pro-Soviet line adopted in Mao's July 1 statement was result of Soviet pressure. In his "New Democracy" written in 1940 Mao said, "It is becoming increasingly clear now that, without policy of unity with Soviet, any holding back from alliance with the one Socialist country in world is bound to lead one to policy of alliance with imperialists"; and "As struggle between Socialist country and imperialist countries is becoming sharper and sharper, it becomes absolutely necessary that China make her choice between two camps". Mao in his public statement[s] has consistently followed pro-Soviet line and any increase or decrease emphasis would seem due more to changes in world situation than Soviet pressure on Mao. Commie materials intended for indoctrination of cadres such as Liu Shao-chi's "self-cultivation of a Commie" (series of lectures given at Yenan party school in 1939) place heavy emphasis on Communism as world movement and USSR as leader that movement. It is difficult to believe, in absence strong evidence to contrary, that Mao himself is not convinced of validity of theory of Commie world revolution and consequent necessity for China of close alliance with USSR.

Sent Department 1795, repeated Shanghai 996, Embassy Canton 758. Department pass Peiping 334.

JONES

---

[82] Department of State, *United States Relations With China* (Government Printing Office, 1949).
[83] Not printed.

893.00/8–1549 : Telegram

The Chargé in China (Clark) to the Secretary of State

CANTON, August 15, 1949—8 p. m.
[Received August 16—4: 51 a. m.]

Cantel 956. Reference our airgram A–39, July 26,[84] reporting earlier interview with General Ma Hung-kuei, Governor Ninghsia and Deputy Commander now Northwest Political-Military Command.

We called on General Ma again August 15 and found General interested in talking about only one thing—bullets. General Ma, gesticulating and signing in vigorous demonstration his professed feeling complete frustration, said he could not fight Communists without bullets: that his bullets were just about exhausted, and that Central Government absolutely refused send him even one empty cartridge. He stated that he had asked Central Government officials Canton and Generalissimo in Formosa for bullets, but answer was invariably no. He said he even proposed borrowing bullets with promise return them when fighting was over, but answer was same. Asked what excuse was given for refusal allot bullets, General Ma, his voice reeking with disgust, said: "They give no excuse: they simply say they have none." General Ma asked specifically that his statements be reported Washington and stressed point that US, if it intends help China fight Communists, must do so "now, not wait until 1950 or 1951". Clear implication this statement was of course that US should give immediate and direct aid to Ma Hung-kuei, view which General Ma has long held and which was fully reported in reference airgram. General Ma was assured that conversation would be reported, our response in other respects being purely non-committal.

Asked about results high-level military conference now in progress Canton, General Ma called for piece of paper and brush and forthwith sketched positions now held by Nationalist and Communist forces in Lanchow–Tienshu–Ninghsia area. His sketch showed Communist three-pronged drive on Lanchow and contained arrows indicating how Nationalist forces could chop up Communists: Ma Pu-fang's forces striking out from Lanchow and driving wedges between the three advancing Communist columns, Ma Hung-kuei's forces attacking Communist right flank, and Hu Tsung-nan's forces attacking Communist left flank and rear. General Ma pointed out that Communists in that area are now outnumbered by some 300,000 to little over 200,000. With very expressive twist of wrist, he claimed that Communists could be "ground" to bits if the Central Government would only supply bullets. Implementation of counter-attack, said General, awaits only allotment of necessary bullets by Central Government.

CLARK

---

[84] Not printed.

893.00B/8–1649 : Telegram

The Counselor of Embassy in China (Jones) to the Secretary of State

NANKING, August 16, 1949—4 p. m.
[Received August 16—11 : 41 a. m.]

1806. Movement to streamline government organizations and promote austerity now being vigorously pushed throughout Commie China illustrated financial crisis facing Commies. Rapid growth their army to present size some 4 million men and recent takeover many large cities have created enormous financial burden on their meager resources. In effort to avoid unlimited resort to printing press, which brought disaster to Kmt, Commies are adopting only feasible alternative—reduction in government expenditures, increase in government revenue and reduction population of large cities. Last measure in itself reduces pressure for increased note issue as need for currency less in rural areas than cities. Dispersal expenses held at minimum by relying on traditional Chinese social security system whereby relatives in villages and small towns expected assume support of bulk of former city dwellers. In their urgent need of revenue Commies will not hesitate squeeze upper and middle classes in cities until all are reduced to common minimum living standard as has already taken place in many country areas.

Advantage long held by Commies over Kmt has been their small budget, resulting from relative lack of corruption, limited number government employees and notoriously frugal mode of living of cadres all levels. However, Commie entry into cities and absorption Kmt armies brought about rapid increase in number government employees with consequent strain on budget. Hence current desperate efforts increase revenue coupled with streamlining and austerity program designed to bring country mode living into city.

There are indications that takeover cities has brought in its wake increasing problems of morale and discipline even in ranks of Commies. Recent resolution of CCP Central China Bureau stated "government organizations show signs of extravagance after entering cities" and decreed "steadily growing tendency among cadres to covet enjoyment and crave position". Published self-criticism from other cities such as Peiping and Nanking demonstrate such tendencies exist generally although not yet to serious degree. Therefore, important subsidiary purpose of austerity movement is to maintain purity of revolutionary discipline against blandishments of city.

Kmt never had moral courage to carry out effective taxation and reduction of government expenditures. Result was financial debacle. Commie policy is ruthless and determined, apparently paying no heed to number of jobless former Nationalist Government employees or middle classes it may ruin. Immediate objective is to win war as quickly as possible. Chou En-lai frankly stated to recently-returned delegate to All-China Scientific Workers Conference that financial problem is most serious and that it is imperative to win war quickly in order be able demobilize army.

It seems unlikely, however, that even drastic measures employed by Commies can avert increasing budgetary deficits, greater resort to printing press and mounting inflation. Bare fact is impoverished Commie China can not afford civil war on present scale. The longer war continues the more taxable reserves will be depleted. Furthermore Commie efforts through police measures to continuous growing peasant resistance against heavy exactions will presumably continue cause heavy drain on CCP resources. In short Commies are facing financial crisis they feel they can surmount only by bringing early end to war and they are now employing every resource toward that end.

We are inclined to doubt that even end of war will in fact bring relief to tax-ridden Chinese. Demobilization is traditionally difficult in China and CCP will also probably feel continuing need of large army to maintain internal order and provide for national defense. Further clue to future contained in recent statement of CCP Central China Bureau that "after war is ended austerity must still be relied on to accumulate capital and enter on large scale industrial construction".

Sent Department 1806, repeated Shanghai 1006, Embassy Canton 767.

JONES

893.00/8–1649 : Telegram

The Chargé in China (Clark) to the Secretary of State [85]

CANTON, August 16, 1949—8 p. m.
[Received August 17—2 : 12 a. m.]

Cantel 964. Chu Chang-wei, Secretary-General President's office and political advisor Li Tsung-jen, made further plea today for support Li when inevitable split with Generalissimo comes. He says Li has endeavored play role "great moderator" in his efforts bring together all elements in resistance Communism. In demeaning himself to compromise with Generalissimo, Li has sought set example others and discourage clique and individual bickering. Conference other day Canton between Ma Pu-fang, Ma Hung-kuei and Hu Tsung-nan had been called by Li in effort put stop their differences which, Chu says, are based on mutual distrust, but Li's efforts met with only moderate success. Ma Pu-fang, says Chu, is most ambitious and thoroughly disgruntled at appointment Ma Hung-kuei Governor Kansu, which incidentally Chu says was Generalissimo appointment. In other words, we

[85] Text printed from corrected copy received August 18, 2 a. m.

552–963—78——32

can expect continued bickering northwest to benefit Communist purpose.

Situation Canton, which was already bad, has, according Chu, been aggravated by Generalissimo's insistence appointment Li Chi-lan [as] garrison commander Canton, which has caused indignation on part Yu Han-mou, Commander Pacification Headquarters Canton, and Hsueh Yueh, Governor Kwangtung, and in resignation and alienation Yeh Shao, former garrison commander closely allied with underground, and Li Fu-lan, who controls pirating and smuggling activities Pearl River delta.

Chu admitted quite frankly that Pai Chung-hsi planned fight only rear guard action, conserving his troops and supplies for last ditch stand southwest China. He said it was not at all certain that government would move Chungking when Canton becomes untenable. Kunming, Yunnan, is definitely being considered, Chu saying situation there was nothing like as bad as some people thought and he left me with definite impression [garble] is in consultation with Lu Han, Governor Yunnan, reestablishing temporary capital Kunming. Should Kunming become untenable, Li envisages establishing capital Kweiyang, Kweichow, or somewhere in Kwangsi. Chu says Pai Chung-hsi will hold Kwangchowwan and Pakhoi at all costs so as have access sea.

With this background, Chu admitted Li would under no circumstances go Taiwan [and be] subservient Generalissimo. He envisages that time will come when Generalissimo will rule resistance forces Taiwan and Li Tsung-jen will rule similar forces southwest China. Li hopes desperately that we will support him in Southwest China equally with Generalissimo in Taiwan and that we will not let diplomatic and legalistic niceties lead US different course. Obviously Li fears when time comes for him set up his government southwest China, present government may disintegrate with many seeking sanctuary under aegis Generalissimo. Li feels he represents liberal forces and has much better chance rallying eventual forces resistance on mainland than has Generalissimo. It is for this reason he spoke as he did to me as reported Cantel 886, August 6, repeated Nanking 584, Shanghai 479, Taipei 97, and that he wrote Dr. Stuart in similar vein on August 9.

As I prepare leave China, therefore, course immediate future events seems clear: The land in northwest can be written off as of no other than nuisance value. Szechuan, where Chang Chun is bickering with Governor Wang and each of about 12 war lords is fending for himself, can be written off whenever Communists attack. There is slight possibility that Li Tsung-jen, supported by armies Pai Chung-hsi, will succeed in establishing himself with claim to legitimacy as head of government somewhere in southwest China. Generalissimo will remain entrenched on Taiwan with his Kmt Director General's office, which with its 8 sections is in fact a government and which may through emergence Generalissimo that time have semblance at least of legitimacy. We may find ourselves confronted with necessity choosing between two, yet with traditional ability Chinese adapt themselves to unusual situation, Li and Generalissimo may adjust themselves in some way and save us that embarrassment.

Sent Department Cantel 964, repeated Nanking 635, Shanghai 501, Taipei 128.

CLARK

893.00 Yunnan/8–1649 : Telegram

The Chargé in China (Clark) to the Secretary of State

CANTON, August 16, 1949—8 p. m.
[Received August 17—3 : 17 a. m.]

Cantel 965. James Brennan of CAT [86] stated August 16 that CAT's Chinese representatives in Kunming—ex-Tai Li [87] men—came from Kunming to Canton August 15 and stated Yunnan Governor Lu Han is preparing go over to Communists. He has up to now been reported sitting on the fence. They anticipate his defection may take place within a week. Vice President Willauer of CAT has flown to Kunming, where CAT has extensive installations.

Sent Department, repeated Kunming 18.

CLARK

893.00/8–1749 : Telegram

The Chargé in China (Clark) to the Secretary of State

CANTON, August 17, 1949—5 p. m.
[Received August 17—10 : 35 a. m.]

Cantel 977. Ma Pu-fang is returning Lanchow tomorrow August 18 in disgust. In brief conversation this morning, Ma said his short visit Canton and Formosa (where he and Hu Tsung-nan saw Generalissimo) for purpose obtaining arms and ammunition has been complete flop. With complete frankness he volunteered view Canton Government is totally worthless, hopeless organization, expert only in passing bureaucratic buck. Expressing appreciation for US concern over China, Ma said US must not give further aid to Central Government but to individual commanders who, like himself, care about common people and have shown they can fight Communists.

[86] Civil Air Transport.
[87] Deputy Director of the Bureau of Investigation and Statistics (security), Chinese National Commission of Military Affairs, killed in an airplane crash, 1946.

Ma said simply he is going back to Lanchow to fight Communists with what he has. Admitting that Hu Tsung-nan was "little lacking" in cooperative spirit, Ma said Hu must fight—or else.

CLARK

893.00/8–1749 : Telegram

The Consul General at Taipei (Macdonald) to the Secretary of State

TAIPEI, August 17, 1949—5 p. m.
[Received August 17—12:17 p. m.]

393. Reference Canton's telegram 923, August 11 to Department, repeated Taipei 112. On August 15 Chiang Yun-tien (Democratic Socialist Party) called and inquired what US attitude would be towards true democratic party and if it could expect US assistance. His statements were remarkably similar to ones mentioned in second paragraph Canton's telegram 923 to Department.

I told Chiang US is most anxious to see a democratic government that will resist Communism and govern the country in best interests of China and its people. In my estimation, I added, such a government [would?] receive sympathetic consideration by the US Government in connection with American assistance.

Chiang Yun-tien previously unknown to me. He claims to have been an advisor to the Acting President but now inactive Taipei.

Sent Department 393, repeated Canton 187.

MACDONALD

893.00/8–1849 : Telegram

The Consul General at Hong Kong (Hopper) to the Secretary of State

HONG KONG, August 18, 1949—9 a. m.
[Received 12:21 p. m.]

578. On August 14, Hong Kong group headed by Hwang Shao-hsiung,[88] Chang Chien-hua and Liu Fei [89] issued manifesto attacking Generalissimo as betrayer Sun Yat-sen revolution and advocating cooperation with CCP in interest peace and achievement *San Min Chu I*[90] through new democracy of Mao Tse-tung. Manifesto, generally restrained in tone. Had 44 signatures among which were those of 5 Whampoa generals and contained no references to US. Received highly favorable editorial comment in *Ta Kung Pao* and extensive writeup in CCP-controlled *Huah Siang Pao*. Pouching full details.

[88] Governor of Chekiang, 1937–47; member of Chinese Legislative Yuan.
[89] Deputy Chief of Chinese General Staff, 1948–49.
[90] Three People's Principles of Sun Yat-sen.

It is our impression that main purpose manifesto is pave way for signatories reach collective agreement with Communists whereby they can participate as group if possible or as individuals if necessary in coalition government. Since initial response of Communists apparently favorable, highly possible group may gain adherence others similarly situated. For example, we understand group former Kmt generals, including Chang Fa-kuei,[91] approved manifesto in principle, but refused to sign pending further consideration. Since group strongly desires reach working arrangement with Communists, its failure make reference in manifesto to "American imperialism" taken by us as indication its fundamentally pro-American orientation, especially since manifesto stresses Chinese independence.

Sent Department 578, repeated Nanking 42, Shanghai 119, Department pass Peiping unnumbered.

HOPPER

893.00/8–1849 : Telegram

The Consul General at Hong Kong (Hopper) to the Secretary of State

HONG KONG, August 18, 1949—noon.
[Received 12 : 32 p. m.]

581. On August 15 . . . source was informed by usually reliable informant . . . [that] manifesto referred to in ConGen telegram 578,[92] . . . was essentially propaganda for CCP consumption, aiming persuade Communists enlist support of signers in new coalition government. Initial Communist response leads signers believe move possibly successful. If Communists agree, they plan join new government, if possible as bloc, and will try gain adherence all remnants Kmt not attached KmtRC.[93] Also plan throw all possible support behind Chou En-lai whom they characterize as leader CCP faction favoring accommodation with western powers. Hope secure political appointments southwest China, mainly Kwangsi and Yunnan, and try create base in that area. Hope secure military support in Communist army through connections Whampoa generals who signed manifesto.

Informant stated group pro-American and hoped to be bridge between Chou En-lai and U.S. However, if necessary to convince Communists of their sincerity, they will temporarily adopt anti-American propaganda line. Informant claimed position taken in manifesto was gaining large support from prominent non-Communist personalities, particularly military men and it was intended these persons and others join with manifesto signers formally form political party.

---

[91] Commander in Chief of Chinese Army, 1948–49.
[92] August 18, *supra.*
[93] Kuomintang Revolutionary Committee.

In conclusion, informants stated he and colleagues had noted with great interest expressed intention American Government aid democratic groups China. Considered he and colleagues qualified this denomination and said believed logic of situation would sooner or later force US cooperate with movement of which he part. Said anxious maintain contacts American officials on information level, but also anxious explore in tangible and practical way possibilities for covert cooperative political activity.

Source expressed appreciation for above information, promised report to Department and stated would continue maintain contact and devise means keep same if informant and colleagues should leave Hong Kong. Source received distinct impression informant and friends not in close or direct contact with Hong Kong CCP leaders.

HOPPER

893.00B/8–1849 : Telegram

The Consul General at Hong Kong (Hopper) to the Secretary of State

HONG KONG, August 18, 1949—1 p. m.
[Received August 18—10 a. m.]

582. There is increasing evidence that Li Tsung-jen, probably mainly at instigation Pai Chung-hsi, has rejected idea of accommodation with Communists and plans continue hostilities longest possible (re Shanghai telegram 3224, August 13 to Department). This attitude sharp contrast to that of Liu Fei, Huang Shao-hsiung, Chang Chien-hua and other former close supporters [garble] Hong Kong who strongly advocate peaceful settlement and advise Li capitulate. Thus, in our view, we can no longer properly speak of "Hong Kong group Li Tsung-jen supporters". Although door still open Li join this group, believe time past when Li could surrender on terms acceptable both Communists and himself.

Sent Department 582, repeated Nanking 43, Shanghai 120, Department pass Peiping unnumbered.

HOPPER

893.00/8–1849 : Telegram

The Consul General at Peiping (Clubb) to the Secretary of State

PEIPING, August 18, 1949—4 p. m.
[Received August 18—11 a. m.]

1369. Re Contel 1080, June 27 to Department. For AMilAt [94] from Barrett.[95] Following from Keon: [96]

---

[94] Brig. Gen. Robert H. Soule, American Military Attaché.
[95] Col. David D. Barrett, Assistant Military Attaché in China.
[96] Michael Keon, Australian newspaperman in China employed by the United Press.

Evening August 15 after careful briefing on procedure to be followed he was taken with much cloak and dagger atmosphere to house in north city where he saw Chang, Secretary to Chou En-lai, previously mentioned re Chou *démarche*. Chang extremely nervous, has aged visibly in past 2 months and kept repeating he was taking big risk in seeing Keon. Chang told Keon substantially the following:

[1.] Po Yi-po [97] has worked an elaborate case against Keon with view arresting him on charge being spy and through him striking at Barrett whom he not in position to touch. Plan is bring Keon to an at least partially public trial in which evidence both manufactured and partially true will sound convincing even to foreign newspaper reporter. At present final action this case awaiting decision highest authority presumably Mao Tse-tung to whom all evidence has been presented. Is possible decision of highest authority will be [to] run Keon out, perhaps under humiliating circumstances, but Po may at any moment break case into open by arresting Keon, thus committing party to action from which recession would be difficult. In the party Po can be controlled by Mao alone but even so Po is no longer own master, implication being that he under control of Soviets. If Keon tried, will undoubtedly be convicted and probably sentenced to long prison term but he not likely get death sentence. If arrested, will be forced reveal all circumstances his connection with Chou *démarche* about which Po fully informed.

2. CCP at present torn with bitterest internal strife. Chou group has only slight chance of winning. Whole picture of party since Keon knew it in Nanking and Shantung 1946 and 1947 has changed. Chang convinced Soviets have weapon equal atomic bomb and Chang knows war coming soon but refused hazard guess to more exact time. Chang refused answer question as to state of Mao's health but reaction to question appeared indicate that chairman seriously ill.

3. Soviet hatred of Americans unlimited and will crack whip over CCP in every possible way hurt us. Anti-US action may be expected all over Asia. Had Chou *démarche* not leaked, some other pretext would have been found for Soviet assumption strong hand in Chinese affairs.

4. Chang advised Keon attempt secure exit permit now before final decision highest authority has been made this case. Even now may be unable secure permission to leave. Chang suggested possibility Keon's friends in Chou faction might be able arrange for him be run out under humiliating circumstances but could offer no assurance Keon would know in whose hands he was if such action taken against him. Once final decision as to action to be taken has been made will be unable leave if arrest included.

Comment: Convinced Keon telling story as heard it. He badly frightened over possibility smouldering [*mouldering*] in Commie dungeon. As Keon already declared his eagerness leave town, I do not believe any one trying scare him into going. I can afford to take calmer view of case than Keon but I believe that if case has really been

---

[97] Communist leader in Shansi.

presented to Mao he will give Keon chance to leave but the savagery of Po and possibility of Soviet pressure cannot be disregarded. If he tried, might get suspended sentence as did Jimmy Young in Tokyo just before Pearl Harbor.[98]

Sent Nanking 987, repeated Canton 267, Department 1369. [Barrett.]

[CLUBB]

893.00/8–1949 : Telegram

The Vice Consul at Chungking (McGeary) to the Secretary of State

CHUNGKING, August 19, 1949—7 a. m.
[Received August 19—1 : 14 a. m.]

162. From Strong. [In] view of vacillation of Nationalist Government with regard move to Chungking, feel desirable express own views re military situation West China. Although Communist timetable obscure, there are several seriously limiting factors affecting plans for attack on Szechuan, such as need to complete campaign in NW China, existence Pai Chung-hsi and Ma Pu-fang forces intact as military threats on flanks which must be eliminated or securely contained, need for regrouping of forces in both Southeast and Northwest, long supply lines and need to change direction of flow of supplies, very difficult terrain with few and bad roads, addition 2 months of great heat, desirability of two-prolonged [*pronged*] attack from both North and East, and fact that although bulk Nationalist soldiers this area may not be well-trained or have real will to fight there are large forces being gathered under loyal generals which capable of delaying Communists.

Seems reasonable to expect no sudden Communist attack or collapse Nationalists in near future. Despite dissension in Szechuan and Sikang and unpopularity of Nationalist Government, there is little reason to believe internal coup possible until Communists' intrusion into Szechuan obviously successful.

Thus feel situation can string along for several uncertain months before end becomes apparent. Experience gained in close observation of several major campaigns in North China supports idea that, although final results inevitable, events take their own time, longer than would seem normal to western observers. An exception in Szechuan would be surprising.

Sent Department, repeated OffEmb Canton 115. [Strong.]

MCGEARY

---

[98] See *Foreign Relations*, 1940, vol. IV, pp. 995–1002.

893.00 Manchuria/8–1949 : Telegram

The Ambassador in the Soviet Union (Kirk) to the Secretary of State

Moscow, August 19, 1949—4 p. m.
[Received August 20—3 a. m.]

2092. French Ambassador here states French Embassy Nanking reports that during June relations between military forces Manchuria and those North China became so acute that Mao and Manchurian commander appealed to Moscow to arrange *modus vivendi*. In response that appeal one Sokolikov despatched from Moscow and arranged an agreement substantially as follows:

(1) Manchurian troops would not move south, and North China troops would not move north of the Great Wall without specific mutual agreement.
(2) At time of establishment of Central Chinese Communist Government, in consideration of special position of Northeast China a special agreement on relations between Manchuria and central authorities will be worked out.

This Embassy has no information re Sokolikov. Please protect source this report.

Sent Department; repeated Nanking 89.

KIRK

893.00/8–2249 : Telegram

The Consul General at Hong Kong (Hopper) to the Secretary of State

HONG KONG, August 22, 1949—4 p. m.
[Received 4 : 53 p. m.]

602. . . . Source informed . . . that Huang and followers going almost any lengths get and keep good will CCP. Group leaders inform members western powers inimical China's political and economic development. Only true friend China is USSR.

Contact believes main motivation group members is wish get appointments coalition government. Thinks group incapable independently constructive political action in new government even if leaders so disposed. Feels CCP presently using group win over Kmt political and military officials useful completing conquest China and will reject or strictly control it when military operations concluded.

Source points out contradiction above and third paragraph Hong Kong telegram 581 to Department,[99] quoting statement member of group. Source believes group leadership incompetent, confused, fundamentally acting from personally selfish motives despite claims larger aims. Only slight, though some possibility play significant or inde-

---

[99] August 18, p. 495.

pendent role in coalition government. To become effective political force would need much outside guidance.

HOPPER

893.00/8–2349 : Telegram

The Consul at Shanghai (McConaughy) to the Secretary of State

SHANGHAI, August 23, 1949—5 p. m.
[Received August 23—8 : 45 a. m.]

3399. In first public mention of Chen Yun (labor trouble-shooter sent from Peiping whose presence Shanghai hitherto kept secret), *Ta Kung Pao* August 1 reports Chen previous day addressed meeting industrial leaders, analyzing and suggesting solution for Shanghai's difficulties which he termed only temporary. Stressed need maintain activities of major industries and "tide over existing difficulties" and assured that "both public and private enterprises will have every chance develop" and city's manufactured goods will soon "be shipped all parts of country for consumption".

Sent Department 3399, repeated Nanking 1822.

McCONAUGHY

893.00B/8–2349 : Telegram

The Counselor of Embassy in China (Jones) to the Secretary of State

NANKING, August 23, 1949—5 p. m.
[Received August 24—1 : 54 a. m.]

1878. Four months of CCP occupation has failed to convince Nanking people of merits of Communist regime. Primary cause of widespread discontent among all classes is severe economic depression which Communists unable to alleviate. Important aggravating factors are ruthless discharge of former Nationalist Government employees and heavy taxation. "Streamlining" campaign recently embarked upon by Communists has added to ranks of jobless hundreds of persons who take small comfort from Communist injunction to return to country and produce. Business and vehicle taxes introduced within past month affect large number of persons including even such impecunious groups as pedicab drivers, sidewalk junk-sellers and vegetable peddlers.

Among bitterest critics of Communist regime are those intellectuals at first favorably impressed but now disillusioned. They have nothing good to say for Communists and repeat with relish stories of Communist difficulties. Merchants, apprentices, industrialists and unemployed laborers all affected by deep economic slump, share common resentment against "liberators" and compare unfavorably present conditions with Kmt days. Servants also express dissatisfaction with new regime perhaps because of Communist bias against them as "unproductive" class, but more likely because of close ties most of them maintain with country and their knowledge of oppressive Communist policy there. It is probably no exaggeration to say that at least 90 percent of population (excluding, of course, CCP and PLA) are dissatisfied and feel they were better off before "liberation".

However, there is small group of intellectuals, among them number of younger college professors, who admit economic situation is bad but consider it inevitable at this stage and do not blame Communists for it. They are impressed by discipline of PLA, frugal mode of living of cadres, and relative absence of corruption. They point to stability of prices during past few weeks as good augury for future. On other hand they criticize one-sided reporting of world news in Communist press and Communist inefficient use of personnel which lays more stress on person's political thought than technical ability for job at hand.

A third group, very small indeed, are those wholeheartedly convinced that in CCP lies salvation of China. This consists primarily of students and those who have actively joined CCP program whether from reasons of idealism or personal advantage. They refuse to admit any faults in CCP's program and outdo CCP itself in proclaiming party line.

It is significant that dissatisfaction with Communist regime results to very large extent from economic pressure. There is little criticism of CCP regimentation and thought control partly because such measures are not very severe nor widespread in Nanking and partly because average Chinese has always been more deeply concerned with earning his daily bread than with freedom of thought. There is no sign as yet that grumbling heard on every hand in Nanking is likely to find expression in organized direct action such as has been reported from some country districts.

Sent Department; repeated OffEmb Canton 788, Shanghai 1032.

JONES

893.001/8–2349 : Telegram

The Chargé in China (Clark) to the Secretary of State

CANTON, August 23, 1949—8 p. m.
[Received August 23—3 : 18 p. m.]

Cantel 1012. When I called on Acting President Li Tsung-jen to say good-bye and introduce Strong,[1] found him closeted with Pai

---

[1] Robert C. Strong, First Secretary of Embassy in China on detail to Chungking, was slated to succeed Mr. Clark as Chargé when latter returned home; for further documentation, see pp. 811 ff.

Chung-hsi. Pai is quite proud of his recent victories in Hunan and stated that forces on mainland were boiling down to those willing to fight. He intimated that, if other armies were as good as his 3 Kwangsi armies, defeating Communists would be easy.

For first time, Li Tsung-jen evidenced considerable ire over frustration he has suffered at hands Gimo. He said reform was needed and he had done his best, but that so long as Gimo held purse strings there was nothing he could do. If he anatagonized man who held purse strings, he would have no money for continued resistance Communists. He was therefore completely stymied and making best of it.

He and Pai feel unless we make the best of a bad bargain and come to aid of existing government, corrupt as it is, Communist domination of all China is inevitable and liberalism will die. They desperately seek liberation from the dead hand of Gimo control through his control of Treasury and they hope as stated Cantel 886, August 6 repeated Shanghai 479, Nanking 584, in some way we can find it possible to help them even if we decide that Gimo and his supporters fight on without further assistance. Obviously, what they fear is that situation may develop on mainland impelling Gimo reemerge as President and leaving Li leader of autonomous regional administration.

They are confident that Pai's 3 armies plus the guerrilla outfits on the Anhwei–Honan–Hupeh border, for which Pai claims credit, saying he left officers behind for that purpose, can form nucleus of victorious advance over communism provided they can obtain aid from US direct and not through any machinery controlled by Gimo. In this regard, Chu Chang-wei, Gimo [Li] advisor, pleaded with me give him list military supplies now being delivered Taiwan, indicating Li's efforts obtain such list through Minister National Defense met with failure.

Finally, President and Pai stated they were anxious welcome another General Stilwell [2] to train and even actually command their troops; they all would give a warm welcome to American advisors.

Sent Department Cantel 1002, repeated Nanking 653, Shanghai 515, Taipei 141.

CLARK

893.00B/8–2449 : Telegram

The Counselor of Embassy in China (Jones) to the Secretary of State

NANKING, August 24, 1949—3 p. m.
[Received August 24—9 : 40 a. m.]

1885. Bearing upon extent to which CCP draws inspiration from Sun Yat-sen doctrine as against Marxism–Leninism–Stalinism, we

---

[2] Lt. Gen. Joseph W. Stilwell, Commanding General, U.S. Army Forces in China, Burma, India, and Chief of Staff to Generalissimo Chiang Kai-shek, 1942–1944.

note that to best of our knowledge Chinese Communists have held no commemoratory services or celebrations at Sun Yat-sen mausoleum since their take-over of Nanking last April. Neither have we heard of Sun's picture being used at public meetings as are those of Lenin, Stalin, Mao and Chu.[3]

Sent Department 1885; repeated Shanghai 1036, Canton 793.

JONES

893.00B/8-949 : Telegram

The Secretary of State to the Chargé in China (Strong), at Canton

WASHINGTON, August 24, 1949—6 p. m.

TelCan 618. Dept sympathetic Han Li-wu's views reported Cantel 912 Aug 9 as he believed typify best type enlightened patriotic honest capable official who has made valiant effort prevent development present situation. Suggest you reply along fol lines:

US Govt does desire support in China measures taken by Chinese themselves build independent nation free from outside interference and domination. Cannot be too strongly emphasized, however, measures must be indigenous and to be effective must be based on Chi initiative and not dependent upon external assistance. US Govt wld, of course, welcome rallying of effective resistance which wld give hope of opposition to Commie domination China and is interested in any plans to that end.

Suggest you indicate reply ur personal views but that Dept has expressed interest in Han's efforts and wld be interested in his plans.

ACHESON

893.00/8-2449

The Consul at Taipei (Edgar) to the Secretary of State

No. 48   TAIPEI, August 24, 1949.
[Received September 3.]

SIR: I have the honor to report that during the absence of Consul General Macdonald in Canton on consultation, Hsia Tao-sheng called at this office stating that he is a member of the Standing Committee of the Young China Party and concurrently Minister of Organization of the Party, which currently has a membership of 300,000 in China, mostly in the West and requesting opportunity of discussing the White Paper [4] which he had read in USIS [5] summary form. His interpreter was a Mr. Emile Hsia.

---

[3] Chu Teh, Commander in Chief of Chinese Communist armies.
[4] Department of State. *United States Relations With China* (Washington, Government Printing Office, 1949).
[5] United States Information Service.

Hsia started the discussion with a statement of his satisfaction with the White Paper conclusion that the Chinese Communists were in fact Communists and not agrarian reformers and that the current troubles in China were more than a local civil war. He said that this was a great step forward for the State Department and was encouraging to all factions in free China. He then followed with the opinion that all that was said about graft, corruption, and inefficiency in the Kmt [6] was correct and could be expanded.

These things he said led Chinese to the hope that the United States would announce a new China policy, but the White Paper had failed to give clear indication of the probable direction. He was interested in knowing what direction Washington current thinking was taking subsequent to the publication of the White Paper. Since the rapid growth of the Chinese Communist Party after the war gave conclusive proof of foreign support, he believed that any opposing democratic force would need comparable foreign support. In his opinion China could still be saved and it would be disastrous if American aid were withheld until after the entire mainland was lost. Recovery would be harder than retention. But, he emphasized, the time is very late and prompt steps must be taken.

He then came to the main point of his visit and asked if the United States had already selected the democratic force that it was willing to support in substitution for the Gimo and the Kmt. His party, he claimed, had had no defections to the Communists, was well organized, represented the most liberal elements and stood for the most democratic principles. But, unlike the situation in the United States and the European countries, no democratic force can have any effect on the Chinese national picture while it is out of power. Only when in power can any party be effectual in any degree. He hoped that America would give consideration to the possibilities of his party. It was already larger than the Communist Party had been after the war.

In reply to these statements and questions I replied that in my opinion there was no great change of view regarding the CCP and the civil war. Undue publicity given certain individuals' statements had confused many regarding the official American attitude toward the problem. The White Paper attempted to clarify this, not make public new and radical evaluations. As regards the morality of the Kmt, I expressed the personal opinion that graft, corruption, and poor government had all become characteristics of China long before the creation of the Kmt, but that as the Kmt had become more firmly entrenched these had only become more open and prevalent and that consideration for the welfare of the people had given way to prime consideration for the Kmt party. But I had no personal illusions that any new party which might come to power would be naturally free

---

[6] Kuomintang (Nationalist Party).

of the tendency. So long as government failed to pay adequate compensation to government employees, including the military, the employees had necessarily to augment their incomes in some way. I said that any correction of this greatest curse would result only from a concerted campaign to correct both the psychological and economic causes. So long as the people of the country countenanced graft and corruption in government it would continue. The problem was one of education of the masses since the evil now went down to the smallest of hsien officials and was generally accepted. It was only more evident at the national level.

As comment on his claim that the CCP had succeeded only because it had received outside support, I pointed out that the CCP had probably not received a fraction of the support the United States had poured out to the Kmt. The difference in the outcome was the fact that the Kmt had lost the leadership of the people and no longer fired their imagination nor offered salvation from their troubles. Disregarding the reaction of the people who found themselves far behind Communist lines where true Communist practices and policies began to be understood and disliked, the people of China in general who found themselves in a position to choose between the CCP and the Kmt chose the former. I cited the many merchants in Shanghai who had said nothing could be worse than the Kmt. This, not outside support, was causing the defection of villages, towns, provinces, and armies. I said that any new group that wanted to lead the nation to the democratic way of life could not hope for success solely on the basis of outside support. It must rekindle the flame among the people and build up support from the bottom, not from the top among a handful of men educated abroad and resident in the cities with little or no contact with the people who can aid or sabotage a military operation with or without arms.

Hsia Tao-sheng then asked if the American Government had written China off in its consideration of world policy.

I replied that such was not my understanding, that the White Paper was a factual summary of past developments, that new policy was under consideration, and that the White Paper itself stated that the administration was constantly prepared to support any democratic elements which could and would work for a free, united, strong and democratic China and would resist the extension of Communism, or combat it from within the Communist areas.

Hsia said that his party was very disappointed that a statement of new United States policy was so slow in coming. He hoped that when it was developed consideration would be given to the fact that just as our 1918 isolationism in the West had lost us the advantages of the

Wilson 14 points,[7] so desertion of China now would lose us the advantages of the Four Freedoms.[8] To him it appeared that our withdrawal from the China scene was a desertion of the Open Door Policy and that whereas we had in the 19th century paid more attention to China and less to Europe, we were in the 20th century reversing this at a time when China most needed help. Did we feel that we had reaped the full advantages of the Open Door Policy and were therefore discarding it?

I pointed out that when the West first came into contact with China across the Pacific it was a weak and crumbling empire, a ready prey for the imperialistic designs of more powerful states. The purpose of the Open Door Policy was and continued to be to give China time to restore itself to its former power and prestige so that it could defend itself against any and all comers. With great persistence we had continued on that path over the years. We had checked Russian inroads, Japanese inroads, as well as British, French, and German. By investment in China and her cities, we and the other powers had subsidized China for the last hundred years and more, putting more in than we had taken out. President Roosevelt alone and against strong opposition had given China the status of one of the Big Five powers of the world.

Despite these continuing efforts to help China find and establish her place in the world, the people of China and its politicians and warlords continued to play at their medieval games and lead their medieval life. In my opinion, China had deserted the United States rather than that the United States had deserted China. China had turned her back on the proffered helping hand. Any future move would be better and more convincing coming from China. The question was "What is China's policy?" not "What is America's policy?"

I said that it was my belief that the American Government had no intention of laying itself open to the charge of intervention by fostering a revolutionary movement against the Gimo and his Kmt followers, that it was not selecting any one so-called democratic group to support in this way. But that it still looked hopefully for some signs of a real and potent democratic movement which could and would resist Communism and that once in power the leaders of such a movement, if national in scope, could count on the continued interest and support of the United States.

Hsia Tao-sheng closed the conversation, which lasted two and one-half hours, with the statement that he was relieved to learn that it was my understanding that no particular group had yet been selected for American support. At the same time he emphasized that time was

---

[7] See address by President Wilson to the joint session of Congress, January 8, 1918, *Foreign Relations*, 1918, Supplement I, vol. I, p. 12.

[8] See address by President Roosevelt to Congress, January 6, 1941, Department of State, *Peace and War: United States Foreign Policy, 1931–1941* (Washington, Government Printing Office, 1943), p. 608.

running short and if anything was to be saved, prompt action must be taken. There was no time to "wait and see" nor to "let the dust settle." He asked me to remind my Government that the transition of France from the Bourbons to republicanism had required eighty years with many intermediate ups and downs, and that China was now less than forty years along this path.

Coming so shortly after the visit reported in our telegram of August 17, 5:00 p. m. (No. 393) it would appear that more than one political group is hopefully awaiting some move from the United States which it can interpret to its own benefit. I believe that it should be made clear to them why in our opinion the Kmt ultimately failed after so brilliant a start. They should also, I believe, be made to understand that our criticism of the Kmt is not superficial and political but that we believe after bitter experience that it lost its base support and that any other political group without a solid foundation holds no real attraction for us.

One thing that I told Hsia which I find I have failed to include in the above account is that I suspect that the Chinese people as a result of years of military and economic attrition are spiritually, and morally, as well as economically bankrupt, and that before whatever indications of effort to throw off the Communist yoke as may appear can be galvanized into a national movement which will lead them to that national unity and strength, which is their due, there must be formulated a new Chinese philosophy incorporating all the good of the past from the time of Confucius and including much of the principles of Sun Yat-sen but adapted so as to solve the problems of contact and cooperation with the democratic western world. Without some such catalyst, attempts to overthrow Communist domination will be sporadic and futile, and even though superficially successful will be but temporary in nature.

Hsia Tao-sheng is also a member of the Legislative Yuan from Anhwei Province.

Respectfully yours,   DONALD D. EDGAR

893.00B/8-2549 : Telegram

The Consul at Shanghai (*McConaughy*) *to the Secretary of State*

SHANGHAI, August 25, 1949—11 a. m.
[Received August 25—9 : 21 a. m.]

3435. Reliable American has informed officer ConGen that he has just been shown text of intra-governmental "report" very recently issued Peiping stating that despite hostile nature of American Government policies, "People's Government" will follow policy of protecting Americans and further trade with USA. Source twice repeated this information at request ConGen officer who wished thus ensure he got it accurately. Source regretted he could not reveal identity of Chinese who showed him document "in strictest confidence" beyond fact "they" are trusted contacts, nor identity of authorities who signed document beyond fact they were "highest level" (clearly implying Mao Tse-tung was included).

During same talk source mentioned having very recently seen (1) Madame Sun Yat-sen and Madame Chou En-lai (old friends of his) and (2) close high business associate who has just received letter from Chen Shu-tung at Peiping reporting recent talks which Chen had with Mao; and we strongly surmise it was one of these two quarters which showed him document. Thus have every reason believe document did emanate from highest level Peiping authorities and that it was not planted on source unless planting was work of those very authorities.

Source feels that possibilities for "driving wedges" to pry Communists from Kremlin are by no means hopeless; that, however, present American Government policies are not well calculated to achieve results in this direction. He feels that present policies involving in his conception inflexibly negative attitude to Communists, no exploratory steps towards possibility *modus vivendi*, manner of treatment of blockade, unclarified stand toward [garble] and toward Taiwan serve to push Communists increasingly into subservience Moscow.

(This connection ConGen has received separately from several good sources indications Communists seek following from USA as prerequisite to relations (1) early recognition following formation "government"; (2) abrogation all treaties, agreements with Kmt (possibly only those negotiated since dissolution PCC[9]); (3) complete withdrawal all US naval military forces from China and Chinese waters including Taiwan. They feel particularly sensitive on Taiwan issue and demand its prompt "restoration" to Chinese, i.e., Communist sovereignty.

Despite obvious debatability source's conclusions, we consider his views worth reporting not only by reason of his own reputation as keen observer with excellent contacts but also because as suggested in previous telegrams from ConGen, his views believed substantially representative of considerable section of local intelligent American and other foreign opinion.

Sent Department, repeated Nanking 1833, EmbOff Canton. Department pass Peiping 282.

McConaughy

---

[9] Political Consultative Conference.

893.00/8–2549 : Telegram

The Counselor of Embassy in China (Jones) to the Secretary of State

NANKING, August 25, 1949.
[Received August 25—10:39 a. m.]

1895. *Hsin Min Pao* August 23 published Li Chi-shen address to Peiping branch of KmtRC in which he said in part:

"Formerly our principal task was to weaken and sabotage rule of reactionary government. Therefore, we encouraged and established association with anyone willing to work for KmtRC and sow confusion in reactionary group. As a result, it has been unavoidable that some bad characters join committee. Hereafter, we must demand that understanding and activities of each member be up to standard and must select members with more care.

There are now three types of persons in committee: 1st, those who understand facts and principles clearly; 2d, those who simply opposed Chiang; and 3d, opportunists, who seeing crisis facing Chiang regime secretly established relationship with committee for their own benefit.

Comrades of first type should assume responsibility of leadership and education, those of second type should be encouraged to learn, while those of third type should have their actions subjected to strict review. Those guilty of actions contravening public opinion should not be permitted to reregister. Preparations for reregistration are being made first by Peiping branch and we hope will serve as example to other branches."

Sent Department, repeated Shanghai unnumbered.

JONES

893.00/8–2849 : Telegram

The Chargé in China (Strong) to the Secretary of State

CANTON, August 28, 1949—3 p. m.
[Received August 28—8:20 a. m.]

Cantel 1040. Following statements were made by Chu Chang-wei yesterday.

Northwest China: It seems certain Ma Pu-fang withdrew his forces intact from Lanchow during afternoon August 26. This step was necessary view failure of Ma Hung-kwei's troops to arrive from Ninghsia and failure Hu Tsung-nan render any measure support. Chu remarked that Hu can be relied upon for nothing.

Southeast China: Chu claims that East River situation could possibly be expected improve within 2 or 3 days provided Nationalist troops in area were properly deployed, but since this involves close coordination between two generals, outcome is, of course, uncertain. He insisted strongly that there was no danger of local turnover to Communists in or about Canton, and on more than one occasion referred to "over-emphasis" on possibility of such development particularly by American military observers and newsmen and Hong Kong newspapers. According Chu, Yu Han-mou will, without question, remain loyal, whereas any actions of Hsueh Yueh are of no significance. Chang Fa-kwei was stated to have informed President Li that at such time as his government broke cleanly with Generalissimo he would whole-heartedly enter into cooperation with Li.

The Generalissimo: Chu stated that upon Generalissimo's most recent visit Canton, President Li again attempted persuade him take initiative in installing Pai Chung-hsi as Minister National Defense. Generalissimo as usual did not refuse but temporized. Chu says Li intends upon Generalissimo's return from West China to take up matter again, and, failing positive action on part Generalissimo, will request, and if necessary order, Yen Hsi-shan to vacate his concurrent post of Minister National Defense and install Pai on his own responsibility regardless of consequences. He stated this move could no longer be delayed in view of grossly unequal division available military supplies and money among various field commanders. For example, whereas Pai claims 300,000 troops and supposedly actually has that many, Soong Hsi-liang claims have 300,000 men in Hupeh and Hu Tsung-nan draws supplies and money on basis of 450,000 men. These figures for Soong and Hu are obviously considerably padded, but they are receiving supplies proportionate to forces claimed.

Generalissimo indicated he would spend approximately 2 weeks in West China. Although his itinerary is not definitely known, it is believed he will visit Hanchung and Sining and possibly other points. Chu asserted during Generalissimo's present visit Chungking he is continuing his favorite old game of playing off various leaders against each other. Chang Chun definitely desires resign, but Generalissimo has insisted he remain in office, without granting him any additional authority.

Re Cantel 1012, August 23, repeated Nanking 653, Shanghai 515, Taipei 141, Chu again expressed keen desire of President Li to obtain details on military cargo landed Taiwan from US.

Sent Department Cantel 1040; repeated Shanghai 521, Taipei 150, Nanking 660.

STRONG

893.00/8–3049 : Telegram

The Vice Consul at Chungking (McGeary) to the Secretary of State

CHUNGKING, August 30, 1949—1 p. m.
[Received August 30—4 : 02 a. m.]

179. L. K. Taylor, American, President [of] Chennault's[10] International Supplies Corp., China, passed through Chungking today from Sining; he states Sining expected fall to Communists within 2 days and Chungking will be behind Iron Curtain in not more than 5 to 6 weeks; Hu Tsung-nan double-crossed Ma Pu-fang in Lanchow battle; both generals were to attack in defence Lanchow August 18; Ma did and put up big battle; inflicted large number casualties on Communists, lost some himself; Ma spokesman told Taylor for every 2100 Communists killed he cannot afford lose even 700; Hu did not attack and Taylor states Hu cannot be depended upon defend Szechuan for he and his men unable and unwilling fight; he states heaviest fighting equipment Nationalists had were light machine guns and at same time were short of ammunition; Communists had heavy mortars (Japanese) [garble] ammunition into Sining.

Sent Department; repeated Nanking 163, OffEmb Canton 135.

McGEARY

893.00B/8–3049 : Telegram

The Chargé in China (Strong) to the Secretary of State

CANTON, August 30, 1949—9 p. m.
[Received August 31—3 : 27 a. m.]

Cantel 1053. Contents of telCan 618, August 24, were today communicated to Han Li-wu in manner suggested therein.

Han stated that he is not being subjected to supervision by any other government organ or official in his battle for the Chinese mind, but he is going ahead as his conscience dictates, making it plain to both Generalissimo and Li factions that he considers they should unite at this late stage. Although his program is limited by unavailability of significant sums of money, he feels that what he is able to obtain is adequate in view of the great caution with which he is obliged to select and utilize personnel. He also recognizes that even if the US were to contribute financially to the Chinese Government specifically for his program, it is doubtful that more than a portion of the funds would be passed on for his use. Han volunteered his understanding that it was first up to China to show success in these measures before raising question of assistance.

---

[10] Maj. Gen. Claire L. Chennault (ret.), Chairman of the Board of China Civil Air Transport (CAT).

According to Han, Hu Shih has already edited one pamphlet of "Free China" and has himself written another. However, before undertaking further writing of this type, Hu desires to be released from his nominal post as Minister of Foreign Affairs, and has asked Han to speak to President Li with this in view. Han asserts that Hu will then devote considerable effort in this direction.

Han declares CAF now carrying out air drops his written material in Communist territory at points en route to bombing objectives and also over such objectives. So far no special flights have been made for the purpose disseminating propaganda. Pamphlets have also been mailed to important personages in Communist territory, but, as expected, few apparently reached the addressees view of the absence of responses.

STRONG

894A.00/8-3149 : Telegram

The Consul General at Taipei (Macdonald) to the Secretary of State

TAIPEI, August 31, 1949—1 p. m.
[Received September 2—5:20 a. m.]

Following observations from 4-day visit Amoy 2 [*23?*]-27 August. General alarm over impending Communist attack Amoy. Local business and foreign sources expect Communist capture city first or second week September. New Fukien Governor, General Tang En-po, stated Chinese Nationalists not to evacuate Amoy but take offensive and attempt recapture Foochow. Plans include joint Army–Navy occupation of Fukien coastal islands as bases for naval blockade Fukien. However, river junk traffic indicating withdrawal Nationalist troops from interior. C–3 sources report removal certain units of 22nd Group Army from Amoy. Air reconnaissance over Amoy entrance islands including Quemoy and Little Quemoy Islands revealed no important troop dispositions. Twelve recently-built pillboxes noted along west coast of Quemoy islands. Numerous pillboxes observed along Kulangsu and Amoy Island coastlines. Chinese Navy slowly evacuating Amoy. LST *Chung Lien* alongside Butterfield and Swire wharf loading Chinese Naval Academy gear. One-third of student personnel already transferred Tsoying. Amoy Naval Dockyard equipment and stock largely crated, awaiting shipment Taiwan. 26 August Chinese Navy source reported Amoy naval patrol station including radio station ordered Quemoy Islands. Small marines unit officially reported quartered Quemoy. Navy drilling wells there insure fresh water supply. Chinese Navy to clear Fukien waters of all large junks in order to forestall Communist landings on Amoy and coastal islands occupied by Nationalists. Communists reported to have concentrated troops and junks at Putien in preparation landing Amoy. 26 August RCS[*PG?*] *Chu Kuan* returned Amoy after one day's reconnaissance Fukien coast. Naval vessels present 23–27 August: AMS *Nan An*, *Yung Sheng*, LST *Chung Lien*, LSM *Mei Ho*, PG *Chu Kuan*, ex-Japanese vessel *Wu Ling*. Source C–3 reported upwards dozen Japanese minecasings shipped Takao from Amoy. Official Navy stated 30 Japanese torpedoes in storage launching tubes. Signed Shahin.[11]

Department pass CNO/DNI [12] and for information to Com-NavFe,[13] Com7thTaskFlt,[14] CinCPac; [15] repeated ALUSNA,[16] Nanking AstALUSNA [17] Canton.

MACDONALD

893.00B/8–3149 : Telegram

The Consul General at Peiping (Clubb) to the Secretary of State

PEIPING, August 31, 1949—5 p. m.
[Received September 2—7:45 p. m.]

1456. Re Contel 1412, August 25 [*24*],[18] Chin Ting-chih, closely connected Chou Ching-wen, informed me variously August 29 and today Communists are encountering difficulties in bringing Democratic persons definitely into camp, that Chang Tung-sun, Lo Lung-chi and Chou Ching-wen particularly might lead Democrats in move nonparticipation new PCC. One of primary points difference between Communists and Democrats is question foreign relations. Democrats oppose Communist policies following exclusively pro-USSR line, contending this would be justified only in war, that otherwise China should maintain at least as close economic and political relations with USA and Britain as does USSR. Chin said today possibility break had increased, that it seemed "good possibility". Chin noted persons belonging no organizations like Yenching and Tsinghua could not but subscribe to general condemnation "American imperialism" but that few Democrats are coming forward individually take same stand (but see Contel 1399, August 20[18] and others).

Per Chin, also Li Chi-shen is now so closely "protected" by Communists that would-be visitors are turned away.

Chin says Democrats were aware USSR was consolidating its position Manchuria but USSR in thus acting was following way of Japan which had "clasped bomb to bosom", and would eventually get into

---

[11] Lt. (jg.) Edward S. Shahin.
[12] Chief of Naval Operations, Office of Naval Intelligence.
[13] Commander, U.S. Naval Forces, Far East.
[14] Commander, 7th Task Fleet.
[15] Commander in Chief, U.S. Naval Forces in the Pacific.
[16] Naval Attaché for Air in China.
[17] Assistant Naval Attaché for Air in China.
[18] Not printed.

trouble with USA. I noted that when Japan occupied Manchuria, China had objected but now they (1) went through motions approving Soviet actions Manchuria and (2) daily asserted USA was enemy.

Chin said Democrats felt balance military power Europe had shifted recently in favor USSR (Contels 1276, August 1, and 1316, August 8 [20]), that however by March USA might be expected take strong stand against USSR. He opined that if USSR in such case retreated, CCP would be badly shaken. He still showed belief war might come end this or beginning next year. One might deduce from his statements Democrats less sure now.

Chin opined pause in Communist advance toward Canton results from Communist deliberations now in progress re what action to be taken against (1) Hong Kong, (2) Formosa. He pointed out re Hong Kong that Communists were filled with confidence as result their "victory over imperialism" Shanghai and opined Hong Kong be attacked after capture Canton. He voluntarily conceded this would create serious situation. He seemed feel USA would somehow assist Nationalists hold Formosa.

Chin reiterated previous forecast Communists would soon be asking for American food. See Contel 1452 this date.[21]

Believe skepticism is indicated re Chin's report of possible Democratic bolt. Granted Democratic dissatisfactions, they have no place to go. Their craven adherence to Communist propaganda line would indicate little inclination to follow another road, even if offered, if danger were to be faced en route. Until facts prove contrary, assume Chin's report this regard reflects Democrats' desire appear in somewhat better light reflected in their public utterances, and maintain some connections.

Unconfirmed reports indicate Chou En-lai now bears primary administrative responsibility Communist set-up, that is, has taken over much load from Mao Tse-tung. New report Mao seriously ill but note he went to station [to] meet Mme. Sun Yat-sen August 28.

Sent Department; repeated Nanking 1053, Shanghai 943.

CLUBB

893.00B/9–149 : Telegram

The Consul at Shanghai (McConaughy) to the Secretary of State

SHANGHAI, September 1, 1949—11 a. m.
[Received September 1—2 : 25 a. m.]

3584. Re press reports of Mme. Sun Yat-sen's recent arrival and impressive welcome Peiping. Same American source who told us re

---

[20] Neither printed.
[21] Not printed; it reported efforts to avert famine in Hopei (893.48/8–3149).

Mme. Sun's decision bow to Communist pressure to get her to Peiping (Contel 2717, July 12) states that during many years he has known Mme. Sun and Mme. Chou En-lai he has never seen either one looking so badly as she did on eve of Mme. Sun's departure north. Mme. Sun confided to source that her home was becoming so much used by comrades and their various meetings that she no longer felt [she] had home of her own.

Sent Department 3584, repeated Nanking 1882, Embassy Canton 1063, Peiping 293.

McConaughy

893.00B/9–149 : Telegram

The Counselor of Embassy in China (Jones) to the Secretary of State

Nanking, September 1, 1949—5 p. m.
[Received 11 : 39 p. m.]

1975. Re Embtel 1951, August 30 to Department.[22] Manner in which CCP has seized bull by horns in connection with current Soviet campaign against Titoism confirms that Chinese Communist leaders are extremely sensitive to threat which Chinese nationalism offers to their own program of unconditional subservience to USSR.

CCP press coverage of this Soviet-Yugoslav dispute is all out of proportion to importance it holds for China. Thunderous denunciations of Titoism by New China News Agency, "democratic personages" and mass organizations show CCP to be more Papist than Pope as respects leading role of Soviet Union in "Anti-imperialist camp". General effect of this press campaign is to anathematize all utterances, whether private or public, against pro-Soviet orientation of CCP. It may also be inspired in part by CCP determination to intimidate and suppress forces of Chinese democratic individualism as defined in White Paper.

It is to be noted that no top rank Chinese Communist has yet expressed himself publicly on this subject. Quite possibly they consider it unnecessary in view of July 1948 resolution of Central Committee of CCP on question of Communist Party of Yugoslavia.

Sent Department, repeated Shanghai 1072, OffEmb Canton 811, Moscow 62.

Jones

---

[22] Not printed.

893.00/9–249 : Telegram

The Consul General at Taipei (Macdonald) to the Secretary of State

TAIPEI, September 2, 1949—4 p. m.
[Received September 2—2:44 p. m.]

443. A member of Chinese Islamic National Federation called today as representative of General Ma Pu-fang with following message and request:

General Ma plans to keep his army intact and withdraw to Sikang Province where he hopes to re-equip and train his troops. In this connection he sent his representative to request US assistance. He wants American military advisers to train his army, and military supplies from US. The representative stated that General Ma wants this US assistance given directly to him and not through the Central Government. Recently Ma's request to the Generalissimo for supplies was refused and he apparently feels any aid sent through the Central Government would not reach him. I explained to the General's representative that the United States cannot negotiate or deal with individual army commanders and any aid would have to be granted to the Central Government and distributed through its organizations. He said he understood and so did General Ma but the General hopes that in the event of a total collapse of the Central Government the US will be willing to help him as an individual Army Commander resisting the Communists and give him advisers and supplies. I assured the General's representative that I would transmit his message to Washington.

Some sort of reply to the effect that the US will consider General Ma's request but making no definite commitments if the Central Government collapses would be a great boost to General Ma's morale and determination to carry on the fight against Communism. The Department's comments would be appreciated.

MACDONALD

893.00/9–249

The Vice Consul at Kunming (Lutkins) to the Secretary of State

No. 74   KUNMING, September 2, 1949.
[Received September 18.]

SIR: I have the honor to report concerning a two-hour interview which I had with Governor Lu Han on August 31st, in the course of which he expressed his views on the present situation in South China and Yunnan and commented on the developments of the past four years in China.

Summary—The Governor believed that after capturing Canton the Communists would probably strike westward into Kwangsi in an attempt to crush the forces of Pai Ch'ung-hsi. The latter would probably attempt resistance, but Governor Lu indicated that he considered a successful defense to be unlikely.

In the Governor's opinion, if General Pai continued to fight on and the Nationalists resolved to undertake a protracted resistance in West China, attempts would inevitably be made to convert Yunnan into a Nationalist stronghold. However, he did not expect the arrival of any additional Nationalist troops in the province until such time as the Communist advance had pushed the Government armies back into western Kweichow and Kwangsi.

Over half of the interview was devoted to a discussion, initiated by the Governor, of the developments of the past four years in China and America's present China policy. In response to his questions I stated that as a personal observer my impression was that no further American aid would be forthcoming to Nationalist China, but that at the same time our policy toward the Communists appeared to be hardening. The Governor agreed that it was now too late for the United States to furnish any effective aid.

Governor Lu believed that the principal error of America's postwar policy in China has been not to compel the Generalissimo and the Kmt reactionaries by force or threats to accept the arrangements for a coalition government and a unified army, which had been worked out at the time of the Marshall Mission.[23] He emphasized the traditional friendship existing between the Chinese and American peoples on all levels and declared that the anti-American sentiment prevalent in China during the last few years was limited to a small group. He concluded by stating that the Chinese people had always distrusted the Russians and that in the long run they would reject both Communism and a pro-Russian orientation in national policy.

The Governor stated in reply to my opening question that he considered a protracted defense of Canton unlikely in view of the fact that the Nationalist troops were greatly outnumbered. If and when Canton fell, he thought, the Communists would probably not proceed immediately to launch an attack on Taiwan which might involve them in conflict with the United States [24] and which would involve considerable preparation. Instead he thought that they would almost certainly move west and endeavor to crush remaining Government forces in Kwangsi, Kweichow, and the South-West.

[Here follows detailed report on interview.]

Respectfully yours,

LaRue R. Lutkins

---

[23] See *Foreign Relations*, 1946, volumes IX and X.
[24] Marginal notation: "Apparently wide-spread Chinese belief."

893.00/9–349 : Telegram

The Vice Consul at Chungking (McGeary) to the Secretary of State

CHUNGKING, September 3, 1949—8 a. m.
[Received September 3—4:50 a. m.]

182. Wong Wei, Georgia-born Chinese Negro presently flying for CAT,[25] says he and balance CAT planes personnel evacuated Sining yesterday; that Sining in all probability fell to Communists today; (mytel 179, August 30). Colonel Poston of office of Military Attaché, Hong Kong, told me at airport Sunday, August 28, that General Ma Pu-fang passed through Chungking from Sining Sunday en route Taipei; that Ma did not see Generalissimo; that he talked with Ma's fourth wife who had evacuated Sining and was en route Ninghsia; Poston mailed report of conversation to Military Attaché, Hong Kong.

Wong states Ma left his son, Ma Chi-yuan, in charge his troops when he left; Ma Chi-yuan arrived Chungking yesterday from Sining having abandoned father's troops; that Ma sent cavalry toward Lanchow to fight Communists; that they turned about-face and retreated to Sining; that Hu Tsung-nan's army has simply stood by and watched the Ma generals fight and given no assistance whatsoever; that Ma's troops have been evacuating to Sining in large numbers and may be expected to disperse in hills beyond since departure of their deputy commander; that troops, some of whom had worked for General Ma for 17 years, are greatly disappointed in departure of both their commanders. Wong stated further that Communists have already started for Ninghsia 3 days by road from Lanchow to liquidate Ma Hung-kwei's troops; he saw Ma Hung-kwei in Sining recently and Ma looked terrible; his eyes swollen as though he had been crying; he was unable stand alone; two aides assisted him to stand. Wong believes Communists able take Ninghsia within next 2 to 3 weeks in spite desert terrain with no water or food and difficulties crossing Yellow River 30 miles from Ninghsia by raft as there is no bridge and after Ma generals liquidated Communists should have free access to Szechuan for Wong states Hu Tsung-nan's troops have stood by and watched Ma brothers fight Communists; Hu and his men have lost will to fight. Wong states foreigners nonplussed at rapid defeat of Ma generals in northwest; after meeting of Ma's with Generalissimo in Taipei, will to fight changed to complete defeatism.

Sent Department; repeated Nanking 166, OffEmb Canton 139.

McGEARY

---

[25] Civil Air Transport.

893.00 Yunnan/9–349 : Telegram

The Vice Consul at Kunming (Lutkins) to the Secretary of State

KUNMING, September 3, 1949—10 a. m.
[Received September 3—4:41 a. m.]

146. Kunming tense with rumors of National troops converging on city and possible clash between them and provincial forces. Chiang Ching-kuo [26] also rumored to be here attempting to dissuade Lu Han from turning over. French ConGen and I consider such an incident or attempted coup by Lu unlikely at this time.

CAT received orders this morning to evacuate all foreign personnel immediately because of information received from high Chinese Government official in Canton that there would be turn-over in Kunming on September 6. Please check and reply soonest. Have requested radio schedules for Sunday and Monday.

Sent OffEmb Hong Kong 54, repeated Department 146.

LUTKINS

893.00/9–349 : Telegram

The Counselor of Embassy in China (Jones) to the Secretary of State

NANKING, September 3, 1949—1 p. m.
[Received September 5—2:43 a. m.]

1994. We believe recent history of China justifies drawing these three conclusions:

1. CCP is here to stay for some time. We must not mistake already apparent widespread dissatisfaction and disillusionment with Communist regime or revolutionary situation which will lead to its early overthrow. CCP has more than 20 years' experience. It has large, well-disciplined party, large and effective (by Chinese standards) fighting force and more than rudiments of secret police system. It is incomparably stronger than Bolsheviks at time they seized power. It is futile to expect Chinese Communists to be overthrown by economic distress, scattered peasant revolts or diminishing resistance of Kmt. Sun Yat-sen tried and failed for more than decade before organizing revolution successful in overturning decadent Manchurian rule. Corrupt and defeated Russian Empire suppressed abortive 1905 revolts and only disastrous major war weakened it to point of permitting successful revolution against it. Bolsheviks, although beset with calamitous economic conditions, civil war and foreign intervention, yet managed retain power through early years Soviets' regime. Mussolini and Hitler were only overthrown after invasion of their countries by foreign armies. Seizure of power is extraordinarily difficult task, requiring dogged

---

[26] Eldest son of Generalissimo Chiang Kai-shek and chairman of Taiwan Provincial Kuomintang Headquarters.

determination, exacting organizational work and spirit of self-sacrifice. As Marx put it, "revolution is an art".

2. Any successful resistance movement must be purely Chinese. Any group which must depend for its continued existence upon foreign aid is unlikely to prove savior of China. When conditions are truly ripe for revolution, an indigenous resistance group can find means for its support among masses of discontented population. When it has proved its ability to exist independently and steadily expand its influence, then and only then can our assistance be effective.

3. There is now on horizon no anti-Communist Chinese leader who is suited by temperament or experience to lead successful revolution against CCP. In White Paper [27] we admitted failure of Generalissimo and, in effect, washed our hands of Kmt. We doubt whether Li Tsung-jen and Pai Chung-hsi are suitable leaders of such a movement, although they might conceivably contribute to it (reEmbtel 1922, August 28 [28]). Despite their undoubted sincerity and patriotism, we have little confidence that such men as Ku Meng-yu or Han Li-wu (reCantels 923, August 11 and 912, August 9 to Department) would make successful revolutionary leaders.

It is on these three premises, we believe, that we must base our fundamental policy toward China. Simply stated, that policy should be to prevent China from becoming reinforcement to Soviet power. To achieve this end, we must wait for development of Chinese form "Titoism", meanwhile doing nothing to encourage growth of strong Communist China. Policy of outright hostility toward rulers of China and overt support of subversive activity against them, while it undoubtedly would hinder consolidation CCP power, would be unlikely to contribute toward detachment of China from USSR because it would conflict with, rather than make use of, Chinese chauvinism.

This policy of awaiting development "Titoism" has disadvantage that at this stage it is largely negative. It will be criticized as lacking force. Yet, as our three premises show, present time is not propitious for positive action on our part. Conciliatory gestures now of economic or diplomatic nature would not only be opposed by large portion of American public but would simply be interpreted by CCP as bearing out Communist theory of inner weakness of USA. It would be explained as having been forced upon US by coming depression and desperate need for markets and raw materials.

Our optimum policy therefore has following quality:

1. Let CCP learn by experience that USSR has little aid to offer, that Soviet friendship is always one-sided, that China will lose much more than it will gain by such association, that it will receive no assistance from US as long as it is satellite of USSR. CCP is going to have to learn these facts the hard way. While CCP is doing this, we may not be able to avoid acrimonious public exchanges over instances

---

[27] Department of State, *United States Relations With China* (Washington, Government Printing Office, 1949).
[28] Vol. IX, p. 541.

of clear-cut discrimination against US interests, but we should endeavor to minimize open clashes to avoid diverting public attention from growing encroachments of USSR. Soviet actions injurious to China's if [own?] interests must be made to stand out more sharply in contrast to our own proper behavior. We should constantly look for signs of friction between CCP and USSR and seek means to increase it particularly by publicizing Soviet actions which reveal true intention of Kremlin toward China. During this period we should also watch closely for emergence of dynamic revolutionary groups but not be hasty in aiding potential revolutionaries before they have proven in some degree their worth.

2. Let US do nothing to contribute to comfort of new bed which CCP has made for China. Short of war or open hostility we can do little now to hurt CCP. However, this is not necessarily true in future. We have many potential weapons: Economic sanctions, abrogation of GATT [29] benefits, Taiwan, or Japan policy, diplomatic recognition, UN membership, immigrant remittances, air and sea transportation, loans. Eventually time will come when we can and should use these weapons effectively.[30]

Sent Department 1994, repeated OffEmb Canton 818, Shanghai 1083.

JONES

893.20/9–349 : Telegram

The Chargé in China (Strong) to the Secretary of State

CANTON, September 3, 1949—5 p. m.
[Received September 3—12:28 p. m.]

Cantel 1066. Chu Chang-wei today made following statements of interest: Supreme Policy Committee requested Generalissimo transfer one army Taiwan to Kwangtung as necessary and adequate defend Canton area. Generalissimo refused. Thus news reports of reinforcements from Taiwan completely false.

Fu Tso-yi "escaped" from Peiping in some style with regiment his troops and about 20 staff members and officers. Chu believes Communists arranged departure order allow Fu to take over 90,000 troops now controlled by Governor Suiyuan and probably confident Fu will then remain neutral or quiescent, thus eliminating a troublesome area for Communists. Nationalist Government hopes win Fu over and President Li has offered meet him. Although his message sent 3 days ago, no reply yet received.

Sent Department Cantel 1066, repeated Nanking 644, Shanghai 524.

STRONG

---

[29] General Agreement on Tariffs and Trade, signed at Geneva, October 30, 1947.
[30] The Secretary of State in telegram No. 1098, September 14, 7 p. m., informed the Counselor of Embassy that his telegram was found to be "most helpful in crystallization of Dept's views" for discussion in impending conversations with the British Secretary of State for Foreign Affairs (Bevin) ; for documentation on those conversations, see vol. IX, pp. 1 ff.

893.00/9–749 : Telegram

The Vice Consul at Chungking (McGeary) to the Secretary of State

CHUNGKING, September 7, 1949—4 p. m.
[Received September 7—9 : 54 a. m.]

188. Following gist conversation between self and Mayor Yang Sen of Chungking this morning regarding fire which started downtown Chungking Friday September 2, 3 p. m. and burned until yesterday:

Casualties 24,780 wounded to date; 10,000 serious; 2,513 buried by municipal government to date; so far 5,728 families have registered as having lost homes, which believed small fraction total; Chungking comprised 18 districts; 1, 2 and 3 are most heavily populated; fire burned out two-thirds of first district comprising 21 streets, estimated population 110,000, not including boat people; damage estimated to be greater than Japanese bombings May 2 and 3, 1939; richest portion city burned destroying godowns, money shops, banks, merchandising establishments; great loss commodities particularly cotton; no military supplies; fire was started by Communists who plan destroying government center operations southwest; fire started five places at once, including cottage on yellow hill on south bank, formerly Generalissimo's residence; mayor has in hand documents indicating Communist organization in Chungking comprising two corps with daily plans burn Chungking to ground; Canton to be burned as well; two fire bugs already shot, others arrested; cutting of water pipes, pouring gasoline into water pumps, and setting off gasoline-soaked rags in hotel room are indicative of intention burn city; numerous new fires broke out in widely separated areas September 3, 4, 5, 6; mayor received telephone call from Luhsien that large fire started there yesterday near water front in small alleys where difficult bring in fire fighting equipment as was case in Chungking; mayor believes Communists wish burn city to ground as it is center of political, military and economic activity of southwest; desire neutralize any effort Nationalists organize new offensive here; cost Generalissimo his face; and break up scheduled V–J Day anti-Communist parade demonstration Saturday September 3 to be witnessed by Generalissimo.

Generalissimo ordered parade called off. Street talk Monday blamed Generalissimo's presence for fire. Yesterday People's Council of Chungking reportedly petitioned Generalissimo remain here. Mayor informed me that Yunnan Governor Lu Han departed Kunming yesterday by plane at 2:20 p. m. arrived Chungking 4:45 p. m., is guest Generalissimo at Santung, official residence near Lin Sen's [31] tomb; Chiang Ching-kuo is with his father at Santung.

---

[31] President of the National Government of the Republic of China, December 1931–August 1943.

Sent Department 188, repeated Nanking 168, Canton 142, Kunming 7.

McGEARY

893.00/9–249 : Telegram

The Secretary of State to the Consul General at Taipei (Macdonald)

WASHINGTON, September 8, 1949—8 p. m.

294. Ur 443 Sept 2 reporting conversation with representative Ma Pu-fang, which Dept has rptd Canton.

For ur confidential info Dept fol with interest plans and capabilities regional leaders to oppose Commies. Because reported stability his regime until recently, strength his forces and geographic position, Ma Pu-fang has been considered one of most promising such leaders. However, recent reports of Commie successes in northwest and deterioration morale Ma's troops tend to cast doubt Ma's capability maintain sustained defense against Commies. Dept desires maintain friendly interest Ma's plans capabilities without at this time committing US Govt to any direct assistance.

Dept suggests that if Ma or his representative again approaches you, you state that you reported previous conversation to Dept which endorsed remarks you had made and expressed its interest in Ma's plans and capabilities to carry on sustained resistance to Commies.

ACHESON

893.00/9–949 : Telegram

The Chargé in China (Strong) to the Secretary of State

CANTON, September 9, 1949—4 p. m.
[Received September 9—2 : 07 p. m.]

1075. Adviser Li Tsung-jen tells us Ma Pu-fang put up strong resistance before Lanchow but was overwhelmed due superior numbers Reds and lack ammunition. Li thinking of rebuking Hu Tsung-nan publicly for retreat which caused such debacle. Ma Hung-kwei has shown no interest in war at all, leading many believe he is negotiating with Reds for "non-belligerent" status.

Same source states Ma Pu-fang has less than 20,000 men left and, though still a fighter and still loyal [to] government, has decided situation northwest is hopeless and plans go Near East as emissary Chinese Moslems.

Time correspondent (believed reliable observer, and with combat experience USMC[32]), who left Lanchow 4 days before fall, states

---

[32] U.S. Marine Corps.

552–963—78——34

Reds only 4 miles away from city at that time, but had not yet begun attacks on extensive defenses mountain perimeter. Moslem troops were in high spirits and had prepared excellent earthworks but had almost no heavy weapons or even mortars and very little ammunition. This source believes that if troops actually fought it was very short, sharp battle until ammunition gave out. Believes Moslems probably retreated from Lanchow into Tsinghai in good order with heavy fight. In any event, unless Ma Pu-fang has troops and ammunition in some as yet unrevealed citadel, northwest seems to be finished except for nuisance value as area where Reds will have difficulty maintaining firm control. Red radio states fall Lanchow-Sining has cleared way for major drive on Chungking.

STRONG

893.00 Manchuria/9–949 : Telegram

The Consul at Shanghai (McConaughy) to the Secretary of State

SHANGHAI, September 9, 1949—5 p. m.
[Received September 9—7 : 23 a. m.]

3748. Consulate General officer informed by reliable Chinese source (prominent newspaper policy advisor close to Communists) that authorities much disturbed by widespread criticism of Soviet position Manchuria. Criticism runs as follows: Soviet insistence on taking over Port Arthur, Dairen and joint control over Chinese Eastern Railway and even removal Manchurian machinery justifiable so long as danger Manchuria might be controlled by Kmt under domination America which would in effect put hostile power on Soviet border. However, no excuse for Soviet retention these privileges now that China almost liberated.

As result such criticism source states *Ta Kung Pao* instructed by authorities to write editorial answering critics who appeared September 7 under title "Soviet Union and northeast" (re mytel 3731, September 9 [33]), with object quieting popular resentment against Soviet encroachments. This paper chosen as being safer than official *Chieh Fang Jih Pao*. Source believed editorial poorly done and could only result in deepening people's suspicions vis-à-vis Soviet aims in Manchu[ria]. (Above information of incidental interest as confirming our previous understanding that *Ta Kung Pao* and other "independent" newspapers being utilized by authorities for feeling out public opinion and issuing trial balloons which authorities not prepared launch themselves.)

Pass VOA [34] for information. Department pass Peiping 328.

McCONAUGHY

---

[33] Not printed.
[34] Voice of America.

893.00/9–1149 : Telegram

The Chargé in China (Strong) to the Secretary of State

CANTON, September 11, 1949—11 a. m.
[Received September 13—12 : 46 a. m.]

Cantel 1085. Optimism regarding Nationalists' future is markedly higher in Canton now. Ability to have surmounted Chanisna [*sic*] defections and recent apparent settlement of Lu Han "coup" at Kunming have encouraged Nationalists greatly. Another important factor is Wu Tieh-cheng's [35] report on his talk with MacArthur [36] who, Wu says, assured him that Nationalists would receive US aid if they held Canton a few months longer. Director [American?] section Foreign Office expressed to member this Embassy much interest in Congressional proposals for US aid to China, and requested further information on details and likelihood enactment various proposals. Basis for Nationalists' hopefulness about their cause is not any apparent reversal trend military defeats, but belief US aid is forthcoming within relatively short period if Nationalists can hold out that long.

Sent Department Cantel 1085, repeated Nanking 672, Shanghai 530, Taipei 158.

STRONG

893.00B/9–1249 : Telegram

The Consul General at Peiping (Clubb) to the Secretary of State

PEIPING, September 12, 1949—noon.
[Received September 11—11 : 29 p. m.]

1464. Was informed August 31 by reliable source who got information from adjutant [to] Fu Tso-yi that Fu left Peiping about August 26, proceeded Kweisui. This with consent Communists. Condition precedent was that Fu should not undertake any military action.

Previously well connected person yesterday confirmed this information, that Fu's functions are to "put Suiyuan in order". Fu has 20 to 30 Communists with him to give administration "directive" so that Suiyuan developments in general will accord those North China, Suiyuan not to be independent, but basic principle of arrangement is that there is to be no Communist interference in Fu's running of province and particularly none re military affairs. Fu to reestablish control over Chairman Tung Chi-wu. Boundary line between Fu and Communist territory runs north–south through Chihuaying.

---

[35] Chinese Minister without Portfolio.
[36] General of the Army Douglas MacArthur, Supreme Commander, Allied Powers in Japan.

Per these reports Fu can hardly be considered to have "escaped" as reported Chungking radio. Move may actually be fulfillment final clause original agreement for Peiping turn-over. Indications are Fu will ultimately be discovered somewhere in Communist camp quite rehabilitated "general [garble] note" consequence immobilization Suiyuan forces naturally guarantee Communist flanks in northwest from threat from Suiyuan.

Teng Pao-chan and Chu Hsi-chun still Peiping.

Sent Department 1464, repeated Nanking 1058, Shanghai 945.

CLUBB

893.00 Yunnan/9–1549 : Telegram

The Vice Consul at Kunming (Lutkins) to the Secretary of State

KUNMING, September 15, 1949.
[Received September 15—2 : 06 a. m.]

159. Arrests of "reactionary elements" continuing. Midnight curfew in force for indefinite period and all meetings banned. All universities and middle schools, public and private, dissolved on orders of Executive Yuan pending screening of teachers and students and reorganization.

Sent OffEmb Hong Kong 62; repeated Department 159, American Consul Chungking 9.

[LUTKINS]

893.00B/9–1549 : Telegram

The Chargé in China (Strong) to the Secretary of State

CANTON, September 15, 1949—6 p. m.
[Received September 16—1 : 08 p. m.]

Cantel 1112. Embassy has following comments on Nanking telegram 1994 to Department, repeated Shanghai 1083, September 3. In view of long record of Nationalists' failures against Communists, the premises and conclusions as to US action strike a most responsive chord.

Yet despite our pessimism over chances for Nationalist political and economic survival on continent in next year or two, the Communists have not so far won complete victory and still have considerable task ahead of them to do so. It is thus not quite time to concede them the entire field.

A strong acceptable anti-Communist leader is not in sight and circumstances do not favor appearance of a great new name. On other hand we need to think in terms not only of "revolution" and "counterattack" against Communists but also negatively of merely stopping their advance, in order to preserve part of China. While it appears now improbable that this limited objective can be achieved, sight should not be lost of its value. Communists have many problems and limitations placed upon them which are perhaps even more important than capabilities or incapabilities of the Nationalists.

Nanking is surrounded by signs of Communists' strength and unity while we daily see Nationalists' weakness and diversion. We are not visionary, nor are we even hopeful. Yet fighting is still going on and the field is narrowing down, the footing under the aggressors is not so firm as earlier and victories will be harder to earn. It is not in our tradition to concede that all is lost before defeat is complete. However divided, the Nationalists have not quit yet either.

Various Nationalist commanders have in past for various reasons proved broken reeds, such as Wang Yao-wu, Fu Tso-yi and Ma Pu-fang. In fact the more attention the US paid to them and the more they were built up in the public mind, the sooner and harder they seemed to fall. From precedent it might be predicted that Pai Chung-hsi will go the way of his predecessors in fame. Time will tell, but time is not working entirely in favor of the Communists.

Foregoing should not be regarded as plea for aid to Nationalists now or at any time that it demonstrably would be wasted. It merely proposed that instead of focussing solely on problem of dealing with Communists we should occasionally cast an eye on the Nationalists to see how they are doing and whether we can effectively help ourselves by helping them. We should not install inflexible policy of "wait and see" and "let the Communists learn" but be prepared to back any combination able to stop the Communists. We are skeptical that such a combination will appear. Nevertheless, the stakes are so large that we should not entirely remove ourselves from the scene.

Sent Department Cantel 1112, Nanking 678, Shanghai 539.

STRONG

893.00/9–1649 : Telegram

The Chargé in China (Strong) to the Secretary of State

CANTON, September 16, 1949—noon.
[Received 9 : 27 p. m.]

Cantel 1113. Chu Chang-wei yesterday stated Communists concentrating almost exclusively against Pai Chung-hsi forces in effort destroy Pai or force him out of Hengyang. Entire Li Tsung-jen faction apparently considers major crisis in its fate is now nearing. Chu tried impress me with immediate urgency of US aid.

Chu claimed Generalissimo has ordered troops under his control north of Canton to fall back on city. All commanders involved are said to regard this as suicidal and have so far indicated intention dis-obey. Chu attributes Generalissimo order to jealousy over recent Pai successes and ability to stand ground; to prevent Pai from gaining favor with US on basis his firm resistance, Generalissimo seems willing destroy Nationalist position north of Canton in order ruin Pai and continue myth that Generalissimo is only man able save China. Gen-eralissimo also said to have transferred to Chungking for [from?] Hengyang, without notice to Pai, three CAF bombers on which Pai was depending for destruction of bridges to hamper Communists' sup-ply and troop movements.

Yen Hsi-shan, according to Chu, made recent trip to Chungking to request more funds from Generalissimo since Canton Government flat broke. Central Bank said to have no funds. Yen apparently unable present specific details when Generalissimo said he knew Canton Gov-ernment still had money. As result Hsu Kan going to Chungking to present accounting and beg for remittance from Taiwan; inciden-tally, Chu said Senator Connally's remarks reference Generalissimo absconding with funds would have been more effective [if] he had cited true facts of Generalissimo's illegal control over government re-sources. Chu continued that no one in Canton accused Generalissimo of using government foreign exchange for own benefit.

Regarding Yunnan, Chu stated President Li sending an army from Kweichow to that province to assure maintenance of Nationalist con-trol. He said Canton Government considers Nationalist influence very tenuous and temporary, apparently feeling repressive measures and paper currency will cause strong reaction in support of autonomy un-der Lu Han or Lung Yun.

Sent Department Cantel 1113, repeated Taipei 168, Hong Kong by hand.

STRONG

893.00/9–1749 : Telegram

The Consul General at Hong Kong (Rankin) to the Secretary of State

HONG KONG, September 17, 1949—11 a. m.
[Received September 19—7 : 03 a. m.]

709. In September 16 interview with officer of ConGen, Chu Chang-wei stated that Gimo has given orders through Ku Chu-tung for Nationalist forces along Hunan–Kwangtung border to retire to pre-pared position on outskirts Canton municipality. Since this move would uncover his entire right flank, Pai Chung-hsi protested. Since they believed this move only preparatory onward movement main forces concerned to Taiwan and Hainan, Hsueh Yueh and Yu Han-mou also protested and have informed Li Tsung-jen that they wish

cooperate with him in defense South China. Attitude of General Liu An-chi who directly commands best units concerned is unclear, but Li believes that he will also cooperate. If Liu obeys order, Pai will be forced withdraw [to] Kwangsi and Communist take-over Kwangtung will be greatly facilitated.

Chu also said above act of Gimo, plus his withdrawal air support from Pai, convinces Kwangsi leaders time has approached when they must make overt break with Gimo. They feel that he has deliberate intention sacrifice them in order that he may survive as sole possible repository American aid. Kwangtung leaders also hold similar conviction and now offer Li their political and military support. Both groups now consulting on future moves. Inclined to believe recent activities Gimo Szechuan make it desirable alter earlier plans move government to Chungking when Canton threatened.

Financial factor also likely precipitate break. Government has been largely financed since movement Canton by purchase silver with its foreign currency reserves, which were under control Finance Ministry plus sale 200,000 ounces gold given by Gimo from Taiwan reserve. Foreign currency and proceeds gold sale now exhausted and Gimo unable part with more gold if he is to finance defense Taiwan.

In conclusion, Chu said position South China leaders critically precarious, and if held to be effective, [aid] must be forthcoming immediately. Pai still full of confidence can beat Communists with material aid. With 6 armies which he can recruit in Kwangsi, he will be able retake Nanking.

Interviewing officer expressed sympathies for plight of President Li and promised transmit above data to Department forthwith.

Sent Department, repeated Shanghai 250. Department pass Nanking 49, Peiping unnumbered; pouched Embassy office.

RANKIN

893.00/9–2049 : Telegram

The Chargé in China (Strong) to the Secretary of State

CANTON, September 20, 1949—6 p. m.
[Received September 21—2 : 52 p. m.]

Cantel 1129. Foreign diplomats and correspondents Canton now talking in terms of minimum 2-months' additional lease on life that city and possibility much longer period. They believe gloom still exists on front despite official talk of large Communist offensive and feel minor Communist penetration not of serious importance. Possibility of local turnover now disregarded completely, [garble] theory that Communists sweep along coast through Amoy and Swatow might force withdrawal of forces north of Canton. This route thought to present too many natural difficulties even if Nationalist opposition only light.

Embassy comment: Although situation north of Canton has hopeful elements, it can be changed in few weeks if Communists succeed in splitting Nationalist defenders. Also must not overlook possibility that direct Generalissimo pressure on his loyal subordinates north of China [*Canton?*], probably to be exerted in person following his return to Canton, may result in turning existing coordination between Pai's forces on left and Generalissimo's forces on right. As yet Pai and President Li have little in way of tangible reward to offer these other commanders for continuing cooperation against Generalissimo's orders and pressure. We can readily believe President Li's statement that Generalissimo willing go any lengths prevent Pai Chung-hsi from becoming hero. (Cantel 1113, September 15 [*16*], repeated Taipei 168, Hong Kong unnumbered; Cantel 1114, September 16 [37] and Hong Kong telegram 709, September 17, repeated Shanghai 250).

Embassy's own estimate is minimum of 6 weeks; factors which would lead to estimate of longer life for Canton not yet determined.

Sent Department Cantel 1129; repeated Taipei 170; Shanghai 540; by hand Hong Kong.

STRONG

893.001 Chiang Kai-shek/9–2149 : Telegram

The Consul General at Taipei (Macdonald) to the Secretary of State

TAIPEI, September 21, 1949—9 a. m.
[Received 11 : 39 p. m.]

500. Prolonged absence Generalissimo from Taiwan causes some speculation. Yesterday it seemed during conversation with Hollington Tong and K. C. Wu that they were slightly concerned, but Wu finally said that Generalissimo had settled pressing matters Szechwan and will be returning here within few days.

French Consul told me last night he heard from reliable source that Acting President Li and others, presumably Pai Chung-hsi, doing everything possible to make Generalissimo stay in Chungking or Chengtu, even going so far perhaps as instigating local trouble there to keep him occupied. This report possibly true. Generalissimo's attitude towards Pai, as reported Cantel 1113, September 16 to Department, repeated Taipei as 168, very likely reason for such action on part of Li and Pai and followers.

MACDONALD

---

[37] Vol. IX, p. 548.

893.00B/9–2349 : Telegram

The Consul General at Peiping (Clubb) to the Secretary of State

PEIPING, September 23, 1949.
[Received September 23—5 a. m.]

1592. All Suiyuan Province now nominally under Communist control as result Tung Chi-wu's telegram of September 19 to Mao–Chu [38] declaring severance connection with Kmt and "desire to participate in people's democratic camp". In Ninghsia Province, press to date has only reported liberation on September 14 of Chungning, on Yellow River 90 miles south Ninghsia city. Ninghsia Province now almost cut off by PLA Kansu advance. Status Ma Hung-kuei unreported in press.

Jen Min Jih Pao September 18 reported that in early September a joint message was sent to Tihwa by Kmt Deputy Army Commanders Chao Sui and two division commanders Ma Chen-wui and Tan Chenghsiang, who crossed over to PLA middle August. This message called on Ma Yun-chang, Kmt Mayor, and Ma Pu-fang's 5th Cavalry Army now in Sinkiang to cease fighting and come over to side of Chinese people. Stated that, since PLA liberation of Tsinghai, people have equality and religious freedom as compared previous suppression and exploitation of Kmt and Ma Pu-fang. Expressed hope that officers, troops in Sinkiang will realize the situation, revolt to side of people to avoid meaningless sacrifice.

To Tientsin by mail.

CLUBB

VII. MEETING AT PEIPING OF THE COMMUNIST-SPONSORED PEOPLE'S POLITICAL CONSULTATIVE CONFERENCE (PCC); ESTABLISHMENT AT PEIPING OF THE "CENTRAL PEOPLE'S GOVERNMENT OF THE PEOPLE'S REPUBLIC OF CHINA" (SEPTEMBER 24–OCTOBER 3)

893.00/9–2449 : Telegram

The Consul General at Peiping (Clubb) to the Secretary of State

PEIPING, September 24, 1949.
[Received September 24—7 : 39 a. m.]

1610. Following are 21 members of standing committee of PCC [39] Preparatory Committee. (This committee was set up June 19 and, with 5 subcommittees, has done basic work drafting documents for submission PCC and drawing up list of delegates during past 3 months.)

---

[38] Mao Tse-tung and Chu Teh.
[39] Political Consultative Conference.

Mao Tse-tung,[40] Chu Teh,[41] Li Chi-shen,[42] Li Li-san,[43] Shen Chun-ju,[44] Shen Yen-ping (Mao Tun),[45] Chou En-lai,[46] Lin Tsu-han,[47] Ma Yin-chu,[48] Ma Hsu-lun,[49] U Lan-fu (Yun Tse),[50] Chang Po-chun,[51] Chang Lan,[52] Chang Hsi-jo,[53] Kuo Mo-jo,[54] Chen Shu-tung,[55] Tan Kah-ki,[56] Huang Yen-pei,[57] Tsai Ting-kai,[58] Tsai Chang,[59] Tan Ping-shan.[60] Mao [Tse-tung, chairman], Chou En-lai, Li Chi-shen, Shen Chun-ju, Kuo Mo-jo, and Chen Shu-tung, vice chairmen.

Sent Department 1610; repeated Shanghai 1002.

CLUBB

893.00/9–2449 : Telegram

The Consul General at Peiping (Clubb) to the Secretary of State

PEIPING, September 24, 1949.
[Received September 24—8:33 a. m.]

1611. Chinese People's PCC opened evening meeting September 21 with 636 delegates, alternates, specially invited delegates representing 45 units attending. Mao's opening speech (reported [by] NCNA [61] September 21) stated PCC "declares that it exercises the functions of National People's Congress", PCC thus, in fact, acting as ad interim governing body, will enact powers and function of All-China People's Congress before calling of Congress. Other opening session speeches by Liu Shao-chi,[62] Madame Sun Yat-sen,[63] Ho Hsiang-ning (Madame Liao Chung-kai [64]) of Kmt [65] Revolutionary Committee, Chang Lan

---

[40] Chairman of Central Committee of Chinese Communist Party (CCP).
[41] Commander in Chief of Chinese Communist armies.
[42] Leader of Kuomintang Revolutionary Committee (KmtRC).
[43] Vice Chairman of Communist All-China Federation of Labor (ACFL).
[44] Chinese Democratic League (CDL) leader.
[45] Novelist.
[46] Member of Central Committee of Chinese Communist Party and of Politburo; vice chairman of Chinese People's Revolutionary Military Affairs Committee.
[47] Known also as Lin Po-chu, member of Central Committee of Chinese Communist Party.
[48] Author and member of Academia Sinica.
[49] Former Chinese Vice Minister of Education.
[50] Chairman of Communist regime in Inner Mongolia.
[51] Leader of Chinese Peasants and Workers Democratic Party.
[52] Titular leader of Democratic League.
[53] Professor at Tsinghua University.
[54] Poet and writer.
[55] Founder of Commercial Press, Shanghai.
[56] Overseas delegate.
[57] People's League leader.
[58] Member of Kuomintang Revolutionary Committee.
[59] Woman revolutionary.
[60] Revolutionary.
[61] Communist New China News Agency.
[62] Vice Chairman of Central Committee of Chinese Communist Party.
[63] Sister of Madame Chiang Kai-shek, Mrs. H. H. Kung, and T. V. Soong.
[64] Widow of leftist leader of the Kuomintang (Nationalist Party) before his execution in 1925.
[65] Kuomintang.

(CDL), Kao Kang (new People's Government),[66] Chen Yi[67] (PLA[68]), Huang Yen-pei (Democratic National Construction Association), Li Li-san (ACFL), Sai Fu-ting[69] (Sinkiang), Chang Chih-chung[70] and Cheng Chi-sen (specially invited delegates), and Ssu-tu Mei-tang (Overseas China). Liu and Mme. Sun speeches complete in NCNA broadcast September 22. Other speeches summarized in NCNA September 22 and Contel 1605, Sept. 24.[71]

Praesidium of PCC is composed 89 members as listed NCNA September 22. Secretary-General is Lin Tsu-han.

Sent Department 1611, repeated Shanghai 1003; by mail Tientsin.

CLUBB

893.00/9–2449 : Telegram

The Consul General at Peiping (Clubb) to the Secretary of State

PEIPING, September 24, 1949.
[Received September 25—11: 53 a. m.]

1615. Report of CCP CC[72] Politburo member Tung Pi-wu to PCC on drafting and contents organic statute Central People's Government, September 22, was summarized in NCNA English language release September 23. In view its importance full translation report as printed *Kuang Ming Jih Pao*, September 23, follows:

Draft organic statute of Central People's Government was drawn up by subcommittee, 25 members including myself, committee chairman (Tung Pi-wu) and vice chairman. Except for Democratic persons cultural educational field, all other units participating PCC preparatory committee, 23 in all, including Democratic parties and groups, people's organizations and professors, were represented on drafting committee. Group called first full meeting June 18, at which time views were exchanged and Chang Chih-jang and six others were designated to map out outline for discussions. On basis outline submitted by outline drafting committee, "basic questions concerning organic statute of Government", discussions were held by group in its second full meeting July 8. Views expressed by members were basically in agreement. Tung Pi-wu, Chang Hsi-jo, Yen Pao-hang, Wang Kun-lun, and Chang Chih-jang were designated to make preliminary draft of organic statute government. Drafting committee had three meetings in all and succeeded in writing first draft of statute, views of such experts

[66] Chairman of "People's Government of the Northeast" since August 1949.
[67] Communist mayor of Shanghai.
[68] Communist People's Liberation Army.
[69] Leader of Ili uprising in northwest Sinkiang, 1944.
[70] Former Chinese Governor of Sinkiang and Military and Political Affairs Director for Northwest China.
[71] Latter not printed.
[72] Central Committee of the Chinese Communist Party.

as Chien Tuan-tshang, Wang Chih-hsiang and Teng Chu-min were sought on draft. On August 17 group had third plenary meeting at which time amendments were made to first draft of statute. This was then submitted to standing committee of new PCC HKE [*sic*] committee. On August 27, at fourth regular meeting standing committee new PCC preparatory committee, Huang Yen-pei, Ma Hsu-lun, Chang Hsi-jo, Li Li-san and I were designated further to amend draft. After some changes in wording in "draft organic statute of Central People's Government of People's Republic China" at fifth standing committee meeting September 13, draft was passed in principle at second plenary session new PCC preparatory committee September 17. Tung then proceeded to explanation various points concerning draft organic statute stating:

(1) Question of name of state. We have adopted name "People's Republic of China" because term "Republic" explains our political entity and term "people" signifies today's new democratic China of working class, peasant class, petty bourgeoisie and national bourgeoisie and implies people's democratic dictatorship. It is thus unnecessary to repeat term "democratic" in the name.

(2) Question of characteristics of state. State is instrument used by ruling class to repress ruled classes. Hence we must explain clearly interrelationships among various classes under people's democratic dictatorship of today. Outstanding characteristic of new democracy of China lies in alliance four class[es], based on alliance worker and peasant classes led by working class. On this point all were in agreement.

(3) Principles governing organization government. Principle—is democratic centralism. It has as its concrete form a government based on system people's representative assemblies. In other words the people exercise state power through various levels of people's representative assemblies and various levels of people's government. People's representative assemblies are elected by means universal suffrage and people's governments in turn are elected by the assemblies. During adjournment of various strata of people's representative assemblies, various levels of People's Government will be authority exercising the state powers. Supreme state authority of nation is the national people's representative congress. Principle of democratic centralism is in contradistinction to separation of powers of old democracy. Parliamentary system is one by which part of bourgeoisie in power allow[s] another small group, so-called opposition, to air their empty talk in conferences, while people in power hold tight their administrative prerogatives and maintain rule to their own advantage. It is trick played by exploiting class before eyes of broad masses people for facilitating sharing of spoils, and sort of democratic system purposing swindling the people. Nominal independence judicial power in fact similarly serves interests ruling class. We do not want have this kind system. Our system is one combining legislative and executive and centralization of all powers in government of people's representative congress.

(4) Pending convocation all-China people's congress, which will be elected by universal suffrage, plenary meeting of Chinese people's PCC

will exercise functions and powers of people's congress, elect Central People's Government council of People's Republic of China, and exercise powers of state. After Central People's Government council has been elected, national committee elected by Chinese people's PCC will become consultative body of various parties and groups and people's organizations outside organs of state power.

(5) Functions and powers of Central People's Government council stipulated by draft organic statute are 10 in number. Externally council represents People's Republic of China and internally it directs exercise state power.

(6) Draft organic statute stipulates that Central People's Government council shall set up political affairs council as highest executive organ of state, people's revolutionary military committee as highest military organ of state, supreme people's court and office procurator general.

Tung Pi-wu then dealt with several questions concerning organization and functions and powers of Central People's Government council. He declared that as stipulated in draft, council shall be composed of chairman, several vice chairmen, number of members to be elected by plenary session people's PCC, and secretary general to be elected by council itself. Chief of political affairs council shall be called premier. Central People's Government council shall make appointments or approve appointments of chairman, vice chairmen and principal administrative personnel of various administrative areas, and of various provincial and municipal people's governments at proposal political affairs council. The term "approval" is used because chairman and vice chairmen in certain administrative areas and provincial and muncipal governments may be placed in office by election in which case all Central People's Government will do is to endorse their appointments. Finally Tung Pi-wu touched on question organization political affairs council. He said that according to draft, council shall comprise premier, several vice premiers, secretary general, and members to be appointed by Central People's Government council. Members of council may serve in concurrent capacity as ministers or chairmen various committees. Premier shall control affairs of council. Vice premiers and secretary general shall assist premier in performance his duties. Political affairs council shall have under it political and legal committee, financial and economic committee, cultural and educational committee, people's supervisory committee, and 30 ministries (secretaries), committees, yuan offices and bureau[x]. The four above-mentioned committees shall be responsible for direction ministries, committees, yuan offices, bureaux with which they are related in performance their duties.

Regarding this Tung explained:

(1) Members political affairs council may fill in concurrent capacity posts minister or chairman various committees. In other words ministers and chairmen committees are not necessarily members coun-

cil. Political affairs council will have under it 30 ministries, committees, yuan offices and bureaux. If all chiefs were appointed council members in addition to members of council without portfolio, council membership would be too big and it would be difficult conduct meetings council satisfactorily.

(2) Political and legal, financial and economic, cultural and educational committees have been placed on same plane in order facilitate their giving assistance to political affairs council and maintaining liaison and direction over various competent organizations in performance their duties. Various organizations are thus subject to direction from two sides, namely direction political affairs council on one hand and direction committee to which they properly belong on other.

(3) Duties of people's supervisory committee lie in investigation as to whether or not administrative personnel satisfactorily discharge their duties; it is different from office of procurator in that the subordination of the committee to political affairs council enables it to keep in closer contact with and have better knowledge of various administrative organs and makes its performance of duties much easier than (office of procurator) which is under direct control centridas [government council?].

(4) There will be established under political affairs council 30 organs exclusively in charge administrative affairs. This is because, in order shift its efforts of construction, our People's Republic must set up a few more organs to assume charge financial and economic affairs. There is provided in our organic draft stipulation, however, to effect that Central People's Government council is authorized when necessary to effect addition or reduction or amalgamation of members, ministries, committees, yuan offices, bureaux or offices of political affairs council upon resolution that effect. Since we have drawn up such a flexible stipulation, work of government will be much easier.

Sent Dept, repeated Shanghai 1006; Tientsin by mail.

CLUBB

893.00/9–2449 : Telegram

The Consul General at Peiping (Clubb) to the Secretary of State

PEIPING, September 24 [26?], 1949—noon.
[Received September 27—2:40 a. m.]

1618. As of possible interest and passing interest in connection current PCC following: Liu Shao-chi has reappeared after absence from public scene 2 or 3 months. It was suggested earlier he had gone Moscow. Note relative soberness his speech PCC session in course which he (1) refrained from making heavy attack on "imperialists" and (2) indicated it would take long time for Chinese achieve stages socialism, then Communism. Liu incidentally was listed before Chou En-lai in CCP Politbureau line-up.

If Liu has in fact been Moscow, his temperance which is matched by perceptible falling off Chinese press attacks on USA past 10 days might reflect either new estimate given Chinese Commission [*Commu-*

nists?] war time table or Soviet advice Communists cannot expect any substantial material aid from USSR. It should, of course, not by itself be taken as signifying any fundamental Communist change of heart.

Note that speeches given before PCC to date alike are remarkable for their temperance in respect to matter foreign relations. Even Kuo Mo-jo, who has not yet been called on to make major speech, in short published command [*comment?*] for first time refrained from his usual vilification USA. Pixs displayed behind conference platform are those Mao Tse-tung and Sun Yat-sen. CCP at moment seems be making effort avoid appearance dominating scene.

Concomitant with convocation PCC by report there were arrested number former members Democratic Socialist party, Kmt Youth Corps. Same report indicated authorities intend pick upon present for "indoctrination" all major "individualists". Such action which, of course, would shortly be public knowledge would naturally cause conference delegations be reluctant show any signs "individualism" at PCC. There are still no signs PCC will see real debate. Communists, nevertheless, apparently desire present good front to world generally.

Sent Department; Department pass Shanghai 1009.

CLUBB

711.93/9–2749 : Telegram

The Consul General at Peiping (Clubb) to the Secretary of State

PEIPING, September 27, 1949—10 a. m.
[Received September 28—8 : 48 a. m.]

1619. Was informed September 24 by L. K. Tao,[73] known to Ambassador Stuart,[74] he had recently met with Lo Lung-chi[75] who had conversation September 20 with Mao Tse-tung. Mao told Lo, re Sino-American relations, USA would have to choose finally between maintenance relations with Kmt Government or establishing relations with new government Peiping, Lo considered Mao's attitude regarding general question Sino-American relations moderate, that Mao realist, not Communist extremist, said it could not be expected CCP in view recent relations could change quickly its attitude toward USA.

Per Tao, Lo himself presented no ideas to Mao regarding matter in point. Lo stated (presumably for transmittal myself) that he realized it was not to be expected USA could break off relations with Nationalists at once but he offered following ideas:

---

[73] Known also as Tao Meng-huo, director of the Institute of Social Sciences (Academia Sinica).

[74] Dr. John Leighton Stuart returned home on leave early in August from Nanking; for further documentation, see pp. 723 ff.

[75] Leader of the Democratic League.

1. USA should discontinue aid in arms and material to Chungking Government "as proposed by MacArthur",[76]
2. Even after break with Chungking it could not be expected American relations with CCP Government would for next year or two be as close as Soviet relations same government.

Tao brought forward, as if his own idea, concept that it might prove possible with establishment new government effect changes regarding foreign policy. I agreed this technically possible, noting establishment of government on "coalition" basis facilitated such policy shifts "in line with majority will" if desired.

Tao quoted Lo as saying Mao "unable accept American aid" which acceptance would arouse Soviet suspicion. I asked what kind of aid Lo had in mind and Tao replied this signified "economic cooperation". I said economic cooperation was proposed under President Truman's Point 4 program.[77] He went on to say however that Lo thought it good idea if USA could extend certain relief as to present famine refugees without however attaching any conditions whatsoever including any regarding American control. I informed Tao that it seemed to me hardly likely American Congress would propose relief when Communists have stigmatized such relief as "imperialistic manipulations" as in Peiping library exhibit (Contel 1607, September 24 [78] and see telegram now in preparation) and Communist press continued daily attacks on USA and allies' works. I said that if CCP side itself however desired make request for aid, supplying data regarding numbers affected, etc., I would pass request on. Tao asked whether it would be satisfactory if request came from Chinese individuals. I opined such move would be pointless, for reasons indicated previously and because Communists would have to have cognizance of matter and USA could hardly be expected endeavor smuggle in flour by shipload pretending they hoped Communists would not notice. Tao said question Communist face would be involved in any request from government. I remarked that that request for aid would have better chance success if it followed change of policy vis-à-vis USA which could of course technically be effected upon establishment new government along lines suggested by Tao himself. I reminded Tao that I was not making proposal, that matter was one for Chinese decision, that I could give no assurances, that I simply desired indicate regarding previous statement that I would not indicate door was shut in advance to any appeal for aid. I said adoption by government of more friendly attitude toward USA would naturally facilitate better trade and general relations. Tao said he proposed discuss matter with Lo.

---

[76] General of the Army Douglas MacArthur, Supreme Commander, Allied Powers in Japan (SCAP).
[77] Technical assistance plan proposed by President Truman in his inaugural address, January 20, 1949, Department of State *Bulletin*, January 30, 1949, pp. 123–126.
[78] Not printed.

Tao communicated also from Lo suggestion it would be helpful if Americans refrained from open announcement support Chinese democratic elements saying he, Lo, particularly felt he would have enjoyed more influential position in PCC had there not been statement regarding democratic individualism in Acheson letter,[79] stated further there was to have been setup foreign relations committee headed by Chou En-lai with Lo and Chang Tung-sun [80] participating but that project had been abandoned after issuance White Paper.

Lo incidentally asked whether we could supply him with copy White Paper, but desired it not be sent him direct to avoid suspicion attaching.

Tao further communicated information that position Hong Kong (see Contel 1456, August 31) could presently be considered safe, it having been decided in PCC subcommittees (that is, by CCP) that all treaties signed before Kmt would be accepted while those signed after that period would be made subject study. I pointed out to Tao incongruity in view circumstances treaties by virtue of which China recovered extraterritorial rights in main were all signed after 1928.

Comment: Position Lo essentially same as that reported Contel 1195, July 19, re both Sino-American relations and American aid. His basic proposal is USA should not expect return for anything given. His proposal in (2) might even seem suggest USA should bear patiently with all Communist vilifications and restrictions for that period of time which may in Communist estimate remain before outbreak of war, while per his suggestion re relief USA would contribute gratis Communist cause. Lo seemed indulging himself in favorite Chinese pastime of eating cake but proposing have it too. Question recognition will be treated separately, but re question American aid point out here : (1) Lo speaks with even less authority than previously and not even himself thought to come around personally and make formal proposal but acted in way to permit him complete repudiation (see case Chou En-lai, Contel 1080, June 27), (2) Communists themselves publicly condemn acceptance American relief foodstuffs particularly, and (3) Communists have expressed full adherence USSR while taking all steps possible root out from China so-called "American–UK imperialistic influences" which in their minds seems include all American influence. That Lo set forth his position right after meeting with Mao may indicate Mao okeh. I maintain strongly convictions set for[th in] tel 1427, August 25,[81] and again would recommend as once before regarding Lo in Conreftel July 19 that his unauthoritative suggestions be disregarded.

---

[79] Letter of transmittal, dated July 30, Department of State, *United States Relations With China* (Washington, Government Printing Office, 1949), pp. III, XVI.

[80] Member of Democratic League.

[81] Not printed.

Remark in passing that though true Lo has been by-passed at PCC in favor septuagenarian Shen Chun-ju this seems be quite in line with Communist policy putting forward to speak second-party persons who are completely subservient to Communist line (and it has been reported that Lo has spoken to Communists in favor of policy maintaining good relations with other powers than USSR), and that Chinese Communists obviously follow usual Communist policy of pursuing their objectives, using any excuses which might come to hand—or inventing them if unavailable.

CLUBB

893.00/9–2849 : Telegram

The Chargé in China (Strong) to the Secretary of State

CANTON, September 28, 1949—2 p. m.
[Received September 28—12:12 p. m.]

Cantel 1147. Chu Chang-wei [82] informed Embassy that after heated debate Generalissimo [83] agreed permit forces under his control remain north of Canton in present line of defense and will move in additional numbers of Liu An-chi's troops from Hainan to vicinity Canton. This is major gain for President Li Tsung-jen.

Chu states Yu Han-mou [84] and Hsueh Yueh [85] have pledged loyalty to Li Tsung-jen. From general conversation it may be concluded Li and Pai Chung-hsi [86] are attempting win, and hopeful of doing so, Liu An-chi to their side. Liu, regarded as key to maintenance of current defense line, described as torn between sentimental loyalty to Generalissimo and realistic understanding of importance cooperation with Pai Chung-hsi forces. Pai stated to have advised Liu that any distribution of material and money he may be in position make later on will include Liu on equitable basis.

Reference Generalissimo, Chu declared President Li again insisting on appointment Pai as Minister National Defense. Generalissimo said to be balking again on grounds generals would not accept order from Pai and would prefer resignation. Chu said: "Let them resign", and added that Generalissimo knows such resignations would seriously weaken his influence. Li remaining firm in refusing confirm appointment of Tang En-po [87] in Fukien; has returned commission to Executive Yuan with written refusal. Chu believes Generalissimo will simply continue Tang in his position, but this will place responsibility

---

[82] Secretary and political adviser to Acting President Li Tsung-jen.
[83] Chiang Kai-shek, who retired as President on January 21, 1949.
[84] Military and Political Affairs Director for South China.
[85] Governor of Kwangtung.
[86] Military and Political Affairs Director for Central China and former Chinese Minister of National Defense.
[87] Deputy Director of Military and Political Affairs for Southeast China.

squarely on Generalissimo for his failure. Nationalist camp believes Communists will require lengthy pause after capture Amoy before beginning further advance. Absence roads Fukien–Kwangtung will alone delay them.

Chu stated Chang Chun,[88] who still Canton, says Generalissimo resolved nothing Szechuan, that former impasse between Chang and Governor Wang Ling-chi still as bad as ever; impasse created by Generalissimo who now unable settle it. Chu does admit Generalissimo made gain in Yunnan but Lu Han [89] not to be trusted for long, thus necessary move loyal troops in. Pai and Li want to do so whenever can be spared from front north of Canton and thus hope obtain control of province for last ditch stand, together with Kweichow, Kwangsi and parts of Hunan and Kwangtung. Chu indicated that if capital must be moved from Canton, Chungking is not now regarded as the place for it.

Chu renewed plea for expression of US support for Li and Pai and stated that immediately after such assurance received Li would break with Generalissimo and take own independent action at head of "liberals"; felt many generals nominally loyal to Generalissimo would come into Li and Pai camp since they dissatisfied with Generalissimo activities and attitude; claimed Generalissimo able pay way only few months longer but admitted Generalissimo now intends support forces and government on continent for further period.

Chu concluded with plea that Military Attaché [90] be assigned remain with Pai's forces to observe and report on their quality and capacity. Reiterated that Li desires have high ranking US military officer make survey and urged that US "take a chance" on backing Li, who would put forth real effort against Communists.

Sent Department Cantel 1147, repeated Shanghai 549, Taipei 177, by hand to Hong Kong unnumbered.

STRONG

893.01/9–2849 : Telegram

The Consul General at Peiping (Clubb) to the Secretary of State

PEIPING, September 28, 1949—4 p. m.
[Received September 28—8 : 01 a. m.]

1631. ReContel 1576, September 20.[91] Chinese informant stated September 20 that new government to be established October 1. This fits in with other reports date has been stepped up, but without confirmation. Note, however, mass celebration being organized for October 2

---

[88] Military and Political Affairs Director for Southwest China.
[89] Governor of Yunnan.
[90] Brig. Gen. Robert H. Soule.
[91] Not printed.

for International Peace Day and "Birth People's Republic of China".
Sent Department 1631, Department pass Shanghai 1018.

CLUBB

893.00/9–2949 : Telegram

The Consul General at Tientsin (Smyth) to the Secretary of State

TIENTSIN, September 29, 1949—9 a. m.
[Received September 30—4 : 39 a. m.]

793. L. K. Tao, friend of Ambassador Stuart and now living in Philip Fugh's [92] house Peiping, called late today. Tao was adviser to Mayor Tientsin in 1947 and 1948, a position I understand obtained for him by Ambassador Stuart.

Tao said he talked with Lo Lung-chi (Democratic League) in Peiping few days ago. Lo said US White Paper had made his position difficult in view Paper's hope "democratic individuals" would work against Communism.

Tao said Lo told him he (Lo) invited by Mao Tse-tung for a talk September 20. During talk, Mao implied Communists could have relations with United States if US "gave up" Generalissimo and Nationalist Government.

Tao said Lo Lung-chi considered it important that recent policy pronouncements of PCC, now meeting Peiping, stated Socialism and Communism something for future rather than present.

I inquired of Tao why our ConGen staff in Mukden had not yet been allowed to leave.[93] Tao said that, although he did not know reason, Manchuria was "different" and Chinese Communists did not seem to have free hand there; he implied Russians were responsible.

Above information reported for what it may be worth.

SMYTH

893.00/9–2949 : Telegram

The Second Secretary of Embassy in China (Bacon) to the Secretary of State

NANKING, September 29, 1949—3 p. m.
[Received September 29—5 : 30 a. m.]

2190. Although CCP and PLA as such allotted only 18 seats on 89-man Presidium of PCC, careful study of same list reveals at least 35 Presidium members are known members CCP.

Sent Department; repeated Peiping 375.

BACON

---

[92] Chinese personal secretary who accompanied the Ambassador on his return to the United States.
[93] See pp. 933 ff.

893.00/9–2949 : Telegram

The Consul General at Peiping (Clubb) to the Secretary of State

PEIPING, September 29, 1949.
[Received September 29—6 : 23 a. m.]

1644. ReContel 1638, September 28.[94] PCC session September 27 passed six basic resolutions by unanimous vote :

(1) Organization statute of Chinese People's PCC;
(2) Organization statute of Central People's Government of People's Republic China;
(3) Capital of People's Republic China shall be Peiping, renamed Peking;
(4) Western calendar to be used in dating, i.e. this year is 1949;
(5) *March of the Volunteers* to be used temporarily as national anthem pending formal selection;
(6) National flag adopted has red background, five-pointed golden star in upper corner near staff flanked by arc of four smaller golden stars.

At this sixth session 25 speakers expressed unanimous support all measures under consideration:
[Here follow names of speakers.]
PCC recessed one day September 28, with various unity [*units?*] and committee on draft common program holding separate meetings in afternoon.

Sent Department, repeated Shanghai 1020.

CLUBB

893.00/9–3049 : Telegram

The Consul General at Peiping (Clubb) to the Secretary of State

PEIPING, September 30, 1949.
[Received September 30—8 : 38 a. m.]

1658. ReContel 1644, September 29. Common program of Chinese People's PCC unanimously passed by PCC September 29. Common program covers organization of state power, military system, economic policy, cultural and educational policy, policy toward nationalities, and foreign policy. Unofficial English version full text given NCNA September 29. Session also passed provisions for electing National Committee of Chinese People's PCC and Central Government Council. Latter will have chairman, 6 vice-chairmen, 56 members. Peiping press September 30 carried full Chinese texts of organization statutes of PCC and Central People's Government. October 1–3 de-

---

[94] Not printed.

clared official 3-day holiday celebrate establishment here of "Central People's Government of Chinese People's Republic".

Repeated Shanghai 1028.

CLUBB

893.01/10-149 : Telegram

The Consul General at Peiping (Clubb) to the Secretary of State

PEIPING, October 1, 1949.
[Received October 2—7:16 a. m.]

1666. Following is text in translation public statement October 1:

"Proclamation of the Central People's Government of the People's Republic of China.

Since the reactionary Kmt Government of Chiang Kai-shek revolted against our Fatherland, joined in collusion with imperialism, and began the counter-revolutionary war, the people of the whole country have been in grievous circumstances. Fortunately, in order to protect the territorial sovereignty of our Fatherland, to protect the lives and property of the people, to eliminate the sufferings of the people and to attain the people's victory, our People's Liberation Army with the aid of the people of the whole country has struggled selflessly, fought valiantly, and succeeded in destroying the reactionary armies and overthrowing the reactionary rule of the Kmt Government. The people's liberation war has now achieved basic victory, and the majority of the people in the entire country has already attained liberation.

On this foundation, the plenary session of the people's PCC organized from representatives of democratic parties and groups, all people's organizations, the People's Liberation Army, all areas, all races, overseas Chinese, and other patriotic democratic elements, of the whole country has already met and, representing the will of the people of the whole country, enacted the organization statute of the Central People's Government of the People's Republic of China, and elected:

As chairman of the Central People's Government: Mao Tse-tung;

As Vice Chairmen: Chu Teh, Liu Shao-chi, Soong Ching-ling (Madame Sun Yat-sen), Li Chi-shen, Chang Lan, and Kao Kang;

And as Council members: Chen Yi, Ho Lung, Li Li-san, Lin Po-chu (Tsu-han), Yeh Chien-ying, Ho Hsiang-ning (Madame Liao Chung-kai), Lin Piao, Peng Te-huai, Liu Po-cheng, Wu Yu-chang, Hsu Hsiang-chien, Po Yi-po, Nieh Jung-chen, Chou En-lai, Tung Pi-wu, Sai Fu-ting, Jao Shu-shih, Tan Kah-kee, Lo Jung-huan, Teng Tzu-hui, Ulanfu (Yun Tse), Hsu Te-li, Tsai Chang, Liu Ke-ping, Ma Yin-chu, Chen Yun, Kang Sheng, Lin Feng, Ma Hsu-lun, Kuo Mo-jo, Chang Yun-yi, Teng Hsiao-ping, Kao Chung-min, Shen Chun-ju, Shen Yen-ping (Mao Tun), Chen Shu-tung, Ssu-tu Mei-tang, Li Hsi-chiu, Huang Yen-pei, Tsai Ting-kai, Hsi Chung-hsun, Peng Tse-min, Chang Chih-chung, Fu Tso-yi, Li Chu-chen, Li Chang-ta, Chang Po-chun, Cheng Chien, Chang Hsi-jo, Chen Shu-ming, Tan

Ping-shang, Chang Nan-hsien, Liu Ya-tzu, Chang Tung-sun, and Lung Yun.

Has organized the Central People's Government Council; has proclaimed the establishment of the People's Republic of China; and has fixed Peking to be the capital of the People's Republic of China.

The Central People's Government Council of the People's Republic of China today took office in the capital and unanimously decided to proclaim the establishment of the Central People's Government of the People's Republic of China and to accept the common program of the Chinese People's Political Consultative Council as the course of action for the government.

Elected from among the Council members Lin Po-chu to be Secretary-General of the Central People's Government Council;

Appointed Chou En-lai to be Premier of the Administrative Council of the Central People's Government and concurrently Minister of Foreign Affairs;

Appointed Mao Tse-tung to be chairman of the People's Revolutionary Military Council of the Central People's Government.

Appointed Chu Teh to be Commander in Chief of the PLA;

Appointed Shen Chun-ju as head of the Supreme People's Court of the Central People's Government;

Appointed Lo Jung-huan as head of the Office of the People's Procurator General of the Central People's Government; and charged them with responsibility for setting up all government organs and putting into operation all government activities as rapidly as possible.

At the same time it was decided to proclaim to the governments of all countries that this government is sole legal government representing all of the people of the People's Republic of China. This government alike is willing to establish diplomatic relations with any and all governments of foreign countries which wish to observe principles of equality, mutual benefit, and mutual respect for territorial sovereignty.

Mao Tse-tung, Chairman Central People's Government, People's Republic of China, October 1, 1949." [95]

Per NCNA item October 1 published *Hsin Min Pao* October 2;

"Foreign Minister Chou En-lai of the Central People's Government today sent Chairman Mao Tze-tung's public statement by letter to all foreign governments.

Minister Chou sent it by official notes to all old [garble] Consular offices of various countries in Peking, requesting them to transmit to their countries' governments. In cases of those without Consulates in Peking but having Embassies or Legations in Nanking, then they were sent to the old Embassies or Legations of various countries in Nanking." (Here *Hsin Min Pao* prints text covering letter, carries also text public statement.)

Tientsin by mail. Repeated Nanking 1127, Shanghai 1032.

CLUBB

---

[95] Notation by Troy L. Perkins, of the Division of Chinese Affairs: "Copy Mao statement handed British and French Emb. repr. 10–3–49. To Belgian, Italian, and Dutch on 10–4–49."

893.01/10–349 : Telegram

The Consul General at Taipei (Macdonald) to the Secretary of State

TAIPEI, October 3, 1949—2 p. m.
[Received October 3—7: 21 a. m.]

546. During call this morning K. C. Wu [96] expressed concern and alarm over Soviet recognition Communist China. Said he expects all Russian satellites to follow suit and fears that Britain will grant Communist *de facto* recognition and influence India do same.

Wu next referred to serious split between Gimo and Acting President re appointment General Tang En-po as commander of Fukien, saying it is a disgraceful, disgusting mess. He claims both sides at fault and that General Chen Cheng [97] supported by Gimo should not have appointed Tang without consulting Acting President but that due to emergency and urgent need for commander Fukien Acting President should have approved appointment on understanding he would be consulted in future re appointments. Wu feels Acting President placed himself in vulnerable position by refusing to approve appointment as he cannot produce anyone better than Tang.

Gimo's protracted absence from his headquarters [98] and close involvement official bickerings resented by Wu who was critical of Gimo saying he would be better off remain in his headquarters here with advisors. Here he would get better perspective overall situation. In reply my question when Gimo would return Taipei, Wu said he was due return by September 10 but that nobody knows what his present plans are and sounded as though he wanted to say, "nor do I care". It has just been announced now that Gimo returned unexpectedly from Canton at 9 : 30 a. m. today with most of his entourage.

MACDONALD

893.00/10–349 : Telegram

The Consul General at Peiping (Clubb) to the Secretary of State

PEIPING, October 3, 1949.
[Received October 3—7 : 42 a. m.]

1667. ReContel 1658, September 30. Final session PCC September 30 unanimously elected Mao Tze-tung chairman of Central People's Government of People's Republic of China and six vice chairmen Chang Lan, Chu Teh, Kao Kang, Li Chi-shen, Liu Shao-chi and Madame Sun Yat-sen. Central organ of state authority is People's Government Council with 56 members as given by NCNA October 1. September 30 final session also elected 180 members of National Committee Chinese People's PCC of which 18 seats reserved for areas to be

---

[96] Former Mayor of Shanghai.
[97] Governor of Taiwan.
[98] As Chairman of Kuomintang Supreme Council.

liberated, and passed final declaration (NCNA September 30). PCC closing speech delivered by Chu Teh (NCNA October 1). Central People's Government of People's Republic of China established here October 1 with formal proclamation by Chairman Mao (NCNA English October 1).

Mao stated Central People's Government Council took office October 1 and unanimously made following decision:

(1) Proclamation of formation of Central People's Government.
(2) Adoption common program of Chinese People's PCC as policy for new government.
(3) Election of Lin Po-chu as Secretary-General of Central People's Government Council.
(4) Appointment of Chou En-lai as Premier of State Administration Council [con]currently Foreign Minister; Mao Tze-tung as [Chairman of] Chinese People's Republic Military Council; Chu Teh as CinC of PLA; Shen Chun-ju as Chief Justice Supreme People's Court; Lo Jung-huan as Procurator General.

Mao proclamation further stated Central People's Government Council decided to declare to governments all other countries that this government is the sole legal government representing all peoples of People's Republic of China. (ReContel 1666, October 2 [1].) Aforecited NCNA English version of second sentence final paragraph of proclamation reads "this government is willing to establish diplomatic relations with any foreign Government which is willing to observe the principles of equality, mutual benefit and mutual respect of territorial integrity and sovereignty." [99]

Sent to Department, repeated Shanghai 1833, Tientsin by mail.

CLUBB

VIII. DISINTEGRATION OF NATIONALIST ARMIES ON MAINLAND; FALL OF CANTON, CHUNGKING, AND KUNMING; REMOVAL OF NATIONALIST CAPITAL TO TAIPEI; CONTINUED IMPASSE BETWEEN GENERALISSIMO CHIANG KAI-SHEK AND ACTING PRESIDENT LI TSUNG-JEN; LATTER'S VISIT TO THE UNITED STATES FOR MEDICAL TREATMENT; COMMUNIST WARNING REGARDING INDOCHINA FRONTIER; VISIT OF MAO TSE-TUNG TO MOSCOW (OCTOBER 7– DECEMBER 31)

893.001 Chiang Kai-shek/10–749 : Telegram

The Chargé in China (Strong) to the Secretary of State

HONG KONG [*Canton?*], October 7, 1949—10 a. m.
[Received 10 : 12 a. m.]

Cantel 1171. In private conversation with me Han Li-wu, Minister Education, on October 4 stated that Gimo [1] definitely becoming more

---

[99] For further documentation on question of recognition, see vol. IX, pp. 1 ff.
[1] Generalissimo Chiang Kai-shek, who retired as President on January 21, 1949, Chairman of the Kuomintang (Nationalist Party) Supreme Council.

cooperative with President.[2] Han and Wang Shih-chieh,[3] who has confidence of Gimo, are working hard on Gimo toward this end and believe they will succeed in persuading Li and Pai [4] to assume rather full authority and direction on continent while Gimo retains control Taiwan and possibly Hainan, but Li and Pai cannot control continent if Gimo out of whole picture. Han declared Li Tsung-jen must show moderation to assure this development and say this possible but handicapped by "little men around Li and particularly one little man" (meaning Chu Chang-wei [5]) who creating trouble. As an example, Han said, Li should have handled more carefully his refusal confirm appointment Tang En-po; [6] Li in May gave full authority in writing to Minister National Defense to appoint field commanders without consulting him; thus Li had no right, no matter how bad the appointment of Tang, summarily to refuse it. Li is good man who does make good decisions if he thinks them out himself.

Han said he himself appointed by Li and he supported him but did not feel Li should always be considered right and Gimo wrong; feels Gimo sincere and has much to contribute. Gimo's last visit to Canton resulted in big step toward more harmony, and next visit in near future should make further advance.

Han throughout 2-hour talk emphasized time and again moderation in Gimo attitude toward Li and Pai and optimism that his own influence, with that of Wang Shih-chieh, with whom he working closely, expected to bring Gimo around fully. Han is patriot working for unity as only effective way of stopping Communists and hopes persuade US enter Chinese scene again by showing unity exists.

Gimo, according to Han, has agreed defend north Kwangtung because original concept of defense of Fukien coast impossible with swift fall of Foochow and imminent fall of Amoy.

Han claims has trustworthy reports from friends who went Chungking with Gimo that people of that city did in fact give Gimo big spontaneous welcome, completely unorganized, and that "Gimo was moved to tears".

Regarding finance, Han said currency collapse with its disastrous effects might well precede any military collapse which could be precipitated by disunity. Funds on Taiwan earmarked for 8 months were consumed in 3 months. Government might be obliged resort to printing press again unless Premier [7] able obtain local revenues. (This may be one reason Gimo more willing to cooperate since his hold on financial

---

[2] General Li Tsung-jen, Acting President, Vice Chairman of the Kuomintang Supreme Council.
[3] Former Chinese Minister for Foreign Affairs.
[4] General Pai Chung-hsi, Military and Political Affairs Director for Central China, former Chinese Minister of National Defense.
[5] Secretary and political adviser to Acting President Li.
[6] Deputy Director of Military and Political Affairs for Southeast China.
[7] General Yen Hsi-shan.

resources has given him control in past but now Li and Pai control large area which can produce considerable income.)

Sent Department Cantel 1171, repeated Shanghai 558, Taipei 187, to Hong Kong by hand.

STRONG

893.00/10–949 : Telegram

The Chargé in China (Strong) to the Secretary of State

HONG KONG [*Canton?*], October 9, 1949—10 a. m.
[Received October 11—12 : 26 p. m.]

Cantel 1180. Despite general feeling Canton will be entered by Communists in 2 weeks time, city remains calm. In usual Chinese style, recriminations are now filling political atmosphere, one side claiming Generalissimo by interference and failure promptly to grant Pai full military authority had made Pai's position untenable, while other side accuses Pai of pulling back intentionally. Talk of greater unity prevalent few days ago has ended. So far Nationalists have preserved main forces intact.

Chang Chun [8] stated October 7 that, unless events of next 4 or 5 days favorable, government would move to Chungking in much less than month. Foreign Office Oct. 8 declared definitely that, at such time as decision made leave Canton, government would proceed Chungking. Li–Pai faction does not wish move government Chungking, and hinting to foreign correspondents outside chance for Kunming. Our feeling is government will have no choice; Generalissimo has chosen Chungking. Unless situation stabilized north of Canton, Foreign Office will probably inform diplomats of move shortly after Double Tenth,[9] which to be celebrated by reception given by President Li and cocktail party by Minister Foreign Affairs.[10]

Sent Department Cantel 1180, repeated Shanghai 561, Taipei 192, by hand Hong Kong.

STRONG

893.00/10–949 : Telegram

The Chargé in China (Strong) to the Secretary of State

HONG KONG [*Canton?*], October 9, 1949—2 p. m.
[Received October 11—7 : 45 a. m.]

Cantel 1184. Chang Chun on October 7 compared situation southeast China with that in southwest. Said the two were not similar in

---

[8] Military and Political Affairs Director for Southwest China and Chinese Minister without Portfolio.
[9] October 10, 1911, beginning of the Chinese Revolution.
[10] George Kung-chao Yeh.

that military unity prevailed in southwest, and that political disunity between government and leaders of people's councils was not serious because government had the force and military unity to retain full control. Claimed Yunnan was now being thoroughly stabilized on a gradual basis, and that military campaign against Communist guerrillas should be completed within 2 months. Said no serious problems remaining unsettled in southwest.

Although Chang would not be specific on southeast, he obviously indicated that in both military and political affairs there has been nothing but disunity.

Chang feels Communists will attack Szechuan both from southeast and north, with Kweiyang very probably becoming major strategic point as crossroads between Kwangsi, Yunnan and Szechuan.

Sent Department Cantel 1184, repeated Taipei 195, Shanghai 563, by hand Hong Kong.

STRONG

893.458/10–1049 : Telegram

President Truman to Acting President Li Tsung-jen of China

WASHINGTON, October 10, 1949—5 p. m.

On this national anniversary I extend to Your Excellency and to the people of China the sincere good wishes of the people of the United States.

HARRY S. TRUMAN

893.00/10–1149 : Telegram

The Consul General at Hong Kong (Rankin) to the Secretary of State

HONG KONG, October 11, 1949—1 p. m.
[Received October 11—7 : 42 a. m.]

814. Although Nationalist Government claims pouring Taiwan troops into Swatow and Canton for defense Kwangtung, complete lack activity Whampoa dock area indicates this not true Canton. Officer Consulate October 6 able freely inspect area. Found few troops, few ships and no loading or unloading equipment. This sharp contrast visits July, August when carefully guarded port crowded with ships, clogged with troops who escaped from Shanghai via Chekiang–Kiangsi and Canton–Hankow railroad, plus heavy construction equipment, small tanks, all moving to Taiwan.

RANKIN

893.00/10–1249

Memorandum by the Consul at Taipei (Martin) to the Consul General at Taipei (Macdonald)[11]

TAIPEI, October 11, 1949.

Since the recognition of the Communist regime in Peiping by the USSR there has been a very sharp change in the tone of Chinese Nationalist propaganda, which, while not surprising, is still worthy of attention. One thing that has always struck me in reading the Chinese press during the past few years is how often the United States is blamed for the troubles of the world and how little attention has been paid to the Russian shortcomings—this despite continued U.S. aid to China and Russian inspiration for the Chinese Communists. The Chinese Government itself has always shown extreme timidity in accusing Russia or even of mentioning obvious wrongs such as the manner in which Dairen has been handled. This pussy-footing approach by the National Government and the very foggy approach of much of the Nationalist press has meant that the Nationalists have heretofore almost completely neglected the very effective propaganda weapon of identifying one's opponents with foreign aggressors. The Communists, of course, have exploited this weapon to the limit, and very effectively, too.

But at long last (and undoubtedly much too late) the Nationalists have finally woken up, and lately the semi-official press has been plastered with anti-Soviet articles summarizing Soviet injuries to China and the subservient role of the Chinese Reds. Another instance is the display in a very prominent position on the reviewing stand for the Double Tenth parade yesterday of a gigantic banner carrying the following slogan: "Ta tao Su Lien Ti Kuo Chu I"—Down with Soviet Imperialism! This is a slogan which I expect will become increasingly popular and will furnish an excellent counterpart to the Communists "Down with American Imperialism". In this connection I think I have detected a more vigorous and patriotic air about the local press attacks on the Chinese Reds than was apparent in the mainland press six months ago. This, I feel, may be attributed to the injection of the "foreign aggression" issue into Nationalist propaganda. It provides a chance to appeal to nationalism and patriotism, far more powerful stimuli than the largely negative slogans, such as "Suppress the Bandits" which have been the mainstay of Nationalist propaganda.

Incidentally, did you notice that the Gimo's Double Tenth statement was entirely devoted to the anti-Soviet aggression theme? In its recital of recent diplomatic history it resembles a Foreign Office note

---

[11] Copy transmitted to the Department by the Consul General at Taipei in his despatch No. 73, October 12; received October 24.

more than an anniversary speech, which makes me think that undoubtedly Wang Shih-chieh had a hand in drafting it. In view of its style and content I would say this statement was designed primarily for foreign consumption though it does fit in very closely with the present trend of domestic propaganda.

In conclusion I should say that the current Nationalist propaganda line is a far more effective weapon against the Reds than anything they have had so far, but in view of the continued deterioration of the Nationalist military position it has come too late to be of much immediate value. In the long run, however, it should prove to be one of the keys to rallying resistance to Communist rule.

[EDWIN W. MARTIN]

893.00B/10-1749 : Telegram

The Secretary of State to the Consul General at Peiping (Clubb)

WASHINGTON, October 17, 1949—3 p. m.

718. Dept desires clarification composition of CCP [12] Politburo. Presently accepts fol[lowing] as correct: Mao Tse-tung, Chu Te, Chou En-lai, Liu Shao-chi, Jen Pi-shih, Kao Kang, Peng Chen, Chen Yun, Peng Te-huai, Lin Tsu-han, Tung Pi-wu, Kang Sheng. Various sources also list Wang Chia-hsiang, Chen Shao-yu, Chang Wen-tien, Li Fu-chun, Li Wei-han, Wu Liang-ping. Pls comment.

ACHESON

893.00/10-1849 : Telegram

The Chargé in China (Strong) to the Secretary of State

CHUNGKING, October 18, 1949—2 p. m.
[Received October 18—1:54 p. m.]

Cantel 1165. Herewith our Cantel 1165 sent by hand to Hong Kong October 5, 6 p. m. This telegram written October 2.

Tillman Durdin of *New York Times* had interview with Li Tsung-jen October 1, notes from which Durdin at once turned over to me. Durdin's article will probably include all major points made by Li who now apparently feels it necessary go to press for expression of views previously presented privately. It is noteworthy that Durdin claims Li embarrassed by question regarding assets on Taiwan, merely stating he doing his best to get hold of them. Asked regarding relations with Generalissimo, [Li] admitted there were difficulties but he trying to solve them.

[12] Chinese Communist Party.

Following interview Chu Chang-wei, apparently instructed by Li, followed up on many points Li not willing discuss personally. He complained that, although Generalissimo agreed move two more of Liu An-chi's divisions from Hainan to Canton area, Generalissimo has failed provide necessary money and ships. Same thing regarding troops of Hu Lien at Tinghai which Generalissimo promised send Canton.

Chu reviewed old complaint that Soong Hsi-lien [13] and Hu Tsung-nan [14] draw inordinate portion of resources as compared with Pai Chung-hsi. He revealed Generalissimo was overruled on his order that Liu An-chi should withdraw from area Kwangtung; that Generalissimo gave his reason for order his opinion Nationalists too strung out and must be concentrated; that, in opinion of Li-Pai camp, Generalissimo desires undercut Pai of whom he is jealous.

With regard Taiwan gold, Chu said Generalissimo not control it personally, but controls persons and agencies through which it must pass to reach Canton. Said Yen Hsi-shan's statement in reply to Connally [15] about Generalissimo and funds was drafted Taipei and Yen was virtually ordered to issue it. In original form was bitter and scornful of US but Yen toned it down; Yen felt had to issue it because was on point of approaching Generalissimo in Chungking for more money; Yen is old and tired and not able stand up to Generalissimo on politics and appointments. Chu claimed Li and his government were hurt seriously by Connally statement since it convinced Generalissimo that Washington is against him and he thus more reluctant than ever to release money; Washington preference for Li makes Generalissimo's own survival more than ever dependent on his keeping the money. Hsu Kan's resignation,[16] according to Chu, forced by Generalissimo who dissatisfied with him. (Foreign Office officials state Kuan Chi-yu appointed by Yen Hsi-shan, has been in charge of Tibetan and Mongolian affairs and "shows great courage" in stepping in as Minister Finance; normally a taciturn man, "he will have to do some shouting".)

Chu concluded situation getting desperate; troops not yet paid for September; Generalissimo gives in driblets and in way to favor own forces; struggle for control Hainan in progress; Li recognizes its importance and trying keep it through Governor Chen Chi-tang who "at the moment" is loyal to Li; Li's main dilemma caused by Washington which says must be unity in Nationalist camp but at same time show dislike of Generalissimo; Li cannot maintain army and get rid of Generalissimo; also Washington says Li must make good before aid

---

[13] Deputy Director of Military and Political Affairs for Central China.
[14] Pacification Commissioner for Shensi.
[15] Senator Tom Connally, Chairman of the Senate Committee on Foreign Relations. In a debate in the Senate on September 7, 1949, Senator Connally spoke of Generalissimo Chiang Kai-shek having "absconded" to Formosa with Chinese Government funds; *Congressional Record*, vol. 95, pt. 10, p. 12636.
[16] As Chinese Minister of Finance.

forthcoming, but we cannot under present circumstances make good without aid; Li's position like that of sick man who cannot be told "get up and walk and then we shall give you medicine"; medicine must come first, at least a glass of milk and a couple of pills; Li can make good only by striking out on his own but he cannot do so because Generalissimo has the money.

Foregoing passed on to Department [in] view Embassy lack knowledge how much of Chu's remarks Durdin will include. Although portion is repetition of previous Embassy reports, some new information is included. Most interesting is fact reporter given such plain statement by Chu with no limitation on what he may print so far as Embassy knows.

Impasse seems to be real and basic and although real crisis exists between Li and Generalissimo now, prospects are that it will deepen until something snaps, doubtless with serious consequences.

Sent Department Cantel 1165; repeated Taipei 184; Shanghai 556; by hand to Hong Kong unnumbered.

STRONG

893.20/10–1949 : Telegram

The Chargé in China (Strong) to the Secretary of State

CHUNGKING, October 19, 1949—4 p. m.
[Received October 19—7 : 09 a. m.]

Cantel 1213. At private dinner early October, Vice Admiral Kwei Yung-ching stated intention strongly hold Chinmen Tao [17] off Amoy as means interdicting activity there connection invasion of Taiwan.

STRONG

893.01/10–1949 : Telegram

The Chargé in China (Strong) to the Secretary of State

CHUNGKING, October 19, 1949—5 a. m. [*p. m.?*]
[Received October 19—7 : 03 a. m.]

Cantel 1214. Chu Chang-wei confirms that Kunming selected as alternate capital by Executive Yuan. Says no steps yet being taken make preparations there and government will stay Chungking long as possible. Yunnan, according to Chu, will be site of last-ditch stand. Says government feels will lose Szechuan but can hold out long time in Yunnan.

STRONG

[17] Quemoy Island.

893.00/10–2149 : Telegram

The Consul General at Hong Kong (Rankin) to the Secretary of State

HONG KONG, October 21, 1949—1 p. m.
[Received October 24—1 : 45 p. m.]

910. . . . Source information by American missionary and Chinese Christian leader, both with wide acquaintance Chinese Shanghai
and North China bankers and industrialists presently refugees
Hong Kong, that bulk such persons making arrangements return Communist China resume business activities. Fall Canton,
impending fall Kweilin and lack confidence in Taiwan Government convinces refugee businessmen impossible Nationalists return power in foreseeable future, if ever. Communist progress formation new government, and news received from private sources
Communist China, persuades them that they can have constructive, if
not personally profitable, careers under new government. Many these
persons have large personal fortunes in Hong Kong and States. Their
return not prompted by economic need but rather feeling that they as
Chinese should participate in building of "New China". While they
not without apprehension over future, feel constrained proceed as
indicated from sense duty to country.

In our opinion this only natural development. Since crossing
Yangtze, Kmt [18] has been guilty same gross ineptitude as in previous
3 years, so that Communists succeeding virtually by default. Substantial, able persons mentioned previous paragraph, whose services rejected and advice neglected by Kmt, are increasingly aware they must
accommodate themselves to new order, or remain permanently in refugee status. Despite real and implied short and long term dangers in
former, they feel this preferable to latter, especially since no other
alternatives visible.

Sent Department 910, repeated Shanghai 174, Taipei unnumbered,
Department pass. Peiping unnumbered.

RANKIN

893.01/10–2149 : Telegram

The Chargé in China (Strong) to the Secretary of State

CHUNGKING, October 21, 1949—3 p. m.
[Received October 21—10 : 05 a. m.]

Cantel 1215. Although government just settling down in Chungking, there is already much discussion on "next move". Few people
seem to feel city will be secure beyond new year. Pessimism and gloom
pervade all ranks, stemming not only from military aspects but also

---

[18] Kuomintang (Nationalist Party).

from economic conditions. Assume that many government officials [un]willing accompany government in future move.

Interest shown by Yen Hsi-shan and Chang Chun in commencing land reform Yunnan and withdrawal Kwangsi Provincial Government from Kweilin leave little doubt Kunming to be next capital. Movement troops into Yunnan and from NE to SE Szechuan are indication government now fears attack from SE more than from north and that strategy will be to defend approaches Yunnan and maintain corridor between Yunnan and SW Kwangsi.

Considerable interest here reference US intentions toward Formosa. Recent broadcast from Peiping stating Communists devoting efforts toward Formosa, thus delaying entry SW China, has been subject much discussion. Despite additional "lease on life" which might be expected this area, people are no less gloomy over future. Feel US hand will be forced in Formosa.

STRONG

893.00B/10-2149 : Telegram

The Consul General at Peiping (Clubb) to the Secretary of State

PEIPING, October 21, 1949—4 p. m.
[Received October 22—3 : 54 a. m.]

1800. Re Deptel 718, October 17, Department listing CCP Politburo 12 names Mao through Kang Sheng accurate except Peng Te-huai. Wang Chia-hsiang, Chen Shao-yu, Chang Wen-tien also known Politburo members. Status Peng Te-huai, Li Fu-chun, Li Wei-han, Wu Liang-ping unclear. Mao is chairman Politburo, Liu Shao-chi vice chairman, Chang Wen-tien secretary-general.

Sent Department 1800; Department pass Shanghai 1085.

CLUBB

893.5123/10-2249 : Telegram

The Chargé in China (Strong) to the Secretary of State

CHUNGKING, October 22, 1949—1 p. m.
[Received October 22—7 : 13 a. m.]

Cantel 1218. Nationalist Government preparing plan sponsored by Premier Yen return part tax revenues to provinces. In turn provinces to maintain total 1,750,000 troops, serving only in native provinces. Central Government maintain 750,000 troops going from place to place to support provincial forces under Communist threat. Plan effective November 1. Minister Finance Kuan trying have total troops reduced to 2 million.

To obtain revenue certain tax collection changes proposed. Plan use high grade men and pay them well. Also plan float loans and create more [garble] through compulsory methods in China persuasion overseas Chinese. Total government outgo under this military program approximately $38 million silver monthly. Kuan said "part can come from Taiwan" and observed that previous Minister Finance's trouble was inadequate provisions for collection current revenues. Consequently Taiwan hoard dissipated faster than anticipated.

His remarks confirm other reports Hsu Kan spent Generalissimo's advances at great rate instead trying meet expenditures from current taxes. High Foreign Office official said Hsu in three and half months spent 11 months' allotment which was 200,000 ounces gold monthly from Generalissimo. Moreover, Hsu left deficit which wiped out 2 months' allotment given Minister Finance Kuan.

Generalissimo's reluctance release funds attributed to fiscal caution necessitated by diminishing gold and currency holdings.

[STRONG]

893.00B/10–2249 : Telegram

The Consul General at Shanghai (McConaughy) to the Secretary of State

SHANGHAI, October 22, 1949—2 p. m.
[Received October 22—6:18 a. m.]

4486. Information reaching us from various private sources re conditions countryside in provinces this part of China has revealed increasingly strong and now virtually unanimous testimony that general situation such areas is substantially worse than in Shanghai and other large cities. Chinese contacts who quite ready admit Communists have scored some creditable achievements in Shanghai have entirely different view of their accomplishments in country. While we have as yet little concrete evidence to support this thesis, testimony to general fact of rural distress is becoming so persistent and universal that it must have considerable factual basis. From relatively meager information to date, we would tentatively list following as among possible causes of trouble:

(1) Landowning farmers and landlords, fearing eventual dispossession under Communist land re-division program, are sacrificing normal long range care of property for immediate profits with consequent drop in morale and in farm productivity.

(2) Poorer tenant farmers who anxiously await long-promised re-division, becoming restless as program not yet activated.

(3) Chinese peasants who traditionally resist change have little faith in Communist land reform measures as relatively small indi-

vidual portions presently held in crowded Yangtze basin area not suited for effective redistribution.

(4) Farmers resent constant interference private life by Communist cadre workers. Dislike endless compulsory attendance meetings. Formerly local government not much in evidence in small rural communities with few officials seen. Communists have transformed simple rural government into elaborate regulatory system through which surveillance, restrictions and regimentation of populace is exercised to extent not yet apparent in cities. Strict control travel (with even trips to nearby towns requiring permits), together with frequent home visitations by police to verify presence all members household, results widespread feeling apprehension and insecurity.

(5) Peasants confused by high pressure Communist propaganda, which one day tells them they are backbone of revolution and next day indicates they play second fiddle to industrial workers in cities.

(6) Defaulting by landlords on tax payments (some of whom prefer surrender land rather than pay heavy assessments on property they expected shortly lose anyway) has placed tax burden directly on many tenants. In recent years Kmt farmers theoretically supposed to pay about 15 percent of produce in taxes or if tenant about 30 percent in rental. In practice both rental and taxation largely ignored or nullified through inflation and through payments in inferior goods. Farmers now held strictly accountable for prompt payment taxes in best quality rice and other produce.

(7) Large quantities rice "donated" by peasants to Communist authorities immediately after "liberation" on understanding that rice thus taken would be deducted from autumn taxes. However, at meetings of people's representatives in various localities this area it was decided that in order support war front, spring "taxes" should not be deducted from autumn payment and receipts for advanced spring payments should be returned to government for cancellation. Farmers resentful that authorities have gone back on word.

(8) Rice and other stocks depleted by heavy rainfall, floods and typhoon making future prospects dim. Some superstitious farmers believe catastrophes signify divine disapproval of Communists.

(9) During Kmt inflation farmers could count on high prices which merchants and traders were willing to pay for food in expectation of charging even higher prices in cities. Farmers would thus hoard rice in anticipation favorable price levels. Communist authorities in seeking create artificial abundance in cities at expense countryside insist that farmers sell all rice immediately after harvest at prices determined by prevailing demand. This forces prices down and creates unfavorable market which farmers cannot avoid.

(10) Desire of Communists to take care rice needs of industrial workers in cities has led them to press various austerity measures on peasant population in some instances even going so far as to insist that peasants change from rice staple to flour and other foods. Peasant response is to hide rice for own use. Communist attempts to recover such caches could hardly avoid causing resentment on part of farmers who fail to understand why they should change diet for sake of city stomachs.

(11) Farmers now deprived of income from subsidiary occupations such as basket weaving, furniture making, carpentry, masonry, etc.,

by prevailing stagnation business and drying up of former markets these goods in cities through departure foreigners and other consumers.

(13) [*sic*] Former credit relationship between farmers on one hand, landlords and merchants on other broken down with no adequate system having yet been installed to replace it. Communists trying to utilize banks and cooperative societies for purpose with indifferent success to date.

(14) Communists widely heralded program repatriation of "refugees" from cities to countryside for "production" burdens already greatly overcrowded farming areas with surplus population which has nothing to produce. Strenuous opposition by farmers has caused at least temporary halt to repatriation program and many "refugees" have returned to cities.

(15) Peasants most vociferous in supporting Communists are generally least successful farmers who hope gain through Communist land reform what they could not achieve in normal competition with other farmers. Their support discredits entire Communist movement in mind of more able farmers who feel that any peasant should by ordinary application and diligence become self-sufficient within two generations.

(16) Communist Party workers in countryside definitely inferior calibre to those in cities and not as likely attract support.

For positive side of ledger, reportedly some farmers favorably impressed with Communist attempts keep down interest rates and willingness Communists to modify programs in light of experience. Also feel Communists achieved considerable success in mobilizing farmers to cooperate in rectifying damage caused by floods and typhoon. Communist efforts to improve hygiene, health measures and setting up service stations for assistance in fertilization and irrigation methods also appreciated. Too early for such measures to have appreciable effect on over-all discontent, however. By same token dissatisfaction has not yet approached stage of violent resistance, although rumored that farmers in several areas are passively opposing individual Communist regulations. (Reports also indicate continued activity by bands of guerrilla Kmt forces now operating under name "Paichun" (White Army) in many districts but we believe such reports tend to be exaggerated.)

Believe also well to keep in mind that present situation is product initial Communist efforts effect far-reaching changes in face tremendous obstacles and it is impossible at this early confused stage to estimate to what extent Communists may eventually succeed in carrying out rural program to point where system functions effectively with sufficient support of majority peasants to preclude likelihood continuous significant opposition.

Sent Department, repeated Taipei 401, Hong Kong 332.

McCONAUGHY

893.20/10–2349 : Telegram

The Chargé in China (Strong) to the Secretary of State

CHUNGKING, October 23, 1949—10 a. m.
[Received October 24—1 : 40 a. m.]

Cantel 1219. Late yesterday afternoon at interview requested by Chu Chang-wei he inquired as to status of US plans for China aid. Upon being told substance of telCan 728, October 17,[19] he said that President Li had directed him to request Embassy urgently inform Department that Li desires in very near future proceed to US to make personal appeal to President Truman, Secretary Acheson and "other high government officials" for aid. Chu said Li hoped US Government would invite him make trip and provide US Government aircraft for the journey.

According to Chu, if US Government does not extend invitation Li will soon visit US anyhow "for thorough medical examination" and will use trip as opportunity to make appeal even though the physical examination pretext for going to US may be regarded as obvious.

Chu repeatedly emphasized that this trip did not mean Li intended give up fight. He asserted Li, together with Pai Chung-hsi, intended fight to finish.

On behalf President Li, Chu requested earliest possible reply.

STRONG

893.00/10–2349 : Telegram

The Chargé in China (Strong) to the Secretary of State

CHUNGKING, October 23, 1949.
[Received October 24—12 : 44 a. m.]

Cantel 1220. During same conversation referred to in next preceding Cantel,[20] Chu Chang-wei stated Indochina Communist forces had at unnamed point or points crossed border into Kwangsi and that this done on order of Ho Chi Minh[21] at request of Chinese Communists. He said Pai Chung-hsi was considering despatching troops which would not only drive Indochinese Communists out of Kwangsi but would as punitive measure pursue them into Indochinese territory. Troops would then remain Indochina as precautionary measure.

Chu stated he was authorized by President Li to request good offices of US Government to persuade French Government agree to entry of Pai's forces into Indochina and remain there apparently indefinitely and said Chinese Government not approaching French Government.

---

[19] Vol. IX, p. 556.
[20] *Supra.*
[21] Indochinese Communist leader.

Embassy acceded to his request to transmit foregoing to Department. Only comment made by Embassy was that information as to specific points at which Kwangsi border violated might be provided.

At first glance this rather amazing proposal appears designed to give legal means of escape for forces of Pai and to be an attempt to involve US by likely resultant Chinese Communist violation of Indochinese frontier. Pai of course is in position create same situation without French consent. In this connection it is interesting that Chu stated flatly that Pai would not retreat into Kweichow and thence into Yunnan. If this is true, it may logically be expected that failing to halt Communist advance many Pai troops would cross into Indochina.

Department pass Paris.

STRONG

893.01/10–2349 : Telegram

The Chargé in China (Strong) to the Secretary of State

CHUNGKING, October 23, 1949—6 p. m.
[Received October 26—11:28 a. m.]

Cantel 1227. Measure referred to in Cantel 1225, October 25,[22] although represented as response to local governor's demand for greater powers and responsibility, actually is manifestation of Nationalist Government bankruptcy. Unable support its administrations, it is forced shift burden to local administration. Indicating transferred revenues far below new added expense is statement Szechuan Finance Commissioner October 20 that in past Nationalist Government's subsidy accounted for 80 percent all Province revenues but that Nationalist tax items transferred constitute subsidy equal only 25 percent Province income. Thus acute financial distress anticipated.

Similar situation obtains Yunnan which is presently asking increased subsidy from central government [on] account heavy military outlay that province recent months. Moreover tax collections will be most difficult since southwest has been unwilling be involved in civil war and its burdens.

STRONG

---

[22] Not printed; it reported inception of a new tax measure by which provincial and municipal governments would be entrusted with collection of national taxes (893.512/10–2549).

893.00/10–2449 : Telegram

The Chargé in China (Strong) to the Secretary of State

CHUNGKING, October 24, 1949—3 p. m.
[Received October 24—7 : 43 a. m.]

Cantel 1222. In explanation sudden fall Canton, Chu Chang-wei stated President Li with concurrence Yu Han-mou [23] and Hsueh Yueh,[24] but with most reluctant consent of Gimo, appointed Pai Chung-hsi over-all commander central and south China areas. Ku Chu-tung [25] failed issue necessary order for several days, thus Pai unable commence direction all troops. Pai intended have Soong Hsi-lien protect west Hunan flank with capture of Yuanling and move Hulien forces west to support east flank; Pai would then have been able use own forces defend Kukong which key to defense of Canton; Soong refused move, claiming inadequate forces, and as result when Communists began all-out offensive Pai obliged withdraw Seventh Army from Kukong toward Hengyang; failure Soong cover left flank and capture Kukong by Communists forced Pai retreat; Seventh Army plus one division disobeyed orders not to stand against Communists and were surrounded with loss of two divisions; and that Liu An-chi forces failed to fight at all and their present whereabouts unknown.

Major blames for Canton debacle placed on meddling by Gimo which made concerted defense plans impossible.

Chu then declared Pai would defend Kwangsi borders long as possible but that view fact Communists able approach Kweilin from at least four directions he unable concentrate his forces; thus last line of defense would be near Nanning, including Luichow Peninsula, and to Kweichow; on this line Pai would be able achieve desired concentration.

According to Chu, who spent several days Kweilin and saw Pai several times before coming Chungking October 21, Pai will, without question, oppose Communists to the end, there being no thought of compromise or surrender in his mind (telCan 730, October 19 [26]). Pai is still in position to fight major battle and will do so on final line of defense.

Desperate shortage of time for US aid to save situation was pleaded by Chu, who gave impression some immediate catastrophe hanging over Chinese Govt. Embassy considers possible Pai may have set time limit which he able hold out against Communists if they launch major attack. As yet they have not reached Kwangsi border. We seriously doubt Pai is considering turn-over to Communists.

[23] Military and Political Affairs Director for South China.
[24] Governor of Kwangtung.
[25] Chief of the Chinese General Staff.
[26] Not printed; it reported a rumor to this effect (893.00/10–1949).

It is noteworthy that no mention made by Chu of future guerrilla activities by Pai forces. Impression he left was that all would be over if Communists defeated Pai at final line of defense. Also of interest were statements that Pai would not withdraw into final bastion of Yunnan and that other generals under his direct command withdrew their forces with his into Kwangsi and remain loyal to him.

STRONG

893.20/10–2349

Memorandum by the Assistant Secretary of State for Far Eastern Affairs (Butterworth) to the Secretary of State

[WASHINGTON,] October 24, 1949.

Subject: President Li Tsung-jen's Request for an Invitation to the United States to Discuss Aid

Discussion:

Attached is Chungking's telegram no. 1219 of October 23 [27] in which the Chargé d'Affaires reports a request from President Li that he be invited to the U.S. to make a personal appeal to the President, you and other high U.S. officials for aid. The telegram indicates that if such an invitation is not forthcoming President Li intends to visit the U.S. for a medical examination and use the trip as an opportunity to make his appeal for aid. President Li asks for the earliest possible reply.

It is possible that this request from President Li represents an effort on his part to force the issue on the use of the $75 million recently authorized by the Congress and that he would interpret U.S. encouragement for his visit as an indication that the $75 million would be used for military aid to his and General Pai Chung-hsi's forces. Conversely, failure to encourage his visit to the U.S. might be construed by him as indication that his chances of obtaining such military aid were slight. However, his visit to the U.S. at this time would probably be generally interpreted as an indication that the U.S. planned to extend large scale military aid to his forces and would thus be undesirable both from his standpoint and from the viewpoint of the U.S. If he came to the U.S. and did not obtain such assistance, it would probably mean the end of what prestige he now has and the collapse of his powers of resistance to the Chinese Communists.

Recommendation:

It is recommended that you sign the attached telegram to Chungking [28] authorizing the Chargé d'Affaires to inform President Li that

---

[27] *Ante*, p. 560.
[28] See telegram No. telCan 735, October 26, 5 p.m., p. 566.

this Government cannot assume the responsibility for his visit to the U.S. at this time in view of the critical situation and the inevitable misinterpretation that such a visit would create.

893.00/10–2449: Telegram

The Chargé in China (Strong) to the Secretary of State

CHUNGKING, October 24, 1949—4 p. m.
[Received October 25—2:01 a. m.]

Cantel 1223. In addition to matters in several preceding telegrams, Chu Chang-wei made number remarks which seem entitled to credence. Perhaps requests he made of Embassy and prospect of trip to US led him make more factual statements.

Following are gist of Chu's remarks: Situation in Szechuan much more favorable than were given understand in Canton. Although Generalissimo accomplished little during late trip this area except in relation Hu Tsung-nan and Soong Hsi-lien (details unknown), there seems be considerable support for President Li. Dissident leaders at Chengtu called on President soon after his arrival and exhibited keen desire to be of service. In contrast same leaders refused visit Generalissimo. Chungking Mayor Yang Sen is working closely with President (which is important because of his control of Twentieth Army, 16th hsien in and around Chungking and local Kmt headquarters). Yang is apparently transferring allegiance from Generalissimo to Li. Even Governor Wang Ling-chi is willing cooperate with Li to considerable degree.

Premier Yen Hsi-shan is regarded as weak link in organization. He frequently talks too much and is afraid take any action Generalissimo may not approve. Impasse frequently results because Yen must countersign official actions of President. President urged appoint Yang Sen [as] Chungking garrison commander in place of Sun Chen but Yen said only he would think it over and has pigeonholed question. As mentioned Cantel 1170, October 6,[29] Yen's days as Premier may be numbered.

Ku Chu-tung is still Chief of Staff. Although Hsiao Yi-hsu appointment as acting Chief of Staff has been confirmed, Ku is being given opportunity quietly to leave scene. At Canton it had been arranged among all parties that not long after Pai Chung-hsi assumed overall command of central and south China areas he would become Minister National Defense.

Open US distrust of Generalissimo and determination not to channel further China aid through him places President in bad situation in that Generalissimo holds on harder than ever to his treasury, know-

---

[29] Not printed.

ing he will not share in further US largesse, whereas President unable cut loose from Generalissimo for lack of own resources. Generalissimo is "devil" and Li does not wish to compromise with devil because in doing so he has lost and continues to lose support from liberals. All grants of treasury to government [garble] are hard won. On last trip Taiwan, Yen got 200,000 ounces gold which enough for 2 months. Generalissimo's current holdings estimated at US $200 million (this believed high). Generalissimo expected visit Chungking near future. In fact President Li sent him telegram inviting him (this seems curious unless it is face-saving device to make it appear Generalissimo's visit due to invitation or unless Li wishes confront him with great measure support he receiving and thus force show-down or larger cuts from Generalissimo).

STRONG

893.01/10–2449 : Telegram

The Consul General at Peiping (Clubb) to the Secretary of State

PEIPING, October 24, 1949—5 p. m.
[Received October 26—1:18 p. m.]

1826. Re Contel 1667, October 3.[30] Preliminary analysis of Chinese People's Government shows clear balance power retained by CCP. Non-Communist[s] are liberally scattered throughout various government organs but few hold key positions in important government organs.

Communists hold following key positions: Chairman Government Council, Premier State Council, Chairman Military Council, Procurator General, Director General's Office, Chairman of Committee Political and Legal Affairs of State Council, Chairman of Committee of Finance and Economic of State Council.

Non-Communists hold only positions: Chief Justice, Chairman of Committee on Culture and Education of State Council, Chairman of Committee of People's Control of State Council.

In Ministries, Commissions and Administrations of State Administrative Council, CCP members hold 17 of 30 positions with rank of Minister. Although 13 non-Communists were appointed with ministerial rank, control of even these ministries by Communist Vice Ministers is evident in most cases. In all 13 ministries headed by non-Communist Ministers, at least one and in several cases all Vice Ministers are CCP members. Total of 35 of 62 Vice Ministerial positions are held by Communists. As example control those ministries, note case of Ministry Health where Li Teh-chuan (Madame Feng Yu-

---

[30] *Ante*, p. 546.

hsiang [31]) is Minister and figurehead while Communist Vice Ministers Ho Chang and Ssu Ching-kuan actively direct Ministry affairs. Important to note complete Communist domination, by holding all official positions, in Ministries Foreign Affairs, Public Security, Information Administration, Food, in Bank of China; also major domination of official positions in Ministries Interior, Finance Trade, Heavy Industry, Fuel Industry, Textile Industry, Railway, Labor, Law, Commerce, Commission of Offices of Nationalities, Maritime Customs and News Administration.

So far as concerns memberships of various major organs of government, there are 27 known and 3 probable Communists of total 56 members Government Council, 6 known Communists of total 15 members State Administrative Council, 16 known Communists of 22 members in People's Republic Military Council, 7 known Communists of 11 members Procurator General's Committee, 5 known Communists of 14 members of Supreme People's Court. On numerical basis it is certain that CCP controls voting in Government Council, Military Council and Procurator General Committee, stipulated parliamentary procedure requiring simple majority vote of quorum, which consists of one over half total members, to pass any measure.

This analysis does not take into consideration fact that non-Communist officials, Council members and committee members are committed to follow CCP policy. This has not only been stated but is also clearly illustrated by their unanimous support of measures passed by PCC.[32] This substantiates previous indications that CCP is making doubly sure of their control of government policy and administration.

Sent Department 1836; Department pass Shanghai 1096.

CLUBB

893.20/10–2349 : Telegram

The Secretary of State to the Chargé in China (Strong)[33]

WASHINGTON, October 26, 1949—5 p. m.

TelCan 735. Urtel 1219 Oct 23. In reply Pres Li request communicated thru Chu Chang-wei you shld orally inform Li as follows:

At this critical stage situation China US Govt cannot assume responsibility inviting Pres Li leave China for visit to US. Such invitation wld be misinterpreted, either as indication Pres Li fleeing China or as sign US had made firm decision extend large scale mil assistance Nat Govt. Question of use $75 million authorized by Congress for expenditure in general area of China now under careful consideration and Pres Li's presence here wld have no bearing on decision re use these funds. Same considerations apply to Pres Li's visit to US even tho not at invitation of US Govt. In any event, as Pres Li is aware, total funds available for assistance in general area of China limited to $75 million.

ACHESON

893.00/10–2349 : Telegram

The Secretary of State to the Chargé in China (Strong) [34]

WASHINGTON, October 26, 1949—5 p. m.

TelCan 736. Urtel 1220 Oct 23. In reply Pres Li request for US good offices vis-à-vis French Govt re entry Pai's forces Indochina, you shld inform him orally that in view diplomatic relations between French and Chi Govts and presence Chungking French reps and Paris Chi Govt reps US Govt considers this matter one for direct discussion between French and Chi Govts and not one calling for good offices third power.

ACHESON

893.00B/10–2749 : Telegram

The Chargé in China (Strong) to the Secretary of State

CHUNGKING, October 27, 1949—3 p. m.
[Received 10 : 54 p. m.]

Cantel 1233. Reference telCan 734, October 26, 1 p.m.[35] Best information here indicates Communist troops had not crossed Kweichow border at any point. On contrary, Nationalists claim minor successes in West Hunan by troops based Kweichow.

As stated Cantel 1224, October 25,[36] it may be expected Nationalists will make serious effort hold Kweichow and its approaches.

Reliable source also states Communists have not yet entered Kwangsi.

Sent Department Cantel 1233. Department pass Kunming 34.

STRONG

---

[34] Notation by the Secretary of State: "Approved by the President. D. A."
[35] Not printed; it requested information regarding report of capture by Communist General Lin Piao of Kweiyang (893.20/10–2649).
[36] Not printed.

893.01/10–2849 : Telegram

The Consul General at Peiping (Clubb) to the Secretary of State

PEIPING, October 28, 1949
[Received October 28—8 : 04 a. m.]

1843. *Jen Min Jih Pao* October 26 reported State Administration Council held second meeting October 25 with Premier Chou En-lai presiding and all members present except Tseng Shan. Principal decisions passed were:

(1) Committee headed by Chen Yun and including Tung Pi-wu, Shao Li-tzu, Huang Shao-hsiung, Chang Nai-chi, five others set up for taking over personnel, files, and property of former Kmt Central Government organs.

(2) To request chairman of Central People's Government [37] to issue order winding up work of North Chinese People's Government.

Organs of the new Central Government will set up their respective working organs on foundation of organs of North China Government and will officially begin work November 1. Five provinces (Hopei, Shansi, Chahar, Suiyuan, Pingyuan) and two municipalities (Peiping, Tientsin) formerly under North China Government will now come under direct administration Central Government.

Sent Department; repeated Shanghai 1109. Mail to Tientsin.

CLUBB

893.00/10–2849 : Telegram

The Chargé in China (Strong) to the Secretary of State

CHUNGKING, October 28, 1949—2 p. m.
[Received October 28—8 : 52 a. m.]

Cantel 1238. AP representative Moosa has received report, which concurs with previously formed opinion of Embassy, that Wang Ling-chi may be removed from post as Governor Szechwan and be replaced by Chang Chun who would hold concurrently his present post of Director of Southwest Military and Political Administration.

Gimo may be expected oppose such action but strength other local leaders believed enough to assure removal of Wang who seems to be only person of standing in Szechwan not fully committed to join Li Tsung-jen "bandwagon" (Cantel 1223, October 24). Assumption Governorship by Chang Chun would be major step toward badly needed unity.

STRONG

[37] Mao Tse-tung.

893.00/10–2849 : Telegram

The Vice Consul at Kunming (Lutkins) to the Secretary of State

KUNMING, October 28, 1949—3 p. m.
[Received October 29—4 : 02 a. m.]

209. In interview yesterday Lu Han [38] expressed opinion that Communists will push into Kwangsi soonest in effort to knock out Pai and end war. He was pessimistic as to possibility of effective resistance by Pai whom he described as outnumbered at least two to one and lacking in funds; thought Pai would retreat into southeast Yunnan. He did not expect major fighting in north Szechwan due approach winter; Kweichow defences very weak but no Communist thrust expected there in near future.

Governor stated Communists would not be halted by mountainous terrain southwest like Japs due apathy people who do not regard them as invaders. Painted black picture in view continued Generalissimo–Li split and Nationalist lack of funds and troops, estimated resistance could be maintained in West China for 6 months.

Lu bitterly critical Generalissimo whose stupidity, stubbornness and selfishness he blamed for Nationalists' debacle. Thought situation not completely lost as disillusionment and war weariness widespread among civilians and troops in Communist areas and one major reverse could turn tide. He believed even small scale US aid, such as recently appropriated 75 million dollars, would effectively stop Communists and give time to prepare counterattack but only on two conditions: One, that a US military mission strictly control and supervise its uses; two, that it not be scattered among various areas and leaders but be used entirely in Kwangsi region. If no such aid forthcoming, he said, everything would be over in few months.

Governor claimed there was continuing evidence of contact and cooperation between Yunnanese and Indochinese and Burmese Communists. Though [*Thought?*] it a certainty that once resistance in China crushed, Communists would furnish arms, advisers and manpower to Communists in southeast Asia. Considered it a mistake to count on development Chinese Titoism [39] in foreseeable future because of strong hold Soviets appear to have over Mao, Chou, etc.

Sent OffEmb Chungking 78; repeated Department 209, Department pass Chungking.

LUTKINS

[38] Governor of Yunnan.
[39] Marshal Josip Broz Tito, head of Yugoslav State and Communist Party, defected from Cominform in June 1948.

893.00/10–2849 : Telegram

The Chargé in China (Strong) to the Secretary of State

CHUNGKING, October 28, 1949—5 p. m.
[Received October 28—3 : 07 p. m.]

Cantel 1240. Minister Education Han Li-wu today stated privately President Li Tsung-jen in his recent telegram to Generalissimo, mentioned Cantel 1223, October 24, requested Generalissimo reassume Presidency. Han then said in conferences Taiwan, Generalissimo and his advisors agreed Generalissimo should not reassume that office but, as spiritual leader, should give full measure of support to Li as Chief of State and seek to eliminate existing friction. As evidence Generalissimo's good intentions this regard, he plans remain Chungking for some time.

In response query as to what effect visit of Generalissimo to Szechwan at this time would have, Han thought result would be beneficial in that there is respect in province for both Generalissimo and Li. He added that desire exists on part of Generalissimo and Li to work in cooperation but a few men around each of them were disruptive influences.

As example of new attitude conciliation on part of Generalissimo, Han said just before recent major victory Chinese Nationalists, Generalissimo ordered removal of Tang En-po as commander and his replacement by General (unnamed) whose troops actually doing fighting. Whether change will occur now that Tang has finally won a victory remains to be seen.

Implications of foregoing, together with current important military and political confabs and projected policy shuffles, seem highly significant. We shall watch closely for any signs that Li and Generalissimo are capable of establishing "a new era of cooperation" as well as for major political and military shifts now supposedly under discussion.

STRONG

893.00/10–2949 : Telegram

The Chargé in China (Strong) to the Secretary of State

CHUNGKING, October 29, 1949—10 p. m. [a. m.?]
[Received October 28—10 : 43 p. m.]

Cantel 1241. Embassy on October 28 instructed, telCan 736, October 26, orally give Chu Chang-wei Department's reply and requested he convey it to President Li.

Chu thereupon informed Embassy that Li had now authorized him have Minister Foreign Affairs take up Indochina border question directly with French and that he would do so.

STRONG

893.00/10–2949 : Telegram

The Chargé in China (Strong) to the Secretary of State

CHUNGKING, October 29, 1949—1 p. m.
[Received October 29—4:05 a. m.]

Cantel 1244. Chang Chun has informed Chu Chang-wei that in his opinion Lu Han is now completely reliable. Chang told Chu that Lu has carried out every one of the 10 conditions he imposed.

Repeated Kunming 35 (Department pass).

STRONG

893.20/10–2949 : Telegram

The Chargé in China (Strong) to the Secretary of State

CHUNGKING, October 29, 1949—1 p. m.
[Received October 31—1:59 a. m.]

Cantel 1245. Understand from Chu Chang-wei that at recent military conference Haikou [*Hainan*] Yu Han-mou and Hsueh Yueh agreed defend southwest Kwangtung, Pai to defend south Kwangsi and Chen Chi-tang, Hainan. With regard latter, Chu stated not much to be expected view lack of forces at his disposal. No estimate of forces commanded by Yu and Hsueh.

STRONG

711.93/10–2949 : Telegram

The Chargé in China (Strong) to the Secretary of State

CHUNGKING, October 29, 1949—2 p. m.
[Received October 29—4:22 a. m.]

Cantel 1246. During courtesy call by Rinden [40] and myself October 27, Premier Yen Hsi-shan, while avoiding entirely any question US aid, dwelt on historic Sino–American amity and fact US now main friend. He stated efforts by Chinese Government in past had been as practical as an attempt drive an automobile over the ocean. Now Premier declared Chinese Government was exchanging auto for a ship, and if they could not have a steamship they would at least have sailing vessel.

Yen asserted that military methods alone were insufficient to defeat Communists who mobilized entire population. Three main areas [of] endeavor by Nationalist Government in future were to be: (1) teaching people that Communists carrying on class warfare; (2) improving condition of people and (3) removing causes for hatred by the people for their overlords, the upper classes.

[40] Robert W. Rinden, appointed Consul at Batavia, at this time on 3 months special detail to the Embassy at Chungking.

Despite appearance of feebleness, Yen showed full mental alertness and at times humor.

STRONG

894A.00/10-2949 : Telegram

The Chargé in China (Strong) to the Secretary of State

CHUNGKING, October 29, 1949—7 p. m.
[Received October 31—3 : 44 a. m.]

Cantel 1248. October 26 Chu Chang-wei in conversation at Embassy said a Chinese Communist offensive against Taiwan would be mounted "soon" and although many Communists had been killed in Chinmen Tao battle they had secured beachhead and Nationalists would lose Chinmen before long. Accordingly he urged US decision on Taiwan policy (Cantel 1221, October 23 [41]) in view length time required for negotiations with Chinese Government and implementation agreement. He reiterated President Li preferred see Taiwan in hands of friendly country to its capture by Communists.

At military conference held few days ago at Hainan, according to Chu, "former" Chief of Staff Ku Chu-tung told Pai Chung-hsi that Generalissimo had decided appoint him Minister National Defense. Said to have replied "too late ", that he could now accomplish nothing. Chu said President Li has also lost enthusiasm for this appointment.

Conference of most military men in Nationalist China being convened here soon is to determine over-all defense strategy, Chu stated.

STRONG

893.20/10-3149 : Telegram

The Chargé in China (Strong) to the Secretary of State

CHUNGKING, October 31, 1949—noon.
[Received October 31—7 : 14 a. m.]

Cantel 1250. TelCan 735, October 26. Department's reply orally communicated to President Li October 29 through Chu Chang-wei.

Chu stated Li understood possible misinterpretation departure from China at this time and Li was sure to appreciate statement US Government giving careful consideration to use of $75 million.

No indication given by Chu as to next move by Li except that matter had intentionally been kept out of hands of Foreign Office (probably to avoid any leak in event plans dropped).

We believe Li will not proceed US. There is possibility that his approach re trip was intended primarily to sound out US attitude

---

[41] Vol. IX, p. 400.

toward him in order assist him in choosing course of action vis-à-vis Generalissimo.

STRONG

893.00/11–149 : Telegram

The Chargé in China (Strong) to the Secretary of State

CHUNGKING, November 1, 1949—3 p. m.
[Received November 1—7 : 12 a. m.]

Cantel 1252. During our call October 31 Chang Chun expressed belief that despite diversity of opinions among various sections and leaders of Szechuan, problem of their relations with government can be settled. He did not say they will be settled. Militarily he said government has complete internal control of Szechuan.

Chang asserted present defensive line from Kwangtung to Kansu involving three separate fronts was greatly over-extended and left impression that there will be some consolidation. He is counting on mountainous areas to slow up Communist advance and he too asserted Kweiyang currently most strategic point.

Chang expressed belief that Yunnan is now secure for Central Government; although silver notes are not yet in use there Nationalist Government will introduce them whenever silver coins available to assure convertibility.

We are impressed by Chang's inner calmness and air of quiet resignation. Nevertheless he is still endeavoring to extend life to a dying government.

STRONG

893.00B/11–149

The Ambassador in Korea (Muccio) to the Secretary of State

No. 685
SEOUL, November 1, 1949.
[Received November 17.]

The Ambassador has the honor to enclose, for the Department's information, a copy of a paper recently given to him by President Rhee [42] which purports to set forth the terms of two agreements allegedly entered into between the Chinese Communists and the Soviet Union. President Rhee informed the Ambassador that the paper came to him from a "Chinese source", presumably the Chinese Ambassador, Mr. Shao Yu-lin. It appears that the material was handed President Rhee in the Chinese language and that a Korean translator prepared the English-language translations enclosed.

---

[42] Syngman Rhee, President of the Republic of Korea.

It will be observed that the enclosed material concerns what are termed "Harbin" and "Moscow" agreements between the Chinese Communists and the USSR.

The Embassy has no way of passing on the authenticity of the alleged agreements. It would appear, however, that certain of the provisions set forth in the agreements have long since been implemented or are now in the course of being implemented.

Regarding point 13 of the "Harbin" agreement, it may be mentioned that the Embassy is in receipt of persistent and presumably fairly reliable reports that two divisions of the Chinese Communist Army in Manchuria, the 164th and the 166th divisions, composed of 10,000 men each of Korean descent, have, within the past three months, entered North Korea and are now stationed in the Sinuiju and Nanam areas in North Korea.

[Enclosure 1]

Text of Alleged Soviet-Chinese Communist Agreement

HARBIN AGREEMENT
(Translation From Chinese Source)

1. Soviet Russia supports entirely the Communist China in all diplomatic and military aspects.

2. Soviet Russia cooperates with the Communist China in the economic development of North-Eastern area.

3. The Communist China gives the privilege to Soviet Russia of the communication by land and air in North-Eastern area.

4. Soviet Russia supplies 50 planes of air force to the Communist China in the long range.

5. Soviet Russia transfers to the Communist China half of arms captured from Japanese troops.

6. Soviet Russia sells various types of arms and its supplies to the Communist China at a reasonable price.

7. In case that a serious situation should occur in North-Eastern area, leading the Communist China Army to the risk, they will retreat to Soviet zone taking the road of North Korea.

8. Should the Nationalist Army of China succeed to attack and land the North-Eastern area, Soviet Russia will promptly assist the red army in secret.

9. Soviet Russia approves the Communist China Army to establish air force training institute in Juktap with North Korea.

10. The Communist China Furnishes Soviet Russia with informations regarding to Nationalist China and U.S.A.

11. Soy bean, cotton and other products of fuel, necessary in strategic, after deduction of the demands in its area, will be sent to Soviet Russia.

12. Soviet Russia cooperates with the Communist China to extend the power of the latter in Sinkiang.

13. Within the boundaries of Yoryung [*Liaotung?*] and Kwantung, a special ZONE shall be established for the station of North Korean Army.

[Enclosure 2]

Text of Alleged Soviet-Chinese Communist Agreement

MOSCOW AGREEMENT

1. The Communist China gives priority to Soviet Russia upon proprietorship of mines in China territory. A Russo-China joint company will be established and its executive right will be transferred too.

2. The Communist China approves the stationing of Soviet Russia Army in Sinkiang of [*and?*] North-Eastern area.

3. Should world war break out, the Communist China Army will cooperate with Soviet Russia under the latter's supreme commanding, and the sub-commanding power will be held by the Communist China Army.

4. Soviet Russia cooperates with Communist China in the establishment of Russo-China Air Force jointly.

5. The organization of the Communist China shall be extended to the formation in China of the Cominform in the Far East.

6. Should war break out in Europe and Soviet Russia becomes a combat zone, the Communist China despatches an expeditionary of 100,000 forces and one million labor[er]s to cooperate with Soviet Russia.

7. Soviet Russia supplies army equipments of the latest and trains 11 corps of the Communist China Army.

893.00/11–349 : Telegram

The Chargé in China (Strong) to the Secretary of State

CHUNGKING, November 3, 1949—3 p. m.
[Received November 3—2 : 34 p. m.]

Cantel 1255. Generalissimo not expected Chungking until mid-November, according Han Li-wu, who boxing terms said Generalissimo waiting for "early rounds" in Szechuan to be fought out without him, for full information as to exact nature and status of difficulties, whereupon he will appear for "final round".

In meantime, Han admitted, precious time is passing and basic decisions being delayed. Top generals gathered here are dispersing since they cannot afford to wait so long; Szechuan leaders, who originally refused wait to meet Generalissimo but finally agreed to do so, have returned to Chengtu, doubtless feeling miffed at double dealing.

As indication of current impasse, Wang Chuan-hsu, influential Szechuanese, has resigned as deputy director of SWMPA.[43] Although his post was merely nominal his acceptance of title at least helped create façade. Last July Wang told me he would resign if could not get satisfaction from Generalissimo on role for Szechuan leaders. Chang Chun doubtless was able persuade him stay on in hope of something better. Wang's resignation at this time seems indicate he has given up that hope which included removal of Wang Ling-chi as governor.

Resubmission of resignation by Chang Chun as director of SWMPA appears to reinforce view that prospect for settlement of political differences in Szechuan is dim. Only unity in Szechuan is in Chungking and surrounding country districts where Yang Sen has been mayor and head of Kmt and now has been appointed defense commander.

Thus Generalissimo continuing old game of dividing and ruling regardless of cost. Sop in form of return of Tang En-po to Taiwan, leaving Hu Lien in command at Chinmen Tao, which he has thrown to government on continent is of no importance here.

Sent Department Cantel 1255, pouched Hong Kong, Kunming, Taipei.

STRONG

893.01/11–349

The Consul General at Hong Kong (Rankin) to the Secretary of State

No. 309   HONG KONG, November 3, 1949.
                                       [Received November 14.]

SIR: I have the honor to report that in contrast to the relatively uneventful preceding month, October brought a series of important developments affecting the political and economic position of Hong Kong. The earliest of these was the setting up in Peking on October 1 of a Communist regime, which Soviet Russia promptly recognized as the *de jure* Government of China. Neither action occasioned surprise in the Crown Colony, but they brought home to everyone the fact that time was running out, and that the United Kingdom might at any moment be forced to take a formal position on recognizing Communist China.

The early days of October brought reports that the Communist advance on Canton had begun in earnest. By the "Double Tenth" (October 10) they were only seventy miles from the Kwangtung

---

[43] Southwest Military and Political Affairs.

capital, along the Canton–Hankow Railway. Such progress influenced the celebration of this major Chinese holiday in Hong Kong, with the local Communists attempting to make it appear as a Red Field Day and the Chinese Nationalists also putting on a brave front. The Hong Kong police took extra precautions and outdoor demonstrations were banned, with the result that no incidents of consequence were reported. Rallies and receptions were held indoors, however, and the huge Kam Ling Restaurant accommodated both a Nationalist meeting on one floor and a Communist women's celebration two floors above. The food at both affairs was doubtless equally expensive.

A local Communist daily on October 10 included a supplement in the form of a red paper flag, which accounted for a considerable portion of the Communist emblems displayed on the streets. The British have never insisted that private persons fly the Union Jack along with other flags in Hong Kong, and the net result on the Double Tenth was a more or less equal number of Nationalist and Communist flags on display with the majority of the population evidently indifferent to the whole matter. (They refer to the Chinese Communist flag as "Chinese-Russian"). President Truman's telegram of congratulations to Acting President Li Tsung-jen,[44] and Chiang's message to the nation were both prominently featured in the press.

The Communist armies reached Canton on October 15 and all regular means of communication with Hong Kong, by rail, river and air, were suspended. Such reports as came through indicated that the turnover had been orderly on the whole. The police remained on duty and looting was not serious, while no one appears to have molested the remaining foreigners, who included some fifty Americans. The only immediate catastrophe was the demolition of the steel highway bridge across the Pearl River, which appears to have been carried out by the retreating Nationalists and occasioned heavy civilian casualties.

While the occupation of Canton passed off as peacefully as could have been expected, developments along the Hong Kong frontier were even more gratifying to the British authorities. Only a handful of Nationalist soldiers sought refuge in the Colony, while regular Communist troops apparently did not approach closer than twenty-five miles from the frontier. Communist guerrilla units occupied the Chinese border posts but caused no trouble. During the first week after the fall of Canton some 18,000 refugees were recorded as entering the Colony; this number dropped to 900 the following week and a net outward movement was in prospect. At the close of October no regular Communist formations had appeared at the frontier, and all was quiet. However, British efforts to obtain Communist agreement on reopening rail service to Canton had produced no results, and it was feared that such action might be made contingent upon British recognition of

---

[44] October 10, p. 550

the Peking regime. The negotiations in this case were handled by a British railway official, who went to Canton for the purpose. Meanwhile, Hong Kong was following with great interest press reports of more formal negotiations between British and Chinese officials in Peking.

The suspension of normal transportation facilities between Hong Kong and Canton by no means stopped all movement between these cities. The Police Commissioner informed me that a general exodus of prominent Communists from Hong Kong occurred after the fall of Canton. In fact, he said that they had combed out the faithful with great care and had included everyone of any value in order to fill administrative posts in Kwangtung. The Commissioner regarded this as a good riddance for Hong Kong and seemed more than ever confident of his ability to prevent serious internal disorders. He fears nothing from local students and does not believe that the rank and file of labor will support political strikes on a large scale.

The arrival in Hong Kong on October 21 of no less than eight foreign ambassadors from Nanking, via Shanghai, inevitably started a new crop of rumors as to Chinese Communist intentions, and more particularly as to the possibilities of early recognition by the Western Powers of the Communist regime. In conversation with me, both the British Ambassador[45] (whom I knew in Belgrade in 1945) and the Australian Ambassador were non-committal, but others quote them as having admitted that they were recommending recognition as soon as possible. Neither gave any comfort to the personal representative in Hong Kong of Acting President Li Tsung-jen, who had been instructed to interview them privately. He (General S. K. Yee) informed me subsequently, however, that Sir Ralph Stevenson did not expect the British Government to act favorably on his recommendations as to recognition for some weeks at least.

An interesting prediction was made by the Indian Ambassador[46] in private conversation with the Australian Trade Commissioner. It was that the Chinese Communist regime would soon demand publicly the return of Dairen-Port Arthur to full Chinese sovereignty; the Soviets would then immediately accede, ostensibly at least, and the way would be prepared for a similar demand that the British hand over Hong Kong. The Indian Ambassador also is quoted as favoring early recognition of the Chinese Communists.

An official whose opinion on the political situation was not sought arrived from Canton on October 12—the erstwhile Soviet Chargé d'Affaires, Vladimir Varshov, whose transit through the Colony with his staff was facilitated on urgent instructions from London.

---

[45] Sir Ralph Stevenson.
[46] Sarkar K. M. Panikkar.

The Belgian Ambassador, Edouard le Ghait, who was Spaak's [47] *Chef de Cabinet* when I was stationed in Brussels, elaborated his views to me at considerable length. An intelligent man, with no apparent Communistic leanings, he is convinced that Mao and his confreres will not remain subservient to Moscow. He described the discipline and honesty of the Communist armies as unprecedented for China. He favors recognition and believes that we should try to get along with them. The Ambassador indicated that these views represented the consensus of opinion among his colleagues from Nanking.

All of which suggests that the possibility of Red China's taking a line independent of Red Russia should not be excluded. But in view of Mao's own pronouncements and actions to date, there would appear to be more tangible grounds for assuming that Communist China will follow, for an indefinite period, the pattern established by Russia. Certainly it would seem only common prudence to expect the second alternative, and to plan accordingly, while hoping that the first may materialize and preparing to take advantage of it in that event. A British official in Hong Kong suggested to me that some of the Nanking diplomats may have been too close to the Chinese problem of late; the bamboo curtain may have obscured their view of the larger issues of world Communism.

Hong Kong continued to receive visits from important visitors from London. In the last days of October both Field Marshal Sir William Slim, Chief of the Imperial General Staff, and Mr. David Rees-Williams, Under Secretary of State for the Colonies, were in the Colony at the same time. Their presence inspired further confidence in the intentions of the British Government to maintain its position in Hong Kong, However, they made no statements which would support the remarks credited to Australian Foreign Minister Evatt on October 25, to the effect that Communist China must agree to respect the territorial integrity of its neighbors, "notably Hong Kong", as a prerequisite to recognition; also that the United Kingdom, the United States and Australia were in "complete accord" on their attitudes toward the New Chinese regime.

Respectfully yours,

K. L. RANKIN

893.001/11–449 : Telegram

The Chargé in China (Strong) to the Secretary of State

CHUNGKING, November 4, 1949—10 a. m.
[Received November 3—11 : 20 p. m.]

Cantel 1256. President Li accompanied by Chang Chun flew to Kunming afternoon November 3. From Chu Chang-wei we gather

---

[47] Paul-Henri Spaak, Belgian Premier.

main purpose of trip is to spread influence of Li in Yunnan by his physical presence there for several days.

According to Chu, resignation of Chang Chun as director SWMPA will be considered only in connection with governorship of Szechwan. Chu says Generalissimo will agree switch Chang for Wang Ling-chi only [if] good job first found for Wang who does have many assets, among them firm resolution to resist Communists.

Sent Department Cantel 1256, repeated Kunming 36. Department pass Kunming from OffEmb Chungking. Pouched Hong Kong, Taipei.

STRONG

893.00/11–449 : Telegram

The Chargé in China (Strong) to the Secretary of State

CHUNGKING, November 4, 1949—11 a. m.
[Received November 4—3 : 14 a. m.]

Cantel 1257. Minister of Interior, Li Han-hun, called at Embassy November 3 and proceeded for a full hour to make plea for US support for Li-Pai group.

In arguing his case he stated Pai forces were only ones on continent able fight Communists and thus aid should be given directly to them. He stated flatly that, although considerable quantities military supplies believed exist Taiwan, Generalissimo would never release them, nor money, to Pai.

In political field Li asserted Generalissimo would never cooperate with Li Tsung-jen but would continue to run things for his personal aggrandizement only.

Sent Department Cantel 1257; pouched Hong Kong, Kunming, Taipei.

STRONG

893.00/11–749 : Telegram

The Vice Consul at Kunming (Lutkins) to the Secretary of State

KUNMING, November 7, 1949.
[Received November 7—1 : 55 a. m.]

220. Acting President Li in address November 5 called on Yunnanese people to re-enact their traditional record of self-sacrificing patriotism so as to ensure success of rebellion suppression and national reconstruction. Defined struggle as between democracy and totalitarianism, saying Nationalist Government had dedicated itself to task of preserving people's freedom and nation's independent sovereignty. Argued struggle was one against aggression just as anti-Japanese war. Admitted seriousness of situation and acknowledged faults of the

Nationalist Government but professed faith in ultimate victory if faith and determination retained.

Sent Chungking 84, repeated Department.

LUTKINS

893.01/11–749 : Telegram

The Chargé in China (Strong) to the Secretary of State

CHUNGKING, November 7, 1949—3 p. m.
[Received November 7—9 : 30 a. m.]

Cantel 1261. Recent public and private denials of intent to move capital to Kunming may possibly be based on the theory that Szechwan better able support large military forces. However, there are indications denials may be intended reassure Szechwan leaders and people they will be defended and thus gain greater local support for government. We understand that publicity over projected removal to Kunming has been undermining government cause in Szechwan.

Whether capital moved Kunming or remains Szechwan to end may be dictated by Communists, and not remain free choice of Nationalists. If Communists able take Kweiyang in next month or two, move to Kunming would seem questionable.

Sent Department Cantel 1261. Department pass Hong Kong 53, Kunming 37, Taipei 206.

STRONG

893.00/11–949 : Telegram

The Chargé in China (Strong) to the Secretary of State

CHUNGKING, November 9, 1949—4 p. m.
[Received November 9—2 : 37 p. m.]

Cantel 1268. Foreign Minister Yeh states he going Taiwan in few days to see Generalissimo. Claims will repeat to Generalissimo what he has urged in past that southwest China including Szechuan, Yunnan, Kweichow and part of Kwangsi be considered locale of "last stand", that all resources of China be devoted to this end and that idea of turning Taiwan into final bastion following loss of all mainland be abandoned. Says government now divided into two distinct camps on this question.

Yeh described southwest as shield for southeast Asia. In addition he felt Government would be fiction if had no hold on continent and said "apart from legal aspects" island could not long be held. He referred to hopes of many that MacArthur would wish assure security of Taiwan, that US would underwrite its defense. Thinks Air Force and Navy should be given up and savings be devoted to southwest and first line troops now Taiwan should be used southwest.

In closing subject Yeh said hoped all friendly nations would refrain from expressing belief either in public statements or by individual representatives that Taiwan can be made impregnable. Anything of this nature would end any slight hope of centering major effort on continent. Although Foreign Office supposedly controlled by Generalissimo, during past month Yeh has given several indications not entirely overtly that his thinking is much closer to Li-Pai group than to Generalissimo. Foregoing is another such evidence.

Sent Department Cantel 1268; repeated Taipei 209; Department pass Taipei; pouched Hong Kong, Kunming.

STRONG

893.00 Yunnan/11–949 : Telegram

The Vice Consul at Kunming (Lutkins) to the Secretary of State

KUNMING, November 9, 1949—6 p. m.
[Received November 10—6 : 25 p. m.]

224. This telegram summarizes following despatch on political developments during past six [weeks?].

[Here follows summary.]

Like most observers here, I feel Commies can take Yunnan when they wish; time depends only on their plans and food supply problems. I am convinced that mountainous terrain will offer no effective obstacle. Province may go within 2 months and there is little hope of effective Nationalist resistance here for more than 6.

Department pass OffEmb Chungking as 85.

LUTKINS

893.00/11–1049 : Telegram

The Chargé in China (Strong) to the Secretary of State

CHUNGKING, November 10, 1949—2 p. m.
[Received November 10—5 : 43 a. m.]

Cantel 1271. We see in recent Chinese Government proposal to French that fugitive Annamese leaders be installed in Indochina north border regions (Cantel 1266, November 9, 11 a. m.[48]) a second best alternative to original idea of obtaining French assent to entry of Pai Chung-hsi forces into Indochina (Cantel 1220, October 23) which Chinese Government probably felt could never be obtained from French without US initiative and strong support.

---

[48] Not printed.

If basic idea behind these maneuvers is somehow to involve US in international incidents of serious nature (in view White Paper warning to Communists not to violate southeast Asia frontiers [49]) results of which could benefit Nationalist Government, we feel Nationalists must lay foundations in near future for such development. Basis for thinking in these terms is undeniable hope of Nationalists that third world war ("development of international situation" as expressed by Yen Hsi-shan) will occur in time to force US to pull Chinese Government chestnuts out of fire. Since time is running out on them they may well try assist in development of international situation before Chinese Government is defunct on mainland.

Perhaps we are too Machiavellian but we feel it reasonable to suspect that same men who hope US will soon be at war are quite capable of assisting to that end. Also we feel that men who consider it practically a right to receive additional large scale aid from US and who are thoroughly disappointed in this respect may well seek to force trouble on US. They have no future in Communist China nor do they have a future outside it.

STRONG

893.00B/11–1049 : Telegram

The Chargé in China (Strong) to the Secretary of State

CHUNGKING, November 10, 1949—4 p. m.
[Received November 12—5 : 43 a. m.]

Cantel 1273. Minister Interior Li Han-hun stated November 8 four Communist Armies based west Hunan being used in compaign into Kweichow. Claimed Communist forces in Hupeh which recently captured Patung and Enshih are not strong and are not to be considered threat to Szechwan. Said Pai Chung-hsi to strengthen Kweichow which now included in his command. He reiterated remarks made earlier by Foreign Minister Yeh re split of government into island and continental groups. Said, although he and many friends did not feel third stage [*world?*] war near, must stay on mainland in event it does come. He then asked US Government take steps to persuade Generalissimo give up concept of island fortress since continental group unable do so. Said Generalissimo doing poorly on Taiwan and Hainan, conditions being very unhappy.

Li then renewed his earlier plea for US aid to continental group. In his opinion China problem is for US, not China, to solve. He also thinks it is up to US to see that aid given his group does not get into Generalissimo's hands.

---

[49] See letter of transmittal, July 30, by the Secretary of State, Department of State, *United States Relations With China* (Washington, Government Printing Office, 1949), pp. III, XVI.

For some obscure reason, Li says he hopes to have good news for Embassy when he returns from Kunming next week.

Sent Department; pouched Hong Kong, Kunming.

STRONG

893.00B/11–1149 : Telegram

The Chargé in China (Strong) to the Secretary of State

CHUNGKING, November 11, 1949—4 p. m.
[Received November 12—4 : 22 a. m.]

Cantel 1276. Chu Chang-wei today informed AstAMilAtt [50] Commies had reached Kweiting just east of Kweiyang and unless things improved Commies would be near Chungking in 10 days.

Chu indicated there is no agreement yet on what government will do. Premier Yen wishes stay Chungking regardless. Others feel it futile move Kunming. Shortage of commercial aircraft (suspension CNAC [51] and CATC [52] flights) of course renders any move difficult.

President Li is going Kweilin today from Kunming, according to Chu, to discuss next measures with Pai Chung-hsi. Apparently Pai's Forty-sixth Army is supposed to move up to Kweiyang from Liuchow.

We are trying get authentic information from government leaders on future plans. If no move to be made from Chungking or if move is to Taiwan, we shall request attaché plane from Taiwan and proceed to Hong Kong at such time as seems necessary and await orders from Department.

Embassy recommends Rozier [53] be authorized at once to close Consulate at his discretion.

Department pass to Taipei 215, Hong Kong 58, Kunming 38.

STRONG

893.00/11–1249 : Telegram

The Chargé in China (Strong) to the Secretary of State

CHUNGKING, November 12, 1949—9 a. m.
[Received November 12—1 : 51 a. m.]

Cantel 1277. We visited Chang Chun afternoon November 11 view our belief he is best balanced source information in Chungking.

Chang stated threat to Chungking need not be expected within 2 to 3 weeks and thus government had not yet considered further move. He discounted possibility further important defections and added

---

[50] Assistant American Military Attaché.
[51] China National Aviation Corporation.
[52] Central Air Transport Corporation.
[53] John W. Rozier, Vice Consul at Chungking.

that it would probably be government decision, which Pai obliged accept, that Pai should move forces into Kweichow and Yunnan. Every effort, he said, would be made to hold Kweichow and Yunnan. Apparently he hopes movement of Pai forces northwest into Kweichow will slow Communists down.

This connection, Chang declared, defence of Taiwan equally as important as defence of southwest. He felt mistake to employ one against other, and added that Generalissimo and Li to confer "very soon".

In explanation his resignation as head of SWMPA, Chang said latter lost much importance with presence of Nationalist Government. He prefers devote entire energies to Executive Yuan and Supreme Emergency Council of Kmt.

In general, we gain impression Chang believes days of government Chungking are numbered and that he thinks move to Kunming may be possible.

Sent Department Cantel 1277. Department pass Taipei 216, Hong Kong 59.

STRONG

893.00 Yunnan/11–1449 : Telegram

The Vice Consul at Kunming (Lutkins) to the Secretary of State

KUNMING, November 14, 1949—11 a. m.
[Received November 15—10 : 32 p. m.]

229. [To Chungking:] This telegram summarizes following despatch [54] giving information available here on degree of contact and cooperation between Yunnanese Communists and Viet Minh.

French and Chinese sources agree Yunnan Communists have received training at Hagiang.[55] Viet Minh may also have supplied them with small quantity arms and ammunition. Orders sent to Yunnanese through Hagiang radio.

Provincial government authorities have approached French consul general as to French action in event Chinese troops retreat to Indochina. Some indication that Nationalist troops in Yunnan may do so.

Sent OffEmb Chungking 89, repeated Department 229, Saigon unnumbered (Department pass Chungking, Saigon).

LUTKINS

---

[54] Not found in Department of State files.
[55] North Indochina.

893.001 Chiang Kai-shek/11-1449

The Consul General at Taipei (Macdonald) to the Secretary of State

TAIPEI, November 14, 1949—1 p. m.
[Received November 14—3:29 a. m.]

696. During past several weeks numerous unconfirmed reports have reached this ConGen from diverse sources that Generalissimo was seriously considering transferring his headquarters from Taipei to southwest (see Hong Kong's 1001 to Department [56]) where he would assume active direct leadership. Recent developments may, of course, have changed such plans if they did, in fact, exist.

Sent Department, repeated Hong Kong 72.

MACDONALD

893.00/11-1449 : Telegram

The Consul General at Shanghai (McConaughy) to the Secretary of State

SHANGHAI, November 14, 1949—2 p. m.
[Received 12:29 p. m.]

4782. Reference recent Contels regarding Soviet relations with new regime, including especially 4329, October 14 and 4501, October 24.[57]

Past 7 weeks' fanfare over Chinese Communist–Soviet love, as witnessed Shanghai in exhausting orgy of public demonstrations (celebrating establishment new regime, Soviet recognition, "International Peace Day", PLA military victories, recent visit Soviet Cultural Delegation and October Revolution [58]) and in press publicity propaganda crescendo which accompanied them, leaves no doubt that, at least from standpoint officially manifested policy and other surface signs, Communist China's advent to nationhood on basis all-out friendship cooperation with Soviet international leadership has been impressively fulfilled. Beneath the display, however, there have been various undertones and indications in disharmony with superficial picture:

1. While Soviet Cultural Delegation's visit stimulated officially sponsored machinery and programs for propagandizing Sino-Soviet solidarity, weight of evidence indicates that from viewpoint immediate popular feeling, it aggravated rather than improved relations. Sudden unexplained departure of delegation leader, Fadeyev, for Moscow few hours after his arrival Shanghai mystified Chinese circles who suspected it meant Kremlin displeasure over some *faux pas* made in Peiping (local Russian sources unknown reliability that offense consisted in loud drunken toast "down with Anglo-Saxons" at large

[56] Not printed.
[57] Neither printed.
[58] November 7, 1917.

Peiping function). Other four or five top delegates seem to have impressed their Shanghai-Chinese hosts fairly favorably, but delegation's forty-odd lesser personnel (Red Army troupe and other artistic performers, five workers, etc.) were apparently regarded as rather mediocre crude types. Has been widespread criticism of delegation for lavishness of its hotel accommodations and "open house" entertaining therein; for its indulgence in champagne and flashiest local limousines; and for avid purchasing clothes, etc., in Shanghai stores. Occasional cordoning of entire streets used by delegation also aroused some resentment and private comment that "American parades had never required such things". Our Chinese contacts, who attended festivities, admitted daily decline enthusiasm with growing surfeit of endlessly repetitious toasting and "perfect unselfish love" talk, boringly complicated by language difficulties. Program conspicuously bolstered by strict official directives compelling attendance functions regardless ill-health or advanced age.

Widely stated in Chinese circles that delegates utilized visit to voice strong criticism of Communist-Shanghai efforts. Aside from criticising local political-economic measures as too lax, they reportedly berated local Communists for their hectic overwork to complete neglect of health as wasteful, inefficient and advised normal living, rest, recreation.

Local Russian sources assert delegation left 5 days ahead schedule because bad Chinese reaction. We believe this quite possible as local press play-up prior delegation's arrival had given impression visit was to be longer. We surmise that any further Soviet group visitations made on similarly ceremonial social level will be gingerly handled by both sides.

2. Considerable feeling has been aroused over officially decreed spectacularity of display portraits Stalin [59] and Lenin,[60] especially when given precedence over Chinese leaders. Two Chinese sources report incident where one unit, marching out of race course to join big parade October 8, was forced by crowd onlookers to change sequence of large portraits from Stalin, Mao, Chu,[61] Sun [62] (order observed by most portrait-bearing units, including official Red Army unit) to Sun, Mao, Chu, Stalin. Reliable American also reports noting overnight switch of portraits displayed Hongkew Park. *Ta Kung Pao* October 11 published "letter from reader" which referred to "large numbers of people" whose inquiries as to reason necessity display portraits Soviet leaders reveal their "ignorance" of Soviet aid to

---

[59] Josif Vissarionovich Stalin, Chairman of the Council of Ministers of the Soviet Union.
[60] Communist premier, 1917–24.
[61] Chu Teh, Commander in Chief of Chinese Communist armies.
[62] Sun Yat-sen, founder of the Chinese Republic at Nanking, January 1, 1912, and of the Kuomintang.

China. Paper proceeded to "explain" how "People's revolutionary movement" and new regime owe all to Marxism and Soviet Union led by Lenin, Stalin. Has been other evidence of letters complaint written to local press. Also, local authorities October 15 published in all papers rules for display Sino-Soviet flags and portraits, tone of which suggested authority's awareness need for calming population's anxiety (Contel 4397, October 18[63]). Day after Soviet delegation's departure, four large portraits Stalin, Mao, Chu, Sun set up in Canidrome were reduced to two—Mao and Sun.

3. Exceptionally well-informed Chinese contacts tell us that "pretty heated issue" is developing over steps being taken to implement "Soviet-backed" principle that urban factory workers (only "4 percent" of Chinese population) should dominate government ahead of peasant masses ("80 percent"). He analyzes Russian angle about as follows:

Moscow's chief Chinese objectives are (a) maintain economic and strategic controls north peripheral areas, especially Manchuria, and (b) keep Chinese from deviationist laxities, safely in line with Soviet leadership based on proletariat internationalism peace fiction. To best achieve both aims, Russia must win over Chinese urban factory, business and railway workers and maintain them as dictators of China. Peasant masses are too cumbersome, inaccessible and basically bourgeois due home loving for ready convertibility to good Communists interested in Soviet collaboration and accepting idea of subservience to Moscow-led internationalism. If, however, Soviets can help compact, readily organized and influenced Chinese city workers to gain dominant position and can secure their gratitude by such help and by "unselfish international wise comradeship collaboration" in Manchuria's industries and in China's general worker spheres, they can thereby acquire natural easily-controlled vehicle for (a) protecting their economic strategic advance through Manchuria, and (b) ensuring China's non-deviating adherence to "selfless internationalism" which veneers Moscow's new imperialism. To confirm chain of its authority, Moscow seeks not only to ensure Chinese population's domination by urban workers (leavened with radical intellectuals) but also, "following European satellite pattern", to bring about situation (not yet achieved in China) where workers' representatives (such as Li Li-san and Chen Yun) are concurrently both the top government officials and the delegates to Moscow-bossed Comintern or successor organization. That some such strategy being pushed by Moscow and arousing dissension within Chinese circles is also suggested by such sign[s] as: Frequently reported Soviet interest in strengthening Shanghai labor; Soviet Cultural Delegation's and Soviet cameramen's stress on Chinese labor aspects and apparent neglect of countryside; reports that farmers

---

[63] Not printed.

resent being subordinated to workers and exploited for industry's higher priority; and occasional press items. For example, *Ta Kung Pao* October 28, in reporting proceedings of South Kiangsu People's Representatives' Conference, recorded that "common political program was discussed this morning with special emphasis on why working class should lead people's democratic dictatorship and why China should lean to side Soviet".

Also revealing in this connection is stress on need for industrialization of China with Soviet help noted in recent Chinese Communist utterances (such as Liu Shao-chi's October 5 address at inauguration Sino-Soviet Friendship Association, Peiping) and strenuous official press campaign to popularize Sino-Soviet industrial collaboration, especially in Manchuria.

Chinese suspicious resentment over Soviet role in Manchuria has been increasingly noticeable here in recent months. It has been aroused by Manchurian-Soviet trade pact which many Shanghai circles consider harmful to Shanghai manufacturing industries and foodstuff needs; and by disturbing news from Manchuria (frequently brought by travelers from there and North China) such as reports that General Malinovsky [64] brought military mission to Harbin about early September (reliably confirmed); that Soviets are taking over much of Manchurian railway operation; that they have failed keep promises regarding delivery machinery, etc., though vaunting their "generosity" in returning worthless portions of equipment they removed in 1945; and that in general they are steadily acquiring control most important industries and resources. Such news has excited widespread and often outspoken complaints (reflected in many letters to newspapers) against trade pact and against USSR's manifested unwillingness surrender preferred position in Manchuria despite substitution there of friendly Communist for hostile Kmt regime.

This wave of popular anxiety has been countered by increasing stream of news and editorial articles in Communist-controlled local press concerning "sensational" production records, technical advances and bustling activity being achieved by Chinese in Manchurian industries (especially Dairen, Port Arthur) with "unselfish aid Soviet friends"; enlistment of groups of Shanghai-Chinese technicians for service northeast; Soviet training of Manchurian Chinese technicians; Soviet assistance in railway development program; Soviet machinery for northeast; and import-export benefits accruing Shanghai from Soviet-Manchurian trade pact and from trade with Russia and Russian-aided Manchuria. In short, this mass of press material clearly reflects major campaign to prove that Chinese workers are playing

---

[64] Soviet military commander in Manchuria, 1945–46.

glorious role in rebuilding "their" Manchuria and that Soviet role (actual domination industries, railways) is unselfish collaboration for benefit China, including Shanghai. Soviets obviously try spread impression that their Manchurian activities are dedicated to expediting "industrialization of China"—thus playing on vanity of cherished Chinese ambitions and distracting attention from sovereignty infringement aspect.

Indications are that few intelligent Chinese are fooled by all this and that suspicion [of] USSR is growing rather than subsiding. Illustrating this is fact that at lectures by prominent Chinese who have recently returned from Northeast, majority of questions asked have been concerned with and reflected worry over Soviet position in Manchuria.

Another obvious device to combat Chinese distrust USSR and rationalize Soviet interest in Manchuria and in Chinese labor dictatorship has been recent increased propaganda stress on need for Chinese to join proletarian internationalism under "selfless Soviet leadership". This is particularly evident in recent announcements regarding necessity developing facilities for study internationalism in army ranks and in directives to army and civil bodies for celebration October Revolution—which should be used "as occasion to launch publicity drive on internationalism as expression friendship toward USSR". A directive to Woosung-Shanghai Garrison stated: "Narrow-minded nationalistic feeling should be removed, portraits of Lenin, Stalin, Mao and Chu are to be hung at gathering places and greatness of Lenin, Stalin should be introduced to members of various army units beforehand". Such evident seriousness of Communist efforts to convince army of blessings of Soviet-guided internationalism is not surprising when one considers that army is composed mostly peasants who might logically be expected to feel that they, and not factory workers nor USSR, won liberation war and who probably do not take kindly to idea of worker dictatorship.

4. Also signs that Chinese dislikes of new regime's all-out pro-Soviet policy is being strengthened by deep-seated factors of Chinese tradition background which includes: (a) Chinese popular goodwill toward America, which continues significant here despite violent anti-American propaganda and genuine unpopularity of aspects recent American policy; (b) traditional Chinese recourse to playing one nation against another and consequent anxiety (revealed by many Shanghai-Chinese) for American recognition if for no other reason than to check Soviet power over Chinese; (c) "stubborn bourgeois mentality" of great majority Chinese population, admitted by Communists who realize such situation must largely continue until present adult population replaced by Communist-indoctrinated younger generation.

As to question how far the above discussed forces and trends toward anti-Sovietism exist within upper Communist ranks, our information has been mostly in nature rumors. However, exceptionally well-informed local American states he has it from two independent "savvy foreign" sources in Peiping that weeks preceding establishment new regime October 1 were marked by bitter intra-Communist dispute before all-out pro-Soviet policy was finally adopted.

While too early to appraise true spirit and progress in this area of officially-proclaimed solidarity and collaboration, one gets distinct initial impression of perfunctory show on much of Chinese side and exploratory go-slow caution on Soviet side. Sino-Soviet Friendship Associations set up [in] Shanghai and several other cities have evidently been created and operated more by command than spontaneity and their officers selected for official prestige rather than any interest in Russia (though these associations do appear have thoroughgoing programs which, if intelligently carried out, might exert influence which should not be underestimated). Press has publicized plans for starting Russian-language courses (virtually nonexistent hitherto Shanghai) which seem thus far resulted in establishment three night schools with total 800 enrolled and moves toward teaching some hundreds students at two universities. All classes appear elementary starting from scratch. Is remarked by Chinese contact who attended tongue-tied functions for Soviet Cultural Delegation, progress toward Sino-Soviet friendship is tremendously handicapped by lack any common educational background—and especially by mere inability to talk resulting from China's long dependence on English language and scarcity of Russian-speaking Chinese. Local Sino-Soviet Friendship Association recently announced itself "sorely in need translators and interpreters in Russian".

This language difficulty would take years for Soviets to overcome and must meanwhile result in virtually all Soviet approaches and propaganda having to be through Chinese translations distributed through press, books, motion pictures and radio. Such translations are already flooding public through vernacular press, bookshops and radios and Soviets seem now working hard on more difficult remaining task of dominating motion picture media.

From limited signs thus far, guess is hazarded that Soviet penetration strategy this area may likely attempt following lines:

(a) Keep Soviet hand in Shanghai much less conspicuous than in Manchuria or even North China.

(b) Go especially slow on developing large bustling conspicuous diplomatic-consulate-military establishments ("such as Nanking AAG with its ubiquitous jeeps"). This connection noteworthy that local Soviet Consulate General has thus far avoided any ceremonious reopening and given general impression of lying low. Understood still nominally closed.

(c) Push cultural, "international ideological" and labor first penetration through intense cultivation and instigation, by carefully-
selected inconspicuous experts, of Shanghai press, cultural, scientific,
student and labor circles. That the press avenue of approach may play
very important part in Soviet setup is suggested among other things
by Tass monopoly of foreign press news reaching China, and by
opinion well-informed Chinese that Rogov's transfer Peiping significant and that he has great influence in field of China's foreign
relations. Keen Chinese observer, who long worked with Rogov, describes him as very able, exceptionally slippery, untrustworthy.

(d) Bring in industrial technicians and more trade specialists on
"humble comradely" level.

(e) Keep local western democratic communities under close surveillance, shorn of influence and in as much trouble with authorities
as possible.

(f) Especially watch and combat trends toward democratic individualism and pro-Americanism which Moscow is said to feel danger-
ously permeates new regime.

(g) Reform Soviet residents community, whose social prestige and
political, cultural dependability is evidently considered inadequate
by Soviet authorities. (Soviet Cultural Delegation members were under orders shun contact with local Soviet residents far as possible.
Delegation's visit has, however, markedly spurred colony's cultural
and other activities.)

(h) In general to feel way cautiously, distrust any even Communist
Chinese and anxious avoid repetition 1927 anti-Soviet reaction caused
by overplay Russian hand.

That the discordant undercurrents and manifestation in current
Sino-Soviet relations discussed in this telegram have, of course, been
to considerable extent aggravated by Kmt agents and/or exaggerated
by Kmt propaganda in no way lessens significance of fact that they
exist. Keen local Chinese observer, bitterly contemptuous of Kmt,
in describing Chinese anti-Soviet feeling to officer of Consulate General, commented that Kmt "propaganda, while in all other respects
failure, has been most effective in fanning popular indignation
against USSR".

Purpose this telegram has been endeavor to produce from available
piecemeal indications a rough tentative pattern of some of the locally-
observable factors and trends which are impeding—and possibly might
ultimately ruin—Pan-Soviet cause in China. No attempt is made
here to gauge present significance and potentialities of such factors
and trends. They should, of course, be viewed against harsh basic
fact that Moscow definitely dominates present Chinese scene with
apparent full approval of Chinese Communist Party and with no
tangible sign of any likely important setback in near future.

Believe, however, that evidence suffices prove at least that Soviet
course in China cannot be plain sailing and that it faces many obstacles and risks which cannot be quickly or easily passed and which

offer excellent opportunities for intelligent exploitation by the American side.

Please pass VOA[65] for background.

Sent Department 4782. Department pass Moscow.

McConaughy

893.00/11–1549 : Telegram

The Chargé in China (Strong) to the Secretary of State

Chungking, November 15, 1949—11 a. m.
[Received November 15—4 : 13 a. m.]

Cantel 1281. Chungking's overcast skies are more than matched by gloom and depression caused by political and military failures.

Earlier hopes of high officials that substantial progress could be made in southwest toward political unity and military unity and reform have been blasted. Postponement by Generalissimo of his visit to Chungking scheduled for early November has served waste valuable time, antagonize local leaders and discourage government officials of all ranks.

Military scene is still one of retreat; defection; uncorrelated commands; long lines of "defense" with great gaps; inadequate pay, food and clothing for troops; financial and material stringency and mutual distrust.

Political scene is one of continuing deep division between Generalissimo and Li–Pai groups with no prospect of any healing of the breach; heightening of financial crises as result of lack of local support; gradually inflating silver paper currency which will soon no doubt enter an uninterrupted nose dive; and failure to satisfy local leaders on questions of governorship, their participation in affairs of state, self-defense organization and taxation.

US aid and/or third World War are regarded as only means of saving remnants of government and some of its territory. Which is considered more possible is hard to guess. We are constantly bombarded with argument that even though US aid was squandered in past and is lying on Taiwan unused US has obligation pour in more aid, that China is a US problem, not Chinese problem. A final hope, equally as unfounded as other two, is that Generalissimo will at this last moment be persuaded to throw Taiwan resources into southwest for final stand.

Disintegration is apparent in all fields and may increase in geometrical progression. It is unclear whether attempt will be made to hold Chungking to end, whether government will be able move Kunming, or whether some less well-known city such as Kwangsi temporary

---

[65] Voice of America.

capital of Nanning or Hsichang in southeast Sikang will be next seat of government. Pai Chung-hsi holds key to question of length of time Yunnan can be held. If he centers efforts in Kwangsi, Yunnan fate will soon be sealed. If he heeds desire of government that he move into Kweichow and Yunnan, latter can stand for additional period. His movements to date would indicate former course. Pai's forces may fall apart at seams with further retreat and defections.

At such time as government leaves Chungking, whether for other continental point, for Hainan or for Taiwan, many officials, particularly of lower ranks, we feel will no longer follow. If move is not to Taiwan, many other officials will leave government for Taiwan.

Once government no longer can maintain foothold on continent, it may be expected that it will have to be thoroughly reconstituted by Generalissimo because of belief of many of present ranking officials that a Chinese Government on Taiwan would have no meaning or real purpose and they would not continue with it. Also Generalissimo will desire have own men in office at that time.

Thus we feel that whereas enough of a government may exist while on continent for Embassy to follow and maintain contact new decision by Department will be required with regard to relations with island government.

Sent Department Cantel 1281, Department pass Hong Kong, Taipei, Kunming, Shanghai.

STRONG

893.00/11–1549 : Telegram

The Vice Consul at Kunming (Lutkins) to the Secretary of State

KUNMING, November 15, 1949—2 p. m.
[Received November 15—5 : 50 a. m.]

233. I have just been approached by a leading Yunnanese businessman who claims to represent a group of top-ranking local government officials and businessmen. This group points to President Truman's statement that US Government would aid any group in China which actively opposed Communism. It guarantees that if America issues statement promising to defend Yunnanese independence and territorial integrity it will do anything desired by US Government. It is willing to break with Central Government, accept American protectorate and American troops, and to follow orders of American military, political and economic advisers. If desired, it would issue public statement requesting US Government to intervene and defend Yunnan against Communism.

This group believes that despite extent to which situation has deteriorated, an American statement guaranteeing Yunnanese independence would save Yunnan from Communists and at least give breathing spell until military aid and advisers were forthcoming. An unstated quantity of arms and other military equipment would be required; group does not ask US Government to send American troops but would welcome them if we chose to send them.

Group emphasizes strategic importance of Yunnan as possible bulwark against expansion of Communism into Southeast Asia.

Group's representative not willing at present time to name members of group but inferred it included top Yunnanese officials. If US Government indicates interest in proposal, then names of members will be given to me plus more detailed requests for aid. Otherwise, no need for further discussion. Group believes Yunnan will fall in 2 months if US aid not forthcoming.

This individual is highly reliable and I feel sure that his story is truthful, especially in view desperate situation.

Group requests US Government reply to proposition as soon as possible.

Sent Department 233. Department pass Chungking 91.

LUTKINS

893.001 Chiang Kai-shek/11–1549 : Telegram

The Chargé in China (Strong) to the Secretary of State

CHUNGKING, November 15, 1949.
[Received November 15—10:43 a. m.]

Cantel 1284. Sudden arrival afternoon November 14 of Generalissimo found President Li flying Nanning from Kweilin for 3-day visit despite phone call from Premier Yen urging him return to discuss all problems with Generalissimo. Li appears to be playing "hard to get" as has Generalissimo during past 2 weeks.

Li may be showing deep interest in Kwangsi at this time as a means of forcing greater concessions out of Generalissimo for continuing government somewhere in southwest or he may be deciding at this late date whether situation Kwangsi justifies breaking away and establishing in Kwangsi a government of members of own group plus few independents. Situation appears ripe for a split of government right down the middle.

By arriving during absence of Li and by summoning him to return, Generalissimo has made it clear he has not come at invitation of Li (final paragraph Cantel 1223, October 24). Although Generalissimo's presence earlier would not have altered ultimate outcome, he has definitely come too late to achieve even a slowing down of the current crumbling process. Kweiyang is said to have fallen November 14 as did Pengshui in southeast Szechuan to inferior Communist forces. Hu Tsung-nan has moved headquarters from Haichung back to Chengtu and is withdrawing several armies into central Szechuan in face of rumblings Communist thunder in Kansu and Shensi.

We feel government must take decision within week on next move or on regrouping forces to "defend" sizeable area of Szechuan. We doubt Generalissimo can force decision in absence of Li, strength of whose position should increase if he remains full 3 days in Kwangsi.

Absence of Li at this time may also be connected with desire prevent Generalissimo from returning to Taiwan in time to see Senator Knowland [66] who now understood plans visit there November 22 to 25 but not Chungking.

As thought probable earlier, Ministries now being required prune personnel for discharge as economy measure from 10,000 to 4,000. Presumably those dismissed who wish proceed place of safety must do so without aid of government.

Sent Department Cantel 1284, repeated Taipei 220, Hong Kong 65, Kunming 42. Department pass Taipei, Hong Kong, Kunming.

STRONG

893.20/11–1549 : Telegram

The Consul General at Hong Kong (Rankin) to the Secretary of State

HONG KONG, November 15, 1949—6 p. m.
[Received November 15—11:26 a. m.]

1050. We are informed by American journalists recently Hainan that there are about 100,000 Nationalist troops in Hoihow area who are refugees from adjacent mainland. Troops are virtually out of control, units mixed and discipline bad, with crimes of violence common.

Chen Chi-tang [67] informed journalists he lacks rice feed these troops and funds pay them. Has been supporting local government from private funds which are almost exhausted. Has unsuccessfully applied to Generalissimo for help meet this situation.

RANKIN

---

[66] Senator William F. Knowland, of California.
[67] Governor of Hainan Island.

893.00/11–1549

Memorandum of Conversation, by the Acting Deputy Director of the Office of Chinese Affairs (Freeman)

[WASHINGTON,] November 15, 1949.

Participants: Dr. T. V. Soong [68]
    Mr. Thomas Corcoran [69]
    Ambassador James Bruce, S/MDA [70]
    Mr. Jack Ohly, S/MDA [71]
    Mr. Fulton Freeman, CA

At a small luncheon today given by Ambassador Bruce at the Mayflower Hotel for Dr. T. V. Soong, the latter discussed several points of interest with regard to the situation in China. Some of these remarks were in answer to questions; others Dr. Soong volunteered himself. A summary of Dr. Soong's principal points follows:

1. The recent victory of the Nationalist forces at Quemoy Island is an indication of Sun Li-jen's ability to fight the Communists and is also an indication of the willingness to fight of the troops which will be called upon to defend Taiwan. In the neighborhood of 20,000 Communist troops were either killed or captured in the battle for Quemoy.

2. There are now some 700,000 Nationalist guerrillas behind the bamboo curtain who continue to harass the Communists.

3. In May of this year General Liu Fei,[72] who had already defected to the Communists, held an unpublicized meeting with General Cheng K'ai-ming [73] in Hong Kong and endeavored to convince General Cheng that he had no future with the Nationalists and should also go over to the Communist side. Liu pointed out that, although Cheng was high on the Communist list of war criminals he would be welcomed with open arms because of his "connections." In turning down the suggestion, Cheng stated that he did not wish to become a Soviet puppet and indicated that Communist China, having already lost Manchuria, was fast becoming merely a Soviet satellite. Liu tacitly admitted the temporary loss of China north of the 40th parallel to the Soviets, but he pointed out that China would have her big chance during the imminent third world war while Russia was busy in Europe. At that time, Liu indicated, China would send out several groups of expeditionary forces: 50,000 to Indochina; 200,000 to Malaya and Singapore; 20,000 each to Siam and Burma; and 400,000 to India and Pakistan. After conquering these countries, Liu stated, Communist governments would be established which would look to China rather than to Russia as the parent power. In this way the power of the Kremlin in the Far East would be counterbalanced and China would have the last laugh at the Western Powers as well as full control of Southeast Asia.

---

[68] Brother-in-law of Generalissimo Chiang Kai-shek and former President of the Chinese Executive Yuan.
[69] Partner of Corcoran, Youngman, and Rowe, Washington law firm.
[70] Director of Mutual Defense Assistance Program; formerly Ambassador to Argentina.
[71] John H. Ohly, Deputy Director of Mutual Defense Assistance Program.
[72] Former Deputy Chief of the Chinese General Staff.
[73] Chinese Vice Minister of National Defense.

4. Plans have now been made by Pai Chung-hsi to transfer his headquarters from Kwangsi to Hainan Island which will be the "impregnable" eastern end of a Nationalist corridor running through the Luichow Peninsula and Kwangsi to Kunming. The shift of Pai's headquarters to Hainan does not mean that Kwangsi will not be defended; it will rather make defense of the Luichow Peninsula and therefore access to Kwangsi and Yunnan more easy. Although Hainan does not grow a sufficient amount of food to feed the troops that will be stationed there, agreement has been reached with the Generalissimo that rice will be shipped to Hainan from Taiwan. (The growing of sugar on Taiwan is to be discontinued and rice will be planted in its place.)

5. General Sun Li-jen is in actual as well as nominal control of all ground forces on Taiwan and has the full support of the Generalissimo. General Chou Chih-jou who is in command of the airforce, while nominally responsive to Chen Cheng as governor, is actually on bad terms with Chen but is cooperating with Sun. Arrangements have been made for Taiwan to provide the necessary air and naval support to General Pai in Hainan.

6. The principal difficulty on Taiwan at the present time is the lack of sufficient arms and equipment for the ground defense forces. Six of Sun Li-jen's divisions are fully trained and fully equipped with US arms; six additional divisions, however, while also fully trained are completely lacking in equipment. Dr. Soong estimated that it would require approximately US$20,000,000 to equip these six divisions with US arms, but that such an expenditure would make Taiwan invincible for some time to come. He reiterated that the Generalissimo would not interfere with Sun's plans to defend the Island. (At one point Mr. Corcoran said that there was one statement which he would make which Dr. Soong in his position could not make, namely, that neither he nor Dr. Soong "had ever gotten along very well with Chiang Kai-shek." This remark brought forth only a trace of a smile from Dr. Soong which communicated nothing.)

7. If it becomes necessary to move the capital from Chungking, it will probably be shifted to Kunming and not to Taiwan, at least for the time being.

Mr. Corcoran brought up the subject of the recent defection of 12 CNAC and CATC planes from Hong Kong, strongly implying that the US Government should have done something to prevent their going to the Communists. He stated, as if it were an announced fact, that the British Government would recognize the Chinese Communists on December 15 and pointed out that if the remaining CNAC and CATC planes were still in Hong Kong on that date, title would automatically pass to the Communists. Mr. Freeman remarked in this connection that there had been no American citizens involved in the defection of Chinese commercial planes and crews and that the matter appeared to be one for discussion between the Chinese and Hong Kong authorities. He suggested that it might be well for the Chinese Government, rather than to insist on the freezing of CNAC and CATC assets in Hong Kong, to request permission to have the remaining planes flown to Taiwan or Hainan by reliable crews in order to reduce the possibility of having a large number of planes in Hong Kong when and if the British recognized the Chinese Communists. Dr. Soong appeared to recognize the dangers inherent in the present situation and indicated that he would bring the matter to the attention of the Chinese Government.

There was no discussion of the $75 million fund for expenditure in the general area of China per se, and the only oblique request for US assistance brought forward by Dr. Soong was the suggestion that $20 million was needed to arm and equip Sun Li-jen's additional six divisions in Taiwan to insure the defense of that Island. Ambassador Bruce listened sympathetically to Dr. Soong throughout, but made no commitments.

893.00/11–1649 : Telegram

The Vice Consul at Kunming (Lutkins) to the Secretary of State

KUNMING, November 16, 1949—3 p. m.
[Received November 17—12:47 a. m.]

239. Individual mentioned mytel 233,[74] repeated OffEmb 91, called again this morning to report a meeting of group last night. Group wished to emphasize its unconditional acceptance of any American demands and willingness to accept complete American control rather than be overrun by Communism. As he put it, local authorities would go right or left as instructed by US Government. Group also stated their proposal was not merely that of a small unrepresentative body but represented the genuine desire of Yunnanese people to escape Communist yoke.

He again said that if and when US Government expressed serious interest in proposal the whole plan would immediately be made public.

Sent Department 239; Department pass OffEmb Chungking 92.

LUTKINS

893.00/11–1649 : Telegram

The Chargé in China (Strong) to the Secretary of State

CHUNGKING, November 16, 1949—6 p. m.
[Received November 17—9:17 a. m.]

Cantel 1285. In private talk last evening, Chang Tu-lun, chief of political section SWMPA, stated Gimo here not to discuss move of capital but rather measures to improve conditions in army and regrouping of forces to defend Szechuan. He said he and other[s] like him feel most keenly the present impasse between President Li and Gimo.

---

[74] November 15, 2 p.m., p. 594.

In discussing site of capital, Chang felt Kunming out of question with very slight likelihood on Nanning, Paoshan (Yunnan) or Hsichaichang (Sikang). Said Paoshan could support only 30,000 troops and Hsichang 100,000 at very maximum. In his opinion Chungking is essential.

With regard guerrilla warfare, Chang said possible lay plans but fighters must have something behind them; although possible favor group of liberals to form guiding committee, he seemed feel rather futile and said that resistance would have to generate itself in local areas and could not be prearranged. He indicated that present emphasis is on using trained men to help locals organize in those areas where people of themselves wished resist.

Chang mirrored prevailing gloom and depression and feeling of nearness of end.

Pouched Taipei, Hong Kong, Kunming.

STRONG

893.00/11-1749 : Telegram

The Chargé in China (Strong) to the Secretary of State

CHUNGKING, November 17, 1949—2 p. m.
[Received November 17—1 : 56 p. m.]

Cantel 1287. Rinden and I interviewed Chu Chang-wei afternoon November 16. Chu began by saying military situation very, very bad and "unless miracle happens Chungking cannot hold more than 1 week"; he feared same thing as at Canton, simply a route march for Communists with no resistance, saying Tsunyi was lost November 15. Chu thought Communists would drive for Pichieho, hence equally easy attack toward Kunming, Chengtu or Chungking. Formerly he said had been planned resist on two fronts but after arrival here Generalissimo decided only Szechuan could be defended.

When in Kunming, President Li had decided make that city capital but fall of Kweiyang nullified that hope, Chu said, and added that in same manner as at Canton plans for shifting Pai's forces into Kweichow in order hold Kweiyang for time and slow Communist advance to west came too late to mature. Pai now falling back on line based on Liuchow though appears Communist plan first go after Kunming then attack Pai.

Chu then said Generalissimo did not intend resume Presidency and admitted government would split on question going Formosa or remaining continent, say at Nanning. Who might follow Li to latter point Chu could not guess, the line not yet having been at all clearly drawn. President Li he hoped would return "in a day or so"; he had sent several urgent wires asking him come back.

Chu was obviously worried about transport out of Chungking. He said no CAT planes had arrived here in past 3 days and remarked "it is a long way to Nanning" and that his own plans were far from clear.

With attitude "it was nice while it lasted but it is all over now", Chu expressed appreciation for our presence in Canton and at Chungking and suggested that we make own arrangements to leave. He promised at once to advise any decisions regarding government.

Sent Department Cantel 1287; repeated Taipei 222, Hong Kong 67, Kunming 44, Shanghai 572; Department pass Taipei, Hong Kong, Kunming, Shanghai.

STRONG

893.00/11–1749 : Telegram

The Chargé in China (Strong) to the Secretary of State

CHUNGKING, November 17, 1949—5 p. m.
[Received 9 : 47 p. m.]

Cantel 1290. It seems probable that President Li is absenting himself from Chungking in knowledge decision of majority will be to seek refuge Taiwan and in desire not to associate himself with such decision.

However, we feel that by staying away at this crucial time he will lose any hope of drawing group with him to Nanning if he plans set up shop there. Most of those who might have been attracted to his standard cannot very well follow a man who does not appear to plead their cause.

We believe high policy decision being taken today in meetings of Supreme Emergency Council, Executive Yuan and CEC of Kmt.[75] If decision Taiwan, as seems probable, we feel it is end of this Chinese Government as presently constituted.

Sent Department Cantel 1290; repeated Hong Kong 68, Kunming 45, Taipei 223; Department pass Hong Kong, Kunming, Taipei.

STRONG

893.01/11–1849 : Telegram

The Chargé in China (Strong) to the Secretary of State

CHUNGKING, November 18, 1949—7 p. m.
[Received November 19—12 : 55 a. m.]

Cantel 1293. It becomes apparent that move of Generalissimo-selected Chinese Government personnel to Taiwan is about to begin and

---

[75] Central Executive Committee of Kuomintang (Nationalist Party).

it is expected that, if Chungking becomes insecure before movement of personnel completed, Chengtu will be used as staging point, despite its greater distance from Taipei, in view fact it can be held longer.

Recent refusal of Szechwan "leaders" return Chungking from Chengtu to see Generalissimo would indicate their belief in futility of attempting improve matters now. It may be expected that they will endeavor play ball with Communists in every way.

An increasingly independent attitude on part of the various military leaders will doubtless show itself before long, each seeking in best way preserve forces and position. Friction between population and troops in western Szechwan will heighten and before end there may even be clashes between different groups of Nationalist forces.

We now believe President Li Tsung-jen will not attempt attract enough men of caliber to form government in Nanning. It seems more likely that, although for face purposes he may return briefly to Chungking, he will regard it as useless to attempt create rump government. Unless he could get numbers of capable men to join him and be sure of outside financial help, he would merely be increasing overhead expenses without achieving object. Provincial Government of Kwangsi is quite adequate for purely local purposes of Li and Pai Chung-hsi.

Headlines in leading paper today supporting current rumors that Generalissimo may soon resume presidency seem entitled credence as logical move in view virtual abdication by Li, who is being criticized even by friends for neither returning nor resigning. A brief absence might have increased strength of his position but failure join issue in crisis has decreased his stature.

SWMPA now controls all travel and cargo out of Chungking. Tickets sold only by China Travel Service, which must have prior clearance each case.

Sent Department; repeated Taipei 225, Hong Kong 70, Shanghai 574. Department pass Taipei, Hong Kong, Shanghai.

STRONG

893.00/11–1949 : Telegram

The Vice Consul at Kunming (Lutkins) to the Secretary of State

KUNMING, November 19, 1949—3 p. m.
[Received November 19—6 : 43 a. m.]

249. French Consul General reports story from source he calls reliable that Li Tsung-jen on recent visit there tried to persuade Lu Han to desert Generalissimo and form bloc with Pai and him. This bloc would then negotiate with Communists and, if latter's terms unacceptable, fight on together. According to source, Lu felt unable to accept proposition at time.

Sent Department 249; repeated OffEmb Hong Kong telCan 96; Department pass OffEmb Hong Kong.

LUTKINS

893.001/11–2149 : Telegram

The Consul General at Hong Kong (Rankin) to the Secretary of State

HONG KONG, November 21, 1949—11 a. m.
[Received November 21—3 : 35 a. m.]

1093. Son of Li Tsung-jen informs officer of Consulate General that Li desires go to States in his official capacity to seek medical treatment. Li would like to travel with entourage, extent of which yet unknown, by official American aircraft as did Madame Chiang Kai-shek. Will Department please advise soonest reference visas and transportation.

RANKIN

893.00/11–2149 : Telegram

The Consul General at Hong Kong (Rankin) to the Secretary of State

HONG KONG, November 21, 1949—1 p. m.
[Received 4 :10 p.m.]

1097. . . . Source . . . reports that Li refused go Chungking and came Hong Kong because Generalissimo determined directly order him give up presidency. Li still undecided overtly break with Generalissimo [and] set up own party because consequences this act would be deprive Pai Chung-hsi of continuation air support and possibility financial help. Li unwilling continue as Acting President on same basis past few months because Generalissimo increasing usurpation presidential powers and "meddling" Yen Hsi-shan. Thus Li inclined toward decision temporarily stay Hong Kong seek promise direct and substantial support from MacArthur, which, if forthcoming, would allow Kwangsi clique organize own political party independent of Generalissimo and continue civil war. No firm decision on above had been reached as of 1000 hours November 21st. Person furnishing above information did not mention Li approach to Consul General of visa and transportation America but volunteered opinion Li might try go States.

RANKIN

893.001/11–2149 : Telegram

The Consul General at Hong Kong (Rankin) to the Secretary of State

HONG KONG, November 21, 1949—2 p. m.
[Received 4:29 p. m.]

1100. Reference Contel 1093 of November 21. Li Tsung-jen advised Consulate General officer today his desire to go US official capacity for medical treatment duodenal ulcer. In course conversation, he indicates other reasons for trip: (1) To plead for US aid to group headed by Li and including Pai Chung-hsi, Chen Chi-t'ang, Hsueh Yueh *et al*, (2) To force Generalissimo's hand; Li has resisted intense Generalissimo pressure go Chungking, resign office and request Generalissimo assume Presidency. Consulate General opinion while Li in need medical treatment this tertiary to other motives. Li desires go US soonest possible in American official plane if possible. His entourage numbers 10 persons. He instructed Foreign Minister Yeh cable Koo transmit Li desires to Department, but fears Generalissimo has countermanded instructions. Li emphasized intends return China and carry on war against Communists. Li seriously concerned over attempts Generalissimo propaganda make him scapegoat impending Nationalist military defeats Szechuan. Generalissimo has put intense pressure on Pai Chung-hsi assume post chief MND [76] but Pai adamant in refusal. Strong has informed us Li's previous request.

RANKIN

893.00/11–1649 : Telegram

The Acting Secretary of State to the Vice Consul at Kunming (Lutkins)

WASHINGTON, November 22, 1949—7 p. m.

127. Urtels 233 Nov 15 (passed Chungking), 239 Nov 16. For ur info. On Aug 15 Chi Amb presented request milit ec aid proposing defense line China mainland.[77] Substance JCS [78] comment fols:

"Obviously impracticable for Natlist armed forces hold this line in face superior Commie forces, irrespective of provision US mil aid in amounts requested. Further, it wld be impossible, in view of compartments of terrain and concentration capabilities of Commies, for Nat armed forces prevent enemy from piercing stronger defensive lines further to West, although such mil operations wld not necessarily result in wresting from Nat control area of West China as a whole".

Subsequent milit developments have borne out foregoing estimate and there is no ground for now assuming milit assistance forces

[76] Ministry of National Defense.
[77] Vol. IX, p. 678.
[78] Joint Chiefs of Staff.

Yunnan wld enable them maintain themselves against overwhelming strength Commies who wld almost inevitably be ultimate recipients materiel provided. Possibility development successful resistance movement Yunnan under present govt or successor considered too remote justify US involvement proposed in reftel. Urdes 38 Apr 8, 47 May 7, 57 Jul 14, 58 Jul 17 [79] indicated Yunnan neither militarily, politically suited development such movement, though Jul 17 des reported improvement polit situation. In any event US Govt obviously cld not issue statement guaranteeing Yunnanese independence which wld represent commitment this Govt not in position fulfill.

Suggest you not volunteer any reply proposal. If asked reply you shld state while this Govt sympathetic to desire all peoples avoid domination by alien-controlled regimes, US Govt cannot undertake guarantee which would represent far-reaching commitment involving direct intervention internal affairs China and use US troops fulfill such commitment.

WEBB

893.00/11–2349 : Telegram

The Consul General at Taipei (Macdonald) to the Secretary of State

TAIPEI, November 23, 1949—noon.
[Received November 23—4 : 15 a. m.]

740. During call this morning K. C. Wu [80] criticized Acting President Li severely for refusing proceed Chungking to confer with Generalissimo. According Wu, Li is not seriously ill and merely used illness as excuse for refusing see Generalissimo.

Wu said that he (Wu) had written off the mainland early last summer but that Generalissimo believed southwest could be held, but after fall of Canton Generalissimo also wrote off mainland. Wu describes Generalissimo's present visit to Chungking as burial service of mainland.

"Conditions on Hainan Island are much more serious than most people realize," said Wu. The command there is divided and Wu does not expect the island to hold out much longer.

With respect to Taiwan, Wu said that at least there is a unified command. He said that, although he and other people do not approve of many of General Chen Cheng's decisions, they at least support him and do not put obstacles in his way. He remarked that Governor Chen's greatest fault is his narrowness and depending entirely too much on his old cronies.

---

[79] None printed.
[80] Former mayor of Shanghai.

Wu is leaving tomorrow for Hong Kong where he will join Senator Knowland and accompany him to Chungking where Knowland will meet the Generalissimo. Morale is, according to Wu, getting lower and lower and defeatism spreading rapidly even in Taiwan. If US is going to give any increased aid to Taiwan, Wu said that it must come before end of year in order to be of any good whatsoever. The future is definitely black and Wu made no attempt paint an optimistic picture this morning.

Sent Department 740; repeated OffEmb Hong Kong 222.

MACDONALD

893.001/11–2349

Memorandum of Conversation, by the Director of the Office of Chinese Affairs (Sprouse)

[WASHINGTON,] November 23, 1949.

Minister Tan [81] called by appointment this afternoon and said that Ambassador Koo had asked him to transmit to the Department on instructions from the Chinese Foreign Office a request from Acting President Li Tsung-jen that appropriate action be taken to facilitate his proposed trip to the United States for purposes of obtaining medical treatment. Minister Tan emphasized that the Acting President was coming to the United States solely for medical reasons and that he would return to China immediately after obtaining the necessary treatment in order to carry on the fight against communism. He explained that the assistance requested was in connection with visa formalities and his entry into the United States and that the Acting President indicated that he would be accompanied by a party of ten. Minister Tan expressed as his personal opinion considerable doubt as to the desirability or necessity for such an entourage. He further stated that the Acting President had indicated that he would not desire any official hospitality in the U.S. since his trip was solely for medical reasons.

I informed Minister Tan that I would look into the matter and let him know what steps should be taken to assist the Acting President.

893.001/11–2149 : Telegram

The Acting Secretary of State to the Consul General at Hong Kong (Rankin)

WASHINGTON, November 23, 1949—7 p. m.

1429. Urtels 1093 and 1100, Nov 21. Dept wld be glad extend all appropriate assistance to Pres Li Tsung-jen re proposed trip to US

---

[81] Dr. Shao-hwa Tan, Chinese Minister-Counselor in the United States.

for purpose medical treatment and to members family or such personal party as wld be commensurate with this objective. However, as Dept previously advised Strong in connection with earlier proposal for Li trip, US Govt cannot assume responsibility for extending invitation for visit during present critical situation in China. There are no official Amer transportation facilities available for this purpose.

Although Pres Li as head of friendly state shld be immed issued dipl visa on application, Dept suggests applications made by party accompanying Li be urgently referred to Dept with ur comments prior taking final action.

WEBB

893.00/11–2549 : Telegram

The Chargé in China (Strong) to the Secretary of State

HONG KONG, November 25, 1949—3 p. m.
[Received November 25—2 : 17 p. m.]

Cantel 1300. Early in evening November 23 while I was drafting immediately preceding Cantel,[82] Foreign Minister Yeh telephoned me at hotel to inquire whether President Li during interview that afternoon broached subject of trip to US. On receiving reply in affirmative, Yeh said Li, on arrival in Hong Kong, had asked him approach US authorities on matter; he had refused to do so, stating he must communicate first with Chungking; Premier Yen in return had requested him persuade Li return Chungking and promised bring American doctor to China; government could not afford have Li permit personal desire take precedence at this critical stage when there was hope of *rapprochement* between Generalissimo and Li; Chinese Embassy was being advised that Chinese Government wished Department delay acquiescence to Li's visit, which White House would have to give before Li could make trip. Yeh asked whether I had made reply to request by Li; I answered I was not in position to do so. We [He?] then asked if Li had requested transmission of message to Department, which I affirmed. Next, he inquired whether Li had referred to Yeh's refusal take matter up with Embassy. This I denied. Yeh said he was seeing Li at 8 : 00 (November 23) and needed this background and added he hoped Department would not encourage Li to take trip.

At noon on November 24 Yeh called at my hotel to state he had quite forcibly told Li that he must not take trip to US and resign there; that is, if he wished go US for medical attention, he should first proceed seat of government and resign presidency; then, as Vice

---

[82] Not printed; it reported a conversation with Acting President Li regarding his proposed trip to the United States.

President, he could go US for operation since Embassy in Washington had been instructed not to take matter of visit up with Department.

In this conversation, Yeh contradicted statement made earlier by phone, to effect there was hope of reconciliation between Generalissimo and Li. He admitted his sole purpose was to prevent Li from resigning in US; that Li was sick; that Li could hope for nothing from Generalissimo at any time; that if he were Li, he would not return to Chungking.

Yeh expressed belief that, if Li resigns, Generalissimo will resume presidency. He also said it is useless for Foreign Office and himself to join "mobile cabinet", without proper means of communication with outside world. We believe he will be quite content to remain Hong Kong as long as possible in connection with airlines, National Resources Commission and BOTRA [83] property disposition.

In Yeh's opinion British will recognize Communists during recess of UNGA.[84]

Sent Department Cantel 1300, by hand Hong Kong.

STRONG

893.00/11–2549 : Telegram

The Chargé in China (Strong) to the Secretary of State

HONG KONG, November 25, 1949—5 p. m.
[Received November 26—2 : 34 p. m.]

Cantel 1304. In conversation with President Li Tsung-jen November 23 we asked him for views on future of Chinese Government in light of deterioration in southwest and departures of some government personnel for Taiwan.

Admitting serious split between those wishing capital in Taipei and those preferring continent, Li said it was his intention eventually establish government Nanning; he would never agree to government on Taiwan. Generalissimo, Li maintained, would not reassume Presidency but only wished continue his control behind scenes. Constitutionally, therefore, Li claims right approve appointments and site of government.

Prior to evacuation from west China, Li declared government would retreat to Chengtu and later probably Hsichang (Sikang province) which would provide several weeks' grace before essential establish it Nanning. That period he would use regain health; already numbers of his supporters are moving overland to Nanning and by time of

---

[83] Board of Trustees for Rehabilitation Affairs.
[84] United Nations General Assembly.

evacuation from Szechuan or Sikang he will have enough "liberals" and independents to form government; Chu Chang-wei has been instructed remain with government to maintain contacts; united front among Yu Han-mou, Hsueh Yueh, Chen Chi-tang, Lu Han and Li group is practically accomplished; their hope is to hold portions Yunnan, Kweichow, Kwangsi, Kwangtung and Hainan.

How optimistic Li really is over achieving his goal we cannot gauge. Certain serious questions may be raised.

First, is whether Li can retain loyalty and services of competent persons during an extended absence; with uncertainty whether he is really coming back or not. Chinese do not seem noted for trust in leaders under such circumstances. Pai Chung-hsi may be able give appropriate assurances.

Second, combination involving people like Lu Han (if he stays in it), Yu Han-mou and Hsueh Yueh is not necessarily attractive to "liberals".

Third, Li still needs more [money?] badly and will need more if he is to have government at Nanning. Li criticized Generalissimo for recently moving 700,000 taels of gold from Kweiyang, Chungking and Chengtu to Taiwan, feeling this treasure should have been left in mainland, presumably at Nanning. Generalissimo thus has same hold on Li that he always has had and Li has no better means of breaking away than before.

Fourth, Li may be trying attract support by claiming he is only one qualified for US aid and that he may get it if he shows he is protecting Indochina border. Pai's strategy seems to be to keep back to that border and to a seaport.

Fifth, in back of his mind is doubtless intention move to Hainan as last resort, thus he too may become exponent of island government based Taiwan.

We find it hard to believe that current impasse can be broken in favor of Li. Generalissimo holds far better cards and knows how to play them. That any number of competent men will, under the circumstances, choose to support Li in a going cause on mainland seems doubtful.

Generalissimo may feel some necessity for bolstering Li if he feels it politically unwise to resume Presidency in view of unfavorable US attitude toward him and fact he would be heading a losing cause. If Generalissimo does not resume office, then he needs Li to fulfill certain constitutional functions. We cannot believe that this late date Generalissimo will give Li what latter wants and needs. The time for doing so was months ago, not now.

We are [un]certain of extent of hold Li has on Generalissimo that makes his return to Chungking so necessary. Face important, constitutional procedures are desirable, but would scarcely seem overwhelming; a façade of unity is perhaps important to Generalissimo but at this stage not to anyone else; Pai Chung-hsi's forces are only ones on mainland with any ability and coherence, but they are facing over-whelming odds, and seem heretofore to have been regarded by Generalissimo as rivals; Generalissimo has never shown any interest in type of people supporting Li.

We can only conclude that Generalissimo wants someone else to continue "holding the bag" for him and to take public responsibility for loss of mainland.

Sent Department Cantel 1304, repeated Taipei 228, Shanghai 567, Hong Kong by hand.

STRONG

893.00/11–2649 : Telegram

The Chargé in China (Strong) to the Secretary of State

HONG KONG, November 26, 1949—11 a. m.
[Received November 26—5 : 15 a. m.]

Cantel 1307. After due deliberation, we have reached conclusion that in remarking on desire prevent President Li Tsung-jen from resigning in US (Cantel 1300, November 25) Foreign Minister Yeh may well have made remark in hope that it would reach Department and create suspicion in Department as regards Li's motives in visiting US and thus would enhance possibility of unfavorable response by Department.

Sent Department Cantel 1307, by hand Hong Kong.

STRONG

893.001/11–2649 : Telegram

The Consul General at Hong Kong (Rankin) to the Secretary of State

HONG KONG, November 26, 1949—1 p. m.
[Received November 26—4 : 19 a. m.]

1131. ReDeptel 1429.[85] Li Tsung-jen informed this date of Department's decision. Li stated understood US Government not assume responsibility for invitation and decision entirely his own. Li hopes depart Hong Kong by commercial air within 1 week going directly New York for hospitalization. Li doubts Foreign Office acting Generalissimo's instructions will issue passports to entourage and requests our attitude this matter. Li emphasized he not going resign office.

RANKIN

[85] November 23, p. 606.

893.001/11–2849 : Telegram

The Consul General at Hong Kong (Rankin) to the Secretary of State

HONG KONG, November 28, 1949—1 p. m.
[Received November 28—12 : 56 p. m.]

1137. Re Contel 1131.[86] Li Tsung-jen states he wishes include following in entourage in addition to wife, two sons, Li Yu-lin aged 31 and Li Chih-shen aged 11: Li Han-hun, former Minister of Interior; Huang Hsueh-tse, Chief of Political Bureau of President's office; Wang Chih, military aide; Sun Ying-kian, personal physician; Huang Ying-lan, secretary to Mrs. Li.

Li Tsung-jen and elder son have valid passports, while wife and younger son have not. Wang Chih has passport valid Japan only and others do not have passports due refusal Generalissimo-controlled Foreign Office issue them.

We perceive no objection any above persons and if Department desires will draw up travel affidavits for each here. Please advise soonest.

RANKIN

893.00/11–2849

Memorandum by the Ambassador to China (Stuart) to the Assistant Secretary of State for Far Eastern Affairs (Butterworth)

[WASHINGTON,] November 28, 1949.

The source for the following information is in my opinion entirely trustworthy:

1. He reports that he made a trip to Peiping last month and saw Li [87] and Liu.[88] Li says that CCP pro-Soviet extremists do not want U.S. recognition. That Liu is totally under Soviet dictation. Li is now accusing Liu as not being sufficiently leftist although he has heretofore been regarded as the leader of the doctrinaire pro-Soviet faction in the Peiping CCP. The CCP complains that the present American administration is reactionary but that they can cooperate with the American people.

2. . . . . remarked that the White Paper [89] caused great embarrassment to liberal Shao Li-tse and himself because of its reference to democratic individuals. All such liberals came therefore under CCP suspicion. He mentioned especially a list of 10 names including . . .

---

[86] *Supra.*
[87] Li Li-san, Vice Chairman of the Communist All-China Federation of Labor.
[88] Liu Shao-chi, Vice Chairman of the Central Committee of the Chinese Communist Party (CCP).
[89] Department of State, *United States Relations With China* (Washington, Government Printing Office, 1949).

who are all worried. They question whether USA wants them to continue their past efforts by thus exposing them to danger.

3. These men all agree that the anti-American propaganda has been intensified since the arrival within the past few months of more Russian advisors. This is not approved by Chou En-lai [90] and other relatively liberal CCP leaders, but their position is becoming steadily weaker.

4. My source tried to see Chou 5 times; to see Yeh Chien-ying [91] 3 times; to see Wang Ping-nan [92] 7 times but could never get any response. This seems to indicate their caution against further criticism.

5. . . . said that there were no CCP members on the Yenching faculty although two subordinates man and wife and office secretary J. C. Yang had admitted that they were members. Yang who originally had been quiet has now become very active on the campus. . . . and the others mentioned above regarded the treatment of Philip Fugh's [93] family as evidence of unfriendliness toward me. Their home has been searched four times. Some of his art objects were confiscated. He is accused of being a "running dog of Americans, etc." . . . is pessimistic about the outlook for Yenching and similar institutions. He fears that the pressure upon them will begin sometime next year.

893.00/11–2849 : Telegram

The Consul General at Peiping (Clubb) to the Secretary of State

PEIPING, November 28, 1948—2 p. m.
[Received November 29—5 : 06 p. m.]

2110. In course conversation November 23 Chang Tung-sun [94] expressed serious concern re political situation. I said it appeared economic problems were at present probably more exigent. Chang agreed re seriousness economic situation but reverted politics, stating he feared international political questions would in due course constitute grave domestic problem for Chinese leaders.

Chang reported that there was never any discussion either high level or low of major political problems in Government, that neither Communist leaders nor Soviet talked to "us" (democratic personages?) re either major policy or current matters major import; they just went ahead and did things and Government was confronted with results. Chang agreed this procedure was facilitated by absence laws and rules,

---

[90] Member of the Central Committee of the Chinese Communist Party and of the Politburo; Vice Chairman of the Chinese People's Revolutionary Military Affairs Committee, and Premier since October 1, 1949.

[91] Communist mayor of Peiping.

[92] Member of Chou En-lai's delegation during 1946 negotiations with the Chinese Government.

[93] Chinese personal secretary to Ambassador Stuart.

[94] Member of the Democratic League.

thought situation on other hand was seriously complicated by attempt to do everything at once.

He said ultimate problem in essence was whether China would proceed with its own solutions and handling of affairs, or whether it would merely follow direction from outside. He agreed difficulties here being experienced with ignorant cadres in respect to political orientations, but said that even some democratic personages still failed realize implications developments. Others, however, "even some at top", are beginning see difficult situation without knowing what to do about it.

Chang agreed situation most critical in that respect in Manchuria. He professed ignorance respecting amount of grain shipment and other operations under Manchu[ria]–USSR trade pact, stating none had seen text pact and none Peiping knew what was shipped out or in, none had seen machinery presumably obtained from USSR in exchange, none knew how commodity values were determined in implementation pact. USSR, he agreed, was still advancing in Manchuria.

[Garble] gave Chang copy brochure containing Yugoslav–USSR CP correspondence and he showed awareness [garble] position China and that Yugoslavia 1948, particularly with respect advisors, technicians.

Italian source reports "second Borodin" [95] resides in quarters adjoining Soviet Embassy which have guard posted outside gate (which remains without signboard indicating agency within). Sovietized White Russian, whose duties take him there occasionally, reports that his account with personage residing therein is only in name "Mr. X".

Information believed reliable indicates 563 special aliens resident certificates were issued up to about middle November.

Sent Department 2110, Department pass Shanghai 1230.

CLUBB

893.00/11–2849 : Telegram

The Vice Consul at Kumming (Lutkins) to the Secretary of State

KUNMING, November 28, 1949—6 p. m.
[Received November 29—2 : 33 a. m.]

263. Reply Deptel 127, November 22 conveyed to group representative. He called again today to report a further meeting which decided to make a final approach to US Government. Group wished to emphasize belief that any aid would prove effective and would not be necessary to send US troops. Secondly, stated that group willing to declare Yunnan's independence first and then ask US protection; argue this would then not be intervention.

---

[95] Meaning chief political adviser from Moscow; Mikhail (Michael) Markovich Borodin was active in China, 1924–1927.

Implied provincial independence would be declared in any case. Local authorities would then negotiate with US Government and Communists. If unable secure favorable terms from either side, would then retreat into Burma and await aid there. Representative stated Governor Lu Han fully aware of and sympathetic to movement.

I strongly doubt that any full scale retreat into Burma will materialize. Settlement with Communists far more probable.

Sent Department 263; Department pass OffEmb Hong Kong telCan 100.

LUTKINS

893.001/11–2949 : Telegram

The Chargé in China (Strong) to the Secretary of State

HONG KONG, November 29, 1949—noon.
[Received November 29—6 : 46 a. m.]

Cantel 1312. Foreign Minister Yeh on November 28 stated he thought question of relations of President Li with Chungking Government were near solution though he had not seen final terms brought to Hong Kong yesterday by Vice Premier Chu Chia-hua.

With relation to travel documentation for members of presidential entourage, he hoped US Government would settle question by provision of "entrance facilities" for the group. In any event he said he could not issue passports for some 2 or 3 days, and then only if matter settled satisfactorily.

Yeh again insisted he does not want Li resign while in US (Cantel 1307, November 26) though he disclaims interest in internal Chinese politics and denies need to play Generalissimo's game. When asked whether he believed Li really intended resign in US, he stated emphatically that upon arrival here Li told him his purpose in going to US was to resign there and that accounted for his (Yeh's) refusal take matter up with US Government. This probably accounts for bitterness of Li against Yeh who had previously indicated he favored Li group.

Sent Department Cantel 1312, by hand Hong Kong.

STRONG

893.001/11–2849 : Telegram

The Secretary of State to the Consul General at Hong Kong (Rankin)

WASHINGTON, November 29, 1949—7 p. m.

1458. Re ur 1137 Nov 28, Dept perceives no objection to use of travel affidavits for such members of Li's party as appear to be accompanying him in connection with stated purpose of visit. Since Pres Li has made it known on several occasions that sole purpose of trip which wld be of limited duration is medical treatment, Dept fails perceive close connection with this objective of such members of his party as former Min of Interior and Li's Chief of Polit Bureau and wld desire satisfactory clarification this point before authorizing issuance visas these two.

ACHESON

893.00/11–3049 : Telegram

The Consul General at Peiping (Clubb) to the Secretary of State

PEIPING, November 30, 1949—11 a. m.
[Received November 30—2 : 38 a. m.]

2128. At 2220 last night received by messenger hand letter yesterday's date from Wang Pin-nan as chief General Affairs Section Peiping Foreign Office, signed and sealed by Wang, addressed me personally stating:

"In accordance with order Chou En-lai, Minister of this Ministry, there is now especially forwarded to you, sir, one copy of statement with hope you will transmit to your Government."

Letter in official note form used usual honorifics.

Note in ConGen translation slight variation from NCNA [96] English language text.

Text enclosure given in next telegram Peiping No. series. French Consul requests text be passed his Embassy Washington for transmission Foreign Office Paris.

Sent Department 2128; Department pass Shanghai 1238, Nanking 1189.

CLUBB

893.00/11–3049 : Telegram

The Consul General at Peiping (Clubb) to the Secretary of State

PEIPING, November 30, 1949.
[Received November 30—4 : 01 a. m.]

2129. Following text is translation November 29 statement Chou En-lai:

"The People's Liberation Army of the People's Republic of China, which is presently swiftly continuing to wipe out the remnant reactionary bandit forces of the Kuomintang, under conditions where it retreated vast areas of our south and southwest China, is on this day pressing near the southwest border of our country. The Kuomintang reactionary bandit horde headed by Chiang Kai-shek, Li Tsung-jen,

[96] New China News Agency (Communist).

Pai Chung-hsi and Yu Han-mou is turning their hopes toward Annam and other places adjoining the frontiers of China, planning to make these places an asylum for their battered troops and officers and preparing to turn them into bases for staging a comeback at an opportune moment. In view of this, I, on behalf of the Central People's Government of the People's Republic of China, solemnly point out to the Government of France and the governments of countries adjoining the frontiers of China that the thorough wiping out of all reactionary armed forces of the Kuomintang is the unshakeable [resolve?] of our government. No matter where the defeated Kuomintang reactionary forces flee, the Central People's Government of the People's Republic of China reserves the right to take up this matter, and the government of any country which gives shelter [and aid] to the Kuomintang reactionary armed forces must take responsibility in this regard and moreover must accept all consequences arising therefrom."

Sent Department 2129, Nanking 1190, Shanghai 1239, to Tientsin by mail.

CLUBB

893.001/11-2949 : Telegram

The Secretary of State to the Consul General at Hong Kong (Rankin)

WASHINGTON, November 30, 1949—7 p. m.

TelCan 777. Re Cantel 1300 Nov 25 and 1312 Nov 29. Pls arrange to see Li Tsung-jen as soon as possible and state, as under instrs from ur Govt, that reports have come to us that Pres Li might resign during his visit to US, and that if resignation shld be or become his intention it is our desire that it be carried out either prior or subsequent to his trip and not while he is in US. You shld point out his resignation while in this country wld inevitably be interpreted as instigated or inspired by US Govt, an interpretation which this Govt definitely does not wish to be made.

ACHESON

893.00/11-2849 : Telegram

The Secretary of State to the Vice Consul at Kunming (Lutkins)

WASHINGTON, November 30, 1949—7 p. m.

131. Urtel 263.[97] For US Govt to encourage declaration independence by Yunnan wld place US Govt position encouraging break up Nat Govt and defection substantial portion remaining forces, wld constitute intervention internal affairs China.

Info contained reftel does not change views expressed Deptel 127 Nov 15 [22].

ACHESON

[97] November 28, p. 613.

893.00/12–149 : Telegram

The Consul General at Peiping (Clubb) to the Secretary of State

PEIPING, December 1, 1949—3 p. m.
[Received December 1—1 : 50 p. m.]

2149. French, British, Netherlands Consuls confirmed [they] received likewise Chou's statement mytel 2128, November 30, but Belgium and Italy in non-receipt.

Acknowledged receipt letter addressed Wang Ping-nan personally yesterday, informing him also had transmitted statement as requested that date.

Sent Department 2149; Department pass Shanghai 1247, Nanking 1197.

CLUBB

893.001/12–249 : Telegram

The Chargé in China (Strong) to the Secretary of State

HONG KONG, December 2, 1949—1 p. m.
[Received December 2—5 : 11 a. m.]

Cantel 1316. In accordance telCan 777, November 30, I today expressed to President Li US Government's views on question of possible resignation in US.

Li declared very definitely that he does not intend resign at all, that he is returning to China after his US visit and that he is determined to hold his present post. He added that Generalissimo will not reassume presidency and has so stated to him.

STRONG

893.01/12–249 : Telegram

The Chargé in China (Strong) to the Secretary of State

HONG KONG, December 2, 1949—3 p. m.
[Received December 2—1 : 47 p. m.]

Cantel 1318. Foreign Office protocol chief [who] recently arrived Hong Kong declares belief widespread among responsible officers of Chinese Government that government should remain on mainland as long as possible. Although he questions whether government will retreat to Hsichang when Chengtu untenable he claims Premier Yen determined remain on continent. Source declares Yen recently declared occupation of Taiwan by Chinese Government was most unfortunate event of postwar period in that it diverted thought and effort from mainland and created "island bastion" outlook. We may therefore see an attempt to keep a corner of mainland such as Luichow Peninsula, with its relatively narrow neck as main defense line, as haven for government. We question whether Pai Chung-hsi can long hold Nanning.

Source also stated Executive Yuan did not organize move to Chengtu but each ministry or other organ "scrambled" for itself. Only with greatest difficulty did he finally charter plane to bring French, Italian and Korean diplomats to Hong Kong. He congratulated US Embassy for leaving when it did, on its own means of transportation.

Sent Department Cantel 1318, repeated Taipei 230, Hong Kong by hand.

STRONG

893.01/12–349 : Telegram

The Consul General at Peiping (Clubb) to the Secretary of State

PEIPING, December 3, 1949—10 a. m.
[Received December 5—4 : 06 p. m.]

2194. Met December 1 with Chang Tung-sun who reported he had seen Chou En-lai at conference November 30 (mytel 2110, November 29 [*28*]). Chou acknowledged receipt letter but "didn't mention" Mukden matter. Chang still in nonreceipt reply to letter. Chang evinced interest in Mukden matter, opined settlement would be improvement. He said, however, saw little chance for general improvement Sino-American relations due political orientations. Reply question, however, he said Soviets not "controlling" all China; they were concentrating on Manchuria. He expressed belief Soviets were preparing for war; in which event, he opined, Soviets would move much of their industry Manchuria. (This seems farfetched hypothesis, probably reflects Chinese hope get something out of developments.) Chang admitted Soviets take strong attitude Manchuria, but less strong stand in China Proper. He said Chinese leaders experiencing much "bitterness" regarding matter but are without recourse: they lack force with which oppose. Lin Piao and others in south unaware course events and in any event few Chinese troops remain Manchuria. Said China, by itself, would be unable solve problem Manchuria; that problem could be solved only by (1) settlement American–USSR differences or (2) war between USA and USSR with former winning. He admitted China, in present political circumstances, unable call in outside support against USSR.

Looks like Chinese Communists beginning discover what imperialism is really like.

Sent Department 2194; Department pass Shanghai 1267.

CLUBB

893.01/12–349 : Telegram

The Chargé in China (Strong) to the Secretary of State

HONG KONG, December 3, 1949—noon.
[Received 3 : 22 p. m.]

Cantel 1321. In discussion on future of Chinese Government, Foreign Minister Yeh on December 2 stated Foreign Office Chengtu, which now cut to 14, still has no communications and he unable make contact; claimed practically all records now at Taichung on Taiwan and that Foreign Office could not continue to be included in "mobile cabinet". He intimated that before long Foreign Office might be set up in at least relatively secure place with own communications, and would keep only liaison unit with government if latter not move Taiwan. This subject he apparently discussed with Vice Premier Chu Chia-hua on second trip of latter to Hong Kong. According to Yeh, he was to have gone to Chengtu today but cannot see much reason now to do so, thus expects remain here in connection National Government property interests. Yeh claims to have told Generalissimo he would not serve in government based Taiwan, and additionally that he threatened that if Generalissimo not come across with funds for Waichiaopu [98] he would resign and would be followed by majority of senior Waichiaopu officers who cannot be replaced easily. In this connection Yeh said Chinese Government maintains 142 establishments abroad, total budget cut while in Canton to US dollars half million monthly, and now cut by 30 percent more by staff reductions, most personnel still remain unpaid since August. It may be expected from remarks made by Yeh that if he resigns he will desire obtain visa for US. His two children are in school in Davis, California, and are understood to have been there several years.

Sent Department Cantel 1321, repeated Taipei 233, Hong Kong by hand.

STRONG

893.01/12–349 : Telegram

The Chargé in China (Strong) to the Secretary of State

HONG KONG, December 3, 1949—1 p. m.
[Received December 3—3 :19 a. m.]

Cantel 1322. Embassy on December 2 placed diplomatic visa on *laisser-passer* issued by Foreign Minister Yeh in favor President Li, his wife, and his 11-year-old son. Yeh stated he unable issue diplomatic passports to President and Mrs. Li simply because office of special commissioner at Hong Kong had none in stock. He then went on to

---

[98] Chinese Foreign Office.

express resentment at report that had been spread about that he would refuse to issue travel documents to President and family, stoutly maintained he was neither a Li man nor a Generalissimo man, and asserted he had not consulted with Generalissimo nor had been consulted by Generalissimo with regard travel documentation for Li.

We assured him that American officials had no part in spreading any rumors of foregoing nature.

Sent Department Cantel 1322, Hong Kong by hand.

STRONG

893.001/12–449 : Telegram

The Vice Consul at Kunming (Lutkins) to the Secretary of State

KUNMING, December 4, 1949—2 p. m.
[Received December 5—3 : 49 a. m.]

266. Lu Han told me in interview yesterday that he is under great pressure from local elements to leave Yunnan and allow them to surrender to Communists. He states he has refused to do so until situation becomes much worse.

He thought it highly unlikely that Kunming would be endangered within next 2 weeks and promised to give me 3 days' notice if advisable for me to leave sooner than planned. Also promised to instruct trusted subordinates who will remain after he leaves to protect American and other foreign lives and property from looting or molestation during interim period before Communists' arrival.

LUTKINS

893.00/11–2349 : Telegram

The Assistant Secretary of State for Far Eastern Affairs (Butterworth) to Dr. Kan Chieh-hou, Personal Representative of Acting President Li Tsung-jen

WASHINGTON, December 5, 1949.

DEAR DR. KAN : I refer to your letter of November 23, 1949 to the Secretary of State,[99] in connection with the projected unofficial visit to the United States of Acting President Li Tsung-jen for the purpose of medical examination and treatment.

In reply, I wish to inform you that the Department of State has already instructed its representatives in Hong Kong to facilitate the issuance of visas and other travel documents as may be necessary for the travel of Acting President Li and his party.

Sincerely yours,   W. WALTON BUTTERWORTH

---

[99] Not printed.

893.6363/12–549 : Telegram

The Chargé in China (Strong) to the Secretary of State

Hong Kong, December 5, 1949—4 p. m.
[Received December 6—5 : 23 a. m.]

Cantel 1326. While waiting for telephone call to Admiral Kwei [1] (telCan 1324, December 5 [2]), Yeh discussed on several subjects, interesting of which are briefly stated below :

1. Private reports indicate Asiatic Petroleum Company has closed deal with Chinese Communists for 100 million Hong Kong dollars' worth of petroleum products, payments to be made in New York from European sources. No indication of duration of contract.

2. Just prior to departure of Li Tsung-jen for US this morning, he advised President not to make direct statements to press or public but to do so through his secretary, view fact US Government understands trip is for medical reasons only. (Incidentally at airfield Li practically ignored Yeh who had to seize President's arm and draw him aside for one very brief conversation.)

3. Yeh proposed recently in cable to Generalissimo that government remain Luichow peninsula except Foreign Office which should be Hainan with rapid communications between them. Generalissimo failed reply. All Foreign Office personnel from Chengtu now being sent Taiwan via Hainan apparently at Generalissimo's orders, except Vice Minister, 3 secretaries and 2 code clerks.

4. Foreign Office officials, far from being Generalissimo enthusiasts, are unanimous in "cursing" Generalissimo.

5. Recent refusal local authorities clear further CAT flights arose from frequent failures by CAT to observe regulations, rather [than?] from political causes. Apparently CAT has straightened matter out.

6. Chinese Government will attempt transfer assets of CNAC and CATC to other company or form new foreign company to take them over. As last resort will try destroy them rather than let Communists have them. Yeh feels this in accord with US aviation policy toward Chinese Communists.

7. Yeh would like to know whether Indian Government has actually notified US Government of intention recognize Chinese Communists this month as recently report[ed] by United Press.

Sent Dept Cantel 1326, repeated Shanghai 578, Taipei 236, Hong Kong by hand.

STRONG

893.00/12–649 : Telegram

The Vice Consul at Kunming (Lutkins) to the Secretary of State

Kunming, December 6, 1949—10 a. m.
[Received December 7—6 : 54 a. m.]

269. Spokesman Yunnanese group called again today. Stated declaration Yunnanese independence being seriously considered despite

[1] Vice Admiral Yung-ching Kwei, Commander in Chief of the Chinese Navy.
[2] Vol. ix, p. 1180.

response Deptels 127 and 131.[3] Said chief headache was financial problem. Asked whether I thought United States Government might buy Yunnanese opium for medical use. I told him I thought this most unlikely. He asked whether I thought United States aid might be forthcoming after Yunnanese independence declared. I replied this also seemed highly improbable in view reference Deptels.

In spite of unreceptive United States Government attitude, I consider it quite possible that Yunnanese independence may be declared within next 10 days.

Sent Department 269. Department pass OffEmb Hong Kong telCan 101.

LUTKINS

893.00/12–649 : Telegram

The Consul General at Saigon (Abbott) to the Secretary of State

SAIGON, December 6, 1949—6 p. m.
[Received December 6—7:50 a. m.]

428. From conversation with Diplomatic Counselor Dugardier, obvious local officials worried over implications Chou En-lai "ultimatum" re Nationalist refugees since it is almost sure that, in spite all efforts French, some Nationalist troops will manage cross frontier. They are somewhat encouraged by present indications that General Pai plans retreat to Hainan and has recently pushed Communists back from Luichow Peninsula. Dugardier also pointed out that area along Tonkin frontier is largely in hands guerrilla bands now calling themselves Communists which would offer serious obstacle passage any small units Nationalist troops. He added he had requested Chinese Consul General [at] Saigon advise any Nationalist officials whom he might still be able to contact against attempts refugee troops to retreat into Tonkin. Dugardier hopes Paris will publicly reply to Chou En-lai (and I gathered he hoped we would also).

Exchange of messages between Ho Chi Minh and Mao Tse-tung considered less serious although added new factor to problem French recognition Mao regime and even forecast possibility of recognition of Ho government by Chinese Commies.

While Chou En-lai message and Ho–Mao exchange featured local press, little independent comment in native papers other than reiteration Vietnam wants no Chinese any type any time.

Sent Department 428. Pouched Hanoi; Department pass Paris, Hong Kong, Taipei.

ABBOTT

[3] November 22, 7 p.m., and November 30, 7 p. m., pp. 604 and 616, respectively.

893.00/12–749 : Telegram

The Consul General at Peiping (Clubb) to the Secretary of State

PEIPING, December 7, 1949—5 p. m.
[Received December 7—1 : 37 a. m.]

2221. French Consul General Breal informs me re Contel 2149, December 1, it is projected he make statement French position to Peiping authorities; action presently being temporarily held up to await clearance from Indochina authorities. Position per international law, foreign armed forces which might try retreat into Indochina would be repulsed or disarmed and interned.

CLUBB

893.00/11–3049

Memorandum by the Director of the Office of Chinese Affairs (Sprouse) to the Assistant Secretary of State for Far Eastern Affairs (Butterworth)

[WASHINGTON,] December 7, 1949.

Chou En-lai's note as reported in Peiping's telegram No. 2129 November 30 is not entirely clear. There would seem to be no objection to the statement that no matter where the defeated troops of the National Government flee, the Communists reserve "the right to take up this matter." But his subsequent statement that the government of any country which "gives shelter" to Nationalist armed forces must take responsibility in this regard and must accept all consequences arising therefrom, is ambiguous in that it is not clear whether he refers to shelter to armed forces which have been disarmed and interned by the neighboring country or whether he has in mind shelter to armed forces which retain their arms and independent command structure. From his earlier reference to bases for staging a comeback at an opportune moment, the latter might be inferred.

From a discussion with Mr. Snow in L[4] and Dr. Bacon,[5] it appears that the legal aspects of the matter may be summarized as follows: Countries adjoining China are under obligation to disarm and intern Chinese armed forces of either side which cross into their territories. The French are informing Chou En-lai that they will take these steps. However, it is reasonably certain that considerable portions of the frontier between Indochina and China are not under effective French control and there is some doubt that the French would in all cases be able to carry out this action promptly, if at all. The legal situation which would arise in the event that the French did not so disarm and

---

[4] Conrad E. Snow, Assistant Legal Adviser for Political Affairs.
[5] Ruth E. Bacon, United Nations Adviser of the Bureau of Far Eastern Affairs.

intern Chinese armed forces entering their territory is not clear-cut. It is believed that French failure to take this action would constitute grounds for a complaint by the Chinese against the French authorities. In some cases failure of an adjacent country to prevent the use of its territory for the assembling of armed forces hostile to a neighbor has been used to justify action by the other party, as for example in the case of the US and Mexico in connection with Villa.[6]

The legal situation is somewhat further confused by the fact that neither the French nor the US recognize the Chinese Communist regime. Consequently neither the US nor French would from a strictly legal standpoint consider that that regime has any rights as a government. However, from a practical standpoint, it is believed that the views outlined above remain applicable. Certainly we could not hope to impress the Chinese Communists with a legal argument based on their not being a government and not enjoying any rights as such.

It is believed that under the circumstances no reply should be made to the note in question[7] for the following reasons: (1) The legal situation is not clear-cut and any attempt to bring to Chou's attention the principles of international law applicable to the case would be so hedged and qualified as to impress him little and would almost inevitably lead us into a discussion of French obligations to disarm and intern retreating armed forces—an obligation which the French may not be able to discharge and which we perhaps should not emphasize; (2) We are not *directly* a party of interest in the matter, and the French, who have replied to the note, have not asked for our assistance or support.

It is not believed that our failure to reply could be properly construed as acquiescence, since (1) We do not recognize the Communist regime and are consequently under no obligation of any sort to reply to its notes; and (2) the wording of the note itself is so ambiguous as to permit differing interpretations.

893.00/12–949 : Telegram

The Chargé in China (Strong) to the Secretary of State

HONG KONG, December 9, 1949—1 p. m.
[Received December 10—2 : 30 a. m.]

Cantel 1329. On December 8 Foreign Minister stated he had planned fly Chengtu that day but learned just in time that Government in process of evacuating to Taiwan. Said expected notify diplomatic corps in next 3 to 4 days that Foreign Office to function Taipei.

---

[6] For documentation, see *Foreign Relations*, 1916, pp. 483 ff.
[7] Marginal notation by the Deputy Assistant Secretary of State for Far Eastern Affairs (Merchant) : "I agree. LM".

In view of press announcement today that Chinese Government beginning functions Taipei today, foregoing is excellent indication of manner in which Government operating almost on hour to hour basis and of fact Foreign Office is more or less a stepchild.

Would appreciate instructions as to my course of action.

Should Department order me to Taipei, request be advised whether O'Grady [8] should also proceed there in light of possible increase in code traffic.

Sent Department Cantel 1329, repeated Taipei 237, Hong Kong by hand.

STRONG

893.00/12–1049 : Telegram

The Consul General at Hong Kong (Rankin) to the Secretary of State

HONG KONG, December 10, 1949.
[Received December 10—4 : 25 a. m.]

1214. CAT reports Kunming changed hands night 9 December 1949 and controlled either by Communists or their local representatives. Guard put on airfield, immediately trapping 4 CAT aircraft, 1 TAA, and 1 C–54 of POAS on charter to CAT, plus unknown number CAF planes. Guards withdrawn temporarily unknown reason allowing above C–54 embark for Haiphong with 45 passengers, including unknown number Americans aboard. Expected arrive Hong Kong 5 p. m., 10 December. No information now re Lutkins and Knowlson but appears doubtful they aboard. Expect answer to radio enquiry Haiphong re Lutkins soon. If negative, will explore other means.

Sent Department, repeated Hanoi.

RANKIN

893.00/12–1249 : Telegram

The Consul General at Saigon (Abbott) to the Secretary of State

SAIGON, December 12, 1949—noon.
[Received December 12—7 : 08 a. m.]

437. Following signed statement issued [by] Pignon [9] over weekend:

"Am authorized by French and Vietnam Governments announce following position:

French and Vietnam Governments feel need announce their position in case Chinese military formations should be tempted to try penetration Indochina, particularly Vietnam. Instructions given

---

[8] Walter J. O'Grady, clerk assigned to the Embassy office.
[9] Leon M. Pignon, French High Commissioner in Indochina.

troops French Union are to oppose entry Indochina any foreign troops which appear at frontier under arms. If such case occurs elements which cross frontier will be ejected or disarmed and interned. In no case will French and Vietnam Governments permit Vietnam or other French Union territory be used as refuge by elements which might influence security frontier region or good neighborly relations with border states."

Evident Pignon not as confident on border situation as his press condemn Bao Dai departure indicated (Contel 436, December 12).[10] Pouched Hanoi. Department pass Paris, Hong Kong.

ABBOTT

893.00B/12–1249 : Telegram

The Consul General at Shanghai (McConaughy) to the Secretary of State

SHANGHAI, December 12, 1949—3 p. m.
[Received December 12—9 : 18 a. m.]

5169. Would Jessup [11] be interested in possibility of meeting Hong Kong in purely informal conversation a Communist representative from Peiping? If interested, think there is possibility of making approach here on very high level through person who we have excellent reason believe would be most sympathetic to idea and could be depended upon for great discretion in making such approach if she felt in position to undertake it. In strictest secrecy, person is Madame Sun Yat-sen.

McCONAUGHY

893.00/12–1349 : Telegram

The Consul General at Saigon (Abbott) to the Secretary of State

SAIGON, December 13, 1949—11 a. m.
[Received December 13—6 : 34 a. m.]

441. Pignon states communiqué re Chinese refugee troops in Indochina (Contel 437, December 12) issued on instructions Paris and identical message delivered same day to Chinese Communist authorities by French Consul General [at] Peking as reply to Chou En-lai note of end November.

Said actual situation on frontier much improved by disintegration General Pai's army. Confident French troops can easily disarm such small bands as may now cross frontier. He admitted French had been

---

[10] Not printed; Bao Dai, Chief of State of Vietnam since June 14, 1949, departed for France.

[11] Philip C. Jessup, Ambassador at Large, who was to make a tour of U.S. missions in the Far East.

extremely worried till last few days since it would have been impossible stop any organized withdrawal into Tonkin and even if troops submitted to disarmament, facilities for feeding, housing and guarding a hundred thousand or more men did not exist.

Pass Paris, Hong Kong. Pouched Hanoi.

ABBOTT

893.00B/12–1349 : Telegram

The Consul General at Shanghai (McConaughy) to the Secretary of State

SHANGHAI, December 13, 1949—11 a. m. [*p. m.?*]
[Received December 14—12 : 47 a. m.]

5200. In course of long conversation at dinner party December 10, Cheng Kang-chi (remytel 5191, December 13 [12]), former Nationalist career diplomat now acting as advisor to Communist Alien Affairs Bureau here, told me that Communist regime still suffering acutely from lack of experienced and qualified personnel in diplomatic field. Chou En-lai and Chang Han-fu said to be screening carefully Chinese Nationalist Foreign Service list. Contrary to general impression in Chinese Nationalist diplomatic circles, not all Chinese diplomatic and consular officers who defect will be retained by Communists. Some who have already made overtures to Communists have been marked for rejection as politically undependable or too closely identified with high Kmt policy.

Presumably, Vice Minister-Designate Chang Han-fu depends to certain extent on Cheng Kang-chi for information and advice on even elementary procedural matters, although it is clear that Communists do not fully trust Cheng Kang-chi and do not seek his advice in matters basic policy. I gather that Cheng Kang-chi has shown considerable courage in trying, although apparently without much success, to correct some of the fundamental misconceptions of Communists in area of foreign relationships and diplomatic history.

Cheng says, for example, that Communists inclined to regard everything in terms of all black or all white. They consider everything done by Nationalist Government during past 22 years must have been wholly evil. Cheng says he has gone to great lengths to convince them that, while Nationalist Government has many sins to answer for, there were some devoted and able public servants in positions of authority in the Nationalist Government who took some actions and made some agreements which were greatly in the interest of the Chinese people.

---

[12] Not printed.

Cheng says Communists convinced every treaty and other international agreement entered into by Kmt must somehow be constituted betrayal of Chinese people. If they could not find any clause in a treaty as promulgated to which they can object, then they are convinced that there must be "secret protocol" attached which sells Chinese people down the river. Cheng indicates that they are obsessed with this idea of secret clauses to treaties and that this partly accounts for their reluctance to take stand as to which treaties they intend to respect.

Cheng declares there is woeful lack of archives, reference material and scholarship available to Communist Foreign Office. He says Nationalist Foreign Office either evacuated or destroyed its archives including certified copies of treaties ratified by China. Communist regime has been entirely unsuccessful in its efforts to assemble authentic texts of treaties to which Cheng [China] is a party. He says that they literally do not know what treaty obligations they have inherited and cannot be sure they have true texts of those treaties which they know about. He believes this will delay settlement of question of treaty obligations.

A useful purpose might be served if Communist regime could be provided with authentic texts of valid Chinese treaties and other international agreements with all countries. Cheng says Chang Han-fu seems to have accepted his idea that "reasonable period" must elapse before Communists can expect action on their recognition bid of October 1. Communist officials pressing him periodically for precise definition of "reasonable period". He assures them that no exact time limit can be set. They have been somewhat discomfited by his reminder that US did not recognize Soviet Government for 16 years after October Revolution,[13] and that Czarist Government did not recognize American independence for some years after American Revolution.

McCONAUGHY

893.00B/12–1349 : Airgram

The Chargé in the United Kingdom (Holmes) to the Secretary of State

LONDON, December 13, 1949.
[Received December 15—11:15 a. m.]

A–2347. Following is a rough translation from the French of the text of a telegram said to have been addressed by Mao Tse-tung to Ho Chi-minh in response to a congratulatory message addressed by Ho Chi-minh to Mao Tse-tung by Radio Vietminh early in December.

---

[13] For documentation on recognition of the Soviet Union by the United States on November 16, 1933, see *Foreign Relations*, 1933, vol. II, pp. 778 ff.

The French text of this message was supplied the Embassy informally by M. Jean Le Roy, Counselor of the French Embassy in London:

Thank you sincerely for your telegram dedicated to the occasion of the installation of the democratic government of China. China and Vietnam are both at the front of the anti-imperialist struggle developing victoriously; the struggle of the two peoples for their liberty will certainly render from day to day even closer the relationship between our two nations. May I express my best wishes for the consolidation of the unity between the Chinese and Vietnamese peoples? My best wishes also for the complete success of the cause of independence and democracy of the Republic of Vietnam.

HOLMES

893.00B/12–1249 : Telegram

The Secretary of State to the Consul General at Shanghai (McConaughy)

WASHINGTON, December 14, 1949—10 a. m.

2417. Answer to question put in first sentence ur 5169 Dec 12 is affirmative. Re sentences 2 and 3 this Govt is not prepared take initiative in suggesting any such mtg and in any discussions which may arise out of interchanges which led urtel under reference this shld be made clear though fact remains Amb Jessup will stay for few days Hong Kong and if suitably approached wld be available for informal discussion.

ACHESON

893.00/12–1549 : Telegram

The Chargé in China (Strong) to the Secretary of State

HONG KONG, December 15, 1949—noon.
[Received December 15—8 : 55 a. m.]

Cantel 1335. Transfer of Liu An-chi and his forces from Hainan to Formosa may indicate:

1. Pai Chung-hsi given free hand in Luichow Peninsula and Hainan with no or at least minimum support from Generalissimo. Li Tsung-jen may thus be retaining office solely in hope that if US to supply military or financial aid he will be in position influence delivery to Pai direct. Li may bring up question in US of developing Hainan resources, as means increasing income for military purposes. Li previously raised this problem with Embassy Chungking.

2. Generalissimo feels that need for Liu An-chi on Formosa as means checking any ideas Sun Li-jen [14] and his friends may have on seizing power. Liu has proved thoroughly faithful to Generalissimo,

---

[14] Commander in Chief, Taiwan Defense Headquarters and Deputy Director of Military and Political Affairs for southeast China.

who now has to consider his control of Formosa more important than checking Pai Chung-hsi whose prospects, while still dismal, have improved perhaps 10 percent with departure Liu An-chi forces.

Sent Department Cantel 1335, repeated Taipei 245.

STRONG

893.00/12–1549

Memorandum of Conversation, by the Ambassador at Large (Jessup)

[NEW YORK,] December 15, 1949.

By appointment arranged through his physician, Dr. Frank Meleney, I called on President Li Tsung-jen at the Harkness Pavilion of the Presbyterian Hospital at 6:00 PM. Recalling the reports of Madame Chiang's entire floor during her stay in the same place, it may be worth noting that President Li occupies a simple single room on the third floor. Dr. Meleney met me at the desk and took me to the room where we found Dr. Kan with Li. Dr. Meleney asked me if I wished him to leave and put the same question in Chinese to President Li. We both told him we had no objection to his remaining. Dr. Kan acted as interpreter.

I began by saying that I greatly appreciated the President's courtesy in allowing me to call upon him to pay my respects, despite his illness. I said I wished to express my sympathy for his illness and my hopes that he would speedily recover. Li replied that he had long wished to visit the United States but his duty in China had made it impossible. It was hard for him to have left his country during the present difficulties but his health required it. He had looked forward when he visited the United States to meeting all of the leading personalities in our government but I was the first official person he had met and he was very pleased to see me. He continued that he regretted that the troubles of his country had led to the serious situation in the Far East which had led to my trip which he hoped would be successful.

I said that I regretted that it was illness which had brought him to this country. I had, in planning my trip[,] looked forward to meeting him there but appreciated the opportunity he gave me to meet him here before I left in two hours' time to start my journey. Just as illness had brought him here so it was true, as he suggested, that a great political illness was taking me to the Far East.

President Li said that the Government of China was very much to blame for the unfortunate situation which had developed. They had failed to take the steps necessary to hold the confidence of the people of China and this was the cause of the success of the Communists. He would be glad to answer any questions I wished to ask since he hardly knew where to begin on so large a question.

I said I had no specific questions but would be grateful for any information or suggestions which he cared to give me.

President Li then analyzed the situation in China. Due to the mistakes of the National Government the Communists had at first been able to persuade many people that Communism would afford the solution they sought. The situation was comparable to that twenty-odd years ago when the people similarly rallied around the Kuomintang. But people were rapidly becoming disillusioned. He was receiving frequent reports to this effect. Liberal leaders of the Democratic League and others were sending him word that they had made a mistake in joining the Communists. The manager (?) of the Manchurian railways had escaped and had come to Li to tell him that the Communists were unable to fulfill their promises. He reported that the people of Manchuria were now wishing the Japanese were back since under them they had a little freedom while under the Communists they had none. The Communists used their principle of "struggle" to liquidate great numbers of people. The National Government had been very remiss in not putting land reform into effect. They had many plans but had not carried them into effect. The Communists had started land reform but their method had been to liquidate by "struggle" not only the large landholders but even the humblest peasant who had any land. They charged that all the peasants were capitalists at heart because they sought each year to accumulate something in order to buy more land. The peasants were thus turned against the Communists and would now be ready for and welcome the true reforms which the National Government planned. Unfortunately the Government no longer had any area in which they could carry them out. The Communists were also losing the people by severe taxes and heavy requisitions to feed their armies. Their armies included very many national troops who had been "forced to surrender". These troops were not trusted but were guarded by Communist troops and were virtual prisoners. Labor too was dissatisfied because the Communists due to lack of foreign trade and the Nationalist blockade were unable to get the raw materials to keep the factories going. All of these elements were ready to rise against the Communists if only they had hope. At present they had none. (The implication was made obvious but there was no direct reference to United States aid.) If this situation were allowed to continue the Communists would in five years or so liquidate all possible leaders.

I thanked President Li for this information and analysis of the situation which I was sure would be very helpful. I was confident that under care of my old friend and doctor, Dr. Meleney, he would soon be well again.

Dr. Kan walked out with me to the elevator and asked if I were going to China. I said I was waiting to arrange my itinerary after I reached Japan, that I would of course like to visit China but did not wish to be another "Ward Case".[15] Neither Kan nor Li mentioned Formosa or the Generalissimo.

Dr. Meleney told me they expect to operate on Monday.

PHILIP C. JESSUP

761.93/12–1649 : Telegram

The Consul General at Shanghai (McConaughy) to the Secretary of State

SHANGHAI, December 16, 1949—10 a. m.
[Received December 16—8 a. m.]

5250. Re Contels 4782, November 14 and 5251, December 16.[16] Information reaching Consulate General from many quarters shows rapidly swelling tide Chinese charges and bitterness re Soviet greed, encroachments. Soviet "crimes" now chief topic on tongues our Chinese contacts, many whom literally bursting to tell us latest. Even those closest new regime more and more unreserved, elated in their attacks. One contact through whom we have been regularly supply[ing] SMCC Foreign Affairs Bureau with much material (American papers, press releases, Acheson [and] Jessup statements, Department's Soviet affairs notes series, etc.) recently urged: "Don't be afraid of giving them anti-Soviet material; they are glad to get it".

Selection of more reliable significant items follows. As will be noted, present Chinese ire is direct[ed] especially but by no means exclusively at Russian demands for Chinese foodstocks:

1. Source: . . . Enraged to find it "definitely true" that North China has shipped many trains of its food to Russia when China's own food needs great and he himself found people eating grass, bark in very suburbs Peiping. Said authorities sought excuse on grounds China all-dependent on Russia, must do what she wants; and that Siberia has severe famine. Consulate General notes item in Department Bulletin No. 282, December 1, that "Office of Foreign Agriculture Relations says Russia's 1948–49 crop produced more bread-grain than all four biggest grain countries combined . . ."[17] Reported having noted that posters put up by Peiping authorities to explain rise food prices as being due demands of armies and newly liberated areas, etc., had superimposed handwriting (scrawled at night) reading: "Price rise is due to food shipments to supply big [garble] (Russians)". On every side he heard reports of Soviets' high living in Peiping, Tientsin—insistence on best houses, best clothes, etc. Found whole attitude toward new regime more critical than at Shanghai.

---

[15] For documentation regarding the detention of Angus Ward, Consul General at Mukden, and his staff, pp. 933 ff.
[16] Latter not printed.
[17] Omission indicated in the source text.

2. Source: American bank manager quoting two Chinese informants . . . who told him some 2 weeks ago there was pending shipment one million bags wheat flour from Shanghai to Tientsin or further north, which one informant believed "probably destined for USSR as North China people too poor to buy". Comment: Tientsin postwar has imported up to 300 to 500 thousand bags Shanghai wheat flour monthly from time to time, and rail shipments flour though costly might be undertaken by state trading companies to meet North China shortage. (Note million bags roughly 850 freight cars or 21 trains 40 cars each.)

3. Source: . . . Last spring Chiaotung University graduating class in railway administration, as result of visit their institution by Lu Cheng-chiao, well-known Communist General [in] Manchuria, recently appointed Vice Minister Railways, eagerly petitioned for trip to Manchuria which Lu duly arranged. Group (63 graduates) left Shanghai about September full enthusiasm for new regime (as personally observed by source). After finishing 2 months' apprentice study work on Manchurian railways, returned Shanghai December 9 utterly revolted. Source has just seen 3 members of group who reported: (a) Entire group is bitterly against Russians and pro-Russian policies; (b) "whole Manchurian people" similarly minded; (c) every northward train group saw was filled with food for Russia; (d) 5 members of group had watches or pens "borrowed" by Russian rail workers; (e) invitation for group to stay on working Manchuria was rejected to a man. Comment: Consulate General hopes get more on this. While something should be allowed for presumable youthful emotional exaggeration, consider information most significant.

4. Source: . . . Friend of source returned later November from Manchuria told him that Mukden, Changchun, Harbin authorities collecting of wheat flour stocks there for shipment USSR were being stubbornly opposed by local people who saw no justification for shipments when "China itself short of food".

5. Source. . . . Soviets promised return stolen machinery to Manchuria soon as Kmt expelled. Have not done so. Chinese Communists also indignant over greed displayed by Soviets in taking ("according to source's friend, Minister of Heavy Industries Peking") 100 percent profit on "the 100,000 tons of steel rails of West German origin" which they sent China, having priced rails at $150 per ton compared half that cost for Soviets. (Press item reported to Department by Consulate General some time ago mentioned USSR as having supplied 500 kilometers of rails to new regime, evidently some time between spring and autumn 1949.) Soviets have not been fulfilling terms three recent barter agreements (one with Manchuria and two "with East China" but "negotiated in Manchuria"), their deliveries to date being mainly confined to paper, some textiles and small quanti-

ties machine tools and steel plates. True that Soviets seek monopoly soybean trade and already have it to point where other buyers must approach Moscow rather than China. China thus deprived of both exports and foreign exchange to buy imports from west. (These items tally generally with information from other sources.) As result of Soviet bad faith and rising Chinese opposition, further implementation of pacts is more or less at standstill.

6. Source: . . . Seems increasingly clear that recent Soviet "cultural" delegation was avid in buying up metals, etc., while in Shanghai and securing Chinese commitments for goods such as bristles for Soviet use or speculative profit with *quid pro quo* largely vague promises "whose failure to be kept will become plain before long and cause violent Chinese reaction".

7. Source: . . . Friend just back from North China, Manchuria with "Shanghai industrial inspection group" says press giving false information re northeast. Dairen population decreasing. People most unhappy under Russian influence.

8. Source: . . . Is positively set against accepting post or returning Peiping as long as Soviet dominance prevails. Soviet have advisors in Ministry Justice with great influence (confirmed by source 7) and with other organs. Even Chinese non-Communist leaders, in order see high Communist leaders, must first clear with liaison office which contains Soviet advisors; and none can travel to Peiping from Shanghai unless can prove good reasons to satisfaction that office. Mao Tse-tung has retired to Western Hills to "escape pressures". Comment: Our sources differ considerably re degree Soviet influence Peiping, most asserting such influence great, but some claiming recent decline. All agree, however, on Soviet's powerful position Manchuria, and most assert "personal conviction" that Soviets primarily responsible for Ward case.

9. Source: . . . Issue of whether to recognize Yugoslav recognition was warmly debated in his office, some favoring such recognition on grounds China should have independent foreign policy.

10. Source: . . . "Everywhere in Shantung" (recently visted by source) as well as Shanghai, people greatly concerned for Soviet encroachments. Chinese now refer to Stalin as "stepfather" with everything that term implies.

11. Source: Several. The signs of increasingly manifested resentment criticism Soviet Union in schools, colleges reported in Con-Gen telegram 4887, November 22 [18] continue. For example, officer of Consulate General informed by Chinese friends in . . . Law School that professor there, in introducing to his class in comparative court systems the subject of Soviet courts, which authorities now require as main phase of the course (in place of former stress British, Ameri-

---

[18] Not printed.

can and Chinese systems), said: "It will all sound very nice, but there is no way of checking". Many more questions now being debated in class than formerly, with large, very vocal non-Communist group no longer browbeaten by pro-Moscow minority.

12. Source: . . . Soviet efforts to acquire former Czarist Russian bank building at 15 The Bund are being obstinately resisted by local authorities.

13. Source. . . . Chinese people, including Communist leaders, feel bitterly re Soviet treatment Manchuria, Outer Mongolia, Sinkiang. Mao has been doing best to maintain Chinese influence in Manchuria, Sinkiang. Has managed do something in Manchuria thanks to communication facilities, but remoter Sinkiang much more difficult. Recent attempted plane trip of Sinkiang leaders to Peiping was Mao's scheme for strengthening ties by showing honor, friendship to Sinkiang patriots most likely stand up to Soviet aggression and by appointing them in their posts. Mao deeply shocked when all killed in plane crash, was first to wire their families. Asked whether he suspected foul play, source admitted at least possibility. Source also stated, as "certain fact", that Tan Kah-kee "great Chinese industrial patriot", had actually wept on Mao's shoulder in complaining to him of Soviet encroachments especially Manchuria, and that Mao comforted him by assurance that "this would be corrected in time".

Aside from above types of more reliable information, Consulate General has been getting flood of less vouched material. Such includes, for example, reports:

That Chinese delegation to Moscow had interview with Stalin in which he stated bluntly that China and USSR must cooperate even more closely and implied that if every [ever?] Mao Tse-tung should stand in the way of this, it would be duty of Chinese people to liquidate him;
That one million Chinese youths are to go to Russia for training;
That (in keeping with their boastful superiority) "Russians slap better than anyone else" (sarcastic jibe arising from manner in which Soviet movie director Gerasimov is said to have manhandled Shanghai crowds while shooting his pictures) ;
That no Soviet organs pay any taxes in Manchuria;
That Soviet soldiers constantly rape Manchurian women;
That Russian naval personnel is supervising erection coast defenses for Shanghai and Foochow;
That China (especially north) is being flooded with Soviet agents;
That Soviet technicians are only skilled workmen, with inadequate technical training.

Even such less credible reports derive significance in mere fact of their general and eager circulation and consequent effect in further exciting Chinese feeling.

Almost nothing favorable to Soviets has been heard by Consulate General aside from wholly propagandist press blasts (and, with exception of ultra pro-Soviet *Ta Kung Pao*, even they show cooling tendency of late). For sake fairness, however, such as we have is summarized:

1. Source: . . . PPCC delegation member new regime's Economic Finance Commission, recently returned from North China, Manchuria. Remains strong supporter new regime policies. Told American friend he found Mukden, Dairen people fairly employed, fed, definitely better than under Kmt, 80 percent factories operating thanks partly to Russians, who have supplied steel plates and other materials to keep them going and "are sending machine tools and machines in return for soybeans". He himself saw "some" Russian lathes. Soviet technicians have only been accepted on contractual conditions: (*a*) Same wages as Chinese, (*b*) won't interfere in politics, (*c*) will return USSR when job finished. True that Soviets have some influence, but are Socialist nation and only one helping new regime, so only natural. Peiping little dominated by Soviets.

2. Source: . . . Soviet technicians did good work repairing some railway bridges, "showing up" foreign-trained Chinese engineers.

To recapitulate, great weight of Consulate General's evidence indicates rapidly developing indignation and obstructionist spirit against USSR, in which Chinese Communists [them]selves seem showing increasing tendency to join.

Sent Department. Department pass Moscow 17.

McCONAUGHY

761.93/12–1749 : Telegram

The Ambassador in the Soviet Union (Kirk) to the Secretary of State

Moscow, December 17, 1949—noon.
[Received December 17—5 : 26 a. m.]

3123. Press prominently reports arrival Mao Tze-tung Moscow yesterday accompanied by Professor Chen Po-ta and others unnamed. Was received same day at Kremlin by Stalin, Molotov,[20] Malenkov,[21] Bulganin[22] and Vishinsky.[23] At railroad station to meet him were following: Molotov, Bulganin, Menshikov,[24] Gromyko,[25] Moscow Com-

---

[20] V. M. Molotov, Senior Deputy Chairman of the Council of Ministers of the Soviet Union.
[21] G. M. Malenkov, Deputy Chairman of the Council of Ministers of the Soviet Union.
[22] Marshal N. A. Bulganin, Deputy Chairman of the Council of Ministers of the Soviet Union.
[23] A. Ya. Vyshinsky, Soviet Minister for Foreign Affairs.
[24] Mikhail Alexeyevich Menshikov, Soviet Minister of Foreign Trade.
[25] A. A. Gromyko, Soviet First Deputy Minister for Foreign Affairs.

mandant Sinilov, Chief First FE Section, MFA, Kuryukov, Acting Chief Protocol Section, MFA, B.U. Shuyev, Chinese Ambassador and staff, Czech, Korean, Bulgarian, Rumanian, Hungarian, Mongolian, Albanian Ambassadors, Polish Chargé and acting head German Diplomatic Mission.[26]

Press states Mao was met at USSR border by Deputy Foreign Minister Lavrentyev and others and that Roschin [27] arrived Moscow "simultaneously with Mao".

At station Mao made brief radio speech. Large photo of group at station shows Mao fleshier than usual pictures.

KIRK

761.93/12–1849 : Telegram

The Ambassador in the Soviet Union (Kirk) to the Secretary of State

Moscow, December 18, 1949—2 p. m.
[Received December 18—11 : 24 a. m.]

3135. In connection arrival Mao Tze-tung Moscow 16th, following are Embassy comments:

1. Primary purpose probably signing by Mao and Stalin of friendship, commercial, and possibly mutual assistance (military) pacts. Presumably 1945 treaty [28] to be replaced by another cementing China to USSR along lines conventional satellite treaties, but with Japan as principal possible aggressive menace.

2. Arrival Mao in time participate Stalin birthday celebrations is nicely timed. Russians gratified to see Stalin accorded this respect by the outstandingly successful non-Russian Communist of the day. In effect, Mao personally reporting to "throne" acquisition of vast new territories and hundred[s] of millions people for Stalin empire. Stupendous birthday gift for Stalin. From Chinese Communist viewpoint, significance of Stalin and USSR in Communist world can be demonstrated by Mao's trip, perhaps helping Chinese Communists to put across to Chinese people reason for fanfare on occasion Stalin's birthday. As Chinese by "old custom" recognize decade birthdays in advanced age as occasion for special celebration, Mao's visit readily understandable such mentalities.

3. Visit will focus attention Communist world on tremendous significance attached to China victory.

4. It is possible that Mao is the first of several satellite chiefs of state to arrive at Moscow for the birthday celebrations. There has as

---

[26] All Communist representatives.
[27] N. V. Roschin, Soviet Ambassador in China successively to the National Government and to the Chinese Communist regime at Peiping.
[28] Signed at Moscow, August 14, 1945; United Nations Treaty Series, vol. x, p. 300.

yet been no indication that others will be present. If there should be such a gathering, Mao's visit would furnish Stalin with an opportunity to introduce Mao to the family.

5. Stalin thus afforded opportunity exert his personal magnetism on Mao under impressive conditions attendant these birthday celebrations. Moscow being decorated and Stalin will be recipient of most profuse declarations of affection, remarkable and extravagant presents (often bizarre), and protestations of universal love as greatest living man. In establishing personal relationship with Mao, these proprieties can be expected to assist Stalin as practical evidence confirming his overwhelming stature in the Communist movement.

6. If Chinese popular resentment of Soviet influence and action in China is serious, as reported Shanghai's 5250 and 5251, December 16, Stalin may be expected to do utmost to reassure Mao of righteousness Soviet motives and necessity Chinese Communists convince people correctness accepting Kremlin leadership.

7. Barely possible Mao may discuss Chinese situation very frankly with Stalin and recommend less obtrusive Soviet influence China Proper at present in interest long-term goals. Danger of such candor obvious, but Mao feels forced by circumstances to discuss matter if anti-Soviet feeling in China reaching proportions serious enough to compromise success of new government.

8. Mao's visit, of course, provides material for pointing up CCP subservience USSR and other obvious angles.

9. Although there are rumors that Chu Teh [29] also is here, Embassy unable presently to confirm. In view his stature in CCP movement, next only to Mao, if Chu is here it is difficult to explain absence of publicity.

10. Chen Po-ta only member Mao's party mentioned by name in press. More names may be published on occasion official reception which might be given Mao prior "great day", otherwise on that day itself.

11. In brief announcement of reception by Stalin of Mao, no mention made of Chinese Ambassador being present. US correspondents here consider this means no other Chinese was present during meeting, and that only those persons named in press report, i.e., Molotov, Malenkov, Bulganin and Vyshinski, were on hand when Mao met Stalin Friday.

Sent Department; Department pass London 343, Paris 441, Shanghai 21, Peiping 23.

KIRK

---

[29] Commander in Chief of Chinese Communist armies.

893.00/12–1949 : Telegram

The Second Secretary of Embassy in China (Bacon) to the Secretary of State

NANKING, December 19, 1949—2 p. m.
[Received December 19—3 : 52 a. m.]

2615. In November former Chinese professor at . . . visited home . . . for first time since 1937. Painted bleak picture of region which in Communist hands for 10 years, stating most persons worse off than before war. Land redistribution has given each individual in village approximately one and one-half *mou* which insufficient maintain livelihood as taxes now 10 times prewar. This enforced equalization landholding means class of persons who formerly able maintain selves partly from profitable intensive small gardening and partly from peddling or handicrafts now have plot of land large enough to demand all their time but too small support them. Only group better off than before those with children in PLA who entitled tax reduction and labor assistance contributed by other members of village. Class struggle has created new small class "public slaves" composed former landlords who dispossessed of everything and forced eke out meager living working for others.

Floods this year greatly aggravated already bad situation. Informant anticipates by February next year practically no grain left throughout large areas resulting widespread starvation. Refugees streaming out of Shantung by tens of thousands mostly to Manchuria and Shansi. *Hsien* government at Yenchow issued 3,000 travel permits daily for past 2 months.

Sent Department 2625; Department pass Shanghai 1278.

BACON

893.003/12–2149 : Telegram

The Consul General at Shanghai (McConaughy) to the Secretary of State

SHANGHAI, December 21, 1949—3 p. m.
[Received December 21—6 : 28 a. m.]

5330. 1. Trusted American exceptionally well posted on Peiping Communist developments has given officer ConGen following information as coming from high official of Chinese Communist regime:

Liu Shao-chi and Kao Kang [30] preceded Mao to Moscow for preliminary talks to stage-set Mao's visit. Mao left for Moscow following Liu's return Peiping. (Not known whether Kao Kang has yet returned to Peiping or Manchuria.)

---

[30] Vice Chairman and member of the Central Committee of the Chinese Communist Party.

Chou En-lai will probably leave Peiping very soon—our source's inference being that Chou has been alerted to be ready proceed Moscow to handle routine drafting and other details for Soviet-Chinese Communist agreements as soon as basic terms settled.

Chen Shu-tung, non-Communist Shanghai industrialist who has enjoyed Mao's favor [and] confidence, opposed Mao's going Moscow and Mao answered him in letter explaining necessity for trip. (American source lacked information whether other high government officials had voiced opposition.)

Comment: Advance sending of Liu and Kao would seem suggest that most difficult points have already been settled through them sufficiently to ensure strong probability that Stalin–Mao agreement will be quickly reached.

Choice of Liu as pathmaker (presumably the most difficult and responsible task) and Chou as follow-up routine man would seem reflect (a) Moscow's preference for Liu and/or (b) Liu's higher rank and influence in CCP.

Selection Kao Kang strengthens logical surmise that Manchuria plays extremely important part in discussions.

2. Liu Hua-jui (now assisting ECA [31] disposal plans), who is astute, well-informed observer, gives us following explanation:

While Mao's visit Moscow was to be expected, indications are that his decision for trip this particular juncture came as result strong and rather sudden Moscow pressure; that Moscow was dissatisfied with Chinese Communist performance and their manifestations of loyalty; and that timing of visit was related to British and other western nation "moves" toward recognition "including perhaps even Jessup's trip to Far East",[32] and to Kremlin's desire to "nail down" its objectives while Chinese Communists still manageable and before Soviet position weakened by development of western influence and anti-Russian trends in Chinese Communist regime.

3. Han Ming in talk with officer ConGen today expressed similar views. Said that Mao's trip would probably have awaited some "climaxing" event such as Chinese Communist conquest of Taiwan, but that Moscow's dissatisfaction with Chinese Communists and signs of early western relations with new regime caused sudden Soviet insistence on immediate visit. Han believes Moscow has "put strong heat" on Mao.

4. As also of interest in above connection may be mentioned that officer ConGen was told yesterday by local Swedish Consular official that a Swedish newspaper recently carried article reporting Molotov

---

[31] Economic Cooperation Administration.
[32] For White House announcement of forthcoming trip to Bangkok in January 1950, see Department of State *Bulletin*, November 28, 1949, p. 800.

having completed 2-month visit in Manchuria. (Rumors current here some time ago also had Molotov in Manchuria.) Should Dept lack text this article, ConGen will seek further details.

Sent Dept, Dept pass Moscow 20, Peiping 533.

McConaughy

893.00B/12–2149 : Telegram

The Consul at Tientsin (*Wellborn*) *to the Secretary of State*

Tientsin, December 21, 1949—4 p. m.
[Received December 28—5 : 49 a. m.]

1070. Sent Department as 1070, Department pass to Peiping as 338 and Shanghai as 458. Although indications here are Communists continuing consolidate their control over all phases people's activities local Chinese in no way recently have shown no [*any?*] desire play USSR game. (1) Flow of flour to USSR (ourtel 972–A, November 25 [33]) resulted much bitter comment; (2) University students have lost some enthusiasm for Communists and we informed teachers of newly inaugurated courses in Communist dialectics and materialism posed embarrassing questions by students re Soviet aims and activities Chinese; (3) Large portrait Stalin paired off with portrait Mao Tzetung at entrance Tientsin industrial exhibit (opened November 4) removed after 2 days because of quips by public re inappropriateness giving "foreigner" such prominence; (4) No. prominent Chinese canvassed re joining Sino-Soviet friendship society resentful implied element coercion.

Chinese traditionally consider themselves apart from government and that they must protect personal interests against encroachments government. Non-Communist Chinese continue refer to Communists as "they"; conversely Communist propaganda aims at identifying people with government. We should continue seize every opportunity particularly through VOA [34] drive wedge between Chinese people and Communist authorities and emphasize incompatibility interests Chinese and Soviets. Suggest stressing forced loan aspects of victory bonds. Current effort Communist press play up projected celebrations Stalin's birthday also presents opportunity point up Soviet encroachments.

Wellborn

---

[33] Not printed.
[34] Voice of America (radio broadcasts).

761.93/12–2149

The Ambassador in the Soviet Union (Kirk) to the Secretary of State

No. 802   Moscow, December 21, 1949.
                                    [Received January 6, 1950.]

The Ambassador has the honor to enclose a copy in translation of the speech [35] read by Mao Tse-tung immediately after his arrival at the Moscow Yaroslavl railway station on December 10 [*16*], 1949. The text of Mao's speech was published in all Moscow newspapers on December 17: it was broadcast by Radio Moscow at 11:30 p. m. on December 16.

In his brief remarks at the railway station, Mao Tse-tung unmistakably conveys the impression that he comes to Moscow representing a great nation, bringing greetings from the people of one great nation to the people of another. While paying tribute to the leadership of Stalin in world communism, Mao avoids obsequiousness. There is an impression in western diplomatic and press circles in Moscow that the Chinese communist leader tactfully indicated that his country does not expect to be relegated to the satellite relationship which has been allotted to the eastern European governments. While this impression may be the result of wishful thinking, it is apparent that Mao did not indulge in the type of fulsome homage which has become so typical of the European satellite leaders.

893.00B/12–2249 : Telegram

The Consul General at Peiping (Clubb) to the Secretary of State

                              PEIPING, December 22, 1949—noon.
                              [Received December 23—5:09 a. m.]

2334. Translation requested Deptel 883, December 7 sent mytel 2322, December 21.[36] Comment on phrase "Agri-socialism entirely wrong even reactionary["] follows:

Term agri-socialism first appeared in speech by Mao at Shansi-Suiyuan cadre conference in spring 1948, detailed interpretation of [*made?*] public by NCNA in August same year. Agri-socialism was at time interpreted as signifying equal apportionment of real property among peasants on basis of private ownership with implication of permanent preservation these conditions of equality. Revised concept however now recognizes that maintenance such conditions is imprac-

---

[35] Not printed.
[36] Neither printed; the Department requested clarification of Chinese Communist Party statement that "agricultural socialism is entirely wrong" (893.00B/11–2149).

ticable owing different natural environment (soil and climate), discrepancies individual capabilities and attitudes, unforeseeable effects, natural calamities, etc. New class differentiation follows and reform is therefore deemed inevitable and must ever be approved and encouraged in order to provide peasants with productive stimulus. That is, say, free competition among peasants and consequent appearance new rich peasants or capitalistic farmers must be emphasized as means of raising national productivity. This will constitute first stage in agri-socialization process with concomitant and significant difference as compared with pure capitalism of necessity for existence effective central government control and direction. Former totalitarian concept of agri-socialism hence is now regarded as fanciful and even reactionary, and criticism of land reform on basis that at its completion unequal conditions of land ownership continue to exist as similarly ill-informed.

Department pass Shanghai 1343.

CLUBB

893.00B/12–2349 : Telegram

The Consul General at Peiping (Clubb) to the Secretary of State

PEIPING, December 23, 1949—6 p. m.
[Received December 24—9 : 13 a. m.]

2341. Comment as follows re travel Mao Tze-tung Moscow, reEmbtel 3135, Moscow 23, December 18.

Mao's departure was untold China in advance. Unclear whether he and Roschin departed in company. Names accompanying staff ungiven in full. In short, travel undertaken in high degree local security.

. . . told me today Mao accompanied by large staff including Chu Teh and wife Chi Chao-ting, others unknown. Mao will discuss Moscow signature treaty, draft of which brought here by Roschin. Treaty comprises three sections: Military, economic and trading. . . . unable make detailed inquiry but thought military section covered training Chinese troops, trading would be along lines usual barter agreements between USSR and satellites, accorded suggestion economic section might provide for Soviet participation Chinese enterprises (re Sinkiang pattern). . . . now opined, reContel 2320, December 20,[37] figure one million for troops China required provide in case war too small, three million might be nearer.

Mao desires obtain in Moscow, if possible, (1) return all Manchuria and particularly Dairen to control China, and (2) loan 300 million but in what currency unclear to . . . . Expects in return be called on give *quid pro quo* comprising particularly employment additional Soviet advisors in railroad, transportation, communications, military organi-

---

[37] Not printed.

zation, "municipal planning". (Presumably this is Chinese estimate of least to be demanded of them.)

. . . said Soviet tactics clear to see. They desired maintain breach between China and USA at least until they could tie China in Soviet camp by deal along lines USSR–Bulgar treaty, but China however felt need for closer relations with US for both economic and political reasons.

Comment: Believe . . . main contact for above probably Chi Chaoting. Motives either or both perhaps open to question but if there be some emphasis on dark aspects situation this is essentially problem for Communist purpose speeding American recognition and thus getting (1) American counterbalance to Soviet machinations, and (2) American economic aid (see later message).

To me seems unlikely Soviets would consent to replacement 1945 treaty prior to legal determination end war with Japan, more probable that it would be supplemented by another act along lines USSR–Mongolia treaty 1936 [38] or, as . . . suggests, USSR satellite. If as per Contel 2320, December 20, there already is "verbal agreement", treaty covering all China would be simply expansion formalization Communist accord already existing in prototype. It would probably go farther than foreseen by . . . .

Some clauses such agreement, however, would probably be kept secret. Note particularly re Contel 2300, December 17[39] that West Manchuria now has status which would facilitate its incorporation in visible future into Mongolian People's Republic. Current reports indicate that parts of China and Suiyuan will also be demarcated at [*as?*] "Inner Mongolia" but whether as part "Inner Mongolia" this would, of course, make possible still greater accretion territory to MPR, and Inner Mongolian cordon like MPR itself would then connect on west with politically unstable Sinkiang where there can logically be expected renewal Soviet expansion along 1933–42 lines.

Mao would naturally desire expansion Sino-Soviet trade which to date falling short expectations. Diversion trade from old channels to new proving more difficult than first thought. Note report that Soviets demanded Chinese 5-year plan for purpose coordination trade needs and when Chinese said best they could do was plan 2 years ahead Soviets said nothing doing without 5-year plan. Experience seems support belief that in China as in Sinkiang and Manchuria Soviets may try get Soviet participation in certain Chinese enterprises with aim getting eventual control.

In sum probabilities seem be developments Moscow will follow lines contrary both Chinese *amour-propre* and self-interest. Mao, as

---

[38] Signed at Ulan Bator (Urga), March 12, 1936; *British and Foreign State Papers*, vol.cxl, p. 666.
[39] Not printed.

most Chinese, deeply nationalistic. Communist adulation "great leader Stalin" goes against grain many otherwise strong supporters Chinese Communist regime. It would go even more against Chinese grain for them because give up territory and rights traditionally regarded as Chinese. Mao knows this.

In circumstances it could logically be expected Mao might return from Moscow somewhat beaten down, perhaps somewhat disillusioned. This not to suggest he would be on verge Titoism: Soviets undoubtedly have ever in mind example 1927 and are steeled check any such development ruthlessly. They hold stick over Chinese by being able threaten "separatist movement" Manchuria, and location capital Peiping with main Chinese forces far away in south makes quite feasible Soviet brandishing big stick. Chinese have always preferred others do their fighting with big powers, but non-Soviet friends presently unavailable. In theory Mao might with decision and vigor now react as Tito against USSR but in fact developments too unlikely. Also unlikely in view Communist discipline and strict surveillance personnel there will yet occur any major split in military ranks with some leader exploiting national misery in coup against Mao's leadership. Nevertheless it is not to be thought impossible that Mao and his government should try draw somewhat away from USSR along lines perhaps foreshadowed Contel 917, June 1.[40] Peiping regime can now presumably look forward with reasonable assurance to recognition by certain non-Soviet states near future, which may seem to them to offer opportunity maintain measure of independence from Soviet octopus. Nationalistic Chinese Communist elements might now feel urge resume fence-straddling in world politics. Modern experience seems show they could hardly hold their precarious balance in that position under Soviet attack, and would probably be forced in time make sterner choice.

[To] Moscow at Department's discretion.

Sent Department 2341, Department pass AmPolAd [41] Tokyo.

CLUBB

893.00/12–2449 : Telegram

The Consul General at Shanghai (McConaughy) to the Secretary of State

SHANGHAI, December 24, 1949—noon.
[Received December 24—6 : 28 a. m.]

5369. Local government making strenuous efforts eliminate "excess population" from Shanghai. Widespread rumor current that recent

---

[40] *Ante*, p. 357.
[41] American Political Adviser to the Supreme Commander, Allied Powers in Japan.

beggar and refugee roundup (remytel 5296, December 19 [42]) included not only vagrants and the like who were thrust into "labor-production-education centers" but large numbers men around military age, not gainfully employed, who were drafted into PLA. (While there is possible need for recruits to supply manpower for contemplated attacks on Chusan and Taiwan Islands, difficult to see why already huge army of at least 5 million men constantly being augmented with defeated or defected Nationalist troops would not be equal to task if properly equipped.) Consulate General has heard several instances where individuals reportedly given 48 hours to find employment or leave town. Jobless houseboy formerly employed by Consulate General approached Consulate General officer begging for job even without salary as he feared what would happen if authorities discovered him unemployed. Apparently former Kmt officials not yet reemployed are especially concerned, and one source reports many "white collar class" desperate for any job irrespective pay to escape draft.

City census taking inaugurated December 20 (remytel 5319, December 20 [42]) also generally believed aimed mainly at collecting excess and floating population for triple purpose of security control, removal surplus population and army-labor conscription.

That it is logical to expect drastic action by authorities along lines such as above reports suggest also indicated by various other factors. Generally admitted even by official quarters that Government's repatriation policy announced shortly after take-over has failed miserably. Official sources attribute this to devastation of farm lands by floods and consequent food shortages in countryside which have forced farmers seek refuge in city. However, additional causes may be:

1. Excesses in countryside by Communist cadre members (said to be of rather low calibre) have stimulated movement from land to city.
2. Anticipated eventual confiscation measure distribution of land, as well as desire to avoid taxes have led many farmers to abandon land-holdings and head for city.
3. Many merchants fleeing from Canton to escape levies imposed on them by new authorities are reported to have made their way to Shanghai. Hence, city has greater population now than before activation of repatriation policy, which even at its peak probably failed keep pace with birth rate. Downtown pedestrian and vehicle traffic, automobiles excepted, have noticeably reached pre-takeover proportions, with ever-increasing numbers beggars soliciting alms on streets. With approach of winter, press already carrying reports of dead bodies littering streets in numbers seemingly undiminished from Kmt-rule days. Government's evident policy (attested to by many sources) of keeping city supplied with food at expense of rural areas in danger of being nullified by increased news of swelling stream refugees flowing into Shanghai. Government policy of buying up and dumping food as balancing

---

[42] Not printed.

factor to prevent extreme price fluctuations also imperiled by impending food shortage. According to Tsao Men-chih, Director Shanghai Civilian Affairs Bureau (remytel 5296, December 19), there has been influx into Shanghai and surrounding areas of 550,000 refugees since September, not to mention large numbers unemployed, destitute normally present in city.

No Chinese daily news [*North China Daily News?*] item reported same telegram that "winter camps" and other relief centers can handle approximately 40,000. Problem of disposing of the balance remains as major "headache" new regime. (Van Oss [43]).

Sent Department 5369, repeated Taipei 585, Hong Kong 436.

McCONAUGHY

711.93/12–3049

Memorandum by the Assistant Secretary of State for Far Eastern Affairs (Butterworth) to the Under Secretary of State (Webb)

[WASHINGTON,] December 30, 1949.

You may recall having referred some time ago to the President's having expressed an interest in the extent of U.S. interests in China. I am attaching hereto a memorandum setting forth briefly the nature and magnitude of our interests in China which may be of use to you should the President again express an interest in this subject.

[Annex]

Memorandum on United States Interests in China

Broadly speaking, United States interests in China include (1) American citizens, (2) private property and investments of American citizens, (3) trade, (4) United States Government property, (5) credits due to the United States Government by the Chinese Government, (6) United States Foreign Service establishments, (7) United States influence.

1. *American Citizens.* According to the latest information, 3,227 Americans are now residing in China. Of this total 241 are officials or employees of the United States Government and their dependents and 2,986 are private citizens. It is estimated that 3,018 Americans are now residing in areas under Communist control and 211 in areas still under Chinese Government control. It should be noted that an unknown but certainly substantial part of the persons listed above are in fact of Chinese or mixed Chinese race whose permanent home is in China and to whom American citizenship is largely a matter of convenience.

---

[43] Hendrik Van Oss, Vice Consul at Shanghai.

2. *Private Property and Investments.* The latest comprehensive survey of privately owned American assets in China was made by the Treasury Department in 1943. According to this survey the value of such assets was approximately $122.2 million. Although information is not currently available upon which to make exact estimates, according to best available information the present value of privately owned American assets is between $100 and $200 million. This amount is almost evenly divided between direct investments in business enterprises, direct investments in philanthropic organizations and indirect investments including securities, notes, accounts receivable, and claims.

3. *Trade.* In the pre-war period the total value of United States trade with China fluctuated between $100 million and $125 million a year. The following table sets forth in millions of dollars the value of exports to and imports from China during representative pre-war and post-war years.

	Exports	Imports
1934	92.7	32
1937	55–65	68.5
1946	465	92.7
1947	353.5	116.7
1948	240	120.5

(Export figures for post-war years include UNRRA,[45] Relief, ECA, and military assistance shipments.) Imports from Communist China for March 1949 through October 1949 were valued at approximately 10 million dollars. The value of American exports to Communist China during this period is not known but it is believed to be considerably smaller.

The proportion of United States total foreign trade accounted for by trade with China has been consistently small, never exceeding 1.9 per cent of total United States exports or 3.4 of total United States imports in the pre-war period and never exceeding 4.8 per cent total United States exports or 2 per cent of total United States imports in the post-war period.

In the pre-war period the United States supplied from 15 to 25 per cent of all China's imports and took from 11 to 26 per cent of China's total exports, being in fact China's most important trading partner. In the post-war period 1946–48 the United States has accounted for a much larger percentage of China's foreign trade, supplying 48 to 57 per cent of her total imports and taking 20 to 38 per cent of her total exports. This was due to abnormal post-war economic conditions and has been changing steadily to a more normal pattern as China's alternative suppliers re-enter the market.

The loss of the China market would not be important for American producers as a whole, although producers of a few commodities (e.g.

---

[45] United Nations Relief and Rehabilitation Administration.

leaf tobacco, raw cotton, and timber) might feel the reduction in the market. A few articles (e.g. tung oil, bristles, tungsten ore, antimony, carpet wools) are of importance to certain sectors of our economy, but there is no article produced by China which is of predominant importance to the United States. Conversely China can in general obtain from alternative suppliers adequate quantities of articles essential to it.[46]

4. *United States Government Property.* The total purchase cost of United States Government real property in China is $11.8 million. (Of this total, properties costing $11.2 million were purchased with local currency made available under the terms of the bulk surplus property agreement of August 30, 1946.[47]) These properties include buildings for Foreign Service establishments in China and certain property purchased at Tsingtao and Shanghai at the instance of the United States Navy.

5. *Credits Due the United States Government by the Chinese Government.* Outstanding obligations of the Chinese Government to the United States Government resulting from financial assistance directed primarily toward economic rehabilitation, amount to $157.5 million. Such obligations resulting from financial assistance primarily of a political character amount to $642 million. The two governments have not yet agreed upon terms of settlement for most of the latter obligations.[48]

6. *United States Foreign Service Establishments.* The United States has Foreign Service establishments at Peiping, Tientsin, Shanghai, Nanking and Taipei. Offices at Hankow, Tsingtao and Kunming have closed and the staffs have been or are being evacuated. Foreign Service establishments constitute important interests of this Government in China because of the services which they perform for American citizens and the measure of protection which they have afforded Americans and their properties. Furthermore, they provide valuable sources of information regarding developments in the country and important channels of American influence.[49]

7. *United States Influence.* Throughout the past one hundred years, American influence has grown steadily in China and, notwithstanding setbacks during the past year or so, it remains one of our most valuable assets in that country. American championship of and support for expanding educational facilities have contributed much to this development. American founded and supported institutions of higher education including Yenching University, Peiping Union Medical College, the University of Nanking, Ginling College, Lingnan University,

---

[46] See also vol. ix, pp. 817 ff.
[47] Signed at Shanghai; Department of State Publication No. 2655, *Report to Congress on Foreign Surplus Disposal* (October 1946), pp. 40–45.
[48] See also vol. ix, pp. 729 ff.
[49] See pp. 933 ff.

St. Johns University, Fujen University and Hangchow Christian College, enjoy an outstanding reputation in Chinese scholastic circles. Many influential officials in both the Nationalist and the Communist camps have been educated in these or other American institutions, while Chinese presently studying in such institutions will supply much of their country's future leadership. This is particularly true in China where the opportunities for higher education are relatively few and there is a scarcity of men with a background of advanced education. The remission for educational purposes of the punitive portion of this country's share of the Boxer indemnity and, more recently, use of Fulbright funds for similar purposes have further contributed to the reservoir of educated Chinese oriented toward the United States. American mission activities involving direct contact with large numbers of Chinese and including the maintenance of schools and hospitals have likewise contributed and are contributing to the spread of American influence, as have American business men and technical personnel in their daily contacts with Chinese. Finally these activities have been favored by American policy toward China which traditionally has sought to preserve the integrity and independence of the country, has opposed the seeking of special rights and privileges and has taken the lead in renouncing extraterritorial privilege. Consequently, the Chinese have seen less danger of exploitation in American activities of this nature than in similar activities of other countries and have been correspondingly less hostile to American influence.

China is approximately as large as the United States and has a population three times as great. With this in mind, it is evident from the foregoing that the monetary value of our stake in China is comparatively small. But from the standpoint of our national interests much more important than the dollar value of our trade with China and of the physical assets of American missionary and educational institutions, American business and industrial organizations and American Foreign Service establishments is the importance of these as purveyors of American influence, as symbols of American interest in the Chinese people and as sources of information. Their value to us in this sense represents the accretion of more than a century of governmental and private endeavor. It is in this sense that they are one of our principal assets in China today.

761.9311/12–3149 : Telegram

The Consul General at Peiping (*Clubb*) *to the Secretary of State*

PEIPING, December 31, 1949—noon.
[Received December 31—5 : 08 a. m.]

2380. Sent Department 2380; Department pass Moscow, AmPolAd Tokyo. . . . December 29 also reported Contel 2341, December 23, negotiations were in progress Moscow for signature Sino-Soviet treaty alliance. Said present trials Japanese war criminals USSR designed as backdrop for new move. Opined ex-Emperor, Pu Yi, would shortly be extradited China for trial. Confirmed reports other sources party Chinese war criminals are now being tried without publicity, stripped of all possessions where adjudged guilty and turned out on streets with beggar's bowl.

. . . offered opinion that return Mao Tze-tung would be sole way changing Communist attitude toward Americans [and] Chinese for better or worse.

At dinner attended December 30 by Van Putten,[50] . . . subject Mao visit Moscow arose. Following information presented by various persons Chinese side : Draft of treaty as brought Peiping by Roschin unacceptable in some respects Mao and other more nationalistic Chinese and it was therefore decided matter be discussed Moscow at same time as other affairs. Treaty provisions included following (besides information previously reported) :

(1) Chinese and USSR would be allies in event war.
(2) Besides troops as previously reported, Chinese to furnish 5 million workers as manpower.
(3) Transport to be placed under Soviet supervision, supported by railway guards and
(4) Interior Department also to be under Soviet supervision.

This treaty designed to replace "arbitration agreement".

CLUBB

---

[50] James D. Van Putten, Consul at Peiping.

SUCCESSIVE MOVES OF THE EMBASSY OFFICE IN CHINA IN EFFORT TO REMAIN NEAR THE HEADQUARTERS OF THE CHINESE GOVERNMENT [1]

893.01/1-1549 : Telegram

The Ambassador in China (Stuart) to the Secretary of State

NANKING, January 15, 1949—1 p. m.
[Received January 16—11 : 55 a. m.]

117. Government preparations to move from Nanking have become increasingly apparent during week. Despite difficulty concealment move this magnitude, Government's decision still shrouded in secrecy. Consequently, reports are in detail conflicting. They, however, indicate implementation in initial stages evacuation of Government to points south in face of increasing military threat to Nanking. Places most generally mentioned are Canton area and Taiwan.

Foreign Office admitted in confidence Vice Ministers met January 11 to discuss plans for evacuation archives of various Ministries and tentative plans, requiring Cabinet approval, for removal of Ministries themselves from Nanking in event extreme emergency. No attempt to conceal packing of archives in Foreign Office though official insisted he did not yet know their destination and denied any final decision taken re movement personnel.

Other sources indicate all Ministries ordered to pack their archives for delivery to Ministry of Communications this week for shipment south. Re personnel, one reliable source reports recent order 80 percent of Government personnel must choose to resign and receive 3 months' salary or be evacuated from Nanking. Remaining 20 percent, regarded key personnel, will remain Nanking and be airlifted out at last minute. Source continued that in general, administrative sections of Government including banks are being moved to Canton or points along railways en route. Air Force, Navy and ground troops in training are being moved to Taiwan, he continued, where Government's gold and silver reserves now are. Legislative Yuan is not now in session, its members are scattered and not scheduled to meet again until early February although some individual members have appeared Taiwan.

Foregoing would apparently support two conclusions. First, if and when Communists or coalition takes over Nanking and governing

---

[1] For previous documentation on the subject of the possible move of the Embassy, see *Foreign Relations*, 1948, vol. VII, pp. 850 ff.

responsibility for expanded area, its administrative difficulties will be substantial and far greater than originally anticipated as result wholesale removal archives and dispersion of experienced personnel. This estimate might well moderately reduce such incentive as exists for Communists to negotiate at this time since Nationalist negotiators would no longer be in position to offer intact administrative machinery.

Second conclusion is that odds have increased that diplomatic corps will be faced with last-minute request by Nationalist Government to evacuate with Government from Nanking. Physical problems connected with any attempt to comply greatly increased by apparent Government intention to hold only key personnel here and evacuate by air at last minute. Moreover, scattering of archives and Government personnel over South China and Taiwan make it difficult visualize how Government could be conducted. If diplomatic corps were to move in accordance with prospective request, we assume it would follow Foreign Minister [2] and Foreign Office whose destination would, from present indications, be Canton.

To sum up, chances of our being asked to move have increased. While present phase of Government's move indicates widespread dispersal of archives and personnel, it must be admitted that adoption and implementation of plan to move capital now, may give Nationalists time to establish Government in south with sufficient degree of continuing authority to warrant at least sending diplomatic representatives with it. In accordance with instructions, we will immediately report any request by Nationalist Government that we accompany it elsewhere, giving at such time relevant facts and our recommendation. Pending arrival or in absence of instructions we will remain Nanking as previously directed. General sentiment in rest of diplomatic corps seems to be still further hardening on remaining Nanking under any circumstances though many assuredly are waiting to follow our lead, whatever it may be.

STUART

701.0093/1–1749

Memorandum of Conversation, by the Deputy Director of the Office of Far Eastern Affairs (Allison)

[WASHINGTON,] January 17, 1949.

Mr. Collins [3] called this morning to seek such information as we could give him with regard to the American policy toward the removal of foreign Embassies from Nanking in the event that the Chinese Government left that city. He said that the Chinese Ambassador in

---

[2] Wu Te-chen.
[3] Ralph E. Collins, Second Secretary of the Canadian Embassy.

Ottawa had made a formal request to the Canadians last Friday, January 14, that the Canadian Ambassador and staff in Nanking be instructed to move with the Chinese Government to Canton at such time as the Chinese Government evacuated Nanking. The Chinese Ambassador stated that quarters would be made available to the foreign diplomatic corps at Canton and that this was the place where the Chinese Foreign Office would be located. According to Mr. Collins, the Canadian representative in Nanking had recommended that the Canadian Embassy not leave Nanking and had stated that this was in accord with the general sentiment prevailing among the diplomatic corps in Nanking. Mr. Collins said that Ottawa is not convinced that it is the best policy for the Embassies to remain in Nanking and feels that there is definite advantage in having the Ambassadors move with the Chinese Government. They point out that if this is done it will:

(1) Encourage the Chinese Government to continue such resistance as is possible and thus delay complete Communist domination of China,
(2) Postpone the necessity of making a decision as to the possible recognition of a Communist-controlled Chinese Government,
(3) Give the remaining free territories of Southeast Asia more time to make plans for such action as may be deemed possible and necessary to ward off Communist infiltration into their territories, and
(4) Postpone the time when a Chinese Communist-dominated government can claim to represent China in the UN [4] and when Chinese Communist officials will be attached to Chinese Government missions abroad.

I told Mr. Collins that we had been approached informally by Dr. Tan [5] of the Chinese Embassy and that he had been informed that this Government was not prepared at this time to make a decision on the basis of such uncertain information as the Chinese Government is now able to give as to the timing and place of removal of the capital. Mr. Collins was further informed that our Embassy in Nanking had been instructed to take no decision in this matter until further instructed by the State Department [6] and to report at once any decisions in this matter by the Chinese Government and any requests from it that the foreign missions accompany the Government when it leaves Nanking. I stated that this Government would then make its final decision based upon circumstances prevailing at the time such a request was finally made.

Mr. Collins said that his Government would want to keep in line with the United States Government on this matter and requested that he be kept informed of our thoughts on this subject. I assured him that we would keep him so informed.

---

[4] United Nations.

[5] Dr. Shao-hwa Tan, Chinese Minister-Counselor of Embassy.

[6] See telegram No. 1639, November 16, 1948, 7 p. m., to Ambassador Stuart, *Foreign Relations*, 1948, vol. VII, p. 853.

893.01/1–1849 : Telegram

The Ambassador in China (Stuart) to the Secretary of State

NANKING, January 18, 1949—11 a. m.
[Received January 18—2:17 a. m.]

134. British, Canadian and Indian Governments have according their Ambassadors here been approached by Chinese Envoy their respective capitals to ascertain if appropriate instructions have been issued for movement their Diplomatic Missions to South China when National Government decides to move. I have informed colleagues here that as far as I know similar approach has not been made US Government (see Embtels 117, January 15 and 134, January 18 to Department). Yesterday in conversation with one of my staff, Vice Minister [7] Foreign Office said if peace negotiations failed Foreign Office would move Canton; that plans were almost complete to transport archives all Diplomatic Missions to that city. He said we would be officially notified in about 3 days that Government was ready transport archives Canton; that Government had secured adequate housing there for Diplomatic Corps (houses for about 800 people). He added we probably would want to leave caretaker staff Nanking protect interests here.

Above are first definite indications Government is making plans move Diplomatic Corps in time Canton and by its foresight make it difficult for any Mission accredited National Government to refuse. We should be prepared receive early invitation follow Government to provisional capital in south. We will of course refer invitation to Department reporting our views Government's future role national scene.

Sent Department 134, repeated Shanghai 65, Canton 4.

STUART

893.01/1–1849 : Telegram

The Acting Secretary of State to the Ambassador in China (Stuart)

WASHINGTON, January 18, 1949—8 p. m.

67. When Chi Emb approached Dept re subject matter your 134 Jan 18 it did so by way of confirmation and approach allegedly already made by Chi FonOff to AmEmb. Dept indicated it had not yet recd report of such conversation.

ChiEmb was very vague merely indicating ChiGovt had to contemplate possibility of removal of capital from Nanking; had no info as to probable new location. It did vouchsafe offer of transportation facilities for personnel and archives (sic) and residence in guest

---

[7] George K. C. Yeh.

house. ChiEmb seemed to regard this offer as applying to ConGen Shanghai as well but readily agreed that this could not be intended since consular officers and staffs invariably remained within their consular districts to perform their traditional functions. Dept requested further details pointing out necessity of knowing at appropriate time locus of new capital and facts relating to removal of Govt as whole there as well as info as to extent and adequacy of facilities which might be provided.

Today Chi Min-Counselor informed Dept FonOff telegraphed that Canton was point selected for removal of Govt but he was seemingly unable to provide more specific info even on point as to whether Govt as whole was to be located in Canton or whether some of its integral parts were to be as suggested in press in Formosa, Fukien Province or even Chungking.

Dept has been informed in confidence by member of French Emb that Amb Meyrier has recd instructions from Paris to remain in Nanking.

LOVETT

893.01/1–1949 : Telegram

The Ambassador in China (Stuart) to the Secretary of State

NANKING, January 19, 1949—11 a. m.
[Received January 19—1 : 25 a. m.]

143. Officially notified by Chief Protocol, Foreign Office, that National Government is moving Canton beginning January 21 and have been officially requested to follow Government Canton. Further details with our recommendations will follow.

STUART

893.01/1–1949 : Telegram

The Consul General at Canton (Ludden) to the Secretary of State

CANTON, January 19, 1949—6 p. m.
[Received January 19—8 : 24 a. m.]

9. On January 16 local representative FonOff intimated that early move FonOff Canton was possible but he said he had not received specific information (reference Embtel 134, January 18, 11 a. m. to Dept, repeated Shanghai 65, Canton 4).

I am at loss to understand Vice Minister's statement "adequate housing" for about 800 people of diplomatic corps has been secured here. My information is to effect that, aside from inadequate quartering arrangements made tentatively at Oikwan Hotel, FonOff representatives have made no efforts obtain housing for full diplomatic missions.

Incidentally it is of some interest that on evening January 16 Rau-Yang Chu, Mayor of Canton, assaulted, mauled, threatened with death and forcibly evicted from Mayor's official residence the special delegate of Ministry Foreign Affairs. I am not aware of all of the underlying animosity between these two individuals but it may be a reflection of the Mayor's increasing irritability as the influx of officials from the north increases.

Sent AmEmb Nanking 14, repeated Department 9, Shanghai 17.

LUDDEN

124.93/1–1949 : Telegram

The Ambassador in China (*Stuart*) *to the Secretary of State*

NANKING, January 19, 1949—10 p. m.
[Received January 20—1 : 04 a. m.]

146. Further conversation Foreign Office re move to Canton leaves impression government has no definite plans itself for southward movement but would like to evacuate Diplomatic Corps and see it safely established Canton before emergency move Foreign Office and other vital Ministries becomes necessary. (See Embtel 143, January 19.) We told Foreign Office official that its invitation to proceed Canton must be referred Washington; that in order for Department to give serious consideration and intelligent reply it must have certain detailed information, such as when Foreign Minister will proceed Canton, when Foreign Office will begin functioning effectively in provisional capital, when and where Executive Yuan will go, and where Prime Minister [8] will take up residence. We also expressed view that future movement of Legislative Yuan would be important consideration. Of less importance but of interest would be schedule and future seat of Judicial and Control Yuans. Foreign Office official was unable to answer any of these questions, said he would try to obtain replies but expressed doubt that any decisions, particularly with respect to dates on above points, had yet been determined.

He explained government was seeking means for peaceful settlement of civil war and present move by Foreign Office vis-à-vis Diplomatic Corps was primarily "preventative" in event peace formula failed. He expressed Foreign Office concern for safety of Diplomatic Corps in face of increasing military threat to national capital. We expressed appreciation this thought but pointed out that our Government would hardly condone our moving to Canton for reasons of personal safety while leaving Nationalist Government to which we were accredited in Nanking; that obviously any decision we might

---

[8] Sun Fo.

make would be greatly influenced by Government's schedule and movement. We will report pertinent details as they become available.

Apart from above considerations, following elements appear to us important. On the one hand this contemplated move is additional evidence that Government is disintegrating and its authority, prestige and military power diminishing by the week. Any foreign government which follows it into exile risks its relationship on any kind of workable basis with successor Nationalist Government dominated by Communists. On other hand this may be effectively balanced and more by maintaining prestige domestically and internationally of recognized Government of China which for moment at least maintains nominal authority over vast amount of Chinese territory and which continues to show every intention to resist Communism in territories under its control. More important from standpoint of free countries of world is that our continuing recognition of Nationalist Government of China, even in provisional capital in south, will assure us for that length of time a continuing friendly vote in Security Council and friendly voice in world's international assemblies.

Our preliminary recommendations are, therefore, that:

1. We do not accept government's invitation until at least Foreign Minister and majority of Cabinet have moved to Canton.

2. When this has been accomplished Minister Clark,[9] with a small selected staff, immediately follows government Canton.

3. At time of his departure we inform Foreign Office, and if desirable give out to press, that a portion of staff is proceeding to Canton to establish Embassy, make initial preparations for housing and working facilities, and that timing Ambassador's movements will be reserved later consideration.

4. Depending upon subsequent military and political developments decision can then be made by Department whether Ambassador with remainder of his staff (except Consulate) should proceed to Canton, if ever.

Sent Department; repeated Shanghai 76.

STUART

701.0093/1–1949 : Telegram

The Ambassador in China (Stuart) to the Secretary of State

NANKING, January 19, 1949—11 p. m.
[Received January 24—12 : 11 a. m.]

149. At a meeting this afternoon of "North Atlantic group"[10] the Chiefs of Mission of UK, France, Netherlands, Belgium, Canada and

---

[9] Lewis Clark, Minister-Counselor of Embassy in China.
[10] For list of governments which negotiated establishment of the North Atlantic Treaty Organization, see the North Atlantic Treaty signed at Washington, April 4, 1949; Department of State Treaties and Other International Acts Series No. 1964, or 63 Stat. (pt. 2) 2241.

myself discussed at length Chinese Government request that Diplomatic Corps follow it Canton (see mytel 146, January 19). It was immediately obvious that none of other Ambassadors wanted to go to Canton and there was almost unanimous sentiment for procrastination in replying to Chinese. There was complete unanimity that group stick together and present united front to National Government.

It was finally agreed that each Chief of Mission would recommend to his government (1) That no move be made without more evidence of real intention part of Government to move to Canton and (2) That should Government actually move to Canton each Ambassador send senior officer of his staff, possibly accompanied by others to Canton, to maintain contact preserving position of Ambassador himself for future consideration.

British and French Ambassadors emphasized need for unanimity. Dutch and Canadian Ambassadors agreed. We have been told separately by Siamese, Indian and Egyptian Ambassadors that they will follow Anglo-American lead in this decision. We are inclined to believe today's press reports that Soviet Ambassador, Czech and Polish Chargés will follow Government to Canton when invited.

Sent Department, repeated Shanghai 78.

STUART

701.0093/1–2049 : Telegram

The Ambassador in China (Stuart) to the Secretary of State

NANKING, January 20, 1949—1 p. m.
[Received January 20—4 : 17 a. m.]

153. Obviously news of meetings North Atlantic group has spread (see our 149, January 19). Philippine Counselor informs us Burmese Ambassador called meeting 19th Egyptian, Indian and Philippine Ambassadors to discuss Foreign Office request removal Canton. Each agreed recommend his government that Ambassador remain Nanking, sending senior subordinate Canton after Chinese Government had effectively removed there.

STUART

893.01/1–2149

The Chinese Ambassador (Koo) to the Secretary of State

MEMORANDUM

The Chinese Ambassador presents his compliments to the Secretary of State and, pursuant to instructions, has the honor to inform him that the Chinese Government intends to move the capital from Nanking to Canton should it be found impossible to reach satisfactory terms with the Communist Party for the restoration of peace. It is requested, as also of the governments of the other Powers maintaining diplomatic missions in Nanking, that, in that event, the Ambassador of the United States accredited to the Chinese Government, his staff, and members of their families will also move to Canton in order to be near to the seat of the Government. Transportation facilities from Nanking to Canton and suitable living quarters in the latter city will be provided by the Chinese Government without charge. It is understood, however, that the number of staff members of the United States Mission to remain in Nanking to attend to matters dealing with the protection of United States nationals is to be decided by the United States Government.

WASHINGTON, January 21, 1949.

124.936/1–2249 : Telegram

The Ambassador in China (Stuart) to the Secretary of State

NANKING, January 22, 1949—noon.
[Received January 22—8 : 19 a. m.]

187. In view attitude of Communists toward Consul General [at] Mukden [11] and indications of similar attitude in Tientsin, we believe time has come to review our policy re size of staffs permitted to go behind Iron Curtain. Should government actually move Canton and should we send mission with it, those remaining Nanking would have little to do until arrival Communists. Even then it appears considerable time may elapse before establishment successor [to] Nationalist government with which Embassy could deal. If staff is to be kept incommunicado and Communists treat personnel as private individuals pending recognition by US of Communist government as may be indicated, there would seem little need retain large staff Nanking. This would appear particularly true if our interests should dictate continuing support National regime or others resisting Communism. Should events lead to recognition Communist government, staff could later be strengthened. In meantime services of personnel which would be surplus under such conditions could be used elsewhere. Accordingly should situation develop as we envisage, we recommend following:

(1) Clark would take to Canton with him: Lancaster, Link, Norton, Woodworth, Waseman, Moses, Maeliang and Dr. Ho.

(2) Available for transfer would be: Terry, Anner, Coty, Doucette, Fer, Gibson, Green, Hall, Hordern, Krueger, Mead, Pond, Kierman, Sullivan, Swierczek, Thomson and Mincey.

---

[11] For further documentation, see pp. 933 ff.

Status Merchant [12] presents special problem. Behind Iron Curtain Nanking, his talents would be wasted. Should our policy result in continued support Nationalist Government in Canton and resistance forces elsewhere, his services in Canton could prove of extreme value. Accordingly we recommend that he proceed on provisional basis to Canton with Clark.

There would in our opinion still remain Nanking adequate staff to carry on until situation clarified.

Sent Department 187, repeated Shanghai 92 (for Cabot).

STUART

701.5193/1–2349 : Telegram

The Ambassador in France (Caffery) to the Secretary of State

PARIS, January 23, 1949—5 p. m.
[Received 6:21 p. m.]

293. Foreign Office source advises that if Communists establish government at Nanking, French Ambassador will probably be instructed proceed to Shanghai. French thinking is that his continued presence Nanking would be an implied *de facto* recognition Communist government and would prove embarrassing if latter requests seat on Security Council.[13]

Foreign Office considers Shanghai most advantageous as offering communications with France and possibility maintaining contact with Nanking and perhaps Canton (just prior to Chiang's [14] withdrawal, Foreign Office received note from Chinese Embassy here "inviting" French Ambassador to follow government to Canton).

CAFFERY

893.00/1–2549 : Telegram

The Ambassador in China (Stuart) to the Secretary of State

NANKING, January 25, 1949—5 p. m.
[Received January 25—7:44 a. m.]

213. New Director American Department Foreign Office [15] tells us Foreign Office moving immediate and almost in its entirety to Canton. American Department will be closed in Nanking tomorrow and director leaves day following for Canton. After tomorrow only Foreign Office officials left Nanking will be Minister, two vice ministers and their secretaries. Dr. Chen added that same situation obtains in other

---

[12] Livingston T. Merchant, Counselor of Embassy in China.
[13] Of the United Nations.
[14] President Chiang Kai-shek retired on January 21 in favor of Vice President Li Tsung-jen as Acting President of the Republic of China.
[15] Chen Tai-chu.

ministries Nanking. Military and Air Attachés confirmed this re Minister National Defense [16] and Hu Shih [17] gives similar confirmation Education Ministry. Nanking is in fact assuming aspect dead city. Government meets this afternoon establish date Foreign Office and Government will begin functioning Canton. It seems obvious all Government personnel except very top few in each ministry is departing immediately. Hu Shih says those remaining can be removed two ministries per plane.

Lapham [18] called on Acting President this morning re China aid problems. During conversation Li Tsung-jen told him he would not surrender to Communists; that if he could not negotiate reasonable settlement he would move southwest with Government and continue resistance. He had come on scene too late to prevent Communist crossing Yangtze River.

Troops are now passing through Nanking for south, indication being destination Fukien area. Best information is there will be no defense Nanking; that pattern of Peiping may be repeated; and that if efforts to negotiate settlement fail, Communists can take Nanking with little effort. Upon breakdown peace negotiations or when Nanking falls, whichever comes first, we may expect hurried removal remaining government personnel southward.

Either Li Tsung-jen will continue to carry on in Canton or Kweilin, or Generalissimo [19] will reappear upon scene, resuming his functions as President and Commander in Chief, using Canton as seat of Government and possibly Foochow as military headquarters.

In light of above and of Communists' imminent arrival north bank Yangtze from whence they can interdict use all Nanking air fields, it seems to us feasibility evacuation portion of Embassy to provisional capital is daily lessened. If, as we assume, it is US policy to support any legitimate national government which will continue to resist Communist encroachment militarily, or Communist-domination politically, time has come, we believe, for prompt action to assure US diplomatic representation Canton, at least along lines suggested our 187, January 22. Foreign Office tells us we will have tomorrow formal written request removal Canton, giving us date Government will begin functioning there. Upon receipt note we will immediately report further. However, if Embassy contingent has not left Nanking by Thursday or Friday of this week, departure may be impossible through Communist interdiction use air fields.

STUART

[16] General Ho Ying-chin.
[17] Chinese Minister of Education; former Chinese Ambassador to the United States.
[18] Roger D. Lapham, Chief of the China Mission of the Economic Cooperation Administration.
[19] Chiang Kai-shek.

701.5193/1–2349 : Telegram

The Secretary of State to the Ambassador in China (Stuart)

WASHINGTON, January 25, 1949—6 p. m.

91. Following Paris telegram 293 January 23: [Here follows text of telegram printed on page 661.]

French Emb here conveyed similar info Dept Jan 22, saying Schuman [20] had requested Emb ascertain Dept views re desirability removal Ambs to Shanghai for reasons given in foregoing tel and also since Shanghai would provide easy exit from China if desired withdraw Amb. Dept replied would consider suggestion but in view withdrawal Gimo, reported efforts open peace negotiations and absence evidence Chi Govt actually moving Canton no decision re removal foreign embs Canton seemed necessary this juncture.[21]

ACHESON

893.00/1–2649 : Telegram

The Ambassador in China (Stuart) to the Secretary of State

NANKING, January 26, 1949—noon.
[Received January 26—12 : 37 a. m.]

217. Formal note received [from] Foreign Office announcing removal Government to Canton which becomes legal seat Government February 5. We are requested to follow Government and Foreign Office offers assistance this regard. Foreign Office advises us orally Government will cease function Nanking February 3.

In view situation outlined our 213, January 25, request immediate authorization as suggested our 187, January 22, except that Clark would take Mincey instead of Link.

It is obvious that after February 3 those remaining Nanking will have nothing to do until arrival Communist[s].

STUART

393.1115/1–2249 : Telegram

The Secretary of State to the Ambassador in China (Stuart)

WASHINGTON, January 26, 1949—noon.

95. In making recommendations contained (2) your 187 Jan 22 have you taken into consideration repercussions particularly on Amer community Shanghai which would result therefrom? You will recall (penultimate sentence para 1 Deptel 1691 Nov 23 and ultimate para

---

[20] Robert Schuman, French Minister for Foreign Affairs.
[21] This section of telegram was repeated to the Ambassador in France as No. 203, January 25, 5 p. m.

Deptel 2078 Dec 2 [22]) that it has been made clear both in this country and in China that this Govt intended maintain at full strength its diplomatic and consular representation in China and that in any unforeseen evacuation *in extremis* US business and missionary personnel would be accorded same facilities as official personnel.

ACHESON

---

123 Stuart, J. Leighton

Memorandum by the Director of the Office of Far Eastern Affairs (Butterworth) to the Under Secretary of State (Lovett) [23]

[WASHINGTON,] January 26, 1949.

Subject: Status of the Ambassador and the Embassy at Nanking

[Here follows résumé of the following telegrams on the above subject: No. 1639, November 16, 1948, from the Ambassador in China, *Foreign Relations*, 1948, volume VII, page 853; Department's No. 1777, December 7, 1948, to the Ambassador in China, *ibid.*, page 859; No. 134, January 18, from the Ambassador; No. 143, January 19, from the Ambassador; No. 9, January 19, from the Consul General at Canton; No. 146, January 19, from the Ambassador; No. 149, January 19, from the Ambassador; and No. 153, January 20, from the Ambassador.]

The Ambassador recommended (1) that the invitation to move to Canton not be accepted until at least the Foreign Minister and the majority of the cabinet should have moved to that city; (2) that when this occurred, the Minister-Counselor, with a small staff, should immediately proceed to Canton; and (3) at that time the Embassy would inform the Foreign Office, and if desirable the press, that a portion of the Embassy staff was proceeding to Canton to establish the Embassy, make initial preparations for housing and working facilities and that the timing of the Ambassador's movements would be reserved for later consideration.

Several considerations are pertinent to this matter. You will recall that reports from the Embassy, the consular offices and the U.S. military representatives in China indicate that there is little likelihood that the National Government can effectively oppose a determined Communist advance into south China since it has little strength in terms of regular forces south of the Yangtze, except for those being withdrawn in the Nanking area. The Embassy has stated that the scattering of archives and governmental personnel over south China

---

[22] *Foreign Relations*, 1948, vol. VIII, pp. 892 and 907, respectively.
[23] Notation by Mr. Butterworth: "Seen by the Secretary, 1/26/49."

and Taiwan makes it difficult to visualize how government could be conducted.

If the Ambassador should remain at Nanking after the withdrawal of the National Government and if the U.S. should continue military and economic aid to a National Government-controlled south China, his status and that of our Embassy would be somewhat anomalous and very difficult. This would, of course, also be true of our consular offices in Communist areas and the position of U.S. businessmen in such areas would likewise be affected. The Ambassador's presence in Nanking would in a sense be interpreted as recognition of the *de facto* authority of any successor regime regardless of our intentions. At the same time, the Ambassador's presence in Nanking could be advantageous. He speaks Chinese with great fluency; he is acquainted with the leaders of all factions in China; and, as former President of Yenching University, approximately fifty percent of whose graduates are reportedly in the Communist camp, he occupies the traditional position of the teacher vis-à-vis the pupil in his relationships with many Chinese.

On the other hand, the Ambassador's withdrawal from Nanking would be taken as indication that the U.S. was prepared to continue support and recognition of the evacuating Government and the U.S. would logically be expected to continue aid to that Government under such circumstances. In that event, the position of U.S. businessmen and missionaries in Communist areas would obviously be difficult, if not untenable, not to mention the remaining portion of our Embassy staff and of our consular offices. It should not be overlooked that with the fall of Nanking the Communists will have the capability of occuping Shanghai and that Communist control of the lower Yangtze valley, whether by military or political means, appears to be shortly forthcoming. When that occurs, the Communists will have under their control the major centers of population from Manchuria to the Yangtze valley. In these areas are located the majority of U.S. interests and U.S. businessmen and missionaries in China. If the U.S. is to afford any protection to or promote U.S. interests in these areas, it must have official representation which can get in touch with the central governing authorities of the area.

It may be expected that domestic reaction in the United States from some Congressional quarters and newspapers will be highly critical of any decision not to direct the Ambassador to follow the Chinese Government to Canton. These quarters are, however, not aware of the hopelessness of the situation as described by General Barr, Director of the Joint U.S. Military Advisory Group. General Barr has stated that only a policy of unlimited U.S. assistance, including the immediate employment of U.S. Armed Forces to block the southern advance of the Communists, which he emphatically does not recommend, would enable the National Government to maintain a foothold in south China against a determined Communist advance.

Pertinent also to the problem is the withdrawal of Generalissimo Chiang Kai-shek from Nanking and the temporary assumption of the President's powers by Vice President Li Tsung-jen. The latter is endeavoring to open peace negotiations with the Chinese Communists, failing which he may be expected to withdraw to the south and continue resistance. The manner in which the Generalissimo withdrew—that is, the vagueness of his farewell statement which seems to leave the way open for his return to power, his concentration of the Government's assets on Taiwan, the indications that he is building up Taiwan as a bastion to which he may withdraw to continue the struggle and his reported withdrawal of his "personally loyal" troops toward Fukien Province—indicates that he may be expected to reenter the scene and continue resistance from Taiwan and those areas on the mainland still under his control. Should the peace negotiations fail or should they result in such terms for the Government that the Generalissimo could reject any agreement as a "national betrayal", he would be in a position to resume the Presidency and attempt to rally all remaining resistance forces. If the past can proclaim the future, he has some such plan in mind. It is not expected, however, that the Generalissimo himself would proceed to Canton. The chiefs of foreign missions would not, therefore, even in Canton be in touch with the head of the government to which they are accredited.

In this general connection, it should be noted that the Soviet Ambassador [24] has been recalled to Moscow for consultation, thus enabling the USSR to avoid sending its Ambassador with the Chinese Government. The Embassy at Nanking has reported that the Polish and Czech Chargés d'Affaires are expected to follow the Chinese Government and the USSR may take similar action.

In his telegram no. 213 of January 25 the Ambassador reports that all Government personnel except for the very top few in each Ministry is departing from Nanking immediately for Canton and that the remaining personnel is expected to be evacuated if the peace negotiations break down or when Nanking falls, whichever comes first. The Ambassador points out that in view of the current military situation and of the imminent arrival of Communist forces on the north bank of the Yangtze River, from which point they can interdict the use of all airfields at Nanking, the feasibility of the evacuation of a portion of the Embassy staff to the provisional capital is daily lessened. He suggests, therefore, that prompt action be taken to assure U.S. diplomatic representation at Canton, along the lines previously recommended by him whereby the Minister-Counselor with a selected group of necessary staff assistants would proceed immediately to Canton.

---

[24] N. V. Roschin.

It is recommended that, pursuant to the Embassy's suggestions, the Minister-Counselor with a small selected staff immediately follow the Government to Canton and that the Ambassador remain at Nanking. It is also recommended that the Department inform the concerned Embassies here, for communication to their governments, of the U.S. Government's decision to send the Minister-Counselor with a small staff to Canton to maintain contact with the Chinese Government, preserving the position of the Ambassador himself for future consideration, as was agreed by the chiefs of mission of the U.K., France, Netherlands, Belgium, Canada and the U.S. at Nanking on January 19 (Embassy's telegram no. 149 of January 19). Should future developments make desirable the withdrawal of the Ambassador from Nanking, the presence there of a U.S. Navy transport, together with a small complement of U.S. Marines serving as Embassy guards, would provide the necessary facilities for his departure.

A draft telegram in the sense of the foregoing recommendations is attached.[25]

W. W[ALTON] B[UTTERWORTH]

893.021/1–2649 : Telegram

The Ambassador in China (Stuart) to the Secretary of State

NANKING, January 26, 1949—6 p. m.
[Received January 27—3 : 35 a. m.]

229. Note just received from Foreign Office states they will stop receiving communications on February 3 at 5 p. m. Note adds that Foreign Office will stop work February 4 and resume work February 5 at 8 a. m. at No. 68 [–70] Fuhsing Road, Shameen, Canton.

Sent Department 229; repeated Canton 10.

STUART

701.0093/1–1949 : Telegram

The Secretary of State to the Ambassador in China (Stuart)

WASHINGTON, January 26, 1949—9 p. m.

103. Next following telegram has been authorized by Pres[ident] on understanding that these instructions will be carried out in concert with "North Atlantic group" as indicated in your 149 January 19, it being particularly important that you be not alone in remaining in Nanking when Chinese Communists take over but remain together with other Chiefs of Mission.

---

[25] Not attached to file copy; see telegram No. 104, January 26, 9 p. m., to the Ambassador in China, p. 668.

British Embassy here has been advised of US Government's decision as has French Embassy. Other Embassies will be contacted forthwith. As regards French tentative suggestion that consideration be given to question of Ambassadors going to Shanghai Department is of opinion which apparently shared by British FonOff that such course of action offers few if any advantages and that logical place for Ambassadors to stay is at Embassies in Nanking.

Department also particularly has in mind fact that when lower part of Yangtze Valley falls to Chinese Communists they will control main centers where Americans and their interests are located. While having in mind considerations enumerated in Deptel 1852 December 17 [26] it is important you draw upon your personal influence with view to protecting positions and alleviating conditions of Americans now in Communist territory and of maintaining contact with Peiping and reestablishing contact with Mukden and Tientsin.

ACHESON

---

123 Clark, Lewis: Telegram

The Secretary of State to the Ambassador in China (Stuart)

WASHINGTON, January 26, 1949—9 p. m.

104. Urtel 213 Jan 25. Min-Counselor Clark with personnel named urtel 187 Jan 22 should proceed Canton with Chi Govt. As suggested urtel 146 Jan 19, you should inform FonMin Min-Counselor with portion staff proceeding Canton pursuant Chi Govt request establish office and housing facilities and maintain contact with Govt.

Prior approaching FonMin you should inform chiefs missions with whom you discussed matter Jan 19 this Govt's decision along lines agreed by chiefs missions urtel 149. Dept similarly informing those Embs here.

Evacuation travel orders should be issued cover Min-Counselor and personnel accompanying him.

Inform all Consulates, and Lapham.

See immediately preceding telegram.

ACHESON

124.93/1-2749: Telegram

The Ambassador in China (Stuart) to the Secretary of State

NANKING, January 27, 1949—noon.
[Received January 27—2:08 a. m.]

240. In recommendations contained Embtel 187 January 22, we did take into consideration factor raised in Deptel 95, January 26. Our

---

[26] *Foreign Relations*, 1948, vol. VII, p. 658.

intention which we strongly reaffirm is a sensible reduction in Embassy staff to level commensurate with what need or can be done in backwater which Nanking promises soon to become. Latter as probability reinforced by Li Tsung-jen's personal approval last night transfer legal capital to Canton and decision to accompany or follow it himself.

We emphasize our recommendations were not for purpose evacuation. Orderly reduction in force to prospective workload would of course simplify any emergency evacuation for US representatives and any business, missionary personnel if such should later be necessary.

STUART

124.93/1–2749 : Circular telegram

The Ambassador in China (Stuart) to the Secretary of State

NANKING, January 27, 1949—5 p. m.
[Received 10:30 p. m.]

In compliance Department's instructions, Minister-Counselor Clark with requisite staff is proceeding Canton with Chinese Government and will establish section of Embassy there to be functioning not later than February 5, being date upon which Foreign Office states Government will begin functioning Canton. Ambassador will, for time being, remain Nanking with bulk Embassy staff. Shanghai please instruct Lapham.

Sent Consulates circular; repeated Department. Department pass Tientsin.

STUART

124.93/1–2749 : Telegram

The Ambassador in China (Stuart) to the Secretary of State

NANKING, January 27, 1949—6 p. m.
[Received January 27—10:11 a. m.]

249. At meeting North Atlantic group today I informed them of our decision re government's move Canton (Deptel 104, January 26), Belgian, Canadian and Netherlands Ambassadors said their instructions were to follow our lead. British expressed concurrence our decision and indication recommend strongly his Government do likewise. French Ambassador took same position, but indicated possibility which he did not believe likely his Government might require him go Shanghai. In absence Foreign Minister, I have advised senior Vice Minister Foreign Office of our decision. As press will undoubtedly become aware

of our move, we plan to state simply that Clark is proceeding with requisite staff to Canton for purpose of establishing section Embassy there and, if queried re Ambassador's movements, will say merely that he is remaining Nanking for time being. North Atlantic group agreed unanimously this policy in respect of press.

As use of airfields Nanking may be interdicted at Communists' will, Clark will plan his departure with staff on our best estimate Communist intentions.

STUART

893.01/1–2749

Memorandum by the Deputy Director of the Office of Far Eastern Affairs (Allison) to the Director of That Office (Butterworth)

[WASHINGTON,] January 27, 1949.

Mr. Daridan [27] called to say that he had been in touch with Paris on the telephone last night and has been informed that the French Ambassador in Nanking is being instructed to stay there and that the First Counselor of the French Embassy with suitable staff will proceed to Canton. Paris suggests that the Ambassadors inform the Chinese Foreign Minister that the Counselors are being sent to make preliminary preparations and that the question of the Ambassadors following will be for later decision.

As Daridan says, this is practically the same as the American position.

701.4193/1–2749

Memorandum of a Telephone Conversation, by the Chief of the Division of Chinese Affairs (Sprouse)

[WASHINGTON,] January 27, 1949.

Mr. Graves [28] telephoned this afternoon to inform me that the British Embassy had just received a message from the Foreign Office stating that instructions had been issued to the British Ambassador at Nanking to remain at that city and send the British Counselor to Canton with the Chinese Government. Mr. Graves added that the sense of instructions was similar to those he had discussed with Mr. Butterworth and me yesterday. Mr. Graves also said that the Foreign Office had informed his Embassy that the "Brussels Treaty [29] Min-

---

[27] Jean Daridan, Counselor of the French Embassy.
[28] Hubert A. Graves, Counselor of the British Embassy.
[29] Treaty for collaboration in economic, social, and cultural matters and for collective self-defence signed at Brussels, March 17, 1948; United Nations Treaty Series, vol. XIX, p. 51.

isters", now meeting in London, had issued similar instructions to their Ambassadors at Nanking. By way of clarification, he said that these were the Belgian, French and Netherlands Ministers.

124.93/1–2749 : Telegram

The Secretary of State to the Ambassador in China (Stuart)

WASHINGTON, January 27, 1949—7 p. m.

116. In view ur 240 Jan 27 Dept will act on recommendations contained in (2) urtel 187 Jan 22 as amended by second para urtel 217 Jan 26. Telegraphic instruction going out tonight.

In view considerations mentioned Deptel 95 Jan 26 you are instructed implement these transfers in manner to draw as little notice as possible and in association with movement to Canton.

ACHESON

124.93/1–2749

The Chinese Ambassador (Koo) to the Secretary of State

The Chinese Ambassador presents his compliments to the Secretary of State and, referring to the Ambassador's memorandum of January 21, 1949, has the honor to inform the Secretary that the Chinese Government has decided to move the Capital from Nanking to Canton, and that effective from February 5, 1949, Canton will be the legal seat of the Chinese Government. Every effort will be made by the Ministry of Foreign Affairs to assist the several diplomatic missions in their change of residence. To that end all the missions have been asked to send representatives to the Ministry of Foreign Affairs at their earliest convenience for consultation in regard to such removal and related matters. It is requested that the United States Government will instruct its Ambassador to China to take up his residence in Canton as soon as possible.

Pursuant to the determination of the Chinese Government to restore peace, the Executive Yuan has decided to issue cease-fire orders to its troops and designated representatives to undertake peace negotiations. However, after the lapse of six days there is still no response from the Communist Party. Instead, its armies are still exploiting every opportunity to advance. As a measure of precaution the Government has of necessity to move the Capital to the south, though it will continue to persevere in the effort to bring peace to the nation.

WASHINGTON, January 27, 1949.

124.93/2–149 : Telegram

The Ambassador in France (Caffery) to the Secretary of State

PARIS, February 1, 1949—1 p. m.
[Received 7:37 p. m.]

395. According Foreign Office, Soviet Ambassador, Nanking, informed French Ambassador January 30, he had received instructions to accompany Chinese Government to Canton. We had previously informed Foreign Office contents Deptel 104, January 26 to Nanking, repeated Paris 236, and Foreign Office would appreciate being informed whether we contemplate any changes as result Soviet decision.[30]

CAFFERY

893.01/2–349

The Chinese Ambassador (Koo) to the Secretary of State

The Chinese Ambassador presents his compliments to the Secretary of State, and, pursuant to instructions, has the honor to refer to the Ambassador's Memorandum of January 21, 1949, and note of January 27, 1949, concerning the transfer of the Capital of China from Nanking to Canton, and to inform the Secretary that the Ministry of Foreign Affairs will cease to function at Nanking as from February 3, 1949, at five o'clock P. M., and that beginning from February 5th it will resume its duties at the new office located in No. 68–70 Fu Hsing Road, Canton. All diplomatic missions are requested to conduct their business with the Chinese Government at Canton from the latter date. The Shanghai Office of the Ministry of Foreign Affairs is also to be closed on February 3rd.

Beginning February 5th, Nanking and Shanghai will be considered as military areas. The local military and police forces will do their utmost to render due protection to the lives and property of the foreign diplomatic and consular personnel. The Chinese Government earnestly hopes that the foreign diplomatic and consular officers in the above-mentioned places will endeavor to cooperate with the local military and police authorities so as to ensure their fullest personal safety.

After February 5th, all foreign diplomatic and consular representatives remaining in Nanking and Shanghai are requested to deal with the municipal governments in matters of a local nature.

It is hoped that all the diplomatic missions will complete their transfer to Canton by February 8th.

WASHINGTON, February 3, 1949.

---

[30] In his telegram No. 321, February 3, 5 p. m., the Secretary of State responded that the Department did not contemplate any change.

124.93/2–449 : Circular telegram

The Ambassador in China (Stuart) to the Secretary of State

NANKING, February 4, 1949.
[Received February 4—12:05 a. m.]

308. (1) Minister Clark on January 31 established "Office of the Embassy, Canton". Foreign Office will open Canton February 5 and hereafter all communications requesting representations to Foreign Office or other National Government office should be addressed Canton.

(2) Consulates should address all communications intended for that office "AmEmbassy Canton" in order distinguish from communications for Consulate General, Canton and should use separate number series.

(3) Administrative matters will continue to be handled by American Embassy, Nanking.

(4) Reduction staff Nanking makes impossible handling normal flow press telegrams and preparation weekly press review. Therefore, request telegrams quoting local vernacular or English press be sent directly Department, repeating Nanking for information as long as possible.

Circular February 4, repeated Department 308.

STUART

701.4193/2–1849 : Telegram

The Ambassador in China (Stuart) to the Secretary of State

NANKING, February 18, 1949—9 p. m.
[Received February 19—5:27 a. m.]

422. On call of French Ambassador as *doyen*, British, French, Canadian, Netherlands, Belgian Ambassadors and I met informally again February 16. British Ambassador accompanied by Lamb [31] and I by Merchant.

Meeting obviously inspired by British Ambassador who launched carefully prepared argument designed to secure agreement all present that they should remain Nanking through take-over and shortly thereafter, having accomplished personally whatever possible to protect their national interests and citizens, be recalled by their governments for consultation.

Discussion following recommendation revealed high degree unanimity. I reserved, however, my position regarding possible move or character recommendations I might later make to Department on this subject.

I was interested to observe whereas French Ambassador personally sympathized British views expressed he made plain that, in light prob-

---

[31] Lionel H. Lamb, British Minister in China.

lem and contiguity of French Indochina, his Government held firmly
to belief that Nationalist Government should be supported as long
as it continued resistance to Communists and that continued resistance
if only for matter of months might be of unpredictable value.

Repeated OffEmb Canton 85.

STUART

893.00/3-1749 : Telegram

The Ambassador in China (Stuart) to the Secretary of State

NANKING, March 17, 1949—11 a. m.
[Received March 17—1 : 13 a.m.]

587. Recent meeting North Atlantic Group discussed withdrawal
or reduction foreign missions' representation in Canton. Meeting apparently called at suggestion British Ambassador who showed active
interest in topic. He seemed to feel not more than merest token was
necessary which may be personal or one more indication his Government's pragmatic attitude toward Chinese political changes.

I argued for postponement any general action though each mission
was of course free to make any shifts in personnel. I felt it would be
premature make any significant changes at least until new Cabinet [32]
officially announces its intention to be located Nanking and informs us
what units will be retained Canton. There is also possibility prospective
peace negotiations may fail and National Government move south.
Moreover, there would be political consequences to various Chinese
factions including those within Kmt [33] if we seemed to be committing
ourselves by any departure from present arrangements.

All present agreed to call new problem to attention their governments but suggest there be no significant change until more is known
of possible developments.

Sent Department, repeated Canton 165, Shanghai 267.

STUART

893.00/4-149 : Telegram

*The Minister-Counselor of Embassy in China (Clark) to the Secretary
of State*

CANTON, April 1, 1949—2 p. m.
[Received 9 : 35 p. m.]

Cantel 183. Foreign Office unable confirm press report Executive
Yuan decision chiefs of mission and Political Vice Minister to be

---

[32] For documentation on formation of the Cabinet under General Ho Ying-chin,
see pp. 180 ff.
[33] Kuomintang (Nationalist Party).

stationed Nanking, leaving administrative Vice Ministers and administrative units Canton. Am informed George Yeh, Political Vice Minister, Foreign Office, coming Canton next week and that definite decision Foreign Office will be taken that time.

Even though press reports prove correct, it would seem necessary retain office Embassy Canton carry on routine business. Also pending clarification peace negotiations situation, believe I should remain here. Considerations originally making desirable my removal Canton appear still valid. I continue convinced inevitable failure peace negotiations with likely resulting forced move Government from Nanking in which case someone should be free and available continue US representation.

Sent Department Cantel 183, repeated Nanking 169.

CLARK

701.4193/4–949

Memorandum of Conversation, by the Chief of the Division of Chinese Affairs (Sprouse)

[WASHINGTON,] April 9, 1949.

Subject: Status of Foreign Chiefs of Mission at Nanking

Mr. Graves called by appointment this morning to inform me of the British Embassy's receipt of a telegram from the British Foreign Office regarding a further meeting of the North Atlantic group of chiefs of mission at Nanking. He handed me a paper (attached) containing pertinent excerpts from the Foreign Office telegram and explained that the British continued to maintain the position that the chiefs of mission should remain at Nanking in the event of a breakdown of the negotiations between the National Government and the Communists. He emphasized that it was considered of great importance that a common front be maintained in regard to this question.

In reply to his inquiry, I stated that Ambassador Stuart had not reported the results of this meeting at Nanking but that he was under a standing directive to seek the Department's instructions in the event that circumstances should warrant reconsideration of this question. I added that the Department's position in this regard had not changed and that it was still contemplated that Ambassador Stuart would remain in Nanking in the event of a breakdown in the negotiations. I concluded that I would, however, discuss the matter with Mr. Butterworth during the weekend and get in touch with him on Monday to confirm that there had been no change in the Department's position.

[Annex]

The British Embassy to the Department of State

1. We consider it to be of great importance that a common front should be maintained in regard to the question of the locale of our representation in China.

2. The probable consequences of premature abandonment of our position at Nanking would be that we would jeopardise our chance of establishing satisfactory relations with a communist dominated China, and we should be abandoning our commercial interests in the areas already over-run by them. The position of our Consulates in communist occupied areas might become intolerable and we might have to withdraw them.

3. In the view of His Majesty's Government there still remains no prospect that, if the National Government were to move in its entirety to the south, it would be capable of setting up an effective administration which could resist the communist advance. In these circumstances we very much hope that the United States Government will feel disposed to instruct its representative to remain in Nanking subject to discretion being given to withdraw in a case of exceptional emergency.

893.00/4–1149 : Telegram

The Secretary of State to the Ambassador in China (Stuart)

WASHINGTON, April 11, 1949—9 p. m.

447. British, French and Canadian Embs Washington inform Dept at recent meeting North Atlantic group chiefs mission Nanking general agreement reached chiefs mission would remain Nanking regardless outcome current peace negotiations. British Govt expresses hope US Govt will instruct you remain Nanking subject discretion being given withdraw in case of exceptional emergency and also indicates importance attached to maintaining common front re location chiefs of mission in China.

Dept has informed these Embs US Govt position remains unchanged and that it expects you remain Nanking along with other foreign chiefs mission.

ACHESON

123 Stuart, J. Leighton : Telegram

The Ambassador in China (Stuart) to the Secretary of State

NANKING, April 12, 1949—5 p. m.
[Received April 12—9 : 04 a. m.]

750. Recent developments seem to make desirable review our policy should I be requested by Acting President [34] to accompany him south after breakdown peace negotiations (Deptel 103, January 26). New factors are involved which were not present at time Chinese Government moved to Canton and I and other chiefs of mission of North Atlantic community decided to stay Nanking. Briefly new factors are:

(1) Anticipated invitation this time will come in earnest from Acting President and not technically as it did last January. It is assumed request will not come until Li himself is ready to leave Nanking with his cabinet. With such departure there will be no national authority left in the capital to which diplomatic corps might be accredited.

(2) While there was no support for Generalissimo and Sun Fo Government last January among people in any thing but peace policy, we must recognize increased stature of and political support for Li Tsung-jen which he might well maintain into resistance phase if forced to defend militarily national territory by deliberate attack from Communists such as crossing Yangtze during peace negotiations.

(3) Treatment of our consular officers by Communist officials in north as well as development of Chinese Communists' foreign policy in their public pronouncements has in past 6 weeks only added confirmation of their hostility to occident beginning with USA. If Communists have in all this period refused recognize official status of consular officers, how much less may they be expected to recognize official status of diplomatic corps accredited to another government or have any dealings with it.

Factors which conditioned my recommendations and Department's decision in January that I remain in Nanking with other chiefs of mission and which are still valid are :

(1) Little possibility of effective military resistance on national scale to Communists once they successfully cross Yangtze in force.

(2) Move of chiefs of diplomatic missions to Canton would undoubtedly strengthen Li's Government and give its supporters moral encouragement but would not by itself have effect of creating will to resist in south.

(3) Move of chiefs of mission to Canton might have serious repercussions on foreign nationals and interests in Yangtze basin and be considered by Americans remaining here as abandonment by their government of them and their interests.

(4) Presence Diplomatic Corps in Nanking might have salutary effect on Communists when they over-run lower and middle Yangtze cities. It is likely to be embarrassment to Communists.

[34] Li Tsung-jen.

(5) We might lose friendly relationship with Chinese people by identifying ourselves in move to Canton with political party that has so completely lost public support, particularly should Generalissimo again take over leadership of Government if and when Li's peace efforts fail. Certainly my transfer to Canton under such circumstances would end for all time any personal influence I might have in Chinese thinking circles and make it impossible for me to ameliorate conditions under which Americans may live in Communist-dominated China.

(6) While recognizing likelihood of being ignored and object of studied slights from local Communist authorities in remaining Nanking, onus for bad relationship would clearly be on Communists which would not be lost on those Chinese who also remain behind.

In reviewing this situation and recommending it for Department's consideration I have very much in mind heavy responsibility which rests on US Government in decision to leave Nanking with National Government or await Communists. Whatever decision I make will most assuredly be followed by other chiefs of mission of North Atlantic community, and what that group decides will set the pattern for most if not all of rest of corps. It is greatest concern among my colleagues that we follow similar course and particularly that British and ourselves keep in step.

There are three possible courses of action open to me:

(1) That I accept Li's invitation and follow him in flight to Canton,
(2) That I remain in Nanking, regardless of Li's movements, with other chiefs of mission,
(3) That I be recalled to Washington for consultation at time Li asks me to move south and before occupation Nanking.

I have discussed this problem with Clark and Merchant who have been in Nanking week end. Clark favors third alternative, Merchant was inclined to second though he has not seen this telegram. Jones [35] considers either first or third alternative preferable to second. My personal inclination is to remain in Nanking (second course) for same reasons that brought me to that decision last January and outlined above.

While Acting President has made no suggestion of move or his future plans, I anticipate invitation to Diplomatic Corps as soon as peace negotiations clearly break down. I would be grateful for Department's guidance earliest.

Sent Department 750, repeated AmEmbassy Canton 244, Shanghai 363, Taipei.

STUART

---

[35] J. Wesley Jones, Counselor of Embassy in China.

893.00/4–1249 : Telegram

The Secretary of State to the Ambassador in China (Stuart)

WASHINGTON, April 12, 1949—7 p. m.

451. Urtel 750 Apr 12 apparently crossed Deptel 447 Apr 11. Dept concurs ur recommendation remain Nanking for reasons outlined Emb reftel.

ACHESON

893.00/4–1349 : Telegram

The Ambassador in China (Stuart) to the Secretary of State

NANKING, April 13, 1949—10 a. m.
[Received April 12—11 : 27 p. m.]

756. It was not my understanding that any agreement, general or otherwise, was reached at last meeting (April 6) of North Atlantic group chiefs mission Nanking or recommendations to respective governments in event peace negotiations broke down and Acting President invited us follow him south. (Deptel 447, April 11.) While my British colleague pressed hard for agreement on recommendation that chief of mission remain Nanking, meeting was primarily devoted to discussion of Communist ultimatum (see mytel 716, April 6, repeated Canton 228 [36]) in light this development it was agreed to defer decision on any recommendations for few days. Review of pertinent factors, new developments with alternative courses and recommendations have been sent in separate telegram [37] which I commend to Department's consideration before making final decision my future movements.

Sent Department 756, repeated OffEmb Canton 245.

STUART

123 Stuart, J. Leighton : Telegram

The Minister-Counselor of Embassy in China (Clark) to the Secretary of State

CANTON, April 14, 1949—4 p. m.
[Received 9 : 22 p. m.]

Cantel 213. My reasoning in preferring third alternative regarding Ambassador's movements, Nanking's 750, April 12 to Department, repeated Canton 244, Shanghai 363, Taipei unnumbered, is as follows :

---

[36] *Ante*, p. 229.
[37] Telegram No. 750, April 12, 5 p. m., p. 677.

Should Ambassador remain Nanking despite invitation Acting President accompany him Canton, such action would unquestionably have adverse effect on morale those advocating further resistance and tend discredit Nationalist Government. Agree, however, that for Ambassador accept invitation and proceed Canton would likely end for all time any personal influence he might have in Chinese thinking circles and make it impossible for him assist Americans remaining Communist-dominated China. On the other hand, should he remain Nanking we may anticipate that he will be subjected to indignity of being ignored while treated with correctness as private individual. In view action Communists in respect of Consular offices North China, find it difficult believe presence Ambassador Nanking after departure Acting President and Government would accomplish any purpose other than that which I gather is envisaged by Dr. Stuart; namely, to demonstrate to Chinese coming under Communist domination our availability to Communist approach in effort reach some *modus vivendi* with resulting discredit to Communists when they fail take advantage opportunity.

Third course of action seems offer avoidance discrediting Nationalist Government, avoiding subjecting Ambassador to indignities or prejudicing his position while at same time holding him available on consultation in US ready to return either to Canton or to Communist-dominated territory as circumstances and our interests seem to dictate.

I agree desirability agree action among principally interested nations, particularly North Atlantic community, yet feel all with possible exception British seek our guidance.

Sent Department, repeated Nanking 188, Shanghai 138, Taipei 3.

CLARK

893.00/4–1949 : Telegram

The Ambassador in China (Stuart) to the Secretary of State

NANKING, April 19, 1949—3 p. m.
[Received April 19—7 : 17 a. m.]

792. Acting President has sent Embassy message re his future plans in face of unacceptable Commie peace terms. President Li will stay Nanking as long as possible and then will go Canton. He expressed hope that I would go with him at that time. (See Deptel 447, April 11.) Li said while he recognized French Ambassador was Dean of Corps he was addressing informal invitation to me first because he felt sure others would follow US lead. In his message to me Li used arguments ranging from personal considerations for my comfort and welfare to official responsibilities toward his Government. I intend to send oral reply that I do not make these decisions myself; that my instructions

since move of Government to Canton early February have not been altered, that I will report his suggestion to my Government and that I have most sympathetic understanding of his problem.

Sent Dept; repeated AmEmbassy Canton 266, Shanghai 394.

STUART

---

123 Stuart, J. Leighton : Telegram

The Ambassador in China (Stuart) to the Secretary of State

NANKING, April 22, 1949—11 a. m.
[Received April 21—11:22 p. m.]

813. Prime Minister telephoned early this morning to tell me Communist forces have already crossed Yangtze at Chiangyin. He advised that I proceed first to Shanghai, adding that Government would go to Canton very shortly. Subsequently Vice Minister Foreign Affairs called with similar message and added that Ministry was informing other missions Nanking similarly suggesting they also move Canton.

Sent Department 813; repeated Shanghai 409, OffEmb Canton 276.

STUART

701.0093/4–2249 : Telegram

The Ambassador in China (Stuart) to the Secretary of State

NANKING, April 22, 1949—3 p. m.
[Received April 22—7:51 a. m.]

822. I attended meeting this morning called by Dean of Diplomatic Corps of all chiefs of mission yet Nanking. French Ambassador read brief communication from Chinese Foreign Office Canton inviting attention of foreign Embassies to earlier communication re move of Govt to Canton February 5. Foreign Office note continued that in light of grave developments military situation making Nanking war area and concern of Foreign Office for safety welfare of chiefs of mission and other members Diplomatic Corps their attention is again called to earlier note regarding present seat of Chinese Government. I and several other chiefs mission stated that we had no change in earlier instructions to remain Nanking for time being. That seemed to be general sense of instructions to other chiefs of mission. Meeting ended with implied understanding that chiefs of mission would remain in capital. Those present were French, British, Belgian, Netherlands, Indian, Iranian, Burmese, Egyptian and American Ambassadors, Portugese and Afghan Ministers, Swiss and Philippine Chargés and Canadian First Secretary representing Ambassador.

Sent Department 822, repeated Shanghai 413, AmEmb Canton 278.

STUART

123 Stuart, J. Leighton

Memorandum by the Assistant Secretary of State for United Nations Affairs (Rusk) to the Secretary of State

[WASHINGTON,] April 22, 1949.

Mr. Butterworth has recommended the attached telegram [38] to Nanking. It instructs Ambassador Stuart to return to the United States for consultation after Communist occupation of Nanking. Mr. Butterworth wishes you to know that his primary purpose in making this recommendation is to help meet the domestic political situation in this country which would be created by leaving Ambassador Stuart in Nanking indefinitely following upon Communist occupation.

Although I have had misgivings about Ambassador Stuart's remaining in Nanking, I have concurred on the ground that he might be of some use in establishing contacts with and getting information from Communist authorities and might, in addition, offer effective protection to American lives and property in Communist-held areas.

I concur in the attached telegram.

___

123 Stuart, J. Leighton : Telegram

The Secretary of State to the Ambassador in China (Stuart)

WASHINGTON, April 22, 1949—7 p. m.

510. ReDeptel 451, Apr 12. After further consideration various points raised urtel 750, Apr 12, Dept continues concur ur position you shld remain Nanking during Commie takeover as was agreed with Nanking reps other powers with which you have been acting in concert. Foll firm establishment Commie regime Nanking, however, Dept desires you proceed Washington under TO 9–14712 [38a] Apr 21 for period consultation. On occupation Nanking by Commies, therefore, Dept intends make announcement to press along foll lines: Amb Stuart has remained Nanking during takeover by Commies in order extend insofar as possible appropriate protection Amer civilians and Emb staff. He has been instructed proceed Washington for consultation in event Commie occupation as soon as he is assured re safety welfare Amer community.

You are authorized inform interested Ambs US intention this regard in order enable those powers take similar action if they so desire. Dept informing Washington representatives those powers. Means egress foll Commie occupation necessarily left ur discretion, but Dept prefers you not proceed via Canton or Taiwan. On departing China you shld proceed to US by most direct expeditious route available (preferably by air) and shld not make any comment re situation

___

[38] No. 510, *infra.*
[38a] Travel Order.

China pending consultations Washington. Clark will act as Chargé in Canton during ur absence China.

ACHESON

124.93/4–2349 : Telegram

The Minister-Counselor of Embassy in China (Clark) to the Secretary of State

CANTON, April 23, 1949—9 a. m.
[Received April 23—1 : 03 a. m.]

Cantel 254. Received today urgent FonOff note referring note January 25 and urging that because Nanking has become war area, Embassy take action move Canton as requested previous note.

Sent Department, repeated Nanking 213.

CLARK

---

123 Stuart, J. Leighton : Telegram

The Secretary of State to the Ambassador in China (Stuart)

WASHINGTON, April 23, 1949—11 a. m.

513. Dept wishes to be sure that implications of its 510 Apr 22 are not misunderstood : It assumes you will not depart from China before communicating with it for final confirmatory instructions unless communications are entirely severed.

ACHESON

124.936/4–2349 : Telegram

The Ambassador in China (Stuart) to the Secretary of State

NANKING, April 23, 1949—5 p. m.
[Received April 23—8 : 59 a. m.]

840. April 23 burned bulk of classified files. Small amount classified material, currently needed codes and code machine not being destroyed for time being.

Sent Department; repeated Shanghai 426, AmEmb Canton 288.

STUART

---

123 Stuart, J. Leighton : Telegram

The Ambassador in China (Stuart) to the Secretary of State

NANKING, April 23, 1949—6 p. m.
[Received April 23—7 : 24 a. m.]

841. I shall of course comply with Department's instructions but feel moral position in Chinese people's eyes achieved by my remaining

Nanking during take-over would be largely vitiated if my departure after establishment Communist authorities were precipitate. In addition to assuring myself of the safety and welfare of the American community following the establishment of Communist authorities, I would also like to remain sufficient period to give any high ranking Communist authorities opportunity to approach me should they desire.

Estimating 1 week firm establishment Communist regime Nanking and allowing 2 weeks thereafter for above considerations, securing transportation and arranging exit, I suggest departure from here for US approximately May 14. Does Department approve this timetable? Urgent reply requested.

Sent Department, repeated OffEmb Canton 289, Shanghai 428, Canton pass Taipei 45.

STUART

123 Stuart, J. Leighton: Telegram

The Secretary of State to the Ambassador in China (Stuart)

WASHINGTON, April 23, 1949—1 p. m.

515. You will have seen from Deptel 513 Apr 23 which crossed your 841 Apr 23 that it is not Dept's intention that you should make precipitous departure from China following Commie takeover. On contrary Dept attaches greatest importance your attempting informally to regularize situation of Amer communities in Commie territory and of Amer Cons therein.

ACHESON

123 Stuart, J. Leighton: Telegram

The Ambassador in China (Stuart) to the Secretary of State

NANKING, April 24, 1949—11 a. m.
[Received April 23—11:52 p. m.]

850. Acting President sent me personal message Saturday [39] morning through Minister of Education renewing his plea that I leave for Shanghai and expressing concern for my personal safety. French Ambassador as Dean of Corps also received renewed invitation from Acting Foreign Minister to follow Government. He replied, after consultation with me and my British colleague, that the Chiefs of Mission had decided to remain in Nanking for the present and that in any event it was probably too late to do otherwise.

Sent Department 850; repeated OffEmb Canton 296, Shanghai 436.

STUART

[39] April 23.

701.0093/4–2449 : Telegram

The Ambassador in China (Stuart) to the Secretary of State

NANKING, April 24, 1949—noon.
[Received April 24—1:36 a. m.]

851. At meeting Chiefs of Mission North Atlantic Community last week question our position under Communist local regime discussed. It was considered desirable that representatives of North Atlantic Community, if possible, of all other countries maintaining Missions here, follow similar line of conduct vis-à-vis new authorities. It was suggested and generally agreed that after establishment Communist regime Nanking each Mission would send representative to highest local authority notifying him of existence of Chief of Mission and his staff in Nanking and handing him list of Government owned or occupied properties. Only point of discussion which we agreed to refer to our Governments for decision was whether representative should be diplomatic officer or consular officer. Since relations with local authorities are generally carried on by consular officer and since no question of recognition is necessarily involved in contacts between consular officers and local *de facto* authorities, it was argued that each Mission should use consular officer as its spokesman. On other side it was argued that consular officers had received short shrift in North China from Communists; that Diplomatic Corps was something new for Communists and they should therefore be approached on diplomatic level and that communication to them would merely be notification of Diplomatic Mission's presence in Nanking and where its properties were, with no request for recognition, contact et cetera. Those in favor this position pointed out that this would not preclude usual approach by local consular officers on protection of foreign residents, their property, et cetera.

If Department has any suggestions or considers question approach by consular or diplomatic officer important, I would be grateful for immediate guidance. Since I have three officers with consular commissions (Bacon,[40] Clough,[41] and Cory[42]), I can easily use one of them which is what I have normally done when communicating with municipal administration in past.

Sent Department 851, repeated OffEmb Canton 297.

STUART

---

[40] Leonard L. Bacon, Second Secretary of Embassy in China and Consul at Nanking.
[41] Ralph N. Clough, Second Secretary of Embassy in China and Consul at Nanking.
[42] Thomas J. Cory, Second Secretary of Embassy in China and Consul at Nanking.

701.0093/4–2449 : Telegram

The Secretary of State to the Ambassador in China (Stuart)

WASHINGTON, April 25, 1949—1 p. m.

518. Urtel 851, Apr 24. Dept has no strong opinion re line of conduct vis-à-vis local Chi authorities and wishes leave matter in ur discretion after consultation with Fon colleagues in order you may have freedom action if necessary establish common front with other Fon missions.

For your guidance this matter, Dept believes desirable Emb representative sent establish contact with ranking local Chi authorities shld be one of consular officers named Reftel, preferably Chi speaking, who wld make approach both in consular and diplomatic capacity. Apart from question recognition involved in contacts with local Chi authorities, pattern Commie takeover Peiping and Tientsin indicates likelihood initial approach by chiefs mission themselves or by high ranking diplomatic officer wld leave diplomatic missions open to rebuff and possible loss face through refusal permit Fon representatives see other than low ranking Commie officials. In any event, unless point is carefully and clearly made, Commie authorities unlikely understand distinction between diplomatic and consular functions officers serving Fon missions.

ACHESON

701.0093/4–2549 : Telegram

The Ambassador in China (Stuart) to the Secretary of State

NANKING, April 25, 1949—7 p. m.
[Received April 25—10 : 47 a. m.]

864. At meeting of North Atlantic mission chiefs this afternoon I told them in confidence of my instructions to return to US for consultation after I had assured myself re American Consulates and communities. I told them that my most recent instruction gave me more latitude in time than I had originally understood (Deptel 515, April 23, repeated Canton Telcan 107, Shanghai 734.) British Ambassador said, in speaking for Commonwealth, that he attached greatest importance to unanimity of action of all powers represented at meeting, that he would regret action by any one country which would break this united front. The others agreed with him and it was decided that we would recommend to our governments that we should all take unanimous action with respect to Ambassadors remaining Nanking or returning home for consultation at appropriate time.

When pressed on his views on what position chiefs of mission should be, Stevenson said he felt Ambassadors should remain Nanking as long as necessary to complete their mission but this is not part of agreed recommendation.

Sent Department 864, repeated Embassy Canton 306, Shanghai 446.

STUART

[For further documentation on the continuance of Ambassador Stuart and the seat of the Embassy in China at Nanking, see pages 723 ff.]

893.00/5–649 : Telegram

The Ambassador in France (Caffery) to the Secretary of State

PARIS, May 6, 1949—2 p. m.
[Received May 6—11 : 09 a. m.]

1842. In view press reports of rapid Chinese Communist advance toward Canton, Director Far Eastern Section, Foreign Office, called us today to inquire whether our Chargé [sic] would be instructed to follow government should it be compelled to leave that city for another haven, presumably Formosa. He expressed personal view that representatives should follow government as long as we extend recognition to it, although Foreign Office would like obtain our views before final decision.

CAFFERY

893.00/5–649 : Telegram

The Secretary of State to the Ambassador in France (Caffery)

WASHINGTON, May 10, 1949—7 p. m.

1517. Urtel 1842, May 6. Too early state at this time what steps US Govt will take re diplomatic reps Canton shld Chi Govt again move capital. Decision will be made at proper moment in light *inter alia* of location new capital. Dept keeping in touch with Fr Emb Washington re this and other related matters.

ACHESON

893.01/5–1049 : Telegram

The Secretary of State to the Minister-Counselor of Embassy in China (Clark), at Canton

WASHINGTON, May 10, 1949—7 p. m.

TelCan 160. Emb Paris has forwarded inquiry from Fr FonOff re steps US Govt expects take in event Chi Govt moves capital from

Canton. Fr Emb Washington has indicated Fr considering recalling Chargé from Canton and assigning diplomatic officer "of lesser rank" to follow Govt, presumably to Taipei. Dept has informed Fr that decision not yet reached but will be made at proper moment in light *inter alia* of location new capital. Ur comments requested.[43]

ACHESON

124.93/5–1249 : Telegram

The Minister-Counselor of Embassy in China (Clark) to the Secretary of State

CANTON, May 12, 1949—4 p. m.
[Received May 13—6 : 09 a. m.]

Cantel 368. Reliable sources inform us Liu Po-cheng [44] presently has total 9 armies in vicinity Nanfeng, in eastern central Kiangsi Province. There are no reliable nor battle-tested Nationalist troops to south of this concentration. Consequently, it appears that Communists have capability take Canton within about 4 weeks, if not sooner.

In order that we may make necessary plans for evacuation Embassy Office, would appreciate you inform us if you can furnish LST or similar vessel stand by Canton for movement Embassy Office personnel, files and effects to place of safety should it become necessary.

Repeated ComNavWesPac.[45]

CLARK

893.01/5–1449 : Telegram

The Ambassador in China (Stuart) to the Secretary of State

NANKING, May 14, 1949—5 p. m.
[Received May 14—9 : 09 a. m.]

1023. In light of probability last-ditch defense tactics between Generalissimo and Li factions at time of abandonment of Canton, might it not be most practical as well as politic to have OffEmb Canton withdraw to Hong Kong to await developments. (DeptelCan 160, May 10, repeated Nanking 57, Shanghai 895.) Could appropriately be explained we were awaiting accommodations new provisional capital.

Sent Department 1023, repeated AmEmb Canton 415, Shanghai 573.

STUART

---

[43] For Minister Clark's reply, see his telegram Cantel No. 379, May 14, noon, p. 316.
[44] Chinese Communist commander in Central China.
[45] Commander, U.S. Naval Forces, Western Pacific, Vice Adm. Oscar C. Badger.

893.01/5–1849 : Telegram

The Minister-Counselor of Embassy in China (Clark) to the Secretary of State

CANTON, May 18, 1949—9 p. m.
[Received May 18—6 : 53 p. m.]

Cantel 404. Despite continuing efforts both sides, there remains little or no likelihood Generalissimo and Li Tsung-jen factions can compose their differences to point where Nationalist China will again have effective functioning government. Mutual distrust is too deep-seated to permit unified action and everyone seems to be going around in circles.

It now appears that Li plans move Government Chungking when Canton becomes untenable. Many Government functionaries in lower levels have been refusing come Canton from Shanghai and there is increasing evidence that lower echelons in Government circles will remain Canton, come what may; thus only ranking officials would proceed Chungking. From Chungking Li will attempt continue resistance based on southwest.

In view Communist superior military potential, length tenure this transplanted administration is almost wholly at pleasure Communist military leaders. Li himself is well aware insecurity his position and is even better aware comparative security Generalissimo faction with its control Taiwan. Both groups appreciate defensive value Formosa Strait and both believe that our strategic requirements will compel us keep Taiwan in hands non-Communists' administration.

While Li continues efforts organize resistance in hope of establishing bargaining position with Communists, his basic concern appears to be question of ultimate leadership of anti-Communist resistance movement which will have some hope, however remote, of forming successor government to forthcoming Communist regime. He greatly fears that when this time comes Generalissimo and his followers will be firmly entrenched Taiwan under our protection while he and his followers will be dispersed group political refugees.

These factors should, we believe, be taken into account in making decision re character our future diplomatic representation Nationalist China. To follow to new interior capital when Li leaves Canton would do much convince him our genuine concern for success his efforts and allay his present fears that we regard Generalissimo and his followers as legal, logical and desirable political heirs non-Communist China. However, in our judgment, this advantage would be outweighted by fact that appearance of support of Li such mission would inevitably give would serve as occasion for requests for more tangible evidence in terms of material aid of our desire that Li succeed. Our failure respond favorably such requests would doubtless vitiate any improvement Li's morale resulting from dispatching mission in first instance. Also, military capabilities seem guarantee that Li's efforts resistance southwest may be short-lived at best. To encourage him, however tacitly, attempt course action for which he lacks capabilities will be in long run to gain his ill-will. Finally, transplanted Government will be no more than administrative façade and doubtless will be forced flee again at will Communists so that our continued close association with it might develop comic aspects. For these reasons it seems to us difficult to perceive developments that would warrant planning for OffEmb accompanying Government when it leaves for interior.

There is another aspect, however. When Li moves west it seems evident considerable portion those at present supporting regime will choose security under Generalissimo [on] Taiwan and that others will seek safety Hong Kong, Macao or elsewhere. It is entirely possible, though we believe unlikely, that Generalissimo may choose resume presidency at time Li Tsung-jen leaves Canton, or he may bide his time until Li is forced from his new capital in Chungking and then resume authority. Even though Generalissimo should emerge when Canton falls, we think it would be great mistake for mission proceed Taiwan. To do so would not only have disastrous effect on Li faction, but would confirm Generalissimo and followers in conviction circumstances forced us protect and preserve them against any contingency and despite their own shortcomings.

In this situation it appears at this stage that our best policy would be to close Embassy office Canton when Government leaves this city and that whatever further relations are maintained with Nationalist Government or its constituent parts be carried out through appropriate consular officers. Final decision must of necessity await the event, but we felt the above views might help the Department in its planning.

Sent Department Cantel 404; repeated Nanking 296, Shanghai 250.

CLARK

701.0093/5–1949 : Telegram

The Minister-Counselor of Embassy in China (Clark) to the Secretary of State

CANTON, May 19, 1949—9 a. m.
[Received 12:04 p. m.]

Cantel 414. FonOff now in process burning portion their files and packing remainder for shipment. Junior officers have been told that bulk of them are to go Chungking with small number sent Taipei.

Section FonOff which arranged movement Diplomatic Corps Canton states their belief Chinese Government does not now have facilities move even small number diplomats presently Canton to Chungking. Sent Department Cantel 414; repeated Nanking 304, Shanghai 256.

CLARK

124.93/5–2049 : Telegram

The Secretary of State to the Minister-Counselor in China (Clark), at Canton

WASHINGTON, May 20, 1949—7 p. m.

TelCan 215. For ur info only Dept's tentative view generally coincides with conclusions reached final par Cantel 404, May 18 (rptd Nanking 296, Shanghai 250) but Dept is of opinion US Govt shld continue avoid acting unilaterally. You are therefore authorized sound out as on ur own initiative dipl reps other friendly Fon powers now stationed Canton with view establishing line concerted action. Inform Dept results ur discussions. You shld meanwhile give consideration question adequate consular representation Chungking in event Chi Govt or substantial portion thereof moves there. Wld appear desirable send in necessary personnel before move announced in order transportation may be assured. Having in mind Van den Arend [46] now on stat leave and no language officer at post, Dept wld appreciate ur suggestion re suitable and available personnel who might be transferred or detailed Chungking.

ACHESON

701.0093/5–2549 : Telegram

The Ambassador in China (Stuart) to the Secretary of State

NANKING, May 25, 1949—4 p. m.
[Received May 26—2 : 54 a. m.]

1109. [To Canton:] Papal internuncio favors sending his representative now Canton to Hong Kong when Nationalist Government evacuates provisional capital, to await developments there (re Cantel [TelCan] 215, May 20 to [from] you, repeated Nanking 621, Shanghai 1015). Australians have indicated similar plans. No indication from other Missions their plans but many have asked us. If you would like us to assist here in sounding out view of Chiefs of Mission in compliance Department's reftel, please let us know.

Sent OffEmb Canton 462, repeated Department.

STUART

---

[46] Frederik van den Arend, Consul General at Chungking.

124.93/5-2549 : Telegram

The Ambassador in China (Stuart) to the Secretary of State

NANKING, May 25, 1949—5 p. m.
[Received May 26—2 : 29 a. m.]

1115. We wish to commend Clark's excellent analysis Nationalist Government present situation, future moves and express agreement with conclusions reached regarding future OffEmb Canton (see Cantel 404, May 18 to Department, repeated Nanking 296, Shanghai 250). While we had felt Hong Kong offered ready interim refuge US representation Nationalist Government (see Embtel 1023 to Department May 14, repeated Canton 415, Shanghai 573), we agree with reasons so well stated by Canton that OffEmb might equally well be closed when Nationalist Government is forced to evacuate present provisional capital and that we maintain in future our relations with remnants Nationalist Government through Consulates. As suggested in Deptel 215, May 20 to Canton, repeated Nanking 621, Shanghai 1015, Consulate Chungking should be strengthened. Edgar,[47] Taipei, may also need assistance.

Under arrangement envisaged above, it is assumed Embassy would remain Nanking and that contact with Nationalist Government could be maintained by it through appropriate Consulates as long as Embassy has access to communication facilities. In a technical sense at least such an arrangement could be said to avoid hiatus diplomatic relations with a Chinese Government.

All indications are that Communists are in no hurry to establish Central Government. We anticipate lapse of several months before there is anything to recognize on national scale even informally on Communist side. Regardless of where PCC[48] may be held or ["]government" established, we believe it useful providing of course new authorities permit to maintain Embassy establishment at Nanking after departure Ambassador (ReCantel 337 to Department May 9,[49] repeated Nanking 259, Shanghai 217). Physically Embassy to China is in Nanking and it would seem appropriate for remnant of it at least to remain in capital until (1) it can move with deliberateness and facility to new capital, or (2) enter into formal relations with new government in Nanking, or (3) be withdrawn from China altogether after efforts have been made and failed to establish formal friendly relations on *de jure* basis. There is every indication that even when Chiefs of Mission are withdrawn for consultation respective countries, their staffs will remain and that some kind of diplomatic establishments

---

[47] Donald D. Edgar, Consul at Taipei.
[48] Political Consultative Conference.
[49] *Post*, p. 740.

will continue to be maintained by other powers here. Presumably we would not wish to take unilateral action in closing out our diplomatic establishment in China.

We would be grateful for Department's views on this problem involving our future arrangements and Department's plans for Ambassador after period consultation Washington.

Sent Department; repeated OffEmb Canton 464, Shanghai 628.

STUART

893.01/5–2649 : Telegram

The Minister-Counselor of Embassy in China (Clark) to the Secretary of State

CANTON, May 26, 1949—3 p. m.
[Received May 27—8 : 47 a. m.]

Cantel 477. Grateful Department tentative views contained TelCan 215, May 20; repeated Nanking 621, Shanghai 1015, re removal Government. Had already been casually canvassing colleagues on subject. British Ambassador has, subject Foreign Office approval, directed Counselor [at] Canton proceed Hong Hong at time Government moves and await developments there. Understand from President Li Tsung-jen that Soviet representative has orders return Moscow about June 1st. Czechoslovak representative confirms this and says Soviet Counselor will likely remain Canton await "liberation." Czechoslovak instructions to follow Soviets. Position Netherlands representative complicated by concurrent position as ConGen Canton. He has tentative orders remain Canton but is requesting review. Canvass remaining members Diplomatic Corps indicates that those with instructions contemplate following US–UK lead and hope problem will not be made more difficult by differing action US, UK. French still hold to idea sending junior officer Chungking. Final decisions will of course be made respective Foreign Offices.

Believe British idea has merit and if situation develops as envisaged Cantel 404, May 18, it would be desirable that I be directed proceed Hong Kong with entire staff in order give Department time survey situation and make decision. If Department approves such action and can, through respective Foreign Offices, persuade UK, France do likewise, believe others, except Iron Curtain countries, will fall into line. Have discussed matter with Admiral Badger who will have US vessel in readiness Hong Kong accommodate personnel pending decision and onward transportation.

In response Department request suggesting strengthening representation Chungking, can only suggest that if services someone such as

Ringwalt [50] unavailable, then possibly Rice [51] may be spared from Manila. Understand he has required qualifications. Millet [52] should be available that time replace Rice if felt necessary.

Agree desirability immediate transfer person chosen as seems inevitable at least portion Government will move Szechuan when Canton seriously threatened. (In this connection and tending confirm my belief Taipei should also be strengthened is word from unimpeachable source that bulk Foreign Office archives are being shipped Taipei.) Chungking could be further strengthened by transfer from Embassy of cryptographic personnel to be chosen from those available at time. We are having difficulty this regard Canton as most assignees seem to resign when confronted with prospects [of leaving?] Canton. Re Taipei, see Cantel 417, May 19.[53]

Sent Department; repeated Nanking 328, Shanghai 281.

CLARK

893.01/6–149 : Telegram

The Minister-Counselor of Embassy in China (Clark) to the Secretary of State

CANTON, June 1, 1949—11 a. m.
[Received 12:55 p. m.]

Cantel 512. Called informal meeting North Atlantic Canton representatives yesterday to discuss prospective move Government from Canton. Present were British, French, Italian and Dutch representatives, Cantel 477, May 26, repeated Nanking 328, Shanghai 281. Portuguese was absent but it is known that his instructions are to follow US–UK lead.

There was complete agreement that Government would be compelled move near future; that Chungking would most likely be next capital; that Government would be most unwelcome there as inviting Communist attack; and after move Government would be mere façade of senior Ministers with no real support; that after short period time at will [of] Communist[s] Government would be forced flee further; and that move would then be Taiwan.

These conclusions are based on agreement that distrust between Generalissimo and Li Tsung-jen and their supporters is so deep as to be insurmountable; on evidence that majority Legislative Yuan, operational sections of certain Ministries and majority subordinate per-

---

[50] Arthur R. Ringwalt, former Chief of the Division of Chinese Affairs, on detail to the Naval War College.
[51] Edward E. Rice, former Assistant Chief of the Division of Chinese Affairs, Consul at Manila.
[52] Charles S. Millet, Consul at Shanghai.
[53] Not printed; it concerned reassignment of personnel to Chungking and Taipei (125.925/5–1949).

sonnel all Ministries are en route or planning to go to Taiwan, thus indicating to us that Chinese themselves admit temporary character move Chungking. It seems to us that Generalissimo is fostering move by offering some of his treasure in hope that Communists will be enticed westward, thus delaying attack Taiwan.

In light of above it was unanimously agreed that we would recommend our Governments that when confronted with request Government follow it Chungking, we be instructed reply that we would request instructions our Governments and that in meantime we would remove to Hong Kong to avoid falling into hands Communists. Such action would give our Governments opportunity survey situation and make unhurried decision re future representation Nationalist Government. At same time it would avoid discouraging forces resistance by telling them frankly we had no intention removing Chungking. Should appreciate Department's further reaction this suggestion.

British instructions remain unchanged. He has his Ambassador's direction, still unapproved by Foreign Office, to proceed Hong Kong and await developments. French [Counselor] has opened Consulate Taipei and his instructions are proceed Hong Kong and if Government removes Taipei proceed France. France had not envisaged transfer capital Chungking and he is now suggesting strengthening Consulate there and modification his instructions so as to authorize him proceed homeward in event Government moves Chungking. Position Dutch complicated by fact he is Consul General [at] Canton and his instructions are that he remain Canton. Italian, though without instructions, indicated belief he would be directed follow US–UK lead. He is recommending he be directed do so and authorized open Consulate Canton with jurisdiction Taiwan as well as west China, thus permitting him send consular representative Chungking.

If North Atlantic group is in agreement on action suggested, it is belief others, with exception Iron Curtain countries, will follow. Soviet Ambassador departed May 31 for Moscow on consultation and is not expected return.

Sent Department Cantel 512, repeated Nanking 349, Shanghai 300.

CLARK

701.5193/6–749 : Telegram

The Minister-Counselor of Embassy in China (Clark) to the Secretary of State

CANTON, June 7, 1949—5 p. m.
[Received June 8—12 : 07 a. m.]

Cantel 545. French Counselor has instructions remove to Hong Kong when requested follow government, Cantel 512, June 1, repeated Nanking 349, Shanghai 300; but French still intend send subordinate diplomatic officer Chungking. They apparently feel such action will ease blow to National Government and also permit handling some delicate problems re Indochina.

Italian Counselor has received instructions detail consular representatives Chungking. Portuguese has recommended he withdraw to Macao when requested move and says he will do so unless otherwise directed [by] Lisbon. He anticipates he will move Macao.

Sent Department; repeated Nanking 369, Shanghai 315.

CLARK

124.93/6–1049 : Telegram

The Acting Secretary of State to the Minister-Counselor of Embassy in China (Clark), at Canton

WASHINGTON, June 10, 1949—8 p. m.

TelCan 315. ReCantel 512, June 1, rptd Nanking 349, Shanghai 300. On effective withdrawal Chi Govt from Canton, you are instructed close Emb Off Canton and proceed with staff to Hong Kong under emergency evacuation orders to await further instructions re disposition staff (i.e., transfer or stat leave orders). This connection, Dept considering assignments suggested Cantel 417, May 19,[54] re strengthening staffs Taipei and Chungking.

While Dept appreciates probability any move Chi Govt to Chungking would as stated reftel be "mere façade of senior Ministers with no real support", Dept of opinion withdrawal contact with Chi Govt on diplomatic level wld be undesirable. Dept therefore assigning Strong[55] to Off Emb as First Secretary detailed to Chungking. Strong will not have dual status Chungking and will not therefore assume charge of ConGen. McGeary[56] will continue temporarily in charge but shld function under general supervision Strong in matters of policy. Strong shld occupy ConGen's residence in capacity senior Amer official Chungking. Dept desires Strong proceed immed to Canton for brief period consultation with Clark prior continuing to Chungking, but authorizes family proceed Chungking direct under emergency evacuation orders issued by Off Emb if considered advisable. Canton shld instruct Strong and inform Chungking. (Depending on local circumstances and availability transportation, Emb Off might wish authorize Strong accompany family Chungking in order arrange accommodations returning to Canton for period consultation.) Orders transferring Strong to Off Emb will be issued within week.

---

[54] Not printed.
[55] Robert C. Strong, Consul at Tsingtao.
[56] Stanley A. McGeary, Vice Consul at Chungking.

You are authorized inform at such time as you deem desirable concerned Fon Reps with whom you have been discussing matter of US plans continue diplomatic contact with Chi Govt through Strong and endeavor encourage similar action on part other Fon powers.

WEBB

893.01/6–1149

Memorandum of Telephone Conversation, by the Chief of the Division of Chinese Affairs (Sprouse)

[WASHINGTON,] June 11, 1949.

Mr. Tsui [57] telephoned this morning and stated that the Chinese Embassy had been instructed by the Foreign Office at Canton to communicate to the Department orally the following information:

In view of the military situation in south China, various Chinese Government ministries and commissions have begun the establishment of offices at Chungking in order to make appropriate preparations for the removal of the Government from Canton to that city in the future. The Chief of Protocol has informed the accredited foreign diplomatic representatives at Canton of the foregoing and has asked them to send officers from their staffs to make the necessary preliminary preparations for removal to Chungking. The Ministry of Foreign Affairs will render all possible assistance to the foreign diplomatic establishments and will pay the expenses of air transportation for travel from Canton to Chungking. Canton still remains the seat of the Government but because of the possibility of the spread of warfare to the Canton area the Chinese Government must make these preparations. In the event that the National Govenment should decide to move to Chungking, sufficient advance notice of such a decision will be given to the foreign diplomatic representatives and assistance will be given to them in moving from Canton. The Foreign Office desires that instructions be given by the concerned governments to their diplomatic representatives to accompany the Chinese Government at the time of its removal from Canton. The Foreign Office is giving no publicity to this action and would appreciate the Department's treating this information as confidential.

---

[57] Tswen-ling Tsui, Counselor of the Chinese Embassy.

893.01/6–1149 : Telegram

The Minister-Counselor of Embassy in China (Clark) to the Secretary of State

CANTON, June 11, 1949—2 p. m.
[Received June 12—3:49 a. m.]

Cantel 567. Chief Protocol Section Foreign Office called this morning under instructions Acting Minister to say in confidence that all important Ministries are proceeding immediately to establish offices in Chungking against possibility government may be compelled evacuate Canton. Ministers themselves and senior subordinates would remain Canton for present, but alerted and ready depart Chungking on very short notice.

Dr. Wang conveyed request that I arrange accompany government should it move and offered transportation as well as services Foreign Office in locating housing Chungking. Restricted my comment to expressing regret situation had deteriorated so far and promised report request Department for consideration.

Situation East River area continues deteriorate and preparations Communists Kiangsi for drive south continue with active operations on large scale expected almost any time. Reports indicate Pai Chung-hsi has insufficient money pay troops and is most discouraged. Also, in spite of reliable information previously given me to contrary, am now convinced Generalissimo has not released any his gold. Anticipate therefore final request move Chungking will likely be made early or middle July.

Sent Department, repeated Nanking 378.

CLARK

124.93/6–1349 : Telegram

The Minister-Counselor of Embassy in China (Clark) to the Secretary of State

CANTON, June 13, 1949—noon.
[Received June 13—9:12 a. m.]

Cantel 576. Have been giving further thought to action we should take when Nationalist Government finally moves Chungking (Cantel 512, June 1, repeated Nanking 349). There may be elements in situation of which I am unaware yet from here; am coming to conviction there may be some advantage in French idea of maintaining diplomatic representation Chungking at subordinate level.

Communists have publicly stated they will not recognize any government maintaining relations with Nationalist Government and, if we send no one Chungking when Govt moves, it is conceivable Communists will interpret such action in nature appeasement and greatly increase their pretensions, possibly even to extent demanding China's seat international councils immediately provisional government formed. On other hand, if we maintain representation Chungking we not only avoid possible death blow Nationalist Government, but we also demonstrate to Communists that we intend ignore their threat and will consider recognition Communist govt only upon demonstration Communist willingness and capacity meet usual international requirements. At same time we assure retention friendly Chinese vote international councils. That Nationalist Government realizes advantage this point would seem evident from action Acting Foreign Minister in endeavoring impress me intention Chinese Government henceforth almost slavishly follow our policy regarding Japan (Cantel 558, June 10 [58]). Such action might improve our position in negotiations with Communists and it might not, but thought Dept should be informed my present thinking on subject.

In early days Kmt Government we maintained relations through Consulates General and Counselor Embassy Nanking. Would it not be desirable at this time return to some such arrangement and give Strong concurrent title Secretary of Embassy at time Government moves? Giving Strong diplomatic capacity that time might be wise move for reasons given above and would enable him maintain any contacts needed with remnant Government Chungking. He could be removed elsewhere and Consulate function as heretofore when Government is forced leave Chungking as appears eventually to be inevitable. Even its most ardent supporters give it less than year in Chungking.

Repeated Nanking 383.

CLARK

893.00/6–1449 : Telegram

The Ambassador in Portugal (MacVeagh) to the Secretary of State

LISBON, June 14, 1949—4 p. m.
[Received June 14—2 : 58 p. m.]

216. Foreign Minister [59] assured me this morning that Portuguese Minister Canton has been instructed to conform actions to those of US and UK colleagues (infotel June 13, 4 a.m.[58]) ; if move made to Hong Kong, Minister will leave Consul [in] Canton to take care of Portuguese nationals.

Expressed special interest US efforts encourage western powers continue contact with Chinese Government and reiterated his belief in supreme importance concerted attitude (mytel 187, May 19[60]).

---

[58] Not printed.
[59] Dr. José Caeiro da Mata.
[60] Vol. IX, p. 26.

Added that following apparent crystallization British intention hold Hong Kong Portuguese Government sending four battalions of approximately 1,000 each to Macau, to reinforce present garrison of 2,000 plus 1,000 armed police. Two of new battalions will be Portuguese and two African native.

MACVEAGH

893.01/6–1549 : Telegram

The Minister-Counselor of Embassy in China (Clark) to the Secretary of State

CANTON, June 15, 1949—1 p. m.
[Received June 15—8 : 20 a. m.]

Cantel 592. Called informal meeting North Atlantic group yesterday to reconsider representation near Nationalist Government (TelCan 315, June 10, repeated Nanking 687, Shanghai 1169). Representatives Britain, France, Netherlands, Italy, Portugal attended. All were so enthusiastic at idea sending subordinate diplomatic officers to maintain contact Nationalist Government as to lead to believe they had gone along with previous idea almost solely so as to stay in step with US. Each anticipates some technical difficulty in securing qualified personnel and Netherlands representative feared his Ambassador would remain adamant that Nationalist Government was not worth following, but all agreed recommend strongly following our line. Will mention matter informally to other inquiring colleagues and feel sure our lead will be followed by most. Question advisability discussing matter with Soviets and am not doing so.

My plan is next few days inform Foreign Office that in response its informal request regarding Chungking, Cantel 567, June 11, repeated Nanking 378, we are sending officer Embassy Chungking to look around and make arrangements against possibility Government may move there.

Under emergency evacuation orders, am directing Strong proceed Chungking with family soon as transportation available, anticipate around June 20, and will direct him return Canton for consultation later. He has already spent 1 day with me in Canton and if things develop too quickly for him return for further consultation, no great harm will be done.

Sent Department Cantel 592, repeated Nanking 395, Shanghai 337.

CLARK

124.93/6–1849 : Telegram

The Ambassador in China (Stuart) to the Secretary of State

NANKING, June 18, 1949—6 p. m.
[Received June 19—4:51 a. m.]

1321. I have some misgivings re Department's proposal to assign Diplomatic Secretary Chungking maintain contact remnants Nationalist Government. (ReDeptel 687, June 10, sent telCan 315, repeated Shanghai 1169, and 705 June 16,[62] repeated telCan 342, Shanghai 1213.) Some of my colleagues here, particularly British Commonwealth, have been upset by this decision and obviously feel we have gotten out of line on what they consider was generally agreed policy to close offices Embassies Canton and maintain relations remnant Nationalist Government through Consular Officers. British Ambassador sent long telegram last night requesting his Government suggest US reconsider in consultation British Government.

I can see advantages to maintaining diplomatic contact with Nationalist Government as long as possible. On other hand, I feel relations could be maintained through our Consul Chungking and perhaps subsequently Taipei acting in dual capacity if considered desirable but with emphasis on Consular establishment. I recommend Strong be appointed Consul Chungking and placed in charge Consul[ate] there; that, incidentally and during time Nationalist Government would be in Chungking, he be given dual commission as Consul and First Secretary to represent Embassy near Nationalist Government; that, if and when Government moves Taipei, our Consul there be given similar dual status. I feel that our relations with diminishing Nationalist Government would be better understood in China and by Chinese people if they were maintained through already established Consulates in Chungking, etc.; that incidental commissioning of our Consul as Diplomatic Representative would be technical device, which important to Nationalist Government but not the significant factor. Britain, I believe, would go along with this.

One other factor adding my uneasiness is that we might find ourselves with only French maintaining diplomatic representation Nationalist Government Chungking. French impress me as willing to make any sacrifice their China policy in order to protect colonial holdings Southeast Asia and I would regret to see US associated with French policy Far East even by implication.

Sent Department 1321, repeated OffEmb Canton 549, Shanghai 716.

STUART

---

[62] For latter, see p. 758.

893.01/6–2249 : Circular telegram

The Secretary of State to Certain Diplomatic and Consular Offices [63]

WASHINGTON, June 22, 1949—4 a. m.

Fol for your background info:

(1) Original decision leave Amb Nanking and estab Off of Emb Canton under Min Coun was preceded by full discussion among Chiefs of Mission Nanking except Sovs and satellites and reflected general policy evolved during discussions to leave Chiefs of Mission Nanking and send ranking subordinate Canton. Shortly prior fall Nanking to Commies, Dept instructed Amb to return Washington for consultation at some future date after he had assured himself safety wellbeing Amer citizens lower Yangtze valley area. No date has been set for Amb's return to US on consultation which may be timed coincide with completion withdrawal Amer staff Mukden.

(2) Chi Govt now making active plans removal Canton to Chungking but all evidence indicates move will involve mere façade senior Mins without real support. Furthermore, no indication disappearance rift between Li Tsung-jen and Gimo factions. Consequently when Govt moves Chungking Min Coun now in charge Off Emb Canton will close office, withdraw with staff to Hong Kong while contact on dipl level with Govt at Chungking will be maintained through First Secy detailed Chungking for that purpose. Similar steps contemplated by most other dipl missions Canton with exception USSR and satellites whose plans unknown.

(3) Although Chinese Communists have not yet established regime purporting be Central Govt China, discussions and exchanges of views respecting recognition such regime if and when established have been taking place among non-Commie powers with dipl representation China. Our view which has obtained general support other powers during these discussions is (1) that concerned powers should not evidence eagerness extend recognition but that initiative this respect shld be left to Commies and (2) that countries having similar interests in China shld work out common course of action respecting recognition, commerce and protection interests guarding against efforts Commies play one country off against another to ultimate detriment all.

Sent to all China posts.

ACHESON

---

[63] Sent to the Embassy in China and Consular posts at Canton, Chungking, Dairen, Hankow, Hong Kong, Kunming, Peiping, Shanghai, Taipei, Tientsin, Tihwa, and Tsingtao.

124.93/6–2849 : Telegram

The Ambassador in China (Stuart) to the Secretary of State

NANKING, June 28, 1949—2 p. m.
[Received June 28—8:18 a. m.]

1391. ReDepcirtel June 22, 4 a. m. summarizing concise coherent manner position US Embassy China and US policy possible recognition Chinese Communist Central Government.

Only one statement, however, not in accord Embassy's understanding situation: That is last sentence paragraph 2. So far as Embassy knows, only French and US Governments have thus far decided maintain contact on diplomatic level with Government at Chungking through secretary of Embassy. (See Embtel 1321, June 18 to Department, repeated Canton 549.) If Department has confirmation this procedure from other governments, we would appreciate being informed.

Sent Department; repeated Canton 587.

STUART

893.01/6–2849 : Telegram

The Ambassador in China (Stuart) to the Secretary of State

NANKING, June 28, 1949—4 p. m.
[Received June 28—8:56 a. m.]

1396. Cantel 596, June 16,[64] repeated Nanking 398, strengthens my conviction that we should not emphasize relations at diplomatic level with Nationalist Government after it is forced to move from Canton. Inference drawn from reference telegram is that as disintegration Nationalist Government continues, there will be less apparent reason for it to move Chungking en route Taiwan. We should look carefully at what portions of Government go to Chungking eventually before sending diplomatic representative there. I again recommend Department's consideration mytel 1321, June 18 to Department, repeated Canton 549, suggesting consular officer in charge Chungking be given diplomatic status if and when Nationalist Government moves Chungking. This same device would then be useful Taiwan when Government eventually moves there. Emphasis would thus be on consular establishments in Chungking and Taipei and would not have appearance of US diplomatic representative "following" Government from one post to another. This also seems to be position generally of other diplomatic missions here.

Sent Department 1396, repeated Embassy Canton 592.

STUART

---

[64] *Ante,* p. 388.

893.01/6–2849 : Telegram

The Secretary of State to the Ambassador in China (Stuart)

WASHINGTON, June 30, 1949—3 p. m.

763. Urtel 1396, June 28. Decision detail Strong [to] Chungking prior to movement Natl Govt and solely in dipl capacity taken by Dept only after mature consideration all pertinent factors including US public opinion. Action also related to notification from FonOff of Chi Govt intention move to Chungking when situation required. Moreover, as reported in Cantel 592, June 15 (rptd Nanking 395), Canton reps Brit, Fr, Neth, Ital and Port all enthusiastic over idea and agreed recommend strongly that their Govts adopt similar procedure. Dept has recd no further info from Canton indicating Govts concerned unwilling follow US lead this matter.

Regardless action taken by other govts, however, Dept of opinion that continuity of contact on dipl level shld be maintained with Natl Govt as long as that Govt continues function on mainland and enjoy internatl recognition as sole Govt China. Shld transfer Govt to Chungking prove abortive Strong's dipl status cld be withdrawn and he assigned as Consul; but for present Dept intends proceed as outlined telCan 315 June 10 (rptd Nanking as 687).

ACHESON

124.93/7–549 : Telegram

The Minister-Counselor of Embassy in China (Clark) to the Secretary of State

CANTON, July 5, 1949—3 p. m.
[Received July 5—10: 15 a. m.]

Cantel 688. Informal survey here indicates practically all nations represented here plan send mission Chungking should Government move there, telCan 406, June 30, repeated Nanking 763.[65] French, Italian, Portuguese and Vatican representatives have received definite instructions to do so. Britain anticipates following lead, but says there is diversion in Nanking toward thought giving officer dual commission. Australians and Philippines have no instructions. Netherlands situation is complicated by recent transfer Counselor and ConGen to Hong Kong as ConGen to fill vacancy there. Burmese, Turkish and Iranian representatives expect follow our lead.

Sent Dept Cantel 688, repeated Nanking 461.

CLARK

---

[65] *Supra.*

124.93/7-849 : Telegram

The Ambassador in China (Stuart) to the Secretary of State

NANKING, July 8, 1949—11 a. m.
[Received July 8—9:25 a. m.]

1457. Apparently there is difference of opinion on type of representation Chungking between representatives Canton and Chiefs of Mission Nanking. British Ambassador frankly admits he and his Counselor Canton differ in their views desirability sending diplomatic representatives to Chungking when Government moves there (re Canton telegram 688, July 5 to Department, repeated Nanking 461). Netherlands' situation is complicated by lack of personnel, although Netherlands' Ambassador here does not personally approve of diplomatic representative ultimately Chungking. So far as I can ascertain, that seems to be view of most other Ambassadors here, many of whom are practically incommunicado and whose views are probably not known by their respective governments or vice versa.

Sent Department 1457, repeated OffEmb Canton 613.

STUART

701.4193/7-2149 : Telegram

The Minister-Counselor of Embassy in China (Clark) to the Secretary of State

CANTON, July 21, 1949—8 p. m.
[Received July 22—2:27 p. m.]

Cantel 796. British here inform me decision definitely taken have diplomatic representation Chungking through Consul General with full capacity First Secretary.

Sent Department Cantel 796, repeated Nanking 529.

CLARK

---

123 Stuart, J. Leighton : Telegram

The Chargé in China (Clark) to the Secretary of State

CANTON, August 5, 1949.
[Received August 8—4:58 p. m.]

Cantel 880. Ambassador having departed from China opening business August 2, I assumed charge that time.

Sent Department Cantel 880, repeated circular to Nanking and all Consulates China.

CLARK

124.93/8–1149 : Telegram

The Chargé in China (Clark) to the Secretary of State

CANTON, August 11, 1949—noon.
[Received 2 : 05 p. m.]

Cantel 893. Military situation deteriorating so rapidly we may be compelled leave Canton prior August 15.[66] Suggest therefore desirability expediting decision posed Cantel 883, August 5 [67] re closing Canton Consulate.

CLARK

124.936/8–1249 : Telegram

The Chargé in China (Clark) to the Secretary of State

CANTON, August 12, 1949—2 p. m.
[Received August 13—9 : 35 a. m.]

Cantel 931. After discussion matter with Nanking it appears interests all concerned best served by division supervisory responsibilities Chinese Consulates and Hong Kong between two branches Embassy with Consulates outside Red China reporting personnel changes, administrative problems, visa policy, etc., to Canton, and those inside curtain continuing report Nanking. We have been dividing responsibilities on informal basis since fall Nanking. Department has already authorized Nanking issue local travel orders posts Communist areas, with Canton issuing orders for those outside.

This telegram serves as authority Taipei, Kunming, Chungking and Hong Kong report directly us for advice and supervision. We also supervising closure Tihwa.

Nanking inform Consulates Red China.

Sent Nanking 617, repeated Department Cantel 931, Taipei 116, pouched Chungking 14, Hong Kong 40.

CLARK

124.93/8–1449 : Telegram

The Chargé in China (Clark) to the Secretary of State

CANTON, August 14, 1949—5 p. m.
[Received August 15—3 : 51 a. m.]

Cantel 938. Appreciate discretion Department re closure OffEmb Canton contained telCan 553, August 12.[68] There has been slowdown

---

[66] In telCan No. 553, August 12, p. 1313, the Department authorized closing the Embassy office "whenever in your judgment this move desirable".
[67] *Post*, p. 1308.
[68] *Post*, p. 1313.

in military advance and believe we will have longer period Canton than originally anticipated.

Discussed situation with Admiral Badger August 7 in Hong Kong and as result he is making available Hong Kong USS *Dixie* to house Embassy staff whenever I remove from Canton. Nationalist Government will have its personnel reduced to minimum by August 20 and ready for removal Chungking on very short notice. They have promised give me ample notice, yet local turnover or excitement of moment may not permit them do so.

Best military advice available indicated maximum 2 weeks likely elapse between fall either Hengyang or Kanhsien and fall Canton. There will always be danger of course overnight turnover Canton garrison as Communist troops approach city. Accordingly, I plan, unless Department directs contrary, to move personnel OffEmb Hong Kong aboard *Dixie* when either Kanhsien or Hengyang falls to Communists. Would plan commute daily Canton with nucleus staff, thus keeping OffEmb open and minimizing embarrassment Chinese Government. When Chinese Government finally requests we remove Chungking, I could merely cease coming Canton at that time. Sincerely hope Department will have ready instructions for me and staff avoiding prolonged stay Hong Kong (Cantel 919, August 10 [69]).

Sent Department, repeated Nanking 619, Hong Kong 41.

CLARK

124.93/8–1549 : Telegram

The Chargé in China (Clark) to the Secretary of State

CANTON, August 15, 1949—8 p. m.
[Received August 16—7 : 09 a. m.]

Cantel 955. Communists have surrounded Kanhsien and some elements have moved eastward indicating possibility joining with Chen Yi armies for drive East River area where conflagration may resemble prairie fire. My military advisors tell me we would run unwarranted risk were we remain Canton more than 1 week from today. Accordingly, plan begin movement Embassy personnel to *Dixie* Hong Kong Friday, August 19, operations to be completed 20th (Cantel 938, August 13 [*14*], repeated Nanking 619, Hong Kong 41), synchronizing removal with Consulate General which will report its program in separate telegram.

Office will be kept open NCB Building Canton and members staff will commute daily maintain contact Nationalist Government. Final closure Embassy will be deferred until Government requests US move

---

[69] Not printed ; it concerned reassignment of personnel (123 Lancaster, Bruce).

Chungking or elsewhere. Rumors have it, although confirmation lacking, request will be forthcoming next week.

Sent Department Cantel 955, repeated Nanking 629.

CLARK

---

123 Clark, Lewis: Telegram

The Chargé in China (Clark) to the Secretary of State

CANTON, August 17, 1949—5 p. m.

[Received August 17—10 : 57 a. m.]

Cantel 976. For Butterworth. If developments are to be as suggested your telCan 565, August 13,[70] believe I should not delay my departure later than Badger plane, etc., Manila August 28. This being so, suggest desirability directing Strong report me aboard *Dixie* early next week in order afford opportunity introduce him contacts Foreign Office and assure continuity representation near Nationalist Government. He could carry on from *Dixie* and proceed Chungking or elsewhere when Government moves, which I still anticipate may be some time next week. Have recommended [to] Strong he evacuate family because housing situation Chungking and this recommendation seems reinforced by fluidity situation China. If you agree, I will issue necessary instructions under authority already granted me. Please advise urgently.

CLARK

---

123 Clark, Lewis: Telegram

The Secretary of State to the Chargé in China (Clark), at Canton

WASHINGTON, August 17, 1949—7 p. m.

TelCan 592. From Butterworth. In light Cantel 976 Aug 17 agree desirable your departure via Badger plane about Aug 28. Well in advance departure you should call Strong to *Dixie* for purpose introducing him Foreign Office other officials explaining that you are being recalled to serve with US Delegation to UNGA.[71] Assume you will arrange Strong retain small but adequate staff presumably including China language officer in order adequately to support him in his assignment. [Butterworth.]

ACHESON

---

[70] Not printed; it requested Mr. Clark to proceed to Washington to take up a "certain appointment".

[71] United Nations General Assembly.

124.93/8–1949 : Telegram

The Chargé in China (Clark) to the Secretary of State

CANTON, August 19, 1949.
[Received August 19—1:11 a. m.]

Cantel 990. Following statement released to press at 0100 Gmt,[72] this date.[73]

"In view of the present Communist threat to this region, the American Embassy is evacuating its staff to Hong Kong. Officers of the Embassy, however, will commute daily to Canton to carry out their normal duties so long as the situation permits.

"The American Consulate General, in accordance with instructions from the Department of State, will close today and begin evacuation of its American staff. Consular officers, however, will be available to assist American citizens to evacuate and to perform for them essential consular services as long as possible. Thereafter the American Consulate General at Hong Kong will assume the functions of this Consulate General."

CLARK

124.936/8–2249 : Circular telegram

The Counselor of Embassy in China (Jones) to the Secretary of State

NANKING, August 22, 1949—3 p. m.
[Received August 22—8:05 a. m.]

1857. Deptel 969, August 16 [74] approves division Embassy's supervisory functions following basis: Consulates Communist-occupied regions continue report personnel changes, administrative problems, visa policy, etc., to Nanking, while consulates in Nationalist areas report to Embassy Canton-Hong Kong for advice and supervision.

Sent circular Shanghai, Peiping, Dairen, Embassy Canton; repeated Department and Hankow. Department pass Tientsin, Tsingtao.

JONES

---

123 Strong, Robert C.: Telegram

The Chargé in China (Strong) to the Secretary of State

CANTON, August 26, 1949—8 p. m.
[Received August 26—4:07 p. m.]

Cantel 1027. ReCantel 1014, August 23 [24].[74] Clark departed this afternoon. I assumed charge as of cob[75] August 25.

STRONG

---

[72] Greenwich mean time.
[73] This press release had been cleared with the Department on August 17.
[74] Not printed.
[75] Close of business.

124.936/9-149 : Telegram

The Chargé in China (Strong) to the Secretary of State

CANTON, September 1, 1949—2 p. m.
[Received September 1—8:21 a. m.]

Cantel 1059. Foreign Office requests OffEmb install coat of arms over USIS building Canton as symbol that US still carrying on diplomatic relations with Nationalist Government. Replied I could see no objection view almost daily visits of OffEmb staff members to Canton, using USIS building as base and as place to receive calls and written communications.

Have taken no action. Request Department's instruction, particularly view statement made August 31 by Acting Foreign Minister Yeh to British Counselor that "US Embassy returning to Canton very soon".

STRONG

124.93/9-349 : Telegram

The Chargé in China (Strong) to the Secretary of State

CANTON, September 3, 1949—5 p. m.
[Received September 3—2:14 p. m.]

Cantel 1064. Acting Foreign Minister today again guaranteed he would give 10 days' notice prior to any move Nationalist Government from Canton. However, he added that it is not yet time for him even to begin thinking about giving such notice. (In this connection it was today noted that police guard on Shameen has been considerably augmented and for first time troops were seen drilling on the island.) Acting Foreign Minister expressed unhappiness that Embassy had not accepted his assurances of ample notice and stated that diplomatic representatives other smaller countries had been noticeably affected by our decision evacuate Canton.

He went on to effect that for foreign consumption it was important that Nationalist Government hold Canton area, it being their last major exit to sea, thus much more important than Szechuan. Government still intends move Chungking if necessary. He considers best answer Nationalist Government can give to White Paper [76] will be securing Canton area against Communists.

STRONG

---

[76] Department of State, *United States Relations With China* (Washington, Government Printing Office, 1949). For documentation on the subject of the "China White Paper", see vol. IX, pp. 1365 ff.

124.931/9–349 : Telegram

The Chargé in China (Strong) to the Secretary of State

CANTON, September 3, 1949—8 p. m.
[Received September 3—1 : 19 p. m.]

Cantel 1065. Reference Cantel 1049, August 30 and 1056, August 31.[77] Personnel of Embassy and Consulate General Canton have succeeded finding acceptable temporary quarters ashore effective September 4, thus eliminating problem originally posed by departure *Dixie*.[78]

Coding machine being installed Consulate General Hong Kong afternoon September 4 under direction regional security supervisor Beman. Embassy office work apart from coding will be performed in residence [to] be occupied by Strong and Lancaster.[79] All classified files be shipped Taipei first opportunity.

STRONG

124.936/9–149 : Telegram

The Secretary of State to the Chargé in China (Strong), at Canton

WASHINGTON, September 6, 1949—6 p. m.

TelCan 651. Cantel 1059 Sept 1. Dept perceives no objection installing coat of arms, since bldg is in fact place where OffEmb carries on its official business.

Actg FonMin's statement represents of course nothing more than his own view.

ACHESON

124.93/9–1549 : Telegram

The Chargé in China (Strong) to the Secretary of State

CANTON, September 15, 1949—5 p. m.
[Received September 16—7 : 47 p. m.]

Cantel 1109. Chief of Administrative Section of FonOff yesterday dwelt at length on dissatisfaction of Chinese Government with its contacts with Embassy since had moved personnel to Hong Kong. He was very insistent that we return to Canton, with at least skeleton staff,

---

[77] Neither printed : telegram Cantel No. 1049 had to do with housing and travel problems of personnel at Hong Kong awaiting reassignment (124.93/8–3049), and telegram Cantel No. 1056 contained a recommendation that the code machine be sent to Taipei (119.25 MCA/8–3149).

[78] A regularly scheduled sailing of the *Dixie* by the Navy caused some concern to the Embassy Office because of its use of the vessel both for business and living quarters (124.93/8–2849).

[79] Bruce Lancaster, Third Secretary of Embassy in China, on detail with the Embassy Office since January.

saying current situation was highly anomalous. He cited several delays and inconveniences over important matters and stated that in these difficult times contact should be possible with Embassy at all hours. He regretted US Government unwillingness accept FonOff assurances of security of Embassy personnel Canton and of ample notice should situation deteriorate. He seemed feel Embassy coat of arms was only reluctantly installed over USIS building entrance Shameen.

This is third or fourth time he has raised question but on this occasion he made it a major subject of conversation and a real issue. Acting Foreign Minister also dwelt briefly on subject earlier.

I assured him that no one was more aware of disadvantages and discomforts of our juxtaposition than we were; that many items of business were delayed by our distance from Canton; that confusion could occur on complicated issues from the necessity for using different Embassy officer to travel to Canton during any given week; that frequent trips to Canton were debilitating in the current heat; that after making a trip to Canton I often was obliged to work until midnight catching up on the day's business, and as a matter of personal importance to me, if some officers in the Department did not understand the handicaps under which we were working and thus the delays and errors which could easily ensue, my own reputation would suffer.

I also informed him that the decision to move to Canton [*Hong Kong*] was based on sound judgment at the time; that the move having been made, it was no simple matter to reverse the decision; that we were not violating British hospitality in that all our business with the Chinese Government was conducted on Chinese soil; that we were available by telephone in Hong Kong and could upon occasion set up an out-of-schedule flight by Attaché plane (we have average 4 flights a week to Canton, by commercial plane on Mondays, Wednesdays, ar.d Fridays and remainder by Air Attaché plane taking off 9 in the morning and returning to Hong Kong on 4 p. m. flight). I then advised him that return to Canton with a skeleton staff would not materially improve matters in view of the communications problem that would ensue; if we were to return to Canton we would have to do so prepared to leave on a few hours' notice; we could not re-establish our radio station, telegrams to the US and even Hong Kong were very expensive, so that it would then be more practical to have a daily courier by air to carry radio traffic back and forth and that frequently such a procedure would entail even greater delays and inefficiencies than were being created now; that we had certain administrative functions which made it difficult to cut staff below its present level until, say, a move was made to Chungking where we could use the Consular staff as an administrative unit.

He recognized the validity of the arguments but insisted that the prime function of the Embassy was its relations with Chinese Government and that Chinese Government was not satisfied. I stated that his views would be reported to Department but that I did not feel it possible to recommend to Department a return to Canton with reduced staff; despite confidence I felt that Canton would be held for some time and that there would be no local turnover.

I do feel that in near future we should make some small concession to Chinese Government susceptibilities in matter. It can be stated with reasonable confidence that any threat of local turnover has been negated and that military fronts to north and east offer no immediate threat to Canton. Thus it seems that to mollify Chinese Government we might after waiting, say, 1 week, have an Embassy officer spend 3 consecutive days in Canton followed by another officer who would spend the next 3 days, and continue this procedure for some time until there has been sufficient lapse of time to determine future course. Thus would not commence to return to Canton, would answer Chinese Government argument re availability of Embassy at all times, would entail little increase in commuting and communication crews and would not throw entire burden on one officer. Adequate quarters and food are available on Shameen. Procedure indicated would also greatly enhance our coverage of Chinese affairs, which must necessarily be spotty under present circumstances and our contacts, which are now very limited, would usefully be extended. As it is, on each trip we have only about 5 hours in which to carry on all activities, and most officers are unavailable during 3 of those hours.

Request Department consider foregoing recommendation in light of this rather lengthy exposition and reply at as early date as possible.

Sent Department, repeated Hong Kong 49.

STRONG

124.93/9–1549 : Telegram

The Acting Secretary of State to the Chargé in China (Strong), at Canton

WASHINGTON, September 20, 1949—7 p. m.

TelCan 692, Cantel 1109 Sept 15. Dept's instructions to EmbOff were that office close sufficiently in advance Commie takeover permit orderly withdrawal staff. Timing and manner left discretion principal officer. Removal office to Canton and commuting members staff to maintain contact Chi Govt undertaken initiative EmbOff and shld not prevent members staff overnighting in Canton if our judgment this desirable and will not result in (1) members staff remaining after Commie takeover; (2) substantially greater telegraphic or other expenses.

WEBB

124.936/9–2149 : Telegram

The Acting Secretary of State to the Chargé in China (Strong), at Canton

WASHINGTON, September 28, 1949—1 p. m.

TelCan 704. ReCantel 1140, Sept 21.[80] FYI [81] during call on Deputy Under Secy Rusk [82] on Sept 21, Amb Koo alluded to a report that Dept had on occasion instructed our ConGen in Taipei to take up matters of a dipl character with Chi Govt. Amb Koo indicated that such practice wld be highly undesirable and merely serve conflict with established channels dipl intercourse which were through FonOff Canton. It was explained to Amb Koo that only on one or two occasions had Dept requested ConGen take up dipl matters with Taiwan auths and that in each case it had been action parallel or supplementary to that already taken Canton; purpose these occasions had been expedite action urgent matters and was no way bypassing established channels Canton. Amb Koo appeared satisfied with explanation.

WEBB

124.936/9–2949 : Circular telegram

The Acting Secretary of State to Certain Diplomatic and Consular Offices in China

WASHINGTON, September 29, 1949—1 a. m.

Dept believes time has arrived when necessary delineate duties of Emb Offices Commie China and Nationalist China. Therefore, fol instrs will guide officers in China:

OffEmb Nanking already informed due staff reduction Nanking not expected exercise admin supervision over other China posts. Bacon considered prin off Emb Off Nanking.

Strong designated Chargé near Natl Govt with primary duty fol that Govt negotiate therewith and report polit matters pertinent to Natl Govt. This does not presume Strong in supervisory position other China posts as his staff small and must be relieved all admin supervisory responsibilities. Therefore, posts Natl China fol same procedures set forth for posts Commie China with no admin supervision from Emb.

(Shanghai inform Hankow if possible.)

WEBB

---

[80] Not printed; it reported Chinese Foreign Office complaint regarding the taking up of diplomatic matters with Chinese officials at Taipei.
[81] For your information.
[82] Dean Rusk.

124.936/9–3049 : Telegram

The Chargé in China (Strong) to the Secretary of State

CANTON, September 30, 1949—9 a. m.
[Received October 1—9 : 10 a. m.]

Cantel 1150. Reference telCan 704, September 28, repeated Taipei 344. We made almost identical verbal explanation to Foreign Office September 23. Foreign Office apparently satisfied.

Sent Department; repeated Taipei 178.

STRONG

701.0093/10–1[11]49 : Telegram

The Chargé in China (Strong) to the Secretary of State

HONG KONG, October 1 [11], 1949—1 p. m.
[Received October 11—4 : 57 a. m.]

Cantel 1189. During Minister Foreign Affairs subdued cocktail party evening October 10 Protocol Chief informed each diplomatic mission separately date departure Canton set for October 15. Minister himself later stated October 20 as date for commencement Ministry Foreign Affairs full functions Chungking. Formal written notice received October 11 almost immediately following which FonOff verbally advised "situation changed" and whole FonOff leaving for Chungking and Hong Kong October 12.

We plan proceed Chungking October 15 or 16.

STRONG

124.93/10–1249 : Telegram

The Chargé in China (Strong) to the Secretary of State

HONG KONG, October 12, 1949.
[Received October 12—6 : 03 a. m.]

Cantel 1192. All Embassy staff safely out of Canton and now at Hong Kong.

STRONG

123 Rinden, Robert W.: Telegram

The Chargé in China (Strong) to the Secretary of State

CHUNGKING, October 18, 1949.
[Received October 18—3 : 45 a. m.]

Cantel 1210. Rinden,[83] Norton [84] and Strong arrived Chungking October 17, recommencing office functions today.

STRONG

893.01/10–2149: Telegram

The Chargé in China (Strong) to the Secretary of State

CHUNGKING, October 21, 1949—4 p. m.
[Received October 21—7 : 25 a. m.]

Cantel 1216. British Consulate [*Consul*] General today called on Foreign Office to state he received authority from his government to "maintain official contact with Foreign Office but without diplomatic status".

We inquired whether his successor, due to arrive shortly, would not have diplomatic status. Answer reluctantly given that successor would have consular status only but would maintain official contact with Foreign Office.

We have noted delay in arrival Chungking diplomatic representatives other governments, and reluctance Chinese Foreign Office to be specific as to which representatives have arranged to come and on which dates. Recent British actions on question recognition [85] may be resulting in slower and more cautious approach by other governments of representation in Chungking.

STRONG

701.5193/10–2749: Telegram

The Chargé in China (Strong) to the Secretary of State

CHUNGKING, October 27, 1949—4 p. m.
[Received 11 : 18 p. m.]

Cantel 1236. French and Italian second secretaries have arrived Chungking. Korean Ambassador expected from Taiwan in few days. No definite word that diplomatic representatives other nations planning come Chungking although an Australian representative seems to be hoped for soon.

STRONG

---

[83] Robert W. Rinden, appointed Consul at Batavia, on temporary detail to Chungking.

[84] Lawrence H. Norton, communications supervisor of the Embassy Office in China.

[85] See memorandum of October 7, vol. IX, p. 108, and subsequent documents.

124.93/11–1749 : Telegram

The Chargé in China (Strong) to the Secretary of State

CHUNGKING, November 17, 1949—3 p. m.
[Received November 17—6 : 56 a. m.]

Cantel 1288. We are planning notify Foreign Office Friday November 18 of our intention leave within next few days, destination depending on Chinese Government, decisions and ensuing developments. Shall also advise foreign press same day.

STRONG

124.93/11–1749 : Telegram

The Secretary of State to the Chargé in China (Strong), at Chungking

WASHINGTON, November 17, 1949—7 p. m.

TelCan 762. Department spokesman made following statement noon today result queries over Chungking despatches reporting closure :

"The U.S. Embassy office and the American Consulate in Chungking are being closed in view of the imminence of the Communist threat to that area. The American staff will be evacuated as soon as the situation warrants. The American Consulate at Kunming also is making preliminary plans to close but probably will not determine the exact date for that action pending further developments. The Department authorized the American Consuls at both places to close at their discretion at any time when Communist occupation of those cities was threatened. In this connection, it should be recalled that the Chinese Communists have thus far in areas under their control demonstrated in many cases an inability or unwillingness to afford adequate freedom of movement and have prevented our consular personnel from carrying out their normal duties. It is expected that some of the Chungking staff will begin evacuation from Chungking tomorrow. All Americans in the area were warned several months ago of our contemplated action to close the Consulates when it became necessary. At the same time, the Department informed missionary and business interests of its intentions so that all American citizens in the area could take appropriate action."

ACHESON

124.93/11–1749 : Telegram

The Secretary of State to the Chargé in China (Strong), at Chungking

WASHINGTON, November 17, 1949—7 p. m.

TelCan 763. Re Cantel 1288, Nov 17. In view Dept intention close Consulate Kunming immed future, you are instructed to proceed with personnel Emb office to Hong Kong to await further instructions when you consider move from Chungking necessary.

ACHESON

124.93/11–1849 : Telegram

The Chargé in China (Strong) to the Secretary of State

CHUNGKING, November 18, 1949—4 p. m.
[Received 11:55 p. m.]

Cantel 1292. This morning we informed Chen Tai-chu, director American Department Foreign Office, decision leave for Hong Kong November 20, explaining we considered relatively same military situation had arisen here as at Canton at time Nanking fell; Communists about 4 days march or at most 2 days by truck from Chungking; whereas easy to evacuate Canton, several days required arrange leave Chungking and we did not wish get involved in last-minute rush.

Chen of course expressed regret at our decision, said Foreign Office and Government considered situation secure and had every intention give ample notice and facilities for departure (French Embassy representative here said Foreign Office today told him it unable arrange air passage to Hong Kong although he has orders return there). He said Government not considering next move yet because situation does not warrant.

In reply we stated we recognized Chungking might remain secure for additional period but elements of situation were such we felt obliged leave not from unfriendliness or desire affect Chinese Government adversely. We said we would keep contact with special commissioner of Foreign Office [in] Hong Kong and keep US Government informed of Chinese Government's decision and subsequent developments which would have to determine our future course of action.

Chen said he sympathized with our viewpoint and hoped impression would be avoided that we no longer maintained relations with Chinese Government. We replied we could not set up formal office Hong Kong but would maintain informal contact.

With regard to British, Chen claimed very recent telegrams from Chinese Embassy indicated change on [in?] British attitude and British recognition of Communist regime in near future seemed very unlikely.

STRONG

124.93/11–2949 : Telegram

The Chargé in China (Strong) to the Secretary of State

HONG KONG, November 29, 1949—3 p. m.
[Received November 29—9 : 37 a. m.]

Cantel 1314. TelCan 763, November 17. Apparent determination of nucleus of Chinese Government to move from place to place in West

China during next few weeks would seem to rule out efforts for time being by this Embassy to remain with it on the spot.

We cannot predict whether, after West China phase is ended as far as maintenance of Government there is concerned, a legal regime will be installed in Kwangsi which may remain secure little longer than, for example, Hsichang, or whether Government will be based somewhere on Hainan, or at Taipei.

We also are unaware of Department's thinking with regard to question of continuance of diplomatic relations with Chinese Government under various circumstances which may arise.

After discussion of the several possibilities with Rinden, I recommend with his concurrence that he be released from his temporary detail with Embassy. There is not sufficient worth-while work to keep two officers busy in Hong Kong, and it is my feeling that should Embassy at later date again follow Chinese Government one officer will be adequate to perform necessary functions, or, in event of a regime in Kwangsi or Hainan, a junior officer with special language qualifications might be detailed.

Inasmuch as O'Grady [86] can obtain field cryptographic indoctrination at Hong Kong, Norton will proceed on home leave in near future.

STRONG

---

123 Strong, Robert C.

Memorandum of Telephone Conversation, by the Deputy Director of the Office of Chinese Affairs (Freeman)

[WASHINGTON,] December 15, 1949.

I telephoned Mr. Ford of the British Embassy and Mr. Daridan of the French Embassy [87] today to inform them of the decision reached in the Department to instruct Mr. Strong, our Chargé d'Affaires to China temporarily residing in Hong Kong, to proceed to Taipei under the following conditions: (1) in the event that we receive official notification from the Chinese Government of the removal of the capital to Taipei, and (2) if Foreign Minister George Yeh no longer remains in Hong Kong in that capacity.

---

[86] Walter J. O'Grady, clerk assigned to the Embassy office.
[87] J. F. Ford, First Secretary of the British Embassy, and Jean Daridan, Counselor of the French Embassy.

124.93/12–1549 : Telegram

The Chargé in China (Strong) to the Secretary of State

HONG KONG, December 15, 1949—5 p. m.
[Received December 15—2:16 p. m.]

Cantel 1336. Deptel 1546, December 13 to Hong Kong.[88] Following letter dated December 13 received December 15 from special Commissioner of Ministry Foreign Affairs:

"I am instructed to transmit to you following message from Ministry Foreign Affairs:

'Ministry Foreign Affairs presents its compliments to American Embassy and has honor to state that seat of Nationalist Government of China is now in Taipei, China.
'I am also instructed to inform you that Chinese Government would arrange for accommodations to be made available to your Embassy in Taipei and for transport facilities to Taiwan if you and your Embassy staff should require them. I await your advice.' "

Am not making formal reply to above quoted letter, but shall advise Foreign Office in writing when begin functioning Taipei.

Am planning arrange own transportation for O'Grady and self. Shall notify Department departure date when firm, probably December 20.

Sent Department Cantel 1336, repeated Taipei 240, Hong Kong by hand.

STRONG

893.01/12–1549

The Chinese Ambassador (Koo) to the Secretary of State

The Chinese Ambassador presents his compliments to the Secretary of State and has the honor to inform him that the seat of the National Government of the Republic of China has been transferred to Taipeh, Taiwan (Formosa) and that the Executive Yuan and the Ministry of Foreign Affairs have been functioning there since December 9, 1949.

The headquarters of the Commander-in-Chief of the Military, Naval and Air Forces for the purpose of directing military operations on the mainland of China are now established at Sichang, Sikang Province.

WASHINGTON, December 15, 1949.

---

[88] Not printed; it concerned reassignment of personnel (123 MacDonald, John J.).

123 Strong, Robert C. : Telegram

The Chargé in China (Strong) to the Secretary of State

HONG KONG, December 16, 1949—4 p. m.
[Received December 16—9:39 a. m.]

Cantel 1337. Reference Cantel 1336, December 15, repeated Taipei 247. Am proceeding Taipei with O'Grady on SS *Shenking*, departing Hong Kong December 20, arriving Keelung December 22.

Request Department circularize interested posts to direct telegraphic communications for Embassy to Taipei from December 19.

Sent Department Cantel 1337, repeated Taipei 248.

STRONG

890.20/12–2749 : Telegram

The Chargé in China (Strong) to the Secretary of State

TAIPEI, December 27, 1949—1 p. m.
[Received December 27—12:45 p. m.]

Cantel 1343. During initial call on FonMin Yeh December 26 found him brimming with self-confident good humor. He lost little time in pointing out he was now member of 3-man standing committee of Executive Yuan, said committee in constant session, really running Central Government; added Generalissimo had turned over to him house only 50 yards from Generalissimo's own residence. In response to question whether he then planned remain in Central Government, Yeh replied he would stay until "Government reshuffled", after which he would take needed rest.

Conclusion is to be drawn that Yeh now feels more important, is getting established in inner circles and thus does not want to quit, as he did earlier. It seems doubtful that any big reshuffle will occur but merely a continuation in the series of changes which have taken place already over period of time. Thus he may be attempting justify failure live up to earlier statements. It might be added that Yeh told L. K. Little [89] recently and me that he telling Generalissimo [that] Taiwan not defensible alone over extended period and that either Luichow peninsula must be held or landing made on China coast. With what means either to be achieved he did not say. He says he opposes conscription of Taiwanese to begin January, but "guesses that is Chen Cheng's [90] problem for decisions".

Yeh also told Little that chances are now 60 to 40 that US aid would be forthcoming soon.

STRONG

---

[89] American who recently resigned as Inspector General of the Chinese Maritime Customs.
[90] Military and Political Affairs Director for Southeast China.

890.20/12–2749 : Telegram

The Chargé in China (Strong) to the Secretary of State

TAIPEI, December 27, 1949—2 p. m.
[Received December 27—3 : 55 a. m.]

Cantel 1344. Foreign Office still in mess and key personnel missing. In view fact Yeh will probably give minimum time to Waichiaopu [91] (Cantel 1343, December 27) and is only man in that office able make decisions, we feel that while form should be followed in taking up all matters with Foreign Office, we should also approach military authorities simultaneously on questions which concern them.

Reference Cantel 1342, December 27.[92] Fact Governor Wu [93] was unwilling discuss question of entry of British relief vessel into Shanghai but rather referred me to Foreign Office is indication that there is little point in bringing up with him intergovernmental affairs.

STRONG

---

123 Strong, Robert C. : Telegram

The Secretary of State to the Consul at Taipei (Edgar)

WASHINGTON, December 30, 1949—7 p. m.

598. Robert C. Strong transferred Taipei Chargé d'Affaires (First Secretary) EmbOff Taipei and Consul [at] ConGen Taipei effective day following receipt this telegram. Submit 353 showing effective date. TO 0–13341 Dec 30 OA–238220 authorizes transportation effects Hong Kong to Taipei. If no effects to be shipped under this order please notify Department by telegram so that TO can be canceled.

ACHESON

---

[91] Chinese Foreign Office.
[92] Not printed.
[93] K. C. Wu, Governor of Taiwan.

THE EMBASSY IN CHINA AFTER OCCUPATION OF NANKING BY CHINESE COMMUNISTS

I. VIOLATION OF AMBASSADOR STUART'S RESIDENCE; CHINESE COMMUNIST REFUSAL TO RECOGNIZE OFFICIAL STATUS OF DIPLOMATIC PERSONNEL; DEPARTURE OF THE AMBASSADOR FROM CHINA (APRIL 25–AUGUST 3)

124.931/4–2549 : Telegram

The Ambassador in China (Stuart) to the Secretary of State

NANKING, April 25, 1949.
[Received April 25—3:01 a. m.]

856. The Ambassador's residence was violated this morning at 6:45 by 12 armed Communist soldiers. They persuaded the Chinese porter to open the front gate of the compound and then came in the back door of the residence where they asked the servants how many Chinese and how many foreigners lived in the residence and where the Ambassador was. On receiving reply to the last question, the soldiers all mounted the stairway promptly, went to the Ambassador's room and entered. The Ambassador was not quite awake at that hour and their appearance in his bedroom was something of a shock. While they did not threaten him, the first to enter room spoke in loud and angry tones. Those that followed were more civil and said that they had come to "look around". They wandered about the bedroom inspecting its contents and making remarks to effect that all this would eventually go to people to whom it should belong anyway.

They questioned Mr. Fugh[1] but did not inspect his room. They refused to let Anderberg[2] into the Ambassador's bedroom and forced him back into his own room at the point of a gun. They inspected his room and asked him his nationality; after which inspected other bedrooms. They then left the house and the compound without having removed anything. They told one of the servants that the Ambassador should not leave the compound but this was not conveyed to the Ambassador or any member of his official staff. No other houses in the compound were visited.

Sent Department, repeated OffEmb Canton 301, Shanghai 440, Peiping 133.

STUART

---

[1] Philip Fugh, Chinese personal secretary to Ambassador Stuart.
[2] Edward Anderberg, Jr., Economic Analyst of the Embassy.

124.931/4–2549 : Telegram

The Secretary of State to the Ambassador in China (Stuart)

WASHINGTON, April 25, 1949—1 p. m.

516. Urtel 856 Apr 25. You are instructed have MA [3] immed approach highest available Commie mil auths Nanking and enter strong oral protest against action Commie soldiers violating Ambs residence, indicating he is doing so on instructions from his Govt. Suggest he might in ur discretion support such protest with memo setting forth factual acct incident.

Emb should follow up with approach to Commie civil auths when they are established Nanking.

Did Commie soldiers use threats or show of arms to compel Chi porter open gate?

ACHESON

124.931/4–2549 : Telegram

The Secretary of State to the Consul General at Peiping (Clubb)

WASHINGTON, April 25, 1949—1 p. m.

230. You are instructed immed approach highest available Commie auths Peiping and enter strong protest in manner deemed by you most appropriate against violation Ambs residence Nanking as reported Embtel 856 Apr 25 to Dept (rptd Peiping as 133), indicating you are doing so on instructions from ur Govt. Suggest you hand Commie auths memorandum containing factual account.

Emb being instructed in separate tel have MA take similar action vis-à-vis Commie mil auths Nanking and approach Commie civil officials when established Nanking.

ACHESON

124.936/4–2649 : Telegram

The Ambassador in China (Stuart) to the Secretary of State

NANKING, April 26, 1949.
[Received April 26—12:03 a. m.]

866. This morning Embassy personnel attempting to come to work from Ambassador's and adjacent compound were stopped by armed soldiers and ordered to return to compound and not attempt to ride or walk out of compounds. Personnel entering compounds likewise

---

[3] Military Attaché in China, Brig. Gen. Robert H. Soule.

not permitted to leave.   However, some American employees Attaché staffs driving jeeps and walking were allowed free passage.   Will keep you advised as situation develops.

Sent Department 866, repeated OffEmb Canton 308; Shanghai 448; Peiping 136.

STUART

124.931/4–2649 : Telegram

The Ambassador in China (Stuart) to the Secretary of State

NANKING, April 26, 1949—11 a. m.
[Received 1 :06 p. m.]

868. ReEmbtel 856, April 25 to Department.   Same day delivered to Ma Ching-yuan, letter addressed "Chairman, Nanking Peace Preservation Committee" and signed by Jones as Counselor of Embassy requesting Committee call to attention responsible authorities this violation diplomatic immunity.   Ma said he had discussed today with high-ranking Communist officials question entry Communist soldiers into British Embassy compound last night.   According to Ma, Communists stated categorically soldiers had no orders to enter property of diplomatic missions and that they undoubtedly did so simply because they did not understand situation in Nanking.   Ma added Communists expressed concern for protection diplomatic missions and he said circular would go out shortly to all missions assuring them protection.   He promised to pass Embassy's letter to Communists and discuss with them.

Sent Department 868, repeated AmEmb Canton 309, Shanghai 449, Peiping 137.

STUART

893.00/4–2649 : Telegram

The Ambassador in China (Stuart) to the Secretary of State

NANKING, April 26, 1949—11 a. m.
[Received 1 : 22 p. m.]

869. Embassy informed by *Times* correspondent that spokesman for South Yangtze advance army headquarters has announced that foreigners should confine movements to necessary journeys only, and will be protected provided they do not violate military secrets or engage in espionage; that those who are guilty such acts will be deported, and that radio stations must be registered.

Stoppage of motor car circulation on part Diplomatic Corps becoming general. Australian Ambassador prevented leaving residence but told he could proceed to Chancery if he would submit both car and brief case to search. Wife of Netherlands First Secretary deprived of car while on personal errand; car and chauffeur taken into custody. Two members British Embassy prevented leaving residences; others except Naval Attaché staff not stopped. Wife of Italian Ambassador prevented leaving residence although on foot.

Two female American missionaries this area have been approached for contribution to purchase fodder and straw Communist army. Embassy has instructed them to temporize on ground they neutral (1) as American citizens, (2) as missionaries, and to refer all persons making demands this nature to Embassy.

Sent Department 869, repeated Shanghai 450, AmEmb Canton 310, Peiping 138.

STUART

701.0093/4–2649 : Telegram

The Ambassador in China (Stuart) to the Secretary of State

NANKING, April 26, 1949—1 p. m.
[Received 1 : 35 p. m.]

870. Embassy officer called on Peace Preservation Committee to ascertain reason for interdiction traffic at Shanghai Road compounds. Chairman in meeting and unavailable but other officer of committee suggested direct approach military authorities. Embassy officer then went military headquarters where unable see any responsible official, but told that while military phase continued Nanking foreign diplomats should stay off street for own protection. Soldier who carried message refused request for copy of formal order prohibiting circulation foreign diplomats and was unable explain inconsistencies in application of order. Embassy officer returned to Committee where official tried arrange by telephone interview with Communist political officer but failed. He commented Communist military headquarters in state of confusion making it difficult get things done. Also said Communist officials below top rank afraid take any action on or even discuss matters relating to foreign affairs without order from above. He promised inquire of Ma re circular letter mentioned yesterday was to be sent foreign missions, and inform Embassy.

Returning to office Embassy officer stopped by Communist soldiers who told him to get off street as circulation all foreigners was forbidden.

We believe order has been issued at high level to prohibit circulation foreigners and that inconsistency in application due simply to state of confusion prevailing during first days of take-over. We expect situation to be clarified once Military Control Commission takes over, probably within few days. As yet no guards posted Chancery compound, but personnel are being instructed stay off streets unless absolutely necessary go out. No interference thus far with entry and exit Chinese from any compound.

Sent Department 870, repeated Canton 311, Shanghai 451.

STUART

893.00/4–2649 : Telegram

The Ambassador in China (Stuart) to the Secretary of State

NANKING, April 26, 1949—2 p. m.
[Received April 26—11 :53 a. m.]

874. E. Youde, Third Secretary of British Embassy, April 24 returned from his mission north of Yangtze on which he fruitlessly attempted to establish contact with Communist authorities and arrange withdrawal of British vessel *Amethyst* to either Nanking or Shanghai from her present position.[4]

He crossed river at Pukow April 21 and spent night there. Following day while walking toward battle line at Puchen suddenly found himself in middle of machine-gun battle. He waited until shooting ceased, and then surrendered to Communist troops. He explained to them purpose of his mission and was escorted back from lines, passing through successively higher echelons until he reached district commander and finally area commander. They listened to him, but persistently and pointedly regarded him as having capacity of only private British subject and lacking any diplomatic or official status. Area commander told him Communists would help extricate *Amethyst* only on condition she support Communist crossing of Yangtze. To this, of course, Youde replied in negative. Communists were much incensed by casualties British Navy had inflicted upon their troops.

Comment: This experience of Youde is first indication Communists intend to deny official status to diplomatic personnel as they have done to consular personnel.

Sent Department, repeated Shanghai 454, EmbOff Canton 312.

STUART

---

[4] H.M.S. *Amethyst* had been disabled by Chinese Communist gunfire.

124.931/4–2749 : Telegram

The Ambassador in China (Stuart) to the Secretary of State

NANKING, April 27, 1949—9 a. m.
[Received April 26—10 : 58 p. m.]

879. ReDeptel 516, April 25, repeated American Embassy Canton 108, Shanghai 738. Military Attaché called at former OMEA [5] headquarters at 4:30, April 26, to make oral protest reftel and leave memo if necessary. These headquarters believed political branch PLA [6] but are only offices yet known to Embassy. After 20-minute delay, received by Captain who said his battalion commander unwilling talk to Americans and that anything we had to say could be said to him. He then launched into political tirade denouncing Americans as aiding Kmt,[7] imperialists, etc. Attaché left card with phone number saying would return if given appointment with officer rank of general or better. Attaché received only evasive answers to questions on location general headquarters and name Supreme Commander, Nanking. Efforts to locate headquarters will be renewed today.

Sent Department 879, repeated OffEmb Canton 318, Shanghai 460.

STUART

701.0093/4–2749 : Telegram

The Ambassador in China (Stuart) to the Secretary of State

NANKING, April 27, 1949—6 p. m.
[Received April 27—8 : 45 a. m.]

886. Re Deptel 518, April 25.[8] Although too early express definitive judgment, as Military Control Commission not yet functioning, experience in attempting contact responsible Communist officials here parallels that Peiping and Tientsin, and indicates such direct personal contacts may be difficult if not impossible for some time to come. We agree initial approach by Chief of Mission or high ranking diplomatic official would leave mission open to rebuff. In fact Military Attaché has already experienced such rebuff in attempting to carry out instructions contained Deptel 516, April 25. We now trying through Peace Preservation Committee arrange appointment for Military Attaché with high ranking Communist military official but not sanguine favorable outcome. If this approach fails establish direct contact, we will use Committee as channel communication (though

---

[5] Officers Moral Endeavor Association.
[6] People's Liberation Army (Communist).
[7] Kuomintang (Nationalist Party).
[8] *Ante*, p. 686.

so far has proved to be one way only) until establishment control commission creates top Communist local organ with which to deal. At that time Chinese-speaking officer of second secretary rank will make initial approach.

Sent Dept. 886, repeated Embassy Canton 324, Shanghai 46.

STUART

124.936/4–2749 : Telegram

The Ambassador in China (Stuart) to the Secretary of State

NANKING, April 27, 1949.
[Received April 27—8 : 57 a. m.]

887. Commencing 26th Embassy operations and personnel seriously crippled by increasing restriction on movements.

Ambassador, Jones, Cory,[9] Kierman,[10] Anderberg and Anderson[11] now rigidly confined residence compound as result additional guard posted noon 27th permitting no one to leave. At same time officers residing Chancery compound (Bacon,[12] Clough,[13] Harris,[14] Hinderer[15]) on call to handle groups Communist soldiers demanding electric cable, electric current, water, et cetera, or merely entrance to satisfy curiosity. Usually such groups disposed of without difficulty; but one threatened to break down gate if not admitted and left only after being shown Chen Yi's[16] proclamation on protection foreign properties. Embassy has now made telephone request to a number (said to be competent headquarters) supplied by Peace Preservation Committee for investigation incident and for appropriate Communist posters directing troops to leave Embassy premises undisturbed. Other protection problems (such as 5 Ninghsia and 47 Ninghai[17]) apparently on way to solution. With establishment Control Commission anticipate fewer such emergency problems will arise. Bennett[18] and Harris have so far been able to function without restriction at their offices situated elsewhere in city. No interference with alien government or domestic employees reported, and their morale considerably improved since week end. American morale never better.

Sent Department 887, repeated AmEmbassy Canton 325. Shanghai 465, Peiping 140.

STUART

---

[9] Thomas J. Cory, Second Secretary of Embassy.
[10] Frank A. Kierman, Assistant Attaché.
[11] Robert Anderson, Assistant Attaché.
[12] Leonard L. Bacon, Second Secretary of Embassy.
[13] Ralph N. Clough, Second Secretary of Embassy.
[14] George L. Harris Attaché.
[15] Harry A. Hinderer, Attaché.
[16] Chinese Communist commander in the Nanking area.
[17] Embassy properties in Nanking.
[18] Josiah W. Bennett, Assistant Attaché.

124.931/4–2849 : Telegram

The Consul General at Peiping (*Clubb*) *to the Secretary of State*

PEIPING, April 28, 1949—4 p. m.
[Received April 30—5 :01 a. m.]

730. Following is the text of my communication of April 27 to the Commander-in-Chief of the People's Liberation Army:

"General Chu Teh, Commander in Chief, Sir: Under instructions from my Government, I invite your attention to the circumstances that there has occurred at Nanking the violation of the American Ambassador's residence at 6 :45 a. m. April 25 by members of the Chinese Communists' armed forces. The circumstances of that violation are as set forth below.

At the indicated hour 12 armed Chinese Communist soldiers caused the Chinese porter to open the front gate of the compound. The soldiers entered the back door of the Ambassador's residence, asked the servants how many Chinese and foreigners lived in the residence, and where the Ambassador was. When they were informed where the Ambassador was, the soldiers went up to the second floor of [the residence?] and entered the American Ambassador's bedroom. The first soldier to enter the room spoke in loud and angry tone. Those soldiers who followed the first one were more civil and said that they had come to 'look around'. They wandered about the bedroom inspecting the contents and making remarks to the effect that all this would eventually go to the people to whom it should belong anyway.

The soldiers prevented the Ambassador's secretary, Mr. Edward Anderberg, from entering the Ambassador's bedroom and forced him back into his own room at the point of a gun. They inspected his room and asked his nationality, after which they inspected other bedrooms. They then left the house and compound. No other houses in the compound were visited.

Since the above reported violation of the residence of the American Ambassador by armed Chinese Communist soldiers was in clear contravention of established international law and custom and in full disregard of the courtesy always due an Ambassador, I have been instructed by the United States Government to bring the matter to the attention of the highest Chinese Communists' authorities at Peiping and to enter strong protest against that violation.

In view of the reputation of the People's Liberation Army for strict discipline, and particularly in light of the specific assurance given in item 6 of the Proclamation of April 24 [of?] the Political Section of the East China area headquarters of the People's Liberation Army that embassies and consular establishments would be protected— which assuredly must mean that they will be accorded the type of treatment and protection due them by international law and custom— it is presumed that the action [mentioned?] must have been without the authorization of the command of [the People's] Liberation Army; and it is requested that your headquarters take prompt action to the end that the matter shall be appropriately adjusted and that similar unfortunate incidents of violating of American diplomatic immunity shall not occur in future.

I should appreciate receiving an early reply for communication to my Government. Signed American Consul General."

CLUBB

124.93/4–2949 : Telegram

The Ambassador in China (Stuart) to the Secretary of State

NANKING, April 29, 1949—noon.
[Received April 29—6:23 a. m.]

897. Guard placed at Chancery compound April 28 obstructed entry and exit American personnel for a time, but eventually permitted all who desired to enter or leave on foot if not carrying anything. Commissary supplies, bicycle, girl's coat and handbag among articles prohibited exit. He obviously operating under orders which are neither clear-cut nor clearly understood and his actions of permitting or forbidding entry and exit were sometimes overruled by gang of unarmed comrades from same unit lounging on sidewalk across street. Jones succeeded in establishing system of checking in and out satisfactory to guards at Ambassador's compound but was stopped at corner and turned back before reaching Chancery by several rude and angry PLA soldiers. Capriciousness of Communist soldiers compounded of ignorance, hostility to Americans and desire demonstrate authority.

In effort obtain passes to permit personnel go to and from Chancery to work or at very least statement of conditions under which we being confined and reasons therefor, Clough and Harris called at newly established Military Control Commission located former Executive Yuan building. They permitted to proceed inward after long discussion with officers in charge unit guarding Chancery. Commission building in great disorder more resembling barracks than government office and clerk who received officers said Liu Po-cheng, Chairman, and Sung Jen-chiung, Vice Chairman of Commission, had not yet come Nanking, newspapers' statements to contrary notwithstanding. He took to some higher official letters containing lists of US Government property and Embassy personnel but after 20 minutes returned and said no one as yet able discuss question passes or confinement diplomatic personnel. Would not say when responsible official might be available. Clough will call at Commission again today carrying letter requesting audience for me with Liu Po-cheng as soon as latter reaches Nanking in order protest intrusion Ambassador's residence. Hope by daily attempting trips to Commission even though likely to be barren of results to establish precedent with Chancery guards that Embassy entitled to free access to highest Communist organ in city.

Sent Department, repeated OffEmb Canton 330, Shanghai 475.

STUART

893.00/4–2949

Memorandum of Conversation, by Mr. Robert N. Magill of the Division of Chinese Affairs

[WASHINGTON,] April 29, 1949.

Participants: Mr. Hubert Graves, Counselor of the British Embassy
Mr. Philip D. Sprouse [19]—CA
Mr. Fulton Freeman [20]—CA
Mr. Robert N. Magill—CA

Mr. Graves called this afternoon by appointment under instructions from the British Foreign Office to present and discuss an Oral Communication (copy attached)[21] with regard to problems currently facing our two Governments in China.

In discussing the question of our diplomatic representatives at Nanking, it was pointed out to Mr. Graves that the Department does not consider its recent action in authorizing Ambassador Stuart to return to Washington for consultation at some time in the future as constituting a departure from the position previously adopted by joint decision of certain foreign powers in Nanking to retain top representation during a Communist take-over. Mr. Graves was also informed that the Department appreciated the desirability of acting in concert with other interested powers in matters of this nature, and it was suggested that Mr. Graves might wish to ascertain whether the British Government was giving consideration to taking similar action to that contemplated by the Department. Mr. Graves stated that he had not as yet received any indication that his Government was planning to recall the British Ambassador for consultation but that he would forward a discreet inquiry and inform the Department of any reaction received.

With regard to the question of stationing foreign warships in the Yangtze and the Whangpoo, Mr. Sprouse assured Mr. Graves that our reports indicated that there had been continuing and extended consultation between the United States and British representatives in Shanghai and Nanking on this subject. Mr. Sprouse also pointed out that all United States Naval vessels have now withdrawn from the Whangpoo to a point in the mouth of the Yangtze east of Woosung and that reports indicated that the British were adopting a similar course of action.[22]

---

[19] Chief of the Division of Chinese Affairs.
[20] Assistant Chief of the Division of Chinese Affairs.
[21] *Infra.*
[22] For documentation on this subject, see vol. IX, pp. 1098 ff.

Mr. Graves was assured that no decision had been made to cut off ECA [23] supplies from Shanghai because of the impending Communist takeover; that ECA intended to continue the importation of petroleum for utility and other essential requirements and of the United States cereals contribution under the rationing program until Communist control of the city had taken place. It was pointed out that we wished to keep to a minimum the quantity of such commodities that would fall to the Communists, and that ECA's diversion of cotton shipments should be considered in that light. Mr. Sprouse explained that the recent China aid legislation makes it mandatory that ECA shipments cease as soon as the Communists gain control of Shanghai, but that the United States Government would not attempt to stop the importation of petroleum and other commodities through private channels thereafter.[24]

In response to Mr. Graves' queries regarding the present commodity stock position in Shanghai, it was stated that according to our latest information (1) cotton stocks were at a 2–1/2 month level since the fall of Wusih, (2) ECA was maintaining ten-day stocks for its share of the ration program, and (3) Shanghai Power had about a two weeks' supply of petroleum.

With regard to paragraph numbered 6 of the attachment, Mr. Sprouse indicated that the question of what might be stated to the Communists by United States and British officials when they come into Shanghai is a matter he would have to discuss with other officials of the Department, and that we would give it immediate attention.

893.00/4–2949

The British Embassy to the Department of State

ORAL COMMUNICATION

Now that Nanking has fallen to the Communists, while Shanghai is threatened with a possible battle, His Majesty's Government think that the time has come to take stock and to consult with other Governments as to whether any steps should be taken to meet the situation which confronts them.

2. *Representatives at Nanking.*

His Majesty's Government hope that the State Department will be disposed to agree that it is of great importance that the common front which has so far been presented in this connexion should be maintained. They trust that the public announcement of the intention to recall the United States Ambassador for consultation does not indi-

---

[23] Economic Cooperation Administration.
[24] For documentation regarding economic aid, see vol. IX, pp. 599 ff.

cate any departure from the position hitherto adopted by the Atlantic Group on retention of representation. It is to be expected that the Communists will try to break up the common front, and though it is impossible to predict what will happen, it is thought that any such attempt should be resisted for as long as possible. Such indications as have been received from His Majesty's Ambassador at Nanking [25] do not suggest that the Communists are as yet contemplating any drastic steps towards Foreign Missions.

3. *Warships in the Yangtze*

Though through force of circumstances there was not time for consultation between Governments, Governments seem to have reached the same conclusion about the retention of warships in the Whangpoo. Further clashes between warships and the Communist forces would be very likely to have an adverse effect upon the position of our respective representatives and communities. It is also desirable to avoid being put in a position where our ships are bottled up and can only withdraw with the permission, or under the orders of, the Communists.

4. *Shanghai*

It is the situation in Shanghai which causes His Majesty's Government the most serious concern. A battle for Shanghai can, in their view, in no way alter the fate of the National Government. On the other hand, it would be an act of criminal folly to involve this densely populated area in the conflict, since quite apart from battle casualties the effect upon the economy and welfare of the people can only be disastrous.

5. Even without a battle, recent reports show that the economic situation in Shanghai is parlous to a degree. His Majesty's Government are not sure how the United States Government view this matter, but think that they would agree that it would be inadvisable to withhold supplies from the Shanghai area which will enable it to function at any rate to some degree and which can be paid for. The Chinese Minister stated to the Foreign Office this morning that United States deliveries of cotton are being diverted from Shanghai. If this were to result in large-scale unemployment for operatives in cotton factories, a critical situation might develop. Similarly the withholding of other vital supplies (in particular, of course, rice) might cause a breakdown of public utilities, and finally the total collapse of law and order.

6. It may be that, when the Communists occupy Shanghai, our Governments should point out to them at an early stage that they will have to depend on outside resources to maintain the life of the city, and that unless they treat foreign business interests in quite a different way from the treatment accorded to such interests in Tien-

---

[25] Sir Ralph Stevenson.

tsin, there will be a complete breakdown for which the Communists themselves will be held responsible by the entire population. But we think we must be careful not to contribute to such a breakdown before the Communists arrive, because then we shall be held responsible.

7. The Foreign Office would be grateful to learn the views of the State Department on these and related questions as soon as possible.

[WASHINGTON,] 29 April, 1949.

124.93/4–3049 : Telegram

The Ambassador in China (Stuart) to the Secretary of State

NANKING, April 30, 1949.
[Received April 30—3 : 37 a. m.]

906. After negotiations with guard at residence compound resulting in signed stipulation guard would not be held responsible for any mishap to them, Jones, Cory and Anderson were released a. m. 29th and succeeded reaching Chancery compound. Guard at Chancery side entrance established for first time, but disappeared after few hours, possibly because of bad weather. Same true of residence Assistant Naval Attaché Kutchera,[26] with no one allowed leave or enter during afternoon. However, control at main entrance Chancery considerably relaxed, believed owing to: 1. Change of guard personnel; 2. Cold rain and wind; 3. Capriciousness. Embassy has been canvassing missionaries so far as possible by telephone and has had no report of any interference with them either at homes or offices, although several have been warned to get off streets by sentries at certain intersections.

On 29th Clough made second trip to Control Commission and presented new letter requesting interview for Military Attaché with Liu Po-cheng. Also asked urgently for interview with responsible official to discuss question isolation Beebe House where for 2 days occupants have been prevented from sending out for food and fuel. Was told responsible official not in office at that time but that matter would be reported him and he would telephone Embassy. Expect official will not telephone and if Embassy unable obtain action by telephoning will attempt negotiate on spot with guards or with their immediate superiors, if such can be found.

Report received a. m. 30th [that] guard blockading house, Associated Press Correspondent Seymour Topping has disappeared and

---

[26] Lt. (jg.) Dean J. Kutchera.

that Australian and British Ambassadors now permitted use automobiles.

Sent Department 906, repeated Canton 336, Shanghai 483.

STUART

124.931/4–3049 : Telegram

The Ambassador in China (Stuart) to the Secretary of State

NANKING, April 30, 1949—5 p. m.
[Received April 30—5 : 30 a. m.]

908. ReDeptel 516, April 25. Communist soldiers were armed. Porter first sought advice from Ambassador's house boy [*chauffeur*], but on returning to gate was frightened to such extent by soldiers' manner and language as to unlock gate.

STUART

124.93/5–249 : Telegram

The Ambassador in China (Stuart) to the Secretary of State

NANKING, May 2, 1949—5 p. m.
[Received May 3—12 : 20 a. m.]

916. Close confinement diplomatic personnel greatly relaxed by May 2. American Ambassador's compound still guarded, but all personnel except Ambassador permitted come to Chancery. Ambassador for first time tried come to Chancery, but guards, who knew his identity, said that for his own protection he should not leave compound. Italian Ambassador who lives across street also turned back. Guards at Chancery compound removed and personnel moving freely in and out on foot. Embassy officer in jeep travelled downtown and back without being challenged. However, Military Attaché in sedan stopped coming out of his office compound which on same side street as Ambassador's compound, but permitted proceed after orally assuring guards they would not be responsible for anything that might happen as result. Letter now being sent Military Control Commission requesting instructions be issued guards at Ambassador's residence to permit him go to and from office, pointing out present situation prevents him carrying out official duties.

Sent Department; repeated OffEmb Canton 339, Shanghai 485.

STUART

123 [Stuart, J. Leighton] : Telegram

The Secretary of State to the Ambassador in China (Stuart)

WASHINGTON, May 3, 1949—1 p. m.

538. Dept notes urtel 906 Apr 30 Brit and Austral Ambs now permitted use their automobiles. Pls report whether you are restricted to ur residence compound and denied freedom movement about city.

ACHESON

124.936/5–349 : Telegram

The Ambassador in China (Stuart) to the Secretary of State

NANKING, May 3, 1949—2 p. m.
[Received May 3—4 :13 a. m.]

923. Canadian Ambassador has asked that our recent telegrams on situation Nanking, particularly with respect restrictions, attitude toward Diplomatic Corps by new authorities, be shown to Canadian Embassy, Washington, for info his Government.

Sent Department 923; repeated Ottawa 1.

STUART

---

123 Stuart, J. Leighton : Telegram

The Ambassador in China (Stuart) to the Secretary of State

NANKING, May 3, 1949—4 p. m.
[Received May 3—8 : 04 a. m.]

924. For first time today Ambassador permitted by guards at this compound to visit Chancery. Embassy personnel also travelled about with little interference, some in cars. A few were challenged on street but permitted proceed upon identification.

Repeated OffEmb Canton 344, Shanghai 419.

STUART

124.931/5–449 : Telegram

The Ambassador in China (Stuart) to the Secretary of State

NANKING, May 4, 1949—4 p. m.
[Received May 5—1 : 05 a. m.]

935. We have taken following steps with respect to intrusion at Ambassador's residence:

(1) Written protest made day following incident to Peace Preservation Committee with request it be called to attention appropriate military authorities;

(2) Following receipt Deptel 516, April 25, AMilAt [27] approached 35th Army headquarters but unable reach anyone in authority;
(3) Written request made to Military Control Commission for appointment for AMilAt with Liu Po-cheng.

As these approaches have brought no reply and since likely impossible in near future deliver oral protest to highest military authority Nanking, suggest we present strong written protest addressed Chairman Military Control Commission.

Sent Department; repeated Shanghai 500, AmEmb Canton 352.

STUART

---

123 Stuart, J. Leighton : Telegram

The Ambassador in China (Stuart) to the Secretary of State

NANKING, May 4, 1949—6 p. m.
[Received May 5—2 : 02 a. m.]

938. Embassy officer today called on Ch'en Ying, Chief General Affairs Section of newly established Aliens Affairs Office, a department of Nanking Military Control Commission, to discuss question of Ambassador's free access to Chancery and occupation US Government-owned houses by Communist troops. Interview resulted in no positive action other than Ch'en's statement he would investigate and inform us, but following points appear significant:

1. Ch'en said PLA does not wish interfere with free movement foreign nationals Nanking (this borne out by notable relaxation restrictions on foreigners' movements last few days);
2. Ch'en said PLA soldiers should not move into foreign property;
3. Ch'en prefaced remarks with statement that no diplomatic relations exist between our Governments and studiously avoided using title Ambassador or referring to diplomats in other terms than "foreign nationals".

Sent Department; repeated Shanghai 502, OffEmb Canton 354.

STUART

---

123 Stuart, J. Leighton : Telegram

The Minister-Counselor of Embassy in China (Clark) to the Secretary of State

CANTON, May 6, 1949—3 p. m.
[Received 3 :23 p. m.]

Cantel 324. Director American Section, Foreign Office, under instructions his superiors, asked me to express earnest hope U.S. Government that Ambassador Stuart visit Canton prior returning

---

[27] Military Attaché, Brig. Gen. Robert H. Soule.

US for consultation. In agreeing transmit request, I pointed out that, in granting departure Ambassador, Communists might stipulate different itinerary. Knowing Department's desires this regard, shall continue avoid definite reply Foreign Office.

Sent Nanking 250, repeated Department Cantel 324.

[CLARK]

---

123 Stuart, J. Leighton : Telegram

The Ambassador in China (Stuart) to the Secretary of State

NANKING, May 7, 1949—10 a. m.
[Received May 7—6 :30 a. m.]

954. ReDeptel 538, May 3. I have been coming regularly to Chancery once a day without hindrance since May 3, and have been several other places in city. Guards were removed from my compound morning of May 6. There appears to be no obstacle now to my moving freely about city except after dark, when Communists reportedly stop both Chinese and foreign, although they have not announced a curfew.

Sent Department, repeated OffEmb Canton 366, Shanghai 518.

STUART

124.936/5–749 : Telegram

The Ambassador in China (Stuart) to the Secretary of State

NANKING, May 7, 1949—10 a. m.
[Received May 7—7 a. m.]

955. Aliens Affairs Office has informed Embassy it cannot accept communications on Embassy letterhead or signed by officers using either diplomatic or consular title. Will accept only communications on plain paper signed by officer in "personal capacity". Obvious intent is to avoid even tacit admission that diplomatic personnel have any special status other than that which may be accorded "foreign nationals" in general. Our refusal to adopt prescribed procedure would in all likelihood close only channel so far available for negotiating local problems. Would our acceptance this procedure, in Dept's opinion, prejudice our position, already stated orally to official of Aliens Affairs Office, that diplomatic missions have special position, universally recognized under international law even where diplomatic relations may not exist between governments involved? We will withhold further communications to Commies pending Dept's reply.

Sent Department; repeated AmEmb Canton 367, Shanghai 519.

STUART

124.93/5–949 : Telegram

The Minister-Counselor of Embassy in China (Clark) to the Secretary of State

CANTON, May 9, 1949—7 p. m.
[Received May 11—7 :20 a. m.]

Cantel 337. At this stage it seems matter small importance whether communications Communist officials omit mention diplomatic or consular capacity writer, Nanking's 955, May 7, repeated Canton 367, Shanghai 519. Feel status of Consulates' officers will be recognized later when Communists recognize need services they perform. Status diplomatic officers of Embassy, Nanking, it seems to me, is entirely different. They are accredited to Government unrepresented Nanking and it would seem difficult to establish under international law any claim other than that of safe conduct out of country and protection from molestation of themselves and property in meantime. For this reason I wonder whether Department has given consideration to desirability arranging for departure from Nanking, along with Ambassador, of all except staff sufficient functioning consular office and protection property to be left behind. I find it difficult believe that Communists will recognize any diplomatic capacity of officers remaining until such time as we have given *de jure* recognition to a Communist government. As there are no indications at this stage of intention establish government Nanking, consular officers Peiping would seem more likely channel any tentative discussions on *de facto* basis with Communists.

Sent Department, repeated Nanking 259, Shanghai 217.

CLARK

124.936/5–1049

Memorandum of Conversation, by the Chief of the Division of Chinese Affairs (Sprouse)

[WASHINGTON,] May 10, 1949.

Mr. Tsui [28] called by appointment this afternoon and said that he had been requested by the Ambassador, pursuant to instructions from Acting Foreign Minister George Yeh, to suggest the desirability of the Department's directing Minister-Counselor Clark at Canton not to transmit to Ambassador Stuart at Nanking any communications regarding matters concerning the Ministry of Foreign Affairs. Mr. Tsui presented this suggestion somewhat apologetically.

I informed Mr. Tsui that Minister-Counselor Clark was in communication with Ambassador Stuart only by radio, as are the De-

---

[28] Tswen-ling Tsui, Counselor of the Chinese Embassy.

partment and Consulate General at Shanghai, and I did not understand the concern of the Acting Foreign Minister with respect to communications between Mr. Clark and the Ambassador. I gave no indication that we would even consider complying with such a request.

893.00B/5–1149 : Telegram

The Ambassador in China (Stuart) to the Secretary of State

NANKING, May 11, 1949—noon.
[Received May 11—6 :18 a. m.]

994. As Department aware, Huang Hua, member Communist staff former Executive Headquarters, is presently Chief Aliens Affairs Office, Nanking Military Control Council. Immediately prior to his advent Nanking, he held same position Communist municipal government Peiping. He is alumnus Yenching University and classmate Philip Fugh. Last week Fugh telephoned Foreign Office where Huang set up offices, leaving his name. Huang returned call next day, said it was "inconvenient" for him to call on Fugh, asked if latter would visit him which Fugh did. Huang received him cordially and asked after their "old college President".[29] Although he referred to me several times during course of conversation, he was careful to avoid use of my official title. He said he did not recognize me as Ambassador nor any other Ambassadors in Nanking because we were accredited to Kmt Government. He added that it would be up to USA, when time came, to make first move in establishment relations with People's Democratic Government. He emphasized this a second time later on in conversation.

He launched into a tirade against US foreign policy, its assistance to Kmt, its consequent responsibility for civil war, giving reasons why CCP[30] considers USA "an enemy". He did, however, admit favorable impression from Secretary's letter March 15[31] to Connally.[32] He said the CCP was bringing a "new democracy"to Chinese people quite different from old democracy known in USA and Britain. Objectives of CCP were to eliminate (1) feudalism and (2) American, British imperialism, China. In referring to HMS *Amethyst* incident, which he insisted fired first shot, elaborated CCP British policy as follows:

(1) British must pay indemnity for hundreds of Communist casualties.

(2) Must promise never to repeat incident.

---

[29] Ambassador Stuart was President of Yenching University at Peiping, 1919–46.
[30] Chinese Communist Party.
[31] Vol. IX, p. 607.
[32] Tom Connally of Texas, Chairman of the Senate Committee on Foreign Relations.

(3) Must agree to discuss Hong Kong question.
(4) Must withdraw all troops, ships, planes from Chinese territories and waters.

Huang said CCP intended to hold Political Consultative Conference in June either Peiping or Nanking; that Nationalist [*national?*] government would be established in early autumn. When Fugh inquired about delay, Huang replied necessary to achieve one-mindedness re new government. Li Chi-sen,[33] he said, would soon come Nanking [as] recognized head of Kmt.

Fugh suggested propriety of Huang calling on his "old college President". Huang agreed he would like to do so but not immediately. During course conversation Fugh twice brought up Communist soldiers' intrusion Ambassador's bedroom April 25. On second reference Huang obliquely acknowledged it by saying he brought message from Chou En-lai [34] saying latter was distressed by incident. Interview lasted one hour during which Huang did most of talking. Attitude toward Fugh most friendly, Huang accompanying him all the way to street gate of former Waichiaopu; [35] said he would telephone. Fugh will not attempt to see him again unless initiative comes from other side.

Department pass to Peiping and Tientsin in its discretion.

Sent Department, repeated OffEmb Canton 395, Shanghai 552.

STUART

893.00/5–1249 : Telegram

The Ambassador in China (Stuart) to the Secretary of State

NANKING, May 12, 1949—6 p. m.
[Received May 13—3:21 a. m.]

1010. Aliens Affairs Office yesterday summoned Embassy officer and told him orally following four regulations re conduct foreigners: [36]

1. No one to be on streets during curfew hours 11 p. m. to 5 a. m. except in emergency;
2. For time being no foreigners to go outside city walls without permit from Public Safety Bureau;
3. No military uniforms to be worn on streets or arms carried;
4. Pending completion preparations for registration automobiles they may be freely used within city.

---

[33] Previously head of Kuomintang Revolutionary Committee (KmtRC) at Hong Kong; at Peiping since end of 1948.
[34] Chinese Communist Party representative during 1945–46 negotiations and member of the Central Committee of the Party.
[35] Chinese Foreign Office.
[36] For information concerning the Chinese Communist occupation of Nanking, see telegram No. 848, April 24, from the Ambassador in China, p. 269.

Other Embassies' representatives called in individually and given same information orally. Imparting of information orally and individually apparently selected in order avoid inference Communists recognizing special status Foreign Missions. Embassy informing all Americans.

Sent Department, repeated Shanghai 562, OffEmb Canton 402.

STUART

124.931/5–449 : Telegram

The Secretary of State to the Ambassador in China (Stuart)

WASHINGTON, May 12, 1949—7 p. m.

576. Written protest to Chairman Mil Control Comm recommended Embtel 935, May 4, authorized. Tel text to Dept.

ACHESON

124.936/5–749 : Telegram

The Secretary of State to the Ambassador in China (Stuart)

WASHINGTON, May 13, 1949—2 p. m.

583. Urtel 955 May 7. Dept believes most important consideration is establishment practical channel for essential communications in manner not construable as recognition Commie regime. Possibly difficulty outlined reftel can be avoided by use memoranda (unsigned, initialed, or signed Emb officer with or without title) delivered Alien Affairs Office by Emb officer. In event it necessary communicate Commie auths by ltr, ltr shld be addressed to Commie auths by name without title and may be signed by officer of Emb either with or without official title. However Dept believes insofar as practicable Amb himself shld not sign communications Commie auths without inclusion his official title. Suggest you discuss with other friendly missions Nanking.

ACHESON

893.01/5–1349 : Telegram

The Ambassador in China (Stuart) to the Secretary of State

NANKING, May 13, 1949—4 p. m.
[Received May 14—1 : 50 a. m.]

1019. After reviewing of problem of status of Embassies and Consulates in face of Nationalist Government approaching defeat and possible extinction, plus intransigent attitude Communists on recognition as matter absolute reciprocity, Embassy's views developing as follows: (see Embtel 979, May 10, repeated Canton 389, Shanghai 542 [37]).

1. So long as Nationalist Government exists and is recognized by US, diplomatic status all FS [38] personnel China remains unchanged. Such status created by agreement US and Nationalist Governments, cannot be destroyed piecemeal and is unaffected by Communist current military successes. Continued residence our Ambassadors Brussels 1914–1917 [39] provides analogy if needed.

2. Until Nationalist Government obviously extinct, our approaches to Communists should be limited to inquiries, protests regarding welfare, property Americans.

3. After extinction Nationalist Government our status analogous diplomatic personnel in country from which US has withdrawn recognition. Status continues until reasonable time for departure has elapsed after unequivocal notice to depart received from new authorities.

4. In period following extinction Nationalist Government we may, on Department's authorization, confer informally with Communists on general matters, and endeavor ascertain whether *de facto* government exists. We assume that by this time Communists will have announced provisional government, called constituent assembly and organized foreign office. Any act our part implying recognition to be avoided.

5. If existence *de facto* government is ascertained, Embassy will report same to Department and if requested suggest stipulations regarded desirable as conditions to *de jure* recognition, e.g., protection American lives and interests, treaty obligations, etc.

6. Embassy feels Communist attitude regarding absolute and immediate reciprocity on question recognition typically Communist position adopted either for propaganda purposes or on theory foreign embassies and consulates perform no important function benefiting Chinese interests. Communists apparently unaware these offices are existing agencies best suited to determine facts regarding existence *de facto* Communist government and desirability recognition. Meanwhile Communists seem to regard toleration of foreign diplomatic personnel as yielding of hard-won sovereignty which ought not to be sacrificed without immediate counter-concessions. They appear to consider continued presence diplomatic offices places their regime in inferior position and are apparently unaware diplomatic inferiority their position exists in any case from moment new government is formed until it receives general recognition.

---

[37] Vol. IX, p. 19.
[38] Foreign Service.
[39] For documentation on continued residence of the American Minister in Brussels after German occupation, see *Foreign Relations*, 1914, Supplement, The World War, pp. 45–47, 49, 65, 67, 69, 73–74, 76.

7. Embassy believes that if Communists are convinced diplomatic and consular personnel chiefly engaged political, commercial, espionage and propaganda, Communist attitude regarding reciprocity likely to continue. Some evidence accumulating, however, that attitude towards embassies based also on embarrassment their presence and uncertainty regarding procedure.

8. There have been recent indications that Nanking may be retained as capital under Communist regime and we believe good possibility new government will establish itself here following PCC. (ReCantel 337, May 9 to Department, repeated Nanking 259, Shanghai 217.) Consequently we feel office of Embassy should be retained Nanking after departure of Ambassador until assured capital will not be Nanking or until Communists ask us to leave. Even if government establishes itself permanently elsewhere, there is ample precedent for office of Embassy remaining ex-capital until move to new capital can conveniently be made.

Sent Department, repeated OffEmb Canton 412, Shanghai 570.

STUART

893.00B/5–1449 : Telegram

The Ambassador in China (Stuart) to the Secretary of State

NANKING, May 14, 1949—4[*1?*] p. m.
[Received May 14—7: 54 a. m.]

1021. Subordinate of Huang Hua and former Yenching student called on me yesterday on personal basis. Conversation soon turned to political problems and we discussed such varied subjects as position our Consulates in Communist-occupied China and *Amethyst* incident. (Conversation regarding latter revealed basic misconception at least locally and as result thereof British Ambassador is presenting to Communists new and detailed account of entire tragic affair.) Following our conversation my young friend reported promptly to Huang Hua who later asked for appointment with me. (See mytel 994 to Department May 11, repeated Canton 395, Shanghai 552.) I now suspect principal reason for call was to ascertain if I would be receptive to visit from Huang.

Huang called my residence last evening remaining almost 2 hours. Our conversation was friendly and informal. I refrained from political remarks until he opened way which he did after few personal exchanges. I then spoke earnestly of great desire that peoples of all countries had for peace, including, emphatically, my own, of dangerous situation developing despite this universal popular will; of indescribable horrors of next war; of my conviction that much, but not all, present tension due to misunderstandings, fears, suspicions which could be cleared away by mutual frankness; of fears Americans and other non-Communists had of Marxist-Leninist doctrine, subscribed to by CCP, that world revolution and overthrow of capitalistic governments necessary, thus proclaiming subversive interference or armed invasion as fixed policy. Huang spoke of Chinese people's resentment at American aid to Kmt and other "mistakes" of US policy to which I briefly replied.

Huang asked about my plans and I told him of my instructions,[40] adding that I was glad to stay long enough for symbolic purpose of demonstrating American people's interest in welfare of Chinese people as whole; that I wished to maintain friendly relations of past; that being near end of my active life I hoped to be able somewhat to help restore these relations as I knew my Government and people desired; that my aim was unity, peace, truly democratic government and international good will for which Huang knew I had worked all my life in China.

Huang expressed much interest in recognition of Communist China by USA on terms of equality and mutual benefit. I replied that such terms together with accepted international practice with respect to treaties would be only proper basis. He was greatly surprised at my explanation of status of armed forces in China particularly Marines in Shanghai. Our side of story, that is desire to protect American lives during civil disturbances and chaotic conditions brought on by war, appeared never to have occurred to him. He was obviously impressed. I explained question of national government was internal; that Communists themselves at present had none; that it was customary to recognize whatever government clearly had support of people of country and was able and willing to perform its international obligations; that therefore USA and other countries could do nothing but await developments in China. I hinted that most other nations would tend to follow our lead. I explained functions of foreign consulates in maintaining informal relations with *de facto* regional authorities.

Huang expounded upon needs of China for commercial and other relations with foreign countries. He said instructions had been issued to all military units to protect safety and interests of foreigners. Intrusion into my bedroom was discussed and he promised to do his best in constantly shifting military situation to trace offenders. He explained that first Communist troops in city had not been prepared or properly instructed on treatment of foreigners.

I inquired about our mutual acquaintances among CCP. Their plans for PCC [41] and formation of coalition government seem still rather inchoate; I received impression Communists are confused by

---

[40] See telegram No. 510, April 22, 7 p.m., p. 682, and subsequent documents.
[41] Political Consultative Conference.

being ahead of schedule and particularly worried about responsibilities, administrative implications of Shanghai take-over.

Repeated Canton 413, Shanghai 571.

STUART

---

123 Stuart, J. Leighton : Telegram

The Ambassador in China (Stuart) to the Secretary of State

NANKING, May 14, 1949—2 p. m.
[Received May 14—9 : 07 a. m.]

1022. Embassy official called to Aliens Affairs Office May 12 and handed written communication addressed to him personally stating Commie authorities had considered earlier request for access to Air Attaché plane and had decided to permit plane to be repaired and when repairs completed flown out of Nanking. Persons other than original pilot and crew might leave only if they obtain written permit from Military Control Commission. Letter added that if pilot does not wish to depart, plane would be placed in custody of Military Control Commission which would not be responsible for any subsequent damage.

During course of my discussions with director Aliens Affairs Office, local Military Control Commission last night (see Embtel 1021, May 14), we discussed status Air Attaché's plane. I explained that it had been retained here solely for purpose of transporting me out of Nanking at appropriate time. Huang appeared to accept this explanation and I anticipate no major difficulties when time comes for my return to USA on consultation.

Sent Department 1022, repeated Shanghai 572, AmEmb Canton 414.

STUART

893.00B/5–1649 : Telegram

The Ambassador in China (Stuart) to the Secretary of State

NANKING, May 16, 1949—5 p. m.
[Received 10 : 52 p. m.]

1037. Underling of Huang Hua mentioned by telegram 1021 to Department May 14, repeated Canton 413, Shanghai 571, is Peng Shujen, a member of Chinese diplomatic service for number of years and recently returned here from Australia. He reports he was left Nanking by George Yeh in charge of Foreign Office turnover to Communists. Peng told me he still undecided whether return National territory or remain and work with Communists.

We infer from several indications that Huang Hua communicated Peiping after conversation with Fugh (see Embtel 994 to Department May 11, repeated Canton 395, Shanghai 552) and did not make his call on me until after it had been cleared, approved in the north.

Sent Department 1037, repeated OffEmb Canton 425, Shanghai 584.

STUART

124.931/5–1849 : Telegram

The Ambassador in China (Stuart) to the Secretary of State

NANKING, May 18, 1949—5 p. m.
[Received 10:49 p.m.]

1059. AMilAt and EmbOff today called at Aliens Affairs Office to present written protest (Deptel 576, May 12). Document was returned with statement military authorities now arranging interview in near future with Embassy officer concerning incident. From this development it appears may soon be possible present both oral and written protest direct to military authorities.

STUART

124.931/5–2249 : Telegram

The Ambassador in China (Stuart) to the Secretary of State

NANKING, May 22, 1949—10 a. m.
[Received May 22—1:43 a. m.]

1083. Interview with military authorities reported being arranged Embtel 1059, May 18, turned out to be for purpose returning to Embassy officer his original written request for interview between AMilAt and Liu Po-cheng with statement matter should be taken up through Aliens Affairs Commission. Accordingly Embassy official called May 19 on Huang Hua to present written protest for forwarding to highest military authority Nanking. Huang unwilling accept document for transmission on ground lack of instructions and instead requested oral account of incident which was given him. He then replied he was authorized to make statement and proceeded by referring to PLA's excellent discipline and Communist proclamation guaranteeing protect foreigners and asserted when he first heard of incident he was much surprised as Communist soldiers do not act this way. Now he had been formally informed of facts he will investigate. Embassy official pointed out Embassy's instructions went beyond recital of facts; we had been directed to protest incident to highest military authority in Nanking. Huang replied he could take no action on matter at that time, but would consult with superiors. Huang was requested inform Embassy soonest of results his consultation.

Incident obviously great embarrassment to Communists. They hesitate accept protest as implying recognition Ambassador's official status, but at same time reluctant reject protest outright and thus laying selves open to charge of denying responsibility for incident for which in eyes of world they assuredly cannot escape.

In compliance Huang's suggestion, Embassy has subsequently submitted written statement of facts to assist in Communist investigation incident. I feel that we should not push protest further; that we have pressed our advantage to maximum point and that further initiative may well force unfavorable reaction detrimental to our present, future position here. As I reported to Department, incident is known and undoubtedly cause of embarrassment to Communist High Command (see Embtels 994, May 11 and 1021, May 14 to Department and Peiping's 730 to Department April 28). We have been informed on good authority that General Liu Po-cheng was "very angry" when informed of incident.

If Department agrees we will take no further steps at this end to press question of protest, either oral or written. We will not, of course, discourage any initiative which Communists themselves may take in this regard and will cooperate in any investigation which may require our assistance.

Repeated to Peiping.

STUART

124.936/5–2449 : Telegram

The Ambassador in China (Stuart) to the Secretary of State

NANKING, May 24, 1949—5 p. m.
[Received May 24—8:25 a. m.]

1102. As our experience somewhat different from Peiping, would comment as follows on Peiping's 860 [*896*] to Department: [42]

Important consideration is maintenance channel communication, rather than form of document. Communist authorities Nanking refuse accept letter or memo signed with title. Embassy therefore using primarily unaddressed memos signed without title and handed to Aliens Affairs Office. When use letter desirable, it is addressed to Communist official by name without title and signed without title. Form in Chinese is that of letter between private individuals. Communists have not objected to inclusion in text language which makes obvious official character of representation and it appears unlikely that inclusion or omission official title either side likely seriously

---

[42] May 18, 5 p. m., p. 1084.

influence effectiveness Communist action in response to such representations. However, we see no objection to using titles both sides if considered preferable in local situation, as Communist official addressed would in any case be local official and question implied recognition National Government would not arise. Believe question can usually be side-stepped by use of unaddressed memo delivered to Aliens Affairs Office with oral or textual request it be transmitted to appropriate authorities. Embassy agrees consular officers, as opposed diplomatic, should use official title in all cases where intercourse will not thereby be impeded. By so doing we maintain our position that consular officers are always competent to deal with any local authorities while diplomatic intercourse limited to National authorities.

Sent Department 1102; repeated AmEmb Canton 459; Shanghai 624; Peiping 179.

STUART

124.931/5–2249 : Telegram

The Acting Secretary of State to the Ambassador in China (Stuart)

WASHINGTON, May 24, 1949—9 p. m.

634. Urtel 1083, May 22. Dept wishes commend Emb on efficient and exhaustive manner in which it has proceeded re transmission protest Commie auths. Dept predisposed believe Commies shld not be allowed forget incident or necessity satisfactory reply to protest, but willing give Emb discretion it requires in accordance final para reftel.

WEBB

893.00/6–649 : Telegram

The Ambassador in China (Stuart) to the Secretary of State

NANKING, June 6, 1949—9 a. m.
[Received June 7—12:36 a. m.]

1215. Lo Hai-sha [43] June 3 brought message to me from Chen Ming-shu, Shanghai representative of Li Chi-sen, and leaders Shanghai KmtRC.[44] Latter has been very active in Shanghai, Hong Kong, Canton in rallying Kmt liberals to join with him in strengthening their point of view in prospective new Chinese government. He intends strongly to advocate friendly relations with USA. He has

[43] Nanking representative of General Chen Ming-shu.
[44] Kuomintang Revolutionary Committee.

acceded to pressure to go to Peiping because of realization that high policy discussions can only be fruitful at top level. He feels talking with even men like Chen Yi, new mayor Shanghai, is of only slight value.

Chen Ming-shu plans to call on me on his way north. Lo himself was surprised when I gave him facts about US aid to Nationalist Government and explained why shipments of munitions are still coming. During our discussion of Taiwan and US position I remarked to Lo that perhaps simplest thing would be to ask CCP leaders to look at facts. We could have included Taiwan in SCAP [45] or even claimed it as our share of postwar settlement as USSR did with Sakhalin and Kuriles, to say nothing of Manchuria. Actually we have even limited ECA activities to a few projects directly benefiting native farmers. Lo pointed out that both he and Chen will have to be very careful in not seeming to plead America's case before men as suspicious as CCP leaders.

Embassy undertaking to gather some factual material on US-Sino relations and US aid to China to assist Chen in his discussions Peiping.

Sent Department 1215; repeated Shanghai 658, AmbEmb Canton 500, Peiping 200.

STUART

---

123 Stuart, J. Leighton : Telegram

The Ambassador in China (Stuart) to the Secretary of State

NANKING, June 8, 1949—noon.
[Received June 8—1 : 09 a. m.]

1234. I, of course, wish to visit Shanghai before returning to US on consultation and I have made arrangements to do so June 11 to 14, inclusive. Trip has been cleared with local Communist authorities who will send representative with me. I shall also be accompanied by Attaché Kierman and Philip Fugh. I plan to travel on night train (sleeper) to Shanghai June 11, returning Nanking same manner night June 14.

I am making my trip subject of local press release to US correspondents, basing it on Department's instructions to assure myself of welfare of American citizens in Yangtze basin before returning to US on consultation.

Sent Department; repeated OffEmb Canton 610, Shanghai 663.

STUART

---

[45] Supreme Commander, Allied Powers in Japan (MacArthur).

711.93/6–849 : Telegram

The Ambassador in China (Stuart) to the Secretary of State

NANKING, June 8, 1949—noon.
[Received June 8—6 :46 a.m.]

1235. Huang Hua invited me to tea June 6. Only other persons present were his assistant Ling Ke-yi (Yenching alumnus) and Philip Fugh. Conversation chiefly followed Huang's lead. It soon turned to relation between China and foreign countries with more particular reference to breaking off relations with Nationalist Government. I received two definite impressions from this discussion :

(1) CCP is extremely anxious to have foreign governments, particularly USA, discard a government which as Huang put it has completely lost the support of Chinese people, is in flight and will be further dispersed whenever Communist troops reach Canton.

(2) Deep sensitivity as to China's right to make her own decision in international field.

Huang had raised question of foreign relations in our first encounter (see Embtel 1021, May 14 to Department, repeated Canton 413, Shanghai 571) and I explained again why USA had to be passive; that politico-military development China was purely internal issue in which other countries should not interfere; that on emergence of new government we would want to ascertain whether it really represented people of China and was both willing and able maintain hitherto accepted international standards. I continued that after all Communist regime was at present nothing more than People's Liberation Army defeating Kuomintang troops and occupying steadily enlarging parts of country; that there were still very large areas nominally under Nationalist Government and that there was as yet not even pretense on Communists' part of administrative agency on national scale with which it would be possible for foreign countries to deal. I pointed out that presence in Nanking of chiefs of diplomatic missions (with exception of Soviet) after arrival of PLA could be regarded by CCP as significant. He quoted Mao's New Democracy to effect that CCP was willing to recognize any nation on terms of equality, mutual benefit and respect for each other's territorial and other sovereign rights.

I reminded him that this worked both ways; that while we fully acknowledged right of Chinese people to have any form of government they desired, yet if such Chinese Government had policy which threatened not to be mutually beneficial or which was committed to overthrow governments of other countries, then obviously this became something beyond purely Chinese issue.

I made further effort to explain position of consulates in occupied territory but without too much success. Huang Hua reiterated that CCP attitude toward consulates was based on latter's original establishment under and relationship with Kuomintang Government (see Embtel 1205, June 6,[46] re Soviet attitude). When asked our action should not [*National*] Government move Taiwan, I replied that in all probability we would not follow it there with diplomatic mission and that I felt that was position of other foreign countries concerned. He dodged such questions as should China be communized or industrialized first or would coalition government be as inclusive as possible to bring in Kmt liberals and other public spirited persons by replying in each case that was purely question for Chinese people to decide for themselves.

Following discussion of need of economic recovery of China, I asked what I might do to further mutual relations between our two countries which had long been my chief concern. Almost brusquely he replied that China needed to be allowed to work out her own destiny without interference; that all CCP wanted from US was stoppage of aid and severance of relations with "Kmt Government". As previously he harped on "past mistakes" of US Government, its miscalculation re strength of Kmt, its maintenance of AAG,[47] its continuing aid to Kmt, etc. Having reviewed 1948 China Aid Act [48] in earlier conversation, I merely pointed out that some shipments had been delayed and that continuing arrival of aid was result of circumstances now outside control of US Government.

I continued that, speaking for many Americans, there was widespread fear re Communist doctrine apparently supported by CCP which advocated world revolution by violence until all other nations had been communized by that process or by highly organized subversive activity; that this fear explained considerable in American attitude.

Conversation lasted about 2 hours. Certain other topics which were discussed will be reported in separate telegrams. Conversation was frank and at times almost beyond usual Chinese amenities. However, both men were very friendly to me and expressed their personal attitude of friendliness in various small ways.

Sent Department 1235, repeated OffEmb Canton 511, Shanghai 664.

Stuart

---

[46] Not printed.
[47] Army Advisory Group.
[48] Approved April 3, 1948 ; 62 Stat. 158.

123 Stuart, J. Leighton : Telegram

The Ambassador in China (Stuart) to the Secretary of State

NANKING, June 8, 1949—6 p. m.
[Received June 8—9:38 a. m.]

1241. In recent conversation with Huang Hua I was pressed for definite details regarding my departure for consultation including date. Huang referred several times to July 1 which was date I had tentatively mentioned on our first meeting. I avoided direct answers by replying that my departure was closely related to progress negotiations for closing Mukden Consulate General.[49] However, since permission to repair Air Attaché plane here, in which I hope to exit, is related in Communist minds to date my departure, it would be useful if I could receive Department's confirmation its instructions for me to proceed US consultation within next 30 days (see Deptel 513, April 23, repeated Canton 106 [50]).

In preparation for departure it would be convenient to have some idea Department's intentions my future. Dept will doubtless be informed recent exchange views between my British colleague and his Foreign Office to effect once Chief of Mission leaves here he or his successor should not return until prospective Chinese Govt will have been formally recognized. Logic of this is irrefutable, yet in my special case I am of opinion that if I can be of any further service my Government it will be by returning here after sufficient period Washington. If Department agrees, perhaps some formula could be worked out for my return without violating international proprieties.

My reasons for desiring return are indicated in recent Peiping and Nanking telegrams regarding internal conditions CCP together with my belief liberals within or without Kmt are ready in large numbers to associate themselves with new regime if it can be persuaded to take more independent nationalistic as against pro-Soviet line. Am convinced our own most hopeful policy lies in this direction. In view of artificially inflamed anti-American feeling, my continuing presence here has also certain symbolic value.

Related to this question of course is future remaining Embassy staff Nanking (see Embtel 1115, May 25 [51]) and whether Department desires maintain office of Embassy in Nanking after my departure or to reduce it to status and size of consulate.

Repeated OffEmb Canton 513.

STUART

---

[49] For documentation on this subject, see pp. 933 ff.
[50] *Ante*, p. 683.
[51] *Ante*, p. 692.

701.0093/6–1349 : Telegram

The Ambassador in China (Stuart) to the Secretary of State [52]

NANKING, June 13, 1949—2 p. m.
[Received June 13—7 : 48 a. m.]

1275. Diplomatic Corps has been subjected series restrictive measures which is beginning make many chiefs mission doubt wisdom remaining here longer. First, official automobiles were required registered in name of individual. In case of each ambassador, he was required add after his title "acting in capacity of foreign national". Following registration, automobiles were limited on purely arbitrary basis, from 1 to 5 cars each mission depending on its size. For most missions this is crippling and constitutes direct interference in official activities. Finally and most important, since resumption of commercial telegraphic facilities overseas, diplomatic missions have been unable to send coded messages. This has been made subject of informal protest to local Aliens Affairs Office by at least one mission without result.

There has been some agitation for meeting Diplomatic Corps and concerted action by that body vis-à-vis local authorities. However, Dean of Diplomatic Corps, who is French,[53] is unwilling to take initiative or responsibility for political reasons involving French-Chinese relations. At his suggestion, however, series of small meetings including all chiefs mission who remained Nanking were held last week at four embassies to discuss individual but parallel action. Plan of approach to local authorities on basis generally recognized privileges and immunities of diplomatic missions, drawn up by French Ambassador and approved by British, Indian and myself, met sufficient opposition from other colleagues to be discarded. Strongest objection was that if Corps approaches local authorities on this basis and receives rebuff or flat negative answer, chiefs mission, at least, would be forced to withdraw or find their position even more intolerable. Since all are not prepared to take this step now or are uninformed of their governments' desires in this connection, there is sufficient lack of unanimity to make parallel approach impractical. Abortive attempt of Diplomatic Corps to assert itself may have following beneficial results, however: (1) will inspire those chiefs mission without instructions concerning their future moves to request them and (2) quiet temporarily those chiefs mission who have been most vociferous in their complaints and demands for concerted action.

Sent Department 1275, repeated AmEmb Canton 528, Shanghai 688.

STUART

---

[52] The Ambassador was away from Nanking June 11–16 on a trip to Shanghai (see telegram No. 1325, June 19, noon, p. 763). Telegrams from Nanking during this period were sent in his name.
[53] Jacques Meyrier, French Ambassador in China.

893.00/6–1349 : Telegram

The Ambassador in China (Stuart) to the Secretary of State

NANKING, June 13, 1949—5 p. m.
[Received June 14—11 : 39 a. m.]

1280. Chen Ming-shu dined with me June 10 en route Peiping. He was accompanied by his wife and Lo Hai-sha (see Embtel 1215, June 6 to Department, repeated Shanghai 658, Canton 500, Peiping 200).

Chen is thoroughly committed to broadening of CCP administrative personnel and program including international as against narrowly Soviet relations. He recognizes need for friendly relations with USA. Chen is conscious of CCP dogmatic intolerance as well as its conscious need of technical workers.

I gave Chen and Lo factual material prepared and translated by Embassy, including such things as abstract comparing Sino-Soviet treaties and Sino-American treaties; Sino-American trade figures showing importance to China of trade with USA and relative unimportance to US of foreign trade with China; brief history of Sino-American relations, et cetera. It was against this background that I did most of talking, feeling it unique opportunity to explain American position to non-Communist Chinese whose party will participate in pre-PCC reportedly convening Peiping next few days. In general my comment revolved around five points:

(1) Americans believe states with different ideologies can live together in peaceful world.

(2) We are primarily concerned in Chinese people rather than form of government they choose themselves, provided only government has support of whole nation and is willing and able to maintain accepted international standards. We are particularly interested in two features prospective CCP-dominated government: (*a*) Would it really maintain human rights as set forth in UN declaration, or would it follow usual procedure of totalitarian or police state? (*b*) Was it committed to world revolution by violence based on Marxist-Leninist theory? If so this position must be recognized as virtually open declaration of aggression both by subversive tactics and armed force and would be regarded by rest of world as the real imperialism threatening it.

(3) Indications of CCP foreign policy (yet unannounced officially) are disconcerting, to say least, to those who desire to maintain friendly relations hitherto maintained between US and China.

(4) CCP economic program, except most general terms, is likewise unannounced, although such official utterances as have been made appear discouraging to trade with USA.

(5) US attitude is one of waiting, observing. However, fact of my remaining Nanking together with other chiefs of mission (except Soviet) has significance which must surely be appreciated by CCP.

I emphasized that what US Government had more than once publicly announced as its policy toward China (sovereign independence, internal unity and peace, economic progress, truly democratic form of government) was precisely what almost all Chinese desired for China; that obstacle was alien factor which it was hoped Chinese statesmanship could solve.

Chen and Lo expect to be back in Nanking in about 4 weeks. In view of importance of my securing first-hand knowledge reaction of CCP top leaders to Chen's position I am inclined to feel that I should await his return before making my trip to US. I should be grateful for Department's comments thereon.

As interesting sidelight Lo related experiences their previous evening at dinner with General Liu Po-cheng. He referred to 16-course dinner, abundance of motor cars for guests, in fact everything up to old mandarin or Kmt standard. General Liu had confessed to them that economic outlook CCP territory was so serious he saw no solution. That the more they applied Marxist tenets the more difficult did their situation seem to become. In referring to difficulties in working out coalition government, Liu said CCP did not trust any one outside the party, yet it required expert help which CCP unable solely to provide.

Sent Department 1280, repeated Off Emb Canton 529, Shanghai 693, Peiping 215.

Stuart

701.0093/6–1549 : Telegram

The Ambassador in China (Stuart) to the Secretary of State

Nanking, June 15, 1949—4 p. m.
[Received June 15—8:32 a. m.]

1292. British Ambassador has drawn up and circulated among Commonwealth colleagues his résumé situation in which chiefs of mission find themselves as result failure plan for concerted representations on privileges and immunities (refEmbtel 1275, June 13, repeated Canton, Shanghai). Summary of résumé as follows:

1. Powers will not withdraw recognition from Nationalists until recognizable successor government exists, since UN Security Council cannot function without Chinese member.

2. Powers desire act in concert and with caution.

3. Powers will consult first with Nanking envoys and therefore must ultimately recall them.

4. If envoys not recalled their presence in China embarrassing to powers while question recognition under debate.

5. As new government will not be constitutional successor to old, new agreements will be necessary. Powers desiring reappoint present envoys will scarcely wish envoys remain China while new government

debating their acceptability.   Such envoys cannot be expected ask for own agreements and risk refusal.

6. If senior officers now Canton do not accompany Nationalists to Chungking, retention chiefs mission at Nanking may appear abandonment neutrality.   Nevertheless can be argued chiefs should not leave Nanking until Nationalists leave Canton.

7. So long as powers continue recognize Nationalists, Communists will refuse even *de facto* relations and ignore Diplomatic Corps.

8. Nanking no longer capital and missions comparatively isolated. Without confidential telegraph and courier service their usefulness doubtful.

9. Although no official declaration made, Communists by acts and informal statements indicate no intention accord diplomatic immunities or prerogatives.   For time being position of Corps is undignified but still tolerable.

10. All objectives envisaged by retention heads of mission at Nanking have been attained or are now no longer attainable merely by continuing retain heads here.

British Ambassador concludes points 3 to 10 inclusive must all be considered in determining date of recall.   Envoys now can do no more than clarify for their governments situation in respect immunities, telegraph and code service and other prerogatives.   Until such clarification obtained powers cannot well determine whether envoys should be left in position outlined points 7, 8 and 9.   Immediate clarification therefore desirable but negative Communist response would of course not be deciding factor in powers' final decision.   Certain envoys desire side-step issue in belief negative response would compel their governments to act precipitately in recalling them immediately.   This view sufficiently well-founded to make concerted action all heads of mission impossible and British Ambassador concludes proposal must therefore be dropped.

Repeated Canton 539, Shanghai 703.

STUART

---

123 Stuart, J. Leighton : Telegram

The Acting Secretary of State to the Ambassador in China (Stuart)

WASHINGTON, June 16, 1949—7 p. m.

705. Reurtel 1241, June 8.   Dept of opinion suitable time for your return Washington on consultation wld be when satisfactory withdrawal staff Mukden ConGen effected.   Particularly since you have in conversation with Huang Hua related ur departure with closing Mukden ConGen, earlier departure might indicate to Commies US not primarily concerned with evacuation Mukden staff and might result in further delaying their withdrawal.   Dept approves ur utilizing Attaché plane for departure China but desires you change to com-

mercial flight or MATS [54] on reaching first transfer point (e.g. Okinawa). As you undoubtedly aware, news correspondents will make every endeavor obtain statement from you at first point outside China and en route Washington. Suggested this regard you follow time-tested formula of informing correspondents you are proceeding to Washington to make report to SecState and can give no info or statement prior submitting report.

While there wld be obvious usefulness ur conferring with Clark Canton prior ur return Washington, Dept of opinion such visit necessitating calls Acting Pres Li and other high Chi officials wld excite speculation and misinterpretation. Having in mind possible repercussions such visit (including possibility Commies might block ur return China in any capacity), Dept wld appreciate ur comments and those of Clark re desirability such visit.

Re question future plans for you subsequent consultation, decision this matter will be reached by President in consultation with Secy Acheson and must therefore wait until Secy's return from Paris. Dept, however, very appreciative ur willingness continue serving in capacity you have so ably filled; for its part doubts whether feasible you return China in capacity Amb as long as Chi Commie regime unrecognized.

Re remaining Emb staff Nanking, Dept no present intention of reducing office to status or size consulate on ur departure for Washington. Emb shld continue functioning as at present under direction Counselor Jones who will assume charge, while Clark will be appointed Chargé d'Affaires in Canton. Dept's tentative view is that on departure from Canton of Clark (telCan 315, June 10 [55]), Strong [56] wld be apptd Chargé d'Affaires in Chungking.

Dept has recd no info re plans other major powers to recall ambassadors for consultation (reDeptel 510, Apr 22 [57]). Pls report present status their plans this regard.

Dept shld be consulted re exact date ur intended departure before plans finalized.

WEBB

---

123 Stuart, J. Leighton : Telegram

The Ambassador in China (Stuart) to the Secretary of State

NANKING, June 17, 1949—5 p. m.
[Received June 17—9:01 a. m.]

1312. I returned Nanking by Shanghai night train arriving here this morning 7 a. m. Trip without incident except half-hour delay

---

[54] Military Air Transport Service.
[55] *Ante*, p. 696.
[56] Robert C. Strong, First Secretary of Embassy.
[57] *Ante*, p. 682.

city gates Nanking while passes were checked. Department will recall Nanking railroad station outside city walls. Luggage, three unclassified pouches were not subjected to inspection.

Sent Dept 1312, repeated Embassy Canton 545, Shanghai 712.

STUART

---

123 Stuart, J. Leighton : Telegram

The Ambassador in China (Stuart) to the Secretary of State

NANKING, June 18, 1949—1 p. m.
[Received June 19—1 :54 a. m.]

1317. When I first received Department's instructions to return US for consultation (Deptel 510, April 22,[58] repeated telCan 103, Shanghai 727), I requested Admiral Badger's [59] assistance in trans-Pacific flight in view uncertainties availability commercial transport from China. Badger promptly replied by offering 4-motor plane his personal disposition (the one which flew Madame Chiang to US last autumn). Badger has still kept this offer open as seen by statements his recent press conference Tokyo.

Since I have staff airplane capable of making Pacific trip and because of obvious convenience of being accompanied by members my own staff, I prefer to use my Air Attaché's B–17 presently based Canton. (ReDeptel 705, June 16, repeated telCan 342, Shanghai 1213.) This plane would meet me in Okinawa after I had flown out of Nanking in Air Attaché's C–47. It could bring Minister Clark from Canton where I could have much-needed consultation with him at Okinawa without misinterpretation which would surely be attached to any visit of mine to Canton at this stage. Clark could return to Canton from Okinawa in C–47 which would then be based Canton. I see no special reason for keeping B–17 China once C–47 is released from here, and after it has transported me Washington it could be reassigned there by Air Force to more useful post.

If, however, flight of B–17 to USA at this time for this purpose is not agreeable to Air Force, I intend to accept Admiral Badger's offer his very comfortable plane which he has stated will be available to me on 24 hours notice whenever I request it.

Would be grateful for Department's comments.

Sent Department; repeated OffEmb Canton 547, Shanghai 714.

STUART

---

[58] *Ante,* p. 682.
[59] Vice Adm. Oscar C. Badger, Commander, U.S. Naval Forces, Western Pacific.

123 Stuart, J. Leighton : Telegram

The Ambassador in China (*Stuart*) *to the Secretary of State*

NANKING, June 18, 1949—7 p. m.
[Received June 19—2 :01 a. m.]

1322. Now that I have completed Shanghai visit only remaining major problem before my departure China is safety, withdrawal Mukden ConGen staff. Although wall of silence finally broken, progress this problem slow, doubtful. These [*There*] is also reported pre-Political Consultative Conference Peiping which I surmise Chen Ming-shu and others have gone north to attend. I should like to obtain some firsthand information on it before my return Washington. Chang Tung-sun,[60] who may still visit me Nanking en route Shanghai next month, will be delegate. (See Peiping's 644, June 9, repeated Department 969,[61] Canton 155.) Consequently if there is not too great discrepancy between happy conclusion Mukden affair and termination pre-PCC, I should like to delay my departure China until I can have received firsthand accounts of Communist position, possible future coalition government from some of my old friends in attendance. (See Embtel 1280, June 13, repeated Canton 529, Shanghai 693.) In any event I shall comply with Department's instruction to consult re exact date my intended departure within next few weeks.

Present status plans other major powers to recall Ambassadors for consultation are as follows:

1. Netherlands Ambassador expects recall and will not return China. (For Department's confidential information, I believe he is resisting recall.)

2. British Ambassador has no specific instructions to return but convinced it is HMG's intention recall him eventually and before formation Communist Nationalist [*National?*] Government. HMS *Amethyst* affair is of course holding Stevenson here as Mukden affair detains me.

3. French Ambassador has no instructions to return and on contrary believes his Government desires him remain China until France has worked out details recognition Chinese Communist Government. (Department may wish to try to bring French Government into line with others since it is absurd to believe that Communist aspirations French Indochina will be influenced by appeasement policy followed by French Ambassador, Nanking.)

4. Canadian Ambassador plans to return Canada for normal home leave this summer.

5. Belgian, Italian and Portuguese have no instructions, but Italian Ambassador is suggesting his return Rome during summer and following my departure. Believe Portuguese will follow our [and] British lead.

---

[60] Professor at Yenching University, Peiping ; member of the Democratic League.
[61] *Ante*, p. 376.

6. Indian and Burmese Ambassadors apparently have authority to leave at any time and are planning to return their respective countries as soon as exit permit facilities established and transportation available.

7. Thailand Ambassador instructed close Embassy Nanking and return Bangkok.

8. Afghan Minister recalled Kabul, leaving First Secretary in charge Nanking.

Sent Department; repeated OffEmb Canton 550, Shanghai 717.

STUART

---

123 Stuart, J. Leighton : Telegram

The Minister-Counselor of Embassy in China (Clark) to the Secretary of State

CANTON, June 19, 1949—10 a. m.
[Received 11 :49 p. m.]

Cantel 612. Agree that visit Ambassador [to] Canton en route Washington for consultation will excite speculation and misinterpretation (Department's 705, June 16 to Nanking, telCan 342, Shanghai 1213). In answer to inquiry which have received from various Government sources, have invariably replied felt sure Ambassador would wish visit Canton but feared Communists might refuse him exit permit except on condition he proceed direct US. Regardless Communist attitude, believe disadvantages possible repercussions Ambassador's visit here outweigh advantages conferring with me prior return Washington. From my telegrams he is aware trend my thinking. Also there is increasing evidence disintegration Kmt Government. By appointing Strong First Secretary and detailing him Chungking [62] we will give Government great boost morale. For Ambassador come south would, I believe, be overdoing it.

Am inclined agree Department's tentative view that in event simultaneous absence China [of] Ambassador and myself Strong should be appointed Chargé d'Affaires, Chungking. Both Soviet and Czech Missions in absence chiefs missions have appointed Canton representative Chargé and it may yet develop that both will move Chungking with Government. After all it will be Strong who will be representing US Government near Chinese Government and to let it be known that someone Nanking was assuming charge in absence Ambassador might lead embarrassing publicity as well as detract from gesture of support incident maintaining diplomatic contact Chungking.

Sent Department; repeated Nanking 409, Shanghai 348.

CLARK

---

[62] See telegram telCan No. 315, June 10, p. 696.

893.00B/6–1949 : Telegram

The Ambassador in China (Stuart) to the Secretary of State

NANKING, June 19, 1949—noon.
[Received June 20—7:24 a. m.]

1325. I left for Shanghai evening June 11 returning by night train June 16. Trip seemed very worth while. Immediate purpose was have conferences American businessmen and missionaries. I met each group separately with about 25 present each case. They seemed pleased this opportunity as I certainly was myself. I met individuals or smaller groups each type when discussion went along same lines. Also had several contacts with Chinese: One with Yenching graduates, another with Christian leaders. Of more practical value perhaps were visits, very confidentially, from certain politically active Chinese. One was Lo Lung-chi, Vice Chairman Democratic League, another with Li Chen, one of peace delegation.

Philip Fugh went with me, had long talk with Chang Han-fu,[63] opposite number to Huang Hua here. . . .

Foreign and Chinese employers alike apt worry over labor troubles. They have been precipitated by Communist propaganda in past, but new authorities thus far seem more conservative than employees in individual factories. Trade Unions seem somewhat between the two. Unless CCP leaders can adopt more realistic and tolerant course than their earlier theoretical approach, they may alienate both management and labor.

This trip to Shanghai gave me ample evidence local CCP authorities very anxious develop international trade and make utmost use Shanghai for promoting industry, communications, production, reconstruction. To this end they especially want friendly relations with USA. They very curious as to why I had made trip, what my impressions of their take-over had been and what my general attitude was to these issues. How much this is merely effort solve local problems or represents purely temporary tactical shift it [*is*] open question. They are hampered by strictness their own system and in way that subordinates have of overreaching their authority they seem to foreign merchants to be indifferent, incompetent. My impression is this largely due to regimentation which gives very little discretion and makes person concerned more anxious follow instructions than get results. Of greater importance is indication this trip afforded me of veering toward national interests in economic recovery with international help, at least among one influential element of CCP leaders. This gives us an opportunity to influence their policies by

[63] Director of Alien Affairs Office of Communist Military Control Commission at Shanghai.

firm but tactful insistence on principles which we believe essential to any satisfactory cooperation.

Sent Department 1325, repeated Canton 561, Shanghai 720.

STUART

---

123 Stuart, J. Leighton : Telegram

The Secretary of State to the Ambassador in China (Stuart)

WASHINGTON, June 23, 1949—8 p. m.

736. Urtel 1317, June 18. Dept understands Dept Air Force intends order Air Attaché's B–17 return US prior reassignment Canada. Dept informed Air Force instructing Air Attaché adjust plans for flight suit your schedule. Understand Air Force bearing cost trip as normal operational transfer. In view above no objection ur utilizing return of B–17 for trip to Washington. Suggest you coordinate plans Air Attaché keeping Dept informed. Dept wld not be disposed approve trip in Adm Badger's plane as costs, whether chargeable Navy or State, wld be excessive and wld rightly subject Navy, State and yourself to public criticism.

ACHESON

---

123 Stuart, J. Leighton : Telegram

The Ambassador in China (Stuart) to the Secretary of State

NANKING, June 24, 1949—5 p. m.
[Received June 24—10:27 a. m.]

1371. I have had word indirectly from Chen Ming-shu that he has already had conversations with Mao Tse-tung [64] and Chou En-lai which he regards as completely satisfactory. He reports that he will hasten his return to Shanghai via Nanking and expresses hope that I will delay my departure for US accordingly (see Embtel 1322, June 18). Further comment will be made after I have heard directly from Chen but I consider it significant that he saw these two top Communist leaders so promptly and advanced date return south with their approval.

STUART

---

[64] Chairman of the Central Committee of the Chinese Communist Party.

701.5193/6–2849

Memorandum of Conversation, by the Assistant Chief of the Division of Chinese Affairs (Freeman)

[WASHINGTON,] June 28, 1949.

Mr. Daridan [65] called today at his request and referred to a question which I had asked on a previous occasion with regard to any plans which the French Government might have to recall Ambassador Meyrier in Nanking to Paris for consultation. Mr. Daridan stated that he had queried Paris on this point and had received a non-committal reply from the Foreign Office. The French Government took the view, according to Mr. Daridan, that, as there was little likelihood of early diplomatic recognition of the Chinese Communist regime, no harm would be done by Ambassador Meyrier's remaining in Nanking for the time being.

It was obvious from other remarks of Mr. Daridan that the principal reason for the reluctance of the French Government to withdraw their Ambassador at this time was based on the increasing Communist threat to southeast Asia and the possible necessity of dealing with the Chinese Communists in this regard. I gained the impression that the French Government is of the opinion that it must maintain all of the contacts which it presently has with the Chinese Communists in order to protect French interests insofar as possible.

In commenting on the situation in China, Mr. Daridan stated at one point that nothing can now be done to save the Nationalist Government in China—that no military, political or economic assistance would be of any use. He also gave as his opinion that the Communists have the capability of occupying Yunnan Province at any time and of proceeding across the border into Indo-China. Discounting the feasibility or advisability of employing military force, Mr. Daridan suggested that the U.S. Government give consideration to employing economic warfare techniques against the Chinese Communists should they give indication of plans to invade Indo-China or Siam.

I pointed out to Mr. Daridan the probability that the Communists would require a considerable period of assimilation following their conquest of China proper before they would consider the invasion of foreign countries. I stated, however, that the U.S. had for some time been considering the application of certain controls over trade with Communist China, not primarily with the idea that such controls would be utilized immediately but in order that the machinery would be available for use at any time when such action might be considered necessary. Mr. Daridan indicated interest in the progress of discussions on this matter and I assured him that he would be informed

---

[65] Jean Daridan, Counselor of the French Embassy.

prior to any public announcement which might be made on this subject.[66]

---

123 Stuart, J. Leighton : Telegram

The Ambassador in China (Stuart) to the Secretary of State

NANKING, June 30, 1949—noon.
[Received June 30—5 :38 a. m.]

1410. Huang Hua called on me by appointment June 28. He reported that he had received message from Mao Tse-tung and Chou En-lai assuring me that they would welcome me to Peiping if I wished to visit Yenching University. Background of this suggestion is as follows:

In early June Philip Fugh, in one of his conversations with Huang, asked casually, and not under instructions from me, if it would be possible for me to travel to Peiping to visit my old University as had been my habit in previous years on my birthday and Commencement. At that time Huang made no comment. However, 2 weeks later, June 18 to be precise, in discussing my return to Washington for consultation, Huang himself raised question with Fugh of whether time permitted my making trip to Peiping. Fugh made no commitment, commenting only that he himself had made this suggestion 2 weeks earlier. Neither Fugh nor I followed up this suggestion but apparently Huang did. Present message (almost an invitation) is reply.

Regardless whether initiation this suggestion is considered [by] Peiping to have come from me or from Communists, I can only regard Huang's message as veiled invitation from Mao and Chou to talk with them while ostensibly visiting Yenching. To accept would undoubtedly be gratifying to them, would give me chance to describe American policy; its anxieties regarding Communism and world revolution; its desires for China's future; and would enable me to carry to Washington most authoritative information regarding CCP intentions. Such trip would be step toward better mutual understanding and should strengthen more liberal anti-Soviet element in CCP. It would provide unique opportunity for American official to talk to top Chinese Communists in informal manner which may not again present itself. It would be imaginative, adventurous indication of US open-minded attitude towards changing political trends in China and would probably have beneficial effect on future Sino-American relations.

---

[66] For documentation regarding trade controls, see vol. IX, pp. 817 ff.

On negative side, trip to Peiping before my return to US on consultation would undoubtedly start rumors and speculations in China and might conceivably embarrass Department because of American criticism. It would probably be misunderstood by my colleagues in Diplomatic Corps who might feel that US representative was first to break united front policy which we have sponsored toward Communist regime and might prove beginning of trek of chiefs of mission to Peiping on one pretext or another. Trip to Peiping at this time invariably suggests idea of making similar one to Canton before my return to US.

While visiting both capitals might effectively dramatize American interest in Chinese people as a whole, it might also appear as peacemaking gesture, unwarranted interference in China's internal affairs, and would probably be misunderstood by Chinese Communists, thus undoing any beneficial effects of visit north. Finally, trip of US Ambassador to Peiping at this time would enhance greatly prestige, national and international, of Chinese Communists and Mao himself and in a sense would be second step on our part (first having been my remaining Nanking) toward recognition Communist regime.

I received clear impression that Mao, Chou and Huang are very much hoping that I make this trip, whatever their motives. I, of course, gave Huang no answer to Mao's message, replying that, while I enjoyed going back to Yenching, this year had assumed it would be out of question, that I had already delayed longer than intended my departure for Washington; that travel on as yet incompletely restored railway line to Peiping might be taxing for "feeble old man", et cetera. Question of using my airplane was raised. Huang objected on ground danger from Communists' anti-aircraft batteries; that it would take couple days at least to give proper instructions and that there would always be some risk. He continued Peiping trip can now be made in less than 3 days by train, adding that all facilities of railway would be put at my disposal. I could, if thought desirable, make airplane travel condition to visit Peiping and it is not to be excluded that permission would be granted. There is consideration that prestige of travel Peiping my own plane would somewhat offset negative features outlined above.

I have made this rather full statement of case for Department's consideration and decision. I am, of course, ready to make journey by either means should Department consider it desirable, and should be grateful for instructions earliest and nature of reply to Huang.

Sent Department, repeated Shanghai 780, OffEmb Canton 594, Peiping 243.

STUART

123 Stuart, J. Leighton

Memorandum by Mr. John P. Davies of the Policy Planning Staff to the Director of the Staff (Kennan) [67]

[WASHINGTON,] June 30, 1949.

Walt [68] is very anxious that you see the underlying message from Stuart.[69] It strikes me as being extremely significant—even more so than the *démarche* made by Chou.[70] (It may even be an explanation of why Chou turned down the approach from Clubb through an intermediary.)

Obviously, the Communists would try to make as much capital as they could out of such a visit. All of the objections raised in the message are valid.

The utility of the visit to my mind is less what Stuart would learn—which would probably be a great deal—than what he could under our instructions tell the Communists. And that should be plenty. He should give them a curtain lecture in even stronger terms than that presented by Bedell Smith [71] to Stalin.[72]

What worries Walt most is the domestic reaction in this country to such a move. And that reaction could be violent. Walt's formula is that Stuart should accept only on the basis that he will fly in his own plane to Mukden to (*a*) make sure that all facilities were made available for the departure of the staff there and (*b*) bring Mr. and Mrs. Ward [73] back in his plane, stopping off at Peiping en route to see Mao and Chou. Walt feels, and I think rightly, that this would make a lot of face for us in Asia and that it would be a justification in the eyes of the American public for the visit.

The hooker in this is that such terms might well be quite unacceptable to the Communists and the opportunity for conversations would be lost by making it contingent upon such terms.

It seems to me that the problem of American public criticism could be met in a large measure by a statement which would be issued by the Department following the conversations in which we would make clear that Stuart had not gone to Peiping to play footy-footy with the Communists but had gone there, as would be the fact, to read them the riot act.

---

[67] Notation by Mr. Kennan for the Deputy Under Secretary of State (Rusk): "7/1/49-Mr. Rusk—Dean–Since I am leaving this afternoon thought you might like to see this. G.F.K." Notation by the Assistant Chief of the Division of Chinese Affairs (Freeman): "Shown to the Secretary 7/1/49 by Mr. Rusk." Notation by the Director of the Office of Far Eastern Affairs (Butterworth): "Absent from Dept 7/1/49 seen 7/5/49 WWB".

[68] W. Walton Butterworth.

[69] Telegram No. 1410, June 30, *supra*.

[70] For documentation, see pp. 357 ff.

[71] Ambassador in the Soviet Union, 1946–49.

[72] Marshal Josif Vissarionovich Stalin, Soviet Prime Minister and Chairman of the Council of Ministers of the Soviet Union.

[73] Angus Ward, Consul General at Mukden.

Walt's position is that the ultimate decision turns on an estimate of American domestic reaction and that that is a factor which he is not competent to judge. It must be weighed by the Secretary and a decision made by him.

---

123 Stuart, J. Leighton : Telegram

The Consul General at Shanghai (Cabot) to the Secretary of State

SHANGHAI, July 1, 1949—4 p. m.
[Received July 1—11:29 a. m.]

2585. ReEmbtel 780, June 30, noon.[74] I suspect one of reasons Mao and Chou may wish see Ambassador is to discuss increasingly difficult situation prevailing Shanghai. Telegrams already sent by Consul General and two now being drafted show how Communists have found themselves involved in unexpected and unwanted snarls with foreigners and how seriously they must be concerned at course of economic developments in Shanghai.[75]

With regard attitude of other friendly powers, we strongly suspect Western interest in Shanghai would welcome Ambassador's proposed trip with open arms as first means of putting West viewpoint before top Communist leaders and therefore of protecting those interests. All West representatives here both official and private are suffering from severe case of pessimism and frustration. Although British might feel some pangs of jealousy at American Ambassador having first top-level talks, I believe this would be much more than counterbalanced by their anxiety to have something effective done to protect their immense commercial stake in China.

Sent Department, repeated Nanking 1424.

CABOT

---

123 Stuart, J. Leighton : Telegram

The Secretary of State to the Ambassador in China (Stuart)

WASHINGTON, July 1, 1949—6 p. m.

775. Following highest level consideration urtel 1410,[76] you are instructed under no circumstances to make visit Peiping. Principal reasons for negative decision are those contained urtel.

ACHESON

---

[74] Same as telegram No. 1410 from Nanking, p. 766.
[75] For documentation on conditions in Shanghai, see pp. 1155 ff.
[76] Dated June 30, noon, p. 766.

123 Stuart, J. Leighton : Telegram

The Minister-Counselor of Embassy in China (Clark) to the
Secretary of State

CANTON, July 2, 1949—6 p. m.
[Received July 3—1 : 30 a. m.]

Cantel 681. Advantages Ambassador visit Peiping seem obvious (Nanking's 1410, June 30, to Department, repeated Shanghai 780, Canton 594, Peiping 243). However, in making decision for or against, Department should bear in mind numerous requests I have received that Dr. Stuart visit Canton prior his return US. For Ambassador visit Peiping and not Canton would be taken here as unfriendly act and would be terrific blow prestige Government which has not much prestige left.

Sent Department Cantel 681; repeated Nanking 457, Shanghai 394, Peiping 12.

CLARK

---

123 Stuart, J. Leighton : Telegram

The Ambassador in China (Stuart) to the Secretary of State

NANKING, July 6, 1949—11 a. m.
[Received July 6—2 : 28 a. m.]

1442. For purposes of making test flight of Embassy plane, Air Attaché is informing local authorities that I hope to leave Nanking for US around July 15. I have had word from Chen Ming-shu that he will be in Nanking July 12–13 en route from Peiping back to Shanghai. (See Embtel 1322, June 18 to Department, repeated Canton 550, Shanghai 717.) After my conversation with him I will be ready to return to US on consultation and should like to leave between 15th and 20th this month.

Mukden affair still drags on. Fugh spoke to Huang Hua about it again last week (see Embtel 1441, July 5 to Department,[77] repeated Canton 609, Shanghai 800). While latter was noncommittal, inference Fugh drew was favorable to ultimate settlement. If I could have indication from Ward within next 10 days that he were making progress with packers, skippers [*shippers*], transportation, I would feel that I could do little more for him here and could myself depart with some degree of satisfaction.

Since considerable planning is involved at this end and Communist inexperience, native suspicion will work toward delays, does Department approve my setting target date for departure on or about July 15? (Deptel 705, June 16, repeated telCan 342, Shanghai 1213.[)]

---

[77] Not printed.

If no progress Mukden, target date can be advanced from time to time. For security reason, prefer actual date of my departure be kept secret until after arrival first stop, that is Okinawa.

Sent Department, repeated OffEmb Canton 610, Shanghai 802.

STUART

893.00/6–2249

Memorandum by General Chen Ming-shu, Chairman of the Shanghai Board of the Kuomintang Revolutionary Committee (KmtRC)[78]

SUPPLEMENTARY MEMO TO CONVERSATION WITH MR. L. STUART

As I have a long standing friendship with the Chinese Communist authorities and I also have with you a recent friendship of a special nature, I had personal conversations with you several times at your invitation and was commissioned by you to discuss them with the Chinese Communist authorities. I now wish to inform you of the important points in the replies which I received as a result of my conversations with the Chinese Communist authorities.

Before reporting what they said I first want to tell you, with complete objectivity and lack of prejudice, what I personally gained from my observations. We must both put aside our national concepts—only thus will it be easy to gain a true insight. The results of my observations may be divided into five points:

1. *Chinese revolutionary history is divided into periods.*

[Here follows historical discourse. It concludes that success of present revolution is merely military success in war and political construction will be much more difficult.]

2. *The people's century is beginning to appear in China.*

What does it mean to say that the people's century is beginning to appear in China? It may be proved by the following points:

(*a*) In my contacts with all classes in China it may be said without exception, no bureaucratic attitudes are to be observed, still less bureaucratic habits. From administrative organs through the various social groups, all give evidence of having thoroughly destroyed bureaucracy. While in Peiping at this time I observed that from Chairman Mao on down they all had eradicated *official calls* and similar empty forms. If you had an important matter and asked to see someone then a time would be fixed for an interview or they might not wait for a request for an interview but go themselves to see you. There

---

[78] Handed to the Ambassador in China and carried by him on his return to the United States; received in the Department about August 15. The Chief of the Division of Chinese Affairs (Sprouse) in a memorandum on August 25 described this as "of considerable interest as indicative of the thinking of the Chinese Communists and also at least of one non-Communist Chinese". (893.00/8–2549)

was absolutely no "polite conversation". Talk was confined to discussion or solution of actual problems. There was not one among them who did not display the aspect of the most ordinary man, particularly Mr. Mao. Immediately upon seeing his friendly attitude one unconsciously felt "this is truly a leader of the people". It might be said that if you draw apart from the people you cannot see Mao Tse-tung. Mao is the people. Also, if you draw apart from the people you cannot see the Communist Party. The Communist Party is the people. Their spirit of study, the rigid execution of their system of criticism and self-criticism, particularly as it hastens political reform and as a motive power for construction, I will not take time to elucidate in detail.

(b) What is the secret of success of the People's Liberation Army's high discipline and high education? It is in causing each officer and soldier to understand not only the object of the revolution but to understand that his duty is to act for the people and that acting for the people is acting for himself. The people are the owners of the land, that is to say, he himself is owner of the land although the portion belonging to him may be extremely small. However, without struggling to establish the correct position of the whole body of land, his small portion might be lost. Therefore, the sole policy and objective of the PLA is to fight for the attainment of the rights of all the people. In contrast, the men in Chiang Kai-shek's army do not know why they are fighting. They fight blindly and without purpose. It is this which determines victory or defeat, prosperity or adversity.

(c) The People's Liberation Army, both behind the lines and at the front, creates all kinds of lines of support through the organized strength and the great contributions of the "People's auxiliaries". This is a veritable miracle. The 600,000 people's auxiliaries organized by the present Vice-Governor of Shantung, General Kuo Tzu-hua, may be cited as evidence. This enormous unit of people's auxiliaries with innumerable camels, horses and carts was initiated, brought together, apportioned, sent forward, controlled and managed by the people themselves without any need for supervision by soldiers and without any case of desertion. According to what General Kuo told me when I passed through Tsinan on my way north, at the present time there are 50,000 people's auxiliaries who have crossed the Yangtze with the Army and have not yet returned from south of the river. This amazing kind of organization and enormous strength seems almost unbelievable. If it is not a miracle what is it? Another instance was that of the Tientsin–Pukow railway where, except for the bridge across the Yellow River, almost all of the steel bridges along the route had been destroyed by Chiang's army, but the army and the people's auxiliaries worked day and night to restore them so that section by section through traffic was resumed. Finally, because the great steel bridge across the Huai River had been blown up, another crossing spot was found and by the use of wood alone in place of steel, within a very short time they were successful in restoring through traffic. This also was almost unbelievable. These two things are proof of the immense strength of the people and its inexhaustibility.

(d) On my trip south from Peiping between Hsuchow, Pengpu and Nanking I saw the whole body of civil and military public employees, troops and aroused people struggling day and night against the floods. Everywhere newspapers were full of the struggle for flood prevention. This again is sufficient proof of the cooperation of Army and people, and the unity of the officials and the people. Officials and army do not exist outside the ranks of the people. The four facts which I have cited are confirmation that my assertion that the people's century is beginning to appear in China is not merely empty words.

3. *The importance of this great manifestation of the Chinese People's Revolution in influencing the world situation.*

This point need not be dwelt upon at length. I shall mention briefly two recent illustrations. First, are the successive meetings in Europe in the last six months of the World Peace Congress, the World Federation of Trade Unions, and other labor and professional bodies, all of which unanimously announced their recognition of the influence on the world situation of the victory of the Chinese People's Liberation Army, expressing their highest hopes for the Chinese Revolution and submitting valuable criticisms. Second, is the revolutionary success of Mr. Mao Tse-tung's doctrine of progression from agrarianism to urbanism, which was not contained in earlier Marxist-Leninist thought. As it gradually enters upon its period of success, we first see the extraordinary contribution of his theory to Marxism–Leninism. Thus, it may be called a Sinicized Marxism–Leninism. Mr. Stalin also has told his comrades that the Soviet Union was not aiding the Chinese Communist Party, but we should study the excellent discoveries made by the CCP. It may be seen that the success of the present revolution exercises an influence, not only on international bodies, as shown above, but on Russia as well. This is of great importance.

We must thoroughly explain the essence and content of the foregoing three points in order to avoid any misconception of the Chinese Communist political line and to make clear that that line *has always been definite, unalterable and correct. The phrase, "leaning to one-side" indicates this, but on no account can "leaning to one side" be mis-interpreted as implying dependence on others. To understand the phrase in that way would be an insult.* It must be understood that *our political line is entirely our own.* It must be further understood *as regards our national independence there can never be any question of dependence on others.*

Furthermore, *national position and political line must not be confused.* These two questions *basically are one, but they also stand opposite to each other.* For example, during the Second World War, *the political line of Russia was not the same as that of England and America; yet, from the point of view of national position, Russia could fight shoulder to shoulder with England and America.* Another example is the *sympathy manifested by your Mr. Wallace* [79] *for the people's front, naturally, in opposition to the position of President Truman. Notwithstanding, Mr. Wallace cannot be said to differ with President Truman on the question of American national standing, since in this matter he is necessarily profoundly patriotic. China's present revolution, aside from uprooting feudal and compradore influences and casting off all foreign bonds, must uphold the dignity of the nation's independence and sovereignty. We must obtain a long period of peaceful construction and achieve a strong position.*

It is essential that we understand thoroughly the unity and the opposition of the foregoing two propositions in order to understand the kind of mission with regard to China's future being undertaken by Mr. Mao Tse-tung and the party led by him. I offer these explanations to assist you in judging soundly because your remarks with respect to Mr. Mao's statements to the opening session of the Preparatory Committee of the new PCC and on the anniversary of the founding of the Chinese Communist Party on July 1, indicated disagreement and doubt. What I have said above is in accordance with Mr. Mao's comment, *"In politics, severity is necessary. In economics, give-and-take is permissible."* In our conversation yesterday, because of considerations of time, I was unable to complete my remarks, and I agreed to write a supplementary memorandum for your reference. The four points which Mr. Chou En-lai asked me to convey to you, I have already stated in detail in our conversation and have also recorded them on a separate sheet.

CH'EN MING-SHU, July 10 [1949].

[Annex 1]

Memoranda by Mr. Lo Hai-sha for General Chen Ming-shu

1. Chou (En-lai) and Yeh (Chien-ying) [80] repeated last year's telegraphic request for continued liaison.
2. Mao (Tse-tung) was still able to name the date of the Stuart–Ch'en talks last year.

---

[79] Henry A. Wallace, Vice President of the United States, 1941–1945; Progressive Party nominee for President in 1948.
[80] Communist Mayor of Peiping.

3. The emphasis they placed on studying the documents and (the way) they mentioned comparative figures.

4. Praise for Mr. Stuart's spirit during the Japanese period and his accomplishments during several decades of educational work in China.

5. The friendship of President Roosevelt, General Stilwell,[81] and Mr. Wallace for China.

6. They sent Mr. Stuart their most important hopes for the future.

The importance attached by the CCP to future Sino-American relations as evidenced by the above 6 points.

Moreover, it can be said with respect to the very great hopes sent Mr. Stuart that these are the very great hopes for future Sino-American relations. What they mean by "hopes" is of course not that the U.S. walk the road of the Soviet Union or enter the embrace of the Soviet Union, but they hope that hereafter the U.S. will not again aid the reactionary government of Chiang Kai-shek in China; and they hope that she will be able to act and formulate policies in the manner of President Roosevelt, General Stilwell and Mr. Wallace. If the U.S. can treat the future China like this, China will naturally treat the U.S. with similar friendship. This of course will depend upon Mr. Stuart's efforts after he returns to his country. (Signed) Lo Hai-sha

1. Looking at their general propaganda Mr. Mao spoke personally to Mr. Ch'en asking that Mr. Stuart read his statement of June 20,[82] from which he would know his (Mao's) attitude. Of course what he referred to was the last section, in which he hoped that China would open diplomatic and commercial relations with all countries on the basis of independence and sovereignty.

2. The July 1 article was of course a sort of statement for his own party [83] and cannot be viewed in a purely political light. Furthermore, in the sixth paragraph from the end he clearly admits that the realization of socialism will still require a long time and that it can be said that China is a special case.

3. The July 7 message to the Preparatory Committee for the New Political Consultative Council commemorates Japanese aggression against China. Since Japan today is under American leadership, America is mentioned at many points. Their way of talking about America should be divided into two types. The first type, constituting 7 or 8 tenths, uses only the word "America". The second type, only about 2 or 3 tenths, uses "American imperialism." From this we can see that they discriminate in their method of speaking. Ref-

---

[81] Lt. Gen. Joseph W. Stilwell, Commanding General, U.S. Army Forces in the China–Burma–India Theater, 1942–44, and Chief of Staff to Generalissimo Chiang Kai-shek.

[82] See telegram No. 1045, June 20, from the Consul General at Peiping, p. 392.

[83] See telegram No. 1443, July 6,, 1 p.m., from the Ambassador in China, p. 405.

erences to "America" means the great part of the American administration which is friendly to China. Reference to "American imperialism" means the bad part of the American Government. This is like the case of the Kmt, where they cooperate with the KmtRC but stand in opposition to the Kmt reactionary clique. This is a very clear fact.

Judging from the above three points, as soon as formal diplomatic relations are established between the U.S. and China, a different attitude will be manifest in their propaganda. (Signed) Lo Hai-sha.

Regarding the individual treatment of foreigners according to what their authorities told Mr. Ch'en, they dispose of Soviet citizens infringing the law in the Northeast uniformly in accordance with Chinese methods. Hence, they will treat the individual nationals of other countries in the same way. This point is also a general phenomenon in sovereign and independent states and cannot, of course, be considered as a specially hostile attitude.

Concerning the disposition on this occasion of the American cotton in Shanghai, the CCP has not issued one word. In my opinion, this is because it is not proper for them to speak in the absence of formal diplomatic relations. At the same time, pressed by personal consideration for Mr. Stuart, I think that even without going through formal diplomatic procedures, if America publicizes this affair, they will of course not deny it. (Signed) Lo Hai-sha

[Annex 2]

Two Talks With Mr. Chou En-lai

I. The Revolution has been forced upon us.

The breaking of the peace originated with the U.S. Because the U.S. wanted dictatorial rule, she supported reactionaries.

Nobody can interfere with the self-determination of the people's democracies.

Interference has taken place in countries such as Greece, Italy, and China.

Today has come about because there has been supporting of reaction and disruption of unity.

Mr. Mao Tse-tung's four steps for dealing with the enemy:

1. Control others by letting them have the initiative;
2. To retire and not seek a struggle (in the face of superior force);
3. To requite good with good (and bad with bad);
4. In dealing with others, use their own methods.

That the supporters of peace should be opposed to aggression, interference, and monopoly is because of their freely made decision.

Our peace front has been built by all peoples.   This is the first idea.

II. 1. In the time of Yuan Shih-k'ai the Soviet Union was the first to establish friendly relations with the Kuomintang of Sun Yat-sen.[84]

2. The Soviet Union was the first to recognize the Chinese Revolution.

3. Also in the anti-Japanese War, the Soviet Union was the first to give aid to China.

4. The U.S. in the beginning gave Japan material aid—such as scrap iron, etc.

5. The U.S. aided Chiang Kai-shek.

6. The Soviet Union respected Sino-Soviet treaties.

7. We will always remember the friendship accorded us in the period after the war by President Roosevelt, General Stilwell, and Mr. Wallace.

8. The plan of Marshall [85] and Wedemeyer [86] to aid Chiang.   Great virtue never commits transgressions; small virtue may transgress.

America's many good points pertain to small matters, Soviet Russia's to large.

III. With respect to the question of Mr. Stuart himself, we must estimate virtue and measure power.   Of course, he is a representative of imperialism—people in government carry out the policies of their government.   But the personal qualities he displayed during the time he was confined in Japan (*sic*)[87] very much deserve respect.   In the present case too, we must listen to his words and observe his actions.

IV. When he says that China depends upon the American economy and that America does not depend upon China, he is completely wrong.

His statistics are reliable, but his conclusion is the reverse of the truth.

He says the U.S. has no need at all for t'ung oil, raw silk, pig's bristles, etc.

1937   69,000,000 (dollars) [U.S. imports from China] [88]

---

[84] President Yuan Shih-kai (1912–1916) died in June 1916; in 1923 Moscow's representative in China A. A. Joffe issued a joint statement at Shanghai with Sun Yat-sen, leader of the Kuomintang. This preceded the sending of Soviet Ambassador L. M. Karakhan to Peiping.

[85] General of the Army George C. Marshall, President Truman's Special Representative with rank of Ambassador in China, December 1945–January 1947.

[86] Lt. Gen. Albert C. Wedemeyer, President Truman's Special Representative in China, July–September 1947.

[87] Mr. Stuart, at the time President of Yenching University, was held in Japanese military custody at Peiping from 1941 to 1945.

[88] Brackets appear in the source text.

Imports he says cannot be done without: Petroleum, steel, machinery, cotton, timber, automobiles, paper, photographic supplies, etc. U.S. $55,000,000 [Chinese imports from U.S.][88a]

1947   Imports: U.S. $233,000,000
       Exports: U.S. $46,000,000

The result is quite the opposite (of what he says).

The U.S. wants to relieve its crisis and is exporting in great quantity. Its stomach is sick with glut, ours with hunger. It is not at all equivalent to there being no market for our exports—goods not purchased would not exceed $46,000,000. (US $69,000,000 is less than the value of a million tons of soy beans.) In expanding its production, China does not fear lack of markets. For example, England and Russia want t'ung oil. England is the most important buyer of pig's bristles. Other countries all want our vegetable oil, eggs, handicrafts, tungsten ore, etc.

IMPORTS

Such things as tobacco we can plant for ourselves and don't need to seek outside. As for iron and steel, there are the factories at An-shan, Ta-ming, Shih-ching-shan, etc. We also don't depend (on the outside) for paper, cotton, or timber. That leaves petroleum, machinery, automobiles, and photographic materials which must be imported. But in 1937 these four classes (of goods) which were imported from the U.S. amounted to only U.S. [$]11,000,000.

FOOD

North of the Yangtze (this problem) was solved in two years, so that this area is now more than self-sufficient, with land reform production increasing daily. South of the Yangtze we have not yet investigated the problem.

HEAVY INDUSTRY

When the tide is in flood the boat is high. Agricultural production has increased. Cotton production has improved and increased. Within five years it will be possible to start on the road of construction of heavy industry.

PETROLEUM PRODUCTS

After new lands have been opened up, we will export on a big scale. These exports will be exchanged for machine goods. (In 1937 imports of American machine goods amounted to U.S. $3,000,000 and were 6% of U.S. exports.)

(Production of) food in the Northeast is 11,000,000 tons (sic). This year's plan calls for production [increase?] of 1,500,000 tons.

---

[88] Brackets appear in the source text.

In future years we will be able to return to the figure of the time of the Japanese (occupation).

(American) exports last year included $13,000,000,000 of Marshall Plan (aid). The $353,000,000, including relief goods, which entered China amounted to 2.6%.

We must still *base ourselves on the principle of equal advantage.*

We must reject unplanned economic surplus material.

No special rights, no monopolies, equal advantage, when the tide is in flood the boat is high.

In conclusion, I do not depend upon you, you depend upon me.

If you should seek to come in a private capacity, it is possible that you would be able to meet a person in responsible position.

893.00/7–1149 : Telegram

The Consul General at Peiping (Clubb) to the Secretary of State

PEIPING, July 11, 1949—11 a. m.
[Received July 11—6 : 41 a. m.]

1153. ReEmbtel 1410, June 30. On basis experience to date this office with Commie regime, respectfully offer following comments [on] reported trip Ambassador [to] Peiping:

1. Commies undoubtedly desirous increasing their prestige in every possible manner and would desire if there be any contact between Commie and American side that it be so as to enhance their prestige (Contel 869, May 20 [89]).

2. Experience re Chou note (Contel 1080, June 27 [90]), however, would indicate Commies presently in fact chary of such contact, this deduction fitting in with what seems to be official Commie position that they will have contacts only if official recognition has come from abroad.

3. In circumstances, therefore, would recommend most earnestly that Ambassador proceed Peiping with plan and appearance to meet with Mao Tse-tung and Chou En-lai only if and when there might be categorical assurance from Commie side that meeting arranged. Invite attention to serious loss to American prestige which would follow upon Mao-Chou refusal see Ambassador if he made trip Peiping with apparent intent meeting with them.

Note this connection was told July 8 . . . it was currently rumored in town Ambassador was proceeding Peiping after trip USA for purpose according recognition Commie regime.

---

[89] Not printed.
[90] *Ante,* p. 398.

552-963—78——50

Note further, for what it is worth, in this connection Keon [91] reports to Barrett [92] on basis information given him, Keon, by Chinese Commie girl with whom he intimate, that Commies charge he bungled matter Chou note by failing (1) make clear no specific reply expected and (2) keep Chou En-lai's name out of matter, Chou being undesirous of being brought into it personally. Keon, however, confirmed that (1) Barrett's notes of Keon's report were faithful record of meeting as experienced by Keon and (2) Chou had said without hesitation Barrett would know from whom message came. Commie said moreover, per same source, is now disturbed by what they view "Ambassador's efforts contact Chou through other sources" for presumed purpose endeavoring still deliver American reply. Keon expressed opinion Chou himself is "on the spot" as result denouement.

Believe that experiences Mukden, Peiping, Nanking and now Shanghai are clear proof present hostility Commie leaders toward USA. I have limited self to comment on only one aspect matter in point, but would express firm conviction that it is most undesirable make moves in Commie direction which could be interpreted as signs American weakness.

Repeated Nanking 823, OffEmb Canton 210, Shanghai 777.

CLUBB

---

123 Clark, Lewis : Telegram

The Ambassador in China (Stuart) to the Secretary of State

NANKING, July 11, 1949—noon.
[Received July 11—2:11 a. m.]

1472. I would appreciate if Department would instruct Lewis Clark to meet me Okinawa for consultation on or about July 18.

Sent Department; repeated OffEmb Canton 617.

STUART

---

123 Stuart, J. Leighton

Memorandum by the Secretary of State of a Conversation With the President

[WASHINGTON,] July 11, 1949.

RETURN OF AMBASSADOR STUART

The President agrees that Ambassador Stuart should not arrive in this country prior to issuance of the White Paper.[93]

---

[91] Michael Keon, Australian newspaperman in China employed by the United Press.
[92] Col. David D. Barrett, Assistant Military Attaché in China.
[93] Department of State, *United States Relations With China* (Washington, Government Printing Office, 1949). For documentation on the publication of the China White Paper, see vol. IX, pp. 1365 ff.

The President also believes that it is important and desirable for the Ambassador to visit Canton before returning. He believes that it would not be understood in the United States for the Ambassador to return after being out of touch for so long with the Government to which he is accredited.

125.633/7–1149 : Telegram

The Ambassador in China (Stuart) to the Secretary of State

NANKING, July 11, 1949—4 p. m.
[Received July 12—1 :11 a. m.]

1475. From Peiping's 803, July 7, repeated Department 1136,[94] Canton 203, Shanghai 765, infer that Ward feels he is making progress closure Mukden Consulate General and I am inclined to believe that there is little my continued presence can contribute to expedite handling Mukden closure, withdrawal. (See Embtel 1442, July 6, repeated Canton 710, Shanghai 802.) Consequently I have set confidential date July 18 for my departure Nanking and would appreciate Department's earliest confirmation its approval. Persons accompanying me will be those listed in Embtel 1468, July 9 to Department, repeated Canton 616, Shanghai 818.[95]

Sent Department; repeated Embassy Canton 620, Shanghai 823, Peiping 260.

STUART

---

123 Stuart, J. Leighton : Telegram

The Secretary of State to the Ambassador in China (Stuart)

WASHINGTON, July 12, 1949—6 p. m.

819. In accordance urtel 1475 Jul 11, you are authorized depart from Nanking on Jul 18.

ACHESON

---

123 Stuart, J. Leighton : Telegram

The Secretary of State to the Ambassador in China (Stuart)[96]

WASHINGTON, July 12, 1949—6 p. m.

820. As indicated in Deptel 819 [97] you are to depart from Nanking on Jul 18 for Okinawa.

---

[94] Not printed.
[95] *Post*, p. 894.
[96] Repeated to the Minister-Counselor at Canton as telCan 446.
[97] *Supra*.

Pres and I desire that upon arrival Okinawa you proceed thence to Canton for brief visit since you have been so long out of touch with govt to which you are accredited. You will leave in Okinawa all passengers including Philip Fugh and you will proceed to Canton alone with Air Attaché and crew. It is understood that B–17 will be available in Hong Kong or Canton on which you can return via Okinawa to U.S. You should depart on B–17 on Jul 23 (Hong Kong time). I wish you to know but I do not wish info communicated to any Chinese and to no one except Jones and Clark that Depts White Paper on China is scheduled be made available to press on Jul 23 Wash time for publication morning of Jul 25 Wash time and therefore it is imperative that you will have taken off for US by time its release to press.

It is equally imperative that effect of issuance of this White Paper be in no way confused or diminished by any other press statement either while you are in Canton or en route to US. Therefore I wish you to instruct all members of your party to refrain from giving any interviews or indulging in any conversations which by any chance could indirectly result in interviews and when questioned by the press you will in accordance with Depts suggestion contained in its 510 to Nanking Apr 22 [98] merely state that you are returning to US to report to Secy of State and that until you have done so you have no statement to make. As you are aware particular care will have to be taken during your overstops in Honolulu and San Francisco.

It is obviously highly desirable that in your visits with officials of ChiGovt in Canton you vouchsafe no info or views but indicate that you have come to Canton to acquaint yourself with views of ChiGovt prior to returning to Wash. Same applies equally to your contact with such of your foreign diplo colleagues as are now residing in Canton.

ACHESON

---

123 Stuart, J. Leighton : Telegram

The Ambassador in China (Stuart) to the Secretary of State

NANKING, July 13, 1949—4 p. m.
[Received July 13—7:31 a. m.]

1500. Chen Ming-shu called on me July 1 [*12?*] en route from Peiping to Shanghai (see Embtel 1442, July 6, to Department). In view of my imminent departure from China, I shall report on these conversations after my arrival in Department. I shall bring with me memoranda of conversations.[99] Suffice it to say that Mr. Chen

---

[98] *Ante*, p. 682.
[99] See memorandum of July 10 by General Chen Ming-shu, p. 771.

was well received in Peiping and returned south enthusiastic about dynamic quality of new leadership (Communist). Despite Chen's enthusiasm, which is not without underlying awareness of Communist menace to his party and to China, his report in general was discouraging to me. There is no hint of any deviation from present political course set, including relations with USA. There is expression of naive hope that despite political relations, economic relations can and will be established between China and the West.

STUART

---

123 Stuart, J. Leighton : Telegram

The Ambassador in China (Stuart) to the Secretary of State

NANKING, July 13, 1949—6 p. m.
[Received July 13—1:56 p. m.]

1516. I of course will comply with instructions contained in Deptel 820, July 12; repeated telCan 446. In reaching decision that I visit Canton en route Washington I assume you had in mind negative aspects of such visit set forth in Canton's telegram 612, June 19 to Department; repeated Nanking 409, with which I agreed (see mytel 1317, June 18; repeated Canton 547).

I suggest my new itinerary not be given to press either here, Washington or at Canton until after my departure Nanking. While neither I nor any of my party including plane crew have yet received our exit visas, I still hope to leave Nanking 18th and maintain schedule established Deptel under reference.

Sent Department; repeated Canton [for] Clark.

STUART

---

123 Stuart, J. Leighton : Telegram

The Secretary of State to the Ambassador in China (Stuart)[1]

WASHINGTON, July 14, 1949—1 p. m.

828. ReDeptel 820 July 12 rptd telCan 446. Presume Emb has given consideration possibility AirAtt[2] plane being intercepted en route Okinawa by CAF[3] planes as well as possibility drawing ground fire from Chi Commie forces China mainland particularly if both sides given no prior info re flight plans. Dept recommends, therefore, Emb take steps through ConGens Shanghai and Taipei[4] and OffEmb Can-

---

[1] Repeated to the Minister-Counselor at Canton as telCan 451.
[2] Air Attaché.
[3] Chinese Air Force.
[4] John M. Cabot, Consul General at Shanghai, and Donald D. Edgar, Consul at Taipei.

ton to acquaint local Commie and Natl Govt auths re details ETD [5] and route to be fol, requesting at same time safe passage for plane. Dept suggests such info might be transmitted local Commie auths without any indication passenger list or future flight plans plane after arrival Okinawa as being in accordance their instrs AirAtt plane depart China. Natl Govt auths shld be informed re further flight plans after plane reaches Okinawa. Clark, Edgar and Cabot shld be instructed, however, not prior Amb's arrival Okinawa in any way give indication his plans visit Canton as disclosing such info if leaked to Commies might result in inability Amb and party depart Nanking.

ACHESON

123 Stuart, J. Leighton : Telegram

The Ambassador in China (Stuart) to the Secretary of State

NANKING, July 14, 1949—3 p. m.
[Received July 17—11:33 p. m.]

1522. In retrospect I feel that Communist leaders picked up chance suggestion that I might like to spend my birthday again this year at Yenching with extraordinary alacrity and I can only interpret it as earnest desire that I take initiative to travel to Peiping and be available for conversations with some of them. Not only did Huang Hua raise question twice here, but, according to my friends in Peiping, Mao openly stated that I would be welcome in Peiping if I wished to visit my old university. From other sources I have received reports that Mao–Chou [6] counted on entertaining me and talking to me during this ostensibly private visit to Peiping. Cabot reported on July 8 from Shanghai that "Chinese friend informed me he has word from Peiping that you asked Chou En-lai whether you might visit Yenching and see him and that Chou replied noncommittally".

When I refused to go I feel that they all lost some face but particularly Huang Hua who first took initiative here. My suspicions this respect are confirmed by recent remark of Huang Hua's number two, Ch'en Ying, who, in connection with some difficulties I and my party are having in obtaining our exit permits from China, said to Fugh, "If Stuart had gone Peiping all these little questions would have been easily settled". Fugh feels that since time when I told Huang of my belief that I would not be able to go to Peiping attitude of Communist authorities from top down has changed and hardened, including our personal relations locally. I am inclined to agree there has been change but whether it comes from chagrin over my

[5] Estimated time of departure.
[6] Mao Tse-tung and Chou En-lai.

refusal to visit Peiping or general reflection of orthodox line laid down in Mao's July 1 article [7] I cannot say.

Sent Department; repeated OffEmb Canton 635, Shanghai 854. Department pass Peiping 272.

STUART

___

123 Stuart, J. Leighton : Telegram

The Ambassador in China (Stuart) to the Secretary of State

NANKING, July 14, 1949—6 p. m.
[Received July 14—3 : 14 a. m.]

1526. Feel I must advise Department I am running into difficulties obtaining exit permits myself and party and warn that I may not be able to depart on 18th as planned. Exit permit forms were available to us only July 11. They provide for "shop guarantee" (guarantee by local commercial firm that departing foreigner leaves behind no debts, unpaid taxes, civil or criminal charge pending and also guarantor assumes liability for any unlawful act committed by person leaving China during period prior to his actual departure). We have assumed this would not be required of myself and my party all of whom are members of Embassy. Communist authorities however are insisting on this point as well, at least with respect to other members of my party, and we have over past 24 hours made discreet inquiries among local banks and Embassy contractors to ascertain if they would act as guarantors for Cabot, Hinderer, Air Attaché and members of crew, thus far without success. We have now inquired if American firm, such as Socony-Vacuum, CalTex, etc., would be acceptable and have had no reply from Aliens Affairs Office. With respect to myself, Huang Hua said he would waive requirement to extent of not requiring "shop guarantee" but "personal guarantee of some friend". I inferred Huang himself would sign as my guarantor which would in effect be waiving of this requirement.

I have not reported this complication earlier hoping that it would be treated as formality and not develop into major issue. However, as only 3 days remain before my intended departure I am becoming more concerned that we might be unable to find any local guarantors for members of my party and that even in my case requirement will not be waived as I had originally understood. Fugh has been unable to get in touch with Huang Hua for past 2 days to discuss this and other less important matters concerned with my departure. Thus we are unable to get to anyone in authority. I assume Department will agree that I should not comply with Communists' request for guarantor, personal or otherwise, if Huang Hua himself does not undertake

___

[7] See telegram No. 1443, July 6, 1 p. m., from the Ambassador, p. 405.

this formality. On other hand Department might consider my departure on schedule and avoidance of further complications with Communist authorities sufficiently desirable to authorize member of my staff remaining Nanking to act as guarantor for us all. I am not at all sure that this would be acceptable.

Unless instructed to contrary and if feasible locally I shall proceed with obtaining of "shop guarantees" for other members my party which I have hopes will result in more lenient attitude toward my own application for exit. I should be very grateful for Department's guidance earliest and shall report developments this regard promptly.

Sent Department; repeated Canton 638, Shanghai 857.

STUART

---

123 Stuart, J. Leighton : Telegram

The Ambassador in China (Stuart) to the Secretary of State

NANKING, July 15, 1949—2 p. m.
[Received July 15—5 : 15 a. m.]

1531. Morning radio reports that Generalissimo [8] has arrived Canton to pay his long-anticipated visit to seat of government (Canton's 728, July 13 to Department [9]). I assume he will remain several days and that my visit to Canton (if I depart Nanking on schedule) will coincide with his (see Deptel 820, July 12 to Nanking, repeated telCan 446). From this end I consider speculation, misinterpretation which would inevitably result most undesirable and to be avoided if at all possible. It will be impossible to convince world public opinion that Generalissimo's and my visits to Canton this time are pure coincidence; Communists will make all possible political capital out of it and undoubtedly consider that in my departure plans I have not been entirely ingenuous; even my colleagues Diplomatic Corps will hardly be convinced that our simultaneous appearances in Canton are not by design. At small luncheon yesterday with my colleagues British Commonwealth they spoke of Generalissimo's recent visit to Philippines,[10] President Rhee's [11] invitation to Generalissimo to visit Korea and said that my departure from Communist China at this time would undoubtedly be linked with those events in Communists' mind since their press is already branding Baguio meeting as "American imperialistic plot". My colleagues considered this an unfortunate coincidence. They of course had no intimation of my proposed visit to Canton in addition. I feel I must bring above considerations to your

---

[8] Chiang Kai-shek, President of China until January 21, 1949, when he retired in favor of Vice President Li Tsung-jen as Acting President.
[9] Not printed.
[10] For documentation on this subject, see vol. VII, Part 2, pp. 1115 ff.
[11] President Syngman Rhee of Korea.

attention. Any changes in my instructions as result thereof could reach me in Okinawa as late as July 18 which is still only target date as our exit permits have not yet been approved.

Sent Department; repeated OffEmb Canton 641.

STUART

---

123 Stuart, J. Leighton : Telegram

The Ambassador in China (Stuart) to the Secretary of State

NANKING, July 15, 1949—2 p. m.
[Received July 15—5:45 a. m.]

1532. Embassy has already informed local Communist authorities details flight plans, including maps and E.T.D., of Air Attaché's plane as far as Okinawa and we have every confidence Communist Armed Forces will be appropriately alerted. Air Attaché made successful test flight yesterday.

Air Attaché and I had considered possibility notifying Nationalist Government but had discarded it as unnecessary and even involving some security risk. However, in light recommendations in Deptel 828, July 14, agree appropriate to inform CAF at Canton and Taipei and request assurances safe conduct. We will not, however, delay trip for receipt such assurances.

Following for Clark and Edgar: Please inform appropriate authorities Headquarters CAF your post that I plan depart Nanking 0800 hours July 18 in American aircraft C–47. Course will be set from Nanking 96 degrees to 25 miles at sea for turning point to 137 degrees Naha, Okinawa, altitude 10,000. This course will take plane approximately 50 miles north Shanghai. Since delay obtaining exit permits myself and party now foreseen, possible plane may be delayed one or two days. Consequently appropriate Chinese Armed Forces should be alerted for 19th and 20th as well. We will communicate promptly any change above schedule.

Sent Department; repeated OffEmb Canton 642, Taipei 63.

STUART

---

123 Stuart, J. Leighton : Telegram

The Secretary of State to the Ambassador in China (Stuart)

WASHINGTON, July 15, 1949—5 p. m.

833. Urtel 1526, Jul 14. Dept greatly disturbed over "shop guarantee" requirements for Amb and other official passengers AirAtt plane and believes dangerous precedent wld be set if "shop guarantees" from either Chi or Amer firms for official dipl or con personnel

were provided Chi Commie auths under any conditions. If this shld prove not local but attempt to impose countrywide procedure, its application to such outlying places as Mukden for example wld be virtually impossible fulfillment. While Dept of opinion any undue delay Amb's departure wld be unfortunate, question of "shop guarantees" believed of sufficient importance warrant postponing departure until requirement such guarantees waived for official US personnel. For ur info, Chi Commie requirement "shop guarantees" believed unique and no similar restrictions applied in [iron] curtain countries Eastern Europe.

Dept also of opinion similar guarantees by Emb or individual Emb officers extremely undesirable and might lead to endless complications resulting from trumped up charges brought against Olive [12] or other members party fol their departure.

Dept has considered possibility giving wide publicity to planned date Amb's departure and list passengers accompanying in attempt to effect permission departure as planned without requiring "shop guarantees", but concerned lest such action might make Commies even more obdurate and leave no room for face saving retreat. Wld appreciate Emb's comments this point.

Emb shld in meantime point out to Commies unprecedented nature their demand (and only reminiscent of tactics Manchu Li Fanyuan [13]), which completely contrary accepted internatl custom and usage with regard dipl and consular officials, and inform them under instructions US Govt Emb can under no circumstances accede. Emb might also in its discretion give Commies understand any unreasonable delay in departure will be full responsibility Commie auths and wide publicity re reasons for delay not unlikely.

ConGen Peiping instructed make similar representations Chi Commie auths there.

ACHESON

---

123 Stuart, J. Leighton : Telegram

The Ambassador in China (Stuart) to the Secretary of State

NANKING, July 16, 1949—1 p. m.
[Received July 16—2:23 a. m.]

1537. In compliance Deptel 833, July 15, we informed Director Alien Affairs Office this morning that, under instructions US Government, Embassy could under no circumstances accede to requirement

---

[12] For documentation on the case of Vice Consul William M. Olive at Shanghai, see pp. 1155 ff.
[13] The Li-fan Yuan, established in 1638, was a Manchu board in charge of affairs relating to Koreans and Mongols.

of "shop guarantees" for myself and official party. Huang Hua replied that such decision was out of his competence and that he would refer entire matter to Peiping urgently. Suggest Department give no publicity to these difficulties until Peiping authorities have had opportunity to reply this reference.

In light of this development and approaching week end I see no possibility of maintaining original schedule. Consequently I will now plan to depart Nanking morning of July 19 circumstances permitting.

Consul General Cabot, Vice Consul Olive and wife arrived from Shanghai this morning. (Deptel 832, July 14.[14]) We will not be assured of latter's exit China until we have submitted applications for exit entire party, presently being delayed by "shop guarantee" requirement.

Sent Department, repeated OffEmb Canton 645, Taipei 64, Department pass Peiping 277.

STUART

---

123 Stuart, J. Leighton : Telegram

The Minister-Counselor of Embassy in China (Clark) to the Secretary of State

CANTON, July 16, 1949—6 p. m.
[Received July 16—6:37 a. m.]

Cantel 749. Although impossible obtain reliable information regarding duration Generalissimo's visit Canton, best I can get is week–10 days (Nanking's 1531, July 15 to Department, repeated OffEmb 641). Included [*Inclined*] agree impossible convince public visit Ambassador and Generalissimo Canton simultaneously was pure coincidence. Fact remains, however, that henceforth Generalissimo may be expected assume more public control and a motivation Department's instructions Ambassador come Canton may be unaffected by his presence here. Feel we can be sure Communists will take full advantage visit regardless whether Generalissimo present.

Sent Department; repeated Nanking 495.

CLARK

---

[14] Not printed.

123 Stuart, J. Leighton : Telegram

The Consul at Taipei (Edgar) to the Secretary of State

TAIPEI, July 18, 1949—11 a. m.
[Received July 17—11:04 p. m.]

294. Information on Ambassador flight given personally [to] General Chou Chi-jou [15] who assures me appropriate orders would be issued at once. Please advise if 19th schedule postponed.

Sent Nanking 183; repeated Department 294; Canton 128.

EDGAR

---

123 Stuart, J. Leighton : Telegram

The Consul General at Peiping (Clubb) to the Secretary of State

PEIPING, July 18, 1949—noon.
[Received July 18—7:49 a. m.]

1189. RefDeptel 453, July 16.[16]   Matter taken up in brief yesterday with Joseph Chang [17] with request he ascertain whether Chang Tung-sun, then in town, would be prepared communicate Communist authorities. Gave Chang 8 o'clock this morning memorandum making representations as outlined Depreftel but omitting, however, comments set forth penultimate paragraph. Father will act.

Chang informed me father and Lo Lung-chi [18] when acquainted with matter yesterday gave two possible explanations: (1) Peiping Communist authorities were aware and approved requirement established re Ambassador's travel possibly desiring delay his departure perhaps with idea communicating some message (see later message) or (2) Nanking authorities instructed and proceeding in manner unapproved by higher Communist authorities as I opined when I handed Chang memo was possible explanation.

Chang informed me he would probably be able report by 4 o'clock today whether communicated higher Communist authorities. Am withholding further action pending receipt that information.

Sent Department, repeated Nanking 843.

[CLUBB]

---

[15] Commanding the Chinese Air Force.
[16] This telegram repeated pertinent excerpts from telegram No. 833, July 15, 5 p.m., to the Ambassador in China, p. 787.
[17] Son of Professor Chang Tung-sun of Yenching University, member of the Democratic League.
[18] A leader of the Democratic League.

123 Stuart, J. Leighton : Telegram

The Ambassador in China (Stuart) to the Secretary of State

NANKING, July 18, 1949—1 p. m.
[Received 7:02 p. m.]

1546. I am daily strengthened in my conviction that visit to Canton at this time is undesirable from every aspect known to me and should be avoided. All reports that I have from Peiping and indications from local Commie authorities confirm that Mao and Chou have lost face, are chagrined at my rejection of their "invitation" to visit Peiping and consider it clear indication of American policy. While I do not deny that this may be salutary, it is certain that visit to Canton and meeting with Generalissimo (which could not be avoided) promptly following my refusal to travel to Peiping would appear to Commies studied insult to which they might be expected to react vigorously. Whatever influence I have with Commie leaders is on purely personal basis. My flying to Canton to see their arch enemy would certainly never be forgiven me and any future usefulness I might have had in Commie China entirely vitiated. Once it is known here that I have gone to Canton rather than directly to Washington difficulties which Americans are now facing in Shanghai, Hankow may be expected to increase and extend to Nanking and cities in north. I do not preclude retaliatory measures against Embassy and other official establishments in Commie China.

My trip to Canton at this time would inevitably add to Generalissimo's triumph and prestige (see Cantel 741, July 15 to Dept.[19]) at time when that of acting President Li is definitely on wane. While I concur in Dept's decision that I not travel to Peiping with hat in hand to call on Chairman Mao, by same token I feel it unwise to change my course and pay visit to Chairman Chiang.[20] I trust Dept will appreciate my anxiety over issues involved and will want to have benefit these further views before replying Embtel 1531, July 15, repeated Canton 641.

Sent Department 1546, repeated AmEmb Canton for Clark as 647.

STUART

---

123 Stuart, J. Leighton : Telegram

The Ambassador in China (Stuart) to the Secretary of State

NANKING, July 18, 1949—4 p.m.
[Received July 18—5:16 a. m.]

1547. No reply from Peiping authorities and I am again forced to change my ETD. I will not depart morning of 19th (Embtel 1537,

---

[19] Not printed; it dealt with a Voice of America press summary.
[20] Generalissimo Chiang Kai-shek was leader of the Kuomintang (Nationalist Party).

July 16 to Department, repeated Canton 645, Taipei 64) as planned and will inform you promptly of new ETD as soon as decision reached on our exit permits.

Sent Department; repeated OffEmb Canton 648, Taipei 65.

STUART

---

123 Stuart, J. Leighton : Telegram

The Secretary of State to the Consul at Shanghai (McConaughy)

WASHINGTON, July 18, 1949—8 p. m.

1428. *NY Times* Shanghai Jul 17 Lieberman [21] story reports shop guarantee question delaying departure Amb and party incl Cabot, Olive in Air Attaché plane says "According telephoned report from Nanking this morning Emb officials now trying iron out question 'shop guarantees' whereby merchants undertake responsibility for debts or any other outstanding obligations left unsettled by those leaving Chi. Problem involves getting Chi businessmen endorse departing Amers amid obviously anti-Amer atmosphere and under conditions where responsibilities employers to laborers often have proved sticky and enduring" adds same question involved fon businessmen who may elect leave when transportation available from Shanghai. Story then reviews Gould–Miner affair.[22]

View fact all details arrangements Ambs departure most carefully handled secret basis Dept fails understand why this info allowed reach press especially since resolution problem thereby made more difficult. For urinfo Dept had considered publicity but withheld awaiting Ambs comments whether publicity increase rather than diminish his problem.

Queried on basis Lieberman story Dept spokesman today attempted minimize as "local problem" with details which we unfamiliar. Spokesman recalled Amb for some time been authorized leave said "This is evidently something that has come up in his making arrangements for departure".

ACHESON

---

123 Stuart, J. Leighton

Memorandum by the Director of the Office of Far Eastern Affairs (Butterworth) to the Secretary of State

[WASHINGTON,] July 18, 1949.

There are attached copies of two priority telegrams from Ambassador Stuart in Nanking (No. 1531 of July 15, Tab A, and No. 1546

---

[21] Henry Lieberman, *New York Times* correspondent at Shanghai.
[22] For documentation on details concerning Americans involved at Shanghai, see pp. 1155 ff.

of July 18, Tab B)[23] which I believe you may want to show to the President as a matter of urgency in which he sets forth anew his recommendation that he be not instructed to visit Canton en route to the United States.

There is another aspect to this question—one which has not been mentioned by Ambassador Stuart and which he may not have consciously had in mind—which should be given consideration. That is the personal question of Ambassador Stuart's future. Having been born in China and having spent over fifty years in that country, he will naturally want to return in a private capacity at some future date. It is seriously doubted, however, whether he would ever be permitted to return to a China dominated by the Communists if, having refused their invitation to visit Peiping, he were now to proceed to Canton.

893.00/7–1849

Memorandum by the Secretary of State of a Conversation With the President

[WASHINGTON,] July 18, 1949.

AMBASSADOR STUART'S RETURN

I reported to the President on the difficulties which were being put in the way of the Ambassador's obtaining an exit program [*permit?*] by the Communists and also the problem which might arise if he should obtain an exit permit in the next day or two. This problem is that if he proceeds immediately to Canton, the Generalissimo will be there, and if he delays too long the White Paper will be out.

We left it that as soon as we heard as to when the Ambassador would return I should consult the President again.

D[EAN] A[CHESON]

---

123 Stuart, J. Leighton : Telegram

The Minister-Counselor of Embassy in China (Clark) to the Secretary of State

CANTON, July 19, 1949—3 p. m.
[Received July 19—6 : 04 a. m.]

Cantel 779. Am unaware all reasons motivating Department's desire Dr. Stuart visit Canton. On other hand, I have deep sympathy for him in his predicament (Nanking 1546, July 18 to Department, repeated Canton 647). He has given his life to Yenching and he

---

[23] *Ante*, pp. 786 and 791, respectively.

envisages the loss of any personal influence he might later bring to bear with Communists in protection Yenching and I have been sufficiently closely associated with him past 2 years to be aware his mental torture. As loyal servant of public he appears willing come Canton if necessary in interests of US despite fact that to do so will be negation of everything for which he has stood through his long life in China.

If US domestic requirements will be satisfied thereby, I am most willing proceed Okinawa and meet Dr. Stuart there. I have seen everyone in authority in Canton recently and it might well be said that in order avoid overwearying Ambassador who is no longer young, I had been directed meet him Okinawa give him views Chinese Government.

CLARK

---

123 Stuart, J. Leighton : Telegram

The Secretary of State to the Ambassador in China (Stuart)[24]

WASHINGTON, July 20, 1949—1 p. m.

852. In accordance with recommendations made urtels 1531 Jul 15 and 1546 Jul 18, you may disregard that part of Deptel 820 Jul 12 which had to do with your proceeding to Canton and you may remain in Okinawa and consult with Clark there regarding the latest developments with respect to Natl Govt and thence proceed to US. Pls arrange with Clark to meet you and caution him not to make his plans prematurely known. Pls also inform Dept as soon as you can date of your actual arrival in Okinawa so that Dept may give full publicity to fact that Clark is meeting you there to apprise you of developments within Natl Govt China. You will be informed if due to technical considerations there is any change in the publication date of White Paper.

ACHESON

---

123 Stuart, J. Leighton : Telegram

The Consul General at Peiping (Clubb) to the Secretary of State

PEIPING, July 21, 1949—9 a. m.
[Received July 21—5 : 42 a. m.]

1204. [To Nanking:] July 20, 2 p.m. ReContel 843, July 18.[25] Joseph Chang informed me by phone last night message delivered July 18; action unknown.

---

[24] Repeated to the Minister-Counselor at Canton as telCan No. 470. Notation by the Director of the Executive Secretariat (Humelsine) : "Cleared with President by phone."
[25] Same as telegram No. 1189 from Peiping, p. 790.

Sent Nanking 853; repeated Department, Shanghai 813.

CLUBB

---

123 Stuart, J. Leighton : Telegram

The Ambassador in China (Stuart) to the Secretary of State

NANKING, July 21, 1949—9 p. m.
[Received July 21—1 : 09 p. m.]

1571. I regret publicity US "shop guarantee" question and agree that premature release our difficulties exit permits may make solution more difficult (Deptel 1428 to Shanghai July 18, repeated Nanking 843, Canton 463, Taipei 187 and Embtel 1537, July 16 to Department, repeated Canton 645, Taipei 64). When *New York Times'* string man Nanking called Embassy July 20, he already had full story my difficulties "shop guarantees". We were noncommittal. Explained for his background information that it was unwise to give any publicity to present negotiations for my departure which might have adverse effect upon Communist authorities. All we could say for his use was that my plans to depart were proceeding and that there was no ETD as yet. I can only assume local *New York Times'* correspondent obtained his information from other Embassy. Last week I had several small informal conferences with my diplomatic colleagues to say farewell. Because of their obvious interest in details of my departure, I felt it only fair to advise them of Communists' requirements and of progress on my negotiations to reach satisfactory conclusion. I assume that this confidence was not respected in all instances.

We are waiting from day to day for call from Aliens Affairs Office regarding our exit permits. Apparently no new instructions have been received from Peiping (see Peiping's telegram 853, July 20 to Nanking, repeated Department 1204,[26] Shanghai 813). I feel we should not display too much impatience as evidence to Communists of our weakening over question of "shop guarantees", other immunities connected with my departure. Obviously however delay cannot be permitted to drag on indefinitely and Department may wish prepare statement for release to press when we here feel that no advantage to further waiting or if negative instructions from Peiping received. I would suggest that any release state obvious; that despite absence diplomatic relations, one right which we all possess, and which should be beyond question, is our right to leave in same manner that we entered China.

Before making release Department may wish to inform Embassies other foreign governments having representation Nanking with suggestion those governments may themselves wish to take official

---

[26] July 21, 9 a. m., *supra.*

cognizance this denial most fundamental right of exit to foreign representative sovereign state.

Repeated Canton 660, Shanghai 881, Taipei 67.

STUART

---

123 Stuart, J. Leighton : Telegram

The Secretary of State to the Ambassador in China (Stuart)

WASHINGTON, July 22, 1949—6 p. m.

871. Urtel 1571 July 21. Since any statement made by Dept re "shop guarantee" and ur departure wld be designed for Chi consumption rather than world or US, Dept desires you prepare and forward soonest draft statement for release by Dept when you feel time propitious or when negative reply recd from Commies. Statement shld be designed facilitate ur own departure as well as future movements US cit[izen]s desiring leave or travel within China.

ACHESON

---

123 Stuart, J. Leighton : Telegram

The Minister-Counselor of Embassy in China (Clark) to the Secretary of State

CANTON, July 22, 1949—9 p. m.
[Received 10:30 p. m.]

Cantel 801. Urge desirability advance information Canton for release here at proper time by Connors[27] of publicity contemplated Deptel 825, July 20 to Nanking, repeated Canton telCan 470. Advance knowledge details Department's plans and *en clair* message re release would be most valuable.

CLARK

124.931/7–2349 : Telegram

The Ambassador in China (Stuart) to the Secretary of State

NANKING, July 23, 1949—1 p. m.
[Received July 23—6:42 a. m.]

1590. Afternoon of fire (see Embtel 1585, July 22 to Department, repeated Canton 664, Shanghai 887[28]) in Service Attaché's compound (adjoining mine) Huang Hua telephoned to inquire of my safety and to assure me that he had ordered all fire fighting equipment Nanking to scene to prevent fire spreading my compound. At same time

---

[27] W. Bradley Connors, Attaché in China.
[28] Not printed; the Embassy repeated a Nanking newspaper story of a fire on the Embassy premises (124.931/7–2249).

he referred my departure and gave us to understand that Bureau Public Safety had been unduly zealous; that some of its requirements had been included on exit permit form without knowledge Aliens Affairs Bureau. He suggested we call Public Safety Bureau next day and that he would have ground prepared for our reception and early solution our problems. Yesterday morning Air Attaché and Embassy Officer called Public Safety Bureau and received following assurances:

(1) Official and personal mail would not be subjected to inspection.
(2) My baggage exempted from inspection but this not applicable to other members of party (we do not object to this procedure).
(3) Exit permit Ambassador not required bear "shop guarantee".

However all other exit permits were returned to Embassy Officer with statement that "shop guarantees" were required of them and that their forms were therefore not complete.

Fugh attempted all afternoon yesterday to communicate with Huang Hua without success. We wish to ascertain if Public Safety Bureau had not understood Huang's instructions or if, as is probably case, only I am to be exempted from "shop guarantee" requirement. We will inform Department promptly when position Director Alien Affairs Office is clarified. However, since appears Communist authorities remaining adamant on "shop guarantee" requirement for members my party (all entitled to diplomatic immunity), I would be grateful for Department's guidance on course of action to follow. (Deptel 833, July 15).

Sent Department, repeated Canton 666, Shanghai 890.

STUART

124.936/7-2349 : Telegram

The Ambassador in China (Stuart) to the Secretary of State

NANKING, July 23, 1949.
[Received July 23—5 : 33 p. m.]

1595. Following is text note received today by Director Nanking USIS [29] from MCC.[30]

"As the United States Information Service is a part of the United States Department of State organization, and since the People's Government has no diplomatic or consular relations with the United States, the United States Information Service must cease its activities as from today. Such activities include the printing and distribution of news bulletins, the exhibition and presentation of books and papers, exhibition of illustrated posters, movie showings, holding of musical

---

[29] Josiah W. Bennett, Assistant Attaché, Director of United States Information Service.
[30] Military Control Commission.

concerts and all other public activities. It is hoped that you will comply without fail." [31]

Sent Department 1595, OffEmb Canton 668, ConGen Shanghai 893, Hankow 56, Peiping 290, Tientsin 62, ConGen Canton 40.

STUART

124.936/7–2349 : Telegram

The Ambassador in China (Stuart) to the Secretary of State

NANKING, July 23, 1949—9 p. m.
[Received July 24—4 :03 a. m.]

1596. Rumor circulating local Communists received instructions close all foreign transmitters Nanking. While we doubt reliability sources, such step would be logical successor closing USIS Communist China and we feel probability after Ambassador departs China. Suggest therefore Department may wish consider policy toward FS establishments in China should their present community's [*communication*] facilities all be denied them. We are unable to extend protection to Americans. We are hardly able to protect ourselves. Our only remaining function is that of reporting and should that be denied us there would appear to be no reason for our continued existence. We submit for Department's consideration desirability in event of closure our transmitters, of prompt announcement of Department's intention to withdraw its diplomatic and consular establishments (with possible exception Peiping) in Communist China because of denial of last facility for performing normal functions. In any event it would seem necessary precaution to undertake immediate consideration of understood plan between Department and various establishments involved in order that they may work conjointly once confidential communications are severed.

Sent Department, repeated OffEmb Canton 670, Shanghai 895.

STUART

124.931/7–2349 : Airgram

The Ambassador in China (Stuart) to the Secretary of State

NANKING, July 23, 1949.
[Received August 10—5 :10 p. m.]

A–89. Reference Department's telegram 634, May 24, to Nanking. Several weeks ago Huang Hua telephoned Philip Fugh and asked latter to call on him urgently. When Fugh arrived, he found General

---

[31] The Ambassador in China stated in his telegram No. 1589, July 23, not printed : "USIS Nanking today discontinued public activities as result notification from Nanking Alien Affairs Bureau." (124.936/7–2349)

Liu Po-cheng, Director Nanking Military Control Council and Mayor. Fugh, who had never met General Liu before, had impression their meeting in Huang's office was not pure coincidence. After exchange of the usual amenities, General Liu said he understood Dr. Stuart's privacy had been violated by Communist soldiers in early days of Nanking "liberation". When Fugh confirmed this, General Liu continued that he had been most sorry to hear of this unfortunate incident, that he had regretted it exceedingly, and that the officer and soldiers responsible had been returned to Peiping for further indoctrination. (We understand that "to be returned North for further indoctrination" is roughly equivalent to our military being returned to base for corrective instruction and, as such, a form of degradation.) The remainder of the conversation was of general and insignificant import, and we suspect that General Liu created this occasion to express in an indirect way his regret for the incident involving the violation of the Ambassador's premises.

STUART

---

123 Stuart, J. Leighton : Telegram

The Ambassador in China (Stuart) to the Secretary of State

NANKING, July 24, 1949—2 p. m.
[Received July 24—3:51 a. m.]

1603. Fugh saw Huang Hua this morning preparatory to a conference with me Monday afternoon 4 o'clock (4 a. m., Washington time) to discuss my departure, principally question of "shop guarantees". After Fugh had restated US position (see Deptel 833, July 15), Huang replied that Communists feel that they had already made great and special concessions my case in permitting me to leave with confidential mail, immunity from baggage search and waiver of any guarantee; that to deviate further from a procedure which they have established for exit of foreigners during transitional period of non-recognition would establish precedent for other foreign diplomats for which they are unprepared. He begged Fugh to impress upon me their own dilemma and to express the hope that we would help them in finding satisfactory solution. Huang Hua feels that he has made every possible concession to facilitate my departure and I am inclined to believe that within the framework of his own limitations this is true. The principal point at issue was requirement of "shop guarantee" for other members of my party which he insists is only a formality and should not be magnified by US into a major controversy. (See Embtel 1590 July 23).

Certainly our case before the Chinese people and in world public opinion is considerably weakened in light of concessions already made for Chief of Mission. The local authorities have already agreed that "an American" can sign as guarantor. We now find that American Foreign Service and army officers leaving Peiping in March and April complied with requirement of "shop guarantee" in order to exit Communist China under Department's instructions (i.e., for man transferred to Shanghai, Major Moyer [32] transferred to Nanking), also that members of ConGen staff Shanghai going on leave under orders have already obtained "shop guarantees" pursuant to local requirements which are similar to those in Nanking. The only Chief of Mission leaving Nanking with permission to exit China (Afghanistan Minister) complied with "shop guarantee" requirement to extent of having his Chargé sign guarantee.

We recognize force of the Department's arguments in its telegram 833 and the dangers which compliance with these requirements might hold for other American officials. On the other hand it should be considered that a rigid adherence to our stand may in itself act as a barrier to the exit of any US official personnel for an indefinite period through their inability to comply with exit requirements. As of [for] Mukden, Ward reports that members his staff are planning depart for Peiping next week and has reported no trouble over their exit permits. Among my colleagues I find that their principal concern has been over treatment Chief of Mission and I am inclined to believe that they would not consider it unreasonable if members of their staff obtained a guarantee. Thus we may well find that regardless of our position many others will comply with the guarantee requirements for members of their staffs. The mere fact of my exit without a guarantor would be a welcome precedent for my colleagues. Department should therefore consider possibility that at a later date it may be compelled by general procedure to reverse its position and accede to Communist demands in order to enable members Foreign Service to depart and that it may face a morale problem of critical proportions among its personnel in China, once transportation is available.

In light of the above and desirability of my departure in compliance Department's instructions at earliest possible date I recommend I be authorized to tell Huang when I see him tomorrow afternoon that as a special concession my Government has agreed that the Embassy Nanking will act as guarantor for the other members of my party. This in effect is what the Embassy would normally do in an informal manner for any members of its staff who inadvertently might have left debts or other unsettled obligations and would seem the most appropriate exit from the present impasse. If Huang agrees this arrangement and we thus reach solution on basis of mutual concessions, I feel that it will have a beneficial effect not only upon the

---

[32] Maj. Maynard G. Moyer, on duty in China for the Department of the Army.

Embassy's relations with him in future but also on position of Americans generally in this area. Department will appreciate need for most urgent reply if I am to discuss matter with Huang Hua Monday afternoon on any new basis.

STUART

---

123 Stuart, J. Leighton : Telegram

The Secretary of State to the Ambassador in China (Stuart)

WASHINGTON, July 24, 1949—noon.

876. Dept studying subject urtel 1603 July 24, which requires most careful consideration. As it doubtful you will receive further instructions in time your Monday meeting Huang Hua you may wish so inform him.

ACHESON

---

123 Stuart, J. Leighton : Telegram

The Ambassador in China (Stuart) to the Secretary of State

NANKING, July 26, 1949—5 p. m.
[Received July 26—12 :38 p. m.]

1625. I talked one and half hours July 25 with Huang Hua. Our personal relations were cordial as usual, but I came away with feeling of discomfiture. His Communist mind is impermeable to argument and even to facts.

I began with "shop guarantee" issue, expressing appreciation of special treatment accorded me and explaining at length views of my Government. He described reasons for this provisional arrangement and admitted that Communists had not thought of peculiar problems affecting diplomatic personnel. He implied that he might give matter further consideration (see Deptel 876, July 24 to Nanking). I said that before my departure it would be helpful to know whether CCP [33] wished our consulates closed and nationals withdrawn, stating that incessant denunciation of our "imperialism" and experiences of individuals especially in Shanghai had led many Americans to ask this question. He quoted Mao's June 15 speech as evidence that Americans and others who stay in China on Mao's terms would be welcome.

He reviewed again CCP grievances against USA, chiefly for aiding and continuing recognize Chiang Government. I countered by enlarging as previously on American desire for peace and fear of aggression and war springing from CCP-avowed advocacy of world revolution. There was nothing new in any of this and I doubt if

---

[33] Chinese Communist Party.

either one changed other's opinions. When he charged USA as being behind Chiang–Quirino [34]–S. Rhee alliance,[35] I referred to explicit denials of State Department. He retorted that anyhow they were all our protégés. I pointed out in what sense this was true of each one, and asked what hope there was of better relations when CCP surmises were treated as facts.

As to future he said that best American policy would be to keep hands off China, that any merchant, peasant, student would agree to this. He said China could face her industrial and other problems unaided. He was also quite unrealistic in describing gains thus far in support of the People's Government by rural farmers, urban workers, small-scale capitalists and intellectuals.

Sent Department 1625, repeated Shanghai 909, Canton 680.

STUART

393.1115/7–2649 : Telegram

The Ambassador in China (Stuart) to the Secretary of State

NANKING, July 26, 1949—8 p. m.
[Received July 26—1:42 p. m.]

1628. In effort to seek concerted action on protests to Communist authorities over lack of protection, miscarriage of justice in cases involving Americans, Embassy requests Department's opinion of following proposed circular telegram to all posts in Communist China:

"In all cases involving Americans in your district where clear evidence exists lack protection afforded by Communist authorities, you are instructed (1) attempt protest through most effective or feasible channels to local authorities citing circumstances, (2) provide Consulate General Peiping with details in order it may attempt lodge similar protest with headquarters Communist authorities, (3) provide same information to Nanking which will attempt protest as [an] Embassy, (4) repeat information to Department."

STUART

---

123 Stuart, J. Leighton : Telegram

The Ambassador in China (Stuart) to the Secretary of State

NANKING, July 27, 1949—11 a. m.
[Received July 27—12:03 a. m.]

1629. Unless Embassy has reply to its telegram 1603, July 24, within 24 hours, is doubtful that it will be possible to complete all arrange-

---

[34] President Elpidio Quirino of the Philippines.
[35] For documentation on a proposed Pacific pact, see vol. VII, Part 2, pp. 1115 ff.

ments for departure of Ambassador and party prior to deadline established in Deptel 875, July 23, repeated Canton telCan 490.[36]
Sent Department; repeated OffEmb Canton 682.

STUART

893.00B/7–2749 : Telegram

The Secretary of State to the Consul General at Peiping (Clubb)

WASHINGTON, July 27, 1949—3 p. m.

490. Dept considering instructing Amb to present *aide mémoire* to Huang Hua on eve of departure reciting intolerable actions and inquiring whether these perpetrated with view to making untenable position Amer reps in China and stating if so notification hereby given we are prepared close Emb and progressively Consulates as interests in area permit.

Dept wishes receive urgently your reaction and main outlines of character of note you wld advocate having not only current situation in mind but also that which will come to pass when Chi Commie auths organize themselves as govt, invite recognition and it is not readily forthcoming from US.

Wld not Dept be well advised seek opportunity to close Emb Nanking fol Ambs departure in view of likelihood Peiping being new capital and attempt make advantage out of eventual necessity?

ACHESON

---

123 Stuart, J. Leighton : Telegram

The Secretary of State to the Ambassador in China (Stuart)[37]

WASHINGTON, July 27, 1949—7 p. m.

890. Urtel 1603 Jul 24 brings out facts re previous compliance by Amer and fon official personnel with "shop guarantee" demands which Dept previously unaware. Dept remains concerned at implications any official compliance these demands. It knows no auth of law or availability appropriated funds whereby Emb in behalf US Govt may be permitted assume responsibility possible personal obligations, if any, of its personnel. Nevertheless, it wld appear we are being subj[ected] to duress requiring *ad hoc* measures to meet a situation involving possible safety, well-being Amer personnel. To meet this extremity, Dept authorizes fol procedure: Emb sign as guarantor. In event financial loss resulting procedures, Dept will consider use funds

---

[36] Not printed; the deadline was August 1.
[37] Notation by the Secretary of State: "Approved by the President. D. A."

for emergencies arising dipl and consular service for purpose relieving any expenditure involved in obligations. Where personal liability established for individuals concerned Govt wld reserve right of recovery from them expenditures made their account.

If FonServ personnel remaining at post required sign on personal, unofficial basis (in keeping with Commie insistence they do not recognize FonServ Officers' official status and capacity act), this action wld be considered by US Govt official act of US Govt employees.

In complying this procedure Emb shld emphasize to local auths that this treatment of US Govt reps is considered contrary to internatl custom and usage and does not constitute a waiver of any rights under such internatl usage.

It shld be stressed that status of dipl personnel in internatl law is clear. Internatl practice contemplates that such personnel are exempt from the jurisdiction of the country in which stationed, not being amenable to civil or criminal process. They partake of a sovereign character and any interference with the freedom of their movement or the discharge of responsibility in the manner demanded is considered repugnant to internatl custom and usage.

ACHESON

---

123 Stuart, J. Leighton : Telegram

The Ambassador in China (Stuart) to the Secretary of State

NANKING, July 29, 1949—5 p. m.
[Received July 29—5 : 26 a. m.]

1644. Please inform appropriate authorities CAF that I intend depart Nanking for Okinawa in Embassy plane Monday August 1, 8 a.m. (see Embtel 1532, July 15 to Department, repeated Canton 642, Taipei 63). Information contained in reftel still holds.

Sent OffEmb Canton 692, Taipei 70, repeated Department.

STUART

---

123 Stuart, J. Leighton : Telegram

The Ambassador in China (Stuart) to the Secretary of State

NANKING, July 29, 1949—5 p. m.
[Received July 29—6 :28 a. m.]

1645. I informed Huang Hua yesterday of Department's concession in permitting Embassy to sign as guarantor of members my party (Deptel 890, July 27). He said he would have to refer matter to Peiping. Today we are informed that local public safety bureau will accept Embassy as guarantor. Consequently applications for exit permits are being submitted to public safety this afternoon with Embassy's "chop" and signature of Embassy certifying officer (Bacon). Statement of US Government's position in acceding to this requirement (Deptel under reference) will be made to Huang Hua tomorrow when I expect to have final interview with him.

I have tentatively set date my departure Monday, August 1, 8 a. m., arriving Okinawa 12:30 same day. While Huang expressed some doubt that this "early date" would give him time to make necessary preparations, he agreed to try. It may be necessary for me to postpone departure one day. I shall keep Department regularly informed.

Sent Department; repeated OffEmb Canton 693, Shanghai 916, Taipei 71.

STUART

893.00/7–2949 : Telegram

The Consul General at Peiping (Clubb) to the Secretary of State

PEIPING, July 29, 1949—5 p. m.
[Received July 29—2:59 p. m.]

1263. ReDeptel 490, July 27. International political situation worse for Communists generally due failure re Berlin,[38] re Atlantic Pact.[39] Overall political situation therefore worse for Chinese Communists who could have been right in following virulent anti-American line past 3 years only if war near when they thought, to win if USSR won but not lose if USSR lost. USSR has used them as pawns and may still advise Soviet war imminent (see Contel Nanking [garbled group]) but Communists may now suspect international political game going badly. I believe this probable. Note Lo Lung-chi's leading questions (see Contel 1195, July 19 [20]) [40].

Economically Communists were wrong from beginning in attempting too much. Economic situation steadily deteriorating, grave shortages both food and industrial materials can be expected develop before 1950 harvest with resultant famine industrial breakdown. Economic failure would weaken Communist political authority, reduce China's usefulness to USSR.

In present circumstances Communists could logically be expected withdraw somewhat from extreme anti-foreign position originally taken. Such retreat quite fitting in Communists' own logic, hampered only by natural reluctance admit errors even implicitly, innate Chi-

---

[38] This reference is to the Berlin airlift operation when the western sector was closed off from western Germany.
[39] North Atlantic Treaty signed at Washington, April 4, 1949; Department of State Treaties and Other International Acts Series No. 1964, or 63 Stat. (pt. 2) 2241.
[40] *Ante*, p. 443.

nese xenophobia, stupidity in lower party command, these Communists who sought cheap victories in international field now face necessity trying repair damage done good relations. They probably now appreciate significance of their plans of absence Sino-Japanese trade, closure Mukden Consulate, of Embassy's warning to Americans, reduction missionary funds. Finally Lo Lung-chi's attempt make it appear Mao Tse-tung is powerful and would lash back if baited, Communist line unpopular with many intellectuals and with increasing economic distress shows signs becoming more unpopular with masses.

Note inconclusive but possibly significant sign Communist change tactics. Since July 7 there has been notable lightening of anti-USA press attacks. Recently even such items US printed have in greater proportion than before been reprints from Soviet press. Also about July 21, there was perceptible change in attitude Bureau Public Safety in direction greater ease, more courtesy, less argument connected with application consular officials for registration with regard questioning, acceptance, notations reference to consular occupation titles, presumably by directive. Soviet regrets expressed French and Belgians regarding social non-attendance (Contel 1237, July 25 [41]) of possible parallel significance.

In view all circumstances would myself recommend following approach: Assuredly take advantage Ambassador's departure make démarche vis-à-vis Communists but refrain from playing all cards at once or giving hand away in advance, undertaking now only limited objective as major Communist shift hardly to be achieved one blow however heavy and better got through series lighter but wearing blows. Would draft aide-mémoire on following lines: Note outstanding cases violation rights person, residence, trade, missionary effort, travel of American officials and citizens as established by treaty and international law and practice, but omitting question whether Communists aim make diplomatic position untenable; omit also threatened closure Consulates but inform Communists that in existing circumstances Ambassador will not return at this time and US Government will mould its future policies regarding its representatives, nationals and interests in Communist China according to actual developments under Communist administration; give essence first two paragraphs message projected Deptel 367, June 14,[42] stiffening it somewhat and particularly in second paragraph changing "hope" to "had expected" (recommend for psychological reasons Ambassador give no indication aide-mémoire incorporates any part of message intended for Chou En-lai) and referring to significance USIS work for development understanding between two nations; and conclude

---

[41] Not printed.
[42] Ante, p. 384.

with short statement to effect USA will judge Communist *bona fides* by actions not words and be guided accordingly.

After departure Ambassador and after having given message time sink in, Department could then, insofar as administratively and politically desirable, undertake progressive reduction Nanking establishment to point consonant with current demands on it, using at least some personnel to strengthen other China posts if Communist policies permit their profitable functioning.

Believe this approach gives full flexibility to USA for actions designed to meet developments in fluid situation, including making ready for time when Communists have organized central government and put selves in position "accept" recognition, and at same time keeps Communists in dark as to American intentions. As indicated Contel 296 [769?], May 12,[43] this desirable.

CLUBB

---

123 Stuart, J. Leighton : Telegram

The Secretary of State to the Minister-Counselor of Embassy in China (Clark), at Canton

WASHINGTON, July 29, 1949—6 p. m.

TelCan 513. Re ur 801 Jul 22. Dept plans press release merely stating as follows:

"Amb Stuart departed by air on (date) en route to Washington for consultation. During a brief stop-over in Okinawa, the Amb will meet Min Counselor Lewis Clark who is proceeding from Canton for the purpose of apprising him of recent developments within areas held by Chi Govt. Fol these discussions, the Amb will continue to the US and Min Counselor Clark will return to his post at Canton."

Dept will inform you when statement released to press.

ACHESON

---

123 Stuart, J. Leighton : Telegram

The Consul General at Taipei (Macdonald) to the Secretary of State

TAIPEI, July 30, 1949—9 a. m.
[Received 10:31 a. m.]

335. Information urtel 70, July 29 [44] given personally General Chou Chi-jou who is issuing orders.

Sent Nanking 190, repeated Department 335, Canton 146.

MACDONALD

---

[43] Not printed.
[44] Same as telegram No. 1644 from Nanking, p. 804.

123 Stuart, J. Leighton : Telegram

The Ambassador in China (Stuart) to the Secretary of State

NANKING, July 30, 1949—5 p. m.
[Received July 30—6:16 a. m.]

1662. As soon as exit permits members my party granted and my ETD firm, I intend to release to local American and foreign correspondents following press statement:

"The American Ambassador to China, The Honorable J. Leighton Stuart, is proceeding to the US for consultation in compliance with instructions received from his Government the latter part of April. Ambassador Stuart plans to leave Nanking in the Embassy's aircraft on August blank. He intends to proceed directly to the US except for normal stopovers and a change of plane en route as required for trans-Pacific travel. It is anticipated that he will arrive in Washington about August blank.

"The pilot and co-pilot of the plane are Air Attaché Colonel John A. Dunning and Assistant Air Attaché Major Robert Van Ausdall. Crew members are Sergeants Edward Memczer and Charles Fillingame, members of the Air Attaché's staff. In addition to the pilots and crew, the Ambassador's party will consist of: Mr. John M. Cabot, Counselor of Embassy and Consul General in Shanghai; Mr. Harry A. Hinderer, Embassy Administrative Officer; Vice Consul and Mrs. William M. Olive; Mr. Philip Fugh, the Ambassador's private Chinese secretary."

If I do not hear from Department to contrary, I will assume it concurs.

Sent Department, repeated Shanghai 921, OffEmb Canton 696 for Connors.

STUART

---

123 Stuart, J. Leighton : Telegram

The Ambassador in China (Stuart) to the Secretary of State

NANKING, July 30, 1949—10 p. m.
[Received July 30—11:33 a. m.]

1663. Exit permits being issued today and local Communist authorities have tentatively fixed Tuesday morning August 2 as date for my departure Nanking (see Embtel 1645 of July 29). Consequently that will by [be] my ETD unless I advise to the contrary. Time of take-off 8 a. m.

Taipei and Canton please inform appropriate authorities CAF change my ETD.

Sent Department 1663, repeated EmbOff Canton 697, Shanghai 922, Taipei 73.

STUART

123 Stuart, J. Leighton : Telegram

The Ambassador in China (Stuart) to the Secretary of State

NANKING, July 30, 1949—10 p. m.
[Received July 30—11:20 a. m.]

1664. With reference Deptel 875, July 23,[45] I am making every effort to depart not later than morning August 2. (See Embtel 1663, July 30.) Communist authorities declare they require time properly to alert their armed forces along aircraft's course and that August 2 is only tentative ETD. They said I will not be delayed longer than August 3 in any event.

STUART

123 Stuart, J. Leighton : Telegram

The Ambassador in China (Stuart) to the Secretary of State

NANKING, August 1, 1949—3 p. m.
[Received August 1—12:47 p. m.]

1671. Philip Fugh July 20 handed Huang Hua written memorandum stating US Government position with regard to shop guarantee procedure as stated Deptel 890, July 27. Huang read memorandum but returned it on usual ground no diplomatic relations between US and People's Government.

STUART

123 Stuart, J. Leighton : Telegram

The Ambassador in China (Stuart) to the Secretary of State

NANKING, August 2, 1949.
[Received August 2—3:20 a. m.]

1679. Relinquished charge and departed Nanking August 2, 1949 via Air Attaché plane due Okinawa same day.
Sent Department 1679; repeated all China posts circular.

STUART

123 Jones, J. Wesley : Telegram

The Counselor of Embassy in China (Jones) to the Secretary of State

NANKING, August 2, 1949.
[Received August 2—1:24 a. m.]

1680. I have assumed charge of the office of the American Embassy at Nanking as of today, August 2, 1949.
Sent Department, repeated circular to all China posts.

JONES

[45] Not printed.

123 [Stuart, J. Leighton] : Telegram

The Secretary of State to the Chargé in China (Clark), at Canton

WASHINGTON, August 2, 1949—2 p. m.

TelCan 525. Dept this morning released to press statement previously transmitted you re departure Ambassador.[46]

ACHESON

---

123 Stuart, J. Leighton : Telegram

The Counselor of Embassy in China (Jones) to the Secretary of State

NANKING, August 2, 1949—6 p. m.
[Received August 2—4 :41 p. m.]

1693. When exit permits in form described Embtel 1645, July 29 were presented Public Safety Bureau, they refused accept Embassy as guarantor on ground Embassy no longer existed in official capacity because no diplomatic relations. Public Safety Bureau then was requested telephone Huang Hua which they did and reported Huang confirmed Embassy guarantee not acceptable. Embassy shop [*chop?*] therefore cancelled, leaving only certifying officer Bacon's personal signature, authorized Deptel 890, July 27.

From other cases of which Embassy has knowledge it appears Communists will accept either shop guarantee or personal guarantee by an individual. They will not, however, accept the guarantee of diplomatic or consular establishment.

We are at loss to understand Huang Hua's apparent sudden reversal of position and are inclined to attribute it either to possible mutual misunderstanding or conflict of views between Aliens Affairs Office and Public Safety Bureau, with latter winning out.

Sent Department 1693, repeated Canton 708, Shanghai 935.

JONES

393.1115/7–2649 : Telegram

The Secretary of State to the Counselor of Embassy in China (Jones)

WASHINGTON, August 3, 1949—5 p. m.

913. Dept concurs that Emb, ConGen Peiping, and Dept shld be informed immed when cases subject of urtel 1628 Jul 26 arise. However, is possible some cases may be settled satisfactorily and without undue delay locally and circumstances be such that protests on higher level might serve only irritate local Commie auths concerned. Suggest cirtel be changed to fol:

---

[46] See telegram telCan No. 513, July 29, p. 807.

"In all cases involving Amers in ur district where clear evidence exists lack protection afforded by Commie auths, you are instructed (1) attempt protest through most effective or feasible channels to local auths citing circumstances (2) provide ConGen Peiping and Emb Nanking with details and recommendation whether or not those posts shld at that time attempt lodge similar protest with Commie auths Peiping, Nanking (3) rpt info Dept. You shld keep Emb, Peiping and Dept informed re outcome such cases. Re cases concerning which you have initially recommended Emb and Peiping not attempt protest, you shld at any subsequent time you feel such protest desirable recommend such, repeating message to Dept. Emb to keep Dept, Peiping and post concerned informed re protests. Peiping to keep Emb, Dept and post concerned informed re protests."

ACHESON

II. DIFFICULTIES OF THE DIPLOMATIC COMMUNITY AFTER THE DEPARTURE OF AMBASSADOR STUART; CHINESE COMMUNIST OBSTRUCTIONIST TACTICS TO PREVENT DEPARTURE OF THE AMERICAN MILITARY ATTACHÉ (AUGUST 5–DECEMBER 31)

701.0093/8–549 : Telegram

The Counselor of Embassy in China (Jones) to the Secretary of State

NANKING, August 5, 1949—8 p. m.
[Received August 5—12 :29 p. m.]

1722. Within Nanking's Diplomatic Corps there is currently considerable speculation whether Ambassador Stuart's departure is going to be followed by new Communist transgressions against foreign diplomatic missions and nationals. By his mere presence in Nanking, this great and understanding friend of China undoubtedly extended a certain mantle of protection to all foreigners here. Now that he has left China it is not excluded that Communists will close our transmitters, prohibit code messages over commercial facilities, initiate arbitrary arrests and humiliations à la Olive,[47] aggravate our labor troubles by supporting extortionate demands [by] employees of foreigners, incite ex-employees of AAG [48] to claim severance pay from this Embassy, increase our cost of living by various financial taxation maneuvers, and in general make our hold here untenable. Altho these persecutions have so far touched Nanking lightly as compared with Shanghai, whole trend of developments points toward their increase. This would be even more probable if Chen Yi [49] takes over adminis-

---

[47] For documentation on the case of William M. Olive, Vice Consul at Shanghai, see pp. 1155 ff.
[48] Army Advisory Group.
[49] Communist general and Mayor of Shanghai.

tration Nanking. Communist reaction against escape of *Amethyst* [50] may also increase pressure against us.

Despite (1) example set by departure of American Ambassador, (2) local pessimism regarding immediate future of diplomatic missions in Nanking and (3) inactivity of those missions which lack radio communication with outside world, apparently few governments have thought through question of withdrawing from Nanking their chiefs of mission or their staffs either in part or *in toto*.

We assume it is in best interests of US Government now for other chiefs of mission to be withdrawn or at latest before formation CCP [51] national government. This would accord with the "common front" policy of the Western Powers vis-à-vis the CCP and would strengthen bargaining position of these powers if and when they commence negotiation regarding diplomatic recognition of new CCP government. Unfortunately, however, there is little we in Nanking can do to encourage or facilitate departure of these chiefs of mission. At present whole question is still hypothetical because of absence of onward transportation out of Shanghai. British Ambassador [52] is still without instructions to leave Nanking and his example affects other chiefs of mission. However, Canadian Ambassador has been instructed return Ottawa. We regret to say that one or two other chiefs to be [*sic*] are opposed to leaving Nanking near future for what appear to be personal reasons.

Department may wish discuss question of withdrawal of other chiefs of mission directly with other governments, placing emphasis on importance of "common front", and bleak future facing missions in Nanking. It could take this opportunity to suggest that coordinated plan should be developed for diplomatic personnel Nanking as well for respective nationals Shanghai desiring evacuation. (See Deptel 1502, to Shanghai July 30, repeated Nanking 903.[53]) Chiefs of mission who still remain Nanking are: British, French, Italian, Belgian, Austrian, Burmese, Siamese, Canadian, Australian, Portuguese, Indian, Dutch, Egyptian, Iranian, Holy See. Missions presently headed by Chargé d'Affaires are: Swiss, Turk, Afghan, Polish and Philippine. USSR has Office Embassy headed by Counselor.

Repeated Shanghai 948, Canton 719, Department pass Peiping 322.

JONES

---

[50] H.M.S. *Amethyst*, British naval ship, crippled by Chinese Communist gunfire on the Yangtze off Nanking in April; at this time it had escaped downriver to Shanghai and thence to the open sea.
[51] Chinese Communist Party.
[52] Sir Ralph Stevenson.
[53] Vol. IX, p. 1278.

701.4193/8–649 : Telegram

The Counselor of Embassy in China (Jones) to the Secretary of State

NANKING, August 6, 1949—3 p. m.
[Received 11:23 p. m.]

1729. Re Embtel 1722, August 5 to Department, repeated Shanghai 948, Canton 719. British Ambassador recommending his Government that he depart China for consultation London after Nationalist Government has moved from Canton. He is further recommending that British Government make early announcement that he will be recalled for consultation some time before formation government in Commie China.

Stevenson has always hoped to delay his departure Nanking long enough to avoid nomination Chargé d'Affaires, Canton.

Sent Department, repeated Embassy Canton 722, Shanghai 950, London 2.

JONES

701.0093/8–949 : Telegram

The Ambassador in the United Kingdom (Douglas) to the Secretary of State

LONDON, August 9, 1949—7 p. m.
[Received August 9—4:14 p. m.]

3137. According Dening,[54] Foreign Office, Canadian Ambassador originally suggested those ambassadors remaining China announce concurrently their impending withdrawal but timing departure left convenience individual ambassador. British Ambassador so informed Foreign Office and recommended concurrence (Nanking 12 [2], August 6[55]). Foreign Office reaction unfavorable as placing too much importance on "unrecognition". No decision, however, in absence Bevin.[56]

Repeated Nanking, Canton.

DOUGLAS

---

[54] Maberly E. Dening, British Assistant Under-Secretary of State for Foreign Affairs (Far East).
[55] Same as telegram No. 1729 from Nanking, *supra*.
[56] Ernest Bevin, British Secretary of State for Foreign Affairs.

701.0093/8–1549 : Telegram

The Counselor of Embassy in China (Jones) to the Secretary of State

NANKING, August 15, 1949—10 a. m.
[Received August 15—4:23 a. m.]

1787. Most recent obstacle imposed by local Communists to establishment informal relations with *de facto* authorities is requirement that Embassy official when calling Alien Affairs Office described himself on appointment slip as either "official of former American Embassy" or as "foreign national". As Department is aware, appointment slip must also describe purpose of visit which gives Communist official opportunity to be "busy" or "out" if it is subject he prefers not discuss. Coming at this relatively late date, after representatives various diplomatic missions fairly well-known at AA Office, this most recent effort to force local diplomats to disassociate themselves in writing from their representative capacities can only be considered further evidence that Communists have no intention relaxing their present policy of nonrecognition foreign representatives during interregnum.

Sent Department 1787; repeated OffEmb Canton 750, Shanghai 991.

JONES

701.0093/8–1549 : Telegram

The Counselor of Embassy in China (Jones) to the Secretary of State

NANKING, August 15, 1949—11 a. m.
[Received 11:20 a. m.]

1788. Consistency shown by CCP in denying official representative character of diplomatic missions Nanking and consulates in Communist China leaves no doubt it is deliberate policy (see Embtel 1787, August 15). All Communist officials from top to bottom mouth same phrase about absence of diplomatic relations and obviously have been well indoctrinated. Whether this is purely CCP policy or whether it has been arrived at in agreement with Moscow is unkown. It is clear, however, that in its implementation Soviets cooperate fully. (Re closure their consulates Peiping, Shanghai and transfer Soviet Ambassador [57] and major Embassy staff out of Nanking prior Communist occupation.) If Communist policy of nonrecognition on *de facto* basis arrived at by agreement with Moscow, it would be of course even more inflexible than if independent policy.

Several reasons suggest themselves for this revolutionary concept of attitude of *de facto* authorities toward official representatives of established sovereign states:

---

[57] N. V. Roschin.

1. By stubbornly refusing to permit establishment informal relations by slightest act or word with foreign diplomatic representatives, CCP hopes to force *de jure* recognition on its own terms immediately central government is established. Interim period probably considered softening up process which will make individual diplomat and his government that much more anxious to regularize position through establishment formal relations as soon as this becomes possibility.

2. This is Soviet concept of international relations prior formal recognition and has been suggested by USSR. It not only appeals to xenophobic "middle kingdom" mentality of China but is most useful instrument for Soviets in diminishing western influence, official and private in China. As a part of this policy CCP utilizes present position of missions to impress upon Communist officialdom and Chinese public in general apparent helplessness of foreign governments in face of Communist power.

3. CCP is not anxious for relations with West either formal or informal in early stages of Communist regime. It has deep distrust of anything non-Communist and when Mao [58] refers to willingness to establish diplomatic relations with all nations on basis equality, mutual benefit, etc., he is talking only in terms of CCP conditions for recognition which would obviously be impossible of acceptance to any non-Communist government of the West.

If any above analyses correct, would appear continued maintenance diplomatic establishment Nanking worse than useless. Not only is diplomatic mission unable to carry out its representative function on even most informal basis, but mere presence diplomatic personnel, particularly chiefs mission, gratuitously provides Communist authorities means of pressure to impel establishment formal diplomatic relations on Communist terms. Western powers may find themselves more and more restricted politically in their freedom of action toward Chinese Communist regime by presence official personnel here.

We must admit that Communists have whip hand in this situation, and that they will not hesitate to use it to their advantage. Longer we remain here and more we attempt to deal with local authorities, more we are all convinced that we cannot have it both ways. There are only two courses: Either we stay and take it, lending ourselves to this new interpretation of international relations, or we withdraw until such time as we can return with recognition and assurances of ability to function. It is, of course, for Department's decision whether our usefulness here in present circumstances outweighs considerations of our anomalous position.

Sent Department 1788, repeated AmEmbassy Canton 751.

JONES

---

[58] Mao Tse-tung, Chairman of the Central Committee of the Chinese Communist Party.

124.933/8–1849 : Telegram

The Counselor of Embassy in China (Jones) to the Secretary of State

NANKING, August 18, 1949—4 p. m.
[Received August 18—11:40 a. m.]

1825. ReDepcirtel August 9.[59] Notice today given 8 USIS employees their services terminated as of close business September 3. Balance of staff informed decision their cases pending. Final determination number and names persons terminated will be made when reply [to] Embtel 1766, August 12 [60] (to Canton 739, Shanghai 967) received. No action yet severance pay but expect demands from terminated employees shortly.

Sent Department 1825, repeated OffEmb Canton 777, Shanghai 1012.

JONES

124.933/8–1949 : Telegram

The Counselor of Embassy in China (Jones) to the Secretary of State

NANKING, June [*August*] 19, 1949—5 p. m.
[Received August 19—8:47 a. m.]

1838. Following is text of dismissal notice handed each of 8 USIS employees (Embtel 1825, August 18) :

"It is with regret must inform you owing obligatory closure USIS public activities by Nanking MCC,[61] Embassy unable make use your services after September 3 which to be considered your termination date.

In accordance permanent policy US Government, preference will be given in new employment in future to former employees whose record and relations with Embassy have been satisfactory to the Government. Those whose employment interrupted by Japanese war know this has been actual practice. For protection such employees, Embassy setting up preferred list of Chinese staff who qualify and who must be separated for reasons beyond Embassy's control. This list will be made available to all American Consulates and other US Government agencies which may need to employ at any time additional Chinese staff. In case employment sought from private American firms or international organizations functioning in China, such employees may also refer prospective employer to preferred list."

[59] Not printed; it reported the situation with regard to the United States Information Service in Nanking (125.0093/7–3049).
[60] Not printed; the Embassy recommended allowing posts to retain a limited staff for custodial purposes in the USIS situation (124.933/8–1249).
[61] Military Control Commission.

Employees Committee has not yet presented demands but we expect take following initial bargaining position:

(1) Any employee may stand on existing terms employment and upon separation now or later will be entitled accrued leave pay and retirement accumulations with interest.

(2) Dissatisfied employees will be considered to have renounced US Government provisions for separation *in toto* and must negotiate for Communist-sponsored 1 to 3 months' severance allowance in place of, and not in addition to, US Government provisions.

(3) Except possibly in case of employees paid less than US $50 monthly and employed less than 1 year, employees who unwilling honor their agreement with US Government cannot be considered have satisfactory record or relation with Government and therefore ineligible preferred list.

Senior employees appear to have already decided independently that they wish to have nothing to do with Communist-encouraged group. One has already offered resignation in fear his claim to full pension next year may be jeopardized. This split in ranks has had good effect in impressing on all personnel that US Government separation provisions and policy are (at least in normal circumstances) infinitely superior to Communist counterparts.

Sent Department, repeated Canton 781, Shanghai 1016.

JONES

124.93/8–2049 : Telegram

The Counselor of Embassy in China (Jones) to the Secretary of State

NANKING, August 20, 1949—noon.
[Received August 20—3 :09 a. m.]

1843. ReEmbtel 1835, August 19.[62] Would like to inform other friendly missions, particularly North Atlantic group, Department's decision drastically reduce OffEmb Nanking. (Deptel 975, August 17.[63]) However, there are no secrets Diplomatic Corps Nanking and Department should be prepared for leak to press if I am authorized inform colleagues this new development. Please instruct.

JONES

---

[62] Not printed; it reported in detail the Embassy's recommendations on the personnel situation (124.936/8–1949).
[63] Not printed; it dealt with more technical aspects of personnel reduction which marked a decision to begin a process of attrition with respect to the duties and strength of the Embassy's staff (124.93/7–2749).

124.933/8–2349 : Telegram

The Counselor of Embassy in China (Jones) to the Secretary of State

NANKING, August 23, 1949—11 a. m.
[Received August 23—6 :43 a. m.]

1873. ReEmbtel 1838, August 19, 5 p. m. Employees' committee Saturday formally stated "hope", not "demand", that Embassy would settle with dismissed employees now and in future on following terms: (1) 1 year's pay; (2) additional allowance US $300 to each employee earning less than $1000 annually; (3) special additional consideration to be given employees with more than 1 year's service; (4) foregoing to be in addition to lump sum payment accrued leave and retirement deductions; (5) all benefits to be paid immediately on separation and on US draft; (6) on resumption normal operations, severed employees to be reemployed. Year's pay explained on basis US dollar now worth in commodities only 30 percent its value before take-over.

Embassy's position as outlined reftel given to committee for digestion over week end and all discussion of committee terms deferred until adjourned meeting August 22. Meantime Shanghai MCC rules governing settlement labor disputes in newly reopened enterprises published providing, *inter alia*, that in case of dismissal terms of employment contract must be adhered to and where no contract exists employee is entitled to 1 month's notice and 1 to 3 months' pay, depending on length of service. August 22 committee requested deferment meeting until 23rd.

Sent Department; repeated OffEmb Canton 786, Shanghai 1030.

JONES

124.93/8–2049 : Telegram

*The Secretary of State to the Counselor of Embassy in China (Jones),
at Nanking*

WASHINGTON, August 24, 1949—5 p. m.

1009. Urtel 1843, Aug 20. You may in ur discretion inform heads friendly missions on confidential basis decision re reduction Emb staff. This wld appear to be in order in view our endeavor achieve common action among certain powers on dipl moves. In any case Emb staff applications for exit permits wld probably soon make our decision common knowledge.

ACHESON

701.5193/8–2749 : Telegram

The Counselor of Embassy in China (Jones) to the Secretary of State

NANKING, August 27, 1949—noon.
[Received August 28—2:50 a. m]

1913. In informing heads of mission of Department's plans to drastically reduce Embassy office Nanking (Deptel 1009, August 24), fo¹ lowing information re their plans of interest:

(1) French Ambassador [64] presently Shanghai has been recalled Paris for consultation. He plans return Nanking for brief period prior departing China. He hopes depart before formation new government Peiping. Method of exit not yet arranged but Embassy hopes French boat may be permitted enter Shanghai. He will leave Embassy Nanking in charge of counselor with staff approximately seven officers and seven clerks (exclusive Service Attaché Staff).

(2) British Ambassador still plans leave China after fall Canton and before formation new government. Understood he plans exit by British naval vessel waiting outside territorial waters which can be reached by small British river launch from Shanghai. Ministry Council [*Minister Counselor?*] [65] has arranged for exit visa and hopes to depart *Gordon*. British Embassy will not be further reduced according to Stevenson who would like to keep it "intact for move to Peiping". After departure of Stevenson and Lamb, First Secretary will be in charge and officer complement will be approximately seven (exclusive of service attachés).

(3) Canadian Ambassador has reservation on *Gordon* to return home. He plans recommend withdrawal entire staff in Nanking, Military Attaché, leaving local interests property in care of Canadian Consulate General, Shanghai. Davis has likewise recommended Canadian Consulate General, Shanghai, be reduced to skeleton staff.

(4) Portuguese Minister, while hoping someone else will take lead, has his orders and is prepared to leave on first available transport to Europe. He plans close legation on departure.

(5) Italian Ambassador without instructions but he believes once French Ambassador leaves he too will be instructed depart. (Department may wish inquire Italian Government its plans particularly in light specific instructions and plans most his colleagues North Atlantic community.)

(6) Netherlands Ambassador has instructions return home preparatory retirement. Departure plans, however, indefinite because lack transportation Europe and personal disinclination. He will leave Embassy Nanking intact with Counselor in charge, First Secretary and two attachés (all Sinologues), Chancellor and clerk.

---

[64] Jacques Meyrier.
[65] Lionel Henry Lamb.

(7) Belgian Ambassador has general instructions giving him wide latitude. He does not wish to depart before British or French Ambassador. When he leaves, however, he plans take his staff with him, leaving local affairs in care Belgian Consul General, Shanghai.

Sent Department, repeated OffEmb Canton 805.

JONES

124.93/8–2749 : Telegram

The Counselor of Embassy in China (Jones) to the Secretary of State

NANKING, August 27, 1949—6 p. m.
[Received August 28—4 ;35 a. m.]

1915. Embassy has interviewed Woo Yun-chih recently nominated Judge of People's Court for service probably Nanking or Shanghai but temporarily advisor on international law to Communist authorities Peiping. Introduced by AstAMilAt Beebe,[66] [as] formerly editor *World Culture* and graduate Soochow Law School. Says authorities reconsidering question status foreign diplomatic and consular personnel. Discussed with him memo on recognition and status prepared in Embassy May 9 [67] with which Ambassador is familiar. Woo appeared genuinely interested and asked for copy to take Peiping to which we agreed. Impressed on him that our prime interest in status question not personal immunities and courtesies but :

(1) Right to represent American citizens in their personal and property rights. (2) Right to access to Communist officials. (3) Right to confidential communications. (4) Right to travel to and from posts. Woo apparently already engaged question taxation Government property (Depcirtel August 26, 6 a. m.[68]) and seems to share generally accepted views this point.

Sent Department 1915, repeated Shanghai 1050.

JONES

123 Stuart, J. Leighton : Telegram

The Counselor of Embassy in China (Jones) to the Secretary of State

NANKING, August 31, 1949—6 p. m.
[Received 11 :20 p. m.]

1964. Lo Hai-sha [69] requests Ambassador Stuart be informed (1) relaxation Communist exit requirements facilitating Ambassador's departure was due to number of telegrams and letters sent by Chen

[66] Maj. John E. Beebe, Jr., Assistant Military Attaché in China.
[67] Not found in Department of State files.
[68] Not printed.
[69] Nanking representative of General Chen Ming-shu, Shanghai representative of Marshal Li Chi-shen, head of the Kuomintang Revolutionary Committee (KmtRC) at Peiping.

Ming-shu to Mao Tse-tung; (2) Chen has agreed take up Bender–Smith matter [70] on present trip to Peiping, Lo also requests Ambassador's attention called to Chen's statement on White Paper (Embtel 1963, August 31).[71]

JONES

701.4193/9–149 : Telegram

The Counselor of Embassy in China (Jones) to the Secretary of State

NANKING, September 1, 1949—8 p. m.
[Received September 2—3 :37 a. m.]

1979. Further information re future British Embassy Nanking (see Embtel 1913, August 27, to Department, repeated Embassy Canton 805) :

Upon departure of Minister Lamb (sailing on SS *General Gordon* end of September) and Ambassador Stevenson (who presently plans depart Nanking after fall of Canton), British Embassy Nanking will be headed by Minister Hutchison (presently Minister-Counselor for Commercial Affairs stationed in Shanghai). Military Attaché with rank of Lieutenant Colonel plans remain; NA,[72] however, departing on *Gordon*. Retention of relatively large Embassy staff Nanking explained on basis that Embassy acts as personnel reservoir for all China; that Peiping office is greatly understaffed having only one consular officer (newly arrived) and one clerk.

Re future Indian Embassy Nanking, Indian Ambassador [73] admitted for first time that he expects remain Nanking until after formation Communist government and probably until establishment relations therewith. While Panikkar's instructions are sufficiently broad that they permit him to depart whenever he considers it appropriate, he informed me in confidence that Nehru's [74] oral instructions to him were to "stick it out as long as possible". On this basis Panikkar feels that unless life Nanking becomes quite intolerable for him and staff he should and will remain. There is possibility that his instructions may be modified, however, following Acheson–Bevin's conversations Washington.[75] Panikkar admitted that Indian Government's attitude would be influenced by results those conversations on China policy.

Sent Department, repeated OffEmb Canton 813, Shanghai 1074, London 14, New Delhi 11.

JONES

---

[70] See footnote 31, p. 384.

[71] Telegram No. 1963 not printed ; for documentation regarding the publication of the China White Paper, see vol. IX, pp. 1365 ff.

[72] Naval Attaché.

[73] K. M. Panikkar.

[74] Jawaharlal Nehru, Indian Prime Minister and Minister for External Affairs.

[75] For documentation regarding conversations between the Secretary of State and the British Secretary of State for Foreign Affairs, see vol. IX, pp. 1 ff.

702.4193/9–349 : Telegram

The Counselor of Embassy in China (Jones) to the Secretary of State

NANKING, September 3, 1949—noon.
[Received September 4—4:07 a. m.]

1991. Re Shanghai telegram 3495, August 26,[76] repeated Nanking only. British Embassy advise that their ConGen Shanghai paid taxes on ConGen without prior consultation Embassy and that FonOff can object only on basis former practice in China and not on grounds comity since British municipal taxes appear to be collected from foreign consulates and even embassies. Nevertheless British Embassy still desires that consulates in China resist payment similar direct taxes.

Embassy has received house tax bills for two rented and three government-owned premises. Bills returned promptly to tax office, one group August 1 and second group August 17, with explanation premises owned by people of US and held for their benefit by US Government; and in case rented property that landlord bound under lease pay all taxes and further that under international law foreign government relieved from payment taxes this description. Nothing further heard to date in respect these properties and no new bills for neighboring properties received. While other missions have declared their intention resist taxation government-owned premises, British say they consider it politic to pay house tax on rented premises in order avoid appearance complete uncooperativeness. In all cases assessments extremely trifling; US cents 25 to 150 for 2-month period.

Sent Department; repeated Shanghai 1082, Hankow 73. Department pass Peiping 356.

JONES

124.933/9–549 : Telegram

The Counselor of Embassy in China (Jones) to the Secretary of State

NANKING, September 5, 1949—4 p. m.
[Received September 5—9:10 a. m.]

2005. At adjourned meeting, August 23, (Embtel 1873, August 23) Embassy Employees' Committee indicated no change their position and Embassy expressed view matter must be brought to attention General Labor Union. August 24 splinter group proposed whole matter be deferred await results Shanghai negotiations. Meantime Committee obtained signatures great majority employees (including all separated USIS staff) take no step individually. Embassy pre-

---

[76] *Post*, p. 1284.

pared letter to Union setting forth general terms Government provisions, accumulated accrued leave, retirement deductions and effect application each separated employee. Although Committee known to have been consulting Union informally, pressing of case by Embassy produced new conferences August 29–31 with final September 1, at which Embassy without making offer requested Committee's views Shanghai terms (Shanghai's 3312, August 18 [77]) and suggested discussion these terms applied in reverse might be fruitful as Embassy considered special circumstances warranted giving proportionately greatest benefits to those employees with smallest accumulations. Committee retired, then proposed bonuses equal 8 months' salary all employees plus $100 those earning between 1,000–1500 annually and $200 to those earning less. Committee also requested payment maintenance at full salary, pending dispute, from September 3 onward and agreement not to dismiss, pending dispute, any additional employees. Embassy naturally obliged reject all proposals, and delivered reference letter to Union September 2. Union expressed interest but stated unable accept letter or act on request it state its views as to whether employment contract existed or whether dismissal notices valid, on ground only employees can ask Union to take any action. Union then indicated Embassy's proper course was to take up matter with Aliens Affairs Office. Memo requesting AAO to take cognizance dispute and forward letter to Union delivered to AAO morning 3rd. AAO stated it provisionally obliged reject memo because (1) objected to statement dismissals resulted from closure USIS public activities, (2) had not received communication from employees and therefore not familiar with all facts, (3) both parties should continue negotiate directly with each other and reach settlement. Meantime Committee indicated own intention approach Union but it is believed it has not yet done so.

Sent Dept; repeated Shanghai 1089, Taipei 88.

JONES

124.933/9–949 : Telegram

The Counselor of Embassy in China (Jones) to the Secretary of State

NANKING, September 9, 1949—5 p. m.
[Received September 10—6 a. m.]

2043. Following developments labor front since Embtel 2005, September 5, repeated Shanghai 1089, Taipei 88:

Despite Embassy instructions to watchman at 5 Ninghai to admit no one to premises beginning September 6, discharged employees prevailed on him to admit them and spent working hours September

---

[77] Not printed.

6, 7 and 8 in compound, leaving one employee overnight to readmit them each morning. Efforts persuade them leave unavailing. We have informed them we consider their notices of termination valid, and since they are no longer Embassy employees, they have no right occupy US Government property. They insist employment not terminated until agreement reached on separation terms, and are supported in this view by General Labor Union and American Embassy Employees' Committee.

Clough [78] went September 8 with employee representatives to AAO in further effort to bring dispute formally to attention authorities. AAO representative Tsui stated General Labor Union already in contact with employees, and will represent them in direct negotiations with employer. GLU will set time for opening negotiations. Tsui referred to Bennett [79] as employer but after being informed (1) that USIS integral part of US State Department operations in China, as MCC itself recognized in notice to USIS to terminate; (2) that discharged employees on Embassy payroll and under jurisdiction Embassy personnel office, he did not press point beyond usual formal declaration that People's Government does not recognize USIS or Embassy, and it seems likely Clough will be able continue to negotiate on behalf Embassy.

Tsui also stated while negotiations in progress employer: Not discharge employees and latter have obligation continue work for employer. When asked for pertinent regulation, he referred to Shanghai provisional labor regulations published Nanking *Hsin Hua Jih Pao* September 6. However, he would not state that these regulations are binding in Nanking, but said merely that they could be used for "reference purposes" in negotiations.

Tsui refused to discuss our contention that employees' employment terminated September 3, and they had no right enter US Government property without our permission. He said this question as well as that of proper amount of severance pay could only be discussed directly with GLU.

At opening of negotiations with GLU, Embassy will take following position:

1. Occupation US Government property by discharged employees form of duress making it impossible for us to negotiate while it continues;

2. Embassy does have right to discharge employees and latter cannot continue employment at will simply by making exorbitant demands;

3. Embassy has contract with employees providing terms of severance. This contract must be taken into consideration in discussion of additional demands employees have made.

---

[78] Ralph N. Clough, Second Secretary of Embassy in China.
[79] Director of United States Information Service.

Initial meeting with GLU representative will be of exploratory nature to feel out his attitude. Embassy does not expect make any concessions at this meeting beyond Shanghai offer referred to Embtel 2005, September 5.

We have been informed by senior employee that present attitude of Embassy Employees' Committee is to mark time pending Shanghai settlement, following which they will demand same treatment. We will continue push for separate settlement although, if GLU adopts delaying tactics, there is little we can do to expedite matters.

We are closing building at 5 Ninghai and withdrawing librarian who has been working there in order strengthen our contention that discharged USIS employees no longer working. If we succeed, discharged employees will then have access only to gatehouse and courtyard.

Sent Department 2043; repeated Shanghai 1108, Taipei 92.

JONES

701.0093/9–949 : Telegram

The Counselor of Embassy in China (Jones) to the Secretary of State

NANKING, September 9, 1949—5 p. m.
[Received September 10—9 :10 a. m.]

2044. One aspect of our "united front" policy toward Communist China is continued presence of chiefs of mission North Atlantic Powers in Communist territory as formation Central Government Peiping becomes imminent. While French and Netherlands Ambassadors are under instructions from their Governments to leave by first available transport (probably SS *Marechal Joffre* October 15 if permitted enter Shanghai), the other western European representatives are torn with indecision, awaiting move from British Ambassador. The latter has become key figure in plans for general exodus of chiefs of mission Nanking and he shows no inclination to leave.

Stevenson informed me this morning his instructions are that he should leave Nanking when formation of Communist government appears imminent. These, of course, give wide latitude, and lack of regular transport makes precision timing of departure impossible. I have impression that Stevenson has no intention of leaving China near future, rather that he intends to stay to await future developments here and that he will not be particularly embarrassed finding himself in Communist territory after formation of Central Government. This attitude is supported by recent conversation with Australian Ambassador who likewise felt formation Central Government Peiping before his departure China was more technical than practical political problem.

We have heard from authoritative British source that about 2 weeks ago British, Australian and Indian Ambassadors met and took decision not leave Communist China before formation Central Communist Government; that since that time their actions and future plans have been based on that decision. This is somewhat confirmed by attitude expressed by Indian Ambassador last week (see Embtel 1976 to Department; [80] repeated Embassy Canton 812, September 1). Likewise Australian Ambassador has no definite plans for leaving China although he has expressed intentions of proceeding Shanghai at time formation Central Government Peiping as ostensibly en route out of country.

Representatives of small powers are bewildered and unhappy over what appears to them divergence policy between US and UK. While some may be persuaded by departure French Ambassador to leave, many will remain until British Ambassador's plans clarify. If Department considers continued present [*presence*] friendly chiefs of mission Nanking after formation Communist Central Government, Peiping, has important political significance, it may wish to clarify British stand during visit Foreign Secretary [to] Washington. Their continued presence after formation Communist Central Government may be considered another step toward early recognition that regime. Certainly departure chiefs of mission Communist China after establishment new government will have much greater political significance than could be attached to such action during present period to [*of?*] local military control commissions.

Sent Department 2044; repeated Embassy Canton 825.

JONES

124.936/9–1249 : Circular telegram

The Counselor of Embassy in China (Jones) to the Secretary of State

NANKING, September 12, 1949—noon.
[Received September 12—3:24 a. m.]

2065. Because of drastic staff reductions Nanking will be unable handle large volume political telegrams presently received here. Request effective immediately no political telegrams be repeated Nanking unless of particular interest this office. Press telegrams heretofore regularly repeated Nanking by most posts must also be discontinued. Political reporting from Nanking will be limited to developments this district. Instructions economic reporting given Embassy cirtel September 2, repeated Department 1983.[81] Sharp cutback necessary both classified and unclassified traffic since navy radio facilities being closed and teletype operation discontinued.

[80] September 1, vol. IX, p. 70.
[81] Not printed.

Sent circular, repeated Department 206 [*2065*], Department pass Hankow, Tientsin, Tsingtao.

JONES

---

123 Jones, J. Wesley: Telegram

The Counselor of Embassy in China (Jones) to the Secretary of State

NANKING, September 13, 1949—10 a. m.
[Received September 13—4:52 a. m.]

2071. Exit permits for USIS Director Bennett and myself [82] are being delayed by Nanking Public Safety Bureau because current labor dispute alien employees. When I responded along with other Embassy officers to invitation from PSB [83] to pick up my completed exit permit September 10, I was told there would be some delay in my case, that there was unsettled labor dispute at Embassy; that Embassy employees' representatives had asked PSB in writing to withhold exit permits from Bennett, Bacon [84] and me until labor dispute settled. Suggestion was made however that if my guarantor willing accept responsibility and that arrangement satisfactory to employees permit would be issued.

I immediately convened Embassy Committee who admitted they had written PSB September 2 as result decision mass meeting employees August 25. I was assured, however, step taken because general fear all officers leaving and no responsible official remaining Nanking settle claims. When I explained Bacon would assume charge my departure and have full authority responsible all Embassy activities they appeared to be satisfied and agreed that I could so state and that they would so indicate to Public Safety Bureau when approached. On my second call Public Safety Bureau September 12, I found neither side had moved and case same status. After discussions, long consultations with each other Public Safety Bureau suggested another letter from employees withdrawing September 2 letter or agreeing to assumption responsibility by guarantor. I then had second meeting with Embassy Committee, told them what Public Safety Bureau required from them and stated I expected that they would comply. Again they appeared to agree Bacon's assumption charge met their requirements. Three of Committee left meeting to call at PSB ostensibly to counteract effect September 2 letter but subsequent report confirms our suspicions Committee has no intention of taking positive action to relieve situation.

---

[82] In telegram No. 1762, August 11, Mr. Jones requested transfer out of China, in view of the fact that he had been separated from his family for more than the maximum period of one year for officers in China. (123 Cory, Thomas J.)
[83] Public Safety Bureau (Communist).
[84] Leonard L. Bacon, Second Secretary of Embassy.

I feel we have exhausted all reasonable channels of finding amicable solution problem our exit permits and must now place responsibility on local authorities for their refusal issue. Consequently plan call PSB and Aliens Affairs September 13 to protest delay issuance Bennett's and my permits. Will report further at which time Department may wish consider giving appropriate publicity. Also suggest immediate assistance Peiping ConGen in bringing this official acquiescence in blackmail tactics to attention central authorities.

Sent Department 2071; repeated Shanghai 1120.

JONES

121.5493/9–1349 : Telegram

The Military Attaché in China (Soule) to the Secretary of State [85]

NANKING, September 13, 1949.
[Received September 13—6 :12 a. m.]

9611. Capt. John J. Christensen, Asst. AMilAt, Nanking, attempted discharge two servants 9 September for refusal take vaccination and dishonesty. While discussing termination settlement, Mrs. Christensen padlocked compound gate believing servants were planning departing with Christensen property. Gate locked from 1800 to 1915 hours when Capt. Christensen removed padlock in presence one servant. Servants remained on premises 21 Yi Ho Road overnight and following morning Capt. Christensen was requested telephonically by Foreign Affairs Section [of] Public Safety Bureau to appear with servants. Christensen then discovered servants had lodged complaint against him they were locked in from 1800 hours 9 September to 0800 hours 10 September, depriving them of their liberty during this entire period. Public Safety officials refused consider Christensen allegations against servants and questioned him from 1030 until 1600 hours without break. Christensen accompanied by Chinese interpreter remained in same room where no telephone available. No opportunity given them eat lunch or phone Embassy but Christensen did not request recess or use of phone. Christensen was requested sign confession and finally signed approximately as follows:

"I, John J. Christensen, admit that the gate at 21 Yi Ho Lu was locked during the hours of 1800 to 1915 hours on the evening of 9 September with the intention of retaining Wang, Chen, Tsai and Chiang. I admit that this was a violation of the Nanking People's Law."

The authorities refused to accept earlier draft including reason for locking gate and statement that case would be regarded leniently and

---

[85] Sent via Department of the Army.

concluded. Latter statement was originally stipulated but after statement signed Christensen told case was not closed. Statement finally signed after Christensen tired, thirsty, hungry. Christensen was never told could not leave or under detention or arrest but Public Safety asked for guarantor that Christensen would not leave Nanking and appear when summoned. After first suggesting Christensen send note by messenger for signature guarantee by Bacon, Public Safety then suggested he could go with messenger following to bring back guarantee. Christensen departed, followed in jeep by unarmed Public Safety officer. Without being informed of confession Bacon signed guarantee that Christensen would be available for questioning after eliminating word "summoned" and after being informed by PSB that guarantee did not imply Christensen under arrest, Christensen permitted depart. Public Safety, General Labor Union and Foreign Residents' Employees Association insist servants remain on premises until case settled. Servants not performing duties and one attempted kill Christensen puppy dog evening 9 Sept. Whole day 11 September spent in fruitless discussion with Servants' Union official. Unable agree basis for negotiation because official unable decide whether Christensen justified in discharging servants and even who were discharged as Union regards all servants discharged. Request being made to Alien Affairs Office to arrange basis for negotiation and get servants off premises. Christensen offered pay their maintenance without prejudice to their claims if they would move out but they refused and Union insists they remain. Servants demand 6 months' pay.

Possible propaganda will be made by Communists on lock-in. Settlement of lock-in case and servant dispute being linked by Communists. We are trying keep two issues separate.

[SOULE]

---

123 Jones, J. Wesley : Telegram

The Secretary of State to the Consul General at Peiping (Clubb)

WASHINGTON, September 13, 1949—8 p. m.

630. [Here follows text of telegram No. 2071, September 13, 10 a.m., printed on page 827.]

Pls bring foregoing immed attn Peiping auths, pointing out this is serious example failure local auths afford protection promised fons in what appears to be official acquiescence by those auths in unreasonable and coercive tactics against fons.

ACHESON

123 Jones, J. Wesley : Telegram

The Counselor of Embassy in China (Jones) to the Secretary of State

NANKING, September 13, 1949—8 p. m.
[Received September 14—5 :02 a. m.]

2077. Bennett and I were courteously received at Public Safety Bureau this morning with further reference our exit permits (Embtel 2071, September 13). Substance of long discussion during which I attempted to establish responsibility for issuance or denial exit visa squarely on PSB as controlling authority was that my permit had not been denied but was merely delayed because of written intervention of Embassy employees and that PSB was continuing to investigate to determine whether my departure would in fact affect settlement of existing labor dispute. Under circumstances I did not make protest but confined my remarks to statement that I was concerned over continuing delay; that I was sure that my Government would take grave view of any continuing delay which would prevent my departing on *General Gordon;* that with PSB concurrency I intended to take up question of delay with AAO.

Subsequently at Aliens Affairs Office I was received by one of Huang Hua's [86] assistants. After listening to my story (which I felt he already knew by heart) he assured me that an investigation of my application was proceeding and that AAO had consulted both with PSB and Labor Union. I have feeling local authorities do not wish to make issue my case or have it become subject widespread publicity and that probabilities of some face-saving formula will be found in time to permit my exit on *Gordon.* No promises were, however, given and both offices suggested easiest way to obtain permit would be prompt and satisfactory settlement of pending labor dispute. Our impression is that they therefore intend delay issuance as long as they dare and hence Peiping pressure would be decisive.

As Department is aware, Bennett's exit permit is being delayed over settlement of payment of rent of former USIS premises (Embtel 1948, August 30 [87]). Since landlord has been found Shanghai, that obstacle we hope will be entirely and satisfactorily eliminated by end of week. However, at PSB this morning Director admitted that Bennett had second hurdle, namely employees letter regarding labor dispute. When we raised delay in Bennett's exit permit at AAO this morning, official agreed that this was case similar to mine and implied investigation my case would include that of Bennett also.

Sent Department 2077; repeated Shanghai 1126.

JONES

---

[86] Chief of the Alien Affairs Office, Nanking Military Control Council.
[87] Not printed.

121.5493/9–1449 : Telegram

The Counselor of Embassy in China (Jones) to the Secretary of State

NANKING, September 14, 1949—8 p. m.
[Received September 14—6 :44 p. m.]

2094. Re 9611 from AMilAt September 13. In view fact Christensen responded voluntarily to telephone call from Bureau Public Safety September 10 and executed confession without being under apparent restraint or other compulsion by Bureau, and at no time attempted communicate with Embassy, we have seen no clear way protest Bureau action. When asked give guarantee, Bacon (not informed of previous execution confession) obtained categorical statement that language of guarantee did not imply Christensen under arrest, and on his objection he could not guarantee Christensen's appearance whenever "summoned" without Department's approval, Bureau eliminated objectionable term and substituted guarantee that Christensen would be "available at any time for questioning". Bureau has not since recalled him. Memo handed today to Aliens Affairs Office requesting prompt action conclude dispute with Christensen and servants and pointing out intolerable situation resulting continued residence servants his premises. We consider Government's interest as well as Christensen's personal interest best protected by continuing treat matter as unsettled labor dispute in which he is endeavoring cooperate with both police and labor authorities.

JONES

---

123 Jones, J. Wesley : Telegram

The Counselor of Embassy in China (Jones) to the Secretary of State

NANKING, September 15, 1949.
[Received September 15—12 :48 p. m.]

2106. Following memorandum was presented Nanking Aliens Affairs Office this morning :

"John Wesley Jones, American FSO with rank of Counselor of Embassy, made application to Nanking Public Safety Bureau for permission depart China September 2, 1949. Mr. Jones has complied with all requirements of PSB in making application to exit but has thus far failed to receive approved permit. He plans to leave Nanking on Sunday, September 18 for Shanghai and to sail from that port September 24 on SS *General Gordon.*

"Mr. Jones, who entered China 1 year ago with full diplomatic immunity, expects that he will be permitted to return to his country without hindrance or further delay."

Similar memorandum *mutatis mutandis* concerning Bennett submitted same time. Both notes returned with statement absence diplomatic relations written communication mentioning diplomatic immunity could not be accepted with reference exit permits. Official added that question was under study.

Sent Department 2106, repeated Shanghai 1146, and Peiping 369.

JONES

124.933/9–1549 : Telegram

The Counselor of Embassy in China (Jones) to the Secretary of State

NANKING, September 15, 1949—4 p. m.
[Received September 17—3 :46 a. m.]

2107. Embtel 2106, September 15 refers to Embtel 2077, September 13. Aliens Affairs Office summoned Bennett, myself this morning. Official stated after conference with Embassy employees AAO felt it desirable to settle as quickly as possible labor dispute pending Embassy. He therefore suggested we meet with employees at Labor Union today. I asked if subject of our present discussion was labor dispute or my exit permit. Official replied former. I said that Embassy was most anxious settle labor dispute and would of course send representative to Labor Union at any time latter so designated. We added that neither Bennett nor I had been involved in labor discussions with Embassy Committee and therefore we personally would not appear but that qualified representative of Embassy, to deal on behalf of Department with employees, would be present. AAO official emphasized desirability my and Bennett's presence. We reiterated that we would send qualified representative; and that Embassy must reserve right to decide who would represent it in labor discussions. AAO replied that settlement of labor dispute was most important issue and hoped that I would make every effort to bring dispute to early conclusion; he added that he had just received call from Labor Union and that Embassy employees' representatives. were waiting there to discuss dispute.

I then asked if I could discuss question of my exit permit to which official consented on condition I be brief since Embassy employees were already waiting for us as pointed out. Briefly I emphasized point that I had made application for exit permit, that I had demonstrated clearly both to AAO and Embassy employees full authority and responsibility of Bacon to conduct and settle any labor dispute after my departure from China; and that my presence in, or absence from, China would have no effect on final settlement of labor dispute and that I would regret very much to see my departure from China tied closely to final settlement of pending labor dispute of Embassy.

Official replied that since labor dispute was in process of negotiation he was unable to make any comment on my statement.[88]

Department please pass information Peiping.

Sent Department 2107; repeated Shanghai 1147.

JONES

124.933/9–2449 : Telegram

The Counselor of Embassy in China (Jones) to the Secretary of State

NANKING, September 24, 1949.
[Received September 24—2:18 p. m.]

2168. Following is termination agreement reached with employees, dated as of September 17:

This termination agreement is hereby entered into between representatives by the American Embassy (hereinafter referred to as the employer) and representatives of the Preparatory Committee of the Chinese Employees Union of the American Embassy (hereinafter referred to as the employees). The following termination terms have been negotiated and agreed upon between the employer and the employees. All employees of the Embassy proper and affiliated organization, the United States Information Service, regardless of whether they are already terminated or to be terminated in the future, shall abide by the terms of the present agreement.

(1) When the employer terminates any employee, written notice shall be served 1 month in advance.

(2) In addition to lump sum leave pay and retirement deductions, to which the employees are entitled and which shall be handled in accordance with the standing regulations, the employer shall issue severance pay to terminated employees.

(3) (*a*) Severance pay equivalent to 2 months' salary shall be issued to terminated employees whose length of service is less than 2 years, to be calculated according to the value of 1 United States dollar in terms of parity units.

(*b*) For employees whose length of service is 2 years or more, an additional severance pay equivalent to 1 month's salary shall be issued, to be calculated in the same manner as that referred to in the preceding paragraph.

(*c*) If the total amount of parity pay and the salary of the last bi-weekly payment together come to less than 200 United States dollars, the employer shall make it up to 200 United States dollars.

(4) The method of calculation of parity pay shall be based on the parity unit rate and United States dollar official exchange rate announced by the People's Government. The factor for calculation has been determined by agreement between the employer and the employees to be 1 United States dollar equals 6.23 parity unit. In the future, if due to fluctuation of the parity unit rate and the United States dollar official exchange rate, the parity value of each United

---

[88] In telegram No. 2126, September 18, the Counselor reported exit permits for himself and Mr. Bennett were received the evening of September 17 (123 Bennett).

States dollar in people's notes at the official exchange rate is less than actual United States dollar converted into people's note at the official exchange rate, the parity pay shall be calculated on the basis of actual dollar pay converted into people's note at the official exchange rate. If the parity value is higher than an actual United States dollar in people's notes at the official exchange rate, parity pay shall not exceed 140 percent of actual United States dollar pay.

(5) Parity pay shall be calculated according to the official quotation of the parity unit rate at Nanking on the date of termination of the employee and shall be issued not later than 2 days after the date of termination. If United States dollar drafts can be sold locally, parity pay shall be calculated and issued on the date of termination.

(6) The above terms are determined in accordance with the spirit of the terms concluded between the employer and the employees of the United States Information Service at Shanghai on September 16, 1949. If at a future date they should be found to be at variance with the latter's actual termination practice, they shall be modified as occasions warrant.

(7) The present agreement shall be prepared and signed in duplicate, one copy each being kept by employer and employees.

(8) The present agreement shall come into effect as of September 17, 1949.

Representatives of the American Embassy:
Representatives of the Preparatory Committee of the Chinese Employees Union of the American Embassy:
Nanking, September 17, 1949.

Sent Department, repeated Shanghai 1174.

JONES

---

123 Jones, J. Wesley: Telegram

The Counselor of Embassy in China (Jones) to the Secretary of State

NANKING, September 25, 1949.
[Received September 30—1:30 a. m.]

2172. China Post Circular. Embassy cirtel September 20, repeated Department 2140.[89] Relinquished charge office Embassy Nanking to Bacon today September 25, and depart China.

JONES

---

[89] Not printed.

701.4193/9–2849 : Telegram

The Second Secretary of Embassy in China (Bacon) to the Secretary of State

NANKING, September 28, 1949—10 a. m.
[Received September 28—5 :10 a. m.]

2185. British Ambassador advised me September 26 that he has now agreed with Foreign Office that on his departure Coghill,[90] presently Canton, be appointed Chargé; Hutchison, presently Shanghai, will be transferred Nanking as officer in charge office of Embassy Nanking and French Ambassador advises that First Counsellor Roux, presently Canton, will be Chargé and Second Counsellor Royère will be in charge of Nanking Office of Embassy as well as principal officer Shanghai Consulate General.

Since American Embassy, Nanking, presently performing few functions other than Consular, question continuance diplomatic status may soon be under consideration by Department. Question presumably will become acute on announcement organization Communist Central Government and recognition thereof one or more powers. We nevertheless urge Department postpone possible reclassification Nanking until joint action can be taken with Britain and France because (1) as Consulate, our relations with existing missions would be awkward; (2) reclassification Embassy properties into Consulate premises might reopen question taxability which apparently dormant; (3) reclassification for administrative reasons certain to be construed as political step and ought not to be made until political purpose thereby served.

BACON

124.931/10–1149 : Telegram

The Second Secretary of Embassy in China (Bacon) to the Secretary of State

NANKING, October 11, 1949—10 a. m.
[Received October 11—5 :52 a. m.]

2244. Municipal Tax Bureau returned October 6 house tax bills (Embtel 1991, September 3) with exception bill rented premises Chung Shan Lu, formerly USIS and surrendered owner September 17. Bureau repeats demand taxes be paid and further asks submission leases and deeds; also advises bills other properties not yet rendered may be expected.

Embassy replied October 7 stating hope authorities would express views our objections listed our letter August 1 and adding: "It is

---

[90] John Percival Coghill, Consul General with diplomatic status attached to the British Embassy.

especially appropriate this be done this time since authorities Peking have recently acknowledged presence official representatives foreign governments at both Nanking and Peking".[91]   Also pointed out tax on 1–A Lang Ya Lu (leased by AMilAt) should be cancelled as being in same category as Chung Shan premises.

Possible but doubtful that re-reissuance these bills connected with bid for diplomatic recognition. Re-issuance suggests bills not to be considered feelers only; however as these for period May–June and originally issued July, July–August bills now overdue and reason for delay unknown.

Sent Department 2244. Department pass Shanghai 1177.

BACON

121.5493/10–1149 : Telegram

The Second Secretary of Embassy in China (Bacon) to the Secretary of State

NANKING, October 11, 1949—noon.
[Received October 11—7:07 a. m.]

2247. Service Attachés have offered equivalent two and three-quarters to three and three-quarters months' pay as separation allowances [garbled group] 50 alien employees terminated as of October 31.   Employees' Committee agreed October 7 and 12 employees standing by agreement. Majority remainder dissatisfied insisting on US $200 minimum as in case Chancery employees.

While negotiating a. m. October 8 Major Moyer[92] prevented by group 30 employees from leaving Attaché compound for Chancery and told could not go until after arrival Union official. Moyer called Public Safety Bureau, representative of which arrived within hour, talked to employees and obtained Moyer's release.

Meanwhile, Frankel,[93] Clough and myself went to AAO to report and protest detention. AAO representative Tsui allowed us wait 30 minutes, and after being told facts stated: (1) if there was complaint to make Moyer must make it in person. On our objection this an impossibility he left room and returned in 15 minutes to state this police matter in which AAO had no interest. Interview then ended.

Same afternoon Sgt. Abramson detained at home by domestic servants in similar dispute. PSB representative accompanied by Union representative promptly responded and released him.

---

[91] See telegram No. 1665, October 2, 1 p. m., from the Consul General at Peiping, vol. IX, p. 93.
[92] Maj. Maynard G. Moyer, Department of the Army officer on duty in China.
[93] Capt. Samuel B. Frankel, Naval Attaché and Naval Attaché for Air in China.

Moyer's subsequent interview Miss Chiang at PSB leads him believe police disturbed unauthorized action employees and now anxious step in before situation out of hand. Also noteworthy is current report Peiping has indicated dissatisfaction treatment given foreigners by police and local governments. CCP publicity on repatriation ship *Gordon* and others libels [*labels?*] passengers as parasites and adventurers from which possible infer Communists surprised if not dismayed numbers departing. On other hand attitude local AAO grows steadily worse. Its uncooperativeness likely due in part anxiety avoid responsibility for any positive action; but when it does act immediate result many cases to turn foreigner's minor difficulties into major ones. Net effect current seemingly contradictory policies PSB and AAO to emphasize [garbled group] capabilities CCP on one hand and disadvantages absence formal diplomatic relations on other.

BACON

124.93/10–2049

Memorandum by the Director of the Office of Chinese Affairs (Sprouse) to the Deputy Assistant Secretary of State (Merchant)[94]

[WASHINGTON,] October 20, 1949.

With reference to your question as to the possible downgrading of the Embassy at Nanking to a Consulate General or Consulate now that the Communist "government" has been formed and invited recognition, there is attached a copy of Nanking's telegram no. 2185 of September 28[95] which anticipated this problem and recommended, for reasons which CA[96] considers cogent, that no action be taken except on the basis of joint action with the U.K. and France.

In addition to the reasons given by Nanking for retention of the status of Embassy, it is our opinion that it might be politically unwise to take any steps to change the status of our office at this time. Such action, if publicized, would be sure to be interpreted as indicating a basic change in our attitude toward the Chinese Communists along the following lines: (1) that the U.S. had no intention, now or in the future, of recognizing the Communist regime and was therefore cutting all remnants of diplomatic ties with Communist-occupied China; or (2) that the U.S. was paving the way for recognition by the removal of our Embassy office at Nanking for the purpose of raising our Consulate General in Peiping to an Embassy. Speculation along either of these channels would, we feel, be unfortunate, and it is our opinion that we would be well advised to let the present situation continue undisturbed.

---

[94] Notation by the Assistant Secretary of State for Far Eastern Affairs (Butterworth) : "I agree. W.W.B."
[95] *Ante,* p. 835.
[96] Office of Chinese Affairs.

As far as precedents for such action are concerned, you will recall that at the time of Pearl Harbor we had three functioning Embassy establishments in China: one in Japanese-occupied Peiping with a Counselor as principal officer; one in the puppet capital of Nanking with a Second Secretary in charge; and one in the Nationalist capital of Chungking where the Ambassador was in residence.

121.5493/10–2049 : Telegram

The Secretary of State to the Consul General at Peiping (Clubb)

WASHINGTON, October 20, 1949—5 p. m.

725. Nanking Public Safety Bureau has refused issue exit permit Gen Soule, MA Nanking, who thereby forced cancel passage Hong Kong on Brit ship scheduled sail from Shanghai Oct 19. Soule completed all necessary procedures, including newspaper ad and application for permit Oct 6. Soule also furnished PSB with written statements (1) naming persons responsible for negots with Chi employees Asst MA after Soule's departure, (2) setting forth principles on which negots being conducted effect final settlement with employees. Soule also explained to PSB officials during personal call that Maj Moyer remaining behind represent Soule and that all Attaché offices had disbursing officers staying behind capable making payments when settlement reached.

PSB recd ltr Oct 15 a.m. from certain US Govt employees (including ALUSNA [97] personnel neither paid nor employed by Asst MA) requesting Soule be refused permission leave Nanking until termination pay negots completed. PSB stated it desired investigate entire matter and refused exit permit on grounds employees whether Army Navy or Air considered Soule senior Attaché responsible for negots. All efforts determine identity ltr writers no avail.

Dept desires you address ltr to "General Chou En-lai,[98] Peiping" setting forth above facts and pointing out (1) Gen Soule has stated orally and in writing responsible officers Asst MA and other Attaché offices remaining behind with full auth negotiate and make final payments; (2) neither Gen Soule nor his rep is responsible for negots with Navy and Air employees who are among signers ltr requesting detention; (3) US takes serious view of attempt by local auths at Nanking, on basis flimsy pretext, to prevent departure of Amer official from China, in contravention recognized principles internatl law; (4) US Govt does not countenance negot under duress and will not authorize its rep submit thereto.

---

[97] Office of Naval Attaché.
[98] Communist "Premier and Foreign Minister of the Central People's Government of the People's Republic of China".

Conclusion of ltr shld request assurance Soule will be issued exit permit promptly and will be permitted depart by first available transportation.

Pls comment if you perceive objection this protest. Tele Dept text any communication sent.

ACHESON

121.5493/10–2449 : Telegram

The Consul General at Peiping (Clubb) to the Secretary of State

PEIPING, October 24, 1949—11 a. m.
[Received October 24—3 :52 a. m.]

1805. ReDeptel 725, Oct. 20. Note pending matters include Soule's departure following: Removal Mukden personnel, Smith–Bender, closure Consulates (Depcirtel October 13 [99]). Believe circumstances warrant making direct approach Foreign Office, contemplated Contel 1757, October 17,[1] if feasible. Would recommend that if possible visit, if made, should carry some implicit promise advancing matters of interest Communist side. There might also well be discussed matter of Consulate contacts with local authorities (though I feel basic improvement position improbable prior recognition).

Am temporarily holding up action. Please instruct priority.

CLUBB

121.5493/10–2749 : Telegram

The Second Secretary of Embassy in China (Bacon) to the Secretary of State

NANKING, October 27, 1949—9 a. m.
[Received October 27—1 :22 a. m.]

2316. Reference Military Attaché's 9700, October 25.[2] Following memo sent registered mail to Aliens Affairs Office October 26 after interview refused on ground Bacon had no interest General Soule's exit permit :

"Robert H. Soule, American General officer with title of Military Attaché, applied on October 10 to Nanking Public Safety Bureau for permission depart from China. He understands that he has complied with all requirements of PSB connected with application but has thus far failed to receive his permit. He was informed on October 15 that certain persons had objected to his departure pending settlement of dispute involving him as employer. Although no such dispute now

---

[99] *Post*, p. 1323.
[1] *Post*, p. 982.
[2] Not found in Department of State files.

exists he was informed on October 25 that 'three or four matters' remain unsettled and that permit must be withheld for time being. He is unaware what matters are referred to and is unable to obtain any explanation from PSB.

"General Soule, who entered China with full diplomatic immunity, expects that he will be permitted to depart from China without hindrance or further delay."

Soule intends present personal protest October 27. At present impossible determine whether refusal both PS and Aliens Affairs discuss matter due uncertainty their own position caused by instructions higher authority merely (1) discrimination against Americans or (2) intention force settlement some undisclosed matter involving OMA.[3] Urgently renew request that Consulate General, Peiping, be instructed protest detention and that publicity be given matter (Embtel 2280, October 18 [4]).

BACON

121.5493/10–2449 : Telegram

The Secretary of State to the Consul General at Peiping (*Clubb*)

WASHINGTON, October 27, 1949—6 p. m.

744. Dept is giving consideration subj matter urtel 1805 Oct 24.

ACHESON

124.936/10–2749 : Telegram

The Second Secretary of Embassy in China (*Bacon*) *to the Secretary of State*

NANKING, October 27, 1949.
[Received October 28—1:21 a. m.]

2323. We are finding it increasingly difficult secure protection for US Government property due to adamant stand of Public Safety Bureau that they will deal only with owner of property, or in case foreign government-owned property, only with resident of premises. They refuse admit Embassy officer US Government as owner. In recent case where Clough tried to report burglary in occupied house, he was told only Chinese watchman residing on the premises could make report. PSB attitude is based on doctrine that since US has no diplomatic relations with Peiping Government, no American in China can represent US Government interests here. Doctrine leads to absurdity that only Chinese watchman can deal with PSB in matters concerning protection of unoccupied US Government-owned property

---

[3] Office of Military Attaché.
[4] Not printed.

where he happens to be stationed. We have taken position that as officials of US Government we have responsibility for its property and we consider PSB, as agency responsible for law enforcement in Nanking, has obligation to act on reported violations of law, whoever reports them. Fortunately, local police and PLA [5] soldiers have shown higher sense of public responsibility, and in robbery case cited above, acted promptly to apprehend thieves without inquiring as to whether reporting individual owned or resided in property involved. We have informed PSB of our satisfaction with this prompt action and our hope that police will respond similarly should other cases occur. We made clear that we consider PSB fully responsible for police protection US Government-owned property in Nanking.

Sent Department, repeated Shanghai 1210, Peiping 381.

BACON

124.936/10–2849 : Telegram

The Second Secretary of Embassy in China (Bacon) to the Secretary of State

NANKING, October 28, 1949—9 a. m.
[Received October 28—1 :11 a. m.]

2324. Since dispatch Embtel 2247, October 11, our relations with PSB have taken turn for worse and increasingly stiff attitude on part of both PSB and authorities apparent. Rejection of official character of Embassy officers and insistence on dealing only with individual whom Communist authorities consider directly involved has been carried to ridiculous lengths as in case Embassy property cited Embtel 2323, October 27, and Moyer lock-in case (Embtel 2247, October 11). We suspect this trend will continue as recognition fails materialize. There is some evidence of discrimination against American officials; for example, Indian Embassy officer recently took up with PSB matter of Indian Government coal at certain property and PSB did not object that officer concerned did not reside on property.

Sent Department 2324. Department pass Shanghai 1211, Peiping 382.

BACON

---

[5] People's Liberation Army (Communist).

121.5493/10–2849 : Telegram

The Military Attaché in China (Soule) to the Secretary of State [6]

NANKING, October 28, 1949.
[Received October 28—9 :38 a. m.]

683. ReEmb 2316.[7] Part 1: Morning 27 October Soule called at Alien Affairs Office submitted verbal protest and letter as follows:

"It is desired protest my detention in Nanking by the Nanking Public Safety Bureau. To the best of my knowledge and belief I complied with all People's Government laws and applied for an exit permit. On 15 October I was informed that my exit permit could not be issued until final settlement of separation allowance with Army, Navy and Air Attaché employees who had protested my departure. I was not advised who these employees were though I inquired. Settlement was made with all Attaché employees and all employees have signed a statement accepting same as satisfactory and full payment of all outstanding claims.

An interpreter was sent to secure my exit permit daily. On 24 October he returned stating permit was still withheld because of 3 or 4 unsettled matters. The chief translator of my office was sent to the Public Safety Bureau on the afternoon of 24 October to try and determine what matters remained unsettled. He returned without any definite information.

On 25 October I called at the Public Safety Bureau with Mr. Bacon and the chief interpreter and asked to see the section chief to determine why issuance of my exit permit was still withheld. I was informed that the section chief was absent and would not return until Thursday. I tried to determine what matters under my jurisdiction were considered still unsettled but received no definite reply.

As other diplomatic officials including the American Naval Attaché have been permitted to depart Nanking it appears I am being discriminated against and detained in Nanking. I feel it only just that I be given a clear statement of the reasons my exit permit is being held up, or that I be issued the exit permit and allowed to depart. Your assistance is requested in securing my exit permit."

Mr. Kang read the letter, informed me statement the People's Government was detaining me in Nanking was in error as the government was not detaining any foreigners. He claimed the statement in the letter that other diplomatic officials have been permitted depart was proof that no one being detained. He claimed statement I was being discriminated against was wrong, that when I saw the chief section Public Safety Bureau the reason exit visa held up would be explained. He refused accept letter or copy of memorandum signed by Mr. Bacon, senior Embassy officer, which I presented but read them both. Kang [is] a new official in Alien Affairs Office whom I met for first time. It evident that his main mission was get rid of me.

Part 2: On afternoon 27 October called at Public Safety Bureau with Mr. Bacon and interpreter. After considerable wait managed

---

[6] Sent via Department of the Army.
[7] October 27, 9 a. m., p. 839.

interview with Miss Chang, Chief of Section. Chang went into various reasons Soule's exit permit withheld. Finally she agreed only two things remained unsettled, to wit: demands of defunct Embassy club employees for separation pay and claims three former servants employed by Sergeants Abramson and Fox for exorbitant separation pay. Mr. Bacon and I called attention fact she had letter signed by Mr. Bacon and myself stating he assumed all responsibility for settlement club employees dispute, that I had ceased as member of board governors and had no more responsibility club matters than any former members most whom received exit permits. She read letter dated 24 October claiming was signed by 5 club employees which mentioned Frankel, Soule, Moyer, Kutchera as responsible effecting settlement. Chang stated employees claimed Soule was head board governors of club, therefore letter from Mr. Bacon could not be accepted as legal or valid. She said Public Safety Bureau considered Soule responsible because of employees' letter and matter should be settled prior to his departure. When it pointed out that other members of club and board governors were permitted leave Nanking and this was discrimination against Soule, she denied it on grounds employees had not objected prior departure of some and in Captain Frankel's case he was not leaving China but only going Shanghai. Chang refused accept statements Soule could not negotiate club employees dispute, claimed Soule should present statement signed by all club employees he not responsible for settlement. With respect the three servants of sergeants, it was pointed out these were hired as personal servants and their claims were against individuals and not Military Attaché. She agreed make further investigation of case.

[SOULE]

121.5493/10–2749 : Telegram

The Secretary of State to the Second Secretary of Embassy in China (Bacon), at Nanking

WASHINGTON, October 31, 1949—1 p. m.

1197. Re final sentence ur 2316 Oct 27, full publicity given this case in Secy's press conference Oct 26.[8] ConGen Peiping instructed protest detention, which will be done soonest practicable time.

ACHESON

---

[8] Press release No. 825, "Obstructions in issuance of exit permits in Communist-occupied China", was made public at this conference. It said in part: "The Department takes a serious view of the flimsy pretext used by the local authorities to prevent departure of an American official from China in contravention of generally recognized principles of international law. The United States Government does not countenance negotiations under duress and will not authorize its representatives in China to submit to such pressure."

121.5493/11–249 : Telegram

The Second Secretary of Embassy in China (Bacon) to the Secretary of State

NANKING, November 2, 1949.
[Received November 2—12:51 p. m.]

2355. Re MilAts 683 October 28 (not repeated Peiping). At [*On*] October 29 delegation club employees asked see Soule who received them and stated he not member board and could not negotiate as such; also that their letter October 24 to Public Safety Bureau constituted form duress making any negotiations with signers impossible. At same interview Clough stated Bacon was sole remaining board member and as such had authority effect settlement and had designated Clough as negotiator, but that no further negotiations possible until letter withdrawn. Delegation departed without indicating intentions re letter. Following letter dated October 31 thereupon sent each employee by Bacon:

[Here follows text of letter explaining situation.]

Section chief made following comment: (1) PSB has only Soule's and Bacon's statements that Soule not board member and these statements insufficient in law to establish fact; (2) employees had been endeavoring contact Soule without success and as late [*last?*] resort had filed letter of October 24; (3) an earlier communication had been received October 11 from employees but since Soule had not inquired about it, has not considered necessary to disclose it to him; (4) phraseology statement by Secretary of State "improper" and menacing"; that PSB only following its regulations; and that she would retain the letter for a short time in order to bring it to attention higher authority.

Sent Department 2355, repeated Peiping 386. Please pass Department of Army.

BACON

121.5493/11–449 : Telegram

The Second Secretary of Embassy in China (Bacon) to the Secretary of State

NANKING, November 4, 1949.
[Received November 4—1:29 p. m.]

2364. Embtel 2355, November 2. Following petition delivered November 4 to Aliens Affairs Office by Bacon as chairman board governors former Embassy club after rejection previous day similar communication on ground not in form petition:

"I have the honor to submit this petition and to state that former American Embassy club, a private organization whose members drawn primarily from Diplomatic Corps, Nanking, was closed October 1 due to departure large number members and consequent impossibility further financing its operations. As sole remaining member board governors in Nanking I have been conducting negotiations with employees through my representative Major Moyer in effort reach equitable agreement as to separation allowance to be paid them. To date no settlement reached because employees insist they be paid separation allowance on same basis as official employees of US Embassy. Because impasse reached after more than 6 weeks negotiations I desire that matter be brought before Labor Bureau of Municipal Government and settled through established procedures. Major Moyer is preparing depart and I have therefore designated Clough as my representative this matter. Your attention to matter respectfully requested."

Kang of Alien Affairs Office declared petition acceptable and asked for immediate oral statement on full course of negotiations. Bacon declined on ground had not personally taken part in negotiations and in any event preferred submit written statement. Kang then declared petition not entitled consideration if Bacon refused give account negotiations. After further argument Kang said he would have to call in employees to hear their side. Bacon expressed hearty agreement and inquired whether written statement his part desired. Kang said not necessary and that Bacon would be informed of next step to be taken by him.

Pass Army Department.

Sent Department; repeated Peiping 388.

BACON

121.5493/11–549 : Telegram

The Military Attaché in China (Soule) to the Secretary of State [9]

NANKING, November 5, 1949.
[Received November 5—7:18 a. m.]

9710. Attention invited Embassy Nanking 2355 dated 2 November to State reference club employees.

3 November received letter from Foreign Service Employees (clerks and laborers) Association of Nanking stating representatives all club employees desired appointment with me 10:00 a. m. Met 5 representatives club employees as requested 10 o'clock in presence Mr. Clough. Advised them Mr. Bacon responsible club negotiations, Mr. Clough his representative, that I without authority negotiate dispute; furthermore their letter to Public Safety Bureau causing my detention Nanking under duress which was additional bar my interceding in negotiations, suggested they withdraw letter at PSB. Representatives stated letter had been filed in response advertisement as they afraid no one would be left responsible for club; that respon-

---

[9] Sent via Department of the Army.

sibility for detaining me Nanking was PSB but did not promise withdraw letter.

[Soule]

121.5493/11–749 : Telegram

The Consul General at Peiping (Clubb) to the Secretary of State

PEIPING, November 7, 1949—4 p. m.
[Received November 7—4 :38 a. m.]

1932. ReDeptel 725, October 20. In view interim developments and particularly settlement labor dispute Attaché offices and Bacon's undertaking get mediation of club employees dispute, of course assume Peiping would be authorized make appropriate changes text letter Chou En-lai but propose answer on basis general reasoning to be set forth early telegram eliminate references "flimsy [pre]text" and "USA would not countenance negotiations under duress".

Please authorize.

CLUBB

121.5493/11–849 : Telegram

The Consul General at Peiping (Clubb) to the Secretary of State

PEIPING, November 8, 1949—8 p. m.
[Received 11 :35 p. m.]

1941. ReDeptels 725, October 20, and 759, November 1,[10] next two telegrams Peiping No. series [11] give English texts notes addressed Chou En-lai on two subjects, Assistant [Am.] Military Attaché Soule exit permit and American Government real property Tsingtao under respective dates November 7 and 8, both dispatched today. Recommend no publicity for present.

Department please inform Nanking, Tsingtao appropriately, also Tientsin at discretion.

CLUBB

121.5493/11–849 : Telegram

The Consul General at Peiping (Clubb) to the Secretary of State

PEIPING, November 8, 1949.
[Received November 9—3 :20 a. m.]

1942. Following is text letter November 7 re Soule exit permit :

"Under instructions of my Government, I invite your attention to the fact that the Nanking Bureau of Public Safety has refused to

---

[10] For latter, see p. 1149.
[11] Telegrams Nos. 1942 and 1943 printed *infra* and p. 1151, respectively.

issue an exit permit to Brigadier General Robert H. Soule, American Military Attaché, forcing him to cancel his passage to Hong Kong on a British ship which had been scheduled to sail from Shanghai on October 19, 1949. General Soule had made application for an exit permit on October 6. There was at that time an unsettled labor-management dispute with employees in the Military Attaché's office, but General Soule had furnished the Bureau of Public Safety with a written statement (1) naming the American official responsible for negotiations with the Chinese employees after his departure, and (2) setting forth principles on which the negotiations for final settlement with the employees were being conducted. He explained further than [that] an authorized representative remained behind and that there was attached to the office a disbursing officer capable of making payments when a settlement had been reached.

On October 15th the Bureau of Public Safety received from certain alien United States Government employees, including personnel of the Office of the Naval Attaché, who were neither employed nor paid by the Military Attaché, a request that General Soule not be permitted to depart from Nanking until the completion of negotiations for separation pay. The Bureau stated that it desired to investigate the entire matter, and refused to issue an exit permit on the grounds that those employees whether of the Military, Naval or Air Attaché Offices considered General Soule to be Senior Attaché and responsible for such negotiations. The identities of the persons writing the letter were not disclosed.

It is understood that this particular labor-management dispute has now been satisfactorily settled but that former Chinese employees of the American Embassy Club now claim likewise that General Soule is responsible for their pay and that consequently General Soule has not yet received his exit permit, or assurances that he will, prior to the settlement of those new disputes. The dispute concerning the former Attaché employees having now been settled, it will not be dealt with here.

Quite apart from the question of the propriety in international law of the refusal of local authorities to permit the exit from a country of a diplomatic official on the grounds that there is an unsettled labor dispute involving members of his staff, particularly when responsible administrative officers are remaining behind, it is observed that in the present instance the responsible chairman of governing board of the American Embassy Club is American Foreign Service Officer Leonard L. Bacon and not General Soule, who resigned from his position as board member prior to October 12, 1949.

The United States Government takes a serious view of the refusal of the Nanking authorities to permit the departure from China of that American Embassy official, on the grounds that there exists an unsettled labor dispute in an organization for which he does not even have responsibility in contravention to the recognized principles of international law. It is not understood that this action by the concerned local officials has the approval of superior authority. It is requested that you kindly bring this matter to the attention of the appropriate high authorities with a request for investigation and appropriate action, to the end that General Soule will be promptly issued the desired exit permit and permitted to depart by the first available transportation.["]

Sent Department, Nanking 1149.

CLUBB

124.933/11–1449 : Telegram

The Second Secretary of Embassy in China (Bacon) to the Secretary of State

NANKING, November 14, 1949.
[Received November 13—9 : 39 p. m.]

2412. Prior to termination September 30 employment of American Embassy club workers, board governors offered to each worker 1 month's pay in lieu of notice and 1 month's separation pay. Board considered this reasonable and in accordance Shanghai labor regulations governing separation allowances, since club had been opened only December 1948, no employee had worked more than 10 months and some less than 6. Board dissolved early October. But Bacon as chairman has continued to keep offer open. Three employees have accepted offer and have been paid off. Majority employees, however, through their committee, originally demanded separation allowance amounting to approximate equivalent US $200 for each, regardless salary or length of service. On November 8 employees reduced demand to amounts ranging from equivalent US $50 to US $200, equal to approximately 6 months' pay for each employee and in addition maintenance at full salary from October 1 to date dispute settled. Meantime Bacon has ascertained that board's original offer was not only reasonable and in accordance with law but more generous than law requires. On October 5 Peking Labor Bureau mediated case of former USIS employees and decided that separation allowances should be paid in accordance with Shanghai regulations and that rate was to be one-half month's pay for each 6 months of employment, maximum 3 months' pay and that where no allowance had been offered maintenance should be paid during pendency dispute at rate of one-half former salary. It is presumed that this decision is known to labor and administrative authorities at Nanking. Yet to date Nanking general labor union has failed to intervene in Embassy club case despite requests from both sides; and Nanking Aliens Affairs Office has declined to act on formal request November 4 that Nanking Bureau of Labor proceed to mediate case. By insisting that direct negotiations with the employees be resumed, the Aliens Affairs Office has avoided assuming any responsibility for the expeditious settlement of the case. At same time Nanking Public Safety Bureau continues encourage employees to demand more than provided for in Shanghai regulations or Peking decision by continuing withhold Soule's exist permit.

Pass Army Department.

Sent Department 2412, repeated Peiping 395.

BACON

121.5493/11-1449 : Telegram

The Second Secretary of Embassy in China (Bacon) to the Secretary of State

NANKING, November 14, 1949—9 a. m.
[Received November 13—10:42 p. m.]

2413. Miss Chang's transparent efforts obtain from Soule written statement containing admission continuing responsibility for settlement club dispute (Embtel 2411, November 14 [12]) indicates she has been advised bolster Communist position Soule primarily responsible and presence necessary final settlement. We consider this result of Peiping protest (Contel 1942, November 8).

Urgently recommend Peiping file soonest supplementary protest on basis facts stated Embtel 2412, November 14, repeated Peiping 395. This probably only opportunity get merits of case before Peiping authorities.

Pass Army Department.

Sent Department 2413, repeated Peiping 396.

BACON

121.5493/11-1449 : Telegram

The Consul General at Peiping (Clubb) to the Secretary of State

PEIPING, November 14, 1949—4 p. m.
[Received November 14—12:15 p. m.]

1992. Re Embtel [my] 1941, November 8. Letter November 7 to Chou En-lai re Military Attaché Soule exit permit was returned by mail today without acknowledgement or comment.

Re Embtel 396, November 14,[13] believe in circumstances new note to Chou at this stage would be fruitless. Believe it would be better await further developments Nanking. Effect of any note to Peiping authorities should shortly be discernible Nanking and if communication quite without effect new note would be for present useless. Re Embtel 394, November 14,[12] suggest Bacon apply formally direct Labor Bureau as "representative" club if feasible.

---

[12] Not printed.
[13] Same as telegram No. 2413 from Nanking, *supra.*

Department's instructions requested.

Sent Department 1992. Department pass Nanking 1155.

CLUBB

121.5493/11–1449 : Telegram

The Acting Secretary of State to the Consul General at Peiping
(Clubb)

Washington, November 15, 1949—noon.

793. Re Embtel 396, Nov 14.[15] If you perceive no objection pls file supplementary protest suggested Embtel 395, Nov 14.[16]

WEBB

121.5493/11–1449 : Telegram

The Secretary of State to the Consul General at Peiping (Clubb)

Washington, November 16, 1949—6 p. m.

796. Ur 1992 Nov 14, Deptel 793 Nov 14. Although delivery supplementary protest may prove fruitless, this channel appears offer only possibility getting to central auths additional facts in situation which they may well not have. Consequently, pls endeavor pass to auths info outlined Embtel 395.[16]

Pls inform Dept whether ltr Nov 7 opened by Commie auths.

Dept concurs your suggestion Bacon, if he perceives no objection, apply formally Labor Bureau as "representative" club.

ACHESON

121.5493/11–2649 : Telegram

The Consul General at Peiping (Clubb) to the Secretary of State

PEIPING, November 26, 1949.
[Received November 26—7 :03 a. m.]

2098. Following is text letter November 25 re exit permit American Military Attaché Soule :

"With reference to my letter of November 7, 1949, regarding the refusal of the Nanking authorities to grant an exit permit to Brigadier General Robert H. Soule, American Military Attaché, because of an unsettled management-labor dispute in the American Embassy Club in that city, under instructions of my Government I invite your attention to the circumstance that the matter is still unsettled.

---

[15] Same as telegram No. 2413 from Nanking, p. 849.
[16] Same as telegram No. 2412 from Nanking, p. 848.

"It is to be noted in this general connection that, despite extended discussions from November 7 through November 14 both directly with the employee side and at the Nanking Aliens Affairs Office and the Foreign Affairs Section of the Nanking Bureau of Public Safety, as of November 14 the Nanking General Labor Union had failed to intervene in the management-labor dispute despite requests from both sides and the Aliens Affairs Office had declined to act on the formal request of November 4 that the Bureau of Labor proceed with mediation of the dispute. Contrariwise, by insisting that direct negotiations with the employees be resumed, the Aliens Affairs Office had avoided taking any responsibility for the expeditious settlement of the case, and the Chief of the Foreign Affairs Section of the Bureau of Public Safety had demonstrated an evident intent that General Soule should be advanced [sic].

"It is noteworthy that the section chief rejected as unacceptable two different letters offered by the management side—in response to her own suggestion—showing full delegation by General Soule of any club responsibility he might bear to American Foreign Service Officer Leonard L. Bacon, chairman of the Board of the club, and that the section chief declared that the management side was responsible for payment of the employees' wages for the duration of the dispute; but when the management side observed that it considered that the Bureau of Labor would be the organ responsible for determining whether wages as well as severance allowances were payable and asked for a written order, the section chief refused to supply such order. Further, when the management side cited the case of mediation at Peiping of the labor-management dispute involving certain former USIS employees, the section chief stated that North China cases were not to be taken as precedents for the East China Military District. This, be it noted, seems to be in contradiction to the fact that the ruling of the Peiping Bureau of Labor embodied in the aforementioned Peiping mediation agreement of October 5, 1949, was itself based in part on the provisional measures for the administration of disputes regarding resumption of work and resumption of enterprises as promulgated by the Shanghai Military Control Commission, as published in the *People's Daily News* of September 6 and supported by a New China News Agency editorial of the same date.

"There would also seem to arise a question of the propriety of the assumption by the Foreign Affairs Section of the Bureau of Public Safety of jurisdiction of labor-management disputes (which would presumably ordinarily fall within the province of the Bureau of Labor) without its being willing to assume final responsibility for settlement of such disputes. The negotiations appear [to] have reached a stalemate at that stage. It is apparent that the Nanking authorities are failing to facilitate the settlement of the dispute in question, which the management side has repeatedly suggested be referred to the presumed responsible organs, the General Labor Union and the Bureau of Labor. It is evident likewise that, as indicated in my reference letter of November 7, the local authorities in contravention of existing international law and amity are preventing the American Military Attaché from leaving China using as an excuse, a problem, the solution of which they have failed thus far to facilitate. In the circumstances, in accord with the instructions of my Government, I must again request that the matter be given your early attention, to the end that General Soule be given his exit permit and permitted to depart by the first available means."

Sent Department 2098; repeated Nanking 1180; Shanghai 1221.

CLUBB

121.5493/12–149 : Telegram

The Second Secretary of Embassy in China (Bacon) to the Secretary of State

NANKING, December 1, 1949—4 p. m.

[Received 5:40 p. m.]

2520. Embtel 2482, November 26.[18] Bacon and Clough attended hearing re Labor Union after receiving phone call from Aliens Affairs Office stating Union desired appearance Soule and Bacon. Soule's absence not commented on nor name mentioned at hearing. Employees' demand for separation allowance reduced to 2 months but maintenance and other demands renewed plus demand that all payments based on wage scale be recalculated according to rise cost of living. At conclusion Union official stated case transferred to Labor Bureau which would begin preliminary investigation possibly December 3.

Inform Peiping.

Pass Army.

BACON

121.5493/12–749 : Telegram

The Secretary of State to the Second Secretary of Embassy in China (Bacon), at Nanking

WASHINGTON, December 7, 1949—5 p. m.

1277. Dept Defense has requested this Dept make representations Chi Commie auths obtain exit permits Gen Soule, Maj Moyer and take necessary action obtain exit permits balance Army personnel Nanking, including dependents.

Request info status above cases and recommendations as to further appropriate action re Soule, Moyer.

ACHESON

---

[18] Not printed.

121.5493/12–849 : Telegram

The Second Secretary of Embassy in China (Bacon) to the Secretary of State

NANKING, December 8, 1949.
[Received December 8—5:30 a. m.]

2556. Re Embtel 2520, December 1. Aliens Affairs Office requested Soule December 5 by telephone to [go?] Labor Bureau December 6 a. m. Soule, Clough, and I appeared and found Employees' Committee, Labor Union and AAO officials present, plus 9 stenographers and several photographers. Clough and I registered but Soule did not. Chang for Labor Bureau announced Bureau had been requested by Union to mediate and asked if we agreed. We raised question of necessity Soule's presence and after great argument Chang declared Soule was responsible party. We requested written decision to that effect, which Chang promised to give at end of hearing.

Resuming after lunch, Chang immediately asked for employees to state case. Union officials read long statement including claims for 2 months' separation pay, 1 month's pay in lieu of New Year's bonus, maintenance at full wages from October 1, leave pay at rate of 1 day per week, all payments to be recalculated according to rise in cost of living since September 30, standard being number of parity units purchasable that day by PBN [18a] equivalent of each employee's US dollar salary. He also alleged long hours, hardships, et cetera. I requested copy of statement but none was given. I then introduced employees' statement giving copies to Union and AAO officials. Principal point made was that extra demands not covered either by terms of employment or labor regulations. During afternoon session Bureau official, Chang, directed most of his questions at Soule, who referred them to me. At close of session Chang announced Bureau's recommendations—namely, 1–½ months' separation pay, 1 month's pay in lieu of New Year's bonus, full maintenance from October 1, all payments to be recalculated according to rise in cost of living. I requested recess to afternoon December 7 in order to determine whether club able to pay and renewed my objections to demands which appeared to be outside amounts covered by regulations.

Resuming hearing December 7, succeeded only in reducing mediator's recommendation New Year's bonus proportionately to number of months served. Draft agreement then prepared by mediator which mentioned only Soule as responsible board member and provided for signature by one representative each party. After extended argument clause referring to responsible board member was amended to read as

---

[18a] People's Bank Notes.

follows: "Soule and Bacon, responsible members of the board of the former American Embassy Club".

Terms stated were:

(1) 1–½ months' separation pay.
(2) New Year's bonus equal to 1–½ months' pay for each month employed.
(3) Full maintenance from October 1.
(4) All payments to be recalculated according to rise in cost of living.

Mediator then asked whether we agreed. I replied that employer agreed. Employees Committee likewise assented. Mediator asked whether Soule had any statement to make. He then prepared to read text of letter which appears below. Mediator, however, called recess for preparing final copies agreement and meantime indirectly ascertained nature of Soule's statement.

On resuming hearing, head of Labor Bureau for first time joined conference and new copies of final agreement were given to parties. Union official then announced that my name should not appear in text of agreement and that Soule must sign. Based statement on fact employees had alleged Soule was responsible person and in petition to Labor Bureau had referred to Soule only. Soule then read following statement:

"As I have previously stated, upon dissolution of former 'American Embassy Club' at end of September, I delegated all my responsibility as former member of board of governors to Mr. Bacon, Chairman. I have taken no part in ensuing labor dispute negotiations. I have attended mediation proceedings in Bureau of Labor at request of AAO, but I have no authority from former board to agree to any settlements. Such authority is vested solely in Mr. Bacon. If, in view of Bureau of Labor, my signature is necessary to confirm Bureau's decision, I can affix my signature only under protest."

Head of Bureau immediately declared that question Soule's responsibility had already been determined by Bureau, that his protest was evidence bad faith, that mediation proceeding had ended; next step would be arbitration and that Soule was responsible for mediation failure. I inquired of Chang when arbitration would take place and he stated "very quickly", and that Arbitration Committee would be composed of three persons selected by Labor Bureau.

Nanking Military Control Commission on October 21 promulgated pertinent Shanghai regulations for application in Nanking. Provisions for arbitration are as follows:

"If mediation proves to be of no avail, Labor Bureau shall then render an arbitration in accordance with law. Decision of Arbitration Board shall be signed by its chairman and after approval by Director of Labor Bureau it shall be notified to both labor and capitalist for execution. If either party of labor and capitalist offers objection to arbitration, he shall notify Labor Bureau within 5 days after receipt of arbitration decision and shall request court to deal with it; otherwise arbitration decision shall have legal binding force."

Sent Department; repeated Peiping 424, Shanghai 1260; Department pass Army.

BACON

121.5493/12–849 : Telegram

The Second Secretary of Embassy in China (Bacon) to the Secretary of State

NANKING, December 8, 1949—5 p. m.
[Received December 8—5:06 a. m.]

2561. ReEmbtel 2556, December 8. Expect Arbitration Committee will find Soule to be person primarily, if not solely, responsible for settling club labor dispute. Believe that if such decision handed down by government organ, Soule would have little choice but to accept and comply. Alternatives would be carry matter People's Court on own initiative or await police action when arbitration decision becomes legally binding after 5-day limit. Alternatives not attractive particularly in light Ward experience.[19] Please instruct soonest. Soule concurs.

BACON

125.5461/12–849 : Telegram

The Secretary of State to the Second Secretary of Embassy in China (Bacon), at Nanking

WASHINGTON, December 9, 1949—8 p. m.

1291. RefEmbtel 2561 Dec. 8. Dept's opinion little would be gained by refusing accept Arbitration Comite decision and carrying question responsibility settlement club labor dispute to People's Court. Likely that such action wld merely prolong Soule's detention since doubtful People's Court wld reverse Arbitration Comite position. Dept and Army recommend acceptance decision Arbitration Comite re responsibility for settlement. No objection ur compliance terms as outlined Embtel 2556, Dec. 8.

ACHESON

---

[19] For documentation concerning the case of Consul General Angus Ward at Mukden, see pp. 933 ff.

121.5493/12–1549 : Telegram

The Second Secretary of Embassy in China (Bacon) to the Secretary of State

NANKING, December 15, 1949.
[Received December 15—1:41 p. m.]

2596. Embtel 2556, December 8. On telephonic notification to Soule from Aliens Affairs Office a. m. December 14, Soule, Clough and I appeared Labor Bureau 3 p. m. to attend arbitration. In anticipation of possibility receiving oral decision only, I had invited one representative from Canadian Embassy and two from Dutch who accompanied us as spectators. Although they declared their interest in proceedings as former club members, their admission refused after 20 minutes' delay on ground no invitation given them by Labor Bureau.

Five-man arbitration committee composed of Labor Bureau Deputy Director Feng, two representatives AAO, one representative General Labor Union, and one other representative Labor Bureau. Each side given 10 minutes present arguments. Employees merely stated they wished eliminate from terms agreed on December 7 provision for recalculation wages according to cost of living because difficult explain substitution of parity unit to other employees. (During intervening 7 days parity unit had risen less than 8 percent while dollar exchange had risen 20 percent.) I then stated had always urged actual wage was proper basis for payment and employer agreed to modification terms as proposed by employees. (This change eliminates slight saving resulting from current rate fluctuations but also eliminates one speculative feature of agreement and avoids dangerous precedent.) I further stated that I understand both sides had agreed to terms of settlement and only question for arbitration was which individual required to execute agreement, and that on that point employer had already stated his full case.

After short recess Feng read preliminary statement summarized as follows: (1) Soule is wholly responsible for settlement dispute because (*a*) he was responsible member of board at time dispute arose, (*b*) his statements regarding resignation self-contradictory, (2) he refused negotiate and therefore responsible for delay in settlement, (3) Labor Bureau succeeded bringing both sides to agreement on terms, (4) at least moment Soule wrecked mediation proceedings by declaring he could sign agreement only under protest.

Feng then read Arbitration Committee's decision which in general repeated foregoing and fixed terms of settlement as follows: (1) one and half months' separation pay in view long hours and no vacations, (2) maintenance full wages from October 1 to December 14 and (3) New Year's bonus one-twelfth month's pay each month's service; said written copies of decision would be delivered a. m. December 15, after which each party had 5 days either to report dissatisfaction to Labor [or] appeal to People's Court.

Full text of decision will follow as soon as received and translated.

Sent Department 2596, repeated Shanghai 1271, Peiping 428.

BACON

121.5493/12–1549 : Telegram

The Second Secretary of Embassy in China (Bacon) to the Secretary of State

NANKING, December 15, 1949—3 p. m.
[Received 6:34 p. m.]

2599. Deptel 1291, December 9 and Embtel 2596, December 15. Atmosphere arbitration hearing notably better than at mediation where attitude officialdom extremely hostile. Decision itself unexpectedly moderate in language. No new conditions or penalties imposed nor do we see where Soule will be compelled sign any agreement. Decision will be published local press. It fails to disclose any hints regarding length of service, terms of employment, terms original offer, exact terms employees' demands nor my efforts obtain action from Labor Bureau. However, abundantly emphasizes Soule's continued refusal negotiate and assume responsibility for settlement even though Soule and I presented as artful dodgers. I am preparing pay off employees December 16 after which Soule will renew inquiry re exit permit.

We concur People's Court unlikely reduce award. Embtel 2561, December 8 intended only as request permission submit to jurisdiction arbitration commission as distinguished from mediation proceedings.

Footnote: British at first agreed send representative to arbitration hearing but later withdrew, saying could not risk involvement without Foreign Office's prior permission. As previously indicated, their personnel extremely anxious avoid any complications which might delay transfer to Peiping.

Pass Peiping Department's discretion.

Pass Army.

Sent Department 2599, Department pass Shanghai 1272.

BACON

121.5493/12–1749 : Telegram

The Second Secretary of Embassy in China (Bacon) to the Secretary of State

NANKING, December 17, 1949.
[Received December 16—9 :16 p. m.]

2609. All club employees (Embtel 2596, December 15) paid off. Formal written decision not yet received but payment made on basis written statement from Labor Bureau December 15 announcing terms arbitration award in accordance reftel.

Pass Army Department.

Sent Department 2609, repeated Shanghai 1274, Peiping 430.

BACON

893.111/12–1949 : Telegram

The Second Secretary of Embassy in China (Bacon) to the Secretary of State

NANKING, December 19, 1949.
[Received December 19—7 :16 a. m.]

2620. Soule received exit permit a. m. December 19. Only pending permits are now Captain John J. Christensen (whose application filed and accepted December 19 after completion advertising) and Ast-ALUSNA [20] Lieutenant Dean Kutchera. November 7 Kutchera applied for permission proceed Shanghai and establish residence there. Repeated inquiries elicited only reply that matter under consideration. December 2 cancelled this application and applied for permit exit to States. Paid fee and was instructed proceed with advertising notice intent. Upon completion advertising December 5 made formal application for exit permit. Eight-day period for presentation claims expired December 13, at which time Kutchera again requested issuance permit. Frequent subsequent inquiries result only in statement "matter still under consideration higher authorities" and no reason given for withholding permit. Kutchera had been named by former club employees as "responsible officer" with request his exit permit be withheld, but that dispute completely liquidated Dec. 17. Permit still withheld December 19.

Sent Department 2620, repeated Shanghai 1284, Peiping 432.

BACON

---

[20] Assistant Naval Attaché.

121.5493/12–3049 : Telegram

The Consul General at Shanghai (*McConaughy*) *to the Secretary of State*

SHANGHAI, December 30, 1949—4 p. m.
[Received December 31—12:10 a. m.]

5451. Sent Department, repeated Taipei 607. Pass Department of Army, AstAMAt[21] Taipei from Soule. Cite 125. Captain J. J. Christensen and family arrived Shanghai 29 December. This completes evacuation all DA[22] and AF[23] personnel from Nanking.

Shipping situation Shanghai extremely tight. Attention invited to Shanghai ConGen 5441 and 5442, December 29[24] and Taipei 1342, December 27 to State.[25] Assume DA familiar with situation and providing all possible support to effect evacuation DA personnel.

Request advise DA policy reference evacuation personnel on blockade runners in event any successful entering Shanghai. Alternate possibilities for evacuation are to secure Communist permission for special cars or train to Tientsin, Canton or other less closely blockaded port. Present restrictions on travel Americans in Communist China make it unlikely such permission will be secured. Repeated requests in Nanking for Sgt. Fox to depart China via Tientsin all refused.[26]

MCCONAUGHY

---

[21] Assistant Military Attaché.
[22] Department of the Army.
[23] Department of the Air Force.
[24] For telegram No. 5441, see vol. IX, p. 1362; for telegram No. 5442, see *ibid.*, p. 1188.
[25] Not printed.
[26] For information on closing of Embassy at Nanking on March 5, 1950, see Department of State *Bulletin*, March 20, 1950, pp. 462 and 463. For arrangement to evacuate official American personnel in Communist-occupied China by way of Tientsin in late April 1950, see *ibid.*, May 15, 1950, p. 755.

INCREASING DIFFICULTIES OF THE CONSULATE AT DAIREN DUE TO ACTIONS OF SOVIET AND CHINESE COMMUNIST AUTHORITIES; CLOSURE OF THE CONSULATE [1]

123 Gleysteen, Culver : Telegram

The Consul at Dairen (Paddock) to the Secretary of State

DAIREN, January 11, 1949—6 p. m.
[Received January 13—10:45 p. m.]

12. Soviet refusal issue Gleysteen [2] pass (re immediate preceding telegram [3]) highlights Consulate difficulties arising from peculiar international status Dairen.

On one hand is Soviet interpretation their rights here and US compliance with that interpretation—for example, acquiescence to Soviet refusal allow US ship come here with couriers. On other hand is fact Kwantung government has dual nature by being both a Soviet puppet and an extension of Chinese Communist government at Harbin.

Until recently Soviets and Chinese Communists sensitive about Sino-Soviet agreement on Dairen [4] which provided for Chinese civil administration of this port. They implied this fulfilled by "people's democratic government" organized after "refusal" of Chinese National Government take over civil administration of Dairen 1946. However, dating from fall Mukden this sensitivity rapidly disappeared. When Chinese Communist government is formally established and given Soviet recognition, their present collaboration in Dairen probably will be conducted publicly.

It pointed out that even should US recognize Chinese Communist government it still not certain Soviet would then allow Consulate personnel or couriers enter Port Arthur naval base area [to] commute Mukden. Although value of Dairen Consulate as possible link with Mukden, as emphasized in previous telegrams, still remains, Embassy and Department should note Soviet disinclination allow Consulate personnel have slightest contact with naval base area. All requests

---

[1] For previous documentation regarding the Consulate at Dairen, see *Foreign Relations*, 1948, vol. VII, pp. 787 ff.
[2] Culver Gleysteen, Vice Consul at Dairen.
[3] Not printed.
[4] Signed at Moscow, August 14, 1945, United Nations Treaty Series, vol. 10, p. 354.

of present Consulate officers for passes to leave Dairen city for picnics into nearby country not even answered by Soviet Kommandatura.

It believed Embassy or Department have never given Consulate directive on how to regard Soviet occupation authorities and Kwantung government. Although Consulate obviously not able to dispute legality of Soviet-Chinese composition and although every effort made comply quietly with many irritating restrictions, there is still a sphere where Consulate doubtful how to act. Pattern of Soviet and Chinese Communist behavior in relation to Consulate emphasizes their enmity and lack of cooperation. Examples are Contels 84 to Nanking November 4, repeated Department 192,[5] Moscow 71; 104 to Nanking November 22, repeated Department 219,[6] Moscow 88.

In previous cases I have noted Department's custom to draw up periodically a concise description of its overall policy for each country of [or] area. If no objection, it would be appreciated if Department would telegraph Consulate review of its policy re Dairen and Port Arthur naval base area. Such a guide will help Consulate during present changing times here. Consulate anxious to act correctly in accepting or protesting Soviet interpretation their rights, in recognizing or not recognizing jurisdiction of Kwantung government in various fields, and in doing nothing which might become unfortunate precedent for time when Chinese Communists may take over Kwantung government openly.

Sent Nanking 10, Department 12, repeated Shanghai 14, Moscow 9.

PADDOCK

---

123 Gleysteen, Culver : Telegram

The Secretary of State to the Consul at Dairen (Paddock)

WASHINGTON, February 1, 1949—noon.

11. Urtel 12 Jan 11 rptd Nanking 10, Shanghai 14, Moscow 9. Following Dept views. Status Soviets Port Arthur naval base area and Dairen determined by agreement accompanying Sino-Soviet Treaty 1945.[7] Soviets contend Dairen subject military supervision or control established Port Arthur naval base areas pending formal termination war with Japan. Nat Govt of China does not agree that such is meaning intent of agreement and it is palpably absurd to maintain that other than a fictitious state of war exists after unconditional surrender and occupation of Japan. US of course not party to this agreement. This Govt has taken formal cognizance undesirable situ-

---

[5] Not printed.
[6] *Foreign Relations*, 1948, vol. VII, p. 803.
[7] Signed at Moscow, August 14, 1945, United Nations Treaty Series, vol. 10, p. 300.

ation Dairen in notes to Sov and Chi Govts in Jan 1947[8] urging prompt consideration by those Govts current unsatisfactory situation Dairen with view implementing pertinent provisions Sino-Soviet agreements re Dairen and adding US Govt perceives no reason further delay reopening port international commerce under Chinese administration as contemplated in agreements. In Note Aug 14, 1947 to Sov Govt[9] US reiterated these views, expressed hope Sov and Chi Govts would soon be able reconcile differing views and added in interim Sov Govt would be held responsible treatment accorded American interests Dairen. Latter responsibility Sovs categorically rejected. Basis approaching Chinese and Sovs each case US responsibility to American interests in area. From standpoint practical operating procedure it recognized Sov exercise *de facto* control Dairen and you will have to deal with them. In such dealings you should endeavor treat them as military authority exercising *de facto* control in area without attempting pass on legality control.

Notwithstanding special concessions to Sovs in area, sovereignty Kwantung remains Chinese. Kwantung civil administration has existed in defiance Govt of China recognized by US and should be treated as unrecognized authority. Continued functioning of consulate in area under control unrecognized authorities or dispatch of consular officers such territory does not itself imply recognition but in any course of action it most important leave no doubt recognition by this Govt not implied and Consul acting entirely in consular capacity. Relations with unrecognized local officials should be maintained insofar as possible on informal and personal basis. Social invitations of private nature may be accepted in discretion principal officer but acceptance should be in personal not official capacity. In general invitations to social functions of official nature should be filed without formal acknowledgement and such functions should not be attended. Foregoing applies to Kwantung govt or any successor which not established by Govt of China recognized by US.

American policy with respect Dairen has been directed toward establishment of Chinese civil administration responsible to Nat Govt China and free port open to commerce and shipping all nations, as provided Sino-Soviet agreements. While it unrealistic expect Nat Govt can under present circumstances establish civil administration Dairen, implementation free port provision agreement remains US objective. Furthermore Dept considers continued maintenance Consulate Dairen highly desirable standpoint American interests in area and believes importance office will increase with cessation hostilities

---

[8] See telegram No. 18, January 3, 1947, 6 p. m., from the Ambassador in the Soviet Union and telegram No. 28, January 6, 1947, 5 p. m., from the Ambassador in China, *Foreign Relations*, 1947, vol. VII, p. 482; and telegram No. 1252, December 31, 1946, to the Ambassador in China, *ibid.*, 1946, vol. x, p. 1200.

[9] See telegram No. 1588, August 12, 1947, 5 p. m., to the Ambassador in the Soviet Union, *ibid.*, 1947, vol. VII, p. 535.

Manchuria, reestablishment communications and general reconstruction. It may be possible work out arrangement whereby personnel Dairen and Mukden interchangeable. Whatever may be the legal basis present control and administration Dairen, Dept realizes control by Sovs and Kwantung civil administration is reality and must be accepted as such in working out practical operating procedure Dairen.

ACHESON

893.00/3–2449 : Telegram

The Ambassador in China (Stuart) to the Secretary of State

NANKING, March 24, 1949—11 a. m.
[Received 11:56 p. m.]

643. Re penultimate paragraph Peiping telegram 440 to Department March 19 [*20*] [10] which translated CCP [11] article as explaining Soviet occupation of Dairen and Port Arthur as motivated by intention "to protect them from Japanese aggression". In English Morse cast [*English broadcast?*] monitored by Embassy, Soviet occupation Dairen and Port Arthur was explained rather as move to protect them against "imperialist aggression in Far East" which, judging by tenor of article, refers principally to US.

Sent Department, repeated OffEmb Canton 188, Shanghai 294, Peiping 99.

STUART

893.00B/4–249 : Telegram

The Consul at Dairen (Paddock) to the Secretary of State

DAIREN, April 2, 1949.
[Received April 2—6:52 a. m.]

92. Re two immediate preceding telegrams dated April 1, [12] Kwantung Chinese Communist Party has come out of glass hiding place as of today and ostensibly assumed responsibility for Kwantung government. Contel sent Nanking 51, repeated Department 79,[10] Shanghai 77, Moscow 37, March 19. Heretofore Kwantung government publicly blamed, not top part of Communist China, and this position upheld by Soviets.

All public buildings, police stations, Soviet and Kwantung government-controlled commercial camps et cetera decorated today with Soviet flags and with what is apparently Chinese Communist flag (red field; yellow hammer, sickle and yellow outline of star), formerly

---

[10] Not printed.
[11] Chinese Communist Party.
[12] Apparently Nos. 89 and 91, neither printed.

Chinese national flag crossed with Soviet flag on public occasions. In many cases "white star on blue field["] of Chinese national flag merely cut out and hammer, sickle, star sewed in its place.

Sent Department 92, repeated Nanking, Shanghai 86, Moscow 45, Seoul 15, Peiping 2.

PADDOCK

893.00B/4–1049 : Telegram

The Ambassador in China (Stuart) to the Secretary of State

NANKING, April 10, 1949—noon.
[Received April 10—5:15 a. m.]

739. Re Dairen telegram 92, April 2, to Department, repeated Shanghai 86, Hankow 45, Seoul 15, Peiping 2. Following, as it does, only some 2 weeks upon second Plenary Session Central Committee elected by 7th CCP Congress, emergence CCP in Dairen gives support our belief that that Session probably reached as yet unannounced important decisions. Parenthetically, another decision which has come to light past few days as at least having been reaffirmed is that of rejecting any compromise with Nationalists.

It seems to us that whole pattern of behavior indicates Soviets may have obtained some very important *quid pro quo* to induce them thus modify their position Dairen and make this exception their policy "correctness" toward National Government. It is worth noting that, despite obvious temptations, CCP propaganda has so far failed capitalize upon CCP achievement Dairen.

Sent Department 739, repeated Shanghai 353, OffEmb Canton 236, Dairen 23, passed Moscow 24, Seoul 6.

STUART

893.00B/4–1249 : Telegram

The Consul at Dairen (Paddock) to the Secretary of State

DAIREN, April 12, 1949—3 p. m.
[Received April 13—11:22 p. m.]

106. Emergence of Chinese Communist Party in Kwantung and admission that it attached to Northeast Bureau of Chinese Communist Party not yet followed by any formal recognition of Kwantung administration.

Actual control this local government apparatus in Chinese Communist hands since established 1946 (re Consulate Report 10, October 15, pages 16–18 [14]). To make it purely Communist, only puppet

---

[14] Not printed.

figureheads need be removed although change may also bring to power new cadres "to cope with new conditions".

First indication that avowed Chinese Communists may hold top positions as well those of real power was resignation puppet Mayor Hsu and replaced by Chinese Communist Mao (re immediately preceding telegram.[15])

Mao referred to as "mayor" in press last few weeks but press only today announced change. Even now Mao is only Acting Mayor.

It possible Soviets and Chinese Communists awaiting some famous day like May Day to effect formal changes in Kwantung government. They perhaps also postponing action pending imple[menta]tion larger plans of Chinese Communists (re paragraph 2, Nanking telegram 739 to Department, April 10, repeated Canton, Shanghai, Moscow, Peiping, Seoul).

Sent Nanking 70; repeated Department 106, Shanghai 102, Embassy Canton 19, Moscow 55, Seoul 17, Peiping 5.

PADDOCK

---

123 Gleysteen, Culver : Telegram

The Consul at Dairen (Paddock) to the Secretary of State

DAIREN, April 15, 1949—4 p. m.
[Received April 16—8 :44 p. m.]

108. Early evening April 12, two Chinese police and two Soviet soldiers arrested Vice Consul Gleysteen at point of land near Rokotan where we picnic periodically. He held 4 hours.

April 13 I discussed arrest with Soviet Consul. I agreed this not his jurisdiction but pointed out practice of Chief Soviet Kommandatura not answering my previous request for appointments. Soviet Consul said he would see regarding appointment. No word from him and today I sent formal letter to Soviet Consul reviewing arrest:

(1) Rokotan not restricted area; (2) Gleysteen there only to enjoy scenery; (3) Chinese policeman tried forcibly pull him from jeep; (4) Gleysteen taken first Povva prison nearby, then Chinese police same area, then Soviet camp in another part of Dairen, then Kommandatura headquarters; (5) not permitted telephone; (6) Kommandatura Soviet Colonel first interviewed him; then left and after hour returned with Soviet junior officer (obviously MVD) ; (7) this officer cross-examined Gleysteen in detail why he at Rokotan; (8) during examination, he said Gleysteen signalling with auto lights out to sea; Gleysteen said auto parked away from sea and besides lights off as still daylight; police ran up few minutes after he arrived; (9) signalling charge not pressed further and Gleysteen let go with excuse police protecting him "from being thrown in sea by bandits"; (10) in conclusion letter emphasized Gleysteen broke no regulation

---

[15] Telegram No. 105, April 12, not printed.

but held 4 hours; not allowed telephone; I said most serious aspect was signalling charge even though dropped; I asked for information which regulation Gleysteen violated thus leading to arrest.

It possible I receive answer but do not expect any.

Except for incidents of Consulate report wire July 26 "military activity at Lao-sun" and despatch 32 to Nanking August 26 "description of trip to Ta Ho Shang," [16] this only time Consulate officer arrested at Dairen. Consulate anxious not give impression this was major affair. Soviets may regard it as unimportant and routine.

However, Consulate feels incident clear-cut example of Soviets in wrong and that Gleysteen acted calmly, correctly.

Consulate would like Department instruct Moscow Embassy protest Foreign Office as matter record and principle unless this believed impolitic.

Sent Department 108, repeated Nanking, Embassy Canton 21, Shanghai 105, Moscow 59.

PADDOCK

---

123 Gleysteen, Culver : Telegram

The Consul at Dairen (Paddock) to the Secretary of State

DAIREN, April 16, 1949—1 a. m.
[Received 7:27 p. m.]

109. Chief Soviet Kommandatura today said I receive 2 or 3 days answer to points re Gleysteen arrest (reference immediately preceding telegram) ; thus no need action last paragraph as yet.

Sent Department 109; repeated Nanking 75, Moscow 6.

PADDOCK

---

123 Gleysteen, Culver : Telegram

The Ambassador in China (Stuart) to the Secretary of State

NANKING, April 20, 1949—4 p. m.
[Received April] 20—6:50 a. m.]

803. Provided Dairen concurs, Embassy urges Department give fullest publicity facts stated Dairen's 108 to Department April 17 [15] preferably at time protest despatched to Foreign Office Moscow (reference Dairen's 109 to Department April 16, repeated Nanking, Moscow) : That arrest made with assistance Soviet soldiers, that Gleysteen held incommunicado at Soviet camp and at Kom[manda]tura, and that he interrogated there by two Soviet officers are all examples of Soviet official abrogation [arrogation?] of authority in Dairen. Such

---

[16] Neither printed.

examples would bring home to Chinese public China's loss of sovereignty Dairen area and real meaning Sino-Soviet treaty and would provide picture future Soviet domination wherever Soviet administration officials allowed to penetrate.

Sent Department 803, repeated Dairen 28, OffEmb Canton 271, Shanghai 401, passed Moscow 26.

STUART

---

123 Bacon, Leonard Lee : Telegram

The Secretary of State to the Consul General at Shanghai (Cabot) [17]

WASHINGTON, April 21, 1949—6 p. m.

709. Dept apprehensive possible Commie capture Shanghai wld complicate travel Bacon and Colling [18] Dairen. Pls report present status applications Soviet transit visas and travel arrangements and take such follow-up action to expedite consideration applications as appears desirable. Can Dept be any assistance this connection?

ACHESON

---

123 [Gleysteen, Culver] : Telegram

The Secretary of State to the Consul at Dairen (Paddock) [19]

WASHINGTON, April 22, 1949—6 p. m.

54. Re Dairen's 108 April 15 and 109 April 16 to Dept, Dept has pursuant Dairen recommendation latter reftel deferred instructing Moscow protest Gleysteen detention pending reply Soviet Kommandatura Dairen. However Dept reluctant defer this action more than stipulated 2 or 3 days; accordingly requests Dairen report present status reply.

Dept inclined concur Nanking tel 803 April 20 to Dept recommending fullest publicity Gleysteen detention at time protest despatched Moscow FonOff and requests urgently views Moscow Dairen re desirability this action.

ACHESON

---

[17] Repeated as No. 244 to the Ambassador in the Soviet Union.
[18] Leonard L. Bacon and Guy Thomas Colling, assigned to relieve Messrs. Paddock and Gleysteen at Dairen.
[19] Repeated as No. 250 to the Ambassador in the Soviet Union.

123 Gleysteen, Culver : Telegram

The Consul at Dairen (Paddock) to the Secretary of State

DAIREN, April 23, 1949—11 a. m.
[Received April 24—9 :28 a. m.]

117. No answer as yet from Chief Soviet Kom[manda]tura regarding Gleysteen arrest (Contel 109, April 16, repeated Moscow 60, and immediately preceding telegram April 15, repeated all addressees).

At interview April 16 he said Gleysteen did not have identification. This true. I replied I had asked Soviet Consul last summer for identification but nothing done. Since November we had carried Soviet Komtura curfew pass (for use after 11 p. m.) but this had expired April 1; although Consul had written March 23 for renewal, no answer. (New passes issued us day after arrest and apparently only because of arrest.) Actually Gleysteen arrest first time any identification ever asked for.

Only identification Chief Soviet Komtura could suggest for us was driving license. I said Consul had written local police chief last summer but no answer; also tried several times since then see police but no success; result we still do not have licenses. He said I should try again. Accordingly this week Consul wrote police for driving tests; we may or may not get reply.

Excuse of Chief Soviet Komtura that Gleysteen had no identification thus believed irrelevant. Soviet Colonel of paragraph 6, April 15 telegram [20] knew Gleysteen and subject of identification never raised by him; yet Gleysteen held and questioned in Komtura for 2 hours after meeting him.

Chief Soviet Komtura said Gleysteen never under arrest. I objected, pointing out conditions under which Gleysteen held tantamount arrest. Chief made no further comment.

Nearest chief came to giving a reason for Gleysteen arrest was statement that seashores patrolled after dark. I said Dairen not part of PA [21] naval base area and shores of Dairen city never termed restricted area.

Protest to Soviet Foreign Office plus publicity regarding this incident, in which Soviets wholly in wrong, may result in more respect to Consul in day-to-day affairs. Thus Consul concurs Embassy suggestion Nanking telegram 803, April 20, Moscow 26.

In its consideration this problem Department should note that apparently last time Dairen discussed with Soviet Foreign Office (except visas and special ship last March–April to bring personnel here) was refusal let newspapermen ashore from courier ship January 1947

---

[20] Telegram No. 108, p. 865.
[21] Port Arthur.

[*December 1946* [22]]. It perhaps of future value to use Gleysteen case as excuse reaffirm Department's position regarding Dairen, particularly as local administration now in process of change.

Note: During first 2 hours of Gleysteen arrest he remained in Consulate jeep under armed guard (two Soviet soldiers with tommyguns, one Soviet officer and one Chinese police officer). Gleysteen ordered drive to Soviet guardhouse, Chinese police station at Rokotan and Soviet camp in west part Dairen before being taken Soviet Komtura.

Repeated Nanking 83, Moscow 65, OffEmb Canton 27, Shanghai 113.

PADDOCK

125.351/4–2349 : Telegram

The Consul at Dairen (*Paddock*) *to the Secretary of State*

DAIREN, April 23, 1949—noon.
[Received April 24—8:49 a. m.]

118. In last half year treatment of consular auto by Chinese traffic police of the Kwantung administration has been highly discriminatory and rude. Incidents increasing when auto stopped and chauffeur (or Consular officer if driving) subjected to 10 minutes harangue for alleged violation traffic regulations.

By now, reasons given for stopping car so picayune, it assumed police instructed step up program of petty annoyances on American Consulate. In past 3 weeks 4 such incidents when no traffic regulation broken.

Increased police pressure drove away another servant from my household only few weeks ago.

I wrote Chief Soviet Kommandatura April 9 for interview to discuss traffic police. No reply, but Gleysteen arrest produced interview April 16 which afforded opportunity bring up subject of Kwantung police. I emphasized Kwantung police are direct Soviet responsibility. He said his reply on this problem would be sent "in 2 or 3 days". No reply yet received.

Unwarranted discourtesy and discrimination of police reported now merely for Department's information and to give background (re immediately preceding telegram, of another phase of Soviet administration of Dairen).

Sent Department 118, repeated Nanking 84, AmEmbassy Canton 28, Shanghai 114, Moscow 66.

PADDOCK

---

[22] See telegram No. 2538, December 23, 1946, noon, from the Consul General at Shanghai, and subsequent documents, *Foreign Relations*, 1946, vol. x, pp. 1194 ff.

123 Gleysteen, Culver : Telegram

The Chargé in the Soviet Union (Kohler) to the Secretary of State

Moscow, April 23, 1949—2 p. m.
[Received April 23—9 :10 a. m.]

1018. Embassy believes propaganda value Far East of publicity Gleysteen detention and protest (Deptel 250, April 22 [23]) should be overriding consideration. Consequently we concur Nanking and Department views regarding protest and are prepared transmit note to Foreign Office upon receipt Department instructions.

Repeated Dairen 21, Nanking 45, Shanghai 8, Canton 13.

KOHLER

---

123 Bacon, Leonard Lee : Telegram

The Chargé in the Soviet Union (Kohler) to the Secretary of State

Moscow, April 23, 1949—2 p. m.
[Received April 23—9 :21 a. m.]

1020. Still unable elicit answer Bacon visa, reDeptel 244, 21st.[24] Not informed of date Colling application but have sent note Foreign Office. Doubtful Colling visa can be obtained prior next sailing *Smolny*, exact date of which unknown here, but will continue press.

Repeated Shanghai 9, Dairen 22, Nanking 46.

KOHLER

---

123 Gleysteen, Culver : Telegram

The Consul at Dairen (Paddock) to the Secretary of State

DAIREN, April 26, 1949—4 p. m.
[Received April 27—11 :47 p. m.]

120. Chief of Civil Administration Office of Kommandatura, Major General Levushkin, granted me interview today. He informed me on behalf Commanding General Soviet Dairen Garrison (believed to be Colonel Usachuk) that Gleysteen detained because (1) he had no identification; (2) seashores restricted area after dark. He refused commit himself regarding date seashore regulation put in effect other than "early April". No announcement of such restricted area in press.

I reviewed actual facts regarding main points but no further comment by him. These facts already sent Department (Contel 117 [25]).

---

[23] Same as telegram No. 54 to Dairen, p. 867.
[24] Same as telegram No. 709 to Shanghai, *ibid.*
[25] Dated April 23, 11 a. m., p. 868.

He suggested we apply to Chinese Police Chief of Kwantung administration for identification cards; I said he [we] would do so.

This dismissal of Gleysteen case by Soviets and irresponsibility regarding facts would seem justify action contemplated by Department in its telegram 54, April 22.

Sent Department; repeated Nanking 85, OffEmb Canton 29, Shanghai 116, Moscow 68.

PADDOCK

---

123 Gleysteen, Culver : Telegram

The Consul at Dairen (Paddock) to the Secretary of State

DAIREN, April 26, 1949—5 p. m.
[Received April 27—11:35 p. m.]

121. It uncertain if my application to Chinese police of Kwantung administration for identification cards (re immediately preceding telegram) will be considered by Department as a form of recognition of Kwantung administration.

In short discussion regarding Chinese police, Levushkin, at same interview, said they responsible maintain order and are not under Soviet control. I replied I considered Kwantung police merely a branch of Soviet administration and that Soviets, as military authorities, are responsible for area; it was on this basis Consulate had written police for driving licenses and other matters in past year. He made no comment.

Sent Department 121; repeated Nanking 86, OffEmb Canton 30, Shanghai 117, Moscow 69.

PADDOCK

---

123 [Gleysteen, Culver] : Telegram

The Secretary of State to the Chargé in the Soviet Union (Kohler)

WASHINGTON, April 28, 1949—2 p. m.

273. Dept desires you protest to Sov FonOff in appropriate terms detention Gleysteen (Dairen tels 108 Apr 15, 109 Apr 16, 117 Apr 23 to Dept rptd all addresses) by Sov officials Dairen. Dept believes that after outlining circumstances Gleysteen's seizure and detention, refusal permit communication Consulate by telephone and his lengthy interrogation, you shld point out Gleysteen exercises his consular duties Dairen in accordance internatl law and practice and seizure detention of him carried out on terr[itory] Republic of China. You shld not bring up at this time question right of Sovs exercise auth in Dairen but shld base protest on arbitrariness detention and violation privileges and immunities Consuls established in internatl law and

usage. You shld request explanation this arbitrary action and assurances non-recurrence. Pls transmit text protest to Dept with view to its release here and inform when delivered.

Dept plans issue full statement re detention Gleysteen including statement AmEmbassy Moscow has been instructed protest to Sov FonOff. Since publicity likely prove more effective in China if conveys impression Sovs violating Chi territorial sovereignty, phrase re incident occurring "on territory Republic of China" shld be prominent in note, particularly since Tass may release text.

ACHESON

---

123 Gleysteen, Culver : Telegram

The Consul at Dairen (Paddock) to the Secretary of State

DAIREN, April 29, 1949—5 p. m.
[Received May 1—7:24 a. m.]

129. Traffic police yesterday stopped Consulate auto in Dairen commercial district for alleged traffic violation. Consulate chauffeur driving and Vice Consul Gleysteen only passenger. Police insisted chauffeur admit he had violated traffic regulations. As he definitely had not, chauffeur refused.

Gleysteen did not intervene because sudden congregation four extra police at crossroad (where known that Consulate auto would pass) and their extraordinary insulting manner indicated auto possibly halted as deliberate provocation.

When police ordered chauffeur drive to police station, Gleysteen requested them postpone [to] evening. They did not answer but entered car without permission and instructed chauffeur drive to station.

Gleysteen waited in car while chauffeur detained 20 minutes. Chauffeur on return said he had agreed with police regarding their version of facts. Obviously he had done so only to protect self.

American flag on car.

Today I sent letter protest to chief Soviet Kommandatura.

Incident possibly soured police reaction to previous Consulate protest Contel 118, April 23, to which no reply received. Status of police mentioned Contel 121, April 26.

Chauffeur said two plain-clothes men came his house late last night and questioned him how felt re his work.

It is not known if Department has reached decision whether to protest at Moscow re Gleysteen detention, Contel 108, April 15 and 117, April 23. In this connection Department should note Consulate working conditions are daily more hampered. Most recent development is response of Soviets and police re true facts of these successive incidents.

In official Soviet reply re Gleysteen detention (Contel 120, April 26) their distortion actual facts is in itself a [garbled group] provocation.

Consulate believes advisable warn Department of possibility of some truly serious incident occurring any time under prevailing conditions. Consulate unable judge if protest by Department re Gleysteen detention and effective publicity, as considered by Department at the time Deptel 54, April 22, will decrease this possibility.

Sent Department 129; repeated Nanking 9, American Embassy Canton 36, Shanghai 122, Moscow 75.

PADDOCK

---

123 [Gleysteen, Culver] : Telegram

The Secretary of State to the Consul at Dairen (*Paddock*)

WASHINGTON, April 29, 1949—8 p. m.

58. Ur 121 Apr 26. Dept realizes it inevitable you have to apply Kwantung authorities time to time and does not consider your application Chi police as such a form recognition Kwantung administration. To avoid possibility misunderstanding this connection you should when possible direct ur requests to appropriate official by name without title or to appropriate official by title without name, for example, to Chief Police, Dairen.

ACHESON

---

123 Gleysteen, Culver : Telegram

The Chargé in the Soviet Union (*Kohler*) *to the Secretary of State*

Moscow, April 30, 1949—11 a. m.
[Received April 30—9:23 a. m.]

1096. Following note delivered to Foreign Office today (Deptel 273, April 28):

The Embassy of the US presents compliments to Foreign Minister and has honor state that in early evening April 12, 1949, Vice Consul Culver Gleysteen, official of American Consul[ate] General at Dairen, China, was arrested by 2 Chinese police and 2 Soviet soldiers at a point of land near Rokotan near Dairen. After being taken to a Soviet guardhouse nearby, to a Chinese police station in the same area, and to a Soviet camp in another part of Dairen, Vice Consul Gleysteen was finally taken to Soviet Kommandatura headquarters, where he was interrogated at length by Soviet officers.

Vice Consul Gleysteen was detained for a period of 4 hours during which time he was not permitted to telephone the American Consul General. The area where Vice Consul Gleysteen was arrested has never been publicly designated as a restricted area and he violated no known law or regulation.

The Embassy desires to point out that Vice Consul Gleysteen exercises his consular duties in Dairen in accordance with international law and practice and to emphasize that his arbitrary seizure and detention by Soviet authorities was carried out on the territory of the Republic of China.

The Government of the US protests this arbitrary violation of the privileges and immunities of Consuls established by international law and usage and requests from the Government of the USSR an explanation of this action and assurances that it will not recur.

Sent Department 1096, repeated Dairen 23, Nanking 50, Shanghai 10, Canton 17.

[KOHLER]

125.3513/4–3049 : Telegram

The Consul at Dairen (Paddock) to the Secretary of State

DAIREN, April 30, 1949—noon.
[Received May 1—7 :31 a. m.]

131. Clerk Chao (who sleeps office) says police last night midnight broke down door his house and searched house 3 hours. Took two English language books.

Contel 62, March 3 and Nanking telegram 858 to Department April 25 [26] describe his situation here.

Police have made series visits his house questioning wife why he works American Consulate; 2 days ago he called to police station and himself questioned. He says he usually followed by plain clothesman.

Department requested instruct Consulate re action it should take in event Chao or other member staff arrested or detained by police. In such event Consulate would prefer not have to wait to communicate with Department before protesting local authorities.

Note that police visited house of chauffeur night before last, Contel 129, April 29.

Sent Department 13; repeated Nanking 93, American Embassy Canton 37, Shanghai 123, Moscow 76.

PADDOCK

---

123 Bacon, Leonard Lee : Telegram

The Consul General at Shanghai (Cabot) to the Secretary of State

SHANGHAI, May 3, 1949—4 p. m.
[Received May 3—8 :31 a. m.]

1488. ReDeptel 709, April 21. Soviet Consul General awaiting instructions Moscow on Bacon and Colling visa applications. Soviet Consul said he understood decision deferred depending outcome ne-

---

[26] Neither printed.

gotiations Washington. Nothing can be done here expedite issuance. If visas forthcoming, space will be reserved on *Smolny* whose next sailing date uncertain. Vessel has just left Hong Kong for Vladivostok and Dairen without calling Shanghai.

Moscow please notify Shanghai if Foreign Office needs more information regarding Colling application which filed after Bacon's.

Repeated Nanking 837, Dairen 38 and Moscow 10.

CABOT

893.00/5–449 : Telegram

The Consul at Dairen (Paddock) to the Secretary of State

DAIREN, May 4, 1949—9 a. m.
[Received 10 p. m.]

134. Political changes here seem now completed. Others not expected until conditions in rest of China stabilize. Purpose this telegram to outline major steps involved in these changes and summarize information sent by Consulate in miscellaneous telegrams.

1. March 19 Preparatory Committee of New Democratic Youth Corps formed in accordance resolve of CCP Central Committee. This first public admission by a Chinese body in Kwantung of Communist connect[ion]s and hinted CCP would soon emerge here.

2. March 31 *Kwantung Jih Pao* (organ of Kwantung Administration) announced it would cease publication; *Dairen Jih Pao* (Labor Union organ) stated it would become an apparatus paged under name *Jen Min Daily*.

3. April 1 CCP emerged from underground in Kwantung and announced it subordinate to NE bureau of CCP. Front agencies changed names or admitted Communist connections.

4. April 12 puppet Dairen Mayor Hsu granted long leave absence. This first sign of formal changes in Kwantung Administration.

5. April 22 puppet Chairman of Kwantung Administration Chih announced resignation. People's Republic Conference summoned by Vice Chairman and leaders of "democratic groups" (all Communists) to elect new chairman and officers.

6. April 25 elections to conference held, only "democratic organs" voted which controlled by CCP.

7. April 28, April 27 conference held; positions of former puppets filled by CCP members. Name Kwantung administration changed to P[ort]A[rthur]–Dairen Executive Administration. Regional CCP Secretary Ou-yang stated PA-Dairen is part CCP liberated area; he indicated Soviets remain PA naval base area but avoided reference to Soviet-occupied Dairen.

Summary: CCP now openly controls local government. Soviet civil administration, Soviet garrison and other Soviet organs remain in Dairen. Thus CCP-Soviet local relations appear unchanged. However, without former restraints necessitated by Soviet policy of "correctness" toward National Government, CCP expected carry out now same economic, political, social program as in Manchuria.

Sent Canton 41, repeated Department 134, Nanking 95, Shanghai 127, Peiping 12, Moscow 80, Seoul 26.

PADDOCK

---

123 Bacon, Leonard Lee : Telegram

The Ambassador in China (Stuart) to the Secretary of State

NANKING, May 7, 1949—noon.
[Received May 7—6:57 a. m.]

956. In view Commie occupation Nanking and lapse nearly 10 weeks without Soviet response to Bacon visa application, we suggested Dept instruct Peiping ConGen to apply legal authorities for authorization Bacon and Boorman [27] travel overland to Dairen via Manchuria or by sea on Chinese vessel out of Tientsin. Commies have announced Tientsin–Pukow railroad will be operable by June 1. Soviets may intend to base visa refusal on ground travel via Vladivostok north no longer necessary, but this argument would be invalid if application to Chinese Commies has been refused or unanswered. Same considerations would apply Colling when Shanghai falls.

Re Peiping's 164, April 30, repeated Dept 733.[28] Embassy recommends assignment Boorman [to] Dairen soonest so that application can be made at once basis actual assignment.

Sent Dept; repeated Shanghai 520, AmEmb Canton 369, Dairen 30, Peiping 148, Moscow 27.

STUART

125.351/5–749 : Telegram

The Ambassador in China (Stuart) to the Secretary of State

NANKING, May 7, 1949—noon.
[Received May 7—6:57 a. m.]

957. Re Embtel 956, May 7. We feel bound to observe that, while we earnestly desire retain Dairen Consulate, our position there is becoming increasingly untenable as result Communist persecution of Consular staff, difficulties in maintaining courier and telegraphic communications and difficulties in replacing personnel. We assume Department is currently considering means, if any, to improve our position there, though in light of such telegrams as Dairen's 121, May 1 [April 26] to Department we are beginning to question usefulness of maintaining Consulate Dairen in circumstances of increasing isolation.

---

[27] Howard L. Boorman, Vice Consul at Peiping.
[28] Not printed.

Department pass Peiping, Moscow in discretion.

Sent Department, repeated OffEmb Canton 370, Shanghai 521, Dairen 31.

STUART

---

123 Paddock, Paul : Telegram

The Consul at Dairen (Paddock) to the Secretary of State

DAIREN, May 10, 1949—4 p. m.
[Received May 11—11:17 p. m.]

141. Yesterday Gleysteen and I had picnic same place Gleysteen arrested April 12. When we returned to car at 2:30 p. m. Soviet officer and guards who had been waiting said Soviet Kommandatura ordered them escort us there.

Deputy Commander Dairen Garrison received us and asked re our permit go Rokotan implying it not part of Dairen city. I said no permit necessary based on information from Soviet authorities (Contel 120, April 26) but that I would discuss matter with General Levushkin, Chief Dairen Civil Administration. I now trying get interview with him.

It was evident yesterday Soviet officers acting on prearranged instructions from Kommandatura.

Sent Department, repeated Nanking 99, Canton 46, Moscow 84.

PADDOCK

125.3513/4–3049 : Telegram

The Secretary of State to the Consul at Dairen (Paddock)

WASHINGTON, May 13, 1949—6 p. m.

64. Urtel 131, April 30. In event Chao or other member alien staff arrested or detained by police you should request info re nature of charges and date of trial and permission interview him. Experience in other areas has tended to show that an informal and oral initial approach is most satisfactory. If no reply received within reasonable time your inquiry or if reply unsatisfactory and you convinced purpose arrest detention is embarrassment Consulate you may protest action as unwarranted interference Consulate in its legitimate functions.

In event you convinced detention for purpose embarrassment Consulate Dept would consider upon ur recommendation placing alien concerned leave without pay status with continuing payment in lieu compensation to him from other funds.

ACHESON

761.93/5-1449 : Telegram

The Consul at Dairen (Paddock) to the Secretary of State

DAIREN, May 14, 1949—5 p. m.
[Received 11:33 p. m.]

143. Local speculation that Soviets preparing withdraw to P[ort] A[rthur] Naval Base area, that Dairen port will be opened, and that Dairen will be incorporated into Manchuria administratively as well as politically reached point last week where merchants perturbed and gold price started to rise.

Such rumors recurrent since CCP emergence April 1 but had died down with government reorganization before May Day. Their strong revival now reputedly based on observations of overt actions of Soviets and CCP indicating arrangements under way for such a move. However, Consulate has not itself observed any such actions.

Any Soviet retreat, if only to position actually accorded them in 1945 Treaty, probably will be dressed up as voluntary renunciation of their "right". Similar propaganda device in Kwantung when re-equipment of some factories (stripped by Soviets 1945) gave chance to pretend USSR had donated this equipment for sake Sino-Soviet friendship. Soviets also "donate" raw materials to Kwantung but export of goods to USSR not mentioned. Local Chinese Communist press supports these ruses.

If Soviet's military forces do leave Dairen, Consulate assumes they leave behind effective organizations to guarantee continued economic control including bulk of large industries and port facilities.

Sent Nanking 101, repeated Department, Canton 48, Moscow 86, Shanghai 134, Peiping 14, Seoul 30.

PADDOCK

761.93/5-1749 : Telegram

The Ambassador in China (Stuart) to the Secretary of State

NANKING, May 17, 1949—1 p. m.
[Received May 17—5:39 a. m.]

1044. Re Dairen's 41, May 5 [4] to Embassy Canton, repeated Department 134, Shanghai 127. Suggest you may wish to mention to Nationalist Government that it is missing opportunity to capitalize on emergence of CCP in Port Arthur–Dairen area despite hypocritical Soviet recognition Nationalist sovereignty there. That organized CCP has long functioned there was succinctly announced April 19 by Peiping radio which, in referring to "conference of active elements of CCP from April 1–3 in Dairen", stated "work of CP in area during past 3 years was discussed and CP of area was made public"; also on May 12 Peiping radio announced "workers in Port Arthur and Dairen have made great headway in rehabilitation and reconstruction during past 3 years under leadership of CCP organization there".

Sent Embassy Canton 430; repeated Department 1044, Shanghai 591.

STUART

125.3516/5-2049 : Telegram

The Consul at Dairen (Paddock) to the Secretary of State

DAIREN, May 20, 1949—noon.
[Received May 22—1 a. m.]

148. Ten p. m. last night four Chinese police came Consulate residence to "investigate the population" (interrogate Chinese staff). I told them I could not allow such irregular nocturnal visits. Although police said they would not enter house by force, they obtained reinforcements of about 14 men who surrounded building.

Eventually a superior officer arrived with whom after lengthy debate it was agreed police could come in daytime to interrogate Chinese staff residing here but they were to enter only room such as sleeping quarters of staff. Police then withdrew at 2 a. m.

In letter to this officer today I reviewed our conversation and repeated I did not wish interfere regular duties of police re Chinese population but that this building due its official character could not be treated as ordinary Dairen residence.

Affair several times threatened ugly turn and police rude and insulting.

Although interview with officer closed amicably, it [is] apparent solution of this latest example of police persecution of our Chinese staff is at best temporary.

Situation now is police able enter Consulate residence (where security room located with shield over door) any time during day even when none present, although they supposed go only sleeping quarters of Chinese staff. Due exposed position of Consulate and lack of appropriate protection by Soviets or Chinese authorities, it believed no other solution possible.

Sent Department 148; repeated Nanking 106, OffEmb Canton 51, Moscow 88.

PADDOCK

123 Gleysteen, Culver : Telegram

The Chargé in the Soviet Union (Kohler) to the Secretary of State

Moscow, May 20, 1949—4 p. m.
[Received May 20—10:01 a. m.]

1308. Following note No. 48 dated May 19 received [from] Foreign Office (re Embtel 1096, April 30) :

Minister Foreign Affairs . . .[29] with reference Embassy note No. 219, April 30 has honor state following:

"On evening April 12, 1949 at oncoming darkness in a forbidden zone of naval base of Port Arthur there was detained by Soviet military authorities guarding this base a stranger who from shore was making light signals seawards with headlights of automobile. Detainee did not present documents establishing his identity and did not present pass for automobile.

"In military Kommandatura where violator of regulations of forbidden zone was brought it was established that this person was Am. Vice Consul in City of Dalny, Mr. Culver Gleysteen.

"Upon establishment of his identity Gleysteen was released.

"Minister will be grateful to Embassy for assurances that such actions of Gleysteen will not be repeated."

Sent Department 1308; repeated Dairen 24, Nanking 58, Shanghai 11, Canton 24.

KOHLER

---

123 [Gleysteen, Culver] : Telegram

The Acting Secretary of State to the Consul at Dairen (Paddock)

WASHINGTON, May 23, 1949—8 p. m.

67. Re Moscow tel 1308 May 20 to Dept rptd Dairen 24, Dept considers it unwise permit Soviet assertions re Gleysteen remain uncorrected. Before instructing Moscow transmit reply to Sov FonOff, Dept desires receive any info not previously reported which might be useful refuting Soviet assertions.

WEBB

---

123 Gleysteen, Culver : Telegram

The Consul at Dairen (Paddock) to the Secretary of State

DAIREN, May 23, 1949.
[Received May 24—11:57 a. m.]

154. Reference Soviet Foreign Office note regarding Gleysteen detention (Moscow telegram 1308, May 20), Department will recall long confusion regarding boundary of PA naval base area and Dairen city.

---

[29] Omission indicated in the source text.

Claim that Rokotan area is in base (made now for first time so far as Consul aware, Contel 141, May 10) again advances boundary considerably.

Note that Rokotan not isolated village, people of Dairen accept it as part of their city and it is serviced by Dairen streetcars; along chief route to it one never leaves built-up section of city. No barriers or other indication of base boundary. Doubtful if possible go there from base proper except through Dairen municipal center.

Aside from political significance, this subject is important to Consul since Rokotan and Fukusho (on coast between Rokotan and neck of peninsula) are only two beaches and picnic places left to Americans.

Attempts of Consul get identification cards and driving licenses from Chinese police, as suggested by Levushkin Contel 120 April 26, never answered. We still without proper identification.

Consulate's officers will not go again to Rokotan or Fukusho until Department gives permission but it hoped Department will soon do so even though this leads to possibility of detention. Throughout incident Soviets have acted in wrong, have misstated facts, and now note officially repeats serious charge of Gleysteen signaling and ignores his detention and questioning for 2 hours after identification as Consulate officer.

Repeated Nanking 111, Canton 55, Moscow 90.

PADDOCK

---

123 [Bacon, Leonard L.] : Telegram

The Acting Secretary of State to the Ambassador in China (Stuart)

WASHINGTON, May 25, 1949—5 p. m.

636. Ur 956 May 7. Dept agrees desirability request Commies authorize Bacon travel Dairen via Manchuria or Chinese vessel ex Tientsin (likewise Colling if Shanghai falls). Dept suggests however that application permission more properly made Nanking since Bacon now there.

Dept deferring assignment Boorman Dairen to allow completion language course July.

WEBB

---

123 Gleysteen, Culver : Telegram

The Ambassador in China (Stuart) to the Secretary of State

NANKING, May 25, 1949—5 p. m.
[Received May 26—1 a. m.]

1112. Re Moscow telegram sent Department 1308, May 20. Would appreciate learning whether Department has ever released story of arrest of Gleysteen at Dairen. If not, recommend Department release text of Soviet FonOff note of May 19 while simultaneously pointing out that (1) Gleysteen was arrested during daytime when he could not possibly have been signalling with automobile headlights and (2) he was detained not within Port Arthur area but within Dairen area which by Sino-Soviet treaty of August 14, 1945 is free port under Chinese administration.

In general it is our conclusion that persecution of our Consulate at Dairen just as our ConGen at Mukden is of Soviet rather than CCP inspiration (Embtel 1076, May 21 [30]). Consequently short of closing Consulate at Dairen we believe our sole defense at present time lies in prompt and effective publicity of every violation by joint Soviet and CCP police power of our Consular rights at Dairen. In this connection suggest Department may also wish to publicize latest violation recounted in Dairen telegram sent Department 148, May 22 [*20*].

Sent Department, repeated Shanghai 626, OffEmb Canton 463, Dairen 34, Moscow 30.

STUART

---

123 Gleysteen, Culver : Telegram

The Consul at Dairen (Paddock) to the Secretary of State

DAIREN, May 28, 1949—7 p. m.
[Received May 30—7 :31 p. m.]

162. Consulate has no details to add to its 154, May 23 re Soviet note re Gleysteen detention. ReDeptel 67, May 23, received today.

Sent Department 162; repeated Moscow 93, Nanking 117, Canton 61.

PADDOCK

---

123 Gleysteen, Culver : Telegram

The Acting Secretary of State to the Consul at Dairen (Paddock)

WASHINGTON, May 31, 1949—7 p. m.

72. Ur 162 May 28. Dept desires most specific info possible re fol points for use in replying Sov note Gleysteen detention: (1) time of arrest, (2) name Sov Col referred to ur 117 April 23 who knew Gleysteen.

WEBB

---

[30] Not printed.

123 Gleysteen, Culver : Telegram

The Consul at Dairen (Paddock) to the Secretary of State

DAIREN, June 2, 1949—1 p. m.
[Received June 3—12:54 a. m.]

163. ReDeptel 72. Time of arrest between 7:30 and 8. It was dusk but not dark. Consular jeep parked facing inland, headlights off. Gleysteen had used lights on Rokotan Streets as safety precaution but turned them off when out of built-up section as they unnecessary because it still daylight. Thus lights never used when jeep facing open sea while approaching parking place. Police and Soviet soldiers ran up within few minutes after Gleysteen arrived.

Question of identity as American official never raised after initial request. "American Consul General" is prominently painted on front of jeep; police and soldiers accepted Gleysteen as American official.

Name of Soviet officer who first questioned Gleysteen at Soviet Kommandatura is Ocadchuk, his rank is Lieutenant Colonel; title is Commander Dairen garrison. He never asked Gleysteen who he was but definitely greeted him as acquaintance. Gleysteen had met him at Army day reception at Soviet Consulate General last November. Later MVD officer brought up question identity but only if Gleysteen Consul or Vice Consul. He tacitly admitted Gleysteen's arrest was mistaken by saying it took place because soldiers ignorant and trying protect him from bandits.

PADDOCK

---

123 Bacon, Leonard Lee : Telegram

The Ambassador in China (Stuart) to the Secretary of State

NANKING, June 3, 1949—noon.
[Received 11:34 p. m.]

1182. Deptel 636, May 25, repeated Shanghai, OffEmb Canton, Dairen, Peiping. Application for necessary travel documents Bacon and wife, Nanking [to] Dairen to replace Paddock as Consul filed June 2 with Aliens Affairs Office Nanking. Director of office stated no permit now available for travel as individual since areas under military control and travel regulations foreigners not established. Also stated his office not competent discuss travel as official of government and could not transmit application to competent authority; moreover he could not indicate any authority to which application could be made.

Embassy therefore urges Department request Moscow renew pressure FonOff Soviet transit visa for use *Smolny* ex-Shanghai or Hong Kong.

Sent Department; repeated Shanghai 642, OffEmb Canton 484, Moscow 34, Dairen 35, Peiping 193.

STUART

123 Gleysteen, Culver: Telegram

The Acting Secretary of State to the Chargé in the Soviet Union (Kohler)

WASHINGTON, June 7, 1949—6 p. m.

409. Dept considers it undesirable permit assertions Sov note (Embtel 1308 May 20) re Gleysteen remain uncorrected and desires that unless you perceive objection thereto you reply to Sov note along fol lines: US Govt denies categorically Sov assertion Gleysteen making light signals seawards with headlights of automobile. Headlights were not on at any time when Gleysteen in area where taken into custody.

With respect to identification, AmCon Dairen has repeatedly endeavored without success obtain from Sov authorities and from local regime Dairen identification documents for himself and staff. Furthermore immed after being taken to Dairen mil Kommandatura Gleysteen interviewed by Commander of Dairen garrison who had previously met Gleysteen and apparently recognized him. Notwithstanding this Gleysteen held 2 hours, denied permission telephone AmCon which would have quickly established identity.

With respect Sov assertion Gleysteen in forbidden zone, US Govt points out no notification ever recd AmConsul Dairen or, insofar as known, made publicly that place Gleysteen taken into custody a forbidden zone. Furthermore, no sign, barricade or guards along road travelled Gleysteen to indicate he entering restricted zone.

With respect last para Sov note, US Govt assures Sov Govt Amer consular officers stationed Dairen have not knowingly entered restricted mil areas without appropriate pass from authorities and will not do so in future. On other hand US Govt expects Sov assurances that Amer consular officers Dairen will in future be free from arbitrary arrest or detention and will be permitted carry out legitimate duties accordance gen accepted standards internatl usage.

For ur info no press release re Gleysteen incident has been made as yet.

WEBB

893.00/6–949 : Telegram

The Consul at Dairen (Paddock) to the Secretary of State

DAIREN, June 9, 1949—8 a. m.
[Received June 10—11:51 p. m.]

168. In May 30 address to educational workers conference here CCP PA–Dairen committee secretary Ou-yang Chin stated that Dairen City is included in sphere occupied "by Soviet Army for 30 years until the Japanese peace treaty is signed", *Jen Min Daily* June 6.

This statement not related to context of rest of speech. It possible that Ou-yang deliberately publicized it to end the numerous rumors that Soviet Army will soon withdraw from Dairen City.

Sent Nanking 122, repeated Dept 168, Canton 65, Shanghai 142, Peiping 18, Seoul 35.

PADDOCK

123 Gleysteen, Culver : Telegram

The Chargé in the Soviet Union (Kohler) to the Secretary of State

Moscow, June 9, 1949—5 p.m.
[Received June 9—11:28 a. m.]

1490. Note sent Foreign Office today re Gleysteen arrest accordance Department instructions Deptel 409, June 2.

Sent Department 1490, repeated Dairen 26, Nanking 65, Canton 31.

KOHLER

123 Bacon, Leonard Lee : Telegram

The Chargé in the Soviet Union (Kohler) to the Secretary of State

Moscow, June 9, 1949—6 p. m.
[Received June 9—12:32 p. m.]

1491. [To Nanking:] If Embassy to be requested renew efforts re Bacon visas (reurtel 1182 to Department,[31] repeated 35[34?] Moscow), desirable have any information available re probable sailing date and point of departure.

Sent Nanking 66, repeated Department 1491.

KOHLER

[31] June 3, p. 883

123 Gleysteen, Culver : Telegram

The Ambassador in China (Stuart) to the Secretary of State

NANKING, June 11, 1949—noon.
[Received 1 :20 p. m.]

1265. We suggest desirability at least from Far Eastern standpoint of releasing to press stories on Gleysteen incident and efforts withdraw Mukden staff. (ReDeptel 409, June 7 to Moscow, repeated Dairen 74, Nanking 678, OffEmb Canton 304 and Shanghai's telegram 2141 June 7 to Department,[32] repeated Nanking 1112). Implications of Soviet authority and pressure on Chinese soil should be emphasized.

Sent Department 1265, repeated OffEmb Canton 525, Shanghai 682, Dairen 36, Moscow 40.

STUART

125.3516/6–1449 : Telegram

The Consul at Dairen (Paddock) to the Secretary of State

DAIREN, June 14, 1949—2 p. m.
[Received June 15—8 :16 a. m.]

171–A. To keep Embassy informed re current situation Consulate: Police never returned house to examine Chinese staff after incident of Contel 148 to Department, May 20, repeated Nanking 106. Also, no other incidents in last weeks with local authorities; not even difficulties with traffic police.

Sent Department, repeated Nanking 125, Canton 69, Shanghai 14, Moscow 98.

PADDOCK

893.00B/6–2349 : Telegram

The Consul at Dairen (Paddock) to the Secretary of State

DAIREN, June 23, 1949—1 p. m.
[Received 9 :37 p. m.]

181. Workers of all ranks in all Soviet and Chinese Communist trusts must attend "political studies" classes several hours each week after work. It understood Mukden American Consulate spy story currently being stressed at these classes to emphasize every American Consulate "nest of spies" and to warn Soviets and Chinese against any contact with this Consulate.

Recently Soviet clerk in Soviet department store (Churin) chatted with Consulate officer about 5 minutes during purchase. After latter

---

[32] Post, p. 961.

left two Soviet Kommandatura officers reprimanded clerk for being friendly to "our enemy" and threatened punishment if repeated.

Sent Nanking 132; repeated Department 181, Canton 75, Shanghai 152, Moscow 102.

PADDOCK

125.3516/6–2649 : Telegram

The Consul at Dairen (*Paddock*) *to the Secretary of State*

DAIREN, June 26, 1949—2 p. m.
[Received June 27—7 :53 a. m.]

187. [To Nanking:] 9 :30 p. m., June 24 Consul chauffeur Ma taken from his house by five Chinese plain-clothesmen and driven to countryside. He interrogated re his role "in espionage like American Consul, Mukden", if other Chinese on Consul staff involved, and if he had observed secret movements of consular officers. Political police released Ma at midnight but warned they "not through with him".

Soviet accusation Gleysteen signaling to sea when arrested at Rokotan recalled Anna Bukar book on "spying" of American Embassy, Moscow, featured in Soviet bookstore. Contel 132, June 23, repeated Department 181, mentioned emphasis in local political classes that every American Consulate is "nest of spies".

Embtel 957, May 7, to Department "questioned usefulness of maintaining Consulate Dairen in circumstances of increasing isolation". Not known if Department commented on this telegram.

Consul would appreciate views of Embassy (or for Embassy take up subject with Department) re future plans for this post. Ma incident, due timing and implication of possible future public accusation whether Consul able operate indefinitely in face Soviet harassment.

Soviets still directly responsible for Dairen and for Consular difficulties here. Working conditions of Consul after USSR recognizes future CCP government cannot be foreseen. However, Soviet control of Dairen likely until Japanese treaty concluded.

Gleysteen and myself able cope with successive difficulties but morale Chinese staff deteriorating due exposed position. Nervous tension of many months has had effect.

It believed Consul can do nothing locally to improve situation and that only Department and Moscow Embassy (through effects of pressure at Foreign Office, publicity or other means) can restore and maintain workable conditions for this office.

Sent Nanking 138, repeated Canton 80, Shanghai 157, Moscow 106.

PADDOCK

125.3513/6–2849 : Telegram

The Consul at Dairen (Paddock) to the Secretary of State

DAIREN, June 28, 1949—9 a. m.
[Received June 29—1:17 a. m.]

192. Clerk Chao has not gone home last 2 months due fear difficulties with Soviet and CCP police (Contel 40, March 3, repeated 62 [33]). Rarely leaves Consulate premises. Now learned for first time his 19-year-old son arrested 3 weeks ago and just released from prison. Son was asked give information father's work at Consulate; warned that unless he told all he knew regarding father's spying activities he would suffer serious consequences.

As result pressure used on him in prison, son's mind affected.

Sent Nanking 141, repeated Department, Canton 182, Shanghai 159, Moscow 108.

PADDOCK

893.00/7–149 : Telegram

The Consul at Dairen (Paddock) to the Secretary of State

DAIREN, July 1, 1949—10 a. m.
[Received July 2—5:42 a. m.]

199. 1. Port Arthur–Dairen executive administration announced June 15 all anti-people or anti-democratic individuals, elements or organizations must register with police within 1 month and at same time surrender their documents, member lists, correspondence codes, weapons, funds, etc. Persons formerly but not now members such organizations also must register. Informers about those failing comply promised ample rewards. *Jen Min Daily* June 15.

2. Since such organizations not named it thus left to individual to determine member such organization.

3. Order issued just before "exposure espionage AmCon Mukden" June 18. Content and timing suggest likelihood it connected that affair.

4. Local press reported no sensational finds and on June 25 *Jen Min Daily* editorial urged reactionaries voluntarily report, promising them lenient treatment.

5. Consulate chauffeur Ma who [is] Catholic says members that church pressured register on grounds Roman Catholic Church is a world-wide anti-people and espionage apparatus.

6. Gleysteen's servant urged by his police residence area chief to register as employee of reactionary organization but no serious pressure when he declined.

---

[33] Not printed.

Sent Nanking 146; repeated Department; Canton 86, Peiping 23, Shanghai 165, Moscow 110.

PADDOCK

125.3516/7–449 : Telegram

The Ambassador in China (Stuart) to the Secretary of State

NANKING, July 4, 1949—4 p. m.
[Received July 4—11:50 a. m.]

1431. We have racked our brains for solutions to problems of communications, supplies, personnel which beset our Consulate Dairen, but must confess we still find no answers. We doubt whether it would be possible to use Japanese repatriation vessel for purposes envisaged in Dairen telegram 190, June 29 to Department [34] because of time element, possibility Soviets may refuse clearance for passengers and pouches to land, and fact that replacement personnel for Dairen cannot now leave China.

1. Communications: Telegraphic communications with Dairen are still open, although there are of course no assurances that we will continue to enjoy this privilege indefinitely. As respects courier service, there seems little hope of reestablishing it in near future. Last year it was difficult, expensive operation to send couriers from Shanghai via Vladivostok but even that is no longer possible now that Soviet vessels have ceased run between Vladivostok and Chinese ports (Dairen telegram 173, June 16 [15] to Department [34]).

2. Supplies: Apparently Consulate Dairen is running low on commissary official supplies (besides dollar exchange and fresh codes). Our only suggestion here is that Department in cooperation with Foreign Service establishments Japan, Manila, Hong Kong, Singapore might learn of sailing some foreign vessel to Dairen sufficiently in advance to arrange for purchases and shipment. Our Consul occasionally hears of presence of such foreign vessels in Dairen but he is never permitted visit them (Dairen telegram 183, June 23 to Department [34]). In this connection we might also observe that Foreign Service establishments in Communist-occupied areas of China would have few supplies to spare even if direct shipping from Shanghai or Tientsin to Dairen were available. Whether such supplies would be allowed duty-free entry Dairen is moot question.

3. We can think of only four logical ways by which replacement personnel could travel to Dairen:

a. From Shanghai (Colling), Nanking (Bacon), and Peiping (Boorman) by Chinese vessel across Yellow Sea or by rail via Man-

---

[34] Not printed.

churia. Chinese Communists have already refused cooperation in this project on grounds they have no diplomatic relations with US and no inter-port travel regulations. In this connection we might add it is unlikely they will have diplomatic relation with US before next year.

b. From Hong Kong (or Shanghai when port reopens) on Soviet motorship *Smolny* to Vladivostok for transshipment to Dairen. Soviets have refused cooperation in this project by failure to act on Bacon's visa application which was filed February 23 or on Colling's filed April. Also no sailings of Soviet vessels from China to Vladivostok are now even scheduled as far as we can ascertain.

c. From Japan by unarmed LCI or other small US naval vessel, unarmed plane or chartered vessel. Soviets have already shown reluctance to assist in this project by issuing visas last December for courier travel via Vladivostok in preference to permitting carrier entry in Dairen. Presumably Chinese Communists, now that they have theoretically taken over responsibilities administration Dairen area, would also object to such entry on grounds they have no diplomatic relations with US.

d. Reassignment of entire new staff from USA or Europe and travel across USSR via Vladivostok and thence to Dairen by Soviet ship. This approach might seem more promising in view facts that Bacon, Boorman, Colling are now immobilized in China, Boorman has not yet even been assigned Dairen pending completion his language course and Colling has presumably acquired bad name with CCP result his persecution on trumped-up charges brutality toward disgruntled former Chinese employee Consulate General Shanghai (see Shanghai's 2408, June 22 to Department [36]). Probabilities, however, are that Soviets would also refuse transit visas for trans-Siberian travel new Foreign Service personnel.

We clearly perceive advantages retaining our last toe hold Manchuria, not least of which are that Dairen is open port in which we are fully entitled maintain Consulate office and that Dairen is only vantage point from which to observe day-to-day joint Soviet-CCP administration. However, we reluctantly conclude that under present circumstances these advantages are outweighed by struggle expense, humiliation, danger involved in keeping post open. Indefinite continuance of Consulate in present status is unfair to Paddock, Gleysteen who have already exceeded their anticipated tours of duty. American consular officers Dairen are now hardly more than hostages awaiting Soviet retaliation against such American moves as Gubitchev arrest.[37] Due solely to Soviet and CCP police measures, Consulate Dairen has for some time been more productive in administrative-personnel headaches than political-economic reporting. It is for these reasons that we find it difficult agree with theme expressed Moscow

---

[36] *Post,* p. 1174.

[37] For documentation on the rejection of the claim to diplomatic immunity for Valentin Alexeyevich Gubichev, arrested and tried for espionage, 1949–50, see vol. v, pp. 776 ff.

telegram 27, June 29, to Dairen,[38] repeated Nanking 72, Canton 37, Shanghai 13, that since Soviets apparently want US to close post we should endeavor keep it open. It seems to us rather that main issue is whether, under existing circumstances beyond control, we ourselves stand to gain more than we lose by maintaining post.

We fully endorse statements in Dairen telegram 187, June 27[26] to Department that "Soviets are still directly responsible for Dairen and for Consulate difficulties" and that "Soviet control of Dairen likely until Japanese treaty concluded". In Dairen, at least as much as in Mukden, we are dealing with Soviets. We therefore recommend that if Department and Embassy Moscow are still not convinced of futility of continuing our efforts re Dairen, we should make one final approach to Soviet Foreign Office informing that (1) CCP authorities have no facilities or inter-port regulations for travel to Dairen (thus forestalling possibility of Soviets shifting onus onto CCP), and (2) we therefore request Soviets promptly either to issue transit visas to Bacon, Boorman, Colling for use on first available ship from China to Vladivostok or to authorize their entrance into Dairen on unarmed US Government carrier out of Japan as soon as they are able to leave China with simultaneous exit permits and visas for Paddock and Gleysteen. If this approach meets with no success by August 15, we believe Department should then proceed without further delay to close office, at same time giving maximum publicity to Soviet restrictions which forced us to take step. Principal theme of such publicity should be that, following closely on heels of Mukden closure, US Government experience in Dairen constitutes impressive evidence of Soviet domination Manchuria and CCP complaisance.

For our own guidance would appreciate brief statement re Department reaction to this telegram, previous Embassy and Dairen telegrams on same subject.

Sent Department 1431; repeated Shanghai 795, Embassy Canton 607, Moscow 46, Dairen 40.

STUART

125.3516/7–649 : Telegram

The Consul at Dairen (Paddock) to the Secretary of State

DAIREN, July 6, 1949—3 p. m.
[Received July 9—4:25 a. m.]

201. Nanking telegram 1431, July 4, regarding Consulate difficulties obviously drafted after thoughtful review of Dairen telegrams

---

[38] Not printed; it reported that, since the Soviet Government would probably welcome the Consulate's departure from Dairen, the Embassy in Moscow considered it preferable to hold on as long as possible.

of past year.   Unfortunately Consulate seems to have failed empha-size to Embassy basic change in Consulate problems.   Until early spring Consulate difficulties primarily regarding couriers, supplies, replacements.   Now chief question if Consulate physically able op-erate even when courier service resumed and replacement arrives.

Protection of Chinese staff most important problem; Consulate anxious it not be neglected midst administrative problems of servicing or closing post (hence this telegram for consideration of Department re last paragraph Nanking telegram).   Consulate now unable assure staff slightest help if arrested.   Deptel 64, May 16 [*13*], has little application here regarding getting their release from police.

Clerk Chao and radio operator Chao live Consulate residence and rarely leave.   Yet police able enter any time to arrest them; this ex-pected eventually.   Meanwhile police terrorizing family of former and his son's mind affected after one course of police treatment. Contels 131, April 30 and 192, June 28.   Department's attention again drawn to his service of nearly 27 years and outstanding record when Japanese police pressure applied.

Urgency of replacement for radio operator Chao far more import-ant than for Americans.   USIS [39] promised he be replaced and leave Dairen by January 1 which was basis he willing come here.   Since up to this spring conditions similar to those of last couple years, promise could have been kept if proper arrangements had been made in advance to get his replacement here.   Interest of police in chauffeur Ma noted Contel 187, June 26.

Presumably Department also unable protect staff thru channels outside Dairen.

Plans to send additional personnel, as outlined Nanking telegram, need be expanded to assure office can be operated if Chinese staff resign or arrested.   American radio operator should be sent in addi-tion to American clerk.   Plans also should include utmost effort arrange departure of two Chaos when present Americans leave.

Other possible difficulties envisaged regarding Consulate operation next couple months:

(1) Exchange of dollars: Dealers already so frightened to buy Consulate dollars that getting local cy is constant problem;

(2) Access to press: Last couple weeks Consulate unable buy ga-zette of PA–Dairen administration.   Also delivery boy of *Shih Hua Daily* 2 days ago said he forbidden deliver paper to Consulate (deliv-ery however not yet stopped).   Such tactics also open to other two papers.

(3) Purchase of food and other supplies: Fear of merchants to deal with Americans (8 characters omitted).   Equally true in gov-ernment-owned stores.   See second paragraph Contel 139, May 7.[40]

---

[39] United States Information Service.
[40] Not printed.

(4) Insults: All ranks classes trained to be rude to Consulate personnel or else do so for self protection. Messenger has ceased wear Consulate uniform. Department should note that anti-American propaganda definitely success here.

(5) Servants: So far they not unduly troubled by police but always latent threat they become frightened and leave. Two already done so.

(6) Social isolation: Half dozen foreigners who still willing come Consulate residence are desperately trying leave Dairen. When they succeed, isolation of Consulate complete. Most information in Contels regarding local events derived from them. On their departure Consulate reduced to press and street observations for news sources. As mentioned, press may also be eliminated.

(7) Exit visas: Soviets now blandly claim police have sole jurisdiction over exit visas for foreigners. Consulate fears trouble regarding this when couriers arrive here.

(8) Telegrams: See paragraph 1 of Nanking telegram.

(9) Some manufactured publicity incident as at Mukden: US Government then would be on defensive when Consulate closed.

(10) Official contacts: There is no official, Soviet or CCP, to whom Consulate has access. In time of trouble Consulate unable negotiate with or channel its opinion to persons of responsibility.

Importance keep post at this strategic point obvious and Consulate sincerely hopes Department able solve present difficulties. It realized other posts in Communist China probably having parallel troubles or soon will, although various Embtels seem indicate exposed position of Dairen Consulate unique.

However, Consulate discouraged regarding present and future worth of this post. Its value cannot be restored until Department able enforce Soviets to allow workable conditions here including physical protection to Chinese staff. Otherwise it appears better to close Consulate on own initiative with dignity and then perhaps Chinese staff can be withdrawn.

Nevertheless closing office also will cause many problems as Mukden shows: Exit visas, Soviet visas via Vladivostok, transport on Soviet vessels including freight at exorbitant cost, and efforts take out Chinese staff. Only efficient and cheap means close Consulate is to send special ship here to remove all staff and large amount of good office and residence furniture.

Moscow telegram 27 to Dairen June 29,[41] not repeated Department, points out Soviet pleasure if Consulate closed. As yet Soviets may be unaware of extent of success of their pressure program. Thus, should Department decide close post, this situation might be exploited by Department in order to obtain favorable conditions for closing post including withdrawal of Chinese staff.

Sent Department 201, repeated Nanking 148, Moscow 112, Shanghai 166, Canton 87.

PADDOCK

---

[41] See footnote 38, p. 891.

123 Bacon, Leonard L. : Telegram

The Ambassador in China (Stuart) to the Secretary of State

NANKING, July 9, 1949—8 p. m.
[Received July 9—3 :27 p. m.]

1468. ReDeptel 794, July 7.[42] As may be readily verified by Embtel 1431, July 4, we hold fast as strongly as Department re necessity of relieving Paddock at Dairen and we are in complete agreement that Bacon is logical desirable replacement. However, as we pointed out in that telegram, responsibility for Bacon's difficulties in reaching Dairen rests squarely with Soviets and, as far as we know, their obstructionism is still unresolved. Bacon has still received no reply to his Soviet visa application for travel via Vladivostok. Consequently, until some assurances are forthcoming that Soviets will cooperate, we do not believe it is worth while for Bacon to initiate his travel at this stage.

As far as we are aware, there is no shipping service between either Hong Kong or Japan and Vladivostok or Dairen. Furthermore there is little reason to feel assured that CCP authorities in Dairen will permit Bacon to replace Paddock any more than they have permitted American consular replacements in other cities under their occupation. We believe there is good chance that if Bacon were to proceed to Hong Kong (or to Japan which is more promising takeoff point for his jump to Dairen), he would merely cool his heels there indefinitely.

Finally Bacon is vitally needed here during this critical period. As Department aware, Nanking staff has been reduced to bare minimum over period past 6 months by establishing Embassy Office Canton, normal attrition, and we unable to date to receive any replacements. Even those caught Shanghai en route here still unable obtain permits enter Nanking. We are therefore most reluctant to release any key personnel and Bacon's departure this time would be keenly felt. He has excellent command consular duties, his legal background has proven most valuable and, with incidents involving foreigners on increase, will be even more so. Furthermore, he is capable assuming supervisory functions administrative officer when Hinderer [43] departs and until latter's successor permitted enter Communist China (see Embtel 1467, July 9 [44]).

Unless Department has reasons unknown to Embassy to believe that Soviet visa can be shortly obtained, or if Department contemplates use of chartered merchant vessel or unarmed naval craft in attempt transport Bacon [to] Dairen direct from Japan, we urgently

---

[42] Not printed; it instructed the Ambassador to arrange transportation for Consul Bacon to Hong Kong to await further travel arrangements from there to Dairen.
[43] Harry A. Hinderer, Attaché of the Embassy at Nanking.
[44] Not printed.

request that Department reconsider its instruction re Bacon's departure and authorize us retain him until way for his travel is more open, if it ever opens at all, and until Department has given fuller study to reftel July 4.

As far as accommodations on plane are concerned, we could include Mr. and Mrs. Bacon on flight to Okinawa if desired, although with limited amount luggage for them and us all. I had already planned to take Cabot out with me and am delighted Department contemplates issuing him order for this flight. I have been in communication with him and will apply for his exit visa here on Monday.

Because of looting of Air Attaché plane during turn over, involving loss seats, safety equipment, passengers' accommodations C–47 limited. In consultation my Air Attaché, I had planned following passenger list out of Nanking in addition to myself, which I do not intend to enlarge unless Department directs otherwise:

(1) Consul General Cabot, (2) Attaché Hinderer, (3) personal secretary Fugh, (4) Air Attaché Colonel Dunning, (5) co-pilot Vanaus Dall, and crew of two.

Sent Department 1468, repeated Embassy Canton 616, Shanghai 818, Canton pouch Hong Kong 39.

STUART

---

123 Bacon, Leonard Lee: Telegram

The Secretary of State to the Ambassador in China (Stuart)

WASHINGTON, July 11, 1949—8 p. m.

814. Urtel 1468, July 9. Dept's intention in recommending departure Bacon and wife on plane with Amb (Deptel 794 July 7 [45]) was to explore possibility chartering merchant vessel for trip Dairen. If suitable vessel available (possibly SCAJAP [46] vessel from Japan), efforts arrange permission enter Dairen bringing new staff and supplies and evacuating Paddock, Gleysteen and certain of Chinese staff wld represent final effort maintain post at Dairen. In event these efforts fail, Dept will promptly give serious consideration closing Consulate Dairen and withdrawing all staff by most practicable means.

[Here follows recommendation regarding travel of Foreign Service personnel, including application of travel permit for Consul Bacon by way of Peiping.]

ACHESON

---

[45] Not printed.
[46] Shipping Control Administration, Japan.

893.00/7–2249 : Telegram

The Consul at Dairen (Paddock) to the Secretary of State

DAIREN, July 22, 1949—3 p. m.
[Received July 24—6:17 a. m.]

216. Radio operator Chao compelled attend 2-hour "meeting" yesterday obviously staged just to threaten him to register as reactionary (Contel 146, July 1, repeated Dept 199).

Police said American spies and running dogs of imperialism must register [(] these categories omitted in press) and must sign voluntarily by August 1 deadline, or be arrested.

All Consulate staff and servants refuse register as they realize it is against their interests.

Sent Nanking 160, repeated Department 216, Canton 96, Shanghai 173, Moscow 118.

PADDOCK

---

123 Gleysteen, Culver : Telegram

The Consul at Dairen (Paddock) to the Secretary of State

DAIREN, July 22, 1949—4 p. m.
[Received July 24—6:59 a. m.]

217. One of the five persons with whom Consulate has cordial relations rumored arrested week ago and people who called his house turned away by police. Past evening I asked Gleysteen go there verify rumor man had returned home.

Police admitted Gleysteen, took his identification papers (retained only with difficulty) and took him under guard to district police station (branch of Port Arthur–Dairen Executive Administration). There he was treated insultingly and police refused recognize his official position (calling him merely "overseas American["]) and refused let him telephone American Consulate. Fortunately in 15 minutes telephone instructions received by police from superiors and Gleysteen released.

I wrote Chief of Civil Administration today protesting this treatment by police agents of Soviet authorities as violation international law in line with Deptel 273 to Moscow April 28, repeated Nanking 531.

Sent Nanking 161, repeated Department, Nanking 97, Shanghai 174, Moscow 119.

PADDOCK

123 Gleysteen, Culver : Telegram

The Consul at Dairen (Paddock) to the Secretary of State

DAIREN, August 1, 1949—3 p. m.
[Received August 2—9:59 p. m.]

227. Last information regarding communication to Soviet Foreign Office re Gleysteen detention was Moscow's 1490 to Department, repeated Nanking 65.[47] Consulate wonders if any new development regarding this matter.

Sent Department 227, repeated Moscow 121, Nanking 164.

PADDOCK

123 Bacon, Leonard Lee : Telegram

The Counselor of Embassy in China (Jones) to the Secretary of State

NANKING, August 4, 1949.
[Received August 4—4:27 p. m.]

1712. Re Deptel 479, July 23 [22][48]. Bacon's application exit permit via Tientsin, destination Dairen by way of Tokyo, filed August 3. Application received for consideration only. Statement made that foreigners travel Nanking–Tientsin not yet authorized. Similar statement made to AMilAt[49] Beebe August 1.

Sent Department 1712 repeated Peiping 317 Dairen 46.

JONES

123 Gleysteen, Culver : Telegram

The Ambassador in the Soviet Union (Kirk) to the Secretary of State

Moscow, August 6, 1949—2 p. m.
[Received August 6—10:16 a. m.]

1966. Embassy has not received reply its note June 9 to Soviet Foreign Office re Gleysteen (Dairen's 121, August 2, sent Department as 227[50]) nor does it expect reply unless possibly as result further note specifically reiterating request assurances re treatment US Consular officers mentioned last sentence June 9 note. However, should be pointed out that maximum to be expected in event request for assurances were repeated would be Soviet reply to effect that of course they treat foreign consuls accordance generally accepted standards in usage as long as consuls act properly within scope legitimate duties, et cetera, with implication Gleysteen was not so acting.

[47] Dated June 9, 5 p.m., p. 885.
[48] Not printed.
[49] Office of Military Attaché in China.
[50] August 1, above.

If Consulate Dairen to be closed soon with accompanying publicity re treatment our staff, it might be well to leave matters stand as they are, i.e. with Soviet Foreign Office having failed to give assurances requested. A second note revealing our continued interest in treatment Consulate Dairen would probably be interpreted by Soviets as indicating our intention stay Dairen and "fight it out". Such interpretation might lend [lead] Soviets and their Chinese Communist friends to make position of our Consulate more untenable than ever and thus endeavor force closing Consulate under humiliating conditions.

Though this Embassy has felt in past that pleasure which closing our Dairen Consulate would afford Soviets was good reason persist in maintenance Consulate, we now believe that since overall situation China will probably force us close down Dairen sooner or later in any event, we should seriously consider whether present time not most propitious for graceful exit on basis failure receive Soviet assurances.

Sent Department 1966; repeated Dairen 28, Nanking 86.

KIRK

125.3513/8–1349 : Telegram

The Consul at Dairen (Paddock) to the Secretary of State

DAIREN, August 13, 1949—1 p. m.
[Received August 13—7:21 a. m.]

240. Concern of Consulate for departure of radio operator Chao and clerk Chao and family emphasized previous telegrams.

Situation now is Soviet transit visas through Vladivostok applied for but not expected. Consulate has taken all preparations which were taken June 1948 for departure of former radio operator who also of Chinese nationality.

Consulate told Soviets that Consulate is planning for Chaos go with next couriers through Vladivostok and not await replacements. Soviets possibly let them go just to reduce office efficiency but this not counted on.

Best chance for them go is by one of freighters, Contel 167, August 5, repeated Department 232.[51] Consulate intends asking Tokyo, Seoul, Manila to rearrange passage for them on freighter calling here. Consulate will then make all possible efforts get them away. Similar efforts if special ship diverted here with couriers Bangkok, telegram 699 to Department August 9,[51] not repeated Nanking. If departure prevented, it will be on basis Chinese police refuse exit

---

[51] Not printed.

permits. Same time it assured Soviets will disclaim all responsibility re such permits, Contel 154, repeated Department 207, July 11. Soviets already have made similar assertion re police action in various incidents affecting Consulate.

Before beginning affair of two Chaos, Consulate would appreciate following information from Embassy or Department:

1. Is Consulate's opinion correct that Soviets are in fact still responsible, from US Government viewpoint, in event two Chaos not allowed leave Dairen after passage arranged?

2. If opinion correct, is there any form of help or pressure which Embassy or Department able exert to enable them leave later (whenever passage again arranged)?

3. Is American Consulate position in Dairen sufficiently analogous to Soviet Mission in Japan to justify and warrant pressure in that direction (such as on arrival and departure of Soviet personnel and courier visitors)?

Soviets contend Dairen is subject to military control pending Japanese peace treaty, hence American Consulate must submit to Soviet military regulations. US also in military occupation of Japan until peace treaty and Soviets there presumably obliged abide by military regulations. It would seem that if Consulate personnel prevented move in and out of "free port" of Dairen similar restrictions could be applied to Soviets [in] Japan.

It realized Embassy and Department may not wish express opinion these points until proven two Chaos unable leave Dairen. However, same points are important re couriers as police may possibly refuse allow them land at Dairen if they do not come via Vladivostok, that is, if they come on diverted vessel or commercial ship such as in Tokyo telegram 276 to Department August 4 [5][52] not repeated Nanking. If such situation develops, no time telegraph Department. Hence it seems advisable for Consulate receive reaction of Embassy and Department now to points raised this telegram. Consulate then able avoid incorrect action if difficulties develop re two Chaos or couriers or both.

Sent Nanking 172; repeated Department, Moscow 12.

PADDOCK

---

123 Bacon, Leonard Lee : Telegram

The Counselor of Embassy in China (Jones) to the Secretary of State

NANKING, August 13, 1949—3 p. m.
[Received August 13—8:32 a. m.]

1777. As reported Embtel 1712, August 4, Bacon complied with recommendation made in Deptel 814, July 11 for him to apply for

---

[52] Not printed.

travel permits himself and wife to proceed Tientsin as first leg on journey to Dairen. This application has met with no success. Alien Affairs Office August 12 again indicated his exit from Nanking must be through Shanghai and stated that no permits are being granted foreigners for overland travel from Shanghai area to North China. To Embassy's best knowledge, no such permits have been granted. Difficulties confronting foreigners attempting leave China via Shanghai are, of course, already well known.

It being apparent that this effort has failed, we suggest Department now give serious consideration closing Consulate Dairen and withdrawing all staff by most practicable means as stated in Department's reference telegram. In this connection, we refer also to Moscow telegram 1966, August 6 to Department which suggests that now may be more propitious time to close Consulate Dairen.

We further refer to Depinfotel August 8 [54] which reports that four tankers, presumably either American or British, are now en route Dairen from Constanza. If Consulate is to be closed, we suggest that cheap and effective way to withdraw Paddock and Gleysteen would be on board one of these vessels.

Sent Department 1777, repeated Shanghai 982, Canton 744, Moscow 56, Dairen 49.

Pass Peiping 328.

JONES

---

123 Gleysteen, Culver: Telegram

The Consul at Dairen (Paddock) to the Secretary of State

DAIREN, August 13, 1949—4 p. m.
[Received August 14—3:04 a. m.]

242. Consulate agrees with Moscow Embassy's reasons against pressing for answer from Soviet Foreign Office regarding Gleysteen detention (Moscow telegram 1966 to Department, repeated Nanking 86, August 6).

However, while subject still alive, it well point out that as result series of unpleasant incidents, Consulate officers now hesitate go outside two-square-mile area bounded by residence, office and main shopping district. Any movement outside threatens difficulties with Soviets (whose military activities throughout Dairen peninsula continue) and with Chinese police (for whose actions Soviet disclaim responsibility).

Only exception is main road to Fukusho public beach; auto also has been stopped for examination on this road but without irritating incident.

Sent Nanking 174; repeated Department 242, Moscow 130.

PADDOCK

---

[54] Not printed.

125.351/8–1949 : Telegram

The Ambassador in the Soviet Union (Kirk) to the Secretary of State

Moscow, August 19, 1949—4 p. m.
[Received August 19—12 :32 p. m.]

2093. If Department decides close Dairen (Nanking's 1777, August 13 to Department), Embassy strongly assumes that our actions this respect will be carefully planned with view to (1) minimum impairment US dignity and prestige; and (2) maximum public and diplomatic exploitation reasons for our withdrawal to disadvantage Soviet and Chinese Communists. Embassy believes achievement these ends could be accomplished by notification to Soviet Foreign Office at appropriate time US decision close Consulate on account unreasonable and onerous restrictions and vexations imposed by Soviet-dominated regime (including pertinent details) and failure Soviet Government give assurances requested in Embassy note June 9 (Embtel 1490, June 9) that our consular staff would be treated in accordance international law and practice. Our note should be given full publicity in due course.

Embassy also recommends that serious consideration be given to use US naval vessel for physical withdrawal consular staff and effects and that our intention to dispatch such vessel this purpose be included in proposed note Soviet Foreign Office. Evacuation by this means would not only have advantages from standpoint US dignity and prestige but would also simplify otherwise difficult transportation problems. It might also enable US save faithful alien employees from unhappy fate at hands Chinese Communists.

It might be well inform Soviets that use naval vessel necessary to obviate "well-known difficulties and delays now prevailing with respect to ordinary means of travel into and out of Dairen area." Whether Soviets would place obstacles in way implementation such plan problematical. Although last request for permission send courier Dairen US naval vessel turned down by Soviet Foreign Office on ground alternative facilities via Vladivostok available (Embtel 2751, November 27, 1948 [55]) Soviets would this time have difficulty suggesting feasible alternatives and furthermore might view final "withdrawal" voyage in different light from previous requests for periodic courier service. If Soviets should flatly refuse permit vessel enter Port Dairen, arrangement off-shore embarkation similar that which took place on withdrawal mission from Albania in 1946 might be feasible.

Sent Department 2093, repeated Dairen 31, Nanking 90.

KIRK

---

[55] *Foreign Relations*, 1948, vol. VII, p. 805.

893.111/8–2549 : Telegram

The Consul at Dairen (Paddock) to the Secretary of State

DAIREN, August 25, 1949—4 p. m.
[Received August 27—5 :16 a. m.]

252. Chinese police refused exit permits to 11 Germans and 1 Italian listed Tokyo telegram 76 [*276*] to Department,[56] repeated Berlin only. SS *Harpalycus* sailed yesterday.

Group made determined efforts get permits. Soviets insisted that although they willing for group to go decision lay with Chinese police. Only reason given by Chinese police for refusal was that they had not yet investigated Dairen foreigners enough.

For parallel case of only foreigner allowed so far to leave, see Contel 154 to Nanking, July 11, repeated Department 207,[57] Moscow 116, Tokyo 18.

Department might consider advisability suggesting that Italian Ambassador at Moscow protest detention his national here—Carlo Polesello, Italian passenger, No. 746188–P issued April 21 last year by Italian CG,[58] Shanghai, address Valletri 24, Rome.

Tripartite agreement June 25 (authorizing French Embassy, Nanking, to document and handle other questions affecting repatriation of Germans from China to Western Germany) may not be sufficient basis for French Ambassador at Moscow to query refusal of Soviets to allow these Germans to leave for Western Germany. However, situation would seem warrant such query at least in Berlin.

Note that passage on *Harpalycus* already paid Dairen to Liverpool, exit visas through UK arranged, and each of Germans possessed proper document to enter Western Germany. All details thus settled but still they not allowed leave.

Year and half ago Soviets told these and other foreigners they could leave Dairen whenever transport arranged. When Soviets turned over exit permits to Chinese police last May, each member this group again made proper application to that office but no answer received.

Consulate is not sending this telegram in behalf of this group. Matter has direct bearing on Contel 172 to Nanking, August 12, repeated Department 240, Moscow 128 re Consulate plans for departure its alien employees and re possible complications re courier entry and departure.

Also pertinent that Soviets seem be trying hard make Chinese in Dairen, and perhaps in China generally, believe that Chinese, not Soviets, are administering Dairen. Yet all evidence verifies Soviet

---

[56] Dated August 5, not printed.
[57] Not printed.
[58] Consul General.

domination all phases Dairen life. Depending on Department's answer to Contel last paragraph, is perhaps worth while to emphasize whenever possible Soviet responsibility for Dairen.

It should be difficult for Soviets to justify their refusal (that is, of their agents, the police) to let this group foreigners leave despite previous Soviet promises they could go when transportation available.

Sent Department; repeated Nanking 181, Moscow 134, Tokyo 3, Berlin unnumbered.

PADDOCK

125.3513/8–2849 : Telegram

The Consul at Dairen (Paddock) to the Secretary of State

DAIREN, August 28, 1949—4 p. m.
[Received August 29—6:22 a. m.]

257. Person believed to be at Soviet Kommandatura telephoned yesterday to say Soviets not responsible Chinese police. This was answer to Consulate's letter last paragraph Contel 161 to Nanking, July 22, repeated Department 217. I stated Consulate unable accept telephone call as reply and requested letter giving whatever information desired.

Regardless if such letter received, Consulate anxious for Department to reply Contel 172 to Nanking, repeated Department 240, August 12[*13*].

Sent Department 257, repeated Nanking 183.

PADDOCK

125.351/9–149 : Telegram

The Secretary of State to the Consul at Dairen (Paddock) [59]

WASHINGTON, September 1, 1949—noon.

131. Dept has reached decision to close Consulate at Dairen as soon as necessary arrangements can be made. No publication yet being given to closure therefore you shld not make closure known to other than yourself and Gleysteen.

Dept is particularly anxious that all possible measures be taken to assure the departure of loyal Chi employees and their families simultaneously with the Amers. Propose if possible transfer Chi staff including radio operator to other China post. However, give no promise continued employment after evacuation. Could Chi staff be evacuated before announcement made of closing.

---

[59] Repeated to the Ambassador in the Soviet Union as telegram No. 613.

Inform Dept possibility obtaining exit visas for Chi and Amer staff, transportation facilities available, proposed routes of travel, whether difficulties anticipated obtaining exit visas for Chi staff, recommendations on possibilities selling, evacuation or storing Govt-owned property. View cost evacuating Govt property do not anticipate evacuation property where evacuation cost exceeds value property. What do you recommend on Brit interest Dairen.

Courier not being sent Dairen. Inform Bangkok disposition desired mail supplies held for Dairen.

Closing instrs will fol soonest after receipt ur recommendations.

Sent Dairen. Rptd Nanking, Shanghai, OffEmb-Canton, Moscow, Tokyo, Bangkok.

ACHESON

125.351/9–149 : Telegram

The Secretary of State to the Ambassador in the United Kingdom (Douglas)

WASHINGTON, September 1, 1949—6 p. m.

3154. Inform FonOff Dairen and Hankow Consulates have been ordered closed. No public announcement by Dept of closing Dairen at present. Will announce closing Hankow as soon as formal reply from Brit (Deptel 3067 Aug 26 [60]) received.

AmCon Dairen now has custody Brit Con there. Also paying salaries caretakers. Ask FonOff what disposition should be made Brit interests by AmCon upon closing his office.

ACHESON

120.34 Transportation/9–349 : Telegram

The Consul at Dairen (Paddock) to the Secretary of State

DAIREN, September 3, 1949—2 p.m.
[Received September 3—11 :05 p.m.]

262. ReDeptel 131, September 2 [*1*], repeated Moscow 613.
1. Transportation facilities:

(a) Soviet ship to Vladivostok, thence Soviet plane to Tokyo or trans-Siberia to Moscow or Soviet ship. Plane ordinarily difficult due our possibly large party and personal effects. Cost exorbitant. No Soviet ship now out of Vladivostok as shown by courier difficulties. No Government-owned property worth sending via Vladivostok.

(b) One of foreign freighters calling here under Soviet charter. Impossible for Consul see captain arrange passage. No time for representatives to try contact ship before arrival and not certain Soviets

---

[60] Not printed.

even then allow our departure on it. Soviets however may allow it if it is made part of any discussions with them re closing posts.

(c) Diversion special ship by Department. This is cheapest due size party and considerable amount good pieces office and house furniture and equipment for use by American post at first port of call. Whether Soviets able prevent such ship is not known.

2. Department please inform if confidential files should be destroyed or taken, also non-confidential files.

3. Due lack funds Consulate must sell jeep with trailer, Oldsmobile, transmitter, radios, coal supply, in order close office properly. Please authorize. No other inventory items to be sold due bad market.

4. If we go via Vladivostok, Moscow must arrange pay all our expenses there as we will arrive without funds.

5. Moscow Embassy should arrange *laissez passer* for Americans take personal effects out at Dairen and in and out of Vladivostok without examination; also for Soviets to recognize us as couriers (Consulate will issue courier letter).

6. Regardless transport used, Consulate will take out effects of British couriers and assume British Government will pay costs but Department please verify Consulate should do this.

Deptel garbled; if additional information requested Consulate will answer after request.

Sent Department 262, repeated Moscow 140, Nanking 188.

PADDOCK

120.34 Transportation/9–549 : Telegram

The Consul at Dairen (Paddock) to the Secretary of State

DAIREN, September 5, 1949—6 p. m.
[Received September 5—1 :37 a. m.]

263. This continues immediately preceding telegram.

7. Chinese staff consists clerk Chao Shou-yu [with] no family, clerk Chao Yi-hsien with family of 5, messenger Lee Yun-ssu [with] no family, chauffeur Ma Hing-hwa with family of 5. Thus 14 Chinese and 2 Americans (not known if Lee and Ma will wish go).

8. All Chinese without passports except [Chao] Shou-yu who has expired Chinese passport. He and [Chao] Yi-hsien family have new passports in courier mail but these, of course, cannot now be received. These all must use some sort certificate which Soviets will recognize in lieu of passport.

9. Without couriers to accompany them, sufficient funds or passports, it useless now try get Chinese out ahead of Americans.

10. Soviet transit visa through Vladivostok for both Chinese and Americans, delays and difficulties are well known.

11. Re exit visa from Dairen, if decision is left to Chinese police, answer will be refusal re our Chinese staff (and possibly also for Americans). Local Soviets will not override that refusal unless instructed by Moscow.

12. Thus Consulate believes best if closing of Consulate first broached to Soviets at Washington or Moscow. Consulate will then inform local Soviets re closing and will apply for exit visas. However, Consulate should know type of transport to be used and how exit visas requested.

[13.] Specifically we want from Soviets:

(*a*) Permission leave Dairen on whatever transport Department selects.
(*b*) Exit visa for all staff who wish leave.
(*c*) Recognition of certificate in lieu of passport for Chinese.
(*d*) *Laissez-passer* to avoid customs examination for Americans.
(*e*) Recognition Americans as couriers.
(*f*) Transit visas through Vladivostok if we go that route.

14. Consulate is unable suggest effective approach to Soviets to ensure we receive all of above. Problem of exit visas described Contel 172, August 12,[61] repeated Moscow 128. Background of Soviet military occupation of Dairen given Deptel 49 to Moscow January [*February*] 1.[62]

15. Closure of this Consulate may receive much publicity on basis isolation of Consulate, cooperation of Soviets, and exposed position of Consulate staff. Although propaganda along these lines effective in US and non-Communist Asia, it is uncertain if Soviet Government will consider issue important.

16. However, Soviet position with Chinese public possibly hurt by propaganda emphasizing their anomalous position, Dairen:

(*a*) Military occupation due no Jap treaty.
(*b*) Diplomatic relations with Nationalist China but no Nationalist officials allowed here.
(*c*) Status of its Port Arthur–Dairen Executive Administration never explained. Some of its officials are in Northeast people's government. Communist Party and other local organizations are mere branches of parent bodies in NE.
(*d*) Soviets try make local populace believe this administration ruling Dairen and disclaim all responsibility out [*about*] such things as exit visas.
(*e*) Yet Soviet civil administration office unchanged and no decreases in Soviet personnel. When Soviets give order, officials of Executive Administration obey. Whatever friction may develop from this situation, currently it is accepted.

17. Closing of Consulate affects paragraph 16 [garbled group]. If visas refused to Chinese staff, it would seem Department has legitimate

[61] Not found in Department of State files.
[62] See telegram No. 11, February 1, noon, to the Consul at Dairen, p. 861.

basis for publicizing points in that paragraph. It thus appears to Soviet advantage to "persuade" Chinese police issue visas and arrange for all staff leave Dairen quietly. If Department believes this line of reasoning correct, it may provide arguable point with Soviets in arranging these visas.

18. Consulate hopes Department can arrange in 10 days the two problems of type of transport to be used and exit visas for Chinese staff.

19. Basis of Consulate desire for haste is recognition by Soviets of CCP soon as central government organized. Perhaps Department aware this not imminent but locally it constantly [apparent omission]. Since Chinese Communists regard Dairen as extension of Manchuria, we expect be kept in quarters after Soviet recognition of CCP same as apparently done to Mukden Consulate. As our provisions are exhausted and we bankrupt, we foresee long difficult period before Department arranges our departure. Since decision now made to close Consulate, we anxious leave before such recognition.

20. Moscow telegram 2093, August 19 should be given careful consideration. If Soviets hesitate to arrange for Chinese police to issue exit visas for our passportless Chinese staff, it is possible they could be persuaded do so if pointed out that without encumbrance of Chinese staff Department is much freer to arrange evacuation of Americans either by special diverted freighter or by naval vessel. If naval vessel of adequate size used, it could have useful propaganda effect not only here but throughout Manchuria.

Sent Department 263, repeated Nanking 189, Moscow 141.

PADDOCK

125.351/9–849 : Telegram

The Consul at Dairen (Paddock) to the Secretary of State

DAIREN, September 8, 1949—11 a. m.
[Received 9 :54 p. m.]

276. Events past 2 days eliminate time margin for selecting most suitable method for withdrawal Consulate staff, propaganda effect, etc.

Contel 272, September 6 [63] described projected change in status Dairen City. If this occurs before staff gets away, closure possibly not effected for many months.

When restraint placed on local CCP by Soviet diplomatic requirement is removed, Consulate will be as exposed as Mukden Consulate.

---

[63] Not printed; it reported possibility of Dairen's detachment administratively from the rest of the Kwantung area which would affect the city's international status (893.00/9–649).

Lack supplies and funds plus precedent of long record unpleasant incidents, in which helplessness of Consulate proved, are expected make Consulate position worse than Mukden Consulate. Nothing in experience Mukden to indicate Department can arrange departure of staff quickly under such conditions.

Either due announcement of change in Dairen City or merely as another recurring wave, another series petty incidents involving Consulate with Chinese police began 2 days ago.

Consulate began efforts sell jeep as it is most saleable item without awaiting Department authorization. So far, limited circle who able buy it afraid even discuss purchase with American Consulate. Perhaps sale possible later but this factor re difficulties heretofore not realized as so serious.

Thus Consulate needs to insist on last minute Department arranging departure of Consulate staff (Contels 262, and 263, September 3). No couriers here since April 1. Problem of closing Consulate before Department for several months. Situation now such that Department has no alternative but to act immediately and decisively.

In past Moscow Embassy often hampered by difficulty in getting appointment with responsible Soviet official. Accordingly, Consulate recommends Department itself take up problem of departure of Dairen staff at most effective level in Washington within 24 hours after receipt this telegram.

Until notified to contrary by Department, Consulate will plan on Department arranging for Consulate staff to leave Dairen by Soviet ship to Vladivostok, by foreign freighter under Soviet charter (couple such ships in harbor now including Panamanian which has not yet begun unload), by specially chartered vessel from Korea, by specially diverted freighter, or by naval vessel within 10 days.

As Department has now decided to close Consulate and since announcement made of reorganization of Dairen City administration, Department should not postpone, for any reason whatever, departure of Consulate staff.

PADDOCK

125.351/9–949 : Telegram

The Ambassador in the Soviet Union (Kirk) to the Secretary of State

Moscow, September 9, 1949—6 p. m.
[Received September 9—1:59 p. m.]

2255. Reference Department's decision close Consulate Dairen (Deptel 613, September 1 [64]), Embassy suggests that as alternative

---

[64] Same as telegram No. 131 to Dairen, p. 903.

use naval vessel for evacuation personnel and effects (Embtel 2093, August 19) consideration be given despatch one or more planes for this purpose. Since use military planes less likely receive Soviet approval, perhaps arrangements could be made charter commercial plane or planes.

Embassy notes Dairen funds virtually exhausted (Dairen's 256, August 29 to Department [65]) and wonders whether as precautionary measure advantage should not be taken of recent Soviet offer provide air transportation couriers Tokyo–Vladivostok (Deptel 605, August 30 [65]) prior to making any public or formal move re closing Dairen. This would ensure availability funds during what might be protracted period of negotiations re evacuation personnel and would also enable carefully selected courier (preferably a Russian area expert like McSweeney) to make survey Dairen situation in consultation with Paddock and Gleysteen who have been working under handicap of almost complete isolation from outside world for more than year. Upon completion this task, courier could proceed Tokyo or other appropriate post to act as principal field coordinator in implementation evacuation plan. Principal courier might be accompanied by assistant qualified in technical aspects air transportation if that means evacuation to be given serious consideration. Embassy recognizes that round-trip couriers might take several weeks and thus appear delay closing Consulate, but from standpoint funds and morale Dairen courier project might well be indispensable preliminary evacuation.

Embassy agrees with Dairen that only by pressure on Soviet Foreign Office (Dairen's 263, September 3 [5] to Department) is there any likelihood obtaining exit visas for Chinese employees Consulate and is prepared to raise this question when Department authorizes transmission note Soviet Foreign Office re closing Dairen (Embtel 2093). This connection Embassy would appreciate fullest information re length service with US Government of Chinese employees, posts at which service rendered and post to which Soviet may be told employees are being transferred. Even though transfer only hypothetical, suggest choice Hong Kong for obvious reasons. Re chauffeur and messenger (Dairen's 263 to Department), Embassy seriously doubts wisdom trying to evacuate these locally employed Chinese who presumably are long time residents Dairen. To include them may jeopardize possibility obtaining exit visas for the Chaos, who present much better case and to whom Embassy understands certain commitments were made at the time their assignment Dairen.

Sent Department 2255, repeated Dairen 33, Nanking 96, Tokyo 37, Hong Kong 2.

KIRK

---

[65] Not printed.

125.351/9–849 : Telegram

The Secretary of State to the Ambassador in the Soviet Union
(Kirk) [66]

WASHINGTON, September 9, 1949—9 p. m.

635. Dairen tel 276 Sept 8 to Dept being rptd separately to you urges immed action re closing Consulate and withdrawal staff in view expected change in status Dairen city, which if carried out prior withdrawal staff wld probably greatly complicate problem.

Pls convey personally message along fol lines Vyshinsky [67] or in his absence Acting FonMin.

Owing to obstacles to functioning US consulate Dairen, including extreme difficulty or impossibility effecting transfers personnel, maintaining courier service, sending supplies and funds, US Govt has instructed Consul Paddock Dairen close consulate and withdraw immed with staff from Dairen. In view this decision US Govt requests Sov Govt instruct officials Dairen facilitate closing office departure staff.

Specifically US Govt requests Sov cooperation in issuance exit permits Consul Paul Paddock, Vice Consul Culver Gleysteen, and Chi members staff of consulate. Consul Paddock and Vice Consul Gleysteen will travel as couriers and will be provided with identification as such. It is assumed that their personal and official baggage will be exempt from customs examination. Chi staff members referred to above will fol[lowing] their departure from Dairen be assigned other Amer consular posts. Those not possessing valid Chi passports owing difficulty communications with Dairen will be provided by Consulate Dairen with suitable identifying documents in lieu passports.

With respect transportation facilities from Dairen, US Govt wld appreciate being informed as matter of urgency whether Sov Govt prefers Consul Paddock and staff depart by means of (*a*) Sov vessel, (*b*) fon vessel under Sov charter, or (*c*) unarmed US Govt vessel. If departure by means (*a*) or (*b*) it is requested Sov Govt make necessary arrangements immed and if vessel proceeding via Vladivostok or other Sov port, that Sov Govt issue appropriate transit visas, *laissez passers* and courier lists. If departure by means (*b*) it suggested Panamanian vessel under Sov charter now reportedly in Dairen be used.

Owing urgency and importance which it attaches this matter, Dept considers it desirable that Amb deliver message along foregoing lines soonest and press for immed reply. If Amb unable obtain appointment or if other evidence Sov stalling, pls inform Dept at once in order that Dept can convey similar message to Sov Amb Wash.[68]

ACHESON

---

[66] Repeated to the Consul at Dairen as telegram No. 137.
[67] A. Ya. Vyshinsky, Soviet Minister for Foreign Affairs.
[68] A. S. Panyushkin.

125.351/9–1049 : Telegram

The Secretary of State to the Consul at Dairen (Paddock)

WASHINGTON, September 10, 1949—2 p. m.

138. ReDeptel 131, Sept 2 [1]. Fol instrs for guidance closing ur post.

Auth[orized] evacuate or sell motor vehicles, typewriters and other office machines, office and household furniture. Deposit proceeds sale passenger-carrying vehicles special deposit Acct 19F5796, proceeds trucks, jeeps, typewriters, other office machines Acct 1906690, proceeds other items Misc Receipts Acct 195196. If unable evacuate or sell auth place custody friendly fon power US Govt property left behind. Inform Dept re this. Dept doubts advisability evacuation large pieces furniture equipment since evacuation costs probably greater than value property.

In ur discretion, evacuate or destroy seals, stamps, blank passports, blank certificates identity registration, fee stamps, crypto material, stationery bearing official insignia, letterheads, files and archives. Furnish Dept certificates on items destroyed. Evacuate all accts, especially those not cleared GAO for protection clearance financial responsibilities.

Auth evacuate Chi staff imported to Dairen and such other loyal local employees whose life wld be endangered and otherwise jeopardized by remaining Dairen result working for Cons. However, Dept believes preferable personnel employed locally Dairen might be discharged there. For employees discharged, make lump sum payments accordance FSRegs. Auth make severance payments local employees based local custom, i.e., severance payment approx 2 or 3 months salary those discharged; no lump sum or severance payments payable those evacuated. Dept will attempt place evacuated Chi employees Taipei or Hongkong. Tel Dept soonest names local employees being evacuated and possible destinations.

To enable you refund Civil Service retirement deductions plus interest immed to local employees being discharged, tel full name each employee carried on payroll followed by gross dollar amt retirement deductions Dec 26, 1948 through probable date separation. Dept will compute total deduction and interest for period service and inform by tel amt to be refunded by post. Full instrs for payment by post accordance FSS 726, Aug 21, 1947 will be given when payment auth. State n[umbe]r years service for each local employee and indicate if additional service credit purchased.

As of date post officially closed furnish Dept, if possible, form FS–354 reporting departure personnel, termination allowances ur post; submit that time statement unobligated balances remaining each allotment by object class for withdrawal by Dept.

Maintain radio contact until departure; if impossible evacuate radio, destruction auth. Do not permit radio equipment fall into Commie hands intact.

[In] view shortage funds ur post cld Dept transfer needed amts for local needs by tel through local bank or Moscow bank. If necessary and feasible, inform Dept amt to be transferred. Also inform Dept need for funds at Vladivostok or other port entry after departure Dairen so that Dept can arrange transfer funds to you that point if necessary.

Charge expenses closing office allotment OA–223043 (and OM–423043 for any USIE payments) except lump sum payments, refund retirement deductions, severance pay local employees. Use local employee salary allotment for lump sum and severance payments. Allotment for refund CS retirement deductions will be given after receipt urtel giving amts deductions requested above.

TO's covering consultation Dept Paddock Gleysteen being telegraphed separately however do not delay departure awaiting orders.

If unable follow completely above procedure, auth proceed most feasible means close office ur discretion.

Keep Dept informed and indicate when last message sent.

Inform Nanking names destinations local employees to be evacuated so that Nanking can issue evacuation TO's.

If possible, ascertain tel Dept next destination Panamanian vessel in port. If SCAP [69] clearance forthcoming immed cld German refugees depart this or other vessel?

Sent Dairen, repeated Moscow, Nanking.

ACHESON

125.351/9–1049 : Telegram

The Ambassador in the Soviet Union (Kirk) to the Secretary of State

Moscow, September 10, 1949—8 p. m.
[Received September 10—3 :19 p. m.]

2274. Handed note on Dairen Consulate to Vyshinsky at 2005 (urtel 635, September 9) and explained briefly its contents. Emphasized clearly our desire for prompt reply and importance we attached to Soviet action, which Vyshinsky acknowledged as evident by my personal intervention. He assured me matter would be dealt with as rapidly as possible, and that he would avail himself of my offer to come personally to receive their answer.

KIRK

---

[69] Supreme Commander, Allied Powers in Japan (MacArthur).

125.353/9–1449 : Telegram

The Consul at Dairen (Paddock) to the Secretary of State

DAIREN, September 14, 1949—6 p. m.
[Received September 16—3 :47 a. m.]

289. Consulate informed Chinese staff today re closing post but instructed them not repeat this information (except for this and landlord's agent no publicity given by Consulate re closing).

It verified that Chao Yi-hsien and Chao Shou-yu definitely want go with us.

Talks with chauffeur and messenger indicated they probably able withdraw into general Chinese population without too serious difficulty with police. Hence, Consulate did not suggest possibility of their evacuation. They will be discharged upon closing post.

Moscow telegram 2255, September 9 to Department received only today. Following points in reply to last paragraph: Chao Yi-hsien employed 1922 by American Consulate Antung which closed 1927. Next year he employed Dairen Consulate, remaining until now. Thus, approximately 27 years (minus war years when Consulate closed). Consul Chase [70] in special despatch cited [him for his?] able work when post under considerable pressure by Japanese police. After Americans repatriated he was in Japanese jail long time.

Chao Shou-yu has worked for USIS since war in Shanghai and was transferred here on basis of being replaced within 6 months.

Sent Dept 289. Dept pass Moscow 156, Nanking 202.

PADDOCK

125.3513/9–1649 : Telegram

The Consul at Dairen (Paddock) to the Secretary of State

DAIREN, September 16, 1949—3 p. m.
[Received September 18—4 :10 a. m.]

290. Last night 7 p. m. Chinese police from station for this residence area summoned clerk Chao Yi-hsien accompany them. I did not learn of this until 2 hours later and then sent Gleysteen to police station to inquire reasons for police action. Police told him they had asked Chao few questions and released him before 8 p. m.

However, Chao has not returned. It is assumed he is in hands of police, whether Soviet or Chinese not known.

This morning I sent letter to Chief of Soviet Civil Administration asking on what grounds Chao detained. I urgently requested reply today by letter or interview. However, only reply was telephone call

---

[70] Augustus Sabin Chase, Consul at Dairen, 1939–December 7, 1941.

by junior officer who said chief refused both letter and interview and merely insisted matter for Chinese police without Soviet responsibility.

I have written saying Consulate cannot accept telephone call as official reply and again requesting letter in reply or interview. Deptel 64, May 13 designed for emergency of Chao arrest was commented on in Contel 201, July 6.

Consul unable suggest action to secure Chao release as Soviets acting on direct orders Moscow or else will not release him except on such instructions. It is feared if arrest is not protested effectively and immediately Soviets will be in still better position to prevent evacuation of radio operator Chao Shou-yu.

Sent Department. Department pass Nanking 203, Moscow.

PADDOCK

125.3513/9–1649 : Telegram

The Consul at Dairen (*Paddock*) *to the Secretary of State*

DAIREN, September 16, 1949—4 p. m.
[Received September 18—4:50 a. m.]

291. Re immediately preceding telegram re arrest Chao Yi-hsien.

Contel 240, August 12 [*13*], asking Department's opinion as to Soviet-Chinese police relations, not answered. See also Contels 252, August 25 and 257, August 28.

In event of interview with Chief of Civil Administration, I shall say it is Consulate's opinion Soviets are responsible for all actions against American Consulate whether carried out by Soviets or through Chinese police. Latter regarded as branch of Soviet administration. Last Soviet statement re Dairen known to Consulate is that Soviets will remain in military occupation of Dairen until Japanese treaty. Deference to Soviet authority in Dairen City itself evident from presence of Soviet troops, Kommandatura and civil administration. Soviet relations with Nationalist China unchanged as Soviet Embassy still in Canton and Soviet ConGen continues functioning in Dairen although in Communist China Soviet Consulates closed. No public announcement ever made that Soviets have turned over control Dairen City to PA–Dairen Executive Administration to which Chinese police claim to be subject.

Sent Department; Department pass Nanking 204, Moscow 158.

PADDOCK

125.3513/9–1649 : Telegram

The Secretary of State to the Ambassador in the Soviet Union
(Kirk)[71]

WASHINGTON, September 18, 1949—1 p. m.

661. ReDeptel 635, Sept 9, and Dairen's 290, Sept 16 to Dept rptd Moscow. See also Dairen's 201, July 6, to Dept rptd Moscow 112. In view Dairen's failure elicit satis reply to representations Chao's behalf, request Emb protest in most effective and expeditious manner possible this most recent unwarranted interference Consulate in its legitimate functioning by local auths Dairen. Pls rpt text any note presented to Dept and Dairen.

ACHESON

125.3513/9–1949 : Telegram

The Ambassador in the Soviet Union (Kirk) to the Secretary of State

Moscow, September 19, 1949—11 p. m.
[Received September 19—6:13 p. m.]

2358. Reference Deptel 661, September 18. Note addressed Acting Minister Foreign Affairs as follows delivered by Barbour [72] 10 p. m., Moscow time, to Saksin,[72a] head American Section, who promised bring attention Gromyko [73] tonight.

"I have honor to refer to my note No. 518 of September 10, 1949, in which Soviet Government was informed of decision of my Government to close American Consulate at Dairen, in which Soviet Government was requested to instruct its officials in Dairen to facilitate closure of Consulate and departure of its staff. Although reply to this note has not yet been received, it will be recalled that at time of my delivery of this note to Foreign Minister Vyshinsky on September 10, 1949, I pointed out that my Government urgently desired cooperation of Soviet Government in this matter, that Foreign Minister assured me that reply to my note would be forthcoming expeditiously.

"Meanwhile, on September 15, 1949, Mr. Chao Yi-hsien, Senior Chinese clerical employee of American Consulate at Dairen, has been arrested by local police, his whereabouts is unknown. Repeated efforts of Consul Paddock to communicate with Mr. Chao have proved fruitless, Soviet authorities at Dairen have refused to receive Consul Paddock or to accept any communication from him in connection with this case. Clerk Chao Yi-hsien has been an employee of US Government for past 27 years.

"In light of these circumstances, and of position maintained by Soviet Government in Dairen, it is impossible for Soviet Government to avoid ultimate responsibility for Mr. Chao's detention and con-

---

[71] Repeated to the Consul at Dairen as telegram No. 146.
[72] Walworth Barbour, Minister-Counselor of Embassy in the Soviet Union.
[72a] Georgy Filippovich Saksin.
[73] A. A. Gromyko, Soviet Acting Minister for Foreign Affairs.

tinued absence from his duties in American Consulate. Accordingly, in protesting this most recent interference by local authorities with legitimate functioning of Consulate and attitude of Soviet authorities in Dairen in refusing to permit Consulate to communicate with or to interview clerk Chao, my Government has instructed me to impress upon Soviet Government importance of latter's urgent intervention in this matter with view to ascertaining Mr. Chao's whereabouts, effecting his release, and, as requested in my note under reference, arranging for early departure from Dairen of Consul Paul Paddock, Vice Consul Culver Gleysteen, and Chinese members of Consulate staff which includes clerk Chao Yi-hsien and his five family dependents, and clerk Chao Shou-yu.

"Please accept, Excellency, renewed assurance of my highest consideration."

Sent Department 2358; Department pass Dairen 37.

KIRK

125.351/9–2149 : Telegram

The Consul at Dairen (Paddock) to the Secretary of State

DAIREN, September 21, 1949—noon.
[Received September 21—10:47 a. m.]

296. First Jap repatriation ship already left Dairen. Other one, September 28.

"Several" British and other freighters, according Tokyo, due Dairen this month to take soybeans to Japan under transaction especially approved by SCAP.

Unless plans definitely maturing for even sooner transport, it recommended Department and Embassy press for our evacuees either means.

No answer to note presented by Ambassador Kirk Sept. 10 altho arrest of Chao Sept. 15 might be regarded as one form of answer. Surveillance past week of Consulate officer residence auto and officers on foot is more intensive and ostentatious than ever before. Soviets perhaps stalling in order turn over problem to China later. For this see Contels 276 and 291, repeated Moscow 158. Danger of further arrests of Chinese staff exists.

Financial crisis of Consulate worsening. No items yet sold. Consulate cannot even pay money due staff upon closing.

It is suggested that unless Department can obtain assurances from Soviets that Consulate evacuation can be made at latest on second Jap repatriation ship (due here 2 days after Dairen City conference closes), consideration be given to retaliatory measures re this area— such as obstructing further soybean transactions with Japan and if possible discourage British, French, etc., ships coming here under

Soviet charter. See Contel 172, August 12 [74] re possibly analogous position of Soviet Mission at Tokyo.

Regardless route which Soviets may finally permit, office will not be closed until specifically informed by Department that no further efforts being made obtain release of Chao and therefore Consulate should not delay departure his behalf.

Also, unless local or Moscow Soviets promise no examination of official mail or of personal luggage of Americans and no restriction as to departure of radio operator Chao with us, we will refuse leave until Department instructs me acquiesce to such examinations and the abandonment of radio operator Chao.

Sent Department 296 (Department pass Moscow 159).

PADDOCK

125.3515 : Telegram

The Acting Secretary of State to the Consul at Dairen (Paddock)

WASHINGTON, September 21, 1949—7 p. m.

148. Dept concerned ur need funds and anxious assist any way possible. Pls advise on fol points:

1. Can you cash drafts?
2. Any way funds remittable through local banks?
3. Shld we approach Soviets with view getting them transfer funds?
4. Any other way you can suggest?

If 1 or 2 possible, state rates as Dept would not consider unfeasible even though exchange rates unfavorable in view costs difficulties transmitting funds by courier and fact office being closed.

Dept anxious about welfare you and staff. Pls inform Dept any additional steps possible here expedite ur departure.

Sent to Dairen, rptd to Moscow.

WEBB

125.351/9–2349 : Telegram

The Ambassador in the Soviet Union (Kirk) to the Secretary of State

MOSCOW, September 23, 1949.
[Received September 23—6 :20 a. m.]

2392. Following is text note from Foreign Office dated September 22 delivered by messenger to Embassy this morning (reDeptel 635, September 9, 9 p. m., repeated Dairen 137 and Embtel 2274, September 10, 8 p. m., repeated Dairen 36).

---

[74] Not found in Department of State files.

"In connection with your note of September 10 of this year, containing the request of the Government of the USA to the Government of the USSR to give instructions to its officials in the city of Dairen to facilitate the closing of the American Consulate in that city and the departure of the employees of the Consulate, I inform that corresponding instructions have been given to the Soviet Military Command.

"As for your assertion, in the note of September 19 of this year, that the Soviet authorities were apparently responsible for the arrest by the local police of an employee of the American Consulate in the city of Dairen, the Chinese citizen Chao Yi-hsien, I am obliged to reject it, inasmuch as questions concerning Chinese citizens enter into the competence of the Chinese authorities.

"Accept (etc.), (Signed) A. Gromyko."

Embassy will endeavor to learn from Saksin today competent Soviet military organ or official Dairen authorized to handle details with Paddock, and will press for release Chao. Meanwhile, suggest Paddock endeavor directly contact Soviet Commander.

ReDeptel 675, September 21, 7 p. m., repeated Dairen 148. Embassy is approaching Soviet bank today to request TT of funds to Dairen and will report results. Please advise amount local funds desired.

Sent Department 2392. Department pass Dairen 39.

Kirk

125.351/9-2549 : Telegram

The Consul at Dairen (Paddock) to the Secretary of State

DAIREN, September 25, 1949—11 a. m.
[Received September 26—10:21 p. m.]

301. As result Moscow's 2392, September 23, I today sent letter to Chief of Civil Administration; following is summary.

Ambassador Kirk in personal call September 10 informed Vishinski of Consulate's closing and requested Soviets facilitate departure of staff and give preference as to transport for their departure—Soviet ship, foreign freighter under Soviet charter, unarmed American naval vessel.

Soviet note of September 22 stated appropriate instructions sent Soviet Military Command. Since no preference re transport given in note, I assume it immaterial to Soviets which type transport used. Thus Civil Administration requested either itself arrange passage for Consulate staff on one of foreign freighters now here or allow me contact captains personally; if Soviet ship leaving earlier, it is satisfactory with me go that route.

Ambassador pointed out to Vishinski that Gleysteen and I traveling as couriers and official mail thus exempt from examination; also our personal baggage should be exempt.

Chao Shou-yu to go with me; question of release and departure from Dairen of Chao Yi-hsien is being taken up by Moscow Embassy. Reply by letter or interview requested. End of summary.

Department: In event we in fact free go next few days, Department's statements re last two paragraphs Contel 296, September 21 requested urgently.

Sent Department, Department pass Moscow 161.

PADDOCK

125.351/9–2749 : Telegram

The Consul at Dairen (Paddock) to the Secretary of State

DAIREN, September 27, 1949—6 p. m.
[Received September 28—5 :36 p. m.]

303. Chief of Civil Administration today in interview said departure of Americans of Consulate staff would be arranged on foreign freighter due here "in first days of October". Matter of examination of official mail and personal luggage not yet decided. Departure of Chinese clerk Chao Shou-yu for Chinese police to decide, not Soviets. He did not know name or destination of freighter.

I said it certain Department would not permit me leave if official mail subject to examination; personal luggage, however, matter of international courtesy and I could not insist on exemption. Also I absolutely unable go without Chao Shou-yu; however, I said I would have him make application for exit visa at Chinese police at a branch of Soviet Administration in Dairen.

Although Chief definite about our departure on this ship, Department should note that it presumably still for captain to decide if he gives us passage. It hoped matters now arranged for our departure but it realized many opportunities for Soviets to delay it until CCP government organized.

Answers still needed last paragraph Contel 301.

Sent Department 303. Department pass Moscow 163.

PADDOCK

393.6215/9–2849 : Telegram

The Consul at Dairen (Paddock) to the Secretary of State

DAIREN, September 28, 1949—noon.
[Received September 29—10 :25 p. m.]

304. All foreigners including German group refused exit visas. Thus none to go on repatriation ship.

German representatives told officially by Chinese police their names had been sent to Northeast Administrative Committee, Mukden; this committee had sent names to Central Revolution Committee, Peiping; only after Peiping gives permit will local foreigners be allowed leave Dairen.

Intermittent claims of Soviets of no responsibility over Chinese police reported various previous telegrams.

Consul yesterday wrote Chief Civil Administration for verification above and asking information on following points:

1. If above true, on what basis Peiping allowed by Soviets to decide matter of exit visas, or any other question regarding Dairen, since USSR diplomatic relations with Nationalist China unchanged as evidenced by continued functioning Soviet ConGen Dairen and since USSR announced its military occupation of Dairen until Japanese treaty.

2. On what basis Soviet citizens able travel freely in and out Dairen to Vladivostok and Manchuria but citizens of other countries unable leave city.

3. On what basis Civil Administration able in its own name give permit to Japanese residents of Dairen to be repatriated when it denies permit to citizens of other countries.

Consul requested Soviet authorities reconsider departure these foreigners. In case of Germans due type of small ships coming here Consul pointed out no chance again arrange transportation in foreseeable future except with great difficulties and delays: Whereas if allowed go now they home in few days.

Consul's opinion of Soviet responsibility for exit visas reaffirmed. No answer to letter expected.

Consul might have added to above queries why civil administration able permit departure of myself and Gleysteen but not other foreigners.

Nanking please pass to French Embassy. It is hoped French Embassy will accept its responsibility of initiating vigorous protest in Moscow that this group German residents in China prevented by Soviets from using repatriation facilities especially arranged for it; in Dairen all action by American Consulate in this connection done in name of French Embassy.

Sent Department; Department pass Tokyo 34, Frankfort unnumbered, Moscow 164, Nanking 205.

Paddock

125.351/9–2149 : Telegram

The Acting Secretary of State to the Consul at Dairen (Paddock)

Washington, September 28, 1949—7 p. m.

157. Re Contel 296 Sept 21 passed Moscow 159. Penultimate para: Dept agrees not close office until every effort obtain release Chao Yi-hsien exhausted. This connection Dept requests Moscow report any further results its representations and you continue local efforts ob-

tain release. Dept, appreciating your desire depart soonest, commends your loyalty to Chinese staff, likewise realizes may be forced eventually abandon Chao, in which case decision will be made by Dept.

Last para: Dept considers highly unlikely local or Moscow Soviets will give such promises, in which case:

a. Under no circumstances submit to exam official mail or other official documents.

b. If absolutely unavoidable you may acquiesce exam pers[onal] luggage.

c. Refuse depart unless Chao Shou-yu accompanies you.

WEBB

125.351/9–2949 : Telegram

The Consul at Dairen (Paddock) to the Secretary of State

DAIREN, September 29, 1949—6 p. m.
[Received September 29—2:52 p. m.]

305. After reviewing my interview with Chief Civil Administrator (Contel 303, September 27, repeated Moscow 163) and after analyzing Soviet and Chinese policy subterfuges and broken promises in refusing exit visas to foreigners (re immediately preceding telegram), I am convinced real danger exists that Consulate staff unable leave Dairen "in first days of October" as promised by chief. It definitely certain Chao Shou-yu unable go under present circumstances; run-around as to exit visa already begun.

Following points pertinent:

1. No reason why Soviets should ask us await some particular future ship as foreign freighters in harbor now.

2. No reason why chief should be unwilling give details re this ship; as result we completely in Soviet hands as to "unforeseen delays".

3. No way for Soviets to know now if captain of this ship is willing and able take passengers.

4. Most important is subject of exit visas for foreigners. My opinion is that relations between Soviets and local Chinese have become so "touchy" on this matter that Soviets may well believe only way to escape difficulties with Chinese is to postpone departure for all foreigners for time being; this may well include us.

5. No indication what future of Dairen will be after CCP government formed. Press states Chairman of PA–D Executive Administration exhorted Dairen Municipal Conference to be prepared obey gladly all laws of new government as soon as it formed. I cannot emphasize too much that all evidence indicates Chinese police will deal harshly both with Chinese and American members of staff. American Government's helplessness re Mukden staff has provided good propaganda for CCP prestige; similar prolonged situations perhaps of value to Communists and Soviets here.

To prevent any chance of Consulate staff remaining here beyond next week, it is recommended Department act on top priority basis along following lines:

1. If Department has itself definite information (that is, no need to query various posts) of foreign freighter arriving Dairen harbor by October 4, Department is requested to establish by wireless with captain that he agrees to accept Consulate staff as passengers; it is necessary to agree before arrival as once in Dairen he isolated like American Consulate.

2. If no information of such ship at Department or if no agreement with captain in 24 hours, Department is requested to instruct Seoul arrange special freighter to come Dairen in order arrive here by October 4. Unimportant how small ship may be.

3. Department is requested have Moscow Embassy inform Foreign Office (and Consulate do same Chief Civil Administrator) along following lines:

(a) Department appreciates assurances of Chief Civil Administrator that local Soviets will facilitate departure of Consulate staff and that it will arrange evacuation in first days of October.

(b) However, it noted that Soviet plans as reported to American Consulate are vague—no specific information re name or destination of vessel, no assurances as to exemption of official mail or personal baggage of officers, no assurances of permit for Chao Shou-yu accompany.

(c) Department reiterates its position that USSR as military occupying power of Dairen with [apparent omission] and for exemption customs examination.

(d) Because it seems no definite arrangements yet made for transport of Consulate staff from Dairen, Department has itself arranged for special ship to call at Dairen by October 4 to evacuate Americans and Chao (or else has arranged with captain of freighter to accept staff as passengers).

If impasse should then arise that Soviets refuse admit ship or allow us board it or refuse departure of Chao, it will be necessary for Department finally to take definite and public stand on status of Dairen. It realized Department's ability protest behalf Consulate weakened by not raising issue when Soviets first claimed no responsibility when Chinese police began persecution of Consulate. A review of Contels will show, however, that Soviet position at Dairen is highly vulnerable and that Department should be able exploit it effectively.

Sent Department 305, Department pass Moscow 165.

PADDOCK

125.351/9–3049 : Telegram

The Consul at Dairen (Paddock) to the Secretary of State

DAIREN, September 30, 1949—7 p. m.
[Received October 1—4 :08 p. m.]

306. Contel 296, September 21 sent when still hope effecting release Chao Yi-hsien. This now realized as impossible unless Department utilizes means other than now being tried.

Contel 305, September 28 sent when still believed departure Chao Shou-yu could be arranged. Now realized definitely impossible get exit visa for him unless Department able force Soviets to order Chinese police to issue it.

We thus at following impasse: (1) Yi-hsien cannot be freed; (2) Shou-yu cannot leave Dairen; (3) If he left behind by Americans, he immediately seized by police; (4) If Americans remain, he probably arrested anyway; (5) If Americans remain, local authorities will soon place even more stringent restrictions on them whether on basis of Dairen incorporation into CCP China or other excuse; (6) We not prepared for siege in Mukden style as stores long ago exhausted; (7) Although Soviets promised transportation for American officers to leave Dairen "in first days of October", little reason to expect promise to be kept; (8) No assurance of exemption official mail from customs examination as well as personal luggage of Americans; (9) If luggage examined, it possible considerable humiliation will result as well as confiscation of whatever takes fancy of inspectors (see Contel 207, July 11 [75]).

Consulate has no suggestion for solving impasse. Concerning specific point of Shou-yu, it would seem situation re Chinese staff at other posts is pertinent. However, it probable Chinese police here more vicious than elsewhere due Soviet training plus thorough indoctrination with anti-American propaganda.

It is believed advisable for Department to scrap all previous decisions and instructions re Dairen, review pertinent Contels, and decide next course of action. As stated in previous telegrams, Consulate believes Soviet position in Dairen to be highly vulnerable. It is difficult to believe that examination of that position would not reveal lever that would force Soviets to let Shou-yu go.

It is hoped Department will reply to this telegram within 12 hours after receipt. Consulate still convinced [deadline] to be date CCP government is established and Soviets grant recognition. Thus Consulate suggestions of Contel 305 still in order.

Sent Department 306, Department pass Moscow 166.

PADDOCK

---

[75] Not printed.

125.351/10–149 : Telegram

The Acting Secretary of State to the Ambassador in the Soviet Union (Kirk) [76]

WASHINGTON, October 1, 1949—2 p. m.

717. Re Dept's tel [1023] to Hong Kong of Oct 1 [77] rptd Moscow as [716], Dept desires you inform FonOff at once US Govt negotiating diversion Butterfield and Swire merchant vessel from north China or Korean port to Dairen purpose evacuating staff Am Consulate Dairen and expects if negotiations successful vessel will arrive Dairen within next 3 or 4 days. Request FonOff as matter of urgency inform appropriate officials Dairen expedite issuance exit permits and clearances vessel.

WEBB

125.351/10–249 : Telegram

The Ambassador in the Soviet Union (Kirk) to the Secretary of State

MOSCOW, October 2, 1949—6 p. m.
[Received October 2—1:04 p. m.]

2481. Following note (reDeptel 717, October 1, 2 p. m., repeated Dairen 163) delivered to Foreign Office 5:45 p. m. today:

"No. 570. Excellency: I have the honor to refer to my notes numbers 518, 538 of September 10 and September 19, 1949, in which Your Excellency's Government was informed of the decision of the United States Government to close the American Consulate at Dairen, and in which your Government was requested to facilitate this closure and the departure of the American and alien members of the Consulate's staff, and their dependents. In my note of September 19, 1949, I brought to your attention the arrest on September 15, 1949, of the senior Chinese clerical employee of the Consulate, Mr. Chao Yi-hsien, and requested the assistance of the Soviet authorities at Dairen in obtaining his release.

"As a result of receipt by the Soviet authorities at Dairen of instructions referred to in your note on September 22, 1949, Consul Paul Paddock was informed by the competent Soviet authorities on September 27, 1947 [*1949*], that departure would be arranged by vessel from Dairen in the first days of this month. As no information could be obtained from the authorities as to the exact vessel or the date of departure, in order to facilitate closure of the Dairen Consulate and the departure of its staff my Government is arranging for a merchant vessel operated by the British firm of Butterfield and Swire to be diverted from a North China or Korean port and to call at Dairen for this purpose within the next 3 or 4 days.

"In view of the imminent arrival at Dairen of this British merchant vessel to take aboard the American Consul and his staff, it will be appreciated if Your Excellency's Government, as a matter of urgency,

---
[76] Repeated to the Consul at Dairen as telegram No. 163.
[77] Not printed.

will inform the appropriate officials at Dairen, requesting them to expedite clearance for the vessel and the issuance of exit permits to Consul Paddock, Vice Consul Gleysteen, and the alien staff members and their dependents.

"Please accept, Excellency, etc."

Sent Department 2481, repeated Dairen 41.

KIRK

125.3513/10–349 : Telegram

The Consul at Dairen (Paddock) to the Secretary of State

DAIREN, October 3, 1949—9 a. m.
[Received October 4—5 :03 a. m.]

307. For the record, following is summary of Consulate's efforts on behalf Chao Shou-yu exit visa :

September 27 I told Chief Civil Administration Chao would apply visa at Chinese police (Contel 303). September 28 Chao accompanied by Gleysteen called at Port Arthur–Dairen police headquarters and were referred to Dairen municipal police and then local police station. At latter they told come back several times succeeding days. Each time official not there for appointment. Chao was informed last time "it not certain if he ever would be there".

September 29 Consulate wrote Chief Civil Administration reviewing difficulties and asking him to request proper authorities to accept and expedite visa application. No answer and impossible arrange interview with Chief.

September 30 Gleysteen called Port Arthur–Dairen police headquarters; not allowed past guard but talked with minor official who reiterated application must be made at local police station.

October 1 Chao went local police alone (due belief Gleysteen's presence may have prejudiced previous efforts). He unable see official and was told all government offices closed 3 days in honor new CCP government. This first time Chao out of house alone for many months.

During these days Gleysteen repeatedly tried contact police official who once said (during one of our incidents) to telephone him if in need. As usual he unavailable.

No effort made see other Chinese officials as they consistently have refused receive Consulate officers.

Thus Soviets disclaim responsibility for Chao visa and Chinese police refuse even permit him make application.

Sent Department 307. Department pass Moscow 168.

[PADDOCK]

125.351/10–349 : Telegram

The Consul General at Hong Kong (Rankin) to the Secretary of State

HONG KONG, October 3, 1949—3 p. m.
[Received October 3—9:10 a. m.]

788. Diversion *Soochow* not practicable, reference Department's 1023, October 1, 2 p. m., to Hong Kong.[78] Diversion *Hupeh* arrangeable provided assured early departure Dairen. *Hupeh* is coal burner and if delayed Dairen could run out of fuel, water and food. Definite diversion also subject confirmation Tientsin office Butterfield and Swire and has been requested.

Failing *Hupeh*, B and S suggests *Shansi* due sail Taku Bar October 19. Please confirm reasonable assurance Dairen authorities will not delay *Hupeh* beyond time required embark passengers and load freight, which should not exceed 48 hours.

Sent Department 788. Department pass Dairen unnumbered, Seoul unnumbered, Moscow unnumbered.

RANKIN

125.351/10–349 : Telegram

The Acting Secretary of State to the Consul at Dairen (Paddock)

WASHINGTON, October 3, 1949—6 p. m.

164. Assume you answering Hong Kong's 788 to Dept Oct 3 re assurances requested.

WEBB

125.3513/10–449 : Telegram

The Acting Secretary of State to the Consul at Dairen (Paddock) [79]

WASHINGTON, October 4, 1949—2 p. m.

166. If evac ship plans reported to you in recent tels materialize and if Chaos unable leave aboard such ship, Dept reluctantly of opinion your [and] Gleysteen's departure shld not be delayed if exit permits Chaos not forthcoming. Publicity only lever which might be effective this situation, but Dept of opinion such pressure wld not result in favorable action re either Chao, wld probably have undesirable effect further jeopardizing your departure and possibly make more difficult position Chaos if they have to remain Dairen. Pressure through SCAP believed impossible.

---

[78] Not printed.
[79] Repeated to the Ambassador in the Soviet Union as telegram No. 729.

When time comes to leave you shld therefore make payments Shou-yu and family Yi-hsien accordance instructions separate tels.

As for official documents, you already authorized destroy all classified material. This shld leave only accts which may be examined provided (1) exam cannot be avoided and your departure wld otherwise be impossible (2) you destroy or render innocuous all compromising material.

WEBB

125.3513/10–449 : Telegram

The Acting Secretary of State to the Consul at Dairen (*Paddock*)

WASHINGTON, October 4, 1949—2 p. m.

167. Since due arrest Chao Yi-hsien you will probably be unable make lump sum severance payments and dire needs his family auth[orize] payment not exceeding $500 in lieu lump sum salary severance payment to family chargeable allotment OK–138220, Approp 1900522 emergencies arising Diplomatic Consular Service 1950.

Inform Dept action taken.

Chao Yi-hsien eligible for annuity upon receipt his application. Suggest you inform family of this matter. This connection inform Dept details his case requested Deptel 149, Sep 22.[80]

WEBB

125.351/10–549 : Telegram

The Consul at Dairen (*Paddock*) *to the Secretary of State*

DAIREN, October 5, 1949—noon.
[Received October 6—10:14 p. m.]

310. Consulate staff can embark with few hours notice, Deptel 164. However, unable give assurances as to possible delays arising from local authorities. As emphasized previous telegrams, they act only on basis orders from Moscow. Thus it would seem Department is in better position answer Hong Kong telegram than Consulate.

It is hoped Department's action re diversion ship has not been held up by referring subject to Consul: Telegram was transmitted without priority rating.

USSR recognition of CCP government expected to alter situation here radically. However, as Soviets not yet withdrawn military occupation of Dairen, presumably advisable for Department continue plan evacuate Consulate staff on basis Soviets are responsible for city and port.

---

[80] Not printed.

Contel 306, September 30 unanswered; thus Consulate will continue act on basis Deptel 157, September 28.

PADDOCK

125.351/10–749 : Telegram

The Ambassador in the Soviet Union (Kirk) to the Secretary of State

Moscow, October 7, 1949—11 p. m.
[Received October 7—3:35 a. m.]

2531. Note from FonOff dated October 6 just received states no objection to Butterfield and Swire vessel (reDeptel 717, October 1, 2 p.m., repeated Dairen 163, and Embtel 2481, October 2, 6 p. m., repeated Dairen 41) calling at Dairen to pick up staff Consulate. Note reiterates authority Chinese police in Chao Yi-hsien case.

Sent Department, Department pass Hong Kong 5, Dairen 41.

KIRK

125.3513/10–849 : Telegram

The Consul at Dairen (Paddock) to the Secretary of State

DAIREN, October 8, 1949—10 a. m.
[Received October 9—12:54 a. m.]

316. Chao Shou-yu states Chinese secret police met him nights of October 6 and 7. Second night he signed 4 statements under threat personal safety. In summary:

1. He works for American imperialism.
2. American Consuls in China are here for aggressive purposes.
3. He will tell all he knows re Dairen Consulate.
4. He will not tell of interviews.

I did not blame his actions. Without signing, his position hopeless; perhaps this way he has chance survive.

His next meeting October 10.

Possibility exists of course of similar statements by Chao Yi-hsien. Neither Chao ever had contact with confidential material.

This possibly build-up for spy charges similar to Mukden Consulate. Department should note that Mukden spy story of immense propaganda value; still used regularly in political classes in factories, etc. Temptation to Soviets and Chinese Communists to repeat their success here is obvious.

Three-day meeting of highest local officials reported now at Port Arthur. Perhaps this to determine new Soviet-Chinese relations in naval base and particularly Dairen.

Recurrent rumors refer Soviet soybean ship leaving Dairen next couple days for Japan. If Soviets intend for us to use this or any other ship, no indication.

No information from Department why its plans evacuate staff by ship from Korea by October 4 not materialized.

Sent Department, Department pass Moscow 170.

PADDOCK

125.351/10–849 : Telegram

The Consul at Dairen (Paddock) to the Secretary of State

DAIREN, October 8, 1949—11 a. m.
[Received October 9—1 :03 a. m.]

317. No information of any kind from Soviets re our departure since Contel 303, September 27, repeated Moscow 163.

Regardless assurances Kommandatura might give that official mail will not be examined at customs, it realized there may be trouble with Chinese at customs without opportunity to return pouches to Consulate for burning. Also Chao Shou-yu affair (immediately preceding telegram) makes future developments highly uncertain.

To be freer to meet contingencies and because believed unwise postpone action longer, Consulate today burned its files both classified and unclassified.

There remains only small packet current material of which Department does not have copies, copies of Consulate letters to local authorities, and accounts.

Matter of examination still important, however, for 7 months' accumulation Consulate mail.

Sent Department. Department pass Moscow 171.

PADDOCK

125.351/10–1549 : Telegram

The Secretary of State to the Consul General at Hong Kong (Rankin) [81]

WASHINGTON, October 15, 1949—noon.

1125. Reurtel 858 to Dept Oct 15.[82] Moscow's 2531 to Dept Oct 7 rptd Hong Kong 5 stated Sov FonOff has no objection ButSwire vessel calling Dairen pick up Cons staff. Dept's 1064 to Hong Kong Oct 7 [82] noted Dairen Cons staff can embark with few hours notice. Dept believes these factors constitute reasonable assurance *Shansi*

---

[81] Repeated to the Consul at Dairen as telegram No. 175 and to the Ambassador in the Soviet Union as telegram No. 759.
[82] Not printed.

will not be delayed Dairen beyond 48 hours. However, if embarkation impossible within 48 hrs, you authorized inform ButSwire *Shansi* free leave Dairen without Cons staff if necessary in view considerations enumerated ur 788 to Dept Oct 3. On other hand, if necessary and in event *Shansi* able remain in Dairen beyond 48 hr limit, you authorized pay demurrage other fees long as total cost diversion does not exceed maximum authorized Dept's 1023 to Hong Kong Oct 1.[83]

Dept emphasizes absolutely imperative *Shansi* be diverted to Dairen. Proceed make final arrangements urgently without further delay. Inform Dept rpt Dairen by tel

(a) *Shansi's* ETA [84] Dairen
(b) itinerary after leaving Dairen.

ACHESON

761.93/10–2449 : Telegram

The Ambassador in Korea (Muccio) to the Secretary of State

SEOUL, October 24, 1949—3 p. m.
[Received October 24—3 :56 a. m.]

1312. From Paddock. Press conference this morning reviewed Sino-Soviet relations at Dairen. Provisions of 1945 treaty agreements outlined. No interpretation of provisions given other than factual irregularities of Soviets including:

1. Communization of Dairen began immediately Soviet occupation in disregard Nationalist Government laws.
2. Nationalist Government officials not admitted although Nationalist Government sovereignty recognized.
3. Communist Party came above ground April 1 admitting publicly it has operated in Dairen since before war and it subordinate to Northeast Bureau CCP. Nationalist flags replaced by CCP flag.
4. When Port Arthur–Dairen Executive Administration established April 28, 1949, puppets dropped and all important posts filled by Communists.
5. Soviet ConGen continued functioning in Dairen although elsewhere in CCP Chinese [*China?*] Soviet Consulates closed.
6. Foreign freighters entered Dairen despite Nationalist decree closing port.

Also outlined extent of control over populace by Chinese *gendarmerie*, which more stifling to personal freedom than *pao chia* system which CCP attacked in past propaganda.

Stated that whereas Chinese given jurisdiction over Chinese populace, Soviet retained control over foreigners and that Soviet Komtura and Civil Administration still function in Dairen City. [Paddock.]

MUCCIO

---

[83] Not printed.
[84] Estimated time of arrival.

125.351/10–2549 : Telegram

The Ambassador in Korea (Muccio) to the Secretary of State

SEOUL, October 25, 1949—3 p. m.
[Received October 25—4:42 a. m.]

1323. From Paddock: Reference last paragraph Deptel 898, October 24 to Seoul.[85] I sent plain language telegram October 21 from Dairen through usual Soviet Consulate General channel, saying we embarking that day. Soon as ship left harbor, I sent telegram to American Embassy, Seoul, to relay to Department (radio operator said this fastest method) stating we had embarked without difficulties and requesting Department notify interested posts Consulate closed as of October 21. Now find Embassy never received this telegram. [Paddock.]

MUCCIO

125.351/10–2649 : Telegram

The Acting Political Adviser in Japan (Sebald) to the Secretary of State

TOKYO, October 26, 1949.
[Received October 26—6:31 a. m.]

445. From Paddock. Summary of press conference at Tokyo on afternoon October 26th. Three Seoul conferences on Soviet treatment of Consulate Dairen, Sino-Soviet relations in Dairen, and Kwantung economy were summarized for newsmen.

(1) Chief difficulties were servicing post, isolation of Consulate officers and harassment of staff. Soviets controlled servicing post by permitting entry couriers and replacement only through Vladivostok. Due failure issue transit visas, Soviets prevented more than average of one courier trip per 4 months and only replacements since period of opening post were Paddock and Gleysteen in June 1948. Staff members assigned Dairen waited 4 to 6 months for Soviet transit visas, mostly without Soviets taking any action.

During past 14 months we had mail from outside only twice. Office supplies and funds ran short. Soviets imposed many other forms restrictions on Consulate staff—such as stopping car, jamming broadcasts of our intels from Taipei, et cetera. These restrictions petty but over long period built up to impressive total, which definitely hampered all operations of Consulate.

Most serious was persecution of Chinese staff of [*by?*] Chinese *gendarmerie*. When I protested to Soviet authorities, they disclaimed any responsibility for actions Chinese local government. Since be-

---

[85] Not printed.

ginning year, 2 Chinese staff members arrested; we had to abandon third when Consulate closed. Soviet official in charge Dairen, Chief of Civil Administration, altogether received me five times and never answered written communications of Consulate.

Repeated story of Gleysteen detention incommunicado by Soviet Kommandatura in April on trumped-up charge of signalling with jeep lights to sea. Two weeks later we both arrested by Soviet officers.

Due above restrictions, Consulate officers effectively isolated to small triangle of several square miles from Consulate office–resident–main shipping area.

Newsman asked since all functions curtailed if Consulate remained Dairen only for observation. Replied that Consulate like hardware store where one can go to get all sort of things; however, restrictions on Consulate became more constant and embarrassing comparatively recently.

(2) Sino-Soviet relations in Kwantung summarized most briefly. I said Soviets in military occupation in complete control for practical purposes but that Port Arthur–Dairen Executive Administration handled matters affecting Chinese. Executive Administration only recently admitted connection with Chinese Communist Party government in China; but Communists who control it said publicly on April 13 subordinate to Northeast Bureau in Mukden. They also described Port Arthur–Dairen as "liberated area".

Questioned on attitude on Chinese Communists in Dairen on Soviets. Answered that I could [not?] reply specifically but that according local press Han Kuang, Chairman of Executive Administration, was native Heilungkiang and studied in Moscow during war.

Questioned whether Dairen connection with Soviet recognition of Peiping regime. Replied there no way to answer such questions because we had no communication with China or even Manchuria.

(3) Survey of Kwantung economy identical to Seoul press conference on same subject, reported in telegram from Seoul October 25 [24]. [Paddock.]

SEBALD

125.351/10–2649 : Circular telegram

The Secretary of State to Certain Diplomatic and Consular Offices in China

WASHINGTON, October 26, 1949—5 p. m.

Consulate Dairen closed Oct 21. All Amer personnel departed.

ACHESON

PROBLEMS OF UNITED STATES CONSULATES IN AREAS OCCUPIED BY THE CHINESE COMMUNISTS

,I. MUKDEN CONSULATE GENERAL: REPRESENTATIONS BY THE UNITED STATES REGARDING ISOLATION OF CONSULATE GENERAL; DELAYS AND OBSTRUCTIONS TO DEPARTURE OF STAFF AFTER DECISION TO WITHDRAW; SPY CHARGES AGAINST CONSULATE GENERAL; UNITED STATES PROTESTS AGAINST ARREST AND TRIAL OF MEMBERS OF STAFF; WITHDRAWAL AND CLOSURE [1]

125.633/1–549 : Telegram

The Ambassador in China (Stuart) to the Secretary of State

NANKING, January 5, 1949—4 p. m.
[Received January 6—1 :15 a. m.]

39. Following is pertinent portion Hong Kong's 1, January 3, to Embassy:

"Chiao Mu [2] today said he had learned from 'traveler from Shanghai' that 'all personnel Mukden American Consulate General are well'. In further remarks Chiao Mu said question of communications for Mukden Consulate General is part of larger question of US attitudes toward new government and toward Kmt [3] Government clearly indicating granting of any facilities to Consulate General would depend on future course US policy. This contrasted sharply with his original (apparently personal) emphatic stand immediate restoration communication facilities desirable, and suggests today's statement represent[s] official view. Subject was introduced by him in today's conversation. Elsewhere in conversation he [de]scribed essential difference in Communist view of US missionary organizations and consular establishments, saying former are dedicated to helping Chinese people while latter are offices of US Government, thus in entirely different status. Said Communists take broad view of non-political mission activity especially schools, hospitals, et cetera."

In our opinion attitude adopted by Chinese Communists toward American Consulate General in Mukden, not to speak of more neutral British and French Consulate Generals there, is little short of blackmail. It is among most convincing evidence yet that Chinese Communist leaders are basically British [*sic*] bigots out of Bolshevik mold.

This newly expressed attitude of theirs toward foreign consular offices, incidentally, is in startling contrast to fine promises of fair treat-

---

[1] For previous documentation respecting the situation at Mukden, see *Foreign Relations*, 1948, vol. VII, pp. 809 ff.
[2] Head of local branch of the Communist New China News Agency, Hong Kong.
[3] Kuomintang (Nationalist Party).

ment of foreigners which they have recently made in Tsinan, Mukden, Peiping, Tsingtao, Shanghai, et cetera.

Solitary humorous note but significant one is found in the recantation by this naive Hong Kong Communist of his former decent and optimistic attitude toward communication problem of our Consulate General.   Doubtless he was himself surprised by the highhandedness of CCP [4] leaders.

Sent Department, repeated Shanghai 23, Mukden 1.

STUART

125.6336/1–1249 : Telegram

The Ambassador in China (Stuart) to the Secretary of State

NANKING, January 12, 1949—5 p. m.
[Received January 13—9 :23 a. m.]

95. We have drafted joint statement on Chinese Communist denial of communication facilities to British, French and American Consulates General in Mukden as suggested in Deptel 1876, December 23,[5] but have been unable to sell idea to British and French Ambassadors.[6] British Ambassador does not wish to make joint statement and instead proposes that American Embassy give story to foreign correspondents suggesting that they apply to British and French Embassies for further details about British and French Consulates General.

French Ambassador is reluctant make joint statement and although he has agreed to request instructions from Paris, he is not recommending any action. According to French Ambassador, his reluctance is based on following reasons :

(1) He still hopes to reestablish contact with his Consulate General via Hong Kong, Saigon, or Chinese messenger.

(2) He thinks joint statement might prejudice rather than help his Consul General.

(3) French Foreign Office has issued strict instructions that diplomatic officers abroad should issue no press statements.

We have told British and French Ambassadors of Embtel 39, January 5 to Department and informed them that in our judgment CCP statement that "question of communications for Mukden Consulate General is part of larger question of US attitude toward new Government and toward Kmt Government" is little short of blackmail. While expressing sympathy and concern British and French Ambassadors still refuse cooperate in joint statement which we believe occasion warrants. It is apparent that these local representatives are quite

---

[4] Chinese Communist Party.
[5] *Foreign Relations,* 1948, vol. VII, p. 849.
[6] Sir Ralph Stevenson and Jacques Meyrier, respectively.

content to ride along on coattails of US without appearing to take any positive action which might compromise future dealings themselves or their nationals in CCP-occupied China. Unless Department believes their noncooperation and opportunism are important enough to be contested in London and Paris and in order to avoid delay, we recommend as preliminary step Department approve our giving story for attribution to AP or *New York Times* correspondent in Nanking.

In response to this correspondent's query we would:

(1) Express our serious concern about safety since November 18 of American personnel and interests in Mukden.[7]

(2) Point out this is ominous portent of CCP policy toward USA.

(3) State that act of holding incommunicado consular offices of sovereign countries is contrary to international usage and principles guiding relations between civilised communities.

(4) Reveal attitude of CCP authorities as reported in Embtel 39, January 5 and emphasize that we consider solution to communication blockade of our Mukden Consulate General is unrelated to broad question of American policy in China.

(5) Point out that CCP could offer American Consulate General ample outgoing communication facilities to Hong Kong, Dairen and Moscow over American transmission required during and after war and over commercial radio stations.

(6) Recall that following their capture of Tsinan, CCP North Shensi radio broadcast safety and welfare messages from missionaries in that city.

(7) Suggest correspondent inquire of British or French Embassies for detail re status their Consulates General in Mukden.

Sent Department 95, pouched Shanghai, repeated Paris 3, London 2.

STUART

125.6336/1–1249 : Telegram

The Acting Secretary of State to the Ambassador in China (Stuart)

WASHINGTON, January 19, 1949—5 p. m.

69. Embtel 95 Jan 12 rptd Paris 3 London 2. Having in mind current situation Tientsin[8] and unwillingness British and French join in press statement Dept believes issuance press statement re denial communication facilities ConGen Mukden unwise at this time.

LOVETT

---

[7] Mukden was occupied by Chinese Communist forces on November 2, 1948, the Consulate General's radio was closed by Communists on November 18, and the Consulate General's staff was placed under virtual house arrest on November 20.

[8] Tientsin was occupied by the Chinese Communists on January 15; for documentation regarding problems of the Consulate General at Tientsin after the occupation, see pp. 1051 ff.

119.2/2–849 : Telegram

The Consul General at Peiping (*Clubb*) *to the Secretary of State*

PEIPING, February 8, 1949.
[Received February 8—1:22 a. m.]

192. According statement by former foreign employee Chinese Secret Service to member this office, Communists closed Mukden radio primarily because they found messages being transmitted through that radio behalf Chinese Government orders.

Consul General, of course, in no position check but reports as of possible interest that soon after Communist occupation Peiping Kmt official local central government organization asked this office transmit message to Nanking although regular telecommunications there still maintained. Request refused.

Repeated Nanking, Canton, Shanghai.

CLUBB

125.6336/2–1249 : Telegram

The Consul General at Peiping (*Clubb*) *to the Secretary of State*

PEIPING, February 12, 1949—8 a. m.
[Received February 12—2:32 a. m.]

218. ReContel 208, February 10.[9] On basis personal experience Mukden conditions, adduce following possible alternative explanations difficulties Consulate there apparently experiencing: (1) Communists, as previously suggested, may have suspected Consulate transmitting messages for Chinese Government agencies (whether Consulate did so through normal channels would presumably be known Embassy Nanking) or (2) previous . . . connections may have involved Consulate. . . .

ReDeptel 54, January 31.[9] Believe it inadvisable until position Consulate clarified send Manhard[10] or other officer now: (1) Seems clear personnel Mukden unable perform fruitful work at present and (2) new officer arriving might fall in same position as officers already there. Understand persons traveling Manchuria must have Manchurian residence certificates, request authority if feasible send Chinese messenger, preferably former Mukden employee if willing, to check on position Consulate and return to report. This procedure would be adopted after making local representations regarding Mukden–Tientsin communications and coordination Tientsin.

Repeated Nanking 175.

CLUBB

---

[9] Not printed.
[10] Philip W. Manhard, Vice Consul at Peiping.

119.2/2–1449 : Telegram

The Consul General at Shanghai (Cabot) to the Secretary of State

SHANGHAI, February 14, 1949—1 p. m.
[Received February 14—4 :04 a. m.]

515. No radio communications any kind ever transmitted behalf Chinese Government over Mukden radio circuit (Peiping 192, February [8]). Complete file all traffic held Shanghai control station.

Sent Department 515; repeated Canton 56, Peiping 36, pouched Nanking 362.

CABOT

125.6333/2–549 : Telegram

The Secretary of State to the Consul General at Peiping (Clubb)

WASHINGTON, February 16, 1949—1 p. m.

80. Dept agrees para 2 urtel 218 Feb 12 (reurtel 185 Feb 5 [11]) preferable send Chinese messenger for survey and report before Amer officers travel Mukden. In your discretion send Mukden employee if willing undertake journey.

Prevent employee remaining Mukden; if you feel he might decide remain there rather than return Peiping, it might be advisable offer him gratuity upon return Peiping. If you deem it necessary you are authorized offer gratuity not exceeding $50 US currency such dangerous activity after return Peiping chargeable appropriation 1990522 allotment 9K–135353 obligation 706.

ACHESON

125.6336/2–1849 : Telegram

The Ambassador in China (Stuart) to the Secretary of State

NANKING, February 18, 1949—noon.
[Received February 18—4 :57 a. m.]

412. We do not believe Chinese messenger is satisfactory substitute for despatch of FSO [12] to Mukden to relieve officer there and break Consulate's long period silence. It would, of course, be necessary apply appropriate permits, including Manchurian, to local authorities and if granted will permit Manhard and colleague access to Mukden and to consular compound which has thus far been denied apparently to all Chinese (see Peiping's 208, February 10 to Department [13]). Re-

[11] Latter not printed.
[12] Foreign Service Officer.
[13] Not printed.

fusal permits would at least further clarify Communist attitude US official function areas China occupied by them (re Peiping's 218, February 12).

We feel if it is not possible to relieve Ward's [16] staff by Manhard or other officer or otherwise communicate with him, Department should give serious consideration to withdrawal of our consular staff Mukden as hazardous to health, welfare American officers [and] employees, undignified sovereign power continue submit such treatment, and useless expenditure public funds and waste of Foreign Service personnel.

Re Peiping's unnumbered telegram February 8, 2 a.m.[16a] to Department, repeated Nanking, Canton, Shanghai, and Peiping's 218 to Department, Embassy has no knowledge of Ward having used his radio equipment for transmission messages behalf Chinese Government agencies prior its seizure November 18.

Sent Department, repeated Peiping 55.

STUART

124.936/2–2249 : Telegram

The Secretary of State to the Ambassador in China (Stuart)[17]

WASHINGTON, February 22, 1949—noon.

252. AP story datelined Nanking Feb 21 reports Emb spokesman as confirming that "it has been impossible to contact ConGen Angus Ward or any member Mukden staff since Nov 18" and states staff restricted to consular compound without electricity, water service, or telephone. Report also states all efforts communicate with Ward from Nanking, Washington, Moscow, Peiping, and Dairen have failed. Dept replying to inquiries by acknowledging absence communications since Nov 18 and stating Dept making every effort reestablish communications.

Dept fails perceive any advantage gained by dissemination stories portions of which are at best unconfirmed rumors re treatment ConGen staff Mukden or by outlining efforts made establish direct contact with Mukden and believes such stories may have effect complicating any future approach Commies this subject.

Dept contemplating instructing ConGens Peiping and Hong Kong inform Comms US consular officers Mukden have now been denied communications US Govt since Nov 18, such denial understandable during period mil operations and adjustments related transfer local authority, long absence communications however contrary established

---

[16] Angus I. Ward, Consul General at Mukden.

[16a] See telegram 192, February 8, p. 936.

[17] Repeated to the Minister-Counselor of Embassy in China (Clark) at Canton as telCan No. 27 and to the Consul General at Shanghai (Cabot) as telegram No. 333.

international practice governing functioning consular offices in territory under unrecognized govts, and if this procedure settled Comm policy, US Govt must give serious consideration withdrawal Consulate from Mukden.

Embs views re such approach and its estimate precedent implications requested urgently. In meantime Emb instructed withhold addtl handouts or comments this subject.

ACHESON

125.6336/2–2349 : Telegram

The Minister-Counselor of Embassy in China (Clark) to the Secretary of State

CANTON, February 23, 1949—5 p. m.
[Received 11:16 p. m.]

Cantel 76. I think we can safely assume that Communists will tolerate functioning our Consular establishments in areas controlled by them only so long as functioning those establishments serves Communist interests (Department telCan 27, sent Nanking 252,[18] repeated Shanghai 333, February 22). It seems to me unconscionable that they should have maintained our Consular establishment in Mukden incommunicado since November 18 and that in Tientsin since January 23. What we know of their difficulties as well as those of Clubb in Peiping to establish contact with local Communist authorities in accordance international practice under unrecognized governments seems rather strongly to indicate Communist intention to use recognition of consular functions as *quid pro quo* for obtaining *de jure* recognition of National Communist government. In the circumstances, it would seem mistake to admit justification keeping our people incommunicado even during period military operations and adjustment, particularly when our own radio circuits were established and being used solely for official government business. Threat to withdraw Consulate Mukden at this stage would appear play into Communist hands and should not be made lightly. So long as our people are not in physical danger, it is only reasonable to assume they are acquiring knowledge which will be of value later even though they cannot report for time being. Should we threaten to withdraw Consulate Mukden and later have to withdraw, we would prejudice, I believe, our position in other areas China and might find ourselves, as in Soviet Union, without listening posts other than in capital.

May I venture suggestion our best policy would be have Consulates General Peiping and Hong Kong express at every opportunity our concern at continued absence communications with our Consulates

---

[18] Dated February 22, noon, *supra*.

Mukden and Tientsin and our expectation that communications will be restored forthwith. We may not get anywhere with such arguments, but at least we will not be condoning even temporary suspension communication facilities in contravention international practice.

Sent Department; repeated Nanking 72, Shanghai 44.

CLARK

125.6336/2–2449 : Telegram

The Consul General at Peiping (Clubb) to the Secretary of State

PEIPING, February 24, 1949—noon.
[Received February 24—2 : 50 a. m.]

285. This office would favor try approach Communists Peiping regarding Mukden case although would note that as Department will appreciate from recent communications, situation regarding local contacts very difficult. Believe Hong Kong channel should also be used. Would try approach matter directly and indirectly by letter and orally; feel nil could be lost by attempted *démarche*.

Would recommend that now be omitted from communication any threat withdraw Consulate from Mukden which "possibly what Communists (and especially Soviets) want" but would instead stress established rights courtesies which receive general recognition international law and practice spite political change; and fact that "recognition" of [*or*] "nonrecognition" has nil do with case; Consulate being primarily concerned protect their citizens and perform certain other well-recognized functions which without reference overall political situation.

ReEmbtel 437, February 21 to Department,[19] would report there has been growing restlessness likewise among foreign correspondents Peiping in face increasing rumors Mukden situation. Peiping correspondents, however, feel under restraints toward caution not now experienced National China.

Sent Department; repeated Nanking.

CLUBB

125.6336/2–2549 : Telegram

The Consul General at Shanghai (Cabot) to the Secretary of State

SHANGHAI, February 25, 1949—1 p. m.
[Received February 25—3 :25 a. m.]

665. I heartily concur Clark's 44, February 23, 5 p. m.[20] It seems to me evident we can secure respect for our Consulates in Communist-

---

[19] Not printed.
[20] Same as Cantel No. 76 from Canton, p. 939.

dominated areas only insofar as Communists find necessary deal with them achieve their own purposes. I trust on this account Department will soon reply mytel 390, February 4, 8 p. m.[21]

I must respectfully differ with Deptel 333, February 22, noon.[22] It seems be fairly well established now our Mukden consular staff has been confined 3 months to consular compound. Among unattractive alternatives I feel best would probably be given maximum publicity this violation immemorial consular prerogatives and affront to US even though our aid program will weaken propaganda effect.

In talks with Democratic League leaders in Shanghai I have emphasized our concern Communist denial communication facilities to our Consulates Mukden and Tientsin and said that this situation can only strengthen hands those in US who advocate all-out aid to Nationalists.

Department has undoubtedly considered in connection with threat withdraw Consul Mukden [that] Communists may refuse permit consular staff to leave. I assume Department may be willing run this risk as indication what we may expect in this and other vastly more important areas as yet not overrun by Communists.

Sent Department; repeated Nanking 437, Canton 95.

CABOT

125.6336/2–2849 : Telegram

The Ambassador in China (Stuart) to the Secretary of State

NANKING, February 28, 1949—noon.
[Received February 28—8:43 a. m.]

479. Embtel 412 (repeated Peiping 55). As I have already reported, I believe our next step to solve Mukden impasse should be for Clubb to attempt to send Manhard and one other officer to Mukden. I would suggest that Clubb be instructed to send note to highest available Peiping authority informing that US Government is seriously concerned over welfare consular personnel Mukden and that it wishes Communists provide facilities travel Mukden [for] Manhard who has been permanently transferred that post and one other officer who proposes make round trip purpose accompanying out of Mukden two or more members consular staff who have been reassigned. Note should continue US Government takes very serious view Communist failure provide communications facilities to Consulate General and that functioning consular offices [may continue?] in territory under unrecognized governments. I believe such note if accepted in first

---

[21] Vol. IX, p. 906.
[22] Same as telegram No. 252 to the Ambassador in China, p. 938.

instance would soon be passed up to top-level authorities. It would be futile to draw Hong Kong Communists into scene because they have demonstrated themselves to be without influence and poor channel of communication. Further believe at this stage no useful purpose would be served by threatening to close American Consulate General but that if Communists still refuse to act on our request by, say, March 15, then in second note Clubb should inform Peiping authorities that we wish to close Consulate General and request their assistance in effecting withdrawal of consular staff.

It would help buttress our application for second officer to make round trip to Mukden if Department were to reassign Stokes [23] or Hubbard [24] and one or two clerks. Communist action on this would also provide indication whether they are actually holding Consular staff as hostages. I assume two or more members could now easily be spared from Mukden staff.

I have already reported in recent telegram [25] Moscow [*Peiping?*] regarding Mukden Consulate General, namely, that in its present status that post is hazardous to health welfare of staff, derogatory to dignity sovereign power and useless waste FS personnel and public funds. In addition I would observe that our patience over unjustifiable Communist behavior in Mukden may well be misconstrued by Communists in such way as to set very unfortunate precedent for posts in future. I am therefore convinced if worst comes to worst, we should not hesitate close post giving our action maximum publicity.

Disadvantages our withdrawal from Mukden would be somewhat mitigated by presence of Consulate at Dairen. Furthermore, it is quite possible Communists regard Mukden as special case and their hostility toward foreign Consulates in China Proper may not prove as great as it has in Mukden. If this is true, firm action on our part re Mukden would perhaps have salutary effect on treatment of our Consulates elsewhere.

Sent Department, repeated Canton, Shanghai, Peiping.

STUART

---

[23] William N. Stokes, Vice Consul at Mukden.
[24] Fred E. Hubbard, Vice Consul at Mukden.
[25] Telegram No. 412, February 18, noon, p. 937.

125.6336/3–249 : Telegram

The Secretary of State to the Consul General at Peiping (Clubb)[26]

WASHINGTON, March 2, 1949—7 p.m.

103. Dept increasingly apprehensive continuing absence communications from Mukden and persistent reports Comm restrictions on staff and desires you seek interview at earliest opportunity with highest Comm authority available to convey message along following lines (message may be delivered orally or in form unsigned memorandum in your discretion but you should state orally that you are conveying message on behalf US Govt) :

Long experience has shown desirability of and international custom has sanctioned continued exercise by resident foreign consuls of their legitimate and proper functions within their consular districts even during periods of non-recognition betw[een] govts. Such functions relating as they do principally to assistance to nationals and facilitating international trade through certification of invoices, assisting merchant shipping and similar duties are generally recognized as benefitting local population as well as country on whose behalf they are exercised and have no relation to recognition as is evidenced by general international practice. It is recognized that confusion arising from transfer administrative control or continuance of military operations in specific areas may temporarily prevent consular officers from communicating with their Govt but it is noted that ConGen Mukden was allowed continue use its transmitter for several weeks during period military operations and it was not until this phase passed that restrictions placed ConGen. The extraordinarily long period which has now passed without communication of any kind from ConGen Mukden and persistent though unconfirmed reports of confinement US consular personnel to their residential quarters have given rise to serious concern on part US Govt and people re welfare consular staff. US Govt is reluctant believe it established policy Comm authorities impose arbitrary restrictions US consular officers in total disregard international comity and practices but under circumstances must inquire whether ConGen staff is in fact confined, whether they are being otherwise prevented from performing their legitimate and proper duties and what arrangements have been or are being made for resumption of communications with ConGen Mukden.

In conveying foregoing you should request prompt reply.

Both Peiping and Hong Kong should take action outlined above.

At same time ConGen Peiping should in his discretion inform Comms that Manhard assigned Mukden replace member of staff there and request provision facilities travel Manhard [to] Mukden accompanied by another member Peiping staff. Dept believes it desirable

---

[26] Repeated to the Ambassador in China as telegram No. 285, to the Consul General at Hong Kong as telegram No. 118, to the Minister-Counselor of Embassy in China as telCan No. 38, and to the Consul General at Shanghai as telegram No. 390.

leave choice latter to ConGen Peiping and decision regarding person whom Manhard would replace to ConGen Mukden. Transfer of member Mukden staff replaced by Manhard would be arranged after arrival Peiping. Person designated by Peiping accompany Manhard would return from Mukden in company person Manhard replaces. Before departure Manhard and companion you should of course obtain firm assurances latter and person relieved Mukden will be allowed return. Report action taken foregoing and name person designated accompany Manhard.

ACHESON

125.6336/3–849 : Telegram

The Consul General at Peiping (Clubb) to the Secretary of State

PEIPING, March 8, 1949—4 p. m.
[Received March 8—9:01 a. m.]

367. ReDeptel 103, March 2. Informed Peiping Foreign Nationals Office March 4 I desired discuss important matter with responsible authorities and requested procedure. They said they unable reply to question without knowing matter to be discussed. I said I would prepare written statement and present it early date. I returned this morning with written statement comprising actually message set forth Depreftel. I then informed petty official who met me I had message to present under instructions American Government. He disappeared without looking at statement, presumably to request instruction, and returned 15 minutes later with request statement be delivered him for inspection. Gave statement in English and Chinese marked "unofficial translation" neither with address or signature. Took statement, returned in 45 minutes with person understood be responsible official that office, one Li Li-hua. Li said sense of statement would be sent Yeh Chien-ying [27] but he was not in position say whether action would be taken since authority his office and municipal government limited Peiping. He said sense of message understood and I should take it back with me. Despite circumstance return to me of message I believe Nationals Office checked with higher authority before receiving message purportedly from US Government. Message was in all probability copied during interim at least in Chinese and possibly English. Message will probably reach high authorities in form intended. I stated categorically to Li that message was from US Government and told Li at end of meeting my Government would appreciate early reply. Li indicated he not in position give any assurances this regard.

---

[27] Communist Mayor of Peiping.

Seemed me desirable concentrate on matter in point. Did not take up matter Manhard assignment. Told Li had another important matter discuss with authorities on instructions my Government (Deptel 60, February 3 [28]) but would await development from present case and prepare written statement as on this occasion and take up that later as it was not urgent. Propose wait few days before taking up Manhard assignment in order let local authorities digest Department's message.

Believe other approach Peiping regarding Mukden matter infeasible present but my request see highest authority discuss matter still technically sound and I shall be in position make new approach if opportunity offers. I believe message can be considered effectively delivered.

Sent Department, repeated Hong Kong, Nanking, Canton, Shanghai.

CLUBB

125.6336/3–949 : Telegram

The Consul General at Hong Kong (Hopper) to the Secretary of State

HONG KONG, March 9, 1949—noon.
[Received March 10—12:12 a. m.]

86. Commies 8th informed Consulate their regulations do not permit official contact with American Government officials owing absence recognition, and senior Commie thus unable meet me (Deptel 118, March 2, repeated Peiping 103, Nanking 285, Canton 96, Shanghai 390).

As matter has been under negotiation with Chiao Mu since receipt reftel March 4, Consulate today delivering memo containing Department's message to Chiao Mu, claims authority maintain informal contact with US Consular officials as local head New China News Agency, with request he deliver memo to most senior local Commie.

Commie refusal seemed probably due standing instructions forbidding contacts; on recognition excuse specious and premature in view non-establishment Commie national government, but probably accurately reflects official Commie policy. Chiao Mu received [no?] hint contents memo during negotiations, but showed great curiosity.

Sent Department 86, repeated Nanking 20, Embassy Canton 6, Shanghai 25, Peiping unnumbered, Nanking pass addressees from Hong Kong.

HOPPER

---

[28] Vol. IX, p. 11.

119.2/3–1449 : Telegram

The Consul General at Hong Kong (Hopper) to the Secretary of State

> HONG KONG, March 14, 1949—2 p. m.
> [Received March 15—3 :11 a. m.]

91. In cover received today Chiao Mu returned Dept's message left with him March 10, with personal informal signed note dated March 12 to Vice Consul Service [28a] explaining "very sorry that I cannot forward such a message". Tone of note was friendly.

Return of message coincides with Peiping action and Consulate assumes text message radioed Communist headquarters.

Sent Department 91, repeated Nanking 21, AmEmb Canton 7, Shanghai 26, Peiping unnumbered.

> HOPPER

125.7146/3–1849 : Telegram

The Consul General at Peiping (Clubb) to the Secretary of State

> PEIPING, March 18 [*17?*], 1949—11 a.m.
> [Received March 17—11 : 56 p. m.]

Unnumbered. ReContel 367, March 8 to Department, asked at Peiping Foreign Affairs Office today I be informed whether there was any reply re matter discussed March 8. Petty official who took in my written request returned stated matters pertaining Consulates outside jurisdiction their office. Attempt get categorical reply to question resulted in unsatisfactory repetition first statement. Further pressure along same line finally brought forth statement that if there was reply I would be informed.

Took up same time question proposed travel two Vice Consuls (unnamed) [to] Mukden (Deptel 103, March 2), was informed matter could not be discussed with me since I was not immediately concerned, that those concerned should approach Bureau Public Safety. Am having Manhard and Armstrong [29] make application latter bureau [for] departure.

Sent Shanghai 296, repeated Department, Nanking, Canton, unnumbered.

> [CLUBB]

[28a] Richard M. Service.
[29] Oscar V. Armstrong, language officer at Peiping.

123 Manhard, Philip W. : Telegram

The Consul General at Peiping (Clubb) to the Secretary of State

PEIPING, March 18 [*17?*], 1949—11 a. m.
[Received March 17—11 : 56 p. m.]

Unnumbered. Re Contel 296, March 16 [*17?*].[30] Manhard and Armstrong applied March 17 Public Safety Bureau for permission proceed Mukden. Informed reply would be made in due course.

Deptel 80, February 16 and Embtel 55, February 18 [31] noting impossibility [*improbability*] early assignment, does Department's authorization send Chinese messenger still hold?

Sent Department; repeated Shanghai 300, for info Nanking, Off-Emb Canton.

CLUBB

121.67/3–1149 : Telegram

The Secretary of State to the Consul at Dairen (Paddock)

WASHINGTON, March 18, 1949—7 p. m.

39. Urtel 72 Mar 11.[32] Fol re communications Mukden, Tientsin and Peiping under present conditions Communist control for your info.

No direct word recd from Mukden since closing ConGen radio Nov. 18. Shanghai continuing blind broadcast selected important messages Mukden but no confirmation such messages recd. ConGens Peiping [and] Hongkong under Dept instruction have approached Commies re restrictions Mukden ConGen. No reply yet recd. Peiping has been instructed at opportune time request permission send two members staff Mukden. Mail service now open Peiping and Tientsin to Mukden but efforts communicate ConGen Mukden this means unsuccessful to date owing apparently isolation office Mukden.

Tientsin ConGen radio closed shortly after Commie takeover; blind broadcasts not successful. However commercial telegraph radio facilities now open Tientsin and outside. Coded messages not accepted. Commercial shipping north China ports and outside partially restored and Dept attempting arrange courier trip Tientsin this means.

Peiping ConGen radio not restricted by Commies to date continuing transmission receipt plain coded messages. Open mail between Nat and Commie China being reestablished.

In view foregoing Dept believes possibilities communication Mukden better via Peiping–Tientsin than Dairen and requests mail held

---

[30] *Supra.*
[31] Latter is the same as telegram No. 412 from the Ambassador in China, p. 937.
[32] Not printed.

for Mukden be returned Shanghai.   However Dept desires you continue efforts (Deptel 24 Feb 18 [33]) send Gleysteen [34] Mukden.

ACHESON

---

123 Manhard, Philip W. : Telegram

The Ambassador in China (Stuart) to the Secretary of State

NANKING, March 24, 1949—noon.
[Received March 25—8:21 a. m.]

644. Re Peiping telegram 300, March 18 to Shanghai, repeated Department unnumbered.   If by April 1, Communists have refused or taken no action Manhard and Armstrong applications proceed Mukden, I hope Department will then give further consideration recommendations made mytel 479, February 28, re withdrawal all or part consular staff in Mukden.   Current status our Mukden Consulate General now well into fifth month.   Our patience must have some limit.

Sent Department 644, repeated Shanghai 295, Peiping 100, Hong Kong 19, OffEmb Canton 189.

STUART

125.3516/3–2549 : Telegram

The Consul at Dairen (Paddock) to the Secretary of State

DAIREN, March 25, 1949—9 a. m.
[Received 9:22 p. m.]

82. White Russian recently returned from Mukden stated US flag flying over American Consulate General and large house opposite it where all US citizens residing.   Guards stationed before both quarters but this also true of Soviet Consulate General (which apparently now exists.   See Moscow telegram 4 to Department, repeated Nanking 2 [35]).

General condition of Mukden "settled down" but some looting and robbery still occurs in outskirts.

Source says Chinese Communists in complete authority and there little evidence of Soviet political activity.

Mukden-Dairen trip made by railroad without changing trains at Kwantung border.

Sent Nanking 53; repeated Department, Nanking, Shanghai, Shanghai 78, Moscow 38.

PADDOCK

---

[33] Not printed.
[34] Culver Gleysteen, Vice Consul at Dairen.
[35] Not printed; in this telegram dated January 2, the Chargé in the Soviet Union (Kohler) stated: "Foreign Office note just received states no Soviet Consulate in Mukden present time."   (702.6193/1–249)

¹ 23 Manhard, Philip W. : Telegram

The Consul General at Peiping (Clubb) to the Secretary of State

PEIPING, March 26, 1949—9 a. m.
[Received March 27—3 :34 a. m.]

488. ReEmbtel 100, March 24.[36] Manhard yesterday asked authorities whether travel pass Mukden yet forthcoming and was told should await communication from Bureau Public Safety.

Please correct second paragraph Contel 300, March 18 [*17?*] [37] to read "improbability" instead of "impossibility" unnoted typing error.

Am addressing new letter Ward personally today.

Re proposal withdrawal contained Embreftel, respectfully offer observations. Governing factors, I believe, are: (1) USSR views Manchuria area as part arena struggle with Western Powers, as strategic area for Soviet expansionism, and desires, if possible, exclude US and our representatives from area; (2) Position British and French Consulates Mukden basically similar to American, difference being primarily one of degree, British and French also lacking full freedom movement and facilities for communication with Governments through confidential mails and confidential codes (French Consul [at] Peiping who had been receiving letter weekly from Mukden colleague says he has received none for 2 weeks, British Consul received Mukden mail today); (3) Position Consulates here very similar to those Mukden and with hypothetical closing this radio station now it would be closer yet to Mukden isolated state (French Vice Consul Perrouche has been waiting in Shanghai for some time to return Peiping).

Believe Mukden is to be viewed as outpost in present struggle against USSR, that withdrawal would (1) lose US observation post of considerable importance and (2) possibly seriously weaken position other Consulates Communist area particularly Peiping, Tientsin. In circumstances I should propose: (1) representations along lines indicated Contel 475, March 24 [38] re position Consulate Generals, (2) consultation at same time with other concerned powers re Mukden and North China situation, (3) joint *démarche* if individual representations fruitless, either (*a*) before United Nations or (*b*) by ultimatum of sorts accompanied by implicit threat economic sanctions (this latter procedure in my opinion should be adopted only after sufficient time had been given for Communist foreign policy to develop further, my feeling being that it now is in process development), and (4) in absence favorable Communist action, joint action to withdraw Consulates if it seems absolutely necessary but at any rate to bring real economic pressure to bear on Communists. (Note Communist eco-

---

[36] Same as telegram No. 644 from the Ambassador in China, p. 948.
[37] Same as unnumbered telegram from the Consul General at Peiping, p. 947.
[38] *Post*, p. 1074.

nomic difficulties already reported by Tientsin, Peiping.)   In event success re Mukden, I feel proposal re-open Changchun and/or Harbin would be warranted.

Chou En-lai [39] reported to have expressed opinion after his return Peiping Communist attitude vis-à-vis foreigners Peiping (particularly) mistaken. Chou was reported some months ago (source now forgotten) to have contended in Community councils that CCP should incline toward USA rather than USSR, because in event war USA would win, but is said to have lost argument to those favoring USSR alignment. One way or another arrival here Chou and Mao [40] (Contel 489, March 26 [41]) will probably bring new developments for foreigners.

Repeated Nanking, Canton, Shanghai.

CLUBB

125.633/4–349 : Telegram

The Ambassador in China (Stuart) to the Secretary of State

NANKING, April 3, 1949—11 a. m.
[Received April 3—6 :02 a. m.]

697. For reasons set forth mytels 479, February 28 and 644, March 24 and despite cogent arguments to contrary, notably those set forth in Peiping's 488, March 27 [*26*] to Department, we still believe that, on balance, our wisest course is to attempt withdrawal our entire staff Mukden Consulate General soon and with maximum publicity. Commie failure to respond by now to Clubb's two approaches re general treatment Consulates, offices and travel of Manhard and Armstrong promise that Commies will not respond in future, merely leaving matter suspended in mid-air which is, we might point out, familiar Soviet trick.

We do not agree that withdrawal Mukden staff would necessarily have adverse effect on remaining Consular offices in Commie territory but feel it would more probably have salutary effect by showing Commies we do not intend to do business with them on any basis inconsistent with our sovereign dignity and self-respect. Also, Chinese Commie foreign policy has during past several months so accelerated its trend of hostility toward US as to leave little basis for supposing that with few more months of patience we can solve impasse.

Sent Department, repeated OffEmb Canton 218, Shanghai 325, Peiping 108.

STUART

---

[39] Member of Central Committee of the Chinese Communist Party.
[40] Mao Tse-tung, Chairman of the Central Committee of the Chinese Communist Party.
[41] Not printed.

702.4193/4–649 : Telegram

The Ambassador in China (Stuart) to the Secretary of State

NANKING, April 6, 1949—4 p. m.
[Received April 6—9 :11 a. m.]

714. Following text of coded letter sent by open mail March 9 by British Consul Mukden to British Consul General Peiping and handed us by British Embassy, Nanking:

"For first 2 weeks after Communist occupation Consulates had 'normal' relations with authorities. On 15th November peremptory letters were received demanding the handing over of wireless transmitters. French Consul and I replied that we had none. US Consul General replied that he could not deliver his transmitter, but would close it and authorities could remove if they wished. On November 19th, French Consul and I received second letter about transmitters, this time addressed to us personally (not as Consul) and referring to 'former' Consulates. On November 20th US Consul General and his staff including servants were confined to their house where they have remained ever since incommunicado. All are believed to be well. At the same time, my light and telephone (and not French Consul's) were cut off.

2. Since then French Consul and I have been officially ignored. Letters are not answered and interviews are evaded. The very few communications we have received e.g. from police about registration have been addressed personally. My light was restored after 5 weeks but telephone is still cut, car is unlicensed, sentry at gate intimidates visitors and till very recently plain-clothes men followed me and the staff everywhere. French Consul has been consistently treated one degree better.

3. Foreigners (except Americans) have however no personal ill-treatment to complain of. Most important damage to British interests has been the occupation of Hong Kong and Shanghai Bank, with the consent of the Russian left in charge, by Government Trading Corp. Missionaries are working without interference.

Present position is therefore that US Consulate General has ceased to exist and British and French can hardly collect information except from the press and are quite unable to protect nationals though their presence does support morale. On the other hand, authorities have never directly stated that they regard the Consulates as closed and I think they do not wish to commit themselves either way. I have therefore (having first made every effort to obtain interview or answer to letters) refrained from pressing the authorities for the past 3 months in hopes of facilitating 'normal' relations should general settlement make them possible later on. I am convinced that while action on my part might well aggravate the situation it could not conceivably improve it. Mukden authorities obviously receive their orders from elsewhere and I do not think any local improvement is likely till agreement is made either in North China or more probably Nanking."

Sent Department 714, repeated Shanghai 340, AmEmbassy Canton 226.

STUART

125.633/4–1549 : Telegram

The Secretary of State to the Consul General at Peiping (Clubb)

WASHINGTON, April 15, 1949—7 p. m.

212. Unless some new development causes in your opinion objection thereto, Dept desires that you utilize channel in your judgment most suitable convey message along following lines to Commie authorities:

One month has now passed since I conveyed message on behalf my Gov't respecting treatment accorded American consular officers, particularly at Mukden. No reply has been rec'd this message. Meanwhile indirect reports from Mukden state that American consular officers that city are confined to their compounds. Owing to blocking by Communist authorities for past 5 months of all communication with American ConGen Mukden it impossible confirm these reports or, if reports true, ascertain from ConGen reasons this extraordinary behavior Commie authorities. Blocking communications with Mukden in itself creates intolerable situation while reported confinement consular staff if true so clearly contrary universally accepted principles international comity that my Gov't can no longer delay clarification situation. I am accordingly instructed by my Gov't to state that unless Communist authorities are prepared promptly correct unsatisfactory situation Mukden and allow American consular officers there facilities universally recognized necessary proper to discharge their duties, American Gov't will have no alternative but to withdraw them. I am further instructed to point out that, in China as elsewhere in world, only presence American consular officers free to discharge their duties responsibilities can in view my Gov't provide services and safeguards essential to trade and commerce with US.

You may add that you have been requested to report to Dept re foregoing matter within next 2 weeks and that you would accordingly appreciate prompt consideration and reply.

In delivering foregoing you should follow procedure outlined Deptel 103 Mar 2.

ACHESON

125.633/4–1549 : Telegram

The Secretary of State to the Consul General at Peiping (Clubb)

WASHINGTON, April 15, 1949—7 p. m.

213. Immediately following tel [42] requests you make further approach Commies re Mukden. If you feel recent joint approach you and ur colleagues re consular facilities Peiping (urtel 611 Apr 14 [43]) makes desirable deferring Mukden issue few days or a week Dept would have no objection thereto but desires be informed thereof.

ACHESON

[42] *Supra.*
[43] *Post,* p. 1077.

125.633/4–1849 : Telegram

The Ambassador in China (Stuart) to the Secretary of State

NANKING, April 18, 1949—3 p. m.
[Received April 18—6:22 a. m.]

783. Reference Embtel 697, April 3. Today, as total eclipse our Mukden ConGen enters its sixth month, we suggest Department reconsider views expressed in Embtel 479, February 28, particularly our recommendation that Clubb be instructed inform Peiping authorities we feel forced to close Mukden ConGen and request their assistance in effecting withdrawal of staff.

In this connection, we suggest Department also refer to Embtel 714, April 6, which quoted official British report from Mukden as stating American consular staff have been confined incommunicado to their houses since November 20 and that American ConGen has "ceased to exist".

Sent Department, repeated Shanghai 386, OffEmb Canton 262, Peiping 128.

STUART

702.0093/4–1949 : Telegram

The Consul General at Peiping (Clubb) to the Secretary of State

PEIPING, April 19, 1949—11 a. m.
[Received April 19—4:15 a. m.]

654. ReDeptels 212 and 213, April 13 [15]. Return by local authorities Consul's note without comment (Contel 646, April 18 [44]) would seem outwardly constitute essential rejection at least temporarily Consul's propositions. Matter will be analysed in separate message [45] but for present purposes this can perhaps be taken as real position. Delay few days or week for reasons connected that *démarche* would therefore not seem warranted.

Would, however, recommend waiting approximately same period see what, if anything, comes of peace negotiations [46] since this may affect overall situation in respect diplomatic and consular relations. Information obtained by Colonel Barrett [47] indicates matters Communist attitude toward foreigners have been discussed in peace negotiations—though probably not as item major importance.

In meantime would appreciate being informed whether there has been any consultation or coordination with British or French regard-

---

[44] *Post*, p. 1080.
[45] Telegram No. 658, April 21, 7 p. m. *ibid.*
[46] For documentation on the so-called peace negotiations between the Chinese Government and the Chinese Communists, see pp. 1 ff.
[47] Col. David G. Barrett, Assistant Military Attaché in China.

ing projected move.[48]   Respectfully invite attention Contel 488, March 26 this regard.

Sent Department, repeated Nanking 408, OffEmb Canton 63, Shanghai 450.

CLUBB

125.633/4-2549 : Telegram

The Consul General at Peiping (Clubb) to the Secretary of State

PEIPING, April 25, 1949—3 p. m.
[Received April 25—11:58 a. m.]

700. Urtel 212, April 15, mytel 659, April 19.[49]   Note that Communist occupation Nanking, probable occupation Shanghai near future constitute important new developments which might due course bring about some change in Communist attitude re Consulates. Consulates may finally be given degree recognition but there is lacking firm assurance this will happen soon or at all prior recognition Communist government yet to be established.   In circumstances therefore would propose message outlined urtel should be communicated Communists on or about April 27.   In consideration, however, of (1) possibility afore-mentioned changed Communist attitude, (2) possible desirability not indicating in advance our proposed line action, invite consideration alternative of omitting from message statement that consular officers will be withdrawn unless position Mukden is rectified. Time limit might be left in message and at end of 2 weeks unless developments in interim seemed to merit different line action, it simply be requested Communists provide facilities for withdrawal those officers in view Communist failure rectify existing conditions.   Am uncertain whether this changed approach offers improvement other than increased flexibility given, but invite attention to situation. Please instruct.

Will explore possibility communicating message direct [to] Yeh Chien-ying or other high authority as well as presenting it at Aliens Affairs Office.   Former approach would probably be more effective if feasible.

Information received week ago from person coming direct from Mukden known this office indicates Ward confined consular office and Mrs. Ward separately in their residence.

Repeated to Nanking 44, Canton 75, and Shanghai 479.

CLUBB

---

[48] The Secretary of State in telegram No. 85, April 29, 8 p. m., informed the Consul General at Tientsin as follows: " 'Projected move' refers approach ConGen Peiping to Commies re conditions Mukden."   (702.0093/4–2949)
[49] Latter not printed.

125.633/4-2549 : Telegram

The Secretary of State to the Consul General at Peiping (Clubb)

WASHINGTON, April 26, 1949—7 p. m.

235. After careful consideration ur 700 April 25 Dept remains of opinion best course re Mukden is inform Commies that unless situation rectified US must withdraw its consular personnel Mukden thereby insuring Commies apprised our intentions prior to deciding issue. Dept not sanguine success but considers chances this approach measurably better than mere repetition earlier plea which Commies so far utterly ignored. In any case it evident situation Mukden cannot be allowed continue indefinitely awaiting Commie change of heart. In view foregoing Dept desires you deliver message substantially as outlined Deptel 212 April 15 as soon as possible and concurs desirability communicating if possible directly Yeh or other high authority as well as Alien Affairs Office.

ACHESON

125.0093/4-3049 : Telegram

The Consul General at Peiping (Clubb) to the Secretary of State

PEIPING, April 30, 1949—11 a. m.
[Received April 30—9 a. m.]

735. ReDeptel 212, April 15, Contel 654, April 19. Registered letter sent express today to Peiping General Headquarters, People's Liberation Army, along lines indicated Department's reference telegram.

Passed Nanking 468, Canton 90, Shanghai 498.

[CLUBB]

125.0090/5-449 : Telegram

The Consul General at Peiping (Clubb) to the Secretary of State

PEIPING, May 4, 1949—5 p. m.
[Received May 5—12 :30 p. m.]

763. Re Contel 734 [*735*], April 30. Sent today double registry letter May 3 addressed Peiping mayor enclosing copy communications sent previously headquarters PLA.[50] This course followed because general unreceptivity Aliens Affairs Office re subject in point.

Passed Nanking 483, OffEmb Canton 96, Shanghai 511.

CLUBB

---

[50] People's Liberation Army.

893.101/5–949 : Telegram

The Consul General at Peiping (Clubb) to the Secretary of State

PEIPING, May 9, 1949—10 a. m.
[Received May 9—5:34 a. m.]

796. ReContel 734 [*735*] April 30. Peiping mayor (Contel 763, May 4) returned yesterday without comment but letter sent headquarters still unreturned.

ReContel 732, April 29 [*30*],[51] particularly last paragraph. Urge action on matter Japan trade before May 15, if possible, because of possible value for Mukden matter.

CLUBB

125.633/5–1749 : Telegram

The Ambassador in China (Stuart) to the Secretary of State

NANKING, May 17, 1949—noon.
[Received May 17—6:14 a. m.]

1042. ReDeptel 235, April 26 to Peiping, repeated Nanking 522. Assuming action has not been taken along following lines, we believe time has now come for Clubb to send short formal note to highest available Peiping authorities informing that in absence of necessary assurances requested in his last communication, US Government has no alternative but to withdraw immediately staff of Consulate General, Mukden, and requesting cooperation Communists to that end.

Sent Department 1042, repeated Peiping 167, Shanghai 587, Embassy Canton 428.

STUART

125.633/5–1749 : Telegram

The Secretary of State to the Ambassador in China (Stuart)

WASHINGTON, May 17, 1949—6 p. m.

600. In separate tel [52] being rptd to you Dept is instructing ConGen Peiping inform Commies our decision close Consulate Mukden and request transportation facilities staff and effects. At same time Dept desires unless you perceive objection thereto that you bring to attn Huang Hua, Chief, Aliens Affairs Office, either through channel mentioned ur 994 May 11 [53] or through personal ltr intolerable conditions which have confronted ConGen Mukden since Nov 18 and efforts this Govt has taken to have conditions improved, referring specifically to

[51] Vol. IX, p. 974.
[52] *Infra.*
[53] *Ante*, p. 741.

two previous approaches Commies by ConGen Peiping and decision this Govt close Mukden office. You may point out that you bringing this matter to his attn since under conditions Peiping impossible ascertain whether previous messages have reached high Commie auths and because of responsibility which you in your position bear for Ward and staff and in the hope that he will bring this matter to the attn of the responsible Commie auths in Peiping.

ACHESON

125.633/5–1749 : Telegram

The Secretary of State to the Consul General at Peiping (Clubb) [54]

[Extract]

WASHINGTON, May 17, 1949—7 p. m.

299. In view time elapsed without reply your approach Commies re Mukden Dept desires you inform Commies that owing their imposition arbitrary unreasonable restrictions ConGen Mukden US Govt withdrawing its staff closing office that city. You should request transportation and other facilities to enable ConGen staff with personal and other effects and such office supplies and equipment other Govt movable property as deemed desirable depart Commie controlled areas. Evacuate via Tientsin or Peiping depending available housing, etc.

Dept considers most satisfactory method inform Mukden this decision and convey necessary instructions would be send Manhard [and] Armstrong [to] Mukden. Following general instructions for assistance Ward closing Mukden office:

Mukden Cons dist[rict] being added Peiping Cons dist.

Prin[cipal]Off[icer] Mukden shld arrange evacuation personnel and effects closely as possible accord FSRegs.[55] However, due situation, Dept must rely his discretion.

. . . .

ACHESON

125.633/5–2149 : Telegram

The Consul General at Peiping (Clubb) to the Secretary of State

PEIPING, May 21, 1949—10 a. m.
[Received May 21—2:13 a. m.]

876. ReDeptel 299, May 17. Letter dated May 19 southeast [*sent*] headquarters PLA, double registry, yesterday in sense directed. Let-

---

[54] Repeated to the Ambassador in China as telegram No. 603, to the Minister-Counselor of Embassy in China as telCan No. 187, to the Consul in Shankhai as telegram No. 967, and to the Consul General at Mukden as telegram No. 23.
[55] Foreign Service Regulations.

ter same date mailed Ward express double registry today, enclosing copies 2 letters headquarters and Depreftel.

Letters to headquarters requested travel facilities for Manhard [and] Armstrong.

ReDeptel 278, May 13,[56] perforce of course addressed headquarters PLA as such. Since proposed in event nonreply however address either Chu Teh [57] or Mao Tse-tung or both re subject, re Contel 860 [896] May 18,[58] please instruct re mode address in present instance.

Copy letter to Ward and enclosure sent Tientsin for information.

Sent Department 876, repeated Nanking 569, OffEmb Canton 129, Shanghai 588.

CLUBB

125.633/5–2549 : Telegram

The Ambassador in China (Stuart) to the Secretary of State

NANKING, May 25, 1949—4 p. m.
[Received May 25—6:16 a. m.]

1111. May 24 delivered to Huang Hua, Chief, Aliens Affairs Office, memo informing Commies of decision close Mukden (Deptel 603, May 17 [59]) and requesting Huang's assistance transmit this information to appropriate authorities Peiping and transmit to Ward detailed instructions for closing office. Huang stated matter outside scope his duties but he would consider and advise us later whether he could assist in personal capacity.

Sent Department; repeated Peiping 182.

STUART

125.633/5–2649 : Telegram

The Acting Secretary of State to the Ambassador in China (Stuart)

WASHINGTON, May 26, 1949—1 p. m.

640. From Butterworth.[60] We are all very disturbed by protracted confinement Ward and other members staff Mukden and wish no stone left unturned to effect their speedy departure. I hope you will find means personally to press this matter to a rapid conclusion. [Butterworth.]

WEBB

---

[56] Same as telegram No. 98 to the Consul General at Tientsin, p. 1082.
[57] Commander in Chief of Chinese Communist armies.
[58] *Post*, p. 1084.
[59] Same as telegram No. 299 to the Consul General at Peiping, p. 957.
[60] W. Walton Butterworth, Director of the Office of Far Eastern Affairs.

125.633/5–3149 : Telegram

The Consul General at Peiping (Clubb) to the Secretary of State

PEIPING, May 31, 1949—5 p. m.
[Received June 1—6 :35 a. m.]

914. ReContel 876, May 21. Consulate has received no reply to either its letter [to] headquarters PLA or from Mukden.

Travel permits Manhard [and] Armstrong still unreceived.

Information available received thus far indicates foreigners generally unpermitted to date leave Manchuria.

Please instruct.

Sent Department 914, repeated Nanking 597, OffEmb Canton 137, Shanghai 610.

CLUBB

---

123 Ward, Angus : Telegram

The Ambassador in China (Stuart) to the Secretary of State

NANKING, June 1, 1949—3 p. m.
[Received June 2—12 :06 a. m.]

1165. For Butterworth. ReDeptel 640, May 26. I also am deeply disturbed about status of Ward and his staff. Thinking that perhaps a personal letter from me to Chou En-lai would be beneficial in this respect I sent Philip Fugh [61] to Huang Hua May 31 to see if latter would transmit such letter. Huang's first reaction was negative. He said normal channel is through Clubb. However, he did promise to give my request further thought. Needless to say, I shall continue my efforts. (See Embtel 1111, May 25).

As respects whole question of Mukden ConGen, Huang insisted that it was outside his jurisdiction, but he did indicate his belief that its present situation may be explicable by other than surface facts. He hinted that Ward may have been doing espionage for Kmt. However, when pressed, he insisted he had no concrete information on this. I fear we must consider this comment revealing of Communists' official attitude toward our Mukden office once they are publicly put on defensive. Huang added that if he were too active in matter he would be suspected by his superiors of yielding to pressure from me as old teacher and thus overstepping his authority. For obvious reasons Huang requested Fugh to keep this conversation strictly confidential.

STUART

---

[61] Chinese personal secretary to the Ambassador in China.

125.633/5-2149 : Telegram

The Acting Secretary of State to the Consul General at Peiping (Clubb) [62]

WASHINGTON, June 3, 1949—7 p. m.

351. Ur 876 May 21. In view Commie non-reply ur letter PLA Headquarters and non-action request travel permits Manhard, Armstrong, Dept desires you obtain personal interview highest ranking member Alien Affairs Bureau available. You should outline orally steps which you have already taken requesting that facilities be granted Ward to permit closing of office Mukden and withdrawal of staff and call attention to non-receipt any reply [from] Commies. You should reiterate this request and add that you have been instructed by your Govt to state that it takes a most serious view of this matter and to request that you be informed at once of the steps which the Commie authorities are taking in order that Ward and staff may depart from Mukden.

Dept desires above action be taken in light of info from Emb reporting informal conversation with Director Alien Affairs Bureau indicating Alien Affairs Bureau Peiping proper channel.

For ur info and such use as you may consider desirable in connection foregoing, delivery by CalTex of tanker fuel oil for Shanghai Power Company has been approved. If use made this info, Dept believes it desirable avoid any suggestion horse-trading which might lead Commies consider pressure on U.S. Consulates profitable means obtain supplies from U.S.

Dept suggests Shanghai also review Mukden situation with appropriate Commie authorities who probably more impressed essentiality fuel oil for SPC [63] than Peiping Commies.

WEBB

125.633/6-649 : Telegram

The Ambassador in China (Stuart) to the Secretary of State

NANKING, June 6, 1949—11 a. m.
[Received June 7—5 :06 a. m.]

1204. ReEmbtel 1111, repeated Peiping 182, May 25. Embassy officer was summoned to Alien Affairs Office June 3 where he was informed by Ch'en Ying that closing of Mukden Consulate outside jurisdiction that office and therefore no action could be taken on our request. However, memo originally handed Huang Hua was not

---

[62] Repeated to the Ambassador in China as No. 669 and to the Consul General at Shanghai as No. 1122.
[63] Shanghai Power Co.

returned. Time elapsed since he first received it suggests he forwarded its substance to Peiping authorities as part of his request for instructions how to handle matter.

Sent Department 1204, repeated Peiping 196.

STUART

125.6336/6–749 : Telegram

The Consul General at Shanghai (Cabot) to the Secretary of State

SHANGHAI, June 7, 1949—6 p. m.
[Received June 7—7:34 a. m.]

2141. *Shanghai Post* editorial commenting on treatment Consul [at] Mukden speculates Soviets may be responsible because of their special interest in Manchuria.

Considering Chinese Commies have shown themselves sensitive to newspaper comment in US on other matters, notably their possible Titoism,[64] it occurs to me now that publicity has been given Mukden affair Department might wish quietly stir some comment in US press along lines *Shanghai Post's* editorial. If there is basis for presumption Soviets are involved, it may well be due to their desire embroil US and Chinese Commies. Comment in US might perhaps end by embroiling Chinese Commies and Soviets.

Sent Department 2141, repeated Nanking 1120.

CABOT

125.633/6–749 : Telegram

The Ambassador in China (Stuart) to the Secretary of State

NANKING, June 7, 1949—6 p. m.
[Received June 7—10:15 a. m.]

1231. Reference Peiping's 914, June 1 [*May 31*] to Department, repeated Canton 137, Shanghai 610. Suggest Department may wish to instruct Consul General [at] Peiping to request Headquarters PLA to authorize Consul General to send to Ward by regular commercial facilities text of Deptel 299, May 17 to Peiping regarding closing of Mukden Consulate General.

Since things move slowly in China, we have not yet abandoned all optimism that we will be able to reach reasonable solution with Communists regarding Mukden impasse. If action suggested above and in Deptel 351, June 3 to Peiping, repeated Nanking 669, proves unfruitful, suggest Department may then wish to instruct Clubb to

---

[64] Marshal Josip Broz Tito, head of Yugoslav Communist Party and State, who broke with Moscow in June 1948.

follow it up shortly by appropriate communication to Chou En-lai and/or Mao Tse-tung.

However, if by June 19 (1 month after Clubb sent his first communication) Communists still maintain their wall of silence, it would then be time, we believe, for top level Department spokesman to make strong detailed statement regarding Communist treatment of our Mukden Consul General with implications possible Soviet instigation, immediately thereafter giving subject fullest play on VOA [65] and USIS.[66] Unless factors relating to recognition of Chinese Communists make it unwise, Department may also wish to have spokesman indicate that Department is giving consideration to raising matter in Security Council.

Repeated Canton 509, Shanghai 662, Peiping 206.

STUART

125.633/6–949 : Telegram

The Ambassador in China (Stuart) to the Secretary of State

NANKING, June 9, 1949—noon.
[Received June 9—5:16 a. m.]

1245. In my conversation with Huang Hua June 6 (see Embtel 1235, June 8 [67]) I took opportunity tell him that I attach great importance solution impasse regarding our Mukden Consulate General; that perhaps my principal duty is assure protection American nationals, and that I would be very reluctant leave China, in compliance my orders to Washington on consultation, until consular staff has been safely withdrawn from Mukden.

Huang replied that this matter outside his province. However, when I pointed out to him that through Clubb we had exhausted every process we could think of without even reply from Peiping authorities, he promised that he would think again about what it would be possible for him to do.

I do not doubt that Huang's reply was governed by fear that if he oversteps his proper bounds his superiors would suspect him of yielding to pressure from me as former student. However, it is reasonable suppose he will report my remarks to Peiping.

Sent Department; repeated Shanghai 668, OffEmb Canton 515, Peiping 210.

STUART

---

[65] Voice of America.
[66] United States Information Service.
[67] *Ante*, p. 752.

125.633/6–949 : Telegram

The Consul General at Peiping (Clubb) to the Secretary of State

PEIPING, June 9, 1949—noon.
[Received June 9—5:57 a. m.]

966. ReDeptel 351, June 3. Called yesterday Alien Affairs Office and submitted application "see high-ranking responsible official your office in order directly discuss matter of decision American Government close American Consulate General, Mukden". Attendant parroted usual Communist phrase indicating I, as Consul General, unknown to them, required that I add to application that I was making request in capacity ordinary alien before it could be considered. In effort accomplish mission, I complied, attendant disappeared into inner office, returned shortly afterwards to reply as follows:

Communists are informed by radio of matter in point and Mukden officers if they desire withdraw should make application locally. When I said had sent letter Mukden reference matter but reply unreceived, attendant stated message could be forwarded by me in private capacity to Mukden officers through Alien Affairs Office if desired.

I pointed out I was under instructions Department discuss matter with high-ranking responsible official. Attendant said what he had just said constituted reply to my request. Interview refused.

In circumstances was unable present matter to responsible official that office along lines proposed Department reftel and of course did not attempt do so to petty office attendant.

Please instruct whether additional message should be sent Mukden through Alien Affairs Office along indicated lines in private capacity.

Re Department reftel. Note that Alien Affairs Office Peiping has previously repeatedly indicated it is without authority over (1) matters outside Peiping and (2) consular affairs; and it would seem that, if response petty official may be taken signify Communists have decided (1) transmit message and (2) possibly permit Mukden personnel act on it, reply still cannot be considered adequate assurance that there will be extended those Consulate officers either customary courtesies or adequate facilities for removal Government property and personal effects. There is possibility that officers by these terms would be caused remove under humiliating, at least, undignified circumstances. ReEmbtel 1231, June 7 to Department. My own recommendation would be that (1) strong representations be made [Huang] Hua, Nanking, and (2) I be authorized make representations along same lines Mao Tse-tung, Peiping. Those representations, if taking note of information received from Alien Affairs Office indicating Mukden personnel should make local applications, should make it clear that American Government unsatisfied with that reply and desires that responsible Communist authorities take appropriate action to end that winding up Mukden affairs shall be in accordance with requisites international law and protocol.

Re Embassy reftel. Believe that as suggested Contels 732, April 28 [*30*],[68] and 838, May 14,[69] most potent threat to be used against Communists lies ready at hand in SCAP [70] control Japanese trade which can be denied Communists until they act in civilized manner. Invite attention this connection Contel 869 May 20,[69] Tientsin 252, May 26 to Department.[71]

Sent Department; repeated Nanking 641, OffEmb Canton 154, Shanghai 648. Department pass Tientsin 59.

CLUBB

125.633/6–1149 : Telegram

The Consul General at Peiping (*Clubb*) *to the Secretary of State*

PEIPING, June 11, 1949.
[Received June 11—7:45 a. m.]

991. ReContel 985, June 11.[69] Following telegram received yesterday from Ward for transmittal American Embassy:

"No. 1, noon, June 8. Copies of Department telegram No. 603 [72] and letter of American Embassy, Nanking, dated May 17 mailed from Peiping received yesterday. Restrictions imposed on Consulate office American official personnel since noon November 20 continue unchanged. Am trying contact mayor to ascertain whether permission can be given for evacuation of staff and purchase of materials for packing. No replies to repeated requests to see mayor made since November 9 and to buy packing materials made following month.

"Last Embassy message received in November is No. 196. Can only send telegrams in Chinese language. Please transmit this telegram to Department as No. 1. Please reply upon receipt."

Sent Nanking 664; Department 991; OffEmb Canton 165; Shanghai 660.

CLUBB

---

[68] Vol. IX, p. 974.
[69] Not printed.
[70] Supreme Commander, Allied Powers in Japan (MacArthur).
[71] Not found in Department of State files.
reported the substance of this agency's article as printed in two Shanghai papers.

811.20293/6–1949 : Telegram

The Consul General at Peiping (Clubb) to the Secretary of State

PEIPING, June 19, 1949.
[Received June 19—5:46 a. m.]

1039. Following is full text NCNA [73] English language service item appearing today under Mukden June 18 datelines: [74]

"Base of big American spy ring brought to light Manchuria has just been disclosed here by Public Security Department of Northeast Administrative Council. Principal espionage agents involved in case are Sasaki, Japanese, Royen-Tsang, Mongolian, and Wu Jen-chieh, Chinese national of Sino-American parents; they have been arrested and will be punished according to law of People's Government.

"They were discovered with 6 American-made transmitting and receiving radio sets of 15 watts, 3 generators, 16 secret code books of American espionage service, 10 gold ingots for espionage expenses, 3 working plans, 4 directives, 13 documents on organization of American T.S. espionage organization and biographical material of its personnel, 28 copies of intelligence and 40 military maps and charts.

"Evidence at hand shows that so-called American Consulate in Mukden and US Army liaison group Mukden are American espionage organs. American espionage service Mukden made use of former Japanese secret service agents and Chinese and Mongolian traitors to conspire against Chinese people and world peace. According to confession of Sasaki, one of principal espionage agents, he engaged in espionage work before complete liberation of Manchuria under direct instructions from so-called US Army liaison group and former American Consulate in Mukden. His job was to collect military, political and economic intelligence in Northeast liberated area and Inner Mongolia.

"Prior to liberation Mukden in October 1948, Sasaki and Tsao Cheng-teh received orders from so-called US Army liaison group and former American Consulate to go 'underground,' set up secret radio station and continue their activities. So-called US Army Liaison Group (ALG) was open title of American Espionage Department in China called External Survey Detachment 44 of US War Department in Shanghai (ESD 44) with headquarters Shanghai. After Japanese surrender ALG moved to Manchuria with Kmt invasion army and set up branch groups Mukden and Changchun. It enlisted former Japanese secret service agents, Mongolian and Chinese traitors to conduct espionage work against Chinese people. One of Japanese special service agents employed by ALG Mukden was Sasaki, called SSK alias Chang Chih-chung in China and Sakuma in Japan.

"He was graduated from Russian Mongolian [garbled group] of Military Academy of Japanese Kwantung army in Hsingan. During Manchoukuo regime, he undermined Northeast People's anti-Japanese war of resistance in Hsinganling area in Heilungkiang province.

"After August 15, 1945, he fled to Mukden and became intelligence agent of Second Office of Kmt Ministry National Defence. Later he

[73] New China News Agency (Communist).
[74] In telegram No. 2351, June 19, not printed, the Consul General at Shanghai reported the substance of this agency's article as printed in two Shanghai papers.

was recommended to work in former American Consulate, Mukden, and ALG as an espionage agent. He maintained direct connections with Nishida, American-Japanese who was an assistant to Senglauf, head of ALG in Mukden, an American German. His job was to absorb remnants of Japanese and Manchoukuo secret service into work of collecting intelligence on Northeast liberated area and Mongolia. He had altogether supplied important intelligence 70 to 80 times to Nishida and directed American espionage group called T. S. according to copy of report to Nishida on locations of the T. S. organization by Sasaki in April 1948, headquarters of espionage department moved to Peiping in February 1948, with branch headquarters in Mukden and Peiping. Mukden branch headquarters had under it 11 intelligence stations set up in Changchun, Harbin, Tsitsihar, Mutankiang, Tumen, Hailar, Manchuli and Hunchun. ALG Changchun enlisted service of Mongolian traitor Po Yen-tsang called TOAS 4 and ordered him to set up intelligence stations Inner Mongolia to collect intelligence and engage in sabotage work.

"In February, 1947, he went to Chengchiatun in Liaoyuan country and asked the Mongolians there to spread rumor that Inner Mongolian problem can only be solved with help of Chiang Kai-shek and America to undermine national unity of China.

"Then he set up intelligence station in Pechengtze (Piuchengtzu) and supplied American espionage department with intelligence of organization and names of leading persons of Inner Mongolian autonomous government. He also supplied American espionage department with brief biographies and accounts of habits of these persons as well as photographs showing political life of Mongolian people.

Another espionage agent, Wu Jen-chieh, was recommended by Barandson, American intelligence agent in Mukden, to establish connections with Walsh in so-called Navy Liaison Branch Group. His job was to pass on intelligence between Mukden and Tientsin. Wu Jen-chieh camouflaged himself by acting at first as English Secretary of Kmt Northeast Administrative [Affairs] Committee and later as merchant. He met Walsh in family of Tovodani Jiroo, Japanese professor of Mukden National Medical College, and after receiving letters containing intelligence he flew to Tientsin and handed them over to Mrs. Kossov, White Russian residing in former Tientsin British concession. When Wu later lost contact with Walsh, he was recommended by Senglauf to work under direction of Hunt, another American intelligence agent.

"On eve of liberation of all Manchuria at end last October, open section of ALG in Mukden prepared to withdraw to Shanghai and Sasaki [and] Tsao Cheng-teh were ordered to draw up plan for working underground. Main point in Sasaki's plan was to make use of influence of the 'third forces'. So-called third forces were the underground remnants of Japanese and puppet Manchoukuo secret services including Arisaka, Takeuchi, Hsiao Yao-ting, Wang Fanghsin, Kuo Cheng-lu, Yana-Giki, Yamamura and Tsao Cheng-teh, Takeuchi and Hsiao Yao-ting took charge of communications between Peiping and Mukden with the Alice Café in Mukden as their meeting place.

Sasaki received from ALG two miniature radio sets, one miniature generator and one secret code book, nine gold ingots, wheat flour, sugar and rice as espionage expenses. [Garbled group] ordered Sasaki and his gang to collect intelligence about garrison forces, traveling regulations, identification cards, etc., in Manchuria and Inner Mongolia. According to 'plan of work of various stations in East Mongolia proper' drawn up by Tsao Cheng-teh, it was planned to set up an intelligence headquarters in Mukden and liaison stations in Wangyemiao, Changchun, Szepingkai, Chinchow, Chengchiatun and Tungliao. Sixteen intelligence agents were to be employed who would camouflage themselves as merchants.

Plan also provided 12,000 Kmt gold yuan for monthly expenses and 2,100 Kmt GY per month for travelling expenses. At same time, ALG headquarters Shanghai sent Myadan to organize underground work of Mongolian traitor Po Yen-tsang and gave him 2 portable miniature American-made radio sets, code books, intelligence expense [garbled group] American dollars and 16 bags of flour.

Hunt in like manner gave Wu Jen-chieh two miniature portable American-made radio sets, one miniature generator, one secret code book, gold ingots and gold bars as espionage expenses. Hunt also told Wu to establish radio connections with Tientsin. After liberation of Mukden, these espionage agents continued their organization of underground espionage activities.

In December 1946, Wu Jen-chieh went with American intelligence agent Barandson in name UNRRA [76] to Tungliao. They collected military intelligence about People's Liberation Army in name of investigation relief conditions and supplied this intelligence to former American Consul in Mukden.

Another American espionage agent known as liaison officer also ordered Wu Jen-chieh to collect intelligence on Northeast liberated area for former American Consul in Mukden. When Japanese were repatriated in 1947, former American Consul retained Sasaki for espionage work and a retention permit No. Cheng Chiao 177 and identification card for Japanese Nationals were issued to Sasaki by Kmt Administrative Affairs Committee. In January 1948, Hunt, who succeeded Walsh in directing Wu Jen-chieh, stayed on first floor of former Mukden American Consulate. He went to see him four times and Hunt told him to visit him there only until after dark.

"On October 27, 1948, Hunt asked Wu to see him in the former Consulate at 8 next morning and when Wu went there, Hunt took a radio set, a generator and a secret code book in a jeep to Wu's home."

Chinese language version in today's local press has following concluding paragraph:

"Facts of whole case and all kinds documentary proof captured show clearly that so-called Consulate of US Government at Mukden and Army Liaison Group are in fact American espionage organizations whose aim was utilization of Japanese special service and Chinese traitors and Mongol traitors for furthering anti-Chinese people plot activities for destruction of Chinese people's revolutionary enterprise and world peace. Our People's Government respecting offenders in that case is going to impose restraints (or 'controls') in accordance with law.["]

CLUBB

---

[76] United Nations Relief and Rehabilitation Administration.

125.6336/6–2049 : Telegram

The Minister-Counselor of Embassy in China (Clark) to the Secretary of State

CANTON, June 20, 1949.
[Received June 20—2:16 a. m.]

Cantel 614. Following statement released press June 20:

"Communist charges that the American Consulate General in Mukden was engaged in espionage are ridiculous and absolutely false. The Communists may have levelled such charges in order to distract attention from the fact that they have held the American Consul General and his staff incommunicado for the past 7 months in violation of international law and custom."

Sent Department; repeated Nanking 412, Shanghai 350.

CLARK

811.20293/6–2049 : Telegram

The Ambassador in China (Stuart) to the Secretary of State

NANKING, June 20, 1949—noon.
[Received June 20—5:38 a. m.]

1330. In response to AP, UP, *New York Times* and AFP [77] requests for comment on Peiping radio June 18 broadcast re alleged American espionage net in Manchuria and involvement of ConGen Mukden, we felt compelled to make brief oral statement for attribution along following lines:

"Embassy lacks sufficient information for full comment. As is known, communications between Embassy and ConGen Mukden have been severed for about 7 months. However, Embassy believes that reference to ConGen Mukden as espionage organ is too fantastic to merit any comment."

We also informed correspondents that perhaps fuller statement will be forthcoming in Washington.

We did not make fuller comment not only because we felt that on such important matter prior approval of Department should be obtained but also because we felt it injudicious in view our present position Nanking. However, we do believe Department should not hesitate to issue additional statement, making it as strong as possible with view to forcing Communists back into defensive position. We suggest comment along following lines:

"Department fully endorses statement issued June 19 by AmEmb Nanking that Chinese Communist allegations that ConGen Mukden served as American espionage organ are too fantastic to deserve com-

---

[77] Agence France Presse.

ment. Department, however, notes similarity between these charges and charges which have been directed at American diplomatic missions and consular offices in other Communist-dominated countries. They are all designed to smear integrity of those establishments and to rationalize arbitrary restrictions placed upon them by Communist authorities. In particular, Department believes Chinese Communist charges against ConGen Mukden are prompted by bad conscience occasioned by uncivilized and totally unjustifiable treatment which Department has good reason to believe Chinese Communists have accorded personnel that office since last November 20.

As Department has made public in previous statements, all communications between ConGen Mukden and outside world were severed on November 18, only 16 days after Mukden was occupied by Chinese Communist forces. According to unofficial reports, it appears that staff of ConGen Mukden has essentially been under house arrest since November 20. Only since June 13 have Chinese Communists relaxed their communications blockade of ConGen Mukden to extent of permitting it to exchange with AmEmb Nanking and AmConGen Peiping a few Chinese language telegrams on purely administrative matters.

Department is pleased to note that Chinese Communists at least have finally broken their long silence re ConGen Mukden, if only by referring to it in their broadcast as 'so-called AmCon' and 'former AmCon'. Department therefore permits itself to hope that Chinese Communists will finally acknowledge and take action on its note of May 19 which was delivered by AmConGen Peiping to Communist authorities in Peiping informing that 'owing to imposition by Chinese Communists of arbitrary and unreasonable restrictions on ConGen Mukden, US Government is withdrawing its staff and closing its office in that city.' In connection with this withdrawal, Department expects that Communist authorities will now facilitate prompt departure of staff of ConGen Mukden by according it full courtesies customarily enjoyed under international law and comity by foreign government officials."

Sent Department, repeated OffEmb Canton 564, Shanghai 724, Peiping 226.

STUART

125.633/6–2149 : Telegram

The Ambassador in China (Stuart) to the Secretary of State

NANKING, June 21, 1949—11 a. m.
[Received June 21—1 a. m.]

1337. We also are apprehensive (Peiping telegram 966, June 9 to Department) that Communist authorities will permit removal of consular staff from Mukden only under humiliating or undignified circumstances. Hwang Hua raised question with Philip Fugh June 18 referring to fact Ward had been permitted communicate with ConGen Peiping. Hwang implied steps taken in Peiping in certain quarters had been effective.

Suggest Department may wish to instruct Clubb to follow up in Peiping with view to impressing upon highest Communist authorities he can reach fact that we expect Ward and staff to be accorded full courtesies customarily received under international law and comity by officers of foreign governments.

Sent Department, repeated Shanghai 730, OffEmb Canton 567, Peiping 228.

STUART

811.20293/6–2149 : Telegram

The Ambassador in China (Stuart) to the Secretary of State

NANKING, June 21, 1949—6 p. m.
[Received June 22—1:16 a. m.]

1341. ReEmbtel 1330, June 30. [Here follows a reference to Chinese Communist allegations about American activities in Manchuria and the question to what extent they were voluntarily terminated as the collapse of Manchuria became more imminent.]

There is also considerable element of falsehood in Communist claims. . . . Activity in Manchuria was directed against USSR, not "Chinese people". Much of it was hang-over from Japanese war and was not at all concerned with CCP. Broadcast partly supports this by reference to American espionage in Inner Mongolia.

On balance it seems to us that probably preponderant factor behind Communist charges are desires to impugn American motives in China, to rationalize their conduct toward staff Consulate General, Mukden, to denigrate reports Ward will make when he leaves Mukden and possibly to smooth way for further restrictions against other American consular offices and perhaps even this Embassy. It seems to us furthermore that whole tenor of charges and attention to detail show Soviet influence.

In latter connection we suggest release of charges at this late date was possibly occasioned by Soviet-controlled Chinese Communists in Mukden feeling impelled to justify to more independent China, that is North China, their arrogant treatment of our consular staff which will redound so to their disadvantage once Ward is free to tell his story. As corollary, possibly Communist accusations signify our Mukden staff is going shortly to receive more assistance in its withdrawal than it has hitherto experienced.

Sent Department 1341, repeated Shanghai 733, OffEmb Canton 569, Peiping 230.

STUART

125.633/6–2349 : Telegram

The Ambassador in China (Stuart) to the Secretary of State

NANKING, June 23, 1949.
[Received June 23—7 :04 a. m.]

1353. Following is translation Mukden's No. 4 to Department (sent Nanking 6) :

"Director Foreign Affairs Office Mukden Municipal Government called this afternoon. Regarding my requested interview with mayor. he states staff and I permitted leave Mukden with movable property of US Government and that on presentation of lists of staff and articles to be evacuated railway transportation will be provided. He asked me to designate departure date for staff and articles. I replied I cannot do so before being permitted contact packers. When conditions permit, it will be possible to evacuate. Signed Ward."

Repeated Shanghai 745, Peiping 233.

STUART

125.633/6–2149 : Telegram

The Secretary of State to the Consul General at Peiping (Clubb)

WASHINGTON, June 23, 1949—5 p. m.

385. Re Nanking's 1337 June 21 to Dept, rptd Peiping 228, Dept assumes you continuing efforts re evacuation of Ward and staff whenever opportunity presents itself without specific instr from Dept.

ACHESON

125.633/6–2949 : Telegram

The Consul General at Shanghai (Cabot) to the Secretary of State

SHANGHAI, June 29, 1949—2 p. m.
[Received, June 29—10 :41 a. m.]

2544. Letter received today from Ward and other members Mukden staff for forwarding. Confirmation copy of telegram to Clubb dated June 6 states: "Entire American and alien staff continue under arrest imposed noon November 20 by Mukden Military Control Committee. All in surprising good health and spirits notwithstanding arduous conditions our incarceration. Have been without requested dental and medical treatment and inoculations and vaccination during confinement.["] In personal letter to me dated June 12 Ward refers to letter I wrote March 4 which was delivered June 4. First communication from outside since November 20. First telegram received June 6. Ward continues that nothing has been or could have been done as yet to pack up and leave. Written communications local authorities have gone unheeded since November 9. Permission requested [in?] April to purchase lumber, nails, et cetera is according to jailers being "studied by appropriate authorities". Letter continues: "Even though we may desire to close this office, I am not at all certain that this desire is reciprocated by all concerned. Our presence here does serve in some measure as a counterbalance. Both my staff and I have enough of Mukden to last us for some time but we are nevertheless willing to remain here until our replacements arrive, therefore failing knowledge of the actual wording of the order regarding the closing of this office I suggest that the order not be categoric but effective upon the final departure of the principal officer. Of course our status of being neither fish nor flesh may go on for some time but we have withstood the stress thus far and can continue to do so for a further period."

From somewhat cryptic references Ward evidently ascribes his incarceration to break between Soviets and US. He says: "Morale is superb along [among?] Americans but not among aliens." Request cancellation TO [79] 9–10589 dated July 28, 1948 because he cannot enter statutory leave status prior to June 30. He requests letter be acknowledged by telegram which we have done. Sends regards to Butterworth.

Repeated Nanking 1390.

CABOT

125.633/8–649 : Telegram

The Counselor of Embassy in China (Jones) to the Secretary of State

NANKING, August 6, 1949.
[Received August 5—11:30 p. m.]

1723. Following is Mukden telegram 24, July 29 to Embassy.

"Press states exit permits now being issued by Mukden Bureau Public Safety to persons proceeding abroad. If Department, Embassy desire I apply here for exit permits for American staff and our dependents to leave China en route abroad, please instruct me, stating country to which we shall proceed. Inasmuch as my statutory leave travel orders expired June 30, I assume new orders for current fiscal year have been or are being issued. Am still without any indication whether or when first group staff and dependents will be permitted proceed Peiping. Department not informed."

Following is Embassy's replicatory telegram 23, August 6 to Mukden:

"Embassy suggests you apply Mukden for exit permits your staff and dependents to leave China. Travel orders have already been issued American personnel for return to US."

JONES

[79] Travel order.

125.633/8–1349 : Telegram

The Counselor of Embassy in China (Jones) to the Secretary of State

NANKING, August 13, 1949.
[Received August 13—3 :48 a. m.]

1780. Reference Embtel 1223 [*1723*], August 6. Following is Mukden telegram 29, August 9 to Embassy:

"Exit permits requested for 10 American staff members, 5 American and 2 alien dependents Mukden–Shanghai. Travel permits requested for 3 FSA employees; no date departure Mukden specified, but shall set date soonest possible."

Sent Department 1780; repeated Shanghai 985, OffEmb Canton 746.

JONES

---

123 [Ward, Angus I.] : Telegram

The Secretary of State to the Counselor of Embassy in China (Jones), at Nanking

WASHINGTON, August 15, 1949—2 p. m.

959. Dept wld suggest that Emb instruct Ward not to press for permits to proceed to Shanghai as indicated your 1780 Aug 13 but to seek permits for himself and his staff proceed to Tientsin with view to his leaving country earliest possible sailing from Taku Bar.[80]

ACHESON

125.633/8–1649 : Telegram

The Counselor of Embassy in China (Jones) to the Secretary of State

NANKING, August 16, 1949.
[Received August 16—2 :41 a. m.]

1802. In Mukden telegram 31, August 12 to Embassy, Ward reported that "I am today informing Mayor Mukden first group staff members and dependents originally scheduled leave Mukden en route Tientsin and Peiping July 27 continue in readiness to travel and it is my desire they depart on Wednesday August 17."

Sent Department; repeated Shanghai 1003, OffEmb Canton 763.

JONES

---

[80] The Counselor of Embassy informed the Department in telegram No. 1816, August 17, 5 p. m., that "Embassy today sent to Mukden telegram recommending Ward seek permits himself and staff to leave China via Tientsin."

125.633/8–1949 : Telegram

The Counselor of Embassy in China (Jones) to the Secretary of State

NANKING, August 19, 1949—4 p. m.
[Received August 19—9:21 a. m.]

1834. British Embassy has shown us report of former British ConGen, Graham, Mukden, who arrived Peiping July 29. It confirms our worst suspicions, namely, that "AmConGen staff have been complete prisoners". On other hand, report continues, British have been entirely at liberty and their position recently has been improving. For instance British ConGen telephone was finally restored July 25, auto license may be granted soon and plain-clothes guards at British ConGen gate seem to have been withdrawn about beginning of July. These guards were previously an intolerable nuisance but British ConGen believes this was due merely to overzealousness of illiterate soldiers since difficulties were usually ironed out after reference to higher Commie authorities.

It seems to us that Graham's report is unjustifiably cheerful for facts remain that during many months he was incommunicado, had no auto, was unable to arrange for his fiancée to join him and must have suffered many humiliations to his official position. It, however, still seems apparent that Commies do not wish to force out British ConGen as they have AmConGen. French ConGen is reportedly in even better situation than British ConGen. Why Commies are showing such relatively favorable consideration to British and French ConGens, given Soviet-type iron curtain which has descended around Manchuria, we are unable to explain.

Sent Department, repeated Shanghai 1013, Embassy Canton 779. Department pass Peiping.

JONES

125.633/8–2349 : Telegram

The Counselor of Embassy in China (Jones) to the Secretary of State

NANKING, August 23, 1949.
[Received August 24—2:05 a. m.]

1879. Following is text Embtel 30, August 23 to Mukden:

"Please report whether first group staff members and dependents originally scheduled to leave Mukden for Peiping July 27 actually departed August 17 as indicated in your telegram 2 [*31*] on August 12.[81] If not, please report reasons therefor in detail as Embassy wishes to keep State Department fully informed.

"Please report also whether local authorities have issued exit permits via Tientsin to all Consulate General staff and dependents."

[81] See telegram No. 1802, August 16, p. 973.

Sent Department, repeated Peiping 344, OffEmb Canton 791, Shanghai 1033.

JONES

---

123 [Ward, Angus I.] : Telegram

The Secretary of State to the Consul General at Peiping (Clubb)

WASHINGTON, August 29, 1949—7 p. m.

588. While noting urtel 1433 Aug 28 [82] re disruption Mukden-Shanhaikuan rail line Dept disturbed delays Ward encountering leaving Mukden and desires facilitate his departure if possible. Wld appreciate ur opinion whether any or all fol steps wld be helpful. You will recall this connection Ward has specifically cautioned against impatience (Peiping tel 1136 Jul 7 to Dept [82]).

(1) Public statement by Dept spokesman calling attention long delays Ward encountering and stating he has been instructed withdraw immediately with his staff and that US Govt fully expects Commies accord him facilities enable his compliance.

(2) Message from you to Ward conveying Dept's instructions he and staff withdraw immediately.

(3) Communication from you to top Commie authorities Peiping conveying under instruction US Govt message along lines (1) above.

Wld likewise appreciate ur suggesting any other steps which might be taken facilitate Ward's departure.

ACHESON

125.633/8–2949 : Telegram

The Counselor of Embassy in China (Jones) to the Secretary of State

NANKING, August 29, 1949.
[Received August 30—12 :47 a. m.]

1939. Following is Mukden telegram 39, August 26 to Embassy replying to Embtel 30, August 24 [*23?*] to Mukden which was repeated to Department as 1879, August 23:

"Reference Nanking telegram 30, August 24, received today noon. My telegram 35, August 18, stated transportation for first group staff members and dependents was not forthcoming on August 17 as requested and that conditions our confinement unchanged but this message refused transmission for unstated reason. In its reference telegram 30, Nanking inquires reasons for failure first group depart on scheduled date August 17, to which inquiry unable reply other than to state all members of group and their accompanying luggage and effects were in readiness but no transportation was forthcoming. In fact, local authorities have not acknowledged receipt of any my

---
[82] Not printed.

requests for first group transportation and have given no indication whether such requested transportation will be forthcoming.

No exit or travel permits have been issued despite my several communications on subject and no indication thus far whether such permits will be issued.

Barring unforeseen delays or abnormal obstructions, I hope to be able inform local authorities on or immediately after September 1st my readiness leave Mukden en route Tientsin, Peiping with entire staff, dependents and government and personal property. Shall make specific application for outward travel and shipping facilities at that time. Shall endeavor keep Nanking informed of developments but refusal transmit my factual telegrams renders fruitfulness my efforts to this end uncertain. Am fully aware of Department interest in our welfare and conditions at this post, but regret that circumstances beyond my control prevent me from keeping Nanking fully informed."

Sent Deprtment 1939, repeated Shanghai 1056 OffEmb Canton 807.

[JONES]

125.633/8–3049 : Telegram

The Counselor of Embassy in China (Jones) to the Secretary of State

NANKING, August 30, 1949.
[Received August 31—1:20 a. m.]

1957. ReEmbtel 1939, August 29 to Department. Following is text Embtel 34, August 30 to Mukden:

"Reurtel 39, August 26.[83] According to local press, rail service between Mukden and Peiping was resumed August 28 after interruption of 23 days due to floods. Embassy assumes from this development that there is now no reason for your staff, dependents and effects not to proceed to Peiping on or immediately after September 1 as stated in your reference telegram. Embassy is notifying State Department accordingly."

Sent Department; repeated Shanghai 1067, OffEmb Canton 808, Peiping 352.

JONES

125.6336/9–249 : Telegram

The Consul General at Peiping (Clubb) to the Secretary of State

PEIPING, September 2, 1949.
[Received September 2—1:13 p. m.]

1468. ReContel 1433, August 28.[84] Following from Ward reContel 19, August 29 to Mukden:

---

[83] See telegram 1939, August 29, from Nanking, *supra.*
[84] Not printed.

"Although we receive copy local newspaper daily are unable glean any information therefrom for reason translating staff has been in funk and useless since publication fantastic spy charges on June 20. Have had no American staff member with working knowledge Chinese since departure Rinden.[85] Shall therefore be grateful any information you may deem useful to us in closing office and making travel plans."

Sent Department, repeated Nanking 1061, to Tientsin by mail.

CLUBB

---

123 Ward, Angus I.: Telegram

The Consul General at Peiping (Clubb) to the Secretary of State

PEIPING, September 3, 1949—noon.
[Received September 3—6:22 a. m.]

1475. ReDeptel 588, August 29. Note that as reported Contel 1467, September 2,[86] Peiping line broken. Believe (1) it would be pointless press for Ward's departure when travel physically impossible, but (2) public statement reviewing situation and noting delay presumably as result interruption rail traffic now warranted, and (3) instructions then could well be sent Ward either direct or via Peiping directing him depart soon as rail line reopened, if needed besides those reported Embtel 1957, August 30.

In view information Contel 1468, September 2, will forward Ward from here any possible hope for information or suggestions, repeating Department.

Believe other steps such as new communication Communists should wait on developments after restoration rail traffic.

Sent Department 1475, repeated Nanking 1064.

CLUBB

702.4193/9–1249: Telegram

The Secretary of State to the Consul General at Peiping (Clubb)

WASHINGTON, September 12, 1949—6 p. m.

625. British have agreed accept custody US property Mukden (Deptel 601[87]). If possible Ward should obtain receipts from British Consul.

ACHESON

---

[85] Robert W. Rinden, Consul at Mukden in 1948.
[86] Not printed.
[87] Dated September 2, 3 p. m.; it reported that the British had been requested to accept custody of U.S. property in Mukden but had not replied (702.4193/9–249).

125.633/9–1549 : Telegram

The Secretary of State to the Consul General at Peiping (Clubb)[88]

WASHINGTON, September 15, 1949—5 p. m.

634. Department released following statement to press September 15:

"Consul General Angus Ward has on several occasions since announced closure American ConGen Mukden May 18, 1949 requested exit visas, travel passes, rail transportation Mukden, Peiping and Tientsin for ConGen staff. Rail freight facilities for government property and personal effects now packed awaiting shipment out of Mukden also requested.

"Chinese Communist authorities Mukden so far refused or failed acknowledge all such requests. While no reason given by them, it assumed from reports available to Department floods during August early September, resulting in disruption rail service south of Mukden, have contributed to delays encountered by Consul General Ward.

"Department has instructed Consul General Ward continue make every effort obtain from local authorities necessary permission and facilities to depart immediately and confidently expects as soon as normal rail traffic between Mukden–Tientsin resumed, Communist authorities will, in accordance law and comity, facilitate departure Consulate General staff."

ACHESON

---

123 [Ward, Angus I.] : Telegram

The Secretary of State to the Consul General at Peiping (Clubb)

WASHINGTON, September 15, 1949—4 p. m.

637. Urtel 1475 repeated Nanking 1064 September 3. Please send Ward substance press release September 15 regarding Mukden along with following message:

"Department fully aware your strenuous efforts and difficulties besetting you. You are instructed continue take all necessary steps arrange departure self entire staff and property soonest following resumption normal rail service."

ACHESON

125.633/9–1549 : Telegram

The Secretary of State to the Consul General at Peiping (Clubb)

WASHINGTON, September 16, 1949—8 p. m.

641. Reurtels 1542 and 1549 Sept 14 and 15.[89] Press release issued [90] Deptel 634 rptd Nanking 1100 Sept 15.

---

[88] Repeated to the Counselor of Embassy at Nanking as telegram No. 1100.
[89] Neither printed.
[90] Department of State *Bulletin*, September 26, 1949, p. 482.

You are authorized send letter to Chu in ur discretion. Send Dept complete text such letter if and when sent for Dept's use in press release if deemed desirable at time.

ACHESON

125.633/9–2349 : Telegram

The Consul General at Peiping (Clubb) to the Secretary of State

PEIPING, September 23, 1949.
[Received September 23—10 :07 a. m.]

1601. Following communications dated September 22 dispatched today to PLA C-in-C Chu Teh re matter evacuation Mukden consular staff and property.

"Acting under instructions of US Government, by letter of May 19, 1949 this ConGen informed general headquarters PLA that due to imposition by Chinese Communist authorities of arbitrary and unreasonable restrictions on American ConGen at Mukden, my Government was withdrawing its staff from and closing its consular office in that city. It was requested that transportation and other facilities be provided to enable consular staff with personal and official effects to depart from Communist-controlled areas via Tientsin or Peiping.

American ConGen at Mukden, Mr. Angus I. Ward, was appropriately instructed by American Department of State. Mukden authorities, through director of Alien Affairs office, on June 21 informed Mr. Ward that he and his staff would be permitted to depart Mukden with moveable property and that upon presentation of lists of staff and property to be evacuated, railway transportation would be provided. Mr. Ward was asked to designate departure date for staff and property.

Mr. Ward on July 19 notified authorities that 13 of his staff were prepared to depart on July 27, others remained behind until there had been completed arrangements for packing and shipment of effects.

Request was renewed on August 12 with departure date fixed for August 17 [as?] transportation facilities were in fact not provided. On September 3 after completion of packing Mr. Ward sent formal letter to mayor of Mukden requesting rail transportation to Peiping and Tientsin for himself and staff and dependents, excepting persons left behind in custodial capacity, with their baggage and American Government property.

To date facilities have not been provided by Mukden authorities. It is appreciated that there was extended interruption in Peiping rail communications in August to September due to flood damage but it is also understood that breaks have now been repaired and normal traffic resumed; there thus can be no further reason for failure to provide requested facilities for travel of American consular personnel in question.

Department of State has again instructed Mr. Ward to take steps to obtain from local authorities necessary facilities for immediate departure from Mukden. US Government fully expects Chinese Communist authorities, in accordance with international law and practice, to provide facilities which would enable him to comply with instruction. In view of delays and difficulties which have attended making of arrangements heretofore, however, I am instructed to bring this matter to your attention with request that you take appropriate measures to cause Mukden authorities to extend promptly transport facilities required for removal from Mukden of personnel of American ConGen at Mukden and their personal and official effects. Your prompt action to this end would be much appreciated."

CLUBB

125.633/9–2949 : Telegram

The Consul General at Peiping (Clubb) to the Secretary of State

PEIPING, September 29, 1949—1 p. m.
[Received September 29—3 :43 a. m.]

1641. ReContel 1601, September 23. In course discussion September 24 with L. K. Tao [91] (Contel 1619, September 27 [92]), I called his attention to Mukden case, noting unfavorable reaction it was producing USA, and recommended strongly that Chinese authorities, for good Sino-American relations, enable Consulate staff remove as requested.

Consulate letter September 22 unacknowledged, unreturned me.

CLUBB

125.633/10–449 : Telegram

The Acting Secretary of State to the Consul General at Peiping (Clubb)

WASHINGTON, October 4, 1949—6 p. m.

682. In view recent developments Peiping [93] Dept believes it desirable, unless you perceive objection thereto, that you informally and in personal capacity approach Chou En-lai [94] by such means as you consider desirable re evacuation Mukden ConGen staff. While Dept leaves substance to ur judgment, it believes that you might call attn to approaching winter and express earnest hope staff be permitted leave prior to incidence cold weather which under existing conditions wld impose extreme hardship endanger health staff.[95]

WEBB

---

[91] Also known as Tao Meng-ho ; author and member of Academia Sinica.
[92] *Ante*, p. 537.
[93] For information on establishment on October 1 of Communist "Central People's Government of the People's Republic of China", see telegram No. 1666, October 1, from the Consul General at Peiping, p. 544.
[94] Premier and Foreign Minister of the Communist regime at Peiping.
[95] For information on action taken, see telegram No. 1707, October 10, 3 p. m., from the Consul General at Peiping, vol. IX, p. 117.

Mukden Consulate General Files, Lot F21

The Consul General at Mukden (Ward) to the Consul General at Peiping (Clubb)[96]

MUKDEN, October 12, 1949.

80. Early yesterday morning Messenger Chi, who had been dismissed for cause on September 28th but had at that time refused accept salary due and cumulative leave payment, was found hiding in office storeroom contrary my orders upon his departure for home on September 28th that he was not to return to office since payment would be made at his residence upon request. I told him he was trespassing and escorted him hand in hand to courtyard. When Accounting Office opened he again refused proffered payment (which did not include severance pay, Department telegram 23 May 17,[97] for reason he was discharged for cause), and demanded refund of retirement pay deductions, which refund outside my competency. Later, when Chi refused leave Accounting Office and I was endeavoring expel him with intention handing him over as trespasser to armed sentry guarding office building, he lay down on stairway and refused move. During this time his brother who is temporary day laborer attacked me with fists and later attempted attack me with cudgel, but in both instances brother was pulled away by Rehberg.[98] Representatives of Municipality, Public Safety Bureau and People's Court appeared and conducted investigation in reply my request that our warden come to office restore order among Chinese staff, who had in meantime attacked Kristan[99] and endeavored attack Cicogna.[1] Chi continued lie on stairway feigning injury. Chi had small scrape on side of head of origin unknown myself or staff, but neither he nor brother was injured by me or any member my staff. Chi was removed from office ostensibly to hospital. Attending physician certified cerebral concussion and loss consciousness. Chinese staff filed complaint attesting Rehberg, Tatsumi,[2] Kristan, Cicogna and I beat Chi and his brother. Upon completion investigation at 16 o'clock I was informed above complaint will be referred to government.

WARD

---

[96] Notation on Mukden post copy of telegram: "Refused transmission & returned Nov. 5." File of post telegrams transmitted to Department after closing of Consulate General in December 1949.

[97] Same as telegram No. 299, May 17, 7 p. m., to the Consul General at Peiping, p. 957; portion of telegram pertaining to this matter not printed.

[98] Ralph C. Rehberg, clerk.

[99] Alfred Kristan, building maintenance technician.

[1] Frank Cicogna, chief technician.

[2] Shiro Tatsumi, mechanic.

125.633/10–1449 : Telegram

The Secretary of State to the Consul General at Peiping (Clubb)

WASHINGTON, October 14, 1949—9 p. m.

711. Dept proposes release statement re Mukden to press early week Oct 17. Ur comments requested.

First para this proposed s[ta]tement contains verbatim text ur reply Chou En-lai dated Oct 8.[3] Second para reads:

"Occasion taken this reply to Mr. Chou's letter make approach to responsible Commie leadership on this matter which wld not reasonably admit of evasion. Chi Commie auths have thus far demonstrated signal lack good faith in failing honor their June 21 promise provide transportation facilities for staff's withdrawal. Time has passed when Chi Commie auths cld plead any extenuating circumstances, such as disruption rail service due floods, for their continued refusal stand by their assurances given voluntarily some 4 months ago."

Third para continues.

"Chi Commie auths by their refusal take any action this case, can hardly expect gain internatl prestige or attract good will of world community. It is extremely difficult see how a regime now bidding for internatl recognition can possibly expect to have its request considered at all seriously by other than Commie states when that regime repeatedly shows by its deeds, in areas presumably under its control, that it unwilling adhere even to minimum standard internatlly recognized good conduct."

ACHESON

125.633/10–1749 : Telegram

The Consul General at Peiping (Clubb) to the Secretary of State

PEIPING, October 17, 1949—1 a. m.
[Received 5 :32 a. m.]

1757. ReDeptel 711, October 14. Respectfully note there have already been several public statements regarding position Mukden Consulate without result. Believe new statement at this time would likewise fail achieve desired result, i.e. removal personnel. Letter to Chou En-lai was sent only week ago, there is still possibility getting results from that move. Last Mukden telegram was dated October 8. There may be some change there one way or another. Am communicating today asking for situation report.

There is another avenue direct approach Chou; after manner either British or French (Contel 1733, October 13 [4]), could request interview

---

[3] See telegram No. 1707, October 10, 3 p. m., from the Consul General at Peiping, vol. IX, p. 117.
[4] Not printed.

with Chou without indication purpose visit. On arrival Foreign Office subject should obviously be more than case Mukden. Department might wish consider advisability making such approach for discussion several matters. Most effective, if deemed advisable at this time, would be request for Communist reaction regarding project for Jessup [5] visit Communist-controlled areas (if this be planned); that is, whether he would be granted entry and contact with Communist officials. Other possible subjects would be on trade, laws and treaties affecting that trade and foreign rights and interests, and Consulate's relations in present interim period. First of three would be of most interest to Communists but leads naturally to other questions including particularly that Mukden. Such conversation would be in line proposal contained Contel 1703 [*1704*], October 8 [6] and might result in more clarification of situation than obtained thus far.

Note finally that Chen Ming-shu [7] earlier promised take up at Peiping the subject (Nanking telegram 1215, June 13 [*6*] [8]) and that I here had proposed to L. K. Tao that those interested in better relations with U.S.A. (as reputedly Lo Lung-chi [9]) would be well advised give early attention Mukden case (Contel 1641, September 29). Chinese are currently very wary of contacts with Americans but am trying contact Chen or Lo regarding matter, otherwise will try take it up with someone Yenching October 22 when visit there planned.

Emphasize my belief such public statement would more probably retard than advance matter at this time. Therefore recommend statement not be issued until after steps outlined above have been taken and such new statement is discovered be only resort.

Will comment on proposed text statement and another point in separate messages.

CLUBB

125.633/10–1749 : Telegram

The Consul General at Peiping (Clubb) to the Secretary of State

PEIPING, October 17, 1949—4 p. m.
[Received October 17—5 a. m.]

1759. Re Contel 1757, October 17. In final analysis it might be found advisable exert economic pressure against Commies. Note Sino-American and Sino-Japanese trade has to date hardly developed to stage where its manipulation would constitute strong leverage: Threat to withhold what is still ungranted in major scale is less effec-

---

[5] Philip C. Jessup, Ambassador at Large.
[6] Vol. IX, p. 111.
[7] Leader of the Kuomintang Revolutionary Committee (KmtRC).
[8] Not printed.
[9] A leader of the Democratic League and member of the Communist regime at Peiping.

tive than actual withholding of something already in being. Suggest however that if in immediate future there are developments re Sino-Jap barter trade for instance, conclusion deal might be held up pending settlement Mukden and Smith–Bender [10] cases pressure. The more that is involved of course the more pressure would be felt. This might well be worked by implication into any conversation at Foreign Office. Feel strongly, particularly in view relatively short period letter sent Chou, that statement should be held up until new avenues explored.

CLUBB

125.633/10–1749 : Telegram

The Consul General at Peiping (Clubb) to the Secretary of State

PEIPING, October 17, 1949—4 p. m.
[Received October 17—4 : 55 a. m.]

1760. ReDeptel 711, October 14, comment on proposed text press release. Re second paragraph, would recommend using title "general" instead of "mister" or alternatively leaving out title altogether.

Re third paragraph, recommend question recognition not be made subject reference in current press release, believing firmly noncommittal attitude re this question gives greatest flexibility and, by keeping Communists in dark re intentions, makes possible our exercise maximum leverage. Public reference here would possibly bring Communist counterattack.

ReContel 1757, October 17, note however my recommendation press release be held up for present in any event pending other action.

CLUBB

---

123 Ward, Angus I. : Telegram

The Consul General at Peiping (Clubb) to the Secretary of State

PEIPING, October 26, 1949.
[Received October 26—1 :42 p. m.]

1827. Mukden Hsin Hua radio Chinese-language broadcast October 25 carried two following news items:

(1) Shenyang [11] despatch. On October 11 there occurred Shenyang incident in which Ward, American national and formerly American Consul General [at] Shenyang during bandit Chiang [12] occupation period, directed mob in beating up worker and caused serious injuries to latter.

---

[10] For information on latter case, see footnote 31, p. 384.
[11] Mukden.
[12] Generalissimo Chiang Kai-shek, President of the Republic of China until his retirement on January 21 in favor of Vice President Li Tsung-jen as Acting President.

Ward had withheld wages Chi Yu-heng [13] and also discharged him without reason. On October 11, Chi Yu-heng went to Ward's office to demand wages due him. Ward not only refused to give wages to him but threw him off on shameless grounds that that place was "an American place" and dismissed worker was "without right to stay there". When Chi attempted to argue with him reasonably, Ward, acting in his imperialistic and barbarous manner, violently beat and insulted Chi Yu-heng and also incited four ex-Consulate employees, German named Kristan, Japanese-American Shiro Tatsumi, Italian Cicogna and American Rehberg, to take Chi into custody and put him in building where he was beaten with fists and feet by group. Chi Yu-feng, younger brother of Chi Yu-heng, who went to rescue was also beaten. After incident, the body of Chinese staff members and workers promptly reported case to People's Government. When people sent by Bureau of Public Security and People's Court of Shenyang People's Government arrived at scene to mediate, laborer Chi Yu-heng had already been seriously injured and was lying at foot of staircase leading to Ward's office. Examination revealed that laborer Chi Yu-heng had sustained concussion of the brain in addition to wound caused by instrument in right side of head and was unconscious. He had lost control of urination and his life was in danger. He was immediately afterwards sent to hospital for medical treatment.

The 35 Chinese staff members and workers of that place have already lodged stern written charge against violent act of Ward in beating Chinese worker by marshalling mob. For purpose upholding law of Chinese People's Republic and safeguarding human rights, Shenyang People's Government and public security organizations will immediately take action to investigate case according law.

(2) Mukden despatch. *Northeast Daily* today published Shovo commentary on incident in which American citizen Ward withheld wages of worker and gathered mob to beat him, thus inflicting serious injuries on him.

Commentary states, "We Chinese people sternly protest against this violent act and will back up People's Government in meting out to criminals headed by Ward legal sanctions due them. Since Chinese people have strength to rid themselves of domination imposed on China by imperialism, so also they have strength to punish imperialist elements who dare to act barbarously and tyrannically within China's boundaries".

Comment further pointed out "violent act of Ward and American special [service] case unearthed short time ago in Shenyang [14] have given us profoundly to understand that American imperialism has determined the enemy of Chinese people and would to end never take defeat willingly, but will create troubles by every conceivable means, do utmost to effect sabotages and open provocations. All kinds of mean and shameless measures might be used. We must increase our vigilance in face of their malicious and shameless plots and must promptly shatter them (plots)."

Sent Department; repeated Shanghai 1097.

CLUBB

---

[13] Chinese messenger at the Consulate General.
[14] See telegram No. 1039, June 19, from the Consul General at Peiping, p. 965.

123 Ward, Angus I.: Telegram

The Consul General at Peiping (Clubb) to the Secretary of State

PEIPING, October 27, 1949.
[Received October 27—2:56 p. m.]

1837. ReContel 1827, October 26. Mukden Hsin Hua radio Chinese language broadcast October 26 carried following items:

(1) (Shenyang despatch) After news that American imperialist element and American national Ward committed an unreasonably violent act and gathered mob to beat up and injure Chinese laborer Chi Yu-heng was published here, people of all walks of life in Shenyang have been exceedingly excited and infuriated. Recalling American espionage case taking place in city short time ago, they hold that incident has once more proved that American imperialists will make troubles with Chinese people to very end by using every conceivable means, which fact merits serious vigilance. Moreover, they unanimously demand that People's Government promptly punish these criminals.

"Strictly suppress espionage activities" meeting, called by branch office of Federation of Labor of Shenyang RR Administration Bureau, decided to issue circular telegram in name of meeting protesting against the violent act of American imperialist element. Workers of various mills of Northeast Machine Control Bureau, who are in midst of eager campaign for creating new records unanimously stated that they would not readily conclude this matter with this imperialist element and that they would exert themselves in production to work for tight coordinated eradication of all imperialist aggressive plots.

Workers of Telecommunications Machine Factory and Northeast Post and Telegraph Administration Bureau, in meetings of all workers, unanimously manifested their determination to support Chi Yu-heng with action. In course of meetings, workers contributed over one million dollars as comfort fund for Chi.

Students of Shenyang Agricultural College and all municipal lower and middle schools also held separate discussion meetings in which they stated that Chinese people no longer tolerate insults and will definitely mete out severe punishment to criminal Ward and struggle to end with American imperialism. Entire body of teachers and students of Shenyang municipal second middle school, over 100 persons, jointly issued statement of protest. Students of Shenyang Agricultural College have meanwhile launched drive for contributions to comfort laborer Chi Yu-heng.

(2) (Shenyang despatch) After occurrence of violent act of American national Ward, responsible member of Shenyang Municipal Federation of Labor gave talk:

"With respect to this kind of provocative and violent behavior of Ward, apart from requesting that People's Government promptly summon him to trial and punish him according to law to uphold national laws, we would once more warn that, if any imperialist elements dare to act in evil manner in territory of our country and in Shenyang, they will definitely meet opposition of wrath of whole of Chinese people as well as legal sanctions of Chinese People's Republic. Let them realize that we great Chinese people are not to be insulted at will."

"On behalf of entire body of workers in Shenyang, we express our intimate consolation for two laborers, Chi Yu-heng and Chi Yu-feng, and moreover pledge ourselves to back them up. We will certainly make Ward bow in apology before working class. Let them realize that Chinese people have already stood up [apparent omission] time for imperialism to behave tyranically in China has already gone for good."

Sent Department 1837, Shanghai 1105, to Tientsin by mail.

CLUBB

---

123 Ward, Angus I. : Telegram

The Consul General at Peiping (Clubb) to the Secretary of State

PEIPING, October 27, 1949—5 p. m.
[Received October 27—6 :30 a. m.]

1838. ReContels 1827, October 26, and 1837, October 27. British Consul [at] Peiping has received wire from colleague [at] Mukden confirming Ward and Rehberg are charged with assault Chinese.

There are several missing numbers in Mukden telegraph series (serviced several days ago). Pertinent messages may have been help [*held*] up. Tentatively estimate that (1) there probably occurred some minor incident involving Chinese laborer Chi Yu-heng; (2) incident as per Commie practice been substantially blown up; (3) Ward and others charged will probably be tried in People's Court; (4) after due sentence "in accord with People's laws" sentences Americans particularly may be suspended and (5) Mukden Consular personnel may then be "expelled" from country in something approaching public disgrace or at least those involved present incident.

ReContel 1805, October 24,[15] recommend I be authorized soonest make projected call Foreign Office to take up this case *inter alia*.

CLUBB

---

123 Ward, Angus I. : Telegram

The Consul General at Peiping (Clubb) to the Secretary of State

PEIPING, October 28, 1949.
[Received October 27—8 :27 p. m.]

1839. ReContel 1837, October 27. Following received late yesterday evening as Mukden's 89, 24th:

"Consul General Ward, Rehberg, Tatsumi and two European employees removed by police for 2 or 3 days connection their alleged as-

---

[15] *Ante*, p. 839.

sault Chinese employee. Sent Washington, repeated Peiping 89. Stokes [16] for Ward."

Repeated hereby despite original routing provide against possible transmittal delay.

Sent Department 1839, Shanghai 1106.

CLUBB

---

123 Ward, Angus I.: Telegram

The Secretary of State to the Consul General at Peiping (Clubb)

WASHINGTON, October 28, 1949—6 p. m.

750. Reurtel 1839 Oct 28, you shld query Stokes at Mukden present situation Ward and other employees removed by police and whether yet released, requesting you be informed continuously all developments, and rpt Dept at once all info recd.

You shld also immed ask for appointment with Chou En-lai or other high official dealing with Fon affairs to make oral representations, quoting info recd from Amer Cons official at Mukden and Chi press reports that Ward and other employees removed by police. Request authoritative info for transmission ur Govt and inquire specifically whether Ward and other employees still held and if so where.

You shld then point out salient facts in this case along lines ur 1601 Sep 23, stressing isolation of staff in Cons compounds for nearly a year, US Govt's decision in May to close Mukden office, continuous efforts since that time withdraw staff, specific assurances June 21 re transportation facilities and continued refusal, without extenuating circumstances, of Mukden auths abide by their assurances or even indicate what their intentions were. Point out in connection present reports that pretext for isolation of staff was itself based upon alleged necessity protect personnel.

Point out that in ur reply Oct 8 [17] to Gen Chou's letter you had taken occasion make approach to responsible Commie leadership which cld not reasonably admit of evasion. Arbitrary action by Chi Commie auths against Amer Cons officials at Mukden and their continued failure to provide facilities for withdrawal even after giving express assurances that regard is viewed by US Govt with greatest concern. Inquire specifically whether these actions, contrary to established principles international comity, are to be considered as manifestation of hostility toward US and its nationals in China, incl the northeastern provinces.

---

[16] William N. Stokes, Vice Consul at Mukden.
[17] See telegram No. 1707, October 10, 3 p. m., from the Consul General at Pieping, vol. IX, p. 117.

In conclusion state that US Govt requests and fully expects highest Chi Commie auths, in accordance international law and practice, take appropriate measures to cause Mukden auths release Ward and other employees immediately, promptly extend transport facilities for removal from Mukden of all personnel Amer ConGen, with their personal and official effects, and afford them full freedom of movement in carrying out their official instructions in this regard.

In view urgent need of action you shld take this matter up individually. Other questions receiving Dept's consideration.

ACHESON

123 Ward, Angus I. : Telegram

The Consul General at Peiping (Clubb) to the Secretary of State

PEIPING, October 29, 1949.
[Received October 29—7:45 a. m.]

1854. ReContel 1853, October 29 and Contel 1847, October 28.[18] *Tung Pei Jih Pao (Northeast Daily*, Mukden) October 25 carried following news item on joint charge filed by 35 Chinese workers and employees against Ward:

After outbreak of incident in which American national Ward committed violent act, 35 Chinese workers and employees of former American Consulate at Shenyang sent out charge. Original text of charge has been secured and is as follows:

"Statement of charge: To Shenyang Municipal People's Government: We beg to bring charge against former American Consul General [at] Shenyang Ward, who unreasonably discharged worker named Chi Yu-heng, refused him annual leave payment, wage deductions, and separation allowance and, moreover, led mob in beating up Chinese worker at 8 a. m., October 1 [*11*], 1949, culminating in incident in which he caused bodily injury to worker. We earnestly request that People's Government try case in accordance with law in order to protect human rights and uphold sovereignty of our fatherland. Such are facts of charge.

On September 27, 1949, Ward ordered workers to dismantle house. There was found therein reinforced concrete pillar. Ward personally handed hammer to Chi Yu-heng, instructing him to demolish it himself without any aid. When Chi, having beaten and hammered at pillar for half day, had exhausted himself and could not continue, workers Wu Han-chang and Yu Yung-pin offered to help Chi. Thereupon, Ward ordered that other persons were not permitted to assist Chi, who should work all by himself. Ward together with Hubbard [19] and others then looked on from upstairs of building and jeered. That Ward forced Chi Yu-heng to do work beyond his physical strength constitutes concrete manifestation of oppressive exactions of Chinese

---

[18] Neither printed.
[19] Fred E. Hubbard, Vice Consul.

people by imperialists. At time when Ward, Hubbard and others were ridiculing Chi in building, latter stated: 'This is really an insult to Chinese people. He made me do this job under unreasonable duress; I really cannot do it.' At this Ward seized opportunity and expelled him from building at No. 38, San Ching Lu. Unable to do anything about it, Chi moved to live in SVOC[20] compound. Next morning, Ward told Chi: 'You refused to work. I have terminated your service. You are now unqualified to remain in American Government buildings.' Chi explained to Ward that it was not that he refused to work but merely that he could not perform work which he was incapable of doing all by himself. Ward paid not the least attention to what he said and violently pushed and dragged him out of his office. In spite of repeated requests by Chi for settlement of wages, annual leave payment, separation allowance, and wage deductions due him, Ward refused to pay anything except some wages on pretext that Chi was discharged on account of delinquency.

On October 10, 1949, when Chi had already lived as guest for 2 weeks in SVOC compound, Ward had still ignored his request. Under circumstances, which Chi was unable to do anything to improve, Chi visited Ward for second time to demand payment of the wages, annual leave payment, and separation allowance due him. Ward still insisted that he would pay him only his wages but not annual leave, separation allowance and wage deductions. He also pushed Chi out of his office. Hence, no results were obtained that evening.

On morning of October 11, after Ward came [to] building at No. 38 San Ching Lu, Cicogna, an Italian national, told Ward that Chi had not left there the previous night. Feeling his dignity thus hurt, Ward summoned Chi Yu-heng at 3:15 [8:15?] a. m. and cursed: 'Muddle-headed egg, get out'. Together with Cicogna, he pushed Chi down cement staircase on west side of former American Consulate building at No. 38, San Ching Lu. When they reached entrance of building downstairs, Shiro Tatsumi also joined group and beat Chi. This was witnessed by workers Chang Chung-ying, Fang Pin-ching and Queh Han-ri [Kuei Han-ji?]. About 9 o'clock, Ward called Chi up to accounts office upstairs, where Rehberg pressed Chi's hand to sign for drawing money. Finding that sum was deficient, Chi asked for payment of whole sum. Rehberg then said, 'If you refuse to take money, get right out.' So saying he pushed Chi violently few steps backward. Seeing that Chi refused to go, he called Ward to place. As soon as Ward appeared he started beating and kicking Chi. When worker Sun Heng-li saw this, he hurried downstairs to tell Chinese workers and employees and asked them to rescue Chi. When they arrived, Chi had already been knocked down in middle of staircase leading to Ward's office. Ward and others were still holding Chi down and beating him. Chi Yu-feng, younger brother of Chi Yu-heng, who intended to go upstairs to mediate, was stopped before staircase and beaten by Rehberg. Kristan in meantime also came and dealt blows to Chi. Seeing that Chi Yu-heng had been severely injured by Ward and others, we hurriedly sent a worker to report case to Shenyang People's Government Bureau of Public Security of Shenyang Municipal People's Government and People's Court then sent their officials to No. 38 San Ching Lu to mediate and investigate on spot. Results of

---

[20] Standard-Vacuum Oil Co.

physical examination made by law court doctor showed that Chi Yu-heng had sustained an injury on his forehead and bruises on his buttocks. Due to concussion of brain from heavy beating on head Chi had become unconscious, lost control over urination and passed water in his trousers. Fact of the beating of Chinese workers by mob led by Ward and of inflicting of serious injuries on this worker was not only witnessed by plaintiff and all Chinese workers and staff members in No. 38 San Ching Lu but has been substantiated by examination of Bureau of Public Security of People's Government and People's Court. May be said that neither witnesses nor evidence are lacking. Ward's beating of Chinese worker and infringement of human rights is consistent with his behavior. When bandit forces of Chiang were still occupying Shenyang, Ward, relying on domination of Kmt reactionary group, had on several occasions violently beaten Chinese workers CPN [sic].

(1) Toward end of March, 1947, Ward arrived in Shenyang by train via the Peiping–Mukden line. On alighting from train at Shenyang north station, in order to find out if his method of enslaving and oppressing the Chinese people characteristic of imperialists, which he frequently had recourse to 15 years ago when he served as the Consul at Shenyang, was still good, no sooner had he stepped down from train than he beat up a porter by name of Yang on railroad platform. This incident was witnessed on spot by worker Sun Heng-li of former Consulate.

(2) On morning following his arrival in Mukden, Ward ordered a Chinese worker Sun Heng-li to Shenyang north station to bring back his baggage. When baggage was brought to No. 38, San Ching Lu, he beat up driver of horse-carriage which carried baggage. Afraid of provoking unfortunate incident, man swallowed his anger and departed. Incident was witnessed by Sun Heng-li, Yueh Shan-yi and Hao Tze-heng who happened to be around.

(3) On June 2, 1947, Ward personally drove off stall-keeper [named?] Sung who ran cigarette stall on south side outside entrance of house No. 38, San Ching Lu. When Sung refused to budge, Ward beat him with fists and feet and kicked over his stall. After chasing stall-keeper all over street, he finally cut shed over stall with knife. This incident was witnessed by Yueh Shan-yi who happened to be on spot.

(4) On June 28, Ward ordered Lo Hsi-luan, worker of former Consulate, to clear away his cigarette stall. When Ward found that Lo had failed to carry out his bidding, he took Lo by ear, led him into his office and kicked him twice. Forthwith, he issued instruction to have Lo discharged. Since there was nowhere to seek redress, Lo left former Consulate in anger without uttering a word. Ward did not pay Lo money due him. Latter had worked for former Consulate for more than 18 years and since time of his discharge, he has neither received retirement money due him nor the retirement deductions made from his monthly wages up to June 28, 1947, when he was discharged. Two years have elapsed up to present throughout which time Ward held office; but Ward has not yet issued to Lo aforementioned deductions.

(5) On February 6, 1948, former Consulate bought some coal. When coal cart pulled into yard of house No. 38 San Ching Lu, Ward for some reason beat up horsedriver. He also broke his whip and flung stick into western courtyard of house No. 38. The incident was witnessed on spot by Yueh Shan-yi, Sun Heng-li and Huo Wei-hsin.

As result of incident in which American national Ward led his alien employees, Kristan, Cicogna, Shiro Tatsumi and Rehberg, in beating Chinese worker Chi Yu-heng and causing him serious injuries, Chi himself, who had sustained excessively serious injuries, Ward sent to hospital for quick remedy. The undersigned, who are all staff members and workers of former American Consulate at Shenyang, can no longer tolerate Ward's persistent oppression and beating of Chinese laborers in general and his imperialist and barbarous act of beating and causing serious injuries to worker Chi Yu-heng in particular. Hence, we are sternly filing this charge with People's Government. It is hoped that People's Government will from standpoint of safeguarding human rights and upholding laws of new China, mete out to Ward and others punishment due them in accordance with law."

Petitioners: Entire body of workers and staff members of No. 38 San Ching Lu, October 11, 1949.

Signatures. (Signatures omitted) Will be forwarded if Department desires.

To Tientsin by mail.

Sent Department 1854, repeated Shanghai 1115.

CLUBB

---

123 Ward, Angus I. : Telegram

The Consul General at Peiping (Clubb) to the Secretary of State

PEIPING, October 29, 1949—1 a. m.
[Received 7:45 a. m.]

1856. ReContels 1838, October 27 and 1853, October 29.[21] Believe it necessary, in light developments, take into consideration possibility efforts will be made demand court action against Ward and others, against whom 35 petitioners will presumably give evidence touching aspects their activities unrelated charge of assault, to show other allegedly evil aspects American consular administration such as espionage (see Contel 1039, June 19).

Letter of October 26 received by British Consul from his Mukden colleague Steventon [22] reports latter on 26th renewed his request local authorities see Ward. First request appears have been made on or about 19th. Steventon notes regarding matter regular presence strong guards outside Consulate and understood presence such guards inside

---

[21] Latter not printed.
[22] Leve Steventon, British Pro-Consul at Mukden.

building as well, which fact would seem make unlikely occurrence any major alteration involving Chinese staff. He reports further local press 26th carried no further publicity on subject but more cartoons showing wild animal labeled "US" being caged.

CLUBB

123 Ward, Angus I.: Telegram

The Consul General at Peiping (Clubb) to the Secretary of State

PEIPING, October 29, 1949.
[Received October 29—5:24 a. m.]

1857. ReContel 1854, October 29. Following messages sent Mukden:

To Ward October 26:

"Shenyang radio report October 25 states incident involving you occurred October 11. Assume that in such case you will report details by mail but please telegraph brief report early date for information Department."

To Stokes October 28:

"Receipt yesterday acknowledged urtel 89, October 24 [23] (urtels 51, 61, 71, 80 [23a] and 84 through 88 missing). Department informed; please inform whether telephone available you and if so phone number."

To Stokes October 29:

"Reurtel 89, October 24. Local press today states Ward and others to be tried by People's court. Have they been returned to their quarters? Please inform continuously all developments for information Department."

No message received from Stokes since his 89, October 24.
To Tientsin by mail.

CLUBB

123 Ward, Angus I.: Telegram

The Consul General at Peiping (Clubb) to the Secretary of State

PEIPING, October 30, 1949—noon.
[Received October 30—8:13 a. m.]

1859. ReDeptel 750, October 28. Am sending letter Chou En-lai early tomorrow asking for interview himself or deputy "under instructions my Government."

---

[23] See telegram No. 1839, October 28, from the Consul General at Peiping, p. 987.
[23a] October 12, not sent; for text, see p. 981.

ReContel 1787, October 21.[24] Last night saw . . . who reported Lo Lung-chi had feared take up Mukden matter direct with Chou but by indirect inquiries had obtained certain information considered by . . . reliable, indicating policy re Mukden is determined and hardly alterable. . . . said (indubitably against background Lo [Lung-chi]) there is difference between authority exercised by Chou in China proper and in Manchuria. Chou would probably be unable do anything change policy; would have to refer question elsewhere, perhaps Mao Tse-tung.[25] Acknowledged in response question perhaps even Soviets might have be consulted. Reason for holding consular staff unclear, but perhaps designed keep them there until certain information they possess has lost its value. Will be released in good time but this probably means end this year or next spring. Indications are authorities have grasped excuse of minor incident bring Ward and others before People's Court. They may now be found guilty, forced make compensation injured party, then sent out of country—which would be good denouncement. . . . concluded that all foreigners of countries failing recognize China will find it harder going henceforth, but Peiping should still be better than Mukden. Indicated that he was for present largely breaking off contacts with such foreigners . . .

Re penultimate paragraph Deptel, note that it has already been publicly announced Ward and others to be tried by People's Court. This was presumably decided even at time matter was first made public October 25, otherwise incident which had occurred 2 weeks before would have passed without publicity. Believe demand in circumstances for immediate release would bring so definitely into play question Communist "sovereignty" and competence court that it could only aggravate situation, fail of aim and perhaps lead to increased sentences. Therefore, request authority change that request to representations pointing to established international law and practice, noting regular presence guards over concerned Americans, indicating case is of such character that it should be possible readily settle matter in accord law and established practice even without court action, requesting that Ward et al. be given opportunity see British Consul-acting on behalf American interests Mukden and that on settlement matter, Ward and other employees and dependents Mukden office will promptly be given transport facilities for withdrawal themselves and effects from China.

Believe also that it would be preferable in present interview (if obtained) omit reference Communist hostility; that efforts should be made in such first interview put matter on reasonable basis and obtain clarification and progress toward our goal of getting Mukden staff

---

[24] Not printed.
[25] Chairman of Central Committee of Chinese Communist Party and of "Central People's Government of the People's Republic of China" at Peiping.

out of China; and that particularly because of possible developments before hypothetical date of interview, my authority should be left flexible to permit me develop matter in interview largely at own discretion. Therefore, likewise recommend restraint in official statements to press, though feel it would be well now review briefly situation to show men have been virtually prisoners for nearly year, that they were under guard at time alleged incident, that certain charges have been made, but their own version unreported, that matter their position was brought attention Communist authorities Peiping after establishment Communist government in note to Chou (which might now be released without further comment), that Department is following new development closely and endeavoring first obtain clarification, and that British consular representative Mukden has asked see Ward and others.

Note possibility Soviets may be behind delay after June 21 and line development present incident. Matter in such case would reflect higher policy directed and still unknown. Real design as regards use to be made of incident respecting consular personnel should shortly be discernable. Note offense of itself, even if as charged, hardly warrants serious action against Ward *et al.*, and that after 1 year of incarceration, it would be hardly congruous try develop espionage charges. One might deduce from sequels to previous similar Communist outbursts that this development may be procedure designed by Communists to get them credit for "ejecting imperialist elements from China". But flexibility on American side seems requisite for immediate present.

Believe, if interview not forthcoming within week, I should make written representations along lines indicated above.

Please instruct.

CLUBB

---

123 Ward, Angus I. : Telegram

The Consul General at Tientsin (Smyth) to the Secretary of State

TIENTSIN, October 31, 1949—3 p. m.
[Received November 2—6:09 a. m.]

890. Items re Ward at Mukden appeared in Tientsin press October 30 similar to those reported in Peiping telegram 1827, October 26.

Some Chinese here privately express opinion present agitation against Ward is build-up preparatory to "expelling" Ward and other members of ConGen staff from Mukden as face-saving device.

SMYTH

123 Ward, Angus I. : Telegram

The Consul General at Shanghai (McConaughy) to the Secretary
of State

SHANGHAI, October 31, 1949—5 p. m.
[Received 7:42 p. m.]

4618. Reference plight Consul General Ward at Mukden. Presumably, Department hesitant to issue strong refutation Communist charges while Ward kept incommunicado and unable to relate true version alleged incident.

If Department is considering issuance strong condemnation Communist action and wishes receive any evidence tending to show that Communists will not scruple to fabricate charges and incidents out of whole cloth when it serves their purposes, experience of this Consul General during siege by ex-Navy employees last July [26] may be of interest. Press accounts at that time as well as at time of arrest of Vice Consul Olive earlier in July [27] offer strong corroboration of theory that Communists do not hesitate to publish out-and-out lies in order to exploit situation at opportune moment.

Best local example of outright mendacity occurred when Shanghai and Nanking press gave their version of interview of undersigned, then Acting Consul General, with representatives ex-Navy employees on afternoon July 29. Actual fact was that at end of my statement to workers, one of them seized letter knife from my desk, worked himself into hysterical frenzy, brandished it about threatening me and then threatened to stab himself with it, shouting that it was better to commit suicide than to starve to death. I stood with my arms folded throughout this exhibition. Press version (see Nanking's 1677, August 1 [28]) was that "deadlock lasted into evening when quite unexpectedly McConaughy revealed countenance of an imperialist and drew out a knife to threaten employees".

If Department wishes to refer to this in official statement or on VOA as example of gross Communist fabrication of alleged incident, Consul General has no objection.

McCONAUGHY

---

123 Ward, Angus I. : Telegram

The Secretary of State to the Consul General at Peiping (Clubb)

WASHINGTON, October 31, 1949—7 p. m.

757. Dept concurs suggestions ur 1859 Oct 30 re modification Deptel 750 Oct 28 and leaves to ur discretion manner in which question Ward's

---

[26] For information on this subject, see telegram No. 2614, July 6, 10 a.m., from the Consul General at Shanghai, p. 1196.
[27] For information on the case of Vice Consul William M. Olive, see telegram No. 2646, July 7, from the Consul General at Shanghai, p. 1202.
[28] Not printed.

position Mukden developed during any discussion with Chou or other Commie officials or in written communication to Chou. Dept of opinion, however, that it undesirable give Commies impression US Govt acquiesces in People's Court exercising jurisdiction over Ward. Also believes you shld *inter alia* request full information re detention Ward and if as implied ur 1857 Oct 29 communications with Mukden again cut you shld request restoration. In view serious nature matter and widespread interest in US regarding it, Dept believes you shld not delay written communication for week if interview not promptly forthcoming.

ACHESON

---

123 Ward, Angus I. : Telegram

The Consul General at Peiping (Clubb) to the Secretary of State

PEIPING, November 2, 1949.
[Received November 2—8 :36 a. m.]

1893. Stokes' 94, October 28 follows:

Please repeat to Department as No. 12, Mukden telegram 89 to Peiping, October 24,[29] inasmuch I today requested telegraph office return copy addressed Department at urgent rate. Urtel 38, October 26 [30] received yesterday evening, Mukden telegram 80 to Peiping, October 12,[30a] contained Consul General Ward account incident day previous: Confirmation copy mailed yesterday. Officer administering confinement this office today called and returning my letter to Ward (Mukden telegram 91, Oct. 26 [31]) stated in translation "Inasmuch Ward has been taken away he is not allowed to receive visitors or communications. No further attempts to visit or communicate with Ward should be undertaken." Officer then stated my letter yesterday (telegram 92 to Peiping yesterday [32]) re inability pay salaries tomorrow without Ward signature had been delivered to mayor.

Sent Dept 1893, repeated Shanghai 1135.

CLUBB

---

123 Ward, Angus I. : Telegram

The Consul General at Peiping (Clubb) to the Secretary of State

PEIPING, November 2, 1949—6 p. m.
[Received November 2—8 :26 a. m.]

1899. ReDeptel 757, October 31, no action yet on request for Chou interview. Communists took four days act on French request for

---

[29] See telegram No. 1839, October 28, from the Consul General at Peiping, p. 987.
[30] Not transmitted to the Department.
[30a] Not sent; for text, see p. 981.
[31] See telegram No. 1900, November 2, from the Consul General at Peiping, p. 999.
[32] Not printed.

interview, two on Dutch. Department's announcement to press October 29 that I was being instructed take up matter high Communist authorities probably monitored here, may cause Communists adopt Moscow policy or refrain Soviet fashion from replying the while they handle Mukden matters as planned. Will forward letter to Chou on subject tomorrow in absence interview.

Will of course not give impression of American acquiescence exercise People's Court jurisdiction, merely feel it injudicious make that point present issue. Since Mukden still has limited telegraphic facilities, believe better omit that for present. ReDeptel October 13, 10 p. m.,[33] also informing re closure offices, as pertinent.

ReContel 1881, November 1,[33] invite attention possibility Soviets causing Chinese thus treat Ward as counter to action taken against Soviet officials USA.[34] Attempt tar him in process might reflect some Soviet animosity against him personally dating back to period his service USSR. Situation of course more dangerous if, despite implied Chinese Communist desire expel him reported Contel 1879, November 1[33] Soviets try pin espionage tag on him.

ReContel 1810, October 24,[33] French Consul Mukden at his last report still in non-receipt permit travel Peiping.

CLUBB

---

123 Ward, Angus I. : Telegram

The Secretary of State to the Consul General at Peiping (Clubb)[35]

WASHINGTON, November 2, 1949—6 p. m.

766. Dept considering instructing Moscow approach Sov FonOff outlining general circumstances re ConGen Mukden and requesting Sovs exercise good offices ascertain reasons continued Commie failure permit Ward and staff depart and to facilitate departure. Ur comments wld be appreciated.

ACHESON

---

[33] Not printed.
[34] For information on revocation of exequatur of Soviet Consul General at New York, see Department of State *Bulletin*, August 29, 1948, pp. 251–253; for information on closing of certain consulates in the United States and the Soviet Union, see *ibid.*, September 26, 1948, p. 408; for information on arrest of Soviet citizen employed by the United Nations Secretariat, see *ibid.*, May 15, 1949, p. 636.
[35] Repeated to the Ambassador in the Soviet Union as telegram No. 814.

123 Ward, Angus I. : Telegram

The Consul General at Peiping (Clubb) to the Secretary of State

PEIPING, November 2, 1949.
[Received November 2—5 :42 p. m.]

1900. Following is Stokes' 91, October 26, just received:

"Officer arresting Consul General Ward, Rehberg, Tatsumi, Cicogna, and Kristan (Mukden telegram 89, October 24 [36]) presented warrants issued by Mukden police commissioner based upon investigation reported Mukden telegram 80, October 12.[36a] Later same day officer returned and stated accused would be held '2 or 3 days'. He accepted individual packages food, clothing, and bedding which addressee received yesterday. Today am preparing further food packages for transmission tomorrow morning.

No reply yet received letter to mayor requesting permission visit Consul General, reference Mukden telegram 90 yesterday.[37] Attempting communicate with Consul General by letter. Delegation Chinese staff (which has not ceased work stoppage initiated October 11, reference Mukden telegram 84, October 19 [37]) today read sight English translation local newspaper article regarding October 11 incident. Indicate transcription article being mailed to you tomorrow. Will report developments by daily telegram. Only telegram sent Department from Mukden this month has been Mukden number 89 to Peking, October 24. Urgent keep Department fully informed."

Tientsin by mail.
Sent Department 1900, Shanghai 1137.

CLUBB

---

123 Ward, Angus I. : Telegram

The Consul General at Peiping (Clubb) to the Secretary of State

PEIPING, November 3, 1949.
[Received November 3—2 :23 a. m.]

1902. ReContel 1901, November 2.[38] *Kuang Ming Jih Pao* November 3 carried Mukden NCNA [39] November 2 despatch translation as follows:

Incident in which American nationals in Shenyang led by Ward assaulted Chinese worker has been transferred from public security organization of People's Government to Shenyang Municipal People's Court for trial in accordance with law. While under detention and interrogation by municipal public security organization, principal offender and accomplices Ward, Kristan, Cicogna, Tatsumi and Rehberg tried every means possible to evade and repudiate their criminal action of every Chinese worker. Public security organization, in

---

[36] See telegram No. 1839, October 28, from the Consul General at Peiping, p. 987.
[36a] Not sent ; for text, see p. 981.
[37] Not transmitted to the Department.
[38] Not printed.
[39] New China News Agency (Communist).

accordance with judicial procedure, on October 31 formally presented case to Shenyang Municipal People's Court for trial. People's Court has formally accepted case and put five criminal offenders led by Ward under detention. Preliminary hearing has already been conducted.

Sent Department 1902, Shanghai 1139; by mail to Tientsin.

CLUBB

---

123 Ward, Angus I.: Telegram

The Consul General at Peiping (Clubb) to the Secretary of State

PEIPING, November 4, 1949—noon.
[Received November 4—3:28 a. m.]

1909. ReContel 1899, November 2. Sent letter Chou En-lai last night. Text by next telegram Peiping number series.[40] Recommend text not be released immediately but suggest Department might now release text letter October 8.[41] Say new communication on subject was sent Chou under date November 3.

ReContel 1759, October 17. Suggest further, time has now come exercise real pressure, if available. Would recommend Department consider desirability of SCAP's [42] temporarily holding up, if feasible, all commercial negotiations and permits regarding trade between China and Japan without explanation or publicity (which would alike commit USA to certain policy and make matter public issue on which USA and Communists would be forced take official stands), pending release Ward and others from police custody and departure personnel from Mukden. Believe Communists would quickly get point without need of explanation, but absence American policy statement would make it possible for USA readily reverse or adjust tactics if found inefficacious.

CLUBB

---

123 Ward, Angus I.: Telegram

The Consul General at Peiping (Clubb) to the Secretary of State

PEIPING, November 4, 1949.
[Received November 4—5:16 a. m.]

1910. Text letter November 3 Ward case follows:

"In my letter of October 8, 1949,[41] I brought to your attention the matter of the isolation, since November 1948, of the American consular

---

[40] *Infra.*
[41] See telegram No. 1707, October 10, 3 p. m., from the Consul General at Peiping, vol. IX, p. 117.
[42] Supreme Commander, Allied Powers in Japan (MacArthur).

compounds at Mukden, of Consul General Angus I. Ward and his entire staff. Under instructions of my Government, I would now invite your attention to the circumstance that, according to information received from a member of the Mukden staff, Mr. Ward, Foreign Service clerk Ralph Rehberg, and mechanic Shiro Tatsumi, and alien employees Franco Cicogna and Alfred Kristan, were removed by police on October 24 on the charge that they had assaulted one of the Chinese personnel of that office. It was stated by the police at the time that they would be held for 2 or 3 days.

"It is requested that I be supplied with authoritative information regarding the matter in point for transmission to my Government. It is requested particularly that I be informed whether Mr. Ward and the other consular employees are still held, if so, where. I invite your attention to the fact that the personnel in question have been isolated in their compounds under guard since November 20, 1948. As a consequence, the United States Government decided in May of this year to close the American Consulate General at that point, which fact I communicated to the General Headquarters of the People's Liberation Army in a communication of May 19, 1949. Mr. Ward was appropriately instructed at the same time by the Department of State. The Mukden authorities, through the director of the Alien Affairs Office, on June 21 informed Mr. Ward that he and his staff would be permitted to depart Mukden with moveable property, and that upon the presentation of lists of staff and property to be evacuated, railway transportation would be provided. Mr. Ward was asked to designate the departure date for staff and property.

"Mr. Ward on July 19 notified the authorities that 13 of his staff were prepared to depart on July 27, the others to remain behind until there had been completed arrangements for the packing and shipment of effects. That request was renewed on August 12, with the departure date fixed for August 17. Those transportation facilities were, in fact, not provided. On September 3, after completion of packing, Mr. Ward sent a formal letter to the Mayor of Mukden requesting rail transportation to Peiping and Tientsin for himself and staff and dependents, excepting persons left behind in custodial capacity, with their baggage and American Government property. To date those facilities have not been provided by the Mukden authorities.

"In short, the Mukden authorities have continued to refuse, without explanation or extenuating circumstances, to abide by their assurances of June 21 or even to indicate their intentions. Acting again under instruction of my Government, on September 22, 1949, I sent a letter to Commander in Chief Chu Teh [43] in respect to the matter in point, requesting that appropriate measures be taken to cause the Mukden authorities to extend promptly the transportation facilities required for the removal from Mukden of the personnel of the Consulate General and their personal and official effects. In my reference letter of October 8, I took occasion to indicate the grave concern with which the United States Government regarded the arbitrary action of detention by the local authorities of American consular officials at Mukden and the continued failure of the Mukden authorities to provide facilities for withdrawal even after giving express assurances.

---

[43] See telegram No. 1601, September 23, from the Consul General at Peiping, p. 979.

"The latest developments render more urgent still the taking of appropriate action to bring the matter to a speedy settlement. It is noted particularly that Mr. Ward and the others charged with the assault were, at the time of the alleged offense, still in close guard, and that they have had no opportunity to report their version of the incident. And, be it noted, the present development follows upon the action of the Mukden authorities in detaining for nearly 1 year the American and non-American personnel of the Consulate General at that point under close guard, which action was in the first instance said to be because of the need [of] according them 'protection', in clear violation of established principles of international comity and practice respecting treatment of foreign consular officials. It is requested that this matter be brought to the attention of the highest authorities to the end that there shall promptly be taken appropriate measure to bring this matter to a speedy settlement. It is requested particularly that the British Consular Representative at Mukden be given the opportunity to see Mr. Ward and the other persons charged with assault, if they are still detained by the police, that the matter be handled in accord with established principles of international law and practice respecting treatment of foreign consular officials, and that the promised transportation facilities for removal from Mukden of the personnel of the Consulate General with their personal and official effects be provided. In view of the serious nature of this matter and the widespread concern it has caused in the United States, I would emphasize my request for prompt action.

"I take this opportunity to inform you of the recent closure of the American consular offices located in Tihwa, Hankow and Dairen and the impending closure of the office at Tsingtao.[45] The office at Mukden will be formally closed as soon as feasible. The British consular authorities in those several points have taken over, or will take over at the time of closure of the related American consular offices, matters pertaining to American interests."

CLUBB

---

123 Ward, Angus I.

Memorandum by the Assistant Secretary of State for Far Eastern Affairs (Butterworth) to the Under Secretary of State (Webb)

[WASHINGTON,] November 4, 1949.

Reference is made to your memorandum of October 31 [46] respecting your conversation with the President regarding the evacuation of American citizens from Formosa and the position of Consul General Ward and his staff at Mukden. The former is being discussed in a separate memorandum.[47] The following comments with respect to Ward's position may be of interest to you and helpful in the event that you discuss the matter again with the President.

---

[45] For documentation concerning the closure of Consulates at Tihwa, Hankow and Tsingtao, and Dairen, see pp. 1303 ff., pp. 1122 ff., and pp. 860 ff., respectively.
[46] Vol. IX, p. 1355.
[47] Not printed.

According to our latest information, Ward with two other American members of his staff and two aliens continues to be held incommunicado by the Chinese Communist police at Mukden.

Consul General Clubb at Peiping included the question of the continued detention of the staff of the Consulate General at Mukden in his letter of October 8 [48] replying to Chou En-lai's letter inviting recognition. Clubb is also endeavoring, so far without success, to discuss the case personally with high Communist officials. On November 3 [49] he again wrote Chou En-lai, reviewing the Mukden situation and making strong representations on Ward's behalf.

The Embassy at Moscow and Consul General Clubb have been asked to comment on the desirability of asking the USSR to exercise its good offices to ascertain the reasons for the long detention of the consular staff at Mukden and to facilitate its departure. Replies have not been received as yet. The possible use of an appeal to the United Nations is likewise being studied as a matter of urgency. It appears unlikely that an immediate remedy can be sought there.

On the basis of previous efforts to facilitate the departure of Ward and his staff from Mudken, there is no special reason for optimism with respect to the measures described above.

There seems to be no means by which a plane could be sent into Mukden, even with some utilization of force, for the purpose of rescuing our people there. They are closely confined and Mukden, of course, is well inland and firmly in the hands of the Communists.

We have, in our examination of the problem, given thought to the threat of force, or if necessary the use of force as a reprisal to effect the release of our staff. There are two outstanding dangers with respect to such measures: (1) reprisal might well beget reprisal of increasing gravity and in a widening circle with the end point outright hostilities; and (2) the immediate effect of the use of force might well be to increase the danger to the persons whom we wish to aid thereby and to increase the danger to other Americans within the reach of Communst power. For these reasons we have considered it desirable to continue our efforts along less drastic lines.

---

123 Ward, Angus I. : Telegram

The Ambassador in the Soviet Union (Kirk) to the Secretary of State

Moscow, November 4, 1949—6 p. m.
[Received November 4—11 :04 a. m.]

2764. Although deeply aware urgently critical situation Consulate General Mukden arising from detention Ward and four staff members

---

[48] See telegram No. 1707, October 10, 3 p. m., from the Consul General at Peiping, vol. IX, p. 117.
[49] See telegram No. 1910, November 4, from the Consul General at Peiping, p. 1000.

(Deptel 766, November 2 to Peiping, repeated Moscow 814), we believe approach to Soviet Foreign Office will in all probability prove fruitless, and aside from opportunity it would give Soviets to proclaim their noninterference Chinese Communist affairs, might even react Ward's disadvantage if Soviets should then feel their interest to support such disclaimer with tangible evidence of Ward's continued imprisonment and persecution.

We note Radio Bulletin report that Clubb has been instructed contact highest authorities Peiping and we think this channel has only possibility success. Presume Clubb will endeavor convey to Chou En-lai impossibility of giving serious consideration to recognition question while CPG [50] continues ignore basic principles international law, for example in treatment accorded our personnel Mukden, stressing pointless damage to CPG position through failure to release personnel and permit them to withdraw from Mukden.

Sent Department 2764; Department pass Peiping 18.

KIRK

---

123 Ward, Angus I. : Telegram

The Secretary of State to the Consul General at Peiping (Clubb)

WASHINGTON, November 4, 1949—8 p. m.

774. From Amb Stuart. Pls transmit orally substance fol to Chang Tung-sun: [51]

"Am appealing to you personally because of my concern over friendly relations our two countries now seriously damaged by unprecedented harsh treatment Angus Ward and all members Mukden Consulate General. Beginning almost a year ago they have been subjected to utterly unwarranted affronts and virtual imprisonment, followed by refusal to permit their departure and closure of Consulate, culminating in outrageous charges obviously intended to inflame popular sentiment against them and the country they represent. Even granting CCP ignore official consular status yet by all standards international relations and human decency they shld have been allowed to depart with safety. It may be difficult to restrain US public resentment longer unless proper settlement earliest possible. Urge you exert your influence to this end." [52]

[Stuart]
ACHESON

---

[50] Central People's Government (Communist).

[51] Professor at Yenching University, Peiping, and a leader of the Democratic Socialist party.

[52] In telegram No. 2010, November 16, 2 p. m., the Consul General at Peiping reported information that a letter would be written by Chang Tung-sun on the Ward case to Chou En-lai.

123 Ward, Angus I. : Telegram

The Consul General at Peiping (Clubb) to the Secretary of State

PEIPING, November 5, 1949—noon.
[Received November 5—3:20 a. m.]

1922. ReDeptel 766, November 2. Believe approach by Moscow Embassy to Soviet FonOff re Mukden case would be useless on following grounds:

(1) Court aspect of case will presumably be over in near future unless Communists propose development espionage angle by "discovery new facts".

(2) As is matter of general repute, Soviet influence Manchuria strong and as suggested Contel 1899, November 2, perhaps Soviets themselves are responsible for manner handling case.

(3) Soviets once previously refused intervene and could be expected refuse at present juncture (if on different grounds) when their China policy is diametrically opposed [to our?] own, and

(4) Such approach would therefore indicate American weakness and possibly bring deterioration rather than improvement situation Mukden personnel. Therefore recommend against proposed line procedure.

Peiping's position is as set forth Contel 1909, November 4.
Department to pass Moscow at discretion.

CLUBB

---

123 Ward, Angus I. : Circular telegram

The Acting Secretary of State to Certain Diplomatic and Consular Offices [53]

WASHINGTON, November 9, 1949—2 a. m.

You and selected members ur staff shld seek every opportunity in conversations with Chi likely have some influence on Chi Coms or source of info of Chi Commies express as ur personal opinion, and not on instrs from Dept, that Commie treatment Ward and staff Mukden certain create deep public indignation in US and that repercussions this aroused widespread feeling will inevitably lead to strong public demands for counter-action some nature. Discussions along these lines shld be conducted in manner to avoid giving impression planned campaign.

WEBB

---

[53] At Hong Kong, Nanking, Peiping, Shanghai, and Tientsin.

893.00B/11–949 : Telegram

The Consul General at Peiping (Clubb) to the Secretary of State

PEIPING, November 9, 1949—3 p. m.
[Received November 9—4:16 a. m.]

1954. ReDeptel 778, November 8.[54]   Agree re desirability releasing at this time text letter November 3 to Chou En-lai.

Letter still unacknowledged and no answer from Foreign Office to my letter of October 31 requesting interview.

CLUBB

123 Ward, Angus I. : Telegram

The Consul General at Peiping (Clubb) to the Secretary of State

PEIPING, November 9, 1949.
[Received November 9—12:46 p. m.]

1958. Stokes' 102, November 3, received Peiping today as follows:

"Deputation staff read short press articles stating Ward and others sent to People's Court October 31 and preliminary investigation has been conducted by Chief Justice in preparation trial accused near future. Press comment uniformly demands Ward and others be found guilty and accorded severe punishment. Still have no access local newspaper and have today requested restoration delivery to American representative which suspended October 11.

"No reply yet received my request attend trial or to application for release accused to quarters pending trial (Mukden telegram 95, October 29 [55]). Remainder foreign staff required, by complete work stoppage all Chinese employees including servants since October 11, perform own cooking, stoking and cleaning as well as office functions including maintenance administration and interpretation. Staff meeting with success by hard work and cooperation."

CLUBB

123 Ward, Angus I. : Telegram

The Consul General at Peiping (Clubb) to the Secretary of State

PEIPING, November 10, 1949.
[Received November 9—11:10 p. m.]

1964. Stokes' 101, November 3, received today as follows:

"Investigation deputation presumably from People's Court yesterday made detailed examination site Chinese incident and had Chinese staff this office reconstruct its testimony regarding events October 11.

---

[54] Not printed; it stated: "Dept will release text ur Nov 3 ltr to Chou En-lai at press conference Nov 9." (893.00B/11–849) See press release of November 10, Department of State *Bulletin*, November 21, 1949, p. 759.
[55] Not printed.

If my untrained interpretation Chinese language statements correct, staff testified Chinese thrown to ground and struck by accused, but both allegations contrary testimony Ward and others during police investigation October 11 (Mukden telegram 80 to Peiping, October 12, conforms to Ward testimony [55a])."

Sent Department 1964, Shanghai 1169.

CLUBB

---

123 Ward, Angus I. : Telegram

The Acting Secretary of State to the United States Representative at the United Nations (Austin)

WASHINGTON, November 10, 1949—8 p. m.

592. From Rusk.[56] Fol is factual situation on ConGen Angus Ward:

ConGen Ward and entire staff of ConGen Mukden have been denied freedom of movement and under strict guard by Chi Commie auths since Nov 18, 1948 at which time all their communications with outside world were cut. Since July 1949 Commies have permitted ConGen limited *en clair* telegraph facilities, but msgs inevitably delayed and many undelivered. Ward and four other staff members were removed by local police from Cons premises on Oct 24, upon basis alleged assault by Ward and other staff members on Chi employee. ConGen Peiping on Nov 3 made written representations high Commie officials Peiping on subject. Ward and others apparently still held in jail incommunicado, our Vice Consul Mukden having repeatedly been denied interview with Ward. Msg just recd states ConGen Peiping has now held one telephone conversation with Vice Consul Mukden who stated still has recd no info from Ward and rest of personnel. No knowledge when trial of jailed personnel contemplated by Commies will take place.

US Govt prepared to use all available pressure in effort to free Ward and colleagues. If forthcoming GA [57] debate on China gives rise to request from Chi Commie auths to send representatives to Lake Success, US Govt wld be faced with most serious difficulties if at time of Chi Commie request for visas Angus Ward and colleagues are still being held in gross violation elementary principles internatl comity. We do not wish to raise technical legal questions of applicability of agreements with UN re persons travelling on UN business nor to try to decide now the degree of misconduct which wld warrant US refusal of visas. We can anticipate very practical problem arising from fact that public feeling in this country is rapidly mounting over Angus Ward situation and that it wld be most difficult for US Govt or UN to

---

[55a] Not sent ; for text, see p. 981.
[56] Dean Rusk, Deputy Under Secretary of State.
[57] General Assembly of the United Nations.

make satisfactory arrangements for safe conduct and personal safety of Chi Commie representatives while Ward and colleagues are still being held.

I believe we have an obligation to SYG [58] to inform him quite confidentially of this anticipated difficulty in order that the event will not catch either him or us by surprise. In discussing it with SYG, I suggest you not raise the legal problem and that if he raises it you reply merely that you are not trying to provide an answer to the legal problem but merely to apprise him in advance of what might be a troublesome situation.

I do not suggest that you ask SYG to take any action although he may himself decide to try to forestall such situation by finding way to urge release of Ward and others. [Rusk.]

WEBB

---

123 Ward, Angus I.

Memorandum by the Under Secretary of State (Webb)[59]

[WASHINGTON,] November 14, 1949.

MEETING WITH THE PRESIDENT, MONDAY, NOVEMBER 14

ANGUS WARD CASE

The President indicated that he had been giving some further thought to the problem of the release of Consul General Angus Ward, that he felt we should thoroughly explore the possibility of blockading the movements of coal down the coast of China to Shanghai. He said he felt that if we prevented the movement of coal from Tientsin and another coal port, and prevented the entry of coal to Shanghai, the Communists would understand that we meant business, and release Ward. He indicated that he thought we would also gain considerable respect by this move internationally, and that this would make it more difficult for the British to act independently in connection with recognition and other problems. He said further that he felt sure we probably had both the ships and planes available in the neighborhood to accomplish this. I asked him how far he would be inclined to go, that is, would he actually use force to stop the coal traffic if they refused to obey orders from our Naval forces, and he said if we meant to go into this matter we should be prepared to sink any vessels which refused to heed our warning.

JAMES E. WEBB

---

[58] Secretary-General of the United Nations (Lie).
[59] Copies transmitted to the Assistant Secretary of State for Far Eastern Affairs (Butterworth) for action and to the Deputy Under Secretary of State (Rusk).

123 Ward, Angus I. : Circular telegram

The Secretary of State to Certain Diplomatic Representatives [60]

WASHINGTON, November 18, 1949—10 a. m.

Pls pass urgently fol personal msg to the FonMin from SecState Acheson:

"I wld like to emphasize the importance of concerted action by those countries which respect internatl law to protest the treatment being accorded U.S. consular personnel in Mukden, China. Since late Nov 1948 the entire U.S. consular staff and their families have been detained under house arrest inside the consular compounds. All communications between the staff and the U.S. Govt have been strictly controlled by the local auths, and there was one period of almost 7 months when no communication of any kind was possible. At the present time communication is permitted only at the will of the local auths, and it is not possible for the consular staff to report their situation in an effective manner.

Because of this kind of treatment it was impossible for the Consulate to perform any of its functions, and on May 19, 1949 [61] the U.S. ConGen at Peiping under instrs from the U.S. Govt notified the appropriate auths there that the Consulate was being closed and asked that arrangements be made for the safe exit of the consular personnel and their families. On June 21, 1949 [62] the Commie auths at Mukden notified the ConGen that he and his staff wld be permitted to depart and that transportation facilities wld be made available.

These assurances have not been honored. On Oct 25 [63] the Chi Commie press and radio announced that ConGen Angus Ward and four members of his staff had been arrested on Oct 24, 1949. So far as is known, they have been in prison since that time. The local auths at Mukden have not permitted the consular staff to make a report concerning the facts in the case. So far as this Govt has been able to determine, the consular staff has not been permitted to get in touch with Mr. Ward or the four members of his staff and has not been informed of the date of any hearings which may be held or permitted to make arrangements to protect Mr. Ward's interest at such hearings. This Govt has not been informed in any way, except by press and radio reports, of the reasons for the arrest of Mr. Ward and the four members of his staff. The efforts of the U.S. ConGen at Peiping to determine the facts in the case and secure the release of Mr. Ward and the others have been completely ignored.

The internatl practice of civilized countries for many years has recognized that consuls shld be accorded all the privileges necessary for the proper conduct of their duties. Although consuls do not have dipl immunity, it has been the universal practice, because of the public

---

[60] The representatives at Ankara, Athens, Bangkok, Bern, Brussels, Cairo, Canberra, Caracas, Copenhagen, Habana, The Hague, Lima, Lisbon, London, Manila, Mexico City, New Delhi, Oslo, Ottawa, Panama City, Paris, Rangoon, Rome, Stockholm, and Vienna. A similar circular telegram dated November 19, 1 a. m., was sent to representatives at Bucharest, Moscow, Praha, Sofia, and Warsaw.

[61] See telegram No. 876, May 21, 10 a. m., from the Consul General at Peiping, p. 957.

[62] See telegram No. 1353, June 23, from the Ambassador in China, p. 971.

[63] See telegram No. 1827, October 26, from the Consul General at Peiping, p. 984.

and official character of their duties, to permit them and their staff freedom of movement, and in the event that any criminal charge is made, to permit them to remain at liberty on proper arrangements for bail, with unlimited freedom to communicate with their gvts with respect to official business.

The treatment accorded to Mr. Ward and to the Amer consular staff in Mukden is in direct violation of the basic concepts of internatl relations which have been developed throughout the centuries. As such, it is of direct and immed concern to all countries interested in dipl intercourse, particularly to those with missions or consulates in China. I ask you, as a matter of urgency, to express to the highest Chi auths in Peiping through such channels as may be available to you the concern which your Govt undoubtedly feels over the treatment of the Amer consular staff in Mukden who have been arbitrarily deprived of their freedom for one year.

I am sending a similar communication to the FonMins of other countries which have reps in China."

Account fluid situation and recent departure many Fon officials from China, in case you uncertain first discreetly ascertain whether country to which you accredited actually has dipl or cons reps in Commie China. If negative, of course take no action.

In transmitting this request to FonMin you shld suggest that if his Govt does not have representation Peiping he shld transmit his message to his Govt's dipl or cons rep Nanking or Shanghai, sending such msgs by commercial facilities in plain language text.

For urinfo and guidance and for use in discussion with FonMin, if this approach does not produce results within reasonable period of time Dept will expect ask FonMin make public his Govt's approach in this matter.

You shld keep Dept informed of action taken by Govt to which you are accredited and transmit to Dept substance or full text of note or msg sent by FonMin to his rep in China.[64]

Dept does not consider approach envisaged this tel can give rise to implication of recognition.

ACHESON

---

[64] Of the 18 countries having representation in Communist-occupied China, 15 protested or agreed to protest (Australia, Austria, Belgium, Canada, Denmark, Egypt, France, Greece, India, Italy, Netherlands, Norway, Philippines, Sweden, and Switzerland) ; 2 were sympathetic but made no protest (Portugal and the United Kingdom) ; 1 made no protest (USSR). Twelve countries without representation in Communist China did not take action on the Department's circular telegram (Bulgaria, Burma, Cuba, Czechoslovakia, Mexico, Panama, Peru, Poland, Roumania, Thailand, Turkey, and Venezuela).

123 [Ward, Angus I.]

*Memorandum by the Chairman of the Joint Chiefs of Staff (Bradley)
to the Secretary of Defense (Johnson)*[65]

WASHINGTON, 18 November 1949.

The following are the views of the Joint Chiefs of Staff in response to your oral question as to what might be done by the Department of Defense to assist the Department of State to extricate Mr. Angus Ward from his predicament in Mukden:

a. The Department of Defense can, at little risk and cost, assist the Department of State to extricate Mr. Angus Ward from Mukden by providing transportation by sea or air for a duly accredited Department of State representative to any point for which diplomatic clearance for the visit has been obtained;

b. Other military alternatives involve either threats by the United States Government, coupled with a present apparent intent to carry out the threatened action, or direct military action as may be necessary in the circumstance. In either of these two courses of action there are military implications of such deep significance that they should be examined in detail;

c. Mukden, the locale of Mr. Ward's confinement, is the seat of government for Manchuria, this government being subordinate to the Chinese Communist Government at Peking. According to intelligence sources, Mukden is also the headquarters of a Chinese Communist army;

d. In accordance with the rights granted under the Sino-Soviet Treaty of 1945,[66] the USSR has established operating facilities for submarines and for surface vessels at Dairen and Port Arthur. Considerable quantities of Manchurian goods are exported from Dairen by sea; lesser quantities of goods are exported from Manchurian ports in the Gulf of Chihli and in Korea Bay. There is no overt United States trade with Manchuria;

e. It is recognized that political considerations could affect the military considerations involved. Such political considerations would include the nature of the warning and the color of authority (United Nations or the duly recognized Chinese Nationalist Government) under which military action might be initiated. Regardless of the political considerations, however, there are, broadly speaking, only two possible courses of military action; namely:

(1) Forcible measures to remove Mr. Angus Ward from Mukden; and

(2) Military redress;

---

[65] Copy transmitted to the Under Secretary of State by the Secretary of Defense in his letter of November 21.

[66] Signed at Moscow, August 14, 1945; for text, see Department of State, *United States Relations With China* (Washington, Government Printing Office, 1949), p. 585, or United Nations Treaty Series, Vol. 10, p. 300.

f. The physical removal of Mr. Ward from Mukden would require the employment of military forces in sufficient strength to force a landing, either by sea or by air, to effect rescue, and to fight their way out of Manchuria or, alternatively, it would require covert operations for the removal of Mr. Ward from Manchuria after forcibly extricating him from custody. The strength of the military forces required to force a landing and overtly to remove Mr. Ward from custody must be adequate, from the inception of the operation, to insure its success under all contingencies, and such strength is probably greater than that presently available. The undertaking of such military action would involve a conflict with the civil forces in that area, and probably the military forces as well. Thus such action might well lead to open war with the Chinese Communist Government. Furthermore, failure of the USSR to become involved, particularly in view of Soviet strategic interests in Manchuria and the presence of USSR units in the Dairen–Port Arthur area, can be regarded only as a remote possibility. In view of the foregoing considerations, there is a likelihood that overt United States military action might lead to global war. It is understood that covert measures to remove Mr. Ward from Manchuria would probably require action beyond the capabilities of the covert strength available to the United States Government. In the case of either overt or covert action for the removal of Mr. Ward, there would be grave doubts as to whether he would be allowed to survive. Moreover covert action, even if successful, would not sustain the attitude of the United States with respect to the treatment of its consular representatives and other nationals, and might be construed as a tacit admission of Mr. Ward's guilt;

g. The second course of action; namely, redress, would involve the application of retortion, reprisal, or some form of sanction such as embargo or blockade;

h. Since there are no diplomatic representatives of the Chinese Communist Government in United States territory, simple retortion is not possible. Retortion, however, could be accomplished through the kidnapping by covert forces of one or more highly placed officials of the Manchurian Government. Even if such an operation were within the capabilities of United States covert forces, this action would establish a highly undesirable precedent in United States international relations and, by the very nature of its covert form, would fail to provide a clear-cut basis for the extrication of Mr. Ward without at least tacit overt approval by the United States of an unfriendly act carried out by covert forces. Furthermore, retortion of this nature might not alter the decision of the Manchurian Government to hold Mr. Ward rather than to negotiate an exchange. In addition, our covert action or our subsequent retortion might jeopardize the safety of other United States nationals in Communist China;

i. Reprisal would call for seizure or destruction of Manchurian property or that of its citizens. Since there is no Manchurian property in the United States or its possessions, acts of reprisal would have to involve military operations directly against Manchuria and this again would probably lead to war;

j. A United States embargo would be futile in the absence of Manchurian trade with this nation or with nations subject to our influence; and

k. Pacific Blockade. A pacific blockade is a blockade established by one or more states against the ports of another to enforce certain demands, without the intention of going to war. As a rule only vessels of states whose ports are blocked are seized. The United States has never been a party to a pacific blockade. It is generally conceded—

(1) That a pacific blockade is a legitimate means of constraint short of war.

(2) Those parties to the blockade are bound by its consequences.

(3) As a matter of policy it might be advisable to resort to pacific blockade in order to avoid declaration of war.

(4) That states not parties to a pacific blockade are in no way bound to observe it.

Currently British interests control the greater percentage of ships entering China ports. They would not be affected by a United States declaration of a pacific blockade.

l. Blockade. A blockade is normally employed only in time of war and its institution is commonly considered a belligerent act. It affects shipping regardless of nationality. Such blockade to be recognized would have to be effective. It would involve either coercion of or prior agreement with the British and might eventually necessitate the commitment of strength adequate to deal with the Soviet naval and air forces in the Far East.

In view of all the foregoing considerations, the Joint Chiefs of Staff are of the opinion that direct military action to assist the Department of State in extricating Mr. Angus Ward from his predicament might lead to war and would not of itself insure his timely and safe extrication. They do, however, point out that the Department of Defense can assist by supplying appropriate transportation for the accredited representatives of the Government to negotiate for Mr. Ward's release. Consideration might also be given to designating a military officer, such as the Commander of the Seventh Task Fleet, to negotiate locally for the release of Mr. Ward.

For the Joint Chiefs of Staff:

OMAR N. BRADLEY

123 Ward, Angus I. : Telegram

The Consul General at Peiping (Clubb) to the Secretary of State

PEIPING, November 19, 1949—1 p. m.
[Received November 21—3 :26 p. m.]

2044. Opinions along general lines indicated Depcirtel November 9, 2 a. m. were early expressed by staff members in private conversations with Chinese. Chinese contacts themselves profess be unable understand reasons for Communist treatment Mukden Consulate personnel. Would, however, invite attention probable truth of matter lately: (1) matter is being handled by Communists in present way for political reasons and, (2) Chinese Communists may not be concerned either alone or primarily, Soviets may be determining factor and Soviet may regard Ward as counter for Gubitchev.[67] In any event, it has to be realized that Communists whether Chinese or other nationality are unresponsive to either reasoning or threats unless they see in compliance economic or political gain or in noncompliance some possible real injury Chinese Communists' design reduce our political power and prestige and economic holdings China, and incidentally to pressure with what they find on ground to get recognition. Appeals to law, logic or humanitarianism will be generally ineffective. Communists will be halted in any given line action against our interests or people only by superior counter force.

Believe turn case has taken on American side unexpected by Communists who may now realize results will be unfavorable to them in long term. There appears to have been some relaxation controls on communications for Mukden personnel since note to Chou. Per reasoning Contel 1859, October 30, long delay in bringing Ward to trial would seem unfavorable but Communists may now find it difficult dismount from tiger. If there are to be any favorable results of American official statements and Changtung's USUN [*Chang Tungsun's*] *démarches*, they should shortly become apparent. Reference matter in UNGA at this time when American recognition regime ungranted achieve no more results than efforts re north Korea, but publicity tending to prejudice Chinese Communists' chances of getting UN membership or at any rate seat on Security Council would probably cause Communist alarm. Communist interest in participating Japanese peace treaty and perhaps getting Japanese reparations should be noted. Peiping uninformed re secret success Meryn case [68] but suggest precedent might be helpful.

---

[67] For documentation on the rejection of the claim to diplomatic immunity for Valentin Alexeyevich Gubichev, arrested and tried for espionage, 1949–50, see vol. v, pp. 776 ff.

[68] Samuel Meryn, an employee of the American Embassy in Czechoslovakia, was arrested in October on charges of espionage activities; for statement by the Secretary of State, see Department of State *Bulletin*, November 7, 1949, p. 710.

Failing release it would seem Ward and others are being held simply as hostages force some desired action. In such case, further public statements or appeals to reason would appear hopeless. Unrecognized consuls on ground can exercise little or no real leverage in own right now denied. Whether Ward, *et al.*, now being used as pawns in game to force recognition of course unknown and can hardly be known without at least contact with high Communist official. Embassy probably now shall [not?] get chance discuss matter with Chou En-lai except incidentally in connection with talk on some subject Communists more desirous of considering. But submit that there exists possibility that without recognition Communists will bow in present case only to force which can make itself felt.

Form sanctions might take of course subject best explored by Department but note that as first step economic pressure proposed Contel 1909, November 4, would seem only weapon which could be used without fanfare and further aggravation political situation but success unassured.

In summation regret state that if present moves fail this office sees no other line of law or logic that would promise results and would consider it clear that more than new representations required to achieve desired results.

CLUBB

711.93112/11-2149

Memorandum by the Secretary of State to the President

WASHINGTON, November 21, 1949.

With reference to the suggestion that the blockade of Communist coal shipments be utilized in the Angus Ward case,[69] there is no evidence that Shanghai is receiving any significant shipments of coal by coastal vessel from Tientsin or Chinwangtao. Shanghai draws its coal supplies from the Hwainan mines in Anhwei Province and from the Kailan mines in Hopei Province. These coal supplies have for some time been moving to Shanghai primarily over inland transport routes, principally rail, a consequence in part of the National Government's port closure. It is reported that the coal thus available to Shanghai is adequate to meet the present minimum requirements of the city for generation of electric power.

The National Government "blockade" of central and south China coastal ports has reduced coast-wise shipping to a low level, most of which is carried on by traditional junk traffic with which it would be extremely difficult, if not impossible, to interfere. A relatively small but active foreign trade is carried on out of Tientsin, the only major coastal port in China proper that is not within the effective scope of

---

[69] See memorandum by the Under Secretary of State, November 14, p. 1008.

the National Government's port closure. A large proportion of this trade is between Hong Kong and Tientsin and is heavily dependent upon foreign-flag vessels, many of which are British. The number of Chinese-owned coastal and ocean-going vessels available to the Chinese Communists is believed to be small by virtue of their earlier transfer by the Nationalists to Hong Kong and Taiwan.

Despite the low level of China's coast-wise and foreign trade, a "blockade" of all shipping out of China ports, if it could be undertaken effectively, would of course hurt the Chinese economy. Nevertheless, in view of the basic self-sufficiency of the Chinese economy at present low standards of living, such action could not create an economic crisis in the Chinese Communist regime. On the contrary, it might well prove useful to the Communists as a propaganda weapon, both at home and abroad, in support of their argument concerning the imperialistic intentions of the United States.

Preliminary examination of our legal position in a blockade of Communist-held ports indicates that a state of belligerency would be necessary for such blockade to be legal. There is some precedent for establishment of a "pacific blockade", i.e., blockade as an act of reprisal without a state of belligerency, but it is clear that such a blockade could be legally effective only as to Chinese Communist vessels and not against the vessels of third powers trading in ports controlled by Chinese Communists. The United States in the past has never resorted to a "pacific blockade". There are strong grounds for believing that such a blockade, even where a party to the UN is not involved, might be inconsistent with the principles of Article 33 of the UN Charter under which the parties to a dispute undertake to seek solution of it short of force.

We strongly recommend against the use of force against other foreign vessels.[70]

DEAN ACHESON

---

123 Ward, Angus I. : Telegram

The Ambassador in the United Kingdom (Douglas) to the Secretary of State

LONDON, November 21, 1949—5 p. m.
[Received November 21—1 :51 p. m.]

4636. Personal message from Secretary to Foreign Minister[71] (Deptcirctel November 18, 10 a. m.) re ConGen Mukden, presented

---

[70] The Secretary of State stated in a memorandum of November 21 to the Assistant Secretary of State (Butterworth) : "I left with the President the memorandum recommending against blockade procedure. It was agreed between us that for the time being we should await the developments following from the circular note sent to the countries having diplomatic or consular representation in China." (123 Ward, Angus)

[71] Ernest Bevin, British Secretary of State for Foreign Affairs.

Scarlett [72] head Far East Department, this afternoon. He was orally informed substance antepenultimate paragraph reftel.

Scarlett stated Foreign Office on 19 had sent instruction British Embassy, Nanking, (*a*) pointing out seriousness with which British Government regards treatment ConGen Mukden, (*b*) indicating what is happening to US officials today may happen to UK officials tomorrow and (*c*) directing appropriate representations on behalf Ward be made to Communist authorities whether at Nanking or at Peiping at discretion British Embassy.

Foreign Office now telegraphing British Embassy withhold action pending receipt detailed instructions based on Secretary's message.

DOUGLAS

702.4193/11–2249 : Telegram

The Consul General at Peiping (*Clubb*) *to the Secretary of State*

PEIPING, November 22, 1949—noon.
[Received November 22—4:48 a. m.]

2058. On basis Deptels 625, September 10 [*12*] and 662, September 26,[73] informed October 4 British Consul, Peiping, that Department had instructed that British FonOff had agreed accept custody American Government property Mukden, sent him copy my letter even date to Ward regarding matter, asked that he arrange British Consular Office, Mukden, be appropriately instructed.

British ConGen has now asked whether agreement was definitive in as much as his Embassy, Nanking, apparently unaware arrangement and tells him his action vis-à-vis Mukden premature. Informed him my information was definite. Department might wish get clarification British side.

Department pass to Nanking 1170.

CLUBB

---

123 Ward, Angus I. : Telegram

The Consul General at Peiping (*Clubb*) *to the Secretary of State*

PEIPING, November 23, 1949.
[Received November 23—12:46 a. m.]

2064. Talked to Mukden 0945 today.[74] Ward and four others who had been arrested have returned to consular compounds. Failed confirm categorically but infer returned yesterday (this inference

---

[72] Peter W. S. Scarlett.
[73] Latter not printed.
[74] See also telegram No. 2074, November 23, 6 p. m., p. 1020.

supported by fact they were not back when I talked to Stokes November 21). Talked to Ward personally who reported as follows:

Court trial concluded. All five found guilty, sentence as follows: Ward 6 months' imprisonment, 1 year parole, sentence commuted to deportation, Rehberg and Kristan 4 months' imprisonment, 1 year parole, commutation to deportation, Tatsumi and Cicogna 3 months' imprisonment, 1 year parole, commutation to deportation. Ward stated that in addition he was charged with certain financial obligations too lengthy to be reported at time. Obligations, however, include compensation to injured, severance pay and salary payments outside provisions existing FSR. Ward noted employees had refused perform duties since October 11.

Ward reported he had delivered telegram to telegraph office 1600 hours yesterday, telegram refused but same telegram accepted for transmittal this morning. Still unreceived here. Above named five are "up and about." Kristan's physical condition yesterday not good, shows improvement today. Tatsumi suffered from mental strain.

Ward opined it would be necessary for him clear up financial matters before departure. Desires appropriate instructions earliest.

Indications are Mukden in nonreceipt several Peiping telegrams, will check and endeavor supply anything missing. Will also send Ward copy Peiping USIS mediation agreement. Will of course transmit Department promptly all information from Ward re "financial obligations" as received.

Sent Department 206, Shanghai 1210, Nanking 1172, Taipei 40; Hong Kong to Tientsin by mail.

CLUBB

---

123 [Ward, Angus I.] : Circular telegram

The Acting Secretary of State to Certain Diplomatic Representatives [75]

WASHINGTON, November 23, 1949—9 a. m.

Re concerned Depcirtel re Ward case [76] and Depintel Nov 23 [77] stating Ward and other staff members released. In event you are approached by FonMin pointing out that release Ward and staff members from prison wld appear make representations by his Govt to Chi Commie auths unnecessary, you shld reply along fol lines:

---

[75] The representatives in Ankara, Athens, Bern, Brussels, Bucharest, Cairo, Canberra, Caracas, Copenhagen, Habana, The Hague, Lima, Lisbon, London, Manila, Mexico City, Moscow, New Delhi, Oslo, Ottawa, Panama City, Paris, Rangoon, Rome, Sofia, Stockholm, Vienna, and Warsaw; also to Peiping for information only.
[76] November 18, 10 a. m., p. 1009.
[77] Not printed, but see telegram No. 2064, November 23, *supra.*

Although Ward and accused staff members now released on parole and subj deportation, no assurances so far recd from Commie auths that transportation facilities and necessary exit permits forthcoming to enable Ward and staff ConGen (including dependents and those not arrested) depart China for US as directed by US Govt on May 19, 1949 and as promised by Commie auths on June 21. Moreover their release from prison this late date in no way affects facts in case re arrest Ward and four staff members or their detention incommunicado for nearly 1 month despite rptd attempts this Govt get in touch with them or ascertain reason for such intolerable treatment. You may also inform FonMin if question raised that during "trial" of Ward and staff members they were refused access to legal counsel, right to produce witnesses for defense, right to question witnesses or plaintiffs, and right to submit rebutting arguments. Dept of opinion, therefore, that release of Ward and staff members on parole in no way obviates desirability concerned nations making appropriate representations to highest Chi Commie auths expressing their concern over this flagrant violation of accepted standards Internatl conduct.

Pls report any approaches by FonMin this subj and their reaction to above line reasoning.

WEBB

702.4193/11–2249 : Telegram

The Acting Secretary of State to the Consul General at Peiping
(Clubb)

WASHINGTON, November 23, 1949—4 p. m.

822. Urtel 2058 Nov 22 rptd Nanking as 1170. Ur understanding correct. Brit FonOff being informed Brit Emb Nanking apparently unaware arrangements for protection US interests Mukden.

Since Ward unable communicate with Brit re takeover and no means existed for transmitting classified info Mukden suggested approach (Deptel 662 [78]) appeared most feasible one that time. Dept assumed FonOff wld in due course issue instrs approp Brit reps China re Mukden.

For ur info FonOff informed AmEmb London Oct 27 that Brit office Mukden now in chg Pro-Consul. Not sure whether Brit Emb Nanking able transmit necessary instrs to him but has asked for report.

Sent Peiping rptd Nanking.

WEBB

---

[78] Not printed.

123 Ward, Angus I. : Telegram

The Consul General at Peiping (Clubb) to the Secretary of State

PEIPING, November 23, 1949—6 p. m.
[Received November 23—7:11 a. m.]

2074. Ward stated further accused were refused legal counsel, refused right produce witnesses for defense, refused right question witnesses or plaintiffs or other rebutting arguments. Re Contel 2064, November 23.

Recommend no interpretive comment on trial and judgement at least until receipt fuller information. Note personnel still without travel permits or schedule.

CLUBB

---

123 Ward, Angus I. : Airgram

The Ambassador in the United Kingdom (Douglas) to the Secretary of State

LONDON, November 23, 1949.
[Received November 25—11:12 a. m.]

A–2186. Following is the substantive portion of a letter of November 22, 1949 from the Foreign Office describing the efforts of the British Pro-Consul in Mukden to assist Consul General Ward and in general protect American interests in Manchuria:

"The present position is as follows. On the 4th October the United States Consul General at Peking, apparently on instructions from the State Department, formally notified Graham, our Consul-General in Peking, that we had agreed to accept custody of United States Government property at Mukden. Our Consulate-General at Mukden has for some time been in charge of a Pro-Consul, and Graham at once wrote to inform him and to say that pending receipt of formal instructions the Pro-Consul would presumably do anything he properly could to assist Ward. On the 19th October the Pro-Consul informed the Chairman of the North-East People's Government accordingly and asked for early permission to interview Ward in order to discuss details of property to be placed in the Pro-Consul's custody. On the 25th or 26th October, immediately after the announcement in the local press that Ward would be tried in the People's Court, the Pro-Consul again wrote to the Chairman renewing his request for an interview and asking permission to assist Ward and his staff and to be present at any hearing of the case. The Pro-Consul has received no reply to either letter, and does not expect to receive one.

Formal instructions are now being issued to the Pro-Consul to do what he can, but I am sure you will realise that it is very doubtful whether he will be able to do anything effective either to help Ward or to look after United States Government property in Mukden. We understand that there are now no United States citizens in Manchuria other than Ward and his staff."

DOUGLAS

123 Ward, Angus I. : Telegram

The Consul General at Peiping (Clubb) to the Secretary of State

PEIPING, November 24, 1949.
[Received November 24—4:46 a. m.]

2075. ReContel 2064, November 23. Ward, by phone today, confirmed return himself and others to consular compound about 2100 hours, November 21. Reported Kristan, who had stood in danger gangrene, had slight relapse but again better; Tatsumi improving.

Poor phone contact but began preliminary work clarification missing messages.

Sent Department 2075; repeated Shanghai 1213, Nanking 1174, Tientsin by mail.

CLUBB

---

123 Stokes, William N. : Telegram

The Consul General at Peiping (Clubb) to the Secretary of State

Peiping, November 26, 1949—11 a. m.
[Received November 25—11:33 p. m.]

2096. Ward informed me this morning Stokes had been taken court 9 a. m. without warrant for hearing re "spying charges" which Ward connected with June 21 report [79] but whether as accused or witness or in other capacity unindicated to Americans. Ward was refused permission accompany.

Will phone Mukden each schedule until Stokes returns.

Sent Department 2096; Department pass Shanghai 1219, Nanking 1178, Tientsin 102.

CLUBB

---

123 Stokes, William N. : Circular telegram

The Acting Secretary of State to Certain Diplomatic Representatives [80]

WASHINGTON, November 26, 1949—1 a .m.

ReDepcirtels Nov 18, 10 A. M., and Nov. 23, 9 A. M., on Ward case, pls inform FonOff fol:

ConGen Ward reported to US ConGen at Peiping that at 9 A. M., Nov 26, Vice Consul William N. Stokes (who was in charge ConGen during imprisonment Ward) had been taken to court by Commie auths without warrant for hearing re "spying charges". It was not indicated to Ward whether Stokes taken as accused or witness or in

---

[79] For information on Communist "spy ring" charges, see telegram No. 1039, June 19, from the Consul General at Peiping, p. 965.
[80] Sent to the diplomatic representatives listed in footnote 75, p. 1018.

other capacity. Ward was refused permission accompany Stokes. At time latest communication from Ward at 3:45 same day no further word had been received from Stokes.

In conveying above info to FonOff state Dept considers this new violation principles of accepted internatl conduct sufficiently serious to justify inclusion in protest to Commie auths or, if protest already made, subj further representations by Govt to which you accredited.

WEBB

---

123 [Stokes, William N.] : Telegram

The Acting Secretary of State to the Consul General at Peiping (Clubb)

WASHINGTON, November 26, 1949—3 p. m.

836. Urtels 2096 and 2103 Nov. 26.[81] You shld immed ask for appointment with Chou En-lai or other high official dealing with fon affairs to make oral representations on basis info recd from Ward. At same time and without waiting for appointment you shld address letter Chou En-lai stating that you are instructed by ur Govt protest in strong terms this further action by local auths Mukden against US ConGen staff Mukden, request authoritative info for transmission US Govt and say that US Govt requests and expects highest Commie auths accordance internatl law and practice take prompt steps to cause Mukden auths release Stokes and furnish transport facilities for withdrawal from Mukden of all personnel US ConGen, with their personal and official effects, and afford them full freedom of movement in carrying out their official instrs this regard.

Inform Dept text ltr sent to Commie auths.

WEBB

---

123 Stokes, William N. : Telegram

The Consul General at Peiping (Clubb) to the Secretary of State

PEIPING, November 26, 1949—4 p. m.
[Received November 26—6:24 a. m.]

2103. Severally at 1430 and 1545 Ward reported still no word from Stokes, reContel 2096, November 26, no further developments during day. Said it is "theatrical season" Mukden, opined Commies might now try find "reason" expel others.

Suggest logical possibility, however, that Commies may be only checking Stokes re his phone statement that Ward case could only

---

[81] Latter printed *infra.*

be understood by reference June 21 news. This especially since Stokes' position so clearly above suspicion.

Next possible phone talk tomorrow 0800 hours.

Ward's message re trial missing.

CLUBB

---

123 Stokes, William N. : Telegram

The Consul General at Peiping (Clubb) to the Secretary of State

PEIPING, November 27, 1949—11 a. m.
[Received November 26—11:26 p. m.]

2104. Ward reported today, re Contel 2096, November 26, Stokes returned to quarters 1500 yesterday after having attended, as observer, trial "American spy ring" of last June. Some thousand persons present. None of Consulate General staff named but either Ward or I referred to by title. No evidence cited of later date than October 28 last year. Persons named all unknown Ward except Berendson and Welch. In particular, never heard of Hunt.

Without having been named, however, all non-Chinese staff Consulate General were sentenced deportation.

Assume story will break tomorrow.

Sent Department, Nanking 1181, Shanghai 1225, Tientsin 103, Am PolAd [82] Tokyo, (Department pass all addressees).

CLUBB

---

123 Stokes, William N. : Telegram

The Consul General at Peiping (Clubb) to the Secretary of State

PEIPING, November 27, 1949—3 p. m.
[Received November 27—5:57 a. m.]

2106. In better connection 1430 Ward reported yesterday's trial, which must have been final hearing because sentences were passed although trial unheard-of before, was of 10 persons of whom 9 in court, 1 dead. Accused were Chinese and Japanese or Koreans, all unknown Americans but presumed persons connected with June charges. Sentences presumed passed on them unknown by Stokes whose translator only gave him part affecting consular personnel.

No date given Stokes for deportation action, either re Ward *et al.* or re personnel affected new action.

Ward remarked trial ending 21st "brings into critical focus" events past year and yesterday's trial makes all clear.

Court judgment Ward trial published locally today, in process translation, will be forwarded soonest.

---

[82] American Acting Political Adviser (Sebald).

Re Deptel 836, November 26, in view information obtained today am holding up action. Recommend also waiting on receipt fuller reports yesterday's trial before either embarking on new move or giving further interpretive comment to press. Present significance of move appears to be, as indicated by Ward, Communists' search for "reason" to justify "expulsion" consular personnel.

Sent Department, Nanking 1183, Shanghai 1227, AmPolAd Tokyo (Department pass all addressees).

CLUBB

---

123 Ward, Angus I.: Telegram

The Consul General at Peiping (Clubb) to the Secretary of State

PEIPING, November 28, 1949—2 p. m.
[Received November 29—12:39 a. m.]

2111. Saw Chang Tung-sun November 23 at which time he said he had sent projected letter Chou En-lai "several days ago" (mytel 2053, November 22 [83]). Chang said he did not give message as coming either from himself or Ambassador but instead purported it represented my attitude.

Chang did not give me text his letter.

Informed Chang of current Mukden denouncement and expressed appreciation rendered by him re matter.

CLUBB

---

123 Ward, Angus I.: Telegram

The Consul General at Peiping (Clubb) to the Secretary of State

PEIPING, November 28, 1949.
[Received November 28—9:29 a. m.]

2113. *Kwang Ming Jih Pao* November 27 carried news item from New China News Agency, Mukden despatch November 26, entitled "American Nationals in Shenyang Given Sentences for Beating Chinese Workman". *Substantial translation follows:*

Verdict in trial of lawsuit involving imperialist elements headed by American national Ward who collectively beat Chi Yu-heng, Chinese laborer, and unreasonably made deductions from his wages, a case which has aroused common indignation of people of Shenyang municipality and all northeast provinces, was announced by People's Court in Shenyang municipality on November 21. Principal criminal Ward was given sentence of 6 months and his accomplices R. C. Rehberg (American) and A. Kristan (German) each a sentence of 4 months, while F. Cicogna (Italian) and S. Tatsumi (Jap-American)

---

[83] Not printed.

each a sentence of 3 months. Sentences of 5 criminals are to be suspended for period of 1 year. Five criminals are to be deported from territory. Ward was ordered to pay Chi Yu-heng US $105 as three and half months' terminal leave pay, US $60 as 2 months severance pay, and US $9 as wages for 9 days. Retirement deductions are to be refunded in their entirety. Above sums of money are to be paid in local currency calculated at market rate. In addition, $1,365,000 local currency for medical expenses and $2,500,000 local currency as compensation for losses of earnings must be paid Chi Yu-heng.

It may be recalled that murderous criminal Ward and company unreasonably and forcibly dismissed Chinese workman Chi Yu-heng on September 29 and collectively assaulted him twice on October 11 when he came to them demanding payment of various wages and allowances due him, and attacked Chi Yu-feng, his brother, who attempted to intervene in dispute. Shenyang Muni Bureau of Public Security, acting on appeal of 35 Chinese employees and workers at No. 38 San Ching Lu, summoned murderous criminal Ward and company for interrogation and detained them. After undergoing series of interrogations, case was given to Shenyang municipal People's Court for trial.

Criminals were interrogated by court total of five times. Victims Chi Yu-heng and Chi Yu-feng also were summoned for questioning. Witnesses Tsou Yuan-chi, Yu Yung-pin, Chi Ti-chih, Keng Chen-tung, Wu Han-chang, Li Chun-fang and Chang Chung-ying were interrogated several times and on two occasions they were summoned to court to confront criminals. Besides utilizing two photographs taken at spot where Ward and his accomplices committed their atrocity, which showed the wounded Chi Yu-heng sprawling on ground and wound on his right temple, medical report concerning wound by court doctor and medical reports by doctors of the municipal hospital as evidence, the chief judge of court also personally visited the locality in question at time of trial in order to make an investigation. Basing its action on bill of indictment of municipal Bureau of Public Security and evidence obtained by court from interrogation and investigations, which were studied carefully, court opened trial at noon, November 21. The verdict was announced at 6 p. m. and trial ended at 7:00 on same day. At conclusion of the trial, Ward and company immediately returned to No. 38 San Ching Lu.

At both final open trial in court and at time of announcement of verdict, over 30 delegates representing Chinese employees and workers at 38 San Ching Lu, Northeast General Trade Union, Shenyang municipal Trade Union and other organizations, as well as William Stokes, American national of No. 38 San Ching Lu, were present as auditors.

Court was opened by Procurator General of Bureau of Public Security [garbled group] Shenyang Municipal People's Government's reading bill of indictment. Then Chang Yun-lung, President [garbled group] currently Chief Judge of the municipal People's Court, and Judges Chang Shih-hsia and Cheng Yuan-yu, proceeded with trial. Victim Chi Yu-heng and witness Yu Yung-pin appeared before court to correct versions of the incident as presented by criminal Ward and accomplices. Evidence in form of individuals and documents were present and case was concluded. The criminals signed their names to their confessions and admitted they had not been maltreated during their detention and that attitude of authorities toward them had been good.

After chief judge had solemnly announced the verdict, criminal Ward and company were silent. With exception of American national Stokes, those who attended the trial as auditors showed joy in their faces and evidently felt very happy. This proves once again that Chinese people are not to be insulted and that laws and codes of Chinese People's Government are dignified. Those who dare to encroach on our people's rights and violate laws and codes of our People's Government shall be given legal punishment that is due them. *End translation.*

Tientsin and Mukden by mail.

Sent Department 2113, repeated Nanking 1186, Shanghai 1231.

CLUBB

---

123 Ward, Angus I.: Telegram

The Consul General at Peiping (Clubb) to the Secretary of State

PEIPING, November 28, 1949.
[Received November 28—2:29 p. m.]

2114. Following is Ward's 136, November 23, as received by phone (therefore probably subject minor corrections) today:

"People's Court Mukden convened new session (?) yesterday for trial Rehberg, Tatsumi, Cicogna, Kristan and Ward. Stokes permitted attend trial as observer, but was refused permission to speak to or in behalf of accused or to make written notes of proceedings. Neither we nor Stokes had any advance notice of date or hour of trial. We were served no copy of writ indictment either before or at trial; writ was read to us in Chinese, which none of us understood, and English translation so unintelligible as to be understood in part only.

Following my request for rereading of English translation, presiding judge assured me English translation would be reread prior to end of trial, but such rereading did not materialize in view of which we have only sketchy knowledge of charges under which indicted. Have today addressed written request to court for copy of writ. Court refused my three requests October 24, November 1 and 2 for permission retain legal counsel, and also refused my request of November 1 and 2 for permission seek and subpoena witnesses for defense, and likewise refused my request November for recognition of Stokes and Hubbard as my [garbled group] court for purpose liaison with court, for seeking and engaging legal counsel and seeking and interviewing witnesses for defense.

Although I was informed by court I could conduct my own defense, [none] of accused was permitted examine any prosecution witness or to produce testimony refuting statements made by such witnesses. Prosecution was permitted present summation but accused not permitted. After adjournment 16 o'clock court reconvened 1800 o'clock and read findings and pronounced judgment. Oral translation and findings and sentence were not clear or fully understood by Stokes or any of us, in view which I requested written copy of findings and sentences of court.

According our best understanding: Ward sentenced 6 months' imprisonment and probation 1 year with sentence commuted to deportation, and to pay to former messenger Chi 9 days' salary for period September 19–28, leave pay, severance pay, refund of retirement deductions collected this office since entry duty March 27, 1946, sum 1.3 million northeast wan [*yuan?*] equivalent today approximately US $7.00 for hospitalization expenses and 2.5 million NE yuan equivalent approximately US $14.00 for loss of time during hospitalization and convalescence. Rehberg and Kristan sentenced 4 months' imprisonment, probation 1 year, sentences commuted to deportation. Tatsumi and Cicogna sentenced 3 months' imprisonment, probation 1 year commuted to deportation. We were returned to our rooms about 19 o'clock and at 1930 were instructed prepare return our respective residences. All arrived home approximately 21 hours.

Were today permitted proceed under guard from residences to office [garbled group] all were kept in solitary confinement from arrest October 24 to release last evening. Quarters unheated for first fortnight and thereafter practically but for most part underheated until afternoon November 17 after which time quarters adequately heated. Prison diet 6 slices bread from 4 by 5 inch loaf daily and hot drinking water 3 ounces daily. All lost weight during 4 weeks' confinement ranging from Tatsumi 10 lb., to Ward 25 lbs. Rehberg and Kristan in better physical condition than others, but Kristan has acute pains in feet induced by cold. Cicogna in poor physical condition because of cold and diet but better than when I previously saw him November 4 at which time he was barely able to stand. Tatsumi suffering from shock and mental strain and incapable rational thought or reasonable speech, but has already given evidence progressive improvement since release. I experienced acute heart pains during period intense cold and still have sharp pains in right arm, both legs and feet and back induced by cold and prolonged exposure and to stupefying cold, but believe have sustained no disability that warmth and normal living conditions will not overcome. Contemplate paying off entire Chinese staff upon receipt requested allotment and Dept authorization refund retirement deductions after which shall again request land transportation to Tientsin–Peiping of mayor of Mukden for American staff and dependents, Cicogna and wife, Kristan and chauffeurs Deidra and Muhammedzan, in hope that mayor will honor understanding made by him on June 21 to furnish us transportation upon my request. Detailed report our arrest, imprisonment, treatment, examination and trial will be submitted when communications facilities permit. Staff and I very appreciative of efforts Dept and others in our behalf. Please pass Dept as 136, November 23."

Mukden today reported further Tatsumi, Rehberg, Kristan, Cicogna and Ward today received documents from court alleged to be copies findings of sentences of trial end September [*November?*] 21 but concerned American unable to read those documents.

Deptel 831, November 25,[84] received Peiping November 26, was transmitted same date. Propose phone contents Mukden tomorrow if telegram still unreceived. Mukden telegram 136, November 23, still unreceived through telegraph office.

Sent Department 2114, Shanghai 1232, Nanking 1187.

CLUBB

125.633/11–2849 : Telegram

The Acting Secretary of State to the Consul General at Peiping (Clubb)

WASHINGTON, November 28, 1949—7 p. m.

842. Re urtel 2104 Nov 27.   In view strong possibility that occasion of departure Mukden ConGen staff will be exploited to full by Commies for propaganda purposes, staging of which may delay departure, you shld at once send letter to Chou En-lai asking that facilities be made available immed for travel in expeditious manner of Cons staff and dependents from Mukden along lines set forth Deptel 836 Nov 26.   At same time request as under instr from ur Govt definite info re date and itinerary in China in connection with departure.

FYI [85] Dept desires learn as far as possible in advance name of port and date arrival party there in order to secure if possible diversion of ship to embark them.

WEBB

---

123 Ward, Angus I. : Telegram

The Ambassador in the United Kingdom (Douglas) to the Secretary of State

LONDON, November 28, 1949—8 p. m.
[Received November 29—12:57 p. m.]

4745. Substance Deptcirc November 23 and 26 re Ward case given Scarlett, Foreign Office, this afternoon.   Scarlett states British Pro-Consul, Mukden, had been about to make representations Communists basis Deptcirc November 18 when on learning of release of Ward had wired for further instructions.   Foreign Office will now direct Pro-Consul make comprehensive representations based in general on information contained three Deptcircs mentioned herein.   Scarlett agreed press reports release Stokes did not alter seriousness case.

DOUGLAS

---

[84] Not printed.
[85] For your information.

123 Stokes, William N. : Telegram

The Consul General at Peiping (Clubb) to the Secretary of State

PEIPING, December 1, 1949.
[Received December 1—3:04 p. m.]

2143. Ward's 148, November 26, received today, follows:

"Stokes was summoned to unspecified court this morning 9 o'clock to attend hearings on spy ring charges. Am uninformed whether Stokes was summoned in capacity of observer, witness, or accused. Translator Chow Yuan-szi who has participated in Chinese staff concerted stoppage of work since close business October 11 was summoned with Stokes. In absence information to contrary, I assume spy ring charges under reference are those given publicity through Hsin Hwa News Agency on or about June 18 this year and published in Mukden press on June 20. My oral request attend court hearings with Stokes was refused."

CLUBB

---

123 Ward, Angus I. : Telegram

The Consul General at Peiping (Clubb) to the Secretary of State

PEIPING, December 1, 1949.
[Received December 1—2:10 p. m.]

2152. Mukden office per phone today remarked VOA broadcast today stating American vessel arriving Tientsin December 11 for removal Ward and staff and dependents. Mukden staff welcomed news but Ward recommended that, if Department contemplates he and staff proceed USA by air from Korea or Japan, in view hardship past year and particularly past month all staff members and dependents be given opportunity for physical check-up and urgently needed dental attention before proceeding beyond Korea or Japan. Ward's request November 22 for access to physician still unfulfilled. Ward still suffering effects treatment, particularly long exposure to cold confinement. Desires make more progress toward recovery and health before resuming active life, therefore suggests he be spared fast trans-Pacific flight at present. Remarks trans-Pacific ocean voyage would probably be beneficial.

Ward informed mayor several days ago he contemplates paying off all Chinese personnel December 3. He today wrote mayor requesting he be informed December 3 of date when he and staff members and dependents under deportation order will be furnished transportation facilities for departure. He requested 3 days' advance notice of departure to enable himself and staff pay off houses, old servants and handle other personal matters.

Sent Department 2152, Shanghai 1248, Nanking 1198, AmPolAd Tokyo, Tientsin by mail.

CLUBB

123 Ward, Angus I. : Telegram

The Consul General at Peiping (Clubb) to the Secretary of State

PEIPING, December 1, 1949.
[Received December 1—3 :33 p. m.]

2154. Ward's 147, November 25 received today as follows:

"Since entry of Chinese Communist armed forces into Mukden on November 1, a year ago, I have signed all official communications to local civil and military authorities over my title American Consul General. Today, however, two letters thus signed to mayor [of] Mukden and dated November 22 and two to same addresses dated November 23 were returned with oral statement that letters thus signed not acceptable. I have again submitted same letters omitting above-mentioned title."

CLUBB

125.633/12–149 : Telegram

The Ambassador in the United Kingdom (Douglas) to the Secretary of State

LONDON, December 1, 1949—6 p. m.
[Received December 1—4 :31 p. m.]

4794. Reference announcement by State Department press officers on November 30 [86] to effect that UK was included among those countries which had protested, or would protest to Chinese Communists re Ward case. Foreign Office news department official telephoned Embassy this morning stating Foreign Office had not actually promised to protest and would forward immediately to Embassy a note giving its position. In afternoon, the news department of Foreign Office telephoned again saying that in answer to questions arising out of Department's press statement, Foreign Office news department was replying that they had instructed British Consul General at Peking to do everything possible to persuade local authorities to accord proper treatment to staff of US Consulate General at Mukden. They were also saying to the press that a note stating the British Government's position had been sent. Text of this note which has just arrived reads as follows:

"Dear Ringwalt: [87] You were good enough to inform me in your letter of 28 November that the United States Government still feel

---

[86] Michael J. McDermott, Special Assistant to the Secretary of State for press relations, commented on a note sent by the Secretary recently to 30 countries having diplomatic representation in China (see circular telegram of November 18, 10 a. m., p. 1009), and named the following 12 countries that had protested or would do so: Australia, Austria, Belgium, Egypt, France, India, Italy, the Netherlands, Norway, Sweden, the United Kingdom, and the Republic of the Philippines.

[87] Arthur R. Ringwalt, First Secretary of Embassy in the United Kingdom.

that despite the release of Mr. Angus Ward some protest should be addressed to the Communist authorities by the powers represented at Peking at the flagrant violation of the accepted standards of international conduct which the circumstances of his arrest and trial represent. The State Department further cited the subsequent arrest of Mr. Stokes as a fresh instance of the Communists' contempt for the principles of the international conduct, though I gather from the press that Mr. Stokes has subsequently been released.

"Most careful and sympathetic consideration has not [now] been given to this request, but we are very doubtful whether, in present circumstances, representations by us on the lines suggested would achieve any purpose. Respect for the accepted standards of international conduct is a matter to which His Majesty's Government naturally attach considerable importance; but, as the State Department are aware, foreign representatives are left, pending recognition, without any official status, and such contacts as they have with the Chinese authorities are at a low level in the hierarchy and on a personal basis. In these circumstances, little purpose is likely to be served by adopting the procedure which would normally be followed if diplomatic relations existed between the Chinese Communist Government and His Majesty's Government in the United Kingdom.

"It will be clear from the Foreign Secretary's letter to Mr. Douglas of November 25 [88] that His Majesty's Consular Officers in Communistic China have done all they could unofficially to help Mr. Ward and his staff and will most surely continue to do so if need arise. We are, nevertheless, instructing H. M. Consul-General in Peking to do anything that may lie within his power to persuade the local authorities to accord proper treatment to the staff of the United States Consulate-General at Mukden. Yours sincerely, P. W. Scarlett."

DOUGLAS

125.633/12–149 : Telegram

The Ambassador in the United Kingdom (Douglas) to the Secretary of State

LONDON, December 1, 1949—6 p. m.
[Received December 1—4:31 p. m.]

4795. Reference immediately preceding telegram re Ward case as well as Embassy's 4745, November 28, same subject. Embassy unable to understand Foreign Office attitude as Scarlett unequivocally stated his Government understood US position and would take action along lines indicated.

It would appear that after reflection concerned Foreign Office officials decided not to jeopardize British position in China through taking too strong a stand in this instance.

Embassy would appreciate guidance in replying to any press inquiries re this case.

DOUGLAS

---

[88] Not printed.

123 [Ward, Angus I.] : Telegram

The Secretary of State to the Consul General at Peiping (Clubb)

WASHINGTON, December 1, 1949—6 p. m.

853. Dept concerned over physical condition Ward others reported urtels 2114 Nov 28 and 2124 Nov 29[89] and will appreciate ur and Ward's estimate and further recommendations all aspects this situation.

Specifically pls ascertain whether medical facilities in Mukden available to ConGen staff. If not, suggest you immed endeavor enlist aid Brit Pro-Cons Mukden. If it appears medical attn will later be needed at Tientsin, Taku Bar or other point of staff's travel, endeavor make arrangements therefor.

Keep Dept fully informed and take whatever action necessary locally without prior reference Dept.

ACHESON

---

123 Ward, Angus I. : Telegram

The Consul General at Peiping (Clubb) to the Secretary of State

PEIPING, December 1, 1949—6 p. m.
[Received 11 :31 p. m.]

2156. Ward's 154, November 29, as received by phone today, follows:

"On October 11, was assaulted and pummelled by Chinese member my staff. Due only to quick action by Rehberg, I was saved from being further assaulted by another Chinese armed with cudgel. Cicogna assaulted by group Chinese members my staff and Kristan was assaulted and befouled and badly beaten by Chinese staff member and other Chinese. Having reported all the foregoing to group Chinese officials principally from Bureau Public Safety and from People's Court of Mukden which came to office during morning October 11 but group dismissed my representations in matter with statement to effect that these events would be treated in accordance with law. Thus far no action known to me has been taken on above recited attempt assault.

On November 22 following my release from confinement, I requested of mayor Mukden access to my physician. Thus far, no action on my request."

Recommend particularly in view Mukden American personnel's exposed position this information not be given publicity until their departure from Communist China.

Sent Department 2156. Department pass Shanghai 1253, Nanking 1202 [*1212?*], Tientsin 107.

CLUBB

---

[89] Latter not printed.

123 Ward, Angus I. : Telegram

The Consul General at Peiping (Clubb) to the Secretary of State

PEIPING, December 2, 1949.
[Received December 2—4 :54 a. m.]

2167. Mukden reported by phone 1545 today they had just been visited by representatives Mukden Municipal Government carrying message to effect that Ward, together with all foreign members consular staff, together with dependents living in Government-owned property Mukden, must depart Mukden within 48 hours after 0800 December 5, deportation via Tientsin. Personal effects to be handled by Bryners. Consulate General has been given permission for one person contact Bryners tomorrow regarding transport.

Sent Department 2163; repeated Shanghai 1254, Nanking 1204, Tokyo, Tientsin by phone and mail.

CLUBB

125.633/12–249 : Circular telegram

The Secretary of State to Certain Diplomatic Representatives [90]

WASHINGTON, December 2, 1949—11 a. m.

Chi Commie auths Mukden have ordered all non-Chinese members Mukden ConGen staff depart Mukden within 48 hrs after 0800 Dec 5, deportation via Tientsin. Commie auths presumably providing rail facilities to Tientsin while Dept and ConGen Tientsin arranging onward sea transportation for return to US.

In passing above info to FonOff of Govt to which you accredited, pls express Dept's appreciation for sympathetic response to Secty's appeal. Dept believes concerted and expeditious action on part these Govts may well have been responsible for effecting early release Mukden personnel.

ACHESON

125.633/12–249 : Telegram

The Secretary of State to the Consul General at Tientsin (Smyth)

WASHINGTON, December 2, 1949—7 p. m.

448. Re impending departure Mukden staff :

1. Pacific Far East Line whose Tientsin agent is Oriental Shipping Agency, 20 Harbin Road, First Area, Tientsin, has two ships calling Taku Bar as fol : *Joplin Victory* Dec 5–7 and *Lakeland Victory* Dec

---

[90] Sent to the diplomatic representatives at Athens, Brussels, Cairo, Canberra, Copenhagen, The Hague, Manila, New Delhi, Oslo, Paris, Rome, Stockholm, and Vienna.

9–11. This co extremely cooperative and has already wired Tientsin agent accommodate any or all Mukden staff aboard either or both ships. Each ship has regular accommodations for 12 passengers but will make room for more. Both ships will proceed from Taku to Yokohama or direct to US depending on wishes Ward and staff. Pls arrange with local agent accordingly. Ward and staff onward transportation from Japan by regular passenger liner or air of course authorized. Ward authorized by previous tels to evacuate 6 alien employees and dependents to Hong Kong, Tokyo, or other nearby posts.

2. Physical condition Ward and others may require medical treatment Tientsin. On other hand may find it more desirable obtain treatment and thorough medical check-up Tokyo or even US. This decision entirely Ward's. Pls advise Dept soonest so appropriate arrangements can be made beyond Tientsin.

3. Re publicity, Dept proposes have Ward speak freely to press after leaving Commie China, as was case with Dairen staff. This connection pls have Ward summarize and transmit Dept by conf tel brief summary highlights experience Mukden since Nov 18, 1948. Dept will then tel comments and instrs to first con office he will reach after departing Tientsin. He shld await these instrs before giving interviews to press.

In view frequent delay communications with Tientsin, ConGen given wide discretionary auth take whatever action necess in line foregoing. Pls keep Dept fully informed.

ACHESON

125.633/12–149 : Telegram

The Secretary of State to the Ambassador in the United Kingdom
(Douglas)

WASHINGTON, December 2, 1949—7 p. m.

4325. Urtels 4794 and 4795 Dec 1. Dept suggests that in reply to any press inquiries re this case you state that Dept's announcement of action by the Brit was based upon attitude of Brit Govt as understood by Emb at that time.

Although info reported in ur 4745 Nov 28 appears clearly to indicate that Brit were taking action responsive to Sec's msg, it is desired that apparent contradiction receive as little publicity as possible and particularly that contention or recrimination be avoided.

Pls express to FonOff Dept's view re publicity.

ACHESON

125.6333/12–349 : Telegram

The Consul General at Peiping (Clubb) to the Secretary of State

PEIPING, December 3, 1949.
[Received December 3—1:40 a. m.]

2170. ReContel 2143, December 1. Peiping *Jen Min Jih Pao* December 2 carried NCNA Mukden December 1 despatch giving full text verdict Mukden Municipal People's Court in criminal case alleged "American espionage agents["] substantial translation as follows, with surnames Japanese names preceding given names throughout:

Defendants: Sasaki, Hirotsune (alias Chang Chih-chung), Nus, Japanese nationality, male, age 34, native of Kagoshima, Japan. American spy. Now under detention. Hus. Hsiao Yao-ting, Chinese nationality, male, age 40, native of Fengyung, Hopei Province. American spy. Now under detention. Sakashita, Kiichi, Japanese nationality, male, age 37, native of Kagoshima, Japan. American spy. Now under detention. Yang Chao-ho (alias Yanai Tomoichi), Chinese nationality, male, age 34, native of Taichung, Taiwan. American spy. Now under detention. Yamamura, Yoshiaki, Japanese nationality, male, age 33, native of Tokyo, Japan. American spy. Now under detention. Takeuchi, Hajime, Japanese nationality, male, age 35, native of Tochigi [prefecture?], Japan. American spy. Now under detention. Tsao Cheng-te, Chinese nationality, male, age 34, native of Wangyehmiao, inner Mongolia. American spy. Died of disease. Po Yen-tsang, Chinese nationality, male, age 43, native of inner Mongolia, living in Lingsiang, Jehol. American spy. Now under detention. Wu Jen-chieh (alias Li Chia-teh), Chinese of Sino-British parents, Chinese nationality, male, age 41, native of Yingkou, Liaotung Province. American spy. Now under detention. Above-mentioned defendants worked as American spies, recruited secret service agents and spies, set up espionage nets in liberated areas, furnished secret and political intelligence, plotted clandestinely to instigate rebellion and uprising and undermined revolutionary enterprise of Chinese people. Criminal suit was detected and unearthed by Bureau Public Safety of Shenyang Municipal People's Government which has indicated [*indicted?*] accused for trial. Suit has been accepted by this court which now declares following verdict:

Sentences: (1) Accused Sasaki Hirotsune, who assumed responsibility of leading and setting up American espionage organizations in territory of China to collect our military and political intelligence and supply it to American espionage organization, with objective of undermining revolutionary enterprise of Chinese people, is to be given sentence of 6 years. Hsiao Yao-ting and Sakashita Kiichi, who worked as American spies and assisted Sasaki Hirotsune in building espionage organizations, furnished military and political intelligence and supplied it to American espionage organization, are each to be given sentence of 3 years. Hsiao Yao-ting is to be deprived of civil rights for period of 5 years. Yang Shao-ho and Yamamura Yoshiaki, who worked as American spies, furnished military and political intelligence and supplied it to American espionage organization, are each to be given sentence of 3 years. Yang Chao-ho is to be deprived of civil rights for period of 4 years. Takeuchi Hajime, who worked as American spy and furnished military and political intelligence, is to be given sentence of 2 years. [Garble] Legal procedures against us are to be suspended. Two sets of American made radios, 1 generator, 1 set American made secret codes, 5 gold ingots, as well as 3 copies of work projects, 4 letters of instructions, 13 copies of work projects, 4 letters of instructions, 13 copies of reports of activities of American espionage organization "T.S.", 28 copies of drafts of information reports, 40 maps and charts and 1 personal identification card which above-mentioned defendants used to commit crimes are to be confiscated.

(2) Accused Po Yen-tsang, who assumed responsibility of leading and setting up American espionage organization in territory of China to collect military and political intelligence and supply it to American espionage organization, with objective of undermining revolutionary enterprise of Chinese people and instigating our military and administrative staff to rebellion and revolt, is to be given sentence of 6 years and deprived of civil rights for 6 years. Two sets of American-made radios, 1 generator and 10 copies of secret codes, possessed by accused, are to be confiscated.

(3) Accused Wu Jen-chieh, who undermined revolutionary enterprise of Chinese people, set up espionage wireless station in his own home and transmitted intelligence for American espionage organization, to be given sentence of 5 years and of civil rights for period of 6 years. Two sets of American-made radios, 1 generator, 5 copies of secret codes and 10 gold ingots, with which accused committed his crimes, are to be confiscated.

(4) All foreign nationals of former "American Consulate General" in Shenyang are to be expelled from national territory of Chinese People's Republic.

[Here follow details of "Facts and reasons".]

It is observed defendants Sasaki Hirotsume, Po Yen-tsang, Wu Jen-chieh et al., regularly received instructions regarding espionage activities at former "American Consulate" in Shenyang and at former ESD branches in Shenyang and Changchun and supplied intelligence which related to state secrets of China. Various above-mentioned facts sufficiently prove that former "American Consulate" in Shenyang and former American [garbled group] branches in Shenyang and Changchun were all directing and concealing espionage organs of imperialism, especially former "American Consulate" as [at] Shenyang which was seat of American ALG (44th External Survey Detachment, American espionage organ) and in which leaders of spy ring (such as Nishida, Walsh, Hunt, et al.) had living accommodations and by which their espionage activities were covered. It (American Consulate) has really become center endangering national welfare of People's Republic of China, plotting against revolutionary enterprise of Chinese people and engaging in criminal activities, which people of People's Republic of China cannot permit nor endure. In order to protect welfare of state and people of People's Republic of China, entire group of foreign personnel of former "American Consulate" at Shenyang should be deported from China. To sum up, with exception of Tsao Cheng-te, defendant, who died of illness which on [garbled group] course of prosecution of law suit and whose trial should be discontinued, and of former "American ESD branches" in

Shenyang and Changchun which have already left borders of People's Republic of China and which discussions are temporarily suspended, judgment as contained in this verdict is re leadership [garbled group]. Criminal Court.

Chief Judge: Hsu Lieu.

Associated Judges: Sun Chien, Chiao Chuang.

First copy of above judgment is certified to be true copy. End of translation. Mailed to Tientsin.

Sent Department 2170, repeated Shanghai 1258, Nanking 1206.

CLUBB

125.6333/12–349 : Telegram

The Consul General at Peiping (Clubb) to the Secretary of State

PEIPING, December 3, 1949.
[Received December 3—4:52 a. m.]

2179. ReContel 2170, December 2. Peiping *Jen Min Jih Pao* December 2 carried NCNA Mukden December 1 despatch re indictment filed by Shenyang Municipal People's Bureau of Public Safety in Shenyang People's Court re NE espionage case. Concluding portion of indictment contains detailed list of alleged evidence of American implication in espionage plot. Transcript of extract as follows:

(1) Two 15-watt AC–DC receiving and sending radio sets (American-made small model RDR type sets). One generator, 1 set secret codes, 5 gold nuggets (usually 1 ounce each) for espionage funds received from Nishida by Sasaki.

(2) Two 15-watt AC–DC receiving and sending radio sets (American-made small model RDR type sets), 1 electric generator, 5 copies secret codes, 10 gold nuggets and 1 case American cigarettes received from Hunt by Wu Jen-chieh.

(3) Two 15-watt AC–DC receiving and sending sets (American-made small model RDR type sets), 1 electric generator, 10 copies secret codes received from McAdam by Po Yen-tsang.

(4) 1 copy Undercover Activities for June and 1 copy Undercover Activities for October drafted by Sasaki by order of Nishida.

(5) 1 copy Undercover Activities in Various Eastern Mongolian Areas by Tsao Cheng-te.

(6) 1 copy Letter of Instructions Regarding Undercover Activities written in September 1948 by Nishida to Sasaki.

(7) 1 copy Letter of Instructions Regarding Investigation of Transportation Facilities of North Manchuria Railway written in September 1948 by Sasaki to Nishida.

(8) 2 Letters Asking for Information from Nishida to Sasaki dated July 22, 1948.

(9) 13 copies Biographical Material re Personnel American Espionage Organization directed by Sasaki as well as reports of and decisions taken following meetings re methods of activities.

(10) 1 Japanese resident certificate (No. L117) issued to Sasaki by Political Affairs Commission of NE Bandit Suppression Headquarters

of Kmt, Nishida having been retained for service by former "American Consulate" at Shenyang.

(11) 40 military maps and army geographic surveys, as well as 28 copies original manuscripts containing various kinds of intelligence. (End of translation.)

Peiping *Jen Min Jih Pao* December 2 front-pages brief Mukden December 2 despatch reporting unanimous support by people all parts NE of decision Mukden Municipal People's Court in trial on American "imperialist element" Ward.

Sent Department 2179, repeated Nanking 211, Shanghai 1261, mailed Tientsin.

CLUBB

---

123 Ward, Angus I. : Telegram

The Consul General at Peiping (Clubb) to the Secretary of State

PEIPING, December 5, 1949.
[Received December 5—3 :22 a. m.]

2187. Ward reports by phone Chinese staff completely paid off December 3, and most have now left ConGen property. Still uninformed when schedule leave Mukden. Party will consist of 27 adults and 1 infant. Ward has information informally that 4 Koreans and 1 German (who was in USIS [91] library at time isolation compounds November last year) also held in compound past year will be included in party. He wishes it understood he has nothing to do with those 5 persons.

British Proconsul [at] Mukden in touch with Ward through Mayor's office but desired personal interview and visit still unobtained.

Consulate has been permitted contact commercial ship re movement personal and Government property, but shipper apparently reluctant undertake task. Bad weather connections [*conditions?*] past 3 days, poor phone connections.

Sent Department; repeated PolAd Tokyo, mailed Tientsin.

CLUBB

---

123 Ward, Angus I. : Telegram

The Consul General at Peiping (Clubb) to the Secretary of State

PEIPING, December 5, 1949.
[Received December 5—7 :05 a. m.]

2201. Mukden reports this afternoon date departure still uncertain but believed will be evening December 6 or morning December 7.

---

[91] United States Information Service.

Party will include 16 Americans, 11 non-Chinese aliens. Comprises 15 men, 9 women, 3 children (including 1 infant), 4 cats, 3 dogs.

Will carry hand luggage plus checked baggage, total 64 pieces or two and one-quarter tons, and will send 121 pieces personal effects total 11 tons by fast freight to Tientsin.

Americans are Angus Ward, and Mrs. Ward, William N. Stokes, Fred E. Hubbard, Ralph Rehberg, Jack Feigal, Mary E. Braden, Elden Berikson, Walter S. Norman, Hugh C. Picard, Shiro Tatsumi and Tatsumi's wife, minor son and daughter. Tatsumi and Ward's Polish maid Mrs. Janita Nowicka will proceed to States. Tatsumi's married daughter Mrs. Chen and infant child, both Americans, proceeding to Japan. Franco Cicogna, Mrs. Nanya Cicogna (both Italians); Alfred Kristan (German); Bladimi Petukhov, Mrtelpolga Ietuchov (mother), Mrs. Elizabeth Bootinsky and Illyshin Bootinsky (father), Sioagatoola Muhamedzan and Mrs. Muhamedzan (all Soviet subjects); and Karel Dedera (Czech); proceeding Japan, Hong Kong or other point Far East in accordance Dept instructions.

Sent Dept; AmPolAd Tokyo, Shanghai 1268, Nanking 1216, Taipei 47. Tientsin by phone and mail.

CLUBB

---

123 Ward, Angus I.: Telegram

The Second Secretary of Embassy in China (Bacon) to the Secretary of State

NANKING, December 5, 1949—3 p. m.
[Received December 5—12:54 p. m.]

2538. Re Peiping telegram 1212, December 2, sent Department 2156 [December 1]. Embassy agrees story should not be broken until Mukden personnel safely outside China. Facts case so shocking demand fullest treatment by way warning American citizens. Embassy recommends Department not only release story to press and foreign governments, but also prepare full blow-by-blow story based complete interrogation all Mukden personnel [in] Japan and including Communist official version and "judgment". Emphasis should be Ward and codefendants never fully informed charges until trial finished, never allowed full freedom present own cause or question any witnesses, not allowed introduce witnesses or retain counsel. Such judicial spectacle not only betrays truth behind Communists' show-trials all over world (since were dealing with persons they did not hope force into false confessions, they simply prevented them from preparing and presenting case), but also indicates China has retrogressed into legal barbarity which originally necessitated extra-territoriality. Lack most elementary safeguards persons in toils of police particularly hazardous, view Communist disregard any facts but those they create and in view anti-foreign sentiment they industriously produce and nourish.

Embassy believes complete story should be circulated soonest by China posts to all Americans, to all representatives other nations here, to press all complexions and to all responsible Communist representatives.

Department pass Peiping, Shanghai, Tientsin in discretion.

BACON

---

123 [Ward, Angus I.] : Telegram

The Secretary of State to the Consul General at Tientsin (Smyth)

WASHINGTON, December 5, 1949—6 p. m.

451. Re departure plans Mukden staff, Department has made no commitments re travel any specific vessel or line. In addition to physician, however, *Lakeland Victory* may carry pool of 3 correspondents if Master so desires. Irrespective these arrangements, Dept strongly recommends Ward and his staff depart on first available US vessel and that party not be broken up on separate vessels. Dept realizes limited accommodations may mean certain discomforts for staff members while en route Yokohama but of opinion overriding consideration is that staff depart China at earliest moment possible and, if at all feasible, in single group. US ships due Taku Bar this week include *Joplin Victory, Pacific Transport, Lakeland Victory* and *China Mail*.

In event time factor such that Dept cannot review summary Ward's Mukden experiences (as first recommended Deptel 448, Dec 2) before Ward meets correspondents, pls give him fol instrs:

As ConGen in charge of Mukden staff, Ward shld act as official spokesman with correspondents. Dept desires give Ward wide discretion re material covered in conferences with press, but recommends he stick to facts and experiences omitting speculative, interpretive and analytical comment. Other members Mukden staff will undoubtedly be queried by correspondents, but while they shld refer all questions of official nature to Ward as spokesman, Dept no objection their discussing matters of personal nature of interest to papers in their home localities.

ACHESON

123 Ward, Angus I. : Telegram

The Secretary of State to the Acting Political Adviser in Japan
(Sebald)

WASHINGTON, December 5, 1949—6 p. m.

630. Dept understands correspondents seek board *Lakeland Victory* Kobe to Tientsin where ship may pick up Ward and party from Mukden. SS Co advised Dept correspondents' efforts. Dept interposed no objections provided accommodations for round trip addition to Ward party but suggested feasible solution might be pool arrangement with one person representing all press radio another all still photographers and third newsreels.

Urgently instruct Kobe brief any correspondents making trip along following lines:

1. Dept unable promise Ward depart via *Lakeland Victory*. Three ships due Tientsin about same time. Commies may make decision for Ward.
2. Must realize calling Commie port and Commies extremely sensitive security. Urge utmost discretion all.
3. Warn photographers strong possibility Commie objections taking pictures and danger arrest seizure films equipment by Commies.
4. Main US interest is get Ward and party safely out and hope none will endanger his departure by trying take pictures or interview him during actual boarding which might result prevention Ward party departure and arrest correspondents.
5. Dept recommends all wait until ship safely at sea.

ACHESON

---

123 Ward, Angus I. : Telegram

The Consul General at Peiping (Clubb) to the Secretary of State

PEIPING, December 6, 1949.
[Received December 5—10:03 p. m.]

2208. Mukden informed by phone today Ward party scheduled leave Mukden 0345 hours December 7.

Sent Department 2208, repeated AmPolAd Tokyo, Shanghai 1271, Nanking 1218, Taipei 48, Tientsin by phone and mail.

CLUBB

125.6331/12–649 : Telegram

The Consul General at Peiping (Clubb) to the Secretary of State

PEIPING, December 6, 1949.
[Received December 6—8:29 a. m.]

2210. Ward states was asked yesterday (December 5) by local authorities for recent deeds or leases (uncertain which) for two pieces

Government real estate Mukden. When Ward stated believed title deeds in Washington, was informed US Government ownership would not be recognized.

Ward has had no further contact with Steventon, British pro-Consul Mukden, re takeover property.

Bryners now removing personal property and moveable Government property.

Tientsin by mail.

CLUBB

125.633/12–649 : Telegram

The Consul General at Peiping (Clubb) to the Secretary of State

PEIPING, December 6, 1949.
[Received December 6—11 :36 p. m.]

2220. *Kuang Ming Jih Pao* today carries brief NCNA Peking December item headed "To protect Fruits Chinese People Revolution and to Suppress Espionage Activities of Imperialism, Whole Body Alien Personnel Former American Consulate Shenyang being Expelled["]. Order fixes time limit for departure Shenyang within 48 hours to exit boundaries China via Tientsin, as follows:

"Public Security organ of Shenyang Municipal People's Government in implementation of judgment directed by Municipal People's Court regarding espionage case of former American Consulate stationed Shenyang has already informed whole body alien personnel former American Consulate stationed Shenyang fixing time limit by order that they should remove from Shenyang within 48 hours from 8 a. m. of the 5th of the current month and exit from the boundaries of China via Tientsin."

Item makes no reference Soviet and Czech citizens now stated not being reported [*deported?*] with other personnel.

Peiping unable get connection with either Ward or British Consul Steventon, Mukden call time 0800–1000 today.

Tientsin by phone and mail.

Sent Department 2220, Shanghai 1280, AmPolAd Tokyo, Nanking 1222, Taipei 51.

CLUBB

---

123 Ward, Angus I. : Telegram

The Consul General at Peiping (Clubb) to the Secretary of State

PEIPING, December 8, 1949.
[Received December 7—10 :58 p. m.]

2233. Following from British Consul Steventon, Mukden, received last night through British Consul [at] Peking:

"01407 No. 1 for Clubb. Made contact yesterday afternoon full party left last night with 2 days food supply my opinion for Tangku. Will do all possible prevent damage loss to property. Many difficulties. Impossible check inventories properly. Acknowledge. Steventon."

Kuang Ming Jih Pao today carries NCNA Mukden item dated December 7 headlined "Ward *et al.* Depart Shenyang in Accordance With Time Limit Order Our Public Safety Organ" as follows: "Under notification of Shenyang Municipal People's Government Public Safety organization's time limit order, 20 persons Ward *et al.* of former American Consulate stationed Shenyang departed Shenyang today at 3:40 a. m. and will exit China boundaries via Tientsin." Tientsin by mail phone.

Sent Department 2233, AmPolAd Tokyo, Shanghai 1288.

CLUBB

702.4193/12–849 : Telegram

The Second Secretary of Embassy in China (Bacon) to the Secretary of State

NANKING, December 8, 1949.
[Received December 8—5:38 a. m.]

2559. Following two messages sent December 1 by British Pro-Consul [at] Mukden:

"Mr. L. Steventon presents his compliments to Chairman of North East People's Government and informs him that he has now received instructions from his Britannic Majesty's Embassy, Nanking, to assume custody of all US Government property and represent their interests in Shenyang. He further brings to chairman's notice that he has not yet received reply to his previous requests for an interview with Mr. Ward or some other responsible member of his staff for purpose of checking inventories of property referred to.

"In order that he may follow instructions of his Embassy, he repeats request for interview and fullest facilities to permit him to perform necessary work involved."

"Mr. L. Steventon presents his compliments to mayor of Shenyang and wishes to inform him that he has been instructed by his Britannic Majesty's Embassy at Nanking to accept custody of all US Government property and to represent American interests in Shenyang.

"Property of US Government in Shenyang is of considerable value and quantity and it is necessary that inventories should be checked by him in company with responsible member of US ConGen. Some of property is in leased flats in British-owned Hong Kong and Shanghai Bank Building which since January, 1949, has been occupied by Transport Company whose employees have taken possession of flats. Flats were fully furnished in November 1948. To trace can only be accomplished by former occupiers.

"In consideration of difficulties likely to be met with in assuming responsibility he requests that permission for an early interview with Mr. Ward be granted and all facilities be given to enable him to carry out such work as is necessary and satisfactory to his Britannic Majesty's Embassy. He would greatly appreciate reply at mayor's earliest convenience".

Sent Department, repeated Peiping 425.

BACON

---

123 Ward, Angus I. : Telegram

The Consul at Tientsin (Wellborn) to the Secretary of State

TIENTSIN, December 9, 1949—10 a. m.
[Received December 9—9:41 a. m.]

1027. Re ourtel 1026, December 9.[92] We were able arrange December 7 with Tientsin Public Safety Bureau, Communist organ in charge Ward and party, for entire group to stay in US Govt houses. Permission given upon signing of guarantee by two (Vice Consul Manhard and myself) that deportees (1) would leave China on or about December 10, (2) appear at any time summoned and (3) would not go outside quarters or receive outsiders. Outsiders construed by PSB as all except regular occupants Govt houses and their servants. Text guarantee in following telegram.[93]

We had originally planned [to] quarter party in greater number houses for more comfort but PSB told us billeting to be limited to two Govt compounds. PSB endeavored impress us Ward party considered criminals and permission for them staying Govt houses great concession by Communists. We sensed Communists wish isolate group to avoid attracting attention and publicity. Local PSB apparently guided by orders from Mukden authorities. Liaison officers from Mukden accompanied Ward party.

WELLBORN

---

123 Ward, Angus I. : Telegram

The Consul at Tientsin (Wellborn) to the Secretary of State

TIENTSIN, December 10, 1949—5 p. m.
[Received December 10—3:49 p. m.]

1033. From Ward: Time too short for Department review summary Mukden experiences and I shall, therefore, follow instructions Deptel 451 to Tientsin, December 5, release factual account reporters *Lakeland Victory* tomorrow. Intend telegraph summary factual account from *Lakeland Victory*, if possible, otherwise Japan.

---

[92] Not printed.
[93] See telegram No. 1048, December 15, from the Consul at Tientsin, p. 1050.

Following brief analysis background Mukden experience submitted to enable Department appreciate many factors not apparent *per se* in factual narration Mukden experiences to be released press.

Sudden and complete collapse Nationalist resistance Mukden following Generalissimo assumption active military command (abruptly abandoning Li Kuang[94] strategy conserve men and arms for prolonged retention Mukden Island) caught CCP[95] unprepared administer Mukden. Mayor did not arrive until third day occupation, financial officials even later and there was no CCP currency until week after occupation. Suddenness Nationalist collapse surely caught CCP officials Mukden without policy directives and lack communications probably required local officials make snap decisions own initiative. Believe decision arrest Consul General of this nature.

Arrest and isolation Consul General was foreshadowed November 6 (although not so interpreted at time) when building adjacent Consulate General office staffed CCP equipment and personnel which bloomed into warden's headquarters date Consul General arrest. During negotiations November 15–20 over seizure Consulate General radio, I insisted ultimately only upon necessity communicate Secretary State for instructions, but this Military Control Committee refused, even via commercial facilities. I suspended radio transmission prior deadline of November 18, offered seal equipment and place it under CCP guard on Consulate General premises, but arrest imposed nevertheless.

Incommunicado Consul General arrest never defended by CCP as punishment failure surrender radio. January 13, Military Control Committee returned me several commercial telegrams to Department, subsequent arrest, with letter stating my telegrams would not be transmitted [as?] "United States and Northeast People's Government lack diplomatic relations".

I am convinced radio controversy mere pretext Consul General arrest which CCP required alleviate its fears Consul General engaged espionage. Badgering interrogation Chinese staff after November 20 plainly revealed CCP assumption Consul General involved. ... During interrogations following our police arrest October 24, prosecutor told Cicogna ... and only means effectively isolate Consul General from undercover operatives was to arrest Consul General and cut off all outside contact.

CCP hostility Westerners Mukden not confined this Consul General, British Consul stated he for months required special CCP permission leave his premises and has been followed everywhere; also entirely unable enter Hong Kong bank premises which under guard

[94] Possibly General Wei Li-huang, Commanding General of Chinese forces in Manchuria in 1948.
[95] Chinese Communist Party.

and occupied by CCP government personnel. November 1948, CCP arrested custodian Hong Kong bank on charge secret weapons and he has since been held incommunicado unknown location.

During year arrest, have come to believe pro-Moscow elements CCP utilized Consul General arrest to drive wedge between United States and sympathetic elements CCP by aggravating conditions arrest to utmost. Chi Yu-heng incident (fabricated insofar Chinese not hit, kicked or otherwise injured) built by CCP into sensation in order drive wedge between American military and Chinese staff (thus blocking possible espionage through the matter our departure) and specially with spy ring trial to blacken us and justify our expulsion, rather than permit us depart pursuant United States protests and representations, which would have weakened their publicized independence "imperialist" influence.

Recent events corroborate my despatch 11 to Department May 11 [97] this subject to be air pouched from Japan.

Sent Department 1032. Department pass Peiping. [Ward.]

WELLBORN

125.633/12–1149 : Telegram

The Ambassador in the Soviet Union (Kirk) to the Secretary of State

Moscow, December 11, 1949—4 p. m.
[Received December 12—9:22 a. m.]

3086. Re Depcirtels November 19, 1 a. m.,[98] and November 26, 2 a. m.,[99] in note No. 8, dated December 11, Gromyko [1] acknowledges receipt Embassy notes of November 21 and 27 and states:

"In accordance with information received by MFA,[2] the former Consul General of USA in Mukden, Mr. Ward, and the group of staff members referred to in the letter of the Secretary of State, received the possibility to leave Mukden and already have left for Tientsin for the further journey to the USA."

Department pass Peiping 22.

KIRK

---

[97] Not printed; it was received by the Department on December 20 and concerned possible Communist motives for confining the Consul General at Mukden. Mr. Ward concluded that the Communists might well have assumed that the American representatives in Mukden were a source of military information to the Chinese Government at Nanking and that strategic information could best be protected by isolating the Consulate General from its presumable agents. He wrote that a second consideration might be to give color to Communist propaganda charges portraying American diplomacy as an evil influence (125.633/5–1149).
[98] Not printed; see similar circular telegram of November 18, 10 a. m., p. 1009.
[99] Not printed; see similar circular telegram of November 26, 1 a. m., p. 1021.
[1] A. A. Gromyko, Soviet Acting Minister for Foreign Affairs.
[2] Minister for Foreign Affairs.

125.6336/12–1149 : Telegram

The Consul General at Mukden (Ward) to the Secretary of State

ON BOARD S. S. "LAKELAND VICTORY", December 11, 1949.
[Received December 13—12 :55 p. m.]

13. Following factual summary Mukden experiences:

November 20 year ago without warning CCP soldiers cordoned ConGen office and both residence compounds, blocking all egress. Telephones and electricity were cut, disrupting office water supply and all lighting. Delegation Military Control Committee Mukden presented letter addressed me without title stating "Your failure surrender radio station constitutes intentional defiance; personnel former American ConGen hereafter forbidden intercourse with outside," notwithstanding my suspension radio traffic and offer place radio equipment under seal or guard, and that I had insisted only upon communication with United States Government before surrendering Government property, authorities refused permission to reactivate our station to request Department instructions regarding surrender. Delegation's denial my official status contradicted mayor's formal call and letters previously addressed me as ConGen by CCP civil and military authorities. Delegation then seized radio transmitters and generators, and also accused me withholding hidden transmitter. After 10 hours continuous bickering, delegation announced ConGen personnel confined residences incommunicado until further notice. I insisted remain with 18 employees in unlighted office, where 22 persons for 30 hours were limited total one bucket water, with warden ignoring appeals for more and guards forbidding even kerosene light. Aged German casual visitor USIS library confined with Americans for more than 1 year without reply his appeals release or access food, clothing and funds his residence. Chinese casuals caught in residences freed only after several months delay.

Military Control Committee orally assured me Nov. 18 it would transmit my official telegrams over Hsin Hua News Agency facilities. November 22 I submitted telegraphic report Department to Military Control Committee for such transmission. This was subsequently returned January 13 with final letter I received from CCP authorities, stating no messages whatever would be transmitted because "United States and Northeast People's Government not in diplomatic relationship". Personal messages staff to families United States returned unsent. June 6 no communication of any type with outside world permitted and in more than year no communication whatever with other Mukden residents. Passersby were even arrested for waving greetings.

Not until December 4 year ago were Americans permitted move between residences and office, then only under guard and when warden chose to approve specific petitions: Such limited movements subsequent year subject exasperating and wasteful delays and frequent failures permit more than single daily round trip to office. My request mayor restore electricity for Christmas was approved, ending 5 weeks' lack running water in crowded office and relieving eyestrain resulting enforced dependence kerosene lamps. Chinese staff subject repeated badgering interrogations aimed establishing espionage suspicions against ConGen and alleging collaboration with ESD.

Warden took our Chinese consular identity cards promising CCP countersignature but cards never returned. He also wheedled our curfew passes, falsely stating curfew revoked. He threatened seal ConGen safe containing office funds but threat never implemented. Warden imposed regular examination packages carried by American en route office, and mayor ignored our request for permission attend Easter services. Warden failed permit emptying overflowing cesspools in American residences. ConGen given consent dollar rate exchange during 7-month period in which official value silver quadrupled. May 17 Department ordered closure Mukden ConGen in telegram received by mail June 7 as incommunicado phase arrest ended.

June 20 local press published spy charges. Next day mayor's aide called (first contact in more than 7 months), stating People's Government approved ConGen request depart Mukden and requiring submittal packing lists goods to be shipped. When he asked I set departure date, I replied lack equipment and packers prevented me from determining departure date until allowed accesss to designated packing firm, and I pointed out lack telephones, recalcitrance of guards and limits on movement ConGen vehicles greatly hampered preparations.

On July 19 I requested facilities departure part staff July 27 and again August 12 but without fruit. Mytel 58 to Nanking September 17, rejected for transmission, reported *inter alia*.

"Authorities have continued refuse my wife access competent dentist known be present Mukden to treat tooth badly broken early in December. My urgent request April 27 services my physician ignored until June 4 and physician not even allowed complete diagnosis. Same physician later allowed 2 minutes consultation, examination, diagnosis, and treatment my wife suffering mild attack appendicitis. I and every American member my staff threatened at least once with firearms. Electric power needed for adequate water supply denied staff compound. Delay of weeks encountered in purchasing modest quantities packing materials and other supplies readily available in market. Refused permission purchase roof repair materials at times when rain heavy and roof leaking badly. Staff and I obliged wait months for overdue routine innoculations. Have been refused services professional packers and thus prevented from preparing household and office property for shipment pursuant Department instructions. Adequate rail facilities available July 27 and 10 days following but authorities did not permit first group staff members depart from Mukden. We are dependent for fresh foods on merchant appointed by authorities and enjoying monopolistic right who has exploited us through prices over open market levels and through inferior quality and shortweight. Notwithstanding urgent pleas our warden protractedly delayed permission deliver coal in dead of winter to Tatsumi residence where his dependents were suffering from cold. Tatsumi was prevented from rejoining his family for more than fortnight after date our arrest, although I had been informed thereon he would be permitted return home next day. Non-American employees detained in office building repeatedly denied permission obtain urgently needed clothing from their homes. Although mayor informed me on November 5 he would accept uncoded telegrams for transmission and Military Control Committee made similar offer Nov. 18, office not permitted communicate with other Foreign Service establishments until June 6. Delivery telegrams from Nanking during past months delayed average 40 hours after receipt Mukden, and several official communications which I have submitted for transmission have been neither sent nor returned to me. I am still denied permission recover Government and staff property on storage former residences November 20".

September 27 FSA Chi Yu-heng in refusing perform assigned task threw down tools and left job saying "I quit". He refused proffered final settlement, whereupon he was instructed leave Government premises permanently inasmuch final payment would be sent his residence upon his request. Chi nevertheless entered ConGen building surreptitiously October 10 without authority. When discovered morning October 11, I took him by hand and pacifically led him to courtyard: When he demanded money I stated he could await opening accounts office but if he refused settlement then he would have to leave building because he was committing trespass. Later same day Chi again refused settlement and when he adamantly refused leave building I took him by hand intending to turn him as trespasser over to armed sentry at street entrance. At no time did I or any member my staff strike, kick or injure Chi in any way. I was victim assault by Chi's brother already reported Department (telegram reference presently not available) and later Kristan and Cicogna suffered beatings described therein. CCP guard witnessing Chinese staff beating Kristan refused Rehberg's demand he intervene. Allegations Chi unconscious, suffered concussion and other serious injury totally unfounded: Police officer using office telephone was overheard ordering Chi's retention hospital over objections doctor. During police physician examination Chi in office none of several Americans present saw any injury other than slight mat burn over right eye (which I and Rehberg saw inflict upon himself), and Chi's own loud protestations immediately after incident belie his unconsciousness.

Atrocious conditions our confinement under police arrest after October 24 and perversions of justice during investigation and so-called trial November 21 reported my telegrams just prior departure Mukden.

Staff and I with dependents departed Mukden under heavy guard 0345 hours December 7, and after 40-hour rail journey (normally requiring 15 hours) in third class car with board shelves as beds, notwithstanding my request first class accommodations arrived Tientsin. All subjected severe cold during first hours of journey, and car entirely without water. All passengers confined to car throughout journey and subjected to constant surveillance by guards.

Much of foregoing information today released to correspondents.

Attitude of Tientsin local authorities toward us much less hostile and their treatment much more considerate than Mukden authorities. Radio equipment and one generator seized November 20 year ago returned by [*our?*] custody. Staff and I embarked at Taku Bar 0800 hours today on steamer *Lakeland Victory*. Shall disembark Kobe or Yokohama whichever first touched.

WARD

125.633/12–1349 : Telegram

The Consul at Tientsin (Wellborn) to the Secretary of State

TIENTSIN, December 13, 1949.
[Received December 15—12:44 a. m.]

1047. From Ward. "Consulate General Mukden declared closed on December 8 at 0800 hours upon my departure from Consular District through Shanhaikuan."

Sent Department 1047; repeated Peiping by mail 332. [Ward.]

WELLBORN

---

123 Ward, Angus I. : Telegram

The Consul at Tientsin (Wellborn) to the Secretary of State

TIENTSIN, December 15, 1949.
[Received December 15—1:29 p. m.]

1048. Following is translation of guarantee form required by Tientsin Public Safety Bureau for relinquishment of Ward and party into our custody during stay in Tientsin:

"The undersigned hereby guarantees that (blank) who are to be deported and are now waiting for transportation at Tientsin and the luggage they have carried with them shall all leave China on board the S.S. *Lakeland Victory* on or about December 10, 1949. While in Tientsin waiting for transportation, they shall temporarily be taken to the private living quarters of (blank) for residence and the undersigned guarantees that they shall appear at any time when they are summoned and shall not receive outsiders nor go out. The undersigned guarantor (blank) shall be entirely responsible for the persons, living, speeches and activities of the guaranteed persons."

Chinese text guarantee signed December at Tientsin railway station on arrival of Ward group by Wellborn and Manhard as guarantors, and by persons guaranteed.

Sent Department 1048; repeated Tientsin by mail as 333.

WELLBORN

II. CONSULATES GENERAL AT PEIPING AND TIENTSIN: REFUSAL OF CHINESE COMMUNISTS TO DEAL WITH CONSULATES WITHOUT RECOGNITION; CLOSING OF OFFICES OF UNITED STATES INFORMATION SERVICE; IMPOSITION OF TAXES ON CONSULAR PROPERTIES; QUESTION OF THE REGISTRATION OF CONSULAR PROPERTIES

893.00/1–1849 : Telegram

The Consul General at Tientsin (Smyth) to the Secretary of State

TIENTSIN, January 18, 1949.
[Received January 18—3 : 47 a. m.]

81. Newspaper Tientsin *Jih Pao* carried following item today : [3]

"Commander Nieh Jung-chen of the Peiping-Tientsin Garrison Headquarters in a joint statement on January 15 with political member Po Yi-po announced that the Liberation Army will accord protection to law-abiding foreign residents in Tientsin, on the condition that they observe the provisions laid down in the proclamations of the People's Government, the Military Commission, and the Garrison Headquarters."

SMYTH

893.00/1–1849 : Telegram

The Consul General at Peiping (Clubb) to the Secretary of State

PEIPING, January 18, 1949—5 p. m.
[Received 10 : 07 p. m.]

60. ReContel 54, January 18,[4] paragraph 4. USIS [5] Director Van Putten [6] reports that during past 2 days persons well-known their office have voluntarily come forward and informed them confidentially that they know certainly there has been formed organization Peiping to commit certain acts damage to foreign property and violence on individuals in case of attack on Peiping. One of contemplated terroristic methods is use gasoline bombs. Those persons who have reasons be friendly USIS and are trusted by USIS have recommended warning foreigners this area take adequate measures self-protection. They

---

[3] For information on Communist occupation of Tientsin, see telegram No. 61, January 14, 10 :45 p. m., p. 48.
[4] Not printed.
[5] United States Information Service.
[6] James D. van Putten, Consul at Peiping.

mentioned particularly Van Putten and me as persons to whom harm might come.

As of possible significance this general connection, report that this office earlier received from three different official quarters suggestion it might be better concentrate all Peiping Americans in Consular compound or ex-Legation quarter. Apart from nominal and possibly real intent these suggestions of assisting in providing protection foreigners, it is considered that incidental result any concentration Americans or other foreigners would be looting their property and occupation their premises. It would appear also possible however that some of those officials also are apprehensive of plans of Generalissimo's[7] special servicemen.

Suggest Embassy might find it desirable as measure precaution to (1) invite attention highest authority Nanking responsible for actions BIS[8] special service personnel to Communist allegation (Contel 58, January 18[9] for text) and, referring to American experience Mukden[10] and Tientsin of discipline and general correctness Communist behavior, (2) point out that any untoward incidents involving terroristic acts committed against American nationals or property Peiping or Shanghai would in circumstances be unusually suspect, and (3) request special service organs in threatened points be strictly instructed to cooperate with local authorities to fullest to end that all possible and appropriate protection be accorded American lives and property.

If further developments make action appear needful, I propose, unless instructed otherwise, inform high local authorities I have received reports purporting to confirm Communist allegation and have appropriately informed by [my] Government.[11]

Repeated Nanking 56, Shanghai 54.

CLUBB

893.00/1–2149 : Telegram

The Consul General at Tientsin (Smyth) to the Secretary of State

TIENTSIN, January 21, 1949—noon.
[Received January 21—7 : 44 a. m.]

104. This morning Jenkins[12] and I had 1-hour talk with Yang Piao, newly arrived head of Foreign Affairs Bureau. He said Bureau was not formally functioning as at present there can be no formal

---

[7] President Chiang Kai-shek.
[8] Chinese Bureau of Investigation and Statistics (Security).
[9] Not printed.
[10] For documentation on this subject, see pp. 933 ff.
[11] The Ambassador in China (Stuart) instructed the Consul General at Peiping in telegram No. 19 (No. 157 to the Department), January 20, 6 p. m.: "suggest you do not take action suggested your last paragraph until so instructed."
[12] Alfred leSesne Jenkins, Vice Consul at Tientsin.

relations with, by inference, countries which do not recognize Communist government. He said, however, that any individual foreigners as private persons, could write to them if they had any problems. (So far in practice they have not always insisted on this and some minor matters have been taken up orally. For example, Yang obtained return of French motor car mentioned ourtel 78, January 17.[13])

We discussed with him question of our radio which Communists under regulations announced yesterday (ourtel 100, January 20 [13]) forbidding operation sending stations after 72 hours from morning of January 20. We pointed out advantages of fact that we had been able to report promptly safety of American and other foreign nationals. We requested we be permitted to continue to operate station. He said he would transmit request to appropriate authorities.

We said for 2 months now there had been no word from our Mukden Consular staff and that we were very much concerned. He said he had no information but would transmit for inquiry to appropriate authorities.

During our talk he made it clear he had no authority to make decisions on matters or answer inquiries raised by us. Thus inability to obtain information on decisions is characteristic of experience of other foreigners with various Communist officials. It is possible that much of this indecision may be due to their inexperience and confusion in initial period. Communists themselves admit they have much to learn but profess they are anxious to learn and to use available talents satisfactory to them).

SMYTH

893.00/1–2449 : Telegram

The Consul General at Peiping (Clubb) to the Secretary of State

PEIPING, January 24, 1949.
[Received January 24—8:06 a. m.]

117. By present reports no Americans were killed or injured in course recent fighting and turnover of PPG.[14] This report includes Americans [at] Tungchow from which point report received today but does not include recent information from either Yenching-Tsinghua area or western suburbs. At last report, however, Americans these two districts were also safe and it is believed their welfare also assured. So far as known at present only foreigners killed or injured were one German killed and one British wounded as previously reported.

Sent Department 117, Nanking 100, Shanghai 100.

CLUBB

---

[13] Not printed.
[14] Peiping. For information on Communist occupation of Peiping, see telegram No. 94, January 20, 5 p. m., p. 59.

124.93/1–3149 : Telegram

The Consul General at Peiping (Clubb) to the Secretary of State

PEIPING [VIA SHANGHAI], January 31, 1949—3 p. m.
[Received February 1—12 : 40 a. m.]

152. Following is substance (in translation) of message relayed by Shanghai from AmConsul [at] Peiping:

1. Communists accord no recognition functions Tientsin Consulates (including Soviets).
2. No communications permitted outside Tientsin.
3. All activities foreigners virtually paralyzed.
4. There exists no possibility establish contact responsible local authorities for discussion difficulties which arise.
5. After basic statement issued re protection foreigners, there are no signs leading to hope normalization soon existing situation.
6. If present unsettled political situation continues, quick determination position foreigners may be forecast and they would unavoidably find themselves in condition interned persons.
7. Consuls are keeping in touch in order prevent repetition situation prevailing Mukden.
8. Up to now nothing perilous has happened re foreign nationals but because lack normal activities serious financial difficulties may at least be anticipated.
9. Living costs increasing vertiginously.

Peiping Consul reports this message brought back by person he sent Tientsin to establish contact, that messenger (foreigner) experienced difficulty returning because of Communist prohibition travel foreigners through central station Tientsin.

This source indicates consular officials not permitted use cars.

Italian Consul here lacks telegraphic facilities, requests above information be transmitted Italian Ambassador, Nanking.

Sent Department 152, repeated Nanking 128, Shanghai 122.

CLUBB

125.7146/2–249 : Telegram

The Consul General at Peiping (Clubb) to the Secretary of State

PEIPING, February 2, 1949—11 a. m.
[Received February 2—6 : 09 a. m.]

163. Mukden experience indicates we may soon expect visit from Communist authorities to check (1) possibility that Nationalist officials may have taken refuge Consular premises; (2) operation radio station; (3) possession arms or munitions.

In view possibility Peiping may be off air at time and Communists might conceivably make propaganda re any of three points, report now for possible future reference that (1) no refuge at Consulate asked by

Chinese official or given; (2) radio station will continue until cessation demanded whereupon when forced station will go off air with Consulate trying at same time obtain regular commercial facilities; (3) Consulate and ECA,[16] both without Govt arms or munitions. Of Govt arms, Office Assistant Military Attaché has 6 carbines, 1 pistol, AstALUSNA [17] 2 pistols, and DALS [18] 25 carbines, 13 pistols. Some other arms held privately. No attempt will be made secrete any those arms. Possession will be explained as (1) partly custodial (AAG),[19] (2) partly preparation possible self defense in uncertain situation. They will be turned over if demanded with request for inventory receipt.

This message shown concerned military offices.

Sent Dept 163, Nanking 138, Shanghai 136, Canton 1.

CLUBB

893.00/2–349 : Telegram

The Consul General at Peiping (Clubb) to the Secretary of State

PEIPING, February 3, 1949.
[Received February 3—9:43 p. m.]

175. Article 7 of proclamation issued February 2 by "PPG-Tientsin front line headquarters Chinese People's Liberation Army" signed by Lin Piao as Commander and Lo Jung-huan as Political Commissioner provides:

"Safety of lives and property of foreign nationals shall be protected. All foreign nationals must observe laws and regulations of this army and democratic government, may not undertake espionage activities and may not act in opposition to matters of Chinese revolution. They may not hide war criminals or anti-revolutionary elements or other criminals. Otherwise they will naturally be handled in accordance with laws this army and People's Government."

Article 4 of proclamation issued February 2 by Nieh Jung-chen as PPG Defense Commander and Po Yi-po as Political Commissioner provides:

"All arms of Kmt [20] government military and civil officials, *pao chia* [21] members and other arms of population whether or not they have received arms permits issued by Kmt government must be alike delivered to this army or to People's Government. None may secrete arms, munitions, radio stations or other articles of military use. Offenders will be handled in accordance with law."

---

[16] Economic Cooperation Administration.
[17] Office of Assistant Naval Attaché for Air.
[18] Department of the Army Language School at Peiping.
[19] Army Advisory Group.
[20] Kuomintang (Nationalist Party).
[21] Local militia.

Article 7 same proclamation provides:

"Nationals of countries must observe laws and regulations Chinese Liberation Army and People's Government. Offenders shall be handled in accordance with laws Chinese People's Government."

Article 8 provides:

"All military and civil personnel must alike strictly observe laws and regulations People's Government and three great disciplines of People's Liberation Army together with eight items for note and regulations governing entry into city. They are, moreover, subject to restrictions garrison inspection corps. Offenders will be handled in accordance with discipline regulations."

Another proclamation same date designates Cheng Tzu-hua as PPG garrison commander and concurrently political commissioner with Peng Ming-chih and Wu Ke-hua as vice commanders and Mo Wen-hua as deputy political commissioner. All these proclamations published *Jen Min Jih Pao* February 2.

Sent Department 175; Nanking 146; Shanghai 148.

CLUBB

125.9376/2–449 : Telegram

The Consul General at Peiping (Clubb) to the Secretary of State

PEIPING, February 4, 1949—3 p. m.
[Received February 4—10 : 52 a. m.]

182. ReContel 162, February 1.[22] Consulate messenger went Tientsin February 2, saw Smyth February 3, returned last night. Reported as follows:

Communist guards placed all residences Consulate personnel for 4 or 5 days after occupation during period when there was much looting, then withdrawn. None now stationed either residence or Consulate. Smyth's opinion, guards stationed first instance purely protection. Americans and aliens have freedom movements. USIS and Consulate open as usual. USIS attendance fair.

Shortly after occupation Communists directed registration all radios. When Consulate contacted liaison officer of "foreign affairs section", Communists said deliver radio within 72 hours. Radio sent police with inventory and official letter. Both returned with statement equipment not confiscated, merely held in custody, necessary however Consulate take Communist word for no receipt would be given. Consulate has experienced no other trouble. Home radios retained.

Communist regulations all cars must be registered and have new licenses before use. Consulate cars' registered licenses unreceived.

---

[22] Not printed.

Main complaint Consuls is absence person of real authority with whom deal. British Consul tried call on mayor, waited hour, no success. Smyth [has] not called.

Smyth expressed desire have such help this office could give re four points: (1) Consuls [at] Tientsin unable contact person bearing real responsibility, desire see person of authority, (2) Informed by very junior liaison officer, their consular status unrecognized pending recognition Communist regime and desire accept their official status, (3) Inter-port travel, telegraphic and mail facilities desired for foreigners, (4) Foreign banks remain closed primarily awaiting contact responsible authority.

No great difficulty get travel pass, only long wait in line. Some [*Same*] bottleneck re tickets. Persons with silver required change at office gate at station. Travel trip took about 4½ hours. Third class only.

ECA messenger also made round trip. Consulate messenger observed no foreigners traveling.

Sent Department 182, Nanking 152, Shanghai 154.

CLUBB

893.00/2–449 : Telegram

The Consul General at Peiping (*Clubb*) *to the Secretary of State*

PEIPING, February 4, 1949—4 p. m.
[Received February 4—11 : 37 a. m.]

177. ReContel 176, February 3.[23] Foreign Consuls [at] Peiping exchanged views February 2 general subject calling on new mayor.[24] French Consul said he proposed call on Yeh Chien-ying soon, being under instructions particularly from his government early invite attention Communist authorities desirability foreign Consuls [at] Tientsin and Mukden be given facilities contact their governments. British, Dutch, Belgian, Italian representatives indicated they wished consider matter further before acting (at time discussion, still unknown whether Yeh had formally assumed duties mayor). Soviet Consul said he would have to await instructions from Embassy before taking action.

There was ruled out from beginning of discussion any project for joint action re matter meeting being for sole purpose exchange views. I stated my position as being: (1) I would assume local authorities would accord us rights and privileges in accordance international law and practice until discovered otherwise; (2) my function was to protect American lives and property and I was expected maintain with local authorities such contacts as necessary for effective fulfillment my

---

[23] Not printed.
[24] General Yeh Chien-ying.

functions; (3) if new mayor took up post I should, in due course, offer pay courtesy call; (4) functions consular officer unconnected in international law with question recognition.

It now appears Yeh has assumed duties as mayor. In practice Communist representatives, as previously reported, proving very elusive but French Consul and I yesterday indirectly requested to call on Yeh his convenience. Dutch did same today.

Assistant Military Attaché Barrett [25] well acquainted new mayor and propose when and if I see Yeh to approach him re meeting Barrett and Assistant ALUSNA Williams [26] informally. [27]

Sent Department, Nanking 149, Shanghai 151.

CLUBB

893.00/2–549 : Telegram

The Consul General at Peiping (Clubb) to the Secretary of State

PEIPING, February 5, 1949.
[Received February 6, 1949—12 : 02 a. m.]

184. *Jen Min Jih Pao*, February 4, carried official proclamation issued in name of Yeh Chien-ying and Hsu Ping as mayor and deputy mayor announcing that Peiping Municipal Government, established effective January 1 in Peiping suburbs, had taken up duties Peiping itself February 2. Press today reports formal takeover municipal government yesterday. *Hsin Min Pao*, in report of speech given by Yeh Chien-ying on that occasion, quoted him as stating *inter alia* as follows:

"In world today socialism is already main current, capitalism surely is going to die. This has already been stated 100 years ago by Marx. Capitalism, however, in the world still can have period of life. Socialism and capitalism can co-exist in world together. Regarding foreign relations of China, henceforth it is only requisite that there be adherence to principles of equality and mutual benefit and we can have mutual exchange of what we have for what we lack with capitalistic states and enter upon treaties for commercial intercourse and trade." (Full text of speech by mail.[28])

Retel 30, February 4 from Shanghai [to Peiping][29], press today reports resumption regular train service as of February 4 from Peiping station to Tientsin with three trains daily and two trains daily

---

[25] Col. David D. Barrett.
[26] Lt. Thomas E. Williams, Assistant Naval Attaché and Assistant Naval Attaché for Air.
[27] The Consul General at Peiping stated in his telegram No. 215, February 10, 5 p. m. to the Department: "French Consul and I were informed by intermediary February 8 that Yeh Chien-ying desired we postpone calls for present (Contel 149 February 4) since arrangements not complete. In communication to French Consul 'technical difficulties' were mentioned."
[28] Despatch No. 30, February 25, from the Consul General at Peiping, not printed.
[29] Not found in Department of State files.

likewise each to Kalgan and Chohsien. Same item reports direct trains to Shanhaikuan will be resumed today. Peiping *Jih Pao* reports exchange rate for gold yuan has been fixed by People's Bank at 1 PB equals 10 gold yuan, that exchange of gold yuan has already been started but that rates for gold and silver still unfixed. *Shih Chieh Jih Pao* reports peace delegates from Shanghai and Ningsia are scheduled proceed Peiping by plane tomorrow. Same general information carried by other papers but matter unconfirmed. Ordinary mail (including registered and express letters) accepted by post office for Tientsin but telegraph office still does not accept telegrams for same point. *Jen Min Jih Pao* today carries protest CEC [30] Chinese Communist Party release Okamura [31] and his return Japan.

Sent Department 184, Nanking 154, Shanghai 157.

CLUBB

893.50 Recovery/2–749 : Telegram

The Consul General at Peiping (Clubb) to the Secretary of State

PEIPING, February 7, 1949—3 p. m.
[Received February 7—4:54 a. m.]

189. ReContel 167, February 2.[32] Application this office to Peiping garrison headquarters [for] permission ECA chartered plane land Peiping with some two tons medical supplies for PUMC [33] and airlift out certain ECA personnel brought response, purportedly by authority garrison commander Cheng Tzu-hua, that no plane regardless nationality or mission would be permitted land Peiping except those from other points Communist-controlled territory.

Matter not being dropped and appears this office some possibility still exists arrangements can be made. This probably cannot be achieved within next few days because (1) position taken by garrison commander, (2) evident circumstance Communist control still not well organized locally. Matter complicated by absence to date effective direct contacts authoritative quarters.

Note however "peace delegation" plane able land Peiping yesterday (after being fired on) and recommend publicity re subject be withheld pending more definite crystallization.

ECA Peiping director Davis [34] reported separately his Shanghai office re matter February 5.

Sent Department 189, Shanghai 160, Nanking 156.

CLUBB

---

[30] Central Executive Committee.
[31] Lt. Gen. Yasutsugu Okamura, Commander in Chief of Japanese armies in China, 1944–45. See telegram 288, February 1, from Nanking, p. 99.
[32] Not printed.
[33] Peking Union Medical College.
[34] Ritchie G. Davis, acting special representative for Chief of ECA Mission (North China).

893.50 Recovery/2–749 : Telegram

The Consul General at Peiping (Clubb) to the Secretary of State

PEIPING, February 7, 1949—3 p. m.
[Received February 7—8 : 05 a. m.]

191. Application February 2 to Peiping garrison headquarters re ECA plane (Contel 189, February 7) elicited incidental statement attributed garrison commander that Communist side has no relations with Ambassadors or Consuls and has nothing to do with them. Attempts February 3, 4 and 5 arrange call Peiping-Tientsin defense headquarters on official business (re Consular radio station) brought statement officer that organization February 5 that his superiors had instructed that in absence diplomatic relations between "Chinese People's Government" and USA there is no need receive me even on official business. British Consul reports his official communications returned.

FonOff representative told me February 5 he met same day with Yeh Chien-ying who indicated that local Communist authorities proposed have relations with foreign Consuls [at] Peiping with reorganization and enlargement present Peiping office, special delegate Foreign Affairs with concentration in that organization of matters previously handled partly by "Foreign Affairs Sections" in Municipal Government, Bureau of Police and NCBSH.[35] Foreign Office representative indicated he and representative Executive Yuan Ministry Information Office were being invited take over task reorganization. He opined that prior to organization such office little could be expected re administration foreign affairs as new organizations were without directives. He thought Yeh would probably see foreign Consuls soon after setting up new organization. Project based on Yeh's concept that (1) coalition government will soon be established Peiping, (2) new government needs foreign relations (Contel 184, February 5) and (3) Communists would observe treaty obligations (unclear from FonOff representative's report whether Yeh meant this principle would be [garble] without exception).

Believe difficulties of contact will continue immediate present as indicated. Believe also Yeh's reputed good intentions may suffer some check from thinking other Communists' quarters induced by past propaganda. Believe finally, however, Communists will probably in due course be forced by hard facts take more practical view "foreign relations" in its various economic and political aspects.

Sent Department 191, Nanking 158, Shanghai 161.

CLUBB

---

[35] North China Bandit-Suppression Headquarters (pre-Communist).

893.00/2–949 : Telegram

The Consul General at Peiping (Clubb) to the Secretary of State

PEIPING, February 9, 1949—2 p. m.
[Received February 10—1 : 46 a. m.]

201. ReContel 117, January 24 [36] seemingly complete information indicates all Americans unharmed in course recent fighting.

Foreigners permitted in out Peiping gates freely and travel been performed variously Tungchow, Yenching and west hills. Group foreign picnickers February 6 west hills, however, approached by representatives Military Affairs Control Committee who said they should have permission school authorities visit area, that military authorities needed advance notice order give protection, that still period military government, and mines and grenades still scattered about. However, soon they would be free go where they pleased. Consul to get definite regulations, if any, on interpost travel foreigners.

Take this opportunity report no panic or alarm among foreigners during period turnover and no last minute demand for evacuation (few Americans left after beginning siege), that Consul staff in particular continued regular performance duties calmly and efficiently under heavy overload office work (particularly code work) despite local uncertainties and inconveniences.

Sent Department 201, repeated Nanking 165, Shanghai 171.

CLUBB

125.7146/2–1049 : Telegram

The Consul General at Peiping (Clubb) to the Secretary of State

PEIPING, February 10, 1949—3 p. m.
[Received February 10—10 : 13 a. m.]

205. ReContel 191, February 7. Though this Consulate had tried unsuccessfully contact appropriate Communist organization and discuss position Consular radio and to date no call from Communists, view public proclamation (Deptel [*my*] 175, February 3) thought advisable indicate US *bona fides* by indicating to Communists that Consulate had radio and would discuss matter if there were any query its operation. Yesterday took up matter with former Foreign Office representative in absence direct contact, told him of unsuccessful attempts make contact, re Consular radio, stating it was hoped due importance communications we could continue operate radio, if any query such operation would discuss with appropriate authorities. Said radio used for official purposes only; in addition was Government property and I would, of course, not be in position hand over such

---

[36] Not printed.

Government property. Stated I assumed original proclamation of Peiping-Tientsin defense headquarters referred primarily to Chinese Government and Party radio but I felt it desirable clarify situation. Sent Department 205, repeated Nanking 169, Shanghai 176.

CLUBB

125.7146/2–1149 : Telegram

The Consul General at Peiping (Clubb) to the Secretary of State

PEIPING, February 11, 1949—4 p. m.
[Received February 12—12 : 35 a. m.]

216. Informed last night by intermediary, who stated categorically he transmitted message "in personal capacity" as local Foreign Office branch now defunct, that Communist authorities gave oral approval continued use Consular radio for present, permission without prejudice question later delivery over of station. Since my position regarding handing over Government property already set forth (see Consular reference telegram [37]), did not consider it appropriate or desirable argue possible later Communist demand now.

Consul General ceased accept press messages effective time Communist occupation Peiping and early issued office order directing care regarding character message sent plain, aim being avoidance giving Communists ground protest. Recommend no publicity.

Repeated Nanking 176, Shanghai 181.

CLUBB

119.2/2–1649 : Telegram

The Consul General at Peiping (Clubb) to the Secretary of State

PEIPING, February 16, 1949—3 p. m.
[Received February 17—4 : 11 a. m.]

245. [To Nanking :] ReEmbtel 43, February 5.[38] No opportunity yet for taking up effectively subject reftel. Foreign Nationals Affairs Office evidently has begun functioning but to date all contacts Communists have brought statement Consular officials Peiping unrecognized. Regarding communications, note that according information received from employee telegraph office by member Consulate General there now exists no telegraph communication between Peiping and any point liberated areas, that only telegraph connections are with Nationalist-controlled areas, that incidentally telegraph operators Peiping consistently propagandize operators Nationalist end. Lack telegraph communications is generally not only for Consular officials Tientsin but Chinese and foreigners all North China except Peiping.

---

[37] *Supra.*
[38] Not found in Department of State files.

Foreign newsmen have received information indicating Communist censor now functions Peiping telegraph office but instead performing duties usual fashion simply destroys displeasing press dispatches. No indication given newsmen of cutting or failure send message.

Peiping chief operator now certain from technical indications that station nearby is monitoring Consular frequencies presumably with old-type receiver as he can hear frequency beat heterodyne.

Sent Nanking 198, repeated Department 245, Embassy Canton 6, Shanghai 206.

CLUBB

893.00/2–1949 : Telegram

The Consul General at Peiping (Clubb) to the Secretary of State

[Extract]

PEIPING, February 19, 1949—4 p. m.
[Received 11 : 52 p. m.]

260. ReContel 245, February 16. Without formal announcement apparently effective February 17 (when signboard put up), Foreign Nationals Affairs Office, Peiping Municipal People's Government, now functioning old Foreign Office delegates' office on Legation Street. Davis, Barrett and I called severally re various matters and alike told since local authorities do not have diplomatic relations with foreign governments, office unable deal with us in official capacities, that office's procedure requires for present, although situation indicated expected improve as office gets going, completion Chinese form identifying caller and setting forth business. With reference official position deleted from form possible get reply queries. My case notation make under occupation simple deleted space left blank which satisfied persons concerned. Will make effort handle matters outstanding that basis. Effectiveness representation this channel remains be seen.

Sent Department, repeated OffEmb Canton 7, Shanghai 223. Shanghai pouched Nanking.

CLUBB

125.7146/2–2349 : Telegram

The Consul General at Peiping (Clubb) to the Secretary of State

PEIPING, February 23, 1949—7 p. m.
[Received 8 : 47 p. m.]

282. Effective this morning "political directive officer" Liu Tso-hung directed this office state manner procedure being established re entrance [and] exit this compound as follows :

1. All persons riding vehicles any nature should dismount to be identified by guard before allowed in.

2. No other foreigner allowed in except Americans with official business this office.

3. Not allowed out of compound. Basis principles governing procedures stated "protection foreign lives, property".

Although have been variations this today, that is effective procedure end day.

I sent Sollenberger [39] request said political officer see me discuss matter which refused do, later discussion procedure petty guard officer resulted no easing situation.

Meeting Consulate officers this afternoon showed essentially same applies other Consulates (excepting Soviet Consul not present as his confirmation his office ceased function, he now has position private citizen, general situation unknown though guards present). Car with Chi[nese] observed entering Soviet compound without requirement dismount. Consuls decided try discover channel joint approach concerned authorities with possibility that regard sending letters report to Foreign Nationals Affairs Office new meeting February 25.

Italian Consul requests Nanking inform his Ambassador.

To date note has generally proven possible foreigners enter Consulate upon identification.

Repeated Nanking, Shanghai.

CLUBB

125.937/2–2449 : Telegram

The Consul General at Tientsin (Smyth) to the Secretary of State

TIENTSIN, February 24, 1949.
[Received February 27—2 : 44 a. m.]

125. All members staff, all other Americans Tientsin well. All have free movement. Despite continued anti-American propaganda newspapers, radio, posters, Americans so far received treatment good as other foreigners. In some ways Americans fared better than some other foreigners as fewer points friction; for example, British [and] Soviets much larger national groups, property interests here, and [there] has been much dissatisfaction their part with billeting troops. So far no troops billeted residences, occupied Americans, but many Soviet, some British residences occupied by troops.

In general, American business men have adopted policy wait-see and majority seem feel Communist inaction, tending to restrain trade and business, may be due more to inexperience, ignorance than to deliberate anti-foreign policy. The two American Missions with American staff

---

[39] Howard Sollenberger, Director of the Army School at Peiping.

(Methodist and American Board) also adopting wait-see policy; they continuing usual activities, including schools with only minor changes in curriculum and administration; these changes so far do not adversely affect Mission pursuits.

Believe it too early for accurate appraisal to be made of future prospects for American and other foreign business and Missions. New regime up to now so busy with take-over problems and coping with situation with which they not familiar and for which they had inadequate trained personnel that have been few indications what policy toward foreigners' affairs or interests will be. One exception is strong consistent anti-American propaganda press, radio, evidences so far this propaganda not too effective city residents but too early judge results, troops seem indoctrinated with propaganda.

SMYTH

702.0093/2–2649 : Telegram

The Consul General at Tientsin (Smyth) to the Secretary of State

TIENTSIN, February 26, 1949—10 a. m.
[Received February 27—6 : 24 a. m.]

124. Communist authorities continue regard local Consuls, including Soviet, as civilians as their countries do not recognize Communists. In accordance Deptins,[39a] we send no letters to local authorities in official capacity. My only contact local authorities was talk with official Foreign Affairs Bureau mentioned mytel 104, January 21. Only letter to local authorities January 31 to Mayor signed "For American Community of Tientsin". This letter similar to letters sent same time to Mayor by other Consulates, except Soviet, protesting hardships imposed foreign community by lack banking, communication facilities. Letters from other Consuls signed official capacities returned with statement that "as Chinese People's Government does not have any diplomatic relationship your government, your letter officially written in capacity of Consul cannot be received and is returned herewith". Reply my letter received from Secretariat People's Government for Tientsin stated foreign residents concerned should approach Director Foreign Affairs Department of People's Government of Tientsin and Foreign Residents Affairs Section of Public Safety Bureau of People's Government Tientsin for negotiations.

Clear local authorities avoiding recognition official status of Consuls and on all occasions when local Consuls approached them it was pointed out that they considered as ordinary citizens and can only deal in their individual capacities. For example, applications made by Consuls for licenses official cars returned with suggestion applications be made in individuals' names. Have obtained licenses for three official

---

[39a] Not printed.

cars in the individual names and working on two jeeps. Other Consuls also got licenses in name individual members staff.

SMYTH

811.20200(D)/2–2749 : Telegram

The Consul General at Peiping (Clubb) to the Secretary of State

PEIPING, February 27, 1949.
[Received February 27—2 : 11 a. m.]

315. USIS this morning received as specific addressee copy of mimeographed communication "Tung No. 1" February 27 sealed and bearing signatures Yeh Chien-ying and Tan Cheng in respective capacities Director and Vice Director Peiping Military Affairs Control Commission, in translation as follows :

"In view circumstances present military period, all foreign news agencies and correspondents (literally, reporters) may alike not carry on activities in this municipality, and all foreign nationals may not operate newspapers or magazines in this municipality.

"Therefore, this commission especially informs the United States Information Service now at Peiping to cease activities of issuance of news file from this date, and all foreign news agencies and correspondents of foreign newspapers and magazines to cease activities of collection of news and dispatching of news telegrams from this date. It is expected that there will be observance (of the above) without infractions."

In light this official notification, USIS is of course stopping immediately issuance news file, pending possible later modification official position this regard. It is understood same official notification has been addressed particularly to all local foreign correspondents.

Sent Department 315, Nanking 225, Canton 10, Shanghai 247.

CLUBB

125.7146/2–2849 : Telegram

The Consul General at Peiping (Clubb) to the Secretary of State

PEIPING, February 28, 1949—4 p. m.
[Received 8 : 45 p. m.]

322. Re Contel 282, February 23. At meeting Consuls February 25 decided since situation consular gates bettering, result sit[uation] same before save Communist soldiers now in place police, *démarche* by Consulates unnecessary. Generally agreed advisable due course express authorities assumption [garble] police not soldiers temporary emergency and that police if anyone would return. Agreement also on indirect approach to Mayor Yeh Chien-ying had elapsed, with takeover

former Foreign Office, new approach should be made via Foreign Nationals Affairs Office. All now submit severally but identical notes requesting this courtesy call. I have presented application. On request subordinate official, indicated [*omitted?*] official position on application, noting request made as ordinary foreign citizen. This accepted. Also stated this time tell chief other instructions discuss with responsible authority important matters, requested be advised procedure.

CLUBB

893.00/3–449 : Telegram

The Consul General at Peiping (Clubb) to the Secretary of State

PEIPING, March 4, 1949—10 a. m.
[Received March 3—11:14 p. m.]

350. ReContel 201, February 9. Although phone communications with Yenching [and] Tsinghua have been restored for about 2 weeks, movements foreigners that general area still under restriction. Foreigners Tsinghua are able come in town with passes (now required for passage through all gates) while Yenching foreigners are confined campus by request Communist authorities, this nominally for their protection.

ECA personnel Peiping informed by Foreign Nationals Office they will be given travel passes when ready to leave. Foreign businessmen who obtained travel passes Bureau Police Tientsin for trip here discovered Peiping police uninstructed, therefore unable issue passes. Americans successfully returned Tientsin but reported back by phone travel to Tientsin without at least Tientsin pass would get into difficulties since controls worse than before.

Oldtime employee Mukden Consulate planning return Mukden confirms general impression travel to Manchuria more difficult than elsewhere.

CLUBB

125.7146/3–849 : Telegram

The Consul General at Peiping (Clubb) to the Secretary of State

PEIPING, March 8, 1949—4 p. m.
[Received March 8—9:12 a. m.]

368. ReContels 329, February 28 [*March 1*], and 347, March 4.[40] Consulate General received request yesterday from British Consul in

---

[40] Neither printed.

view present inacceptability coded messages for transmittal commercial facilities, Contel 362, March 8,[41] there be arranged if feasible transmit by American network of official British messages Tientsin, Peiping, prefaced by code word SPECIAL. Though this done in past under Nationalists, situation is now to be considered different, station now maintained only by temporary sufferance on basis my statement that traffic [limited?] to American official messages only; if granted British under present conditions, presumably should be under moral obligation grant same other Consuls and granting such facilities probably bring closer still date closure particularly since security all officials both ends would keep secret fact of transmittal.

View all circumstances, believe inadvisable grant British request unless Communist approval received. Since practically infeasible obtain such, and approach moreover immediately bring to fore question continued use station, would recommend request be refused this time on grounds we have indicated station for American official use only and we find it desirable adhere that assurance unless Communists willing extend it which thought unlikely.

Please instruct.

Repeated Nanking, Shanghai.

CLUBB

893.00/3–949 : Telegram

The Consul General at Peiping (Clubb) to the Secretary of State

PEIPING, March 9, 1949—5 p. m.
[Received March 9—1 : 46 p. m.]

375. Re Contel 350, March 3[4]. Correcting report contained reference Contel re movement foreigners Yenching, note Americans Yenching stated yesterday phone foreigners there not confined campus although it suggested to them they should not proceed west hills (Contel 201, February 19[9]), that restriction their moves due inability to date obtain passes for Peiping city gates but it is felt passes forthcoming near future.

Official Peiping police bureau called March 5 own volition to inform passes for travel Peiping-Tientsin were obtainable that bureau by application 1 day in advance. Brown [42] Tientsin stated by phone yesterday it takes approximately 5 days to obtain passes Tientsin-Peiping (Brown's own application now pending 5 days).

Above policeman also asked whether Consulate had recently been troubled by armed soldiers endeavoring enter compound or by persons

---

[41] Not printed.
[42] Willard O. Brown, Consul at Tientsin.

desiring borrow articles (well-known Communist habit which must be said usually followed by return articles borrowed). Suggest this apparent solicitude may be another indication changing Communist attitude respecting foreigners and particularly Consulates, Peiping. Repeated Nanking, Shanghai and Canton.

CLUBB

125.7146/3–849 : Telegram

The Secretary of State to the Consul General at Peiping (Clubb)

WASHINGTON, March 11, 1949—6 p. m.

119. Urtel 368 March 8. Dept concurs recommendation last paragraph reftel but since circumstances may arise making desirable transmission occasional coded message urgent nature behalf your consular colleagues Dept prefers not instruct but leave matter your discretion.[43]

ACHESON

893.00B/3–1949 : Telegram

The Consul General at Tientsin (Smyth) to the Secretary of State

TIENTSIN, March 19, 1949—1 p. m.
[Received March 21—5 : 05 a. m.]

144. Methodist and American Board Missions report that during past few weeks Communist agents have been active in their schools. In Methodist school 5 Communist girls attend daily and have private talks with students; school classes now begin and end with Communist songs of anti-foreign nature; students formerly attentive and friendly now growing inattentive and somewhat sullen. American Board reports its school being influenced by Communist propaganda and American teachers not welcomed as before. Students' energies and interest being focused on Communist meetings and away from studies. Communists paying particular attention to brighter students with leadership qualities. Both missions report evangelical work in Tientsin not directly interfered with so far, but their Chinese pastors who have recently made inspection trips from Tientsin to small mission stations in countryside report a falling off in mission activity due to Communist propaganda and actions, though apparently no direct hostile acts. American Board representative reports that Communist leaders in poorer section of Tientsin where his mission located are of inferior education and status and therefore more bigoted and ignorant in the denunciation of "imperialism" and "colonialism"; their

---

[43] In telegram No. 839, May 16, noon, the Consul General informed the Department that he had informed the British Consulate that British code messages would be accepted in case of emergency (125.7146/5–1649).

bitterness has result of making their audience more apprehensive of contacts with his mission.

Both missions are of opinion, from presently unfolding pattern, that prospects for mission work under Communists are not bright.

SMYTH

893.741/3–1949 : Telegram

The Consul General at Peiping (Clubb) to the Secretary of State

PEIPING, March 19, 1949.
[Received March 19—3 : 26 a. m.]

437. Following regulations published in Peiping *Chieh Tang Pao* March 17 covering telegraphic and telephonic communications with places outside liberated area effective March 16:

"Article 1. For convenience of people and merchants, present measures are especially enacted.

Article 2. Telegraph communications as mentioned in present measures include telegraph and telephone messages.

Article 3. Places to which telegraph and telephone communications are open will be announced by North China Telegraph and Telephone Administration in form of public proclamation.

Article 4. Both cablegrams and airgrams shall be handled by telegraph and telephone administration. In case it is necessary to establish exclusive radio station for maintaining connections between sea and land, between land and air, application for permission to establish it may be made and radio station shall be under control telegraph and telephone bureau in locality concerned.

Article 5. In sending telegrams and making telephone calls, following provisions shall not be violated :

a. Sending of telegrams shall be limited to plain language.

b. Telephone calls shall be limited to use ordinary language, and use of secret language and transmission of telegraph code numbers not permitted.

c. In sending telegrams and making telephone calls, state secrets shall not be divulged.

d. Ships radio stations are required to stop telegraph and telephone communications after ships enter into harbor and anchorage, and radio stations in airplanes are required to suspend telegraph and telephone communications after landing on airfield.

Article 6. In case provisions of any of paragraphs of article 5 violated, Telegraph and Telephone Bureau concerned may refuse to accept, or refuse to transmit, his telegram or stop his telephone calls, and person shall be punished according to circumstances of his violation.

Article 7. Telegraph and telephone charges shall be paid by telegram sender and telephone caller respectively. System of pre-payment of charges for reply telegrams is temporarily suspended.

Article 8. Present measures shall become effective on day their promulgation.

Sent Department; repeated Nanking 279, Canton 22, Shanghai 308.

CLUBB

125.7146/3–1949 : Telegram

The Consul General at Peiping (Clubb) to the Secretary of State

PEIPING, March 19, 1949—5 p. m.
[Received March 20—12 : 46 a. m.]

441. ReContel 437, March 19. Belgian Consul states he received call today from representatives Military Control Commission who checked passports and whether Consul possessed arms or radio (whether transmitting station or receiver unindicated by interpreter). Reported, but still unconfirmed, British Consul also visited.

That fact and new regulations particularly would seem indicate move on this station may be near.

In view provision regulations that application be made for commercial radio stations, would Department consider it advisable this office take cognizance those regulations (added to those February 2) and make move obtain formal permission operate station as "Consulate General"? Communist approval, of course, unlikely. Alternative would be await move from Communist side. Our position would be stronger if "recognized". Propose as partial cover in any event ask interview responsible official early date to discuss "matters touching upon Consulate General itself" but should appreciate early instructions whether Department would approve such application for permission if it seems advisable to this office.

Sent Department; repeated Nanking, Shanghai.

CLUBB

125.7146/3–2049 : Telegram

The Consul General at Peiping (Clubb) to the Secretary of State

PEIPING, March 20, 1949—1 p. m.
[Received March 20.]

444. ReContel 441, March 19.⁴⁴ Representative Military Control Commission last evening called consular compound and questioned gateman re various matters pertaining to Consulate including radio. In accord standing instructions, gateman replied uninformed, suggested officer should visit during office hours. Latter stated he would return 0900 Monday.

---

⁴⁴ Not printed.

British Consular [*Consul*] reports still no visit this [*his*] office. Sent Department, repeated Nanking and Shanghai.

CLUBB

125.7146/3–2149 : Telegram

The Consul General at Peiping (*Clubb*) *to the Secretary of State*

PEIPING, March 21, 1949—3 p. m.
[Received March 21—6 : 35 a. m.]

450. ReContel 444, March 20. Received scheduled visit today from "inspector" Peiping-Tientsin garrison headquarters who desired be provided March 23 with following information : List US and alien personnel including family members Americans with basic statistical information, whether Consulate has radio station, all list official and private arms.

This information being prepared for him as requested.

Inspector made no demands and gave no indication re radio station. When he returns, am considering asking whether registration station required and if so what procedure should be followed. Note, however, he obviously only minor official.

CLUBB

121.67/3–2149 : Telegram

The Secretary of State to the Consul General at Peiping (*Clubb*)[45]

WASHINGTON, March 21, 1949—3 p. m.

140. Urtel unnumbered [*129*] March 6 economic conditions since Jan. 15.[46] For action Tientsin Shanghai, would ConGen consider feasible attempt send courier commercial vessels Shanghai–Taku Bar under present conditions. Is pouch exchange Taku Bar or alternate procedure possible. Dept anxious reestablish direct communications. Your opinion requested necessity sending two couriers for security.

ACHESON

125.7146/3–2349 : Telegram

The Consul General at Peiping (*Clubb*) *to the Secretary of State*

PEIPING, March 23, 1949—noon.
[Received March 23—1 : 58 a. m.]

462. ReContel 444, March 21. Requested information was handed inspector 1100 hours today under cover unaddressed memo signed by

---

[45] Repeated to the Consul General at Tientsin as telegram No. 60.
[46] Not printed.

me as Consul General. As regards radio station, it was confirmed Consulate General possessed one "which was of course established according to a pertinent agreement".

Sent Department, repeated Nanking, Shanghai and Canton.

CLUBB

125.9376/3–2349 : Telegram

The Consul General at Tientsin (Smyth) to the Secretary of State

TIENTSIN, March 23, 1949—4 p. m.
[Received March 25—6:47 a. m.]

160. Inquiry made today of local postal administration by Vice Consul Jenkins regarding nondelivery of mail for Consular personnel which arrived Tientsin about 1 month ago. He was told delay occasioned by censorship with view of intercepting any "reactionary" communication; censorship corps slow in being formed, but promised that all mail not inimical to interests local government would be delivered. He was told that fact mail addressed to Consulate was irrelevant; however, we believe this probably causes delay because of censorship; mail addressed to homes may possibly escape this procedure.

In our telegram 147, March 19,[47] we mentioned apparent nontampering with mail between Tientsin and Peiping. Not known whether this will continue to be the case.

SMYTH

893.741/3–1949 : Telegram

The Secretary of State to the Consul General at Peiping (Clubb)[48]

WASHINGTON, March 23, 1949—7 p. m.

151. Urtel 441 Mar 19. Dept notes Mar 17 reg[ulation]s (ur 437 Mar 19) provide for establishment exclusive radio stations only for sea–land and air–land communications, such stations under control Commie Tel and Tel Bureau and transmission restricted plain language. In view these circumstances Dept of opinion unwise now seek formal permission basis these regs operate station as "Consulate General" and believes your proposed interview responsible official discuss matter better course. However view ur familiarity changing local circumstances Dept leaves final decision ur discretion.

ACHESON

---

[47] Not found in Department of State files.
[48] Repeated to the Ambassador in China and to the Consul General at Shanghai as telegrams Nos. 385 and 527, respectively.

125.7146/3–2449 : Telegram

The Consul General at Peiping (Clubb) to the Secretary of State

PEIPING, March 24, 1949—5 p. m.
[Received March 24—7 : 16 a. m.]

475. Re Contel 462, March 23. It is of course now even probable that there will be developments within next few days affecting Peiping radio station. Therefore request prior authorization present at my discretion to Commie authorities Peiping, in best manner possible, position re Consular offices located Commie areas along lines indicated Contel 415, March 15 [49] and Embtel 90, March 19.[50] As indicated Consulate's reference telegram, believe this would be natural first step and such action would not prejudice other than favorably any other action US Govt might later undertake. I should propose inform Consular colleagues, for coordination our actions where possible for mutual support.

Approach would be based on assumption contained final sentence Embtel 90, that it should be made clear to Commies it is advantageous have good relations with USA (and in even greater degree than they get advantage from USSR) and disadvantageous otherwise. This CCP realization would be entering wedge for Chinese type of Titoism.

Re Contel 456, March 22,[51] propose take up early date matter Deptel 60, February 3.[52]

Note that character Commie action re Peiping radio will of course be interesting indication Commie basic attitude re Consulates at this stage.

Chinese source informed me March 22 it was reported Commies presently negotiating with USSR for gasoline but that progress negotiations hampered by certain "conditions" set forth by Soviets as prerequisite. Nature conditions unknown.[53]

Repeated Nanking, Canton, Shanghai, Hong Kong, Tientsin.

CLUBB

125.7146/3–2849 : Telegram

The Secretary of State to the Consul General at Peiping (Clubb)

WASHINGTON, March 28, 1949—6 p. m.

162. B–3 report from Shanghai recd via controlled American source states Commies Peiping suspect AmConGen of harboring Kmt "war

---

[49] Vol. IX, p. 913.
[50] Not found in Department of State files.
[51] Not printed.
[52] Vol. IX, p. 11.
[53] The Secretary of State informed the Consul General at Peiping in telegram No. 159, March 25, 9 p. m. : "Dept authorizes in ur discretion steps outlined ur 475 Mar 24 and assumes if desirable you will coordinate action with Tientsin."

criminals". Source of opinion report may indicate possible pretext for increased restrictions on ConGen.

ACHESON

121.67/3–2949 : Telegram

The Consul General at Tientsin (Smyth) to the Secretary of State

TIENTSIN, March 29, 1949—11 a. m.
[Received March 31—5 : 10 a. m.]

180. Deptel 60, March 21 [54] received March 26. On March 28 ConGen informally approached official Foreign Affairs section Tientsin Military Control Committee regarding possibility officer this ConGen exchange mail with courier at Taku Bar. Official stated that under present condition of nonrecognition Consulates, such special privileges as courier facilities would be in contravention present Committee policy. He suggested use ordinary mail. We had previously discussed with this official questions of receipt by ConGen of only small part of mail since it reasonable assume had been addressed to us and he had replied this matter concerned postal authorities and was one in which he could not intervene. He restated on March 28 he in no position to expedite our receipt mail through regular postal channels.

Attitude authorities precludes resumption of any type courier service at present.

SMYTH

125.7146/4–149 : Telegram

The Consul General at Peiping (Clubb) to the Secretary of State

PEIPING, April 1, 1949.
[Received April 2—1 : 54 a. m.]

530. April 1, yesterday submitted to Foreign Nationals Affairs Office Peiping following application :

"Acting under instructions from the United States Government, I would request a meeting to discuss with appropriate high local authority questions pertaining to the American Consulate General located at Peiping.

"It is noted that unusual difficulties have developed as respects the performance by the American Consular offices in Peiping, Tientsin and Mukden of their official functions.

"It is earnestly hoped that the Chinese Communist authorities will promptly take appropriate steps to the end that American Consular establishments in the areas under their control shall be afforded normal facilities for carrying on their normal functions, those facilities

---

[54] Same as telegram No. 140 to Peiping, p. 1072.

to include, as basic, the usual contacts with the local authorities in their consular districts, the postal and commercial telegraph facilities regularly accorded consular establishments for confidential communication with their own governments, banking channels for the transmittal of official funds, and facilities for official travel.

"It is emphasized that the United States Government is assured, on the basis of international law and practice, that the functioning of consular officials involves no question of legal recognition of governments. The Chinese Communist authorities will appreciate that the consular function is one with recognition and general acceptance in the international law and practice as having to do with promotion of general international trade and intercourse, but as being without reference to the question of recognition between states.

"Because of the circumstance that 2 months have already elapsed since the takeover by the Communist side of the administration of Peiping, but the position of the aforemention consular offices in relationship to the local authorities remains unsettled, it would be much appreciated if I could obtain an early interview with appropriate high local authority for a discussion of this matter in detail, to enable me to report appropriately to my government."

Sent Nanking 331, Canton 37, Shanghai 371, Hong Kong. By mail to Tientsin.

CLUBB

893.504/4–1349 : Telegram

The Consul General at Tientsin (Smyth) to the Secretary of State

TIENTSIN, April 13, 1949—noon.
[Received April 15—4 : 22 a. m.]

238. Since Communist occupation Tientsin 3 months ago foreign companies have had considerable difficulties with labor. Communist authorities have consistently taken side of labor. American firms which have had most trouble are Texas and Karagheusian although nearly all have had some labor trouble.

White, local manager Texaco, in letter dated April 7 addressed to Bieling, Texas manager Shanghai, described Texas labor troubles here. Letter sent by ordinary mail to Shanghai. I suggest ConGen Shanghai obtain copy that letter from Bieling and send copies to Department. If letter does not arrive Shanghai, please inform us and we will summarize.

In dealing with labor troubles of foreign firms, Communist authorities willing to mediate but their decisions very biased in favor of labor. If firm not willing accept decision, Communist authorities then say firm at liberty to settle direct with laborers. As this means firm at mercy of laborers, without police protection, result is firms accept mediation, however unreasonable. Karagheusian has had particularly difficult time.

Number of foreigners, including a few Americans, have been haled into People's Court on labor and other matters. Some decisions fair, but generally biased in favor Chinese. Report on People's Court will be telegraphed shortly.

Sent Dept; repeated Nanking as 154, Shanghai as 159 and Peiping as 101.

SMYTH

702.0093/4–1449 : Telegram

The Consul General at Peiping (Clubb) to the Secretary of State

PEIPING, April 14, 1949.
[Received April 14—3:16 a. m.]

611. ReContel 530, April 1. The following note was addressed under date April 12 jointly by French, American, Belgian, Italian, Dutch, British Consuls and Diplomatic Representatives Peiping to Peiping Mayor Yeh Chien-ying:

"We have honor invite your attention to circumstance undoubtedly already known to you that we severally represent in Peiping our respective Governments in capacity Consular Officers. We have during 2 months since occupation this town by Chinese Communist Army been without those usual contacts with local authorities which would make it possible for us to take up direct with those authorities outstanding official matters of importance and our several attempts to establish such contacts through medium of Aliens Affairs Office have been fruitless.

"We therefore send this joint communication directly to you as the responsible local official to whom we should ordinarily address ourselves.

"Although statutes [*status of?*] Consular office would of course be affected by an international war in which its own country and the country of indication were opposing belligerents, both in international law and practice Consular offices may and usually do continue to perform their regular functions during periods either civil war or revolution. You will be aware that this principle can be supported by ample precedents adduced from records history both in China and many other countries of world. Particularly in view of early public announcements from Chinese Communist side to effect that foreign persons and foreign enterprises in areas coming under Communist control would receive full measure of protection and that they could and should carry on as usual, many of our nationals remained behind in north China to pursue their ordinary vocations. It is understood that the Chinese Communist authorities are not opposed in principle to foreign contacts, whether social or commercial, but your attention is called to circumstance that in practice in Peiping there have developed to date unusual difficulties for both foreign enterprises and foreign officials. The two difficulties are interrelated.

"Functions Consular officers are part of whole complex of social and commercial relationships which comprehends international travel facilities, business contacts, banking and foreign exchange, international shipping and shipping documents, passports and visas, protection of foreign lives and property, etc. Foreign businessmen and others interested in various types of endeavor in Communist-controlled areas naturally expect receive usual services assistance and advice their representative in area; those representatives are present in north China but to date there are certain facilities which they still lack for full performance of their legitimate functions. Communist authorities in Peiping have, it is true, set up Alien Affairs Office for express purpose handling problems foreign nationals but that office itself states that it is not authorized deal with official matters which might be presented to it by Consular officers. It is to be noted moreover that such offices naturally cannot take place of foreign nationals' own Consular officials, cannot (as simple examples) issue passports to those foreign nationals, give visas for entry foreign countries, assist in connection with trade and banking international character or report trade opportunities to prospective foreign merchants residing abroad.

"Certain public statements and promulgation foreign trade regulations indicated desire to promote international commerce with north China. Experience shown that international intercourse is generally facilitated where local representatives of parties concerned are in position meet together on normal basis. It may perhaps be felt that inasmuch as local Consulates still are in position have contacts with their own nationals and issue passports, visas and shipping documents where required such arrangement suffice meet needs of situation. Such, however, is not case for Consular establishments generally are accorded certain additional facilities for carrying on their normal functions.

"The main facilities which we now lack are primarily those usual contacts with local authorities which may be required for the performance of our duties and also postal and commercial telegraphic facilities for the confidential communication of the Consular officials with our own Governments, banking facilities for handling official funds and facilities for official travel within our Consular districts. At present there exist certain shortcomings in these several respects. It is in an effort to effect an amelioration of this situation that we now jointly address ourselves to you in regard to the several matters in point. Having reference to what has already been said above regarding legal position of Consular offices, it is noted that only explanation which has been received from local administrative organs for refusing to deal with Peiping Consular establishments in normal way is that Chinese Communist side is without diplomatic relations. We would emphasize at this point that we are assured that Consular function by international law and practice while having to do with such international matters as promotion of trade and intercourse and with such affairs of mutual interest as assistance and protection of nationals residing abroad is quite without reference to question of formal recognition between states which matter is subject for action of national governments.

"It would be much appreciated if your office would take appropriate action in respect to the subject matter of this letter either to end that needed adjustments be made or give us severally or jointly an early opportunity to discuss this whole matter in order that usual social and commercial interchanges which commonly take place between friendly peoples shall thus be facilitated.

Please accept, Sir, assurances of our high consideration."

Sent Department, repeated Nanking 381, Canton 50, Shanghai 413, Tientsin by mail.

CLUBB

125.7143/4–1549 : Telegram

The Consul General at Peiping (Clubb) to the Secretary of State

PEIPING, April 15, 1949—4 p. m.
[Received April 15—6 : 24 a. m.]

625. Deptel 162, March 28. On night April 13–14 residence USIS director's assistant Chang Tung and other USIS employee Wang Jui-hui was visited by party comprising 2 police, 1 soldier, 7 Communist Party workers. Party was met at door by Wang who, after identifying himself, was told return to quarters and remain there, that matter did not concern him. Quarters Chang thoroughly searched and Chang himself taken away at 2 in morning. Three guards were stationed over residence yesterday and phone inquiries made by USIS when employees failed appear elicited information from unidentified persons Wang was sick and Chang had been caused depart Peiping suddenly on business. Messenger check however disclosed presence 3 guards at gate and showed general nature situation.

Wang returned to work this morning, stated Chang still unreturned but Chang's wife remaining on premises. Guards now withdrawn.

Wang reports he was told by Party member "case very important" without indication why.

Chang was formerly employed by OWI [55] and went from OWI service directly into USIS.

Information obtained from Communist seeking information through alien governmental employee indicated Communists suspicious of Consulate Japanese transcasts [*translator*] Sakimura, considering him "spy".

Same source indicated Communists interested in suspected radio transmittal by Consulate of messages for other Peiping Consulates.

Although doubt there could be discovered slightest evidence to support charge of "harboring Kmt war criminals", that Communists would be able turn up employees with BIS connections of course possible.

Repeated Nanking 389, OffEmb Canton 54, Shanghai 422.

CLUBB

---

[55] Office of War Information.

702.0093/4–1849 : Telegram

The Consul General at Peiping (Clubb) to the Secretary of State

PEIPING, April 18, 1949—5 p. m.
[Received April 18—6 : 38 a. m.]

646. ReContel 611, April 13[*14*]. English and Chinese versions of Consuls' note to mayor, dispatched by express mail April 13, both returned French ConGen (first signator) by messenger today, without comment. Consul meeting tomorrow.

Note significance current peace talks might possibly incidentally bear for position consular offices, given particularly peace settlement of sorts. Note also that Communist side probably desires force *de jure* recognition of its regime prior to permitting regularization position Consuls, and would use its "nonrecognition" policy as lever for that purpose if possible. Either continuation civil war or Communist peace "in Peiping pattern" would presumably [be?] alike soon after [in] bringing new developments for consular offices this area.

Sent Department 646, passed Nanking 402, OffEmb Canton 61, Shanghai 433.

CLUBB

702.0093/4–2149 : Telegram

The Consul General at Peiping (Clubb) to the Secretary of State

PEIPING, April 21, 1949—7 p. m.
[Received April 22—1 : 18 a. m.]

658. [To Nanking:] April 19, 3 p. m. ReContel 646, April 18.[56] Consulate today decided against move now considering it probably be fruitless. Significance US manner Communist return Consulate's note unclear but consensus opinion present peace negotiations if bear fruit might affect Consulate's position. One official remarked reliable report that senior Yenching professor who advising Communist foreign affairs proposed Consulates' function Communist areas essentially unnecessary, matters handled as in Soviet with trade channelized through government organs. If argue that acceptance this doctrine disregards presence in China consider[able] foreign colony certain centers, it might be deduced corollary Communist Prop [*sic*] situation envisages ultimate reduction foreign colony to zero.

Note exit permits granted by Communists with speed, entry permits granted only isolated instances. It must be concluded strict adherence present line would be one natural feature of continued residence of Communist China in Soviet satellite camp.

---

[56] See also telegram No. 654, April 19, 11 a. m., from the Consul General at Peiping, p. 953.

Considered same meeting: 1—Communists perused communication in detail (it was returned in new cover) and possibly gave it serious consideration on high levels; 2—Formal statement or move re Consulates is expected near future; 3—Possibly with matter brought attention Communist senior authorities adjustment in practice some of points brought to Communist attention expected.

Sent Nanking 410, repeated Department Canton 65, Shanghai 453.

CLUBB

125.7146/5–349 : Telegram

The Consul General at Peiping (Clubb) to the Secretary of State

PEIPING, May 3, 1949—3 p. m.
[Received May 3—2:45 p. m.]

752. There have been no appreciable changes in respect to position Consulates Peiping since return joint note (reContel 410, April 19 [57]). Consulates still have guards posted at gates. This office has experienced trouble with such guards only on two or three occasions when either guards had just been changed or some local misunderstanding caused temporary tightening up, but has had better treatment in this regard than Italians or British.

Presence guards over Consulate General naturally intimidates Chinese visitors and probably keeps number of them away.

This Consulate General April 24 received request from two PLA [58] personnel for permission install air raid warning signal on wireless mast. Informed them orally that Consulate General had previously refused similar request from Kmt forces on grounds USA maintains neutral position respect Chinese civil war and that our position was same at present. I asked that any formal request along these lines should be presented in official communication. Personnel concerned indicated they would consider matter and departed and have not returned.

Consulate still has operating permit covered one motor car. No such permits provided either for DALS, Assistant Military Attaché or AstALUSNA. Other Consulate likewise limited one operating permit. Heretofore all requests by Consulate personnel for permits enable them pass through city gates into suburbs have been refused but Vice Consul Farrior has now received permit enabling him make 1-day trip Tsinghua University next weekend. Six foreign PUMC personnel have just received passes valid 1 May for travel Yenching, Tsinghua, Summer Palace.

Persistent anti-American campaign has had as one result stoning of foreigners by Chinese (usually children). To date there have been

---

[57] Same as telegram No. 658, April 21, *supra.*
[58] People's Liberation Army (Communist).

thus struck 6 members American official family. Some incidents have been reported to police or gate guards, AP [*but?*] authorities give appearance of being concerned with matter. Plan send note to Mayor on subject near future.

CLUBB

125.9376/5–749 : Telegram

The Consul General at Tientsin (Smyth) to the Secretary of State

TIENTSIN, May 7, 1949—noon.
[Received May 9—6 : 54 a. m.]

292. Since Communist take-over Consul General has been guided by instructions contained in secret telegram from Embassy [( ]believed circular telegram January 4 [59]) to refrain from taking steps which might constitute or be interpreted as recognition regime particularly to refrain from addressing either formal or informal communications to new officials. Consequently we have taken up all matters orally and informally with local officials. Conversely local officials appear to be under similar instructions since written communications addressed to local officials by your Tientsin Consular colleagues have all been returned.

Consul General however notes that Clubb at Peiping is addressing written communications to new officials and signing as American Consul General. If instructions contained in reference telegram have been amended, we would appreciate being informed as we feel that practice of two Consular Offices should be consistent.

Repeated Nanking 183, Peiping 125.

SMYTH

125.9376/5–749 : Telegram

The Secretary of State to the Consul General at Tientsin (Smyth) [60]

WASHINGTON, May 13, 1949—2 p. m.

98. Dept perceives no objection as general rule to Consuls in Commie areas addressing Commie authorities by letter signed either in personal capacity or over official title (urtel 292 May 7 repeated Nanking 183, Peiping 125), but such authorities shld be addressed personally by name without inclusion official titles. However Dept believes that where circumstances permit it preferable communicate by means memoranda (either unsigned, initialed, or signed with or without consular title) delivered appropriate Commie authorities by consular officers.

ACHESON

---

[59] Not found in Department of State files.
[60] Repeated to the Consul General at Peiping as No. 278.

893.76/5–1649 : Telegram

The Consul General at Tientsin (Smyth) to the Secretary of State

TIENTSIN, May 16, 1949—5 p. m.
[Received May 19—9:45 a. m.]

321. Burdett, British Consul General, tells me confidentially during past week Communists shown great interest opening radio with Hong Kong. Communists forced But[terfield and] Swire vessel in port last week to send number of commercial messages to Hong Kong Government radio but not known whether received or forwarded. Burdett reported details to his Embassy in code via our Peiping radio and matter probably discussed with our Embassy.

Burdett says few days ago, go-betweens for Communists asked him send message to Hong Kong Government urging it to agree maintain radio contact with Communist radio here. Burdett replied must take up with his Embassy and under present rules could only send in plain. Communists proposed he send message to Embassy in Communist military code which he agreed to do. I believe he was most unwise in agreeing send message in Communist code and feel he should have raised point sending in his code.

Question Communists communicating with outside via Hong Kong involves International Telecommunications Union to which British adhere. Suggest matter be discussed with British Government.

Recommend effort be made to establish more united front with British and other governments than heretofore case. In appointed bank matter (see other telegrams) 2 British, 1 Belgian banks accepted appointments although American and French banks not appointed. Suggest before Shanghai falls some common action be decided on before question arises. Communists obviously trying play off British against us and seem to have succeeded somewhat.

Sent Department 321; repeated Nanking 202; Shanghai 224; Peiping 140 and Hong Kong.

SMYTH

125.9371/5–1749 : Telegram

The Consul General at Tientsin (Smyth) to the Secretary of State

TIENTSIN, May 17, 1949—4 a. m.
[Received May 19—9:39 a. m.]

329. Reourtel 320, May 16.[61] If Communists endeavor take over any of our 4 ex-German houses or ex-Jap consular property acquired under

---

[61] Not printed.

bilateral agreement, [62] I feel we should react with some positive action. US has suffered very serious loss of prestige through Communist confinement our Consulate General staff Mukden [by] Communists which fact is generally known in Communist areas. Throwing us out of houses or taking over ex-Jap property here would involve further aid striking loss of prestige and would make position of Consulate General staff here difficult if not impossible. I believe we should exercise patience with Communists but feel this policy should have limitations.

I recommend that if Communists show intention of taking over any of our houses or ex-Jap property to all of which we have full title, I be authorized to inform Communist authorities that such action would result in prompt closing of our Consulate General office and withdrawal of staff; it should be pointed out to Communists that thus far US Government has placed no restrictions on US trade with North China but that Communist action in question would place serious obstacles in way of such trade through absence of Consulate General to issue consular invoices; it should also be intimated that any Communist effort in such case to channel trade between Tientsin and US through Hong Kong would not succeed. In view of Communist desire for trade with US it must be made clear to Communists that action in question on their part would result in stoppage of such trade.

We hope Communists will not raise this question but we feel some course of action should be decided on previously in case they do.

Sent Department 329, repeated Nanking 206, Shanghai 228, Peiping 143.

SMYTH

125.7146/5–1849 : Telegram

The Consul General at Peiping (Clubb) to the Secretary of State

PEIPING, May 18, 1949—5 p. m.
[Received May 19—8 : 48 a. m.]

896. ReDeptel 278, May 13.[63] Respectfully invite attention Department to practical objections to rule that Communist authorities should be addressed by letter if at all only personally by name without inclusion official titles; (1) Letters exchanged between American and Communist side under present conditions where personal contacts absent would lose effectiveness where effectiveness already lacking in large degree in so far as title omitted by either side, (2) Communist organs Peiping have consistently emphasized necessity use Chinese at least as accompanying translation for written matters and elimination from

---

[62] Agreement between the United States and China for the sale of certain surplus war property, signed at Shanghai, August 30, 1946; Department of State, Office of the Foreign Liquidation Commissioner, *Report to Congress on Foreign Surplus Disposal*, October 1946, pp. 40–45.
[63] Same as telegram No. 98 to Tientsin, p. 1082.

text of all reference to official position or title would in Chinese letter give impression either disesteem or calculated rudeness and (3) that approach would be particularly incongruous where efforts consular officials recent months have been to get Communists acquiesce in Consuls' acting in full official capacity. Addressing either civil or military along lines reftel would probably prove less effective even than would otherwise be case.

Disadvantages which would follow adoption indicated procedure seem to promise no commensurate return or advantage. Noting Department indication that it is considered preferable communicate by means memo delivered appropriate Communist authorities, would note that experience Peiping has been that appropriate Communist authorities actually unapproachable. Effective delivery other than communication in letter form for present infeasible. Memo it is true can be given Aliens Affairs Office which has however proved only ineffective and unhelpful in respect to all matters concerning official functions consular officers.

For effective representations about matters such as position Embassy, Nanking (Contel 718, April 27 [64]) and Consulate, Mukden (Contel 735, April 30 [65]) representation should naturally be made either to highest Communist military level or highest level local authorities. Note American legal position during period Jap occupation North China was that consular officers might properly have contacts and negotiate with local authorities for performance their legitimate functions. By international law use of official titles of local or military officials would not in any event suggest recognition. Note further that with expanding control China it is desirable set up now system which will most effectively serve purpose providing communications channel with Communists for months ahead.

Believe adoption of policy handling matters on local *de facto* basis would be most suitable to both practical and legal requirements.

Sent Department; repeated Nanking 553, OffEmb Canton 124.

CLUBB

125.0093/5–2749 : Telegram

The Acting Secretary of State to the Consul General at Peiping
(Clubb)

WASHINGTON, May 27, 1949—3 p. m.

330. Ur [*Our*] 278 May 13 [66] and 299 May 17.[67] Dept desires leave greatest latitude possible consuls in Commie areas China exercise their

[64] Not printed.
[65] *Ante*, p. 955.
[66] Same as telegram No. 98 to Tientsin, p. 1082.
[67] *Ante*, p. 957.

judgment, discretion, dealing with new and unforeseeable circumstances which arise. Dept concurs consular officers may properly have contacts and negotiate with local authorities for performance their legitimate functions and believes it desirable insofar as permitted by local conditions that consular officers addressing written communications such authorities sign communications over their consular title. With respect to addressing such communications Dept believes use of (1) informal memoranda delivered in person to Alien Affairs Office or other appropriate auths (2) letters addressed such auths by name without title or (3) in cases where office addressed existed prior Commie takeover letters addressed to office without name of Commie official exercising duties of office offer adequate channels communication. For your info foregoing means communication used by consuls communicating with "Manchukuo" authorities. Dept notes no assurances exist that letters addressed Commie auths by name and title any more likely reach official so addressed and no indication this method address would be more productive of desired action than one of methods outlined above. Dept believes with Nanking (Embtel 1102 May 24 [68] rptd Peiping 179) important consideration is maintenance channel communications and has suggested forms of address above as possible means communication which contain no suggestion of recognition. However, recognition is more matter of intent than form and Dept has no desire limit Cons to use forms suggested if in using other forms it made clear no recognition intended.

WEBB

893.76/6–249 : Telegram

The Ambassador in China (Stuart) to the Secretary of State

NANKING, June 2, 1949—11 a. m.
[Received June 2—8 : 35 a. m.]

1172. We asked British Embassy this morning present status Commie efforts establish radio communication between Tientsin and Hong Kong (see Tientsin's 321, May 19 [*16*], to Department, repeated Nanking 202, Shanghai 224, Peiping 140, Hong Kong unnumbered). British admitted rather shamefacedly that communications were now open between Hong Kong and Tientsin and that no concessions had been extracted therefor. As result of Commie approach British Consul General [at] Tientsin, local British Embassy recommended to its Foreign Office this occasion be used to ameliorate conditions foreign consuls Tientsin, particularly privilege confidential communications. Subsequently British Embassy began receiving reports of re-establishment of wireless communication between Tientsin and Hong Kong and on

[68] *Ante*, p. 749.

inquiry of governor Hong Kong were informed Cable and Wireless Ltd. had gone ahead without consulting governor and on instruction from home office London to reestablish radio contact with Tientsin on basis Commie request. British Embassy here then promptly queried Foreign Office who admitted somewhat apologetically that official approval had been given without sufficient consideration of all aspects and that now it appeared too late to revoke agreement. Local British Embassy agreed that once communications established they should be permitted to continue, though deploring lost opportunity to extract concessions from Commies, particularly for our Consulates in north.

It may be of interest to ascertain what arrangements C and W has made for payment and how Tientsin hookup fits into international telegraphic arrangements. Hong Kong might try sending coded message to Tientsin via this channel as experiment. If accepted and delivered, might be useful channel for Department to communicate with Tientsin in code, one way traffic. It is assumed Tientsin can use such outgoing facilities for clear language messages at least. We agree with last paragraph Tientsin's telegram under reference and suggest Department may wish to raise with British in energetic manner this additional break of common front as one more evidence of Commies extracting advantages piecemeal from west without giving anything in return.

Sent Department 1172, Peiping 189, Hong Kong 30. Department pass Tientsin 36.

STUART

893.00B/6–449 : Telegram

The Consul General at Tientsin (Smyth) to the Secretary of State

TIENTSIN, June 4, 1949—11 a. m.
[Received June 6—11 a. m.]

385. Number Communist civil officials from Tientsin proceeded Shanghai to be ready on takeover to give benefit experience gained here. Tientsin has been guinea pig for Communists in foreign trade, business, industry and industrial labor, shipping and communications, banking, commercial taxation and many other matters. Communists came here straight from bushes with undeveloped policies and little experience except in rural areas. Their policies and practices here were developed slowly, by trial and error. This has been tough on Tientsin but should make things smoother in many ways in Shanghai. Speed with which Communists restoring shipping and communications Shanghai one example.

As matter interest, we understand Tientsin also guinea pig re consular radio. Communists apparently expected our consular radio to be used to their disadvantage through transmission what they considered "bad reports". However, reports in plain language over consular radio to Department (until radio closed few days after fall Tientsin), and released by Department to press and broadcasters, surprised and favorably impressed Communists, particularly ConGen report that conduct Communist occupation troops "exemplary"; this radio bulletin which was broadcast, commented on several times by Communist official mentioned ourtel 74, January 16.[69] Our request continue operation to Foreign Affairs official (ourtel 104, January 21), referred to higher authorities, not acted on before brief deadline set by occupying military authorities expired. Understand our compliance with Communist regulations re radio (which we considered best course action in circumstances), plus advantages to them from favorable reports on conduct of Communist troops, important factor in later Communist decision to allow Peiping radio to operate. Fact that Communist subsequent takeover Peiping peaceful, not by hard fighting as at Tientsin, also conducive to more considered action.

Unfortunately, once our radio closed, Communists could not, without loss face, allow resumption.

SMYTH

119.2/6–1149 : Telegram

The Consul General at Peiping (Clubb) to the Secretary of State

PEIPING, June 11, 1949—11 a. m.
[Received June 11—3 : 44 a. m.]

990. Retel 161, June 1, from Shanghai [70] asking report on tactics used retain radio. Procedure involved several steps. Shortly after issuance order February 2 by Peiping-Tientsin Defense Hdqrs treating *inter alia* matter radio stations' operation, this office had Chinese employee telephone to ask them receive me (as Consul General) "on official business". Hdqrs refused on 2 separate occasions without asking nature of business.

On February 9 in discussion with former member Foreign Office known be in contact with Communists, I brought up question Consular radio, said it functioned under terms pertinent agreement, was used for official purposes only, that I would of course not be in position deliver over Govt property but if local authorities desired discuss matter with me in any of its aspects should be glad do so (Contel 205, February 10 to Dept). Official in question in due course reported back Communists (understood be mayor's office) had said informally I could

---

[69] Not printed.
[70] Not found in Department of State files.

use radio for time being (Contel 216, February 11). I made no subsequent approach Defense Hdqrs.

New regulations were promulgated March 16 governing telecommunications and giving procedure for established radio stations (Contel 437, March 19).

Received visit from representatives Defense Hdqrs only March 21 when they requested that I supply certain information, including whether Consulate possessed "radio station". March 23, I supplied written statement in affirmative stating incidentally, however, that station "was of course established according to a pertinent agreement" (Contel 462, March 23 to Dept). Despite alarms and excursions, no further approach has been made Consulate in this regard.

In Contel 392, March 11,[71] I suggested to Dept possibility Communists permitted continued operation because Soviets might likewise be operating station. Soviet operations still unconfirmed.

Recommend as basic approach this and similar questions that it be assumed Communists do not intend application any promulgated regulations, or ordinances to Consulates unless it is clearly so stipulated or indicated or there is formal communication or visit conveying that information. Reurtel final paragraph, this Consulate's procedure in similar circumstances therefore would be first to check if possible through reliable intermediary to determine whether Communists interpret provisions regulations as applicable official US Govt radio, otherwise send them official letter regarding matter or await their approach. It may be assumed in first instance they are aware of existence Consulate radio. It may be assumed further that if they desire take action against that radio they will probably proceed to Consulate to take up matter direct. Stipulation in cited regulations possibly refers simply to Chinese Govt and private radio stations and not to foreign govt stations: For one thing, organs foreign govts Communist China are currently "unrecognized".

For further background reference, express belief Communists are desirous avoiding "incidents" or "cases" involving foreign consulates, especially at present juncture.

Suggest Dept repeat Contel 205, February 10 to Shanghai for reference.

Sent Dept 990, repeated Shanghai 659, Nanking 663.

CLUBB

---

[71] Not printed.

119.2/6—1549 : Telegram

The Ambassador in China (Stuart) to the Secretary of State

NANKING, June 15, 1949—2 p. m.
[Received June 15—8 : 04 a. m.]

1289. Reference Peiping telegram 990 to Department June 11. Embassy would appreciate résumé origin China network, agreements with Nationalist Government, et cetera which Department feels would be valuable in any negotiations with Communists for retention of network.

Sent Department; repeated Shanghai 700, AmEmb Canton 538.

STUART

893.00B/6–1649 : Telegram

The Consul General at Peiping (Clubb) to the Secretary of State

PEIPING, June 16, 1949—6 p. m.
[Received June 17—10 : 26 a. m.]

1026. ReContels 970, June 10 and 1021, June 16.[72] Wu Yueh-tsung (W. Y. Wu incorrect) and Shen (not Sheng) Ti-lan, Chinese Christians acting by Communist request as liaison between Communist and Christian groups, spoke June 13 at open meeting foreign missionaries. Following report by Armstrong [73] who attended.

Majority of speeches devoted orthodox Communist ideology terms such as capitalism doomed, West instigating war, with little relation Christianity in Communist China. Following points interspersed in verbiage:

(1) Some Xian schools, hospitals taken over by Communists in Manchuria.

(2) Top Communist leaders have moderate policy but lower ranks more radical or inefficient. Wu urged Communists issue general statement reaffirming religious freedom, but Communists countered would also have to issue statement re freedom anti-religious activities. Communists have recently issued order lower ranks respect religious freedom.

(3) Xian work must undergo change, since some activities dead, some taken over by non-Xian groups, some need modifications meet present situation. But challenge and opportunity Xian work greater under new order.

(4) Catholics in special class, since their orders from Vatican always anti-Communist, anti-Russia, anti-Chinese revolution.

(5) Wu quoted explanation chief Peiping Foreign Residents Bureau re lack of preferential treatment "good" foreigners; action western governments, especially US, has created real hatred among Chinese

---

[72] Neither printed.
[73] Oscar V. Armstrong, language officer.

which will take years to dispel. This hatred reflects on all foreigners. Actually fortunate no anti-foreignism comparable Boxer days.

(6) Possibly less Communist interference evangelism than medicine and education, since latter complete [*compete?*] Communist activities.

Most missionaries disappointed Wu and Shen, feeling they are unqualified represent Xian groups, but wholly gratified this semi-direct contact possible.

Sent Department 1026; repeated Nanking 705, OffEmb Canton 178, Shanghai 686.

CLUBB

119.2/6–1749 : Telegram

The Minister-Counselor of Embassy in China (Clark) to the Secretary of State

CANTON, June 17, 1949—12 a. m.
[Received 10 : 33 a. m.]

Cantel 605. Résumé China net[work] origin requested Embtel 538, June 15, repeated Department 1289, Shanghai 700.

Established late 1944 joint OWI [74]–Army project as OWI–PRO net. Army public relations wanted net facilitate coverage China theater by accredited war correspondents whose only outlet to States was Chungking, Kunming commercial facilities. Net delivered correspondents' stories to points where commercial facilities available. OWI utilized net link its China offices for administration traffic, later added news facilities. Original equipment supplied by Signal Corps, which also authorized frequencies as part its net. First circuit Chengtu, Chungking. Later expanded connect all OWI offices free China.

When war ended, extended cover all major cities where OWI offices established. After OWI merged Department, stations added all consular posts China. All equipment after original installation and all personnel came from OWI resources. Continued operate until early 1946 as part Signal Corps net, in that Signal Corps authorized all frequencies call signs and cleared frequencies, etc., with Chinese Government as integral part its own radio operations China. Same frequencies call signs still in use.

When China theater deactivated, Gen. Marshall [75] arranged Executive Headquarters assume same responsibility when Chinese Government concerned. Nationalist Government after 1946 many times raised question networks operation through Ministry Communications, then Foreign Office, on grounds infringement national sovereignty, commercial facilities available and fact US refused China reciprocal

---

[74] Office of War Information.
[75] General of the Army George C. Marshall, Special Representative of President Truman in China, December 1945–January 1947.

privilege. Matter resolved high level discussions each time, basis view American effort Executive Headquarters and later aid programs that we required special facilities provide speedy communications Embassy and Consulate and commercial facilities inadequate. Marshall–Generalissimo [76] conversation finally required end most pressure on US cease operation.

No formal agreements ever made, and net operation since VJ Day [77] been on flimsy basis noted above.

Sent Nanking 405, repeated Department Cantel 605, Shanghai 345.

CLARK

119.2/6–1549 : Telegram

The Secretary of State to the Ambassador in China (Stuart)

WASHINGTON, June 24, 1949—6 p. m.

741. Ur 1289 June 15. Dept files contain no info re China network origin in addition that supplied by Off Emb Canton in tel 405 June 17, rptd Dept Cantel 605.

ACHESON

893.00B/7–749 : Telegram

The Consul General at Peiping (Clubb) to the Secretary of State

PEIPING, July 7, 1949—7 p. m.
[Received July 9—4 : 32 p. m.]

1138. Noting from Embtel (reEmbtel 242, June 29 [78]) 239, June 24,[79] refusal Alien Affairs Office Nanking concern itself with Colling case, reContel 869, May 21 to Department,[80] take occasion note that representations Alien Affairs Office Peiping re Consulate matters have in practice generally proved fruitless. Barrenness comes naturally from Communist attitude that they "lack diplomatic relations". As suggested Conreftel, Alien Affairs Office appears to be throw back to time when Chinese normally acted in way to humiliate and obstruct foreigners desiring deal with them. Note Barrett [81] report Contel 802, July 7.[82] See also Contel 641, June 9.[83] Note further Mao remark July 1 for need "raising our own (Communist) morale and

---

[76] President Chiang Kai-shek, who retired on January 21.
[77] September 2, 1945.
[78] Not found in Department of State files.
[79] See telegram No. 1368, June 24, 4 p. m., from the Ambassador in China, p. 1180.
[80] Not printed.
[81] Col. David D. Barrett, Assistant Military Attaché in China.
[82] Sent to the Department as telegram No. 1135, not printed.
[83] Same as telegram No. 966 from Peiping, p. 963.

taking down arrogance of enemy". In short, there exists good reason consider office in same category as Manchu Li-fan Yuan.[84]

In meeting yesterday Peiping Consuls generally agreed Alien Affairs Office Peiping largely useless for their purposes. In practice, this office by-passes it insofar as possible in favor direct approach concerned Communist organ such as Bureau Public Safety. Letters addressed municipal government or local military authority may on occasion be returned and none sent by this office has to date been answered but in any event one feels some assurance they are read by competent persons and treatment accorded letters in no respect worse than that received at hands Alien Affairs Office. Note that Tientsin [and] Shanghai Consulates apparently have greater success dealing with Alien Affairs Office; this presumably because their more important relationship commercial matters. Communist practice notably ununiform. Peiping experience reported for possible value as reference.

ReContel 802, July 7, note that offensive anti-foreign posters were generally removed from streets shortly before convocation preparatory committee PCC,[85] one report being this due intervention [Tan] Kahkee [86] pointed fact poster that type still displayed in government office dealing specifically with alien affairs by arrogant flaunting of antiforeignism is clear indication non-co-operative spirit that office respecting American officials particularly. Believe it might be helpful in any discussion general matter relations with Communists indicate to Communists Nanking, Shanghai and/or Peiping, desirability that there be provided channel for more effective handling problems growing importance and concern both sides than offered by Alien Affairs Office. Adduce in this connection point 3 Shanghai's 2600, July 3 to Department [87] at same time express belief Communists if really desirable possessing effective means deal with local problems concerning foreigners they should be prepared as alternative use more direct, authoritative, therefore effective channel than offered by Demo[cratic]-Leaguers.

Sent Nanking 810, repeated Department 1138, Office of the Embassy Canton 205, Shanghai 768.

[CLUBB]

---

[84] The Li-fan Yuan, established in 1638, was a Manchu board in charge of affairs relating to Koreans and Mongols.
[85] Political Consultative Conference.
[86] Member of Standing Committee of PCC and member of Commission of Overseas Chinese Affairs.
[87] *Post*, p. 1193.

893.111/7–1149 : Telegram

The Consul General at Peiping (Clubb) to the Secretary of State

PEIPING, July 11, 1949.
[Received July 12—5 : 27 p. m.]

1155. NCNA [88] English language service yesterday announced that according to notification issued that date by Peiping Military Control Committee all foreign residents Peiping were required register with Bureau Public Safety, Peiping People's Government. Registration procedure as laid down same source requires :

1. Presentation visa residential certificate issued prior liberation Peiping and other identification papers for examination.
2. Supply 6 prints passport photo.
3. Complete application forms provided by Bureau Registration to close July 31. Local Americans being circularized.

Sent Department 1155; Nanking 825; OffEmb Canton, Shanghai, Tientsin by mail.

CLUBB

893.111/7–1449 : Telegram

The Consul General at Peiping (Clubb) to the Secretary of State

PEIPING, July 14, 1949.
[Received July 14—10 : 10 a. m.]

1174. ReContel 1155, July 11. Checking of original text regulations July 10 shows requirement is for submission "passport, residential certificate issued before the liberation of Peiping, or other pertinent certifying document" instead of visa, et cetera.

Application form requires in addition information regarding name, nationality, date, place birth, age, sex, passport number, local address; standard of education and special talents, occupation, place of service, family domicile outside Peiping, principal properties outside China, important properties in China, organizations joined, criminal record, possession arms, camera, automobile, radio receiver, occupation in China, time first trip and total years residence China, residence and objective first trip to China, interior parts China resided in and objective, career before coming China, career after trip to China.

Peiping *Chieh Fang Pao* this date [reports?] after submittal application forms applicants are registered in order and times fixed for interviews.

Repeated Nanking 834, Canton 215, Shanghai 786, to Tientsin by mail.

CLUBB

---

[88] New China News Agency (Communist).

125.7146/7–1949 : Telegram

The Consul General at Peiping (Clubb) to the Secretary of State

PEIPING, July 19, 1949.
[Received July 19—6 : 17 a. m.]

1200. Following is translation communication Tung No. 11 this date addressed USIS by Peiping MCC [89] signed by Yeh Chien-ying in capacity director delivered by messenger today:

"It is observed USIS is section organized by American State Department. Since People's Government has no diplomatic or consular relations with USA, therefore USIS office should effective this date cease activities, including printing and distribution news copy, display and presentation books and periodicals, affixing of charts and pictures, showing of motion pictures, giving of musical concerts, together with all other external activities. It is expected there will be immediate observance without infraction." USIS being closed to public immediately.

Sent Department 1200, Nanking 849, OffEmb Canton 225, Shanghai 809. To Tientsin by mail.

CLUBB

125.7146/7–2049 : Telegram

The Minister-Counselor of Embassy in China (Clark) to the Secretary of State

CANTON, July 20, 1949—2 p. m.
[Received July 20—12 : 42 p. m.]

Cantel 786. Closure Peiping USIE [90] and anticipated similar action Tientsin (probably already taken but unreported due delays communications) and Nanking leaves us with definite impression Communist action designed force our hand re recognition. May be first move in jockeying for position since we have failed succumb their blandishments. Had expected overtures long before now from at least some of powers. Fact US regarded as leader common front nonrecognition may be direct cause closure order attempt embarrass US Government and force our hand since Communists would consider it extreme loss face if they put in position having make overture to foreign imperialists beyond their oft-repeated statement willing establish diplomatic relations any country withdrawing recognition Nationalists.

For these reasons believe protests re closures unsuccessful and only course left US is to sit back and wait developments, meantime re-

---

[89] Military Control Committee.
[90] United States Information and Educational Program.

doubling efforts get American facts before Chinese public in Communist areas through stepped up VOA [91] activities.

Sent Department Cantel 786; repeated Nanking 519.

CLARK

125.7146/7–2049 : Telegram

The Consul General at Peiping (Clubb) to the Secretary of State

PEIPING, July 20, 1949—3 p. m.
[Received July 21—3 : 14 p. m.]

1214. ReContel 1200, July 19, Deptel 450, July 15.[92] Peiping MCC messenger desired Van Putten sign receipt for message in private capacity. Van Putten insisted signing as USIS Director. This perhaps jeopardized Van Putten's remaining Peiping.

In view express character order, no practical alternative to immediate cessation for present external activities USIS. Staff will continue for present with work at hand. USIS has been performing important social service Peiping, being only source for certain types academic cultural material. Will discuss matter with some person having contact with Communist side earliest opportunity but believe no useful purpose would be served by making local protest direct to Communist authorities on basis logical legal points set forth Depreftel. Note that Department release July 18 [93] indicates protest to be made Peiping re Shanghai, Hankow but Depreftel unspecific Peiping action. Please clarify in light present development.

Believe Communists propose use this and possible other measures (1) pressure USA into early *de jure* recognition after formation new government and concomitant withdrawal support to Nationalist Government and (2) in meantime, cut into American political, economic, social prestige and influences as deeply as possible for joint Sino-Soviet benefit.

Note that Communists might use "logic" adduced in the USIS order to close Consulate, when it might suit their convenience. Slow action re Mukden and reference "external activities" in MCC communication alike seem bear possible implication Communists prepared see such offices kept intact for possible use following hypothetical recognition even though all activities stopped for present.

Believe Peiping USIS employees who have been most loyal and efficient should be given every consideration. Note, however, that being placed on leave with pay status would inevitably consume terminal pay they would otherwise get and that when all leave taken problem

---

[91] Voice of America.
[92] Same as telegram No. 1420 to the Consul General at Shanghai, p. 1234.
[93] Department of State *Bulletin*, August 1, 1949, p. 152.

would probably still remain, since early favorable Communist action permitting reopening most unlikely. Staff can be continued on duty status for short period but note that continuation their services for any considerable period after need therefore has ceased might establish precedent to which they could refer as basis for awkward demand they be continued in employment indefinitely. It might be best cut down to skeleton staff as soon as discussions completed, presumably fruitlessly, with assurances to employees they would be given preference if USIS able reopen. Believe serious consideration should be given matter early date.

British Council and Soviet VOKS [94] reading room evidently unaffected.

This message prepared in consultation Van Putten, propose address any protest Yeh Chien-ying as director MCC.

Please instruct.

Sent Department; repeated Nanking 862, OffEmb Canton 231, Shanghai 814.

CLUBB

893.76/6–249 : Telegram

The Secretary of State to the Ambassador in China (Stuart)

WASHINGTON, July 21, 1949—5 p. m.

865. ConGen Tientsin tel 321, May 16, rptd Nanking 202, Shanghai 224, Peiping 140, Hong Kong unnumbered; Embtel 1172 June 2 rptd Peiping 189, Hong Kong 30, Tientsin 36.

Dept not in position object unilateral action Brit firm in establishing Tientsin–Hong Kong radio communications since Dept has indicated to RCA [95] no objection its negotiating with Commie authorities for North China circuit via Manila. No evidence at present Chi Commie discrimination against RCA.

ACHESON

125.8576/7–2249 : Telegram

The Ambassador in China (Stuart) to the Secretary of State

NANKING, July 22, 1949—4 p. m.
[Received July 22—11 : 19 a. m.]

1584. Embassy attempted July 21 deliver to Aliens Affairs Office written protest (text contained Embtel 1583, July 22 [96]) on closure USIS offices Shanghai, Peiping, Hankow and Tientsin. After mes-

---

[94] All-Union Society for Cultural Relations with Foreign Countries.
[95] Radio Corporation of America.
[96] Not printed.

senger had informed higher officials subject of visit was "closure USIS offices", which Embassy officer required state in advance, junior official came down to waiting room to state his superiors not prepared discuss this question. Asked when they would be prepared discuss it, he was noncommittal. He did, however, read text of protest, but returned it, declining take it to his superiors. We feel further attempts present protest would not be fruitful and might hasten closure Nanking USIS.

Sent Department 1584, repeated Shanghai 886, Embassy Canton 663.

STUART

125.9376/7-2349 : Telegram

The Consul General at Tientsin (Smyth) to the Secretary of State

TIENTSIN, July 23, 1949.
[Received July 23—5 : 41 p. m.]

538. Following is translation of text letter dated July 20 received today by USIS here from "Huang Ching, Director Military Control Committee for Tientsin, China People's Liberation Army."

"Inasmuch as the United States Information Service is part of the American State Department organization, and inasmuch as the People's Government has no diplomatic and consular relations with the United States, the United States Information Service shall as of today cease its activities, including the publication and distribution of news service, the exhibition and free distribution of books and newspapers, the circulation and displaying of pictures, the showing of motion pictures, the holding of concerts and any other activities in contact with outside. Compliance is requested."

In view above, USIS office here closed today.

Sent Department 538, repeated Nanking 301, Shanghai 356, Peiping 225, and OffEmb Canton.

SMYTH

125.9376/7-2749 : Telegram

The Consul General at Tientsin (Smyth) to the Secretary of State

TIENTSIN, July 27, 1949—1 p. m.
[Received August 3—11 :13 a. m.]

564. In connection recommendations our telegram 562, July 26,[97] following résumé of difficulties imposed this Consulate General by Communists which we feel we should not take without trying retaliate in order impress Communists with fact, although US Government has

---

[97] Vol. IX, p. 952.

so far exercised forbearance, it not willing indefinitely turn other cheek:

1. Nearly half American personnel this office due home leave, but cannot be released until replacements arrive, which blocked by Communist refusal grant entry permits (see Peiping's telegram 1145, July 9 [98]).

2. Brown's agricultural reporting severely restricted by Communist refusal grant him permit travel Peiping although most other foreigners obtain such permits without undue trouble.

3. Communists close USIS, prevent courier service, tamper with our mail, impose duties on official supplies and personal importations staff on very limited items for which Communists grant import licenses, withhold permission our visit American vessels at Taku Bar on basis we not recognize them, yet continue let us perform services beneficial to them as certification invoices.

SMYTH

125.7146/7–2049 : Telegram

The Secretary of State to the Consul General at Peiping (Clubb)

WASHINGTON, July 28, 1949—7 p. m.

498. Implication Dept release July 18 [99] re protest (urtel 1214 July 20) simply that Peiping deliver protest along lines suggested Deptel 450 July 15.[1] While Dept not sanguine results believe unwise action go unchallenged. Protest should embrace Shanghai, Hankow, Tientsin, Peiping, Nanking closure orders.[2]

Dept endorses Canton proposal[3] present status only suspension USIE activities and retain full local USIE staff on duty status. Use opportunity do many internal USIE or consular jobs neglected in past, but without violation terms closure orders.

ACHESON

125.7146/7–2949 : Telegram

The Consul General at Peiping (Clubb) to the Secretary of State

PEIPING, July 29, 1949—5 p. m.
[Received August 3—1 : 16 p. m.]

1272. Re Contel 752, May 3. For purposes record, note that stoning Americans did not recur after day Consulate reference telegram except

---

[98] Not printed.
[99] Department of State *Bulletin*, August 1, 1949, p. 152.
[1] Same as telegram No. 1420, July 15, to the Consul General at Shanghai, p. 1234.
[2] For information on closure at Shanghai, see telegram No. 2775, July 15, 11 a. m., from the Consul General at Shanghai, p. 1232 ; for information on closure at Hankow and Nanking, see telegram No. 210, July 15, from the Consul General at Hankow, p. 1132, and telegram No. 1595, July 23, from the Ambassador in China, p. 797.
[3] See Cantel No. 786, July 20, 2 p. m., from the Minister-Counselor of Embassy in China, p. 1095.

for one isolated instance. Cessation presumably reflected official concern at action and no note was sent mayor in view amelioration situation.

CLUBB

125.7146/8–949 : Telegram

The Consul General at Peiping (Clubb) to the Secretary of State

PEIPING, August 9, 1949—11 a. m.
[Received August 12—1 : 03 a. m.]

1327. ReDeptel 498, July 28. Letter sent today registered mail Director Peiping MCC, protesting closure indicated USIS offices, asking reopening Peiping office (request limited because of his technically limited authority). Text by despatch.[4]

Michael Lindsay [5] told Barrett closure USIS offices resulted [from] Soviet pressure.

Sent Department; repeated Nanking 952, OffEmb Canton 252, Shanghai 872.

CLUBB

125.0093/7–3049 : Circular telegram

The Secretary of State to Certain Diplomatic and Consular Offices in China [5a]

WASHINGTON, August 9, 1949—7 p. m.

ReDeptel 498, July 28; Nanking's 1653 and 1657, July 30.[6] Dept has reconsidered question retention full USIE local staff in duty status during suspension USIE activities Commie China. Policy stated Deptel 498, July 28 hereby revised.

Dept feels since USIE activities suspended by Commie auth it would be propitious moment to clear from staffs all posts concerned local employees without creation unusual situations as arose Shanghai connection ex-Navy employees.[7] All posts at which USIE employees stationed therefore instructed give discharge notice to USIE local employees and pay them accrued and current annual leave from USIE local employee salary allotment. However, concur Nanking's recommendation (Embtel 1632, July 27 [8]) Nanking, Shanghai, Peiping each may retain one local librarian provided no repercussion anticipated by

---

[4] Despatch No. 110, August 10, not printed.
[5] Australian lecturer and writer.
[5a] Sent to Canton, Hankow, Nanking, Peiping, Shanghai, and Tientsin.
[6] Telegrams Nos. 1653 and 1657 not printed.
[7] For documentation on this subject, see pp. 1155 ff.
[8] Not printed.

which Commie auths may demand retention entire USIE local staff. Dept assumes monitoring distributing bulletin local community can be handled by regular administrative staffs these posts.

While Dept not informed what severance pay may be agreed upon as discussed Nanking's 1653, July 30, Dept feels since activities ordered stopped by Commie auths no greater payment should be made employees being discharged than made by local govt organizations discharging employees. Dept understands certain local govt employees Shanghai, for instance, given 6 weeks' severance pay. At any rate Dept feels not more than 2 months' severance pay shld be granted employees. Dept regards approach outlined Shanghai's 3077, Aug. 6,[9] good one. As with regular program employees Dept desires keep payments USIE employees low as possible order avoid setting undesirable precedent complicating problems other posts. However, final decision this matter discretion prin[cipal] off[icer].

When informing USIE local employees of discharge, be prepared make severance payments immed, obtaining if possible certificate complete satisfaction from employee. If unable obtain such certificate because failure refund retirement deductions auth include in severance payments amounts estimated near as possible to retirement refund which wld be payable by Civil Service.

You will be given severance pay allotment soonest.

This tel does not affect Am[erican] employees USIE program which will be dealt with in later communication.

Pls keep Dept informed.

ACHESON

125.7143/8–1049 : Telegram

The Consul General at Peiping (Clubb) to the Secretary of State

[Extract]

PEIPING, August 10, 1949—11 a. m.
[Received August 10—4 : 11 a. m.]

1302. [To Nanking :] August 4, 1 p. m. Re Embassy's cirtel July 30, repeated Department 1653.[10] Van Putten and I agree it is desirable reduce USIS personnel to skeleton staff in near future in order avoid any creation "prescriptive rights" by keeping them on after need patently passed. Not [*Note?*] that principles indicated Contel 907, July 31 [10] envisaged discharge employees when business may close. In present circumstances USIS being closed by overt order MCC. In circumstances noted, anticipate no difficulty or at most simple requirement that staff be given 1 month's notice and something in nature sep-

---

[9] Not printed; it concerned liquidation of USIE offices (125.0093/8–649).
[10] Not printed.

aration pay (which would be in present case covered by payment retirement funds and terminal leave).

.   .   .   .

CLUBB

125.9371/8–1249 : Telegram

The Consul General at Tientsin (Smyth) to the Secretary of State

TIENTSIN, August 12, 1949—9 a. m.
[Received August 15–6 : 58 a. m.]

618. Re ourtel 568, July 28.[11] Tientsin "People's Government" issued August 9 "provisional measures collection house tax" (for full text see ourtel 619, August 12 [11]). Assessment to be made September 1 and payment September 10 retroactive to January 1. We estimate tax on four Consulate General houses and ex-Japanese Consul building (all US Government-owned) about $620 for period January–June, and $103 monthly thereafter, or total through August about $826.

We plan inform local authorities that as Consulate General properties are government-owned and non-income producing, we assume they exempt this tax in line pertinent section regulations. However in view previous actions local government re "nonrecognized" foreign consuls, not too hopeful exemption. Therefore request prompt instructions re policy if exemption disallowed, as default charges for delayed compliance reporting properties and filing assessment application amounts 50 percent, and penalty delayed payments mounts steeply with arraignment in court after 30 days overdue.

We would appreciate reply by August 20.

Other consuls here asking instructions from their embassies.

Re ourtel 595, August 8.[11] It would be helpful if Department or Embassy could keep this Consulate General informed re taxation matters in other Communist-occupied areas particularly Shanghai.

Sent Department as 618; repeated Nanking as 332, Shanghai as 384. Department pass Peiping as 24.

SMYTH

124.931/8–1949 : Telegram

The Counselor of Embassy in China (Jones) to the Secretary of State

NANKING, August 19, 1949—5 p. m.
[Received August 19—9 : 54 a. m.]

1836. [To Tientsin :] ReContel 332, August 12,[12] received here August 17. Embassy and ConGen Shanghai declining pay house tax on ground property owned by foreign government and used in its service

---

[11] Not printed.
[12] Same as No. 618 to the Department, *supra.*

exempt by international usage and law. Shanghai believes local authorities not yet ready commence eviction or condemnation proceedings, and Embassy incline to agree. Assume Department's instructions already en route to you; however, British and Italian Embassies state they understand assessment date is August 20 and therefore Embassy recommends urgently punctual compliance reporting and assessment procedure with simultaneous expression reservation of rights on any points which might imply a submission by US Government to tax powers of local authorities.

Sent Tientsin 72, repeated Department 1836, Shanghai 1014.

JONES

125.714/8–1849 : Telegram

The Secretary of State to the Consul General at Peiping (Clubb)

WASHINGTON, August 23, 1949—6 p. m.

568. In view proposed staff reductions other China posts Depcirtel Aug 15, 7 a. m., and urtel 1391 Aug 18,[13] Dept had hoped be able transfer to Peiping from other posts surplus personnel not due statutory leave or available assignment new posts. However, appears no present possibility obtaining travel permits authorizing travel such personnel from central to north China or permits for entry into China of new personnel and only source additional personnel for Peiping this time wld be Mukden and Tientsin. Mukden staff being ordered return US and Tientsin being instructed reduce staff by attrition through permitting departure personnel on statutory leave. In view foregoing wld appear only means keeping Peiping staff up to strength wld be through assignment language officers to ur office as they finish their courses. Ur comments requested.[14]

For your info, Dept planning close Dairen, Tsingtao and Hankow in near future and withdraw US personnel as transportation facilities available. Kunming and Chungking have been authorized close and withdraw Amer personnel prior to Commie take-over those cities. Tihwa being closed and personnel now withdrawing.

With departure Min-Counselor Clark when Canton falls Dept desires you assume responsibility for over-all appraisal China scene, rather than restriction to ur consular district or north China, in reporting polit developments. This appears particularly desirable in view increasing importance Peiping as center Commie polit activity. In this connection, ur tels have been extremely helpful to Dept and have been of uniformly outstanding quality.

ACHESON

---

[13] Neither printed.

[14] The Consul General at Peiping stated in his telegram No. 1508, September 8, 11 p. m.: "Estimate that assignment Language FSO's Peiping would enable office maintain essential functions visible future." (125.714/9–849)

701.0693/8–2649 : Circular telegram

The Secretary of State to Certain Diplomatic and Consular Offices in China [14a]

WASHINGTON, August 26, 1949—6 a. m.

Dept concerned over demands Commie auths for payment taxes on US Govt real property used exclusively for Govt functions in occupied China.

Dept concurs Nanking's recommendation (Nanking's 1836, Aug 19) punctual compliance reporting and assessment procedure necessary with simultaneous expression reservations rights on any points which might imply submission by US Govt to tax powers local auths.

Dept has taken position taxes demanded not payable under internatl law as one sovereign govt may not be taxed by another, either recognized or unrecognized, on properties owned and used for govt purposes. For ur own info case is stronger for dipl property than consular property. However, argument shld be made on basis of govt-owned property used for official purposes.

Make no payments without advance clearance Dept if time possibly permits, and unless other Western Powers definitely agreed pay such taxes. Take no initiative in making payment or encouraging other powers make tax payments.

Necessary that posts make every effort retain protect US Govt property without payment of taxes. As a practical matter, however, it may be necessary to pay taxes demanded. Such taxes to be paid only if in discretion principal officer of each post, based on his knowledge local situation, appears imminent threat exists of eviction, condemnation or confiscation or danger to security Amer personnel.

If necessary to make payment of such taxes Dept expects that appropriate written protests will be made to local auths and that matter be reported to Dept in order that appropriate instru[ction]s may be sent Peiping on protests cover all cases.

If taxes on realty are confiscatory in nature this will be an element for consideration by Dept in deciding whether to retain the post.

Inform Dept immed estimated costs involved. Necessary allotments will be authorized.

Keep Dept fully and currently informed.

ACHESON

[14a] Sent to Canton, Hankow, Nanking, Peiping, Shanghai, Tientsin, and Tsingtao.

125.9376/8–2649 : Telegram

The Consul General at Tientsin (Smyth) to the Secretary of State

TIENTSIN, August 26, 1949—11 a. m.
[Received August 28—12 : 03 a. m.]

662. Recently method of Communists' interference with mail sent us by ConGen Peiping has changed. Instead of opening covers and delivering within reasonable time they presently not delivering some. We now missing five Peiping covers sent since August 3.

Since only method of secure communication is to send codes to Peiping by mail for transmittal, situation delays our communications and will be serious if interference intensified.

SMYTH

893.5200/8–3149 : Telegram

The Consul General at Peiping (Clubb) to the Secretary of State

PEIPING, August 31, 1949.
[Received September 1—1 : 10 a. m.]

1447. *Kuang Ming Jih Pao* August 26 carried notice re registration real estate held by aliens in Peiping municipality and suburbs. Text follows :

"In order facilitate control over aliens' property (both buildings and land) in this municipality, Municipal Land Administration Bureau has specially formulated measures for dealing with application for registration of aliens' real estate in Peiping municipality. Measures provide that in respect to all property (buildings and land) owned by aliens in municipality, owner or legal representative bearing a power of attorney should, between September 15 and end of October 1949, get application forms from Bureau and apply for registration. In applying for registration of real estate, aside from referring to measures provided in 'Rules for Registration of Real Estate in Municipal Area', following procedure should be followed :

"(a) Submit for examination complete set of title deeds (all title deeds in foreign languages should be accompanied by Chinese translation, latter to be accepted as correct version). Receipts shall be issued by Bureau.

"(b) Bring applicant's name, seal, and residence certificate.

"(c) If applicant is religious body, school, company, store, social body, or other such organization, procedure shall be handled by responsible person or by designated agent. In addition, foreigners should fill out accurately and in detail facts concerning all their buildings and land, location, house number, use of property, present state of buildings and/or land, and from whom it was acquired, without concealment or omission or fabrication.

"Any property (buildings or land) acquired by a foreigner in name of a Chinese or under any other name shall also be correctly registered without concealing facts. And particularly without committing acts such as concealing enemy or bogus property or invading other public or private property rights. Violators will definitely be dealt with legally."

Sent Department, repeated Nanking 1045, Shanghai 936, mailed Tientsin.

CLUBB

125.7146/9–349 : Telegram

The Consul General at Peiping (Clubb) to the Secretary of State

PEIPING, September 3, 1949—10 a. m.
[Received September 3—6 : 09 a. m.]

1474. ReDeptel 564, August 22.[15] All external USIE work Peiping terminated in accord MCC order July 19. Loan of material would be violation order, everything called in, nothing being issued. Van Putten and I agree strict compliance indicated local groups desirous of having materials and authorities might be quite willing them get such materials if outside USIE channels, but MCC stand is categorical and continued USIE activity would not only fail being credit USIS but probably give excuse for more castigation and perhaps new restrictions.[16] Our interpretation is that we can continue with USIS interofficial activity but nothing more for present, with whole issue presumably awaiting final definition when new government set up and question recognition arises.

Recommend status USIS Peiping be left undefined for present, with continuation lease USIS premises for present term ending November with reconsideration that time. Property reallocated, redecoraration just being completed, desirable property already becoming scarce (Contel 1132, July 7 [15]). Propose all USIE materials and books be retained *in situ* under supervision small part-time staff. Librarian when employed will complete work on card file.

Recommend that in interim Van Putten be given home leave as soon as eligible so as to be ready to return promptly if USIE able reopen. Believe his local contacts and knowledge local conditions make it desirable in event reopening here person in charge be present Peiping.

Prepared in consultation Van Putten.

No reply Consulate letter August 8 to MCC ever received.

Sent Department, repeated Nanking 1063, Shanghai 949, Hong Kong.

CLUBB

---

[15] Not printed.
[16] In telegram No. 632, September 14, 4 p. m., the Department informed the Consul General that it concurred in his decision to comply strictly with this order.

125.937/9–349 : Telegram

The Consul General at Tientsin (Smyth) to the Secretary of State

TIENTSIN, September 3, 1949—noon.
[Received September 4—8 : 14 a. m.]

703. Communist authorities have consistently taken line that Consulates not recognized and that consular personnel and property foreign governments treated as foreign [*non-*]official so long as diplomatic relations not established. Although dismay [*this may?*] not conform international practice we feel from practical viewpoint it must be taken into account and whether or not we like it our course action must be predicated on this fact. We feel mistake to think Communists will heed "diplomatic" protests or arguments based on international comity.

Futility our "vigorous protests to highest Communist authorities" demonstrated number cases, notably that consular staff Mukden remains virtually prisoners; also re USIS closing. "Vigorous protests" look well in American press or over radio but effect on Communists seems nil. Obvious our consular officers in Communist areas are here on Communist sufferance and must comply Communist regulations or suffer consequences. Mukden good example how we at mercy of Communists with apparent inability United States Government assist Consuls.

SMYTH

893.5200/9–649 : Telegram

The Consul General at Peiping (Clubb) to the Secretary of State

PEIPING, September 6, 1949—noon.
[Received 7 : 16 p. m.]

1480. ReContel 1447, August 31. Peiping Consuls September 1 agreed tentatively regulations by use term "aliens" (foreign persons) automatically excluded foreign government property from registration requirement. All concerned are communicating with their Embassies or Government and we propose adjust positions to developments. ReDeptel 137, March 18,[17] note that in most cases deeds would be unavailable, status property having been determined by international agreement. Propose in short refrain from action unless later called for. Please instruct.[18]

---

[17] Not printed ; it suggested that "no action re formal title deeds be taken time being."

[18] The Acting Secretary of State informed the Consul General at Peiping in telegram No. 648, September 20, 3 p. m., that, should regulations when promulgated refer to registration of property of only "aliens", the Department would have no objection to the approach described in telegram No. 1480, September 6, if a majority of the Consuls agreed on it (893.5200/9–1049).

Note proviso regulations applicant shall present resident certificate, permitting interference [*inference*] such certificates will be issued by September 15.

Sent Department, repeated Nanking 1065, Shanghai 950. Department pass Tientsin 85.

CLUBB

125.937/9–949 : Telegram

The Consul General at Tientsin (Smyth) to the Secretary of State

TIENTSIN, September 9, 1949—10 a. m.
[Received September 12—1 : 42 a. m.]

721. ReDeptel 288, September 2, 7 p. m.[20] I feel that under conditions at present and foreseeable future, there is no good reason to maintain more than small staff here.

Tientsin has always been primarily a commercial post, but American business community has now dwindled to a few persons and firms for whom we are able to do little if anything in our present condition of "non-recognition". Trade promotion is hardly possible with government trading companies taking over more and more of foreign commerce and adjusting their trade methods to Communist pattern. Lack of access to official and other sources and absence of published statistics and economics as a rule out report-writing. Such basic analytic and interpretive reports as we could telegraph on economic conditions since Communist take-over 8 months ago are already in Washington. Recent weeks and months have added little, only odd bits which substantiated our earlier observations and interpretations.

Possibilities for political reporting are extremely limited under strict Communist regime. Chinese civilians, who formerly gave information freely on situation, now afraid to talk. Basic facts of general situation have already been reported.

Until month or two ago, staff fairly busy, much time in coding reports. This reporting has markedly decreased for reasons given above. Regular work now confined to issuance Consular invoices and a few passport and other services for small American community remaining here—less than 70 Americans (including ConGen personnel) and some of these plan to leave. Visa work practically ceased (see our telegram 434, June 20 and Deptel 169, June 30[21]). Coding and miscellaneous administrative problems arising from present conditions constitute much of our work. Present staff no longer fully occupied and preferable take away those not needed.

Another factor in general picture is that importance of Tientsin as a post has decreased since delimitation of Tientsin and Peiping

---

[20] Not printed.
[21] Neither printed.

districts by which much of this district turned over to Peiping ConGen. Tientsin district now so restricted I believe Tientsin should be reclassified from ConGen to Consulate.

In my opinion, American staff of this office should be reduced to one Vice Consul (general service), one Vice Consul (Chinese language officer), and one or two clerks.

Present Chinese staff should be retained substantially at present level, as with contemplated strengthening of Peiping ConGen (Deptel 283, September 1 [22]) it can be expected this office would have considerable work handling travel arrangements for official personnel and official shipments through Tientsin. Our experience that with increased red tape under Communist regime many more man hours spent this work than formerly. Retention Chinese custodial employees also necessary maintenance Government-owned properties.

Dept's views are requested, upon receipt of which specific staff recommendations will be made.[23]

SMYTH

893.00B/9–1249 : Telegram

The Consul General at Tientsin (Smyth) to the Secretary of State

TIENTSIN, September 12, 1949—2 p. m.
[Received September 13—8 : 56 a. m.]

726. Communist increasing strictness control here. Chinese doctor, trained in US and one of few Chinese still willing talk (privately and confidentially), states Communists making clear they displeased with Chinese having contacts with foreigners. Chinese showing increasing reluctance contact foreigners. General trend shown by fact Keats Chu, manager large Ten Li Co., whose export business almost entirely with US, just made member committee local Sino-Soviet Friendship Society. Chu, educated US and long special friend Americans, now avoids contacts with Americans and foreigners in general.

Communist control mail growing stricter. No more safe send mail by masters But [terfield &] Swire and Jardine ships allowed. Our mail from Peiping so frequently not received necessary use Americans as couriers.

General controls here much stricter than Peiping. Example, American staff Peiping ConGen able obtain passes visit Tientsin. Here, however, only girl employees able get passes visit Peiping; Brown, McCarthy,[24] Rogatnick [25] unable get passes.

---

[22] Not printed.
[23] The Secretary of State informed the Consul General at Tientsin in telegram No. 312, September 19, 9 p. m. : "Dept agrees with ur suggestions on reduction of Amer staff."
[24] Richard M. McCarthy, Vice Consul.
[25] Joseph H. Rogatnick, Consular Attaché.

Foreigners here subject increasing inconveniences and Communist policy obviously make foreigners lose face. It is growing apparent withholding of exit permits will be used as club over foreigners. New medical examination for applicants' exit permits extremely strict, unreasonable, and possible exit permits may be refused, if Communists desire, on medical rather than political grounds.

With few exceptions, foreigners here increasingly discouraged over business prospects, as passage time evolves Communists here more following Russian Soviet pattern in all matters.

SMYTH

125.9371/9–2149 : Telegram

The Consul General at Tientsin (Smyth) to the Secretary of State

TIENTSIN, September 21, 1949—3 p. m.
[Received September 24—12 : 14 p. m.]

773. Reourtel 715, September 7.[26] As French and British Consuls paid house and sanitation taxes, we felt no option but do likewise. Taxes paid September 14 on four Government-owned houses totaled $75 for January–June period or $3.15 per house per month. Payment made with written protest in accordance Depcirtel August 31.[27] No bill yet received for ex-Japanese property and possible exempted as dilapidated, unused.

Tax bureau replied our letter August 31 requesting tax exemptions for United States Government-owned properties: "According to regulations, house and sanitation taxes should still be levied on foregoing properties."

Communist attitude re nonpayment taxes reported by foreigner who protested amount tax his property; he bluntly informed if taxes not paid property confiscated.

As we have reported on many occasions during past 8 months, most recently in ourtel 703, September 3, Communist authorities have consistently taken line that Consulates not recognized and that consular personnel and property foreign governments will be treated as nonofficial as long as diplomatic relations not established.

SMYTH

---

[26] Not printed.
[27] See circular telegram of August 26, 6 a. m., p. 1104.

125.7146/9–3049 : Telegram

The Consul General at Peiping (Clubb) to the Secretary of State

PEIPING, September 30, 1949—3 p. m.
[Received September 30—5 : 47 a. m.]

1653. ReContel [1476] September 6 [9 a. m.].[28] Difficulty still continues regarding mail addressed Tientsin with tampering and loss additional covers evidently in Tientsin Post Office. Representations Peiping fruitless. This Consulate therefore refraining from despatching messages or other official correspondence by mail to Tientsin.

MacDonald,[29] who discussed matter in course trip Tientsin last week, reported office there unwilling use alien personnel as couriers to get its mail and unable (see Tientsin's 789, September 27 [28]) get passes for travel American personnel.

Peiping, naturally, not in position spare its American personnel for frequent courier duty, believes further that too frequent travel might well lead to added difficulties regarding our own obtaining of travel passes. This office will of course use every available opportunity get Tientsin's messages to it at least twice weekly but irregularity and occasional delay in circumstances be anticipated.

Tientsin's mail to Peiping comes through regularly.

Department pass Tientsin 89.

CLUBB

893.5200/10–1349 : Telegram

The Consul General at Peiping (Clubb) to the Secretary of State

PEIPING, October 13, 1949—noon.
[Received October 14—9 : 20 a. m.]

1738. ReDeptel 648, September 20.[30] Consuls in meeting October 12 again agreed, particularly against background establishment Peiping new government and its bid for recognition, refrain from action re registration government property presently occupied by Consulates on following ground 1) regulations applicable "aliens" (foreign persons), 2) question status particular property in question is one concerning foreign governments and Communists to date evidently unwilling deal with matters concerning governments which have not recognized them and 3) status same property as defined not in title deeds of interest local land bureau but in international treaties validity which per Communist statements is subject study.

Another suggestion was brought forward in meeting proposing that Consulates might, if they had opportunity, meet with authoritative

---

[28] Not printed.
[29] John E. MacDonald, language officer at Peiping.
[30] Not printed, but see footnote 18, p. 1107.

representative People's Government, set forth their position that regulations presumably inapplicable Consulates' property. It was however generally agreed probably better let matter rest in present status on basis assumption Communists probably undesirous now discussing matter and would not desire make trouble for Consulates at this period when they have bid for recognition.

Action taken by private persons register property according new regulations to date discovers Communists apparently have undertaken only first step of matter, that is, ascertaining foreign real property holding (note similarity re registration foreign nationals, still unpossessed of residence certificates, which incidently unrequired re land registration despite regulations). Note length time taken get matter under way under Kmt rule and note further Communists have technically called into question treaties on which rights beneficial ownership based and at same time have presumably abrogated land law as well as other law codes. Matter will undoubtedly go forward only slowly. Because of absence from Peiping various owners, unrepresented here and sometimes even whereabouts unknown, and possible existence title claims unknown Consulates, it would seem desirable for this office make some statement to land bureau reserving rights unknown owners. Of course, doubtful whether bureau would accept but mere approach would be matter record. Please instruct.

CLUBB

125.714/10–1849 : Telegram

The Consul General at Peiping (Clubb) to the Secretary of State

PEIPING, October 18, 1949—1 a. m.
[Received 6 : 22 a. m.]

1769. Note change October 1 of name Peiping to "Peking". Believe conformity by American Foreign Service establishments unobjectionable except on one point Nationalist sensibilities, and conformity would avoid one minor point exacerbation Communist feelings. Please instruct.

CLUBB

125.714/10–1849 : Telegram

The Secretary of State to the Consul General at Peiping (Clubb)[31]

WASHINGTON, October 27, 1949—7 p. m.

746. Urtel 1769 Oct. 18. In consideration our political relations with Chi Govt, denotation carried by name "Peking" and administrative

---

[31] Repeated to the Embassy at Nanking as No. 1195, to the Chargé in China as telCan No. 738, to the Consul General at Shanghai as No. 2180, and to the Consul General at Tientsin as No. 376.

complexities involved, no change being made in Departmental and general FonServ use of "Peiping". Dept perceives no objection, however, to your following local usage this matter and employing in local communications name of city as designated by local auths. For urinfo, Dept will also employ name "Peking" in any open mail or telegraphic communications transmitted to you via commercial facilities.

ACHESON

893.5200/10–1349 : Telegram

The Secretary of State to the Consul General at Peiping (Clubb)

WASHINGTON, November 2, 1949—5 p. m.

764. Dept has no objection procedure described para 1 urtel 1738 Oct 13 for reason numbered 1 but questions strength reasons numbered 2 and 3.

Re para 2 Dept concurs better let matter rest present status.

Re para 3 Dept authorizes ConGen transmit statement local auths reserving rights absent Amer owners real property.

ACHESON

125.0093/11–1549 : Telegram

The Consul General at Peiping (Clubb) to the Secretary of State

PEIPING, November 15, 1949—noon.
[Received November 15—10:31 a. m.]

2001. ReContel 1976, November 10.[32] In meeting Consuls yesterday note was taken of (1) movement local authorities against German property, and (2) inclusive in new proclamation re registration aliens real property reference to "public".

Regulations still make no mention government property held by Soviet Government [in] Peiping. On their face they are applicable simply property "aliens", and "public" might refer schools et cetera. It was, however, considered desirable by all concerned as certain course current developments re government property Shanghai, Nanking, Tientsin and at same time ask instructions our governments. It was considered possibly now desirable for purposes record send identic letters Chou En-lai [33] stating that due note had been taken of regulations; that it appeared regulations were inapplicable government property but that if they were considered applicable, local authorities were informed that property located such and such address was property blank government with title determined by treaty, exchange of

---

[32] Not printed.
[33] "Premier and Foreign Minister of the Central People's Government of the People's Republic of China" at Peiping.

notes, lease or title deed as case might be. It was agreed this had best be done only in official capacity, that is, using official title in communication in order avoid embarrassment and possible attack on title which could follow our action in "unofficial" or private capacity.

It was agreed also that Communist action elsewhere would not necessarily be guide to action here. Nevertheless, request brief survey by Department of situation re position US Government property three above-mentioned posts. Please authorize likewise that I act at my discretion along lines indicated above. Please instruct particularly re title, deeds or treaties to be cited in our case. In this connection note report Miss Helen Popoff, long connected Legation, to effect that despite recent treaty provisions Government had actually purchased land on which Consulate situated.

Specifically, please authorize in case used, inclusion in any general address west Glacis abutting on ex-Marine compound (on basis prescriptive right and our possession building thereon).

Note French, British, Dutch in addressing their notes Chou all used his full title with identification "People's Government China People's Republic" arguing that they were technically safe in so doing since local regime was thus far differentiated from Nationalist Government. ReContel 1992, November 14,[34] believe that my sole title "General" for Chou might have been used as technical justification for return notes and request instruction whether I authorized use same address and courtesy for him, particularly in present instance where I would use own title but also as general procedure.

Please instruct priority.

Sent Department 2001; Department pass Shanghai 182; Tientsin 95; Nanking 1157.

CLUBB

125.0093/11–1849 : Telegram

The Consul General at Peiping (Clubb) to the Secretary of State

PEIPING, November 18, 1949—2 p. m.
[Received November 18—12 : 29 p. m.]

2031. Miss Popoff cited Contel 2001, November 15, recalls FSO Cecil Lyon who was in charge *Decanat* [35] at Peiping stated American Consulate property had been purchased outright and that FSS Mrs. Krenz stated pertinent papers had been sent Department. Acquisition thus of at least part of government property by Popoff version dates back to approximate Boxer times with one Colonel Blandy [*Denby?*][36] being previous owner. Despite recent treaty provision giving occupa-

---

[34] *Ante*, p. 849.
[35] Office of the Dean of the Diplomatic Corps.
[36] Charles Denby, Minister in China, 1885–1897.

tion for official use, believe it would be useful (particularly since Communists presumably challenge validity that treaty) check to clarify previous titles.

Refusal local authorities have any contacts with consuls in latter's official capacities, with refusal for instance even register motor cars in name US Government or representative that Government, of course makes it appear improbable Communists will accept registration in name American Government. Since they must know consuls will probably resist registration as private property, question logically arises as to ultimate Communist purpose. This unknown here but remark again reputed Communist aim to effect eventually removal foreign government representatives from Legation quarter and invite attention therefore possibilities in development Communist pressure on American installations Tsingtao and possibly Peiping, elsewhere. Recommend strongly that in case infringement American Government property rights China by Communists, full compensation be taken through impounding action against Chinese Government real and movable property including cash assets USA at such time as Nationalist Government may have lost control.

CLUBB

125.0093/11–1849 : Telegram

The Second Secretary of Embassy in China (Bacon) to the Secretary of State

NANKING, November 18, 1949—3 p. m.
[Received November 18—6 : 31 a. m.]

2454. [For Peiping:] Contel 2001, November 15. As result joint discussions at Embassy, principal officers missions mentioned below have requested quoted portion this telegram be passed by AmCon Peiping to respective Consulates Peiping and by Department to respective Embassies Washington for transmission Foreign Offices concerned.

"As result meetings November 17 and on 18 of officers in charge British, Netherlands, French, Italian and American Embassies following conclusions reached :

1. We see no objection eventual registration as such since this probably desirable as means protecting rights.

2. Meantime letter proposed by you should be sent not to Chou Enlai but to land administration bureau since (*a*) policy to date has been to approach local administrative authorities rather than Central Government, (*b*) Chou's reply, if any, might well be delayed until after November 30 which case penalties for noncompliance might be applied.

3. Both letter and possible registration application should make clear rights in respect property described are held by government concerned.

4. Whether letter or application is filed, manner of signing seems secondary importance. If document bearing official signature will be

accepted should be signed that manner. But if consulates have reason to believe document liable rejection if so signed should be signed in individual capacity. However, in such case should be made clear signer acting as agent for government concerned.

5. If, but only if, there is evidence that registration preliminary step imposition taxes, application should contain reservation that government concerned does not in effecting registration acquiesce in possible exercise tax powers local authorities in respect such property.

6. We recommend that no reference be made in your letter to deeds, treaties, et cetera, since only few deeds available and since we consider this neither suitable time nor suitable occasion risk raising controversial question validity existing treaties and other intergovernmental agreements."

Department pass to Peiping 402, Shanghai 1238. Peiping pass Tientsin.

BACON

702.0093/11–1949 : Telegram

The Consul General at Peiping (Clubb) to the Secretary of State

PEIPING, November 19, 1949—noon.
[Received November 19—4:47 a. m.]

2043. Consuls met yesterday regarding question land registration (reContel 2029, November 18 [37]). It was agreed most recent development required action and that it should not be taken vis-à-vis Land Bureau instead Chou En-lai. It was considered that particularly because of desirability effecting initial clarification of relations of Consulate to matter in point, parallel letters of acknowledgment should early be directed Land Bureau acknowledging receipt communications, noting that real property at such and such addresses (including those which might be unnamed in Bureau's letter) belong blank government, stating that Consulate would be able act in matter only as "official representative" of that government and instructions were being requested from his government and new communication would be sent when such instruction received. It is planned meet November 21 to reach final decision against background information which may be received in interim from Tientsin with letters to be sent out immediately thereafter. Consulate titles would not be used in signature but text of letter would, as indicated, make clear that person signing was acting only in official capacity. Further agreed most desirable Consulates take parallel action re matter in point.

Mytel 2035, November 18.[37] Note that form does not name "owners" but only "user" and "applicant". Consulate agreed that under heading "user" and "applicant" should be set forth name government and that

---

[37] Not printed.

agent would be consular official. Other Consulates found no objection agent signing form without title but note reputed requirement Tientsin that British Consul in signing as agent should also affix personal Chinese seal. Believe proper position would be that any seal used could only be official Consulate seal. Would be prepared agree that if user and applicant were alike stipulated to be American Government, agents might forego insistence on affixing his title since if local authorities were prepared accept unfrozen agency without protest, presumably omission of title would not constitute our acquiescence in non-official and private status agent. However, request answer particularly on this.

Trouble has reputedly been met Tientsin due demand Land Bureau information submitted on form dictated manner. I feel that application might be submitted in any form applicant found fit and that it would only be after acceptance that Bureau would legally be entitled challenge position indicated by applicant. Therefore believe that application should not be worded to meet Bureau's political desires, that unless authorities prepared accept form as submitted by Consuls, Bureau's rejection of form should be viewed as refusal to consider application.

Mytel 2030, November 18.[38] Believe that on completion form Article 2 of 1943 treaty [39] should be cited as basis title, thus making direct issue of validity that treaty. Believe it will be necessary inform Land Bureau at time impossible give all requested data within time limit set. However, if matter made issue include west Glacis on ground that it constituted part of "the land which has been allocated to Government USA in diplomatic quarter Peiping on parts of which are located buildings belonging to Government USA".

Assume it would be necessary effect detailed survey before there could be determined, for instance, value land, buildings and total value real property involved. Believe forms should be submitted by November 26, if possible. Please instruct priority.

In view felt desirability united stand, Department and Nanking may desire consult representatives concerned governments.

Sent Department 2043; Department pass Shanghai 1202, Tientsin 99, Nanking 1166.

CLUBB

---

[38] Not printed.
[39] Treaty between the United States and China for the relinquishment of extraterritorial rights in China, signed at Washington, January 11, 1943, Department of State, Treaty Series No. 984; 57 Stat. (pt. 2) 767.

702.0093/11–2249 : Telegram

The Consul General at Peiping (Clubb) to the Secretary of State

PEIPING, November 22, 1949—6 p. m.
[Received November 23—12:29 a. m.]

2054. Consuls yesterday took note difficulties by report being experienced re registration government property Tientsin, agreed nevertheless letter in parallel terms should be sent Land Bureau without official signature but text making clear (1) properties involved appertained foreign governments, and (2) consuls acting in their capacities authorized agents "those governments were requesting instructions". Dispatch letters being held up temporarily, probably until 25th.

This preliminary letter reply technically unessential, would be necessary only if it proved infeasible take first steps for application in prescribed procedure by November 30, but was felt desirable in order effect initial clarification matter. Personally feel Communist *bona fides* undependable, and remarkable absence code law for use as reference, therefore consider due care should be taken avoid comprise [*compromise?*] our official character. Re Embtel 406, November 22,[40] particularly feel strongly private Chinese seal should not be used because of implication (especially in Chinese eyes) action performed in other than official capacity.

Reiterate at this time strong belief in desirability maintenance united front here as elsewhere vis-à-vis Communists.

Sent Department 205; Department pass Nanking 1168, Shanghai 1206, Tientsin 100.

CLUBB

702.0093/11–2549 : Telegram

The Consul General at Peiping (Clubb) to the Secretary of State

PEIPING, November 25, 1949—noon.
[Received November 25—2:29 a. m.]

2080. Consuls yesterday decided send letter (Contel 2054, November 23 [*22*]) Land Bureau tomorrow along indicated lines without title, unless in receipt prior contrary instructions. French Consul for present unable act in view instruction from his office Shanghai.

Sent Department 2080; Department pass Nanking 1175, Tientsin 101, Shanghai 1215.

CLUBB

---

[40] Not printed.

893.5200/11–3049 : Telegram

The Consul General at Peiping (Clubb) to the Secretary of State

PEIPING, November 30, 1949.
[Received November 30—8 : 22 a. m.]

2133. Reftel 2108, November 28.[41] Following is text letter sent Peking Bureau Land Administration under date November 29 reserving rights absent Americans re titles real property this municipality:

"With reference to regulations, effective November, of September 15, 1949, re registration of aliens real property and November order Fu Ti I No. 15 extending period for submission of application for such registration, I invite your attention to circumstances that there are probably number of American citizens holding title to real property in this municipality who, however, are presently absent from Peking, and either have not been informed in respect to current regulations, or have been unable to make arrangements to make application for registration as indicated. Under instructions of US Government, I would inform you that my Government therefore makes reservation in respect to rights of nationals of US holding title to real property in area covered by reference regulations, in those cases where concerned Americans may have been unable to comply with reference regulations within time set, because of absence from Peking, or other valid cause."

Letter returned by Bureau shortly afterwards.
Sent Department, Shanghai 1241, Nanking 1192, Tientsin by mail.

CLUBB

125.7141/11–3049 : Telegram

The Consul General at Peiping (Clubb) to the Secretary of State

PEIPING, November 30, 1949—5 p. m.
[Received December 1—11 : 47 a. m.]

2155. Submitted applications for registration property November 30 (mytel 2029, November 18 [41]). Property divided four parts: (1) San Kuan Miao; (2) motor pool; (3) main compound 23 Legation St; (4) Glacis property west of (3), with separate application for each. British, Belgian, Netherlands, Italian consular representatives also applied registration property their governments. French awaiting instructions have not presented applications. All used identical Chinese answers on bureau form as suggested Nanking's 2455, November 18, and 2468, November 22 [42] as far as possible.

Land Administration Bureau raised no question "former" ["*for*"?] American Government or status "Foreign Service Officer". Used Con-

---

[41] Not printed.
[42] Neither printed.

sulate General stamp once on document in nature and register not on application forms. Personal stamp neither supplied nor required. But requested delivery within one week, sketch of property covered in applications including buildings located thereon. Now endeavoring prepare this on basis available information and maps, but will state at time submission it is not survey map. Land Bureau plans independent survey British compound and other Peiping property and may in due course propose survey American Government property.

Under head "Titles or Deeds Submitted" all Consuls used formula Nanking's 406, November 22.[44] Bureau requested copy of such agreements. Paragraph 4 Nanking's 406, November 22, please instruct priority re treaty citation.

Sent Department 2155. Department pass Nanking 1200, Shanghai 1251, Tientsin 107.

CLUBB

125.7141/12–649 : Telegram

The Consul General at Peiping (Clubb) to the Secretary of State

PEIPING, December 6, 1949—6 p. m.
[Received December 7—1 : 15 p. m.]

2227. Consuls meeting today took cognizance previous action at Tientsin re payment house and land taxes and regulations governing matter recently promulgated Peiping (Contels 2165, December 2; 2215, December 6[45]). Agreed themselves not take initiative by approaching Bureau and if themselves approached, (1) not to pay, (2) to present no argument, but simply (3) to refer question to their several governments.

Note December 15 land tax deadline. If Tientsin action be taken as precedent, Consulates here will possibly be approached for payment taxes.

In circumstances, request (1) information re denouncement Shanghai (re Deptel 1419, July 15 to Shanghai; [46] Depcirtel August 26, 6 a. m.; [47] Shanghai's 303, September 1 [48]) and (2) Department's directive re procedure to be followed Peiping, particularly in event local authorities demand such taxes.

Sent Department 2227; Department pass Shanghai 1283, Nanking 1224, Tientsin 108.

CLUBB

---

[44] Not printed.
[45] Neither printed.
[46] *Post*, p. 1233.
[47] *Ante*, p. 1104.
[48] Same as telegram No. 3615, September 2, 3 p. m., p. 1288.

125.7141/11–3049 : Telegram

The Secretary of State to the Consul General at Peiping (Clubb)[49]

WASHINGTON, December 8, 1949—6 p. m.

887. Urtel 2155 Nov 30. Because of deadline suggest you inform local Commie auths Peiping properties acquired by "Final protocol for the settlement of the disturbances of 1900" concluded at Peking, Sept 7, 1901 (Art. VII)[50] and rights thereto confirmed by "Treaty between the United States of America and the Republic of China for the relinquishment of extraterritorial rights in China and the regulation of related matters", which was signed at Washington Jan 11, 1943 and entered into force May 20, 1943 (Art. II).[51] Suggest you concert with colleagues.

ACHESON

125.7141/12–649 : Telegram

The Secretary of State to the Consul General at Peiping (Clubb)[52]

WASHINGTON, December 16, 1949—7 p. m.

909. Urtel 2227, Dec 6. Position taken Depcirtel Aug 26 still prevails. If tax bills recd they shld be returned with statement ConGen assumes bills sent in error. In returning bills ConGen shld state reason for exception viz., "taxes not payable since a sovereign Govt shld not be taxed on property owned by that Govt and used for Govt purposes".

ConGen in its ltrs to Shanghai land admin bureau stated US Govt adheres to internationally accepted principle one country does not tax property of another, US Govt considers itself not liable for payment of taxes.

Suggest you handle tax problem this basis but keep Dept fully informed.

Sent Peiping, rptd Shanghai, Nanking.

ACHESON

---

[49] Repeated to the Embassy at Nanking as No. 1282.
[50] *Foreign Relations*, Appendix, 1901, Affairs in China, pp. 312, 316.
[51] Department of State Treaty Series No. 984, or 57 Stat. (pt. 2) 767, 768.
[52] Repeated to the Consul General at Shanghai as No. 2438 and to the Embassy at Nanking as No. 1300.

III. HANKOW AND TSINGTAO: REFUSAL OF COMMUNISTS TO DEAL WITH CONSULATES; CLOSING OF UNITED STATES INFORMATION SERVICE OFFICES; CLOSURE OF CONSULATE AT HANKOW AND WITHDRAWAL OF STAFF; CLOSURE OF CONSULATE AT TSINGTAO; SEIZURE OF UNITED STATES GOVERNMENT PROPERTY BY COMMUNISTS AT TSINGTAO; DEPARTURE OF STAFF FROM TSINGTAO DELAYED BY COMMUNIST OBSTRUCTIONS

893.00/5–2449 : Telegram

The Consul General at Hankow (Callanan) to the Secretary of State

HANKOW, May 24, 1949—3 p. m.
[Received May 24—5 : 20 a. m.]

157. Last 4 days quiet, uneventful, no formal entry made by Communists.[53] In reply to letter from Commissioner of Police written just before Communists arrived, I sent him, just after Communists arrived, list of American properties Hankow. Same action taken British and French colleagues. Upon verbal request police officer of former Foreign Affairs Section known to Consulate General and still occupying post, a list of American and Chinese staff of Consulate General supplied. He planning submit list when turning over to new officials.

Ferry services resumed and railways being repaired. New mayor Wu Teh-feng reported assumed office May 23. Sian reported taken May 20 and Nanchang 22nd, only confused rumors re Changsha.

Foreigners here using their cars and moving about Wuhan [54] as usual. No regulations or orders have been issued restricting activities in any way.

Sent Department 157, repeated Nanking 119, OffEmb Canton 72.

CALLANAN

893.00/5–2549 : Telegram

The Consul General at Hankow (Callanan) to the Secretary of State

HANKOW, May 25, 1949—9 a. m.
[Received 3 : 03 p. m.]

159. Wuhan garrison headquarters regulations issued through press yesterday. Summary follows:

(1) people to continue normal occupations and observe orders; (2) all anti-Communist organizations dissolved, their officers to register and turn in documents and arms; (3) headquarters will maintain order and punish unlawful acts; (4) disbanded soldiers and stragglers must surrender selves and weapons and will receive lenient treatment; (5) all arms must be delivered PLA [55] and nobody shall conceal arms,

---

[53] For information on Chinese Communist occupation of Hankow, see telegram No. 152, May 19, from the Consul General at Hankow, p. 336.
[54] Wuchang, Hankow, Hanyang.
[55] People's Liberation Army (Communist).

ammunition, radio stations or other military supplies; (6) nobody shall shelter those who destroyed property or committed acts of hostility against PLA; (7) all foreigners shall observe laws and orders promulgated; (8) PLA shall observe orders not fire without reason and shall observe discipline.

Reference points 5 and 7, Consulate General transmitter is not concealed, police aware that staff includes 3 radio operators, therefore am taking no action re radio pending more specific approach by authorities. Department note however Consulate General may be off air in few days with little or no advance notice.

Sent Department 159; repeated Nanking 121, Embassy Canton 73.

CALLANAN

---

123 Blackerby, William: Telegram

The Consul at Tsingtao (Hawthorne) to the Secretary of State

TSINGTAO, June 4, 1949.
[Received June 4—12:01 a. m.]

242. Blackerby [56] proceeded ConGen this morning by bicycle relieve Vice Consul Hein [57] prevented entry by C C [58] guards on building. [59] Hein, who has been forcibly detained office past 24 hours, will attempt proceed home on foot after dispatch message, leaving two alien members staff in building maintain communications.

Troops also permitting no ingress-egress British ConGen.

City quiet with curfew from 8 p. m. to 5 a. m., standard time which has been established.

Making every effort contact responsible officials in effort obtain vehicle passes and eliminate interference Consular functions, withdrawal troops US Government property.

Now understand Tan Hsi-lin in command troops here and that mayor has not arrived. Press reports Tan Hsi-lin's chief of staff is Chao Yi-ting and that Chairman Military Control Committee is Hsiang Ming with Tan Hsi-lin acting as vice chairman.

Sent Nanking 176, repeated Shanghai 94, Department 242.

HAWTHORNE

[56] William W. Blackerby, Consular Clerk at Tsingtao.
[57] George M. Hein.
[58] Chinese Communist.
[59] For information on Chinese Communist occupation of Tsingtao, see telegram No. 238, June 3, from the Consul at Tsingtao, p. 365.

893.00B/6-649 : Telegram

The Consul at Tsingtao (Hawthorne) to the Secretary of State

TSINGTAO, June 6, 1949.
[Received June 5—11 : 53 p. m.]

243. President Soviet Citizens Society, accompanied by Danish Consul, Saturday attempted call CC Military Headquarters apply vehicle passes, refused admission, although reportedly a liaison officer to deal with such matters has been appointed.

Although orders to sentries still somewhat confused, now possible foreigners including American staff enter, leave Consulate General and believe communications can be maintained.

Exchange rate announced today US $1 equals 5.50 PN; [60] Yuan Shihkai $1 ditto; gold bars PN 45,000 per ounce.

Sent Nanking 177; repeated Department 243, Shanghai 95.

HAWTHORNE

125.9536/6-1349 : Telegram

The Consul at Tsingtao (Hawthorne) to the Secretary of State

TSINGTAO, June 13, 1949—1 p. m.
[Received June 13—6 : 37 a. m.]

261. Chinese staff permitted enter Consulate General for duty today for first time; previously radio operators had lived on premises maintain communications.

Expect issuance vehicle passes tomorrow.

By informal memo today protesting occupation US Government property 1 Kwangsi Road, withdrawal troops from premises requested; meantime responsibility protection real estate and Government property stored therein placed on occupying forces (Chinese staff members residing in building have not been evicted and report no property has been removed[)]. Similarly inquiry made regarding whereabouts welfare Bender and Smith [61] and when I may expect them turned over my custody (reDeptel 156, June 4 [62]).

Relatively little anti-American propaganda either by poster, radio or press. On contrary district military leader of area where Consulate General located on June 11, in speech to representatives each family in district, stated "thanks to our American comrades, the Kmt [63] bandits did not destroy public utilities". Presumably he referred to joint

---

[60] People's Notes (Chinese Communist currency).
[61] For information on the case of Elmer C. Bender, U.S. Marines, and William C. Smith, U.S. Navy, see footnote 31, p. 384.
[62] Not printed.
[63] Kuomintang (Nationalist Party).

Consular representations to Liu An-chi,[64] previously reported,[65] when I acted as spokesman.

Repeated Nanking 188, Shanghai 106.

HAWTHORNE

125.9536/6–1449 : Telegram

The Consul at Tsingtao (Hawthorne) to the Secretary of State

TSINGTAO, June 14, 1949—4 p. m.
[Received June 14—6 : 49 a. m.]

264. Foreign Affairs Secretary perused but refused accept informal memos mentioned mytel 261, June 13 in absence diplomatic relations. Yang [66] said "liberation army protects lives and properties all foreign nationals", from which may be inferred he personally at least recognizes status Kwangsi road property. Regarding Bender and Smith, he remained silent.

Re mytel 258, June 11,[67] Yang further stated I am not allowed to move at this time in view order temporarily prohibiting residents from moving.

Reliable contact states higher level Commies here definitely tuning down anti-American propaganda, probably realizing commercial relations with US essential success.

Sent Department 264, repeated Nanking 190, Shanghai 108.

HAWTHORNE

125.9532 : Telegram

The Consul at Tsingtao (Hawthorne) to the Secretary of State

TSINGTAO, June 18, 1949—11 a. m.
[Received June 18—5 : 19 a. m.]

274. Learned that CCMIK [*Chinese Communist Military?*] occupants property concerned propose remove certain fuels therefrom; I caused delivery following unsigned memo to Foreign Affairs section June 17:

"I was pleased to hear the repeated assurances that the People's Army and Government intend to protect foreign properties. In this connection, the gasoline and kerosene stored in the compound at Nr. 1 Kwangsi Road is the property of the American Consulate General

---

[64] Liu An-chi, Chinese Commanding General, Tsingtao Garrison.
[65] Despatch No. 19, June 2, from the Consul at Tsingtao, not printed.
[66] Yang Yin-chiao, Assistant Chief of the Foreign Affairs section of the Communist Military Control Board at Tsingtao.
[67] Not printed; it concerned the Consul's request to move to 9 Shanhaikuan Road. (123 Hawthorne, Carl O.)

at Tsingtao, having been bought and stored at its present location by this office. I therefore trust that this fuel will not be removed from its present place of storage on American Government-owned property. Needless to say, I cannot acquiesce in the removal of this fuel to any other place of storage, and should it be removed without my authority I can only consider such action as confiscation, unless appropriate receipts are given and written authority granted for withdrawals by me of fuels as needed from the new place of storage."

Anticipate increasing difficulties retaining possession US Government properties, equipment and supplies at this post. I received indirect inquiries as to where American Admiral used to live and status property 9 Shanhaikuan Road.[68] I have replied property purchased by Department for FS [69] use but that as courtesy to senior American official Admiral permitted live there. I pointed out that even during his occupancy Department spent some $25,000 furnishing house.

Repeated Nanking 195, Shanghai 112.

HAWTHORNE

125.9531/6–2149 : Telegram

The Consul at Tsingtao (*Hawthorne*) *to the Secretary of State*

TSINGTAO, June 21, 1949—11 a. m.
[Received June 21—6 : 25 a. m.]

281. Yesterday I renewed request permission move to 9 Shanhaikuan Road. Speaking personally, Yang said he believed such permission could not be given till ownership status clarified and that matter would probably be referred by Military Control Board to central authorities (Yang previously informed we hold title deeds this and other properties).

Reference memo quoted in mytel 274, June 18, Yang said, if for reasons safety, Military should consider it necessary remove fuel from compound due protection will be given and nothing lost, adding if, owing absolute necessity, Ministry should use any part fuel we will be compensated "when all such questions as this and property and moving, etc., are settled". Meantime we not even permitted to withdraw fuel from stockpile since ownership thereof as well as 1 Kwangsi Road property questioned.

Reiterating he spoke only as individual, Yang concluded interview by expressing opinion that if and when relations established on higher level all local problems will be easily resolved.

Repeated Nanking 199, Shanghai 116.

HAWTHORNE

---

[68] For documentation concerning withdrawal of U.S. Naval forces from Tsingtao, see vol. IX, pp. 1191 ff.

[69] Foreign Service.

125.4552 : Telegram

The Consul General at Hankow (Callanan) to the Secretary of State

HANKOW, June 24, 1949—3 p. m.
[Received 11 : 40 p. m.]

193. Registration Consular cars refused today unless submitted as for "former American Consulate General" and "former Consul General". British colleague only other similar case same treatment. Registration in personal name without reference to status refused. Possibilities under consideration with Embassy's 65, February 26, to Peiping [70] in mind and no intention denying Consular status.

Sent Department 193; repeated Nanking 148, OffEmb Canton 89.

CALLANAN

693.002/6–2449 : Telegram

The Consul General at Hankow (Callanan) to the Secretary of State

HANKOW, June 24, 1949—4 p. m.
[Received June 25—4 : 48 a. m.]

194. Combined Foreign Chamber Commerce Hankow, comprising British Chamber, British firms nonmembers of latter, Bank Indochina as sole vestige French Chamber and three American firms, organized instrument for approach local authorities in view nonrecognition Consuls, sent Foreign Affairs Bureau letter and follow-up suggesting discussion problems but have been ignored.

As yet no contact between foreigners and authorities except specific instances where authorities desire use port equipment and such matters, and connection applications by several for permission go Kuling for summer and one Shanghai for business. Applicants questioned exhaustively and applications taken under consideration. No replies received though applications made 2 weeks ago.

Sent Department; repeated Nanking 149, OffEmb Canton 90.

CALLANAN

893.01/6–2949 : Telegram

The Consul General at Hankow (Callanan) to the Secretary of State

HANKOW, June 29, 1949—10 a. m.
[Received July 1—6 : 38 a. m.]

197. Mytels 166 and 167, May 31, to Department.[71] Further new developments. Present status Consulates. French Consul sought inter-

---

[70] Not found in Department of State files.
[71] Neither printed.

view Foreign Affairs Bureau, told could not be received, status unrecognized. British Consulate General visited by alleged Foreign Affairs Bureau official who claimed could arrange interview his chief, nothing material yet and Bureau through British Consulate General Chinese clerk disowned alleged officer. Consequently no attempt contact made by me and no incident except rejection letter sent police and refusal car registration reported by 193, June 24. Further study reveals no hope early termination of lay up our cars. Several foreigners wishing travel applied Foreign Affairs Bureau were questioned closely at length regarding their activities and organizations with stenographer taking full notes. Told would be informed but none has yet received permission travel.

Attitudes new government. Chinks have begun appear façade of rectitude presented by new government after liberation. Respective [*Respect for?*] property does not include effort assure property not foreign before occupation and some Consulate properties are occupied by troops. Seems attitude soft in Hankow but harsh in country and smaller centers where Mission properties inhabited by reduced number missionaries have been part occupied. Peasants reported taxed retroactively 11 years are described by one missionary "in despair".

Adopting Communist method of elusive officialdom, foreign business firms, grouped as foreign commercial community, trying channel all matters concerning individual firms through itself to Foreign Affairs Bureau and striving reach joint decisions, individual firms when approached referring questions to Chamber. Similarly recreation club having large grounds and buildings, now unused and being pressured for occupancy, has replaced chairman by governing committee so that onus of opposing wishes of authorities falls on no one person. Success this plan remains doubtful as Foreign Affairs Bureau has ignored letters from commercial community requesting discussion problems.

Administration. Evident lack trained experienced people hampers regime, engenders supercaution business and stifles progress. Government by decree in full swing, 13 separate series totalling 23 notifications promulgated covering subjects from traffic rules and health regulations to financial edicts. Assurances protection capitalists published to stimulate business but with little effect. Search for Kmt assets unremitting and properties used by Kmt taken over including some foreign-owned.

General. Little news these days from outlying areas. Nothing re Sian but recent traveler said economic conditions bad Changsha which still held by Nationalists. Chinese merchants still travel here from Canton with watches, medicine, other luxury items despite intervening front line. In bombing June 1, 51 Chinese killed, 4 wounded and 2 of 5 bombs dropped fell in river 200 yards from Consulate. June 2,

6 Nationalist reconnaissance planes greeted by few bursts anti-aircraft fire and no raid followed.

Sent Department 197, repeated Nanking 151, OffEmb Canton 92.

CALLANAN

125.9531/6–3049 : Telegram

The Consul at Tsingtao (Hawthorne) to the Secretary of State

TSINGTAO, June 30, 1949—10 a. m.
[Received 10 : 16 a. m.]

302. Chinese military yesterday began removing from compound at 1 Kwangsi Road Consulate General's stocks of gas, kerosene and luboil (remytel 281, June 21).

Sent Department 302, repeated Nanking 210, Shanghai 126.

HAWTHORNE

893.4212/6–3049 : Telegram

The Consul at Tsingtao (Hawthorne) to the Secretary of State

TSINGTAO, June 30, 1949—2 p. m.
[Received July 1—11 : 25 a. m.]

304. Cheloo University in Tsinan only Protestant Christian college in Shantung. Prior to Communist occupation major portion students and all faculty members except 30 Chinese, 4 Americans and 2 British evacuated to Hangchow. Evacuated students now permitted return, also professors who have been "cleared", and Chinese President returned Tsinan recently.

Major changes under Communists are, (1) removal of all foreigners from office in university on grounds such institutions should be strictly Chinese; (2) reduction course to 2 years high school and freshman courses; (3) increasing hours study Chinese literature and government at expense English language; and (4) pressure foreclosure theological seminary on grounds religious instruction out of place on campus.

No interference with college's policy borrowing money against outside credits yet experienced.

University pressured into turning over half of campus and all empty residences to Communist propaganda school. Authorities reluctant openly force foreigners out but constant pressure being exerted through petty annoyances prevail upon them leave Tsinan on own volition (reDeptel 157, June 4 [72]).

HAWTHORNE

---

[72] Not printed.

125.9532 : Telegram

The Secretary of State to the Consul at Tsingtao (Hawthorne)

WASHINGTON, July 1, 1949—7 p. m.

177. Dept assumes you have protested to local Aliens Affairs Office (urtel 302, June 30). Shld attempt obtain receipt for such removals signed by officer removing.

ACHESON

125.9532 : Telegram

The Secretary of State to the Consul at Tsingtao (Hawthorne)

WASHINGTON, July 1, 1949—7 p. m.

178. Dept approves action described urtel 274 June 18. In opinion Dept however desirable avoid use even in unsigned memo terms "People's Army and Govt" in order obviate possible attempt Commies infer US recognition. Suggest any Commie agencies be referred to by ConGen simply as Chinese Communists.[73]

ACHESON

125.9533/7–249 : Telegram

The Consul at Tsingtao (Hawthorne) to the Secretary of State

TSINGTAO, July 2, 1949—10 p. m.
[Received July 2—11 : 09 a. m.]

307. Three Chinese staff members of Consulate General residing at 1 Kwangsi Road yesterday ordered by military vacate premises.

Remytel 302, June 30, will report soon as possible quantity and current market value fuel taken by military.

Repeated Nanking 213, Shanghai 129.

HAWTHORNE

125.9532 : Telegram

The Consul at Tsingtao (Hawthorne) to the Secretary of State

TSINGTAO, July 5, 1949—4 p. m.
[Received July 10—1 : 47 p. m.]

316. By unsigned memo July 2 protested to Foreign Affairs section Military Control Board against removal fuel and requested detailed receipt from responsible officer but not hopeful results (reDeptel 177, July 1). For Department's information, our records indicate follow-

---

[73] See also telegram No. 98, May 13, 2 p. m., to the Consul General at Tientsin, p. 1082.

ing property taken (figures representing current market values in US dollars) :

157 drums kerosene valued $11,932; 424 drums luboil valued $44,944; 321 drums gas valued $26,001; 147 cans axle grease valued $220.50; 100 drums mixture gas and kerosene valued $4,000; 31,400 gallons diesel valued $12,000; total value $99,097.50.

For Department's further information, Consulate General actually purchased direct or through Department above property to total value only $5,310 (including kerosene purchases for commissary valued $1,055). Other property transferred from Navy nonreimbursable basis.

Sent Department 316; repeated Nanking 216.

HAWTHORNE

125.9531/7-749 : Telegram

The Secretary of State to the Consul at Tsingtao (Hawthrone)

WASHINGTON, July 7, 1949—9 p. m.

184. Dept assumes ConGen has protested to local Aliens Affairs Office re order vacate premises nr 1 Kwangsi Road (urtel 307, July 2). US Govt has only provisional title this property. However ConGen should inform Commie auths property is regarded as US Govt owned.

ACHESON

125.9532 : Telegram

The Consul at Tsingtao (Hawthorne) to the Secretary of State

TSINGTAO, July 9, 1949—10 a. m.
[Received July 9—2 : 30 a. m.]

324. Under my instructions Chinese member ConGen's staff yesterday called on Yang of Foreign Affairs section. He said memo protesting removal fuel (remytel 316, July 5) was found in order and accepted. He expressed doubt receipt would be issued but reiterated military would keep accurate record property taken and of consumption fuel if any.

He said he had personally seen Bender and Smith end May and that they were safe and well, adding he doubts negotiations for their release can be opened before diplomatic relations established (reDeptel 156, June 4). Remytel 320, July 8,[74] Department may wish appropriately advise Mrs. Smith.

Yang desires it understood he speaking as individual, not officially.

Sent Department; repeated Nanking as 220, Shanghai as 134.

HAWTHORNE

---

[74] Not printed.

125.9531/7–949 : Telegram

The Consul at Tsingtao (Hawthorne) to the Secretary of State

TSINGTAO, July 9, 1949—11 a. m.
[Received July 9—7:41 a. m.]

325. Chinese staff not actually evicted from 1 Kwangsi Road till yesterday, when Consul General protested by unsigned memo (re Deptel 184, July 7). Memo of June 13 protesting against occupation informed Communists property US Government-owned (re mytel 261, that date).

Sent Department 325; repeated Nanking 222.

HAWTHORNE

125.4556/7–1549 : Telegram

The Consul General at Hankow (Callanan) to the Secretary of State

HANKOW, July 15, 1949.
[Received July 15—7:01 a. m.]

210. Director Foreign Affairs Bureau summoned Pao [75] his office this morning and verbally gave order issued by WMCC [76] to stop all functions USIS [77] 1 p. m. today. No reasons for action given other than military situation. Copy of order refused but USIS interpreter allowed on request take down order as dictated. Order observed but will endeavor arrange resume some functions. Complete details upcoming.[78]

Sent Department 210, repeated Nanking 166, OffEmb Canton 99.

CALLANAN

125.4556/7–1849 : Telegram

The Consul General at Hankow (Callanan) to the Secretary of State

HANKOW, July 18, 1949—10 a. m.
[Received 10:30 a. m.]

214. Reur 42, July 15.[79] All USIE [80] activities have ceased 1300 hours July 15. Any other course foolhardy. There is no law other than the Wuhan Military Control Commission. Exploring possibilities re-

---

[75] Chinese news editor of USIS.
[76] Wuhan Military Control Commission.
[77] United States Information Service.
[78] Telegram No. 211, July 16, from the Consul General at Hankow, not printed.
[79] See telegram No. 1420, July 15, 7 p. m., to the Consul General at Shanghai, p. 1234.
[80] United States Information and Educational Program.

stricted activities but unoptimistic. Hudson [81] was not permitted even discuss matter (mytel 211, July 16 [82]) and foregone conclusion protests would be rejected. Reference suggested protest ground (1) local authorities do not recognize existence Consulate here and admit no authority in me to submit anything in official capacity. They have consistently refused accept representations from me or British or French colleagues.

USIE locals on leave with pay except few to aid Pao and assist putting things in order.

No suggestions re Department's statement and VOA publicity.

Sent Department 214; repeated Nanking 671, Embassy Canton 102.

CALLANAN

125.4556/7–1949 : Telegram

The Consul General at Hankow (Callanan) to the Secretary of State

HANKOW, July 19, 1949—3 p. m.
[Received July 19—9 : 14 a. m.]

217. Formal protest suspension USIS Hankow lodged with Foreign Affairs Bureau today, covering points 1 and 2 suggested by Department.[83] Request also made resumption USIS activities.

Director FAB [84] offered see Hudson. Minor Communist official told him fill out application for interview, reminding Hudson he appearing solely as alien individual. Hudson replied, "I am a representative and citizen of the US and matter I have to discuss with FAB director is not personal but concerns my Government." Hudson then offered official protest memorandum for delivery FAB director who refused to accept on ground not addressed specific individual. Hudson replied memorandum addressed FAB which proper place to take up matters re foreign affairs, again offering memorandum which refused. After further argument, permission granted leave memorandum with receptionist, of whom specific request made that it be delivered FAB director. No reaction yet.

Sent Department 217; repeated Nanking 175, Canton 105.

CALLANAN

---

[81] Harry S. Hudson, Vice Consul at Hankow.
[82] Not printed.
[83] See telegram No. 1420, July 15, 7 p. m., to the Consul General at Shanghai, p. 1234.
[84] Foreign Affairs Bureau.

125.4556/7–2049 : Telegram

The Consul General at Hankow (Callanan) to the Secretary of State

HANKOW, July 20, 1949—10 a. m.
[Received July 21—11 : 06 a. m.]

221. Mytel 217. Our written protest returned without comment yesterday. Today following received from WMCC addressed USIS Hankow:

"The USIS is a part of the organization of the State Department of the US. Since the People's Government has no diplomatic and consular relations with the US, the USIS should from today stop its activities, including the printing and distribution of news releases, the exhibition and donation of books and newspapers, the posting of posters, the showing of movies, the giving of concerts, and all other outside activities.

You are requested to obey accordingly and not to contravene."

Document bears chops WMCC director and deputy.

Sent Department, repeated Nanking 179, OffEmb Canton 109, Shanghai 100.

CALLANAN

893.6363/7–2549 : Telegram

The Consul at Tsingtao (Hawthorne) to the Secretary of State

TSINGTAO, July 25, 1949—2 p. m.
[Received July 25—1 : 26 p. m.]

369. Re third paragraph Depcirtel July 13.[85] Caltex [86] experienced labor trouble when attempted discharge five coolies.

Coolies manhandled American district manager and demanded year's salary. Company finally agreed pay 6 months' salary which acceptable to employees but not to labor union. Case unsettled.

Well-informed foreign banker predicts collapse People's Notes within 3 months.

Small quantities Russian poor quality gas entering Chefoo. Buses operating between here and Chefoo losing minimum 7,000 PN per trip basis cost fuel alone.

Sent Nanking 235, repeated Department 369, Shanghai 146.

HAWTHORNE

---

[85] Not printed.
[86] California Texas Oil Co., Ltd.

893.00/7–2949 : Telegram

The Consul General at Hankow (Callanan) to the Secretary of State

HANKOW, July 29, 1949—10 a. m.
[Received July 31—1 : 52 p. m.]

235. Recent developments (mytel 197 to Department June 29) :
Status foreigners: No travel regulations issued, no permits granted though some requests 2 months old. Large sign placed wall British Consulate compound translates "Chinese and Japanese people unite, oppose long American occupation Japan". British Consul General requested authorities remove sign, letter returned without comment and sign remains. Communist teams of 4 or 5 usually including 1 or 2 uniformed women going rounds foreign firms questioning foreigners re work, economic conditions, Chinese friends, hobbies, etc. Consulate not approached so far.

Attitude to US: New China News Agency version Olive [87] case published here and *Shanghai Liberal Daily* editorial July 10 was copied. No other mention except editorial July 14 in *Ta Kang Pao* on general subject foreign residents problems, referring also to [*Shanghai Evening*] *Post* and *Mercury*, theme equal treatment all.

Ta Kang Pao July 24 published so-called refutation dated Peiping July 22 of Assistant Secretary Allen's USIS statement.[88]

USIS suspension regretted verbally by some regular users. Since closure papers, books, magazines, taken by military guards from persons entering and memo protesting and asking that borrowed items be permitted return library was returned without comment. Guards question employees [and] other Chinese entering building.

General: Large troop movements southward through here recent weeks mostly nocturnal, latterly rumored including troops Fu Tso-yi.[89] Feeling of people in general seems rude awakening those who welcomed change and justification those opposed. Discontent at failure rosy Communist picture materialize rapidly said so keen even return disdained Nationalists be welcome.

Sent Department 235, repeated Nanking 185, OffEmb Canton 115.

CALLANAN

---

[87] William M. Olive, Vice Consul at Shanghai; for documentation on his case, see pp. 1155 ff.
[88] For statement by Assistant Secretary of State George V. Allen, see Department of State *Bulletin*, August 1, 1949, p. 152.
[89] Former Chinese Commander in North China who remained in Peiping after Chinese Communist occupation.

125.953/7-2949 : Telegram

The Ambassador in China (Stuart) to the Secretary of State

NANKING, July 29, 1949—3 p. m.
[Received July 29—10 : 20 a. m.]

1642. In view impossibility effective representation for protection American interests, possible future hardship and danger for staff and probable impossibility sending replacements from outside Commie China prior to recognition, recommend consideration be given to closing Tsingtao and Hankow now and Canton when threatened by Commies. (See Embtel 1639, July 28 [90]) Tsingtao now of relatively little importance either from point of reporting or American interests. Hankow more important, but unless replacement can be sent for Callanan within reasonable time and junior language officer assigned from Peiping to permit increase reporting output, we see no advantage to retaining office there. Canton could be closed at time Embassy office withdraws to Hong King in face Commie advance and its reporting functions assumed by one or two officers, preferably Chinese language, assigned Hong Kong with sole duty procuring, analyzing and reporting information on developments South China.

If Department decides to close offices in Commie China, Embassy requests that male personnel these offices suitable for code and file work, disbursing officer, and guards be transferred Nanking since very unlikely personnel assigned Nanking but not arrived will be permitted entry.

If Department decides against closing ConGen Canton ahead of Commie occupation and despite recent experiences our Consulates elsewhere Commie-occupation areas, then recommend, in addition to above, that our personnel now Hong Kong (Scott, Carter, Vasque, Ryan and Clore en route Nanking and Dawson returning to Shanghai from leave and Finnegan now in Canton) move to Canton immediately so they can be captured with city and proceed Nanking and Shanghai when transportation Canton to north reopens.

Sent Department 1642, repeated Shanghai 914, Canton 691.

STUART

893.01/8-349 : Telegram

The Consul at Tsingtao (Hawthorne) to the Secretary of State

TSINGTAO, August 3, 1949—noon.
[Received August 3—8 : 44 a. m.]

394. Reference Depcirtel June 22.[91] Basis persistent local propaganda dispensed meetings inhabitants required attend, not believed

---

[90] *Post*, p. 1304.
[91] Not printed; it summarized situation of Embassy and Consular establishments in China for information of the various posts in China (893.01/6-2249).

Communists either desire or expect US Government recognition. Nor are they believed interested trade with US. Anti-American propaganda awakening latent anti-fore'gn feeling masses and may result physical violence against Americans [and] other occidentals. Expected key members ConGen's Chinese staff will eventually be forced resign severing only contact ConGen has with Foreign Affairs Section, since officials refuse see me. Except for most fanatic missionaries, believed all local Americans would gladly withdraw if possible and that Communists would welcome their departure. As previously reported, believe we will gradually lose all government property acquired under surplus property agreement [92] and may be impossible obtain other office quarters or to transfer radio station.

Under circumstances we wonder whether continued maintenance this ConGen will serve useful purpose.

Sent Department 394; repeated Nanking 222.

HAWTHORNE

893.01/8–349 : Telegram

The Secretary of State to the Consul at Tsingtao (Hawthorne)

WASHINGTON, August 12, 1949—6 p. m.

235. Reurtel 394, Aug 3. Dept has well to fore difficult position ur office and is giving entire question continuing consideration.

Pls inform what travel facilities, rail or ship, wld likely be available for withdrawal Amers generally from ur district, for our reference in case decision later made to close Consulate. Also report situation re exit permits.

ACHESON

125.953/8–1549 : Telegram

The Counselor of Embassy in China (Jones) to the Secretary of State

NANKING, August 15, 1949—3 p. m.
[Received August 15—11:12 a. m.]

1793. Tsingtao's 394, August 3, to Department indicates Commies may be giving special emphasis anti-US propaganda that city because of previous presence US Navy there. Reftel lends weight to our recommendation (Embtel 1642, July 29) ConGen be closed.

JONES

---

[92] Agreement between the United States and China for the sale of certain surplus war property, signed at Shanghai, August 30, 1946; Department of State, Office of the Foreign Liquidation Commissioner, *Report to Congress on Foreign Surplus Disposal*, October 1946, pp. 40–45.

125.455/8–1549 : Telegram

The Secretary of State to the Consul General at Hankow (*Callanan*)

WASHINGTON, August 15, 1949—6 p. m.

56. Dept has decided close ConGen Hankow view impossibility effective representation for protection Amer interests, possible future hardship for staff and probable impossibility sending staff replacements from outside, supplying and communicating with post. Actual closing date subject future decision. However, Dept of opinion closure shld be timed with departure those Amcit[izen]s desiring leave China on any evacuation ship or ships from Shanghai (Deptel 45 Jul 26 [93]). In meantime ConGen shld take steps preparatory closing and shld notify Amcits in ur district availability ConGen assist extent possible those desiring leave and confidentially advise likelihood closure fol completion evacuation. Amcits desiring leave shld be advised make prompt arrangements obtain exit permits enable them depart Shanghai possible evacuation ship about which you will be kept informed, or via north China. Dept desires ur recommendations re disposition Govt property Hankow. Travel orders and admin instr[uction]s subject separate tels.

ACHESON

393.1115/8–1849 : Telegram

The Consul General at Hankow (*Callanan*) *to the Secretary of State*

HANKOW, August 18, 1949—11 a. m.
[Received 12 : 38 p. m.]

271. Deptel 56, August 15. Appears little possibility people this area reaching Shanghai for evacuation mid-September since (1) no travel regulations yet issued and no foreigner yet permitted leave Wuhan and (2) sailings Hankow–Shanghai irregular and danger of attack river steamers considerable.

At least 20 travel applications business people made to Foreign Affairs Bureau but no results yet. Other hand few missionaries other than those due furlough yet felt urge depart.

If closure likelihood mentioned in letters re evacuation to Americans, and it must be, news will be out. Propose send letters next week. Approval requested.

Sent Department 271, Department pass Nanking 211, Shanghai 118, from Hankow.

CALLANAN

---

[93] See vol. IX, p. 1274, footnote 7.

102.22/8–2249 : Telegram

The Consul at Tsingtao (Hawthorne) to the Secretary of State

TSINGTAO, August 22, 1949—11 a. m.
[Received August 22—4 : 34 a. m.]

448. Communists recently questioned certain Chinese formerly employed by US Navy here. All released against shop guarantees but told because connected foreign military forces they must be reeducated. Some objected, saying they mere coolies and pointing out Chinese continued to be employed by ConGen. Communists replied such Chinese spies, for whom they have separate program.

Such news most disquieting ConGen's Chinese staff.

Department pass Nanking its discretion.

HAWTHORNE

393.1115/8–1849 : Telegram

The Secretary of State to the Consul General at Hankow (Callanan)

WASHINGTON, August 23, 1949—7 p. m.

66. Reurtel 271 Aug 18, rptd Nanking 211, Shanghai 118. Despite present unfavorable outlook for travel and issuance exit permits, you shld proceed with notification Amers and preparations closure office. Since there appears no prospect early amelioration of situation, requests for travel permits shld be pressed in endeavor secure departure earliest possible date Amers wishing to leave. What steamer travel Hankow–Nanking is available and wld request of Natl Govt for safe passage vessel to Nanking be necessary?

FYI,[94] APL [95] agent Shanghai in response demand Amers other foreigners shipping space has announced *Gen Gordon* can call Shanghai mid-Sep.[96] Foreigners there now applying exit permits, few of which issued to date. APL agent states Commie auths have agreed entry of vessel but wish more info passengers and freight. FonOff Canton has informed EmbOff no objection call of evacuation vessel Shanghai to take on passengers. Assuming no hitch in permits for entry vessel from Natls and Commies, chief question is whether number exit permits granted will be sufficient warrant vessel's call. Hope is to have further vessels, possibly including coastal steamers from Hong Kong, visit Shanghai this purpose.

ACHESON

[94] For your information.
[95] American President Lines.
[96] See telegram No. 2946, July 28, 7 p. m., from the Consul at Shanghai, vol. IX, p. 1276.

125.455/8–2649 : Telegram

The Consul General at Hankow (Callanan) to the Secretary of State

HANKOW, August 26, 1949—11 a. m.
[Received 1:21 p. m.]

281. Deptel 66, August 23, 7 p. m. Am cautiously informing Americans likelihood closure. Before definite announcement of intention, wish Department appreciate (1) effect on staff and (2) possibility reaction by authorities. Re (1) under existing conditions "local" staff becomes predatory when dismissal looms, outside influence partly blameable. Despite optimism mytel 277, August 22, noon,[97] USIS staff reasserts demand 4 months' severance pay, insisting with some justice because work is scarce and recalling stigma they bear results service with US. Believe they will agree accept not less than granted Shanghai which they still claiming. Same time if closure plan known they will expect basis not less than accorded Consulate staff, though this will be mainly controlled by seniority sliding scale. Assume complete records supplemented by mytel 263, August 15, noon,[97] in Department for retirement senior Chinese. Important be able assure prompt payment annuities where applicable and proper severance for senior employees not pensionable. With closure planned, layoffs as per staff reduction not feasible and all will expect pay until closure date. I recommend Richard Lee should be retained reduced basis after closing as overseer equipment and US-owned compound. After actual closure several staff will be retained for final work estimated 2 weeks. October 1 appears good closure date, not earlier.

Movement citizens need have no bearing closure date as we powerless to help them now with anything more than advice.

Re (2), with actual closure radio stops necessarily but no assurances authorities will not move when closure intention known. Presuming confidential files to be burned, I request authority burn noncurrent files now. It should also be kept in mind that when and if I am permitted depart probably will not be permitted carry uninspected accounts or other official documents. Official attitude to Consulate appears hardening. Visitors French Consulate have been frisked and last evening about 9 clerk Huso was refused egress this building, he having apartment herein.

Re dismissals, I want direct and realistic approach. Situation loaded against us and might produce more than much upleasantness and not worth saving few hundred dollars. May say after strain of past months, especially last 3, our nerves unlikely equal to wrangle with staff over separation.

Sent Department 281, passed Nanking 220, Shanghai 122.

CALLANAN

---

[97] Not printed.

125.9531/8–3049 : Telegram

The Consul at Tsingtao (Hawthorne) to the Secretary of State

TSINGTAO, August 30, 1949—10 a. m.
[Received August 30—3 : 21 a. m.]

459. ReDepcirtel August 26.[98] Estimated land taxes US Government properties Tsingtao reported mytel 424, August 11.[99] As reported mytel 402, August 2,[99] house taxes nominal. Now have good reason believe house tax bill mentioned that telegram deliberately submitted in name former owner. Also that Communists will not press for payment taxes US Government properties here for present. Despite violent anti-American propaganda, high level Communists here apparently hopeful eventual establishment diplomatic relations with US, when ownership properties purchased from Kmt Government under surplus property agreement will definitely be questioned. Meantime they do not wish recognize ownership such properties by collecting taxes from ConGen.

Department pass Nanking its discretion.

HAWTHORNE

125.455/9–149 : Telegram

The Secretary of State to the Ambassador in the United Kingdom (Douglas)[1]

WASHINGTON, September 1, 1949—7 p. m.

3161. If UK agrees request contained Deptel 3067 Aug 26 [99] pls ascertain soonest if FonOff objects immed release to press of fol :

"Dept State today announced Amer ConGen Hankow instructed close and withdraw all personnel and that staffs AmEmb Nanking and Amer ConGen Shanghai to be reduced about one-half. Reductions will be carried out when arrangements completed for transportation from China Amers and other foreigners who wish depart.

Decision take these actions based upon same factors which led decision close Amer ConGen Canton.[2]

Through generous agreement Brit Govt, custody US official property in areas China in which Amer con[sular] estab[lishment]s are closed will be assumed by local Brit Con, which will also extend to Amer cits same protection afforded Brit subjects. Local Amer communities will form committees with which Brit Con offices will deal in routine matters affecting Amer natls in order that added burdens imposed upon Brit officers will be no greater than necessary.

---

[98] *Ante*, p. 1104.
[99] Not printed.
[1] Repeated to the Consul General at Hankow as No. 77.
[2] See telegram telCan No. 553, August 12, 3 p. m., to the Chargé in China, p. 1313.

These arrangements already in effect Canton and Tihwa consular districts and will take effect Hankow district when Amer Con estab that city closed.

Shld other Amer Con estabs China be confronted by situation similar to that which led decision close Amer ConGen Canton, it expected such estabs will also be closed and custody US official property and protection Amer natls be assumed by local Brit Con." [4]

Repeated Hankow for comment text and timing. [5]

ACHESON

125.4553/9–349 : Telegram

The Consul General at Hankow (Callanan) to the Secretary of State

HANKOW, September 3, 1949—noon.
[Received September 3—7 : 06 a. m.]

307. Depcirtel August 19, 2 a. m. [6] Twelve USIS staff terminated C.O.B. [7] today with 3 months' severance pay. No direct threat to security American personnel but it was clearly intimated that failure of settlement would result in picketing our radio. Also failure make quick settlement now would likely have resulted refusal payment and demand salary payment during subsequent period negotiation which could easily exceed month and possibly involve greater final demands at close of period.

Most important is that matter kept out of hands local authorities. Also hoped this sets pattern severance regular staff, leaving room above 3 months' severance pay for just payments those between 5 and 20 years service of whom there are several. Furthermore, impossible proceed closure preparations and separation regular staff with this matter dangling. Chief radio operator King Chao transferred September 3 C.O.B. to regular payroll from USIS payroll.

Sent Department 307, repeated Nanking 239; Shanghai 129.

[CALLANAN]

---

[4] In telegram No. 3547, September 2, 6 p. m., the Chargé in the United Kingdom stated : "Foreign Office has no objection immediate release of statement. Will be released also by Foreign Office as soon as news of release in US received on ticker." (701.4193/9–249)

[5] Telegram No. 315, September 7, 11 a. m., from the Consul General at Hankow, indicated no objection to statement for immediate release (125.455/9–49). Text was released to press on September 9; see Department of State Bulletin, September 19, 1949, p. 442.

[6] Not printed; it concerned severance pay (120.61/8–1949).

[7] Close of business.

893.6363/9–649 : Telegram

The Consul at Tsingtao (Hawthorne) to the Secretary of State

TSINGTAO, September 6, 1949—10 a.m.
[Received September 6—6 : 12 a. m.]

476. Re mytel 471, September 2.[8] Norwegian acting manager Standard Oil Company has transferred firm's interests to committee Chinese employees and will depart when possible. Believed Asiatic Petroleum Company, British, would also withdraw foreign staff except for current controversy with labor union re payment provident fund former Chinese employees.

British manager Hong Kong [and] Shanghai Bank, only foreign bank here, has informed principals his intention withdraw even if this should involve closing bank and/or his dismissal after over 25 years' service.

BAT [9] cigarette factory employing 6 Americans, 3 of them departing on premature home leave when possible, suffering heavy financial losses and will doubtless be forced close when 3 months' stocks exhausted if not before. Communists obviously plan monopolize cigarette industry, to create which expected sell tax free cigarettes while inspiring labor trouble in BAT plant.

Well-informed Chinese businessman convinced Communist policy is to freeze out all foreign interests through excessive taxation. Even Soviets becoming increasingly unhappy and many have left or are endeavoring leave for Manchuria. Average Chinese has also been disillusioned but expected remain apathetic.

Department pass Nanking its discretion.

HAWTHORNE

_____

125.9532 : Telegram

The Consul at Tsingtao (Hawthorne) to the Secretary of State

TSINGTAO, September 7, 1949—10 a. m.
[Received September 7—8 :30 a. m.]

481. Re mytels 316, July 5, reporting loss fuel stockpile, 394, July 30 [*August 3*], reporting certain present and anticipated difficulties of ConGen, and 459, August 30, re Communists' attitude toward US Government property.

Believe it will be impossible obtain fuel for office and residences for coming winter absence some sort recognition or agreement on high level, if factories given preference in purchasing fuel. Any case diesel will not be available for heating ConGen and house at 1 First Taiping

_____

[8] Not printed.
[9] British-American Tobacco Co., Ltd.

Church Road and heating systems these properties must be converted to coal, but Department seems reluctant grant even $100 for repair upkeep Government buildings (see mytel 356, July 21 [10] which, together with all other telegrams requesting additional funds, remains unanswered). Without such recognition or agreement believe US Government properties will be taken over in not distant future. Also that it will continue to be impossible for ConGen contact any responsible Communist official [garble] departure Americans who have resigned or have been granted premature home leave. Owing present conditions, American business community will consist of 4 men, none representing American firms.

Morale my American staff suffering from general feeling frustration, shared by me, departures personnel other friends and narrowing recreational facilities.

Department pass Nanking its discretion.

HAWTHORNE

893.6363/9–849 : Telegram

The Consul at Tsingtao (Hawthorne) to the Secretary of State

TSINGTAO, September 8, 1949—11 a. m.
[Received September 8—7 : 47 a. m.]

483. Remytel 476, September 6. Faber Hospital, only hospital offering anything like modern, sanitary, medical, surgical facilities, faced with early closure owing Communist taxation. Hospital established by Germans prior to First World War and since that was maintained in part by donations from local foreign nationals and firms, which contributions can no longer be expected.

Department pass Nanking its discretion.

HAWTHORNE

125.953/9–949 : Telegram

The Secretary of State to the Consul at Tsingtao (Hawthorne)

WASHINGTON, September 9, 1949—9 p. m.

265. Reurtel 481, Sept. 7. In view conditions reported tel 481, Sept. 7 and independent considerations Dept has decided close ur post as soon as possible obtain exit permits American members ur staff and neces-

---

[10] Not printed.

sary closing arrangements made. Recommend Dept disposition Govt property.

While no public announcement being made to press, you should take preparatory steps notify Amer cits ur District availability ConGen assist extent possible those desiring depart and confidentially advise of closure.

Travel orders and admin instrs subject separate tel upon receipt ur recommendations.

Dept taking up with Brit Govt question informal representation Amer interest ur Cons district upon closure.

ACHESON

125.953/9–1049 : Telegram

The Consul at Tsingtao (Hawthorne) to the Secretary of State

TSINGTAO, September 10, 1949—noon.
[Received September 10—4:59 a. m.]

493. Lest Department misunderstand certain recent telegrams from ConGen, we hasten assure Department we are not only willing but anxious remain at post so long Department feels usefulness our activities, now largely restricted telegraphic reporting, warrant continued expenditure necessary Government funds.

Department pass Nanking its discretion.

HAWTHORNE

125.9533/9–1449 : Telegram

The Consul at Tsingtao (Hawthorne) to the Secretary of State

TSINGTAO, September 14, 1949—11 a. m.
[Received September 14—5:18 a. m.]

503. K. Y. Liu, interpreter this Consulate General, arrested last night ostensibly because misstatements in application for bicycle license. Actually expected he will be questioned at length regarding personalities, activities all members Consulate General's staff. Needless say, Liu has had access to no classified material.

View long development please expedite issuance administrative instructions regarding closure post, pending receipt which no advice being given American citizens for fear radio station may be closed when our intentions become known.

HAWTHORNE

702.4193/9–2249 : Telegram

The Acting Secretary of State to the Consul General at Hankow (Callanan)

WASHINGTON, September 22, 1949—7 p. m.

92. Fol instrs supplement those contained Deptel 74, Sept 1 [11] and previous.

I. Brit have agreed afford US cits Hankow protection (Deptel 2961 Aug 18 to London [12] sent Hankow 62). Specifically Dept has asked Brit perform fol services for Amcits: Financial assistance; welfare whereabouts; in case physical danger or distress render all possible assistance persons previously documented as Amcits; reports of death; conservation personal property; reports of birth upon request; notarials on an accommodation basis. Will require no visa or passport services.

[Here follow detailed instructions.]

WEBB

702.4193/9–2349 : Telegram

The Counselor of Embassy in China (Jones) to the Secretary of State

NANKING, September 23, 1949—4 p. m.
[Received September 23—11 :10 a. m.]

2162. Deptel 1121, September 20.[11] British Embassy has advised that on or before September 14 requested Foreign Office authority issue instructions to Hankow Consulate General regarding custody US property and protection American citizens on same lines instructions already issued British Consulates Kunming, Chungking and Canton.

JONES

125.4556/9–3049 : Telegram

The Consul General at Hankow (Callanan) to the Secretary of State

HANKOW, September 30, 1949.
[Received September 30—8 : 39 a. m.]

363. This is last message, transmitter and receiver closing down today. ConGen closing October 1. Department please inform all China posts.

CALLANAN

---

[11] Not printed.
[12] *Post*, p. 1320.

125.953/9–3049 : Telegram

The Acting Secretary of State to the Consul at Tsingtao (Hawthorne)

WASHINGTON, September 30, 1949—6 p. m.

298. Dept considers it necessary for you close office immed and depart soonest reDeptel 271, Sep 14.[13] Inform Dept soonest when and how you and staff expect depart. Sep[arate] tel fols personnel assignments. Inform Dept whether difficulties encountered in obtaining exit permits or if any Dept action necessary assist departure.

WEBB

125.953/10–249 : Telegram

The Consul at Tsingtao (Hawthorne) to the Secretary of State

TSINGTAO, October 2, 1949—2 p. m.
[Received October 3—4 : 06 a. m.]

536. ReDeptel 298, September 30. Impossible apply exit permits till October 5, date set foreign registration American staff with local police. Applications will be made then or as soon thereafter as possible. Consulate General will be closed c.o.b. October 15, which earliest possible. When and how we expect depart will be reported soonest.

HAWTHORNE

125.953/10–1249 : Telegram

The Consul at Tsingtao (Hawthorne) to the Secretary of State

TSINGTAO, October 12 , 1949—4 p. m.
[Received 11 : 53 p. m.]

560. ConGen's American staff expect learn action taken on their applications for exit permits October 24. Although ConGen officially closing October 15, will then maintain radio contact until eve actual departure, which will likely be by ship for Hong Kong.

Department may wish inform NY office Standard Oil [that] George Sevaldson, Norwegian, until recently charge company's Tsingtao interests, has been trying since August 28 obtain exit permit. No reason given for nonissuance.

HAWTHORNE

---

[13] Not printed.

702.4193/10–1649 : Telegram

The Consul at Tsingtao (Hawthorne) to the Secretary of State

TSINGTAO, October 16, 1949—2 p. m.
[Received October 16—3 : 14 a. m.]

570. ReDeptel circular 46, October 14.[15] Consulate General by informal memo October 15 informed Communists of closure Consulate that date and of handing over to British. Memo returned with oral statement it unacceptable (1) because Communist government affords protection foreign property and nationals and (2) other is no recognized British representative.

Nevertheless, shall try complete turnover British and laying off staff soon as replies mytels 537 and 546 [16] received.

[HAWTHORNE]

702.4193/10–1649 : Telegram

The Secretary of State to the Consul at Tsingtao (Hawthorne)

WASHINGTON, October 18, 1949—5 p. m.

319. Brit FonOff has asked Brit Emb Nanking ensure appropriate arrangements made for assumption US interests in cases where Brit US consular districts do not coincide. Upon turnover lists Amcits (para XI [*II*], Depcirtel Sept 14, 7 a. m.[17]) discuss with Brit to ensure no Amcits property ur district left unprotected by reason differences consular districts. Dept realizes (urtel 570, Oct 16) Brit may be able afford little if any protection.

ACHESON

125.953/10–2949 : Telegram

The Consul at Tsingtao (Hawthorne) to the Secretary of State

TSINGTAO, October 29, 1949—9 a. m.
[Received October 29—2 : 52 a. m.]

594. [Garble] Remytel 591, October 28.[18] Called to Foreign Affairs section MCC 28th, 3 p. m. Informed Communists do not recognize our title to real properties here acquired under surplus property agreement and they propose takeover such properties. Requested furnish separate inventories all movable property each building belonging to former Consulate General and to former owners. Former will not be confiscated if Communists satisfied as to ownership. Replied I no longer

---

[15] For circular telegram of October 13, 8 p. m., see p. 1323.
[16] Neither printed.
[17] Not printed; paragraph II referred to British agreement to afford U.S. citizens protection where U.S. diplomatic and consular offices had closed or might later close and enumerated the various protective services (702.4193/9–1449).
[18] Not printed.

have custody such properties, custody which turned over to British but this unacceptable. Also requested furnish inventories personal effects American staff. Told that when these demands complied with exit permits will be issued immediately. See no alternative to compliance.

British Consul General informed but no action by him, possible view nonrecognition his status as custodian or as Consul General.

Last radio contact will be at 0700 GMT [19] November 1. Will report on arrival Hong Kong.

HAWTHORNE

125.9531/10–2949 : Telegram

The Secretary of State to the Consul at Tsingtao (Hawthorne)

WASHINGTON, October 29, 1949—4 p. m.

328. Urtel 594 October 29. Advise Commies that US, a sovereign nation, owns property, both moveable and immoveable, in full owner-ship and cannot recognize Commie claims thereto. State further that property acquired under surplus property agreement was acquired under internatl agreement by the sovereign US, that properties so acquired are not subject to confiscation by Commies as acquisition was in accord with laws China and International Law and that US expects Commies to recognize our rights of ownership and that US will insist on receiving full compensation if these rights are not fully respected. Also advise Commies that departure Am personnel not to be considered abandonment since Brit have been requested handle US interests Tsingtao Cons Dist.

You may provide Commies with an inventory of property appending thereto a statement identifying the properties acquired under surplus property agreement. Send copies of such material to Dept and to Brit ConGen, Tsingtao and request him to deliver copy to Commies as representing US interests. Endeavor bring out copy.

Suggest you continue radio contact if this matter likely complicate your departure. Tell Dept when last message sent.

ACHESON

125.9531/10–2949 : Telegram

The Secretary of State to the Consul General at Peiping (Clubb)

WASHINGTON, November 1, 1949—7 p. m.

759. Fol tel recd from Tsingtao as 594, Oct 29. [Here follows text of telegram printed on page 1148.]

---

[19] Greenwich Mean Time.

Fol tel sent Tsingtao, Oct 29. [Here follows text of telegram No. 328, printed *supra*.]

You are instructed to enter protest along lines Deptel to Tsingtao with appropriate Commie auths in manner you deem most effective and inform Dept when protest made and substance conversation or text protest if written.

ACHESON

125.9531/11–249 : Telegram

The Consul at Tsingtao (Hawthorne) to the Secretary of State

TSINGTAO, November 2, 1949—3 p. m.
[Received November 2—5 : 59 a. m.]

603. Today handed Foreign Affairs section MCC memo drafted compliance first paragraph Deptel 328, October 29. Yang in my presence phoned gist memo to chairman MCC who informed Yang memo unacceptable. MCC also refused accept inventories US Govt property from British whose custodian recognized. At insistence MCC such inventories delivered by me.

HAWTHORNE

125.953/11–549 : Telegram

The Consul at Tsingtao (Hawthorne) to the Secretary of State

TSINGTAO, November 5, 1949—11 a. m.
[Received November 5—3 : 50 a. m.]

604. Called at Foreign Affairs section MCC today re exit permits. Yang repeated they will definitely be granted, that his office has reported to MCC re question properties but that MCC has referred question to Peiping. This may indicate my memorandum November 2 not ignored. Suggest US Embassy be instructed make similar representations Peiping.

While exit permits delayed pending reply from Peiping on property, Yang expressed opinion we should be able leave by December 1 absence new developments unforeseen by him. Therefore desire bookings 5 adults, including 1 lady, and such effects as we allowed to take in ship mentioned Deptel 332, November 3.[20]

HAWTHORNE

---

[20] Not printed.

125.953/11–749 : Telegram

The Consul at Tsingtao (Hawthorne) to the Secretary of State

TSINGTAO, November 7, 1949.
[Received November 7—3 : 12 a. m.]

605. ReDeptel 333, November 4.[21] Consulate General officially closed and final accounts submitted as of October 15. Funds may be remitted through New York office Hong Kong and Shanghai Banking Corporation.

HAWTHORNE

125.9531/11–849 : Telegram

The Consul General at Peiping (Clubb) to the Secretary of State

PEIPING, November 8, 1949.
[Received November 9—1 :41 a. m.]

1943. Following is text letter November 8 [22] re American Government real property Tsingtao:

"Under instructions of my Government, I would inform you that the American Consulate General at Tsingtao was informed by the Tsingtao Aliens Affairs Office on October 28, 1949 that the local authorities did not recognize the American title to real property acquired at that place by the United States Government under the surplus property agreement, and proposed to take over such property. The United States possesses the real property in question in full ownership in the capacity of a sovereign nation and cannot recognize the claim thereto set forth by the Tsingtao authorities.

"The property in question was acquired by the United States Government under terms of an international agreement, the surplus property agreement, and, the acquisition being in accord with the laws of China and international law, such properties are not subject to confiscation. The United States, therefore, expects the concerned authorities to respect the United States Government's rights [of] ownership. If such rights are not fully respected, the United States Government will insist on full compensation. As you were informed in my letter of November 3, 1949,[23] the American consular office at Tsingtao is about to close. The departure of American personnel, however, is not to be considered abandonment of United States Government property interests. The concerned British consular office has been requested to handle United States interests in the Tsingtao consular district.

"Your attention is invited to the serious nature of the action taken by the Tsingtao authorities aiming at the confiscation of United States Government real property obtained in accordance with the laws of China and international law, and it is requested that you cause

---

[21] Not printed.
[22] Addressed to Chou En-lai, "Premier and Foreign Minister of the Central People's Government of the People's Republic of China," at Peiping.
[23] See telegram No. 1910, November 4, from the Consul General at Peiping, p. 1000.

an appropriate investigation to be made to the end that such threat of confiscation shall be promptly withdrawn."

Sent Department; repeated Nanking 1150, Shanghai 1161, to Tientsin by mail.

CLUBB

125.9531/11–1449 : Telegram

The Consul General at Peiping (Clubb) to the Secretary of State

PEIPING, November 14, 1949—4 p. m.
[Received November 15—2 : 55 a. m.]

1999. Re Contel 1941 [*1943*], November 8. Letter November 8 to Chou En-lai re Tsingtao property returned by mail today without acknowledgment or comment.

For reference, please inform Peiping any developments favorable or otherwise re matter.

Sent Department 1999. Department pass Tsingtao.

CLUBB

125.953/11–549 : Telegram

The Secretary of State to the Consul at Tsingtao (Hawthorne)[24]

WASHINGTON, November 18, 1949—7 p. m.

340. Dept booking passage on *Pacific Transport* as requested urtel 604 Nov 5. Ship scheduled arrive Tsingtao between Dec 6 and 8, thence proceeding Japan. Date subj change in event appears necessary or desirable. As ship will carry with army approval some US Army cargo, and otherwise to assure safe passage, Dept requests Strong make appropriate representations FonOff for safe conduct Tsingtao. Strong shld inform FonOff sole reason for diversion Tsingtao is to evacuate AmConsul staff and personal effects, and there will be no cargo offloaded or onloaded. Suggest Tsingtao inform Commie auth expected arrival ship. Keep Dept informed devel re ur exit permits. If permits unrecd by time *Pacific Transport* departs Taiwan, doubt whether practicable effect diversion.

ACHESON

---

[24] Repeated to the Chargé in China (Strong) as telCan No. 764 and to the Consul General at Hong Kong as No. 1389.

125.953/12–549 : Telegram

The Second Secretary of Embassy in China (Bacon) to the Secretary of State

NANKING, December 5, 1949.
[Received December 5—1 : 44 p. m.]

2543. Following is Tsingtao's 50, December 5 (reEmbtel 2536 to Department December 4 [25]) :

"Your 91, 2nd. All foreigners must now depart China from Shanghai."

Embassy gathers from this and preceding telegrams from Tsingtao that residents Tsingtao are obliged proceed Shanghai and cannot obtain permits for exit at Tsingtao or via Tientsin.

Sent Department 2543, repeated Taipei 108, Hong Kong telCan 842.

BACON

702.4193/12–1749 : Telegram

The Second Secretary of Embassy in China (Bacon) to the Secretary of State

NANKING, December 17, 1949—11 a. m.
[Received December 17—2 : 40 a. m.]

2610. Under date December 1, British Pro-Consul, Tsingtao, reported by mail following to British Embassy :

"American Government property consists 5 large buildings : Consulate General's house, port facilities, Consulate offices, officers club. Attached were 10 Chinese guards (ex-policemen) to look after property. We were expected to keep eye on properties but without any responsibility. We are free from any complications with regard properties as local authorities have taken over. 'Might is right' is motto of authorities and Chinese flag flies over former consulate offices.

All these 5 properties are handsome and substantial. Would seem unlikely they will be left indefinitely in Chinese hands. Properties have been 'takenover', guards dismissed after payment 5 months' wages as from November 30. They appear to have had verbal contract expiring end June. Having been relieved of any cares about properties and Chinese guards, our work has been greatly lightened."

BACON

---

[25] Not printed.

125.9533/12–1949 : Telegram

The Second Secretary of Embassy in China (Bacon) to the Secretary of State

NANKING, December 19, 1949—4 p. m.
[Received December 19—6 : 30 a. m.]

2618. Deptel 1295, December 15.[26] On second try December 19 reached Hawthorne by phone at British ConGen. He said permits delayed because unable produce evidence 10 navy carbines used by former ConGen guards actually destroyed. Carbines in fact destroyed by burning stocks and dumping metal parts in ocean. Still expects early issuance permits. I informed him evacuation ship at Shanghai expected late this month and urged him use it as argument for prompt action. I asked whether he gets any news besides VOA and he abruptly and positively said "no". I conclude Taipei broadcast not received.

ConGen personnel still living respective homes. All 4 well and request Department inform nearest relatives. Hawthorne will send progress reports even if negative every 3 or 4 days.

Sent Department 2618; Department pass Shanghai 1281, Taipei 109.

BACON

125.953/12–2449 : Telegram

The Consul General at Shanghai (McConaughy) to the Secretary of State

SHANGHAI, December 24, 1949—1 p. m.
[Received December 24—2 : 25 a. m.]

5370. Sevaldson, Tsingtao manager Standard-Vacuum, left there December 19, arrived Shanghai December 23, and reported following December 24:

Hawthorne and staff applied exit permits September 15. Mid-October authorities raised issue disposal navy carbines left with ConGen. Sevaldson claims has definite knowledge Hawthorne burned stocks, sank metal parts weapons after Communist regulations issued re registration firearms. Chinese staff ConGen reported weapons to local authorities who have persistently questioned Hawthorne re disposition in connection exit permits but not yet lodged formal charges for violation regulations. Sevaldson of opinion they will try Hawthorne in court and issue deportation order. Hawthorne unable produce evidence or witnesses of disposal. Hawthorne and staff free to move about but closely shadowed. US flag removed from ConGen about 2 weeks ago and replaced by Communist emblem. Sevaldson unaware Hawthorne has established telephone contact Nanking.

---

[26] Not printed.

At Hawthorne's request Sevaldson informed me Hawthorne had received information from Communist Foreign Affairs Bureau first week December that Smith-Bender safe and well, confined at (Tachiang — Great Harbor?) large Communist military base just outside Tsingtao.

Sevaldson claims all foreigners desiring exit China from Tsingtao must first proceed Shanghai. Also reports Tsingtao dead city with shops closing, large number unemployed and population yearning for return of navy and marines.

Re Deptel 2412, December 13,[27] Nanking telegram 2618, December 19.

Sent Department 5370; Department pass Nanking 2072.

McCONAUGHY

125.9533/12–2749 : Telegram

The Second Secretary of Embassy in China (Bacon) to the Secretary of State

NANKING, December 27, 1949.
[Received December 27—1 : 13 p. m.]

2664. Sent Department, repeated Shanghai 1302, Tsingtao unnumbered.

"Situation unchanged. Hawthorne."

(Re Embtel 2636 to Dept, repeated Shanghai 1290, December 21.[27])

BACON

[The Consulate General at Tsingtao was officially closed on January 23, 1950, at the time of the departure of the American personnel.]

IV. SHANGHAI: CLAIMS OF EX-NAVY EMPLOYEES LEADING TO SIEGE AND OCCUPATION OF CONSULATE GENERAL FOR FEW DAYS; COLLING CASE; GOULD–MINER CASE; ARREST OF VICE CONSUL WILLIAM M. OLIVE; CLOSURE OF UNITED STATES INFORMATION SERVICE; QUESTION OF TAXATION OF PROPERTY OWNED BY UNITED STATES GOVERNMENT

893.00/5–2549 : Telegram

The Consul General at Shanghai (Cabot) to the Secretary of State

SHANGHAI, May 25, 1949.
[Received May 25—7 : 08 p. m.]

1830. Americans reached by telephone in western district report all quiet as of 7 : 30 p. m. No vehicles except pedicabs on street. Some

---

[27] Not printed.

pedestrians. Some shops open. No reports of mistreatment foreigners. Numerous Communist posters already put up, many in English.

Communist radio announces all areas south and west of Soochow Creek now occupied.

Previously reported wounded foreigner in Consulate General sick bay now being treated by doctor.

Two machine gun bullets penetrated Consul General's bedroom 6th floor Glenline and numerous others hit building. Entire staff both in Glenline and other section of city O.K.

Sent Department 1830; repeated Nanking 1002; Canton 543, Com-NavWesPac MAQ 25.[29]

CABOT

893.00B/5–2649 : Telegram

The Consul General at Shanghai (Cabot) to the Secretary of State

SHANGHAI, May 26, 1949—noon.
[Received 3 : 26 p. m.]

1836. Headed by former clerical employee of the firm, 30 Communist soldiers appeared in Shanghai power plant office yesterday about noon while fighting still in progress that area. Former employee was most solicitous re welfare staff; gave 6 PB [30] dollars to enable them buy food as well as assurance full protection and aid staff including Americans to carry on. Thus assured, American on duty felt safe in returning his residence for needed rest. (Power plant itself understood still occupied by Nationalist soldiers—operating on greatly reduced load.)

Last evening ConGen learned from Texas Company that entire plant and personnel of its large installations this side of Gough Island, together with those of adjacent Shell Company and China Petroleum Company were in momentary danger of complete destruction as result of shells falling in nearby river next to anchored ammunition barge with 400 tons explosives. ConGen immediately phoned Provisional Police Commissioner Lo who said he would inform Communist military quarters. Twenty minutes later Texas Company reported to us that barge was being towed from danger point. Not certain but quite possible that towing was done by crew sympathetic to Communists under instructions from Communists following receipt ConGen's message.

These and other signs give us initial tentative impression that, aside from their natural urgent desire preserve city installations and assets intact, leaders of Communist Shanghai occupation forces are making

---

[29] Apparently the serial for Commander, U.S. Naval Forces in the Western Pacific.
[30] People's Bank Notes, Chinese Communist currency.

special effort to demonstrate their concern for foreigners, at least from standpoint of their physical welfare. Incidentally, in such casual meetings as our staff members have had thus far with ordinary Communist soldiers, latter have displayed friendly attitude.

Sent Department 1836, Nanking 1005, OffEmb Canton 548.

CABOT

125.8571/5–2649 : Telegram

The Consul General at Shanghai (Cabot) to the Secretary of State

SHANGHAI, May 26, 1949.
[Received May 27—11 : 33 p. m.]

1840. Consulate offices have been repeatedly hit during afternoon by rifle and machine gun fire. All but two possible cases are clearly from Nationalist side. Majority of cases appear accidental if utterly irresponsible, but in several instances it can only be deliberate, despite American flags on pole and both entrances.

Building is barricaded and of course no military activity permitted within it. This morning we asked Canton to have instructions issued to Nationals to respect building. Fortunately no American yet injured though several very very narrow escapes as rooms and stairwell repeatedly hit.

Only man so far injured within the building my house boy as already reported. If Department wishes it can quote me to press as saying Nationals have wantonly fired on American flag; that is the simple fact.

Sent Department 1840, repeated Nanking 1009, OffEmb Canton 552.

CABOT

893.00/5–2749 : Telegram

The Consul General at Shanghai (Cabot) to the Secretary of State

SHANGHAI, May 27, 1949.
[Received May 27—6 : 42 a. m.]

1865. On May 26 two proclamations appeared in papers, over radio and posted on streets, issued by General Headquarters People's Security Corps of Federation of People's organizations of Shanghai.

First proclamation stated: "This corps ordered by authorities maintain order in city pending takeover by PLA" [31] ordered people avoid panic, protect public and private property, and furnish information on war criminals. All Kmt [32] soldiers and party members would be

---

[31] People's Liberation Army (Communist).
[32] Kuomintang (Nationalist Party).

protected, but must turn in military supplies. "All Consulates, their staffs and foreign nationals who obey regulations of Headquarters will be protected, all members of Corps wear special arm bands.["]

Second proclamation issued same day stated Security Corps on duty day and night. Public transportation would continue operation wherever possible. Factories, schools and businesses should resume work. Policemen should report to provisional committees of their stations for duty. Only Military Control Commission has authority to take over any institution and impostors must be reported to Corps. All people's organizations formerly registered with Federation must register again at 627 Nanking Road.

Sent Department, repeated Nanking 1023, Canton, Dairen, VOANY.[33]

CABOT

---

123 Cabot, John M.: Telegram

The Consul General at Shanghai (Cabot) to the Secretary of State

SHANGHAI, May 27, 1949.
[Received May 27—12:32 p. m.]

1866. I issued following statement May 27 in response to request by *North China Daily News* reporter who had previously received similar statement from British Consul General Urquhart. My statement was distributed by USIS [34] to local press in both English and Chinese languages as well as to press in other Chinese cities where USIS represented.

"So far as we have been able to ascertain no Americans have been injured in course of fighting in or around Shanghai. All reports so far indicate that the Communist soldiers have respected Americans and their property despite certain relatively minor difficulties which have arisen in a few instances.

The American community, both business and philanthropic, is carrying on and intends to continue to do so insofar as this is permitted by the new authorities. They feel that their activities are a benefit to China as well as the organizations they represent. They will, I am confident, respect the laws and regulations instituted as required by the new authorities in their public announcements.

It will be necessary to wait until the new authorities have established the policies which they propose to follow before it is possible to say whether the American community can look to the future with optimism, but the community's first reactions have been distinctly favorable. For those who have suffered tragic losses in the hostilities which have swept over Shanghai the American community feels deeply

---

[33] Voice of America, New York.
[34] United States Information Service.

sympathetic; it is fervently thankful for the greater horrors from which Shanghai has happily been spared."

Sent Department 1866, repeated Nanking 1024, to Canton.

CABOT

125.8571/5–2649 : Telegram

The Acting Secretary of State to the Consul General at Shanghai (*Cabot*)

WASHINGTON, May 28, 1949—3 p. m.

1081. Asst. Secy Rusk discussed substance urtel 1840 May 26 with Amb Koo same day quoting ur statement that "Nationalists have wantonly fired on Amer flag". Rusk told Koo Dept did not intend give publicity this matter but indicated Dept's deep concern over report. Koo stated wld immed wire Chi Govt, Canton, urging cessation firing by Nationalists on US Govt property.

WEBB

125.8571/5–3049 : Telegram

The Consul General at Shanghai (Cabot) to the Secretary of State

SHANGHAI, May 30, 1949—11 a. m.
[Received May 30—5 : 11 a. m.]

1887. Deptel 1081, May 28. Department will appreciate that I did not expect publicity regarding my 1840, May 26, but did hope forwarding it, particularly in plain language, might prove useful as it seems to have. Could not explain at time in classified message due to overloaded facilities.

CABOT

893.00/5–3149 : Telegram

The Consul General at Shanghai (Cabot) to the Secretary of State

SHANGHAI, May 31, 1949.
[Received May 31—8 : 09 a. m.]

1907. *North China Daily News*, May 31, reports Chang Han-fu, Chief Foreign Affairs Department, SMCC,[35] announcement that, although Chinese People's Government has not yet established formal relations with other countries protection foreign lives [and] properties assured under article 8 joint declaration Mao Tse-tung [36] and Chu

---

[35] Shanghai Military Control Commission (Communist).
[36] Chairman of the Central Committee of the Chinese Communist Party (CCP).

Teh.[37] All laws, decrees issued by military political authorities will be published *Liberation* daily. Questions re travel and residence may be submitted to Public Safety Bureau Police headquarters. Foreigners visiting these offices to bring own interpreters. SMCC regulations governing conduct foreigners state foreigners must obey all laws, not conduct espionage, oppose liberation Chinese people, protect or harbour Chinese war criminals or counter-revolutionist[s].

Sent Department 1907, repeated Nanking 1042, Canton 583.

CABOT

102.22/6–849 : Telegram

The Consul General at Shanghai (Cabot) to the Secretary of State

SHANGHAI, June 8, 1949—5 p. m.
[Received June 8—6 : 02 a. m.]

2153. ConGen has received petitioning letter and threats of adverse group action from civilian personnel discharged by action order without prior separation notice or two weeks' salary checks upon disestablishment NavPortFac,[38] Shanghai, 27 April 1949. In view current sensitive political situation, ability such elements exploit to utmost threats cannot be disregarded. Re ComNavPortFac's 031533Z [39] May separation documents not received nor salary checks in lieu such notices. See Administration Attaché letter to Lt. Blocher dated 11 May [39] for full details. ConGen also advised by former Navy employees NavPortFac recommended request to BuSandA [40] further 2 weeks' payment lieu separation notice. No information here bona fide employees to be paid if such claims accepted. Advise. AstALUSNA,[41] Shanghai, informed.

Department pass action to ComNavPortFac, Shanghai, information ComNavWesPac, BuSandA.

CABOT

811.20200(D)/6–1049 : Telegram

The Consul General at Shanghai (Cabot) to the Secretary of State

SHANGHAI, June 10, 1949—3 p. m.
[Received June 10—6 : 20 a. m.]

2198. Question has arisen my mind extent which USIS should continue circulate Shanghai, elsewhere, Communist-occupied China, in-

---

[37] Commander in Chief of the Chinese Communist armies.
[38] Naval Port Facilities.
[39] Not found in Department of State files.
[40] Bureau of Supplies and Accounts, U.S. Navy.
[41] Office of Assistant Naval Attaché.

formation material directly attacking Communism. My concern is overly vigorous attacks may result in early shutdown USIS activities. Deputy Acting Director USIS China believes distribution material unfriendly to Russian imperialism or Communism as employed by Soviet for aggression not likely to be cause for shutdown which likely come any case on more general grounds such as in Peiping. Same time feels deletion of such material from USIS news file except for most flagrantly provocative would result in distorted picture American public opinion, a picture too closely in line with that now being painted by CCP propagandists. Believes shutdown preferable. Specific example type material which I regard as dangerous but which USIS distributed after considered judgement was Paul G. Hoffman [42] speech St. Louis, June 7. Deputy Acting Director USIS feels desirable distribute this type material ground it attack on Kremlin, not on Chinese Communists or even abstract principles Marxism. I realize Department has instructed posts they authorized use best judgement deleting material likely antagonize local authorities. Also presume Department made specific decision before sending Hoffman speech realizing it was for distribution Communist China. Nevertheless desire early guidance this general question in as specific terms as may be provided. Pending reply editorial decisions by USIS made extremely difficult. Also desire Connors [43] comment Canton.

Sent Department, repeated OffEmb Canton 679, Nanking 1154.

CABOT

102.22/6–1049 : Telegram

The Consul General at Shanghai (Cabot) to the Secretary of State

SHANGHAI, June 10, 1949—6 p. m.
[Received June 10—7 : 13 a. m.]

2205. Re ConGentel 2153, 8th. Approximately 35 Sikhs, former USN employees NOB,[44] today forced their way into Consulate and personally served petition on Consul General demanding 2 weeks' pay in lieu separation notice and making strong representations for 2 or 3 months' salary bonus on premise (1) that US Government pledged continued employment and (2) ECA [45] and . . . 44 had paid 3 months' separation bonus for long service and 2 months for short service plus lump sum leave payments. Group departed reluctantly led by Indian CG [46] who personally interceded. Even larger number Sikhs may return.

---

[42] Administrator, Economic Cooperation Administration (ECA).
[43] W. Bradley Connors, Consul at Canton and Acting Director of USIS, China.
[44] Naval Operating Base.
[45] Economic Cooperation Administration.
[46] Consul General.

Consul General representing Navy definitely did not pledge other than temporary employment as record discloses. Have verified, however, ECA paid separation bonuses as represented . . .).

Over 300 Chinese ex-Navy employees who petitioned previously for severance payments reportedly organizing balance dismissed employees and making representations local authorities with planned mass visitation and demonstration Consulate General today or tomorrow. Time not propitious intervention Communist authorities who would probably side with laborers, perhaps holding some office of Consulate General liable. Incident might be useable by Communists for propaganda purposes and highly detrimental American interests Shanghai.

Urgently request Department follow through with Navy to (1) provide specific list by telegram soonest ex-Navy employees entitled severance benefits in lieu notice and (2) release funds for payment up to maximum 2-month salary customary separation allowance paid in Shanghai. Would endeavor settle for less but might be forced concede bonus comparable ECA. Suggest possible alternative payment from Department emergency fund reimbursable by Navy.

CABOT

102.22/6–1049 : Telegram

The Acting Secretary of State to the Consul General at Shanghai (Cabot)

WASHINGTON, June 10, 1949—11 p. m.

1172. Urtels 2153 June 8, 2205 Jun 10 sent by Navy to ComNavWesPac for action.

Keep Dept informed.

WEBB

893.043/6–1149 : Telegram

The Consul General at Shanghai (Cabot) to the Secretary of State

SHANGHAI, June 11, 1949—9 a. m.
[Received June 11—12:24 a. m.]

2208. Three recent incidents afford some indication line Communists may follow dealing with foreigners accused infringing their regulations.

May 29 American resident Michael Kilian reported to authorities Kmt troops had been hiding his apartment and turned over weapons they had left, but according Communists Kilian attempted conceal three pistols which he only turned over after investigation. Communists commended Kilian for original report of "Kmt remnants" but reprimanded him for alleged attempt conceal weapons, secured formal apology and gave affair full publicity.

June 7 SS *Shengking*, Butterfield and Swire, brought 21 foreign passengers to Shanghai without authorization. Communist authorities allowed 14 women and children dependents of Shanghai residents to land but demanded remaining 7 return to original port embarkation by same boat. Communist authorities reprimanded firm for bringing unauthorized passengers, secured formal apology and gave affair publicity which played on theme that sanctity of law had been maintained while magnanimous attitude had been adopted in permitting reunion several foreign families.

June 6 British Consul R. T. Callender was engaged in dispute over wages with 2 Chinese servants whom he had attempted to discharge. In course of dispute Callender was alleged to have struck both servants. Communist authorities, appealed to by servants, took statements from all involved, summoned Callender to police station and finally disposed of case by securing public apology from Callender and payment of 6 months' severance allowance for servants' medical expenses and replacement of torn clothing. Communists gave affair much space in *Chieh Fang Jih Pao*, making points that "oppression and assault of others was not allowed", that Callender was thus "liable to legal restraint", but that "in consideration of its being a first offense" he was treated in "magnanimous manner".

From admittedly scanty evidence these incidents it appears Communists will enforce their regulations firmly against foreigners, will make face for themselves and Chinese generally by securing formal public apologies from offending foreigners, will give offenses involving foreigners full publicity and whatever terms of settlement will take credit for both strict maintenance of regulations and paternalistic magnanimity.

Sent Department; repeated Nanking 1162, OffEmb Canton 685.

CABOT

893.00B/6–1149 : Telegram

The Consul General at Shanghai (Cabot) to the Secretary of State

SHANGHAI, June 11, 1949—11 a. m.
[Received June 11—4 : 10 a. m.]

2210. Four Communist plain-clothes representatives reportedly visited home chief Chinese operator China Radio network, H. J. Sheng, approximately 10 a. m., 9th. Mistakenly visited apartment brother H. Y. Sheng (also ConGen radio operator) same building, asking him questions intended for H. J. Sheng, including nature radio work, why work for American organization, et cetera. When finally convinced mistaken identity, proceeded brother's apartment, asking same questions wife of H. J. Sheng. Upon learning H. J. off duty 9 p. m., said would return 10 p. m. Searched both apartments thoroughly, making apparently perfunctory check other apartments same building. Sheng instructed speak frankly, honestly regarding duties since no Chinese employee should have information detrimental his interests or ours or no advantage gained from false position. H. J. not visited yet although waited home until 11 p. m. 9th and 10th.

Sent Department, repeated OffEmb Canton 686.

CABOT

811.20200(D)/6–1349 : Telegram

The Minister-Counselor of Embassy in China (Clark) to the Secretary of State

CANTON, June 13, 1949—6 p. m.
[Received June 13—8 : 37 a. m.]

Cantel 583. At present seems unwise make frontal attack Communism (Shanghai's 2198, 10th to Department, repeated Nanking 1154) and thus incur Red denunciation possibly resulting closure USIS. Rather seems to us more important for posts coming under Communist domination exercise tact and caution this regard avoid shutdown. Perhaps even overcaution best policy avoid arousing resentment during military control commission period. (Hankow's 174, 9th to Department,[48] repeated Nanking 134.) Harder lines to be adopted on Department instructions following establishment civil control individual areas.

Consider criticism of Soviet policies justified in USIS distribution, especially factual account Soviet related satellite countries and Far East.

Greatest emphasis now should be presentation fullest picture American policies and people, not overlooking however interests in Far East, and striving present fullest possible picture our policies China, elsewhere Far East. Blatant Communist attacks on United States must be countered. Distortions and misrepresentations of truth cannot be overlooked and we should not sit silently by if Communists open frontal assault on United States.

We must not permit fear Communist reprisals and possible closure USIS in China to allow us lose sight our own principles and thus distort own picture to point where it might fit too closely that painted by Communist propagandists. To do this would negate entire information effort and best course such circumstances would be termination

---

[48] Not printed.

information program. It seems feasible and possible to us to steer middle course in this early period that will not compromise our principles and at same time will not bow to Communist propaganda. Officers on the spot must be relied on for decisions with regard specific material and as usual have discretion to withhold distribution any material they consider inimical our best interests at the time.

Department requested provide further guidance if necessary and advise posts concerned policy to follow.

Sent Department Cantel 583, repeated Nanking 390, Shanghai 331, Hankow 19.

CLARK

102.22/6–1549 : Telegram

The Consul General at Shanghai (Cabot) to the Secretary of State

SHANGHAI, June 15, 1949—7 p. m.
[Received June 15—10 a. m.]

2284. ReDeptel 1172, 10th. Assume Department received ComNav-PortFacs 100428Z replying ConGentel 2153, 8th, and 130546Z replying ConGentel 2205, June 10.[49]

Although reftels make clear Navy position, ConGen's opinion this position unrealistic in light factual situation.

Tentative representations by group employees indicate probably valid claims certain employees for 2 weeks' termination pay in lieu notice which apparently provided civilian personnel instructions USNavPortFac chapter III B article 12 page 7 irrespective temporary or permanent appointments. These representations also contend chapter V2B7 also provides final payment effected only upon surrender badge and identification by final separation notice neither of which accomplished; hence claim still employees USN entitled regular pay to date plus separation bonus. . . .

ConGen obviously placed very difficult position. Estimated 400–600 ex-employees including NOB Glenline, BOQ [50] race course, Lunghwa Airfield holding meetings. Contacts reported to have been made with Foreign Affairs Bureau for permission stage mass demonstration Glenline. Permission reportedly given on basis ConGen is private individual. Numerous other large American and local business organizations facing same difficulty with threat mob action. Request for 6 months' separation pay, supported by local authorities in at least one instance involving officer British ConGen.

ConGen urgently requests Navy reconsideration of demands from

---

[49] Nos. 100428Z and 130546Z not printed; the Navy position was that employees were hired on temporary basis and no payment was due above wages and pay for accrual leave (102.22/6–1049 and 102.22/6–1549, respectively).
[50] Bachelor Officers Quarters.

standpoint law and equity in order prevent present relatively fluid situation developing into complete and disagreeable impasse.

Present legitimate employees or claimants unknown to ConGen account lack Navy employment records which evacuated. Separation notices mailed 13 May never received. Therefore urgently reiterate request for telegraphic list and funds outlined last paragraph ConGentel 2205, 10th. Upon receipt this information funds and authority to act ConGen might forestall much adverse public criticism American Government and anti-American sentiment. Otherwise most embarrassing consequences may result.

CABOT

893.9111 RR/6–1649 : Telegram

The Consul General at Shanghai (Cabot) to the Secretary of State

SHANGHAI, June 16, 1949.
[Received June 16—3 : 53 a. m.]

2290. Following news about foreigners appearing in local press: *Chieh Fang Jih Pao* June 14 reports incident in which American named Lin Ai-tang refused pay pedicab driver full fare and set dog on latter. Public Safety Station arrested American and reprimanded him. He admitted his fault, apologized to pedicab driver and paid latter medical expenses for injury by dog and living expenses during convalescence period. After settlement, pedicab driver stated, according to paper, "such reasonable penalty to foreigner would never have been possible in days of Kmt's traitorous reactionary rule".

Same paper June 14 reports May 26 incident in which Bredrup, Norwegian Manager of British-owned Union Brewery Ltd., refused request by workers for loan of truck for welcoming PLA and struck one of them on nose. Official of Criminal Section of Foreign Affairs Department of Police Headquarters told Bredrup that he could no longer handle things in imperialistic way of past and should cooperate with workers. Article concluded: "Yet Bredrup didn't repent of his wrong at all." Same paper June 15 reported continuation mediation Bredrup case in SMCC Labor Department, with atmosphere becoming tense as worker struck in nose brought his bloodstained garments to mediation place. Paper reported management had "stubbornly insisted" on discharging 50 workers as "ruse to enable Bredrup evade responsibility for beating up workers".

Same paper June 14 reports 5 stateless Russian women beating up 15-year-old Chinese beggar were taken by soldier to Public Safety Headquarters for disposal. Pedestrians witnessing spectacle stated "Today we have chance give vent to our anger; formerly, we could do practically nothing even if Chinese was beaten to death by foreigners".

Same paper June 15 reports German resident tried remove from possession of Chinese dyeworks employee bolts of cloth which he claimed belonged to ECA, and had been commandeered before liberation by Nationalist troops and thrown in Whangpoo. German reportedly arrogant. After close examination of cloth at Public Safety Police Station, German realized cloth not same and tendered apology to dyeworks employee, promising not make same trouble again.

Sent Department 2290; repeated Nanking 1209, OffEmb Canton.

CABOT

102.22/6–1649 : Telegram

The Consul General at Shanghai (Cabot) to the Secretary of State

SHANGHAI, June 16, 1949.
[Received June 16—6 : 52 p. m.]

2299. Following petition approximately 400 ex-PortFac employees public works, fire department, em[ployees] club, BOQ transportation and MATS [51] personally presented ConGen 15th by representatives "Committee Former Civilian Employees USN ComNavPortFac Shanghai".

"We undersigned former employees US Navy PortFac Shanghai hereby respectfully solicit your kind assistance in forwarding our petition proper authorities for favorable consideration action.

"We have all served US Navy faithfully during periods employment, some ever since establishment as naval operating base autumn 1945. We feel US Navy by sudden departure these shores 22 April 1949 without notice local employees and without making provisions payment termination wages has actually abandoned their men and acted in manner entirely contrary traditional American justice. We wish therefore present our grievances based on following facts.

"(1) In afternoon 27 April 1949 we were paid salaries for period 16–30 April 1949 plus equivalent accrued annual leave due. Were not given any notice separation either verbally, written. These employees with more 1 year's continuous service and who entitled 2 weeks' notice accordance official circular 'notice to new civilian employees' dated 26 October 1948 also not informed termination or separation was in offing. Were simply informed verbally 28 April 1949 that US Navy was leaving and that we were to leave premises by 4 p. m. as trouble anticipated.

"(2) 'Notice to new civilian employees' dated 26 October 1948 specifically states employees terminating employment from US Navy will not be paid final wages until his/her badge has been turned in.

---

[51] Military Air Transport Service.

"We were not required turn in badges when received pay 27 April 1949 although efforts made by Lt. Bobrew and Shore Police guards to forcibly remove badges from civilian employees who left Naval annex between 3 and 4 p. m., 28 April 1949. Despite this breach regulations and direct contravention terms our employment, majority civilian employees still in possession badges.

"(3) ... Furthermore US Army and other US Government-sponsored organizations such UNRRA,[52] ECA provided civilian employees substantial termination pay upon deactivation.

"(4) While comparison odious we feel it necessary mention that British Consulate paid released employees 6 months' wages, not to mention similar generous gestures civilian organizations various nationalities upon release employees during these troublesome times.

"It is therefore our contention that inasmuch as (a) we received no official notice separation from ComNavPortFac through regular channel of civilian personnel office we are still on payroll of US Navy and entitled and justified claiming remuneration for period 1 May 1949 until such time as receive official notice separation Form CP 8; (b) possession of ComNavPortFac civilian badges accordance civilian personnel regulations is proof our services not terminated, consequently no final wages paid and (c) precedent set by US Army, . . . ECA, etc., in matter termination pay and it only justice that same consideration be given ComNavPortFac civilian employees especially in view present hard times by payment 3 months' termination pay calculated from date separation by Form CP 8. This request fully justified by fact that all undersigned have willingly worked many hours overtime whenever workload required without monetary compensation simply because desire to give very best efforts to service of US Navy.

"It respectfully requested our petition be given primary consideration by your good self and that early reply addressed to the Committee of Former Civilian Employees of the US Navy, Lane 291, House 59 Yung Kia Road (ex Route des Sieyes) may be anticipated in near future.

"Thanking you in advance, we are, Yours most respectfully, Committee of Former Civilian Employees of US Naval Port Facilities, Shanghai, China."

Sent Department 2299, repeated ComNavWesPac unnumbered, ComNavPortFac unnumbered.

CABOT

102.22/6–1649 : Telegram

The Consul General at Shanghai (Cabot) to the Secretary of State

SHANGHAI, June 16, 1949—6 p. m.
[Received June 16—9 : 54 a. m.]

2310. Dept pass CNO [53] and ComNavWesPac. Consulate General transmitting separately plain language text of petition dated 14th de-

---

[52] United Nations Relief and Rehabilitation Administration.
[53] Chief of Naval Operations.

livered 15th to Consulate General officers at meeting with 23 representatives former USN shore installation employees. Petition does not include external security force Glenline Building, clerical workers, etc.

Meeting with delegates carried out orderly fashion but undertones ominous. Spokesmen repeatedly stressed urgency immediate action since desperate circumstances some 400 laborers might precipitate uncontrolled mass action unless relief forthcoming by first next week. Accordance reliable intelligence source, this group planning mass visitation Consulate General 22nd or 23rd in absence settlement claims and considering invasion Consulate General commissary Glenline Building and residences administrative officer and AstALUSNA for food until satisfaction achieved.

At meeting with committee representatives Consulate General took position not authorized represent Navy any respect but could serve only as agency for transmission representations to Navy.

ReConGentel 2299, 16th, points 1 and 2 petition seem substantially correct. Most claim did not receive ComNavPortFac mimeographed notices 26 April which follows:

"Due circumstances unforeseen within past month it has become necessary terminate your employment with US Navy on date indicated on your notice of separation. I wish at this time express personally my sincere appreciation for initiative and loyalty you displayed and excellent service you performed while in employment my command. William V. Michaux, Captain US Navy."

Since most employees still have badges and none have received termination notices port facilities regulations, as well as NCPI II 10.2–7, in their view substantiate claim for 2 weeks' pay in lieu separation notice.

. . . .

Regarding point 4, accordance published article British Consulate General officer did pay 6-month bonus personnel employed under police mediation. Separated civilian employees British Consulate General paid 1 month's salary for each year's service not to exceed 3 months' salary. Committee representatives alleged Consulate General paying bonuses ex-Navy Sikhs employed temporarily. When this refuted with facts and representatives informed Sikh problem being handled thru Indian Consulate General (ConGentel 2205, 10th), representatives drew inference they not handled same fashion account lack Chinese Govt recognition.

. . . Further, that since no separation notices served they [the security guards] entitled 1 month's salary bonus for each year service accordance Shanghai practice which Indian Consul General apparently supports. Also that 2 weeks' pay in lieu notice accordance Navy regulations separate and apart from bonus to which entitled.

Original petition office workers additionally state ComNavPortFac officers had recommended 2 weeks' pay in lieu notice and those entitled should call Consulate General to check status this request.

Consulate General again reiterates request for list, with specific instruction regarding any settlement Navy is prepared to make to men involved. Unless these forthcoming immediately, repeat immediately, cannot assume responsibility for consequences altho planning destruction files, crypto equipment, etc., in event forcible entry premises.

CABOT

102.22/6–1649 : Telegram

The Acting Secretary of State to the Consul General at Shanghai (Cabot)

WASHINGTON, June 16, 1949—8 p. m.

1215. Reurtel 2310, June 16, passed CNO and ComNavWesPac. Dept endeavoring work out with Navy equitable procedure for settling legitimate claims laborers and will telegraph further within 24 hours. In meantime you are instructed orally approach highest Commie authority available along fol lines: That ConGen not authorized represent Navy but can act only as agency for transmission representations to Navy; that ConGen informed that procedure for settling any legitimate claims extant being devised and further info forthcoming; that reliable reports received laborers planning mass invasion ConGen properties shortly in absence settlement claims; and that, in accordance with reptd Commie pronouncements re protection fon properties, responsibility for protecting ConGen properties against any mob action this type will rest squarely on local Commie authorities. You might in ur discretion add that world will watch with interest this test of Chi Commie police authority in protecting fon properties against threat mob violence.

WEBB

893.5045/6–1749 : Telegram

The Consul General at Shanghai (Cabot) to the Secretary of State

SHANGHAI, June 17, 1949—11 a. m.
[Received June 17—10 : 27 a. m.]

2313. *Shanghai Evening Post* stoppage June 15 originated over lack formula for settlement wage dispute. Considering workers' demands unfair, editor [54] suggested refer issue to Labor Department of MCC. Latter organ agreed look into matter next morning which

---

[54] Randall Gould, American citizen.

failed satisfy workers and led them block entrance building and detain editor and assistant. After threatening closure paper, editor finally released late evening June 14. June 15 editor left paper on presses including his story of June 14 events which workers objected to publishing. Editor, considering their refusal take paper as made up constituted strike, then left premises saying he would not return work until workers returned work. Matter understood still stalemated.

Consul General hopes matter may be settled quickly with minimum publicity as magnification issue may jeopardize paper and all American correspondents as well as play into hands of elements anxious to embarrass foreign firms and organizations including (Consul General) through encouragement labor demonstrations. To this end suggest that especially desirable that matter not be played up by VOA or AFRS.[55]

Repeated Canton 730, Nanking 1221.

Савот

893.9111 RR/6–1749 : Telegram

The Consul General at Shanghai (Cabot) to the Secretary of State

SHANGHAI, June 17, 1949.
[Received June 17—2 : 01 p. m.]

2316. *China Daily Tribune* (connected with Chen Ming-shu [56]) June 15, carries editorial entitled "Please Stop Acting Like Overlords". Editorial referred to series incidents involving foreigners (remytel 2290, Department June 16) and stated that in Kmt days common for foreigners to insult China with Chinese person always suffering. According to editorial, "kowtow" diplomacy pursued by reactionary government and attitude bogus officials in currying favor with foreigners have cultivated arrogant attitude on part of "foreign masters." Chiang Kai-shek's [57] "equal treaties" were exposed as fakes by humiliating murder of Shanghai rickshaw coolie, rape of Peiping co-ed, and Kowloon incident. Except for Soviet citizens and those of East European democracies who treat Chinese on basis of equality, nationals of all imperialistic countries have considered Chinese lower class before whom they can display air superiority and whom they can insult as they like, and treat in same way as conquerors treat slaves in colonial possessions. This superiority complex so deep-seated that even after liberation Shanghai foreigners still audacious enough hold Chinese people in contempt. Liberated Chinese people cannot tolerate foreigners' special privileges. Foreigners cannot disobey laws People's

---

[55] Armed Forces Radio Station.
[56] A leader of the Kuomintang Revolutionary Committee (KmtRC).
[57] President of the Republic of China, who retired on January 21.

Government and if they continue insult Chinese people shall be subjected to reasonable judgment of law. Editorial continued "we are not advocates of blind anti-foreignism, nor do we support narrow-minded principle of retaliation". Editorial quoted point 8 of PLA proclamation regarding protection lives and property foreigners as proof that People's Government treats Chinese citizens and foreigners on equal basis, and concluded "all those who obey laws are our good friends".

Repeated Nanking 1223, OffEmb, Canton.

CABOT

102.22/6–1749 : Telegram

The Acting Secretary of State to the Consul General at Shanghai *(Cabot)*

WASHINGTON, June 17, 1949—7 p. m.

1232. ReDeptel 1215 Jun 16. Dept informed Navy has sent instrs to AstALUSNA Shanghai directing him to negotiate "equitable settlement" with laborers after consultation with ConGen. Further informed funds being made available by Navy this purpose. Navy instructing Adm Badger [58] furnish ConGen with list former employees.

Dept believes most desirable negots and settlement claims be handled primarily by AstALUSNA, but desires ConGen extend all practicable assistance in examining claims. ConGen shld avoid far as possible giving any indication US Govt acting this matter as result intimidation or "blackmail" tactics laborers but rather that US anxious investigate all charges underpayment former US Govt employees and effect legitimate compensation. This regard recommend careful screening all claims submitted to insure legitimacy and caution be exercised avoid giving impression US Govt an easy touch.

WEBB

102.22/6–1849 : Telegram

The Consul General at Shanghai (Cabot) to the Secretary of State

SHANGHAI, June 18, 1949—1 p. m.
[Received June 19, 1949—2:47 a. m.]

2348. ReDeptel 1215, June 16. Am trying to get appointment with Chen Yi.[59] However, I feel we should not appear to be unduly eager or insistent about speaking with Communist authorities re this situation despite its dangers. In their present cocky mood a plea for protec-

---

[58] Vice Adm. Oscar C. Badger, Commander, U.S. Naval Forces in the Western Pacific (ComNavWesPac).
[59] Communist mayor of Shanghai.

tion is bound to be taken as another manifestation of weakness on our part and increase their haughtiness in other sectors. For same reason I do not wish to see junior official. There is also some danger in appealing to authorities that they themselves may make embarrassing demands on us on behalf of workmen. My thought is that if Chen Yi does not see me and violence does occur we shall immediately appeal for police protection which we are prepared to do at moment's notice.

As I see situation, Communists can scarcely afford to permit serious violence against foreign Consulate General in heart of Shanghai and threats against outlying residences are probably bluffs because futile. More probable if less dangerous course is that workmen will stage peaceful demonstration which will be highly embarrassing to us and give Communist propaganda a royal opportunity. We cannot ask authorities to stop such a demonstration. It is on above reasoning that I have had matter discussed with labor leaders in an effort to forestall any demonstration by assuring men we are doing all that we can by acting as intermediaries to transmit their demands. Without wishing to prejudge issue, I am hopeful that if men are promptly offered just settlement on basis their employment agreements we will sufficiently deflate pressures for more extreme demands to make them no longer dangerous. I must point out, however, that present pressures have developed largely as result of time elapsed since question originally raised May 11 by Consulate General memo to Navy liquidation team. Despite our past efforts situation remains full of dangerous possibilities. It is therefore imperative that we strive to clear it up as quickly as possible.

CABOT

102.22/6–2049 : Telegram

The Consul General at Shanghai (Cabot) to the Secretary of State

SHANGHAI, June 20, 1949—3 p. m.
[Received 10 : 48 p. m.]

2359. ReConGentel 2348, June 18. Mayor has refused my request for interview and referred matter to Foreign Affairs Bureau.

In light of Deptel 1215, June 16, am disinclined at moment to approach local authorities further, at least until we find out what prospects are for working out a settlement with ex-Navy employees. I shall, therefore, take no further action in this unless instructed to contrary by Department, or unless invited to Foreign Affairs Bureau.

CABOT

123 Colling, Guy Thomas: Telegram

The Consul General at Shanghai (Cabot) to the Secretary of State

SHANGHAI, June 22, 1949—4 p. m.
[Received June 22—6 : 44 a. m.]

2408. Morning June 21 Chinese employee Albert R. D. Chen who resigned in lieu preferment charges February 1948 appeared entrance Glenline Building demanding see me personally re settlement grievance of over 1 year's standing which consistently courteously handled by officers my staff. Upon learning could not see me personally, Chen became obstreperous, threatening personal violence ConGen administrative officer and using insulting language to FSS Guy Colling at reception desk. Chen finally left indignantly toward close office hours. He was not touched by Colling or guards at entrance.

Yesterday June 21 two detectives Whangpoo police station accompanied by MCW [*MCC?*] representative called at ConGen with Chen asking Colling proceed with them to Whangpoo police station to appear before Deputy Commissioner. Colling advised to not go unless and until formally summoned on basis written complaint.

Today police detective called to serve subpoena on Colling to appear before Commissioner between 8 and 8 : 30 a. m. tomorrow on charges assault and battery Chen. Acting upon assumption Colling as FSS clerk not immune from prosecution for personal acts, he advised accept subpoena and appear. Detective tended minimize incident but insisted Colling should appear before Commissioner and apologize to Chen.

Would appreciate Dept's instructions particularly regarding two points:

(1) Colling was acting under my personal orders in refusing admittance to Chen and as such was perhaps performing official acts immune from local jurisdiction. I, of course, did not authorize any violence but this is question of fact not law although I am satisfied that no violence occurred. In any case incident occurred on consular premises and as result of Chen's behavior.

(2) Does any question regarding official acts arise from fact that Colling is clerk, not officer of ConGen?

Unless Dept instructs contrary before 8 a. m. Shanghai time tomorrow, Colling will appear before deputy Whangpoo commissioner Hou Chih-wu, former officer PLA and now MCC, accompanied by witnesses and ConGen officers. Colling instructed relate full facts which amply substantiated witnesses but not apologize nor agree any settlement short complete exoneration. Commies may seek to use this alleged incident for propaganda purposes but I propose to take every means in my power to secure Colling's complete exoneration. Already mentioned incident at meeting GOI [*local?*] consular body for which I was leaving at moment summons arrived.

Feel Dept should immediately consider means which might be employed to back up ConGen either in this incident or if matter of ex-Navy employees get out of hand. Frankly see little justification for maintenance of ConGen Shanghai if this will merely result in making us target for humiliating incidents and propaganda. However, I am by no means satisfied this is Commie purpose at moment. On contrary, am inclined to believe they will seek means to avoid incident if we are courteous but firm.

Sent Department; repeated Nanking 1292.

CABOT

---

123 [Colling, Guy Thomas] : Telegram

The Secretary of State to the Consul General at Shanghai (Cabot)

WASHINGTON, June 22, 1949—6 p. m.

1258. Reurtel 2408, June 22. Colling shld not appear before commissioners. Instructions follow immediately.

ACHESON

---

123 [Colling, Guy Thomas] : Telegram

The Secretary of State to the Consul General at Shanghai (Cabot)[60]

WASHINGTON, June 22, 1949—7 p. m.

1259. Reurtel 2408 Jun 22. In absence violence Colling acting in official capacity and consequently, in accordance with normal rule of Internatl Law, action was that of sovereign US which is not amenable to jurisdiction of local authorities. Status as clerk not material as long as Colling acting in official capacity. In view above, suggested Colling not appear before local authority as recommended. Suggest instead you address informal communication in ur discretion to local authorities substantially as fols:

"(Give brief statement facts incident).

Since Colling did not use any violence against Chen and was acting in official capacity as representative of US ConGen Shanghai, does not appear there is need or occasion for Colling to appear before Commissioner.

As municipal authorities undoubtedly aware, official actions of a sovereign govt are not, under universally accepted principles of Internatl Law, cognizable by courts of another authority."

It is suggested that at same time a member of your staff get in touch with Chief of Alien Affairs Bureau and acquaint that official with

---

[60] Repeated to the Ambassador in China as No. 727.

whole matter. Corresponding action should be taken by Emb at Nanking.

ACHESON

---

123 Colling, Guy Thomas: Telegram

The Consul General at Shanghai (Cabot) to the Secretary of State

SHANGHAI, June 23, 1949—noon.
[Received June 23—12:55 a. m.]

2426. Just returned from long interview Chang Han-fu, head of local Foreign Affairs Bureau, reference Colling case. I explained at length facts case and our position regarding Colling. Chang took attitude that foreigners would be protected if they obeyed laws, that since no diplomatic relations existed Colling was here in entirely private capacity and that he must, therefore, obey summons. Despite my efforts find some face-saving device and emphasis that petty matter involving false charges of disgruntled ex-employee might occasion serious international scandal, he stuck doggedly his position.

We have addressed letter to Police Commissioner which we are sending as soon as translated.

Have instructed Colling remain within building and will arrange he be in my office if police come building arrest him. Feel it necessary in view of Department's position make abundantly clear gravity of violation of Consulate premises if one occurs.

Sent Department; repeated Nanking 1309, Peiping.

CABOT

---

123 Colling, Guy Thomas: Telegram

The Consul General at Shanghai (Cabot) to the Secretary of State

SHANGHAI, June 23, 1949—1 p. m.
[Received June 23—1:54 a. m.]

2427. ReConGentel 2426, June 23. Police have phoned repeatedly all morning demanding to know why Colling has not appeared, notwithstanding full oral explanation made to police by Consulate General Chinese interpreter in person at 8 o'clock a. m.

Deadline of 10:30 a. m. fixed by police for appearance Colling at police station.

Colling remaining in Consulate General. Up to 1 p. m. police have not come to get him.

Ambassador [61] and Clubb [62] understood making representations in Nanking and Peiping respectively.

Sent Department, repeated Nanking 1310, Peiping.

CABOT

---

123 Colling, Guy Thomas: Telegram

The Ambassador in China (Stuart) to the Secretary of State

NANKING, June 23, 1949—2 p. m.
[Received June 23—5:11 a. m.]

1354. [To Shanghai:] Whatever outcome of immediate negotiations in compliance Department's instructions Deptel 1259, June 22, repeated Nanking 727, we feel following aspect of general problem should be brought to attention director Aliens Affairs Office Shanghai at opportune moment. You should express concern at apparent threat to fundamental rights American citizens as evidenced by Chen's ability to call innocent American before authorities new regime on trumped-up charge based purely on personal grudge against foreign organization. (Reur to Department June 22 [63] repeated Nanking 1292) you may say that I requested you to inquire if this practice is condoned by public authorities; if not, what assurances Americans, generally, may have in future that they will not be subjected to unwarranted, unjust molestation. You should add that both you and I are concerned over impression apparent denial fundamental human rights accorded foreigners by new regime is having on American Government and American public opinion; that American officials in China cannot help but be unfavorably impressed at apparent acceptance by new authorities of campaign of vilification, humiliation foreigners in Shanghai and that this will inevitably be reflected in their reports to US Government on responsibility, maturity of Commie regime.

I feel that we should react swiftly and vigorously at proper level to this careless disregard of American rights, not only on behalf official but private Americans as well.

Sent Shanghai for Cabot 747, repeated Department, Peiping 234.

STUART

---

[61] J. Leighton Stuart.
[62] O. Edmund Clubb, Consul General at Peiping.
[63] Telegram No. 2408, 4 p. m., p. 1174.

893.6363/6–2349 : Telegram

The Consul General at Shanghai (Cabot) to the Secretary of State

SHANGHAI, June 23, 1949—5 p. m.
[Received June 23—9:20 a. m.]

2442. Offices Standard-Vacuum Oil Company invaded today by large force former temporary employees contractors associated with Standard-Vacuum. Workers demand they be placed on Standard-Vacuum permanent payroll. Several foreign officials barricaded in offices; other officials also threatened. Attitude workers menacing. Labor Department SMCC and police so far have declined intervene. Labor situation here appears to be gradually getting out-of-hand with officials indifferent to situations bordering on anarchy where large industrial firms both foreign and Chinese concerned.

Repeated Nanking 1320, Canton 785.

CABOT

893.6363/6–2349 : Telegram

The Consul General at Shanghai (Cabot) to the Secretary of State

SHANGHAI, June 23, 1949—6 p. m.
[Received June 23—6:50 a. m.]

2448. Re ConGentel 2442, June 23, 5 p. m. Workers who invaded StanVac building have rejected bonus proposal and company offer to negotiate further with Labor Bureau as mediator. Five foreign executives including Coltman caught in building have barricaded selves in offices. Workers in corridors gradually adopting more threatening attitude. No sign police intend to intervene. Inform StanVac Washington representative of both messages for relay New York.

CABOT

893.00/6–2449 : Telegram

The Ambassador in China (Stuart) to the Secretary of State

NANKING, June 24, 1949—noon.
[Received June 24—8:02 a. m.]

1360. Immediately after learning intransigent attitude Shanghai authorities Chen case [64] yesterday morning, Philip Fugh [65] at my request telephoned Aliens Affairs Office Nanking MCC. Director Huang Hua is absent few days (we believe in Peiping) and Fugh spoke to Assistant Chen Ying. Chen Ying was sympathetic, expressed surprise

---

[64] See telegram No. 2408, June 22, 4 p. m., p. 1174.
[65] Chinese personal secretary to Ambassador Stuart.

at action taken by MCC authorities Shanghai, said mistake was obviously in permitting military authorities Shanghai MCC handle case rather than Aliens Affairs Office; concluded he would telephone Chang Han-fu, Shanghai, immediately.

Sent Shanghai 750, repeated Department, Peiping 236.

STUART

---

123 Colling, Guy Thomas: Telegram

The Ambassador in China (Stuart) to the Secretary of State

NANKING, June 24, 1949—noon.
[Received June 24—9: 08 a. m.]

1361. [To Shanghai:] We have repeated all of your and Department's telegrams concerning Chen–Colling incident (urtel 1310, June 23, sent Department 2427) to Peiping for information, action. Suggest all future telegrams this incident be repeated Peiping likewise.

Sent Shanghai 751, repeated Department 1361.

STUART

893.6363/6–2449 : Telegram

The Consul General at Shanghai (Cabot) to the Secretary of State

SHANGHAI, June 24, 1949—2 p. m.
[Received June 24—6: 48 a. m.]

2460. Reference ConGentel 2448, June 23, 6 p. m. Laborer's siege of StanVac office building lifted at 9 last night when Communist army officer attached downtown police station finally appeared and dispersed laborers. He told them while he sympathized their case [they] were presenting it in wrong way. He instructed them present their demands General Labor Union and Labor Bureau Military Control Commission following morning. He then told manager StanVac Article 8 Mao Tse-tung's proclamation regarding protection law-abiding foreigners still in effect and StanVac officials need have no fear mob violence though they would be required accept rulings Labor Bureau SMCC. No explanation offered long-delayed appearance law enforcement officers.

CABOT

123 Colling, Guy Thomas : Telegram

The Ambassador in China (Stuart) to the Secretary of State

NANKING, June 24, 1949—4 p. m.
[Received June 24—8 : 02 a. m.]

1368. ReEmbtel 750, June 24.[66] Delivered memo this morning to Aliens Affairs Office accordance Deptel 727, June 22.[67] However, it was returned on grounds matter outside jurisdiction this office and could only be handled by Shanghai Aliens Affairs Office.

Repeated Shanghai 758, Peiping 239.

STUART

125.8576/6–2449 : Telegram

The Consul General at Shanghai (Cabot) to the Secretary of State

SHANGHAI, June 24, 1949—4 p. m.
[Received June 24—9 : 09 a. m.]

2466. British Consul General has report of unknown reliability that Military Control Commission is considering manufacture incident with assistance of disloyal employees by which mob action against Consulate General would occur, police would intervene and discover framed evidence of contact between Consulate General [and] Nationalists in Consulate General's premises and apartment building at 70 Rte. Doumer, reconstruction of which just being terminated by contractors. Consulate General has already taken virtually all precautions seem feasible against being rushed either by mob or police but we are again examining arrangements.

Sent Department 2466; repeated Nanking 1331.

CABOT

811.42700 (R) /6–2449 : Telegram

The Consul General at Shanghai (Cabot) to the Secretary of State

SHANGHAI, June 24, 1949—7 p. m.
[Received June 25—2 : 39 a. m.]

2475. *Shanghai Evening Post* editor Gould announced liquidation of paper yesterday press conference. Suspension publication June 15 initially due to wage dispute, later issue editorial freedom, after workers refused to print news story giving Gould version *Post* dispute (remytel 2313, June 17). Gould considered continued newspaper operation futile when labor coercion attempted dictate contents of paper.

---

[66] Same as telegram No. 1360 from Nanking, p. 1178.
[67] Same as telegram No. 1259 to Shanghai, p. 1175.

Gould and owner Starr [68] offered workers space in paper to give their version of dispute. Gould's final decision to liquidate based on recent attitude of SMCC authorities regarding foreign papers as shown in *North China Daily News* case reference story of mining Yangtze (remytel 2387, June 21 [69]) in which *NCDN* editor held personally responsible.

VOA for background only.

Sent Department; repeated Nanking 1345, OffEmb Canton 798.

CABOT

893.00B/6–2449 : Telegram

The Consul General at Shanghai (Cabot) to the Secretary of State

SHANGHAI, June 24, 1949—8 p. m.
[Received June 25—9:21 a. m.]

2479. While Consulate General does not wish draw premature conclusions on any phase of regime still in infancy, study of Communist press since take-over Shanghai would appear reveal certain weaknesses in propaganda technique which VOA can perhaps exploit. Communist propaganda machinery formidable weapon when working according to plan based on predictable events as indicated, for example, by ease with which public aroused to take action against silver peddlers (remytel 2227, June 13 [69]). However there are indications machinery too unwieldy to shift gears rapidly when unforeseen events occur (perhaps corresponding to general rigidness Communist dialectics which, in claiming to be able to predict inevitable progression of events in all fields, sometimes must indulge in fancy interpretation to make unexpected occurrences fit dialectic pattern). Communist authorities may find themselves considerably embarrassed by position into which they have been led in past 2 weeks by their propaganda campaign. Study of party and party line press indicates that after initial silence regarding foreigners in Shanghai immediately after take-over, mild but definite anti-foreign trend has become increasingly apparent in last few weeks.

This shown by following (previously reported to Dept):

1. Increase in press coverage of incidents in which foreigners allegedly maltreat Chinese in which foreigners always shown to be aggressor and forced to acknowledge wrong by public apology. Incidents of this sort invariably accompanied by moral that days of imperialism and special privilege in China are over.

2. Initial stage of press attack on foreign-owned utilities for raising rates, accompanied by hints companies should be taken over by people.

---

[68] Cornelius V. Starr, American citizen.
[69] Not printed.

3. Increasing involvement of foreign firms in labor disputes (although these cases have not yet received prominent treatment in press).

4. Increasing reference in press items and editorials to British-American imperialism (foreign news items almost exclusively taken from Tass or Hsin Hua) and increasing number special articles on various phases of Soviet Russian life.

5. Recent "uncovering" in newspapers of USA spy activities in Manchuria.[71]

6. Climax reached in attacks on *North China Daily News* and indirectly on foreign correspondents for publicizing assumed Kmt mining Yangtze channel and accompanying accusation of British-American conspiracy to aid Kmt establishing blockade.[72]

Last few days have produced events obvious to major portion Shanghai populace which in themselves disprove views and motives ascribed to Britain-America by Communist propaganda over Kmt mines incident. It becoming difficult for vernacular press to maintain silence on existence of actual blockade in view official Kmt announcement commencement blockade on June 26. Evidence appearing in English language press that Britain and possibly USA may not submit to Kmt announced blockade, together with logical British-American business interest in keeping Shanghai port open, will make it difficult force imperialist blockade idea down throats of sophisticated Shanghai merchants. Also repeated Communist statements that shipping lines free and nondangerous being disproved by daily Nationalist plane bombing raids which can be seen by everyone in city. Will be interesting to see how Communist press explains away bombing of SS *Anchises* and attacks on American oil installations during these raids.

Should American-British make definite stand against Kmt blockade, which precisely contrary to what dialectics tell Communists these "capitalistic", "imperialistic" nations are bound to do, Communists will be hard put to it to shift stand or make facts fit previous statements. Consequently Dept may wish VOA to stress any British-American acts protesting Kmt blockade or indicating desire to keep shipping lanes open.

On other hand should Britain-America recognize Kmt blockade, this will present Communists with knotty problem of belligerents' rights and duties towards neutrals which tends to lead towards *de facto* recognition Communist regime (involving Communist assumption of international obligations) rather than the *de jure* recognition which Communists apparently desirous of obtaining without interim steps.

Repeated Nanking 1431, Canton 800.

CABOT

---

[71] See telegram No. 1039, June 19, from the Consul General at Peiping, p. 965.
[72] For further documentation regarding closure of certain ports, see vol. IX, pp. 1098 ff.

123 Colling, Guy Thomas : Telegram

The Consul General at Shanghai (Cabot) to the Secretary of State

SHANGHAI, June 25, 1949—noon.
[Received June 25—2 : 04 a. m.]

2486. Re ConGentel 2427, June 23, repeated Nanking 1310. Colling has been asked to come to Foreign Affairs Bureau at 2 this afternoon. Since I believe Foreign Affairs Bureau is proper forum in which to discuss official immunities, I am going with Colling to Foreign Affairs Bureau as requested. Despite possibility of trickery, I feel that we should not miss this possible chance to settle case.

Sent Nanking 1347; repeated Department.

CABOT

102.22/6–2549 : Telegram

The Consul General at Shanghai (Cabot) to the Secretary of State

SHANGHAI, June 25, 1949—noon.
[Received June 29—4 : 32 a. m.]

2487. Consulate General informed majority of ex-Navy employees not disposed to accept Consulate General offer and plan demonstration Monday. Offer is more than any reasonable interpretation their employment agreements albeit less than demands and local custom.

Unless instructed to contrary, I propose to stand firm and not seek police protection unless workers try to force entry into Consulate General. Since minority reported willing to accept offer and since any weakness may lead to further demands, I feel present offer affords as good a chance of settlement as any.

Pursuant to my letter to Chen Yi, I was invited June 22 to Foreign Affairs Bureau and on June 23 in my talk with Chang Han-fu I sketched this matter also. I did not particularly emphasize it in view of considerations set forth mytel 1310 [*2310*, June 16] and fact we were preparing make offer.

Sent Department; repeated Nanking 1348.

CABOT

---

123 Colling, Guy Thomas : Telegram

The Consul General at Shanghai (Cabot) to the Secretary of State

SHANGHAI, June 25, 1949—noon.
[Received June 25—4 : 02 a. m.]

2488. [To Nanking:] Urtel 747, June 23.[73] Feeling that it would not be wise call personally on Chang Han-fu for second time in 24

---

[73] Same as No. 1354 from Nanking, p. 1177.

hours, I am conveying your message to him through Cheng Kang-chi (see mytel 1309, June 23, repeated Department 2426). I expressed your thoughts to Chang Han-fu in slightly less emphatic language in my interview Thursday.

Sent Nanking 1349; repeated Department.

CABOT

---

893 Colling, Guy Thomas: Telegram

The Consul General at Shanghai (Cabot) to the Secretary of State

SHANGHAI, June 25, 1949—4 p. m.
[Received June 25—9 : 20 a. m.]

2493. Have just returned from second session with Chang Han-fu re Colling case. Chang cross-questioned Colling at length re case, told him he had done wrong in disregarding police summons, said that all foreigners in China must obey Chinese law and gave impression that with that he closed case. I had distinct impression that affair was a face-saving device carried out under orders. Chang seemed embarrassed at my presence and tried to cold-shoulder me, at one point rudely, to which I was forced to make tart reply. I answered Chang's point about obeying law by pointing out that foreigners had every intention of so doing but that question in this case was whether Chinese or International Law applied. I twice said we must agree to disagree.

I mention this because my principal concern at moment is that they may publish story that Colling apologized which he did not. I am optimistic that he is in no further personal danger.

Sent Department 2493, repeated Nanking 1353.

CABOT

893.9111 RR/6–2649 : Telegram

The Consul General at Shanghai (Cabot) to the Secretary of State

SHANGHAI, June 26, 1949—1 p. m.
[Received June 27—1 : 16 a. m.]

2497. Press reported incidents of last few weeks involving foreigners have dampened any initial optimism with which foreign colony may have regarded future under Communist rule. Facts in at least three cases grossly misrepresented in vernacular newspapers and methods by which cases resolved do not offer assurances of fair treatment according to western conceptions due process of law. In fact, there is no law as yet and cases being decided by fiat of branches of SMCC Public Safety Department. Actual facts British-owned Union Brewery case (remytel 2290 [74]), according to company official, were that manager Bredrup had attempted run away to avoid being locked in office by employees as part of what is by now familiar Shanghai labor bargaining technique. Chinese employee tripped him, and to save himself from falling Bredrup grabbed Chinese tearing latter's sleeve. Other Chinese struck at Bredrup. Bredrup did not strike any Chinese. In Shanghai Tramway Co. incident (remytel 2425, June 23 [75]) Matheson had verbal altercation with Chinese employee over sick leave. Chinese grabbed Matheson's coat lapels, whereupon Matheson backed away and Chinese fell, striking mouth against desk. Initial worker's protest relatively mild, with no claim that Matheson had struck employee. Later, second protest filed, alleging version of incident reported mytel. Police later removed Matheson from office at gun point, jailed him incommunicado, and insisted that Shanghai Tramway Co. dismiss him, pay indemnity to injured worker, and offer public apology, before case could be considered further. Callender case (mytel 2308 [*2208*], June 11) also one in which Chinese employees appear equally to blame for eventual row.

Method of handling each offense has followed pattern: Storm of protests at bad conduct of foreigner sent to newspapers by fellow employees of plaintiff, by peaceful onlookers, and by people in other occupations however unrelated to original plaintiff, accompanied by many readings of moral that days of imperialism and special privilege in Shanghai are over. Foreigner inevitably found to be wrong, forced to recompense Chinese for damages suffered, and to make public apology promising never to repeat offense. Such chastisement and accompanying publicity in keeping with Chinese ideas of "face" seems designed to humiliate rather than to punish severely.

While above incidents may be explained by natural emphasis on nationalism in newborn revolutionary regime, fact that Communist authorities apparently seizing on slightest pretext to demonstrate their own potence and impotence [of] foreigners significant partly (1) as settlement of old scores against foreigner for his activities under extraterritoriality; (2) as attempt in pulling foreigner from pedestal he so long occupied (and doubtless exploited) to give average Chinese self respect and sense own importance never before enjoyed in this international city; (3) as desire keep foreigner in line by eliminating his sense of security and by impressing him with fact that he dwells Shanghai on sufferance of conquering PLA which will treat him well and protect him so long as he behaves: Good behavior being interpreted as unquestioning acquiescence in any rule or decree, however detrimental to his own interest. Another explanation is that with hard economic times ahead, Communist authorities wish take people's minds off un-

---

[74] June 16, p. 1166.
[75] Not printed.

filled needs and give them something else think about by bringing time-honored foreign scapegoat to their attention. This technique, incidentally, also used by previous Kmt regime.

In fairness, it should be noted that all incidents mentioned above have involved alleged misconduct by foreigners and that Communist authorities have in general adhered to Mao Tse-tung's point 8 in protecting lives and property of foreigners who abide by laws and regulations of PLA, do not engage in espionage activities, et cetera. Communist authorities dispersed workers in StanVac dispute (remytel 2460 of June 24) and, according to British Consul General, also effectively intervened yesterday to prevent violence in dispute involving British company. These somewhat encouraging indications that authorities have decided to curb labor violence. They also support belief that Communist authorities may desire retain modicum good will on part of foreign business community to help restore foreign trade and bring Shanghai economy back to life. Just how they hope to accomplish this and at same time put foreigners in their place is not clear. Increasing mood among American businessmen is that of packing up and leaving Shanghai rather than submit to humiliations and insecurities of present situation.

Sent Department; repeated Nanking 1356, OffEmb Canton 805.

CABOT

102.22/6–2749 : Telegram

The Consul General at Shanghai (Cabot) to the Secretary of State

SHANGHAI, June 27, 1949.
[Received June 27—10:45 a. m.]

This refers previous messages concerning former employees Nav-PortFac Shanghai:

Following memo delivered Friday, 24 June:

"In response to numerous inquiries by former employees of United States Navy Port Facilities, Shanghai, and as agreed by the American Consulate General with certain representatives of former USN Port Facilities employees, the Consulate General has informed the US Navy of the situation and the claims of its former civilian employees.

Following receipt of the Consulate General's report, the Navy has now authorized the Consulate General to pay 1 month's salary in lieu of 2 weeks' separation notice, and as a termination bonus, to those employees having continuous satisfactory service of 1 year or longer prior to April 27, 1949 with US Navy Port Facilities, Shanghai. Two weeks' salary is authorized as a termination bonus for employees of less than 1 year's satisfactory service who were on the payroll as of April 27, 1949.

Arrangements are being made to complete a payroll based upon information supplied by the United States Navy. A notice as to when and where to report to receive payment will be issued as soon as we are in receipt of complete payroll lists from the Navy. The payment, of course, will be made in People's Bank Notes in accordance with the new Chinese regulations.

In authorizing these payments and providing the funds for them, the United States Navy wishes to point out the following facts:

(1) All of the local employees of the Navy were on temporary appointments only, in accordance with USN civilian personnel instructions, which are not governed by regulations or procedures of other US Government agencies or other local civilian employers. This was understood by all employees at the time of their appointments.

(2) Nothing other than the temporary employment outlined in (1) above was ever pledged or implied.

(3) Although formal notices of separation could not be delivered under the circumstances prevailing at the time of departure of the Navy, all hands were well aware of the possibility of NavPortFac's early closure and each employee knew when he accepted his pay on April 27 that the payment was final, particularly since it included a lump sum payment for accumulated leave in accordance with USN regulations. It should be noted that, although the regulations specify that 2 weeks' notice should be given by the employee or the employer prior to termination, such notice is not mandatory under the regulations (even for temporary employees of more than 1 year's service), and there is no provision, pledged or implied, to pay salaries in lieu of such notices. Because of the exigencies under which the Navy departed from Shanghai, delivery of such notices was of course impracticable, as was the collection of official US Navy badges retained for the most part by the employees.

The USN paid among the highest salary rates of any employer in Shanghai. Employees were consistently paid the highest rates obtainable when paid in local currency, and were protected against falling exchange during the chaotic exchange situation rates expressed in terms of US dollars.

It should be clearly understood that the United States Navy, in voluntarily offering this settlement, is doing so in keeping with the policy of the United States Government with respect to fair treatment of all its employees.

It should further be clearly understood that, in accepting this payment, each former employee waives all further claims against the United States Navy or the United States Government by virtue of his former employment, and in accepting this payment, each employee will be required to sign a certificate to that effect. American Consulate General."

Following letter response to Consul General, Shanghai, memo to ex-NavPortFac Shanghai employees received at meeting today:

Shanghai, June 25, 1949. The American Consul General, American Consulate General, 2, Peking Road, Shanghai.

Dear Sir: The committee of former civilian employees of the US Navy do this date acknowledge receipt of your undated memorandum (for all former employees of United States Navy Port Facilities, Shanghai), the contents of which have been carefully noted.

While we fully appreciate the prompt action you have taken in connection with our petition of June 14, 1949, and are indeed grateful for the favorable consideration given same by your good self and the US Navy, we wish to state that your above-mentioned undated memorandum does not constitute a direct reply to our petition and some of the "facts" drawn to our attention are, in our opinion, incorrect and therefore subject to controversy. We shall endeavor to present below our understanding of the "facts" in the order enumerated by you.

(a) Your paragraphs (1) and (2). We fully agree that all local employees were on temporary appointments only and nothing other than temporary employment was ever pledged or implied. However, local employees of ESD 44, US Army, UNRRA, ECA and other US Government agencies were also on temporary appointments and adequate notice and substantial termination pay were given such employees when these agencies deactivated.

(b) Your paragraph (3). While we were indirectly aware of the early closure of NavPortFac, we had not anticipated the end to be so sudden and abrupt. Neither did we expect to be abandoned in the way we were. We were given to understand that the payment of salary on April 27, 1949, plus accrued annual leave due was a precautionary measure and no indication whatever was given that the pay was final and that the US Navy would depart the following day. Inquiries made of officers resulted only in evasive and conflicting replies which served only to further complicate the situation. As an illustration, may we state that employees who had been released and who came for payment of monies due on the morning of April 27, 1949, were turned away and advised to call again on Saturday, April 30, 1949.

We do not agree with your contention, that although the regulations specify that 2 weeks' notice shall be given to employees in the event of separation after 1 year's continuous service, such notice is not mandatory. Employment and separation of local employees by the US Navy have been guided by regulations at all times. Operation of the US Navy and other US Government agencies are governed by regulation. If such regulations are not mandatory, then why are regulations made and why did the US Navy take the trouble in issuing the "Notice to New Employees" and hand one copy each to every new employee? You further claim the exigencies under which the Navy departed from Shanghai made the delivery of separation notices impracticable. If the Navy had given greater consideration to the welfare of their local employees who had served them faithfully, such notice could have been given at the time of payment of salaries on April 27, as there was sufficient time, and if the pay on that date was to be considered final, the collection of official US Navy badges could have been made at the same time.

(c) Your paragraph (4). We are indeed grateful to the US Navy for the generous treatment and remuneration received while we were in their employ and our services required. However, in return they received our best efforts and much over-time work without compensation at all times. We do not wish to appear ungrateful or unreasonable but we would like to again encroach upon your valuable time and solicit your kind assistance in obtaining better terms for us from the US Naval authorities. When the Navy left we were given verbal assurance that some payment would be made to us through the American Consulate General. It is now 2 months that we have waited and nothing concrete has materialized. Your memorandum did not state any specific date when payment would be made. It could be in the near future and yet it could be in the distant future. There are many of us who would have liked to return to our homeland but have not done so only because we have waited for the promised money from the US Navy. In the meantime our funds are running now and by the time we receive the termination bonus as mentioned in your memorandum, such fund might only be sufficient to liquidate our debts. In view of this and the fact that we are all undergoing difficult times owing to the present unstable economic conditions in Shanghai, we have no alternative but to reiterate that a payment to cover salary for from May 1, 1949 to June 24, 1949, the date of receipt of our above-mentioned memorandum, which can be construed as the official notice of separation plus 3 months' termination pay, would be a more appropriate and justifiable compensation under present circumstances.

We feel sure if all concerned are thoroughly familiar with our predicament, they will be sympathetic to our cause and would reconsider the contents of your undated memorandum and would offer more generous terms.

In conclusion we wish to again apologize for the inconvenience caused and to thank you for the courtesies extended to and the kind and valuable assistance given us in this distasteful matter.

Anticipating an early reply, we remain, Yours most respectfully, Committee of Former Civilian Employees of US Navy, Shanghai, China.

[CABOT]

102.22/6–2849 : Telegram

The Consul General at Shanghai (Cabot) to the Secretary of State

SHANGHAI, June 28, 1949—10 a. m.
[Received June 28—2 : 19 a. m.]

2519. AstALUSNA SHAI 270957Z. Transmitting separately to Navy Department texts ConGen memo issued 24th announcing settlement (mytel 2487, 25th, repeated Nanking 1348) and reply employees rejecting proposal.

Three ConGen officers met 25 delegates library former BOQ 3 p. m. 24th to receive reply. During prolonged discussion principally reiteration old arguments their side and position ConGen as transmitting agency, loud mob broke into BOQ lobby, overran grounds shouting for 3 months' pay and otherwise demonstrating force. This followed by orderly withdrawal, all of which apparently staged to demonstrate power of numbers and authority of leaders.

ConGen representatives stood firm on settlement as announced, promising payment as soon as complete lists received from Navy. Also to transmit new representations to Navy but without likelihood favorable reply. When meeting ended, leaders invited ConGen representatives to BOQ garage compound to accept "thanks" entire group Approximately 350 strong arranged disciplined ranks such fashion, again demonstrating strength and control, cheered leaders who reiterated their original demands and urged prompt settlement. ConGen officers then permitted leave without molestation.

Unconfirmed intelligence reports and rumors indicate strong likelihood mass visitation including occupation ConGen premises entire group plus families relatives on pattern established other recent labor incidents foreign establishments. On other hand, have reports 6A groups satisfied announced settlement, refuse take part but these apparent minority and under strong pressure to present united front.

Unless otherwise instructed, ConGen will maintain position that settlement offered 24th generous and that Navy will authorize additional funds this purpose.

Will report developments promptly.

Department pass to CNO, ComNavWesPac, CoMarianas, BuSandA, BuPers.[76]

Sent Department, repeated Nanking 1372.

CABOT

———

893.00/6–2949 : Telegram

The Consul General at Shanghai (Cabot) to the Secretary of State

SHANGHAI, June 29, 1949—10 a. m.
[Received June 29—12 : 15 a. m.]

2536. Swiss ConGen has through intermediary with Communist contacts story substantially similar to that given me by British ConGen (remytel 2466, June 24, repeated Nanking 1331).

While this second warning can obviously not be disregarded, am still inclined regard story as fishy. Nevertheless should anything this nature occur trust Department will immediately issue statement pointing out that ConGen was twice explicitly informed through reliable sources before event of complicity of Communist authorities in incident and that threats of ex-Navy employees were also brought to attention of Communist authorities.

ConGen could use tear gas and fire hose for defense, but will not do so unless so instructed. Navy has also left some firearms in building, these of course will not be used under any circumstances.

Sent Department, repeated Nanking 1382.

CABOT

———

[76] Bureau of Personnel, U.S. Navy.

125.8576/6–2949 : Telegram

The Consul General at Shanghai (Cabot) to the Secretary of State

SHANGHAI, June 29, 1949—1 p. m.
[Received June 29—4 : 32 a. m.]

2539. Pursuant to my general orders a coolie of Consulate General staff this morning removed several offensive posters from walls of Consulate General. Chinese member of Consulate General staff was forced to go to police station regarding matter and was told that I personally should appear at police station at 2 o'clock this afternoon. I am informing Foreign Affairs Bureau of incident and saying that I trust this will end it. I have, of course, no intentions of going to police station.

Sent Department, repeated Nanking 1385.

CABOT

125.8576/6–2949 : Telegram

The Consul General at Shanghai (Cabot) to the Secretary of State

SHANGHAI, June 29, 1949—4 p. m.
[Received June 29—9 : 02 a. m.]

2547. Re mytel 2539, June 29, 1 p. m. Another telephone conversation with police station indicates that, as result of Foreign Affairs Bureau intercession, matter has been dropped.

Sent Department 2547, repeated Nanking 1395.

CABOT

125.8576/6–3049 : Telegram

The Consul General at Shanghai (Cabot) to the Secretary of State

SHANGHAI, June 30, 1949—5 p. m.
[Received June 30—9 : 42 a. m.]

2570. Reliable source states that Chen Yi has recommended tongs being against plan to rush Consulate reported in mytel 2466, June 24, repeated Nanking 1331, and 2536 June 29, repeated Nanking 1382.

Sent Department 2570, repeated Nanking 1409.

CABOT

125.8576/6–2449 : Telegram

The Secretary of State to the Consul General at Shanghai (Cabot)[77]

WASHINGTON, June 30, 1949—8 p. m.

1322. Urtels 2466 June 24, rptd Nanking as 1331 and 2536 June 29, rptd Nanking as 1382. Dept prepared issue statement suggested second para urtel 2536 shld occasion warrant and ConGen so recommend. Dept of opinion use tear gas or fire hose for defense might exacerbate situation and shld be avoided. Recommend police protection be sought if and when necessary. Dept concerned presence firearms in building, assumes precautionary measures being taken prevent their unauthorized use. Dept also assumes whatever steps necessary re their registration, or notification authorities that they are in possession consulate, have been taken.

ACHESON

893.918/7–149 : Telegram

The Consul General at Shanghai (Cabot) to the Secretary of State

SHANGHAI, July 1, 1949—3 p. m.
[Received July 2—3 p. m.]

2597. ReConGentel 1417, July 1, repeated Department 2580.[78] Gould of *SEP*[79] negotiated with his ex-employees in his office from 3 p. m. until 7 : 30 p. m., July 1. R. T. Bryan as attorney and Charles Miner as Treasurer, Starr interests, also participated. Committee of 8 represented workers. Ninety-three additional workers appeared in corridor about 3 : 30 p. m. and blocked doors making it impossible for Gould to leave until they voluntarily dispersed at 11 : 30 p. m. Gould considered that he was being coerced but nevertheless offered June settlement of 72 basic units, 20 percent more than May. Gould pressed workers to submit definitive severance pay proposal which he could transmit to Starr. Workers flatly refused to make any severance proposal, insisting paper could not liquidate and that in any event full pay must continue indefinitely. Asserted only present issue was amount of June pay. They held out for 144 basic units, double Gould offer. Workers refused acknowledge validity Starr's cabled instructions, saying Starr misinformed by Gould, therefore not able make competent decision. Workers revealed they had access to all messages at government cable office. Consulate endeavored unsuccessfully from 8 to 11 p. m. induce police and FAB[80] to afford safe conduct besieged Ameri-

---

[77] Repeated to the Ambassador in China as No. 76.
[78] Not printed; it reported that Randall Gould had received instructions from C. V. Starr to close the *Shanghai Evening Post and Mercury.*
[79] *Shanghai Evening Post.*
[80] Foreign Affairs Bureau.

cans. Both parties refused on grounds Gould had rejected good offices People's Government authorities, therefore they washed hands of whole matter and Gould would have to accept consequences his intransigent attitude.

Gould thinks pressure may shift temporarily to Miner who has Treasury controls funds. However, Miner has no authority to override liquidation decision which Gould says is final. Gould considers he is prisoner here, predicts he will not be permitted leave Shanghai unless settlement satisfactory to new regime is made. Impasse seems complete. Gould maintains every foreigner here who employs labor is now virtually hostage, believes hostage idea accounts for continued delay issuance exit permit regulations for foreigners.

Regardless basic merits issue, Gould's handling of workers has been highly inept and his tactics needlessly provocative. This complicates problem securing protection for him and increasing risk further aggravation situation.

Sent Nanking 1432; repeated Department, OffEmb Canton 847.

CABOT

893.00/7–349 : Telegram

The Consul General at Shanghai (Cabot) to the Secretary of State

SHANGHAI, July 3, 1949—10 a. m.
[Received July 3—3:24 a. m.]

2600. Chase [81] and Thomas [82] had interesting talk Thursday evening with Democratic League leader Han Ming; also participated in by Mr. Amos Wong who helped arrange meeting. Han (who recalls pleasant wartime acquaintance with Vincent,[83] Sprouse,[84] Freeman [85] and other FSO's) seems clearly belong to League's pro-American moderate wing which includes Lo Lung-chi, Chang Tung-sun and Yih Tu-yi; is City Editor of newly reemerged *Hsin Min Jih Pao;* is close friend and frequent contact of FonOff Chief, Chang Han-fu, and Deputy Chief, Hsu Yung-yin. Both he and Amos Wong are much concerned over increasing seriousness Shanghai situation and need for foreign help in coping with it. Han feels that current Shanghai troubles involving foreigners are not due to Communist wishes but to temporarily unavoidable difficulties centering on:

1. General intransigence of labor, whether under foreign or Chinese employment, in exploiting opportunity to extent which Communists disapprove but cannot presently afford suppress, irrespective rights

---

[81] Augustus Sabin Chase, Consul at Shanghai.
[82] Reuben R. Thomas, Administrative Attaché at Shanghai.
[83] John Carter Vincent, then Counselor of Embassy in China.
[84] Philip D. Sprouse, then Third and Second Secretary of Embassy in China.
[85] Fulton Freeman, then Third Secretary of Embassy in China.

and wrongs, for fear seeming to champion capitalists, imperialists and so losing urgently needed mass support.

2. Deeply ingrained suspicion and sensitivity which rank and file Communists have re all American, British actions and which Americans, British fail appreciate.

3. (Especially stressed by Han) Unfortunate lack, pending recognition, of communication channel between Communists and foreign Consuls for proper understanding and discussion troubles, problems. Communist officials reluctant deal with Consul publicly (in offices and office hours). They prefer out-office informal contact but also cautious re that. While genuinely desiring meet foreign representatives, they are accordingly unable find adequate means therefor. Result is misunderstandings and aggravation troubles.

Han indicated that in such circumstances, and especially in pre-recognition period, Democratic Leaguers who understand viewpoints both sides could and should help as intermediary communication channel.

By way illustrate Communist psychology, Han mentioned *North China Daily News* case. He said outburst against paper's publication of items re Nationalists' mining of Yangtze and foreign (British) aid in sweeping for mines came as result Communists' exasperation over what they regarded as old-style imperialistic face-insulting tactics of British authorities in making patronizing offer to clear mines in return for Communist release of British warship *Amethyst*.

He said that as editor himself, he well realized difficulties operating newspaper to satisfaction of Communists. Even *Ta Kung Pao* is perplexed over problem. Communist authorities one day blame papers for not following CP line and next day criticize for slavish imitation.

Han regretted Gould's decision close *Evening Post* and could not help feel Gould not acted wisely. He feels convinced Communists are perturbed over closure; have been anxious have one American and one British paper continue publication. He pointed to ability of *NCDN* to continue publication despite clamor for its closure as evidence to support his conviction.

Chase, Thomas expressed full concurrence re urgent need adequate means communications between Communists and Consuls to prevent misunderstandings and permit disposal potentially dangerous matters before reach serious stage. They mentioned as example ConGen's predicament with respect extensive demands by former Navy employees, pointing out that development of trouble to violent stage could not fail react seriously on all local as well as general relations between new regime and Americans, and mentioning danger that underground anti-Communist agents might likely lose no chance to help stir employees to violence against ConGen for which Communist authorities would be blamed. Had also pointed out that, while it might be somewhat embarrassing for authorities to "champion imperialists" to extent intimating to ex-employees need for refraining from violence, it would be infinitely more embarrassing if violence once started and authorities had to choose between leaving it unchecked or interfering forcibly against laborers. Han apparently impressed and, without any request from Consulate officers, thereupon said he would talk over ConGen's problem with Chang Han-fu at first opportunity and requested background memo re matter (which ConGen has already supplied him).

Throughout talk Han mainly stressed need for communication channel. Believe that he presented views on own initiative rather than by request Communists but that he is nevertheless sufficiently close to local Communists to have good understanding their present line of thinking and desires. ConGen officers much impressed by his intelligent and earnest interest in problem and absence any desire push himself forward.

Sent Department; repeated Nanking 1435, Canton 850, Peiping 189.

CABOT

893.918/7–549 : Telegram

The Consul General at Shanghai (Cabot) to the Secretary of State

SHANGHAI, July 5, 1949—5 p. m.
[Received July 5—11 : 50 p. m.]

2609. [To Nanking:] ReContel 1432 to Nanking, repeated Department 2597. *Shanghai Evening Post* workers, after detaining Gould in downtown office July 1, to discuss wage settlement, finally permitted him and *SEP* Treasurer, Miner, return home at 11 p. m. on condition negotiations would be continued with workers' committee next morning. Following day before Gould dressed, 7 workers knocked loudly on his private apartment door and started force way in. Mr. and Mrs. Gould and Freeman, American employee of Starr's American Underwriters, in apartment at time and latter assisted Goulds to forcibly prevent workers from entering. No real violence and no one injured, but Goulds did use force to keep workers out.

Workers promptly obtained medical certificates re their "injuries" and filed a charge of assault and battery at police station. Police summoned Gould to station and he appeared with his American lawyer Bryan at 2 p. m. Saturday. Police informed him they took very serious view of case and confronted him with 7 affidavits of "victims" of his attack and eye-witnesses. Police indicated that they considered strongest affidavit that of Russian guard, Soviet citizen, hired by *SEP* businessman Douglas, about 1 week before closure. Police triumphantly pointed out facts stated must be true because even foreigner's version agreed with Chinese. Gould replied that workers were forcing entry into private apartment and he resisted in self-defense. Police insisted he would have to make apology. Gould drafted one which indicated workers had used force and police rejected it. Gould then told police to draft one themselves but they refused on ground that it must be in his own words. Compromise draft by Bryan acceptable police limited to general apology without detailed statement circumstances. Police added line "I agree there will be no repetition of incident" which Gould considered very compromising but he had no alternative but to sign. Bryan advised him privately to sign to avoid an almost certain jail sentence, pointing out that apology was meaningless anyway since obtained under duress. Apology appeared following day inconspicuously in *North China Daily News* among ads on back page, more prominently in Chinese papers. Police also ordered Gould apologize in person to all employees SEP at paper's office on July 4.

Saturday morning workers' delegation returned to Miner's office as agreed to continue discussion wages. Remained adamant in stand that only June wage adjustment subject for discussion and paper must continue them on payroll indefinitely after that. They lowered their demands, however, and expressed willingness accept same wage scale as employees of *North China Daily News* which was about one-third higher than Miner had offered them but also [less?] than they had originally demanded. Miner agreed to their request to telegraph this latest demand to Starr in England. Negotiations were then suspended pending receipt Starr's reply. Monday morning police at last minute complied with Gould's request for police protection at meeting he was scheduled to apologize to workers. Gould was under influence sedative administered by his doctor. One officer of SMCC accompanied him to meeting which was held inside paper's offices. Workers orderly and reasonable as Gould read his apology, announced his willingness to negotiate and explained that the final decision would have to rest with Starr. Following meeting Gould, Miner and workers conducted further wage negotiations and Gould offered turn over paper's ready cash as part payment June payroll. Accepted conditionally by workers. Gould permitted leave the premises in afternoon and take with him effects from his editorial office.

Sent Nanking 1441; repeated Department.

CABOT

125.8576/7-649 : Telegram

The Consul General at Shanghai (Cabot) to the Secretary of State

SHANGHAI, July 6, 1949—10 a.m.
[Received July 6—5 : 49 a. m.]

2614. Reourtel 2601.[86] Threatened demonstration ex-Navy employees. Han Ming, mentioned ConGentel 2600, July 3, repeated Nanking

---

[86] Not printed.

1435, wrote letter today [87] to Chang Han-fu, Chief FonAff Bureau, pointing out possibility of hostile demonstration with regrettable consequences. His letter characterized "more than one-half" of demonstrators as direct or indirect agents Kmt Secret Service Bureau. Apparently, Chang took immediate action basis this letter, for two special policemen began patrolling street near Consulate entrance at 1 p. m. today. At 2 p. m. detachment of about 25 Communist soldiers appeared. They are stationed across street from ConGen on both Peking Road and the Bund. They have not interfered in any way with legitimate callers at Consulate. Appear detailed solely for maintenance order. Ex-employees gathered at former Navy Club this morning, but dispersed voluntarily about time military guard assigned to ConGen. Spokesman for employees has made inquiries of ConGen today, but no threats. Undoubtedly stationing of military guard has had restraining effect on ex-employees though results of long continued detail of troops to guard ConGen might be undesirable. Military detail should also prevent violent action by ex-ECA chauffeurs, who renewed their threats this morning. Various small straws tend indicate wind blowing direction tacit Communist acceptance right foreign Consulates to modicum consideration.

Sent Department; repeated Nanking 1445.

CABOT

102.22/7–649 : Telegram

The Consul General at Shanghai (Cabot) to the Secretary of State

SHANGHAI, June [*July*] 6, 1949—5 p. m.
[Received July 6—1: 35 p. m.]

2628. Group of ex-Navy employees have been at entrances to Glen Line Building since noon. They have demanded that we receive large delegation, which we have refused. We have offered to admit not more than 4 but have pointed out that in absence of lists from Navy there is nothing more we can tell them at moment. Ex-employees are evidently mobilized in teams of 25–50 to maintain continuous watch. We have simply closed gates and waited, so it not yet clear whether they would offer violence to Americans seeking to enter or leave. We believe, however, they would try to rush the building if we opened gates. After waiting 2 hours to see whether authorities would act spontaneously, we phoned Foreign Affairs Bureau to inform them of what was happening. I propose if no action taken in meantime to phone FAB at 4 p. m. informing them American [and] Chinese employees leaving building at 4: 30 p. m. and we trust authority will prevent violence.

---

[87] Apparently July 5.

I do not wish to use exit recently built through British compound for fear of getting them involved, but will if necessary.

Sent Department 2628, repeated Nanking 1453.

CABOT

102.22/7–649 : Telegram

The Consul General at Shanghai (Cabot) to the Secretary of State

SHANGHAI, July 6, 1949—8 p. m.
[Received July 6—11 : 48 a. m.]

2639. ReConGentel to Department 2638 [*2628*], July 6, repeated Nanking 1453. At 4 called Foreign Affairs Bureau which claimed no one there with authority to take any action. Called police who promptly said they would send a patrol but as I write at 7 they have not shown up. They claim patrol sent; although conceivably it has been blocked by parade now going on. I believe we are merely getting the run around. I have sent Stelle [88] to police station to make representations on basis of Mao Tse-tung's eighth point.[89]

At 6 a large group headed by me attempted to leave building. Gates were forcibly held against us and at 8 we are still unable leave building. Although I think we could probably break through, I have taken every precaution against violence on our part.

In brief talk at gate, I made it clear that under no circumstances would we talk under threat of violence. We have given facts of case to press to avoid inaccuracies but I think comments should be withheld till we are entirely satisfied that authorities will not intervene.

Sent Department 2639; repeated Nanking 1461.

CABOT

125.8576/6–649 : Telegram

The Ambassador in China (Stuart) to the Secretary of State

NANKING, July 6, 1949—10 p. m.
[Received July 6—1 : 02 p. m.]

1450. We have talked to Cabot by phone twice this evening. At 8 : 30 there was no change his beleaguered position and he and staff were preparing to spend night inside Consulate General. Assume Department has details direct from Consulate General and press. We feel in addition press accounts appearing in US, Department should make its own authoritative statement to press emphasizing complete lack protection from public authorities. In circumstances we believe pub-

---

[88] Charles C. Stelle, appointed First Secretary of Embassy in China, temporarily at Shanghai.
[89] See telegram No. 1701, May 18, from the Consul General at Shanghai, p. 330.

licity our best weapon and full use of it should be made. (Shanghai telegram 2628 July 6 to Department.)

We telephoned Hua [90] at his home this evening to report incident. He offered to telephone Shanghai director Aliens Affairs tomorrow morning. Suggested Cabot himself continue trying to reach Chang Han-fu by telephone tonight and tomorrow morning as best chance early relief. Tomorrow complicated by celebration Shanghai-Nanking occupation and anniversary Marco Polo bridge incident [91] (see Embtel 1447 and 1448, July 6,[92] repeated Shanghai 805 and 806) [10 characters garbled] outrageous incident in keeping with present unreasonable demands of labor principally resulting from provocative Communist propaganda. We can only assume that present near-anarchic conditions Shanghai are out of control of Communist authorities or that they are developing with their connivance, unless Communists are afraid of losing face over retraction their own anti-foreign propaganda.

Repeated Shanghai 808.

STUART

102.22/7–649 : Telegram

The Consul General at Shanghai (Cabot) to the Secretary of State

SHANGHAI, July 6, 1949—midnight.
[Received July 6—12 : 36 p. m.]

2640. After 2 hours' talk with police they are now (11 : 30 p. m.) trying to clear ex-Navy employees from in front of building. We have agreed to send a representative to discuss matter Friday but have made it clear that we cannot accept arbitration, are only acting as intermediaries and will not negotiate under threat of violence.

Please inform Navy.

Sent Department 2640; repeated Nanking 1462.

CABOT

---

123 Olive, William M. : Telegram

The Consul General at Shanghai (Cabot) to the Secretary of State

SHANGHAI, July 7, 1949—11 a. m.
[Received July 7—2 : 42 a. m.]

2641. Vice Consul William Olive arrested yesterday afternoon while en route filling station in jeep, apparently for alleged obstruc-

---

[90] Huang Hua, Director of Communist Aliens Affairs Office at Nanking.
[91] Outbreak of hostilities between Japanese and Chinese forces near Peiping, July 7–8, 1937; see *Foreign Relations*, 1937, vol. III, pp. 128 ff., and *ibid.*, Japan, 1931–1941, vol. I, pp. 313 ff.
[92] *Ante*, pp. 409 and 410, respectively.

tion Communists in parade. Still held incommunicado this morning. Authorities refuse to divulge charge, will not let us see him or take him food. We have report from Sikh eyewitness that he was severely beaten last night after accidently overturning ink bottle. Chase and Supple [93] were rebuffed and insulted at police station this morning, when they went there in effort to ascertain facts and assist him. Separate report their experience follows.

Sent Department 2641; repeated Nanking 1463, Peiping 191.

CABOT

102.22/7–749 : Telegram

The Consul General at Shanghai (Cabot) to the Secretary of State

SHANGHAI, July 7, 1949—1 p. m.
[Received July 7—9 : 27 a. m.]

2643. At 9 : 30 last night police patrol came to Consulate General and were admitted. They wished immediately to discuss matter with Consulate General representatives and leaders of ex-Navy employees, intimating that otherwise they would withdraw. I reiterated that under no circumstances would we talk to employee representatives while they maintained blockade of building but that I would be glad to inform police regarding case. They agreed. Two-hour talk followed, during which we explained case and they asked numerous and generally pertinent questions. We pointed out that we were acting solely as intermediaries, were not directly involved in dispute, could only give what Navy wishes, expected protection from violence in accordance with International Law and Mao Tse-tung's eighth point and that if we were officials we should have special protection, if private citizens as they claimed we clearly had nothing to do with the dispute. They pointed out that many of men still unemployed and consequently suffering, that it was desirable to settle case on basis of local custom, and that further violence might occur if it weren't settled. What they said showed that they had been fully informed since yesterday of developments in matter, hence guards Tuesday. Note that delay their coming yesterday was deliberate. We finally agreed to send a representative tomorrow to Foreign Affairs Section to discuss but not to arbitrate matter. At midnight police finally dispersed men peaceably and staff went home. Police courteous and generally helpful. However, in talking to men, police said no further violence while negotiations in progress, leaving intimation violence permissible if we do not agree to settlement satisfactory to workers.

I am planning a strong protest to Foreign Affairs Bureau tomorrow (today is holiday).

---

[93] William J. Supple, Security Officer at Shanghai.

Department will appreciate that situation now more difficult than ever. Men's tempers inflamed by long delays and not improved by 12 hour vigil in rain. Authorities almost certain to put pressure on us and to wash hands of any violence if we prove intransigent despite any representation on our part. As reported in mytel 2462 [*2642*],[94] although I believe authorities concerned at bitterness of labor disputes, they seem afraid to take firm hand even in flagrant cases of violence and even connive with them to some extent. Men's appetites growing as each further case of violence brings further successes. Pattern followed yesterday if [*of?*] long delay in appearance of police is so similar to that in other cases as to reflect definite policy. It is this atmosphere that we must consider what to do.

Only bright spot is that we have found an April 1948 Navy payroll which will enable us to divide men fairly accurately into categories of more or less than a year's service. We are urgently working on this now. I propose at meeting tomorrow to offer pay on basis present offer on fixed day next week and to transmit further messages to Navy if they reject offer. I frankly doubt that this will satisfy many.

I frankly find it difficult to recommend course of action to Department. Rough estimates indicate that we have some balance in Navy fund with which to increase present offer. I hesitate to increase present offer because (*a*) it is more than equitable under regulations men agreed to when employed, (*b*) I do not like to yield to violence, (*c*) I doubt men would accept even increased offer.

Only other suggestion I have to offer despite obvious objections is that Navy send team of labor experts here to negotiate. I should not like to undertake mission for Navy but (*a*) it would get Consul General out of a mess which is Navy's responsibility, (*b*) it would put Communist authorities on spot re acceptance.

I would greatly appreciate urgent instructions.

Sent Department, repeated Nanking 1463.

CABOT

---

123 Olive, William M. : Telegram

The Counsul General at Shanghai (Cabot) to the Secretary of State

SHANGHAI, July 7, 1949—3 p. m.
[Received July 7—5 : 45 a. m.]

2645. ReConGentel 2641, repeated Nanking 1463, Peiping 191.

Suggest Department release story of jailing and beating Vice Consul William Olive, pointing out it seems part of systematic plan to humiliate foreigners. Correspondents here have filed story, but AP

---

[94] Dated July 7, vol. IX, p. 1261.

correspondent believes transmission may be delayed by radio administration.

Sent Department 2645, repeated Nanking 1467, Peiping 193.

CABOT

---

123 Olive, William M.: Telegram

The Consul General at Shanghai (Cabot) to the Secretary of State

SHANGHAI, July 7, 1949—5 p. m.
[Received July 7—8:51 a. m.]

2646. ReConGentel 2641, repeated Nanking 1463, Peiping 191. On July 6 at 11:30 p. m. Vice Consul William Olive had been missing from Consulate General approximately 10½ hours. Inquiry various police stations by phone disclosed Olive jailed in Wayside police station. William J. Supple accompanied by M. E. Meyer, local stateless employee formerly employed Chinese police, arrived Wayside police station approximately 12:30 a. m. July 7. Refused permission see Olive and police superintendent contacted by telephone refused talk with us and instructed police clerk on night duty not to give us any information. We did learn Olive was brought Wayside police station because he had not obeyed traffic order to go to the other side of the street because of CC parade. Olive booked about 3:15 p. m. at Wayside. Night police clerk further advised that Olive was charged with assault and battery and breaking wristwatch of inspector in charge. Night police clerk advised us to return about 9 a. m. July 7 and that we could bring Olive food.

Approximately 8:30 a. m. July 7, before going to Wayside, Supple learned that an Indian guard, Boor Singh, employed Italian Consulate General, was detained at Wayside during time Olive was brought in. Approximately noon Boor Singh reported verbally to Meyer and Supple:

"Approximately 5 p. m. Olive brought into Wayside station, taken to a back room, approximately 10 minutes later Olive brought back to front counter. Olive argumentative, hit the counter with hands two or three times, several other police officers came in and one took hold of Olive's arm to pull him away, Olive reached for the counter and pulled a letter box off the counter, splashing ink in his own face and over his clothes, also clothes of police officer, whereupon blows and kicks were exchanged between Olive and police officers, Olive being knocked to the floor and handcuffed after which police officers kicked and beat him. Olive kicked back and one police officer drew his gun threatening to shoot, Olive begged for mercy, was told to enter the detention cell with Boor Singh and two Chinese. Olive refused and was picked up bodily and thrown into the cell. Olive later asked to use phone but police refused to listen. Boor Singh stated he was released approximately 6:15 p. m., Olive remaining in the cell." [95]

Nine-thirty this morning Supple went with Meyer by car to Wayside district police station taking breakfast food. Chase for reasons close personal friendship with Olive (rather than official function) accompanied them with idea remaining background in car but available for possible consultation. Upon approaching entrance (Muirhead Road) to police station compound, they found two police and two military sentries at gate. As sentries made no sign objecting to car's entrance and as Supple had brought in car without difficulty previous evening, they drove car into compound and Supple, Meyer entered building. Chase remained in car. Supple, Meyer approached duty police sergeant explaining politely they came from Consulate General with purpose inquire regarding welfare and charges against Olive and requesting if possible see officer in charge. Sergeant referred inquiry to near-by civilian dressed man, evidently political commissar, who answered curtly that they could see nobody. Sergeant repeated statement and refused further talk on ground no interpreter had been brought. When Meyer proved his ability speak Chinese, he said no recognition the American Consulate General and matter "ordinary" affair involving foreigners. Supple, Meyer then asked whether as private citizens they could give their food to Olive and referred to Mao Tze-tung's eighth point regarding protection foreigners. Such approach proved no avail and Supple, Meyer then left building. As they were about to rejoin Chase in car, sentry indicated car would not be permitted to leave compound. Returning to building to inquire reason this action, Meyer met police officer (former acquaintance on Settlement police) who offered to get permission for car leave. At this point, however, order came, apparently from political commissar, summoning Chase, Supple, Meyer to "lecture" room. Here commissar informed them they had been guilty "serious" violation regulations in bringing car into compound rather than first alighting and approaching gate on foot to request permission enter. When Consulate General officers expressed regrets for having been unaware of such regulations of which sentries had given them no indication commissar proceeded harangue them at length in loud and most abusive, insulting manner. Main lines of his attack were:

1. Who do you think you are, behaving thus, having nerve to drive straight into compound? Do you take us for dance hall or public place? What was your idea of coming here in first place? (A simple reply they had come to inquire regarding Olive was ignored and followed by renewed tirade.)

[95] For summary of Mr. Olive's account of affair, see telegram No. 2678, July 9, 7 p.m., from the Consul General at Shanghai, p. 1220.

2. We don't recognize American Consul General and Americans no longer have any voice in China. During Kmt they could assume airs and attitudes, but that is all finished: All foreigners must now obey our laws or be punished—Consulate or no Consulate—which means nothing to us.

3. Do you realize how serious this offense is? We could shoot all of you right now for it. If you had attempted to drive away in car, our sentries should have shot you.

4. If you foreigners want to go back to your countries, so much the better. But first we shall find out if you are good or bad people (implication obvious). At several points Consulate General officers, with careful effort to speak with courtesy and restraint, and believing useless if not dangerous attempt argument, reiterated quietly their regret at having been unaware of violated regulations. Each such "apology" elicited renewed outburst of sarcastic sneers regarding "meaningless apologies" and further vituperation. Was clear that commissar, whether or not considering more extreme action, was determined do everything possible humiliate Consulate General officers before large crowd of police, military personnel, onlookers. More crowd gathered, more loud and aggressive he became. Consulate General officers were addressed as if criminals and kept continuously standing. He finally produced paper and told Chase, Supple, Meyer to write (1) personal history (with details former occupation), (2) explanatory statement why they had ventured visit police station, and (3) apology. He then said such statement would be sent police headquarters ("where full information to verify statement would be available") to verify "whether good or bad people". Said he assumed we wanted go back to car and asked whether would agree write such statements. If so, would be released from detention provided statements seemed to justify. Believing that nominal compliance under duress would satisfy police and be preferable to refusal and incarceration, Consulate General officers and Meyer wrote desired statements about 1½ pages each providing routine facts and statement to effect "it is to be regretted that through unawareness violated regulations". Upon completion statements police constable took them to next room (to which commissar had meanwhile removed) and after about 3 minutes returned to state all three could leave in car. He added that hereafter should clearly realize that any matter for discussion with police should be taken up with Alien Affairs Office Bureau Public Safety and never with police station direct.

During period when written statements being prepared, there was apparently made from next room phone call to police headquarters concerning case. Chase, Supple feel headquarters probably directed prompt release and that without instructions they and Meyer would very likely still be detained.

After departure from police station it was learned from Consulate chauffeur who drove car that he also was quizzed by police. Among other things, they asked him which one of three Consulate General representatives was Consul General (to which he answered "none"

they are all employees) and stated that he was a bad man for working
for the Consulate General.

Repeated Nanking 1468.

Department pass Peiping in its discretion.

CABOT

---

123 [Olive, William M.] : Telegram

The Secretary of State to the Ambassador in China (Stuart)[96]

WASHINGTON, July 7, 1949—6 p. m.

793. Re Shanghai's 2646 Jul 7 rptd Nanking 1468, gist being telegraphed Peiping by Dept.[97] If not already done, Emb shld immediately
make protest to appropriate Chi Commie auths in strong and forceful
term re arrest, beating, detention incommunicado Vice Consul Olive.
Dept recommends immediate oral protest to Alien Affairs Bureau to
be fol by written memo detailing facts in case as outlined by ConGen
Shanghai but leaves final decision as to method protest to discretion
Emb. Emb shld impress on Commie auths that US Govt takes extremely serious view this flagrant violation established internatl law
re treatment consular officials. Emb shld also protest on humanitarian
grounds insulting and arbitrary treatment accorded consular officers
who went to police station merely to inquire re Olive and bring him
food.

ConGen Peiping requested take similar action.[98]

ACHESON

102.22/7–749 : Telegram

The Secretary of State to the Consul General at Shanghai (Cabot)

WASHINGTON, July 7, 1949—9 p. m.

1358. Urtel 2643 July 7. Dept considers procedure you proposed
in para 4 as best move at this time and suggests it be followed.

Navy now has under consideration ur suggestion concerning special
negotiators, which we agree would be desirable if feasible.

ACHESON

---

[96] Repeated to the Consul General at Shanghai as No. 1356 and to the Consul
General at Peiping as No. 417.
[97] Telegram No. 418, July 7, 6 p. m., not printed.
[98] The Consul General at Peiping in telegram No. 1151, July 10, 10 a. m., reported he had sent letter on this matter that day to the Headquarters of the
Communist "People's Liberation Army".

123 Cabot, John M. : Telegram

The Secretary of State to the Consul General at Shanghai (Cabot)

WASHINGTON, July 7, 1949—9 p. m.

1359. Urtel 2627 July 6.[99] Dept inclined view favorably ur departure with Amb [1] on date now tentatively set Jul 15. Chief problem possible unfavorable reaction Amer community Shanghai ur departure this critical stage. Seems little or no likelihood ur successor could arrive Shanghai near future both because absence transportation facilities due closure port and question Commie documentation for his entry.

If decision made authorize ur departure, Dept desires McConaughy [2] assume charge time ur departure. Dept chose McConaughy Shanghai assignment with view having him assume charge during ur temporary absence or interregnum prior arrival ur successor and his executive officer functions given him with such possibility in mind. Subsequent this decision Chase promotion has made latter ur senior subordinate but Dept continues believe McConaughy should assume charge in event ur departure in view his special qualifications and his being chosen for that purpose. Dept certain Chase will appreciate its continuing confidence in him and desire afford him fullest opportunity devote time important polit reporting and problems requiring Chi language officer's special qualifications.

Dept would appreciate ur comments foregoing prior making final decision re ur return US.

ACHESON

701.0993/7–849 : Telegram

The Consul General at Shanghai (Cabot) to the Secretary of State

SHANGHAI, July 8, 1949.
[Received July 8—9 : 27 a. m.]

2656. *Ta Kung Pao* and other local papers including *North China Daily News* July 6 carried the following item :

"Day before yesterday, Alien Affairs Section of Public Safety Bureau of Shanghai City Government set up a station at the North Station for inspecting foreign travellers. The work of this station is to inspect travel permits of foreign travellers going in and out of this city and to assist railway guards to inspect their luggage.

"From now on, Embassy and Consulate staff and newspapermen of imperialistic countries who formerly enjoyed special rights under Kmt

---

[90] Not printed.
[1] For documentation regarding departure of Ambassador Stuart, see pp. 723 ff.
[2] Walter P. McConaughy, Consul at Shanghai.

reactionary rule will be subject to inspection by inspection officers of People's Government."

Sent Department; repeated Nanking 1477, Canton.

CABOT

---

123 Olive, William M. : Telegram

The Consul General at Shanghai (Cabot) to the Secretary of State

SHANGHAI, June [*July*] 8, 1949—5 p. m.

[Received July 8—9 : 58 a. m.]

2658. Chinese reporter for UP was told by guard at Wayside police station this morning that Olive was injured three places on left side in course of fight evening July 6 with police officers. According to this source, Olive's original offense was that his car, along with several others, obstructed line of march Communist parade. Olive was only offender singled out and taken to police station. Report continues [that] Olive objected strongly to this discrimination. He was overruled and sentenced to 24 hours in jail on spot. He protested vigorously and insisted he be permitted pay fine in lieu jail sentence. Again overruled and was being taken away when he apparently overturned desk or table he was trying to hold to. Fight then started with Section Chief. Several policemen came to assistance Section Chief and administered severe beating. Guard added Olive held absolutely incommunicado, not even Chinese unconnected police station can see him. Guard asserts police made persistent efforts July 7 to induce Olive sign complete apology which he steadfastly refused to do, thus compounding offense in Communist view.

Foregoing report, of course, cannot be taken as unimpeachable but probably worthy some credence.

Repeated Nanking 1478, Peiping 196.

CABOT

---

123 Cabot, John M. : Telegram

The Consul General at Shanghai (Cabot) to the Secretary of State

SHANGHAI, July 8, 1949—7 p. m.

[Received July 8—7 : 38 a. m.]

2660. Reurtel 1359, July 7. Greatly appreciate Department's sympathetic views. I believe most of American community here knows that I postponed my departure leave since this was published in May as item to instill confidence during turnover. This plus fact that many in community know I have been recurrently ill for some months should help explain departure. I agree some unfavorable reaction will inevitably result but since community has great confidence in and liking for McConaughy I think such reaction will not be very serious. Despite distinctly unfavorable turn which events have taken since early June, it is still true Consulate General can do but little for Americans and their interests here under present circumstances. Department will appreciate that most serious cases handled by Consulate General have involved Consulate General itself. Chase has taken decision in ingenuous and cooperative spirit.

Should Department contemplate action in accordance with my telegram 2642, July 7,[3] paragraph 11, it might be advisable for me to stay until this operation completed but I have misgivings whether my health will stand up under indefinite strain of present conditions. Although Ambassador's target date is July 15, I think it doubtful he will be able to get off so soon.

CABOT

---

123 Olive, William M.: Telegram

The Consul General at Shanghai (Cabot) to the Secretary of State

SHANGHAI, July 8, 1949—7 p. m.
[Received July 8—12:46 p. m.]

2661. Re Vice Consul W. M. Olive arrest. Afternoon July 7, a consular officer called upon a close foreign contact including police to discuss case. Contact was pessimistic and stated Olive's obstreperous attitude complicated case to extent that effective action could not be taken. He said that since every department in police stations is now under supervision of Communists, police intervention could not be made; since he now could not trust many of his closest former colleagues, inquiry into case would have to proceed with caution. Together consular officer and representative called on a department head of Chinese police at his home and again discussed case. The Chinese was quite shocked at Olive's action and called case hopeless so far as early release is concerned. Stated if Olive insisted on his rights as a Vice Consul and member of American Consulate, case would assume a political color and be immensely implicated [*complicated?*]. He also of opinion that if there are Consulate markings on jeep, that fact would be involved in case.

Both contacts advised strongly that Consulate General consider seriously advisability of treating case as purely civilian incident in which Consulate General has no responsibility. They were of opinion that initial Consulate General interference only magnified case in eyes

---

³ Vol. IX, p. 1261.

of police authorities and any subsequent interference would have no beneficial effect unless case does not assume political importance.

Suggested that only presently effective line of action would be Mrs. Olive write in Chinese petition addressed to Commissioner of Police and deliver to Foreign Affairs Commission of Police by Mrs. Olive in person. This would eventually be given to above Chinese contact who would take whatever action possible as circumstances permit. The petition should be written in sentimental way in which she declares her love, worry, concern for her husband, admits that some trouble must have occurred and that she sincerely apologizes for what he did, indicating his actions were result of his great concern for her health, asserting she has been seriously ill for several weeks. Contacts could not indicate result of such petition but opined it might be of great assistance.

Contacts stated that a doctor would not be permitted to see Olive. They were confident he would be held for several months before sentence and sentence could be several months more or even year.

Consular representative plans dinner with contact tonight at which time official as well as unofficial police version of story will, it is hoped, be provided.

Sent Department, repeated Nanking 1480.

CABOT

102.22/7–849 : Telegram

The Consul General at Shanghai (Cabot) to the Secretary of State

SHANGHAI, July 8, 1949—7 p. m.
[Received July 8—11 : 59 a. m.]

2662. Re mytel 2643, repeated Nanking 1465, 7th. Thomas designated represent Consul General in discussing ex-Navy employees severance pay contacted Foreign Affairs Section Bureau Public Safety through Chinese interpreter 8 : 30 a. m. That office denied any knowledge of appointment, said not within their jurisdiction, should be referred Foreign Affairs Bureau SMCC. Thomas then had Chinese assistant contact officers from Whangpoo station with whom appointment initially made. Latter likewise said affair not within their jurisdiction and referred Consul General back to Foreign Affairs Section BPS. Latter then arranged appointment with SMCC Foreign Affairs Bureau 11 a. m.

Female representative SMCC first met group 6 ex-Navy employees approximately 30 minutes, then called Thomas. First inquired reason of visit and nature of request. Thomas replied meeting arranged pursuant request SMCC officials and Cabot evening 6th when pickets removed from Consulate General. SMCC representative then said since matter not previously reported would like written outline entire matter. Thomas presented brief prepared statement in Chinese. SMCC representative said more detailed statement sequence events and position "capital versus labor" needed for study and decision higher authorities. Thomas pointed out that while glad to discuss matter with claimants and/or authorities with view to early solution Consul General representing sovereign power could not accept decision or arbitration by authorities since such would not conform applicable principles international law. Thomas reiterated Consul General not authorized represent Navy except as transmitting agency and not able act in capacity employer.

SMCC representative replied there are always two parties to every dispute and that in absence of Navy, Consul General should represent capital in matter. Thomas agreed submit new written résumé but pointed out this would involve further delay in effecting any payment whereas Consul General now almost ready effect payment accordance terms outlined AstALUSNA's 270957Z [4] and inquired whether Consul General should proceed such payment next week, mentioning rising commodity prices and increasing evidence bad temper claimants. SMCC representative said first submit written statement and await reaction higher authorities before making settlement. Thomas pointed out that in view increasing pressures claimants as demonstrated 6th further violence might be anticipated meantime unless authorities intervene. SMCC representative said in event such violence or incident report by phone to that office. Thomas replied three such phone reports made afternoon and evening 6th in addition police reports but that no assistance forthcoming until after staff detained approximately 10 hours. SMCC representative replied that holiday 6th and absence from office responsible for lack assistance that day.

Unless instructed to contrary will withhold settlement proposed 270957Z and await developments. However, visualize danger being ordered by authorities to effect settlement along lines demands workers with possibility further violence and prolonged siege Consul General. Even more dangerous possibility is that ex-Navy employees now organized only as each may join one of large labor unions, thereby increasing proportion pressure and possibility larger incidents accordingly. Latter possibility first suggested by SMCC officer night of 6th.

Sent Department 2662, repeated Nanking 1481.

Department pass to CNO & ComNavWesPac.

CABOT

---

[4] Same as No. 2519, June 28, 10 a.m., from the Consul General at Shanghai, p. 1189.

123 Olive, William M. : Telegram

The Ambassador in China (Stuart) to the Secretary of State

NANKING, July 8, 1949—8 p. m.
[Received July 8—12: 35 p. m.]

1460. [To Shanghai :] I attempted to make appointment with Huang Hua this morning to discuss detention Vice Consul Olive (Deptel 793, July 7 to Nanking, repeated Shanghai 1356). Huang asked Philip Fugh to come to see him first in order that he might be prepared for subject of my interview. This seemed reasonable preliminary and I agreed.

After Fugh had recounted briefly predicament Vice Consul Olive and purpose of my anticipated call on Huang, latter replied that CCP would accept no protests from any foreign governments since no diplomatic relations existed between CCP and any foreign nations. He stated that he had no knowledge of circumstances case of Olive but assumed that latter must have violated traffic regulations during military parade July 6 and had thereupon been taken to Public Safety Bureau; that upon arrival there he must have acted "in arrogant manner, insisting on his position", thus aggravating officials of PSB. Huang added that PSB officers are not allowed to strike anyone except in self-defense.

Fugh, knowing that I had intended to ask Huang in my interview to convey circumstances of complaint to Peiping, suggested such action to Huang, to which latter replied that he could not do so without offending authorities in Shanghai; that Shanghai was out of his jurisdiction. When Fugh pointed out that Consulate General Shanghai had been unable to reach Director Aliens Affairs Bureau [5] because Shanghai director was on honeymoon, Huang agreed this was "very unfortunate". He told Fugh that best way to solve Olive case would be (1) to investigate facts of case and determine what actually happened; (2) to take no action based on "one-sided story which might have been sheer fabrication", and (3) case should be left in hands of PSB to settle.

Result of Fugh's conversation is that Huang has in effect refused to do anything in this case and I shall not make further attempts to see him thereon. I likewise consider it useless to send written protest at lower level which would only be rejected without reply on ground that our official status not recognized.

I can only suggest that Cabot continue efforts to see Chang Han-fu personally. Since one of our immediate objectives is to secure medical aid, proper diet and legal counsel for Olive, I suggest initial approach to Chang might better be on humanitarian basis, including request for Consulate General doctor to visit him promptly, suitable food made

---

[5] Chang Han-fu.

regularly available to him, and member of Consulate with legal counsel be permitted to interview him promptly. Protest re flagrant violation established international law and general discussion assurances re future treatment American officials and private citizens Shanghai might well be taken up later after above minimum essentials secured.

Sent Shanghai 817, repeated Department 1460.

STUART

102.22/7–749 : Telegram

The Secretary of State to the Consul General at Shanghai (Cabot)

WASHINGTON, July 8, 1949—8 p. m.

1371. Urtel 2643, July 7, last paragraph. Navy states it is prepared to send Shanghai two men equipped with info and powers negotiate ex-Navy employees: Lt. D. W. Denton, former Asst. Supply Officer Nav Port Fac, and E. A. Sompayrac, civilian of Industrial Relations Dept.

Pls explore and report soonest passport documentation needed, possibilities obtaining permission Commie authorities for entrance and firm assurance exit plane, crew and two men, having in mind adequate local warning and safety plane's arrival Shanghai. Comment on preferable point departure whether Formosa, Korea, Hong Kong or Okinawa.

Navy advises it is willing *in extremis* to make funds available for negotiations on fully equitable basis.

ACHESON

---

123 Cabot, John M. : Telegram

The Secretary of State to the Consul General at Shanghai (Cabot)

WASHINGTON, July 8, 1949—8 p. m.

1374. Fol consideration urtel 2660, July 8, Dept approves ur return Washington on consultation returning US on Attaché plane with Amb. Authorization this travel contained Deptel 1355, July 7.[6]

ACHESON

811.42700(R)/7–949 : Telegram

The Consul General at Shanghai (Cabot) to the Secretary of State

SHANGHAI, July 9, 1949—1 p. m.
[Received July 9—5 : 48 a. m.]

2672. *Liberation Daily* reports today Olive has tendered written apology to police admitting following offenses: Violation of traffic

---

[6] Not printed.

regulations, refusing to report name to police authorities, beating up police officers, damaging property Public Safety Bureau. Apology gives assurance that similar incident will not occur in future and states that during detention Olive had not been given any maltreatment.

I suggest this be played up by VOA as typical example of Communist propaganda. From at least two impartial sources in position to know facts it is clear Olive was severely beaten (although in fairness resisting authority) and that he was placed in filthy cell with other prisoners incommunicado and without being allowed to have food sent him. I believe it is important to let as many people in China as possible know how much one of these apologies is worth.

Pass to VOA New York.

Sent Department; repeated Nanking 1491.

CABOT

---

123 Olive, William M.: Telegram

The Consul General at Shanghai (Cabot) to the Secretary of State

SHANGHAI, July 9, 1949.
[Received July 9—4:02 a. m.]

2674. *Chieh Fang Jih Pao*, July 9, carries following story on arrest Vice Consul Olive:

"As reported yesterday, on July 6, Wm. Olive, American national, refused obey police, violated traffic regulations, and was taken Wayside public safety station for questioning. He attacked policemen during interrogation. Authorities realized he lost his reason and placed him under arrest. After continuous exhortation he formally admitted guilt and said reason for rude arrogant action was that he is American Vice Consul.

"Officer told him no diplomatic relations with any foreign government and so all foreign residents subject People's Government protection and jurisdiction in private capacity. Even after establishment formal diplomatic relations foreign consular officials should not violate laws and regulations People's Government. Olive admitted his fault and personally wrote apology and willingness compensate police officers for damages he caused.

"Apology stated: I, Wm. Olive, former Vice Consul of American Consulate General, admit that while Liberation Army was parading— I violated traffic regulations and was taken to Wayside public safety station. At station I refused give my name, thus preventing officer in charge identifying and handle my case. When told I was to be detained I became so excited I beat up two police officers, damaged station property and acted rudely toward police officers. I committed serious error and admit following offenses: Violated traffic regulations; refused report name to authorities; beat up police officers; and damaged property of station. I am willing tender apology to insulted officers and pay expenses for damages and loss to station. I give assurance that similar incident will not recur in future and that I will abide by laws and regulations of People's Government and behave like law-abiding foreign resident. I beg authorities deal with this case leniently. I realize my fault and after re-examination, regret my actions. During my detention I have not received any maltreatment. (Signed) Wm. Olive."

Sent Department; repeated Nanking 1493, Canton. Department pass VOA, New York.

CABOT

102.22/7–949 : Telegram

The Consul General at Shanghai (Cabot) to the Secretary of State

SHANGHAI, July 9, 1949—4 p. m.
[Received 7 : 04 p. m.]

2677. Consul McConaughy accompanied by interpreter Ernest Tung called Foreign Affairs Bureau July 8 to discuss siege of Consulate building July 6 [by] ex-Navy employees, maltreatment Vice Consul Olive [in] Wayside police station. He had appointment with Director Chang Han-fu who did not appear. Conversation held with Feng Chih-ho, second in command. Verbatim transcript in Chinese made by Communist steno. When McConaughy refused to accede to Feng request that he change designation on appointment slip from "American Consul" to "ex-American Consul", mutually agreed to insert "American citizen" instead.

1. Siege of Consulate building. McConaughy outlined facts ten and half hour siege Glenline building afternoon and evening July 6, stressing lawlessness and irresponsibility action taken by mob; seven and half hour delay of police in taking action notwithstanding repeated phone appeals to both FAB and police officials from 2 p. m.; denial of freedom movement Consular staff which was confined without benefit of suitable eating or sleeping facilities until after midnight.

Feng objected to use of term "mob", actively defending ex-Navy employees. McConaughy pointed out that group used physical force and intimidation to prevent staff from opening Consulate gate; trespassed on Consular premises by forcing way over adjoining roof and wall; stationed lookouts at top barbed wire fence to threaten staff members who might endeavor to leave by adjoining British compound; and were raining blows on back door Consulate General in effort to break it down when police finally arrived. This corresponded to general conception of what constituted a mob.

Feng argued Consulate General erred in not admitting entire throng of demonstrators to Consulate General "for negotiation". He said when we barred our doors against them it amounted to refusal to bargain and put Consulate General entirely in wrong. McConaughy said we had refused and would continue refuse negotiate under duress.

Even though Consulate General was not party to dispute between workers and US Navy and could only act as channel transmission it had never refused discuss issue in orderly way with small group representing workers. Consulate General was still ready talk at any time with appropriate group if no coercive tactics applied. In fact at that moment Mr. Thomas was discussing case in another room this building.

Feng said even though former Consulate General had acted mistakenly police would have come promptly to investigate case in response our appeal had it not been for holiday parades afternoon and evening July 6 which interfered with normal police activity. McConaughy said obligation on authorities to maintain law and order continued on holidays same as working days.

Feng said action of workers did not infringe law or order. McConaughy asked if authorities proposed give workers free hand when disputes not settled to workers' full satisfaction. Feng dodged this query, saying crux of matter was mere question final wage settlement susceptible of immediate settlement without raising any larger issues of protection rights. McConaughy said in his view issue was extent to which authorities would permit workers use violence satisfy their demands. He insisted on reply, saying that Consulate General was entitled to know whether it was exposed to possible renewal of siege so that plans could be made accordingly. Feng said he could not give any assurances workers would be prevented by authorities from renewing siege if we failed to reach settlement with them. There would be no excuse for failure to reach solution and People's Government would not assume responsibility for consequences. McConaughy mentioned his belief that such a stand would have serious and far-reaching consequences for American interests in China and inquired if Feng's position had sanction of principal Communist authorities. Feng replied somewhat obliquely stating Mao Tse-tung never intended first part of his 8 point re protection of law-abiding foreigners to apply to foreigners whose actions were not in harmony with interests of people. Implication seemed to be that since legal codes have been abolished term "law-abiding" is to be construed very loosely and that any person or firm not complying completely with wishes of new regime would be deprived of right to protection.

Throughout interview Feng endeavored to turn discussion to merits of wage dispute while McConaughy persistently brought conversation around to right of Americans to official protection from mob violence and threats of mob violence. McConaughy said he was not there to discuss pros and cons of dispute which were receiving careful and sympathetic attention in Navy Department which would make reasonable offer as soon as payroll records now dispersed could be assembled. He reiterated that regardless of merits of case we took emphatic exception to workers' action and police indifference thereto. Feng said workers had a good case, workers had been terminated very suddenly and were entitled consideration. McConaughy said we were sympathetic to economic plight of workers who are still without employment but he did not suppose Mr. Feng was intimating that US Navy had left too soon or should give them renewed employment.

McConaughy said he thought Communist position was lacking in logic. If Communists acknowledge our official position as they seemed to do by holding us responsible for claims against a US Government agency we were entitled under universally accepted international usage to protection as an agency of US Government; if on other hand Communist maintained we were only "former" Consular officers and were now merely private citizens we could not be held responsible as private citizens for claims against US Government. Furthermore if Mr. Feng persisted in alleging it was the "former US Government" which was involved (a phrase he had used several times) how could he maintain that claims could be enforced against a government not in existence in Communist view? Although Feng showed considerable mental agility throughout interview he stumbled on this one and said "former US Government still exists". When this evoked a laugh he covered up by saying while the "former" American Consular officers here were merely private citizens now they could not escape responsibilities which they inherited from period when they were duly recognized by Kmt Government.

McConaughy ended discussion of this subject by asking it be put on record Consulate General would call on authorities to disperse demonstrators if they should again lay siege to Consulate building and would expect effective action to be taken. Present regime would be responsible for any failure to fulfill its minimum protective obligations.

Feng felt he must have last word; cautioned McConaughy he was only private citizen and could not speak for any "former Consulate General" or "any unrecognized government"; furthermore possibility of renewal of siege was purely hypothetical.

Separate telegram re maltreatment Vice Consul Olive follows.[7]

Department's discretion pass excerpts Peiping.[8]

Sent Department 2677; repeated Nanking 1496.

CABOT

---

[7] See telegram No. 2679, *infra*.
[8] Marginal notation: "Not passed."

123 Olive, William M.: Telegram

The Consul General at Shanghai (Cabot) to the Secretary of State

SHANGHAI, July 9, 1949—8 p. m.
[Received July 9—1:38 p. m.]

2679. Re ConGentel 2677 to Department; repeated Nanking 1496. Following is continuation McConaughy interview with Feng of Foreign Affairs Bureau.

Maltreatment of Vice Consul Olive. Turning to case of detention incommunicado, reported beating Vice Consul William Olive, McConaughy outlined story which Consul General had pieced together from fragments information obtained various private sources. McConaughy made it clear no complete or authoritative account of incident could be given authorities because of their own conspicuous omission to notify Consulate General of incident and give its officers access to Olive and to witnesses. McConaughy said investigations were started by Consulate General at about 11:30 p. m. July 6 when Olive had been missing for about 10 hours. Consulate General had received apparently well-founded unofficial reports Mr. Olive had been severely beaten at Wayside police station after being brought there for minor traffic infraction. McConaughy remarked that refusal of authorities to allow Consulate General to communicate with Olive, concealment of nature of charges, refusal to permit food for him to be brought in from outside and denial of medical attention were all gross violations of international law and usage and well below recognized minimum standard of conduct expected of every member of family of nations.

Feng asked if Mr. Olive was a former American Vice Consul. McConaughy replied that he was an American Vice Consul. Feng said he must be considered as former Vice Consul. Feng asked on what basis McConaughy interceded on Olive's behalf. McConaughy replied he was doing it as a representative of American Government and as an office associate and friend of Mr. Olive's and that Mr. Feng could take his choice of capacity in which he wished to view McConaughy. McConaughy told Feng Olive was an employee of US Government which Mr. Feng in discussing siege case had admitted was still in existence. McConaughy urged he be given an official statement of charges preferred against Mr. Olive. Feng referred to official Communist version of case which appeared in *Liberation Daily News* for July 8. McConaughy asked if it was to be taken as authoritative. Feng said it was merely a newspaper report. McConaughy then said reply was not responsive to his request and again urged he be given official statement concerning case.

Feng said McConaughy was going beyond his prerogatives as friend of Olive's; that McConaughy could not be given any information concerning case; no outsider could assist Mr. Olive and no one but Olive would be informed at this time of exact nature of charges. McConaughy expressed dissatisfaction with answer and reiterated request for official information and right access to accused. Feng said he was unable to comply because matter was exclusively within police jurisdiction; furthermore, he did not know case. McConaughy inquired if it would be fruitful for him to return in afternoon to obtain a reply after Mr. Feng had had an opportunity to investigate case. Feng said this would not be necessary as Mr. Olive had committed a certain offense as a private American citizen and would be dealt with by police without intervention of Foreign Affairs Bureau. McConaughy said Consulate General was greatly disturbed by rumors Mr. Olive had been severely beaten by police; that report increased urgency of request for access to Olive on humanitarian grounds. It was quite possible Olive might need medical care which it was known police stations were seldom able to provide. Feng asked where McConaughy heard rumors that Olive had been beaten. McConaughy said report had come to Consulate General from anonymous sources so persistently and circumstantially it must be given some credence. Feng said rumor should not be credited; that police regularly give very good treatment to persons detained by them. McConaughy asked for official confirmation or denial report Olive had been beaten. Feng said he did not have information on this.

McConaughy mentioned articles 1 and 6 of treaty January 11, 1943 [9] providing that jurisdiction Chinese Government over nationals of US is to be in accordance with principles of international law and practice and that consular offices should be informed whenever their nationals are under detention or arrest or in prison or area waiting trial and shall thereupon be permitted to visit such nationals; and that US nationals shall have right at all times to communicate with consular officers; and that such communications from nationals under detention, arrest or in prison should be forwarded to consular offices by local authorities. McConaughy reminded Feng that this treaty was not included among so-called "treaties of national betrayal" listed by Mao Tse-tung, therefore he presumed it was acceptable to Communists and would be considered binding by them. Feng said it was an "old treaty" and was null and void since it had been negotiated with Kmt. McConaughy asked if all "old treaties" as Feng termed them were considered abrogated. Feng replied yes, any treaty not negotiated by Communist authorities was dead letter unless ratified by Communist Government. McConaughy remarked this slant on treaties had far-reaching implications. He said as to 1943 treaty, if present regime repudiated obligations of treaty, it was not entitled to benefits China derived from treaty which included relinquishment of extraterritorial rights by US Government. Feng said since China was sovereign state,

---

[9] Department of State Treaty Series No. 984, or 57 Stat. (pt. 2) 767, 768, 770.

Communist Government considered that extraterritoriality was illegal from outset and Communist Government did not depend on treaty for its abolition.

McConaughy brought up abusive treatment received by Consul Chase and Attaché Supple when they visited Wayside police station July 7 in effort to see Olive. McConaughy pointed out they were on humane mission, acted correctly and did nothing to warrant threats, insults, rebuff and lecture which they received. Feng said if Chase and Supple had any complaints to register they would have to file them personally with his office.

McConaughy said ranking authorities of present regime in China had indicated desire to establish friendly relations with foreign states. If two cases complained about were representative of manner in which new regime would meet its obligations, serious barriers to establishment of mutually beneficial working relations might be created. Feng said General Mao Tse-tung stated diplomatic relations between China and any foreign country would be founded on basis of equality and that foreigners would have to accord equal treatment Chinese. McConaughy said he believed Chinese were receiving equal treatment in US but in Shanghai some foreigners clearly were not receiving equal treatment; there appeared to be systematic campaign to humiliate foreigners. Feng asserted foreigners were receiving equal treatment and there was no truth to charge that campaign was afoot to humiliate foreigners. McConaughy said he hoped henceforth foreigners would receive fair treatment. Feng insisted they had received fair treatment since Communist takeover. Without arguing point McConaughy repeated he hoped foreigners would receive fair treatment. McConaughy said he wished to use statement for record. He hoped Mr. Feng would take careful note of it and that it would be passed to highest Communist authorities. He then said that under instructions from competent American authorities he was lodging an emphatic protest over maltreatment of Vice Consul Olive and condoning by authorities of lock-in of Consular staff in Consular building. The Government of US took extremely serious view of both these cases. Local regime was considered to have flagrantly violated obligations inescapably assumed by it when it took over government of this city. Disregard of international obligations and basic human rights by this regime could not fail to be noted with apprehension in many foreign capitals where the record of new regime in North and Central China was under close scrutiny. Feng said since there were no diplomatic relations between US and China, he was not prepared take note of these words. (However, his stenographer took statement down verbatim and emphasis and solemnity of statement clearly were not lost on Feng.) Feng then said statement read into record by McConaughy would be transmitted to highest Communist authorities but only as personal views of McConaughy. Feng courteous throughout, maintained slightly quizzical set smile which masked his undoubted realization of seriousness of issues he was required to dodge by mouthing party line clichés.

Sent Department 2679; repeated Nanking 1498.

CABOT

---

123 Olive, William M. : Telegram

The Consul General at Shanghai (Cabot) to the Secretary of State

SHANGHAI, July 9, 1949—7 p. m.
[Received July 9—1 : 15 p. m.]

2678. Five p. m., 8th, plain-clothes officer from Wayside police station called on Mrs. Olive her apartment. Brought letter from Olive wherein he admitted "serious errors", reported "good treatment" and asked for clothes to be sent him and money readied (about US $50) to pay "damage he had caused". Officer tried impress Mrs. Olive husband unhurt, well-treated and intimated hope for speedy settlement his case which was not serious except for fact that "he had to be reeducated". When she asked why neither she nor others had been permitted see him for 2 full days, officer replied Olive had refused give his name so case could not be handled. Said nobody could be present when case came up for decision. However, promised notify Mrs. Olive next day so she could see husband if not already released.

Olive released about noon today, allowed return home accompanied by wife whom police had summoned by phone. Consulate General will shortly submit his detailed story, salient points of which follow:

After leaving Consulate General about 1:30 p. m. of 6th, Olive had crossed Garden Bridge, was proceeding along Broadway, with no parade within sight when police signaled him to turn off small side street. As way blocked by 2 carts he sounded horn, hallway cleared and was about proceed when several heavily armed Communist soldiers apparently infuriated over coolies being forced make way for foreigners came up and compelled him back all way to Broadway. On reaching Broadway he started return to Consulate General and was nearing Garden Bridge when civilian police halted him in rough manner. Same group of soldiers then appeared, harangued him, forced him wait about 2 hours, then took to Wayside police station.

He was held but few minutes at Wayside during which a friendly sergeant (take-over from old regime) warned him he was in for bad time being foreigner and regretted his lack authority permit Olive to phone Consulate General. Then take[n] to Foochow Road central police station Office Alien Affairs where only subordinate in charge (as result parade holiday) characterized matter as "very minor offense" and issued written instruction for return Olive to Wayside station for quick settlement case.

On return Wayside sergeant started reassure Olive regarding release when noted that central police official's written order had been amended by Wayside officer to read "is to be detained". During ensuing talk with sergeant, Olive, while appealing for sergeant's intercession to prevent detention, was gripping and leaning on intervening table edge. Soldiers reappeared and forcibly jerked him away from table, causing him lose balance, knock ink wells and cup from table and himself fall to floor, one arm inadvertently striking soldier as he fell. Soldiers, tempers inflamed, instantly surrounded him, striking him with gun barrels, etc., and terrifying him to point where he resisted in instinctive self defense.

He was then put in handcuffs (which not removed for almost 24 hours), brutally beaten up about body and legs and then hauled to preliminary detention cell (housing 3 other prisoners including Indian information source previously reported by Consulate General). Later was taken to another cell in which were already crowded 15 poor Chinese who treated him kindly, even offering tea.

Next morning he was compelled (with armed soldiers surrounding) to write "full confession" of guilt for various offenses including assault and original traffic "violation" (driving on a street which it appeared was among those declared reserved for parade in announcement made noon of 6th—quite unknown to him). Drafted 3 statements none of which satisfied police who then made him write 4th statement with virtually every word dictated by them. During this and various other humiliating points of his experience he was repeatedly photographed. In connection with this and other shorter statement which he was later forced to sign (including apologies to prison guards and people municipal government) he was also pressed to include denunciation of American Government—which he managed evade fairly well.

Following preparation of his confession he was given farcical "trial" charged with no less than 8 offenses, lectured lengthily (several times) on American Government's sins, manner in which foreigners should conduct themselves under people's regime, etc. Was then compelled write down summary of what had been told him.

Following trial he was taken solitary confinement cell in which, while lying, was not even allowed turn over and while sitting forced maintain painful crouched position for hours—at point of guards' guns.

Only nourishment he received during entire stay police station was bread and water—not enough water.

His requests for doctor examine his injuries were refused. He was not even permitted wash till shortly before release.

Such was severity and brutality of his treatment he cannot even recall clearly sequence and character events during latter part his detention—is hazy for example as to number and differentiation of apologies he was forced sign. He clearly recalls however that subsequent to trial he was twice forced make additions to his original confession: First, that he had been well treated and "suffered no injuries while under detention" (phrasing which Olive finally accepted as at least technically correct—injuries being inflicted before detention) ; and second, that his confession was made voluntarily.

About 3 : 30 afternoon 8th Olive noted sudden marked change in attitude of his jailors (McConaughy called at Foreign Affairs Bureau at 11 that morning) ; they became solicitous even to point offering him foreign cigarettes, asking him write wife, etc. Before his release they had him washed, shaved, barbered.

In connection with his apologies he was forced to make 3 waist-deep bows while photographers took pictures.

Before leaving Olive required pay fine. Actual cash paid over only JMP [10] 30500. But jailors had apparently deducted other amounts for "expenses" from cash on his person.

Preliminary superficial exam indicates Olive's bodily injuries probably not serious; but am of course having him thoroughly examined including X-ray—results to be recorded by physician's certificates supported by photos of injuries. He is naturally in highly exhausted, nerve-shaken state—dreading further arrest and torture; and psychological shock believed probably more serious than bodily wounds.

This grim affair impressively confirms my conviction that no American now safe in China. True that sudden change in police attitude afternoon of 8th probably reflected orders for Olive's release given by higher Communist authorities as result of Embassy's and Consulate General's intensive efforts; but fact that action was finally obtained by such efforts is no grounds of reassurance as to future in face of general dangerous attitude toward foreigners by rank and file Communists' personnel.

Department will appreciate that release of full story may jeopardize Olive but may feel full release nevertheless necessary. My 2 statements reported separately were designed to explode police story without involving Olive.

I suggest Olive be moved from Shanghai as soon as unobtrusively possible—perhaps in the interim stop at Tientsin to ease exit permit question.

Repeated Nanking 1497.

CABOT

---

[10] *Jin min piao* (Chinese Communist currency).

123 Olive, William M. : Telegram

The Consul General at Shanghai (Cabot) to the Secretary of State

SHANGHAI, July 10, 1949.
[Received July 10—1 : 50 a. m.]

2683. I issued the following statement to the press immediately following release of Olive:

"I have instructed Mr. Olive, for his own protection, to make no public statement regarding his case."

After examining Olive, I issued the following statement to the press later in the day:

"I have only the following to add to what I said this morning. I have personally seen Mr. Olive's injuries. We have had him examined medically and have taken photographs. There is no doubt whatever that Mr. Olive was brutally beaten by the police and that any statements such as that which appeared in the *Liberation Daily* this morning were obtained as a result of the barbarous treatment he received. On the other hand, I am gratified and reassured to find that the higher authorities, once the matter was brought to their attention, arranged for his speedy release."

Repeated Canton 867; Nanking 1502.

CABOT

---

123 Olive, William M. : Telegram

The Consul General at Shanghai (Cabot) to the Secretary of State

SHANGHAI, July 10, 1949—4 p. m.
[Received July 10—1 : 58 a. m.]

2684. Several Consular colleagues have suggested to me a joint Consular protest at flagrant violation of Consular status in Olive case. Until I know Department's view I hesitate to find out whether all colleagues would join and how many would seek instructions.

Would appreciate Department's instructions.

CABOT

102.22/7–1049 : Telegram

The Ambassador in China (Stuart) to the Secretary of State

NANKING, July 10, 1949—10 p. m.
[Received July 10—1 p. m.]

1470. [To Shanghai:] Embassy following difficulties with ex-Navy employees [with] closest attention and sympathy and has been endeavoring devise some helpful course action (Contel 2643 to Department

July 7). Embassy offers following suggestions for Consulate General's reference wherever they may appear useful.

Following points should be impressed on authorities:

(1) Members Consulate General as individuals have no responsibilities either to Navy or to Navy employees.
(2) Consulate General as organization is merely channel for transmission requests to US Government and agency to execute Government's instructions.
(3) Claims of Navy employees must be presented in orderly and proper form if Consulate General is to receive and transmit them. Mob action neither orderly nor proper, particularly if bonus is requested as gratuity.
(4) If bonus is demanded as obligation, Navy employees have 2 conceivable avenues approach:

(a) Court action, which, however, not available since Consulate General as agency US Government exempt for jurisdiction and claims against US Government likewise outside jurisdiction.
(b) Approach by local authorities on behalf Chinese nationals.

If Consulate General's attempts settle directly with claimants are finally unsuccessful and it becomes evident that bonus is demanded as US Government obligation, claimants' only lawful recourse is to request local authorities act their behalf in pressing claims against US Navy as agency foreign government. Therefore if authorities consider these claims factually and legally justifiable it is their duty to Chinese nationals to act as their sole representatives and not as mere mediators.

Finally it should be presented most clearly and forcibly to highest available local authorities that obligation to prevent violence rests on them and not on Consulate General. If they should permit violence to occur it would demonstrate unequivocally that they do not intend fulfill their oft-repeated pledges protect property persons foreigners.

Sent Shanghai 819, repeated Department 1470.

STUART

---

123 [Olive, William M.] : Telegram

The Secretary of State to the Consul General at Shanghai (Cabot)[11]

WASHINGTON, July 11, 1949—7 p. m.

1382. Urtel 2678 July 9 rptd Nanking 1497, passed Peiping by Dept. On basis Olive's account his treatment, Emb and ConGens Shanghai [and] Peiping shld make further strong protest to appropriate Commie auths (oral where possible, fol by written memo) against inhumane treatment; extortion from Olive and publication of statements contrary to fact; and conditions of confinement Amer Govt

---

[11] Repeated to the Ambassador in China as No. 813 and to the Consul General at Peiping as No. 423.

official borne out by concrete evidence his physical and psychological state (which obviously at variance with description by local auths) as well as his own testimony. Reemphasize contravention internatl law and failure Commie auths observe customary procedures of an orderly regime.[12]

ACHESON

---

123 Olive, William M.: Telegram

The Consul General at Shanghai (Cabot) to the Secretary of State

SHANGHAI, July 12, 1949—3 p. m.
[Received July 12—4:53 a. m.]

2715. Deptel 1382, July 11, 5 p. m., Olive case. Before lodging further protest, would appreciate urgent reply mytel 2684, July 10, 4 p. m., suggesting possibility joint protest by Consular body.

Sent Department, repeated Nanking 1521, Peiping 201.

CABOT

---

123 Olive, William M.: Telegram

The Secretary of State to the Consul General at Shanghai (Cabot)

WASHINGTON, July 12, 1949—5 p. m.

1389. Urtel 2684 July 10 re possible joint consular protest violation consular status, Dept of opinion concerted action wld have definite advantages but it shld be representative of consular corps and initiative shld not come from ConGen. If consular body decides take action Dept suggests protest take cognizance entire situation Shanghai: Contravention recognized principles internatl law in gross maltreatment consular officials; delay and inadequacy safeguarding consular establishments and free movement their personnel in legitimate activities, fol specific repeated requests; failure provide adequate protection fon properties and foreigners (pursuant Mao's 8th point) desiring conduct legitimate affairs, particularly failure afford protection against coercive and irresponsible acts.

Reurtel 2715 July 12 Dept desires you not delay ConGen's specific protest while awaiting decision on common action.

ACHESON

---

[12] In telegram No. 1180, July 15, 5 p. m., the Consul General at Peiping reported he had made protest in a letter of that date to the Headquarters of the Communist "People's Liberation Army". He added that an unconfirmed report indicated that the Peiping Communist authorities were annoyed at the action of the Shanghai police.

393.1121 Kanady, Dilmus/7–1249 : Telegram

The Consul General at Shanghai (Cabot) to the Secretary of State

SHANGHAI, July 12, 1949—6 p. m.
[Received July 12—9 : 24 a.m.]

2719. Consulate General has sent memorandum to Foreign Affairs Bureau re case American citizen Dilmus Kanady arrested June 27 result minor traffic incident June 26. He was given 48-hour jail sentence by police commissioner apparently without evidence or hearing of any sort. No appeal permitted. Sentence served in small cell without furniture or sanitary facilities.

Memorandum to Foreign Affairs Bureau recites reported facts and inquires if Kanady received trial or given right to appeal.

Sent Department 2719, repeated Nanking 1528.

CABOT

___

125.8571/7–1249 : Telegram

The Consul General at Shanghai (Cabot) to the Secretary of State

SHANGHAI, July 12, 1949—6 p. m.
[Received July 12—7 : 34 a. m.]

2727. Tax Bureau has served demand on Consul General for payment taxes on Glenline building equivalent to more than $8,000 US currency. July 20 set as deadline date.

Endeavoring establish tax exempt status of Consul General building with Communist authorities. Also consulting Consular colleagues, several of whom occupy buildings owned by their governments. Appears we are the only Consulate served with ultimatum so far.

Instructions urgently requested for guidance in case our negotiations fail.

Repeated Nanking 1536.

CABOT

___

893.911/7–1349 : Telegram

The Consul General at Shanghai (Cabot) to the Secretary of State

SHANGHAI, July 13, 1949—3 p. m.
[Received July 13—7 : 18 a. m.]

2740. Miner, American Asiatic Underwriters, local representative of Starr interests, is being held in his office by ex-employees of *Shanghai Post* with threat he will be kept indefinitely until some settlement made.

Police refuse to intervene.

Suggest publicity be given to this further example of labor violence condoned by authorities.

Sent Department 2740, repeated Nanking 1544.

CABOT

---

123 Olive, William M. : Telegram

The Consul General at Shanghai (Cabot) to the Secretary of State

SHANGHAI, July 13, 1949—4 p. m.
[Received July 13—8 : 36 a. m.]

2741. Remytel 2678, July 9. Following is substance combined medical report William Olive by USPHS Surgeon Schram and Shanghai physician McLane: Eighteen physical evidences of violence caused by beating with rifle butts, barrels and kickings. Far more serious than physical injuries are psychic trauma induced by humiliation, indignities, torture mental and physical, leaving him in state emotional instability exhibited by extreme unhappiness and apprehension. Medicos state it urgent and essential his recovery he be removed soonest and placed in area free from any traces of Chinese or Communism.

Repeated Nanking 1545; Department pass Peiping 203.

CABOT

893.911/7–1349 : Telegram

The Secretary of State to the Consul General at Shanghai (Cabot)

WASHINGTON, July 13, 1949—7 p. m.

1401. Urtel 2740. Dept believes time opportune to give publicity Miner as well as similar cases where violence condoned by authorities. Dept would prefer take occasion lodging of joint consular protest for this action. If joint protest unlikely or delayed please inform, in which case Dept will immediately proceed publicity these cases.

ACHESON

---

123 McConaughy, Walter P. : Telegram

The Ambassador in China (Stuart) to the Secretary of State

NANKING, July 14, 1949—noon.
[Received July 14—8 : 37 a. m.]

1520. [To Shanghai:] For Cabot. Reference Shanghai telegrams 2677 and 2679, July 9, to Department. Please inform Consul McConaughy that I was deeply impressed with forceful, intelligent manner in which he handled his July 8 interview at Shanghai Foreign Affairs Bureau regarding siege of Consular building by ex-Navy employees and maltreatment of Vice Consul Olive (Shanghai 1487 [*1497*] to Nanking [13]). I hope excellent presentation of American case will have salubrious effect on Communist authorities and believe that in any case American views have been presented to Communists with clarity, logic and dignity which leave nothing to be desired.

Sent Shanghai 852 for Cabot, repeated Department 1520.

STUART

---

123 Olive, William M.: Telegram

The Consul General at Shanghai (Cabot) to the Secretary of State

SHANGHAI, July 14, 1949—5 p. m.
[Received July 14—1: 49 p. m.]

2764. Re Deptel 1401, July 13. Consular body meeting called for 11 a. m. tomorrow. Beyond informing proponents we will agree to protest, have carefully refrained from any initiative in accordance with Department's instructions. However, Brazilian colleague, who has been particularly active, says he is confident protest will be acceptable to practically all, if not all, Consular body. If too much wavering and abstention occurs, I shall take initiative to prevent ineffective protest. I shall, of course, bear in mind Department's desire to have protest as broad as possible and I feel this will be agreeable to my colleagues.

Sent Department 2764, repeated Nanking 1554.

CABOT

102.22/7–1449: Telegram

The Consul General at Shanghai (Cabot) to the Secretary of State

SHANGHAI, July 14, 1949—9 p. m.
[Received July 14—9: 58 a. m.]

2771. Department pass to CNO and ComNavWesPac. Letter comprising résumé entire affair ex-Navy employees requested [by] FAB July 8 (ConGentel 2662, 8th, repeated Nanking 1481) dated 9th was delivered by interpreter 11th. Latter also conveyed oral message urging immediate settlement basis presently authorized or prompt arrangement visit and negotiation claims by Navy team (Deptel 1371, 8th, repeated Nanking 802).

Although written plain bond and signed without title, letter [was] refused after study account (1) use term American Consul General in absence recognition; (2) use term violence describing incident July 6; (3) position Consul General that under uniformly accepted principles international law Consul General as representative sovereign power could not accept arbitration by foreign government.

---

[13] Same as telegram No. 2678, July 9, to the Department, p. 1220.

Acting my instructions Thomas called FAB 12th asking see female representative who requested letter. Instead was seen by Feng Chih-ho. Feng informed that Consul General at loss how meet objection (1) since letter requested [by] FAB for factual résumé and statement Consul General since Consul General involved only [on] account official capacity and absence Navy and no other name appropriate. Re objection (2), Feng told that Consul General could not find better term describe forcible detention entire staff led by me when angry crowd chained bicycle across gate and held closed with force. Re objection (3), reiterated that Consul General as representative sovereign government could act only under instructions from Department. Furthermore although recognizing Communist wish not recognize Consul General, Consul General bound regard itself as such.

Feng made little comment these points except to insist that letter be rewritten in more acceptable terms. Gave no specific reaction Navy mediation team proposal but stated revised letter would be referred higher authorities for decision.

Interesting sidelight developed when Feng's amanuensis taking full transcription conversation belligerently asserted that had Consul General admitted employee representatives 6th subsequent events would not have transpired and that barring gate their faces constituted insult Chinese people. He informed no insult Chinese people conveyed or intended, instead determination Consul General not submit intimidation. Feng terminated this discussion abruptly, obviously displeased with intercession subordinate.

Revised letter being delivered FAB today substituting "this office" for term "Consul General", eliminating term "violence" and using "forcible detention" instead and stating general terms application principles international law and custom to point of arbitration. Also recommending (1) that FAB instruct employees accept settlement presently authorized since this most expeditious and only course open Consul General now authorized; (2) alternately make immediate arrangements airport facilities and safe conduct Navy mediation team which fully authorized negotiate directly employees. Additionally confirming to FAB that actual payment will depend upon availability local currency from Central Bank or appointed banks in exchange for check or draft and requesting assistance this respect at appropriate time. (ConGentel to Department 2659, repeated Nanking 1779, 8th.[14])

Meantime Supple has unconfirmed report that mass visitation again being planned for 18th or 19th. See no choice but stand by awaiting FAB reaction letter. Will keep Department and Embassy informed.

Sent Department 2771, repeated Nanking 1557.

CABOT

---

[14] Not printed.

893.911/7-1449 : Telegram

The Consul General at Shanghai (Cabot) to the Secretary of State

SHANGHAI, July 14, 1949—10 p. m.
[Received July 15—12 : 34 a. m.]

2773. ReConGentel 2740, July 13, 3 p. m. *Evening Post and Mercury* dispute, Charles Miner locked in office and threatened bodily harm by workers all afternoon and part of evening. Not allowed visit bathroom adjoining his office. Finally allowed go home on promise he would appear at Labor Affairs Bureau this morning. At Labor Bureau he was met by two Communist Army officers who upbraided him severely for not having reached settlement and called both Gould and himself "scoundrels". Officers would not listen to Miner's attempted defense and would not permit him to bring R. T. Bryan, local attorney appointed by Starr as liquidation agent. Officers stated no lawyer could intervene in any dispute and Starr could not designate any agent other than personnel now representing his interests Shanghai. Officers disregarded Miner's statement he was not authorized by Starr settle *Evening Post* dispute with workers.

Officers stated wages workers would be fixed on basis 4.8 shen rice about 20% more than had been offered. Payment wages in arrears must be made July 15. Would rice continue indefinitely at this rate regardless fact plant not operating. Officers stated enterprise cannot liquidate without permission. Application for permission liquidate would have to be made formally in writing and go through prescribed procedure with no indication as to what action might eventually be taken.

Miner urged he be allowed sell part equipment plant in order raise funds pay wages. Officers refused, indicating fixed assets plant could not be impaired.

Miner endeavoring obtain remittance from Hong Kong cover payment required for tomorrow. If this fails he may be in for bad time. Undoubtedly this is instance of extortion practiced by Communist authorities. Gould in hospital taking rest cure. Has asked ConGen for advice. Both he and Miner feel they are at end of their rope, particularly since Starr has telegraphed no more funds will be remitted from US. Starr insists enterprise be liquidated at once and his representatives withdrawn. Starr and some other executives now US apparently do not realize it is impossible American representatives here extricate themselves from bad labor situation simply by closing down, writing off loss and washing hands entire matter. Department may wish remind principals American firms with interests here that their Shanghai representatives are virtual hostages held personally responsible by Communist authorities for continued operation their enterprises or at least their payrolls unless liquidation arrangements have full approval Communist authorities. Such approval most cases undoubtedly difficult obtain at best. Meanwhile American representatives at mercy authorities and their own employees.

I must emphasize this is but first of many similar episodes which almost bound to happen. Department will appreciate need for early decision re repatriation of Americans and re control of remittances, particularly former.

Sent Department; repeated Nanking 1558.

CABOT

811.42700(R)/7–1449 : Telegram

The Consul General at Shanghai (Cabot) to the Secretary of State

SHANGHAI, July 14, 1949—10 p. m.
[Received July 15—3 : 10 a. m.]

2774. Pass VOA, New York. Events past weeks indicate that paramount problem ConGen Shanghai is pressing need of working out formula for protecting Americans now in city. Olive case, siege ConGen by ex-Navy employees, increasing vigor anti-American sentiment in press, and mounting differences on part American firms in meeting demands of employees with attendant threats of violence in varying degrees by latter show that we cannot count on ordinary processes law and justice as commonly understood by western world. Assuming that higher Communist authorities realize undesirability of serious incidents of above type (an assumption which we do make and must make if Americans are voluntarily to stay here at all), it can be taken for granted they will be sensitive to charges that they are unable control subordinates. Reduced prestige which they would suffer under such publicized charges might, it is believed, prove more effective than any representations ConGen could make at Alien Affairs Department. From past experience USA officials who have had contact with Communists during war, many top Communists look upon themselves as scholars, gentlemen and soldiers—not bandits—and are anxious for world to consider them as such. Their fear of loss "face" in eyes of world through breakdown in vaunted party discipline might accomplish what threats of positive action at this juncture would fail to do.

Accordingly, suggest as desirable tactics for immediate employment and continuation as developments may warrant that through VOA, USA press editorial comment as well as in ordinary representations to Communist authorities, following line be stressed :

(1) Communist authorities have lost "face" through their demonstrated inability persuade subordinates to carry out Mao Tze-tung's word that foreigners would be protected;

(2) A main requisite of *de facto* as well as *de jure* government is ability exercise complete control over people in territory it occupies. Such control obviously lacking since Communist authorities evidently unable control laborers or police personnel as demonstrated by events mentioned above. If Communist authorities do in fact control subordinates, must we then infer they willingly condone brutal actions which can only be compared to those committed against foreigners by Japanese in war period?

(3) Public opinion polls in USA indicate that majority American people opposed to recognizing or trading with Communist regime under present conditions. It should be brought home that this feeling can only be intensified by misconduct towards Americans in China. Mention might also be made that Chinese Nationals are delighted at turn of events.

It is not suggested, of course, that Communist policy towards trade with West, foreign business or property interests in China would necessarily be affected by above recommendations; at best we could hope for more humane and understanding treatment of persons.

Sent Department; repeated Nanking 1559, Canton. Department pass Peiping 206.

CABOT

125.8576/7–1549 : Telegram

The Consul General at Shanghai (Cabot) to the Secretary of State

SHANGHAI, July 15, 1949—11 a. m.
[Received July 15—12:36 a. m.]

2775. Henderson [15] called to Foreign Affairs Bureau this morning and formally orally directed [to] stop all activities USIS as of today. Order given aggressively. Order covers Consulate General's movies, concerts, library as well as news and publicity operations. We frankly feel there is definite threat of drastic action if USIS continues activities. Appreciate Department's most urgent instructions.

Sent Department; repeated Nanking 1560, Canton 884, Taipei 207.

CABOT

125.8576/7–1549 : Telegram

The Consul General at Shanghai (Cabot) to the Secretary of State

SHANGHAI, July 15, 1949—3 p. m.
[Received July 15—9:09 a. m.]

2784. Further re Contel 2775, July 15, 11 a. m. Henderson requested by Chinese language phone call 14th to appear Foreign Affairs Bureau between 9 [and] noon today. Called, declined state purpose request. At

---

[15] John W. Henderson, Acting Director of the United States Information Service at Shanghai.

outset of interview Feng who identified self merely as representative Military Control Commission informed Henderson he was there in capacity private individual. Asked Henderson describe detail operations USIS China. Henderson proceeded with description, Feng asked many detailed questions. After more than half hour this, Feng advised Henderson he had been called to receive "notice". Then proceeded to read in Chinese from paper held in his hand from beginning: (translation) : "Since you are one of your Government's institutions and in that China and America have no formal diplomatic relations all your publicity operations, including news distribution, libraries, concerts, movies and all other operations, effective as from today, should cease operations. This is not to be violated." Henderson made no comment and left.

Understand British Information Service received similar notice.

Sent Department 2784, repeated Nanking 1566, Canton 88, Taipei 209.

CABOT

---

123 Olive, William M.: Telegram

The Consul General at Shanghai (Cabot) to the Secretary of State

SHANGHAI, July 15, 1949—6 p. m.
[Received July 15—7 : 29 a. m.]

2789. At meeting of Consular body this morning regarding Olive case, British Consul General stated that he had not had sufficient time consult Ambassador and was therefore not prepared to discuss matter officially. It was finally agreed that I should state case to Consular body and that each would thereafter be able consult his Ambassador [and] Foreign Office if he felt it necessary. Further discussion brought out a certain note of hesitancy among several consular officers despite optimism expressed to me by Brazilian Consul who has been particularly active. (I have naturally been careful to avoid any initiative with colleagues as instructed by Dept.) Final decision was that consular body should await result of our protest regarding Olive case and would then decide what next step to take if any. In meantime, Consuls would have opportunity consult respective authorities.

Repeated Nanking 1571.

CABOT

125.8571/7–1249 : Telegram

The Secretary of State to the Consul General at Shanghai (Cabot)

WASHINGTON, July 15, 1949—6 p. m.

1419. Urtel 2727 July 12. Efforts should be made to re-emphasize proposition US recognizes principle of international law which exempts the public consular property of a foreign state from taxation by the receiving state insofar as used for public purposes. Dept interested whether ultimatums received by consular colleagues under similar circumstances. No event should agreement be made pay taxes without prior approval Dept. Principle involved Glenline building might set precedent large annual tax obligation in China. Keep Dept and Emb informed.

ACHESON

125.8576/7–1549 : Telegram

The Secretary of State to the Consul General at Shanghai (Cabot) [16]

WASHINGTON, July 15, 1949—7 p. m.

1420. Dept gravely concerned implications closure orders (urtel 2775, July 15, Hankow's 210, July 15 [17]), singling out one function consular estab for intimidation tactics. Compliance will seriously weaken USIE [18] position vis-à-vis Soviet satellites worldwide. Dept, however, recognizes primary importance affording physical protection staff and avoiding possible incident. Dept therefore authorizes Consul General determine whether USIE activities shld in view local conditions and consideration staff safety be immed suspended and act accordingly, granting local staff leave with pay until situation clarifies.

Any case Dept recommends protest to Communist auths grounds (1) USIE activities integral part consular estab, (2) this principle recognized worldwide including USSR, (3) (if facts warrant) discrimination against US info activities. Consultation and coordination with British at Shanghai discretionary.

Dept will entertain favorably mission's recommendations transfer USIE locals and Amers other posts. Asks ConGen's recommendations re Dept statement and VOA publicity on matter.

ACHESON

123 Cabot, John M. : Telegram

The Consul at Shanghai (McConaughy) to the Secretary of State

SHANGHAI, July 16, 1949.
[Received July 16—2:45 a. m.]

2798. Cabot, William Olive, Marie Olive, Mason, Kinkoff and one Chinese employee left Shanghai for Nanking by train 10:45 last night. Arrived Nanking 7:15.

Sent Department; repeated Nanking.

McCONAUGHY

---

[16] Repeated to the Consuls General at Hankow and Peiping as Nos 42 and 450, respectively.
[17] For latter, see p. 1132.
[18] United States Information and Educational Exchange Program.

125.8576/7–1749 : Telegram

The Consul at Shanghai (McConaughy) to the Secretary of State

SHANGHAI, July 17, 1949—9 a. m.
[Received July 17—12 : 18 a. m.]

2805. ReDeptel 1420, July 15, repeated Nanking 836, Canton 458, Hankow 42. ConGen aware regrettable consequences compliance USIS closure order. Convinced, however, this defiance would be quixotic. Communists have power to enforce closure order and undoubtedly resolved use force if necessary. Majority Chinese staff would not dare violate order. American staff USIS would be endangered as would other functions ConGen. Am therefore reluctantly complying as from July 16 under protest. Emphatic protest CCMO [*memo*] form will be delivered Communist authorities July 18. Text will be forwarded and might be used on VOA when rejected by Communist authorities. Activities will be termed "suspended" rather than "discontinued". Local staff retained on pay roll for present, but believe early decision re disposition local staff should be made by Department in consultation with Connors.[19] Local staff could be dismissed with serious embarrassment Communist authorities by fixing entire responsibility on them. Such course has much to recommend it but would be exceedingly rough on some loyal Chinese employees who have courageously stayed with program and who can hardly expect to find other employment here. If transferred to Nationalist China, unlikely they can obtain exit permits or transportation near future. While American staff cannot move now either, issuance travel orders might be considered.

ConGen believes this highhanded action Chinese Communists vulnerable to effective broadside which might take form of stinging statement by highest available Department officer. Possible lines statement might take set forth separately.[20]

Sent Department; repeated Nanking 1581, Canton 893, Hankow 54.

McCONAUGHY

---

123 Olive, William M. : Telegram

The Ambassador in China (Stuart) to the Secretary of State

NANKING, June [*July*] 18, 1949—6 p. m.
[Received July 18—9 : 47 a. m.]

1548. Embassy has delayed making further protest to local Communist authorities over treatment Vice Consul Olive (Deptel 1382, July 11 to Shanghai) to avoid conflict with current negotiations Mr. and Mrs. Olive's exit from China. Olive is in Nanking, his exit from

---

[19] W. Bradley Connors, Consul at Canton.
[20] See telegram No. 2807, July 18, 8 p.m., p. 1236.

China hangs in balance along with other members of Ambassador's party awaiting exit permits and Embassy is loath to take any action at this time which might exacerbate already strained situation locally and thus prejudice Olive's chance departing China with Ambassador. If Department concurs we prefer make protest envisaged in Department telegram under reference after Olive has left for US or after negotiations his exit have ended in failure.[21]

Sent Department 1548, repeated Shanghai 865, Dept pass Peiping 28.

[STUART]

125.8576/7–1849 : Telegram

The Consul at Shanghai (McConaughy) to the Secretary of State

SHANGHAI, July 18, 1949—8 p. m.
[Received July 18—2 : 55 a. m.]

2807. ReConGentel sent Department 2805, repeated Nanking 1581, Canton 893. Following are few points which might be raised in Department statement re Communist closure USIS Shanghai. Believe these points should be amplified and others added which may occur to Department.

Pending results of protest, ConGen suspending USIS operations in Shanghai response Communist closure order. This suspension results purely from coercion and Communist-demonstrated willingness to use force in defiance of international usage and civilized custom; it does not result from any recognition by ConGen of Communist right to stop its activities or any portion of them by intimidation tactics and without any sanction of law. The unfriendly action taken by Communist authorities at Shanghai on July 15 in ordering suspension of all USIS activities there serves to confirm Communist tenet that people are not entitled to know truth. In silencing this, one of few remaining sources of impartial factual news in Communist China, new regime has shown that it cannot afford to permit publication of unbiased news.

This drastic action is more restrictive against USIS than any taken in other parts of world, including Soviet Union and satellite countries of Eastern Europe. Regime would not have taken a step which is certain to prove so embarrassing to it unless it had been convinced of the effectiveness of USIS in forging a bond of understanding between the Chinese and American people, a bond which the Chinese Communists for reasons best known to themselves seem bent upon destroying.

Chinese Communists appear to have decided that the seeds of hatred, vilification, distrust and misunderstanding which they seem

---

[21] In telegram No. 846, July 19, 5 p. m., the Department informed the Ambassador that it concurred in this procedure.

determined to sow among Chinese people will not grow in atmosphere of friendly relations which USIS seeks to cultivate.

It is apparent that promotion of friendliness and understanding tends to defeat totalitarian objectives; the fomenting of hatred better serves Communist purposes.

It is clear that this decision was taken arbitrarily and without consideration of interests of Chinese people. The decision was taken before giving USIS an opportunity to explain work and objects of organization. With characteristic cynicism a Communist official required USIS representative to make detailed explanation of purposes and operations of organization, while all the time official was holding in his hand previously prepared closure order, ready to read it the moment explanation was finished. This condemnation without affording opportunity of defence is characteristic of whole attitude and nature of Communism everywhere. There was no regard for rights and interests of the many thousands of Chinese citizens who have voluntarily availed themselves of USIS informational programs and cultural aids such as libraries and moving pictures. The poisonous fear of everything free has corroded Communist mentality and has constrained regime to ban even purely cultural activities of USIS such as concerts and art exhibits.

Communists by this action have denied the right of Chinese people to freedom of information and freedom to pursue culture, two of generally recognized basic rights of peoples. Pretext for this deplorable action was of flimsiest sort, namely absence of diplomatic relations between US and Chinese Communist regime. Informational and cultural activities have never depended on formal diplomatic relations for their existence and this excuse is irrelevant. Furthermore, the entire free world knows that it is not real reason for closure.

The AmConGen in Shanghai has been instructed to protest emphatically against this unwarranted closure order.

Appreciate text any statement issued Department. Suggest Department might desire instruct ConGen deliver text appropriate local authorities.

Sent Department, repeated Nanking 1583, OffEmb Canton 894, Hankow 55.   McCONAUGHY

811.42700(R)/7–1849 : Telegram

The Consul at Shanghai (McConaughy) to the Secretary of State

SHANGHAI, July 18, 1949.
[Received July 18—9 : 51 a. m.]

2816. Local press carries announcement by SMCC July 16 establishing provisional measures for censorship of international telegraphic and radio messages. Substance of regulations as follows:

(1). Telegraphic messages and Voice broadcasts may not give information on weather conditions, places bombed or damage committed in air raids, location and condition of airfields and air defense units, place of garrison, strength, unit, name, numbers and movements of PLA; particulars concerning radio stations and military installations; locations sites govt MCC and PLA political military and public organizations.

(2). Telegraphic messages may be sent out only after being censored and passed by SMCC radiogram censorship section.

(3). Manuscripts of Voice broadcasts must be submitted in advance for censorship.

(4). Objectional words or phrases will be deleted but no addition to or alteration in message may be made.

(5). Persons repeatedly violating article (1) will be punished.

Sent Department 2816, Nanking by mail, operational.

McConaughy

893.111/7-1849 : Telegram

The Consul at Shanghai (McConaughy) to the Secretary of State

Shanghai, July 18, 1949.
[Received July 18—9:51 a. m.]

2817. Shanghai Public Security Bureau July 17 announced following regulations foreigners travelling in China.

(1) Require photos, passports, official application form and fee.

(2) Valid for one round trip within 2 weeks.

(3) No more than two destinations at one time and by specified route approved by authorities.

(4) Illness et cetera requiring change of plans must have approval local authorities.

(5) Arrival, departure 2-week visitors must be reported police by head of household and permission received.

(6) Travellers staying from 2 weeks [to] 3 months must report themselves and get temporary residence and travel permit.

(7) Foreign travellers not reaching destination within validity permits must report [garble] "appropriate decisions in accordance with the actual conditions will be made by this bureau".

(8) Those travelling to other areas and unable return Shanghai within validity permits must apply local authorities for extension and turn in original permit upon return Shanghai.

(9) All luggage foreigners subject inspection without exception.

McConaughy

125.8576/7–1849 : Telegram

The Minister-Counselor of Embassy in China (Clark) to the Secretary of State

CANTON, July 18, 1949—9 p. m.
[Received July 19—7 : 11 a. m.]

Cantel 772. Concur no effort should be made defy Communist order close USIS at this time (Shanghai 2805, July 17 to Dept, repeated Nanking 1581, Hankow 54). Recommend, however, that, while USIS closed to public and no distribution or other public activities carried on pending clarification situation and result protests Communist authorities Nanking, Peiping, all staff be retained on basis Communist order only suspension USIS services. Believe Shanghai staff can be utilized following basis: Library staff process all backlog books, periodicals, et cetera; editorial translation staffs utilized special translations pamphlets, Newsletter material, other special articles, looking to day when can resume normal function; visual media staff continue produce posters et cetera for future use. For balance of staff make work as necessary such as housekeeping duties, inventory, et cetera, or adapt [*adopt*] shorter work week. Hankow follow same example.

Believe essential retain loyalty [and] goodwill our staff who have stuck with us during takeover and present emergency justifies above plan. Discharge local staff might embarrass US more than local Communist authorities since latter might force them make exorbitant demands severance pay et cetera, especially since new employment difficult find and transfers Free China impossible this time due lack transportation.

On whole believe we must for present consider order as only suspension and not final decision force USIE completely out of Communist China. For these reasons urge Dept instruct Shanghai [and] Hankow retain full staff above basis pending further developments. Suggest Department also may wish issue precautionary instructions Tientsin, Peiping.

Sent Department Cantel 772, repeated Nanking 509, Shanghai 436, Hankow 21.

CLARK

125.8576/7–2249 : Telegram

The Consul at Shanghai (McConaughy) to the Secretary of State

SHANGHAI, July 22, 1949.
[Received July 22—3 : 34 a. m.]

2880. Following is text memo dated July 20 mailed Foreign Affairs Bureau July 21 re closure USIS:

"Memorandum to the Director of the Foreign Affairs Bureau

"Reference is made to the oral order issued on July 15 by the Foreign Affairs Bureau to Mr. John W. Henderson, Acting Director of the United States Information Service, at Shanghai, directing the immediate suspension of all cultural, educational and informational activities of the United States Information Service at Shanghai.

"Acting on the instructions of the United States Government and in behalf of that Government, the undersigned lodges an emphatic protest against the suspension of the United States Information Service activities at Shanghai. A grave view is taken of this action which constitutes regrettable interference with the normal functioning of this Consular establishment, of which the United States Information Service comprises an integral part; violates the principle that informational and educational activities form a legitimate part of the work of a Consular establishment, a principle which is recognized in all parts of the world; and discriminates against United States Information Service activities as compared with certain similar activities of the Soviet Union, which are still carried on unimpeded in this city.

"The unfriendly action taken by the local regime in denying the residents of Shanghai the informational, technological, recreational, educational, musical and artistic benefits which such large numbers of them received from the United States Information Service news file, library, concerts, motion pictures and art exhibit in Shanghai, can only be construed as a blow at the interests of the people of this area.

"The cessation of these cultural and technical services of the United States Information Service means a corresponding impoverishment of the cultural and technical resources available to the people of China.

"The reason given by the Military Control Commission for the closure order—namely, the absence of formal diplomatic relations between the United States and the Communist regime in China—appears not well-founded in that the work does not involve any diplomatic negotiations or liaison and does not depend on official diplomatic recognition for its existence.

"The activities of the United States Information Service at Shanghai are being reluctantly suspended under protest, in compliance with the order issued by the Military Control Commission. On the assumption that the suspension order will prove to be temporary, this office is retaining the numerous Chinese employees on the United States Information Service payroll for the time being in order to enable the authorities to have a reasonable period of time in which to reexamine all the implications of this issue.

"It is difficult for the writer to believe that the suspension order is intended as a deliberately unfriendly act against the United States. It is urged that this unfortunate decision be reconsidered in the light of the foregoing observations.

"If the local authorities desire to establish friendship and understanding between the Chinese and American peoples, it is confidently anticipated that this suspension order will be rescinded. (Signed) Walter P. McConaughy."

Sent Department 2880; repeated Nanking 1620, Canton 910, Peiping 216, Tientsin 102.

McConaughy

125.8576/7–2249 : Telegram

The Consul at Shanghai (McConaughy) to the Secretary of State

SHANGHAI, July 22, 1949—10 a. m.
[Received July 22—12 :09 a. m.]

2882. ConGen July 21 sent strong memo protest re closure USIS to Foreign Affairs Bureau double registered mail. Full text contained ConGen plain language telegram 2880, July 22. Believe publicity should be withheld until July 25. Recommend its full use VOA, AFRS and as press release if no favorable action taken by that date.

Sent Department; repeated Nanking 1622, OffEmb Canton 911. Department pass Peiping 217, Tientsin 103.

McCONAUGHY

125.8576/7–2249 : Telegram

The Ambassador in China (Stuart) to the Secretary of State

NANKING, July 22, 1949—2 p. m.
[Received July 22—7: 26 a. m.]

1577. Embassy heartily concurs general sentiments Shanghai's 2807, July 18 to Department (repeated Nanking 1883) but strongly recommends Department postpone release blast along these lines until obvious Communist decision close all USIS offices irrevocable and no room left negotiation or further protest. Embassy believes protest should follow closely recommendations Deptel 1420, July 15, sent Shanghai, repeated Nanking 836, and that unduly emphatic language should at this stage be avoided as of no use and serving possibly harden Communist intransigence subject USIS, particularly in view fact Nanking USIS including news file still operating.

Sent Department, repeated Shanghai 884, Hankow 51, OffEmb Canton 661.

STUART

125.8576/7–2249 : Telegram

The Consul at Shanghai (McConaughy) to the Secretary of State

SHANGHAI, July 22, 1949—4 p. m.
[Received July 22—6: 32 a. m.]

2894. ReConGentel 2882, July 22. Foreign Affairs Bureau has returned memo protest re USIS closure with slip reading in translation "this communication cannot be accepted and should be returned". Recommend immediate publication text given ConGentel 2880, July 22, together with reference to its summary rejection by Communist authorities apparently few minutes after it was received.

ConGen using other channels to get text message unofficially and informally before high Communist authorities.

Sent Department, repeated Nanking 1626, OffEmb Canton 913.

McConaughy

125.8576/7–2249 : Telegram

The Ambassador in China (Stuart) to the Secretary of State

Nanking, July 22, 1949.
[Received July 22—2 : 32 p. m.]

1583. Following is text of protest which Embassy attempted submit Aliens Affairs Office Nanking July 21 :

"Instructions have been received from Government of US of America to protest to highest available authorities closure of USIS offices in Shanghai, Hankow, Peiping and Tientsin.

"The activities of USIS are an integral part of the consular and diplomatic establishment of the US, and, as such, are entitled under generally accepted principles of international law to freedom from interference in performance of their proper duties. The status of USIS as performing an integral foreign service function is generally recognized throughout the world, including the USSR and countries in Eastern Europe where the service functions on a regular basis.

"It is most strongly urged that the authorities reconsider the action they have taken in this case. Such a step would do much to create an impression abroad that the authorities hold in respect the long-established practices of comity among nations. On the other hand, a contrary decision would have a most unhappy effect on public opinion in the US."

Sent Department 1513, Canton 622, Shanghai 885, Hankow 53, Peiping 288.

Stuart

125.8576/7–2249 : Telegram

The Ambassador in China (Stuart) to the Secretary of State

Nanking, July 22, 1949—4 p. m.
[Received July 22—11 : 19 a. m.]

1584. Embassy attempted July 21 deliver to Aliens Affairs Office written protest (text contained Embtel 1583, July 22) on closure USIS offices Shanghai, Peiping, Hankow and Tientsin. After messenger had informed higher officials subject of visit was "closure USIS offices", which Embassy officer required state in advance, junior official came down to waiting room to state his superiors not prepared discuss this question. Asked when they would be prepared discuss it, he was noncommittal. He did, however, read text of protest, but returned it, declining take it to his superiors. We feel further attempts present protest would not be fruitful and might hasten closure Nanking USIS.

Sent Department 1584, repeated Shanghai 886, Embassy Canton 663.

STUART

125.8571/7–2249 : Telegram

The Consul at Shanghai (McConaughy) to the Secretary of State

SHANGHAI, July 22, 1949—5 p. m.
[Received July 22—8 : 33 a. m.]

2895. ReDeptel 1419, July 15, tax assessment Glenline Building. Tax notices covering additional space Glenline Building recently received increase total tax bill months May and June only to equivalent over $10,000.[22] Tax rate per annum Glenline Building therefore is fantastic figure of over $60,000. Smaller but substantial bills have also been received for some of residential properties owned by US Government. British ConGen which occupies second most valuable foreign government owned property so far has not received any tax bill. Several Consuls who occupy small rented quarters have indicated they prepared pay relatively modest sums involved without question. Sentiment informally expressed at meeting consular body July 15 seemed preponderantly opposed lodgment protest against either real estate taxes or auto taxes which at equivalent of $600 per vehicle per annum also exorbitant. Believe attitude consular body toward infringement consular prerogatives as revealed discussion tax matters and Olive case will be spineless.

On July 14 we addressed letter to Foreign Office setting forth claim to exemption from taxation US Government-owned consular property. Memorandum was returned by Foreign Affairs Bureau with notation we should approach Bureau of Finance directly. July 19 we sent same letter to Bureau Finance together with entire sheaf tax notices. No acknowledgment yet received.

I recommend we maintain firmly our right to exemption property tax. Showdown should be on principle involved, not on prohibitive amount assessed.

Commie behavior when cards are down on this issue should tell us something about their immediate intentions.

Sent Department; repeated Nanking 1627.

McCONAUGHY

[22] For correction as to this figure, see telegram No. 3039, August 4, 7 p. m., from the Consul at Shanghai, p. 1266.

893.918/7–2649 : Telegram

The Secretary of State to the Consul at Shanghai (McConaughy)

WASHINGTON, July 26, 1949—7 p. m.

1480. Dept informed that C. V. Starr today recd tel from AAU [23] Shanghai stating Miner and Gould locked in office by employees demanding increased pay; Chi auths refusing further intervention on basis Miner uncomplied their order; so far no physical violence but indications lock-in may be lengthy.

Dept also informed Starr has sent tel to Labor Section Shanghai MCC stating that Miner no power to obtain funds for wages or any other purpose except by sale or mortgage plant and stock in Shanghai; that *Post Mercury* no assets outside Shanghai, is deeply in debt and can obtain no further credit for any purpose whatsoever.

Dept assumes ConGen taking appropriate measures assist Miner and Gould insofar as possible.

ACHESON

893.918/7–2749 : Telegram

The Consul at Shanghai (McConaughy) to the Secretary of State

SHANGHAI, July 27, 1949.
[Received July 27—2 : 27 a. m.]

2920. Reference *Shanghai Evening Post* labor dispute, workers have confined Gould and Miner to office since noon yesterday without food, water or sleep. State they will hold them in this situation until all demands satisfied.

Consulate General reported full facts police yesterday afternoon and urged immediate police action be taken to lift siege. Police promised send representative investigate but did nothing. Gould and Miner kept awake by tremendous din created by workers who beat on doors with various implements all through night.

Increasingly apparent authorities do not plan intervene and plight of Gould and Miner very serious. Messengers with food, water and medicines prescribed by Gould's doctor turned away from building by workers this morning.

Alien Affairs Bureau will not give me appointment or any assurance I will be received but I am proceeding there immediately with intention making emphatic representations.

Sent Department, repeated Nanking 1640.

McCONAUGHY

---

[23] American Asiatic Underwriters.

893.918/7–2749 : Telegram

The Secretary of State to the Ambassador in China (Stuart)

WASHINGTON, July 27, 1949—5 p. m.

885. Re Shanghai's 2920 July 27 rptd Nanking 1640. If you have not already done so, pls make strong representations Gould–Miner case earliest.

ACHESON

_____

893.918/7–2749 : Telegram

The Consul at Shanghai (McConaughy) to the Secretary of State

SHANGHAI, July 27, 1949—10 p. m.
[Received July 28—1 : 51 a. m.]

2932. ReConGentel 2920 to Department, 1640 to Nanking, July 27. I called at Foreign Affairs Bureau at 11 : 30 accompanied by Forman [24] as interpreter to intercede behalf Gould and Miner. I was received ungraciously by Feng Chi-ho whose attitude has hardened notably not already done so, pls make strong representations Gould–Miner lock-in and requested immediate action by authorities lift siege. I stressed fact individuals forcibly detaining Gould and Miner were private citizens, not officials local regime, adding presumably their action was lawless by any standard. Feng said Foreign Affairs Bureau could not recognize my right to speak on behalf Gould and Miner since I had not shown I was connected with case. I told Feng if he wished he could consider me as speaking in capacity of friend of Gould and Miner. He said friendship did not afford valid basis my intervention and FAB could not discuss case with me. I remonstrated pointing out by this line of reasoning no one in Shanghai could speak on behalf Gould and Miner and since they were wrongfully held by disaffected workers, they had no way of speaking for themselves, hence refusal heed my request amounted to denial of all recourse.

Despite Feng's unwillingness to hear me out, I proceeded to outline outrageous circumstances under which two Americans were held: Their lack food, water and sleep for 24 hours; refusal of workers permit messengers deliver anything and helplessness of victims do anything for themselves without assistance of authorities. Feng said he did not believe my account of Gould-Miner plight. I said best way for authorities confirm or refute account was to proceed personally to office where Gould and Miner were held at 17 The Bund and ascertain facts by survey on spot. Feng said authorities could not accept any suggestions from me and brusquely rose to signify interview was terminated. I did not rise immediately. After short interval, I rose

_____

[24] Douglas N. Forman, Vice Consul at Shanghai.

deliberately and raising my voice slightly said local regime would find it highly embarrassing if through negligence of authorities these two Americans came to any harm at hands of workers who were forcibly detaining them. Feng said I had no right make any such statement to representatives [of] People's Government. I said "That is all," without taking any cognizance of Feng's remark. I then strode abruptly from room without endeavoring shake hands, making my displeasure unmistakable. Feng had already made it clear he did not intend to make any move to shake hands.

On appointment slip I wrote as subject for discussion "safety of Mr. Gould and Mr. Miner, American citizens," thereby running risk being refused interview, but if I had not written down subject, I would not have been permitted bring it up at all and fact I was received on that subject is something of tactical gain. At least, it is formally on record now we presented facts this flagrant case to authorities and officially requested redress. Despite bad reception I got, authorities may be alarmed into taking some action this afternoon to lift siege. If they do not, their position is far more indefensible than before I called.

Situation of Gould and Miner will become genuinely serious by tonight or early tomorrow if no relief obtained. I plan try another approach through Democratic League intermediaries late this afternoon if nothing accomplished by then.

Recommend Department be prepared give full publicity this outrage VOA and press if ConGen later recommends such course. This might further jeopardize functioning ConGen but it is risk we must undergo if we are to use only means at our disposal at moment to protect Americans here.

Sent Department, repeated Nanking 1646.

McConaughy

893.918/7–2849 : Telegram

The Consul at Shanghai (McConaughy) to the Secretary of State

Shanghai, July 28, 1949.
[Received July 28—10:08 a. m.]

2943. Re ConGentel 2920, July 27, repeated Nanking 1640. Gould–Miner siege lifted late this afternoon basis following understanding with workers: Increase salaries June and July. Termination of paper recognized as of July 31, termination payments to be negotiated through Labor Bureau. Gould–Miner at liberty.

Food and water were provided for Gould and Miner following our protests of yesterday and police finally appeared at noon today.

Sent Department 2943, repeated Nanking 1648.

McConaughy

893.918/7–2749 : Telegram

The Secretary of State to the Consul General at Peiping (Clubb)

WASHINGTON, July 28, 1949—7 p. m.

499. Gould and Miner, *Shanghai Post and Mercury*, locked in office by laborers July 26–28 without food, water, sleep. ConGen's attempts secure intervention Foreign Affairs Bureau met rebuff, FAB refusing accept representations. Siege lifted when men made commitments, obviously under duress.

Pls make every effort bring situation atten[tion] highest Commie auths, pointing out Shanghai auths refused protection, despite repeated requests therefor, against physical coercion and maltreatment of two men by virtual mob action; that this incident, rpting previous ones, raises serious question ability local auths effectively provide adequate protection fon natls.

ACHESON

102.22/7–2949 : Telegram

The Consul at Shanghai (McConaughy) to the Secretary of State

SHANGHAI, July 29, 1949.
[Received July 29—2 : 58 a. m.]

2959. About 20 ex-Navy employees occupied lobby ConGen building 7 : 20 this morning, mingling with staff members reporting for duty. They pushed guards aside, seized gate keys and refused allow gate to be shut. Very abusive language used to American guard. Unfortunately iron gate guarding stairway to upper floors was necessarily open because elevators still out of order following typhoon. A few workers are sitting on first floor stairway to prevent stairway gate from being closed. So far none have gone higher than first floor. They insist their intentions are peaceable. So far they have not interfered with entry to or egress from building but some have brought food and lock-in later in day is possible. Workers have telephoned their associates asking reinforcements be sent.

Delegation of 8 insists on negotiating with Thomas, Administrative Attaché. I have flatly refused consider any discussion while they occupy any portion ConGen building.

This latest crisis directly attributable Foreign Affairs Bureau which officially requested us defer settlement we have been prepared last 2 weeks to make, settlement which is acceptable to more than half the claimants. Workers claim Foreign Affairs Bureau authorized their entry ConGen building. This so far not verified. At 7 : 45 requested police intervene. Result negative. When called second time at 9 a. m. they declined to intervene, saying workers did not intend violence, that it was merely labor dispute and we should negotiate with workers and with General Labor Union, Thomas will proceed Foreign Affairs Bureau at 9 : 30 a. m. Workers invited send their delegation there also but they refused. Thomas will lay responsibility squarely at doorstep Foreign Affairs Bureau and insist it restrain workers.

We are ill prepared for siege at this time owing failure power, light, and water supply still unrestored following typhoon. Am gradually and unobtrusively sending staff members home, planning to have only skeleton staff here by nightfall. All necessary precautions taken.

Sent Department 2959, repeated Nanking 1654, Peiping 227.

McCONAUGHY

102.22/7–2949 : Telegram

The Ambassador in China (Stuart) to the Secretary of State

NANKING, July 29, 1949—11 a. m.
[Received July 29—12 : 05 p. m.]

1651. [To Peiping:] ConGen Shanghai invaded this a. m. by ex-Navy employees who refuse to leave till settlement their demands (see Shanghai's telegram 227, July 29 to Peiping [25]), force being used to prevent entrance and exit to ConGen building. Approximately 11 officers compelled spend night in office. Local authorities have consistently ignored pleas for intervention, protection. Matter was placed in their hands at their request 2 weeks ago. They assured that employees would make no further disturbances while they were studying case; in any event ConGen has no authority to negotiate on behalf US Navy. Navy has offered to send in representatives to negotiate but Communist officials Shanghai have ignored this suggestion.

Some members mob invading ConGen today have become hysterical acting in irresponsible manner. Because recent typhoon damage, ConGen without lights, water. Officers cut off from commissary by occupation ConGen building.

I suggest you communicate with Joseph Chang [26] or his father earliest and beg him report this outrageous development to Chou [27] or Mao. Point out that local authorities have been completely unresponsive; that regardless of lack of official relations persons besieged are officials of US Government and that situation of this nature if allowed develop may end in tragedy. In any event it cannot fail to have very serious effects on future relations between China and USA and reflect grave discredit on Chinese Communist regime in eyes of civilized world.

Sent Peiping 306, repeated Department 1651, Shanghai 918.

STUART

---

[25] Same as telegram No. 2959, *supra*.
[26] Son of Professor Chang Tung-sun, Yenching University, of the Democratic League.
[27] Chou En-lai, of the Central Committee of the Chinese Communist Party.

102.22/7–2949 : Telegram

The Consul at Shanghai (McConaughy) to the Secretary of State

SHANGHAI, July 29, 1949.
[Received July 29—5 : 39 a. m.]

2963. At 3 p. m. besieging ex-employees growing more restive, number greatly increased by arrival women, children. Lobby and first flight stairs full.

Foreign Affairs Bureau evasive, non-committal despite repeated appeals last 7 hours. So far have done nothing. Police also decline intervene.

At 3 : 30 demonstrators are locking gates, preventing all entry and egress.

Workers insist they will occupy ConGen until demands satisfied. I have flatly refused to discuss anything with them unless and until they vacate building and send small delegation to talk in orderly fashion. Complete impasse this issue.

Sent Department, repeated Nanking 1655, Canton 928, Peiping 228.

McCONAUGHY

102.22/7–2949 : Telegram

The Consul at Shanghai (McConaughy) to the Secretary of State

SHANGHAI, July 29, 1949—4 p. m.
[Received July 29—5 : 22 a. m.]

2965. Ex-Navy employees besieging building now demanding 3 months' pay plus 3 months' separation notice plus 2 weeks' pay in lieu notice. Unless demands agreed today will bring 600 laborers tomorrow and all families next day, prepared stay "until carried out in coffins". Large banners raised on Glenline Building reading "American imperialists fail keep their own regulations try starve people". Commander Slayton [28] and assistant forcibly turned back when tried leave building 3 : 40 p. m.

Estimate 100 Chinese and Sikhs now inside, many more outside. Thirteen male Americans and approximately 35 local employees trapped. I shall continue refuse negotiate under duress.

Sent Department, repeated Nanking 1657, OffEmb Canton 929, Peiping 229.

McCONAUGHY

---

[28] Cmdr. Morgan Slayton, Assistant Naval Attaché in China.

102.22/7–2949 : Telegram

The Consul at Shanghai (McConaughy) to the Secretary of State

SHANGHAI, July 29, 1949.
[Received July 29—12:56 p. m.]

2966. At 9 p. m. siege Consulate General building continues, 13 male American staff members dug in for night, Chinese employees permitted leave building. Acting on constructive suggestion from Cabot [in] Nanking, I met with 6 representatives of workers in first floor office at 5 p. m. ably assisted by Thomas, Supple and alien clerk Meyers interpreter. I made it clear I was there to explain Consul General position, not to discuss merits of case while I was under coercion. I expressed sympathy for plight of those without employment who were reported unable to support their families. I then said with all conviction I had no authority to negotiate, that I could act only as channel transmission and could not do that when under confinement, that Foreign Affairs Bureau was entirely responsible for delay in offering settlement proposed by Navy and that FAB also responsible for failure local regime to authorize entry Navy team with full powers to negotiate as proposed by Navy. I urged them abandon unlawful lock-in as worse than useless and to press FAB for entry permit for Navy team.

Workers rejected all these points as mere stalling. Said they knew Consul General had money and they were out to get it from us to meet their just demands. Said Consul General as representative US Government here must be held responsible for all US Government obligations especially those of Navy since Consul General had inherited some Navy assets. They inquired if US Navy "People's Navy or Imperialist Navy". Definite ideological cast to this statement and others indicate they have been well briefed in party line.

Group had no leadership and was incapable of responsible action. At one point said they would not molest us if we tried leave building. Few minutes later reversed this stand entirely. Said they and their families did not have enough to eat and they would stay in building until they died of starvation when Consul General would be responsible for their deaths.

One of group worked himself into state of hysteria, incited others with his screaming, brandished letter opener threatening suicide, lay down on floor. Many additional workers then crowded into room in threatening mood, blocked door with chairs, creating tight situation for several minutes. Workers refused allow me to leave room to return to upper floor. I strongly remonstrated with them. After several tense minutes they let me return my office on 4th floor. Thomas remained for another hour chatting in desultory fashion with them which greatly eased tension. Workers now drafting petition to Navy which I have promised transmit if they vacate building forthwith.

Repeated Nanking 165, Canton 930, Peiping 230.

[McConaughy]

102.22/7–3049 : Telegram

The Consul at Shanghai (McConaughy) to the Secretary of State

SHANGHAI, July 30, 1949.
[Received July 29—10: 49 p. m.]

2967. Occupation Consulate General building continued without incident through night. Pickets reduced to about 40 this morning all on ground floor. Blockade considerably relaxed. Several American staff members have entered and left building without interference but demonstrators have announced that McConaughy, Thomas and Commander Slayton will not be permitted leave building.

Communist soldier with fixed bayonet intermittently stationed Peking Road opposite Consulate General entrance. Chase handling operations outside building is leaving no stone unturned. He has worked practically without rest and has succeeded in getting matter before some influential people.

Sent Department 2967, repeated Nanking 1659, Embassy Canton 931, Peiping 231.

McConaughy

102.22/7–3049 : Telegram

The Ambassador in China (Stuart) to the Secretary of State

NANKING, July 30, 1949—2 p. m.
[Received July 30—5: 53 a. m.]

1658. [To Shanghai:] Reur telephone conversation with Jones,[29] we suggest that you make following proposal:

(1) You will send telegram to Navy;
(2) You and leaders ex-Navy employees both agree to recommend to Communist authorities that Navy team be permitted enter;
(3) Ex-Navy employees agree you appeal to police for protection for 24 leaders in event of any disposition of rank and file of ex-employees to cause trouble. Regarding proposal of 24 leaders that they stay in building. we believe that you should not accede and that ultimate concession you should make would be to say that if they remain in building it would be without your consent.

Sent Shanghai 919, repeated Department.

STUART

---

[29] J. Wesley Jones, Counselor of Embassy in China.

893.918/7–3049 : Telegram

The Ambassador in China (Stuart) to the Secretary of State

NANKING, July 30, 1949.
[Received July 30—10 : 02 a. m.]

1660. Embassy July 30 presented following protest on Gould and Miner case to Aliens Affairs Office, Nanking:

"Information has been received from Shanghai that Mr. Randall Gould and Mr. Charles F. Miner, American citizens who are editor and representative of the owner, respectively, of *Shanghai Evening Post and Mercury*, were confined to their office from noon on July 26 until July 28 by their employees, in attempt by latter to force management of paper to yield to their demands. During nearly 24 hours, Messrs. Gould and Miner were not only not permitted to have food and water brought to them, but all through night of July 26 they were kept awake by workers who beat on doors with various implements. Messenger bringing medicine prescribed by Gould's doctors also refused entrance.

"American Consul General, Shanghai, reported full facts this incident to police on afternoon of July 26 and later to AAO; Shanghai police promised to send representative to investigate, but no effective action was taken until July 28, when police intervened and Messrs. Gould and Miner were finally released after coming to agreement with workers. Although eventual intervention of police enabling settlement is gratifying, the Government of United States of America has issued instructions that a strong protest be lodged at failure of authorities to take action promptly, once they had been informed of facts. Irrespective of intrinsic merits of dispute, it is difficult to believe that arbitrary use by employees against employers of weapons of hunger, thirst and mental anguish is approved by local authorities. Nor does such action seem in harmony with declarations of highest Communist leaders, that foreign lives and property would be protected. Consequently, failure of Shanghai authorities to intervene promptly and bring about settlement of this dispute by orderly and peaceful processes is most difficult to understand. Certainly, American people will be shocked to learn that in China's largest city two of their fellow citizens were isolated by mob action which continued for more than 48 hours before authorities responsible for maintenance of peace and order consented to intervene.

"It is hoped that the responsible authorities will demonstrate in future that they do not approve of irresponsible mob action for settlement of wage disputes and incidents similar to one involving Messrs. Gould and Miner will not recur."

STUART

893.918/7–3049 : Telegram

The Ambassador in China (Stuart) to the Secretary of State

NANKING, July 30, 1949—5 p. m.
[Received July 31—2 : 21 a. m.]

1661. Protest Gould–Miner case (Embtel 1660, July 30) received by third-ranking official Aliens Affairs Office and taken to inner office where presumably read by his superiors. It then returned to Embassy officer with statement could not be accepted because Shanghai outside jurisdiction Nanking AAO.

Sent Department; repeated Shanghai 920.

STUART

102.22/7–3049 : Telegram

The Ambassador in China (Stuart) to the Secretary of State

NANKING, July 30, 1949—11 p. m.
[Received July 30—12 : 53 p. m.]

1665. McConaughy informs us by telephone that situation Consulate General Shanghai has taken adverse turn. New and vigorous direction has been introduced into mob action of ex-Navy employees. New leader, a politico apparently, has rejected all points counter-proposal suggested Embtel 1658 of July 30 to Department, sent Shanghai 919. He waives aside interest US Navy, Government and insists Consulate General must settle issue locally and promptly. Thomas is being held tonight in room first floor Consulate General virtually as hostage and efforts McConaughy to effect his release unavailing at 9 : 15. McConaughy who is in his office fourth floor fears the "psychological treatment" will be used on Thomas during the night to force him to agree to settlement. We have advised McConaughy to preserve his limited freedom of action and not respond to employees' request that he join Thomas first floor trap. McConaughy feels PLA authorities Shanghai are conniving with, if not actually encouraging, mob action and present leadership; that Aliens Affairs Bureau is deferring to military in this issue.

I feel that some drastic action is required to bring an end to this unexampled treatment of an official establishment of the US Government by the *de facto* authority. In considering ways and means of protecting Foreign Service personnel against further pressure and threats of violence, I suggest, as one possible effective course, the prompt convening of the Security Council to consider the threat to the peace of this callous indifference on the part of the Communist authorities to safety, welfare and dignity of official representation of a sovereign state. It might be pointed out that Chairman Mao in issuing 8th point of his proclamation regarding protection of foreigners in Communist China was either insincere or is presently unable to control his underlings in Shanghai. If reference to Security Council fails to have desired effect or if USSR blocks actions, such reference would at least appear to have advantage of clearing decks for more direct, unilateral action which might subsequently be contemplated.

Sent Department; repeated Shanghai 923.

STUART

102.22/7-3049 : Telegram

The Secretary of State to the Consul General at Peiping (Clubb)

WASHINGTON, July 30, 1949—5 p. m.

508. Following is first para Nanking's 1665 July 30 to Dept. [Here follows text of first paragraph of No. 1665, printed *supra*.]

By whatever means available you should at once make clear to highest possible Communist authorities seriousness with which your Government views this callous indifference on the part of the local Communist authorities in Shanghai to safety, welfare and dignity of official U.S. representatives as indicated in above quotation and in Shanghai tels 2959, 2963, 2965 and 2966 all of July 29 and all repeated Peiping.

ACHESON

102.22/7-3049 : Telegram

The Secretary of State to the Ambassador in China (Stuart)

WASHINGTON, July 30, 1949—5 p. m.

904. Dept believes if you have not already done so you personally should approach Huang Hua and in the strongest possible terms protest the callous indifference on the part of the local Communist authorities in Shanghai to safety, welfare and dignity of American official representatives as outlined in first para your 1665, July 30. Clubb being instructed make similar representations.

ACHESON

102.22/7-3049 : Telegram

The Consul at Shanghai (McConaughy) to the Secretary of State

SHANGHAI, July 30, 1949—midnight.
[Received July 30—7 p. m.]

2972. Besieging ex-employees gradually have increased pressure during day insistently demanding yes or no to ultimatum for six and one-half months' pay.

After consultation with Embassy, indicated to them through Thomas this afternoon that I was prepared accept their tentative offer to lift siege and relinquish control of building if I would telegraph Navy Department text of petition drafted by them.

At this stage situation completely changed by abrupt entry of newcomer, civilian unknown to Consulate General officers, who immediately assumed dominant role. He gave workers decisive leadership for first time. He is obviously political figure with some authority, uses Marxist clichés. He may be from General Labor Union or Labor

Bureau. He left after several hours. About 7 underlings accompanied him.

This man assumed intransigent attitude, summarily rejected conciliatory gesture made by Consulate General, announced workers would not wait for case to be referred to Washington, that workers would collect from Consulate General locally. Thomas was working out withdrawal formula with workers when newcomer entered scene at 6 p. m. Thomas has been held in first floor room since then under continuous questioning. Has not been allowed to leave for meal. We have just sent food to him which workers kept from him saying he could go hungry as they had done since siege started. Indications are he will be kept up all night.

We appealed to police again at 9 p. m. to relieve Thomas of severe physical and psychological coercion. They said they would send a policeman to investigate but 3 hours later have not done so. Demeanor of police indicated they probably had orders not to intervene.

Chase succeeded in getting memorandum and letter re case before Chang Han-fu through Han Ming, Democratic Leaguer. Chase discussed case at length with Han Ming who indicated PLA, probably its political section, was backing the demonstration and directing handling of affair by Foreign Affairs Bureau.[30] Some corroboration other sources.

Chang refused to see Chase but Chase with great difficulty saw subordinate who said he would relay Chase's observations to higher authority.

Apart from Thomas, 9 male American staff members in building all barricaded in restricted areas 4th and 6th floors. I have been invited to present myself before demonstrators presumably in place of Thomas but do not intend to do so voluntarily. Such action in my view would play directly into their hands. Much as I wish to afford relief for Thomas, I believe this is a ruse to get control of principal officer depriving him of ability to fulfill his responsibilities.

I consider developments reported herein increase seriousness of case in all its implications.

Sent Department 2972, repeated Nanking 1660, OffEmb Canton 932. Department pass Peiping 232, CNO ComNavWesPac.

McCONAUGHY

125.8576/7–3149 : Telegram

The Ambassador in China (Stuart) to the Secretary of State

NANKING, July 31, 1949—2 p. m.
[Received July 31—4 : 35 a. m.]

1667. Feeling that my best approach was to the highest Communist authority, I despatched a telegram through Philip Fugh to Mao Tse-

---

[30] For correction, see telegram No. 3025, August 4, 4 p.m., p. 1266.

tung Friday evening calling his attention to lack of protection being afforded our ConGen Shanghai and requesting his personal attention (Deptel 904, July 30). I have not approached Huang Hua on siege of Shanghai ConGen knowing his usual attitude toward anything outside his immediate jurisdiction. I am, however, endeavoring to communicate with him as early as possible in an attempt to comply with Department's instruction in reftel.

I must again emphasize to Department that Embassy, ConGen Shanghai, and Clubb, Peiping, have already taken all steps which seem to have any real possibility of success, that Communist authorities Shanghai are clearly conniving at situation there and that Central authorities have not acted although they have been informed and have had ample time to intervene. There is therefore no reason to suppose that any further action which we might take in China will be effective.

STUART

102.22/7–3149 : Telegram

The Consul at Shanghai (McConaughy) to the Secretary of State

SHANGHAI, July 31, 1949—5 p. m.
[Received July 31—7 : 57 a. m.]

2978. Thomas has now been held by mob in large room 118 Consulate General Building continuously for 24 hours. He was kept awake all night and all morning by teams working in relays which subjected him to continuous barrage senseless questions, prodding him when he was too sleepy to answer.

At 1 : 15 a. m. workers, after much argument among themselves, allowed him to eat sandwiches we had sent down at 9 p. m.

He was allowed to eat breakfast and lunch sent down by us today. Workers holding unwashed plates as evidence their generosity allowing him to eat. Dr. Schramm persuaded workers to let cot be brought into room for Thomas' use this morning, convincing them that he has been under treatment for some time and that his health would be gravely endangered by further denial sleep. Thomas allowed to sleep from 12 noon to 12 : 50 and from 2 p. m. to 3 : 30 p. m., total of 2 hours 20 minutes. Interminable questioning now resumed. Permitted go to washroom several times under continuous guard. No opportunity shave, bathe or change linen.

Chase and Forman made still another appeal without avail to Foochow Road police station this morning. After difficulties and delay they saw an official of medium rank at 10 a. m. who said police could not intervene in labor disputes. When Chase demurred, pointing out serious threat to Thomas' well-being caused by ordeal, police promised to "send a man to see". This promise, of course, they never intended to keep and have not kept.

Lock-in applies only to Thomas, Slayton and myself. All others allowed enter and leave freely.

I have encouraged male staff members and foreign correspondents to come and go freely to room 118 in effort to keep outrage in open far as possible and to give Thomas what moral support we can.

Extremists among demonstrators including some Sikhs arguing they should come to get Slayton and me on barricaded upper floor. So far more cautious elements have restrained them but group is volatile and may suddenly arouse itself to frenzy if stalemate is protracted.

Workers still assert they will extract money from three officers they hold responsible, not specifying extraction method contemplated.

Chase knows that third communication this subject adequately setting forth gravity with which we view calculated dereliction Communist officials this matter now before highest authorities Shanghai. Neither Foreign Affairs Bureau nor any other arm Military Control Commission has to date lifted a finger to break up the siege and occupation.

Am now working with good prospects success on plan to provide full night of uninterrupted sleep in quiet room for Thomas.

Significant that workers closely following VOA and BBC broadcasts this case. Since officials have taken side of mob, there is no reason to restrict publicity, which should be carefully checked for accuracy. Workers assert they are incensed at alleged inaccuracies BBC and VOA broadcasts. I have observed no misstatements of facts in VOA text of July 30.

Fortitude, pertinacity of Thomas beyond praise.

McCONAUGHY

102.22/7–3149 : Telegram

The Consul at Shanghai (McConaughy) to the Secretary of State

SHANGHAI, July 31, 1949—10 p. m.
[Received July 31—1 : 55 p. m.]

2979. First hopeful development siege Glenline Building occurred late this afternoon when it was agreed that Thomas and representatives workers would both call at General Labor Union Shanghai municipality tomorrow morning for review of claims of ex-Navy employees and to consider advisory recommendations General Labor Union. I agreed to permit Thomas make this call contingent on following three conditions, all of which accepted by ex-employees:

(1) Thomas to be released immediately from confinement room 118 and enabled to get long recuperative sleep in atmosphere of complete freedom before meeting takes place,

(2) Thomas to proceed to meeting independently, not escorted by ex-employees,

(3) Consul General not to be bound or committed in any way by recommendations General Labor Union.

Understood that I proposed wire Washington promptly for instructions after reviewing Labor Union's recommendations.

Thomas released from room confinement 6 : 35 p. m., and came immediately 6th floor apartment. He is naturally very tired after ordeal of more than 25 hours but appears otherwise in good condition. He ate a hearty meal and is now sleeping soundly.

Mass of workers have left premises, leaving token force of about 12 men who are remaining unobtrusively in lobby. They might not interfere with Slayton, Thomas and me if we wished to leave building tonight but we have decided make no move to leave tonight.

Tension notably relieved at least for time being. It is possible that nothing will come of survey of situation with Labor Union tomorrow, in which case we will be back where we started, but course adopted offers some promise without any compromise essential principles on which we are standing and affords the relief for Thomas we have been seeking.

Authorities still have not intervened openly though we cannot be sure what has been going on behind scenes in response to weighty representations instigated by Chase. Some dissension clearly exists in ranks ex-employees, some of whom, asserting they are non-Communists, allege that Communist Party workers not belonging to ex-Navy employee category have infiltrated group and usurped leadership.

AstALUSNA today received payroll data for ex-Navy employees of BOQ and En Clubs and recreation center. With this data all payrolls should be completed tomorrow.

Sent Department 2979, repeated 1665, Canton 934, Peiping 234.

McCONAUGHY

125.857/8–149 : Telegram

The Consul at Shanghai (McConaughy) to the Secretary of State

SHANGHAI, August 1, 1949—noon.
[Received August 1—2 : 08 a. m.]

2980. 11 a. m. Due continued occupation Glenline Building by ex-Naval employees, problem of whether we should endeavor open Con-Gen for normal business will arise Tuesday, August 2. ConGen normally would have been closed Saturday, Sunday, Monday, latter due local holiday. Since easing tension due agreement consult Shanghai Labor Office (mytel 2979, July 31, 10 p. m.), occupation building reduced to approximately 20 ex-employees in lobby, about 60 watching building from outside. Workers anxious have ConGen resume normal functions and would like to restore our control of front entrance for everyone except themselves. Workers obviously anxious to maintain fiction peaceful picketing and have removed objectionable signs from ConGen entrance.

In my best judgement, ConGen should remain officially closed to general public as long as even a small portion of mob in unauthorized occupation of any part of ConGen with consent of authorities. Resumption of appearance of normality would play into hands of Communist regime naturally anxious to minimize whole affair. Security precautions could not be observed properly with office functioning. Principal and administrative officers and AstALUSNA could not carry on without risk of being seized at any moment. Although we have had water since late afternoon July 30, we still do not have electric lights or power nor safe access to foodstocks. Sudden reimposition of airtight siege which could easily be effected would place us in serious predicament if entire staff caught there.

Continued closure would give impressive evidence of indignation and extreme gravity with which our Government regards this indefensible transgression. ConGen will, of course, maintain essential reporting through staff American officers and will render necessary services to American nationals on emergency basis. I propose notifying Chinese staff to stay home pending lifting by local authorities of illegal occupation of building except for those required for special duty. I propose to announce publicly merely that ConGen is closed until further notice and to give the correct reason in answer to inquiries. Please advise urgently.

State pass to CNO.

Sent Department; repeated Nanking 1666.

McConaughy

125.857/8–149 : Telegram

The Secretary of State to the Consul at Shanghai (McConaughy)

Washington, August 1, 1949—6 p. m.

1509. Reurtel 2980 Aug 1. Dept concurs ur recommendation official closure ConGen to general public as long as there is any unauthorized occupation any part of ConGen with consent auths. Any public announcement shld contain statement in sense foregoing. Also leaves ur discretion number employees to be on duty in Glen Line Bldg during emergency. As you suggest, protection and necessary services Amer natls on emergency basis shld continue.

Acheson

102.22/8–149 : Telegram

The Secretary of State to the Consul at Shanghai (McConaughy)

WASHINGTON, August 1, 1949—8 p. m.

1511. Dept suggests possibility in negotiations ex-Navy employees that any agreement payment for specified periods might provide for additional amounts at an adjusted rate based on rise in rice or commodity prices. This wld enable payment if necessary of part of larger amounts requested but at a basic rate which would not set unfavorable precedent Amer firms and individuals. Navy states it is not sure this procedure allowable. However, concrete figures passed from Ast-ALUSNA to Navy cld be given consideration. Such offer shld not be made until Navy auth obtained.

ACHESON

102.22/8–249 : Telegram

The Consul at Shanghai (McConaughy) to the Secretary of State

SHANGHAI, August 2, 1949—1 a. m.
[Received August 1—8 : 28 p. m.]

2983. Re ConGentel 2979, July 31, repeated Nanking 1665, invasion of Consulate General premises. Thomas and Smith [31] called at General Labor Union (GLU), semi-official Communist agency, at 1 : 30 p. m. today [August 1] to discuss case and consider recommendations GLU. So-called mediator, named Hsu, designated by GLU. Interview lasted 5 hours, representatives of naval workers were present part time.

Hsu maintained outward air impartiality but had been well briefed by workers and acted as their advocate. He did reject as unreasonable workers' demand for six and one-half months' pay. Tacitly recognized that Consulate General officers were there as US Government officials, not private citizens. Argued that delay of more than 3 months in reaching final settlement justified increased termination bonus. When figure of 3 months' pay for all was mentioned, Hsu observed that the lowest paid coolies could not purchase any substantial amount of rice with such a small sum. Mediator thereupon recommended a minimum payment of $150 US regardless of salary level or length of service. This is most costly feature of mediator's recommendation and would greatly increase total sum payable since many of workers received less than $50 per month.

Thomas of course made it clear to mediator as previously to claimants that he had no authority to make any agreement on the spot; the matter would have to be referred to the Navy Department for decision. He was not at all certain that the Navy Department had the funds to

---

[31] Harry L. Smith, Consul at Shanghai.

cover such a costly settlement. Mediator intimated that details of proposal would not be communicated to claimants yet and if total sum required seemed excessive after estimates based on payrolls had been prepared, he would reexamine his recommendation. Additional meeting is scheduled for 2 p. m. August 2.

Thomas exerted himself to place the position of Navy and Consulate General fully before labor union. He delivered written memorandum setting forth full facts of case including siege of July 6 and invasion and detention currently in progress. He stressed absence of any legal or moral obligation of Navy for further payment, responsibility of Communist regime for delay in consummating settlement worked out several weeks ago and inability of Consulate General to act on its own responsibility or to serve as transmitting medium when it was subjected to occupation and intimidation.

Mediator said he was sure workers would not interfere with free movement of Consular personnel while answer from Washington was being awaited. He did not touch on vital matter of continued occupation of Consulate General lobby by token force of workers.

Shortly after Thomas returned to Consulate General, we received word that all workers had voluntarily vacated building. Guards were ordered to secure outside gate immediately. While they were doing so workers who had just left changed their minds and came back, pushing their way in and again establishing themselves in lobby. European employee of Consulate General who was watching says they returned after talking to two PLA soldiers who were standing across the street. They are here for night. Undoubtedly workers intend to keep force here continuously until they get their money.

While the workers probably would not stop Thomas, Slayton or me if we sought to leave the building tonight, we have decided to remain. With building unlawfully occupied, there is no security and siege must be considered as still in effect.

Situation highly unsatisfactory, not only because of large increase suggested, which is probably now the least amount we can settle for without trouble, but also because of impasse resulting from our firm refusal to make definitive settlement while building is occupied. Workers equally adamant in their refusal to leave before final settlement.

In my view we must resolutely refuse to give an inch on occupation issue.

The amount of total payment is a more debatable question. We all resent the gangster methods used to extort more money from the Navy and we feel amount suggested is unjustifiably high and an undue burden on our taxpayers and on the Naval appropriations. At the same time, it is a fact that separation bonuses of some sort are by custom payable in China as in most foreign countries by government agencies as well as by private firms and that pattern bonuses paid by ECA and ESD Shanghai recently set unfortunate precedent fully known to claimants. Furthermore, price of rice (standard unit of value to low paid workers here) has more than quintupled in terms of US currency since end of April. Therefore it is true that proposed payments will buy less rice for most workers than they could have bought with one month's pay at time dismissal.

It seems to me that this highly controversial payments question can only be determined by Navy Department. AstALUSNA compiling US dollars totals from payrolls on hand accordance recommendation payment, roughly estimates will amount to about $150,000 or more than triple original amount CNO permitted him to expend. He will send priority despatch a. m. tomorrow [32] when totals computed.

I trust Department and Navy Department will bear in mind our earnest desire to reach an equitable, dignified and consistent settlement of this business which will enable the Consulate General to resume its important reporting and protective functions unimpeded at this most critical time for American interests in Shanghai. At the same time essential principles involved are even more important than the uninterrupted functioning of the office. We shall be in some personal jeopardy if the proposal is rejected, but this should not be a governing consideration. We do not wish to yield to intimidation. If amount proposed is found to be entirely outside bounds of reason, I recommend refusal, AstALUSNA concurs.

AstALUSNA and I request instructions within 48 hours if at all possible, as to maximum amount we should agree to. We also request endorsement our position we will not pay one cent until besiegers are removed from Consulate General building.

Department pass to CNO.

Sent Department 2983; repeated Nanking 1667.

McConaughy

102.22/8–249 : Telegram

The Consul at Shanghai (McConaughy) to the Secretary of State

Shanghai, August 2, 1949—1 a. m.
[Received August 1—11: 37 p. m.]

2984. Reference invasion Consulate General building by ex-Naval employees, Chase succeeded today [August 1] in getting message, stressing the seriousness of the situation, to General Chen Ming-shu, head of Shanghai branch of KmtRC.[33] Han Ming was the intermediary.[34] Han informed Chase that he personally saw General Chen just before noon and impressed the gravity of matter upon him. General

---

[32] August 2; this telegram was apparently drafted before midnight on August 1.
[33] Kuomintang Revolutionary Committee.
[34] For correction, see telegram No. 3025, August 4, 4 p.m., p. 1266.

Chen assured Han that he would see General Chen Yi, Mayor of Shanghai and the highest political and military personage in the city, during the day and apprise him of the situation.

Chase also saw General Yang Ho, head of the Green Gang, today. Yang Ho reported to Chase later that he had investigated and was hopeful of an early improvement in the situation.

Yang Ho's present influence is doubtful but the approach to Chen Yi through Chen Ming-shu should have significance. It certainly cannot be alleged later by the Communist regime that it was not informed of the affair. The authorities, political, police and military, have been approached at numerous levels and from numerous directions with urgent requests for intervention accompanied by explanations of the implications of the siege and occupation.

Department pass CNO.

Sent Department 2984; repeated Nanking 1668.

McConaughy

893.00/8–249 : Telegram

The Consul General at Peiping (Clubb) to the Secretary of State

Peiping, August 2, 1949—6 p. m.
[Received August 2—12:15 p. m.]

1270. [To Nanking:] July 31, 11 a. m. Re Embtel 306, July 29.[35] Yesterday discussed matter with Joseph Chang, gave him unsigned memo incorporating essential info and representations suggested reftel as message Ambassador desire him or father communicate Chou or Mao. (Assuming from language reftel some local discretion, made text read "lack official diplomatic relation" as taking him more out of picture and "in tragedy and in that event" as having greater possible effect.)

Chang to see father today, will inform me whether action feasible. Says Communist leaders in conference last week, recently unavailable.

Sent Nanking 906, Shanghai 843.

[Clubb]

102.22/8–249 : Telegram

The Consul at Shanghai (McConaughy) to the Secretary of State

Shanghai, August 2, 1949—7 p. m.
[Received August 2—8:45 a. m.]

2990. Siege ConGen building lifted 5:50 p. m. August 2nd Local Standard Time on order General Labor Union following second ses-

---

[35] Same as telegram No. 1651, July 29, 11 a.m., from the Ambassador in China, p. 1248.

sion with Thomas and Smith this afternoon. Last unauthorized person has left building and outer gate secured. Besieged officers going home for first time since July 29. ConGen plans to open for normal business tomorrow. For details settlement proposed to Navy by General Labor Union, see AstALUSNA telegram to CNO 020940Z.[36]

ComMarianas, please pass to Ambassador Stuart.[37]

Sent Department, repeated Nanking 1670, Canton 936, Peiping 235.

McCONAUGHY

893.00/8–249 : Telegram

The Consul General at Peiping (Clubb) to the Secretary of State

PEIPING, August 2, 1949—11 p. m.
[Received August 2—12:30 p. m.]

1281. [To Nanking:] August 2, 11 a. m. ReContel 906, July 31.[38] Informed Joseph Chang yesterday of latest developments for information father who was seeing various Communist leaders at Army dinner last night.

ReDeptel 508, July 30. Yesterday forwarded letter General Headquarters PLA as organ presumably having final authority over actions Shanghai MCC responsible organ Shanghai. Requested headquarters promptly cause Shanghai military authorities bring immediate stop mob action and direct those authorities that any settlement dispute should be effected through usual channel peaceful negotiations.

ReContel 810, July 8.[39] Case in point good example difficulties conducting negotiations re official matters through Aliens Affairs Office. This fact emphasized July 31 to Chang who said perhaps he and father would suggest to Communists there be provided more suitable channel for handling consular affairs.

Sent Nanking 913; repeated Department 1281, Shanghai 847.

[CLUBB]

102.22/7–3149 : Telegram

The Secretary of State to the Consul at Shanghai (McConaughy)[40]

WASHINGTON, August 3, 1949—4 p. m.

1517. Reurtel 2978, Jul 31, it is suggested ConGen (or Emb) within its discretion endeavor interest Indian representation Shanghai (or

---

[36] Not found in Department of State files.
[37] Ambassador Stuart was en route to the United States.
[38] Same as telegram No. 1270, August 2, from Peiping, p. 1263.
[39] Apparently a telegram to the Embassy at Nanking, not found in Department of State files.
[40] Repeated to the Embassy at Nanking as No. 912.

Nanking) in question Sikh participation ConGen difficulties with ex-Navy employees. Approach would also be applicable to Sikh involvement in other labor disputes where there is incitement by local elements. Point out in connection ConGen siege every endeavor arrive fair settlement made by US Govt; ConGen obviously unable negotiate under duress; Foreign Affairs Bureau expressly requested no settlement until it reviewed case; FAB failure act on Navy team proposal. Request Indian rep bring foregoing attention Sikh leadership Shanghai, pointing out that any situation in China involving disorder, lawlessness affects position all foreigners.

Indian Emb here and AmEmbassy Delhi being informed along foregoing lines with request for action Indian FonOff.

ACHESON

---

123 Olive, William M.: Telegram

The Counselor of Embassy in China (Jones) to the Secretary of State

NANKING, August 3, 1949—6 p. m.
[Received August 3—5 : 26 p. m.]

1703. Re Deptel 813, July 11,[41] and Embtel 1548, July 18. In view long delay Olive's departure and fact that case strongly protested Shanghai, Peiping and via VOA, we feel no useful purpose served by Nanking protest at this late date. Local Aliens Affairs Office would, in any case, simply refuse accept as outside their jurisdiction.

Departure of Ambassador and consequent severing special personal channel to Huang Hua raises question whether in future there is any value in making representations here regarding incidents occurring Shanghai or other cities. We have been clearly informed on various occasions that jurisdiction of local Aliens Affairs Office does not extend to Shanghai, and experience has proved that "protests" relating to Shanghai will be curtly rejected—sometimes without even the formality of reading.

Our considered view is that, if we are successful in reestablishing channel to Huang Hua, we may sometimes usefully seek his informal assistance with regard to matters involving other areas, as we did in Mukden case. However, the presentation for facile rejection of protests pertaining to other areas on which Aliens Affairs Office would feel no responsibility for action, may do more harm than good. (This view supersedes that expressed point 3 Embtel 1628, July 26[42] before Ambassador's departure.)

Sent Department 1703; repeated Shanghai 940.

JONES

---

[41] Same as telegram No. 1382 to Shanghai, p. 1224.
[42] *Ante*, p. 802.

123 McConaughy, Walter P.: Telegram

The Consul at Shanghai (McConaughy) to the Secretary of State

SHANGHAI, August 4, 1949.
[Received August 4—5 : 53 a. m.]

3023. I assumed charge of this Consulate General at COB [43] July 15 when Cabot left for Nanking. Official announcement withheld until Cabot's departure from China.

Sent Department 3023; repeated Nanking 1684, OffEmb Canton 941.

MCCONAUGHY

102.22/8–449 : Telegram

The Consul at Shanghai (McConaughy) to the Secretary of State

SHANGHAI, August 4, 1949—4 p. m.
[Received August 4—12 : 59 p. m.]

3025. As result disguised manner of speaking which I and Chase had to employ in phone talks during workers' seige building, errors occurred in Contels to be corrected as follows:

Contel Department 2972, July 30 (Nanking 1660, Peiping 232). Han Ming did not state that political section PLA was backing demonstration and directing Foreign Affairs Office's handling of affair. When Chase mentioned loss of PLA support as indicating need of approaching some high PLA official, Han was noncommittal. However, 2 days before he had indicated to Chase that Chang Han-fu might have to consult higher official before considering a communication from Chase which Han had delivered to Chang.

Contel [to] Department 2984, August 1 [2] (Nanking 1168). Intermediary who conveyed Chase's message to Chen Ming-shu was not Han Ming but a retired Chinese diplomat of ministerial rank. Green Gang representative seen by Chase was not Yang Hu (who now in Peiping) but his assistant L. P. Sun.

Sent Department 3025, repeated Nanking 1685, Department pass Peiping 240.

MCCONAUGHY

125.8571/8–449 : Telegram

The Consul at Shanghai (McConaughy) to the Secretary of State

SHANGHAI, August 4, 1949—7 p. m.
[Received August 5—2 : 24 a. m.]

3039. ReConGentel 2895, July 22, repeated Nanking 1627, house tax on Government-owned buildings Shanghai. Bureau Finance has rejected any request for exemption US Government owned property

---

[43] Close of business.

from tax. Bureau stated request was inconsistent with provisional measures for collection house tax for months May and June promulgated by Municipal Government. Discovered that through clerical error resulting misplacement decimal point total bill May and June only one-tenth amount previously reported. Correct amount is PN [44] 2,277,000, equivalent US dollars 1,035. Assessment for several Government-owned properties here not yet received.

Although amount involved much less than previously indicated, it is still substantial. Further increase later date is quite possible. If we concede our liability to this tax, it would pave way for later Communist expropriation property without compensation. This purpose would easily be accomplished by tax increases.

Understand Chinese and foreign real estate boards protesting both house taxes and land taxes on valuable properties asserting in many cases owners literally unable to pay. American School has received retroactive land tax bill equivalent US $276,600 covering 3 years 1947–49.

Although we may be forced out of some or all our property here if we refuse to pay, I believe risk will have to be run in order maintain vital principles involved. I doubt if Communists will actually evict us from our properties unless they intend eject US in any case from occupied China. Hence it may well be we have nothing to lose by standing firm. We have better case for exemption from real property taxes [than] from vehicle taxes. Latter paid this week.

While it is a temptation to pay the rather small tax on principal officer's residence on Route Delastre (only US $18) in order to tighten our hold on the property which may be challenged, I believe on principle we must refuse to pay this assessment also.

If same taxation principle being applied our properties in all areas Communist China, representations Peiping covering all cases might serve useful purpose.

Sent Department, repeated Nanking 1690.

McConaughy

893.918/8–549 : Telegram

The Consul General at Peiping (Clubb) to the Secretary of State

Peiping, August 5, 1949—5 p. m.
[Received August 17—11:09 a. m.]

1307. ReDeptel 499, July 28. Appropriate letter sent headquarters PLA under date August 4.

Copy by post.[45]

Sent Department, repeated Nanking 933, Shanghai 859.

Clubb

---

[44] People's Notes (Chinese Communist currency).
[45] Despatch No. 103, August 5, not printed.

811.91293/8–949 : Telegram

The Consul at Shanghai (McConaughy) to the Secretary of State

SHANGHAI, August 9 [*7*], 1949—9 [*11*] a. m.
[Received August 9—3 : 12 a. m.]

3082. Follows a substance information given by Randall Gould to ConGen August 6:

At meeting August 4 workers first demanded severance pay each employee one and one-half year's wages, later reducing this to 9 months' pay for workers, 7 months' for staff, aggregate payment approximately US $100,000. Gould feels that this excessive but in principle took notice of fact that majority workers had given long service and relatively their wages among lowest their group in Shanghai. In light these facts he considers their demands by no means unreasonable.

Following August 4 meeting Gould immediately sent message to Starr reporting workers' demands and asking for immediate reply. To date no word. Gould went to plant August 6 informing workers he deeply regretted delay; again made it clear he cannot bind Starr or guarantee anything. Reiterated offer apply own and wife's resources to utmost if necessary. Workers manifested patience. Evidently expecting deal go through, they promised no more lock-ins.

Gould said if Starr does not approve terms he fears worst for himself and wife without whose moral support he would have already collapsed; he realizes he is temperamently unsuited take type punishment he has experienced; he has almost reached limit his endurance; and rather than suffer more such experience he would almost welcome being jailed. Jailing might have wholesome effect making people back home realize seriousness his predicament.

Position Miner representing all Starr interests including American Asiatic Underwriters Bank, Reliance Motors, Metropolitan Motors, Metropolitan Land even worse than Gould's. While Starr may agree to workers' terms for *Evening Post*, corresponding problems other five Starr organizations developing rapidly and thus far with no basis of hope for settlement. All five organizations in deep water financially, probably forced suspend operations. Workers all five organizations demanding not less than 7 months' severance pay (apparently accepting inevitability closure). Starr's Hong Kong representative has refused consider workers' demands, offered no more than one and one-half month's pay. Miner in impossible position, workers pressuring local authorities to deny him exit visa. Workers [of] Reliance Motors which in particularly bad financial state are extremely tough crowd. Payment of claims of workers of five organizations would total about US $500,000 in addition to US $100,000 for the Post.

Gould said *Post* has additional problem meeting many claims which could probably be paid off by selling some of plant's properties. As indication of impossibility operating newspaper in Shanghai under present conditions, he stated *Post's* pay roll alone would total about US $16,000 per month compared former US $3,500; higher pay roll, other increased expenses would involve net loss probably not less than US $10,000 per month.

Gould expressed appreciation McConaughy for what ConGen had done to assist him. Would appreciate if pertinent points of above information were transmitted to Dept—with suggestion, if thought proper, that Dept contact Starr's Washington representative G. M. Rosse, % Paul V. McNutt, with view reemphasizing to Starr seriousness Gould's and Miner's position and grave need acceptance *Post* workers' terms if further persecution Gould is to be avoided.

Gould pointed out that if USA dollar did not have extremely unrealistic local value wage disputes could be settled fraction cost now indicated.

McConaughy

811.91293/8–749 : Telegram

The Consul at Shanghai (McConaughy) to the Secretary of State

Shanghai, August 7, 1949—2 p. m.
[Received August 7—3 : 40 a. m.]

3086. Gould informs Consulate General telegram just received from Starr states latter meeting Stuart, Cabot [in] Washington Wednesday, 10th, after which will instruct Gould but meantime latter not authorized negotiate settlement basis demands outlined ConGentel 3082, August 7, and suggesting alternative considered is acceptance resignation Gould and resumption publication *Shanghai Evening Post* under Miner.

Gould stresses utter impracticability Miner's operation paper account his already heavy preoccupation with problems other Starr interests Far East, aside from other virtually insurmountable problems confronting foreign publications here, and points out that acceptance Gould's resignation by Starr would have no effect upon Gould's predicament until labor settlement reached.

View pattern wage settlements thus far established Shanghai and experience Consulate General with ex-Navy employees, Consulate General of opinion substantial settlement authorized by Starr least troublesome way out of impasse for all concerned.

Suggest Department pass this and reftel to Cabot prior Wednesday meeting with Ambassador and Starr.

McConaughy

102.22/8–849 : Telegram

The Consul at Shanghai (McConaughy) to the Secretary of State

SHANGHAI, August 8, 1949—9 a. m. [*p. m.?*]
[Received August 9—12 : 16 a. m.]

3117. ReDeptel 1517, August 3, representation to Indian Ambassador re Sikh participation invasion ConGen by ex-Navy employees. Pursuant instructions I called on Indian Ambassador Panikkar now in Shanghai re this matter on August 5. I left with Ambassador list of about 35 Sikhs [who] participated, names of 6 worst offenders being underscored. I told him one of Sikhs, Kundam Singh, was worse offender than any of Chinese. This man was leader of extreme element which on afternoon July 30 urged and almost persuaded entire group to barricade 6th floor ConGen building and take me prisoner. I knew Indian ConGen Shanghai was embarrassed over whole affair and both before and during siege had done what he could to dissuade Sikhs. Hence I softened my approach as much as possible and stressed my appreciation loyalty Sikhs employed by ConGen who were fully prepared defend Consular officers with their lives.

Indian Ambassador expressed great regret at Sikh involvement, mentioned in extenuation following facts:

(1) Sikh local community not organized, has no recognized head and no cohesion. Most Sikhs have been here over 20 years, are married to Chinese, and consider themselves more Chinese than foreign.

(2) Indian ConGen has been working continually since early June keep Sikh ex-Navy employees from taking drastic action. Indian ConGen Uppal has exposed himself to abuse and possible violence at hands Sikhs in his efforts restrain them.

(3) Indian diplomatic representatives in China of course have no police power over Sikhs or anyone else.

(4) Indian Government has been doing everything possible repatriate Sikhs from China, having reduced total number from 7,000 to 300 in last several years. Remainder is hard core difficult to influence.

(5) Sikhs apparently entitled to some separation pay by US Navy and long delay of 3 months in making settlement increased difficulty of restraining them.

(6) British Government, not Indian Government, was responsible for bringing out Sikhs from India to Shanghai. Indian Government would never have allowed Sikhs of this sort to leave India. British brought them out during extra-territorial days [to] act as policemen in furtherance British colonial interests and, if there is any responsibility along this line, British Government should shoulder it rather than Indian Government.

Did not seem fruitful pursue divergent excuses raised by Ambassador so, after pointing out considerations mentioned in Deptel and making suggestion recommended by Department re effect of disorder and lawlessness on position of all foreigners here, I thanked him and departed.

Please inform Embassy New Delhi.
Sent Department, repeated Nanking 1723.

McCONAUGHY

393.1163/8–1049 : Telegram

The Consul at Shanghai (McConaughy) to the Secretary of State

SHANGHAI, August 10, 1949—7 p. m.
[Received August 11—1:52 a. m.]

3166. Following is brief survey certain difficulties facing Protestant missions central China as gleaned from conversations various missionaries supervisory positions, especially Methodist, Baptist, and Presbyterian.

Chief difficulty is limitation on freedom movement. As rule missionaries in interior cannot obtain travel permits to attend Christian conferences other points even when nearby. Chinese Christians have similar difficulty. Numerous missionaries interior points have been unable obtain permits proceed Shanghai and this difficulty may interfere with evacuation missionaries interior points who desire leave. Missionaries supervisory positions Shanghai such as Bishop Ward, Methodist, and Frank Price, Presbyterian, unable obtain travel permits to enable them visit their supervisory areas.

Fine Methodist hospital at Suchow virtually taken over by Communist authorities in absence Director, Dr. F. P. Manget. They were spearheaded by Party member who maneuvered himself into hospital staff on pretext he was expert radiologist. He has intimidated Chinese Executive Board left in charge by Dr. Manget.

Missionaries in worst famine areas such as Nanchang in potentially serious predicament because impossibility sending relief supplies to them for distribution. In some cases cash remittances hard to transmit. Since missionaries unable contribute anything to relief of famine and cannot starve themselves they are in vulnerable position, inviting criticism or worse from Chinese rendered desperate by semi-starvation. Yet in many cases they are unable get permits to leave.

Communist inspectors are showing up in most of mission schools. While Bible can still be taught as elective subject, most schools interior and theological seminaries not yet closed down, grounds already exist for suspicion increasingly unacceptable interferences with curricula will take place.

Hipps at Baptist University of Shanghai already informed courses in Theology, History of Religion, Religious Education, Ethics and Philosophy must be dropped from curriculum. He is convinced Communists intend pervert Christian universities into Communist-indoctrinated institutions. Ironically, Communists still hopeful obtaining remittances from American Christian mission boards to propagate

Marxism and atheism. Hipps of opinion time has about come for boards in US to cease remittances and for Christian teachers to leave. Significant that Communists now are interfering more actively with university curricula than with middle schools, indicating early Marxist indoctrination mature students contemplated.

Intermittent occupation of mission school properties by Communist soldiers, of course, constant problem.

While it is too early generalize, I share forebodings of those missionaries here who feel for sake of Chinese Christians (many of whom feel foreign missionaries temporary liability) as well as for safety of missionaries themselves and to prevent misuse missionary funds from US we must reconcile ourselves to temporary ebb foreign mission activity here—especially educational and evangelical as distinguished from medical, which will have somewhat better prospects if hospitals subject themselves Communist supervision.

Sent Department; repeated Nanking 1737, OffEmb Canton 983.

McConaughy

125.857/8–1149 : Telegram

The Consul at Shanghai (McConaughy) to the Secretary of State

Shanghai, August 11, 1949—9 a. m.
[Received 12 : 26 p. m.]

3185. After mature reflection I have come to firm conclusion time has come to reduce staff ConGen materially. Present work load does not justify retention more than 50 percent American staff. Assuming continuation blockade and indefinite continuance nonrecognition status, prospects are that except for protection and evacuation work, all sections will continue with reduced load through autumn and winter. Routine work in shipping, invoice, notarial units practically nil. Volume visa and citizenship work down over 50 percent with further reduction in prospect if evacuation of foreigners takes place. USIS closed down by authorities, volume of political and economic report greatly reduced by absence mail service. Volume administrative work decreased more or less directly in proportion reduction personnel other sections.

With other posts seriously understaffed, we cannot justify retention large staff with little to do.

Almost equally compelling is welfare argument. Assuming blockade and nonrecognition continue, all signs point to winter of great adversity for foreigners Shanghai. At worst we may be confronted with indiscriminate retaliatory action against foreigners by Communist regime goaded to fury by insoluble economic problems, unfairly blamed on West; food riots turned against foreigners by vindictive Communist propaganda; uncurbed baiting foreign employers by discharged Chinese employees; general denial of equal protection to foreigners with or without consent top Communist authorities; and some limitation on local freedom movement foreigners who may be regarded in some sense as hostages.

At best, under assumptions postulated we can expect winter of privation; acute lack of fuel leaving us alternatives either going cold or spending prohibitive amounts for space heating and hot water; serious lack local transportation; constant petty annoyances, mounting cost of living in terms US dollars probably beyond range post allowances; possibility punitive action at any time by unfriendly authorities; constant badgering from cold and undernourished people bound to be very numerous; continuous possibility eviction office and Government-owned houses for nonpayment Communist imposed taxes; intangible but real and accumulative burden of prolonged isolation in beleaguered city.

While this dark picture would be greatly brightened by lifting of blockade or improvement relations with Communist regime, I believe Department will agree we cannot count on such a turn of events in the near [apparent omission] as inevitable first step retrenchment program. Fifteen of them definitely apprehensive and prefer to leave, 2 on fence, and only 3 desirous of remaining. While we could use a few stenographers to good advantage, there being no male stenographers on staff, we can get along without stenographers and I do not believe the Department will wish to take the responsibility of exposing women to conditions I have outlined when their presence not absolutely necessary. I have no special reason to believe that our women staff members would be in direct danger of personal molestation, but the hardships specified would seem to tip the scales in favor of getting them out. Accordingly, I recommend that immediate TO's [46] be issued to those listed below: Surnames: Brubaker, Burrell, Dodge, Fay, Fisher (TO for Calcutta already requested), Gerathy, Josselyn, Kulbacki, Mayor, McGinnis, Parker, Rex, Robertson, Schilling, Smith, Stannard, Steiner, Turner, Thomson, Sullivan. Following have travel orders, waiting transport out: Gardner, Harrelson, Murchinson, Thompson.

I suggest those due or nearly due for home leave be ordered to US; others to be assigned to posts in Far East so as to keep travel expense at minimum, unless services specifically slated elsewhere as in case Fisher (Calcutta).

It may be impossible to obtain Communist exit permits or to obtain transportation, but we must make the effort, and TO's are essential first step.

---

[46] Travel orders.

I propose reduction approximately 40 in male staff; and large cut in local staff if we can withstand labor crisis which might be precipitated thereby.

Separate telegram elaborating recommendations as to male American staff will follow tomorrow.[47]

Sent Department; repeated Nanking 1746, OffEmb Canton 991.

McCONAUGHY

125.8571/8–1849 : Telegram

The Consul at Shanghai (McConaughy) to the Secretary of State

SHANGHAI, August 18, 1949—3 p. m.
[Received August 18—6 : 56 a. m.]

3306. Notification of August 16 re land taxes provides amendment to original notification to effect that failure to pay land tax within 25 days following receipt of notice results in fine of 1–1/2 percent of tax per day and additional 30 percent in case payment delayed over 40 days. ConGen has received notice for some properties and replied to Land Tax Bureau in same vein as in case house taxes (reConGentel 2895, July 22). No reply yet received.

McCONAUGHY

893.918/8–1849 : Telegram

The Consul at Shanghai (McConaughy) to the Secretary of State

SHANGHAI, August 18, 1949—6 p. m.
[Received 10 : 04 p. m.]

3318. Remytel 2943, July 28. August 18 workers again (Gould case still unsettled) invaded office and held Miner, who was later joined by Gould, for several hours during which time they ransacked desks, taking cigarettes, other small items. Before going to join lock-in, Gould called Labor Bureau to ask assistance in dispersing workers. Was told a police matter, not labor. Assistance refused. After Gould joined Miner, ConGen reported matter to police who replied would refer to military commander. Shortly thereafter, whether on basis our call, his call or other cause, union officials appeared and dispersed crowd after Gould signed statement saying he "hoped" to have funds for the next day. This was compromise on workers' demands for firm promise. August 18 Gould borrowed sufficient funds National City [Bank of New York] on basis stocks newsprint and possible sale of press to meet mid-month pay roll so is clear until September 1. Gould now attempting reach official in Labor Bureau who will lay down terms

---

[47] Telegram No. 3211, August 12, 10 p. m., not printed.

of final termination settlement and conclude sale of property which will realize funds to make 3–month pay off, thus making total of 4 since one already paid. Strong possibility such settlement satisfy workers but if not Starr may be asked put up some additional to ransom Gould.

McConaughy

102.22/8–1949 : Telegram

The Consul at Shanghai (McConaughy) to the Secretary of State

Shanghai, August 19, 1949—3 p. m.
[Received August 19—6 : 26 a. m.]

3333. Usually reliable intelligence sources indicate possibility imminent new invasion ConGen for collection severance pay for approximately 150 ex-US Navy employees retained after departure Navy for varying short periods to guard valuable abandoned Navy property pending its disposition. Department will recall funds provided by CNO this purpose (Deptel 789, April 28 [48]) upon urgent request ConGen were utilized retain security guard force, drivers, skilled laborers, et cetera, until after returned Navy mission team had completed property disposal approximately mid-May.

Although these employees were also included in list given USN severance pay last week, they reportedly now claim separate bonus due account separate ConGen employment.

I propose have Thomas take up matter with General Labor Union mediator pointing out absurdity double bonus claim and suggesting applicability waiver signed by each individual ex-Navy employee when paid bonus last week.

Matter further complicated by persistent representations 13 Sikh guards who employed temporarily for occupied ConGen residences during approximately 2-week period just before and during Commie takeover. These Sikhs who also included in Navy security force claim they entitled bonus account danger to lives, separation from families and loss of other employment during period temporary employment ConGen. Indian CG [49] who asked intervene admits helplessness and suggests only way to end trouble is to meet negotiated demands this group. Since these 13 also among principal agitators group described above and account doubtful support Labor Union our position, urgently request special allotment US dollars 500 for payment special bonus this group. Would represent as double time payment special risks involved and not as separation bonus.

Department pass for information to CNO and ComSeventhTaskFlt. Sent Department, repeated Nanking 1798.

McConaughy

---

[48] Not printed.
[49] Consul General.

125.8571/8–1949 : Telegram

The Consul at Shanghai (McConaughy) to the Secretary of State

SHANGHAI, August 19, 1949—4 p. m.
[Received August 19—5 : 57 a. m.]

3338. Have received bills for house taxes US Government property Shanghai and some land tax bills (urtel 384, August 12 [50]). House tax notices returned with letter stating since, contrary generally accepted principles relations between nations, for one to tax property of other, assumed notices sent in error. Notices returned several days later with comment our stand not accepted. Consulate General took no further action. August 17 five representatives Tax Bureau inspected Consulate General and brought up subject of payment. Given answer along same lines which they asked be confirmed in writing. No reply yet. Land Tax Bureau informed in same vein without returning notices, no reply for past week. Shanghai regulations do not contain clause re court appearance after 30 days overdue nor have we been required to report properties. For Department, would appreciate advice as to stand if called to court for non-payment.

Sent Department, Department pass Tientsin 117, Peiping 270, repeated Nanking 1799.

McCONAUGHY

102.22/8–1949 : Telegram

The Consul at Shanghai (McConaughy) to the Secretary of State

SHANGHAI, August 19, 1949— 6 p. m.
[Received August 21—12 : 56 a. m.]

3344. ReConGentel 2990, August 2. Unfortunate that absence mail service prevents submisison comprehensive report occupation Con-Gen by ex-Navy employees. In order place affair in some perspective and pull together loose ends, following concluding observations submitted:

1. Undoubtedly authorities acting through semi-official agency General Labor Union did order demonstrators from building on August 2. Convincing evidence at hand that SMCC through Aliens Affairs Bureau followed affair closely from considerable distance and was increasingly perturbed by mounting proportions which incident assumed when nothing vital was at stake from Communist viewpoint.

2. Although authorities did finally intervene behind scenes, their extreme reluctance take any public action which might be construed as directed against proletariat is significant indication of lengths to which they will go even in face damaging criticism abroad to maintain appearance solidarity regime with workers.

---

[50] Same as telegram No. 618 from Tientsin, p. 1102.

3. ConGen successfully maintained its stand on basic issue that it would not bow to intimidation by agreeing to any settlement while workers were in unlawful occupation building. Workers evacuated August 2 and settlement offer transmitted to GLU 3 p. m., August 3. ConGen was under no commitment to agree to any settlement before that time.

4. Final settlement was in effect compromise between original Navy offer of 2 weeks' to 1 month's pay and workers demands of 6 months' pay. It is undeniable settlement finally reached, while better than we had any right expect during darkest hours siege, did cost Navy slightly more than 3 times amount originally estimated and violent conduct of workers did indirectly serve increase amount which they received. This is true notwithstanding fact we steadfastly refused yield to pressure tactics while they were actually being applied. From financial and prestige standpoints I am dissatisfied with outcome affair. It is part of price we have to pay for living with regime which, partly perhaps through confused ignorance and unpreparedness re foreign affairs but at least to larger extent by deliberate intent, has thus far grossly violated rights of foreign governments and nationals and which has universally supported exorbitant severance pay demands of increasing hordes dismissed employees in contracting economy. Settlement we made was more favorable than most foreign firms have been able achieve but less favorable than some Chinese settlements made under corresponding conditions here since Communist take-over. Noteworthy that majority foreign community seemed think our tactics sound although small fringe at one extreme argued we should never have paid a cent or dealt with any Communist representative, while fringe other extreme argued we were too firm, arousing needless antagonism Communist authorities by uncompromising stand we took on basic issue.

5. Although authorities eventually intervened in covert manner giving clear indication they did not wish final showdown this issue, they still have given us no redress, they do not openly admit they intervened, of course have expressed no regrets, have not disavowed action officials who refused intervene and have given us no assurances they would behave any differently if we are subjected to similar indignity in future labor crises.

We have no way making effective representations covering lock-in and threatened violence against several senior officers or prejudice to US Government interests occasioned by complete paralyzation of office for 5 days and tie-up of entire staff, American and alien, for that period. We are delivering strongly worded protest to Aliens Affairs Department shortly. After delivery text will be telegraphed.

6. Incident afforded impressive evidence usefulness Chinese intermediaries belonging non-Communist fellow-travelling minority parties, especially Han Ming of Democratic League and General Chen Ming-shu, KmtRC leader. Consul Chase worked unremittingly on outside to have remedial action taken by officials. His many fine Chinese contacts served our interests well. We are indebted to Han Ming in particular for his strenuous and eventually successful efforts activate authorities. Consul Chase played large role in settlement of affair and is deserving special commendation. His painstaking efforts over long period build up useful Chinese contacts paid off handsomely in this

instance as in many others. Account of his efforts over period July 29–August 2 is being rendered separately.[51]

7. Looking back it is now plain most dangerous period was afternoon and evening July 30 when mob was in highly inflammable state which could easily have resulted in violence against responsible ConGen officers and sacking of ConGen building and commissary. Serious developments at this time were probably averted by praiseworthy action of Thomas who voluntarily subjected himself to nonstop 25-hours session with workers and by our offer to transmit to Navy Department for workers message which they had drafted. This offer, while later rejected by them when new and more intransigent mob leader took charge, did syphon off some pent-up fury of mob at critical time.

8. Real turning point in incident came on July 31 when I decided authorize Thomas consult on purely advisory basis with GLU re possible solution. Reasoning back of this decision set forth ConGentel 2979, July 31. Injection good offices GLU into picture gave Communists face-saving formula they needed to extricate themselves and bring pressure to bear on workers through organization only semi-official and in theory partly controlled by labor to evacuate building and scale down their demands appreciably.

Throughout affair my objective was, while adhering to essential principle, to show certain pliancy which would convince Communists in absence coercion they could negotiate with us on local issues on basis which might prove mutually satisfactory to some extent. I hoped thus establish precedent which might be useful for future. I believe this objective was in some measure achieved. Communist officials did sit down across table with ConGen representatives and went through process of reasonable give and take for first time. There is reason to believe this example has not been entirely lost on Communists. Their apparent inclination negotiate such questions as disposal ECA cotton and yarn stocks indicates they may have learned it will be expedient to deal with us on certain issues even though they persist in maintaining fiction we have no consular status. To extent we have achieved this objective, a certain limited amount of good may have come out of this unfortunate affair.

I wish to acknowledge with special gratitude invaluable advice and support I received from Embassy at Nanking. Wise counsel and backing of Ambassador Stuart and Counselors Cabot and Jones fortunately were at my disposition at all times thanks to continued availability of long-distance phone as well as radio communications. Forthright representations Consul General Clubb at Peiping may have had important bearing on change in attitude authorities on August 1 and 2.

It should be borne in mind our emergence virtually unscathed from this crisis does not signify we are exempt from further labor crises. Although this incident seems permanently settled with pay-off of workers and signing of quitclaims by them this week, there are other

---

[51] Not printed.

ominous clouds on labor front and we may have renewed unpleasantness with Chinese and Sikhs who have been and will be discharged by other US Government agencies here. While new labor laws may modify their stand, authorities thus far appear still assert in principle right of employees or ex-employees occupy premises of employer during labor dispute and to confine employer under trying conditions until settlement extorted from him.

Sent Department; repeated Nanking 1801.

McCONAUGHY

893.918/8–2349 : Telegram

The Consul at Shanghai (McConaughy) to the Secretary of State

SHANGHAI, August 23, 1949—6 p. m.
[Received August 23—9 : 26 a. m.]

3400. ReConGentels 3082, August 7, 3086, August 7. Fresh from 3-hour session workers, *Evening Post* labor mediator, Gould reports unsatisfactory conversations. Felt he had been bullied and all decisions made favorable to labor without regard management's side or provisions newly promulgated regulations re labor management relations (refConGentel 3383 and 3384, August 22 [52]). Held to following points :

(1) Gould is personally responsible since he Starr's authorized agent.

(2) Interpret Gould's recommendation in telegram to Starr re 9 months' pay for workers and 7 for staff as promise to workers to pay that amount. Mediator stated since union says he promised, their word accepted and Gould has not lived up to promise. Now state he must pay workers 8 months and staff 6.

(3) Unless settlement made before August 31, must continue pay workers.

(4) Workers are to be considered on payroll until final settlement.

Sum total required by Gould to liquidate approximately $80,000. Part of this (estimated at roughly 50 percent) could probably be raised by sale of plant if workers would vacate promptly but now in belligerent mood. Little likelihood their vacating until demands met. Gould seemed at end of his rope and felt remittance from Starr full amount demanded thus enabling him liquidate and sell was only solution. ConGen believes it important free Gould from continuous threat lock-in, other bullying tactics. When Gould remarked he expected face another lock-in, mediator harshly told him not mention possibility; however, given clearly understand authorities would not be interested or give protection in such event. Obvious authorities do not intend re-

---

[52] Neither printed.

spect own regulations unless it suits them. This based on mediator's statement new regulations do not apply this case.

Department pass to Starr at its discretion.

McCONAUGHY

102.22/8–2449 : Telegram

The Consul at Shanghai (McConaughy) to the Secretary of State

SHANGHAI, August 24, 1949.
[Received August 24—3:46 a. m.]

3408. Following letter of protest of siege of ConGen by ex-Navy employees July 29 to August 2 despatched August 22:

"Mr. Chang Han-fu, Alien Affairs Department, Shanghai Military Control Commission, Broadway Mansions, Shanghai. On Friday, July 29, at 7:30 a. m. a group of approximately 30 to 40 workers representing themselves as delegates of the former employees of the US Navy forced their way into the premises of No. 2 Peking Road, which is owned by the Government of the US, and announced their intention of remaining in occupancy of the building indefinitely until satisfactory settlement of their demands regarding separation pay and severance bonuses had been agreed upon. Since this action constituted an illegal invasion of US Government property and was also in contravention of our understanding of point 8 of Chairman Mao Tse-tung's proclamation regarding the protection of foreign property, we protested this action to the Alien Affairs Department of the Shanghai Military Control Commission. Furthermore, since the continued unauthorized presence of crowds varying from 20 to 80 within the premises of the building constituted a continuing threat to the maintenance of law and order, we also protested this potential violation of the peace to the local public safety officials.

"Below is set forth a record of the attempts which were made to secure intervention by the proper authorities:

"1. At 7:30 a. m., on July 29 the Bureau of Public Security of the Whangpoo police station was informed of the invasion of our premises and the officer on duty indicated that police would be sent over.

"2. At 9:35 a. m., on July 29 Mr. Reuben R. Thomas called upon Mr. Feng of your office and informed him of the developments. He called attention to the fact that the dispute between the workers and the US Navy, in which the representatives of this office were acting merely as go-between, had been fully laid before the Alien Affairs Department in our letter of July 12 and that we had been requested to take no further steps pending advice from your office; and had been assured that no violence would be permitted pending the receipt of such advice. Mr. Feng defended the action of the workers by insisting that, as ex-employees of a former occupant of 2 Peking Road, they had a legitimate right within the premises. Mr. Feng's attention was also called to the fact that invasion of the premises of 2 Peking Road constituted a violation of the most elementary principles of international law and universal practice, since the premises in question were the property of the US Government and used for official purposes.

"3. At approximately 10 o'clock on July 29 a second call to the Whangpoo police station inquiring why police had not arrived was answered by the statement that the police could not intervene in what they termed a labor dispute.

"4. At approximately 11 a. m., on July 29, 2 officers from the Whangpoo police station came to the premises and talked with the workers' delegates, but refused to discuss matters with personnel of this office.

"5. At approximately 2 p. m., on July 29, the Whangpoo police station was again called and again refused to intervene in what they termed a labor dispute.

"6. At approximately 2:30 p. m. the Alien Control Department of the Bureau of Public Security at the Foochow Road central police station was informed of the situation and likewise refused to intervene in what they termed a labor dispute.

"7. At approximately 2:30 p. m., on Saturday July 30, a representative of this office delivered to an official of the Alien Affairs Department in its new offices at Broadway Mansions a communication which set forth the urgency and danger of this situation, and was informed that the communication was provisionally accepted although responsible officials were not available at the moment.

"8. At approximately 8:30 p. m., on Saturday July 30, when the situation within the premises of 2 Peking Road had become critical due to threats of violence by the workers, the Whangpoo police station was again informed of this threat to law and order and again refused to intervene.

"9. At 11:30 a. m., on Sunday July 31, 2 representatives of this office discussed the matter personally with an official of the Foochow Road police station who contended that the police could not interfere on the grounds that no violence had occurred which he interpreted to mean no one had been subjected to bodily violence or had been threatened with a gun. He finally agreed to send someone to investigate, but reiterated that the police could not interfere in a labor dispute and could only take action in case of violence. To the best of our knowledge no investigator ever appeared.

"The final withdrawal of the workers from our premises was not effected until 5:50 p. m., on Tuesday, August 2, after they had occupied the building for more than 4½ days. They were apparently persuaded to withdraw as a result of their having at last been made to realize the fact that their continued presence in the building, implying coercion and intimidation, made it impossible for us to refer to Washington, for the Navy Department's consideration, the terms of settlement proposed by the Shanghai General Labor Union mediator at the meeting between representatives of the workers and our office held on the afternoon of August 1. This office has reason to believe that the final persuasion of the workers to withdraw is attributable to the help of your office.

"This office has recently also been given to understand that the workers had been cautioned from the beginning against violence; that your office was prepared at all times to have assistance rendered to us had actual bodily violence been inflicted by the workers upon officers of our staff; and that your office took steps to keep informed in regard to developments in the situation from that standpoint. I have welcomed these indications that your office took cognizance of the situation and eventually undertook remedial action.

"I must, however, place on record the following points:

"(1). As the above chronology of events makes abundantly clear, no effort was spared by this office to bring the developments noted to the attention of the proper authorities, despite which for over 4 days no positive action was taken by the authorities to protect property or to remove the unauthorized occupants from our premises.

"(2). As it hardly seems necessary for me to repeat, this office had at all times exercised its good offices within the limit of its role as a go-between to reach an amicable and mutually agreeable solution to the problem. On the other hand, this office had from the very beginning also made it clear that it would not negotiate or discuss such problems under threats of force and intimidation.

"(3). In my view, the failure of the local authorities for over 4 days, to take effective action to terminate the illegal occupation of the premises at 2 Peking Road, constitutes a serious repudiation of the minimum standards of international law and comity by condoning the invasion of the property of a sovereign state situated within territory purportedly controlled by those authorities.

"(4). While prepared to recognize the authority [authorities?] reported readiness to stop any actual bodily violence which might be employed by the workers against members of our staff, I must point out that:

"(A). Had actual violence been inflicted upon members of our staff by the workers (as easily could have happened in view of their large numbers and high pitch excitement), the harm would have been done before police could have reached the building:

"(B). The treatment to which Mr. Thomas was subjected by the workers, involving, as it did, unremitting verbal pressure (including threats) and forcing him to go with very little food and sleep for over 24 hours, brought him to a point of nervous and physical exhaustion which was no less serious than bodily injury, and, in our opinion, is properly to be regarded as a form of violence.

"The failure of the authorities to take timely positive steps to insure against violence which might easily have occurred and to rescue Mr. Thomas from the cruel and unusual treatment to which he was actually subject is a further serious breach, not only of international law and comity, but also of universally accepted humanitarian standards.

"In reviewing these points for your attention, I must accordingly protest in the gravest terms the failure of the local authorities to fulfill, in the serious respects noted above, obligations towards protection of life and property which are universally recognized under international law and practice, and which, moreover, the authorities themselves have appeared clearly to recognize in publishing specific assurances by Chairman Mao Tze-tung and in other public pronouncements. Very truly yours, signed Walter P. McConaughy."

Letter returned August 24 with following notation: "No diplomatic relations—your letter returned herewith. Message Center, Aliens Affairs Department August 23."

Sent Department, repeated Nanking 1825.

McConaughy

102.22/8–2549 : Telegram

The Consul at Shanghai (McConaughy) to the Secretary of State

Shanghai, August 25, 1949—1 p. m.
[Received August 25—3 : 49 a. m.]

3445. ReConGentel 3333, 19th, repeated Nanking 1798. Mediator could not or would not see Thomas. Suggested letter outlining facts which submitted same day and receipt taken but no reaction yet.

Meantime 13 Sikhs increasingly insistent, even threatening. Feel that settlement smaller issue which has more valid basis might further weaken case larger group.

Since Sikh delegation returning Monday [53] for "answer", request immediate telegraphic approval funds requested reftel.

Sent Department; repeated Nanking 1836.

McConaughy

893.918/8–2649 : Telegram

The Consul at Shanghai (McConaughy) to the Secretary of State

Shanghai, August 26, 1949—noon.
[Received August 26—4 : 37 a. m.]

3476. Miner–Gould case furnishes apt illustration of vicious circle many American and foreign businessmen caught in at Shanghai.

While Gould's case probably ineptly handled due his initial firm stand on moral and freedom of press grounds, issue has now boiled down to hard economic facts. Gould–Miner being held personally responsible since they here and Starr not. To meet demands workers, Gould must dispose assets. Prospective clients uninterested while workers in occupation premises or capable attaching lien at later date. As result Gould unable clear workers from premises without settlement agreeable to them and likewise unable dispose assets to make settlement while property attached by workers. Complicating this case is great amount sympathetic publicity given to case workers which makes recession from initial demands virtually impossible without serious loss of face for workers and Communist press.

Miner's problems liquidating other Starr assets, while not as notorious, are equally involved and difficult. To meet continued payrolls

---

[53] August 29.

of five enterprises operating at loss, Miner compelled draw remittances from abroad in US currency which he must exchange at very adverse rate. Since terms wages, expenses calculated basis unrealistic price rice, Miner forced dispose dollars at rate per picul of approximately US $25 compared with real value between $5 and $10. In Miner's view this results in forced continued investment of US dollars in losing enterprises. Attempts to liquidate are countered by workers' threats for continuance on payroll pending exorbitant severance pay settlements with the added threat that they in position to enforce indefinite delay in issuance exit permits.

Basic problem in both issues is total absence of any "rule of law". Despite recent issuance of regulations apparently designed to settle these and similar disputes, invariable insertion of a weasel-worded escape clause permits arbitrary interpretation by local authorities leaving employer at whim of arbitrator. Even from short experience it is obvious all decisions, including those of People's Court, are to be made on grounds of political expediency and Communists give no sign of intentions to curb or alienate labor. Net result is free rein given to basic mendacity and greed compounded by a moral communist philosophy that political ends justify any means.

McConaughy

125.8571/8–2649 : Telegram

The Consul at Shanghai (McConaughy) to the Secretary of State

Shanghai, August 26, 1949—7 p. m.
[Received August 26—9:51 a. m.]

3495. Apart from labor demands most immediate threat to unimpeded operation of Consulate General is tax collection (ReConGentel 3073 [*3039?*], August 4 and 3306, August 18). Tax collectors have appeared at various residences, properties owned by Government, including Consul General residence, and in some cases have created unpleasant scenes thru their insistence on immediate payment. Communist regime still does not recognize any right foreign government to exemption from tax on its properties, even those used exclusively for public purposes. Both house and land taxes on Consulate General building and government-owned residences already overdue with substantial penalties accrued. Our position has been undermined by action certain other Consulates which have yielded to constant pressure and paid tax. My understanding is that British Consul General has decided (probably on basis of having paid in past) to accede and will pay shortly under protest, if it has not already done so.

Position further complicated by consistent policy of Communists not to recognize any governmental corporate entity and to hold some individual or individuals personally liable for obligations of entity employing him. Thus our staff members occupying houses may be subjected to eviction, personal indignities or actual court process if they do not pay. Tax law provides that if collection cannot be made from owner, then tenant or occupant is personally liable.

Altho some of my consular colleagues disagree, I believe we are on sound policy grounds in refusing to pay taxes regardless of technicalities which might be cited by Communists in support of their position. If Communists intend to close Consulate General, I believe they will do it regardless whether we pay tax. If we refuse to pay taxes, altho individual staff members may be subjected to unpleasantness, questionable whether Communists will take far-reaching decision close us on [as?] this issue not basically important to them. However, Communist course cannot be predicted with any degree of certainty and it is entirely possible that a major issue may be precipitated by tax question, especially if some over-zealous minor employee Tax Bureau or newspaper publicizes extreme position from which top authorities cannot recede without loss of face.

I am bringing up question again solely insure all ramifications of issue, both policy and legal, carefully considered by Dept in light of events since Deptel 1419, July 15. We are prepared stand firm on issue, but decision should be made in full awareness of possible serious consequences.

Sent Dept, repeated Nanking 1848.

McConaughy

102.22/8–2949 : Telegram

The Consul at Shanghai (McConaughy) to the Secretary of State

SHANGHAI, August 29, 1949—10 a. m.
[Received August 29—1 : 11 a. m.]

3510. Letter of protest to Alien Affairs Department re siege of Glenline Building by ex-Navy employees (reftel 3408, August 22 [24]) was delivered through confidential channel on DPLDay [Friday?], August 26, and retained by Alien Affairs Department.

Sent Department 3510, repeated Nanking 1852.

McConaughy

893.512/8–2949 : Telegram

The Consul at Shanghai (McConaughy) to the Secretary of State

SHANGHAI, August 29, 1949—3 p. m.
[Received August 29—6 : 38 a. m.]

3529. Received following letter from Bureau Finance Shanghai Municipal People's Government (Deptcirtel August 26, 6 a. m.[54]) :

"Urlet dated August 18 requests us to note property of the country concerned is not liable to payment taxes. It is found that your request does not conform measures this municipality governing collection of house tax. Therefore, all house tax involved should be paid. Hope you will take due note."

View consistency all Commie agencies Shanghai re liability US Government payment taxes, recommend question be taken up highest levels Peiping to ascertain whether taxation foreign government properties Commie China is policy of tops or only local policy which could be corrected from above. In raising question PPG [Peiping] could point out if Commies expect to be recognized would come into possession valuable Chinese properties New York, San Francisco and Washington which would be liable taxes retroactive to date taxes collected US properties China. Indication amount taxes in US might show they stand to gain on exemption taxation. This question cannot be indefinitely stalled off view liability occupants of property to payment tax in absence order. However, time probably could be gained if we informed authorities that matter being referred Peiping. Doubt if action will be taken against Glenline Building but anticipate trouble for individuals occupying Government houses Shanghai which could result their "re-education" [and] seizure private property in event lack funds prevented payment. Calculation amount now due in course preparation follows subsequent message.[55]

McCONAUGHY

893.00B/8–3049 : Telegram

The Consul at Shanghai (McConaughy) to the Secretary of State

SHANGHAI, August 30, 1949—1 p. m.
[Received August 30—6 : 36 a. m.]

3551. Following is text Shanghai Military Control Commission proclamation dated August 30, 1949, published *Liberation Daily:*

"Foreign news bulletins established in Shanghai have, one after another, suspended business on their own initiative since liberation.

---

[54] *Ante*, p. 1104.
[55] Telegram No. 3588, September 1, not printed.

However, several individual news bulletins are found to be still operating.

It is now decided by this Commission that all foreign news bulletins shall suspend their business at the end of this month: Beginning from September 1, 1949 any bulletin which is found to be still operating (distributing its news manuscripts), shall be considered as having violated the law and be subject to punishment. It is expected that the public take notice of the same."

Associated Press expects discontinue local distribution as result. Correspondent Fred Hampson says operation unprofitable any case, has continued only to avoid necessity dismissing 15 employees. ConGen informed British Chamber Commerce intends discontinue distribution Reuters news result proclamation.

ConGen does not believe *Wireless Bulletin* Foreign Service Digest, distributed only ConGen American staff, covered by proclamation. Intends continue internal distribution on subject safeguard prevent outside dissemination.

Sent Department 3551, repeated Nanking 1866, Canton 1054.

McConaughy

125.8571/9–149 : Telegram

The Consul at Shanghai (McConaughy) to the Secretary of State

Shanghai, September 1, 1949.
[Received September 1—3 : 12 a. m.]

3585. Following note delivered August 30 to Director Bureau Finance in response to their letter:

"Have received urlet dated August 26, which in reply to mine August 18, in which you state since my request does not conform measures of Shanghai municipality governing collection house tax the Government of US is liable for payment taxes on its property in Shanghai.

"Ur views this question transmitted Department, and am awaiting further instructions. In meantime, take this opportunity informing you since Government of US pays no taxes on its property located foreign countries, no funds appropriated by Congress of US for payment such taxes. Hence no funds presently available here for payment these assessments."

Repeated Nanking 1883, Peiping 294.

McConaughy

125.8571/9–249 : Telegram

The Consul at Shanghai (McConaughy) to the Secretary of State

SHANGHAI, September 2, 1949—3 p. m.
[Received September 2—9 : 21 a. m.]

3615. September 1 several tax bills presented with taxpayer's name given as "former American Government". As unable identify properties from bills, they not accepted and authorities asked check ownership. Bills returned today with information identifying them as US Government-owned. Taxpayer's name as given above crossed out and name F. E. Farnsworth [56] inserted. Am returning bills today stating individual American citizens not liable for payment taxes on US Government-owned properties China; if determined Government liable to payment taxes, payment will be made by Government not by individual citizens; and requesting appropriate correction on bills.

Sent Department 3615, repeated Nanking 1895, Peiping 303.

McCONAUGHY

125.8573/9–449 : Telegram

The Consul at Shanghai (McConaughy) to the Secretary of State

SHANGHAI, September 4, 1949.
[Received September 4—11 : 04 a. m.]

3648. Following text of communication delivered September 2 to Alien Affairs Department, Shanghai Military Control Commission:

"On July 15, the undersigned, as deputy acting director of the USIS, branch of this office, was instructed by you to suspend forthwith activities of the USIS. This order was complied with. On July 20 we addressed to your office a petition protesting arbitrary closure of USIS and requesting reconsideration this decision. To date we have received no reply to above communication.

"On July 15, local employees of USIS were notified officially of suspension orders but were retained on payroll pending final decision from your office regarding our petition for reopening. It was made clear at that time that their services would have to be terminated in view of closure order of authorities unless order were modified. On August 18 we informed local employees of USIS their services would be terminated as of September 3, they would at that time receive their final pay, plus lump sum settlements of accrued leave and refund of retirement savings. We also offered them termination bonus of 2, 4 or 6 weeks, depending on length of service. This offer was rejected by employees who, in turn, demanded minimum severance bonus equivalent to 8 months' pay from which demand they have refused recede.

"After several fruitless attempts reach an agreement, dispute was submitted on August 27 by both parties to Shanghai General Labor Union for advice and counsel. We have been informed by Shanghai

---

[56] Consul at Shanghai.

General Labor Union we should receive notice from Alien Affairs Department as to time and place for hearings of this dispute.

"We have been informed by former local employees of USIS they will refuse recognize their dismissal as effective on date September 3. We have clearly informed employees of our position in this matter in two notices of September 1 and 2 respectively, copies of which attached.

["] In communication of September 1, employees have informed us that notwithstanding dismissal they intend continue coming to office as usual after September 3. Since work of USIS has been completely suspended in accordance with your instructions and the various wind-up tasks have been completed, we can only construe this intention of former USIS employees as attempt to circumvent order of your Department.

"We are calling these matters to your attention merely to place sequence of events on record so you may be fully informed in case any incident should develop."

Sent Department; repeated Nanking 1913, Canton 1078, Peiping 312.

McConaughy

125.8571/9–749 : Telegram

The Consul at Shanghai (McConaughy) to the Secretary of State

SHANGHAI, September 7, 1949—3 p. m.
[Received September 8—12:45 a. m.]

3684. Tax bills mentioned mytel 3615, repeated Nanking 1895, Peiping 303, September 2, have been returned rewritten.

Taxpayer given as "former American Consulate" with extension deadline payment date to September 20. Am acknowledging receipt repeating our regulations that in accordance recognized principle of international comity, property one nation within territory of another tax exempt when used for official purposes.

McConaughy

893.00B/9–849 : Telegram

The Consul at Shanghai (McConaughy) to the Secretary of State

SHANGHAI, September 8, 1949—11 a. m.
[Received September 8—5:53 a. m.]

3706. In interview arranged with John Keswick, Director Jardine, Matheson [57] office, ConGen informed [that] Keswick recently made personal call on Mayor Chen Yi at latter's invitation. Mayor's apparent purpose to discuss local conditions and tell Keswick Communists regret departure so many foreign businessmen from Shanghai and

---

[57] British shipping company.

their desire that foreign merchants remain. Mayor stated if foreigners patient conditions would surely grow more favorable for continuation their businesses. Mayor assures Keswick recent imposition many new taxes not intended force foreigners out but to raise needed revenue and that SMCC was even now considering rescinding tax schedules on churches, charitable institutions, schools and hoped later adopt more lenient attitude. Mayor pointed out many Communist officials foreign educated and acquainted both with foreigners and conditions abroad.

Keswick stated he hopes for series of discussions between foreign businessmen and Communist officials which he hopes initiate within week or 10 days.

At end Keswick's conversation with ConGen he made statement he did not expect Americans fare well under Communist regime but without indication this opinion formed as result conversation with Mayor or otherwise. Probable Keswick discussed matters with Mayor other than those indicated. However, despite Mayor's ostensible concern re departure foreign businessmen and alleged Communist attitude, ConGen has no evidence concrete action taken by Communists ease difficulties encountered at every turn by businessmen or even more lenient exit, entrance permit procedures which would reduce feeling claustrophobia prevalent in foreign community.

From independent source ConGen understands Keswick told Mayor, and quite flatly, Jardine's could not take financial punishment encountered past 2, 3 months indefinitely, resulting largely from labor demands and business inactivity.

Sent Department, repeated Nanking 1937, Canton 1088.

McConaughy

702.0093/9–1049 : Telegram

The Consul at Shanghai (McConaughy) to the Secretary of State

Shanghai, September 10, 1949.
[Received September 10—7 : 24 a. m.]

3762. Consulate General has become increasingly aware of lengths to which Chinese Communists have gone in denying traditional distinction international law between status and function diplomatic and consular officers. Communists here have doggedly maintained consular officers and political agents their governments in same sense as diplomatic officers. On this premise they refuse accept or deal in any way with consular officers in absence diplomatic recognition. They are unmoved by all arguments re permissibility negotiations between consular officers and representatives revolutionary regime on local issues. Numerous precedents along this line (especially Latin Americans) impress them not at all.

It would seem Chinese Communists are following Soviet lead this matter. Soviets obviously anticipated Chinese Communist attitude toward consular officers by nominally closing their consulates before take-over and taking other measures insure they would not become victims embarrassing situation resulting from Communist nonacceptance consular status.

Trend Soviet legal thinking for some time appears to have been in direction erasing distinctions between diplomatic and consular officers. While basic reasons are probably, on one hand, desire to get as many diplomatic immunities for Soviet consular agents abroad as possible, and, on other, distrust of foreign consular officers in Soviet Union and reluctance to let them function in usual way which would bring them close to commercial and industrial circles, they can adduce certain trends in western foreign service practice indirectly supporting their thesis, notably:

Amalgamation diplomatic and consular services most west nations;
Interchange ability diplomatic and consular assignments with senior officers usually having had experience in both fields;
Combined diplomatic and consular offices at many capitals;
Dual commissions and dual status many officers of Western foreign services;
Assignment diplomatic attachés with diplomatic status to consular offices where they are under jurisdiction principal consular officer;
Known fact most large consular offices have political sections which do political reporting along same lines as diplomatic missions;
Occasional necessity for consular officers deal with high officials central government on national issues when such officials absent selves from capitals and maintain office in city where consulate is located.

Owing traditional lack highly centralized government China in past and prevalence semi-autonomous provincial governments, consular officers in China for nearly a century held quasi diplomatic position which perhaps makes more colorable Chinese Communist contention consuls are same species and same genus as diplomats. It is suggested this thesis Communist interpretation international law may be fruitful subject for study by our international lawyers inside and outside Department.

Sent Department 3762; repeated Nanking 1966.

McCONAUGHY

893.00B/9–1149 : Telegram

The Consul at Shanghai (McConaughy) to the Secretary of State

SHANGHAI, September 11, 1949—2 p. m.
[Received September 11—4 : 13 a. m.]

3777. Re ConGentel 3706, September 8, conversation with Keswick. Reference penultimate paragraph "he did not expect Americans fare well under Communist regime", while we have no direct evidence Mayor Chen Yi made this remark to Keswick ConGen is satisfied Mayor did intimate something along this line; otherwise Keswick would not have mentioned it in his conversation with ConGen officer. He would hardly have invented this as bluff to frighten away American competitors. Such remark would tally with known Communist tactics as they have come attention ConGen. On several occasions members ConGen staff have been told by minor Communist officials various requests we have made (permits move residence, travel by rail, transfer gasoline stocks, et cetera) could be acted on more expeditiously if interest involved were not American. It seems be settled Communist practice harass and heckle American citizens especially American Government employees at every turn as means provoking minor incidents which can be used in anti-American propaganda campaign and by discriminatory treatment undermining any tendency toward united front among various western communities Shanghai.

Clearly we would merely be playing into their hands by giving vent to exasperation at petty annoyances put in way of Americans. Large measure forbearance is called for and in general is being displayed by American community.

It would appear reasonable assume Chinese Communists are up to their old device of playing off one group foreigners against another. This borne out by conspicuous absence direct and pointed attacks on British over past 3 or 4 weeks. Bitter anti-British propaganda following escape *Amethyst* quite suddenly ceased after tremendous 3- or 4-day build up. Other indications of attempted contacts between British representatives and Chinese Communists have been previously reported in my telegrams and also telegrams from Peiping and Tientsin.

Divergence British [and] American business interests Shanghai has been apparent for some time with former more inclining to compromise and to hear [bear] current losses in slim hope of recouping in future. Divergencies based partly on different orientation basic policy two governments but principally on difference economic position two business communities with British less able to afford a [to] pull out account their deeper involvement Chinese trade and industry and their inability to reestablish selves in their own country.

British Ambassador coming Shanghai September 12 with intent discuss united front with British, US consular and business representatives during course of week. In view presence Washington high British officials, Department may wish raise this matter and pass on for our guidance in these talks any available information.

Sent Department 3777, repeated Nanking 1976, OffEmb Canton 1103.

McConaughy

125.8571/9–1949 : Telegram

The Consul at Shanghai (McConaughy) to the Secretary of State

Shanghai, September 19, 1949.
[Received September 19—5 : 15 a. m.]

3922. Measures collection house tax July, August, September promulgated September 15, résumé follows:

Payment for leased houses to be paid by lease or occupant. Payment to be made by leasee even though no rentals collected. Persons moving into house responsible for unpaid taxes. Tax on vacant houses double. Caretaker responsible for payment.

Exemptions: Destroyed [houses?]. Occupied by Government (Communist Government) organs for official uses. Public schools. Private schools, government approved philanthropic not including churches having business income may apply for reduction of tax as may factories making necessities if closed due to blockade. Private houses occupied by army.

Owner or occupant may apply for investigation in case disagreement assessment. In case tax evasion the party concerned shall be required make payment double stipulated tax in addition same required to make "special payment for the delay". Tax to be paid within 10 days receipt notice with 1 percent fine per day's delay. Taxpayers failing pay after receipt overdue notice shall have case referred "to bureau of public safety for action by latter". ConGen has received no tax notices for period in question.

McConaughy

811.91293/9–2249 : Telegram

The Consul at Shanghai (McConaughy) to the Secretary of State

Shanghai, September 22, 1949—4 p. m.
[Received September 22—6 : 13 a. m.]

3981. For your information following details settlements disputes Starr's interests furnished ConGen by Chas. Miner.

Shanghai Evening Post–Mercury dispute settled September 8 on basis 5–1/2 months' wages staff employees; 7–1/2 months' workers, coolies; this in addition wages paid through August 31. As result payoff Gould and wife granted exit permits, preparing depart *Gordon*.

Considerable portion plant equipment sold to meet settlement after Union evacuated premises several [apparent omission].

Reliance Motors and Met Motors settled same basis 5-1/2 months' wages staff, 7-1/2 workers, coolies, plus wages for first half September in lieu of notice. No unpleasant publicity re this settlement. Miner now engaged liquidating assets both companies.

McCONAUGHY

125.8571/9–2949 : Telegram

The Consul at Shanghai (McConaughy) to the Secretary of State

SHANGHAI, September 29, 1949—4 p. m.
[Received September 29—6 : 25 a. m.]

4112. Have today received follow-up notice on house tax for Glenline reading:

"It is found you have not yet paid house tax last period. Hope you will make payment in full immediately. Do not permit any further delay! This is important."

Have written on bills for return to Bureau to effect property owned by US Government and used as offices by American Consulate General and question of liability of tax subject of correspondence Bureau and this office and case referred to Department of State. This seemed satisfy subordinate who brought notice. Am addressing letter to director reminding him of previous correspondence and stating since US Government adheres to internationally accepted principle one country does not tax property of other it considers itself not liable. Last sentence reads: "In the event that the local authorities require further information as to tax-exempt status those Government-owned properties I shall be pleased to discuss matter with you".

Will write similar letters as further notices received.

McCONAUGHY

800.91293/10–749 : Telegram

The Consul General at Shanghai (McConaughy) to the Secretary of State

SHANGHAI, October 7, 1949—11 a. m.
[Received October 6—11 : 15 p. m.]

4207. On October 6, representatives of the foreign press in Shanghai were told by CGRA [58] that it could no longer accept press messages.

---

[58] Chinese Government Radio Administration.

For clarification, foreign correspondents were referred to Alien Affairs Department. On October 7, they were handed order of SMCC dated October 6, to following effect:

"Effective from the date of issue of this order, all correspondents in Shanghai, irrespective of whether they are Chinese or foreign, for foreign newspapers and periodicals, news agencies and broadcasting agencies, whose country has not established diplomatic relations with the Chinese People's Republic are to cease acting in their capacity as pressmen, including the filing of press telegrams and radiograms."

According to preliminary survey, Tass has two representatives still in Shanghai, one having gone to Peiping. Other Eastern European countries not represented. This effectively closes out foreign news reporting from Shanghai. Department please pass Peiping at its discretion.

McCONAUGHY

800.91293/10–1149 : Telegram

The Consul General at Shanghai (McConaughy) to the Secretary of State

SHANGHAI, October 11, 1949—9 a. m.
[Received October 11—1 : 11 a. m.]

4257. With suspension activities local foreign press, news agencies and correspondents (reContel 4207, October 7), and [*sic*] news items used on VOA or press handouts based on information from this office not attributable other sources will presumably be considered by Communist authorities to have originated from this office. In view delicate situation with respect maintenance our radio contact, suggest extreme desirability close scrutiny any VOA and other releases concerning Shanghai area or otherwise readily traceable to this ConGen. Special caution desirable on anything which hypersensitive Communists might construe as of military significance.

McCONAUGHY

---

123 Colling, Guy Thomas : Telegram

The Consul General at Shanghai (McConaughy) to the Secretary of State

SHANGHAI, November 5, 1949—1 p. m.
[Received November 5—3 : 40 a. m.]

4682. Re ConGentel 4229, October 10.[59] Colling reapplied for rail travel permit to Nanking November 1 and was again officially refused by Public Safety Bureau on November 4. Colling used virtually iden-

---

[59] Not printed.

tical formula with which Ballachey of Canadian ConGen successful in securing permit and was accompanied by Ernest Tung. In course of application Colling was interviewed at length by higher official of Foreign Affairs section who adopted similar line of questioning previously used with some of our Service Attachés, strongly reminiscent of interrogations of prisoners of war customary during World War II. Obviously official deeply suspicious, being obsessed with espionage idea. While present psychosis of local authorities toward American officials continues, I am convinced that entire US Government staff here effectively prevented traveling outside city limits Shanghai.

Sent Department, Department pass Nanking 2031.

MCCONAUGHY

125.8576/11–1149 : Telegram

The Consul General at Shanghai (McConaughy) to the Secretary of State

SHANGHAI, November 11, 1949—1 p. m.
[Received November 11—5:26 a. m.]

4761. This office finding it increasingly difficult obtain accurate information on political developments other areas China, being restricted almost entirely to material printed in Chinese Communist press which not calculated present factual picture essential for maintaining proper perspective in evaluating and reporting local developments east China liberated area. Have found Peiping Consulate General political telegraphic repeats of greatest value and would accordingly appreciate repeats of telegrams from Chungking, Taipei, Hong Kong and Tientsin reporting political developments of other than purely racial interest (remytel 339, October 26 to Hong Kong, repeated 414 to Taipei [60]). Also appreciate continuing background information on current Department policy in China and related areas.

Sent Department 4761, repeated Hong Kong 368, Taipei 470. Department pass Peiping 444, Chungking 45, Tientsin 145.

MCCONAUGHY

125.8571/11–2149 : Telegram

The Consul General at Shanghai (McConaughy) to the Secretary of State

SHANGHAI, November 21, 1949—10 a. m.
[Received November 21—5:06 a. m.]

4862. Shanghai not yet faced problem registration property. (Deptel [*Reftel?*] 1181, November 15, from Peiping.[60] Authorities Shang-

---

[60] Not found in Department of State files.

hai have not questioned ownership Government properties and for only one property, Glenline Building, have asked see deed. Sole contact authorities here has been on subject payment house and property taxes. ConGen has acknowledged by letter each tax notice, pointing out property owned by Government of US and therefore basis generally accepted principle international comity property one nation situated within territory another exempt taxation we assume bills sent in error. Follow-up notices and personal calls by collector handled same manner with statement question payment taxes subject correspondence two offices and Department. So far this technique successful. Doubtful how long before issue brought to head. Land Bureau has received list of properties citing title deeds in Chinese and Finance Bureau (house taxes) has accepted English version.

November 18 tax collector called saying we should follow example of British, who have paid taxes. Oral check reveals Shanghai representative Ministry Works paid house taxes from beginning without protest. Bills for land taxes ignored.

Department please pass Peiping in discretion.

McCONAUGHY

125.8571/11–2149 : Telegram

The Secretary of State to the Consul General at Shanghai
(McConaughy)

WASHINGTON, December 8, 1949—6 p. m

2391. Stated urtel 4862 Nov 21 "Shanghai not yet faced problem registration property". Have Commie auths Shanghai issued reg[ulation]s re registration property? If so or if auths shld do so, Dept assumes ConGen will tele translation text regs.

For ur info Dept has instructed ConGens Tientsin Peiping,[61] in connection with Commie regs requiring registration real property of aliens those cities by certain dates, transmit to local Commie auths statement reserving rights absentee Amer owners real property. Dept has issued press releases giving this info.[62]

ACHESON

---

[61] See telegram No. 764, November 2, 5 p.m., p. 1113.
[62] See Department of State *Bulletin*, November 21, 1949, p. 760; November 28, 1949, p. 800; December 5, 1949, p. 868a; December 26, 1949, p. 957.

125.8571/12–1249 : Telegram

The Consul General at Shanghai (McConaughy) to the Secretary of State

SHANGHAI, December 12, 1949—3 p. m.
[Received December 12—6 : 09 a. m.]

5168. No denouement (Contel 1283, December 6 from Peiping [64] and 1291, December 8 [65]) re taxes Shanghai. Still receiving notices of taxes and demands for payments which being answered in usual sense. Recently officer required accept and receipt for demand notice was informed by collector in humorous tone "just take notice to 2 Peiping Road; they'll send it back".

Concur agreement first paragraph telegram under acknowledgment and request similar directive last paragraph.

Mytel 5135 of December 9 [66] reported requirement registration properties area Shanghai but no Government property located therein. Notification contains no "regulations" other than requirement to register and "bring all the property evidence and relevant documentary proofs within the time limit".

MCCONAUGHY

———

119.2/12–1449 : Telegram

The Consul General at Shanghai (McConaughy) to the Secretary of State

SHANGHAI, December 14, 1949—3 p. m.
[Received December 14—6 : 07 a. m.]

5211. In conversation on December 10 (ConGentel 5200, Dec. 13 [67]) Cheng Kang-chi told ConGen local Communist authorities acutely aware of existence of ConGen radio and have devoted much thought to question whether they should seal it. Cheng assured ConGen he had used his influence to insure retention our radio facilities. He said he reminded them that operation of radios for official purposes by foreign service establishments of principal power had sanction of long usage and general acceptance. He informed officials studying question that it was customary for American diplomatic and consular offices in various parts of world to operate their own transmitters and receivers. He said American foreign service enjoyed this privilege throughout Latin America (ConGen believes he is mistaken about this).

———

[64] Same as telegram No. 2227 from Shanghai, p. 1120.
[65] No. 2237 to Department, not printed.
[66] Not printed.
[67] *Ante*, p. 627.

Cheng said he also observed that closure of ConGen radio at this time when consulates have no diplomatic pouch privileges and no air mail service would in his opinion so cripple ConGen that it might be closed. Cheng told them that silencing of ConGen would be further exacerbating factor in Chinese Communist relations with US and might farther retard recognition prospects.

ConGen remarked to Cheng that he might also bear in mind that when there was anything favorable to report about record of this regime it went in without bias.

Cheng says authorities are aware of existence of British and French radio sets but think of problem mainly in terms of relations with US.

Cheng confident high level decision has been reached not to molest foreign government radios for present. He believes that during period nonrecognition same position will be taken towards radios all three Governments in all three cities where they are located, namely Shanghai, Peiping and Nanking. He thinks US foreign service radios would be placed in more precarious position if either Britain or France recognizes without similar action on our part. Radios nonrecognizing foreign governments might be banned once united western front as to recognition is broken.

McConaughy

893.111/12–1949 : Telegram

The Consul General at Shanghai (McConaughy) to the Secretary of State

Shanghai, December 19, 1949—5 p. m.
[Received December 19—2 p. m.]

5305. Consulate General would appreciate receipt of information as to Department's policy toward issuance or renewal passports American citizens intending to enter Communist China. Question assumes some urgency because of pressing desire certain mission organizations and business firms to bring replacement personnel. Consulate General does not know of any American organization contemplating expansion at this time but several organizations are anxious bring in new personnel to take place of employees who are sick, suffering from nervous strain, due for leave or retirement or slated for duties elsewhere.

Several mission organizations in particular are feeling need for substitutes in view unusually high average age of remaining missionaries. General feeling is that unless some replacements can be brought in, passage of time will force radical curtailment mission activities even though intention is to maintain present level.

Some uncertainty exists as to whether Department is willing grant passports to replacement personnel of established American organizations operating in Shanghai. A few cases of factual or proposed entry of Americans have been reported but presumably these persons have passports issued some time ago. I have told inquirers that Consulate General has no specific information on subject; knows of no blanket ban of issuance or validation of passports to American citizens intending proceed Communist China; that each case undoubtedly is examined closely and decided on its own merits. I added it was conceivable that dependent women and children would encounter more difficulty in obtaining passports than would individuals who would be employed in their own right.

Of course we have no assurance that Communists will admit American citizens in any event or that they will care whether an American passport is valid or invalid for travel to China. They seem disposed to approve after considerable delay entry applications filed on behalf of dependents of persons already resident here, and certain men with special qualifications or responsibilities.

While it would perhaps not be feasible for us to take steps to prevent travel of women and children already in possession of valid passports who may attempt to come to Shanghai, it would seem regrettable for the successful and difficult evacuation operations of a year ago and again of last September to be undone by influx of dependents and nonessential residents. There are signs that a small trickle of returning wives and small children is about to begin.

While it cannot be said that tangible immediate danger of any unusual nature exists, note that (1) lack of status of our Consulate officers which prevents extension of normal protective services to our nationals; (2) refusal of Communist courts to extend protection of any recognizable standard of law to defendants; (3) special animosity of many Communist officials toward Americans which may become more noticeable if recognition withheld for extended period; (4) frequent unwillingness of police authorities to curb unruly Chinese elements wishing to take action against foreigners; and (5) onerous restrictions on travel and on exit from the country, all point to undesirability of bringing in dependents or persons not replacing key American personnel of stabilized American organizations and firms, at least until our position vis-à-vis this regime has been further clarified. If another evacuation in the face of formidable difficulties should become necessary, it is clear that our problems would be magnified by presence of large numbers of additional dependents.

It will be evident from foregoing that I regard with misgiving the entry of dependents and nonessential citizens. Thought perhaps should be given to the advisability of taking up the passports of all US citizens who return to US from Far East, as invalidating them for travel to Communist China, unless specifically endorsed for such travel. At same time I believe it would be the part of wisdom to facilitate entry of necessary replacements in order to maintain the American position here and to take strain off American citizens holding the fort here who cannot leave until their successors arrive. An indication from the Department to this office that passport applications of such essential replacement personnel will receive favorable consideration will assist mission and business organizations in their personnel planning.

McConaughy

893.111/12–1949 : Telegram

The Secretary of State to the Consul General at Shanghai
(McConaughy)

WASHINGTON, December 23, 1949—6 p. m.

2485. Dept concurs views expressed urtel 5305 Dec 19 re issuance passports Amcits desiring proceed Commie areas China. ConGen correct in belief all applications examined closely and decisions based on merits each case. For reasons enumerated para 6 reftel no passports have been issued for many months past to dependents indicating intention proceed Commie areas. However, in very few instances passports issued individuals presenting reasons Dept has considered valid.

Dept shares ur misgivings re entry dependents and nonessential Amcits and desirability facilitate entry essential replacement personnel establ missionary and business organizations. Accordingly, Dept plans continue refuse passports to dependents and nonessential Amcits but prepared give favorable consideration passport applications essential replacement personnel establ Amer orgs provided applications supported by letter from orgs setting forth satisfactory evidence essential nature of travel.

Dept has considered advisability taking up passports all Amcits returning from Far East and requiring specific endorsement for return to Commie areas, but doubts necessity and feasibility such action present time.

ACHESON

119.2/12–1449 : Telegram

The Secretary of State to the Consul General at Shanghai
(McConaughy)

WASHINGTON, December 28, 1949—1 p. m.

2490. Fol comments for ur background info only re statements made by Cheng Kang-chi concerning operation radio facilities for official purposes FonServ estab (urtel 5211 Dec 14).

Although Brit view use of transmitters by dipl estab as right inherent in dipl usage, US and many other govts do not take this position. Contrary Cheng's opinion, not customary for Amer dipl and cons offices operate own transmitters. In few cases where they in use permission generally obtained with great difficulty and operations continue at sufferance fon govt. US Communications Act 1934 [68] restricts licensing radio transmitters to US cits. Govt does not, therefore, permit fon embs Wash operate radio transmitters any sort. However, no prohibitions re use of receivers.

ACHESON

[68] Approved June 19, 1934; 48 Stat. 1064.

DECISION TO CLOSE CONSULATES IN NATIONALIST-HELD CHINA PRIOR TO OCCUPATION BY CHINESE COMMUNISTS: CANTON, CHUNGKING, KUNMING, AND TIHWA

125.313/7–2249 : Telegram

The Secretary of State to the Minister-Counselor of Embassy in China (Clark), at Canton [1]

WASHINGTON, July 22, 1949—7 p. m.

TelCan 486. In view absence substantial Amer interests in Chungking, Kunming and Tihwa consular districts, Dept considering closing these consulates at such time Commie occupation cities concerned appears imminent. Importance Kunming consulate at zenith during war but has declined steadily since VJ Day.[2] No consular estab was maintained in Chungking from end 1930 until Aug 1938 when became apparent Chi Govt might move Chungking.

Dept also concerned over exposed isolated position Kunming [and] Chungking consulates in event Commie advance into Yunnan [and] Szechuan provinces which might also effectively cut off Tihwa from communications with outside world. Dept therefore contemplating instructing Kunming and Chungking that in event those cities threatened by Commie occupation consulates shld be closed sufficiently in advance takeover by Commies permit orderly withdrawal all Amer personnel and dispersal alien staffs. Dept considering sending similar instructions to Tihwa shld ingress and egress that post be threatened by developments that area.

Dept wld expect, prior to closing any of consulates mentioned, have warning issued all Amer cit[izen]s in areas affected informing them imminent closure consular estabs and recommending their withdrawal.

Wld appreciate ur and Emb's views this question soonest.

ACHESON

---

[1] Repeated on the same date to the Ambassador in China as telegram No. 873.
[2] Surrender of Japan, September 2, 1945.

125.313/7–2449 : Telegram

The Minister-Counselor of Embassy in China (Clark) to the Secretary of State

CANTON, July 24, 1949—5 p. m.
[Received July 24—8 : 19 a. m.]

Cantel 813. Concur desirability closing Chungking [and] Kunming when threatened Communist occupation (telCan 486, July 22, repeated Nanking 873). Present indications are those offices would be unable protect American citizens or interests and they would have little value as listening posts. If travel ever permitted in Communist-controlled area, occasional visit those places might satisfy our need political intelligence.

Tihwa, on contrary, and possibly Lanchow would continue, I should think, to have considerable value as listening posts. Suggest consideration, therefore, of detailing to Lanchow China language officer at time Chungking closes so he might be assigned Tihwa for administrative purposes and should certainly be charged solely with listening post activities unburdened by routine. Should Lanchow fall, he could retire to Tihwa. It seems to me Tihwa, properly staffed, could be most valuable listening post and should be retained as long as possible. Withdrawal should always be possible by some route other than China.

Sent Department Cantel 813; repeated Nanking 539.

CLARK

125.313/7–2849 : Telegram

The Ambassador in China (Stuart) to the Secretary of State

NANKING, July 28, 1949—3 p. m.
[Received July 28—6 : 17 a. m.]

1639. We concur Department's suggestion (Deptel 873, July 22 [3]) that isolated posts Chungking and Kunming be closed when threatened by Communist occupation. Tihwa even more isolated and bloody history of Sinkiang counsels that staff be removed before breakdown of law and order become imminent. Difficulty obtaining Soviet visa makes unlikely exit via USSR in event emergency, leaving only difficult mountain route to India or Afghanistan. Therefore, recommend immediate steps close Tihwa as a Consulate, evacuating women, children and personal effects, storing Government property. Communist advance south from Paochi already threatens momentarily cut highway communications between Kansu and Szechuan but air travel still possible via Lanchow and Chungking. Past experience indicates such travel will require careful planning well in advance. If Department

---

[3] Same as telegram telCan No. 486 to Canton, p. 1303.

considers Tihwa sufficiently valuable as listening post (see Cantel 813, July 24), radio might be maintained and Rinden [4] and Dreesen [5] remain there as long as safe to do so, prepared when necessary to abandon Government equipment remaining and depart over mountains with small amount personal belongings. We agree with Canton that Lanchow might be useful listening post if suitable officer available. He could retire to Tihwa and exit with officers there as conditions required if Tihwa also destined as listening post.

Sent Department, repeated OffEmb Canton 689.

STUART

125.267/7–2949 : Telegram

The Secretary of State to the Minister-Counselor of Embassy in China (Clark), at Canton

WASHINGTON, July 29, 1949—2 p. m.

TelCan 510. Rankin [6] was informed before his departure that Dept wld entertain and give full consideration to recommendation of closing ConGen Canton just prior to Commie takeover if facts justified it and that in any case he should have in mind reduction of his staff since ConGen activities including passport and visa services will no doubt be drastically curtailed.

What is your estimate of number of non-official Amers who will remain and importance of their interests involved? What is your recommendation in light of your Cantel 845, Jul 28,[7] having in mind extent to which ConGen Hong Kong can provide certain essential services?

ACHESON

125.937D/7–2949 : Telegram

The Secretary of State to the Consul at Tihwa (Paxton)[8]

WASHINGTON, July 29, 1949—6 p. m.

101. After careful consideration all factors Dept has decided close Consulate Tihwa. In arriving this decision Dept has had in mind absence private Amers or private Amer interests requiring protection in area and probability increasing threat personal safety staff and

---

[4] Robert W. Rinden, Consul at Shanghai, proposed replacement for John Hall Paxton, Consul at Tihwa.
[5] Robert B. Dreesen, Vice Consul at Tihwa.
[6] Karl L. Rankin, assigned as Consul General at Canton.
[7] Vol. IX, p. 1277.
[8] Repeated to the Ambassador in China, to the Minister-Counselor of Embassy in China at Canton, and to the Consul at Shanghai as telegrams Nos. 900, telCan 517, and 1500, respectively.

impossibility supplying post if already tenuous communications via western China cut.

Travel orders and administrative instrs being sent separate tel. Recommend Off Emb Canton explore possibility special CAT[9] flight Lanchow–Tihwa to afford transportation personnel and personal effects. Tihwa's comments requested re this as well as re feasibility you and staff alternatively proceeding by truck to Lanchow and thence by air. Wld also appreciate ur recommendations re disposition Govt property Tihwa in view probability Consulate will not be reopened in foreseeable future.

Dept desires you proceed orderly liquidation Consulate as rapidly as possible in order you and staff may leave while safe exit remains.

Rinden shld not leave Canton pending further instrs.

ACHESON

125.991H/8–349 : Telegram

The Secretary of State to the Vice Consul at Kunming (Lutkins)[10]

WASHINGTON, August 3, 1949—7 p. m.

56. In view moderate number Amers and relative unimportance Amer investment ur Con district and anticipated difficulties supplying and communicating office if area under Commie control, Dept has decided close offices Kunming [and] Chungking sufficiently in advance Commie takeover permit orderly liquidation, dispersal alien staff and withdrawal Amer staff prior takeover. Administrative instructions and travel orders will be transmitted in separate tel.

Dept desires that no publicity be given decision at this time but is informing you thereof for ur background guidance and in order that forthwith you may unobtrusively take such steps preparatory to closing when Commie advance threatens as may be possible without now indicating decision to close. In this connection Dept desires you issue at once unless you perceive objection thereto warning to Amers contained telCan 475 July 21[11] rptd Chungking 52, Kunming 51, revised as follows: Para 1

"Reference is made to the statement issued by this office on November 16, 1948[12] (suggest Chungking use date April statement[13]), warning Amcits residing in this consular district who were not prepared to remain under possibly hazardous conditions that they should

---

[9] Civil Air Transport.
[10] Repeated on the same date to the Embassy in China, the Embassy Office at Canton, and the Vice Consul at Chungking as telegrams Nos. 917, telCan 530, and 58, respectively.
[11] Vol. IX, p. 1270.
[12] See Department of State *Bulletin*, January 2, 1949, p. 29.
[13] See Note to All American Citizens in the Chungking Consular District, April 25, vol. IX, p. 1250.

plan at once to move to places of safety. In view of hostilities in southern China and the likelihood that hostilities may result in the cutting off of the means of egress from this consular district, this warning is now being repeated in order that Amcits in affected areas may give the most serious consideration to the advisability of evacuation at this time. In this connection Amers are advised to utilize existing transportation facilities while they are still available."

Para 2 unchanged. Para 3 deleted. Warning shld if possible be issued through confidential means in order avoid publicity possibly harmful Chi Govt. If queried by Amers whether Con remaining event Commie takeover, you shld reply no assurances can be given Con will remain.

Pls inform Dept when warning issued and means transportation now available Amers who wish to leave. To what extent wld fall Canton complicate transportation problem Amers wishing leave and eventual evacuation you and staff?

It is recognized that at a certain stage you shld inform Amer cits that ur office will be closed. Dept in authorizing you give this notification will be guided by ur advice and wishes to be consulted before such action is taken.

ACHESON

393.1115/8–549 : Telegram

The Vice Consul at Chungking (McGeary) to the Secretary of State

CHUNGKING, August 5, 1949—9 a. m.
[Received August 5—6 : 59 p. m.]

140. Warning issued American citizens this district today verbatim Deptel 58, August 3, [14] paragraph 2, and delivered by messenger in Chungking; airmailed double registry three other places.

Presently two Chinese commercial airlanes CNAC [15] and CATC [16] have daily flights via Canton to Hong Kong with no backlog. CAT has numerous unscheduled flights to Canton. Believe inadvisable go Canton due difficulties accommodations and possible backlog passengers boats, trains, planes Canton, Hong Kong. Local supply aviation gasoline has been in very short supply for several weeks and there is possibility reduction number flights and even cessation air travel. Chinese commercial airlines increasingly negligent in maintenance, sufficient supply fuel, and safe loading planes. American traveler Hong Kong–Chungking reported recently that drums of gas were carried at each end of plane, were insufficiently tied down and passengers were permitted to smoke.

---

[14] Same as telegram No. 56 to Kunming, *supra*.
[15] China National Aviation Corporation.
[16] Central Aviation Transport Corporation.

Americans now remaining have for most part decided stay come what may, perhaps on basis understanding that Consulate staff do likewise and desire American Government that key personnel remain maintain interests. If American citizens informed Consulate closing, believe many will wish to leave. Therefore, in fairness all concerned strongly recommend that announcement be made on entry Communists into Szechuan Province that Consulate will close. Consulate will advise inquiring Americans that no assurances can be given that Consul will remain.

Sent Department 140; repeated Nanking 143, OffEmb Canton 9.

McGEARY

125.267/8–549 : Telegram

The Chargé in China (Clark) to the Secretary of State

CANTON, August 5, 1949—4 p. m.
[Received August 9—2 : 02 a. m.]

Cantel 883. Shall of course discuss with Rankin on arrival [17] question possible closing ConGen Canton, telCan 510, July 29. Discussed whole problem with Ambassador Stuart [18] and Consul General Cabot [19] in Okinawa. They having experienced living under Communist regime feel more strongly on subject than I who have not suffered that experience. Both Dr. Stuart and Cabot feel that to leave any official personnel in Communist territory is to court insult and to weaken our hand in dealing with Communists. Their experience indicates complete inability of Consular officials perform their functions. To leave them at mercy unfriendly Communist regime is to incur personal danger needlessly. Accordingly they recommend closing all Consular offices in China with possible exception Nanking, Peiping. On Shanghai, gather they are undecided. Possibly our best policy would be to leave nucleus of "expendables" staffing skeleton offices at Peiping, Shanghai. South China could be handled from Hong Kong. I gather that there has grown out of experience in Communist China an increasing realization that it will be impossible to "do business" with Communists on any other than intolerable terms; that the Communists are determined to eliminate American interests and institutions from China when to do so suits their purposes; that no friendly approach on our part will change pattern of events and that as a result our best interests dictate that we treat any forthcoming Communist regime at arm's length and demand fullest compliance with international obliga-

---

[17] Mr. Rankin arrived in Canton on August 6 and assumed charge as Consul General on August 8.
[18] J. Leighton Stuart, who left Nanking on August 2 for the United States.
[19] John M. Cabot, Consul General at Shanghai, who accompanied the Ambassador to the United States.

tions before even considering recognition. Under these assumptions I agree with the Ambassador and Cabot that we should consider well before letting another fully staffed Consular office be "liberated" and that we should take such measures as are available to us to reduce to a minimum or close those offices already "liberated".

If our policy will be directed toward hampering Communist successes in China rather than assisting any government which may be established, probably we would be wise to "clear the decks for action" and remove, to the extent possible, all potential hostages from Communist territory and if that is to be our policy, I suggest advising mission bodies as well as business and professional groups that we plan withdraw official personnel and suggesting that they withdraw their personnel from China to the extent feasible. Communists may of course place many obstacles in way departure from China such people and some businessmen may be financially unable meet Communist demands re exit visas. On the other hand, they may welcome the move. No further Consular offices should be allowed to [be] "liberated", and should international repatriation vessel be arranged, we should withdraw all Consular and diplomatic personnel from Communist-occupied areas. Such action would of course be treated by Communists as indication our policy and their reaction might be violent. On other hand, however, they have minced no words in letting us know we are unwelcome in China.

Above recommendations are made in light considered opinions bestinformed people with whom I have had contact, which tend confirm forecast developments outlined Cantel 829, July 27.[20]

CLARK

393.1115/8–649 : Telegram

The Vice Consul at Kunming (Lutkins) to the Secretary of State

KUNMING, August 6, 1949—3 p. m.
[Received August 10—5 : 38 p. m.]

117. ReDeptel 56, August 3, 7 p. m. Warning contained reftel issued August 5th to American citizens this consular district in covers bearing wax impression seal. Americans were requested not discuss warning with aliens.

Air transportation now available via CNAC, CATC, CAT and Air France, Kunming to Hong Kong, Haiphong and Rangoon. Fall Canton might cut off Hong Kong. However, presume flights Haiphong, Rangoon would continue.

LUTKINS

---

[20] *Ante*, p. 459.

125.267/8–849 : Telegram

The Consul General at Canton (Rankin) to the Secretary of State

CANTON, August 8, 1949—6 p. m.
[Received 7 : 40 p. m.]

267. Concur Clark's recommendation third paragraph Cantel 883 August 5 in event US has decided on policy hampering Chinese Communists by such steps as giving tangible aid to guerrilla leaders and tacitly approving Nationalist sea blockade. In this case, or if US contemplates complete hands off policy for visible future, it would clarify matters if Department made immediate public announcement of intention close all or nearly all US Government offices in China. This should expedite decisions by missionary, business and other American groups on withdrawal their US personnel. In case of Canton it obviously desirable any decision close Consulate General be announced as long as possible before Communist takeover, preferably this week, to permit orderly withdrawal private and official groups. Coordination with British much to be desired but should not delay US action.

Third alternative policy involving early intimation to Communists of US intention recognize their regime under specified conditions might suggest desirability maintaining at least skeleton staff certain consular offices to provide continuity and perhaps lessen practical difficulties of reopening.

Fully appreciate difficulty reaching policy decisions quickly under present circumstances but believe highly desirable that question maintenance Canton Consulate General be decided in light general US policy toward China. In fairness to all American groups here, however, announcement of any decision to close Consulate General should not be delayed. Nearness of Hong Kong would permit that office assume Canton's routine consular functions for this region.

RANKIN

125.313/8–949 : Telegram

The Vice Consul at Chungking (McGeary) to the Secretary of State

CHUNGKING, August 9, 1949—2 p. m.
[Received August 10—1 : 52 p. m.]

147. To implement decision close Consulate and permit liquidation orderly windup affairs and withdrawals staff, I recommend closing out USIE [21] unit and reducing alien staff of Consulate to six including one radio operator c.o.b.[22] September 3. One American officer

---

[21] United States Information and Educational Exchange Program.
[22] Close of business.

will be available for transfer after September 3. Recommend selling after September 3 Consular vehicles, typewriters, refrigerators, rugs, fans and distributing on look basis all USIE material, equipment such as projectors, playbacks, records, films, books immediately upon receipt Department authorization close USIE. No market for furniture. Vice Consul and APAO Theodore Wahl [23] will be available for transfer upon completion of liquidation of USIE which should be completed by September 3.

According Consulate's records, there are presently in Kansu, which is under Communist attack, 78 Americans. In fairness to American citizens who have remained in the district with the solemn assurance that the Consulate expected remain come what may, and that they would receive the same facilities in event of evacuation as Consulate personnel, I believe that American citizens should be advised soonest that Consulate does not expect remain, thereby giving them (an estimated 200 who will not decide until decision regarding Consulate is known) opportunity departing district before Communists take over. Two American officers and one American clerk will be available service American citizens during period liquidation which should be completed by September 17, at which time services remainder alien staff will be terminated, Consulate closed and American members depart.

Plan ship confidential archives Washington via last courier August 14 and unclassified and restricted archives via unaccompanied pouch via Hong Kong soonest.

Present stocks avigas Chungking nil. Shell hopes receive shipment overland 3200 drums now either in Wuchow, Kwangsi, or en route to Liuchow. A maximum of 8,000 pounds of cargo and 2,000 pounds of American personnel totaling 10,000 pounds maximum will be required withdraw staff and effects. Due shortage avigas, prospects orderly departure via Chinese commercial air lines most unpredictable. Departure of large number of Americans and wealthy Chinese may precipitate backlog on commercial lines.

If Department concurs, request authorization (1) approach French or British Consul re custodianship Government-owned compound; (2) special instructions pay alien employees retirement deductions; (3) permission retain two senior alien custodian employees; (4) deposit US currency with French or British custodians pay salaries and essential repairs upkeep through June 30 in view of their chronic difficulties in obtaining funds; (5) openly proceed with orderly liquidation; (6) inform inquirers and Americans that Consulate is closing. Also request travel orders and administrative instructions.

---

[23] Theodore A. Wahl, Vice Consul (Assistant Public Affairs Officer) at Chungking.

Recognize Department may wish Consulate continue function on reduced basis if Nationalist Government move Chungking requires FSO Strong [24] and small clerical staff remain here.

Sent Department 147; repeated OffEmb Canton 102; Nanking 148.

McGEARY

125.313/8–949 : Telegram

The Chargé in China (Clark) to the Secretary of State

CANTON, August 9, 1949—noon.
[Received August 16—3 : 33 a. m.]

Cantel 903. Concur suggestion Chungking that American citizens should be informed Consulate closing at time Communists enter Szechuan province, Chungking's 140, August 5 to Department, repeated Canton 94.

As matter shaping up here, it is entirely possible Government will not move Chungking but that should it do so it will be mere façade with plane standing by to airlift it Taiwan slightest provocation. With Communist armies entering Szechuan, Nationalist Government would likely take announcement withdrawal more as blow at Communists than as lack confidence Nationalist Government.

Sent Department Cantel 903, Chungking 78.

CLARK

125.991H/8–1049 : Telegram

The Vice Consul at Kunming (Lutkins) to the Secretary of State

KUNMING, August 10, 1949—9 a. m.
[Received August 12—3 : 56 p. m.]

122. ReDeptel 56, August 3, 7 p. m. Permission requested to inform in confidence heads various mission groups of closure decision to give them adequate time for making plans.

CAT pilot tells me that closure common knowledge in Canton and Hong Kong. Though I fear damage has been done, I am trying to plug leak with CAT here. Request Canton do same.

Sent Department 122, repeated Office of the Embassy, Canton 38.

LUTKINS

---

[24] Robert C. Strong, First Secretary of Embassy in China, temporarily at Chungking.

125.991H/8–1049 : Telegram

The Vice Consul at Kunming (Lutkins) to the Secretary of State

KUNMING, August 10, 1949—10 a. m.
[Received August 12—1 : 45 p. m.]

123. ReDeptel 56, August 3, 7 p. m. I interpret Department's telegram as meaning that Consulate should remain open as long as possible for reporting and other purposes without risking Communist occupation. Please inform if this view incorrect.

LUTKINS

124.93/8–1149 : Telegram

The Secretary of State to the Chargé in China (Clark), at Canton

WASHINGTON, August 12, 1949—3 p. m.

TelCan 553. ReCantel 893, Aug 11,[25] question whether or not completely close Canton ConGen expected be decided later today in consultation with new advisory group recently appointed to counsel on policy matters.

Meanwhile, you are authorized close EmbOff Canton whenever in your judgment this move desirable and make any necessary preparations departure personnel who shld proceed first to Hong Kong. Re Canton's tel 267 Aug 8, ConGen staff shld be reduced to skeleton framework and preparations made for travel departing personnel. Dept relies ur and Rankin's judgment general lines reduction, but inform Dept soonest for its info. In forefront considerations in selection departing personnel shld be length of duty at post, health and family status. Administrative instrs re closure and future assignment departees will be subject sep[arate] tel.

You shld immed notify Amers ur area by most expeditious means of closure EmbOff and state that no assurance can be given that ConGen will not likewise be closed and staff withdrawn prior to Commie arrival near Canton.

ACHESON

125.267/8–1249 : Telegram

The Secretary of State to the Chargé in China (Clark), at Canton

WASHINGTON, August 12, 1949—7 p. m.

TelCan 557. Re first para telCan 553, Aug 12, entire ConGen Canton shld be closed whenever in ur and Rankin's judgment this move desirable prior arrival Commie forces. Make all necessary preparations

---

[25] Not printed.

departure personnel who shld proceed first to Hong Kong. Administrative instructions re closure and future assignment departees, including Rankin, will be subject sep tel. Pls make necessary notification Amer natls.

ACHESON

125.313/8–949 : Telegram

The Secretary of State to the Vice Consul at Chungking (McGeary) [26]

WASHINGTON, August 12, 1949—7 p. m.

62. Dept concurs view expressed urtel 147 Aug 9 Amcits shld be advised soonest Con does not expect remain event Commie takeover. However, in light announced intention ChiGovt move capital Chungking [27] with fall Canton and recent implementation this plan, Dept believes public announcement this time plan close office shld be avoided. Con therefore auth[orized] confidentially inform Amcits consular district and British, French colleagues [that] Con expects close and withdraw staff prior any Commie takeover city. Con shld inform Amcits office available assist those desiring evacuate now and they shld plan early departure if not intending remain event office closed and area taken over by Commies, as no assurances can be given facilities will be available that time for general evacuation Amcits.

Dept believes decision re date closure shld be deferred pending military developments south and west China and decision ChiGovt re location capital. View foregoing, Con shld take no final steps this time dismissal alien personnel, closing USIE, disposal of properties or public action indicative office to be closed. Suggest, however, making confidential inquiries willingness British colleague assume custodianship Govt-owned compound and payment costs upkeep property.

Con shld ship only those files not necessary current reference use and conduct business of office. Ship to ConGen Hong Kong for forwarding National Archives Wash.

AmConsul Kunming shld take action outlined above where applicable, including confidential warning to Amcits.

ACHESON

---

[26] Repeated on the same date to the Embassy in China, the Chargé in China, the Vice Consul at Kunming, and the Consul General at Hong Kong as telegrams Nos. 953, telCan 558, 61, and 722, respectively.

[27] For documentation on this subject, see pp. 547 ff.

125.991H/8–1049 : Telegram

The Secretary of State to the Vice Consul at Kunming (Lutkins)[28]

WASHINGTON, August 13, 1949—3 p. m.

62. Assume Deptel 61 Aug 12 [29] answers query raised urtel 122 Aug. 10. Re question raised urtel 123, Aug. 10 Dept desires you maintain Consulate long as possible but you shld keep in mind possibility local deal engineered by Lu Han [30] and/or Lung Yun [31] adherents by which peaceful turnover wld occur prior advance Commie troops that area. Such contingency is one which Dept of course in no position foresee and must under these circumstances rely upon ur judgment and estimate situation.

ACHESON

125.267/8–1449 : Telegram

The Chargé in China (Clark) to the Secretary of State

CANTON, August 14, 1949—5 p. m.
[Received August 14—11 : 12 a. m.]

Cantel 944. Re telCan 577 [*557*], August 12 and ConGentel 267, August 8. Rankin taking preliminary steps toward closing ConGen Canton. We have discussed matter from all angles; are convinced that even preliminary measures toward closing will become known and fact of closure become public information very quickly. Order avoid rumor-mongering and irresponsible reporting which almost certain have repercussions damaging to Chinese Government once American community informed, we both feel strongly wisest issue press release immediately either by Department or Embassy along following lines:

"The American Embassy has been instructed to close the American ConGen at Canton and to withdraw all official American personnel should that city be threatened with occupation by Communist forces. No date has been set for the actual closure since it depends on military activities.

This decision is the direct result of the Communists' refusal to permit foreigners to exercise their normal functions in Communist-occupied areas contrary to all precepts of international law and custom. Experience to date in Communist areas has indicated that American consular officers are not permitted to perform any of their normal functions such as protection of American life, property and interests and that the Communist authorities do not afford protection from physical violence or [garble] similar action will be taken in respect

---

[28] Repeated to the Chargé in China and the Vice Consul at Chungking as telegrams Nos. telCan 566 and 65, respectively.
[29] Same as telegram No. 62 to Chungking, *supra.*
[30] Governor of Yunnan.
[31] Governor of Yunnan, 1927–45.

of the American Consulates at Chungking and Kunming should those cities ever be threatened with occupation by Communist forces.

American citizens in all these areas are being warned of this action in order that they may reconsider [garble] decisions regarding departure.

The AmCon at Tihwa already has been instructed to withdraw with his American staff since no other Americans are known to reside in that area."

CLARK

125.267/8–1549

Memorandum by the Chief of the Division of Chinese Affairs (Sprouse) to Mr. Livingston T. Merchant of the Office of Far Eastern Affairs [32]

[WASHINGTON,] August 15, 1949.

It is my understanding that the considerations set forth hereunder in connection with the decision to close the Consulate General at Canton were taken into account at the meeting held in Ambassador Jessup's [33] office on August 12, attended by Mr. Rusk,[34] Ambassador Jessup, Ambassador Stuart, Dr. Fosdick,[35] Consul General Cabot, Mr. Perkins,[36] Mr. Merchant, Mr. Davies [37] and Mr. Sprouse.

Advantages: (1) The U.S. has had official representation at Canton since the late 18th century and we should continue to keep the flag flying as we have in the past regardless of the difficulties surrounding the continued retention of our consular offices in areas occupied by the Chinese Communists. (2) The Canton area has provided the greatest numbers of Chinese emigrants to the United States and American influence is strong in this area. Our continued presence will serve to encourage these Chinese and will indicate to them that we have not "deserted" them and are looking toward the day when our traditionally friendly relations with China can be restored. (3) The withdrawal of our consular office from Canton will be looked upon by other peoples south of China as an indication that we are retreating before the Communist advance and will be detrimental to our prestige both in China and in other areas of Asia.[38]

Disadvantages: (1) Given the pattern of the Chinese Communist attitude toward our official establishments in Shanghai, in particular,

---

[32] Notation by Mr. Merchant to Mr. Sprouse: "Good—I suggest putting this in CA files. Maybe it will be of use to future generations of luckless souls then wrestling with problems in China!"

[33] Philip C. Jessup, Ambassador at Large.

[34] Dean Rusk, Deputy Under Secretary of State.

[35] Raymond B. Fosdick, Consultant to the Department regarding Far Eastern policies.

[36] Troy L. Perkins, formerly Consul at Nanking, detailed to the Department.

[37] John P. Davies, Jr., of the Policy Planning Staff.

[38] Marginal notation by Mr. Merchant: "Also matter of US–UK unity."

and in other Communist-occupied cities, our consular offices will be the target for Communist pressure rather than serve as a means of affording protection and assistance to American citizens. Our consular offices are spending most of their time in defending themselves rather than in protecting and assisting American citizens. (2) The difficulties encountered by our Consulate General at Shanghai and the mob action against the Consulate General without any preventive action on the part of the Communist authorities have served to cause a loss of American prestige, outweighing any loss of prestige connected with the closure of our Consulate General at Canton. The presence of our consular office at Canton would present opportunities for further incidents leading to loss of prestige and serious difficulties. (3) All U.S. business firms are withdrawing their American personnel and the number of Americans remaining in this area and the extent of U.S. interests will be relatively small. The Consulate General at Hong Kong will be in a position to perform the necessary consular services for the American residents who elect to remain in southeast China. (4) The closure of our Consulate General at Canton, which should be accompanied by a public statement of the reasons therefor, will serve as a strong indication to the Chinese Communists that we do not like the treatment that has been accorded our consular offices in Communist-occupied cities and might serve as a jolt to them.

125.267/8–1649 : Telegram

The Chargé in China (Clark) to the Secretary of State

CANTON, August 16, 1949.
[Received August 16—11 : 13 a. m.]

Cantel 967. As we envisaged, story on closure Canton Consulate General has reached press and we of necessity have confirmed closure but have made no comment.

CLARK

393.1115/8–1649 : Telegram

The Secretary of State to the Chargé in China (Clark), at Canton

WASHINGTON, August 16, 1949—5 p. m.

TelCan 580. Dept issued following press release today: [39]

"The following notice was issued on July 26 in Canton to Americans in the provinces of Kwangtung, Kwangsi, Fukien, Kiangsi and Hunan: [40]

---

[39] For statement on the anticipated closing of the Consulate General at Canton, see Department of State *Bulletin*, August 29, 1949, p. 318.

[40] *Ibid.*, August 8, 1949, p. 197.

'Reference is made to the statement issued by the American Consulate General, Canton, on November 16, 1948, warning American citizens residing in this consular district who were not prepared to remain under possibly hazardous conditions that they should plan at once to move to places of safety.[41] In view of the renewal of hostilities in southern China, this warning is now being repeated in order that American citizens in areas which may be affected by the renewal of hostilities in southern China may give the most serious consideration to the possible jeopardy in which they may be placed should they remain in the areas in question.

'In this regard attention is called to the fact that the Chinese Communist authorities have thus far, in areas under their control, demonstrated in many cases an inability or unwillingness to afford adequate protection to foreigners or to safeguard their individual liberties, particularly in connection with arrest, detention, trial and mob action. Moreover, no satisfactory procedure has thus far been afforded foreigners wishing to secure permits for exit from China or even for travel between points in Communist-controlled China.

'In view of the possibility that communications may be seriously disrupted in the near future, Americans are advised to utilize existing transportation facilities while they are still available.'

"The Department of State has now instructed the American Consulate General at Canton to close and to withdraw all official American personnel should that city at any time in the future be threatened with occupation by the Chinese Communist forces.

"This decision has been reached in the light of the failure of the Chinese Communist authorities to comply with the usual requirements of international intercourse and their refusal to permit American consular officials in Communist-occupied areas to perform their normal functions, particularly the protection of American nationals and their interests. The Chinese Communist authorities themselves have in some cases failed to afford protection from physical violence or mob action despite explicit publicly expressed assurances by Chinese Communist leaders that foreign nationals and their property would be given appropriate protection. Moreover, the Communist authorities at Shanghai have not established appropriate and adequate facilities for the issuance of exit permits to American citizens desiring to leave China.

"American citizens in areas which may be threatened with occupation by the Chinese Communist forces are being notified of this action in order that they may reach their decisions with respect to departure in full knowledge of the circumstances."

Canton, Chungking and Kunming should inform American citizens their consular districts.

ACHESON

---

[41] Department of State *Bulletin*, January 2, 1949, pp. 28, 29.

702.4193/8–1649 : Telegram

The Secretary of State to the Ambassador in the United Kingdom (Douglas) [42]

WASHINGTON, August 16, 1949—7 p. m.

2925. Submit formal request FonOff British Consulates accept custody US Govt property at Canton, Tihwa, Chungking, Kunming when our Consulates and Emb close those cities. [43]

Dept will make funds available to British for salaries caretakers and essential upkeep.

If British willing accept this responsibility assume FonOff will so inform its reps China. Request this be done urgently. Keep Dept informed.

ACHESON

125.267/8–1749 : Telegram

The Chargé in China (Clark) to the Secretary of State

CANTON, August 17, 1949—6 p.m.
[Received August 17—12 : 52 p. m.]

Cantel 971. As matter courtesy, I informed George Yeh, acting Foreign Minister, that Consulate General [at] Canton will be closed as of close business Friday, August 19, and that on Saturday, August 20, I would remove to Hong Kong, maintaining Embassy office open and commuting daily to maintain contact with Government.

Yeh was shocked by suddenness disclosure and insists threat Canton is not as great as portrayed by my military advisors. He is making inquiry and will let me know tomorrow Nationalist Government analysis military situation. Doubt this can change matters as his sources will be those tapped by my military advisors.

CLARK

702.4193/8–1849 : Telegram

The Ambassador in the United Kingdom (Douglas) to the Secretary of State

LONDON, August 18, 1949—5 p. m.
[Received August 18—3 : 21 p. m.]

3271. Reference Embtel 3260, August 17, 7 p. m. [44] FonOff today informed Embassy by telephone that FonMin Bevin [45] had approved

---

[42] Repeated to Canton as No. 584, Chungking as No. 70, Kunming as No. 67, and Tihwa as No. 120.

[43] The Ambassador in the United Kingdom replied in telegram No. 3260, August 17, 7 p. m., that a formal request had been submitted to the British Foreign Office on that date (702.4193/8–1749).

[44] Not printed ; see footnote 43, above.

[45] Ernest Bevin, British Secretary of State for Foreign Affairs.

US request that British Consuls, China, take custody US Government properties specified cities. FonOff sending immediate telegraph instructions to its representatives concerned. Formal acceptance of US proposal will be sent later and copy airmailed Department.[46]

DOUGLAS

393.1115/8–1849 : Telegram

The Secretary of State to the Ambassador in the United Kingdom (Douglas)[47]

WASHINGTON, August 18, 1949—7 p. m.

2961. Upon closing any US Govt Dipl or Con estab in China where Brit have Dipl or Con reps Dept would also desire ref Deptel 2925 16th Brit Consulates afford Amcitizens protection similar that afforded Brit natls. Conceivable Amcitizens rendered destitute might also require financial or other assistance but criteria for eligibility receive financial assistance and limitations upon maxima amounts would be details for future solution based upon Brit Consuls' recommendations through FonOff to Dept for its consideration.

Emb requested formally inquire FonOff whether Brit willing undertake this service for AmGovt and if so will inform its Consuls China in foregoing sense. Matter considered urgent. Keep Dept informed.[48]

ACHESON

125.267/8–2049 : Telegram

The Consul General at Canton (Rankin) to the Secretary of State

CANTON, August 20, 1949—8 p. m.
[Received August 20—7 : 35 p. m.]

299. ConGen officially closed 5 : 30 p. m. August 19 but is maintaining skeleton staff time being for emergency services to Americans and winding up administrative details. British ConGen has instructions accept custody official property.

As anticipated, closing ConGen had negligible influence on decision Americans whether remain for Communist occupation. Nearly all US citizens now here represent organs and would leave only upon instruc-

---

[46] Despatch No. 1369, August 19, from the Ambassador in the United Kingdom; received August 24, not printed.

[47] Repeated to the Embassy in China, the Chargé in China, the Vice Consul at Chungking, the Consul General at Hankow, the Vice Consul at Kunming, the Consul General at Peiping, the Consul General at Shanghai, the Consul General at Tientsin, the Vice Consul at Tihwa, and the Consul at Tsingtao as telegrams Nos. 985, telCan 597, 72, 62, 70, 557, 1646, 251, 123, and 243, respectively.

[48] Correspondence with the British Foreign Office by which the arrangement was concluded was transmitted to the Department by the Ambassador in the United Kingdom in his despatch No. 1390, August 24; received August 29, not printed.

tions from their head offices in US. In general business firms have issued such orders while philanthropic organs have not.

ConGen has only two requests for assistance in evacuations; only handful Americans have left for Hong Kong during past week and most of these had previously decided depart.

Once housekeeping details substantially all arranged there will be little if any practical purpose maintaining skeleton staff ConGen Canton, particularly in absence appreciable evacuation movement US citizens and with consular records already in Hong Kong. Canton already threatened in that Communists apparently quite capable reaching city in matter few days or anticipating such advance by organizing local turnover. There is no assurance of course that other objectives may not have preference over Canton and that Communists may not delay entering city for 2 weeks or more. However possibility ConGen skeleton staff being cut off obviously increasing daily. Herrick,[49] Millet,[50] Dunn,[51] Waller,[52] Swayne[53] and Lynch[54] already in Hong Kong and Beck[55] in Taipei. About half remaining 10 Americans on ConGen staff expected fly out Monday and unless instructed to contrary I plan accompany remainder staff to Hong Kong Tuesday or Wednesday.[56]

Clark concurs.

RANKIN

125.937D/8–2449 : Telegram

The Vice Consul at Tihwa (Mackiernan) to the Secretary of State

TIHWA, August 24, 1949—10 a. m.
[Received 10:43 a. m.]

233. Consulate closed to public August 16 and all employees discharged by August 20.

British Consul General advises he has received preliminary instructions re assumption custody US Government property China and expects final notification shortly. In view this and Deptels 120, August 16[57] and 115, August 11,[58] and since nothing evacuated with Paxton and present chances evacuation any archives or equipment almost nil, will proceed at once as follows:

[49] Thaddeus A. Herrick, Vice Consul.
[50] Charles S. Millet, Consul.
[51] William B. Dunn, Vice Consul.
[52] Athlyne B. Waller, construction supervisor, Foreign Buildings Office.
[53] Kingdon W. Swayne, Vice Consul.
[54] Norma R. Lynch, clerk-typist.
[55] Anna C. Beck, secretary.
[56] Mr. Rankin assumed charge as Consul General at Hong Kong at close of business September 15.
[57] Same as telegram No. 2925 to London, p. 1319.
[58] Not printed.

Destroy: All archives, cryptographic material and motion picture films (will retain enough OTP pads for communication with Department during period I remain Tihwa).

Sell if possible: Expendable Government supplies such as stationery supplies and gasoline.

Turn over to British Consulate General: US Government real estate and nonexpendable property.

Advise what receipts and other documents Department requires from British Consulate General when turnover effected.

Sent Department 233; repeated OffEmb Canton.

MACKIERNAN

125.991H/9–649 : Telegram

The Vice Consul at Kunming (Lutkins) to the Secretary of State

KUNMING, September 6, 1949—10 a. m.
[Received September 6—1:57 a. m.]

148. Reurtel 25, 4th.[59] Decision to leave Kunming awaits developments South China (refDeptel 61, August 12,[60] repeated Canton 558). Am making no plans to leave this time since do not expect turn over near future.

CNAC, CAT and CATC received orders no flights in or out of Kunming September 5 and 6; awaiting orders re operations thereafter. Air France operating as usual. CAT leaving five Americans here and hopes continue operations though abandoning Kunming as major service base.

Situation quiet. Unable get definite information re reported Nationalist military movements but seems to be crisis arising from efforts Nationalist Government to force Lu Han off fence. Two provincial delegates sent Chungking to discuss matter with Generalissimo.[61] Believe clash unlikely and that crisis will pass with compromise probably giving Central Government more power.

Sent Department; repeated OffEmb Hong Kong 56, Chungking 4.

LUTKINS

125.937D/10–349 : Circular telegram

The Acting Secretary of State to Certain Diplomatic and Consular Offices

WASHINGTON, October 3, 1949—1 a. m.

Consulate Tihwa closed. All Amer personnel departed.

WEBB

---

[59] Not found in Department of State files.
[60] Same as telegram No. 62 to Chungking, p. 1314.
[61] Chiang Kai-shek who retired as President on January 21, 1949.

125.0093/10–1349 : Circular telegram

The Secretary of State to Certain Diplomatic and Consular Offices [62]

WASHINGTON, October 13, 1949—8 p. m.

Chi Govt being notified re Brit protection US interests China where US Consulates close.

Peiping shld if pos informally notify central Commie auths re closure US Consulate Tihwa, ConGen Hankow, Brit take-over US interests; impending closure Tsingtao, Mukden ConGens, projected Brit take-over. Just prior closure any other offices Commie-occupied areas, Peiping shld make similar informal notification. Central Commie auths shld be currently informed re closure U.S. Consulates Commie-occupied territory, Brit take-over (except Dairen).

Tsingtao shld notify local Commie auths informally, just prior closure, re Brit take-over. View Ward's [63] situation, not necessary he do so. Where possible, other offices closing in Commie-occupied territory shld informally notify local Commie auths.

Brit also being asked notify central Commie auths Peiping and local Commie auths re take-overs.[64]

ACHESON

702.4193/10–1949 : Telegram

The Secretary of State to the Chargé in China (Strong), at Chungking

WASHINGTON, October 19, 1949—6 p. m.

98. Brit FonOff has asked Brit Emb Nanking ensure appropriate arrangements made for assumption US interests in cases where Brit US consular districts do not coincide. To assist this respect forward Chungking list Amcits Kweichow (Deptel 91 Sept 28 para A[65]). Dis-

---

[62] At Nanking, Hong Kong, Chungking, Kunming, Peiping, Shanghai, Taipei, Tientsin, and Tsingtao.

[63] Angus Ward, Consul General at Mukden. For documentation regarding the Mukden Consulate General, see pp. 933 ff.

[64] The Chargé in the United Kingdom, in his despatch No. 1940, December 7, enclosed a copy of a letter of December 6 from the British Foreign Office stating that an informal communication on the closing of the American consular offices at Canton. Hankow, and Tihwa and the assumption by the British of the protection of American interests in those areas which had been addressed to the local Communist authorities in Canton had been returned without comment to the British Consul General there (702.4193/12–749).

[65] Telegram No. 89, September 28, 6 p. m., to the Vice Consul at Chungking; paragraph A referred to British agreement to afford protection to American citizens in China upon closure of U.S. diplomatic and consular offices and named specific services which the Department proposed to ask the British to perform for U.S. citizens. These services included financial assistance, welfare whereabouts, assistance in case of physical danger or distress, reports of death, conservation of personal property, reports of births and notarial service. No visa or passport services would be required.

cuss with Brit Con assuming interests ur district upon closure to ensure no Amcits' property there left unprotected by reason differences consular districts.

ACHESON

119.2/10–2949 : Telegram

The Second Secretary of Embassy in China (Bacon) to the Secretary of State

NANKING, October 29, 1949—noon.
[Received October 29—4 : 15 a. m.]

2330. British Consulate Tihwa has advised British Embassy [that] Sinkiang Provincial Government requests use Tihwa American Consulate radio equipment. Consulate recommends acquiescence subject detailed listing each item with official receipt from authorities and asks for instructions. British Embassy has asked Foreign Office to approach Department to ascertain wishes. We assume custody this equipment given British subject restrictions similar Depcirtel September 14, paragraph 4M.[66] This move on part provincial authorities characteristic Communist policy of taking without giving. We further consider fallacious to hope that compliance would extend life USIS network Communist China. On contrary surrender Tihwa equipment because unused might suggest to Communists that all USIS radio equipment could be taken over by simple expedient closing down remaining stations.

BACON

125.991H/11–1149 : Telegram

The Vice Consul at Kunming (Lutkins) to the Secretary of State

KUNMING, November 11, 1949—9 a. m.
[Received November 11—3 : 32 a. m.]

225. Due continued Communist military advances in Kweichow and Szechwan and deterioration general situation as [garble] airlines flop [*fly?*] over, I am today notifying provincial government of intention to close Consulate. No definite date is yet envisaged but I am proceeding with major liquidation steps such as removal of library to Hanoi.

In future unless Department objects all telegrams dealing with closure of office will be sent *en clair* exception special cases.

Sent Department 225; Department pass Chungking 86.

LUTKINS

---

[63] Circular telegram of September 14, 7 a. m., not printed; paragraph IV (M) stated : "Maintain radio contact till departure. Destruction radio equip then authorized or turn over Brit contingent their agreeing not allow equip fall into Commie hands intact."

119.2/10–2949 : Telegram

The Acting Secretary of State to the Second Secretary of Embassy in China (Bacon), at Nanking

WASHINGTON, November 15, 1949—7 p. m.

1234. Urtel 2330, Oct 29. Trans[fer] radio equipment Commies prohibited by reg[ulation]s and in accordance Depcirtel Sep 14, para 4M.[67] Although refcirtel intended as general Admin instr all China posts, it was not sent Tihwa view earlier closure that office. Therefore, probable Brit Con Tihwa not aware provision that radio equipment shld not be allowed fall into Commie hands intact.

In discussing matter with Brit Emb you may point out that obviously Commies wld use radio equipment to further anti-Amer propaganda. If radio equipment not already mutilated and inexpedient do so now, and if Commies arbitrarily seize, inform Dept.

Dept leaves to ur discretion in consultation Brit Emb nature reply to be sent Brit Con Tihwa. Brit Emb Wash informs Dept Brit Con Tihwa desires instr in plain text, via commercial channels.

WEBB

125.991H/11–1649 : Telegram

The Secretary of State to the Vice Consul at Kunming (Lutkins)

WASHINGTON, November 17, 1949—noon.

118. Reurtel 238, Nov 16.[68] Even though liquidation not completed, Dept believes you and Knowlson [69] shld close office and depart while transportation facilities available and prior Commie occupation. Knowlson shld return Taipei.

Sent Kunming rptd Hong Kong and Chungking.

ACHESON

125.313/11–1949 : Telegram

The Vice Consul at Chungking (Rozier) to the Secretary of State

CHUNGKING, November 19, 1949.
[Received November 19—6 :43 a. m.]

Consulate and radio closed. Last despatch number 62 [*66*], last telegram number 246.[70]

ROZIER

---

[67] See footnote 66, *supra*.
[68] Not printed; it stated: "Now liquidating fastest possible but unlikely can close Consulate before December 10."
[69] Clive E. Knowlson, administrative assistant.
[70] Neither printed.

119.2/11–2549 : Telegram

The Ambassador in the United Kingdom (Douglas) to the Secretary of State

LONDON, November 25, 1949—6 p. m.
[Received November 25—2 : 48 p.m.]

4706. Foreign Office advises British authorities were unable prevent Communist seizure radio equipment (re Deptel 4162, November 18 [71]) US Consulate Tihwa. Foreign Office unaware whether equipment seized intact and unable readily get further details because own communication with British Consulate Tihwa imperfect.

Dept pass AmEmbassy Nanking 3.

DOUGLAS

125.991H/12–149 : Telegram

The Vice Consul at Kunming (Lutkins) to the Secretary of State

KUNMING, December 1, 1949.
[Received December 1—10 : 06 a. m.]

265. Consulate closed for business November 30.

Sent Department 265, repeated American Consuls Hong Kong 45, Taipei 24, Shanghai 81, Nanking 94, Peiping unnumbered, Tientsin unnumbered.

LUTKINS

125.313/12–949

The Consul General at Peiping (Clubb) to the Secretary of State

No. 168

PEIPING, December 9, 1949.
[Received January 24, 1950.]

The Consul General has the honor to enclose, for purposes of record, copies (in English original only) of his letters of December 1 and December 8, 1949 to General Chou En-lai [72] informing the latter of the closure severally of the American consular offices at Chungking, Kunming and Mukden,[73] and of the take-over at the same time by the respective British consular offices of matters pertaining to American interests at those several places.

O. E[DMUND] C[LUBB]

---

[71] Not printed.
[72] Neither printed ; they were addressed to "General Chou En-lai, Peking" and were signed "O. Edmund Clubb" without indication of office. General Chou was Communist "Premier and Foreign Minister of the People's Republic of China".
[73] At close of business on November 19 and 30 and December 6, respectively.

119.2/11–2549 : Airgram

The Secretary of State to the Ambassador in the United Kingdom
(Douglas)

WASHINGTON, December 17, 1949.

A–1295. Reference Embassy's telegram 4706, November 25. In view of the experience at Tihwa the Department is anxious that all possible steps be taken to prevent seizure by Communists of usable United States radio equipment at other posts in China where United States Government property has been or may be in the future placed in British custody.

Since there appears to be no way short of destruction by which the equipment could be made inoperable so that it could not be repaired by the Communists if they should seize it, the Department can see only two alternatives in the disposition of radio equipment at closed posts to prevent the equipment falling into the hands of Commies, viz., (1) destruction (2) sale to British for token payment, or outright donation to British.

Please inform the Department of British reaction to the foregoing alternatives. At the same time, if British agreeable authority hereby granted British to destroy radio equipment left by closed posts or take up as British property. Department would like report on action taken at each post.

For your further information and possible transmission to the British, insofar as is known the following situation prevails as pertains to radio equipment at closed posts in China.

Canton	Presumably evacuated. If any such equipment located at Canton follow above instructions.
Chungking	Presumably evacuated. If any such equipment located at Chungking follow above instructions.
Dairen	Destroyed.
Hankow	Stored rooms 318 and 319 former Consular office in Shell House Hankow.
Kunming	Presumably evacuated. If any such equipment located follow above instructions.
Mukden	Evacuated with ConGen staff.
Tihwa	Seized by Communists.
Tsingtao	Presumably seized by Communists along with other U.S. Government property.

ACHESON

INDEX

INDEX

O